Fodor's

CALIFORNIA

Welcome to California

California's endless wonders, from Yosemite National Park to Disneyland, are both natural and man-made. Soul-satisfying wilderness often lies close to urbane civilization. With the iconic Big Sur coast, dramatic Mojave Desert, and majestic Sierra Nevada mountains, sunny California indulges those in search of great surfing, hiking, and golfing. Other pleasures await, too: superb food in San Francisco, studio tours in Los Angeles, winery visits and spas in Napa and Sonoma. Follow a beach picnic with a city stroll and live the California dream.

TOP REASONS TO GO

★ **Stunning Scenery:** Picture-perfect backdrops from the Golden Gate Bridge to redwoods.

★ **Beaches:** For surfing, swimming, or sunbathing, the state's beaches can't be beat.

★ **Cool Cities:** San Francisco, Los Angeles, San Diego, Palm Springs, and more.

★ **Feasts:** Cutting-edge restaurants, food trucks, fusion flavors, farmers' markets.

★ **Wine Country:** Top-notch whites and reds in Napa, Sonoma, and beyond.

★ **Road Trips:** The Pacific Coast Highway offers spectacular views and thrills aplenty.

Contents

Fodor's Features

Contents

MAPS

Chapter 1

EXPERIENCE CALIFORNIA

25 ULTIMATE EXPERIENCES

California offers terrific experiences that should be on every traveler's list. Here are Fodor's top picks for a memorable trip.

1 Crane Your Neck at Redwood National and State Parks

Redwood National and State Parks is home to the tallest trees on Earth (300–400 feet tall), and hugs 40 miles of California coastline. There are countless things to see and do including camping, hiking, fishing, kayaking, and more. *(Ch. 22)*

2 Find the Weird at Venice Beach

California counterculture can be found at Venice Beach: bodybuilders at Muscle Beach and head shops on the boardwalk, and multi-million-dollar homes along the Venice Canals. *(Ch. 7)*

3 Catch Waves in Malibu

Surfrider Beach is part of a stretch of Malibu that includes the Malibu Pier and is a popular point for surfers and beach bums alike. On Zuma Beach surfers share the water with sea lions. *(Ch. 7)*

4 Suspend Disbelief at Universal Studios

Tour sets like *Jaws* and *Back to the Future*, or visit The Wizarding World of Harry Potter and Jurassic World. *(Ch. 7)*

5 Dive Into History in Chinatown

At the largest Chinatown outside of Asia and the oldest Chinatown in the United States, see Chinatown Dragon Gate and Golden Gate Fortune Cookie Factory. *(Ch. 16)*

6 Spot Whales in Monterey

Depending on the season, you can charter boats to witness gray, humpback, and blue whales spyhopping, breaching, and shooting water out of their spouts. *(Ch. 12)*

7 Drink All the Wine at a Wine Tasting

Up and down the California coast are some of the best winemakers on the planet and the crown jewels reside in Napa and Sonoma counties. *(Ch. 18)*

8 Hike the Hollywood Sign

The iconic Hollywood sign was originally erected in 1923 and read "Hollywoodland." The easiest path starts from the Griffith Park Observatory. *(Ch. 7)*

9 Cross the Golden Gate Bridge

Opened in 1937, this mile-long suspension bridge connects San Francisco to Marin County and is a stunning display of engineering. *(Ch. 16)*

10 Get a Bird's-Eye View of Palm Springs

Ride the Palm Springs Aerial Tramway—the largest rotating tramway in the world. At the top (8,516 feet) are restaurants and hiking trails. *(Ch. 5)*

11 Relive Youth at Disneyland

This truly is the happiest place on Earth. *(Ch. 6)*

12 Find Jaw-Dropping Vistas at Big Sur

Spectacular Highway 1 winds around the Pacific Ocean and through jagged mountains and redwood trees. *(Ch. 11)*

13 Explore the San Diego Safari Park

The San Diego Safari Park is a great way to learn about wildlife without the typical claustrophobic animal cages. *(Ch. 4)*

14 Commune with Nature at Yosemite National Park

Yosemite is known for its giant sequoia trees, epic waterfalls, and abundance of wildlife. *(Ch. 14)*

15 Visit Winchester Mystery House

This Victorian mansion was built in 1884 and is said to be haunted by the ghosts of people killed by Winchester rifles.

16 Camp in Joshua Tree

Just east of Palm Springs is this national park, named for the yucca trees which Mormons named after the biblical Joshua, who raised his hands into the sky. *(Ch. 8)*

17 Traverse Death Valley

One of the hottest places on Earth, Death Valley sits on the eastern edge of California along the border with Nevada. *(Ch. 13)*

18 Spend the Night at the Madonna Inn

San Luis Obispo is home to one of the most eccentric hotels in the country. No two rooms are the same, making each stay unique. *(Ch. 11)*

19 Ski at Mammoth

Near Yosemite National Park, Mammoth Mountain is the largest ski resort in California and is built on a volcano. Approximately 3,500 acres of skiable area hosts millions of skiers and snowboarders each year. *(Ch. 15)*

20 Witness Greatness in Sport

Sports fans can see the Lakers or Dodgers in Los Angeles, the Giants, Golden State Warriors, or '49ers in San Francisco, or the Kings in Sacramento. *(Ch. 7, 16, 17, 20)*

21 Go to a Show Taping in L.A.

Dozens of sitcoms, talk shows, and game shows film every day in Los Angeles, and you can get tickets to be an audience member. *(Ch. 7)*

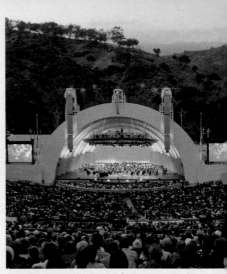

22 See a Concert at the Hollywood Bowl

A live music amphitheater built into the side of the Hollywood Hills, the venue is known for its incredible acoustics. *(Ch. 7)*

23 See Stars on the Hollywood Walk of Fame

The first stars were officially revealed in the early 1960s and today there are more than 2,600 dotting the pavement. *(Ch. 7)*

24 Experience Opulence at the Hearst Castle

Once a celebrity hotspot hosting roaring '20s parties, you can tour the palace's zoo, gold-leaf Roman pool, and priceless art collection. *(Ch. 11)*

25 Get an Adrenaline Rush at Lake Tahoe

Straddling California and Nevada, Lake Tahoe is a summer and winter wonderland for adventure enthusiasts. *(Ch. 21)*

What's New in California

FOODIE PARADISE

In 2019 California passed the 40-million mark in population. The Golden State draws citizens from all over the globe, which is reflected in its diverse culinary scene. Arguably the birthplace of the farm-to-table movement—chef Alice Waters opened Berkeley's Chez Panisse in 1971 emphasizing local, seasonal ingredients and international cooking techniques—California is home to restaurants of every major cuisine. Young chefs up and down the state are challenging old ideas about preparing and presenting food.

The food-truck frenzy of nearly a decade ago has proven more than fad. Gourmet food courts like downtown Sacramento's The Bank, which opened inside an ornate restored former bank, modify the concept indoors. Likewise, pop-up restaurants, with guest chefs offering innovative menus in unconventional settings for a limited time, have moved beyond the trendy phase.

California chefs continue to shop locally for produce and farmer-sourced meat, and many restaurants proudly display the names of their vendors on the menu. Chefs and foodies alike engage in discourse and politicking about food and farming, sometimes for high stakes. During the 2010s, a ban on foie gras was enforced, overturned, and finally reinstated after the U.S. Supreme Court refused in 2019 to intervene.

Sustainably harvested seafood and "snout to tail" cooking, where as much of the animal is used as possible in an attempt to reduce food waste, remain hot topics these days, not to mention the notion that for ethical, health, and climatic reasons we should eschew animal proteins altogether. Even the local steak house is likely to include vegan- and vegetarian-friendly dishes on its menu.

FAMILY FUN

California's theme parks work overtime to keep current. Disneyland stays cutting edge with the mid-2019 debut of Star Wars: Galaxy's Edge, a tech-driven new "land" with major Star Wars–theme attractions, restaurants, and other diversions.

Not to be outdone, LEGOLAND CALIFORNIA, which turned 20 in 2019, introduced an action-filled short film blending 3D computer animation and 4D "real-world" effects.

San Francisco's Exploratorium, the prototype for hands-on science museums, celebrated its 50th anniversary in 2019 with a slew of large and small STEM-oriented exhibits. With trees as tall as they come, the Children's Forest Trail in timeless Humboldt Redwoods State Park is a great place for kids to romp through some awe-inspiring landscapes.

At 12 miles north of San Francisco's Golden Gate Bridge, the redwoods of Muir Woods National Monument are more easily accessed, though be advised that since 2018 a parking or shuttle reservation is required to stroll through these trees.

WINE DISCOVERIES

The move toward sustainable grape growing has also picked up steam, with more than two-thirds of wineries certified for some or all of their vineyards and facilities. As 2019 dawned, Sonoma County was on track to reach its goal of being 100% sustainable by the end of the year. Although together the Napa Valley and Sonoma County produce only 10% of the Golden State's wines, reputation-wise they overshadow other areas. Popular in their own right for high-quality wines, lower prices, and homespun hospitality are Mendocino

County's Anderson Valley, Santa Barbara County, Paso Robles, the Gold Country, and the Lodi area south of Sacramento.

Napa and Sonoma have largely recovered from the October 2017 fires. Unfortunately, the Malibu appellation in Southern California, just establishing itself, was hard hit by fires in late 2018. On the bright side, *Wine Enthusiast* magazine named the Temecula Valley, a 90-minute drive south of Los Angeles and an hour's drive north of San Diego, one of its 10 Best Wine Travel Destinations of 2019 (in the world), high praise for a region many of whose four dozen or so wineries are less than a decade or two old.

ALL ABOARD

A large exhibit in the California State Railroad Museum in Sacramento describes the state's high-speed rail project, which if completed in 2030 as planned will connect San Francisco and Los Angeles in less than three hours. Until then, the best trip is on the luxuriously appointed *Coast Starlight,* a long-distance train with sleeping cars that runs between Seattle and Los Angeles, passing some of California's most beautiful coastline.

Napa Valley Wine Train continues to add themed excursions like murder-mystery dinners. To the east in the Gold Country's Jamestown you can hop aboard a steam train that departs from a historic roundhouse. North of Sonoma in Mendocino County the Skunk Train winds its way through the redwoods, though since 2018 the real treat has been to view the trees pedaling the same rails on two-person, side-by-side reclining bikes outfitted for the track.

BUILDING SPREE

A building spree south of San Francisco's Market Street, most notably the Salesforce Tower, which opened in 2018, has remade the downtown skyline. At 1,070 feet the tower is the city's highest building and the second tallest west of the Mississippi.

Lower to the ground, the Golden State Warriors opened the 2019–20 NBA season at the billion-dollar, beyond-state-of-the-art Chase Center along the waterfront. Down south, Los Angeles Stadium at Hollywood Park, the new home of the NFL's Rams and Chargers, is slated to open in time for the 2020 football season. It's one of many venues preparing to host events at the 2028 Olympics, which in addition to spurring sports-related construction is also bringing changes to transportation infrastructure.

A multiyear expansion of Los Angeles International Airport (LAX) begins in 2020. Already in the works were numerous improvements to the L.A. Metro subway system, a valuable resource for visitors to the West's largest city.

WHAT'S WHERE

1 San Diego. San Diego's Gaslamp Quarter and early California–theme Old Town have a human scale—but big-ticket animal attractions like the San Diego Zoo pull in visitors.

2 Orange County. A diverse destination with premium resorts and restaurants, strollable waterfront communities, and kid-friendly attractions.

3 Los Angeles. Go for the glitz of the entertainment industry, but stay for the rich cultural attributes and communities.

4 The Central Coast. Three of the state's top stops—swanky Santa Barbara, Hearst Castle, and Big Sur—sit along the scenic 200-mile route. A quick boat trip away lies scenic Channel Islands National Park.

5 Palm Springs and the Desert Resorts. Golf on some of the West's most challenging courses, lounge at fabulous resorts, check out mid-century-modern architectural gems, and trek through primitive desert parks.

6 Joshua Tree National Park. Proximity to major urban areas—as well as

NEVADA

UTAH

ARIZONA

moth

O Bishop

O Big Pine

anyon
nal

1

Sequoia
National
Park

ernville

sfield

ACHAPI MTS.

Lancaster
O

Stovepipe
Wells

Furnace Creek

8
Death Valley
Junction

Death Valley
National
Park

China
Lake

O Ridgecrest

MOJAVE
DESERT

15

Barstow

Victorville
O

Wrightwood
O

Lake
Arrowhead

O Pasadena

3

Beach

LOS ANGELES

O Santa Ana

Huntington
Beach

Catalina
Island

Clemente

San
Bernardino

O Riverside

Temecula

Oceanside

Del Mar
La Jolla O

SAN DIEGO
O Tijuana

MEXICO

Las Vegas

Lake
Mead

Baker

Mojave
National
Preserve

Needles

Amboy

Twentynine
Palms

6

Palm
Springs

Joshua Tree
National Park

5

Indio

Desert
Center

10

Blythe

Julian

Salton
Sea

Brawley

El Centro
O

Yuma

8

Mexicali

world-class rock climbing
and nighttime celestial
displays—help make this
one of the most visited
national parks.

7 Mojave Desert.
Material pleasures are in
short supply here, but
Mother Nature's stark
beauty more than
compensates.

**8 Death Valley National
Park.** America's second-
largest national park is
vast, beautiful, and often
the hottest place in the
nation.

9 Eastern Sierra. In the
Mammoth Lakes region,
sawtooth mountains and
deep powdery snowdrifts
create the state's premier
conditions for skiing and
snowboarding.

**10 Yosemite National
Park.** The views immor-
talized by photographer
Ansel Adams—towering
granite monoliths,
verdant glacial valleys,
and lofty waterfalls—are
still camera-ready.

**11 Sequoia and Kings
Canyon National Parks.**
The sight of ancient
redwoods towering above
jagged mountains is
breathtaking.

12 Monterey Bay Area.
Postcard-perfect
Monterey, Victorian-
flavored Pacific Grove,
and exclusive Carmel all
share this stretch of
California coast. To the

WHAT'S WHERE

north, Santa Cruz boasts a boardwalk, a UC campus, ethnic clothing shops, and plenty of surfers.

13 San Francisco.
To see why so many have left their hearts here, you need to visit the city's iconic neighborhoods—posh Pacific Heights, the Hispanic Mission, and gay-friendly Castro.

14 The Bay Area.
The area that rings San Francisco is nothing like the city—but it is home to some of the nation's great universities, fabulous bay views, Silicon Valley, and Alice Waters's Chez Panisse.

15 Napa and Sonoma.
By virtue of award-winning vintages, luxe lodgings, and epicurean eats, Napa and Sonoma counties retain their title as *the* California Wine Country.

16 The North Coast.
The star attractions here are natural ones, from the secluded beaches and wave-battered bluffs of Point Reyes National Seashore to the towering redwood forests.

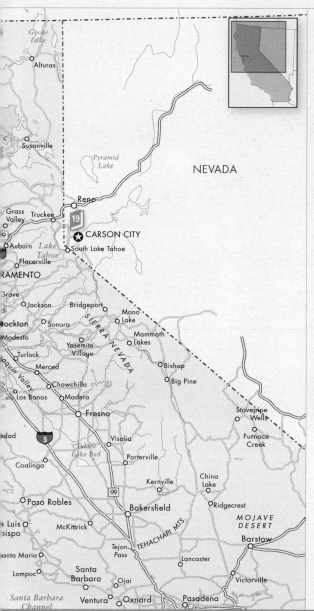

17 Redwood National Park. More than 200 miles of trails, ranging from easy to strenuous, allow visitors to see these spectacular trees in their primitive environments.

18 Sacramento and the Gold Country. The 1849 gold rush that built San Francisco and Sacramento began here, and the former mining camps strung along 185 miles of Highway 49 replay their past to the hilt.

19 Lake Tahoe. With miles of crystalline water reflecting the peaks of the High Sierra, Lake Tahoe is the perfect setting for activities like hiking and golfing in summer and skiing and snowmobiling in winter.

20 The Far North. California's far northeast corner is home to snowcapped Mount Shasta, the pristine Trinity Wilderness, and abundant backwoods character.

What to Eat and Drink in California

Tacos

TACOS
The Mexican influence on California has taken the taco to all new heights. For modern/gourmet fare: Guerrilla Tacos in Los Angeles; for fish tacos: Best Fish Taco in Ensenada; for the "Best Taco in California": Nuestro Mexico in Bakersfield; and for simple and classic: La Taqueria in San Francisco.

SOURDOUGH BREAD
In California, sourdough history is tied to the gold rush, when French bakers set up shop in San Francisco to feed the miners. The perfect loaf can be found at Boudin Bakery in San Francisco where they've been perfecting the sourdough recipe since 1849.

MEZCAL
Mezcal is made from the agave plant, typically in Oaxaca, Mexico, so naturally the best Oaxacan restaurant in L.A. (Guelaguetza) would have a top-shelf selection. Other great spots include modern taco joint Petty Cash, and Madre! in Torrance.

Dim sum

WINE AND BEER
California produces world-class wines, but it is also a hotbed of beer making. Check out Stone Brewing in San Diego, Eagle Rock Brewery in L.A., 21st Amendment in San Francisco, or the ultimate classic Sierra Nevada Brewing in Chico.

FRENCH DIP
Not only was the French Dip invented in Los Angeles, two different restaurants claim its origin. Philippe the Original in Downtown opened in 1908 and is a counter-style diner; Cole's also opened in 1908, is (slightly) more upscale, and features a hidden speakeasy in the back of the restaurant.

MAI TAIS
White rum, dark rum, Curaçao liqueur, orgeat syrup, and lime juice. The drink was invented (allegedly) by Victor Bergeron of Trader Vic's in Oakland, California, though Donn Beach (of Don the Beachcomber fame) claims he invented it in the 1930s in Hollywood.

DONUTS
Donuts in Los Angeles have taken on a life of their own with some of the most inventive and creative sweets around. There's the iconic Randy's Donuts; California Donuts covered with Lucky Charms; Blinkie's Donut Emporium filled with Bavarian cream; or Colorado Donuts where donut design is Instagram-worthy.

DIM SUM
There are more Asian Americans in the San Gabriel Valley than almost any other locale in the United States, and the food culture here rivals the best restaurants in Asia. The most delicious dim sum (dumplings typically eaten at breakfast) can be had at Din Tai Fung.

GARLIC
Gilroy is just south of San Jose and is considered the garlic capital of the world. The city is known for its extensive garlic crop, garlic-themed restaurants, and the annual Gilroy Garlic Festival that takes place every summer.

KOREAN BBQ
Los Angeles has the largest Korean population outside of Korea, and that fact is very much reflected in the food. For traditional Korean BBQ feasts, check out Park's BBQ, Kobawoo House, or Soot Bull Jeep.

Best Wineries in Napa and Sonoma

JOSEPH PHELPS VINEYARDS

In good weather, there are few more glorious tasting spots in the Napa Valley than the terrace at this St. Helena winery. Phelps is known for its Cabernet Sauvignons and Insignia, a Bordeaux blend. The wine-related seminars here are smart and entertaining.

SCRIBE

Two sons of walnut growers established this winery on land in Sonoma first planted to grapes in the late 1850s by a German immigrant. Their food-friendly wines include Riesling, Sylvaner, Chardonnay, Pinot Noir, Syrah, and Cabernet Sauvignon.

RIDGE VINEYARDS

Oenophiles will be familiar with Ridge, which produces some of California's best Cabernet Sauvignon, Chardonnay, and Zinfandel. You can taste wines made from grapes grown here at Ridge's Healdsburg vineyards, and some from its neighbors, along with wines made at its older Santa Cruz Mountains winery.

ASHES AND DIAMONDS

Record producer Kashy Khaledi opened this winery whose splashy glass-and-metal tasting space evokes classic mid-century modern California architecture. In their restrained elegance, the all- Bordeaux wines by two much-heralded pros hark back to 1960s Napa, too.

THE DONUM ESTATE

Single-vineyard Pinot Noirs exhibiting "power yet elegance" made the reputation of this Carneros District winery also known for smooth, balanced Chardonnays. The three dozen–plus large-scale, museum-quality outdoor sculptures by the likes of Anselm Kiefer add a touch of high culture to a visit.

SMITH-MADRONE WINERY

Step back in time at this Spring Mountain winery where two brothers named Smith make wines in a weathered, no-frills redwood barn. Founder Stu has been doing the farming and Charlie has been making the wines for more than four decades at this place with splendid valley views.

SILVER OAK

"Only one wine can be your best," was cofounder Justin Meyer's rationale for Silver Oak's decision to focus solely on Cabernet. The winery pours its two yearly offerings (one from Napa, the other from Sonoma) in a glass-walled eco-friendly tasting room in the Alexander Valley.

Inglenook

INGLENOOK

History buffs won't want to miss Inglenook, which was founded in the 19th century by a Finnish sea captain and rejuvenated over the past several decades by filmmaker Francis Ford Coppola. You can learn all about this fabled property on a tour or while tasting in an opulent salon—or just sip peacefully at a wine bar with a picturesque courtyard.

SCHRAMSBERG

The 19th-century cellars at sparkling wine producer Schramsberg hold millions of bottles. On the fascinating tour you'll learn how the bubblies at this Calistoga mainstay are made using the *méthode traditionelle,* and how the bottles are "riddled" (turned every few days) by hand.

IRON HORSE VINEYARDS

Proof that tasting sparkling wine doesn't have to be stuffy, this winery on the outskirts of Sebastopol pours its selections outdoors, with tremendous views of vine-covered hills that make the top-notch bubblies (and a few still wines) taste even better.

Best Beaches in San Diego

CORONADO

Often praised for its sparkling sand, the island is home to Hotel del Coronado, a 130-year-old luxury hotel perfect for post-beach snacks; Del Beach, which is open to the public; and Dog Beach where pooches can run free sans leash.

MISSION BEACH

Located near SeaWorld San Diego, Mission Beach is home to a bustling board-walk that's frequented by walkers, cyclists, and people-watchers. The bay is popular for water sports such as stand-up paddle boarding and Jet Skiing, but the beach is best known for Belmont Park, its ocean-front amusement park.

WINDANSEA BEACH

Seasoned surfers should head to La Jolla's Windan-sea Beach for powerful waves. Tucked away in a residential area, Windan-sea's entrance is marked by large rocks that make for a great place to watch or dry out, but recreational swimming is not advised here due to the strong surf.

TORREY PINES STATE BEACH

Situated at the base of a 1,500-acre natural reserve, La Jolla's Torrey Pines State Beach offers a long, narrow stretch of pristine beach framed by picturesque sea cliffs. Beachgoers can add a hike to their itinerary that starts or finishes on the sand, with plenty of lookout areas for great photo ops. Beyond the bluffs, a salt marsh provides seclusion from businesses and their associated street noise.

LA JOLLA SHORES

Pack up the whole family for a beach day in La Jolla Shores, which is known for its calm waves, two parks, and playground. Sea caves and underwater canyons that are part of La Jolla Underwater Park and Ecological Reserve—a marine protected area—attract kayakers and scuba divers.

DEL MAR CITY BEACH

In the upscale coastal neighborhood of Del Mar lie two beach parks that are popular for special events because of their stunning views of the Pacific. Seagrove Park is perched on the hill at the end of 15th Street, with benches for ocean gazing and winding paths along the bluffs. Farther north across the railroad tracks, Powerhouse Park offers easy beach access, a playground area, and a volleyball court.

SWAMI'S STATE BEACH

West of the magnificent Self-Realization Fellow-ship Temple and Medita-tion Gardens in Encinitas,

La Jolla Shores

this beach draws surfers and yogis in with its Zen vibes, while others treat the steep staircase leading down to the beach as a workout, with a rewarding view of sea cliffs waiting at the bottom. At low tide, shells and other sea creatures are left behind for beachcombers to easily discover.

FLETCHER COVE BEACH PARK

Nestled in the heart of Solana Beach, Fletcher Cove Beach Park doubles as a recreational park and beach access area. Here you'll find a basketball court, playground, lawn area, and picnic tables. A paved ramp leads down to the crescent-shaped beach that's flanked by cliffs on

both sides. For sweeping views of the ocean, position yourself at one of the lookouts outfitted with seating and/or binoculars—yup, binoculars are waiting for you.

BEACON'S BEACH

Follow the windy dirty path laden with switchbacks down to find Beacon's Beach in Encinitas, a well-known beach spot and favorite locals' hangout; on maps it may be labeled Leucadia State Beach. Since its entrance is hidden below sea cliffs on a one-way residential street, Beacon's Beach has an air of exclusivity. With plenty of space to spread out here, you won't have to infringe on sun-worshipping neighbors.

MOONLIGHT STATE BEACH

Fans of active beach days should head to this Encinitas beach. Volleyball courts, picnic tables, and playgrounds line the beach, with a concession stand, equipment rentals, and free Sunday concerts in high season.

10 Best Photo Ops in San Francisco

THE PALACE OF FINE ARTS

Perched on a swan-filled lagoon near the marina's yacht harbor, this stirringly beautiful terra-cotta-color domed structure has an otherworldly quality about it. Built in 1915, the palace is a San Francisco architect's version of a Roman ruin, and it's been eliciting gasps for almost a century. It's a popular wedding spot if you like happy couples in your photos.

THE PAINTED LADIES

Familiar to fans of the 1990s' TV show "Full House," the so-called Painted Ladies or Seven Sisters are a row of seven gorgeous and beautifully maintained Queen Anne–style houses just off Alamo Square. Take photos at midday for clear city views.

LANDS END COASTAL TRAIL

This 4-mile trail winds and twists along the rugged cliffs of the San Francisco bay, offering stunning views of the Golden Gate Bridge and surprisingly woodsy forest. At the 1.3-mile mark, turn left at the wooden staircase to explore Mile Rock Beach and the Lands End Labyrinth. On a clear day, you can see the Golden Gate Bridge in the distance.

TWIN PEAKS

These two adjacent peaks are at the near geographic center of San Francisco and at an elevation of 925 feet. Especially pretty (and popular) at sunrise and sunset, you'll find sweeping 180-degree views of the Bay Area, with a great view of downtown San Francisco, the Bay Bridge, and the tips of the Golden Gate Bridge.

THE PRESIDIO

As the gateway to the Golden Gate Bridge, San Francisco's 1,500-acre Presidio National Park offers incredible views of the bridge and the sprawling vistas that surround it. The Presidio also abuts Baker Beach, a stretch of sand that lies below the park's western cliffs and offers alternative angles of the Golden Gate Bridge, Baker Beach.

TREASURE ISLAND

Despite its proximity to downtown San Francisco, the tiny, man-made Treasure Island is generally off the tourist track so your photos won't be crowded with selfie-takers. Set right in the middle of San Francisco Bay, it offers gorgeous views and photos of the San Francisco skyline, especially at night when the skyline is lit up.

MUIR WOODS

John Muir wrote, "Most people are on the world, not in it—have no conscious sympathy or relationship to anything about them..." It's hard not to feel connected as you walk the shaded paths of Muir Woods amid the towering majesty of the redwood forests. It will live on in your memories.

HAWK HILL

Located at a high point on the south-facing Marin Headlands, Hawk Hill lies opposite the city and offers views of the Golden Gate Bridge as it enters San Francisco. True to its name, it's also a great spot for nature watching. Hawk Hill is the site of the autumnal raptor migration, and is also a habitat for the Mission Blue Butterfly.

BERNAL HEIGHTS

Pictures of Bernal Heights Hill show a somewhat stumpy-looking hill that rises unenthusiastically above the houses of the surrounding neighborhood. But, pictures taken *from* Bernal Heights Hill offer 360-degree panoramic views. Take a sunset stroll here for stunning San Fran shots.

UNION SQUARE

This lively and central location is a great spot to capture cable cars as they rumble by. Also, the towering pillar of Dewey Monument, topped triumphantly by Nike, the Greek goddess of victory, is a legitimately beautiful sculpture. Relax on the steps and soak in/photograph the city.

10 Best Celebrity Hangouts in L.A.

THE HOLLYWOOD ROOSEVELT

The Hollywood Roosevelt is one of L.A.'s oldest hotels, and has hosted numerous celebrities and dignitaries in its Spanish Colonial Revival rooms. Set in the heart of Hollywood, it offers a convenient location as well as a number of watering holes, including Tropicana Pool & Café and The Spare Room. Incidentally, it's also one of the city's most haunted places, so if you don't spot a celeb, you may bump into a ghost.

THE GROVE

L.A. may be strewn with outdoor malls, but it's The Grove that gets the highest billing, not just for its collection of mid-to high-end shops and restaurants, but also for its next-door neighbor, the Farmers Market. It's also one of the best places to see stars like Lena Headey, Zendaya, and Mario Lopez.

CAFÉ GRATITUDE LARCHMONT

Round out your L.A. vacation with a plantbased meal at local chain, Café Gratitude. For a celeb sighting, head to their Larchmont Blvd. location where Jake Gyllenhaal and Beyoncé, obligingly declare what they're grateful for before digging in.

PINZ BOWLING CENTER

For a bit of family-friendly fun, head to Pinz in Studio City, where bowling is more than just a game, it's also a neon- and black-light party. Every lane comes with an automated ordering system so you can overload on wings and fries without ever leaving your spot. Celebrities often pop in here for bowling night, from A-listers like Vin Diesel and Jessica Alba to performers like Bruno Mars and Missy Elliott.

NOBU MALIBU

Nobu is a known A-list hotspot that's hosted everyone from Keanu Reeves to Kendall Jenner. Even if you don't spot a star, it's still worth the trip for its impeccable sushi and sashimi. Be warned, though: mingling with A-listers doesn't come cheap.

Catch

TOSCANA

Upscale Brentwood is home to many celebrities, and rustic trattoria Toscana is one of their neighborhood haunts. It may not be L.A.'s best Italian restaurant—for that, check out Jon & Vinny's —but for star sightings, it's your best bet. Jennifer Garner, Reese Witherspoon, and Heidi Klum have dined here.

CATCH

Secure a table at the flora-cluttered Catch in West Hollywood and rub elbows with the likes of David Beckham and the Jenner-Kardashian clan. This eatery is as L.A. as you can get, with its al fresco setting, vegan and gluten-free offerings, and locally and sustainably grown ingredients.

CRAIG'S

A West Hollywood dining staple, Craig's plain façade provides a safe haven for the movie industry's most important names and well-known faces like John Legend and Chrissy Teigen. We're not going to lie: this joint is always busy, so you might not even get a table. It's a good thing the food is worth the effort.

RUNYON CANYON

Out of L.A.'s numerous beautiful hiking spots, Runyon Canyon gets the biggest share of celebrity regulars, probably because it's strategically tucked between the Hollywood Hills, where many stars live, and the Hollywood strip. It's also a great venue for getting some fresh air, not to mention an ideal spot to take panoramic sunset photos.

CHATEAU MARMONT

The Chateau Marmont is possibly L.A.'s best-known celebrity haunt. Come for brunch in the garden terrace or drop in at night for the Hollywood-inspired cocktails. Photos not allowed.

What to Watch and Read Before Your Trip

BLADE RUNNER

This iconic piece of '80s cci-fi about a dystopian future L.A. (the year is 2019), has become a cult classic, inspiring a recent sequel set in 2049. The original stars a young Harrison Ford who has the exciting, complicated job of hunting down (and sometimes fighting off) realistic human replicas—and picking them out among other Angelinos.

MULHOLLAND DRIVE

Surreal, psychotic, and artsy, David Lynch's Mulholland Drive paints L.A. as city of scary fun house turns that blur the lines between reality and cuts from a movie. Such dichotomies exist as well in the two main characters: Betty (Naomi Watts), the blond Midwesterner fresh to L.A. and full of dreams, and Rita, an amnesiac whose life seems to be shrouded in violence, darkness and mystery.

TANGERINE

Shot completely with an iPhone camera, this indie film explores the streets of Hollywood with a close lens on a few very moving, human characters. Recently out of prison, a transgender prostitute tries to track down her pimp and his new girlfriend with the help of a friend. It's hard to explain just how much light, humor, and beauty fills this film—you just have to see it for yourself.

THE REVOLT OF THE COCKROACH PEOPLE BY OSCAR ZETA ACOSTA

This story about Chicano radicalization in east Los Angeles is based on very real events, and outlines many aspects of the Chicano movement through the protests, marches, and court cases at its plot. The protagonist lawyer is based on Oscar Zeta Acosta himself, an author, activist, and lawyer/politician with his own fascinating life (and mysterious disappearance), and a key player in the movement.

THE BIRDS

Alfred Hitchcock's 1963 The Birds centers around a small Northern Californian town under attack by swarming, possessed birds. You'll never again look at a crow in quite the same way after watching it. Perhaps the focus on commonly found creatures is what makes this one of the director's most graphic thrillers. When you aren't distracted by the demonic winged creatures, there are breathtaking views of the Sonoma County's coastal drives, and the charming 1960s small town of Bodega Bay, where almost all of the movie was filmed.

THE GIRLS BY EMMA CLINE

In this nuanced story about coming-of-age in the Sonoma County town of Petaluma, the 14-year-old narrator yearns for excitement, attention and beauty—and falls into the violent, psychological mind-trip of a Charles Manson–like cult. Beautiful and gripping, Cline's novel shares a gritty, late 1960s Sonoma County—one that couldn't be further from the world of Cabernets and Pinots—instead full of long hair, VW buses, angst, and seduction.

FAST TIMES AT RIDGEMONT HIGH

This humorous coming-of-age film has become somewhat of a cult classic, but many people don't know it's based on the book and journalistic efforts of Cameron Crowe (the young Rolling Stone prodigy reporter). Cameron spent a year undercover in Clairemont High School in San Diego, and the book and movie tell the account of this wild, adolescent year and the characters he meets.

THE GANGSTER WE ARE ALL LOOKING FOR BY LE THI DIEM THUY

The characters of Thuy's novel are Vietnamese refugees in the late '70s, adjusting to life in crowded bungalows and apartments of Normal Heights, Linda Vista, and east San Diego. The protagonist, a young girl, flees Vietnam with her father and is sponsored by a church-going family in San Diego after their long journey. The novel is based on the author's own childhood.

GUN, WITH OCCASIONAL MUSIC BY JONATHAN LETHEM

Lethem—the recipient of a MacArthur "genius" grant and an accomplished novelist—started his career with a captivating but decidedly weird novel set in San Francisco and Oakland. In the sci-fi noir detective story *Gun, With Occasional Music* people rub elbows with talking, man-sized genetically engineered animals and everyone lives under a monetized "karma" system similar to what modern-day China has begun using to track and influence its residents. It's a compelling, not-quite-dystopian vision set in the near-yet-distant future and highlights what San Francisco might become with just a little (okay, a lot) of rampant genetic experimentation.

BURMA SUPERSTAR BY DESMOND TAN AND KATE LEAHY

Burmese food is an increasingly popular dining option in San Francisco, and Burma Superstar is a hit restaurant drawing in a multitude of diners. Tan and Leahy's cookbook offers a look into the flavor-packed southeast Asian cuisine which is finally starting to get the recognition it deserves. If you're someone who wants to learn more about Burmese food, or are seeking to re-create the joy and bombastic flavors found at this San Francisco restaurant, this is a must-own.

Chapter 2

TRAVEL SMART CALIFORNIA

Updated by
Daniel Mangin

★ **CAPITAL:**
Sacramento

☏ **COUNTRY CODE:**
1

⊘ **TIME:**
Three hours behind New York

⊛ **POPULATION:**
40.1 million

⚠ **EMERGENCIES:**
911

⊕ **WEB RESOURCES:**
www.visitcalifornia.
com, www.parks.ca.gov,
www.dot.ca.gov/cttravel,
travel.state.gov

💬 **LANGUAGE:**
English

🚗 **DRIVING:**
On the right

$ **CURRENCY:**
U.S. dollar

⚡ **ELECTRICITY:**
120-240 v/60 cycles; plugs
have two or three rectangu-
lar prongs

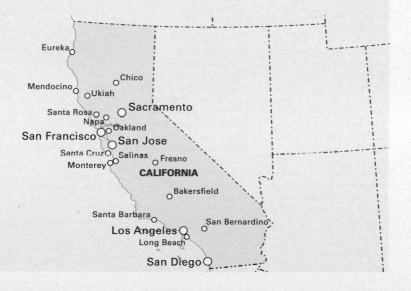

10 Things To Know Before You Go

There are many reasons why the Golden State is the greatest state.: it's huge, diverse, and unique. It has the largest population in America, the most national parks, and the fifth- largest economy in the world? Bottom line, California is incredible, but before you head out there, there are a few things you should really know before you visit the best, biggest, boldest, and baddest state in the Union.

IT AIN'T SMALL

California is the third-largest state behind Alaska and Texas and in square miles is similar in size to France, Spain, Sweden, and Thailand. If you want to drive from San Francisco to Los Angeles, it'll take you about six hours (without traffic). California also has about 40 million people, which ranks it first in the United States and about three million more than the entire country of Canada. It's big.

YOUR WEATHER FORECAST

Depending on where you're going, seasons may be considered optional. Basic lessons: the farther south you go (Los Angeles, Palm Springs, San Diego) the weather tends to be drier and hotter. The farther north (San Jose, San Francisco, Sacramento), cooler and wetter. But with deserts, beaches, mountains, and forests, visitors should prepare for a wide range of climate activity.

SPEAKING OF GEOGRAPHY

Did you know that California has the highest peak in the contiguous United States with Mt. Whitney coming in at 14,505 feet? Did you know that California has the eighth-lowest place on Earth and lowest in the United States with Death Valley coming in at 86 meters below sea level? Did you also know that California has the highest trees on the planet with redwoods reaching over 300 feet high? Did you know!?

TIME TO DRIVE

If there's a downside to exploring the Golden State, it's a lack of high-speed rail to get you around quickly. If you want to see all those deserts, beaches, mountains, and forests, you'll probably want to rent a car. On the plus side, California has some of the most scenic driving spots in the world. Check out the 17-mile drive through the coast of Monterey. Zip along the Pacific Coast Highway which spreads from the beaches of Malibu to the jagged peaks of Big Sur. Or traverse the historic Route 66 from Santa Monica to the Mojave Desert.

CALIFORNIA MAKES STUFF

One of the things that makes California special is its people and their inventiveness. Some of the world's most important inventions hail from this West Coast haven. Heard of blue jeans? California. Apple computers? California. Lasers? California. Skateboards? California. And a few others like sourdough bread, Popsicles, McDonald's, Barbie Dolls, and a little thing called television. Oh, and there's that whole Hollywood entertainment thing that started here as well.

ENTERTAINMENT!

You'd have to be living in a cave to not know that California, specifically Hollywood, is the entertainment capital of the world. But seeing stars isn't the only fun to be had. California packs a big punch on the entertainment front. There's Universal Studios, Disneyland, Disney's California Adventure, Knott's Berry Farm, Six Flags Magic Mountain, California's Great America, Legoland, and Sea World. If you're not having fun here, you're doing it wrong.

PLAY BALL

Because the weather is basically great year-round throughout the state, there's a huge sports culture with spectacular (and often free) outdoor areas and parks to play in.

On top of that, California has incredible surfing, skiing, hiking, biking, and so much more. But because of California's size, it also boasts the most professional sports teams of any state. California has a whopping 16 pro teams including the Los Angeles Lakers, San Francisco '49ers, Golden State Warriors, Los Angeles Dodgers, and many, many more. Any day of the week, you can witness athletic greatness at the highest levels.

IT'S GOT CLASS...AND CULTURE

California has the most museums of any state in America. There are nearly 3,000 museums across the great state that range from classic and modern art to natural and American history, to pop-culture, computers, and cars. If you can think of it, there's a museum for it.

BITES AND SIPS FOR DAYS

When you have the greatest agricultural output, it stands to reason that the food and wine are going to be outstanding. And they are. California is known for some of the world's best wine regions like Napa, Sonoma, and Paso Robles. But California is also a bastion for foodies. The Michelin Guide just announced its first-ever regional guide and chose California for the occasion. And for good reason. California is also the most diverse state in America and with that melting pot of international cultures, the restaurant world from end to end is second to none (yes, even when compared to New York).

CALL OF THE WILDLIFE

Many people naturally think of California's major cities, but because of the state's wide range of geography, it's also the perfect place for animal lovers to see some of the most diverse wildlife in the country. Off the coasts, the state boasts everything from gray and humpback whales to blue whales and orcas. You'll also encounter sea lions, elephant seals, and the occasional shark. Inland, there are forests with black bears and mountain lions, bighorn sheep and bobcats, beavers, and foxes. And for reptile and bird lovers, the desert provides endless fauna to gawk at.

Getting Here and Around

✈ Air Travel

Most national and many international airlines fly to California. Flying time to the state is about 6½ hours from New York and 4¾ hours from Chicago. Travel from London to either Los Angeles or San Francisco is 11½ hours and from Sydney approximately 14 hours. Flying between San Francisco and Los Angeles takes about 90 minutes.

🚌 Bus Travel

Greyhound is the primary bus carrier in California. Regional bus service is available in metropolitan areas.

🚗 Car Travel

A car is essential in most of California, the exceptions being parts of its largest cities, where it can be more convenient to use public transportation, taxis, or ride-sharing services. Two main north–south routes run through California: Interstate 5 through the middle of the state, and U.S. 101, a parallel route closer to the coast. Slower but more scenic is Highway 1, which winds along much of the coast.

From north to south, the state's main east–west routes are Interstate 80, Interstate 15, Interstate 10, and Interstate 8. Much of California is mountainous, and you may encounter winding roads and steep mountain grades.

ROAD CONDITIONS

Rainy weather can make driving along the coast or in the mountains treacherous. Some smaller routes over mountain ranges and in the deserts are prone to flash flooding. Many smaller roads over the Sierra Nevada are closed in

From Los Angeles To:	By Air	By Car
San Diego	55 mins	2 hrs
Death Valley	No flights	5 hrs
San Francisco	1 hr 30 mins	5 hrs 40 mins
Monterey	1 hr 10 mins	5 hrs
Santa Barbara	50 mins	1 hr 40 mins
Big Sur	No flights	5 hrs 40 mins
Sacramento	1 hr 30 mins	5 hrs 30 mins

From San Francisco To:	By Air	By Car
San Jose	No flights	1 hr
Monterey	45 mins	2 hrs
Los Angeles	1 hr 30 mins	5 hrs 40 mins
Portland, OR	1 hr 50 mins	10 hrs
Mendocino	No flights	3 hrs
Yosemite NP/ Fresno	1 hr	4 hrs
Lake Tahoe/ Reno	1 hr	3 hrs 30 mins

winter, and if it's snowing, tire chains may be required on routes that are open. ■TIP➔ It's less expensive to purchase chains before you get to the mountains. Chains or cables generally cost $30–$75, depending on tire size; cables are easier to attach than chains, but chains are more durable. Most rental-car companies prohibit chain installation on their vehicles. If you choose to disregard this rule, your insurance likely will not cover any chains-related damage.

In Northern California uniformed chain installers on Interstate 80 and U.S. 50 will apply chains for about $30 and take them off for half that. Chain installers

From Los Angeles To:	Route	Distance
San Diego	I–5 or I–405	127 miles
Las Vegas	I–10 to I–15	270 miles
Death Valley	I–10 to I–15 to Hwy. 127 to Hwy. 190	290 miles
San Francisco	I–5 to I–580 to I–80	382 miles
Monterey	U.S. 101 to Salinas, Hwy. 68 to Hwy. 1	320 miles
Santa Barbara	U.S. 101	95 miles
Big Sur	U.S. 101 to Hwy. 1	349 miles
Sacramento	I–5	391 miles

From San Francisco to:	Route	Distance
San Jose	U.S. 101	50 miles
Monterey	U.S. 101 to Hwy. 156 to Hwy. 1	120 miles
Los Angeles	U.S. 101 to Hwy. 156 to I–5	382 miles
Portland, OR	I–80 to I–505 to I–5	635 miles
Mendocino	Hwy. 1	174 miles
Yosemite NP	I–80 to I–580 to I–205 to Hwy. 120 east	184 miles
Lake Tahoe/Reno	I–80	220 miles

are independent businesspeople, not highway employees. They are not allowed to sell or rent chains. On smaller roads, you're on your own.

RULES OF THE ROAD

All passengers must wear a seat belt at all times. A child must be secured in a federally approved child passenger restraint system and ride in the back seat until at least eight years of age or until the child is at least 4 feet 9 inches tall. Unless indicated, right turns are allowed at red lights after you've come to a full stop. Drivers with a blood-alcohol level higher than 0.08 who are stopped by police are subject to arrest.

You must turn on your headlights whenever weather conditions require the use of windshield wipers. Texting on a wireless device is illegal. If using a mobile phone while driving it must be hands-free and mounted (i.e., it's not legal having it loose on the seat or your lap). For more driving rules, refer to the Department of Motor Vehicles driver's handbook at ⊕ www.dmv.ca.gov.

CAR RENTAL

When you reserve a car, ask about cancellation penalties, taxes, drop-off charges (to drop off in another city), and surcharges (for age, additional drivers, or driving across state or country borders).

🚆 Train Travel

Amtrak provides rail service within California. On some trips passengers board motor coaches part of the way. The rail service's scenic *Coast Starlight* trip begins in Los Angeles and hugs the Pacific Coast to San Luis Obispo before it turns inland for the rest of its journey to Portland and Seattle.

Before You Go

⊕ Passport

All foreign nationals must possess a valid passport to enter the United States. This includes infants and small children. In most cases, the passport must be valid for at least six months beyond your scheduled return date. Having a valid passport and visa does not guarantee entry to the United States. The final decision about eligibility is made at your place of entry by a U.S. Customs and Border Protection agent.

⊞ Visa

Foreign citizens visiting the United States must have a visa—among the most common being the Nonimmigrant Visitor Visa—unless they belong to one of the three dozen or so nations participating in the Visa Waiver Program. To qualify for the waiver program, visitors need an e-passport with an embedded electronic identification chip and must have an updated Electronic System for Travel Authorization (ESTA). ESTA is the automated system used by the U.S. Department of Homeland Security to determine whether an individual traveler qualifies for the waiver program. Note that even if your home country participates in the waiver program, you may not be eligible if you have recently visited a country on the U.S. terror-prevention list.

✎ Immunizations

The United States has no traveler vaccination requirements. The U.S.-based Centers for Disease Control and Prevention (CDC) maintains a list of current infectious-disease outbreaks within the country. The CDC recommends that prospective U.S. travelers from abroad rely on resources within their home country for health recommendations.

▤ U.S. Embassy/Consulate

Most U.S. embassies are located in host countries' capital cities, with consulates in additional cities. U.S. Foreign Service officers at embassies and consulates are available (usually by appointment) to interview foreign citizens wishing to visit the United States for business, tourism, or other eligible purposes, and paperwork can be filed with them.

▦ When to Go

Expect high summer heat in the desert areas and low winter temperatures in the Sierra Nevada and other inland mountain ranges.

HIGH SEASON $$$–$$$$
High season lasts from May through early September. Expect higher hotel occupancy rates and prices. In Northern California's Wine Country, high season lasts through October. In the Palm Springs desert resorts area, high season extends from mid-December into April.

LOW SEASON $$
From December to March, tourist activity slows. Except in the mountainous areas, which may see snowfall, winters here are mild and hotels are cheaper.

VALUE SEASON $$–$$$
From April to late May and from late September to mid-November the weather is pleasant and hotel prices are reasonable.

Essentials

🛏 Lodging

With just under 5,700 lodgings, California has inns, motels, hotels, and specialty accommodations to suit every traveler's fancy and finances. Retro motels recalling 1950s roadside culture but with 21st-century amenities are a recent popular trend, but you'll also see traditional motels and hotels, along with luxury resorts and boutique properties. Reservations are a good idea throughout the year but especially so in the summer. On weekends at smaller lodgings, minimum-stay requirements of two or three nights are common, though some places are flexible about this in winter. Some accommodations aren't suitable for children, so ask before you book.

The lodgings we review are the top choices in each price category. *For an expanded review of each property, please see www.fodors.com.* We don't specify whether the facilities cost extra; when pricing accommodations, ask what's included and what costs extra. *For price information, see the Planner section in each chapter.*

APARTMENT AND HOUSE RENTALS

You'll find listings for Airbnb and similar rentals throughout California.

BED-AND-BREAKFASTS

California has more than 1,000 bed-and-breakfasts. You'll find everything from simple homestays to lavish luxury lodgings, many in historic hotels and homes. The California Association of Boutique and Breakfast Inns has about 200 member properties that you can locate and book through its website.

HOTELS

Some properties allow you to cancel without any kind of penalty—even if you prepaid to secure a discounted rate—if you cancel at least 24 hours in advance. Others require you to cancel a week in advance or penalize you the cost of one night. Small inns and B&Bs are most likely to require you to cancel far in advance. Most hotels allow children under a certain age to stay in their parents' room at no extra charge, but others charge for them as extra adults; find out the cutoff age for discounts.

🍽 Dining

California has led the pack in bringing natural and organic foods to the forefront of American dining. Though rooted in European cuisine, California cooking sometimes has strong Asian and Latin influences. Wherever you go, you're likely to find that dishes are made with fresh produce and other local ingredients.

The restaurants we list are the cream of the crop in each price category. *For price information, see the Planner section in each chapter.*

DISCOUNTS AND DEALS

The better grocery and specialty-food stores have grab-and-go sections, with prepared foods on a par with restaurant cooking, perfect for picnicking.

MEALS AND MEALTIMES

Lunch is typically served from 11 or 11:30 to 2.30 or 3, with dinner service starting at 5 or 5:30 and lasting until 9 or later. Restaurants that serve breakfast usually open by 7, sometimes earlier, with some serving breakfast through the lunch hour. Most weekend brunches start at 10 or 11 and go at least until 2.

PAYING

Most restaurants take cash or credit cards, though a few don't accept the latter. In most establishments tipping is

Essentials

the norm, but some include the service in the menu price or add it to the bill. *For guidelines on tipping see Tipping, below.*

RESERVATIONS AND DRESS
It's a good idea to make a reservation when possible. Where reservations are indicated as essential, book a week or more ahead in summer and early fall. Large parties should always call ahead to check the reservations policy. Except as noted in individual listings, dress is informal.

🛍 Shopping

California is home to world-class shopping in its big cities, where you'll find all the major designer labels and fine-jewelry establishments represented. The state's northern half was the birthplace of the maker movement, but the sentiment quickly moved south; artisans throughout California craft beautifully made soaps, clothing from organic cotton, fashion jewelry from recycled products, and other handmade products.

In Southern California, Rodeo Drive in Beverly Hills ranks among the world's most famous shopping streets. South Coast Plaza, in the Orange County city of Costa Mesa, is the state's largest luxury mall. Horton Plaza and Fashion Valley have some of San Diego's best brand-name shopping. Head to the Inland Empire for outlet action.

In Northern California, San Francisco's Union Square attracts shopaholics, but far more intriguing are the neighborhood shops of local clothing and jewelry designers. In the Wine Country, check out the compact downtowns of Napa Valley and Sonoma County towns. Look for pottery and other crafts along the coast north and south of San Francisco.

🍸 Nightlife

The good life in California extends to the evening with skilled mixologists serving up farm-to-bar cocktails in big-city night spots, some of them modeled on speakeasies of yore, and regular ole bartenders providing an additional layer of atmosphere to dives in towns large and small.

In Southern California, look for hip hangouts in downtown Los Angeles, Hollywood, Silver Lake, and Los Feliz; for years L.A.'s nightlife revolved around the still popular Sunset Strip in West Hollywood, also known for its bustling gay scene. San Diego's Gaslamp Quarter and neighboring East Village offer numerous options—head to Hillcrest for the LGBT scene. In Santa Barbara, get the night going along State Street's southern stretch; you'll find the best desert nightlife in the town of Palm Springs.

In Northern California, San Francisco has a vibrant nightlife scene, with the broadest selection in Union Square, SoMA, and North Beach but the Mission and other outlying neighborhoods offering dives and diversity. Across the bay, check out Oakland's uptown neighborhood and Berkeley's downtown. Except for downtown Healdsburg and Napa most Wine Country towns are shorter on bar action and especially dancing; ditto for the North Coast and Far North. Santa Cruz has lively spots downtown.

🎭 Performing Arts

With 40 million residents California supplies a built-in audience for touring and homegrown companies from the worlds of dance, opera, theater, comedy, and music of all types. A-list performers appear at venues large and intimate, and numerous cultural festivals fill the calendar.

Catch the Southern California spirit at classic music venues like the Hollywood Bowl amphitheater and the Frank Gehry–designed Walt Disney Concert Hall in downtown Los Angeles. Head to Santa Barbara's historic Arlington and Granada theaters for plays, musicals, opera, symphony, and dance, and San Diego's Old Globe Theatre for regional productions. Each year the Palm Springs area hosts the Coachella Valley Music & Arts Festival, drawing 200,000-plus attendees for superstar performers from Beyoncé to David Byrne.

In Northern California, four historic San Francisco theaters present Broadway musicals and serious plays and comedies; a fifth venue presents opera and ballet, and a newer sixth one the San Francisco Symphony. Across the bay, Berkeley Repertory Theatre is another top troupe. In May, BottleRock Napa Valley, with dozens of rock, hip-hop, indie, and other bands, kicks off a summer of Wine Country concerts, some at wineries of high-profile brands like Robert Mondavi and Rodney Strong.

⊛ Activities

Athletic Californians often boast that it's possible to surf in the morning and ski in the afternoon (or vice versa) in the Golden State, and with thousands of hiking, biking, and horse-riding trails and hundreds of lakes, rivers, and streams for fishing, swimming, and boating—not to mention sandy coastal strands for sunning and surfing and other beaches with dunes or rocks to explore—there's no shortage of outdoor fun to be had. One challenge on many a hiker's bucket list, the Pacific Crest Trail, travels the length of the state. Eight national parks, most notably Yosemite, are in California, along with other National Park Service sites,

and the state park system here is robust. Professional baseball, football, basketball, and hockey are well represented at the major- and minor-league levels.

⊕ Health/Safety

Smoking is illegal in all California bars and restaurants. If you have a medical condition that may require emergency treatment, be aware that many rural and mountain communities have only daytime clinics, not hospitals with 24-hour emergency rooms.

Exercise caution while engaging in outdoor sports. At beaches, heed warnings about high surf and deadly rogue waves. Do not fly within 24 hours of scuba diving. When hiking, stay on trails and pay attention to trailhead warning signs about loose cliffs, predatory animals, and poison oak, which causes a severe rash.

Take the usual precautions to protect your person and belongings. In large cities, ask at your lodging about areas to avoid, and lock valuables in a hotel safe when not using them. Car break-ins are common in some larger cities, but it's always good idea to remove valuables from your car or at least keep them out of sight.

⊞ Hours of Operation

Banks in California are typically open weekdays from 9 to 6; most are open on Saturday but close on Sunday and most holidays. Smaller shops usually operate from 10 or 11 to 5 or 6, with larger stores remaining open until 8 or later. Hours vary for museums, historical sites, and state parks, and many are closed one or more days a week, or for extended periods during off-season months.

Essentials

💲 Money

Metro Los Angeles, San Francisco, and San Diego rank among the nation's most expensive places to live. Along the coast and at desert resorts, expect to pay top dollar for everything from gas and food to lodging and attractions. Prices in the Gold Country, the Far North, and the Death Valley/Mojave Desert region are somewhat lower than on the coast.

TAXES

The base California state sales tax is 7.25%, but local taxes can add as much as 3%. Exceptions include grocery-store food items and some take-out. Hotel taxes vary widely, from about 8% to 16.5%.

📷 Packing

The California lifestyle emphasizes casual wear, and with the generally mild climate you needn't worry about packing cold-weather clothing unless you're going into mountainous areas. Jeans, walking shorts, and T-shirts are fine in most situations. Few restaurants require men to wear a jacket or tie, though a collared shirt is the norm at upscale establishments.

Summer evenings can be cool, especially near the coast, where fog often rolls in. Always pack a sweater or light jacket. Comfortable walking shoes are a must. If you're headed to state or national parks, packing binoculars, clothes that layer, long pants and long-sleeve shirts, sunglasses, and a wide-brimmed hat is wise. You can pick up insect repellant, sunscreen, and a first-aid kit once in-state.

💵 Tipping

Tipping Guidelines for California	
Bartender	$1–$3 per drink, or 15%–20% per round
Bellhop	$2–$3 per bag, depending on the level of the hotel
Hotel Concierge	$5–$10 for advice and reservations, more for difficult tasks
Hotel Doorman	$3–$5 for hailing a cab
Valet Parking Attendant	$3–$5 when you get your car
Hotel Maid	$3–$6 per day (either daily or at the end of your stay, in cash)
Waiter	18%–22% (20%–25% is standard in upscale restaurants); nothing additional if a service charge is added to the bill
Skycap at Airport	$1–$2 per bag
Hotel Room-Service Waiter	15%–20% per delivery, even if a service charge was added since that fee goes to the hotel, not the waiter
Taxi Driver	15%–20%, but round up the fare to the next dollar amount
Tour Guide	15% of the cost of the tour, more depending on quality

Contacts

✈ Air Travel

AIRLINE SECURITY ISSUES
Transportation Security Administration (*TSA*). ☎ *866/289–9673* ⊕ *www.tsa.gov.*

AIRPORTS
NORTHERN CALIFORNIA
Oakland International Airport. ☎ *510/563–3300* ⊕ *www.oaklandairport.com.* **Sacramento International Airport.** ☎ *916/929–5411* ⊕ *www.sacramento.aero/smf.* **San Francisco International Airport.** ☎ *650/821–8211, 800/435–9736* ⊕ *www.flysfo.com.* **San Jose International Airport.** ☎ *408/392–3600* ⊕ *www.flysanjose.com.*

SOUTHERN CALIFORNIA
Hollywood Burbank Airport (*Bob Hope Airport*). ☎ *818/840–8840* ⊕ *www.hollywoodburbankairport.com.* **John Wayne Airport.** ☎ *949/252–5200* ⊕ *www.ocair.com.* **Long Beach Airport.** ☎ *562/570–2600* ⊕ *www.lgb.org.* **Los Angeles International Airport.** ☎ *855/463–5252* ⊕ *www.flylax.com.* **Ontario International Airport.** ☎ *909/937–2700* ⊕ *www.flyontario.com.* **San Diego International Airport.** ☎ *619/400–2400* ⊕ *www.san.org.*

AIRLINES
Air Canada. ☎ *888/247–2262* ⊕ *www.aircanada.com.* **Alaska Airlines/**
Horizon Air. ☎ *800/252–7522* ⊕ *www.alaskaair.com.* **American Airlines.** ☎ *800/433–7300* ⊕ *www.aa.com.* **Delta Airlines.** ☎ *800/221–1212 for U.S. reservations, 800/241–4141 for international reservations* ⊕ *www.delta.com.* **Frontier Airlines.** ☎ *801/401–9000* ⊕ *www.flyfrontier.com.* **JetBlue.** ☎ *800/538–2583* ⊕ *www.jetblue.com.* **Southwest Airlines.** ☎ *800/435–9792* ⊕ *www.southwest.com.* **United Airlines.** ☎ *800/864–8331* ⊕ *www.united.com.*

🚌 Bus Travel

Greyhound. ☎ *800/231–2222* ⊕ *www.greyhound.com.*

🚗 Car Travel

American Automobile Association (*AAA*). ☎ *800/222–4357.*

MAJOR RENTAL AGENCIES
Alamo. ☎ *800/462–5266* ⊕ *www.alamo.com.* **Avis.** ☎ *800/633–3469* ⊕ *www.avis.com.* **Budget.** ☎ *800/218–7992* ⊕ *www.budget.com.* **Hertz.** ☎ *800/654–3131* ⊕ *www.hertz.com.* **National Car Rental.** ☎ *877/222–9058* ⊕ *www.nationalcar.com.*

SPECIALTY CAR AGENCIES
Beverly Hills Rent a Car. ☎ *310/448–2018* ⊕ *www.bhrentacar.com.* **Enterprise Exotic Car Rentals.** ☎ *866/458–9227* ⊕ *exoticcars.enterprise.com.* **MCar** (*Midway Car Rental*). ☎ *866/717–6802* ⊕ *www.midwaycarrental.com.*

INFORMATION
Caltrans Current Highway Conditions. ☎ *800/427–7623* ⊕ *www.dot.ca.gov.* **511 Traffic/Transit Alerts.** ☎ *511.*

🚆 Train Travel

Amtrak. ☎ *800/872–7245* ⊕ *www.amtrak.com.*

➕ Health/Safety

Ambulance, fire, police. ☎ *911 emergency.*

📍 Weather

National Weather Service. ☎ *707/443–6484 northernmost California, 831/656–1725 San Francisco Bay area and central California, 775/673–8100 Reno, Lake Tahoe, and northern Sierra, 805/988–6610 Los Angeles, 858/675–8700 San Diego, 916/979–3051 Sacramento.*

Chapter 3

CALIFORNIA'S BEST ROAD TRIPS

Updated by
Daniel Mangin

Great Itineraries

No trip to California would be complete without a drive through the state's spectacular scenery. However, adding a road trip to your itinerary is not just a romantic idea: it's often a practical one, too. A road trip is a great way to link together more than one urban area (San Francisco to Los Angeles with a drive down the coast, for example) or to venture into some more remote areas of this massive state. Whether you have just a few days or longer to spare, these itineraries will help you hit the road.

The Best of the Northern Coast, 5 Days

Hit the highlights of Northern California in one itinerary: scenic coastal drives, quaint windswept towns, wine tasting, culinary delights, and majestic redwood forests. This route can be done as part of a longer trip north toward the Oregon border, or with a loop back down to San Francisco.

DAY 1: MARIN COUNTY AND POINT REYES NATIONAL SEASHORE

(Without stops, Point Reyes National Seashore is about 1½ hrs by car from San Francisco on Hwy 1. Point Reyes Lighthouse is 45 mins by car from the visitor center.)

As you head out of San Francisco on the Golden Gate Bridge, be sure to pull over at the **scenic lookout** on the north side and take in the spectacular views looking back at the city skyline. If you haven't yet checked out the picturesque harbor community of **Sausalito** just north of the bridge, now is your chance. It will be hard not to linger, but there is much to see today. Bidding San Francisco farewell, you will quickly find yourself in the natural beauty of Marin County. Exit the 101 onto Highway 1 at the chic suburb **Mill Valley,** and head to **Muir Woods National Monument.** Walking among the coastal redwoods, it is hard to imagine San Francisco lies less than a dozen miles away. However, the proximity to the city means that Muir Woods is often crowded, and accessing it can be difficult if you don't make a parking or shuttle reservation a day or two ahead (more in summer).

From Muir Woods, continue on Highway 1 past the laid-back beach towns of **Stinson Beach** and **Bolinas** to **Point Reyes National Seashore.** Spend the remainder of the day at the park tide pooling, kayaking, hiking one of the many trails or exploring the **Point Reyes Lighthouse.** In the winter and early spring, be on the lookout for migrating gray whales.

The town of **Point Reyes Station** offers a selection of shops and dining options, including **Tomales Bay Foods,** a provisions stop favored by foodies. Spend a quiet evening in town and overnight at one of the small inns nearby.

DAY 2: HEALDSBURG

(Point Reyes Station to Healdsburg, via Jenner, is 2 hrs by car.)

Continue north on Highway 1 past the town of **Bodega Bay,** which starred in the 1963 Alfred Hitchcock movie *The Birds.* At Jenner, known for its resident harbor seals, turn east on Highway 116 and follow the Russian River inland, taking time to stop at a winery or two along the way.

Ditch the car in **Healdsburg** and enjoy strolling through the appealing town square with its many tasting rooms and boutiques. The town is home to many acclaimed restaurants and luxurious hotels and is an excellent place to stop for the night. The town's compact layout and quality offerings make Healdsburg a favorite Wine Country destination.

Humboldt
Redwoods State Park
Eureka
Mackerricher State Park
Ferndale
The Avenue of
the Giants
Garberville

PACIFIC
OCEAN

NEVADA

Fort Bragg

Mendocino
Little River
Philo
Anderson Valley
Boonville

Lake
Tahoe

Healdsburg

Bodega Bay
Point Reyes Station
Point Reyes National Seashore
Marin County
Bolinas
Mill Valley
Sausalito
Stinson Beach
San Francisco

DAYS 3 AND 4: ANDERSON VALLEY AND MENDOCINO
(Mendocino is 2 hrs by car from Healdsburg. Budget plenty of time for stops in Anderson Valley, and start early enough to ensure you end this scenic drive before sunset.)

Driving north on the 101 from Healdsburg, pick up Highway 128 at Cloverdale and head into the **Anderson Valley.** This wine region is famous for Pinot Noir and Chardonnay (also Gewürztraminer and other Alsace white varietals), and the laid-back atmosphere of its tasting rooms can be a refreshing alternative to those in Napa Valley. **Pennyroyal Farm, Roederer Estate,** and **Phillips Hill Winery** are all recommended. The small towns of **Boonville** and **Philo** have high-quality dining options, and the latter is home to the **Philo Apple Farm's** beloved farm stand.

Highway 128 follows the Navarro River through several miles of dense and breathtaking redwood forest ending at the ocean. From here you meet up again with Highway 1 as it winds its way along a spectacularly scenic portion of the coast.

With their excellent dining and lodging options, the towns of **Mendocino** and **Little River,** just to the south, are great choices for your overnight stay. (Fort Bragg has

reasonably priced motels and inns, some with full ocean views.) Spend the next day and a half exploring the area. Opportunities for stunning coastal walks abound, including **Van Damme State Park** and the **Fort Bragg Coastal Trail.** Hike through the unique Pygmy Forest in Van Damme and visit **Glass Beach,** part of Fort Bragg's **MacKerricher State Park.** Be sure to save time to explore the town of Mendocino itself with its quaint New England–style architecture and art galleries and boutiques.

DAY 5: HUMBOLDT REDWOODS STATE PARK AND THE AVENUE OF THE GIANTS
(Mendocino to Eureka via The Avenue of the Giants is 3 hrs by car.)

Driving north on Highway 1, the road eventually curves inland and meets up with U.S. 101 near Leggett. Head north on the 101 to reach the redwoods.

A drive through **The Avenue of the Giants** will take your breath away. Pick up a copy of the self-guided tour as you enter the 32-mile stretch of road, also signed as Highway 254, running alongside some of the tallest trees on the planet. The drive weaves through a portion of **Humboldt Redwoods State Park.** Even if in a hurry, make time for a short hike through Founders Grove or Rockefeller Forest.

Great Itineraries

Continue to **Ferndale,** a picturesque town of colorful Victorian buildings. You can overnight here, or carry on to the regional city of **Eureka** for a wider variety of dining and accommodation.

From here, you can continue your way up the coast through the **Redwood National Park** and on to the Oregon border. Alternatively, you can head south on the 101 and either return to **San Francisco** or combine this itinerary with a trip to the **Napa Valley** and inland **Sonoma County.**

Roads Less Traveled: Discovering the Northern Interior, 5 Days

Mountain peaks, alpine lakes, a lush waterfall, and a striking volcanic landscape are all included on this tour of California's far north. The drive packs a big scenic punch in a short amount of time, and without the crowds found elsewhere in California's national parks. The remote roads and high elevations make parts of this route subject to snow closures well into the spring. Check current road conditions before setting out.

DAY 1: SACRAMENTO TO CHICO
(1½ hrs by car.)

Start your trip touring the highlights of California's capital city, **Sacramento.** Wander the cobblestone streets and historic·storefronts of Old Sacramento to get a sense of the city during its gold-rush days. Enjoy a horse-drawn-carriage ride through the historic neighborhood or take a cruise along the riverfront. Train enthusiasts of all ages will enjoy the walk-through exhibits at the nearby **California State Railroad Museum.**

Finally, don't leave town without taking a guided tour of the magnificent **Capitol** building.

Departing Sacramento, drive north on Highway 99 to **Chico.** Overnighting in Chico gets you a jump-start on the next day's drive, with the bonus of spending time in this bustling agricultural university town. Stop at the legendary **Sierra Nevada Brewing Company** for a free tour, or enjoy a meal at the brewpub.

DAYS 2 AND 3: LASSEN VOLCANIC NATIONAL PARK
(1½–2 hrs by car from Chico.)

Get an early start on your day, as spectacular scenery awaits you. From Chico, follow Highway 32 northeast toward Chester, branching northwest at Highway 36 to reach the southern entrance of **Lassen Volcanic National Park.** Spend the next two days exploring the area's geothermal activity and dramatic landscape. Highlights include a hike alongside the bubbling mud pots and hot springs of **Bumpass Hell Trail,** views of **Lassen Peak** from Manzanita Lake, or an ascent of the peak itself. The 185-mile **Lassen Scenic Byway** circles the volcanic park and neighboring Lassen National Forest. If you plan far enough ahead, you might score a reservation at the **Highlands Ranch Resort** or one of the park's campgrounds. Otherwise, you will need to bunk in Chester or another neighboring town. Note: in winter, the park is closed to vehicles, in which case this you can skip it and drive straight to McArthur-Burney Falls from Chico via Highway 299.

DAY 4: MCARTHUR-BURNEY FALLS NATIONAL PARK AND MT. SHASTA
(McArthur-Burney Falls is about 45 mins by car from Manzanita Lake; the start of the Everitt Memorial Hwy. is approximately 1 hr and 10 mins from the falls.)

Follow Highway 89 north out of Lassen to **McArthur-Burney Falls Memorial State Park.** Arrive early on summer holidays and weekends—rangers close the entrance when the park fills to capacity. The 129-foot-high falls, located near the visitor center, are a sight to behold as water cascades over the moss-covered rocks. A hiking trail leads down to the base.

When you've had your fill of the falls, continue north on Highway 89 to **Mt. Shasta.** Drive up the mountain on the Everitt Memorial Highway for incredible views. Time permitting, choose one of the many day hikes along the route. In winter you can hit the slopes at nearby **Mt. Shasta Board & Ski Park.** The charming town of Mount Shasta makes a great place to overnight, though train enthusiasts may prefer to venture 10 miles south to **Dunsmuir** and stay at the **Railroad Park Resort,** a collection of antique cabooses transformed into a motel.

DAY 5: LAKE SHASTA AND REDDING

(The exit for Lake Shasta Caverns is approximately 50 mins by car from the town of Mount Shasta. It's another ½ hr by car to reach Redding.)

Drive south on Interstate 5 to Lakehead and take Exit 695 to the **Lake Shasta Caverns.** The two-hour tour of the glittering caverns also includes a boat ride. Tours are offered throughout the day, more frequently in summer.

Back aboveground, anglers and boating enthusiasts should head to one of the marinas dotting the lakeshore to charter the craft of their choice. Houseboats are plentiful on Lake Shasta, but many rentals come with a two-night minimum. For those more interested in engineering than angling, the hour-long tour of the **Shasta Dam** takes you inside

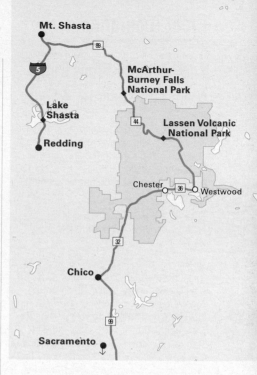

the second-largest concrete dam in the United States. If you are not staying overnight on the lake, drive south and conclude your tour in the nearby city of **Redding** for the best selection of dining and accommodation. Note: this itinerary is designed for those wanting to loop back around to Sacramento and the Bay Area, or to continue to either Lake Tahoe or the North Coast. If you plan on driving north into Oregon, visit Shasta Lake before Mt. Shasta (take Highway 299 west from Burney) and then continue on Interstate 5 north across the state line.

Great Itineraries

The Ultimate Wine Trip: Napa and Sonoma, 4 Days

On this four-day extravaganza, you'll taste well-known and under-the-radar wines, bed down in plush hotels, and dine at restaurants operated by celebrity chefs. Appointments are required for some of the tastings.

DAY 1: SONOMA COUNTY
(1½–2 hrs by car from San Francisco, depending on traffic.)

Begin your tour in Geyserville, about 78 miles north of San Francisco on U.S. 101. Visit **Locals Tasting Room,** which pours the wines of superlative small wineries. Have lunch at nearby **Diavola** or **Catelli's,** then head south on U.S. 101 and Old Redwood Highway to **Healdsburg's Jordan Vineyard & Winery** for a 2 pm Library Tasting. From Jordan head south to **Healdsburg Plaza** downtown. **Hôtel Les Mars** and **Harmon Guest House** are two well-located spots to spend the night. Have dinner at **Chalkboard, Bravas Bar de Tapas,** or **Campo Fina,** all close by.

DAY 2: SONOMA WINERIES
(1 hr by car from Healdsburg to Glen Ellen.)

Wineries dot the countryside surrounding Healdsburg, among them—choose one—**Silver Oak, Arista Winery,** and **Unti Vineyards.** Silver Oak specializes in Cabernet Sauvignon, Arista in Pinot Noir and Chardonnay, and Unti in Zinfandel, Sangiovese, and obscure Italian and Rhône varietals. In the afternoon, head south on U.S. 101 and east on scenic Highway 12 to **Glen Ellen.** Visit **Jack London State Historic Park,** the memorabilia-filled estate of the famous writer, or enjoy a tasting at **Benziger Family Winery, Lasseter Family Winery** or **Loxton Cellars.** Dine at **Glen Ellen**

Star and stay at the **Gaige House + Ryokan** or the **Olea Hotel.**

DAY 3: NAPA VALLEY
(Glen Ellen to St. Helena is about 30 mins by car without traffic. St. Helena to Yountville is about 15 mins by car, without stops.)

On Day 3, head east from Glen Ellen on Trinity Road, which twists and turns over the Mayacamas Mountains, eventually becoming the Oakville Grade. Unless you're driving, bask in the stupendous **Napa Valley** views. At Highway 29, drive north to **St. Helena.** Focus on history and architecture at **Charles Krug Winery** or let the art and wines at **Hall St. Helena** transport you. Take lunch downtown at **Cook St. Helena** or **Market.** Check out St. Helena's Main Street shopping, then head south on Highway 29 to Yountville for more shopping. Start at **Hunter Gatherer,** at Madison and Washington streets, then work your way south down Washington.

Stay overnight at **Bardessono** or the **North Block Hotel,** both within walking distance of Yountville's famous restaurants. A meal at chef Thomas Keller's **The French Laundry** is many visitors' holy grail, but dining at **Bistro Jeanty** or Keller's **Bouchon Bistro** will also leave you feeling well served.

DAY 4: OAKVILLE TO CARNEROS
(Just over 1 hr by car from Napa to San Francisco, without traffic.)

After breakfast, head north on Highway 29 to **Oakville,** where sipping wine at **Silver Oak, Nickel & Nickel,** or **B Cellars** will make clear why collectors covet Oakville Cabernet Sauvignons. Nickel & Nickel is on Highway 29; Silver Oak and B Cellars are east of it on Oakville Cross Road. Have a picnic at **Oakville Grocery,** in business on Highway 29 since 1881, or make reservations at **Mustards Grill.** After your meal, head south on Highway 29, exiting at 1st Street to visit downtown Napa's

CIA at Copia food- and-wine complex. Afterward, backtrack to Highway 29, and head south to Highway 121. Turn west to reach the Carneros District, whose **Domaine Carneros** makes French-style sparkling wines. There's hardly a more elegant way to bid a Wine Country adieu than on the Domaine château's vineyard-view terrace before heading back to San Francisco. Give yourself plenty of time to get to your departure airport; traffic is generally heavy as you close in on the Bay Area.

MODIFYING THE ROUTE FROM SAN FRANCISCO

The above itinerary is useful if traveling to Wine Country from points farther north. If you prefer to make a loop beginning and ending in San Francisco, the itinerary can be easily modified as follows: Day 1: Head north from San Francisco to the town of Sonoma (1 to 1½ hours by car, depending on traffic) and spend some time exploring the restaurants, shops, and tasting rooms lining the downtown plaza. Several excellent wineries operate nearby, including **Bedrock Wine Co.** (wines from old vines) and **Patz & Hall** (Chardonnay and Pinot Noir). From Sonoma, head north to Glen Ellen (15 minutes by car) and pick up the Glen Ellen itinerary described above. Day 2: Continue north to Healdsburg, following the above itinerary in reverse. Overnight in Healdsburg as described. Day 3: Head south on Highway 101 to River Road and then east on Mark Springs Road toward Calistoga (45 minutes by car), a town made famous by its hot springs and mud baths. If time permits, stay overnight at one of Calistoga's luxury spa retreats, among them **Calistoga Ranch, Indian Springs Resort and Spa,** or **Solage Calistoga.** Otherwise, head south to St. Helena (15 minutes by car) and complete the remainder of the road trip as outlined above.

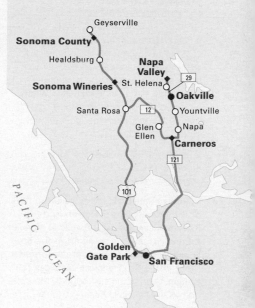

Sierra Riches: Yosemite, Gold Country, and Tahoe, 10 Days

This tour will show you why Tony Bennett left his heart in San Francisco. It also includes some of the most beautiful places in a very scenic state, plus gold-rush-era history, and a chance to hike a trail or two.

DAY 1: SAN FRANCISCO

Straight from the airport, drop your bags at the lighthearted **Hotel Zetta,** south of Market Street (SoMa). A stroll north to Union Square packs a wallop of people-watching, window-shopping, and architecture viewing. **Chinatown,** chock-full of dim sum shops, storefront temples, and open-air markets, promises authentic bites for lunch. Catch

Great Itineraries

a Powell Street **cable car** to the end of the line and get off to see the bay views and the antique arcade games at **Musée Mécanique,** the hidden gem of otherwise mindless **Fisherman's Wharf.** No need to go any farther than cosmopolitan North Beach for cocktail hour, dinner, and live music.

DAY 2: GOLDEN GATE PARK

(15 mins by car or taxi, 45 mins by public transport from Union Square.)

In **Golden Gate Park,** linger amid the flora of the **Conservatory of Flowers** and the **San Francisco Botanical Garden at Strybing Arboretum,** soak up some art at the **de Young Museum,** and find serene refreshment at the **San Francisco Japanese Tea Garden.** The Pacific surf pounds the cliffs below the **Legion of Honor** art museum, which has an exquisite view of the **Golden Gate Bridge**—when the fog stays away. Sunset cocktails at the circa-1909 **Cliff House** include a prospect over Seal Rock (actually occupied by sea lions). Eat dinner elsewhere: Pacific Heights, the Mission, and SoMa teem with excellent restaurants.

DAY 3: INTO THE HIGH SIERRA

(4–5 hrs by car from San Francisco.)

First thing in the morning, pick up your rental car and head for the hills. Arriving in **Yosemite National Park, Bridalveil Fall,** and **El Capitan,** the 350-story granite monolith, greet you on your way to **Yosemite Village.** Ditch the car and pick up information and refreshment before hopping on the shuttle to explore. Justly famous sights cram Yosemite Valley: massive **Half Dome** and **Sentinel Dome,** thundering **Yosemite Falls,** and wispy **Ribbon Fall** and **Nevada Fall.** Invigorating short hikes off the shuttle route lead to numerous vantage points. Celebrate your arrival in one of the world's most sublime spots with dinner in the dramatic **Majestic Yosemite**

Hotel Dining Room (formerly the Ahwahnee) and stay the night there (reserve well in advance).

DAY 4: YOSEMITE NATIONAL PARK

(Yosemite shuttles run every 10–30 mins.)

Ardent hikers consider **John Muir Trail to Half Dome** a must-do, tackling the rigorous 12-hour round-trip to the top of Half Dome in search of life-changing vistas. Mere mortals hike downhill from Glacier Point on Four-Mile Trail or **Panorama Trail,** the latter an all-day trek past waterfalls. Less demanding still is a drive to Wawona for a stroll in the **Mariposa Grove of Big Trees** and lunch at the 19th-century **Big Trees Lodge Dining Room** (formerly the Wawona). In bad weather, take shelter in the **Ansel Adams Gallery** and **Yosemite Museum**; in fair conditions, drive up to **Glacier Point** for a breathtaking sunset view.

DAY 5: GOLD COUNTRY SOUTH

(2½–3 hrs by car from Yosemite.)

Highway 49 traces the mother lode that yielded many fortunes in gold in the 1850s and 1860s. Step into a living gold-rush town at **Columbia State Historic Park,** where you can ride a stagecoach and pan for riches. **Sutter Creek's** well-preserved downtown bursts with shopping opportunities, but the vintage goods displayed at **Monteverde Store Museum** are not for sale. A different sort of vintage powers the present-day bonanza of **Shenandoah Valley,** the heart of the Sierra Foothills Wine Country. Taste your way through Zinfandels at **Turley Wine Cellars,** that varietal plus Rhône-style wines at **Terra Rouge and Easton Wines,** and both plus Barbera and much more at jolly **Jeff Renquist Wines.** Retire in country-boutique comfort at **Rest Hotel Plymouth,** whose owners also operate nearby **Taste** restaurant.

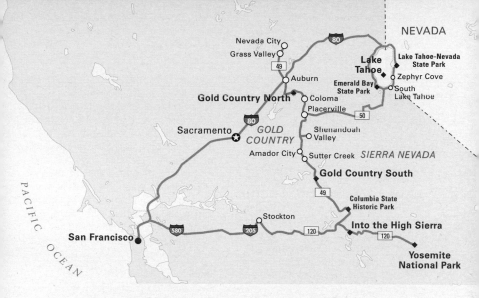

DAY 6: GOLD COUNTRY NORTH
(2 hrs by car from Amador City to Nevada City.)

In **Placerville,** a mine shaft invites investigation at **Hangtown's Gold Bug Mine,** while **Marshall Gold Discovery State Historic Park** encompasses most of **Coloma** and preserves the spot where James Marshall's 1848 find set off the California gold rush. Learn all about El Dorado County wines at **Lava Cap Winery** or **Holly's Hill Vineyards.** Old Town **Auburn,** with its museums and courthouse, makes a good lunch stop. A tour of Grass Valley's **Empire Mine State Historic Park** takes you into a mine, and a few miles away horse-drawn carriages ply the narrow, shop-lined streets of downtown **Nevada City.** Some of Nevada City's bed-and-breakfast inns date back to gold-rush days. For more contemporary accommodations backtrack to Auburn or Placerville.

DAY 7: LAKE TAHOE
(1 hr by car from Nevada City, 2 hrs from Placerville.)

Jewel-like **Lake Tahoe** is a straight shot east of Placerville on Highway 50; stop for picnic provisions in commercial **South Lake Tahoe.** A stroll past the three magnificent estates in **Pope-Baldwin Recreation Area** hints at the sumptuous lakefront summers once enjoyed by the elite. High above a glittering cove, **Emerald Bay State Park** offers one of the best lake views as well as a steep hike down to (and back up from) **Vikingsholm,** a replica 9th-century Scandinavian castle. Another fine old mansion—plus a nature preserve and many hiking trails—lies in **Sugar Pine Point State Park.** Tahoe City offers more history and ample dining and lodging choices. (Interstate 80 east to Highway 89 south to Tahoe City is more convenient if you've spent the previous night in Nevada City and are staying on Lake Tahoe's north shore. If you take this route, reverse the visiting order of the above-mentioned sights.)

DAY 8: EXPLORING LAKE TAHOE
(Sightseeing cruise lasts 2 hrs.)

The picture-perfect beaches and bays of **Lake Tahoe–Nevada State Park** line the Nevada shoreline, a great place to bask in the sun or go mountain biking. For a different perspective of the lake, get out on the azure water aboard the stern-wheeler MS *Dixie II* from **Zephyr Cove.** In South Lake Tahoe, another view unfurls as the **Heavenly Gondola** travels 2½ miles up a mountain. Keep your adrenaline pumping into the evening with some action at the casinos clustered in Stateline, Nevada.

Great Itineraries

DAY 9: RETURN TO SAN FRANCISCO
(About 4 hrs by car from Tahoe City.)

After a long morning of driving, return your rental car in San Francisco and soak up some more urban excitement. Good options include a late lunch at the **Ferry Building,** followed by a visit to the **San Francisco Museum of Modern Art** or lunch in **Japantown.** Head to the **Castro** or the **Haight** for excellent people-watching, then say good-bye to Northern California at a downtown hotel's plush lounge or trendy bar.

DAY 10: DEPARTURE
(SFO is 30 mins from downtown both by BART public transport and by car, without traffic.)

Check the weather and your flight information before you start out for the airport: fog sometimes causes delays at SFO. On a clear day, your flight path might give you one last fabulous glimpse of the City by the Bay.

Monterey Bay, Carmel, and Big Sur, 4 Days

In a nutshell, this drive is all about the jaw-dropping scenery of the Pacific Coast. Visitors pressed for time often make the drive from Monterey through Big Sur in one day, but those who linger can venture off the road and enjoy the solitude of Big Sur once the day-trippers have departed.

DAY 1: MONTEREY
Monterey is the perfect spot to kick off a coastal tour. Start with a visit to the enthralling **Monterey Bay Aquarium.** Exhibits such as the dramatic three-story kelp forest near the entrance give you a true sense of the local marine environment, much of it federally protected.

For an even closer encounter, take to the water on a kayak or whale-watching tour. While undoubtedly touristy, the shops and galleries of **Cannery Row** still make for an interesting diversion, and it's fun to watch the colony of sea lions at **Fisherman's Wharf.** There are plenty of excellent dining and lodging choices within walking distance of downtown, so enjoy a seafood dinner and an evening stroll before hitting the road the next morning.

DAY 2: 17-MILE DRIVE AND CARMEL-BY-THE-SEA
(The 17-Mile Drive's Pacific Grove entrance gate is 15 mins by car from Monterey.)

If your visit falls between October and March, begin your drive with a quick detour to visit the migrating monarch butterflies at the **Monarch Grove Sanctuary** in the charming Victorian town of **Pacific Grove.**

Enter the **17-Mile Drive** through the tollgate ($10.50 per car) off Sunset Drive in Pacific Grove. This scenic road winds its way along the coast through a hushed and refined landscape of stunning homes and the celebrated golf links at **Pebble Beach.** Perhaps the most famous (and photographed) resident is the **Lone Cypress,** which has come to symbolize the solitude and natural beauty of the coast. Even though the drive is only 17 miles, plan on taking your time. If you stop for lunch or souvenir shopping, inquire about a refund on the entry toll.

Upon exiting the drive, continue south to the charming town of **Carmel-by-the-Sea.** Spend the afternoon browsing its boutiques and galleries before walking to **Carmel Beach** for sunset, followed by dinner at one of Carmel's many fine restaurants. Similarly, there is no shortage of stylish,

PACIFIC OCEAN

but pricey, lodging. Venture outside of the village for less expensive accommodation.

DAY 3: BIG SUR
(30 mins by car.)

The drive through coastal **Big Sur** is justifiably one of the most famous stretches of road in the world. The winding curves, endless views, and scenic waypoints are the stuff of road-trip legend. Keep your camera handy, fill up the tank, and prepare to be wowed. Traffic can easily back up along the route, and drivers should take caution navigating the road's twists and turns. While you will only drive about 30 miles today, allow several hours for hikes and stops.

Heading into Big Sur you will first come upon the extremely photogenic **Bixby Creek Bridge.** Pull over in the turnout on the north side of the bridge to get that perfect shot. About 10 miles down the road look for a small cluster of services known as Big Sur Village just before the entrance to **Pfeiffer Big Sur State Park,** a perfect stop for a hike.

One mile south of the park, watch carefully for the sharp turnout and unmarked road leading to **Pfeiffer Beach.** Following the unpaved road 2 miles toward the sea you may question whether you

are lost, but your perseverance will be rewarded when you reach the secluded beach with its signature rocky arch just offshore. Don't miss it!

There are several lodging options around this portion of Big Sur, ranging from rustic to luxurious. If room rates at the legendary **Post Ranch Inn** exceed your budget, consider splurging on the nine-course tasting menu at its spectacular cliff-side **Sierra Mar** restaurant instead. Alternatively, the terrace at **Nepenthe** offers decent food and gorgeous views at a lower price point. Time your dinner reservation to witness the sunset.

DAY 4: BIG SUR TO CAMBRIA
(About 2 hrs by car. Allow ample time for hiking and 2 hrs to tour Hearst Castle.)

Start the morning off with a hike in **Julia Pfeiffer Burns State Park,** a draw for its waterfall tumbling dramatically into the sea. Back on the road, several scenic overlooks will beckon as you head through the southern stretch of Big Sur. A pullout north of the entrance near mile marker 36.2 affords views of **McWay Falls.** If the trail to the falls is open (check the park's website), you can hike in a short way for an up-close view.

Great Itineraries

As you enter **San Simeon,** don't miss the **Piedras Blancas Elephant Seal Rookery.** Depending on your timing, you might catch a late afternoon tour at **Hearst Castle.** If not, you can make a reservation for a tour early the following morning. End the day with a walk at **Moonstone Beach** in the town of **Cambria,** 10 miles south of the castle, and stay overnight in one of the reasonably priced lodgings here.

From here, you can continue your travels south through the central coast to **Santa Barbara.** Or head inland to visit the **Paso Robles** wine region before returning to Monterey via Highway 101.

The Inland Route: San Francisco to Los Angeles via the Sierras, 5 Days

This itinerary provides an alternative to the more frequented coastal route between San Francisco and Los Angeles and takes in the splendid scenery of the Sierras. Though a good survey, this trip barely scratches the surface of all that Yosemite, Kings Canyon, and Sequoia national parks have to offer. Avid naturalists might want to extend their time in the parks. Either way, plan on spending a few days on either end of the road trip to explore California's two most popular cities.

DAY 1: SAN FRANCISCO TO YOSEMITE
(Yosemite is about 4 hrs from San Francisco by car, depending on traffic.)

Hit the road early for the day's long drive to **Yosemite National Park.** As you approach from Route 120, be sure to top up the tank as there are only a few gas stations within the park. Drive straight to the **Valley Visitor Center** to get an overview of the park. Stretch

your legs on the easy loop trail to **Lower Yosemite Falls.** If daylight permits and you are looking for something a bit more strenuous, tackle the **Mist Trail** leading to **Bridalveil and Vernal Falls.** Reserve lodging early at the central valley lodges or campgrounds. Even if you aren't staying there, treat yourself to dinner at the **Majestic Yosemite Hotel Dining Room** (formerly the Ahwahnee).

DAY 2: EXPLORING YOSEMITE
Spend today tackling some of the sights in the northern and central areas of the park. Options include the 8½-mile **Panorama Trail** from **Glacier Point** back down to the valley or a drive along the impossibly scenic Tioga Road to **Tuolumne Meadows.** Alternatively, consider a horseback or photography tour. Hikers looking to tackle the strenuous ascent of **Half Dome** should plan on spending an additional day in the park. While some do attempt to complete the trail in one very long day, many consider camping overnight in Little Yosemite Valley to be preferable. If attempting Half Dome, don't forget to secure your wilderness permit in advance. Spend a second night in Yosemite Valley.

DAY 3: YOSEMITE TO KINGS CANYON
(The Wawona area of the park is about 1 hr by car from Yosemite Valley. From Wawona, Grants Grove Village in Kings Canyon is about 3 hrs by car.)

Make your way south to the **Wawona** section of Yosemite and don't miss the **Mariposa Grove of Big Trees** to see the famous Grizzly Giant before leaving the park. From here, drive south out of Yosemite and link up with Route 180 heading into **Kings Canyon National Park.** Again, remember to get gas along the route. Once inside Kings Canyon, continue along Route 180 for the 30-mile stretch known as the **Kings Canyon Scenic Byway** as it winds between Grant

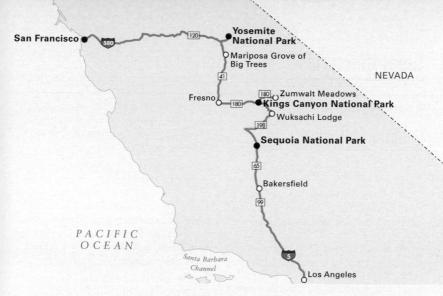

Grove Village and Zumwalt Meadow. There are several vista points or opportunities to stretch your legs en route. Toward the end, enjoy an easy 1½-mile hike along the **Zumwalt Meadows Trail.** Drive back (allow about an hour without stops) and overnight in the Grant Grove area of the park.

DAYS 4 AND 5: KINGS CANYON TO SEQUOIA

(Allow ample time to drive Generals Hwy. as parts are steep and winding, and there are many stops to make on the way. Los Angeles is about 3½–4 hrs by car from the Foothills Visitor Center.)

Spend the next two days exploring **Generals Highway,** the 43-mile scenic route connecting Kings Canyon and Sequoia national parks. Warm up with a hike into Redwood Canyon Grove, one of the largest sequoia groves in the world. You can choose between a short walk to an overlook or longer 6- and 10-mile hikes deep into the grove. From there, continue the drive into **Sequoia National Park** and spend the rest of the day and the majority of the next exploring its highlights, with the **Wuksachi Lodge** serving as your base.

Don't miss the 2-mile **Congress Trail,** an excellent opportunity to walk among the big trees, or the nearby **General Sherman Tree,** a massive specimen. To tour the **Crystal Cave** and its marble interior, purchase tickets in advance online or at the **Lodgepole visitor center.** Challenge your calves on the 350 stone steps of **Moro Rock** and reward your efforts with views over the Middle Fork Canyon. Don't leave the park without making the requisite photo stop at **Tunnel Log,** which, as its name suggests, is a drive-through tunnel carved out of the trunk of a fallen tree. It might take some discipline to pull away from the spectacular scenery, but a 3½-hour drive to Los Angeles awaits. With any luck, an evening arrival will mean you miss much of the city's notorious traffic. Note: intrepid travelers can modify this itinerary to take in **Yosemite and Death Valley national parks** via the **Tioga Pass** and **Mono Lake.** Be aware, though, that Tioga Pass is only open from late spring to early fall—the rest of the time it's snowed in. By the time the pass opens, temperatures in Death Valley are already searing hot and the extreme conditions should not be taken lightly. Always travel with ample drinking water and food, take precautions against the burning sun, limit physical activity, and time outings for early or late in the day.

Great Itineraries

Santa Barbara Wine Country, 3 Days

It has been well over a decade since the movie *Sideways* brought the Santa Barbara Wine Country to the world's attention, and interest in this wine-growing area continues to grow. On this trip you will explore one of the most beautiful cities in the West, enjoy time along the gorgeous coast, and then head inland for a delightful wine-tasting adventure. This itinerary makes a perfect add-on to a trip to Los Angeles, or for those driving the coastal route between Los Angeles and San Francisco.

DAY 1: SANTA BARBARA

(2 hrs by car from LAX to Santa Barbara without traffic.)

Santa Barbara is a gem, combining elegance with a laid-back coastal vibe. It provides a tranquil escape from the congestion of Los Angeles and a dose of sophistication to the largely rural central coast.

Start your day at the beautiful **Old Mission Santa Barbara,** known as the "Queen" of the 21 missions that comprise the California Mission Trail. Plan to spend some time here; if your visit doesn't coincide with one of the 60-minute docent-led tours, self-guided tours are also available. From here, head to the waterfront and spend some time enjoying the wide stretch of sand at **East Beach** and a seafood lunch at one of the restaurants on **Stearns Wharf.** After lunch, consider kicking off your wine tour early by checking out some of the Funk Zone tasting rooms just north of the wharf.

Next stop is a tour of the **Santa Barbara County Courthouse.** Don't miss the murals in the ceremonial chambers or, from the top of the courthouse tower, the incredible views of downtown's beautiful red-tile-roofed buildings and beyond them the Pacific Ocean.

Back on the ground, enjoy superb shopping along **State Street.** Enjoy the lively dining and nightlife scene downtown, or head to tony **Montecito** for an elegant dinner. Splurge on an overnight stay at the posh **Four Seasons Resort The Biltmore Santa Barbara,** or check into the Funk Zone's **Hotel Indigo.**

DAY 2: SANTA RITA HILLS, LOMPOC, AND LOS OLIVOS

(Without stops, this route takes about 2 hrs by car. Plan to linger and to detour down side roads to reach the wineries.)

Take the scenic drive along the coast on Highway 101 before heading inland at Santa Rosa Road for a loop through the Santa Rita Hills. This area's cooler climate produces top-notch Chardonnay and Pinot Noir. Vineyards line the road as you swing west on Santa Rosa Road toward Lompoc and return on Highway 246 to Buellton. A good stop midway along the route is the so-called **Lompoc Wine Ghetto.** Don't let the industrial-park setting deter you—the tasting rooms here include well-regarded producers such as **Longoria.** In Buellton, drop by **Lafond Winery and Vineyards** and **Alma Rosa Winery,** the latter part of the **Industrial Way** food-and-drink complex.

Back on Highway 101, head north about 6 miles before exiting toward **Los Olivos,** where you can park the car and spend the rest of the day exploring on foot. Tasting rooms, galleries, boutiques, and restaurants have made this former stagecoach town quite wine-country chic. **Blair Fox Cellars** and **Coquelicot Estate Vineyard** are just two of the producers with tasting rooms in town. Los Olivos is a good base to dine—**Bear**

and Star at **Fess Parker's Wine Country Inn and Spa** is the star here. Stay at Fess Parker's or just outside town at the lovely **Ballard Inn,** or slip over to nearby **Solvang,** checking into the **Hotel Corque** and dining in its chic locavore **Root 246** restaurant.

DAY 3: SOLVANG, FOXEN CANYON, AND THE SANTA YNEZ VALLEY
(The drive from Santa Ynez to Santa Barbara is about 45 mins by car via Hwy. 154.)

Start the next morning with pastries at the Danish town of **Solvang,** 10 minutes south of Los Olivos. The windmills and distinct half-timber architecture of this village are charming, if a bit touristy. Spend some time exploring the town before hitting the road.

Los Olivos, **Santa Ynez,** and Solvang are located just a few minutes apart, with wineries spread between them in an area known as the Santa Ynez Valley. Heading north from Los Olivos, the Foxen Canyon wine trail extends all the way to Santa Maria and is home to excellent producers. Expect some backtracking along your route today as you wind between the towns and venture into Foxen Canyon. Allow 30 to 45 minutes for the well-conceived walking

tour at **Firestone Vineyard,** a must if you're interested in the wine-making process. Don't blink or you might miss **Santa Ynez,** worth a wander or a stop for lunch. A mile east of the tiny town's commercial drag you'll find **Gainey Vineyard,** whose wines impress major wine critics.

When you've had your fill of the wine region, take scenic Highway 154 over the San Marcos Pass and back to Santa Barbara. Wind down the day with a stroll along the beach, and perhaps one last glass of wine at sunset.

Great Itineraries

Route 66 and the Mojave Desert, 4 Days

Route 66 was the original road trip "from Chicago to L.A.," with California the ultimate destination. The Mother Road travels west from the Arizona border, skirting the Mojave Desert before passing through Los Angeles and ending at the Pacific Ocean. What makes this journey so compelling is actually what it lacks. Desolate stretches of road through windswept towns are reminders of the harsh conditions 1930s pioneers fleeing the central United States dust storms faced, while faded neon signs and abandoned motels offer nostalgic glimpses of Route 66's mid-century heyday. Nearby, the solitary beauty of the Mojave National Preserve beckons with its volcanic rock formations, Joshua trees, and seemingly endless dunes.

DAY 1: SANTA MONICA
By reversing the typical Route 66 journey and traveling from west to east you can hit the road upon arrival at LAX, or spend a few days exploring Los Angeles first. Starting your voyage in **Santa Monica** may feel a bit like eating your dessert first. For road-trippers on Route 66, reaching the Pacific Ocean after a long dusty drive through the desert was certainly a treat. The official end of Route 66 is marked with a plaque in **Palisades Park,** on a bluff overlooking **Santa Monica State Beach.** Soak in the quintessential SoCal beach scene on the wide expanse of sand below before heading to the famous **Santa Monica Pier.** From here, you can rent a bike and cruise south to **Venice Beach** for the ultimate people-watching experience.

In the evening, stroll the pedestrian-only **Third Street Promenade** and neighboring **Santa Monica Place** mall for a good selection of shopping, dining, and entertainment. Relax in luxury at the legendary **Shutters on the Beach.** Or, in keeping with the true Route 66 spirit, opt for the more modest motor-lodge vibe of the **Sea Shore Motel.**

DAY 2: HOLLYWOOD AND PASADENA
(1½ hrs by car from Santa Monica to Pasadena and another 1½–2 hrs by car to Victorville.)

Heading inland through **Beverly Hills** and **Hollywood,** the remnants of Route 66 are quickly overshadowed by the surrounding glitz and glamour. A stop at the **Hollywood Museum** or a stroll along the **Hollywood Walk of Fame** will help transport you back in time to Tinseltown's golden age.

The route continues through **Pasadena,** with its stately homes and spacious gardens. Fans of Craftsman architecture won't want to miss a tour of the **Gamble House,** while a stroll around **Old Town Pasadena** is a great way to stretch your legs before or after you grab a bite to eat.

Depending on your interests and how much sightseeing you've done, you might choose to stay in Pasadena for the night to enjoy the many dining and lodging options. Or, to avoid L.A.'s morning commute traffic, head 75 miles west to **Victorville** and spend the night there.

DAY 3: ROUTE 66
(The drive from Pasadena to Victorville takes about 1¼ hrs, not counting traffic. Driving from Victorville to Barstow takes less than an hr. From there, you can follow as much of Route 66 as time permits.)

Hit the road early if you didn't spend the night in Victorville. First stop is the **California Route 66 Museum** in **Victorville,** where you'll learn all about the history of the Mother Road. Pick up a copy of the museum's self-guided tour book and consult one of the many Route

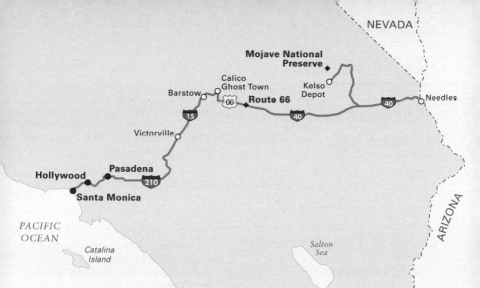

66–related websites, among them ⊕ *www.historic66.com*, to help you navigate the old road as it crosses back and forth alongside Interstate 40 between Barstow and Needles. Abandoned service stations, shuttered motels, and faded signs dot the desert landscape in various states of alluring decay. Grab a meal at the famous **Baghdad Café** in Barstow. For a diversion unrelated to Route 66, spend a few hours exploring **Calico Ghost Town,** a restored old mining town just north of Barstow. In the evening, turn back the hands of time and catch a flick at the **Skyline Drive-In Theatre.**

Accommodations in this area are mostly of the chain-motel variety. Victorville and Barstow are your best bets for lodging unless you follow Route 66 into Arizona, where **Lake Havasu City,** 43 miles south of Needles on Highway 95, offers several options. Staying overnight in nondescript Needles is not recommended.

DAY 4: MOJAVE NATIONAL PRESERVE

(There are several access points to the park along I–15 and I–40. Kelso Dunes Visitor Center is about 1½ hrs by car from Barstow. Within the park stick to paved or gravel roads—others require four-wheel drive.)

In the morning, head north from Route 66 into the beautiful and remote landscape of the **Mojave National Preserve.** Reaching the top of the stunning golden **Kelso Dunes** requires some athleticism, but your efforts will be rewarded with incredible scenery and the eerie sounds of "singing" sand caused by the wind. If you spent the night in Lake Havasu City, explore the volcanic gas formations of **Hole-in-the-Wall** first. Farther north in the park, the Cima Road will bring you to the Teutonia Peak Trailhead and the largest concentration of Joshua trees in the world. Visitor centers at **Kelso Depot** and **Hole-in-the-Wall** provide information on additional sights, hiking trails, and campgrounds in the park.

There are several options for the next leg of your journey. You can drive back to Los Angeles in about three hours or drive onward to **Las Vegas** even faster. If you have more time, you can continue north and spend a few days in **Death Valley National Park,** or head south to **Joshua Tree** and **Palm Springs** before making your way back to **Los Angeles.**

Great Itineraries

Palm Springs and the Desert, 5 Days

Many visitors consider the Palm Springs area pure paradise, and not just for the opportunity to get a good tan or play golf on championship courses. Expect fabulous and funky spas, a dog-friendly atmosphere, and sparkling stars at night.

DAY 1: PALM SPRINGS
(Just over 2 hrs by car from LAX, without traffic.)

Somehow in harmony with the harsh environment, mid-century-modern homes and businesses with clean, low-slung lines define the **Palm Springs** style. Although the desert cities—Cathedral City, Rancho Mirage, Palm Desert, Indian Wells, Indio, and La Quinta—comprise a trendy destination with beautiful hotels, fabulous multicultural food, abundant nightlife, and plenty of culture, a quiet atmosphere prevails. Fans of Palm Springs' legendary architecture won't want to miss the home tours, lectures, and other events at the annual Modernism Week held each February, or the smaller fall preview event in October. If your visit doesn't coincide with these happenings, swing by the Palm Springs Visitor's Center for information on self-guided architecture tours. The city seems far away when you hike in hushed **Tahquitz** or **Indian Canyon**; cliffs and palm trees shelter rock art, irrigation works, and other remnants of Agua Caliente culture. If your boots aren't made for walking, you can always practice your golf game or indulge in spa treatments at an area resort instead. Embrace the Palm Springs vibe and park yourself at the modern-chic **Kimpton Rowan Palm Springs Hotel** or the legendary **Parker Palm Springs.** Alternatively, base yourself at the desert oasis, **La Quinta Resort,** about 40 minutes from downtown Palm Springs.

DAY 2: EXPLORE PALM SPRINGS
(The Aerial Tram is 15 mins by car from central Palm Springs. Plan at least a half day for the excursion.)

If riding a tram up an 8,516-foot mountain for a stroll or even a snowball fight above the desert sounds like fun to you, then show up at the **Palm Springs Aerial Tramway** before the first morning tram leaves (later, the line can get discouragingly long). Dress in layers and wear decent footwear as it can be significantly colder when you reach the top. Afterward stroll through the **Palm Springs Art Museum** where you can see a shimmering display of contemporary studio glass, an array of enormous Native American baskets, and significant 20th-century sculptures by Henry Moore and others. After all that walking you may be ready for an early dinner. Nearly every restaurant in Palm Springs offers a happy hour, when you can sip a cocktail and nosh on a light entrée, usually for half price. Using your hotel as a base, take a few day trips to discover the natural beauty of the desert.

DAY 3: JOSHUA TREE NATIONAL PARK
(1 hr by car from Palm Springs.)

Due to its proximity to Los Angeles and the highway between Las Vegas and coastal cities, **Joshua Tree** is among the most accessible of the national parks. You can see most of it in a day, entering the park at the town of Joshua Tree, exploring sites along **Park Boulevard,** and exiting at **Twentynine Palms.** With the signature trees, piles of rocks, glorious spring wildflowers, starlit skies, and colorful pioneer history, the

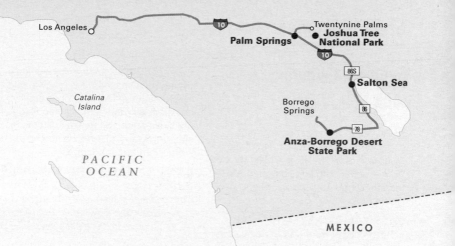

experience is a bit more like the Wild West than Sahara dunes. Whether planning to take a day hike or a scenic drive, load up on drinking water before entering the park.

DAY 4: ANZA-BORREGO DESERT STATE PARK AND THE SALTON SEA
(About 2 hrs by car from Palm Springs.)

The **Salton Sea**, about 60 miles south of Palm Springs via Interstate 10 and Highway 86S, is one of the largest inland seas on earth. Formed by the flooding of the Colorado River in 1905, it attracts thousands of migrating birds and bird-watchers every fall. **Anza-Borrego Desert State Park** to the west, California's largest state park, contains 600,000 acres of mostly untouched wilderness. The springtime wildflower displays here rank among the state's best. Just east of the park lies **Borrego Springs,** a tiny hamlet most notable for its 130 life-size bronze sculptures of animals that roamed this space millions of years ago. The desert is home to an archaeological site, where scientists continue to uncover remnants of prehistoric animals ranging from mastodons to horses. If you have four-wheel drive, a detour down the sandy track

to **Font's Point** rewards the intrepid with spectacular views of the Borrego badlands. However, do not take the challenging road conditions lightly—inquire with park rangers before setting out.

DAY 5: RETURN TO L.A.
(LAX is just over 2 hrs by car from Palm Springs without traffic, but the drive often takes significantly more time.)

If you intend to depart from LAX, plan for a full day of driving from the desert to the airport. Be prepared for heavy traffic at any time of day or night. If possible, fly out of Palm Springs International Airport or Ontario International Airport instead.

Great Itineraries

Southern California with Kids, 7 Days

SoCal offers many opportunities to entertain the kids beyond the Magic Kingdom. LEGOLAND is a blast for kids 12 and under, and families can't beat the San Diego Zoo and San Diego's historic Old Town.

DAYS 1–2: DISNEYLAND
(45 mins by car from LAX to Disneyland.)

Get out of Los Angeles International Airport as fast as you can. Pick up your rental car and head south on the Interstate 405 freeway, which can be congested day or night, toward Orange County (aka the O.C.) and **Disneyland.** Skirt the lines at the box office with advance-purchased tickets in hand and storm the gates of the Magic Kingdom. You can cram the highlights into a single day, but if you get a two-day ticket and stay the night you can see the end-of-day parade and visit **Downtown Disney** before heading south. The **Grand Californian Hotel** is a top choice for lodging within the Disney Resort. If tackling Disneyland after a long flight is too much, head south from LAX to the surfer's haven at **Huntington Beach,** where you can relax at the beach and spend the night in one of several beachfront hotels before heading inland to Anaheim the next morning.

DAY 3: LEGOLAND
(1 to 1½ hrs by car from Huntington Beach or Anaheim, depending on traffic.)

Get an early start for your next roller-coaster ride at **LEGOLAND,** about an hour's drive south of Huntington Beach via the Pacific Coast Highway. Check into the **LEGOLAND Hotel** or the **Sheraton Carlsbad Resort & Spa;** both offer direct access to the park. LEGOLAND has a water park and aquarium in addition to the LEGO-based rides, shows, and roller coasters. The little ones can live out their fairy-tale fantasies and bigger ones can spend all day on waterslides, shooting water pistols, driving boats, or water fighting with pirates.

DAY 4: LA JOLLA AND SAN DIEGO
(La Jolla is just over an hour's drive from Carlsbad along scenic S21, or 40 mins on the I–5 freeway; Downtown San Diego is a 20-min drive from La Jolla.)

Take a leisurely drive south to San Diego by using the "old road," the original Pacific Coast Highway that hugs the shore all the way. It's a slow drive through Leucadia, Encinitas, Solana Beach, and Del Mar, all with popular surfing beaches. When you get to **La Jolla,** swing around the cove to see one of the area's most beautiful beaches. Look, but don't go in the water at the Children's Pool, as it's likely to be filled with barking seals. The **Birch Aquarium at Scripps** here offers a look at how scientists study the oceans.

Hop onto Interstate 5 and head for Downtown **San Diego.** Go straight for the city's nautical heart by exploring the restored ships of the **Maritime Museum** at the waterfront in Downtown. Victorian buildings—and plenty of other tourists—surround you on a stroll through the **Gaslamp Quarter.** Plant yourself at a Downtown hotel and graze your way through the neighborhood's many restaurants.

DAY 5: SAN DIEGO ZOO
(10 mins by car from Downtown San Diego.)

Malayan tapirs in a faux-Asian rain forest, polar bears in an imitation Arctic, and pandas frolicking in the trees—the **San Diego Zoo** maintains a vast and varied collection of creatures in a world-renowned facility comprised of meticulously designed habitats. Come early, and wear comfy shoes. Have dinner in the nearby **Hillcrest** neighborhood or Downtown.

DAY 6: SEAWORLD AND OLD TOWN
(From Downtown San Diego, both Sea-World and Old Town are 10 mins by car.)

Two commercial and touristy sights are on the agenda today. **SeaWorld,** with its walk-through shark tanks, can be a lot of fun if you surrender to the experience. Also touristy, but with genuine historical significance, **Old Town** drips with Mexican and early Californian heritage. Soak it up in the plaza at **Old Town San Diego State Historic Park,** then browse the stalls and shops at **Fiesta de Reyes** and along San Diego Avenue. Unwind after a long day with dinner and margaritas at one of Old Town's many Mexican restaurants.

DAY 7: DEPARTURE FROM SAN DIEGO OR LOS ANGELES
(San Diego Airport is 10 mins by car from Downtown. Depending on traffic, allow 2½–4 hrs to drive from Downtown San Diego to LAX.)

Pack up your Mouseketeer gear and give yourself ample time to reach the airport. San Diego International Airport lies within a 10-minute drive from Old Town. Although you'll be driving on freeways the entire way to LAX, traffic is always heavy and you should allot at least a half day to get there.

Great Itineraries

The Southern Pacific Coast Highway: Sand, Surf, and Sun, 3 Days

This tour along the southern section of the Pacific Coast Highway (PCH) is a beach vacation on wheels, taking in the highlights of the Southern California coast and its world-famous surfer-chic vibe. If at any point the drive feels like something out of a movie, that's because it likely is—this is the California of Hollywood legend. The itinerary is easily combined with the Big Sur and Northern Coast itineraries to do a full run of the legendary coastal route. Roll the top down on the convertible and let the adventure begin.

DAY 1: SANTA BARBARA TO SANTA MONICA
(About 2 hrs by car via the 101 and Hwy. 1. Allow plenty of time for beach stops and be aware of rush-hour traffic as you approach Santa Monica.)

Don't leave **Santa Barbara** without exploring the highlights of this Mediterranean-inspired city. Take a stroll along State Street, through the red-tile-roofed buildings of downtown to the gorgeous **Santa Barbara County Courthouse** and take in the views from its tower. Before leaving town, make a stop at the **Mission Santa Barbara,** widely considered the finest of the 21 California missions.

Heading south out of town the 101 runs along the coast past the low-key beach communities of Carpinteria and Mussel Shoals. Approaching **Ventura** on a clear day, the Channel Islands are visible in the distance. Stretch your legs on the **Ventura Oceanfront** with a walk on San Buenaventura State Beach, or around the picturesque Ventura Harbor. There are several

spots to grab lunch at the harbor, too, including an outpost of Santa Barbara's famous **Brophy Bros.** seafood restaurant.

Leaving Ventura, trade the 101 for Highway 1 and continue south through miles of protected, largely unpopulated coastline. Hike the trails at **Point Mugu State Park,** scout for offshore whales at **Point Dume State Beach,** or ride a wave at **Zuma Beach.** The PCH follows the curve of Santa Monica Bay from Point Mugu through Malibu and on to Santa Monica. Chances are you'll experience déjà vu driving this stretch of road: mountains on one side, ocean on the other, opulent homes perched on hillsides; you've seen this piece of coast countless times on TV and film. As you approach Malibu proper, affectionately known as "the 'bu," be sure to walk out on the **Malibu Pier** for a great photo op, then check out **Surfrider Beach,** with three famous points where perfect waves ignited a worldwide surfing rage in the 1960s.

If you plan to visit the **Getty Villa Malibu,** with its impressive antiquities collection and jaw-dropping setting overlooking the Pacific, you will need to obtain free timed-entry tickets online prior to your arrival. Otherwise, continue the drive to Santa Monica where you can overnight near the **Santa Monica Pier** and grab dinner along the **Third Street Promenade** or at Santa Monica Place.

DAY 2: SANTA MONICA TO NEWPORT BEACH
(About 2 hrs by car without traffic, but plan for traffic.)

Start the day with a morning walk along **Santa Monica State Beach** and, if you didn't visit it the night before, the **Santa Monica Pier.** Rent some beach cruisers and pedal your way south along the bike path to **Venice Beach** (about 3 miles each way) to take in the action along the boardwalk.

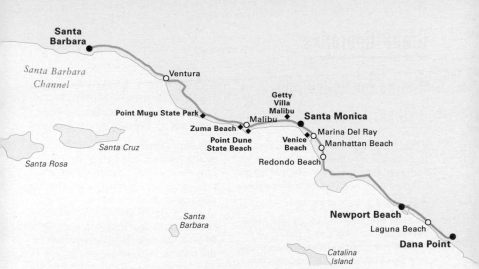

Once you tire of the skateboarders, bodybuilders, and street performers, head inland a few blocks to Abbott Kinney Boulevard for lunch at **Gjelina** and a browse in the local boutiques.

Pedal back to Santa Monica and trade two wheels for four to continue the drive toward Newport Beach. If time permits, you can follow Highway 1 through Marina del Ray and the trio of beach towns well known among beach-volleyball enthusiasts: Manhattan, Hermosa, and Redondo Beach. From here Highway 1 skirts through Long Beach and continues into Orange County. If time is short, skip this section of the PCH in favor of the 405 freeway. However, as is always advisable near L.A., check current traffic reports before choosing your route.

The affluent coastal cities of Orange County (aka the O.C.) are familiar to many thanks to *Arrested Development, The Real Wives of Orange County,* and other TV shows set here. However, the dazzling yachts and multimillion-dollar mansions of Newport Beach still may take you by surprise after the more laid-back brand of luxe found elsewhere on the coast.

Choose from among the many excellent restaurants and overnight at **The Island Hotel.**

DAY 3: NEWPORT BEACH TO DANA POINT
(1 hr by car.)

The next morning, head to Balboa Island in the middle of Newport Harbor. This far quainter (but equally expensive) community is a getaway for locals and tourists alike. Browse the boutiques along Marine Avenue before hopping in a Duffy (electric boat) for a harbor tour. Back on land, don't leave without enjoying a Balboa Bar—the ice-cream treat is virtually mandatory for all Balboa Island visitors. Leaving Newport Beach on the PCH, your next stop is Crystal Cove State Park, 6 miles southeast. If the tide is low, this is a great spot for tide pooling. Otherwise, don't miss the historic beach cottages dating as far back as 1935.

Back on the road, **Laguna Beach** is this journey's final stop. In an area not often noted for its cultural offerings, Laguna Beach is the exception. Browse the art galleries and enjoy a meal in the charming downtown before taking one last walk along the Pacific. The PCH terminates 10 miles south of Laguna Beach near Dana Point, a town famous for its harbor and whale-watching excursions. From here, you can continue to San Diego or return north to Anaheim or Los Angeles via Interstate 5.

Great Itineraries

Hooray for Hollywood, 4 Days

If you are a movie fan, there's no better place to see it all than L.A. Always keep your eyes out for a familiar face: you never know when you might spot a celebrity.

DAY 1: LOS ANGELES

As soon as you land at LAX, make like a local and hit the freeway. Even if L.A.'s top-notch art, history, and science museums don't tempt you, the hodgepodge of art deco, Beaux Arts, and futuristic architecture begs at least a drive-by. Heading east from Santa Monica, Wilshire Boulevard cuts through a historical and cultural cross section of the city. Two stellar sights on its Miracle Mile are the encyclopedic **Los Angeles County Museum of Art** and the fossil-filled **La Brea Tar Pits.** Come evening, the open-air **Farmers Market** and its many eateries hum. Hotels in Beverly Hills or West Hollywood beckon, just a few minutes away.

DAY 2: HOLLYWOOD AND THE MOVIE STUDIOS

(Avoid driving to the studios during rush hour. Studio tours vary in length—plan at least a half day for the excursion.)

Every L.A. tourist should devote at least one day to the movies and take at least one studio tour in the San Fernando Valley. For fun, choose the special-effects theme park at **Universal Studios Hollywood**; for the nitty-gritty, choose **Warner Bros. Studios.** Nostalgic musts in Hollywood include the **Hollywood Walk of Fame** along **Hollywood Boulevard** and the celebrity footprints cast in concrete outside **Grauman's Chinese Theatre** (now known as the TCL Chinese Theater). When evening arrives, the Hollywood scene boasts a bevy of trendy restaurants and nightclubs.

DAYS 3 AND 4: BEVERLY HILLS AND SANTA MONICA

(15–20 mins by car between destinations, but considerably longer in traffic.)

The **Getty Center**'s pavilion architecture, hilltop gardens, and frame-worthy L.A. views make it a dazzling destination—and that's before you experience the extensive art collection. From the museum, descend to the sea via Santa Monica Boulevard for lunch along **Third Street Promenade,** followed by a ride on the historic carousel on the pier. The buff and the bizarre meet at Venice Beach's **Ocean Front Walk**—strap on some Rollerblades if you want to join them! Over in Beverly Hills, **Rodeo Drive** specializes in exhibitionism with a heftier price tag, but voyeurs are still welcome.

Splurge on breakfast or brunch at a posh café in the **Farmers Market,** then stroll through aisles and aisles of gorgeous produce and specialty food before you take a last look at the Pacific Ocean through the camera obscura at **Palisades Park** in Santa Monica.

Chapter 4

SAN DIEGO

Updated by
Claire Deeks Van
Der Lee, Marlise
Kast-Myers,
Jeff Terich, and
Kai Oliver-Kurtin

4

⊙ Sights ★★★★★ 🍴 Restaurants ★★★★★ 🛏 Hotels ★★★★★ 💼 Shopping ★★★★☆ 🍸 Nightlife ★★★☆☆

WELCOME TO SAN DIEGO

TOP REASONS TO GO

★ **Sun and Surf:** Legendary beaches and surfing in La Jolla, Coronado, and Point Loma.

★ **Good Eats:** Brewpubs, a wide mix of ethnic cuisines, fresh seafood and produce, and modern cafés delight diners.

★ **Great Golf:** A concentration of beautiful courses with sweeping ocean views and light breezes.

★ **Stellar Shopping:** From hip boutiques and fine Mexican crafts to the upscale Fashion Valley Mall.

★ **Family Time:** Fun for all ages at LEGOLAND, Balboa Park, the San Diego Zoo, and more.

★ **Outdoor Sports:** A perfect climate for biking, hiking, sailing—anything—outdoors.

1 Downtown. San Diego's Downtown area is delightfully urban and accessible, filled with walkable A-list attractions like the Gaslamp Quarter and the waterfront.

2 Balboa Park, Bankers Hill, and San Diego Zoo. San Diego's cultural heart is where you'll find most of the city's museums and its world-famous zoo.

3 Old Town and Uptown. California's first permanent European settlement is now preserved as a state historic park in Old Town. Uptown is composed of several smaller neighborhoods that showcase a unique blend of historical charm and modern urban community.

4 Mission Bay and the Beaches. Home to 27 miles of shoreline, this 4,600-acre aquatic park is San Diego's monument to sports and fitness.

5 La Jolla. This luxe, bluff-top enclave fittingly means "the jewel" in Spanish. Come here for fantastic upscale shopping and unspoiled stretches of the coast.

6 Point Loma Peninsula. Visit the site of the first European landfall on Point Loma.

7 Coronado. Home to the Hotel Del, Coronado's island-like isthmus is a favorite celebrity haunt.

PACIFIC OCEAN

0		2 mi
0	2 km	

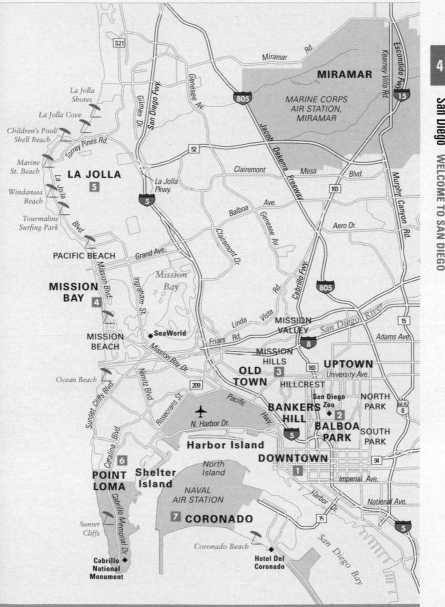

S21

Miramar Rd.

MIRAMAR

805

MARINE CORPS
AIR STATION,
MIRAMAR

Kearney Villa Rd.

Escondido Frwy.

15

La Jolla
Shores

La Jolla Cove

Children's Pool/
Shell Beach

Marine
St. Beach

Windansea
Beach

Tourmaline
Surfing Park

LA JOLLA
5

Torrey Pines Rd.

Gilman Dr.

San Diego Frwy.

Genesee Av.

52

La Jolla
Pkwy.

Clairemont

Mesa

Blvd.

163

Jacob Dekema Freeway

Murphy Canyon Rd.

5

La Jolla Blvd.

Balboa

Ave.

Genesee Av.

Aero Dr.

Clairemont Dr.

PACIFIC BEACH

Grand Ave.

Mission Blvd.

Ingraham St.

Mission
Bay

MISSION
BAY
4

MISSION
BEACH

Mission Bay Dr.

SeaWorld

Friars Rd.

Linda

Vista

Rd.

805

MISSION
VALLEY

San Diego River

8

15

Adams Ave.

Ocean Beach

Sunset Cliffs Blvd.

Nimitz Blvd.

Catalina Blvd.

Rosecrans St.

Pacific

Hwy.

N. Harbor Dr.

209

MISSION
HILLS

OLD
TOWN
3

163

HILLCREST

UPTOWN

University Ave.

BANKERS
HILL

San Diego
Zoo

BALBOA
PARK

5

NORTH
PARK

BUS
8

SOUTH
PARK

2

Harbor Island

Shelter
Island

POINT
LOMA
6

North
Island

NAVAL
AIR STATION

7 CORONADO

DOWNTOWN
1

94

Imperial Ave.

National Ave.

Harbor Dr.

75

5

Sunset
Cliffs

Cabrillo Memorial Dr.

Cabrillo
National
Monument

Coronado Beach

Hotel Del
Coronado

San Diego Bay

San Diego is a vacationer's paradise, complete with idyllic year-round temperatures and 70 miles of pristine coastline. Recognized as one of the nation's leading family destinations, with LEGOLAND and the San Diego Zoo, San Diego is equally attractive to those in search of art, history, world-class shopping, and culinary exploration. San Diego's beaches are legendary, offering family-friendly sands, killer surf breaks, and spectacular scenery. San Diego's cultural sophistication often surprises visitors, as the city is better known for its laid-back vibe. Tourists come for some fun in the sun, only to discover a city with much greater depth.

San Diego is a big California city—second only to Los Angeles in population—with a small-town feel. San Diego's many neighborhoods offer diverse adventures: from the tony boutiques in La Jolla to the yoga and surf shops of Encinitas; from the subtle sophistication of Little Italy to the flashy nightlife of the Downtown Gaslamp Quarter, each community adds flavor and flair to San Diego's personality.

San Diego County also covers a lot of territory, roughly 400 square miles of land and sea. To the north and south of the city are its famed beaches. Inland, a succession of chaparral-covered mesas is punctuated with deep-cut canyons that step up to forested mountains.

Known as the birthplace of California, San Diego was claimed for Spain by explorer Juan Rodríguez Cabrillo in 1542 and eventually came under Mexican rule. You'll find reminders of San Diego's Spanish and Mexican heritage throughout the region—in architecture and place-names, in distinctive Mexican cuisine, and in the historic buildings of Old Town.

In 1867 developer Alonzo Horton, who called the town's bay front "the prettiest place for a city I ever saw," began building a hotel, a plaza, and prefab homes on 960 Downtown acres. A remarkable number of these buildings are preserved in San Diego's historic Gaslamp Quarter today. The city's fate was sealed in the 1920s when the U.S. Navy, impressed by the city's excellent harbor and temperate climate, decided to build a destroyer base on San Diego Bay. Today, the military operates many bases and installations throughout the county (which, added together, form the largest military base in the world) and continues to be a major contributor to the local economy.

Planning

Getting Here and Around

AIR TRAVEL
The major airport is San Diego International Airport (SAN), formerly called Lindbergh Field. Most airlines depart and arrive at Terminal 2. Southwest, Frontier, and Alaska Airlines are reserved for Terminal 1. Free, color-coded shuttles loop the airport and match the parking lot they serve.

AIRPORT San Diego International Airport. ⊠ 3225 N. Harbor Dr., off I–5 ☎ 619/400–2400 ⊕ www.san.org.

AIRPORT TRANSFERS SuperShuttle. ⊠ 123 Caminio de la Riena ☎ 800/258–3826 ⊕ www.supershuttle.com. **San Diego Transit.** ☎ 619/233–3004 ⊕ www.511sd.com.

BUS AND TROLLEY TRAVEL
Under the umbrella of the Metropolitan Transit System, there are two major transit agencies in the area: San Diego Transit and North County Transit District (NCTD). The bright-red trolleys of the San Diego Trolley light-rail system operate on three lines that serve Downtown San Diego, Mission Valley, Old Town, South Bay, the U.S. border, and East County. The trolley system connects with San Diego Transit bus routes—connections are posted at each trolley station.

San Diego Transit bus fares range from $2.25 to $5; North County Transit District bus fares are $4. You must have exact change in coins and/or bills. Pay upon boarding. Transfers are not included; the $5 day pass is the best option for most bus travel and can be purchased on board.

San Diego Trolley tickets cost $2.50 and are good for two hours, but for one-way travel only. For a round-trip journey or longer, day passes are available for $5.

BUS AND TROLLEY INFORMATION North County Transit District. ☎ 760/966–6500 ⊕ www.gonctd.com. **San Diego Transit.** ☎ 619/233–3004 ⊕ www.511sd.com. **Transit Store.** ⊠ 102 Broadway ☎ 619/234–1060 ⊕ www.sdmts.com.

CAR TRAVEL
A car is necessary for getting around greater San Diego on the sprawling freeway system and for visiting the North County beaches, mountains, and desert. Driving around San Diego County is pretty simple: most major attractions are within a few miles of the Pacific Ocean. Interstate 5, which stretches north–south from Oregon to the Mexican border, bisects San Diego. Interstate 8 provides access from Yuma, Arizona, and points east. Drivers coming from the Los Angeles area, Nevada, and the mountain regions beyond can reach San Diego on Interstate 15. During rush hours there are jams on Interstate 5 and on Interstate 15 between Interstate 805 and Escondido.

There are a few border inspection stations along major highways in San Diego County, the largest just north of Oceanside on Interstate 5 near San Clemente. Travel with your driver's license, and passport if you're an international traveler.

TAXI TRAVEL

Fares vary among companies. If you're heading to the airport from a hotel, ask about the flat rate, which varies according to destination; otherwise you'll be charged by the mile (which works out to $20 or so from any Downtown location). Taxi stands are at shopping centers and hotels; otherwise you must call and reserve a cab. For on-demand private transportation, Uber is readily available throughout San Diego County with competitive rates up to 40% less than that of a taxi. The companies listed *below* don't serve all areas of San Diego County. If you're going somewhere other than Downtown, ask if the company serves that area.

TAXI COMPANIES Orange Cab. ☎ 619/223–5555 ⊕ *www.orange-cabsandiego.net.* **Silver Cabs.** ☎ 619/280–5555 ⊕ *www.sandiegosilvercab.com.* **Yellow Cab.** ☎ 619/444–4444 ⊕ *www.driveu.com.*

TRAIN TRAVEL

Amtrak serves Downtown San Diego's Santa Fe Depot with daily trains to and from Los Angeles, Santa Barbara, and San Luis Obispo. Amtrak trains stop in San Diego North County at Solana Beach and Oceanside. Coaster commuter trains, which run between Oceanside and San Diego Monday through Saturday, stop at the same stations as Amtrak as well as others. The frequency is about every half hour during the weekday rush hour, with four trains on Saturday. One-way fares are $4 to $5.50, depending on the distance traveled. The *Sprinter* runs between Oceanside and Escondido, with many stops along the way.

Metrolink operates high-speed rail service ($17) between the Oceanside Transit Center and Union Station in Los Angeles.

INFORMATION Coaster. ☎ 760/966–6500 ⊕ *www.gonctd.com/coaster.* **Metrolink.** ☎ 800/371–5465 ⊕ *www.metrolink-trains.com.*

Activities

San Diego offers bountiful opportunities for bikers, from casual boardwalk cruises to strenuous rides into the hills. The mild climate makes biking in San Diego a year-round delight. Bike culture is respected here, and visitors are often impressed with the miles of designated bike lanes running alongside city streets and coastal roads throughout the county.

If you're a beginner surfer, consider paddling in the waves off Mission Beach, Pacific Beach, Tourmaline Surfing Park, La Jolla Shores, Del Mar, or Oceanside. More experienced surfers usually head for Sunset Cliffs, La Jolla reef breaks, Black's Beach, or Swami's in Encinitas. All necessary equipment is included in the cost of all surfing schools. Beach-area Y's offer surf lessons and surf camp in the summer months and during spring break.

Beaches

San Diego's beaches have a different vibe from their northern counterparts in neighboring Orange County and glitzy Los Angeles farther up the coast. San Diego is more laid-back and less of a scene. Cyclists on cruiser bikes whiz by as surfers saunter toward the waves and sunbathers bronze under the sun, be it July or November.

Even at summer's hottest peak, San Diego's beaches are cool and breezy. Ocean waves are large, and the water will be colder than what you experience at tropical beaches—temperatures range from 55°F to 65°F from October through June, and 65°F to 73°F from July through September.

Finding a parking spot near the ocean can be hard in summer. Del Mar has a pay lot and metered street parking around the 15th Street Beach. La Jolla Shores has free street parking up to two hours. Mission Beach and other large beaches have unmetered parking lots, but space can be limited. Your best bet is to arrive early.

Pay attention to signs listing illegal activities; undercover police often patrol the beaches. Smoking and alcoholic beverages are completely banned on city beaches. Drinking in beach parking lots, on boardwalks, and in landscaped areas is also illegal. Glass containers are not permitted on beaches, cliffs, and walkways, or in park areas and adjacent parking lots. Littering is not tolerated, and skateboarding is prohibited at some beaches. Fires are allowed only in fire rings or elevated barbecue grills. Although it may be tempting to take a sea creature from a tide pool as a souvenir, it may upset the delicate ecological balance, and it's illegal, too.

Year-round, lifeguards are stationed at nine permanent stations from Sunset Cliffs to Black's Beach. All other beaches are covered by roving patrols in the winter, and seasonal towers in the summer. When swimming in the ocean be aware of rip currents, which are common in California shores. For a surf and weather report, call San Diego's Lifeguard Services at ☎ 619/221–8899. Visit ⊕ www.surfline. com for live webcams on surf conditions and water temperature forecasts.

Restaurants

San Diego is an up-and-coming culinary destination, thanks to its stunning Pacific Ocean setting, proximity to Mexico, diverse population, and the area's extraordinary farming community. Increasingly the city's veteran top chefs are being joined by a new generation of talented chefs and restaurateurs who are adding stylish restaurants with innovative food and drink programs to the dining scene at a record pace. Yes, visitors still are drawn to the San Diego Zoo and miles of beaches, but now they come for memorable dining experiences as well.

The city's culinary scene got a significant boost when San Diego emerged as one of the world's top craft beer destinations,

with artisan breweries and gastropubs now in almost every neighborhood. These neighborhoods are also ethnically diverse with modest eateries offering affordable authentic international cuisines that add spice to the dining mix.

The trendy Gaslamp Quarter delights visitors looking for a broad range of innovative and international dining and nightlife, while bustling Little Italy offers a mix of affordable Italian fare and posh new eateries. Modern restaurants and cafés thrive in East Village, amid the luxury condos near PETCO Park. The Uptown neighborhoods centered on Hillcrest—an urbane district with San Francisco flavor—are a mix of bars and independent restaurants, many of which specialize in ethnic cuisine. North Park, in particular, has a happening restaurant and craft beer scene, with just about every kind of cuisine you can think of, and laid-back prices to boot. And scenic La Jolla offers some of the best fine dining in the city with dramatic water views as an added bonus.

PRICES

Meals in San Diego popular dining spots can be pricey, especially in areas like La Jolla, the Gaslamp Quarter, and Coronado. Many other restaurants are very affordable or offer extra value with fixed-price menus, early-dining specials and early and late happy hours.

Restaurant reviews have been shortened. For full information, visit Fodors.com.

What It Costs			
$	$$	$$$	$$$$
RESTAURANTS			
under $18	$18–$27	$28–$35	over $35

Hotels

Sharing the city's postcard-perfect sunny skies are neighborhoods and coastal communities that offer great diversity; San Diego is no longer the sleepy beach town it once was. In action-packed Downtown, luxury hotels cater to solo business travelers and young couples with trendy restaurants and cabana-encircled pools. Budget-friendly options can be found in smaller neighborhoods just outside the Gaslamp Quarter such as Little Italy and Uptown.

You'll need a car if you stay outside Downtown, but the beach communities are rich with lodging options. Across the bridge, Coronado's hotels and resorts offer access to a stretch of glistening white sand that's often recognized as one of the best beaches in the country. La Jolla offers many romantic, upscale ocean-view hotels and some of the area's best restaurants and specialty shopping. But it's easy to find a water view in any price range: surfers make themselves at home at the casual inns and budget stays at Pacific Beach and Mission Bay. If you're planning to fish, check out hotels located near the marinas in Shelter Island, Point Loma, or Coronado.

For families, Uptown, Mission Valley, and Old Town are close to the San Diego Zoo, offering good-value accommodations with extras like sleeper sofas and video games. Mission Valley is ideal for business travelers; there are plenty of well-known chain hotels with conference space, modern business centers, and kitchenettes for extended stays.

When you make reservations, book well in advance and ask about specials. Several properties in the Hotel Circle area of Mission Valley offer reduced rates and even free tickets to the San Diego Zoo and other attractions. You can save on hotels and attractions by visiting the San Diego Tourism Authority website (⊕ www.sandiego.org) for special seasonal offers.

PRICES

Note that even in the most expensive areas, you can find affordable rooms. High season is summer, and rates are lowest in fall. If an ocean view is important, request it when booking, but it will cost you.

Hotel reviews have been shortened. For full information, visit Fodors.com.

WHAT IT COSTS			
$	$$	$$$	$$$$
HOTELS			
under $150	$150–$225	$226–$300	over $300

Nightlife

A couple of decades ago, San Diego scraped by on its superb daytime offerings. Those sleepy-after-dark days are over; San Diego now sizzles when the sun goes down. Of particular interest to beer lovers, the city has become internationally acclaimed for dozens of breweries, beer pubs, and festivals.

The Gaslamp Quarter is still one of the most popular areas to go for a night on the town. Named for actual gaslights that once provided illumination along its once-seedy streets (it housed a number of gambling halls and brothels), the neighborhood bears only a trace of its debauched roots. Between the Gaslamp and nearby East Village, Downtown San Diego mostly comprises chic nightclubs, tourist-heavy pubs, and a handful of live music venues. Even most of the hotels Downtown have a street-level or rooftop bar—so plan on making it a late night if that's where you intend to bunk. On weekends, parking can be tricky; most lots run about $20, and though there is metered parking (free after 6 pm and all day Sunday), motorists don't give up those coveted spots so easily. Some restaurants and clubs offer valet, though that can get pricey.

Hillcrest is a popular area for LGBTQ nightlife and culture, whereas just a little bit east of Hillcrest, ever-expanding North Park features a diverse range of bars and lounges that cater to a twenty- and thirtysomething crowd, bolstering its reputation as the city's hipster capital. Nearby Normal Heights is a slightly less pretentious alternative, though whichever of these neighborhoods strikes your fancy, a cab from Downtown will run about the same price: $15.

Nightlife along the beaches is more of a mixed bag. Where the scene in Pacific Beach might feel like every week is Spring Break, La Jolla veers toward being more cost-prohibitive. And although Point Loma is often seen as a sleeper neighborhood in terms of nightlife, it's coming into its own with some select destinations.

If your drink involves caffeine and not alcohol, there's no shortage of coffeehouses in San Diego, and some of the better ones in Hillcrest and North Park stay open past midnight.

Shopping

San Diego's retail landscape has changed radically in recent years with the opening of several new shopping centers—some in historic buildings—that are focused more on locally owned boutiques than national retailers. Where once the Gaslamp was the place to go for urban apparel and unique home decor, many independently owned boutiques have decided to set up shop in the charming neighborhoods east of Balboa Park known as North Park and South Park. Although Downtown is still thriving, any shopping trip to San Diego should include venturing out to the city's diverse and vibrant neighborhoods. Not far from Downtown, Little Italy is the place to find contemporary art, modern furniture, and home accessories.

Old Town is a must for pottery, ceramics, jewelry, and handcrafted baskets. Uptown is known for its mélange of funky bookstores, offbeat gift shops, and nostalgic collectibles and vintage stores. The beach towns offer the best swimwear and sandals. La Jolla's chic boutiques offer a more intimate shopping experience, along with some of the classiest clothes, jewelry, and shoes in the county. The new La Plaza La Jolla is an open-air shopping center with boutiques and galleries in a Spanish-style building overlooking the cove. Point Loma's Liberty Station shopping area in the former Naval Training Center has art galleries, restaurants, and home stores. Trendsetters will have no trouble finding must-have handbags and designer apparel at the world-class Fashion Valley mall in Mission Valley, a haven for luxury brands such as Hermès, Gucci, and Jimmy Choo.

Enjoy near-perfect weather year-round as you explore shops along the scenic waterfront. The Headquarters at Seaport is a new open-air shopping and dining center in the city's former Police Headquarters building. Here there are some big names, but mostly locally owned boutiques selling everything from gourmet cheese to coastal-inspired home accessories. Just next door, Seaport Village is still the place to go for trinkets and souvenirs. If you don't discover what you're looking for in the boutiques, head to Westfield Horton Plaza, the Downtown mall with more than 120 stores. The sprawling mall completed a major restoration project in 2016 to include a new public plaza, amphitheater, and fountains.

Most malls have free parking in a lot or garage, and parking is not usually a problem. Some of the shops in the Gaslamp Quarter offer validated parking or valet parking.

Tours

BOAT TOURS

Visitors to San Diego can get a great overview of the city from the water. Tour companies offer a range of harbor cruises, from one-hour jaunts to dinner and dancing cruises. In season, whale-watching voyages are another popular option.

Flagship Cruises and Events

BOAT TOURS | One- and two-hour tours of the San Diego Harbor loop north or south from the Broadway Pier throughout the day. Other offerings include dinner and dance cruises, brunch cruises, and winter whale-watching tours December–mid-April. ⊠ 990 N. Harbor Dr., Embarcadero ☎ 619/234–4111 ⊕ www.flagshipsd.com 🖭 From $27.

H&M Landing

BOAT TOURS | From mid-December to March, this outfitter offers three-hour tours to spot migrating gray whales just off the San Diego coast. ⊠ 2803 Emerson St. ☎ 619/222–1144 ⊕ www.hmlanding.com 🖭 From $50.

Hornblower Cruises & Events

BOAT TOURS | One- and two-hour cruises around San Diego Harbor depart from the Embarcadero several times a day and alternate between the northern and southern portion of the bay. If you're hoping to spot some sea lions, take the North Bay route. Dinner and brunch cruises are also offered, as well as whale-watching tours in winter. ⊠ 970 N. Harbor Dr. ☎ 619/686–8700, 888/467–6256 ⊕ www.hornblower.com 🖭 From $27.

San Diego SEAL Tours

BOAT TOURS | This amphibious tour drives along the Embarcadero before splashing into the San Diego Harbor for a cruise. The 90-minute tours depart daily from 10 am to 5 pm from Seaport Village and the Embarcadero. Call for daily departure times and locations. ⊠ 500 Kettner Blvd., Embarcadero ☎ 619/298–8687 ⊕ www.sealtours.com 🖭 $42.

Seaforth Boat Rentals

BOAT TOURS | For those seeking a private tour on the water, this company can provide a skipper along with your boat rental. Options include harbor cruises, whale-watching, and sunset sails. Seaforth has four locations and a diverse fleet of sail and motorboats to choose from. ⊠ 1641 Quivira Rd., Mission Bay ☎ 888/834–2628 ⊕ www.seaforthboatrental.com 🖭 From $160.

BUS AND TROLLEY TOURS

For those looking to cover a lot of ground in a limited time, narrated trolley tours include everything from Balboa Park to Coronado. To venture farther afield, consider a coach tour to the desert, Los Angeles, or even Baja, Mexico.

DayTripper Tours

BUS TOURS | FAMILY | Single- and multiday trips throughout Southern California, the Southwest, and Baja depart from San Diego year-round. Popular day trips include the Getty Museum, and theater performances in Los Angeles. Call or check the website for pickup locations. ☎ 619/334–3394, 800/679–8747 ⊕ www.daytripper.com 🖭 From $89.

Five Star Tours

BUS TOURS | Private and group sightseeing bus tour options around San Diego and beyond include everything from the San Diego Zoo and brewery tours to city tours and trips to Baja, Mexico. ⊠ 1050 Kettner Blvd. ☎ 619/232–5040 ⊕ www.fivestartours.com 🖭 From $50.

Old Town Trolley Tours

GUIDED TOURS | FAMILY | Combining points of interest with local history, trivia, and fun anecdotes, this hop-on, hop-off trolley tour provides an entertaining overview of the city and offers easy access to all the highlights. The tour is narrated, and you can get on and off as you please. Stops include Old Town, Seaport Village, the Gaslamp Quarter, Coronado, Little

Italy, and Balboa Park. The trolley leaves every 30 minutes, operates daily, and takes two hours to make a full loop. ⊠ *San Diego* ☎ *866/754–0966* ⊕ *www. trolleytours.com/san-diego* ⌷ *From $40.*

San Diego Scenic Tours

BUS TOURS | Half- and full-day bus tours of San Diego and Tijuana depart daily, and some include a harbor cruise. Tours depart from several hotels around town. ⊠ *San Diego* ☎ *858/273–8687* ⊕ *www. sandiegoscenictours.com* ⌷ *From $38.*

WALKING TOURS

Several fine walking tours are available on weekdays or weekends; upcoming walks are usually listed in the *San Diego Reader.*

Balboa Park Offshoot Tours

GUIDED TOURS | On Saturday at 10 am, free, hour-long walks start from the Balboa Park Visitor Center. The tour's focus rotates weekly, covering topics such as the park's history, palm trees, and desert vegetation. Reservations are not required, but no tours are scheduled between Thanksgiving and the New Year. ⊠ *Balboa Park Visitor Center, 1549 El Prado, Balboa Park* ☎ *619/239–0512* ⊕ *www. balboapark.org* ⌷ *Free.*

Coronado Walking Tours

WALKING TOURS | Departing from the Glorietta Bay Inn at 11 am Tuesday, Thursday, and Saturday, this 90-minute stroll through Coronado's historic district takes in the island's mansions, old Tent City, the Hotel del Coronado, and the castles and cottages that line the beautiful beach. Reservations are recommended. ⊠ *1630 Glorietta Blvd.* ☎ *619/435–5993* ⊕ *www.coronadowalkingtour.com* ⌷ *$15* ⌸ *Cash only.*

Gaslamp Quarter Historical Foundation

WALKING TOURS | Two-hour walking tours of the Downtown historic district depart from the William Heath Davis House at 11 am on Saturday. ⊠ *410 Island Ave.* ☎ *619/233–4692* ⊕ *gaslampfoundation. org* ⌷ *$20.*

Urban Safaris

GUIDED TOURS | Led by longtime San Diego resident Patty Fares, these two-hour Saturday walks through diverse neighborhoods like Hillcrest, Ocean Beach, and Point Loma are popular with tourists and locals alike. The tours, which always depart from a neighborhood coffeehouse, focus on art, history, and ethnic eateries, among other topics. Reservations are required, and private walks can be arranged during the week. ☎ *619/944–9255* ⊕ *www.walkingtoursofsandiego. com* ⌷ *$15.*

Visitor Information

For general information and brochures before you go, contact the San Diego Tourism Authority, which publishes the helpful *San Diego Visitors Planning Guide.* When you arrive, stop by one of the local visitor centers for general information.

When to Go

San Diego's weather is so ideal that most locals shrug off the high cost of living and relatively lower wages as a "sunshine tax." Along the coast, average temperatures range from the mid-60s to the high 70s, with clear skies and low humidity. Annual rainfall is minimal, less than 10 inches per year.

The peak season for sun seekers is July through October. In July and August, the mercury spikes and everyone spills outside. From mid-December to mid-March, whale-watchers can glimpse migrating gray whales frolicking in the Pacific. In spring and early summer, a marine layer hugs the coastline for much or all of the day (locals call it "June Gloom"), which can be dreary and disappointing for those who were expecting to bask in Southern California sunshine.

Downtown

Nearly written off in the 1970s, today Downtown San Diego is a testament to conservation and urban renewal. Once derelict Victorian storefronts now house the hottest restaurants, and the *Star of India,* the world's oldest active sailing ship, almost lost to scrap, floats regally along the Embarcadero. Like many modern U.S. cities, Downtown San Diego's story is as much about its rebirth as its history. Although many consider Downtown to be the 16½-block Gaslamp Quarter, it's actually comprised of eight neighborhoods, including East Village, Little Italy, and Embarcadero.

Gaslamp Quarter

Considered the liveliest of the Downtown neighborhoods, the Gaslamp Quarter's 4th and 5th avenues are peppered with trendy nightclubs, swanky lounge bars, chic restaurants, and boisterous sports pubs. The Gaslamp has the largest collection of commercial Victorian-style buildings in the country. Despite this, when the move for Downtown redevelopment gained momentum in the 1970s, there was talk of bulldozing them and starting from scratch. In response, concerned history buffs, developers, architects, and artists formed the Gaslamp Quarter Council to clean up and preserve the quarter. The majority of the quarter's landmark buildings are on 4th and 5th avenues, between Island Avenue and Broadway.

👁 Sights

Gaslamp Museum at the Davis-Horton House

HISTORIC SITE | The oldest wooden house in San Diego houses the Gaslamp Quarter Historical Foundation, the district's curator. Before developer Alonzo Horton came to town, Davis, a prominent San Franciscan, had made an unsuccessful attempt to develop the waterfront area. In 1850 he had this prefab saltbox-style house, built in Maine, shipped around Cape Horn, and assembled in San Diego (it originally stood at State and Market streets). Ninety-minute walking tours ($20) of the historic district leave from the house on Thursday at 1 pm (summer only) and Saturday at 11 am (year-round). If you can't time your visit with the tour, a self-guided tour map ($2) is available. ✉ *410 Island Ave., at 4th Ave., Gaslamp Quarter* ☎ *619/233–4692* 🌐 *www.gaslampfoundation.org* 🎟 *$5 self-guided, $10 with audio tour* ⏱ *Closed Mon.*

🍴 Restaurants

Searsucker

$$$ | **AMERICAN** | Since opened by celebrity chef Brian Malarkey a few years ago, this high-energy flagship restaurant has become the Gaslamp's best for food and energetic atmosphere. Foodies from near and far savor the upscale down-home fare like small plates of biscuits with spicy honey, duck fat fries, and shrimp and grits. **Known for:** detailed, home-inspired decor; crispy duck fat fries; late-night menu on Friday and Saturday 11 pm–1 am. [$] *Average main: $30* ✉ *611 5th Ave., Gaslamp Quarter* ☎ *619/233–7327* 🌐 *www.searsucker.com.*

Taka

$$ | **JAPANESE** | Pristine fish imported from around the world and presented creatively attracts crowds nightly to this intimate Gaslamp restaurant. Table service is available inside and outside where an *omakase* (tasting menu) or eight-piece rolls can be shared and savored; take a seat at the bar to watch one of the sushi chefs preparing appetizers. **Known for:** uni sushi topped with wasabi; omakase tasting menu; upscale sake offerings. [$] *Average main: $18* ✉ *555 5th Ave., Gaslamp Quarter* ☎ *619/338–0555* 🌐 *www.takasushi.com* ⏱ *No lunch.*

Hotels

★ Andaz San Diego

$$$$ | **HOTEL** | The lobby of the luxury, Hyatt-managed Andaz—with its dark, sexy vibe, tall columns wrapped in braided leather, buckets of chilled wine awaiting guests, and welcoming service—pretty much sums up the experience here: high-style stay without the attitude. **Pros:** luxurious rooms; romantic vibe; friendly service. **Cons:** noisy on weekends; not a good choice for families; small pool. [$] *Rooms from: $319* ✉ *600 F St., Gaslamp Quarter* ☎ *619/849–1234* 🌐 *www.sandiego.andaz.hyatt.com* 🛏 *159 rooms* 🍴 *No meals.*

★ Kimpton Hotel Solamar

$$$ | **HOTEL** | **FAMILY** | Best known for Upper East Bar, its poolside rooftop bar, and stylish lobby decor, Solamar's guest rooms reflect this urban escape's mixture of luxury and fun, with prints galore and subtle nods to San Diego's happy beach culture. **Pros:** great restaurant; attentive service; upscale rooms. **Cons:** busy valet parking; daily facility fee; no coffeemaker or teakettle in rooms. [$] *Rooms from: $279* ✉ *435 6th Ave., Gaslamp Quarter* ☎ *619/819–9500, 877/230–0300* 🌐 *www.hotelsolamar.com* 🛏 *235 rooms* 🍴 *No meals.*

★ Pendry San Diego

$$$$ | **HOTEL** | Opened in early 2017, the Pendry San Diego is the Gaslamp's newest stunner. **Pros:** well situated in Gaslamp Quarter; excellent dining options; complimentary coffee in the mornings. **Cons:** pricey room rates; meals are expensive; not very family-friendly. [$] *Rooms from: $480* ✉ *550 J St., Gaslamp Quarter* ☎ *619/738–7000* 🌐 *www.pendryhotels.com* 🛏 *317 rooms* 🍴 *No meals.*

★ The Sofia Hotel

$$$ | **HOTEL** | This stylish and centrally located boutique hotel may have small rooms, but it more than compensates with pampering extras like motion-sensor temperature controls, a Zen-like 24-hour yoga studio, an updated lobby, and a brand-new spa suite. **Pros:** upscale amenities; historic building; near shops and restaurants. **Cons:** busy area; small rooms; spotty Wi-Fi. [$] *Rooms from: $259* ✉ *150 W. Broadway, Gaslamp Quarter* ☎ *619/234–9200, 800/826–0009* 🌐 *www.thesofiahotel.com* 🛏 *211 rooms* 🍴 *No meals.*

Nightlife

BARS

★ The Grant Grill

BARS/PUBS | Though the Grant Grill—located on the ground floor of the historic U.S. Grant Hotel—is a full-service restaurant, it's built up a reputation in recent years for stepping up San Diego's craft cocktail game. The cocktail menu is updated seasonally with fresh ingredients and themes (one recently featured a mini "Voodoo" doll frozen inside of a large ice cube), all of which are both innovative and palate pleasant. The atmosphere is comfortable and elegant, even on its busiest nights. ✉ *U.S. Grant Hotel, 326 Broadway, Gaslamp Quarter* ☎ *619/744–2077* 🌐 *www.grantgrill.com.*

★ The Rooftop by STK

DANCE CLUBS | At this rooftop bar and lounge atop the Andaz hotel, a fashionable crowd sips cocktails poolside while gazing at gorgeous views of the city. Thursday through Saturday, the scene heats up with a DJ spinning dance music, while velvet ropes and VIP bottle service please the A-listers (like Prince Harry) in the crowd. ✉ *Andaz San Diego, 600 F St., Gaslamp Quarter* ☎ *619/814–2060* 🌐 *www.hyatt.com/en-US/hotel/california/andaz-san-diego/sanas/dining.*

PIANO BARS

★ Vin de Syrah

WINE BARS—NIGHTLIFE | This "spirit and wine cellar" sends you down a rabbit hole (or at least down some stairs) to a whimsical spot straight out of Alice in Wonderland. Behind a hidden door (look for a handle in the grass wall), you'll find visual delights (grapevines suspended from the ceiling, vintage jars with flittering "fireflies," cozy chairs nestled around a faux fireplace and pastoral vista) that rival the culinary ones—the wine list is approachable and the charcuterie boards are exquisitely curated. ■TIP→ More than just a wine bar, the cocktails are also worth a try. ⊠ *901 5th Ave., Gaslamp Quarter* ☎ *619/234–4166* ⊕ *www.syrahwineparlor.com.*

★ **Westgate Hotel Plaza Bar**
PIANO BARS/LOUNGES | The old-money surroundings, including leather-upholstered seats, marble tabletops, and a grand piano, supply one of the most elegant and romantic settings for a drink in San Diego. ⊠ *1055 2nd Ave., Gaslamp Quarter* ☎ *619/238–1818* ⊕ *www.westgatehotel.com.*

🎭 Performing Arts

DANCE
California Ballet Company
DANCE | The company performs high-quality contemporary and classical works September–May at the **Civic Theatre.** The *Nutcracker* is staged annually around the holiday season. ⊠ *San Diego Civic Theatre, 1100 3rd Ave., Gaslamp Quarter* ☎ *858/560–5676* ⊕ *www.californiaballet.org.*

MUSIC
★ **Copley Symphony Hall**
MUSIC | The great acoustics here are surpassed only by the incredible Spanish baroque interior. Not just the home of the San Diego Symphony Orchestra, the renovated 2,200-seat 1920s-era theater has also hosted major stars like Elvis Costello, Leonard Cohen, and Sting. ⊠ *750 B St., Gaslamp Quarter* ☎ *619/235–0804* ⊕ *www.sandiegosymphony.org.*

San Diego Symphony Orchestra
MUSIC | The orchestra's events include classical concerts and summer and winter pops, nearly all of them at Copley Symphony Hall. The outdoor Summer Pops series is held on the Embarcadero, on North Harbor Drive beyond the convention center. ⊠ *Box office, 750 B St., Gaslamp Quarter* ☎ *619/235–0804* ⊕ *www.sandiegosymphony.org.*

Embarcadero

The Embarcadero cuts a scenic swath along the harbor front and connects today's Downtown San Diego to its maritime routes. The bustle of Embarcadero comes less these days from the activities of fishing folk than from the throngs of tourists, but this waterfront walkway, stretching from the convention center to the Maritime Museum, remains the nautical soul of the city. There are several seafood restaurants here, as well as sea vessels of every variety—cruise ships, ferries, tour boats, and navy destroyers.

A huge revitalization project is under way along the northern Embarcadero. The overhaul seeks to transform the area with large mixed-use development projects, inviting parks, walkways, and public art installations. The redevelopment will eventually head south along the waterfront, with plans under way for a major overhaul of the entire Central Embarcadero and Seaport Village.

👁 Sights

★ **Maritime Museum**
MARINA | FAMILY | From sailing ships to submarines, the Maritime Museum is a must for anyone with an interest in nautical history. This collection of restored and replica ships affords a fascinating glimpse of San Diego during its heyday as a commercial seaport. The jewel of the collection, the *Star of India,* was built in 1863 and made 21 trips around the world in the late 1800s. Saved from the scrap yard and painstakingly restored, the windjammer is the oldest active iron sailing ship in the world. The newly constructed *San Salvador* is a detailed historic replica

of the original ship first sailed into San Diego Bay by explorer Juan Rodriguez Cabrillo back in 1542. And, the popular HMS *Surprise* is a replica of an 18th-century British Royal Navy frigate. The museum's headquarters are on the *Berkeley*, an 1898 steam-driven ferryboat, which served the Southern Pacific Railroad in San Francisco until 1958.

Numerous cruises of San Diego Bay are offered, including a daily 45-minute narrated tour aboard a 1914 pilot boat and three-hour weekend sails aboard the topsail schooner the *Californian,* the state's official tall ship, and 75-minute tours aboard a historic swift boat, which highlights the city's military connection. Partnering with the museum, the renowned yacht *America* also offers sails on the bay, and whale-watching excursions are available in winter. ⊠ *1492 N. Harbor Dr., Embarcadero* ☎ *619/234–9153* ⊕ *www. sdmaritime.org* ⌸ *$18.*

★ Museum of Contemporary Art San Diego (MCASD)

MUSEUM | At the Downtown branch of the city's contemporary art museum, explore the works of international and regional artists in a modern, urban space. The Jacobs Building—formerly the baggage building at the historic Santa Fe Depot—features large gallery spaces, high ceilings, and natural lighting, giving artists the flexibility to create large-scale installations. MCASD's collection includes many pop art, minimalist, and conceptual works from the 1950s to the present. The museum showcases both established and emerging artists in temporary exhibitions, and has permanent, site-specific commissions by Jenny Holzer and Richard Serra. ⊠ *1100 and 1001 Kettner Blvd., Downtown* ☎ *858/454–3541* ⊕ *www. mcasd.org* ⌸ *$10; free 3rd Thurs. of the month 5–7* ☾ *Closed Wed.*

★ The New Children's Museum (NCM)

MUSEUM | FAMILY | The NCM blends contemporary art with unstructured play to create an environment that appeals to children as well as adults. The 50,000-square-foot structure was constructed from recycled building materials, operates on solar energy, and is convection-cooled by an elevator shaft. It also features a nutritious and eco-conscious café. Interactive exhibits include designated areas for toddlers and teens, as well as plenty of activities for the entire family. Several art workshops are offered each day, as well as hands-on studios where visitors are encouraged to create their own art. The studio projects change frequently and the entire museum changes exhibits every 18 to 24 months, so there is always something new to explore. The adjoining 1-acre park and playground is across from the convention center trolley stop. ⊠ *200 W. Island Ave., Embarcadero* ☎ *619/233–8792* ⊕ *www. thinkplaycreate.org* ⌸ *$14* ☾ *Closed Tues.*

Seaport Village

PEDESTRIAN MALL | FAMILY | You'll find some of the best views of the harbor at Seaport Village, three bustling shopping plazas designed to reflect the New England clapboard, and Spanish Mission architectural styles of early California. On a prime stretch of waterfront the dining, shopping, and entertainment complex connects the harbor with hotel towers and the convention center. Specialty shops offer everything from a kite store and swing emporium to a shop devoted to hot sauces. You can dine at snack bars and restaurants, many with harbor views.

Live music can be heard daily from noon to 4 at the main food court. Additional free concerts take place every Sunday from 1 to 4 at the East Plaza Gazebo. The **Seaport Village Carousel** (rides $3) has 54 animals, hand-carved and hand-painted by Charles Looff in 1895. Across the street, the **Headquarters at Seaport Village** converted the historic police headquarters into several trendsetting shops and restaurants. ⊠ *849 W. Harbor Dr., Downtown* ☎ *619/235–4014 office and events hotline* ⊕ *www.seaportvillage.com.*

★ USS *Midway* Museum

MILITARY SITE | FAMILY | After 47 years of worldwide service, the retired USS *Midway* began a new tour of duty on the south side of the Navy pier in 2004. Launched in 1945, the 1,001-foot-long ship was the largest in the world for the first 10 years of its existence. The most visible landmark on the north Embarcadero, it now serves as a floating interactive museum—an appropriate addition to the town that is home to one-third of the Pacific fleet and the birthplace of naval aviation. A free audio tour guides you through the massive ship while offering insight from former sailors. As you clamber through passageways and up and down ladder wells, you'll get a feel for how the *Midway*'s 4,500 crew members lived and worked on this "city at sea."

Though the entire tour is impressive, you'll really be wowed when you step out onto the 4-acre flight deck—not only the best place to get an idea of the ship's scale, but also one of the most interesting vantage points for bay and city skyline views. An F-14 Tomcat jet fighter is just one of many vintage aircraft on display. Free guided tours of the bridge and primary flight control, known as "the Island," depart every 10 minutes from the flight deck. Many of the docents stationed throughout the ship served in the Navy, some even on the *Midway*, and they are eager to answer questions or share stories. The museum also offers multiple flight simulators for an additional fee, climb-aboard cockpits, and interactive exhibits focusing on naval aviation. There is a gift shop and a café with pleasant outdoor seating. This is a wildly popular stop, with most visits lasting several hours. ⚠ **Despite efforts to provide accessibility throughout the ship, some areas can only be reached via fairly steep steps; a video tour of these areas is available on the hangar deck.** ⊠ *910 N. Harbor Dr., Embarcadero* ☎ *619/544–9600* ⊕ *www.midway.org* 🖅 *$21.*

🍴 Restaurants

★ Eddie V's Prime Seafood

$$$ | SEAFOOD | Don't be put off by the name, or that it is part of a small chain. This fine-dining restaurant at the Headquarters at Seaport in Downtown has won a devoted following for classic seafood, casual but sophisticated settings, and nightly live jazz. **Known for:** wallet-friendly happy hour deals; indulgent truffled mac and cheese. Ⓢ *Average main: $34* ⊠ *789 W. Harbor Dr., Embarcadero* ☎ *619/615–0281* ⊕ *www.eddiev. com* ⊘ *No lunch.*

★ Puesto

$ | MEXICAN | Bold graffiti graphics, chandeliers with tangled telephone wires, and beat-heavy music energize this Downtown eatery that celebrates Mexican street food with a modern twist. Settle into one of the interior rooms or the sunny patio under orange umbrellas to sip margaritas and other specialty cocktails, Baja wines, or fruity aguas frescas made daily. **Known for:** taco trio plates; unique Parmesan guacamole; fruit-infused margaritas made in-house. Ⓢ *Average main: $16* ⊠ *789 W. Harbor Dr., Downtown* ☎ *619/233–8880* ⊕ *www. eatpuesto.com.*

🛏 Hotels

Manchester Grand Hyatt San Diego

$$$ | HOTEL | FAMILY | Primarily a draw for business travelers, this hotel between Seaport Village and the convention center also works well for leisure and family travelers. **Pros:** great views; conference facilities; good location; spacious rooms. **Cons:** lots of convention-goers; some trolley noise; not as stylish as many other Downtown hotels. Ⓢ *Rooms from: $259* ⊠ *1 Market Pl., Embarcadero* ☎ *619/232–1234, 800/233–1234* ⊕ *www.manchester. grand.hyatt.com* 🖅 *1628 rooms* ⏻ *No meals.*

🛍 Shopping

★ The Headquarters at Seaport

OUTDOOR/FLEA/GREEN MARKETS | This new upscale shopping and dining center is in the city's former police headquarters, a beautiful and historic Mission-style building featuring an open courtyard with fountains. Restaurants and shops, many locally owned, occupy former jail facilities and offices. Pop into **Urban Beach House** for coastal-inspired fashion from popular surf brands for men and women, including accessories and home decor. Swing by **Madison San Diego** for a great selection of leather goods and accessories, from apparel and handbags to belts and travel accessories. **Dallmann Fine Chocolates** sells truffles in flavors like bananas Foster and coconut curry. **Venissimo Cheese** dishes up the best cheese from around the world, from goat milk chevre filled with Italian truffle salt to French triple crème Brie topped with tangy cranberries. **Geppetto's** has been a San Diego staple for more than 40 years, offering classic toys and games that inspire creativity for the entire family. ✉ *789 W. Harbor Dr., Downtown* ☎ *619/235–4013* 🌐 *theheadquarters.com.*

East Village

The most ambitious of the Downtown projects is East Village, not far from the Gaslamp Quarter, and encompassing 130 blocks between the railroad tracks up to J Street, and from 6th Avenue east to around 10th Street. Sparking the rebirth of this former warehouse district was the 2004 construction of the San Diego Padres' baseball stadium, PETCO Park. The Urban Art Trail has added pizzazz to drab city thoroughfares by transforming such things as trash cans and traffic controller boxes into works of art. As the city's largest Downtown neighborhood, East Village is continually broadening its boundaries with its urban design of redbrick cafés, spacious galleries, rooftop bars, sleek hotels, and warehouse restaurants.

👁 Sights

PETCO Park

SPORTS VENUE | **FAMILY** | PETCO Park is home to the city's major league baseball team, the San Diego Padres. The ballpark is strategically designed to give fans a view of San Diego Bay, the skyline, and Balboa Park. Reflecting San Diego's beauty, the stadium is clad in sandstone from India to evoke the area's cliffs and beaches; the 42,000 seats are dark blue, reminiscent of the ocean, and the exposed steel is painted white to reflect the sails of harbor boats on the bay. The family-friendly lawnlike berm, "Park at the Park," is a popular and affordable place for fans to view the game. The ballpark underwent a huge effort to improve dining in the park, and local food vendors and craft breweries now dominate the dining options. Behind-the-scenes guided tours of PETCO, including the press box and the dugout, are offered throughout the year. ✉ *100 Park Blvd., East Village* ☎ *619/795–5011 tour hotline* 🌐 *sandiego.padres.mlb.com* 🎟 *$20 tour.*

🍴 Restaurants

The Blind Burro

$$ | **MODERN MEXICAN** | **FAMILY** | East Village families, baseball fans heading to or from PETCO Park, and happy-hour bound singles flock to this airy restaurant with Baja-inspired food and drink. Traditional margaritas get a fresh kick from fruit juices or jalapeño peppers; other libations include sangria and Mexican beers, all perfect pairings for house-made guacamole, ceviche, or salsas with chips. **Known for:** house margarita with fruit infusions; surf-and-turf Baja-style tacos; gluten-free menu. [$] *Average main: $18* ✉ *639 J St., East Village* ☎ *619/795–7880* 🌐 *www.theblindburro.com.*

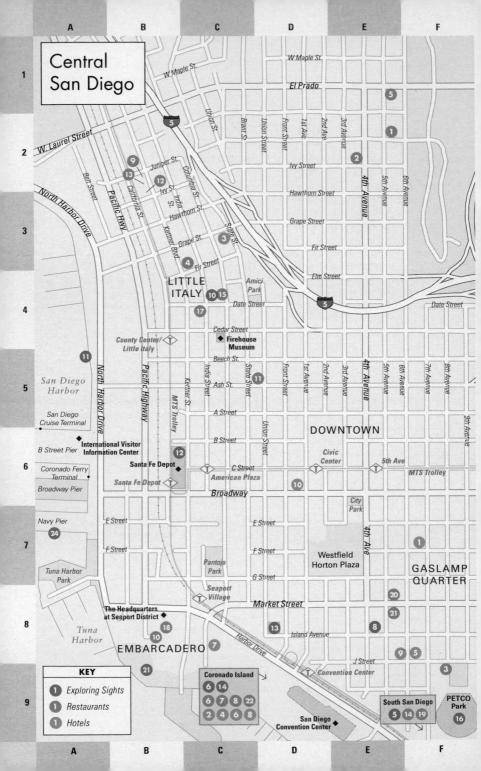

Central San Diego

KEY

- **1** *Exploring Sights*
- **1** *Restaurants*
- **1** *Hotels*

W Maple St.
W Maple St.
El Prado
W. Laurel Street
Juniper St.
Ivy St.
Ivy Street
Hawthorn Street
Grape Street
Fir Street
Elm Street
Date Street
Date Street
Cedar Street
Firehouse Museum
County Center/ Little Italy
Beech St.
Ash St.
A Street
B Street
DOWNTOWN
Civic Center
5th Ave
MTS Trolley
C Street
American Plaza
Broadway
E Street
E Street
F Street
F Street
Westfield Horton Plaza
GASLAMP QUARTER
Pantoja Park
City Park
Seaport Village
The Headquarters at Seaport District
Market Street
Island Avenue
EMBARCADERO
Tuna Harbor
Harbor Drive
Convention Center
J Street
PETCO Park
South San Diego
San Diego Convention Center

Coronado Island

International Visitor Information Center
Santa Fe Depot
Santa Fe Depot

San Diego Harbor
San Diego Cruise Terminal
B Street Pier
Coronado Ferry Terminal
Broadway Pier
Navy Pier
Tuna Harbor Park

North Harbor Drive
Pacific Hwy
Pacific Highway
North Harbor Drive
MTS Trolley

Belt Street
California Street
Columbia St.
India St.
Kettner Blvd.
State St.
Union St.
Brant St.
Union Street
Front Street
1st Ave
2nd Ave
3rd Avenue
4th Avenue
5th Avenue
6th Avenue
7th Avenue
8th Avenue
9th Avenue
Amici Park

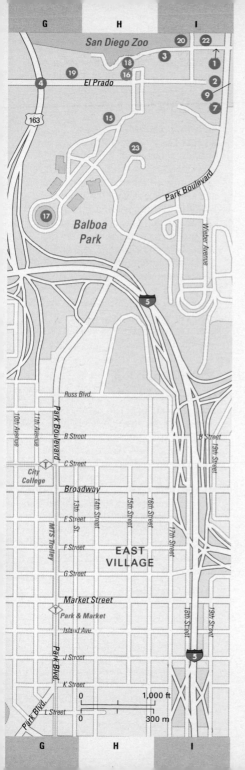

Sights ▼

1 Balboa Park Carousel....I1
2 Bea Evenson Fountain ...I1
3 Botanical Building........I1
4 Cabrillo Bridge G1
5 Chicano Park............. F9
6 Coronado Ferry Landing C9
7 Fleet Science Center.....I1
8 Gaslamp Museum at the Davis-Horton House..... E8
9 Inez Grant Parker Memorial Rose Garden and Desert Garden I1
10 Little Italy Mercato C4
11 Maritime Museum...... A5
12 Museum of Contemporary Art San Diego (MCASD)............... B6
13 The New Children's Museum (NCM)......... D8
14 Orange Avenue C9
15 Palm Canyon H2
16 Petco Park............... F9
17 San Diego Air & Space Museum G3
18 The San Diego Museum of Art H1
19 San Diego Museum of Man G1
20 San Diego Zoo I1
21 Seaport Village.......... B9
22 Spanish Village Art Center...................... I1
23 Spreckels Organ Pavilion H2
24 USS Midway Museum A7

Restaurants ▼

1 Azuki Sushi.............. E2
2 Bankers Hill Bar and Restaurant.............. E2
3 The Blind Burro F9
4 Born and Raised C3
5 Cucina Urbana E1
6 Cafe 1134 .... C9
7 Chez Loma................ C9
8 Coronado Brewing Company................. C9
9 The Crack Shack........ B2
10 Eddie V's Prime Seafood.................. B8
11 Extraordinary Desserts D5
12 Herb & Wood............ B3
13 Juniper and Ivy B2
14 Las Cuatro Milpas F9
15 Little Italy Food Hall...... C4
16 Panama 66............... H1
17 Prep Kitchen Little Italy........................ C4
18 Puesto.................... B8
19 ¡SALUD! F9
20 Searsucker E8
21 Taka E8
22 Tartine.................... C9

Hotels ▼

1 Andaz San Diego F7
2 Coronado Island Marriott Resort & Spa C9
3 Found Hotel............... C3
4 Hotel del Coronado...... C9
5 Kimpton Hotel Solamar................. F8
6 Loews Coronado Bay Resort.................... C9
7 Manchester Grand Hyatt San Diego................. C8
8 1906 Lodge at Coronado Beach......... C9
9 Pendry San Diego E8
10 The Sofia Hotel.......... D6

ⓨ Nightlife

★ Fairweather

BARS/PUBS | Hidden in plain sight next to PETCO Park, Fairweather is an urban tiki oasis with a top-notch cocktail menu that boasts classics like daiquiris and their signature frozen piña colada alongside modern interpretations of old-school tiki drinks like Corpse Revivers and mai tais. ■TIP→ **Come by during Comic-Con in July to view the parade of costumed characters while sipping rum refreshments on the balcony.** ⊠ *793 J St., 2nd fl., East Village* ☎ *619/578–2392* ⊕ *www.fairweatherbar.com.*

★ Noble Experiment

PIANO BARS/LOUNGES | There are a handful of speakeasy-style bars in San Diego, though none deliver so far above and beyond the novelty quite like this cozy-yet-swank cocktail lounge hidden in the back of a burger restaurant. Seek out the hidden door (hint: look for the stack of kegs), tuck into a plush leather booth next to the wall of golden skulls, and sip on the best craft cocktails in the city. ■TIP→ **Reservations are almost always a must, so be sure to call ahead.** ⊠ *777 G St., East Village* ☎ *619/888–4713* ⊕ *nobleexperimentsd.com.*

Little Italy

Home to many in San Diego's design community, Little Italy exudes a sense of urban cool while remaining authentic to its roots and marked by old-country charms: church bells ring on the half hour, and Italians gather daily to play bocce in Amici Park. The main thoroughfare, India Street, is filled with lively cafés, chic shops, and many of the city's trendiest restaurants. Little Italy is one of San Diego's most walkable neighborhoods, and a great spot to wander. Art lovers can browse gallery showrooms, while shoppers adore the Fir Street cottages. The neighborhood bustles each Saturday during the wildly popular Mercato farmers' market.

◉ Sights

Little Italy Mercato

MARKET | Each Saturday tourists and residents alike flock to the Little Italy Mercato, one of the most popular farmers' markets in San Diego. Over 150 vendors line Date Street selling everything from paintings and pottery to flowers and farm-fresh eggs. Come hungry, as several booths and food trucks serve prepared foods. Alternatively, the neighborhood's many cafés and restaurants are just steps away. The Mercato is a great opportunity to experience one of San Diego's most exciting urban neighborhoods. ⊠ *Date and India Sts., Little Italy* ⊕ *www.littleitalysd.com/events/mercato.*

ⓨ Restaurants

★ Born and Raised

$$$$ | **STEAKHOUSE** | The name is cheeky if a little morbid; the title refers to the restaurant's speciality—steak. It's a twist on a classic steak house, with a menu full of aged, prime cuts of beef served with a number of sauces, or perhaps try the table-side-prepared steak Diane with flambéed jus. **Known for:** table-side Caesar salad; aged New York steak; cheeky, glamorous decor. Ⓢ *Average main: $45* ⊠ *1909 India St., Little Italy* ☎ *619/202–4577* ⊕ *www.bornandraisedsteak.com.*

★ The Crack Shack

$ | **AMERICAN** | **FAMILY** | Next to his successful fine dining restaurant, Juniper and Ivy, celebrity chef Richard Blais has opened this more casual eatery complete with a walk-up counter, picnic-style tables, a boccie court, and a giant rooster—a nod to the egg- and chicken-themed menu. Ingredients are sourced from high-quality vendors and used for sandwiches, of which the fried chicken varieties shine, as well as salads and sides like fluffy minibiscuits with a miso-maple butter and a Mexican spin on poutine. **Known for:** Señor Croque fried chicken sandwich with smoked pork belly; biscuits with miso-maple butter; all-outdoor seating with boccie court. $ *Average main: $12* ✉ *2266 Kettner Blvd., Little Italy* ☎ *619/795–3299* ⊕ *www.crackshack.com.*

★ Extraordinary Desserts

$ | CAFÉ | For Paris-perfect cakes and tarts embellished California-style with fresh flowers, head to this sleek, serene branch of Karen Krasne's pastry shop and café. The space with soaring ceilings hosts breakfasts, lunches, and light dinners, accompanied by a wide selection of teas, coffee, organic wines, and craft beers. **Known for:** blueberry coffee cake for breakfast; chocolate dulce de leche cake; house-made dips including onion dip and Parmesan pesto. $ *Average main: $14* ✉ *1430 Union St., Little Italy* ☎ *619/294–7001* ⊕ *www.extraordinarydesserts.com.*

★ Herb & Wood

$$ | AMERICAN | Design lovers will fall for celebrity chef Brian Malarkey's sprawling restaurant, a former art store that has been refashioned into four luxe spaces in one—an entryway lounge, outdoor lounge, fireplace-dotted patio, and the main dining room, which is flanked by beaded chandeliers, lush banquettes, and paintings in rich jewel tones. The menu is heavy on wood-roasted dishes, many of which are apt for sharing like the roasted baby carrots or hiramasa with crispy quinoa. **Known for:** roasted baby carrots with cashew sesame dukkah; pillow-soft oxtail gnocchi; the secret menu Parker House rolls topped with Maldon sea salt. $ *Average main: $20* ✉ *2210 Kettner Blvd., Little Italy* ☎ *619/955–8495* ⊕ *www.herbandwood. com* ☾ *No lunch.*

Juniper and Ivy

$$$ | MODERN AMERICAN | Celebrity chef Richard Blais's addition to San Diego's restaurant scene fills an open-beamed space with seating for 250 and an open stainless-steel dream kitchen where diners can watch the chef and team in action. Blais sources local farm-fresh ingredients for his "left coast cookery" with a molecular gastronomy twist. **Known for:** California-Baja-inspired carne crudo asada topped with quail eggs; off-menu "In & Haute" burger; very shareable Yodel chocolate dessert. $ *Average main: $35* ✉ *2228 Kettner Blvd., Little Italy* ☎ *619/269–9036* ⊕ *www.juniperandivy.com* ☾ *No lunch.*

Little Italy Food Hall

$ | FUSION | FAMILY | A recently opened, chic update on the food court, Food Hall brings together a half dozen different innovative food counters to offer quick bites vastly more interesting than mall fare. Among its offerings are the seafood-centric Single Fin Kitchen and Wicked Maine Lobster, and an update on a local delicacy, Not Not Tacos. **Known for:** fusion tacos; bustling crowds of Mercato shoppers; beer/wine cart dispensing refreshments in the outdoor seating area. $ *Average main: $10* ✉ *550 W. Date St., Suite B, Little Italy* ☎ *619/269–7187* ⊕ *www.littleitalyfoodhall.com.*

★ Prep Kitchen Little Italy

$$ | MODERN AMERICAN | Urbanites craving a hip casual setting and gourmet menu pack architectural salvage–styled Prep Kitchen Little Italy, tucked upstairs above a busy corner in this thriving neighborhood. With first-date cocktails, after-work brews, or birthday champagne, diners relish familiar choices like meatball sandwiches, chops, and pork belly with kimchi Brussels. **Known for:** weekend brunch featuring popular chilaquiles dish; bacon-wrapped dates; $6 tapas during the daily happy hour. $ *Average main: $23* ✉ *1660 India St., Little Italy* ☎ *619/398–8383* ⊕ *www.prepkitchenlittleitaly.com.*

Hotels

Found Hotel

$ | **B&B/INN** | You'll find more amenities at other Downtown hotels but it's hard to beat this property's value and charm. **Pros:** good location; historic property; welcoming staff. **Cons:** some shared baths; no parking; not great for couples or families. [$] *Rooms from: $139* ✉ *505 W. Grape St., Little Italy* ☎ *619/230–1600, 800/518–9930* 🌐 *sandiego.foundhotels.com* 🛏 *23 rooms* 🍴 *Free Breakfast.*

Nightlife

BARS

★ False Idol

BARS/PUBS | A walk-in refrigerator harbors the secret entrance to this tiki-themed speakeasy, which is attached to Craft & Commerce. Beneath fishing nets full of puffer-fish lights and elaborate tiki-head wall carvings, the knowledgeable staff serves up creative takes on tropical classics with the best selection of rums in town. **■ TIP→ The bar fills up quickly, especially on weekends. Make a reservation online a week or more in advance.** ✉ *675 W. Beech St., Little Italy* 🌐 *falseidoltiki.com.*

The Waterfront Bar & Grill

BARS/PUBS | It isn't really *on* the waterfront, but San Diego's oldest bar was once the hangout of Italian fishermen. Most of the collars are now white, and patrons enjoy an excellent selection of beers, along with chili, burgers, fish-and-chips, and other great-tasting grub, including fish tacos. Get here early, as there's almost always a crowd. ✉ *2044 Kettner Blvd., Little Italy* ☎ *619/232–9656* 🌐 *www.waterfrontbarandgrill.com.*

BREWPUBS

★ Ballast Point Brewing Co.

BREWPUBS/BEER GARDENS | Until recently, you had to head to the Miramar/Scripps Ranch area for a tasting at Ballast Point, but now there's a local taproom in Little Italy. The Sculpin IPA is outstanding. ✉ *2215 India St., Little Italy* ☎ *619/255–7213* 🌐 *www.ballastpoint.com.*

Karl Strauss' Brewing Company

BARS/PUBS | San Diego's first microbrewery now has multiple locations, but the original one remains a staple. This locale draws an after-work crowd for pints of Red Trolley Ale and later fills with beer connoisseurs from all walks of life to try Karl's latest concoctions. The German-inspired pub food is above average. ✉ *1157 Columbia St., Little Italy* ☎ *619/234–2739* 🌐 *www.karlstrauss.com.*

MUSIC CLUB

★ The Casbah

MUSIC CLUBS | This small club near the airport, the unofficial headquarters of the city's indie music scene, has a national reputation for showcasing up-and-coming acts of all genres. Nirvana, Smashing Pumpkins, and the White Stripes all played here on the way to stardom. ✉ *2501 Kettner Blvd., Middletown* ☎ *619/232–4355* 🌐 *www.casbahmusic.com.*

Barrio Logan

San Diego's Mexican-American community is centered in Barrio Logan, under the San Diego–Coronado Bay Bridge on the Downtown side. Chicano Park, spread along National Avenue from Dewey to Crosby streets, is the barrio's recreational hub. It's worth taking a short detour to see the huge murals of Mexican history painted on the bridge supports at National Avenue and Dewey Street; they're among the best examples of folk art in the city. Art enthusiasts will also enjoy the burgeoning gallery scene in the Barrio Logan neighborhood, rapidly becoming a hub for artists in San Diego.

GETTING HERE AND AROUND

Barrio Logan is located right off Interstate 5, at the Cesar E. Chavez Parkway exit. Driving is the easiest way to get there, especially coming from Downtown—In fact, it's only a mile from PETCO Park, and easily accessible via Imperial and Logan avenues. However, the Blue Line trolley also stops in Barrio Logan, and several bus lines also cross through the neighborhood, including the 9, 6, 20, 705, and 923.

When staying Downtown, Barrio Logan is also just a 15-minute walk, but with its somewhat isolated location under a bridge, visitors should exercise caution visiting the Chicano Park murals after dark.

⊙ Sights

★ Chicano Park

PUBLIC ART | FAMILY | The cultural center of the Barrio Logan neighborhood, Chicano Park—designated a National Historic Landmark in 2017—was born in 1970 from the activism of local residents who occupied the space after the state rescinded its promise to designate the land a park. Signed into law a year later, the park is now a protected area that brings together families and locals for both public and private events, a welcoming gathering space as well as an outdoor gallery featuring large murals documenting Mexican-American history and Chicano activism. Every year Chicano Park Day is held on April 21, filling the park with the sights and sounds of music, dancers, vintage cars, and food and clothing vendors. ⊠ *Logan Ave. and Cesar Chavez Pkwy., Barrio Logan* ⊕ *chicano-park.com; www.chicanoparksandiego.com.*

🍴 Restaurants

Las Cuatros Milpas

$ | MEXICAN | One of the oldest restaurants in San Diego, having opened in 1933, Las Cuatros Milpas feels like a closely held secret in Barrio Logan. Open daily until 3 pm, it almost inevitably attracts a big lunchtime rush, though the wait is worth it for the homemade tortillas, beans with chorizo, and rolled tacos.

Known for: homemade tortillas; checkered picnic tables; chorizo con huevos. $ *Average main: $5* ⊠ *1857 Logan Ave., Barrio Logan* ☎ *619/234-4460* ⊙ *Closed Sun.* ▤ *No credit cards.*

★ ¡Salud!

$ | MEXICAN | The line that inevitably wraps around the building is indicative of the quality of the tacos and the large selection of local craft beers on tap. Indeed, these are some of the best tacos in all of San Diego, ranging from the classic carne asada and Baja fish tacos to fried-shell beef tacos and Califas, which features french fries inside the tortilla. Just remember—alcohol isn't allowed at the outdoor tables. **Known for:** Baja-style street tacos; Pruno de Piña (beer and fermented pineapple); churros and ice cream. $ *Average main: $3* ⊠ *2196 Logan Ave., Barrio Logan* ☎ *619/255-3856* ⊕ *www.saludsd.com.*

Balboa Park, Bankers Hill, and San Diego Zoo

Overlooking Downtown and the Pacific Ocean, 1,200-acre Balboa Park is the cultural heart of San Diego. Ranked as one of the world's best parks by the Project for Public Spaces, it's also where you can find most of the city's museums, art galleries, the Tony Award–winning Old Globe Theatre, and the world-famous San Diego Zoo. Often referred to as the "Smithsonian of the West" for its concentration of museums, Balboa Park is also a series of botanical gardens, performance spaces, and outdoor playrooms endeared to the hearts of residents and visitors alike.

In addition, the captivating architecture of Balboa's buildings, fountains, and courtyards gives the park an enchanted feel. Historic buildings dating from San Diego's 1915 Panama–California International Exposition are strung along the park's main east–west thoroughfare,

El Prado, which leads from 6th Avenue eastward over the Cabrillo Bridge (formerly the Laurel Street Bridge), the park's official gateway. If you're a cinema fan, many of the buildings may be familiar—Orson Welles used exteriors of several Balboa Park buildings to represent the Xanadu estate of Charles Foster Kane in his 1941 classic, *Citizen Kane*. Prominent among them was the California Building, whose 200-foot tower, housing a 100-bell carillon that tolls the hour, is El Prado's tallest structure. Missing from the black-and-white film, however, was the magnificent blue of its tiled dome shining in the sun.

Bankers Hill is a small neighborhood west of Balboa Park, with gorgeous views ranging from Balboa Park's greenery in the east to the San Diego Bay in the west. It's become one of San Diego's hottest restaurant destinations.

⊙ Sights

★ Balboa Park Carousel

CAROUSEL | FAMILY | Suspended an arm's length away on this antique merry-go-round is the brass ring that could earn you an extra free ride (it's one of the few carousels in the world that continue this bonus tradition). Hand-carved in 1910, the carousel features colorful murals, big-band music, and bobbing animals including zebras, giraffes, and dragons; real horsehair was used for the tails. ⊠ *1889 Zoo Pl., behind zoo parking lot, Balboa Park* ☎ *619/239–0512* ⊕ *www.balboapark.org* ⊠ *$3* ⊙ *Closed weekdays Labor Day–mid-June.*

Bea Evenson Fountain

FOUNTAIN | A favorite of barefoot children, this fountain shoots cool jets of water upwards of 50 feet. Built in 1972 between the Fleet Center and Natural History Museum, the fountain offers plenty of room to sit and watch the crowds go by. ⊠ *Balboa Park* ✛ *East end of El Prado* ⊕ *www.balboapark.org.*

★ Botanical Building

GARDEN | The graceful redwood-lath structure, built for the 1915 Panama–California International Exposition, now houses more than 2,000 types of tropical and subtropical plants plus changing seasonal flower displays. Ceiling-high tree ferns shade fragile orchids and feathery bamboo. There are benches beside miniature waterfalls for resting in the shade. The rectangular pond outside, filled with lotuses and water lilies that bloom in spring and fall, is popular with photographers. ⊠ *1549 El Prado, Balboa Park* ☎ *619/239–0512* ⊕ *www.balboapark.org* ⊠ *Free* ⊙ *Closed Thurs.*

Cabrillo Bridge

BRIDGE/TUNNEL | The official gateway into Balboa Park soars 120 feet above a canyon floor. Pedestrian-friendly, the 1,500-foot bridge provides inspiring views of the California Tower and El Prado beyond. ■TIP→ **This is a great spot for photo-capturing a classic image of the park.** ⊠ *Balboa Park* ✛ *On El Prado, at 6th Ave. park entrance* ⊕ *www.balboapark.org.*

Fleet Science Center

MUSEUM | FAMILY | Interactive exhibits here are artfully educational and for all ages: older kids can get hands-on with inventive projects in Studio X, while the five-and-under set can be easily entertained with interactive play stations like the Ball Wall and Fire Truck in the center's Kid City. The IMAX Dome Theater, which screens exhilarating nature and science films, was the world's first, as was the Fleet's "NanoSeam" (seamless) dome ceiling that doubles as a planetarium. ⊠ *1875 El Prado, Balboa Park* ☎ *619/238–1233* ⊕ *www.rhfleet.org* ⊠ *The Fleet experience includes gallery exhibits and 1 IMAX film $21.95; additional cost for special exhibits or add-on 2nd IMAX film or planetarium show.*

★ Inez Grant Parker Memorial Rose Garden and Desert Garden

GARDEN | These neighboring gardens sit just across the Park Boulevard pedestrian bridge and offer gorgeous views over Florida Canyon. The formal rose garden contains 1,600 roses representing nearly 130 varieties; peak bloom is usually in April and May. The adjacent Desert Garden provides a striking contrast, with 2.5 acres of succulents and desert plants seeming to blend into the landscape of the canyon below. ⊠ *2525 Park Blvd., Balboa Park* ⊕ *www.balboapark.org.*

Palm Canyon

CANYON | Enjoy an instant escape from the buildings and concrete of urban life in this Balboa Park oasis. Lush and tropical, with hundreds of palm trees, the 2-acre canyon has a shaded path perfect for those who love walking through nature. ⊠ *1549 El Prado, south of House of Charm, Balboa Park.*

★ San Diego Air & Space Museum

MUSEUM | FAMILY | By day, the streamlined edifice looks like any other structure in the park; at night, outlined in blue neon, the round building appears—appropriately enough—to be a landed UFO. Every available inch of space in the rotunda is filled with exhibits about aviation and aerospace pioneers, including examples of enemy planes from the world wars. In all, there are more than 60 full-size aircraft on the floor and hanging from the rafters. In addition to exhibits from the dawn of flight to the jet age, the museum displays a growing number of space-age exhibits, including the actual *Apollo 9* command module. To test your own skills, you can ride in a two-seat Max Flight simulator or try out the Talon Racing simulator. Movies in the 3-D/4-D theater are included with admission. ⊠ *2001 Pan American Pl., Balboa Park* ☎ *619/234–8291* ⊕ *www. sandiegoairandspace.org* ⌫ *Museum $19.95 (more for special exhibitions); Flight Simulators $5–$8 extra; restoration tour $5 extra and subject to availability.*

★ San Diego Museum of Art

MUSEUM | Known for its Spanish baroque and Renaissance paintings, including works by El Greco, Goya, Rubens, and van Ruisdael, San Diego's most comprehensive art museum also has strong holdings of South Asian art, Indian miniatures, and contemporary California paintings. The museum's exhibits tend to have broad appeal, and if traveling shows from other cities come to town, you can expect to see them here. Free docent tours are offered throughout the day. An outdoor Sculpture Court and Garden exhibits both traditional and modern pieces. Enjoy the view over a craft beer and some locally sourced food in the adjacent Panama 66 courtyard restaurant. ■ TIP→ **The museum hosts "Art After Hours" most Friday nights, with discounted admission 5–8 pm.** ⊠ *1450 El Prado, Balboa Park* ☎ *619/232–7931* ⊕ *www.sdmart.org* ⌫ *$15; $5 Fri. 5–8 pm; sculpture garden free* ⊗ *Closed Wed.*

★ San Diego Museum of Man

MUSEUM | FAMILY | If the facade of this building—the landmark California Building—looks familiar, it's because filmmaker Orson Welles used it and its dramatic tower as the principal features of the Xanadu estate in his 1941 classic, *Citizen Kane.* Closed for 80 years, the tower was recently reopened for public tours. An additional timed ticket and a climb up 125 steps is required, but the effort will be rewarded with spectacular 360-degree views of the coast, Downtown, and the inland mountains. Back inside, exhibits at this highly respected anthropological museum focus on Southwestern, Mexican, and South American cultures. Carved monuments from the Mayan city of Quirigua in Guatemala, cast from the originals in 1914, are particularly impressive. Exhibits might include examples of intricate beadwork from across the Americas, the history of Egyptian mummies, or the lifestyles of the Kumeyaay peoples, Native Americans who live in the San Diego area. ⊠ *California Bldg., 1350 El Prado, Balboa Park* ☎ *619/239–2001* ⊕ *www.museumofman. org* ⌫ *$13; special exhibits extra; Tower tickets (including museum admission)*

$23 ☞ Tower tours are timed-entry and can be booked in advance through website or on arrival at museum.

★ San Diego Zoo

ZOO | FAMILY | Balboa Park's—and perhaps the city's—most famous attraction is its 100-acre zoo. Nearly 4,000 animals of some 800 diverse species roam in hospitable, expertly crafted habitats that replicate natural environments as closely as possible. The flora in the zoo, including many rare species, is even more dear than the fauna. Walkways wind over bridges and past waterfalls ringed with tropical ferns; elephants in a sandy plateau roam so close you're tempted to pet them.

Exploring the zoo fully requires the stamina of a healthy hiker, but open-air double-decker buses that run throughout the day let you zip through three-quarters of the exhibits on a guided 35- to 40-minute, 3-mile tour. There are also express buses, used for quick transportation, that make five stops around the grounds and include some narration. The Skyfari Aerial Tram, which soars 170 feet above the ground, gives a good overview of the zoo's layout and, on clear days, a panorama of the park, Downtown San Diego, the bay, and the ocean, far beyond the San Diego–Coronado Bridge. ∎ TIP→ Unless you come early, expect to wait for the regular bus, and especially for the top tier—the line can take more than 45 minutes; if you come at midday on a weekend or school holiday, you'll be doing the in-line shuffle for a while.

Don't forget the San Diego Safari Park, the zoo's 1,800-acre extension to the north at Escondido. ⊠ 2920 Zoo Dr., Balboa Park ☎ 619/234–3153, ⊕ www.sandiegozoo. org ☞ $54 adult, $44 children ages 3–11 (includes Skyfari and bus tour).

★ Spanish Village Art Center

MUSEUM | More than 200 local artists, including glassblowers, enamel workers, wood-carvers, sculptors, painters, jewelers, and photographers work and give demonstrations of their craft on a rotating basis in these red tile–roof studio-galleries that were set up for the 1935–36 exposition in the style of an old Spanish village. The center is a great source for memorable gifts. ⊠ 1770 Village Pl., Balboa Park ☎ 619/233–9050 ⊕ www.spanishvillageart.com ☞ Free.

★ Spreckels Organ Pavilion

ARTS VENUE | The 2,400-bench-seat pavilion, dedicated in 1915 by sugar magnates John D. and Adolph B. Spreckels, holds the 4,518-pipe Spreckels Organ, the largest outdoor pipe organ in the world. You can hear this impressive instrument at one of the year-round, free, 2 pm Sunday concerts, regularly performed by the city's civic organist Raúl Prieto Ramírez and guest artists—a highlight of a visit to Balboa Park. On Monday evenings from late June to mid-August, internationally renowned organists play evening concerts. At Christmastime the park's Christmas tree and life-size Nativity display turn the pavilion into a seasonal wonderland. ⊠ 2211 Pan American Rd., Balboa Park ☎ 619/702–8138 ⊕ spreckelsorgan.org.

🍴 Restaurants

★ Azuki Sushi

$$ | SUSHI | Sushi should be a no-brainer when visiting San Diego, especially for tourists from landlocked states who don't often get fresh fish. This menu is based on the seasons, and you'll find innovative sushi, sashimi, and a raw bar, all utilizing the freshest local fish (some is flown in daily from Japan) and produce; there are options for non-sushi fans. **Known for:** reservations recommended; specialty rolls like the R U Kidding Me? (snow crab, diver scallops, tempura asparagus, seared tuna, white truffle oil, and mixed greens, topped with garlic ponzu and flash-fried leaks); surprising pairings with wine and sake. $ Average main: $21 ⊠ 2321 5th Ave., Bankers Hill ☎ 619/238–4760 ⊕ azukisushi.com ⊙ No lunch weekends.

Continued on page 106

Polar bear, San Diego Zoo

LIONS AND TIGERS AND BEARS:
The World-Famous San Diego Zoo

From diving polar bears and 6-ton elephants to swinging great apes, San Diego's most famous attraction has it all. Nearly 4,000 animals representing 800 species roam the 100-acre zoo in expertly crafted habitats that replicate the animals' natural environments. The pandas may have gone home (in 2019), but there are plenty of other cool creatures to see here, from teeny-tiny mantella frogs to two-story-tall giraffes. But it's not all just fun and games. Known for its exemplary conservation programs, the zoo educates visitors on how to go green and explains its efforts to protect endangered species.

SAN DIEGO ZOO TOP ATTRACTIONS

Underwater viewing area at the Hippo Trail

❶ **Children's Zoo (Discovery Outpost).** Goats and sheep beg to be petted, and there is a viewer-friendly nursery where you may see baby animals bottle-feed and sleep peacefully in large cribs.

❷ **Monkey Trails and Forest Tales (Lost Forest).** Follow an elevated trail at treetop level and trek through the forest floor observing African mandrill monkeys, Asia's clouded leopard, the rare pygmy hippopotamus, and Visayan warty pigs.

❸ **Orangutan and Siamang Exhibit (Lost Forest).** Orangutans and siamangs climb and swing in this lush, tropical environment lined with 110-foot-long and 12-foot-high viewing windows.

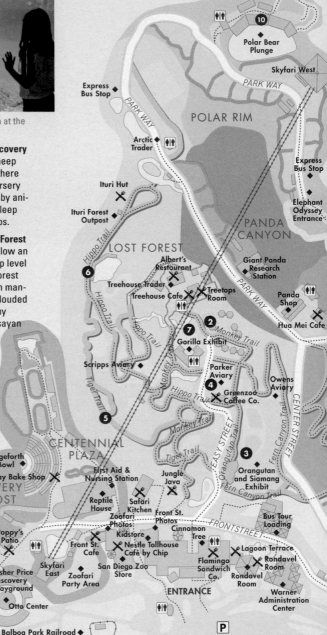

Lories at Owen's Aviary

4 **Scripps, Parker, and Owens Aviaries (Lost Forest).** Wandering paths climb through the enclosed aviaries where brightly colored tropical birds swoop between branches inches from your face.

5 **Tiger Trail (Lost Forest).** The mist-shrouded trails of this simulated rainforest wind down a canyon. Tigers, Malayan tapirs, and Argus pheasants wander among the exotic trees and plants.

6 **Hippo Trail (Lost Forest).** Glimpse huge but surprisingly graceful hippos frolicking in the water through an underwater viewing window and buffalo cavorting with monkeys on dry land.

7 **Gorilla Exhibit (Lost Forest).** The gorillas live in one of the zoo's bioclimatic zone exhibits modeled on their native habitat with waterfalls, climbing areas, and an open meadow. The sounds of the tropical rain forest emerge from a 144-speaker sound system that plays CDs recorded in Africa.

8 **Africa Rocks.** This massive exhibit consists of six different rocky habitats designed to showcase the diversity of topography and species on the African continent. Penguins, meerkats, and a band of baboons are just a few of the animals that call this ambitious exhibit home.

9 **Sun Bear Forest (Asian Passage).** Playful beasts claw apart the trees and shrubs that serve as a natural playground for climbing, jump¬ing, and general merrymaking.

10 **Polar Bear Plunge (Polar Rim).** Watch polar bears take a chilly dive from the underwater viewing room. There are also Siberian reindeer, white foxes, and other Arctic creatures here. Kids can learn about the Arctic and climate change through interactive exhibits.

11 **Elephant Odyssey.** Get a glimpse of the animals that roamed Southern California 12,000 years ago and meet their living counterparts. The 7.5-acre, multispecies habitat features elephants, California condors, jaguars, and more.

12 **Koala Exhibit (Outback).** The San Diego Zoo houses the largest number of koalas outside Australia. Walk through the exhibit for photo ops of these marsupials from Down-Under curled up on their perches or dining on eucalyptus branches.

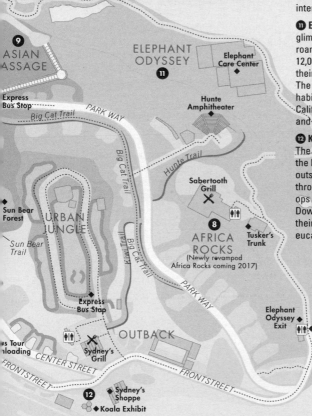

Map labels:

9 ASIAN PASSAGE

Express Bus Stop

Big Cat Trail

PARK WAY

ELEPHANT ODYSSEY **11**

Elephant Care Center

Hunte Amphitheater

Hunte Trail

Big Cat Trail

Sun Bear Forest

URBAN JUNGLE

Sun Bear Trail

Sabertooth Grill

8 AFRICA ROCKS
(Newly revamped Africa Rocks coming 2017)

Tusker's Trunk

PARK WAY

Express Bus Stop

Elephant Odyssey Exit

Express Bus Stop

Bus Tour Unloading

CENTER STREET

Sydney's Grill

OUTBACK

FRONTSTREET

FRONTSTREET

12 Sydney's Shoppe

Koala Exhibit

MUST-SEE ANIMALS

1 GORILLA

This troop of primates engages visitors with their human-like expressions and behavior. The youngsters are sure to delight, especially when hitching a ride on mom's back. Up-close encounters might involve the gorillas using the glass partition as a backrest while peeling cabbage. By dusk the gorillas head inside to their sleeping quarters, so don't save this for your last stop.

2 ELEPHANT

Asian and African elephants coexist at the San Diego Zoo. The larger African elephant is distinguished by its big flapping ears—shaped like the continent of Africa—which it uses to keep cool. An elephant's trunk has over 40,000 muscles in it—that's more than humans have in their whole body.

3 ORANGUTAN

Bornean and Sumatran orangutans have been entertaining San Diego visitors since 1928. The exhibit has rope climbing structures, a man-made "termite mound" that's often filled with treats, rocky caves, and tall "sway poles" that allow the orangutans to swing like they would in trees. Don't be surprised if the orangutans come right up to the glass to observe the humans observing them!

4 KOALA

While this collection of critters is one of the cutest in the zoo, don't expect a lot of activity from the koala habitat. These guys spend most of their day curled up asleep in the branches of the eucalyptus tree—they can sleep up to 20 hours a day. Although eucalyptus leaves are poisonous to most animals, bacteria in koalas' stomachs allow them to break down the toxins.

5 POLAR BEAR

The trio of polar bears is one of the San Diego Zoo's star attractions, and their brand-new exhibit gets you up close and personal. Visitors sometimes worry about polar bears living in the warm San Diego climate, but there is no cause for concern. The San Diego-based bears eat a lean diet, thus reducing their layer of blubber and helping them keep cool.

Did You Know?

Red pandas aren't actually pandas, but more like skunks or raccoons in your backyard. With the giant pandas gone from the San Diego Zoo though, the red pandas are an adorable alternative.

★ Bankers Hill Bar and Restaurant
$$ | **MODERN AMERICAN** | The living wall of succulents, hip warehouse interior, and wine bottle chandeliers suit this vibrant restaurant where good times and great eats meet. An after-work crowd joins residents of this quiet stretch of Bankers Hill for happy hour served from the zinc bar while diners enjoy sophisticated comfort food often with Southwest flair. **Known for:** popular burger with truffle fries; butterscotch pudding topped with shortbread cookies and crème fraîche; living plant wall on the sun-drenched patio. [$] *Average main: $23* ✉ *2202 4th Ave., Bankers Hill* ☎ *619/231–0222* 🌐 *www.bankershillsd.com* 🕓 *No lunch.*

★ Cucina Urbana
$$ | **ITALIAN** | Twentysomethings mingle with boomers in this convivial Bankers Hill dining room and bar, one of the most popular restaurants in town. The open kitchen turns out innovative Italian food with a California sensibility including a selection of small plates and family-style pasta dishes alongside traditional entrées. **Known for:** in-house wineshop with reasonably priced bottles and $9 corkage fee; seasonal polenta with ragu; ricotta-stuffed zucchini blossoms. [$] *Average main: $21* ✉ *505 Laurel St., Bankers Hill* ☎ *619/239–2222* 🌐 *www.cucinaurbana.com* 🕓 *No lunch Sat.–Mon.*

Panama 66
$ | **AMERICAN** | Adding a dose of hip to Balboa Park, this gastropub, located adjacent to the San Diego Museum of Art's sculpture garden, offers a stylish pit stop pretheater or between museum-hopping. The menu features upscale pub fare with several vegan options as well as a weekend brunch. **Known for:** rotating cocktails pegged to museum exhibits; live music most nights; local San Diego and Tijuana brews. [$] *Average main: $12* ✉ *1450 El Prado, Balboa Park* ☎ *619/696–1966* 🌐 *www.panama66.com* 🕓 *No dinner Mon. and Tues. Labor Day–Memorial Day.*

🎟 Performing Arts

THEATER

★ The Old Globe
THEATER | This complex, comprising the Sheryl and Harvey White Theatre, the Lowell Davies Festival Theatre, and the Old Globe Theatre, offers some of the finest theatrical productions in Southern California. Theater classics such as *The Full Monty* and *Dirty Rotten Scoundrels,* both of which went on to Broadway, premiered on these famed stages. The Old Globe presents the family-friendly *How the Grinch Stole Christmas* around the holidays, as well as a renowned summer Shakespeare Festival with three to four plays in repertory. ✉ *1363 Old Globe Way, Balboa Park* ☎ *619/234–5623* 🌐 *www.oldglobe.org.*

Old Town and Uptown

San Diego's Spanish and Mexican roots are most evident in Old Town and the surrounding hillside of Presidio Park. Visitors can experience settlement life in San Diego from Spanish and Mexican rule to the early days of U.S. statehood. Nearby Uptown is composed of several smaller neighborhoods near Downtown and around Balboa Park: the vibrant neighborhoods of Hillcrest, Mission Hills, North Park, and South Park showcase their unique blend of historical charm and modern urban community.

As the first European settlement in Southern California, Old Town began to develop in the 1820s. But its true beginnings took place on a nearby hillside in 1769 with the establishment of a Spanish military outpost and the first of California's missions, San Diego de Alcalá. In 1774 the hilltop was declared a *presidio reál*, a fortress built by the Spanish Empire, and the mission was relocated along the San Diego River. Over time, settlers moved down from the presidio to establish Old Town. A central plaza was laid out, surrounded by adobe and, later, wooden structures. San Diego became an incorporated U.S. city in 1850, with Old Town as its center. In the 1860s, however, the advent of Alonzo Horton's New Town to the southeast caused Old Town to wither. Efforts to preserve the area began early in the 20th century, and Old Town became a state historic park in 1968.

Today Old Town is a lively celebration of history and culture. The Old Town San Diego State Historic Park re-creates life during the early settlement, while San Diego Avenue buzzes with art galleries, gift shops, festive restaurants, and open-air stands selling inexpensive Mexican handicrafts.

◉ Sights

★ Fiesta de Reyes
HISTORIC SITE | FAMILY | North of San Diego's Old Town Plaza lies the area's unofficial center, built to represent a colonial Mexican plaza. The collection of more than a dozen shops and restaurants around a central courtyard in blossom with magenta bougainvillea, scarlet hibiscus, and other flowers in season reflects what early California might have looked like from 1821 to 1872. Mariachi bands and folklorico dance groups frequently perform on the plaza stage—check the website for times and upcoming special events. ■TIP→ Casa de Reyes is a great stop for a margarita and some chips and guacamole. ⊠ 4016 Wallace St., Old Town ☎ 619/297–3100 ⊕ www.fiestadereyes.com.

★ Old Town San Diego State Historic Park
HISTORIC SITE | FAMILY | The six square blocks on the site of San Diego's original pueblo are the heart of Old Town. Most of the 20 historic buildings preserved or re-created by the park cluster around **Old Town Plaza,** bounded by Wallace Street on the west, Calhoun Street on the north, Mason Street on the east, and San Diego Avenue on the south. The plaza is

a pleasant place to rest, plan your tour of the park, and watch passersby. San Diego Avenue is closed to vehicle traffic here.

Some of Old Town's buildings were destroyed in a fire in 1872, but after the site became a state historic park in 1968, reconstruction and restoration of the remaining structures began. Five of the original adobes are still intact.

Facing Old Town Plaza, the **Robinson-Rose House** was the original commercial center of Old San Diego, housing railroad offices, law offices, and the first newspaper press. The largest and most elaborate of the original adobe homes, the **Casa de Estudillo** was occupied by members of the Estudillo family until 1887 and later gained popularity for its billing as "Ramona's Marriage Place" based on a popular novel of the time. Albert Seeley, a stagecoach entrepreneur, opened the **Cosmopolitan Hotel** in 1869 as a way station for travelers on the daylong trip south from Los Angeles. Next door to the Cosmopolitan Hotel, the **Seeley Stable** served as San Diego's stagecoach stop in 1867 and was the transportation hub of Old Town until 1887, when trains became the favored mode of travel.

Several reconstructed buildings serve as restaurants or as shops purveying wares reminiscent of those that might have been available in the original Old Town. **Racine & Laramie,** a painstakingly reproduced version of San Diego's first cigar store in 1868, is especially interesting.

Pamphlets available at the Robinson-Rose House give details about all the historic houses on the plaza and in its vicinity. Free tours of the historic park are offered daily at 11:30 and 2; they depart from the Robinson-Rose House. ■TIP→ The covered wagon located near the intersection of Mason and Calhoun streets provides a great photo op. ⊠ Visitor center (Robinson-Rose House), 4002 Wallace St., Old Town ☎ 619/220–5422 ⊕ www.parks.ca.gov ⌦ Free.

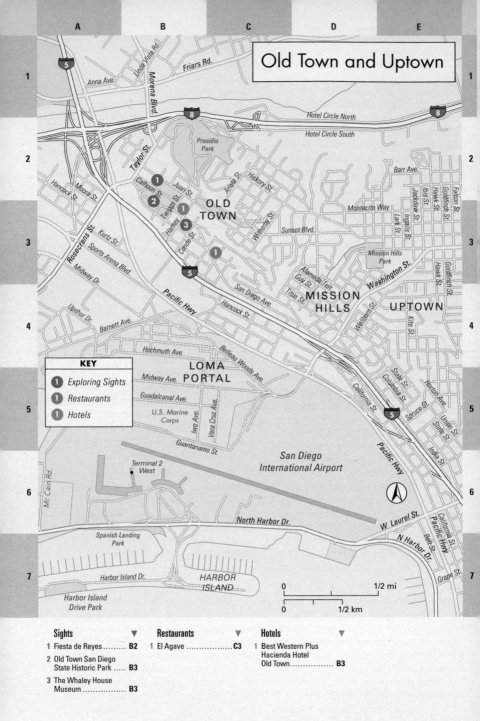

Old Town and Uptown

KEY
- Exploring Sights
- Restaurants
- Hotels

Sights ▼	Restaurants ▼	Hotels ▼
1 Fiesta de Reyes B2	1 El Agave C3	1 Best Western Plus Hacienda Hotel Old Town B3
2 Old Town San Diego State Historic Park B3		
3 The Whaley House Museum B3		

The Whaley House Museum

HISTORIC SITE | A New York entrepreneur, Thomas Whaley came to California during the gold rush. He wanted to provide his East Coast wife with all the comforts of home, so in 1857 he had Southern California's first two-story brick structure built, making it the oldest double-story brick building on the West Coast. The house, which served as the county courthouse and government seat during the 1870s, stands in strong contrast to the Spanish-style adobe residences that surround the nearby historic plaza and marks an early stage of San Diego's "Americanization." A garden out back includes many varieties of prehybrid roses from before 1867. The place is perhaps most famed, however, for the ghosts that are said to inhabit it. You can tour on your own during the day, but must visit by guided tour after 4:30 pm. The evening tours are geared toward the supernatural aspects of the house. Tours start at 6 pm (5 pm on Saturday) and are offered every half hour, with the last tour departing at 9:30 pm. ✉ *2476 San Diego Ave., Old Town* ☎ *619/297–7511* 🌐 *www.whaleyhouse.org* 🎟 *$10 before 5 pm; $13 after 5 pm* 🕒 *Closed Sept.–May and Wed.*

🍴 Restaurants

El Agave

$$$ | **MEXICAN** | Not a typical San Diego taco shop, this Mexican eatery is upstairs in a shopping complex in the middle of a tequila museum with some 2,000 bottles dating from the 1930s. The owners are equally serious about food, calling their cuisine Hispanic-Mexican Gastronomy, which means meat and fish dishes with lots of unusual spicy chilies, herbs, spices, and moles. **Known for:** impressive tequila selection and tequila flights; variety of mole dishes; upscale option in generally casual Old Town. [$] *Average main: $32* ✉ *2304 San Diego Ave., Old Town* ☎ *619/220–0692* 🌐 *www.elagave.com.*

🛏 Hotels

Best Western Plus Hacienda Hotel Old Town

$$ | **HOTEL** | **FAMILY** | Perched on a hill in the heart of Old Town, this hotel is known for its expansive courtyards, outdoor fountains, and maze of stairs that connects eight buildings of guest rooms. **Pros:** airport shuttle; well-maintained outdoor areas; excellent location for exploring Old Town. **Cons:** some rooms need renovating; complicated layout; can be noisy in some areas. [$] *Rooms from: $219* ✉ *4041 Harney St., Old Town* ☎ *800/888–1991* 🌐 *www.haciendahotel-oldtown.com* 🔑 *200 rooms* 🍽 *No meals.*

🛍 Shopping

★ **Bazaar del Mundo Shops**

SHOPPING CENTERS/MALLS | With a Mexican villa theme, the Bazaar hosts riotously colorful gift shops such as **Ariana,** for ethnic and artsy women's fashions; **Artes de Mexico,** which sells handmade Latin American crafts and Guatemalan weavings; and **The Gallery,** which carries handmade jewelry, Native American crafts, collectible glass, and original silk-screen prints. The **Laurel Burch Gallerita** carries the complete collection of its namesake artist's signature jewelry, accessories, and totes. ✉ *4133 Taylor St., at Juan St., Old Town* ☎ *619/296–3161* 🌐 *www.bazaardelmundo.com.*

Mission Valley

Although Mission Valley's charms may not be immediately apparent, it offers many conveniences to visitors and residents alike. One of the area's main attractions is the Fashion Valley mall, with its mix of high-end and mid-range retail stores and dining options, and movie theater. The Mission Basilica San Diego de Alcalá provides a tranquil refuge from the surrounding suburban sprawl.

👁 Sights

★ Mission Basilica San Diego de Alcalá

HISTORIC SITE | It's hard to imagine how remote California's earliest mission must have once been; these days, however, it's accessible by major freeways (I–15 and I–8) and via the San Diego Trolley. The first of a chain of 21 missions stretching northward along the coast, Mission San Diego de Alcalá was established by Father Junípero Serra on Presidio Hill in 1769 and moved to this location in 1774. In 1775, it proved vulnerable to enemy attack, and Padre Luís Jayme, a young friar from Spain, was clubbed to death by the Kumeyaay Indians he had been trying to convert. He was the first of more than a dozen Christians martyred in California. The present church, reconstructed in 1931 following the outline of the 1813 church, is the fifth built on the site. It measures 150 feet long but only 35 feet wide because, without easy means of joining beams, the mission buildings were only as wide as the trees that served as their ceiling supports were tall. Father Jayme is buried in the sanctuary; a small museum named for him documents mission history and exhibits tools and artifacts from the early days; there is also a gift shop. From the peaceful, palm-bedecked gardens out back you can gaze at the 46-foot-high *campanario* (bell tower), the mission's most distinctive feature, with five bells. Mass is celebrated on the weekends. ⊠ *10818 San Diego Mission Rd., Mission Valley* ✚ *From I–8 east, exit and turn left on Mission Gorge Rd., then left on Twain Rd.; mission is on right* 🕾 *619/281–8449* ⊕ *www.mission-sandiego.com* 💲 *$5.*

📺 Nightlife

★ Blanco Tacos + Tequila

BARS/PUBS | Get your margarita skinny, spicy, or standard, with house-made sours and fresh-squeezed juices, at this prime new spot within Fashion Valley Mall. Don't miss Margarita Monday ($5 classic margaritas until 6 pm) or Taco Tuesday ($4 happy hour tacos until 6 pm). ⊠ *Fashion Valley Mall, 7007 Friars Rd., Mission Valley* 🕾 *619/810–2931* ⊕ *www.blancotacostequila.com.*

🛍 Shopping

★ Fashion Valley

SHOPPING CENTERS/MALLS | San Diego's most upscale mall has a contemporary Mission theme, lush landscaping, and more than 200 shops and restaurants. Acclaimed retailers like Nordstrom, Neiman Marcus, Bloomingdale's, and Tiffany & Co. are here, along with boutiques from fashion darlings like Michael Kors, Tory Burch, and Ted Baker. H&M is a favorite of fashionistas in search of edgy and affordable styles. Free wireless Internet service is available throughout the mall. Select "Simon WiFi" from any Wi-Fi–enabled device to log onto the network. ■ TIP➔ If you're visiting from out of state, are a member of the military, or have a AAA membership, you can pick up a complimentary Style Pass at Simon Guest Services (located on the lower level beneath AMC Theaters near Banana Republic), which can get you savings at more than 70 of Fashion Valley's stores and restaurants. ⊠ *7007 Friars Rd., Mission Valley* 🕾 *619/688–9113* ⊕ *www.simon.com/mall/fashion-valley.*

Mission Bay and the Beaches

Mission Bay and the surrounding beaches are the aquatic playground of San Diego. The choice of activities available is astonishing, and the perfect weather makes you want to get out there and play. If you're craving downtime after all the activity, there are plenty of peaceful spots to relax and simply soak up the sunshine.

Mission Bay welcomes visitors with its protected waters and countless opportunities for fun. The 4,600-acre **Mission Bay Park** is the place for water sports like sailing, stand-up paddleboarding, and waterskiing. With 19 miles of beaches and grassy areas, it's also a great place for a picnic.

Mission Beach is a famous and lively fun zone for families and young people; if it isn't party time at the moment, it will be five minutes from now. The pathways in this area are lined with vacation homes, many for rent by the week or month.

North of Mission Beach is the college-packed party town of Pacific Beach, or "PB" as locals call it. The laid-back vibe of this surfer's mecca draws in free-spirited locals who roam the streets on skateboards and beach cruisers. The energy level peaks during happy hour, when PB's cluster of nightclubs, bars, and 150 restaurants open their doors to those ready to party.

◉ Sights

★ Belmont Park
AMUSEMENT PARK/WATER PARK | FAMILY | The once-abandoned amusement park between the bay and Mission Beach Boardwalk is now a shopping, dining, and recreation complex. Twinkling lights outline the **Giant Dipper,** an antique wooden roller coaster on which screaming thrill seekers ride more than 2,600 feet of track and 13 hills (riders must be at least 4 feet, 2 inches tall). Created in 1925 and listed on the National Register of Historic Places, this is one of the few old-time roller coasters left in the United States.

Other Belmont Park attractions include miniature golf, a laser maze, video arcade, bumper cars, a tilt-a-whirl, and an antique carousel. The zip line thrills as it soars over the crowds below, while the rock wall challenges both junior climbers and their elders. ⊠ *3146 Mission Blvd., Mission Bay* ☎ *858/488–1549 for rides*

⊕ *www.belmontpark.com* ☎ *Unlimited ride day package $32 for 48 inches and taller, $22 for under 48 inches, some attractions not included in price; individual ride tickets and other ride/attraction combo packages are also available.*

★ Crystal Pier
BEACH—SIGHT | Stretching out into the ocean from the end of Garnet Avenue, Crystal Pier is Pacific Beach's landmark. A stroll to the end of the pier will likely reveal fishermen hoping for a good catch. Surfers make catches of their own in the waves below. ⊠ *Pacific Beach* ✛ *At end of Garnet Ave.*

★ Mission Bay Park
BEACH—SIGHT | San Diego's monument to sports and fitness, this 4,600-acre aquatic park has 27 miles of shoreline including 19 miles of sandy beaches. Playgrounds and picnic areas abound on the beaches and low, grassy hills. On weekday evenings, joggers, bikers, and skaters take over. In the daytime, swimmers, water-skiers, paddleboarders, anglers, and boaters—some in single-person kayaks, others in crowded powerboats—vie for space in the water. ⊠ *2688 E. Mission Bay Dr., Mission Bay* ✛ *Off I–5 at Exit 22, E. Mission Bay Dr.* ☎ *858/581–7602 park ranger's office* ⊕ *www.sandiego.gov/park-and-recreation* ☎ *Free.*

★ Mission Beach Boardwalk
BEACH—SIGHT | The cement pathway lining the sand from the southern end of Mission Beach north to Pacific Beach is always bustling with activity. Cyclists ping the bells on their beach cruisers to pass walkers out for a stroll alongside the oceanfront homes. Vacationers kick back on their patios, while friends play volleyball in the sand. The activity picks up alongside Belmont Park, where people stop to check out the action at the amusement park and beach bars. ⊠ *Mission Beach* ✛ *Alongside sand from Mission Beach Park to Pacific Beach.*

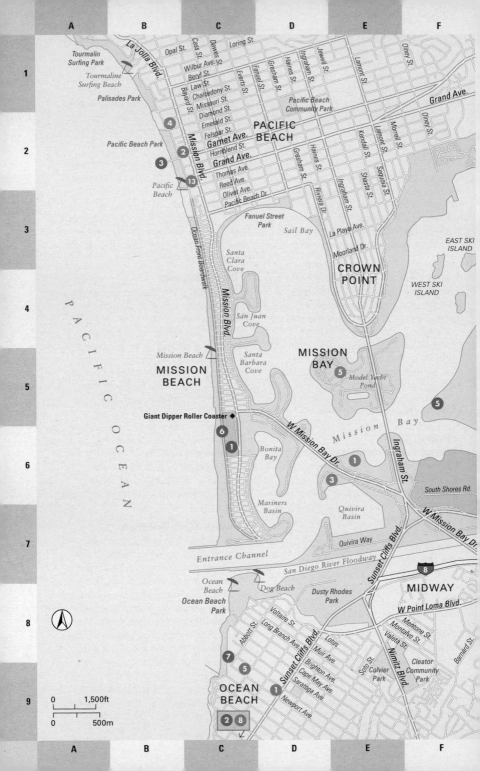

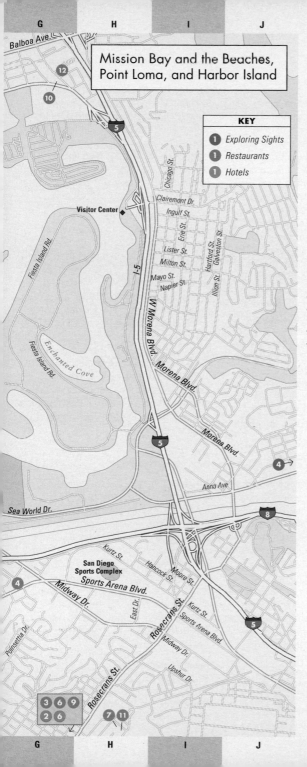

Mission Bay and the Beaches, Point Loma, and Harbor Island

KEY

1 Exploring Sights
1 Restaurants
1 Hotels

Sights ▼

1 Belmont Park.......................**C6**
2 Cabrillo National Monument......**C9**
3 Crystal Pier.........................**B2**
4 Mission Basilica
   San Diego de Alcalá..............**J6**
5 Mission Bay Park..................**F5**
6 Mission Beach Boardwalk........**C6**
7 Ocean Beach Pier.................**C8**

Restaurants ▼

1 Azucar **D9**
2 The Baked Bear...................**C2**
3 Bali Hai...........................**G9**
4 The Cravory **G8**
5 Hodad's **C9**
6 Island Prime and C Level **G9**
7 Liberty Public Market **H9**
8 The Little Lion **C9**
9 Point Loma Seafoods.............**G9**
10 Rubio's Coastal Grill **G1**
11 Stone Brewing World Bistro &
   Gardens...........................**H9**
12 Sushi Ota **G1**
13 Waterbar **C2**

Hotels ▼

1 The Dana on Mission Bay **E6**
2 Homewood Suites
   San Diego Airport
   Liberty Station.....................**G9**
3 Hyatt Regency Mission Bay
   Spa And Marina **E6**
4 Pacific Terrace Hotel.............**B2**
5 Paradise Point Resort & Spa......**E5**
6 The Pearl Hotel **G9**

🏖 Beaches

Mission Beach

BEACH—SIGHT | FAMILY | With a roller coaster, arcade, and hot dog stands, this 2-mile-long beach has a carnival vibe and is the closest thing you'll find to Coney Island on the West Coast. It's lively year-round but draws a huge crowd on hot summer days. A wide boardwalk paralleling the beach is popular with walkers, joggers, skateboarders, and bicyclists. To escape the crowds, head to South Mission Beach. It attracts surfers, swimmers, and volleyball players, who often play competitive pickup games on the courts near the north jetty. The water near the Belmont Park roller coaster can be a bit rough but makes for good bodyboarding and bodysurfing. For free parking, you can try for a spot on the street, but your best bets are the two big lots at Belmont Park. **Amenities:** lifeguards; parking (no fee); showers; toilets. **Best for:** swimming; surfing; walking. ✉ *3000 Mission Blvd., Mission Bay* ✣ *Parking near roller coaster at West Mission Bay Dr.* 🌐 *www.sandiego.gov/lifeguards/beaches/mb.shtml.*

Pacific Beach/North Pacific Beach

BEACH—SIGHT | This beach, known for attracting a young college-age crowd and surfers, runs from the northern end of Mission Beach to Crystal Pier. The scene here is lively on weekends, with nearby restaurants, beach bars, and nightclubs providing a party atmosphere. In PB (as the locals call it) Sundays are known as "Sunday Funday," and pub crawls can last all day. So although drinking is no longer allowed on the beach, it's still likely you'll see people who have had one too many. The mood changes just north of the pier at North Pacific Beach, which attracts families and surfers. Although not quite pillowy, the sand at both beaches is nice and soft, which makes for great sunbathing and sand-castle building. **■ TIP→ Kelp and flies can be a problem on this stretch, so choose your spot wisely.** Parking at Pacific Beach can also be a challenge. A few coveted free angle parking spaces are available along the boardwalk, but you'll most likely have to look for spots in the surrounding neighborhood. **Amenities:** food and drink; lifeguards; parking (no fee); showers, toilets. **Best for:** partiers; swimming; surfing. ✉ *4500 Ocean Blvd., Pacific Beach* 🌐 *www.sandiego.gov/lifeguards/beaches/pb.shtml.*

Tourmaline Surfing Park

BEACH—SIGHT | Offering slow waves and frequent winds, this is one of the most popular beaches for surfers. For windsurfing and kiteboarding, it's only sailable with northwest winds. The 175-space parking lot at the foot of Tourmaline Street normally fills to capacity by midday. Just like Pacific Beach, Tourmaline has soft, tawny-colored sand, but when the tide is in the beach becomes quite narrow, making finding a good sunbathing spot a bit of a challenge. **Amenities:** seasonal lifeguards; parking (no fee); showers; toilets. **Best for:** windsurfing; surfing. ✉ *600 Tourmaline St., Pacific Beach.*

🍴 Restaurants

The Baked Bear

$ | BAKERY | FAMILY | This build-your-own ice cream–sandwich shop a block from Pacific Beach is a local favorite thanks to its homemade cookies and diverse array of ice-cream flavors, from birthday cake to peanut butter fudge. **Known for:** Bear Bowls made of cookies; doughnut ice cream sandwiches; long lines on summer evenings. [$] *Average main: $5* ✉ *4516 Mission Blvd., Suite C, Pacific Beach* ☎ *858/886–7433* 🌐 *www.thebakedbear.com.*

Rubio's Coastal Grill

$ | SEAFOOD | Credited with popularizing fish tacos in the United States, Ralph Rubio brought the Mexican staple to San Diego, opening his first restaurant in Pacific Beach where it still stands today. The original beer-battered fish tacos have fried pollock topped with white sauce, salsa, and cabbage atop a corn tortilla. **Known for:** the original fish taco; Taco Tuesday deal—fish taco and a beer for $5; $7 lunch specials. [$] *Average main: $10* ✉ *4504 Mission Bay Dr., Pacific Beach* ☎ *858/272–2801* 🌐 *www.rubios.com.*

★ Sushi Ota

$$ | SUSHI | One fan called it "a notch above amazing"—an accolade not expected for a Japanese eatery wedged in a strip mall in Pacific Beach. But it's a destination for lovers of high-quality, superfresh raw fish from around San Diego and abroad; reservations strongly encouraged. **Known for:** velvety hamachi belly; sea urchin specials; chef's omakase tasting menu. [$] *Average main: $25* ✉ *4529 Mission Bay Dr., Pacific Beach* ☎ *858/270–5670* 🌐 *www.sushiota.com* ⏲ *No lunch Sat.–Mon.*

★ Waterbar

$$ | SEAFOOD | Occupying a prime oceanfront lot just south of Crystal Pier, the views from the raised dining room are impressive. Throw in an excellent raw bar, a wide selection of shared plates, and a buzzy bar scene and you get Waterbar's "social seafood" concept. **Known for:** late-night "Boardwalk hour" oyster specials; boozy weekend brunch; ocean views. [$] *Average main: $24* ✉ *4325 Ocean Blvd., Pacific Beach* ☎ *858/888–4343* 🌐 *www.waterbarsd.com.*

Hotels

The Dana on Mission Bay

$$$ | RESORT | FAMILY | This waterfront resort, just down the road from SeaWorld, has an ideal location for active leisure travelers. **Pros:** water views; many outdoor activities; shuttle to SeaWorld. **Cons:** expensive resort fee; popular wedding venue; rooms vary in quality and view. [$] *Rooms from: $289* ✉ *1710 W. Mission Bay Dr., Mission Bay* ☎ *619/222–6440, 800/445–3339* 🌐 *www.thedana.com* 🛏 *271 rooms* 🍴 *No meals.*

Hyatt Regency Mission Bay Spa and Marina

$$$ | RESORT | FAMILY | This modern property has many desirable amenities, including balconies with excellent views of the garden, bay, ocean, or swimming pool courtyard. **Pros:** proximity to water sports; 120-foot waterslides in pools, plus kiddie slide; several suite configurations good for families. **Cons:** daily resort fee; not centrally located; some areas in need of updates. [$] *Rooms from: $299* ✉ *1441 Quivira Rd., Mission Bay* ☎ *619/224–1234, 800/233–1234* 🌐 *www.missionbay.regency.hyatt.com* 🛏 *429 rooms* 🍴 *No meals.*

Pacific Terrace Hotel

$$$$ | RESORT | Travelers love this terrific beachfront hotel and the ocean views from most rooms; it's a perfect place for watching sunsets over the Pacific. **Pros:** beach views; large rooms; friendly service. **Cons:** busy and sometimes noisy area; expensive in peak season; resort fee. [$] *Rooms from: $569* ✉ *610 Diamond St., Pacific Beach* ☎ *858/581–3500, 800/344–3370* 🌐 *www.pacificterrace.com* 🛏 *73 rooms* 🍴 *No meals.*

Paradise Point Resort & Spa

$$$ | RESORT | FAMILY | Minutes from SeaWorld but hidden in a quiet part of Mission Bay, the beautiful landscape of this 44-acre resort offers plenty of space for families to play and relax. **Pros:** water views; five pools; good service. **Cons:** not centrally located; motel-thin walls; parking and resort fees. [$] *Rooms from: $296* ✉ *1404 Vacation Rd., Mission Bay* ☎ *858/274–4630, 800/344–2626* 🌐 *www.paradisepoint.com* 🛏 *462 rooms* 🍴 *No meals.*

ⓨ Nightlife

BARS
★ The Grass Skirt

BARS/PUBS | Accessed through a false freezer door inside Good Time Poke, this speakeasy-styled tiki bar serves a wide selection of rum-based tropical cocktails in delightfully kitsch surroundings. The Polynesian-inspired menu features shareable poke and pupus, but call ahead to reserve a table—this hidden gem is no secret! ⊠ *910 Grand Ave., Pacific Beach* ☏ *858/412–5237* ⊕ *www.thegrassskirt.com.*

JRDN

BARS/PUBS | This contemporary lounge (pronounced "Jordan") occupies the ground floor of Pacific Beach's chicest boutique hotel, Tower23, and offers a more sophisticated vibe in what is a very party-happy neighborhood. Sleek walls of windows and an expansive patio overlook the boardwalk. ⊠ *723 Felspar St., Pacific Beach* ☏ *858/270–2323* ⊕ *www.t23hotel.com.*

🏃 Activities

DIVING
Scuba San Diego

SCUBA DIVING | This center is well regarded for its top-notch instruction and certification programs, as well as for guided dive tours. Scuba Adventure classes for non-certified divers are held daily in Mission Bay, meeting near Mission Point. Trips for certified divers depart from La Jolla and include dives to kelp reefs in La Jolla Cove, and night diving at La Jolla Canyon. They also have snorkeling tours to La Jolla's Sea Caves. ⊠ *San Diego Hilton Hotel, 1775 E. Mission Bay Dr., Mission Bay* ☏ *619/260–1880* ⊕ *www.scubasandiego.com* ⌤ *From $70* ⌕ *Scuba Adventure meeting point is 2615 Bayside La. in South Mission Bay, near Mission Point.*

SURFING
Cheap Rentals

SURFING | One block from the boardwalk, this place has good daily and weekly prices for surfboards, paddleboards, kayaks, snorkel gear, skateboards, coolers, umbrellas, chairs, and bike rentals, including beach cruisers, tandems, hybrids, and two-wheeled baby carriers. Kids bikes are also available. Demand is high during the busy season (May through September) so call to reserve equipment ahead of time. ⊠ *3689 Mission Blvd., Mission Beach* ☏ *858/488–9070, 800/941–7761* ⊕ *www.cheap-rentals.com* ⌤ *From $7/hr.*

WATER SPORTS
Mission Bay Aquatic Center

BOATING | **FAMILY** | The world's largest instructional waterfront facility offers lessons in wakeboarding, sailing, surfing, waterskiing, rowing, kayaking, and windsurfing. Equipment rental is also available, but the emphasis is on instruction, and most rentals require a minimum two-hour orientation lesson before you can set out on your own. Reservations are recommended, particularly during the summer. Skippered keelboats and boats for waterskiing or wakeboarding can be hired with reservations. Free parking is available. ⊠ *1001 Santa Clara Pl., Mission Beach* ☏ *858/488–1000* ⊕ *www.mbaquaticcenter.com.*

★ Seaforth Boat Rentals

BOATING | The Mission Bay outpost of this popular rental company offers a wide variety of motorized and nonmotorized craft. Jet Skis, SUPs, kayaks, and fishing skiffs are available alongside sailboats and powerboats of all sizes. For added relaxation, charter a skippered pontoon party boat, some with waterslides for added fun. ⊠ *1641 Quivira Rd., Mission Bay* ☏ *888/834–2628* ⊕ *www.seaforthboatrental.com.*

La Jolla

La Jolla (pronounced La Hoya) means "the jewel" in Spanish and appropriately describes this small, affluent village and its beaches. Some beautiful coastline can be found here, as well as an elegant upscale atmosphere.

Sights

Birch Aquarium at Scripps

ZOO | FAMILY | Affiliated with the world-renowned Scripps Institution of Oceanography, this excellent aquarium sits at the end of a signposted drive leading off North Torrey Pines Road and has sweeping views of La Jolla coast below. More than 60 tanks are filled with colorful saltwater fish, and a 70,000-gallon tank simulates a La Jolla kelp forest. A special exhibit on sea horses features several examples of the species, plus mesmerizing sea dragons and a sea horse nursery. Besides the fish themselves, attractions include interactive educational exhibits based on the institution's ocean-related research and a variety of environmental issues. ⊠ *2300 Expedition Way, La Jolla* ☎ *858/534–3474* ⊕ *www.aquarium.ucsd. edu* ⊠ *$19.50.*

San Diego-La Jolla Underwater Park Ecological Reserve

BODY OF WATER | Four habitats across 6,000 acres make up this underwater park and ecological reserve. When the water is clear, this is a diver's paradise with reefs, kelp beds, sand flats, and a submarine canyon. Plunge deeper to see guitarfish rays, perch, sea bass, anchovies, squid, and hammerhead sharks. Snorkelers, kayakers, and stand-up paddleboarders are likely to spot sea lions, seals, and leopard sharks. The Seven La Jolla Sea Caves, 75-million-year-old sandstone caves, are at the park's edge. ■ TIP→ **While the park can be explored on your own, the best way to view it is with a professional guide.** ⊠ *La Jolla* ✛ *La Jolla Cove.*

★ Torrey Pines State Natural Reserve

NATIONAL/STATE PARK | *Pinus torreyana,* the rarest native pine tree in the United States, enjoys a 1,500-acre sanctuary at the northern edge of La Jolla. About 6,000 of these unusual trees, some as tall as 60 feet, grow on the cliffs here. The park is one of only two places in the world (the other is Santa Rosa Island, off Santa Barbara) where the Torrey pine grows naturally. The reserve has several hiking trails leading to the cliffs, 300 feet above the ocean; trail maps are available at the park station. Wildflowers grow profusely in spring, and the ocean panoramas are always spectacular. From December to March, whales can be spotted from the bluffs. When in this upper part of the park, respect the restrictions. Not permitted: picnicking, smoking, leaving the trails, dogs, alcohol, or collecting plant specimens.

You can unwrap your sandwiches, however, at Torrey Pines State Beach, just below the reserve. When the tide is out, it's possible to walk south all the way past the lifeguard towers to Black's Beach over rocky promontories carved by the waves (avoid the bluffs, however; they're unstable). **Los Peñasquitos Lagoon** at the north end of the reserve is one of the many natural estuaries that flow inland between Del Mar and Oceanside. It's a good place to watch shorebirds. Volunteers lead guided nature walks at 10 and 2 on most weekends and holidays. ⊠ *12600 N. Torrey Pines Rd., La Jolla* ✛ *N. Torrey Pines Rd. exit off I–5 onto Carmel Valley Rd. going west, then turn left (south) on Coast Hwy. 101* ☎ *858/755–2063* ⊕ *www.torreypine. org* ⊠ *Parking $15–$20, varies by day of week and by season.*

⊕ Beaches

Black's Beach

BEACH—SIGHT | The powerful waves at this beach attract world-class surfers, and the strand's relative isolation appeals

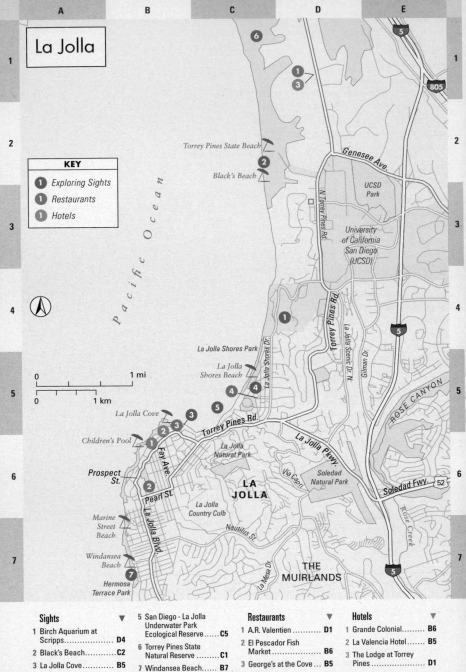

La Jolla

KEY

- ① Exploring Sights
- ① Restaurants
- ① Hotels

Pacific Ocean

Torrey Pines State Beach

Black's Beach

Genesee Ave.

UCSD Park

University of California San Diego (UCSD)

La Jolla Shores Park

La Jolla Shores Beach

Torrey Pines Rd.

La Jolla Cove

Children's Pool

Prospect St.

Fay Ave.

La Jolla Natural Park

La Jolla Pkwy.

Rose Canyon

Via Cap'n

Soledad Natural Park

Pearl St.

La Jolla Blvd.

LA JOLLA

La Jolla Country Culb

Nautilus St.

Soledad Fwy. 52

Rose Creek

Marine Street Beach

Windansea Beach

Hermosa Terrace Park

La Mesa Dr.

THE MUIRLANDS

N Torrey Pines Rd.

Torrey Pines Rd.

La Jolla Scenic Dr. N.

Gilman Dr.

805

5

0   1 mi

0   1 km

to nudist nature lovers (although by law nudity is prohibited) as well as gays and lesbians. Backed by 300-foot-tall cliffs whose colors change with the sun's angle, Black's can be accessed from Torrey Pines State Beach to the north, or by a narrow path descending the cliffs from Torrey Pines Glider Port. Beware the city has posted a "do not use" sign there because the cliff trails are unmaintained and highly dangerous so use at your own risk. If you plan to access Black's from the beaches to the north or south, do so at low tide. High tide and waves can restrict access. Strong rip currents are common—only experienced swimmers should take the plunge. Lifeguards patrol the area only between spring break and mid-October. Also keep your eyes peeled for the hang gliders and paragliders who ascend from atop the cliffs. Parking is available at the Glider Port and Torrey Pines State Beach. **Amenities:** none. **Best for:** solitude; nudists; surfing. ⊠ *Between Torrey Pines State Beach and La Jolla Shores, La Jolla ⊕ 2 miles south of Torrey Pines State Beach parking lot* ⊕ *www.sandiego.gov/lifeguards/beaches/blacks.shtml.*

★ **La Jolla Cove**

BEACH—SIGHT | FAMILY | This shimmering blue-green inlet surrounded by cliffs is what first attracted everyone to La Jolla, from Native Americans to the glitterati. "The Cove," as locals refer to it, beyond where Girard Avenue dead-ends into Coast Boulevard, is marked by towering palms that line a promenade where people strolling in designer clothes are as common as Frisbee throwers. Ellen Browning Scripps Park sits atop cliffs formed by the incessant pounding of the waves and offers a great spot for picnics with a view. The Cove has beautiful white sand that is a bit course near the water's edge, but the beach is still a great place for sunbathing and lounging. At low tide, the pools and cliff caves are a destination for explorers. With visibility at 30-plus feet, this is the best place in San Diego for snorkeling, where bright-orange Garibaldi

fish and other marine life populate the waters of the **San Diego–La Jolla Underwater Park Ecological Reserve.** From above water, it's not uncommon to spot sea lions and birds basking on the rocks, or dolphin fins just offshore. The cove is also a favorite of rough-water swimmers, while the area just north is best for kayakers wanting to explore the Seven La Jolla Sea Caves. **Amenities:** lifeguards; showers; toilets. **Best for:** snorkeling; swimming; walking. ⊠ *1100 Coast Blvd., east of Ellen Browning Scripps Park, La Jolla* ⊕ *www.sandiego.gov/lifeguards/beaches/cove.*

La Jolla Shores

BEACH—SIGHT | FAMILY | This is one of San Diego's most popular beaches due to its wide sandy shore, gentle waves, and incredible views of La Jolla Peninsula. There's also a large grassy park, and adjacent to La Jolla Shores lies the **San Diego-La Jolla Underwater Park Ecological Reserve,** 6,000 acres of protected ocean bottom and tide lands, bordered by the Seven La Jolla Sea Caves. The white powdery sand at La Jolla Sands is some of San Diego's best, and several surf and scuba schools teach here. Kayaks can also be rented nearby. A concrete boardwalk parallels the beach, and a boat launch for small vessels lies 300 yards south of the lifeguard station at Avenida de Playa. Arrive early to get a parking spot in the lot near Kellogg Park at the foot of Calle Frescota. Street parking is limited to one or two hours. **Amenities:** lifeguards; parking (no fee); showers; toilets. **Best for:** surfing; swimming; walking. ⊠ *8200 Camino del Oro, in front of Kellogg Park, La Jolla ⊕ 2 miles north of downtown La Jolla* ⊕ *www.sandiego.gov/lifeguards/beaches/shores.shtml.*

★ **Windansea Beach**

BEACH—SIGHT | With its rocky shoreline and strong shore break, Windansea stands out among San Diego beaches for its dramatic natural beauty. It's one of the best surf spots in San Diego County. Professional surfers love the unusual

A surfer prepares to head out before sunset at La Jolla's Torrey Pines State Beach and Reserve.

A-frame waves the reef break here creates. Although the large sandstone rocks that dot the beach might sound like a hindrance, they actually serve as protective barriers from the wind, making this one of the best beaches in San Diego for sunbathing. The beach's palm-covered surf shack is a protected historical landmark, and a seat here at sunset may just be one of the most romantic spots on the West Coast. The name Windansea comes from a hotel that burned down in the late 1940s. You can usually find nearby street parking. **Amenities:** seasonal lifeguards; toilets. **Best for:** sunset; surfing; solitude. ✉ *Neptune Pl. at Nautilus St., La Jolla* 🌐 *www.sandiego.gov/lifeguards/beaches/windan.shtml.*

🍴 Restaurants

★ A.R. Valentien

$$$$ | **AMERICAN** | Champions of in-season, fresh-today produce, the chefs at this cozy room in the luxurious, Craftsman-style Lodge at Torrey Pines have made A.R. Valentin one of San Diego's top fine dining destinations. **Known for:** red-wine braised short rib; creamy chicken liver pâté; smooth dirty martinis. [$] *Average main: $45* ✉ *The Lodge at Torrey Pines, 11480 N. Torrey Pines Rd., La Jolla* ☎ *858/777–6635* 🌐 *www.arvalentien.com.*

El Pescador Fish Market

$ | **SEAFOOD** | This bustling fish market and café in the heart of La Jolla Village has been popular with locals for its super-fresh fish for more than 30 years. Order the char-grilled, locally caught halibut, swordfish, or yellowtail on a toasted torta roll to enjoy in-house or to go for an oceanfront picnic at nearby La Jolla Cove. **Known for:** clam chowder; bustling on-site fish market; daily-caught cuts to go. [$] *Average main: $15* ✉ *634 Pearl St., La Jolla* ☎ *858/456–2526* 🌐 *www.elpescadorfishmarket.com.*

★ George's at the Cove

$$$$ | **AMERICAN** | La Jolla's ocean-view destination restaurant includes three distinct levels: California Modern on the bottom floor, the Level2 bar in the middle, and Ocean Terrace on the roof. At the sleek main dining room, open only for dinner, give special consideration to the legendary "fish tacos" and the six-course chef's tasting menu; for a more casual and inexpensive lunch or dinner option, head to the outdoor-only Ocean Terrace for spectacular views; for unique craft cocktails, like the "La Jolla" chilled with seaweed-laced ice cubes, and a seasonal happy hour with small bites, cocktails, beer, and wine, it's the Level2 lounge. **Known for:** beef tartare with 67-degree egg; excellent ocean views; attention to detail for special occasion dinners. [$] *Average main: $37* ✉ *1250 Prospect St., La Jolla* ☎ *858/454–4244* 🌐 *www.georgesatthecove.com.*

★ Piatti La Jolla

$$ | MODERN ITALIAN | FAMILY | Blocks from the beach in La Jolla Shores, this comfortably modern dining room and shaded patio hits all the right notes—affordable, polished, and family-friendly. From lunch through close, it bustles with regulars from the neighborhood and visitors from around the world who are guided through the extensive Italian menu by the professional staff, some of whom have worked here for decades. **Known for:** stone-hearth oven pizza; tree-covered patio; house-made ravioli. [$] *Average main: $18* ✉ *2182 Av. de la Playa, La Jolla* ☎ *858/454–1589* 🌐 *www.piatti.com.*

Hotels

★ Grande Colonial

$$$$ | HOTEL | This white wedding cake–style hotel in the heart of La Jolla Village has ocean views and charming European details that include chandeliers, mahogany railings, a wooden elevator, crystal doorknobs, and French doors. **Pros:** great location; superb restaurant; no resort fees. **Cons:** somewhat busy street; no fitness center; valet parking only. [$] *Rooms from: $369* ✉ *910 Prospect St., La Jolla* ☎ *888/828–5498* 🌐 *www.thegrandecolonial.com* 🛏 *93 rooms* 🍴 *No meals.*

La Valencia Hotel

$$$$ | HOTEL | This pink Spanish-Mediterranean confection drew Hollywood film stars in the 1930s and '40s with its setting and views of La Jolla Cove; now it draws the Kardashians. **Pros:** upscale rooms; views; near beach. **Cons:** standard rooms are tiny; lots of traffic outside; strange layout. [$] *Rooms from: $449* ✉ *1132 Prospect St., La Jolla* ☎ *858/454–0771* 🌐 *www.lavalencia.com* 🛏 *114 rooms* 🍴 *No meals.*

★ The Lodge at Torrey Pines

$$$$ | RESORT | Best known for its two 18-hole championship golf courses, this beautiful Craftsman-style lodge sits on a bluff between La Jolla and Del Mar with commanding coastal views, excellent service, a blissful spa, and the upscale A.R. Valentien restaurant (named after a San Diego plein air artist of the early 1900s), which serves farm-to-table California cuisine. **Pros:** spacious upscale rooms; remarkable service; adjacent the famed Torrey Pines Golf Course; warm decor with Craftsman accents and hardwoods. **Cons:** not centrally located; expensive; $30 daily parking fee. [$] *Rooms from: $379* ✉ *11480 N. Torrey Pines Rd., La Jolla* ☎ *858/453–4420, 888/826–0224* 🌐 *www.lodgetorreypines.com* ⛳ *Two 18-hole championship golf courses* 🛏 *170 rooms* 🍴 *No meals.*

Performing Arts

★ La Jolla Playhouse

THEATER | Under the artistic direction of Christopher Ashley, the playhouse presents exciting and innovative plays and musicals on three stages. Many Broadway shows—among them *Memphis, Come From Away, Tommy,* and *Jersey Boys*—have previewed here before their East Coast premieres. Its Without Walls program also ensures that the productions aren't limited to the playhouse, having put on site-specific shows in places like outdoor art spaces, cars, and even the ocean. ✉ *University* of California at San Diego, 2910 La Jolla Village Dr., La Jolla ☎ 858/550–1010 ⊕ www.lajollaplayhouse.org.

🏃 Activities

BIKING

Route S21 (*Coast Highway 101*)
BICYCLING | On many summer days, Route S21, more commonly known as "the 101," from La Jolla to Oceanside looks like a freeway for cyclists. About 24 miles long, it's easily the most popular and scenic bike route around, never straying far from the beach. Although the terrain is fairly easy, the long, steep Torrey Pines grade is famous for weeding out the weak. Another Darwinian challenge is dodging slow-moving pedestrians and cars pulling over to park in towns like Encinitas and Del Mar. ⊠ La Jolla.

GOLF

★ Torrey Pines Golf Course

GOLF | Due to its cliff-top location overlooking the Pacific and its classic championship holes, Torrey Pines is one of the best public golf courses in the United States. The course was the site of the 2008 U.S. Open and has been the home of the Farmers Insurance Open since 1968. The par-72 South Course, redesigned by Rees Jones in 2001, receives rave reviews from touring pros; it is longer, more challenging, and more expensive than the North Course. Tee times may be booked from 8 to 90 days in advance (*858/552–1662*) and are subject to an advance booking fee ($45). ⊠ 11480 N. Torrey Pines Rd., La Jolla ☎ 858/452–3226, 800/985–4653 ⊕ www.torreypinesgolfcourse.com 🏌 South: $202 weekdays, $252 weekends. North: $110 weekdays, $138 weekends; $40 for golf cart 🏌 South: 18 holes, 7227 yards, par 72. North: 18 holes, 7258 yards, par 72.

HIKING AND NATURE TRAILS

Los Peñasquitos Canyon Preserve

HIKING/WALKING | Trails at this inland park north of Mira Mesa accommodate equestrians, runners, walkers, and cyclists as well as leashed dogs. Look at maps for trails specific to bikes and horses. A 7-mile loop passes a small waterfall among large volcanic rock boulders—it's an unexpected oasis amid the arid valley landscape. ⊠ 12020 Black Mountain Rd., Rancho Peñasquitos ✛ From I–15, exit Mercy Rd., and head west to Black Mountain Rd.; turn right then left at first light; follow road to Ranch House parking lot ☎ 858/484–7504 ⊕ www.sdparks.org.

Torrey Pines State Reserve

HIKING/WALKING | Hikers and runners will appreciate this park's many winning features: switchback trails that descend to the sea, an unparalleled view of the Pacific, and a chance to see the Torrey pine tree, one of the rarest pine breeds in the United States. The reserve hosts guided nature walks as well. Dogs and food are prohibited at the reserve. Parking is $15–$20, depending on day and season. ⊠ 12600 N. Torrey Pines Rd., La Jolla ✛ Exit I–5 at Carmel Valley Rd. and head west toward Coast Hwy. 101 until you reach N. Torrey Pines Rd.; turn left. ☎ 858/755–2063 ⊕ www.torreypine.org 🅿 Parking $15–$20.

KAYAKING

Hike Bike Kayak Adventures

KAYAKING | This shop offers several kayak tours, from easy excursions in La Jolla Cove that are well suited to families and beginners to more advanced jaunts. Tours include kayaking the caves off La Jolla coast, and whale-watching (from a safe distance) December through March. Tours last two to three hours and require a minimum of four people. ⊠ 2222 Av. de la Playa, La Jolla ☎ 858/551–9510 ⊕ www.hikebikekayak.com 🚣 From $50.

SURFING

★ Surf Diva Surf School

SURFING | Check out clinics, surf camps, and private lessons especially formulated for girls and women. Most clinics and trips are for women only, but there are some coed options. Guys can also book group or private lessons from the nationally recognized staff. Surf Diva is also home to a boutique that sells surf and stand-up paddleboard equipment. They also offer surf retreats in Costa Rica. ✉ 2160 Ave. de la Playa, La Jolla ☎ 858/454–8273 ⊕ www.surfdiva.com ✉ Group lessons $65; private lessons $90.

Point Loma

The hilly peninsula of Point Loma curves west and south into the Pacific and provides protection for San Diego Bay. Its high elevations and sandy cliffs provide incredible views, and make Point Loma a visible local landmark. Its maritime roots are evident, from its longtime ties to the U.S. Navy to its bustling sportfishing and sailing marinas. The funky community of Ocean Beach coexists alongside the stately homes of Sunset Cliffs and the honored graves at Fort Rosecrans National Cemetery.

At the northern end of Point Loma lies the chilled-out, hippyesque town of Ocean Beach, commonly referred to as "OB." The main thoroughfare of this funky neighborhood is dotted with dive bars, coffeehouses, surf shops, and 1960s diners. OB is a magnet for everyone from surfers to musicians and artists. Fans of OB applaud its resistance to "selling out" to upscale development, whereas detractors lament its somewhat scruffy edges.

◉ Sights

★ Cabrillo National Monument

LIGHTHOUSE | FAMILY | This 166-acre preserve marks the site of the first European visit to San Diego, made by 16th-century Spanish explorer Juan Rodríguez Cabrillo when he landed at this spot on September 15, 1542. Today the site, with its rugged cliffs and shores and outstanding overlooks, is one of the most frequently visited of all the national monuments. There's a good visitor center and useful interpretive stations along the cliff-side walkways. Highlights include the moderately difficult Bayside Trail, the Old Point Loma Lighthouse, and the tide pools. There's also a sheltered viewing station where you can watch the gray whales' yearly migration from Baja California to Alaska (including high-powered telescopes). ✉ 1800 Cabrillo Memorial Dr., Point Loma ☎ 619/557–5450 ⊕ www.nps. gov/cabr ✉ $15 per car, $5 per person on foot/bicycle, entry good for 7 days.

Ocean Beach Pier

MARINA | This T-shaped pier is a popular fishing spot and home to the Ocean Beach Pier Café and a small tackle shop. Constructed in 1966, it is the longest concrete pier on the West Coast and a perfect place to take in views of the harbor, ocean, and Point Loma Peninsula. Surfers flock to the waves that break just below. ✉ 1950 Abbott St., Ocean Beach.

⊙ Beaches

Sunset Cliffs

BEACH—SIGHT | As the name would suggest, this natural park near Point Loma Nazerene University is one of the best places in San Diego to watch the sunset thanks to its cliff-top location and expansive ocean views. Some limited beach access is accessible via an extremely steep stairway at the foot of Ladera Street. Beware of the treacherous cliff trails and pay attention to warning signs. The cliffs are very unstable and several fatalities have occurred over the last few years. If you're going to make your way to the narrow beach below, it's best to go at low tide when the southern end, near Cabrillo Point, reveals tide pools teeming

124

with small sea creatures. Farther north the waves lure surfers, and Osprey Point offers good fishing off the rocks. Keep your eyes peeled for migrating California gray whales during the winter months. Check WaveCast (⊕ *www.wavecast. com/tides*) for tide schedules. **Amenities:** parking (no fee). **Best for:** solitude; sunset; surfing. ✉ *Sunset Cliffs Blvd., between Ladera St. and Adair St., Point Loma* ⊕ *www.sunsetcliffs.info.*

Restaurants

★ Azucar

$ | CUBAN | For a taste of Cuba in San Diego, head to this colorful Ocean Beach bakery where owner Vivian Hernandez Jackson combines her Cuban heritage, Miami childhood, and London culinary training in breakfast and lunch offerings. Morning specialties like raspberry scones with passion fruit icing, a traditional guava-and-cheese puff pastry, and ham-and-spinach quiche can be savored with café con leche, a sweet Cuban espresso with hot milk. **Known for:** tangy, citrus-centric desserts; traditional Cuban pastries; a quick bite before shopping or hitting the beach. $ *Average main: $7* ✉ *4820 Newport Ave., Ocean Beach* ☎ *619/523–2020* ⊕ *www.iloveazucar.com* ☾ *No dinner.*

★ The Cravory

$ | BAKERY | San Diego's best cookies come in crowd-pleasing flavors such as birthday cake, red velvet, and pancakes and bacon. There's also craft sodas, Cravory flavored milks, edible cookie dough, ice cream, and cold brew to round out your snack. **Known for:** amazing cookies; cookie-of-the-month club; ships anywhere. $ *Average main: $5* ✉ *3960 W. Point Loma Blvd., Suite G, Point Loma* ⌖ *next to Souplantation* ☎ *619/795–9077* ⊕ *thecravory.com.*

★ Hodad's

$ | BURGER | FAMILY | Surfers with big appetites chow down on huge, messy burgers, fries, onion rings, and shakes at this funky, hippie-beach joint adorned with beat-up surfboards and license plates from almost every state. Don't be put off by lines out the door, they move quickly and the wait is worth it. **Known for:** legendary bacon-cheeseburgers and thick-cut onion rings; surf-shack vibe; a little sass with your burger. $ *Average main: $9* ✉ *5010 Newport Ave., Ocean Beach* ☎ *619/224–4623* ⊕ *www.hodadies.com.*

★ Liberty Public Market

$ | INTERNATIONAL | FAMILY | The city's former Naval Training Center is now home to more than 30 vendors so even the pickiest of diners will be pleased. Options include tacos and quesadillas at Cecilia's Taqueria; fried rice, pad Thai, and curries at Mama Made Thai; artisan cheeses and charcuteries at Venissimo; lavender lattes from Westbean Coffee Roasters; more than a dozen Argentinian empanadas at Parana Empanadas; and croissants, eclairs, and macarons at Le Parfait Paris. **Known for:** cuisines from around the world; lively kid- and dog-friendly patio; the best regional foods under one roof. $ *Average main: $10* ✉ *2820 Historic Decatur Rd., Liberty Station* ☎ *619/487–9346* ⊕ *www.libertypublicmarket.com.*

★ The Little Lion

$$ | MODERN AMERICAN | Amid surf shacks and hippie beach bars, this restaurant perched on stunning Sunset Cliffs feels like a hidden European bistro. The sisters who run the show come from a long line of successful local restaurateurs and have brought their passed-down expertise to the simple, healthy menu and thoughtful service. **Known for:** light, healthy breakfast fare; cozy bistro setting; flash-fried cauliflower. $ *Average main: $20* ✉ *1424 Sunset Cliffs Blvd., Ocean Beach* ☎ *619/756–6921* ⊕ *www. thelittlelioncafe.com* ☾ *Closed Mon.; no dinner Tues., Wed., and Sun.*

★ Point Loma Seafoods

$ | SEAFOOD | FAMILY | When fishing boats unload their catch on-site, a seafood restaurant and market earns the right to boast that they offer "The Freshest Thing in Town." At first, mostly sport fishermen came here, but word got out about the just-caught fried fish on San Francisco–style sourdough bread and now locals and visitors come to enjoy bay views, sunshine, and a greatly expanded menu of seafood dishes. A friendly efficient crew takes orders for food and drinks at the counter, keeping the wait down even on the busiest days. **Known for:** San Francisco–style seafood on sourdough; dockside bay views; seafood so fresh it's right from the boat. ⓢ *Average main: $15* ⊠ *2805 Emerson St., Point Loma* ☏ *619/223–1109* ⊕ *www.pointlomaseafoods.com.*

★ Stone Brewing World Bistro and Gardens

$$ | ECLECTIC | FAMILY | This 50,000 square-foot monument to beer and good food is a crowd-pleaser, especially for fans of San Diego's nationally known craft beer scene. The global menu features dishes like the Bavarian pretzel and Korean-style BBQ ribs that pair perfectly with on-tap and bottled beers from around the world and Stone's famous IPAs. **Known for:** massive outdoor patio; brew-friendly eats; Meatless Mondays. ⓢ *Average main: $22* ⊠ *2816 Historic Decatur Rd., Liberty Station* ☏ *619/269–2100* ⊕ *www.stonelibertystation.com.*

🛏 Hotels

★ Homewood Suites San Diego Airport Liberty Station

$$$ | HOTEL | FAMILY | Families and business travelers will benefit from the space and amenities at this all-suites hotel. **Pros:** outstanding central location near attractions; close to paths for joggers and bikers; complimentary airport shuttle. **Cons:** breakfast area can get crowded; far from nightlife. ⓢ *Rooms from: $249* ⊠ *2576 Laning Rd., Point*

Loma ☏ *619/222–0500* ⊕ *www.homewoodsuites.com* ⟿ *150 suites* ⦿ *Free Breakfast.*

★ The Pearl Hotel

$$$ | HOTEL | This 1960s Sportsman's Lodge received a mid-century modern makeover, turning it into a retro-chic hangout decorated with kitschy lamps and original, in-room art by local children. **Pros:** near marina; hip bar/restaurant on-site (dinner only, except for seasonal specials); "Oysters and Bubbles" Mondays with $1 oysters and $7 bubbly. **Cons:** not centrally located; one bed in rooms; noise on movie night. ⓢ *Rooms from: $233* ⊠ *1410 Rosecrans St., Point Loma* ☏ *619/226–6100* ⊕ *www.thepearlsd.com* ⟿ *23 rooms* ⦿ *No meals.*

🏃 Activities

★ Bayside Trail at Cabrillo National Monument

HIKING/WALKING | Driving here is a treat in itself, as a vast view of the Pacific unfolds before you. The view is equally enjoyable on Bayside Trail (2 miles round-trip), which is home to the same coastal sagebrush that Juan Rodriguez Cabrillo saw when he first discovered the California coast in the 16th century. After the hike, you can explore nearby tide pools, the monument statue, and the Old Point Loma Lighthouse. Don't worry if you don't see everything on your first visit; your entrance receipt ($15 per car) is good for seven days. ⊠ *1800 Cabrillo Memorial Dr., Point Loma* ✛ *From I–5, take Rosecrans exit and turn right on Canon St. then left on Catalina Blvd. (also known as Cabrillo Memorial Dr.); follow until end* ☏ *619/557–5450* ⊕ *www.nps.gov/cabr* ▱ *Parking $15.*

Shelter Island

In 1950 San Diego's port director decided to raise the shoal that lay off the eastern shore of Point Loma above sea level with the sand and mud dredged up during the course of deepening a ship channel in the 1930s and '40s. The resulting peninsula, **Shelter Island,** became home to several marinas and resorts, many with Polynesian details that still exist today, giving them a retro flair. This reclaimed peninsula now supports towering palms and resorts, restaurants, and side-by-side marinas. A long sidewalk runs past boat brokerages to the hotels and marinas that line the inner shore, facing Point Loma. On the bay side, fishermen launch their boats and families relax at picnic tables along the grass, where there are fire rings and permanent barbeque grills.

🍴 Restaurants

Bali Hai

$$ | **HAWAIIAN** | For more than 50 years, generations of San Diegans and visitors have enjoyed this Polynesian-themed icon with its stunning bay and city skyline views. The menu is a fusion of Hawaiian and Asian cuisines with standouts like the Hawaiian tuna poke, Mongolian lamb with pad Thai, and wok-fried bass. **Known for:** potent Bali Hai mai tais; Sunday brunch buffet with a DIY sundae bar; Hawaiian and Asian-themed menu. [$] *Average main: $25* ✉ *2230 Shelter Island Dr., Shelter Island* ☎ *619/222–1181* 🌐 *www.balihairestaurant.com* ⏲ *No lunch Sun.*

🍸 Nightlife

Humphrey's Concerts by the Bay

MUSIC CLUBS | From June through September this dining and drinking oasis surrounded by water hosts the city's best outdoor jazz, folk, and light-rock concert series and is the stomping ground of such musicians as the Cowboy Junkies, Kenny G, and Chris Isaak. The rest of the year the music moves indoors for first-rate jazz, blues, and more. ✉ *2241 Shelter Island Dr., Shelter Island* ☎ *619/224–3577* 🌐 *www.humphreysconcerts.com.*

Harbor Island

Following the successful creation of Shelter Island, in 1961 the U.S. Navy used the residue from digging berths deep enough to accommodate aircraft carriers to build **Harbor Island**. Restaurants and high-rise hotels dot the inner shore of this 1½-mile-long peninsula adjacent to the airport. Restaurants and high-rise hotels dot the inner shore while the bay's shore is lined with pathways, gardens, and scenic picnic spots. On the west point, the restaurant Tom Ham's Lighthouse has a U.S. Coast Guard–approved beacon shining from its tower and a sweeping view of San Diego's bay front.

🍴 Restaurants

Island Prime and C Level

$$$$ | **MODERN AMERICAN** | Two restaurants in one share this enviable spot on the shore of Harbor Island: the splurge-worthy Island Prime steak house and the relaxed C Level with a choice terrace. Both venues tempt with unrivaled views of Downtown San Diego's skyline. **Known for:** sunset views; popovers served with jalapeño jelly butter; waterfront dining. [$] *Average main: $39* ✉ *880 Harbor Island Dr., Harbor Island* ☎ *619/298–6802* 🌐 *www.cohnrestaurants.com/islandprime* ⏲ *No lunch at Island Prime.*

Tom Ham's Lighthouse

$$$ | **SEAFOOD** | It's hard to top this longtime Harbor Island restaurant's incredible views across San Diego Bay to the Downtown skyline and Coronado Bridge. Now a new alfresco dining deck and a contemporary seafood-focused menu

ensure the dining experience at this working lighthouse doesn't take a back seat to the scenery. **Known for:** bottomless mimosa Sunday brunch; alfresco dining deck with skyline and Coronado bridge views; fresh seafood and beer-battered cod. [$] *Average main: $30* ✉ *2150 Harbor Island Dr., Harbor Island* ☎ *619/291–9110* 🌐 *www.tomhamslighthouse.com* 🕒 *No lunch Sun.*

🍸 Nightlife

Humphrey's Concerts by the Bay
MUSIC CLUBS | From June through September this dining and drinking oasis surrounded by water hosts the city's best outdoor jazz, folk, and light-rock concert series and is the stomping ground of such musicians as the Cowboy Junkies, Kenny G, and Chris Isaak. The rest of the year the music moves indoors for first-rate jazz, blues, and more. ✉ *2241 Shelter Island Dr., Shelter Island* ☎ *619/224–3577* 🌐 *www.humphreysconcerts.com.*

Coronado

As if freeze-framed in the 1950s, Coronado's quaint appeal is captured in its old-fashioned storefronts, well-manicured gardens, and charming **Ferry Landing Marketplace.** The streets of Coronado are wide, quiet, and friendly, and many of today's residents live in grand Victorian homes handed down for generations. Naval Air Station North Island was established in 1911 on Coronado's north end, across from Point Loma, and was the site of Charles Lindbergh's departure on the transcontinental flight that preceded his famous solo flight across the Atlantic. Coronado's long relationship with the U.S. Navy and its desirable real estate have made it an enclave for military personnel; it's said to have more retired admirals per capita than anywhere else in the United States.

Coronado is accessible via the arching blue 2.2-mile-long San Diego–Coronado Bay Bridge, which offers breathtaking views of the harbor and Downtown. Alternatively, pedestrians and bikes can reach Coronado via the popular ferry service. Bus 904 meets the ferry and travels as far as Silver Strand State Beach. Bus 901 runs daily between the Gaslamp Quarter and Coronado.

👁 Sights

Coronado Ferry Landing
STORE/MALL | **FAMILY** | This collection of shops at Ferry Landing is on a smaller scale than the Embarcadero's Seaport Village, but you do get a great view of the Downtown San Diego skyline. The little bay-side shops and restaurants resemble the gingerbread domes of the Hotel Del Coronado. ✉ *1201 1st St., at B Ave., Coronado* 🌐 *www.coronadoferrylanding.com.*

★ **Orange Avenue**
NEIGHBORHOOD | Comprising Coronado's business district and its village-like heart, this avenue is surely one of the most charming spots in Southern California. Slow-paced and very "local" (the city fights against chain stores), it's a blast from the past, although entirely up to date in other respects. The military presence—Coronado is home to the U.S. Navy Sea, Air, and Land (SEAL) forces—is reflected in shops selling military gear and places like **McP's Irish Pub,** at No. 1107. A family-friendly stop for a good, all-American meal, it's the unofficial SEALs headquarters. Many clothing boutiques, home-furnishings stores, and upscale restaurants cater to visitors with deep pockets, but you can buy plumbing supplies, too, or get a genuine military haircut at **Crown Barber Shop,** at No. 947. If you need a break, stop for a latte at the sidewalk café of **Bay Books,** San Diego's largest independent bookstore, at No. 1029. ✉ *Orange Ave., near 9th St., Coronado.*

Beaches

★ Coronado Beach

BEACH—SIGHT | FAMILY | This wide beach is one of San Diego's most picturesque thanks to its soft white sand and sparkly blue water. The historic Hotel Del Coronado serves as a backdrop, and it's perfect for sunbathing, people-watching, and Frisbee tossing. The beach has limited surf, but it's great for bodyboarding and swimming. Exercisers might include Navy SEAL teams or other military units that conduct training runs on beaches in and around Coronado. There are picnic tables, grills, and popular fire rings, but don't bring lacquered wood or pallets. Only natural wood is allowed for burning. There's also a dog beach on the north end. There's free parking along Ocean Boulevard, though it's often hard to snag a space. **Amenities:** food and drink; lifeguards; showers; toilets. **Best for:** walking; swimming. ✉ *Ocean Blvd., between S. O St. and Orange Ave., Coronado* ✥ *From the San Diego–Coronado bridge, turn left on Orange Ave. and follow signs.*

Silver Strand State Beach

BEACH—SIGHT | FAMILY | This quiet beach on a narrow sand-spit allows visitors a unique opportunity to experience both the Pacific Ocean and the San Diego Bay. The 2½ miles of ocean side is great for surfing and other water sports while the bay side, accessible via foot tunnel under Highway 75, has calmer, warmer water and great views of the San Diego skyline. Lifeguards and rangers are on duty year-round, and there are places for biking, volleyball, and fishing. Picnic tables, grills, and firepits are available in summer, and the Silver Strand Beach Cafe is open Memorial Day through Labor Day. The beach is close to Loews Coronado Bay Resort and the Coronado Cays, an exclusive community popular with yacht owners. You can reserve RV sites ($65 beach; $50 inland) online (🌐 *www.reserveamerica.com*). Three day-use parking lots provide room for 800 cars. **Amenities:** food and drink; lifeguards; parking (fee); showers; toilets. **Best for:** walking; swimming; surfing. ✉ *5000 Hwy. 75, Coronado* ✥ *4½ miles south of city of Coronado* ☎ *619/435–5184* 🌐 *www.parks.ca.gov/silverstrand* 🎟 *Parking $10, motor home $30.*

Restaurants

Cafe 1134

$ | CAFÉ | Locals flock to this hip mini-bistro to start the day with flavorful omelets or fresh pastries and coffee. Lunch and dinner patrons enjoy a variety of classic deli sandwiches and salads in a relaxed and friendly atmosphere. **Known for:** hearty breakfast; fresh sandwiches and salads for lunch; friendly service. [$] *Average main: $5* ✉ *1134 Orange Ave., Coronado* ☎ *619/437–1134* 🌐 *www.cafe1134.net* 💳 *No credit cards.*

Chez Loma

$$ | FRENCH | French meets Southern Californian cuisine at this charming historic Victorian home in the heart of Coronado. A favorite of locals and guests at nearby Hotel Del Coronado, the romantic bistro offers French favorites like boeuf bourguignonne and moules marinière as well as California standbys like rockfish ceviche in tomatillo sauce. **Known for:** eclectic Sunday brunch; solid dessert selection; romantic atmosphere. [$] *Average main: $25* ✉ *1132 Loma Ave., Coronado* ☎ *619/435–0661* 🕒 *No lunch.*

Coronado Brewing Company

$ | AMERICAN | FAMILY | Perfect for beer lovers with kids, this popular, laid-back Coronado brewpub offers a menu that features large portions of basic bar food like burgers, sandwiches, pizza, and salads. Enjoy a brew at a pair of sidewalk terraces or belly up to the bar and a new batch being made such as the Islander Pale Ale (IPA) or Mermaid's Red Ale. **Known for:** a good selection of house-crafted beers; kids' menu; more strollers than bar stools. $ *Average main: $12* ✉ *170 Orange Ave., Coronado* ☎ *619/437-4452* ⊕ *www.coronado-brewing.com.*

Tartine

$ | **FRENCH** | **FAMILY** | Dine any time of day at this French-inspired café a block from San Diego Bay, as breakfast commences at 6 am with house-made granola, quiche, and just-baked coffee cakes and croissants. Sandwiches, salads, and soups round out the daytime menu, while dinner highlights include the catch of the day; just be sure be sure to save room for the Paris-pretty desserts. **Known for:** Coronado's best bet for casual but satisfying fare; in-house pastries and desserts; quiche any time of the day. $ *Average main: $15* ✉ *1106 1st St., Coronado* ☎ *619/435-4323* ⊕ *www.tartinecoronado.com.*

 ## Hotels

★ Coronado Island Marriott Resort & Spa

$$$$ | **RESORT** | **FAMILY** | Near San Diego Bay, this snazzy hotel has rooms with great Downtown skyline views. **Pros:** spectacular views; on-site spa; close to water taxis. **Cons:** not in downtown Coronado; resort fee; expensive self-parking. $ *Rooms from: $329* ✉ *2000 2nd St., Coronado* ☎ *619/435-3000* ⊕ *www.marriott.com/hotels/travel/sanci-coronado-island-marriott-resort-and-spa* ⤴ *300 rooms* ⭘| *No meals.*

★ Hotel Del Coronado

$$$$ | **RESORT** | **FAMILY** | As much of a draw today as it was when it opened in 1888, the Victorian-style "Hotel Del" is always alive with activity, as guests—including U.S. presidents and celebrities—and tourists marvel at the fanciful architecture and ocean views. **Pros:** 17 on-site shops; on the beach; well-rounded spa. **Cons:** some rooms are small; expensive dining; hectic public areas. $ *Rooms from: $425* ✉ *1500 Orange Ave.,*

Coronado ☎ *800/468-3533, 619/435-6611* ⊕ *www.hoteldel.com* ⤴ *757 rooms* ⭘| *No meals.*

Loews Coronado Bay Resort

$$$$ | **RESORT** | **FAMILY** | You can park your boat at the 80-slip marina of this romantic retreat set on a secluded 15-acre peninsula on the Silver Strand. **Pros:** great restaurants; lots of activities; all rooms have furnished balconies with water views. **Cons:** far from anything; confusing layout; not ideal for couples. $ *Rooms from: $349* ✉ *4000 Coronado Bay Rd., Coronado* ☎ *619/424-4000, 800/815-6397* ⊕ *www.loewshotels.com/coronado-bay-resort* ⤴ *439 rooms* ⭘| *No meals.*

★ 1906 Lodge at Coronado Beach

$$$$ | **B&B/INN** | Smaller but no less luxurious than the sprawling beach resorts of Coronado, this lodge—whose name alludes to the main building's former life as a boardinghouse built in 1906—welcomes couples for romantic retreats two blocks from the ocean. **Pros:** most suites feature Jacuzzi tubs, fireplaces, and porches; historic property; free underground parking. **Cons:** too quiet for families; no pool; limited on-site dining options. $ *Rooms from: $329* ✉ *1060 Adella Ave., Coronado* ☎ *619/437-1900, 866/435-1906* ⊕ *www.1906lodge.com* ⤴ *17 rooms* ⭘| *Free Breakfast.*

Shopping

SHOPPING CENTER

★ Hotel Del Coronado

SHOPPING CENTERS/MALLS | At the gift shops within the peninsula's main historic attraction, you can purchase sportswear, designer handbags, jewelry, and antiques. **Babcock & Story Emporium** carries an amazing selection of home decor items, garden accessories, and classy gifts. **Blue Octopus** is a children's store featuring creative toys, gifts, and apparel. **Spreckels Sweets & Treats** offers old-time candies, freshly made fudge, and decadent truffles. **Kate's** has designer fashions and accessories, while **Brady's for Men,** with its shirts and sport coats, caters to well-dressed men. **Crown Jewels Coronado** features fine jewelry, some inspired by the sea. ✉ *1500 Orange Ave., Coronado* ☎ *619/435–6611* ⊕ *www.hoteldel.com/coronado-shopping.*

Activities

BIKING

Holland's Bicycles

BICYCLING | This is a great bike rental source on Coronado Island, so you can ride the Silver Strand Bike Path on an electric bike, beach cruiser, road bike, or tandem. ✉ *977 Orange Ave., Coronado* ☎ *619/435–3153* ⊕ *www.hollandsbicycles.com* 🖥 *From $25.*

Chapter 5

PALM SPRINGS

Updated by
Cheryl Crabtree

⊙ Sights	⏱ Restaurants	🛏 Hotels	⬤ Shopping	🍸 Nightlife
★★★★★	★★★★☆	★★★★★	★☆☆☆☆	★☆☆☆☆

WELCOME TO PALM SPRINGS

TOP REASONS TO GO

★ **Year-round sunshine:** The Palm Springs area has 350 days of sun each year, and the weather is usually ideal for playing one of the area's more than 100 golf courses.

★ **Spa under the stars:** Many resorts and small hotels now offer after-dark spa services, including outdoor soaks and treatments you can savor while sipping wine under the clear, starry sky.

★ **Personal pampering:** The resorts here have it all, beautifully appointed rooms packed with amenities, professional staffs, sublime spas, and delicious dining options.

★ **Divine desert scenery:** You'll probably spend a lot of time taking in the gorgeous 360-degree natural panorama, a flat desert floor surrounded by 10,000-foot mountains rising into a brilliant blue sky.

★ **The Hollywood connection:** The Palm Springs area has more celebrity ties than any other resort community. So keep your eyes open for your favorite star.

The Palm Springs resort area is within the Colorado Desert, on the western edge of the Coachella Valley. The area holds seven cities strung out along Highway 111, with Palm Springs at the northwestern end of the strip and Indio at the southeastern end. North of Palm Springs is Desert Hot Springs. Northeast the towns of the Morongo Valley stand along Twentynine Palms Highway, which leads to Joshua Tree National Park. Head south on Highway 86 from Indio to reach Anza-Borrego Desert State Park and the Salton Sea.

1 Palm Springs. A mid-century modern vibe and many restaurants, bars, and galleries line the avenues of Palm Springs. Hiking trails and an aerial tramway lead from the desert floor up to the San Jacinto mountain peaks.

2 Rancho Mirage. An elegant, upscale residential community, Rancho Mirage has resorts, golf courses and gated estates. A main draw here is Annenberg Retreat at Sunnylands, a grand garden estate open to the public for tours.

3 Palm Desert. The mile-long El Paseo shopping and restaurant district is the heart of Palm Desert, a peaceful community also known for its challenging golf courses and the Living Desert Zoo and Gardens.

4 Indian Wells. Exclusive Indian Wells hosts major golf and tennis tournaments at posh resorts, where spas and upscale restaurants pamper players and spectators alike.

5 La Quinta. Coachella Valley's first golf course opened at La Quinta in 1920 and morphed into a quaint town alongside a sprawling resort and club with multiple courses.

6 Indio. The date capital of the nation, Indio lures visitors with date shakes and date palm fields.

7 Desert Hot Springs. A concentrated network of hot mineral springs flows through Desert Hot Springs, where visitors come to soak in the soothing waters and rejuvenate mind and body.

8 Yucca Valley. A laidback roadside city, Yucca Valley is a convenient stop on the way to Joshua Tree National Park. In nearby Pioneertown, Pappy and Harriet's Pioneertown Palace serves classic Western food and big-name musical entertainment.

9 Borrego Springs. Superb wildflower viewing and numerous nature trails are among the draws at Borrego Springs within Anza-Borrego Desert State Park.

10 Salton Sea. Nature lovers retreat to the shores of the Salton Sea, a haven for birdwatching and lakefront activities.

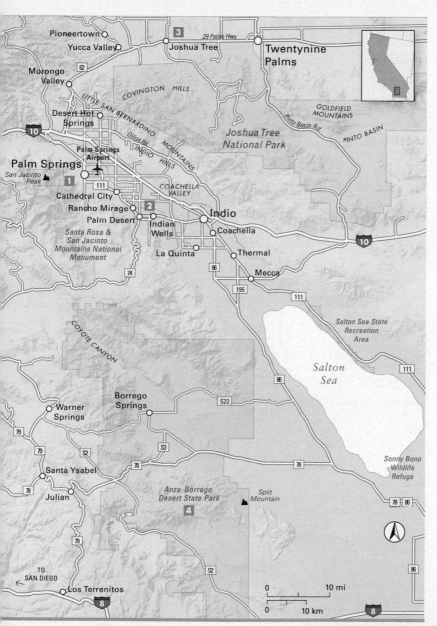

Pioneertown

Yucca Valley

Joshua Tree

3

29 Palms Hwy.

Twentynine Palms

Morongo Valley

62

COVINGTON HILLS

LITTLE SAN BERNARDINO MOUNTAINS

GOLDFIELD MOUNTAINS

Pinto Basin Rd

PINTO BASIN

Desert Hot Springs

10

Dillon Rd

INDIO HILLS

Joshua Tree National Park

Palm Springs Airport

Palm Springs

San Jacinto Peak

1

111

COACHELLA VALLEY

Cathedral City

Rancho Mirage

2

Palm Desert

Indian Wells

Indio

Coachella

Santa Rosa & San Jacinto Mountains National Monument

La Quinta

Thermal

74

86

Mecca

195

111

Salton Sea State Recreation Area

COYOTE CANYON

Salton Sea

86

111

Borrego Springs

Warner Springs

S22

79

79

S2

S3

78

78

Sonny Bono Wildlife Refuge

Santa Ysabel

Julian

Anza-Borrego Desert State Park

4

Split Mountain

78   86

79

TO SAN DIEGO

S2

86

0   10 mi

0   10 km

Los Terrenitos

8

8

With the Palm Springs area's year-round sunshine, luxurious spas, chef-driven restaurants, and see-and-be-seen pool parties, it's no wonder that Hollywood A-listers and weekend warriors make the desert a getaway. Stretching south and east of the city along Highway 111, the desert resort towns—Cathedral City, Rancho Mirage, Palm Desert, Indian Wells, La Quinta, and Indio, along with Desert Hot Springs to the north—teem with resorts, golf courses, and shopping centers. Yucca Valley, Joshua Tree, and other artistic communities lie farther north and northeast. To the south, the wildflowers of Anza-Borrego Desert State Park herald the arrival of spring.

The Palm Springs area has long been a playground for the celebrity elite. In the 1920s Al Capone opened the Two Bunch Palms Hotel in Desert Hot Springs (with multiple tunnels to help him avoid the police); Marilyn Monroe was discovered poolside in the late 1940s at a downtown Palm Springs tennis club; Elvis and Priscilla Presley honeymooned here—the list goes on.

Over the years the desert arts scene has blossomed as spectacularly as the wildflowers of Anza-Borrego. Downtown Palm Springs is laden with urban-chic contemporary artwork (check out the Backstreet Arts District), but the surrounding rural areas are also artist enclaves: Yucca Valley, Joshua Tree, Pioneertown, and Twentynine Palms all have noteworthy galleries, art installations, and natural scenic views. Each April attention centers on Indio, where the Coachella Valley Music and Arts Festival, California's largest outdoor concert, culls droves of Angelenos, and music lovers from all over the world.

Planning

When to Go

Desert weather is best between January and April, the height of the visitor season. The fall months are nearly as lovely, but less crowded and less expensive (although autumn draws many conventions and business travelers). In summer, a popular time with European visitors, daytime temperatures may rise above 110°F (though evenings cool to the mid-70s); some attractions and restaurants close or reduce their hours during this time.

Getting Here and Around

AIR TRAVEL

Palm Springs International Airport serves California's desert communities. Air Canada, Alaska, Allegiant, American, Delta, Flair, Frontier, JetBlue, Sun Country, United, and WestJet all fly to Palm Springs, some only seasonally. Yellow Cab of the Desert and Desert City Cab serve the airport, which is about 3 miles from downtown. The fare is $3 to enter the cab and about $3.12 per mile.

AIRPORT INFORMATION Palm Springs International Airport. ✉ *3200 E. Tahquitz Canyon Way, Palm Springs* ☎ *760/320–3882 info line, 760/318–3800* ⊕ *www. palmspringsairport.com.*

AIRPORT TRANSFERS Desert City Cab. ✉ *3465 E. La Campana Way, Palm Springs* ☎ *760/328–3000* ⊕ *www.desert-citycab.com.* **Yellow Cab of the Desert.** ✉ *75150 St. Charles Pl., Palm Desert* ☎ *760/340–8294* ⊕ *www.yellowcabofthedesert.com.*

BUS TRAVEL

Greyhound provides service to Palm Springs from many cities. SunBus, operated by the SunLine Transit Agency, serves the entire Coachella Valley, from Desert Hot Springs to Mecca.

BUS CONTACTS Greyhound. ☎ *800/231–2222 toll-free in U.S., 214/849–8100 from outside U.S.* ⊕ *www.greyhound.com.* **SunLine Transit Agency.** ☎ *760/343–3451* ⊕ *www.sunline.org.*

CAR TRAVEL

The desert resort communities occupy a 20-mile stretch between Interstate 10 to the east, and Palm Canyon Drive (Highway 111), to the west. The region is about a two-hour drive east of the Los Angeles area and a three-hour drive northeast of San Diego. It can take twice as long to make the trip from Los Angeles to the desert on winter and spring weekends because of heavy traffic. From Los Angeles take the San Bernardino Freeway (Interstate 10) east to Highway 111. From San Diego, Interstate 15 heading north connects with the Pomona Freeway (Highway 60), leading to the San Bernardino Freeway east.

To reach Borrego Springs from Los Angeles, take Interstate 10 east past the desert resorts area to Highway 86 south to the Borrego Salton Seaway (Highway S22) west. You can reach the Borrego area from San Diego via Interstate 8 to Highway 79 through Cuyamaca State Park. This will take you to Highway 78 in Julian, which you follow east to Yaqui Pass Road (S3) into Borrego Springs.

TAXI TRAVEL

Yellow Cab of the Desert and Desert City Cab serve the entire Coachella Valley. The fare is $3 to enter a cab and about $3.12 per mile.

TRAIN TRAVEL

The Amtrak *Sunset Limited*, which runs between Florida and Los Angeles, stops in Palm Springs.

TRAIN CONTACT Amtrak. ☎ *800/872–7245* ⊕ *www.amtrak.com.*

Health and Safety

Never travel alone in the desert. Let someone know your trip route, destination, and estimated time and date of return. Before setting out, make sure your vehicle is in good condition. Stay on main roads, and watch out for horses and range cattle.

Drink at least a gallon of water a day (three gallons if you're hiking or otherwise exerting yourself). Dress in layered clothing and wear comfortable, sturdy shoes and a hat. Keep snacks, sunscreen, and a first-aid kit on hand. If you suddenly have a headache or feel dizzy or nauseous, you could be suffering from dehydration. Get out of the sun immediately and drink plenty of water. Dampen your clothing to lower your body temperature.

Do not enter mine tunnels or shafts. Avoid canyons during rainstorms. Never place your hands or feet where you can't see them: rattlesnakes, scorpions, and black widow spiders may be hiding there.

Restaurants

An influx of talented chefs has expanded the dining possibilities of a formerly staid scene. The meat-and-potatoes crowd still has plenty of options, but you'll also find fresh seafood superbly prepared and contemporary Californian, Asian, Indian, and vegetarian cuisine, and Mexican food abounds. Most restaurants have early-evening happy hours, with discounted drinks and small-plate menus. Restaurants that remain open in July and August frequently discount deeply; others close in July and August or offer limited service. *Restaurant reviews have been shortened. For full information, visit Fodors.com.*

Hotels

In general you can find the widest choice of lodgings in Palm Springs, from tiny bed-and-breakfasts and chain motels to business and resort hotels. Massive resort properties predominate in down-valley communities, such as Palm Desert and Rancho Mirage. You can stay in the desert for as little as $100, or splurge for luxury digs at more than $1,000 a night. Rates vary widely by season and expected occupancy—a $200 room midweek can jump in price to $450 on Saturday.

Hotel and resort prices are frequently 50% cheaper in summer and fall than in winter and early spring. From January through May prices soar, and lodgings book up far in advance. You should book well ahead for stays during events such as Modernism Week or the Coachella and Stagecoach music festivals.

Most resort hotels charge a daily fee of up to $40 that is not included in the room rate; be sure to ask about extra fees when you book. Many hotels are pet-friendly and offer special services, though these also come with additional fees. Small boutique hotels and bed-and-breakfasts have plenty of character and are popular with hipsters and artsy types; discounts are sometimes given for extended stays. Casino hotels often offer good deals on lodging. Take care, though, when considering budget lodgings; other than reliable chains, they may not be up to par. *Hotel reviews have been shortened. For full information, visit Fodors.com.*

WHAT IT COSTS

	$	$$	$$$	$$$$
RESTAURANTS				
	under $16	$16–$22	$23–$30	over $30
HOTELS				
	under $120	$120–$175	$176–$250	over $250

Nightlife

Desert nightlife is concentrated and abundant in Palm Springs, with plenty of bars and clubs, but the action centers on hotel bars and lively pool parties. Arts festivals occur on a regular basis, especially in winter and spring. *Palm Springs Life* magazine (⊕ *www.palmspringslife. com*), available at hotels and visitor centers, has nightlife listings, as does the *Desert Sun* newspaper (⊕ *www. desertsun.com*).

Tours

Best of the Best Tours
GUIDED TOURS | One of the valley's largest outfits leads tours into Andreas Canyon, along the celebrity circuit, or to view windmills up close. ☎ *760/320–1365* ⊕ *www.thebestofthebesttours.com* ✉ *From $40.*

Big Wheel Bike Tours
BICYCLING | This outfit delivers rental mountain, three-speed, and tandem bikes to area hotels. The company also conducts full- and half-day escorted on- and off-road bike tours, and also offers hiking and jeep tours to Joshua Tree National Park and the San Andreas Fault. Guides are first-rate. ✉ *Palm Springs* ☎ *760/779–1837* ⊕ *www.bwbtours.com* ✉ *$105 per person.*

Desert Adventures
SPECIAL-INTEREST | This outfit's three- to six-hour jeep, SUV, or van tours explore Joshua Tree National Park, Indian Canyon, Mecca Hills Painted Canyons, and the San Andreas Fault. The groups are small and the guides are knowledgeable. Departures are from Palm Desert and/or Palm Springs; hotel pickups are available. ☎ *760/324–5337* ⊕ *www.red-jeep.com* ✉ *From $140.*

Trail Discovery Hiking Guides
GUIDED TOURS | For more than two decades, this outfit has been guiding hikers of all abilities through the desert canyons of the Palm Springs area. Tours include Joshua Tree National Park, Indian Canyons, San Jacinto State Park, and sections of the Pacific Crest Trail. ☎ *760/413–1575* ⊕ *www.palmspringshiking.com* ✉ *From $75.*

Palm Springs

A tourist destination since the late 19th century, Palm Springs evolved into an ideal hideaway for early Hollywood celebrities who slipped into town to play tennis, lounge poolside, attend a party or two, and unless things got out of hand, steer clear of gossip columnists. But the area blossomed in the 1930s after actors Charlie Farrell and Ralph Bellamy bought 200 acres of land for $30 an acre and opened the Palm Springs Racquet Club, which soon listed Ginger Rogers, Humphrey Bogart, and Clark Gable among its members.

Today, Palm Springs is embracing its glory days. Owners of resorts, bed-and-breakfasts, and galleries have renovated mid-century modern buildings, luring a new crop of celebs and high-powered executives. LGBTQ travelers, twentysomethings, and families also sojourn here. Pleasantly touristy Palm Canyon Drive is packed with alfresco restaurants, many with views of the bustling sidewalk, along with indoor cafés and semi-chic shops. Farther west is the Uptown Design District, the area's shopping and dining destination. Continuing east on Palm Canyon Drive just outside downtown lie resorts and boutique hotels that host lively pool parties and house exclusive dining establishments and trendy bars.

GETTING HERE AND AROUND
Palm Springs is 90 miles southeast of Los Angeles on Interstate 10. Most visitors arrive in the Palm Springs area by car from the Los Angeles or San

Did You Know?

There are more than 4,000 wind turbines that power all of Palm Springs and the Coachella Valley.

Diego area via this freeway, which intersects with Highway 111 north of Palm Springs. Tahquitz Canyon Way marks the division between north and south on major streets (e.g., North and South Palm Canyon Drive). Once in Palm Springs, take advantage of the free Palm Springs Buzz, an air-conditioned pet-friendly trolley that loops around town Thursday through Sunday every 20 minutes from Via Escuela to Smoketree (⊕ sunline.org).

ESSENTIALS
VISITOR INFORMATION Greater Palm Springs Convention & Visitors Bureau. ✉ Visitor Center, 70–100 Hwy. 111, at Via Florencia, Rancho Mirage ☎ 760/770–9000, 800/967–3367 ⊕ www.visitgreaterpalmsprings.com. **Palm Springs Visitors Center Downtown.** ✉ 100 S. Palm Canyon Dr. ✛ In Welwood Murray Memorial Library ☎ 760/323–8296 ⊕ www.visitpalmsprings.com. **Palm Springs Visitors Center North.** ✉ 2901 N. Palm Canyon Dr. ☎ 760/778–8418, 800/347–7746 ⊕ www.visitpalmsprings.com.

⊙ Sights

Backstreet Art District
MUSEUM | Galleries and live-work studios just off East Canyon Drive showcase the works of a number of highly acclaimed artists. Painter and ceramicist Linda Maxson, innovative digital photographer Taylor Mickle, and new and emerging artists at Galleria Marconi are among the stars here. ■TIP➜ **On the first Wednesday evening of the month, the galleries are open from 5 to 8.** ✉ 2600 S. Cherokee Way ⊕ www.backstreetartdistrict.com ✍ Free ⊙ Most galleries closed Mon. and Tues.

Elvis's Honeymoon Hideaway
HOUSE | The hideaway of the King of rock 'n' roll and his young bride, Priscilla, during their first year of marriage, this house perches on a hilltop abutting the San Jacinto Mountains. A stunning example of local mid-century modern architecture, it is rich in Elvis lore, photos, and furnishings. Docents describe the fabulous parties that took place here, attended by celebrities and local legends. Built in 1962 by Robert Alexander, one of Palm Spring's largest developers, the house consists of four perfect circles, each set on a different level. At the time, Look magazine described the structure as the "house of tomorrow," and indeed many of its features are standard in the homes of today. ✉ 1350 Ladera Circle ☎ 760/322–1192 ⊕ www.elvishoneymoon.com ✍ $35.

★ Indian Canyons
CANYON | FAMILY | The Indian Canyons are the ancestral home of the Agua Caliente, part of the Cahuilla people. You can see remnants of their ancient life, including rock art, house pits and foundations, irrigation ditches, bedrock mortars, pictographs, and stone houses and shelters atop cliff walls. Short easy walks through the canyons reveal palm oases, waterfalls, and, in spring, wildflowers. Tree-shaded picnic areas are abundant. The attraction includes three canyons open for touring: Palm Canyon, noted for its stand of Washingtonia palms; Murray Canyon, home of Peninsula bighorn sheep; and Andreas Canyon, where a stand of fan palms contrasts with sharp rock formations. Ranger-led hikes to Palm and Andreas canyons are offered Friday–Sunday for an additional charge (no dogs allowed). The trading post at the entrance to Palm Canyon has hiking maps and refreshments, as well as Native American art, jewelry, and weaving. ✉ 38520 S. Palm Canyon Dr., south of Acanto Dr. ☎ 760/323–6018 ⊕ www.indian-canyons.com ✍ $9, ranger hikes $3 ⊙ Closed Mon.–Thurs. July–Sept.

Moorten Botanical Garden
GARDEN | In 1938, Chester "Cactus Slim" Moorten and his wife Patricia opened this showpiece for desert

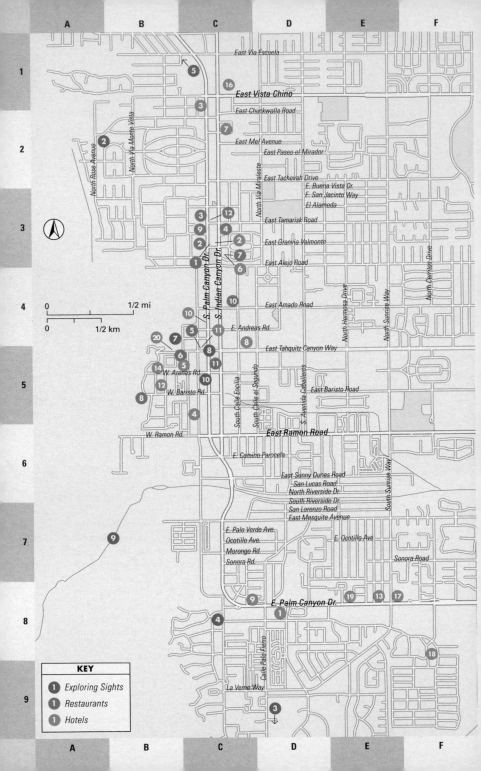

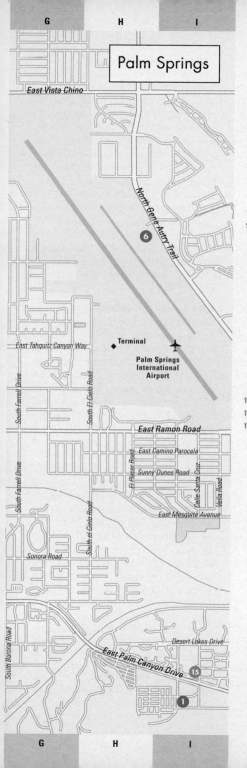

Palm Springs

plants—now numbering in the thousands—that include an ocotillo, a massive elephant tree, a boojum tree, and vine cacti. Their son Clark now operates the garden. ■TIP➜ Take a stroll through the Cactarium to spot rare finds such as the welwitschia, which originated in the Namib Desert in southwestern Africa. ⊠ 1701 S. Palm Canyon Dr. ☎ 760/327–6555 ⊕ www.moortengarden.com ✆ $5 ⊗ Closed Wed.

★ Palm Springs Aerial Tramway

VIEWPOINT | FAMILY | A trip on the tramway provides a 360-degree view of the desert through the picture windows of rotating cars. The 2½-mile ascent through Chino Canyon, the steepest vertical cable ride in the United States, brings you to an elevation of 8,516 feet in less than 20 minutes. On clear days, which are common, the view stretches 75 miles—from the peak of Mt. San Gorgonio in the north to the Salton Sea in the southeast. Stepping out into the snow at the summit is a winter treat. At the top, a bit below the summit of Mt. San Jacinto, are several diversions. Mountain Station has an observation deck, two restaurants, a cocktail lounge, apparel and gift shops, picnic facilities, a small wildlife exhibit, and a theater that screens movies on the history of the tramway and the adjacent Mount San Jacinto State Park and Wilderness. Take advantage of free guided and self-guided nature walks through the state park, or if there's snow on the ground, rent skis, snowshoes, or snow tubes. The tramway generally closes for maintenance in mid-September. ■TIP➜ Ride-and-dine packages are available in late afternoon. The tram is a popular attraction; to avoid a two-hour or longer wait, arrive before the first car leaves in the morning. ⊠ 1 Tramway Rd., off N. Palm Canyon Dr. (Hwy. 111) ☎ 888/515–8726 ⊕ www. pstramway.com ✆ From $26 ⊗ Closed 2 wks in Sept. for maintenance.

★ Palm Springs Air Museum

MUSEUM | FAMILY | This museum's impressive collection of World War II aircraft includes a B-17 Flying Fortress bomber, a P-51 Mustang, a Bell P-63 King Cobra, and a Grumman TBF Avenger. Among the cool exhibits are model warships, a Pearl Harbor diorama, and a Grumman Goose into which kids can crawl. Photos, artifacts, memorabilia, and uniforms are also on display, and educational programs take place on Saturday. Flight demonstrations are scheduled regularly. Rides in a vintage Warbird C-47 Skytrain and P-51D Mustang are also available. ⊠ 745 N. Gene Autry Trail ☎ 760/778–6262 ⊕ palmspringsairmuseum.org ✆ $18.

Palm Springs Art Museum

MUSEUM | This world-class art museum focuses on photography, modern architecture, and the traditional arts of the Americas. Galleries are bright and open. The permanent collection includes shimmering works in glass by Dale Chihuly, Ginny Ruffner, and William Morris. You'll also find handcrafted furniture by the late actor George Montgomery, mid-century modern architectural photos by Julius Shulman, enormous Native American baskets, and works by artists like Allen Houser, Arlo Namingha, and Fritz Scholder. The museum also displays significant works of 20th-century sculpture by Henry Moore, Marino Marina, Deborah Butterfield, and Mark Di Suvero. The Annenberg Theater presents plays, concerts, lectures, operas, and other cultural events. The museum also has a separate Architecture and Design Center at 300 S. Palm Canyon Dr. ⊠ 101 Museum Dr., off W. Tahquitz Canyon Dr. ☎ 760/322–4800 ⊕ www.psmuseum. org ✆ $14, free Thurs. 4–8 and 2nd Sun. each month ⊗ Closed Wed.

Palm Springs Walk of Stars

NEIGHBORHOOD | Along the walk, more than 300 bronze stars are embedded in the sidewalk (à la Hollywood Walk of Fame) to honor celebrities with a Palm Springs connection. Frank, Elvis, Marilyn, Dinah, Lucy, Ginger, Liz, and Liberace have all received their due. Those still around to walk the Walk and see their stars include Nancy Sinatra and Kathy Griffin. ⊠ *Palm Canyon Dr., around Tahquitz Canyon Way, and Tahquitz Canyon Way, between Palm Canyon and Indian Canyon Drs.* ☎ *760/325–1577* ⊕ *www.palmsprings. com/walk-of-stars.*

Tahquitz Canyon

CANYON | On ranger-led tours of this secluded canyon on the Agua Caliente Reservation you can view a spectacular 60-foot waterfall, rock art, ancient irrigation systems, and native wildlife and plants. Tours are conducted several times daily; participants must be able to navigate 100 steep rock steps. (You can also take a self-guided tour of the 1.8-mile trail.) At the visitor center at the canyon entrance, watch a short video, look at artifacts, and pick up a map. ⊠ *500 W. Mesquite Ave., west of S. Palm Canyon Dr.* ☎ *760/416–7044* ⊕ *www.tahquitzcanyon.com* 🖭 *$13* 🕙 *Closed Mon.–Thurs. July–Sept.*

Village Green Heritage Center

MUSEUM | Three small museums at the Village Green Heritage Center illustrate early life in Palm Springs. The centerpiece, the Agua Caliente Cultural Museum, traces the culture and history of the Cahuilla tribe with several exhibits. The **McCallum Adobe** and the **Cornelia White House** hold the collection of the Palm Springs Historical Society. **Ruddy's General Store Museum** is a re-creation of a 1930s general store. ⊠ *219–221 S. Palm Canyon Dr* ☎ *760/323–8297* ⊕ *www.pshistoricalsociety.org* 🖭 *Agua Caliente free, McCallum $2, Ruddy's $1* 🕙 *Closed Tues.*

🍽 Restaurants

★ **Cheeky's**

$ | AMERICAN | The artisanal bacon bar and hangover-halting mimosas attract legions to this breakfast and lunch joint, but brioche French toast and other favorites also contribute to the epic wait on weekends (no reservations accepted). Huevos rancheros, a gem salad with green goddess dressing, and other farm-centric dishes entice the foodie crowd. **Known for:** homemade pastries and sausages; local organic ingredients; grass-fed burger topped with house bacon. 🖭 *Average main: $13* ⊠ *622 N. Palm Canyon Dr., at E. Granvia Valmonte* ☎ *760/327–7595* ⊕ *www.cheekysps. com* 🕙 *Closed Tues. No dinner.*

Copley's on Palm Canyon

$$$$ | MODERN AMERICAN | Chef Manion Copley prepares innovative cuisine in a setting that's straight out of Hollywood—a hacienda once owned by Cary Grant. Dine in the clubby house or under the stars in the garden. **Known for:** romantic patio dining; fresh seafood and meats with innovative flavors; sweet and savory herb ice creams. 🖭 *Average main: $32* ⊠ *621 N. Palm Canyon Dr., at E. Granvia Valmonte* ☎ *760/327–9555* ⊕ *www.copleyspalmsprings.com* 🕙 *Closed July and Aug. No lunch.*

★ **EIGHT4NINE**

$$$ | AMERICAN | The dazzling interior design and eclectic Pacific Coast dishes made from scratch lure locals and visitors alike to this swank yet casual restaurant and lounge in the Uptown Design District. Sink into white patent leather chairs or comfy sofas in the lounge where you can gaze at historic celebrity photos, or choose a table in a grand corridor with a collection of private rooms, or in the outdoor patio with mountain views. **Known for:** nearly everything made from scratch; four-course chef's menu; all-day happy hour in lounge. 🖭 *Average*

main: $28 ✉ 849 N. Palm Canyon Dr. ☎ 760/325–8490 ⊕ eight4nine.com.

El Mirasol at Los Arboles

$$ | **MODERN MEXICAN** | Chef Felipe Castañeda owns two Mexican restaurants in Palm Springs—this one, part of Los Arboles Hotel, is outside on a charming patio set amid flower gardens and shaded by red umbrellas. Castañeda prepares classic combinations of tacos, tamales, and enchiladas, along with specialties such as double-cooked pork and *pollo en pipián* (chicken with a pre-Columbian sauce made of ground roasted pumpkin seeds and dry chilies). **Known for:** classic Mexican dishes; great vegetarian options; garden setting. Ⓢ *Average main: $22* ✉ *266 Via Altamira, off N. Indian Canyon Dr.* ☎ *760/459–3136* ⊕ *www.elmirasolrestaurants.com.*

★ 4 Saints

$$$$ | **CONTEMPORARY** | Perched on the seventh-floor rooftop of the Kimpton Rowan Palm Springs, where stunning views unfold from nearly every table, 4 Saints serves inventive farm-to-table dishes in a slick, hipster dining room and outdoor patio. The eclectic, globally inspired menu focuses on small plates and main dishes made with locally sourced ingredients (e.g., seafood, duck, and short ribs), intended for sharing. **Known for:** creative and classic cocktails; lively social vibe; stellar seafood. Ⓢ *Average main: $43* ✉ *100 W. Tahquitz Cyn. Way* ☎ *760/392–2020* ⊕ *www.4saintspalmsprings.com.*

Le Vallauris

$$$$ | **FRENCH** | A longtime favorite that occupies the historic Roberson House, Le Vallauris is popular with ladies who lunch, all of whom get a hug from the maître d'. The Belgian-French-inspired menu changes daily, and each day it's handwritten on a white board. **Known for:** prix-fixe menus for lunch and dinner; lovely tree-shaded garden; romantic setting. Ⓢ *Average main: $36* ✉ *385 W. Tahquitz Canyon Way, west of Palm Canyon Dr.* ☎ *760/325–5059* ⊕ *www.levallauris.com* ⊗ *Closed July and Aug.*

Purple Palm

$$$$ | **MODERN AMERICAN** | The hottest tables in Palm Springs are those that surround the pool at the Colony Palms Hotel, where the hip and elite pay homage to Purple Gang mobster Al Wertheimer, who reportedly built the hotel in the mid-1930s. Now it's a casual, convivial place where you can dine alfresco surrounded by a tropical garden near the pool. **Known for:** craft cocktails; happy hour and weekend brunch; extensive international wine list. Ⓢ *Average main: $32* ✉ *572 N. Indian Canyon Dr., at E. Granvia Valmonte* ☎ *800/557–2187* ⊕ *www.colonypalmshotel.com.*

Spencer's Restaurant

$$$$ | **MODERN AMERICAN** | The swank dining space inside the Palm Springs Tennis Club Resort occupies a historic mid-century modern structure. Crab cakes, kung pao calamari, and crispy flash-fried oysters are favorite starters. **Known for:** French–Pacific Rim influences; romantic patio; elegant dining room. Ⓢ *Average main: $35* ✉ *701 W. Baristo Rd.* ☎ *760/327–3446* ⊕ *www.spencersrestaurant.com.*

Trio

$$ | **MODERN AMERICAN** | The owners of this high-energy Uptown Design District restaurant claim that it's "where Palm Springs eats," and it certainly seems so on nights when the lines to get in run deep. The menu includes home-style staples such as Yankee pot roast, crawfish pie, and other dishes, along with veggie burgers and other vegetarian and gluten-free items. **Known for:** local artwork; inventive desserts; ample vegetarian and gluten-free options. Ⓢ *Average main: $22* ✉ *707 N. Palm Canyon Dr.* ☎ *760/864–8746* ⊕ *www.triopalmsprings.com.*

The Tropicale

$$$ | **INTERNATIONAL** | Tucked onto a side-street corner, the Tropicale is a mid-century-style watering hole with a contemporary vibe. The bar and main dining room hold cozy leather booths; flowers and water features brighten the outdoor area. **Known for:** globe-trotting menu; happy hour (all night on Wednesday); weekly specials. [$] *Average main: $30* ✉ *330 E. Amado Rd., at N. Calle Encilia* ☎ *760/866–1952* 🌐 *www.thetropicale.com* 🕓 *No lunch.*

★ Tyler's Burgers

$ | **AMERICAN** | **FAMILY** | Families, singles, and couples head to Tyler's for simple lunch fare that appeals to carnivores and vegetarians alike. Expect mid-20th-century America's greatest hits: heaping burgers, stacks of fries, root beer floats, milk shakes; on weekends, be prepared to wait with the masses. **Known for:** house-made cole slaw and potato salad; excellent burgers and fries; delicious shakes. [$] *Average main: $11* ✉ *149 S. Indian Canyon Dr., at La Plaza* ☎ *760/325–2990* 🌐 *www.tylersburgers.com* 🕓 *Closed Sun. late May–mid-Feb. Closed mid-July–early Sept.*

Workshop Kitchen + Bar

$$$$ | **AMERICAN** | Chef Michael Beckman's Uptown Design District hot spot pairs high-quality California cuisine with creative cocktails in a sleek, almost utilitarian setting. The outdoor patio lures the oversize sunglasses Sunday brunch crowd, who slurp cava mimosas and artisanal cocktails; inside, the sleek concrete booths are topped with black leather cushions. **Known for:** most ingredients sourced from within a 100-mile radius; artisanal cocktails; communal seating options. [$] *Average main: $32* ✉ *800 N. Palm Canyon Dr., at E. Tamarisk Rd.* ☎ *760/459–3451* 🌐 *www.workshoppalmsprings.com* 🕓 *No lunch Mon.–Sat.*

🛏 Hotels

Ace Hotel and Swim Club

$$$ | **RESORT** | With the hotel's vintage feel and hippie-chic decor, it would be no surprise to find guests gathered around cozy communal fire pits enjoying feel-good '60s music. **Pros:** Amigo Room has late-night dining; poolside stargazing deck; weekend DJ scene at the pool. **Cons:** party atmosphere not for everyone; limited amenities; casual staff and service. [$] *Rooms from: $189* ✉ *701 E. Palm Canyon Dr.* ☎ *760/325–9900* 🌐 *www.acehotel.com/palmsprings* 🛏 *188 rooms* 🍴 *No meals.*

Alcazar Palm Springs

$$ | **HOTEL** | Tucked at the border of the Uptown Design District and an area known as the Movie Colony, the hip, modern, and affordable Alcazar features ample, blazing-white guest rooms that wrap around a sparkling pool; some rooms have Jacuzzis, and many have private patios or fireplaces. **Pros:** walking distance of downtown; parking on-site; bikes available. **Cons:** limited service; wall air-conditioners; resort fee. [$] *Rooms from: $159* ✉ *622 N. Indian Canyon Dr.* ☎ *760/318–9850* 🌐 *www.alcazarpalmsprings.com* 🛏 *34 rooms* 🍴 *No meals.*

★ ARRIVE

$$$$ | **HOTEL** | During the day, sip cocktails from the indoor outdoor bar (which doubles as the reception desk), and lounge in the pool on an inflatable seahorse, or dance to a live DJ; at night, relax outside in the hot tub and socialize around the communal fire pits (half of the rooms also come with a private patio and fireplace), or cozy up in your king-size bed among tasteful modern furnishings, and wake to sunny mountain views. **Pros:** private cabanas with misting systems; great restaurant, artisanal ice-cream shop, and local coffee shop on-site; easy access to Uptown Design District shops, restaurants, galleries. **Cons:** only

king rooms available; shower offers little privacy; party scene may not suit everyone. $ *Rooms from: $329* ⊠ *1551 N. Palm Canyon Dr.* ☎ *760/507–1650* ⊕ *www.arrivehotels.com* ⇗ *32 rooms* ¶◎¶ *No meals.*

Avalon Hotel Palm Springs
$$$$ | RESORT | With three pools and a spa spread over 4 acres of gardens, the upscale Avalon Hotel Palm Springs calls back to 1960s swanky, with private bungalows, lush gardens, and an emphasis on style. **Pros:** poolside cabanas; complimentary fitness classes; luxurious on-site Estrella Spa and stylish restaurant Chi Chi. **Cons:** popular wedding site. $ *Rooms from: $400* ⊠ *415 S. Belardo Rd.* ☎ *844/328–2566* ⊕ *www. avalonpalmsprings.com* ⇗ *79 rooms* ¶◎¶ *No meals.*

Casa Cody
$$$$ | B&B/INN | An historic 1920s bed-and-breakfast near the Palm Springs Art Museum, Casa Cody has a retro coolness that embodies an old west feel (the founder, Harriet Cody, was Buffalo Bill's cousin). **Pros:** easy walk to restaurants, hikes, museums; relatively affordable rates for location; some rooms come with fireplaces, patios, and/or kitchens. **Cons:** old buildings; limited amenities; office closes in the early evening. $ *Rooms from: $209* ⊠ *175 S. Cahuilla Rd.* ☎ *760/320–9346* ⊕ *www.casacody.com* ⇗ *29 rooms* ¶◎¶ *Breakfast.*

Colony Palms Hotel
$$$$ | HOTEL | This hotel has been a hip place to stay since the 1930s, when gangster Al Wertheimer built it to front his casino, bar, and brothel; it later became the Howard Hotel, owned by local luminaries Robert Stewart Howard (his dad owned the fabled racehorse Seabiscuit) and actress Andrea Leeds (the couple hosted a young Frank Sinatra, Elizabeth Taylor, and Liberace), and today it still attracts a younger crowd. **Pros:** rooms open to pool and gardens

in the central courtyard; attentive staff; fireplaces and whirlpool tubs in many rooms. **Cons:** high noise level outside; some rooms need updating; service sometimes inconsistent. $ *Rooms from: $299* ⊠ *572 N. Indian Canyon Dr.* ☎ *760/969–1800, 800/577–2187* ⊕ *www.colonypalmshotel.com* ⇗ *57 rooms* ¶◎¶ *No meals.*

East Canyon Hotel & Spa
$$$ | B&B/INN | The vibe is social and the rooms are spacious at this classy resort whose gracious hosts welcome LGBTQ and all couples looking for romantic and relaxing getaways. **Pros:** elegant but laid-back feel; attentive service; complimentary poolside cocktails. **Cons:** long walk to downtown; grounds need sprucing up; tiny hot tub. $ *Rooms from: $189* ⊠ *288 E. Camino Monte Vista* ☎ *760/320–1928, 877/324–6835* ⊕ *www.eastcanyonps. com* ⇗ *15 rooms* ¶◎¶ *Breakfast.*

Hilton Palm Springs
$$$ | HOTEL | This venerable hotel across the street from the Spa Casino and a few blocks from the main Palm Canyon dining and shopping scene has spacious rooms decorated in soft desert colors. **Pros:** a short walk to downtown strip; three dining venues; classy full-service spa. **Cons:** not right on Palm Canyon Drive; average service; many business meetings. $ *Rooms from: $189* ⊠ *400 E. Tahquitz Canyon Way* ☎ *760/320–6868, 855/271–3617* ⊕ *www.hiltonpalmsprings. com* ⇗ *260 rooms* ¶◎¶ *No meals.*

★ Hotel California
$$$ | HOTEL | Expect homey accommodations for all budgets at this delightful hotel that's decked out in rustic Mexican furniture. **Pros:** comfortable design; friendly hosts; free off-street parking. **Cons:** far from downtown; property needs updating; fronts a busy road. $ *Rooms from: $185* ⊠ *424 E. Palm Canyon Dr.* ☎ *760/322–8855* ⊕ *www. palmspringshotelcalifornia.com* ⇗ *14 rooms* ¶◎¶ *No meals.*

The Hyatt Palm Springs
$$$ | **HOTEL** | The best-situated downtown hotel in Palm Springs, the Hyatt has spacious suites where you can watch the sun rise over the city, or set behind the mountains from your bedroom's balcony. **Pros:** underground parking; restaurant plus two outdoor bar-lounges; daily sunset hour with free wine, beer, and appetizers. **Cons:** lots of business travelers; some street noise; valet parking only. [$] *Rooms from: $179* ✉ *285 N. Palm Canyon Dr.* ☎ *760/322–9000* 🌐 *palmsprings.hyatt.com* 🛏 *197 suites* 🍴 *No meals.*

★ Kimpton Rowan Palm Springs Hotel
$$$$ | **HOTEL** | One of the newest arrivals on the downtown Palm Springs scene, the Rowan Palm Springs dazzles locals and guests (especially the under-40 set) with stunning views from myriad picture windows and a rooftop deck, and an unpretentious vibe that puts guests of all ages at ease. **Pros:** friendly, attentive service; stunning mountain and valley views; in the heart of downtown. **Cons:** rooftop pool area can get crowded; valet parking only; $35 resort fee. [$] *Rooms from: $259* ✉ *100 W. Tahquitz Canyon Way* ☎ *760/904–5015, 800/532–7320* 🌐 *www.rowanpalmsprings.com* 🛏 *153 rooms* 🍴 *No meals.*

★ Korakia Pensione
$$$ | **B&B/INN** | The painter Gordon Coutts, best known for desert landscapes, constructed this Moroccan villa in 1924 as an artist's studio, and these days creative types gather in the main house and nearby Mediterranean-style villas, spread across 1.5 acres on both sides of the street, to soak up the spirit of that era. **Pros:** two pools; lunch and dinner available on request (fee); yoga on weekends. **Cons:** might not appeal to those who prefer standard resorts; no TVs or phones in rooms; no children under 13. [$] *Rooms from: $249* ✉ *257 S. Patencio Rd.* ☎ *760/864–6411* 🌐 *www.korakia.com* 🛏 *28 rooms* 🍴 *Free Breakfast.*

La Maison
$$$ | **B&B/INN** | Offering all the comforts of home, this small bed-and-breakfast contains large rooms that surround the terra-cotta–tiled and very comfortable pool area, where you can spend quiet time soaking up the sun or taking a dip. **Pros:** restaurants nearby; quiet; genial hosts. **Cons:** on busy Highway 111; rooms open directly onto pool deck; some rooms on the small side. [$] *Rooms from: $239* ✉ *1600 E. Palm Canyon Dr.* ☎ *760/325–1600* 🌐 *www.lamaisonpalmsprings.com* 🛏 *13 rooms* 🍴 *Breakfast.*

★ Orbit In Hotel
$$$ | **B&B/INN** | The architectural style of this hip inn on a quiet backstreet dates back to its 1955 opening—and nearly flat roofs, wide overhangs, glass everywhere—and the period feel continues inside. **Pros:** saltwater pool; Orbitini cocktail hour; free breakfast served poolside. **Cons:** best for couples; style not to everyone's taste; staff not available 24 hours. [$] *Rooms from: $169* ✉ *562 W. Arenas Rd.* ☎ *760/323–3585, 877/996–7248* 🌐 *www.orbitin.com* 🛏 *9 rooms* 🍴 *Breakfast.*

★ The Parker Palm Springs
$$$$ | **RESORT** | A cacophony of color and over-the-top contemporary art assembled by New York City–based designer Jonathan Adler mixes well with the brilliant desert garden, three pools (two outdoor), fire pits, and expansive spa of this hip hotel that attracts a stylish, worldly clientele. **Pros:** celebrity clientele; on-site restaurants, bars, and spa; design-centric. **Cons:** pricey drinks and wine; a bit of a drive from downtown; resort fee ($35). [$] *Rooms from: $399* ✉ *4200 E. Palm Canyon Dr.* ☎ *760/770–5000, 800/543–4300* 🌐 *www.theparkerpalmsprings.com* 🛏 *144 rooms* 🍴 *No meals.*

Riviera Resort & Spa
$$$$ | **RESORT** | A party place built in 1958 and renovated in 2016, the Riviera attracts young, well-heeled, bikini-clad guests who hang out around the pool by day, and

at the Bikini Bar by night. **Pros:** personal fire pits throughout the property; hip vibe; excellent spa. **Cons:** high noise level outdoors; party atmosphere; location at north end of Palm Springs. $ *Rooms from: $300* ✉ *1600 N. Indian Canyon Dr.* ☎ *760/327–8311* ⊕ *rivierapalmsprings.com* 🛏 *449 rooms* ⏹ *No meals.*

★ The Saguaro

$$ | **HOTEL** | A startling, rainbow-hued oasis—the brainchild of Manhattan-based architects Peter Stamberg and Paul Aferiat—the Saguaro caters to young, hip, pet-toting partygoers who appreciate its lively pool party scene. **Pros:** lively pool scene with weekend DJ parties; daily yoga, on-site spa, 24-hour fitness center, beach cruisers; shuttle service to downtown. **Cons:** a few miles from downtown; pool area can be noisy and crowded; $33 resort fee. $ *Rooms from: $169* ✉ *1800 E. Palm Canyon Dr.* ☎ *760/323–1711* ⊕ *thesaguaro.com* 🛏 *244 rooms* ⏹ *No meals.*

Smoke Tree Ranch

$$$$ | **RESORT** | **FAMILY** | A laid-back genteel retreat since the mid-1930s for some of the world's foremost families, including Walt Disney's, the area's most under-the-radar resort complex occupies 385 pristine desert acres surrounded by mountains and unspoiled vistas, and still provides an experience reminiscent of the Old West. **Pros:** priceless privacy; simple luxury; recreational activities like horseback riding and more. **Cons:** no glitz; limited entertainment options; family atmosphere not for everyone. $ *Rooms from: $400* ✉ *1850 Smoke Tree La.* ☎ *760/327–1221, 800/787–3922* ⊕ *www.smoketreeranch.com* ☽ *Closed Apr.–late Oct.* 🛏 *49 cottages, includes 18 suites* ⏹ *All-inclusive.*

Sparrows Lodge

$$$ | **B&B/INN** | Rustic earthiness meets haute design at the adult-centered Sparrows, just off Palm Springs's main drag. **Pros:** unique design; intimate property; private patios. **Cons:** not family-oriented, minimum age 21; daily resort fee; no TVs or phones in rooms. $ *Rooms from: $249* ✉ *1330 E. Palm Canyon Dr.* ☎ *760/327–2300* ⊕ *www.sparrowshotel.com* 🛏 *20 rooms* ⏹ *Breakfast.*

★ Willows Historic Palm Springs Inn

$$$$ | **B&B/INN** | A set of two adjacent opulent Mediterranean-style mansions built in the 1920s to host the rich and famous, this luxurious hillside bed-and-breakfast has gleaming hardwood and slate floors, stone fireplaces, frescoed ceilings, hand-painted tiles, iron balconies, antiques throughout, and a 50-foot waterfall that splashes into a pool outside the dining room. **Pros:** short walk to art museum, restaurants, shops; pool; expansive breakfast and afternoon wine hour. **Cons:** closed from June to September; pricey; some rooms on the small side. $ *Rooms from: $425* ✉ *412 W. Tahquitz Canyon Way* ☎ *760/320–0771* ⊕ *www.thewillowspalmsprings.com* 🛏 *17 rooms* ⏹ *Breakfast.*

Ⓨ Nightlife

BARS AND PUBS

Bootlegger Tiki

BARS/PUBS | Palm Springs tiki-drink traditions, especially during the two daily happy hours (4 to 6 pm and midnight to 2 am), draw loyal patrons to Bootlegger, which occupies the same space as Don the Beachcomber in the 1950s. ✉ *1101 N. Palm Canyon Dr.* ☎ *760/318–4154* ⊕ *www.bootleggertiki.com.*

★ Draughtsman

BARS/PUBS | In the Uptown Design District and part of the ARRIVE hotel, this upscale pub focuses on Palm Springs and SoCal craft beers, classic cocktails, and modern comfort food, as well as classics like chicken potpie and short rib poutine. Hang out in the contemporary indoor space with soaring ceilings and watch sports, or chill on the patio where you can play cornhole or foosball. ✉ *1501 N. Palm Canyon Dr.* ☎ *760/507–1644* ⊕ *draughtsmanpalmsprings.com.*

Palm Springs Modernism

Some of the world's most forward-looking architects designed and constructed buildings around Palm Springs between 1940 and 1970; and modernism, also popular elsewhere in California in the years after World War II, became an ideal fit for desert living, because it minimizes the separation between indoors and outdoors. See-through houses with glass exterior walls are common. Oversize flat roofs provide shade from the sun, and many buildings' sculptural forms reflect nearby landforms. The style is notable for elegant informality, clean lines, and simple landscaping.

Most obvious to visitors are three buildings that are part of the Palm Springs Aerial Tramway complex, built in the 1960s. Albert Frey, a Swiss-born architect, designed the soaring A-frame Tramway Gas Station, visually echoing the pointed peaks behind it. Frey also created the glass-walled Valley Station, from which you get your initial view of the Coachella Valley before you board the tram to the Mountain Station, designed by E. Stewart Williams.

Frey, a Palm Springs resident for more than 60 years, also designed the indoor-outdoor City Hall, Fire Station No. 1, and numerous houses. His second home, perched atop stilts on the hillside above the Palm Springs Art Museum, affords a sweeping view of the Coachella Valley through glass walls. The classy Movie Colony Hotel, one of the first buildings Frey designed in the desert, may seem like a typical 1950s motel with rooms surrounding a swimming pool now, but when it was built in 1935, it was years ahead of its time.

Donald Wexler, who honed his vision with Los Angeles architect Richard Neutra, brought new ideas about the use of materials to the desert, where he teamed up with William Cody on a number of projects, including the terminal at the Palm Springs Airport. Many of Wexler's buildings have soaring overhanging roofs, designed to provide shade from the blazing desert sun. Wexler also experimented with steel framing back in 1961, but the metal proved too expensive. Seven of his steel-frame houses can be seen in a neighborhood off Indian Canyon and Frances drives.

The Palm Springs Modern Committee sponsors Modernism Week in mid-February, when you can visit some of the most remarkable buildings in the area. Visit ⊕ www.psmodcom.org for an app that guides you to the most interesting buildings.

Purple Room Supper Club

BARS/PUBS | In an elegant venue within the Club Trinidad Hotel, this swinging '60s-era supper club offers live entertainment six nights a week. Come for drinks, dinner, and dancing Tuesday through Thursday night (no cover charge, but reservations are recommended). On Friday and Saturday night, dine at 6 pm and watch a scheduled show at 8 pm (reserve tickets in advance). Try to time your visit to catch *The Judy Show*, actor/owner Michael Holmes's Sunday evening comical tribute to Judy Garland, Bette Davis, Katharine Hepburn, and other stars (tickets required). ✉ *1900 E. Palm Canyon Dr.* ☎ *760/322-4422* ⊕ *www.purpleroompalmsprings.com.*

Tonga Hut

BARS/PUBS | The younger sibling of L.A.'s oldest tiki hut (opened in 1958 in North Hollywood), Tonga Hut Palm Springs transports guests to Polynesia with an authentic tiki vibe, pupu platters, and tropical drinks. It's on the second floor of a building in the heart of the downtown strip—try to nab a table on the lanai where you can experience the action from above. The bar and dining area are also fun and lively spaces; ask about the telephone booth that leads to a secret room, available for private parties. ⊠ 254 N. Palm Canyon Dr. ☎ 760/322–4449 ⊕ www.tongahut.com.

★ Village Pub

BARS/PUBS | With live entertainment, DJs, and friendly service, this popular bar caters to a young crowd. Happy hour is fantastic. On weekend days there is live music as well. ⊠ 266 S. Palm Canyon Dr., at Baristo Rd. ☎ 760/323–3265 ⊕ www.palmspringsvillagepub.com.

CASINOS

Casino Morongo

CASINOS | A 20-minute drive west of Palm Springs, this casino has 2,600 slot machines, video games, the Vibe nightclub, plus Vegas-style shows. ⊠ 49500 Seminole Dr., off I–10, Cabazon ☎ 800/252–4499, 951/849–3080 ⊕ www.morongocasinoresort.com.

Spa Resort Casino

CASINOS | This resort holds 1,000 slot machines, blackjack tables, a high-limit room, four restaurants, two bars, and the Cascade Lounge for entertainment. ⊠ 401 E. Amado Rd., at N. Calle Encilia ☎ 888/999–1995 ⊕ www.sparesortcasino.com.

DANCE CLUBS

Zelda's Nightclub

DANCE CLUBS | At this Palm Springs institution, the high-energy DJs, dancing, and drinking are still going strong and the dance floor is still thumping with Latin, hip-hop, and sounds from the '60s, '70s, and '80s. Zelda's offers bottle service in the VIP Sky Box. ⊠ 611 S. Palm Canyon Dr., at E. Camino Parocela ☎ 760/325–2375 ⊕ www.zeldasnightclub.com ⊗ Closed Mon.

GAY AND LESBIAN

The Dinah

FESTIVALS | In late March, when the world's finest female golfers hit the links for the Annual LPGA ANA Inspiration Championship in Rancho Mirage, thousands of lesbians converge on Palm Springs for a four-day party popularly known as The Dinah. ☎ 888/923–4624 ⊕ thedinah.com.

Hunter's Video Bar

DANCE CLUBS | Drawing a young gay and straight crowd, Hunter's is a club-scene mainstay. ⊠ 302 E. Arenas Rd., at Calle Encilia ☎ 760/323–0700 ⊕ huntersnightclubs.com.

★ Toucans Tiki Lounge

BARS/PUBS | A friendly place with a tropical–rain forest setting, Toucans serves festive drinks and hosts live entertainment and theme nights. On Sunday it seems as though all of Palm Springs has turned out for drag night. ⊠ 2100 N. Palm Canyon Dr., at W. Via Escuela ☎ 760/416–7584 ⊕ www.toucanstikilounge.com ⊗ Closed Wed.

White Party Palm Springs

FESTIVALS | Held during spring break, the White Party draws tens of thousands of gay men from around the world for four days of parties and events. ⊠ Palm Springs ☎ 323/782–9924 ⊕ jeffreysanker.com.

THEMED ENTERTAINMENT

★ Ace Hotel and Swim Club

THEMED ENTERTAINMENT | Events are held here nearly every night, including film screenings, full moon parties, live concerts, DJs, and dancing. Many are free, and some are family friendly. The poolside venue makes most events fun and casual. ⊠ 701 E. Palm Canyon Dr., at Calle Palo Fierro ☎ 760/325–9900 ⊕ www.acehotel.com.

🎭 Performing Arts

ARTS CENTERS
Annenberg Theater
CONCERTS | Broadway shows, operas, lectures, Sunday-afternoon chamber concerts, and other events take place at the Palm Springs Art Museum's handsome theater. ✉ 101 N. Museum Dr., at W. Tahquitz Canyon Way ☎ 760/325–4490 ⊕ www.psmuseum.org.

FESTIVALS
Modernism Week
FESTIVALS | Each February the desert communities celebrate the work of the architects and designers who created the Palm Springs "look" in the '40s, '50s, and '60s. Described these days as mid-century modern—you'll also see the term "desert modernism"—these structures were created by Albert Frey, Richard Neutra, William F. Cody, John Lautner, and other notables. The 11-day event features lectures, a modernism show, films, vintage car and trailer shows, galas, and home and garden tours. A shorter preview week happens in October. ✉ Palm Springs ⊕ www. modernismweek.com.

FILM
Palm Springs International Film Festival
FILM | In mid-January this 12-day festival brings stars and nearly 200 feature films from several dozen countries, plus panel discussions, short films, and documentaries, to various venues. The weeklong "Shortfest," celebrating more than 300 short films, takes place in June. ✉ Palm Springs ☎ 760/322–2930, 800/898–7256 ⊕ www.psfilmfest.org.

🛍 Shopping

BOUTIQUES
★ Just Fabulous
LOCAL SPECIALTIES | Find everything from original photography and art, coffee table books, greeting cards, designer home decor, candles, and many other eclectic items at this fun gift shop that celebrates the area's retro-modern lifestyle and desert dolce vita. ✉ 515 N. Palm Canyon Dr. ☎ 760/864–1300 ⊕ bjustfabulous.com.

★ Trina Turk Boutique
CLOTHING | Celebrity designer Trina Turk's empire takes up a city block in the Uptown Design District. Turk, famous for men's and women's outdoor wear, reached out to another celebrity, interior designer Kelly Wearstler, to create adjoining clothing and residential boutiques. Lively fabrics brighten up the many chairs and couches for sale at the residential store, which also carries bowls, paintings, and other fun pieces to spiff up your home. ✉ 891 N. Palm Canyon Dr. ☎ 760/416–2856 ⊕ www.trinaturk.com.

OUTLET MALLS
★ Desert Hills Premium Outlets
OUTLET/DISCOUNT STORES | About 20 miles west of Palm Springs lies one of California's largest outlet centers. The 180 brand-name discount fashion shops include Jimmy Choo, Neiman Marcus, Versace, Saint Laurent Paris, J. Crew, Armani, Gucci, and Prada. ✉ 48400 Seminole Rd., off I-10, Cabazon ☎ 951/849–5018 ⊕ www.premiumoutlets.com.

SHOPPING DISTRICTS
★ Uptown Design District
SHOPPING NEIGHBORHOODS | A loose-knit collection of consignment and second-hand shops, galleries, and lively restaurants extends north of Palm Springs's downtown. The theme here is decidedly retro. Many businesses sell mid-century modern furniture and decorator items, and others carry clothing and estate jewelry. One spot definitely worth a peek is **The Shag Store,** the gallery of fine art painter Josh Agle. For antique costume jewelry check out **Dazzles.** If you dig the mid-mod aesthetic, breeze through the furnishings at **Towne Palm Springs.** ✉ N. Palm Canyon Dr., between Amado Rd. and Vista Chino.

SPAS

★ Estrella Spa at the Avalon Hotel Palm Springs

SPA/BEAUTY | This spa earns top honors each year for the indoor/outdoor experience it offers with a touch of Old Hollywood ambience. You can enjoy your massage in one of four outdoor treatment cabanas in a garden, experience a sugar or salt scrub, get a facial or pedicure fireside, or receive a full-body treatment with a honey-sugar blend. Whatever the treatment, you can use the spa's private pool, take a break for lunch, and order a drink from the hotel's bar. ⊠ Avalon Hotel Palm Springs, 415 S. Belardo Rd. ☎ 760/318–3000 ⊕ www. avalonpalmsprings.com ⚲ Salon. Services: facials, specialty massages, prenatal massages, outdoor treatments, wellness classes. $155, 60-min massage, $260, spa package.

Feel Good Spa at the Ace Hotel

SPA/BEAUTY | The Feel Good Spa within its own dedicated facility at the Ace Hotel has five treatment rooms. The estheticians use local clay, mud, sea algae, and other natural ingredients, which you can purchase at the on-site shop. ⊠ 701 E. Palm Canyon Dr. ☎ 760/866–6188 ⊕ www.acehotel.com/palmsprings ⚲ Fully equipped gym. Services: wraps and scrubs, massage, facials, in-room treatments, salon, wellness classes, yoga. $115, 60-min massage.

Palm Springs Yacht Club

SPA/BEAUTY | It's all about fun at this nautical-theme spa with 15 treatment rooms on the grounds of the Parker estate. Guests receive a complimentary cucumber-infused cocktail while lounging in a poolside tent. Before spa treatments, you can choose music from a playlist and the staff will stream it to your room. Treatments might feature local clay or stones, or a Thai massage. ⊠ 4200 E. Palm Canyon Dr. ☎ 760/321–4606 ⊕ www.theparkerpalmsprings.com/ spa ⚲ Sauna, steam room, indoor pool.

Services: scrubs and wraps, massage, facials, manicures, pedicures, waxing, salon, fitness center with TechnoGym equipment, dining and cocktails. $195, 60-min massage.

Rancho Mirage

4 miles southeast of Cathedral City.

The rich and famous of Rancho Mirage live in beautiful estates and patronize elegant resorts and expensive restaurants. Although many mansions here are concealed behind the walls of gated communities and country clubs, the grandest of them all, Sunnylands, the Annenberg residence, is open to the public as a museum and public garden.

The city's golf courses host many high-profile tournaments. You'll find some of the desert's fanciest resorts in Rancho Mirage, and plenty of peace and quiet.

GETTING HERE AND AROUND

Due east of Cathedral City, Rancho Mirage stretches from Ramon Road on the north to the hills south of Highway 111. The western border is Da Vall Drive, the eastern one Monterey Avenue. Major east–west cross streets are Frank Sinatra Drive and Country Club Drive. Most shopping and dining spots are on Highway 111.

◉ Sights

★ The Annenberg Retreat at Sunnylands

HOUSE | The stunning 25,000-square-foot winter home and retreat of the late Ambassador Walter H. and Leonore Annenberg opened to the public in 2012. You can spend a whole day enjoying the 15 glorious acres of gardens (see website schedule of free guided walks, classes, and other programs), or take a guided 90-minute tour of the residence (reservations essential), a striking mid-century modern edifice designed by A. Quincy Jones. Floor-to-ceiling

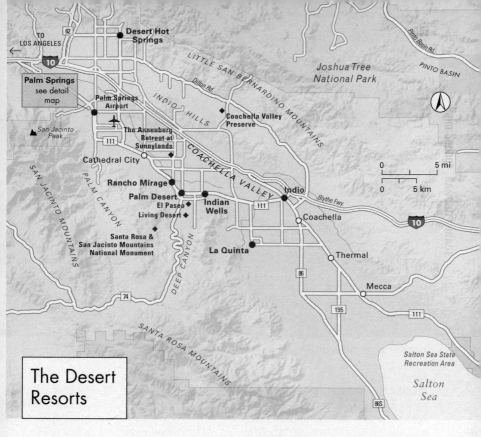

The Desert
Resorts

windows frame views of the gardens
and Mt. San Jacinto, and the expansive
rooms hold furnishings from the 1960s
and later, along with impressionist art
(some original, some replicas). The history
made here is as captivating as the
surroundings. Eight U.S. presidents—
from Dwight Eisenhower to Barack
Obama—and their First Ladies have
visited Sunnylands; Ronald and Nancy
Reagan were frequent guests. Britain's
Queen Elizabeth and Prince Philip also
relaxed here, as did Princess Grace of
Monaco and Japanese Prime Minister
Toshiki Kaifu. Photos, art, letters,
journals, and mementos provide insight
into some of the history that unfolded
here. ⊠ 37–977 Bob Hope Dr., south
of Gerald Ford Dr. ☎ 760/202–2222
⊕ www.sunnylands.org ☞ House tours
$48, tickets available online 2 wks in
advance; guided bird tour $35; open-air
shuttle tour of grounds, $21; visitor
center and gardens free ☾ Closed Mon.
and Tues. Closed June–mid-Sept. and
during retreats.

Children's Discovery Museum of the Desert
MUSEUM | FAMILY | This museum features
more than 80 hands-on exhibits, including
a miniature rock-climbing area, a
magnetic sculpture wall, make-it-and-
take-it-apart projects, a rope maze, and
an area for toddlers. Kids can make
music on oversize drums, chimes, and
a metallophone, work as chefs in the
museum's pizza parlor, assemble their
own cars on a racetrack, and build
pies out of arts and crafts supplies.
⊠ 71–701 Gerald Ford Dr., at Bob Hope
Dr. ☎ 760/321–0602 ⊕ www.cdmod.org
☞ $10 ☾ Closed Mon. Sept.–mid-Nov.

Palm Springs is a golfer's paradise: the area is home to more than 125 courses.

Koffi

RESTAURANT—SIGHT | Locals often hit this chain to get their caffeine fix, and it's a fine pit stop for pastries, premade sandwiches, and bagels. This outpost is the roasting facility, so the beans here are as fresh as they come. ✉ *71–380 Hwy. 111* ☎ *760/340–2444* 🌐 *www.kofficoffee.com.*

🍴 Restaurants

Catalan

$$$ | **MEDITERRANEAN** | At this restaurant known for its beautifully prepared Mediterranean cuisine you can dine inside or under the stars in the atrium. The service here is attentive, and the menu roams Spain, Italy, California and beyond. **Known for:** two-course prix-fixe menu; delicious paella with clams; happy hour with inventive cocktails. [$] *Average main: $28* ✉ *70026 Hwy. 111* ☎ *760/770–9508* 🌐 *www.catalanrestaurant.com* 🕒 *Closed Mon.*

Las Casuelas Nuevas

$$ | **MEXICAN** | **FAMILY** | Hundreds of artifacts from Guadalajara, Mexico, lend festive charm to this casual restaurant, which has an expansive garden patio. Tamales and shellfish dishes are among the specialties—expect more traditional Mexican fare, rather than California-influenced creations. **Known for:** vast tequila menu; weekend live entertainment; lively happy hour. [$] *Average main: $16* ✉ *70–050 Hwy. 111* ☎ *760/328–8844* 🌐 *www.lascasuelasnuevas.com.*

🛏 Hotels

Agua Caliente Casino, Resort, Spa

$$$ | **RESORT** | As in Las Vegas, the Agua Caliente casino is in the lobby, but once you get into the spacious, beautifully appointed rooms of the resort, all of the cacophony at the entrance is forgotten. **Pros:** poolside cabanas outfitted with TV and Wi-Fi; package deals include access to Indian Canyons Golf Course; on-site Sunstone Spa. **Cons:** casino ambience; not appropriate for kids;

some live performances draw huge crowds. $ *Rooms from: $250* ✉ *32–250 Bob Hope Dr.* ☎ *888/999–1995* ⊕ *www. hotwatercasino.com* ☞ *366 rooms* ⦿ *No meals.*

Omni Rancho Las Palmas Resort & Spa

$$$$ | RESORT | FAMILY | The desert's most family-friendly resort, this large venue holds Splashtopia, a huge water-play zone. **Pros:** rooms come with private balconies or patios; trails for hiking and jogging; nightly entertainment. **Cons:** second-floor rooms accessed by very steep stairs; golf course surrounds rooms; resort hosts conventions. $ *Rooms from: $299* ✉ *41-000 Bob Hope Dr.* ☎ *760/568–2727, 888/444–6664* ⊕ *www.rancholaspalmas.com* ☞ *444 rooms* ⦿ *No meals.*

★ **The Ritz Carlton, Rancho Mirage**

$$$$ | RESORT | FAMILY | On a hilltop perch overlooking the Coachella Valley, this luxury resort spoils guests with exemplary service and comforts that include a trio of pools, access to the desert's finest spa, and private outdoor sitting areas for each room. **Pros:** fire pit overlooking Coachella Valley; access to Mission Hills golf courses and tennis; spa that's a destination in itself. **Cons:** hefty rates; some airport noise; resort and parking fees ($40 each). $ *Rooms from: $289* ✉ *68900 Frank Sinatra Dr.* ☎ *760/321–8282* ⊕ *www.ritzcarlton.com* ☞ *244 rooms* ⦿ *No meals.*

The Westin Mission Hills Golf Resort & Spa

$$$$ | RESORT | FAMILY | A sprawling resort on 360 acres, the Westin offers a slew of activities for all ages and is surrounded by fairways and putting greens, two family-friendly pools (one lagoon-style with a 75-foot waterslide) and an adults-only pool. **Pros:** gorgeous grounds; first-class golf facilities; daily activity programs for kids and adults. **Cons:** rooms are spread out; some buildings seem dated; far from town. $ *Rooms from: $369* ✉ *71333 Dinah Shore Dr.* ☎ *760/328–5955, 877/253–0041* ⊕ *www.westinmissionhills.com* ☞ *552 rooms* ⦿ *No meals.*

▽ Nightlife

Agua Caliente Casino

CASINOS | This elegant and surprisingly quiet casino contains 1,300 slot machines, 36 table games, an 18-table poker room, a high-limit room, a no-smoking area, and six restaurants. The Show, the resort's concert theater, presents acts such as The Moody Blues, Joe Bonamassa, Toni Braxton, and Sophia Loren, as well as live sporting events. ✉ *32–250 Bob Hope Dr., at E. Ramon Rd.* ☎ *760/321–2000* ⊕ *www. hotwatercasino.com.*

⚡ Activities

GOLF

ANA Inspiration Championship

GOLF | The best female golfers in the world compete in this championship held in late March or early April. ✉ *Mission Hills Country Club* ☎ *760/834–8872* ⊕ *www.anainspiration.com.*

★ **Westin Mission Hills Resort Golf Club**

GOLF | Golfers at the Westin Mission Hills have two courses to choose from, the Pete Dye and the Gary Player Signature. They're both great, with amazing mountain views and wide fairways, but if you've only got time to play one, choose the Dye. The club is a member of the Troon Golf Institute, and has several teaching facilities, including the Westin Mission Hills Resort Golf Academy and the *Golf Digest* Golf School. ■TIP→ **The resort's Best Available Rate program guarantees golfers (with a few conditions) the best Internet rate possible.** ✉ *71333 Dinah Shore Dr.* ☎ *760/328–3198* ⊕ *www.playmissionhills.com* ☞ *Gary Player, from $74; Pete Dye, from $114* ⚑. *Pete Dye Resort: 18 holes, 5525 yards, par 72; Gary Player Signature: 18 holes, 5327 yards, par 70.*

📷 Shopping

MALL

The River at Rancho Mirage

SHOPPING CENTERS/MALLS | This shopping-dining-entertainment complex holds 20 high-end shops, including the SoCal darling Diane's Beachwear, all fronting a faux river with cascading waterfalls. Also here are a 12-screen cinema, an outdoor amphitheater, and many restaurants including Fleming's Prime Steakhouse & Wine Bar and Babe's Bar-B-Que and Brewery. ⊠ 71–800 Hwy. 111, at Bob Hope Dr. ☎ 760/341-2711 ⊕ www.theriveratranchomirage.com.

SPAS

★ The Ritz Carlton Spa, Rancho Mirage

SPA/BEAUTY | Two hundred–plus suspended quartz crystals guard the entrance of the desert's premier spa. With private men's and women's areas, a co-ed outdoor soaking tub, food service, and some of the kindest spa technicians around, guests can expect pampering par excellence. The signature Spirit of the Mountains treatment, which starts with a full-body exfoliation, includes a massage, and ends with a body wrap and a scalp massage with lavender oil, is a blissful experience. The gym, equipped with state-of-the-art machines, is open 24/7. Private trainers are available to guide your workout; wellness classes are also available. ⊠ 68900 Frank Sinatra Dr. ☎ 760/202-6170 ⊕ www.ritzcarlton. com ⌇ Fully equipped gym. Salon. Services: body wraps, body scrubs, facials, mineral baths, specialty massages, outdoor treatments, waxing, wellness classes. $170, 50-min massage; $340, signature package.

The Spa at Mission Hills

SPA/BEAUTY | The emphasis at this spa in a quiet corner of the Westin Mission Hills Resort is on comfort rather than glitz and glamour. Attentive therapists incorporate coconut lemon balm, thyme, lavender, hydrating honey, and other botanicals into their treatments. Yoga and other wellness classes are also available. ⊠ 71333 Dinah Shore Dr. ☎ 760/770-2180 ⊕ www.spaatmissionhills.com ⌇ Steam room. Gym with: machines, cardio, pool. Services: rubs and scrubs, massages, facials, nail services. $160, 50-min massage.

Palm Desert

2 miles southeast of Rancho Mirage.

Palm Desert is a thriving retail and business community with popular restaurants, private and public golf courses, and premium shopping along the main commercial drag, El Paseo. Each October, the Palm Desert Golf Cart Parade launches "the season" with a procession of 80 golf carts decked out as floats buzzing up and down El Paseo. The town's stellar sight to see is the Living Desert complex.

GETTING HERE AND AROUND

Palm Desert stretches from north of Interstate 10 to the hills south of Highway 111. West–east cross streets north to south are Frank Sinatra Drive, Country Club Drive (lined on both sides with gated golfing communities), and Fred Waring Drive. Monterey Avenue marks the western boundary, and Washington Street forms the eastern edge.

TOURS

Art in Public Places

SELF-GUIDED | Several self-guided tours cover the works in Palm Desert's 150-piece Art in Public Places collection. Each tour is walkable or drivable. Maps and information about guided tours (one Saturday each month) are available at the city's visitor center and online. ⊠ Palm Desert Visitor Center, 73510 Fred Waring Dr. ☎ 760/568-1441 ⊕ www.palm-desert.org/arts-entertainment/public-art ⌇ Free.

Sights

★ El Paseo

PEDESTRIAN MALL | West of and parallel to Highway 111, this mile-long Mediterranean-style shopper's paradise is lined with fountains, courtyards, and upscale boutiques. You'll find shoe salons, jewelry stores, children's shops, two dozen restaurants, and nearly as many art galleries. The strip is a pleasant place to stroll, window-shop, people-watch, and exercise your credit cards. **■ TIP→ In winter and spring a free bright-yellow shuttle ferries shoppers from store to store and back to their cars.** ✉ *Between Monterey and Portola Aves.* ☎ *877/735–7273* 🌐 *www.elpaseo.com.*

★ The Living Desert Zoo and Gardens

GARDEN | **FAMILY** | Come eye-to-eye with wolves, coyotes, mountain lions, cheetahs, bighorn sheep, golden eagles, warthogs, and owls at the Living Desert, which showcases the flora and fauna of the world's deserts. Easy to challenging scenic trails traverse desert terrain populated with plants of the Mojave, Colorado, and Sonoran deserts. In recent years the park has expanded its vision to include Australia and Africa. At the 3-acre African WaTuTu village you'll find a traditional marketplace as well as camels, leopards, hyenas, and other African animals. Children can pet African domesticated animals, including Nigerian dwarf goats, in a "petting kraal." Gecko Gulch is a children's playground with crawl-through underground tunnels, climb-on snake sculptures, a carousel, and a Discovery Center that holds ancient Pleistocene animal bones. Elsewhere, a small aviary hosts seasonal bird exhibits, and a cool model train travels through miniatures of historic California towns. **■ TIP→ Time your visit to begin in the early morning to beat the heat and feed the giraffes.** ✉ *47900 Portola Ave., south from Hwy. 111* ☎ *760/346–5694* 🌐 *www.livingdesert.org* 🎫 *$20.*

Palm Springs Art Museum in Palm Desert

MUSEUM | A satellite branch of the Palm Springs Art Museum, this gallery space tucked into a desert garden at the west entrance to El Paseo exhibits cutting-edge works by contemporary sculptors and painters. The on-site restaurant **Cuistot** (☎ *760/340–1000,* 🌐 *www.cuistotrestaurant.com*) is a splendid, if pricey, place to enjoy French cuisine. ✉ *72–567 Hwy. 111* ✣ *At western entrance to El Paseo* ☎ *760/346–5600* 🌐 *www.psmuseum.org/palm-desert* 🎫 *Free* ⏲ *Closed Mon.*

Santa Rosa and San Jacinto Mountains National Monument

NATURE PRESERVE | Administered by the U.S. Bureau of Land Management, this monument protects Peninsula bighorn sheep and other wildlife on 280,000 acres of desert habitat. Stop by the visitor center for an introduction to the site and information about the natural history of the desert. A landscaped garden displays native plants and frames an impressive view. The well-informed staff can recommend hiking trails that show off the beauties of the desert. **■ TIP→ Free guided hikes are offered on Thursday and Saturday.** ✉ *51–500 Hwy. 74* ☎ *760/862–9984* 🌐 *www.blm.gov* 🎫 *Free.*

Restaurants

★ Bouchee Café & Deli

$ | **AMERICAN** | Devotees of this La Quinta favorite come here for farm-to-table Euro-style meals and deli items. Order the salads or gorgeous sandwiches—the salmon salad is to die for—at the counter, then retire to the French-inspired dining area, or the shaded outdoor terrace. **Known for:** premade dinner to go; gourmet wine and cheese shop; locally sourced ingredients. [$] *Average main: $12* ✉ *72–785 Hwy. 111* ✣ *Off Plaza Way near El Paseo* ☎ *442/666–3296* 🌐 *www.boucheecafeanddeli.com* ⏲ *No dinner.*

Pacifica Seafood

$$$$ | SEAFOOD | Choice seafood and rooftop dining draw locals and visitors to this busy restaurant on the second floor of the Gardens of El Paseo. Seafood that shines in dishes such as twin lobster tails, grilled Pacific swordfish, and barbecued sugar-spiced salmon arrives daily from San Diego; the menu also includes chicken, steaks, and meal-size salads. **Known for:** inventive sauces and glazes; craft cocktails and bourbon; lower-price sunset menu from 3 to 5:30. $ *Average main: $38* ⊠ *73505 El Paseo* ☎ *760/674–8666* ⊕ *www.pacificaseafoodrestaurant.com* ☉ *No lunch June–Aug.*

 Hotels

Desert Springs J. W. Marriott Resort and Spa

$$$ | RESORT | FAMILY | With a dramatic U-shape design, this sprawling hotel, which attract business travelers, couples, and families alike, is set on 450 landscaped acres and wraps around the desert's largest private lake. **Pros:** gondola rides on the lake to restaurants; popular lobby bar; wonderful spa. **Cons:** crowded in-season; high resort fee; long walk from lobby to rooms. $ *Rooms from: $249* ⊠ *74–855 Country Club Dr.* ☎ *760/341–2211, 888/538–9459* ⊕ *www.desertspringsresort.com* ⇩ *884 rooms* ⦿ *No meals.*

Hotel Paseo

$$$$ | HOTEL | FAMILY | A half block from El Paseo's main drag, this hip luxury hotel, which opened in 2018 as a new member of Marriott's Autograph Collection, reflects the mid-century modern history and upscale, yet casual lifestyle of the desert. **Pros:** on-site restaurant owned by famed Palm Springs restaurateurs; full-service spa ; walk to El Paseo restaurants, shops, attractions. **Cons:** some rooms on the small side; pool area can seem small and crowded; street parking unless you pay for valet. $ *Rooms from:*

$289 ⊠ *45400 Larkspur La.* ☎ *760/340–9001* ⊕ *www.hotelpaseo.com* ⇩ *149 rooms* ⦿ *No meals.*

🎟 Performing Arts

McCallum Theatre

THEATER | The principal cultural venue in the desert, this theater hosts productions from fall through spring. *The Phantom of the Opera* has played here; Lily Tomlin and Willie Nelson have performed; and Shen Yun dancers have twirled across the stage. ⊠ *73–000 Fred Waring Dr.* ☎ *760/340–2787* ⊕ *www.mccallumtheatre.com.*

🏃 Activities

BALLOONING
Fantasy Balloon Flights

BALLOONING | Sunrise excursions over the southern end of the Coachella Valley lift off at 6 am and take from 60 to 90 minutes; a traditional champagne toast follows the landing. Afternoon excursions are timed to touch down at sunset. ⊠ *Palm Desert* ☎ *760/568–0997* ⊕ *www.fantasyballoonflight.com* ⧟ *$195.*

GOLF
Desert Willow Golf Resort

GOLF | Praised for its environmentally smart design, this public golf resort planted water-thrifty turf grasses and doesn't use pesticides. The Mountain View course has four configurations; Firecliff is tournament quality with five configurations. A public facility, Desert Willow is one of the country's top-rated golf courses. ⊠ *38–995 Desert Willow Dr., off Country Club Dr.* ☎ *760/346–0015* ⊕ *www.desertwillow.com* ⧟ *Mountain View from $120, Firecliff from $120* ⚐ *Mountain View: 18 holes, 7079 yards, par 72; Firecliff: 18 holes, 7056 yards, par 72.*

Indian Wells

5 miles east of Palm Desert.

For the most part a quiet and exclusive residential enclave, Indian Wells hosts major golf and tennis tournaments throughout the year, including the BNP Paribus Open tennis tournament. Three hotels share access to championship golf and tennis facilities, and there are several noteworthy resort spas and restaurants.

GETTING HERE AND AROUND

Indian Wells lies between Palm Desert and La Quinta, with most resorts, restaurants, and shopping set back from Highway 111.

Restaurants

Vue Grille and Bar at the Indian Wells Golf Resort

$$$$ | AMERICAN | This not-so-private restaurant at the Indian Wells Golf Resort offers a glimpse of how the country-club set lives. The service is impeccable, and the outdoor tables provide views of mountain peaks that seem close enough to touch. **Known for:** farm-to-table cuisine; grilled steaks and seafood; flatbreads and burgers. $ *Average main: $36* ⊠ *44–500 Indian Wells La.* ☎ *760/834–3800* ⊕ *www.vuegrilleandbar.com.*

Hotels

★ Hyatt Grand Regency Indian Wells Resort & Spa

$$$$ | RESORT | FAMILY | This stark-white resort adjacent to the Golf Resort at Indian Wells is one of the grandest in the desert, with seven pools (one with a waterslide and one adults-only), an outdoor game area and a kids club, and a spa. **Pros:** excellent business services; butler service in some rooms; very pet friendly. **Cons:** big and impersonal; spread out over 45 acres; noisy public areas. $ *Rooms from: $370* ⊠ *44–600 Indian Wells La.* ☎ *760/776–1234* ⊕ *indianwells.regency.hyatt.com* ⤳ *520 rooms* ⦿ *No meals.*

Miramonte Resort & Spa

$$$$ | RESORT | Guest rooms at the most intimate of the Indian Wells hotels are in red-roof villas on 11 acres of bougainvillea-filled gardens against a backdrop of the Santa Rosa Mountains. **Pros:** three swimming pools (one adults only); on-site farm-to-fork restaurant and lounge; one of the desert's best spas. **Cons:** extra resort fee; limited resort facilities on-site; long walk to lobby from some rooms. $ *Rooms from: $279* ⊠ *45000 Indian Wells La.* ☎ *760/341–2200* ⊕ *www.miramonteresort.com* ⤳ *215 rooms* ⦿ *No meals.*

Renaissance Indian Wells Resort and Spa

$$$$ | RESORT | FAMILY | The centerpiece of this luxurious resort, adjacent to the Golf Resort at Indian Wells, is an eight-story atrium lobby, onto which most rooms open. **Pros:** adjacent to golf-tennis complex; kids club; bicycles available. **Cons:** higher noise level in rooms surrounding pool; somewhat impersonal ambience. $ *Rooms from: $289* ⊠ *44–400 Indian Wells La.* ☎ *760/773–4444* ⊕ *www.renaissancehotels.com* ⤳ *560 rooms* ⦿ *No meals.*

Activities

GOLF
★ Indian Wells Golf Resort

GOLF | Adjacent to the Hyatt Regency Indian Wells, this complex includes the Celebrity Course, designed by Clive Clark and twice a host to the PGA's Skins game (lots of water here, including streams, lakes, and waterfalls), and the Players Course, designed by John Fought to incorporate views of the surrounding mountain ranges. Both courses consistently rank among the best public courses in California. ■ TIP→ **It's a good idea to book tee times well in advance,** up to 60 days. ⊠ 44–500 Indian Wells La. ☎ 760/346–4653 ⊕ www.indianwells-golfresort.com ⯆ Both courses from $69 🏌. Celebrity Course: 18 holes, 7050 yards, par 72; Players Course: 18 holes, 7376 yards, par 72.

TENNIS

BNP Paribas Open
TENNIS | Drawing 200 of the world's top players, this tennis tournament takes place at Indian Wells Tennis Garden for two weeks in March. Various ticket plans are available, with some packages including stays at the adjoining Hyatt Regency Indian Wells or Renaissance resorts. ⊠ 78200 Miles Ave. ☎ 800/999–1585 ⊕ www.bnpparibasopen.com.

🛍 Shopping

★ The Well Spa
SPA/BEAUTY | A luxurious 12,000-square-foot facility, The Well draws on international treatments and ingredients to indulge the senses and relax the body. Treatments such as hot stone, Himalayan salt, and full-body massages and table yoga are well worth the splurge. Sugar or salt exfoliating scrubs may well restore the soul in addition to the skin. ⊠ Miramonte Resort, 45–000 Indian Wells La. ☎ 866/843–9355 ⊕ www.miramonteresort.com ☞ Services: facials, nail care, solo and couple's massages, scrubs, and other body therapies. $165, 60-min massage.

La Quinta

4 miles south of Indian Wells.

The desert became a Hollywood hideout in the 1920s, when La Quinta Hotel (now La Quinta Resort and Club) opened, introducing the Coachella Valley's first golf course. Old Town La Quinta is a popular attraction; the area holds dining spots, shops, and galleries.

GETTING HERE AND AROUND
Most of La Quinta lies south of Highway 111. The main drag through town is Washington Street.

🍴 Restaurants

Arnold Palmer's
$$$$ | AMERICAN | From the photos on the walls to the trophy-filled display cases, Arnie's essence infuses this restaurant. Families gather in the spacious restaurant for birthdays and Sunday dinners, and the service is always attentive. **Known for:** homemade meat loaf, double-cut pork chops, mac and cheese; top-notch wine list; entertainment most nights. $ Average main: $34 ⊠ 78164 Ave. 52, near Desert Club Dr. ☎ 760/771–4653 ⊕ www.arnoldpalmers-restaurant.com.

★ Lavender Bistro
$$$$ | BISTRO | This romantic bistro with a spacious outdoor atrium decked out with flowers, fountains, and twinkling lights makes diners feel like they've been transported to southern France. Choices on the large menu include steamed mussels, a honey-brine pork chop, and lobster ravioli; for dessert you can't go wrong with the baked apple tart or the banana walnut brioche bread pudding. **Known for:** live music on the patio and in the fireside lounge; organic ingredients; extensive locavore menu. $ Average main: $34 ⊠ 78073 Calle Barcelona ☎ 760/564–5353 ⊕ www.lavenderbistro. com ⯆ Closed June–Sept.

🏨 Hotels

La Quinta Resort and Club
$$$$ | RESORT | FAMILY | Opened in 1926 and now a member of the Waldorf-Astoria Collection, the desert's oldest resort is a lush green oasis with 23 tennis courts and 41 pools set on 45 acres. **Pros:** individual swimming pools in some rooms; gorgeous gardens; pet and family friendly. **Cons:** a party atmosphere

sometimes prevails; spotty housekeeping/maintenance; swimming pools can be crowded. $ *Rooms from: $329* ✉ *49499 Eisenhower Dr.* ☎ *760/564–4111* 🌐 *www.laquintaresort.com* 🛏 *586 rooms, 210 villas* 🍴 *No meals.*

Performing Arts

La Quinta Arts Festival

FESTIVALS | More than 200 artists participate each March in a four-day juried show that's considered one of the best in the West. The event, held at La Quinta Civic Center, includes sculptures, paintings, watercolors, fiber art, and ceramics. ✉ *78495 Calle Tampico* ☎ *760/564–1244* 🌐 *www.lqaf.com* 🎟 *From $17.*

Shopping

SPAS

Spa La Quinta

SPA/BEAUTY | The gorgeous Spa La Quinta may be the grandest spa in the entire desert. At this huge stand-alone facility you'll find everything from massages to facials to salon services and classes, plus a beautiful garden setting with a large fountain, flowers galore, plenty of nooks where you can hide out and enjoy the sanctuary, and a Jacuzzi with a waterfall. ✉ *49499 Eisenhower Dr.* ☎ *760/777–4800* 🌐 *www.laquintaresort.com* ☞ *Fitness center with cardio. Services: aromatherapy, body wraps and scrubs, massage, skin care, salon services, water therapies. $170, 50-min massage; $195, 30-min HydraFacial.*

Activities

GOLF

★ PGA West

GOLF | A world-class golf destination where Phil Mickelson and Jack Nicklaus play, this facility includes five resort courses and four private ones. Courses meander through indigenous desert landscapes, water features, and bunkers. The Norman, Nick Tournament, and TPC Stadium courses are "shot-makers" courses made for pros. TPC highlights include its two lakes, "San Andreas Fault" bunker, and island green called "Alcatraz." The Norman course has tight fairways and small greens. ✉ *49–499 Eisenhower Dr.* ☎ *760/564–5729 for tee times* 🌐 *www.pgawest.com* 🎟 *Mountain Course, from $159; Dunes, from $119; Greg Norman, from $159; TPC Stadium, from $189; Jack Nicklaus Tournament, from $159* ⛳ *Mountain Course: 18 holes, 6732 yards, par 72; Dunes: 18 holes, 6712 yards, par 72; Greg Norman: 18 holes, 7156 yards, par 72; TPC Stadium: 18 holes, 7300 yards, par 72; Jack Nicklaus Tournament: 18 holes, 7204 yards, par 72.*

Indio

5 miles east of Indian Wells.

Indio is the home of the renowned date shake: an extremely thick and sweet milk shake made with dates. The city and surrounding countryside generate 95% of the dates grown and harvested in the United States. If you take a hot-air balloon ride, you will likely drift over the tops of date palm trees.

GETTING HERE AND AROUND

Indio is east of Indian Wells and north of La Quinta. Highway 111 runs right through Indio, and Interstate 10 skirts it to the north.

Sights

National Date Festival and Riverside County Fair

FESTIVAL | **FAMILY** | Indio celebrates its raison d'être each February at its date festival and county fair. The mid-month festivities include an Arabian Nights pageant, camel and ostrich races, and exhibits of local dates, plus monster truck shows, a demolition derby, a nightly musical pageant, and a rodeo. ✉ *Riverside County Fairgrounds, 82–503 Hwy. 111* ☎ *800/811–3247, 760/863–8247* 🌐 *www.datefest.org* 🎫 *$11, parking $10.*

Shields Date Garden and Café
STORE/MALL | Sample, select, and take home some of Shields's locally grown dates. Ten varieties are available, including the giant supersweet royal medjools, along with specialty date products such as date crystals, stuffed dates, confections, and local honey. At the Shields Date Garden Café you can try an iconic date shake, dig into date pancakes, or go exotic with a date tamale. Breakfast and lunch are served daily. ✉ *80–225 Hwy. 111* ☎ *760/347–0996* 🌐 *www.shieldsdate-garden.com* ⏲ *No dinner.*

Restaurants

Ciro's Ristorante and Pizzeria
$$ | SICILIAN | Serving pizza and pasta since the 1960s, this popular casual restaurant has a few unusual pies on the menu, including cashew with three cheeses. The decor is classic pizza joint, with checkered tablecloths and bentwood chairs. **Known for:** daily pasta specials; classic Italian dishes; house-made, hand-tossed pizza dough. *$ Average main: $16* ✉ *81–963 Hwy. 111* ☎ *760/347–6503* 🌐 *www.cirosofindio.com* ⏲ *No lunch weekends.*

Jackalope Ranch
$$$ | AMERICAN | It's worth the drive to Indio to sample flavors of the Old West, 21st-century style. Inside a rambling 21,000-foot building, holding a clutch of indoor/outdoor dining spaces, you may be seated near an open kitchen, a bar, fountains, fireplaces, or waterworks. **Known for:** Western-style barbecue, spicy and savory sauces, and sumptuous desserts; casual, down-home locals hangout; lively vibe. *$ Average main: $30* ✉ *80–400 Hwy. 111* ☎ *760/342–1999* 🌐 *www.thejackaloperanch.com.*

Performing Arts

MUSIC FESTIVALS

★ Coachella Valley Music and Arts Festival
FESTIVALS | Among Southern California's biggest parties, the festival draws hundreds of thousands of rock music fans to Indio each April for two weekends of live concerts. Headliners include acts such as Lady Gaga, Childish Gambino, Ariana Grande, Tame Impala, Kendrick Lamar, Jack Johnson, and Radiohead. Many attendees camp on-site, but to give your ears a rest post-concert you might want to stay at a nearby hotel. **■ TIP→ The festival sells out before the lineup is announced, so expect to pay big bucks if you haven't purchased tickets by late fall.** ✉ *Empire Polo Club, 81–800 Ave. 51* 🌐 *www.coachella.com.*

Coachella Valley Preserve
NATURE PRESERVE | FAMILY | For a glimpse of how the desert appeared before development, head northeast from Palm Springs to this preserve. It has a system of sand dunes and several palm oases that were formed because the San Andreas Fault lines here allow water flowing underground to rise to the surface. A mile-long walk along Thousand Palms Oasis reveals pools supporting the tiny endangered desert pupfish and more than 183 bird species. Families like the relatively flat trail that is mostly shaded. The preserve has a visitor center, nature and equestrian trails, restrooms, and picnic facilities. Guided hikes are offered October–March. **■ TIP→ Be aware that it's exceptionally hot in summer here.** ✉ *29200 Thousand Palms Canyon Rd., Thousand Palms* ☎ *760/343–2733* 🌐 *www.coachellavalleypreserve.org* 🎫 *Free* ⏲ *Visitor center closed May–Sept. Parking lot and hiking closed Aug.*

Desert Hot Springs

9 miles north of Palm Springs.

Desert Hot Springs's famous hot mineral waters, thought by some to have curative powers, bubble up at temperatures of 90°F to 148°F and flow into the wells of more than 40 hotel spas.

GETTING HERE AND AROUND

Desert Hot Springs lies due north of Palm Springs. Take Gene Autry Trail north to Interstate 10, where the street name changes to Palm. Continue north to Pierson Boulevard, the town's center.

Sights

Cabot's Pueblo Museum

MUSEUM | Cabot Yerxa, the man who found the spring that made Desert Hot Springs famous, built a quirky four-story, 35-room pueblo between 1939 and his death in 1965. Now a museum run by the city of Desert Hot Springs, the Hopi-inspired adobe structure is filled with memorabilia of his time as a homesteader; his encounters with Hollywood celebrities at the nearby Bar-H Ranch; his expedition to the Alaskan gold rush; and many other events. The home, much of it crafted out of materials Yerxa recycled from the desert, can only be seen on hour-long tours. Outside, walk the grounds to a lookout with amazing desert views. ✉ *67–616 E. Desert View Ave., at Eliseo Rd.* ☎ *760/329–7610* 🌐 *www.cabotsmuseum.org* 🎟 *$13* 🕒 *Closed Mon. Oct.–May, closed Mon. and Tues. June–Sept.* ☞ *Tours 9:30, 10:30, 11:30, 1:30, 2:30 Oct.–May, and 9:30, 10:30, 11:30 June–Sept. Tours limited to 12 people.*

Hotels

The Spring

$$$ | **HOTEL** | Designed for those who want to detox, lose weight, or chill out in the mineral pools, The Spring delivers quiet and personal service atop a Desert Hot Springs hill. **Pros:** access to mineral pools 24 hours a day; complimentary continental breakfast; spa and lodging packages available. **Cons:** rooms lack character; no TVs or phones; not much poolside privacy. [$] *Rooms from: $239* ✉ *12699 Reposo Way* ☎ *760/251–6700* 🌐 *www.the-spring.com* 🛏 *12 rooms* 🍴 *Breakfast.*

Two Bunch Palms

$$$ | **RESORT** | This adults-only hotel on a gorgeous 72-acre property with stunning views of Mt. San Jacinto provides a luxurious and relaxing experience with full-service access to natural hot springs. **Pros:** on-site restaurant serves breakfast, lunch, and dinner; fresh juice bar open all day; full-service spa, popular since the 1940s. **Cons:** some rooms have no TV; no pets allowed; minimum age 18. [$] *Rooms from: $245* ✉ *67425 Two Bunch Palms Trail* ☎ *760/676–5000* 🌐 *twobunchpalms.com* 🛏 *68 rooms* 🍴 *No meals.*

Yucca Valley

30 miles northeast of Palm Springs.

One of the high desert's fastest-growing cities, Yucca Valley is emerging as a bedroom community for people who work as far away as Ontario, 85 miles to the west. In this suburb you can shop for necessities, get your car serviced, grab coffee or purchase vintage furnishings, and chow down at fast-food outlets. Just up Pioneertown Road you'll find the most-talked-about dining establishment in the desert, Pappy & Harriet's, the famed performance venue that hosts big-name talent.

GETTING HERE AND AROUND

The drive to Yucca Valley on Highway 62/Twentynine Palms Highway passes through the Painted Hills and drops down into a valley. Take Pioneertown Road north to the Old West outpost.

Sights

Hi-Desert Nature Museum

MUSEUM | **FAMILY** | Natural and cultural history of the Morongo Basis and High Desert are the focus here. A small live-animal display includes scorpions, snakes, lizards, and small mammals. You'll also find gems and minerals, fossils from the Paleozoic era, taxidermy, and Native American artifacts. There's also a children's area and art exhibits. ✉ *Yucca Valley Community Center, 57090 Twentynine Palms Hwy.* ☎ *760/369–7212* 🌐 *hidesertnaturemuseum.org* 🎟 *Free* 🕓 *Closed Sun.–Tues.*

Pioneertown

TOWN | In 1946 Roy Rogers, Gene Autry, the Sons of the Pioneers (the music group for whom the town is named), and Russ Hayden built Pioneertown, an 1880s-style Wild West movie set complete with hitching posts, saloon, and an OK Corral. You can stroll past wooden and adobe storefronts and feel like you're back in the Old West. Pappy & Harriet's Pioneertown Palace, now the town's top draw, has evolved into a hip venue for indie and mainstream performers such as Dengue Fever, Neko Case, and Robert Plant. ✉ *53688 Pioneertown Rd., Pioneertown* ✣ *4 miles north of Yucca Valley* 🌐 *pappyandharriets.com.*

Restaurants

★ Pappy & Harriet's Pioneertown Palace

$$$ | **AMERICAN** | **FAMILY** | Smack in the middle of what looks like the set of a Western is this cozy saloon where you can have dinner, relax over a drink at the bar, and catch some great indie bands or legendary artists—Leon Russell, Lorde, Paul McCartney, and Robert Plant have all played here. Pappy & Harriet's may be in the middle of nowhere, but you'll need reservations for dinner on weekends. **Known for:** live music several days/nights a week; Tex-Mex, Santa Maria–style barbecue; fun and lively atmosphere. [$] *Average main: $25* ✉ *53688 Pioneertown Rd., Pioneertown* ☎ *760/365–5956* 🌐 *www.pappyandharriets.com* 🕓 *Closed Tues. and Wed.*

Hotels

Best Western Joshua Tree Hotel & Suites

$$ | **HOTEL** | **FAMILY** | This hotel has spacious, nicely appointed rooms decorated in soft desert colors. **Pros:** convenient to Joshua Tree National Park; pleasant lounge; pool and hot tub. **Cons:** on a busy highway; limited service; some rooms need updating. [$] *Rooms from: $130* ✉ *56525 Twentynine Palms Hwy.* ☎ *760/365–3555* 🌐 *www.bestwestern.com* 🛏 *95 rooms* 🍴 *Breakfast.*

Rimrock Ranch Cabins

$$ | **RENTAL** | The quiet beauty of the surrounding desert attracts Hollywood writers, artists, and musicians to circa-1940s housekeeping cabins, an Airstream trailer, the Hatch House duplex, and lodge rooms. **Pros:** quiet desert hideaway; outdoor fireplaces and fully equipped kitchens; rich music heritage on site. **Cons:** rustic cabins will not appeal to resort seekers; far from most services; some rooms are sparsely furnished. [$] *Rooms from: $120* ✉ *53688 Pioneertown Rd., Pioneertown* ☎ *760/228–0130* 🌐 *www.rimrockranchpioneertown.com* 🛏 *7 rental units* 🍴 *No meals.*

Borrego Springs

59 miles south of Indio.

The permanent population of Borrego Springs, set squarely in the middle of Anza-Borrego Desert State Park, hovers around 2,500. From September through June, when temperatures stay in the '80s and '90s, you can engage in outdoor activities such as hiking, nature study, golfing, tennis, horseback riding, and mountain biking. If winter rains cooperate, Borrego Springs puts on some of the best wildflower displays in the low desert. In some years the desert floor is carpeted with color: yellow dandelions and sunflowers, pink primrose, purple sand verbena, and blue wild heliotrope. The bloom generally lasts from late February through April. For current information on wildflowers around Borrego Springs, call Anza-Borrego Desert State Park's wildflower hotline (☎ 760/767–4684).

GETTING HERE AND AROUND

You can access Anza Borrego by taking the Highway 86 exit from Interstate 10, south of Indio. Highway 86 passes through Coachella and along the western shore of the Salton Sea. Turn west on Highway S22 at Salton City and follow it to Peg Leg Road, where you turn south until you reach Palm Canyon Drive. Turn west and the road leads to the center of Borrego Springs, Christmas Circle, where most major roads come together. Well-marked roads radiating from the circle will take you to the most popular sites in the state park. If coming from the San Diego area, drive east on Interstate 8 to the Cuyamaca Mountains, exit at Highway 79, and enjoy the lovely 23-mile drive through the mountains until you reach Julian; head east on Highway 78 and follow signs to Borrego Springs.

ESSENTIALS

VISITOR INFORMATION Borrego Springs Chamber of Commerce & Visitors Bureau. ✉ 786 Palm Canyon Dr. ☎ 760/767–5555, 800/559–5524 ⊕ www.borregosprings-chamber.com.

◉ Sights

★ Anza-Borrego Desert State Park

NATIONAL/STATE PARK | One of the richest living natural-history museums in the nation, this state park is a vast, nearly uninhabited wilderness where you can step through a field of wildflowers, cool off in a palm-shaded oasis, count

zillions of stars in the black night sky, and listen to coyotes howl at dusk. The landscape, largely undisturbed by humans, reveals a rich natural history. There's evidence of a vast inland sea in the piles of oyster beds near Split Mountain and of the power of natural forces such as earthquakes and flash floods. In addition, recent scientific work has confirmed that the Borrego Badlands, with more than 6,000 meters of exposed fossil-bearing sediments, is likely the richest such deposit in North America, telling the story of 7 million years of climate change, upheaval, and prehistoric animals. Evidence has been unearthed of saber-toothed cats, flamingos, zebras, and the largest flying bird in the northern hemisphere beneath the now-parched sand. Today the desert's most treasured inhabitants are the herds of elusive and endangered native bighorn sheep, or borrego, for which the park is named. Among the strange desert plants you may observe are the gnarly elephant trees. As these are endangered, rangers don't encourage visitors to seek out the secluded grove at Fish Creek, but there are a few examples at the visitor center garden. After a wet winter you can see a short-lived but stunning display of cacti, succulents, and desert wildflowers in bloom.

The park is unusually accessible to visitors. Admission to the park is free, and few areas are off-limits. There are two developed campgrounds, but you can camp anywhere; just follow the trails and pitch a tent wherever you like. There are more than 500 miles of dirt roads, two huge wilderness areas, and 110 miles of riding and hiking trails. Many sites can be seen from paved roads, but some require driving on dirt roads, for which rangers recommend you use a four-wheel-drive vehicle. When you do leave the pavement, carry the appropriate supplies: a cell phone (which may be unreliable in some areas), a shovel and other tools, flares, blankets, and plenty of water. The canyons are susceptible to flash flooding, so inquire about weather conditions (even on sunny days) before entering. ■TIP➔ Borrego resorts, restaurants, and the state park have Wi-Fi, but the service is spotty at best. If you need to talk to someone in the area, it's best to find a phone with a landline.

The sites and hikes listed below are arranged by region of the park and distance from the visitor center: in the valley and hills surrounding Borrego Springs, near Tamarisk Campground, along Highway S2, south of Scissors Crossing, and south of Ocotillo Wells.

Stop by the visitor center to get oriented, to pick up a park map, and to learn about weather, road, and wildlife conditions. Designed to keep cool during the desert's blazing-hot summers, the center is built underground, beneath a demonstration desert garden containing examples of most of the native flora and a little pupfish pond. Displays inside the center illustrate the natural history of the area. Picnic tables are scattered throughout, making this a good place to linger and enjoy the view.

A 1½-mile trail leads to Borrego Palm Canyon, one of the few native palm groves in North America. The canyon, about 1 mile west of the visitor center, holds a grove of more than 1,000 native fan palms, a stream, and a waterfall. Wildlife is abundant along this route. This moderate hike is the most popular in the park.

With a year-round stream and lush plant life, Coyote Canyon, approximately 4½ miles north of Borrego Springs, is one of the best places to see and photograph spring wildflowers. Portions of the canyon road follow a section of the old Anza Trail. This area is closed between June 15 and September 15 to allow native bighorn sheep undisturbed use of the water. The dirt road that gives access to the canyon may be sandy enough to require a four-wheel-drive vehicle.

The late-afternoon vista of the Borrego badlands from Font's Point, 13 miles east of Borrego Springs, is one of the most breathtaking views in the desert, especially when the setting sun casts a golden glow in high relief on the eroded mountain slopes. The road from the Font's Point turnoff can be rough enough to make using a four-wheel-drive vehicle advisable; inquire about road conditions at the visitor center before starting out. Even if you can't make it out on the paved road, you can see some of the view from the highway.

East of Tamarisk Grove campground (13 miles south of Borrego Springs), the Narrows Earth Trail is a short walk off the road. Along the way you can see evidence of the many geologic processes involved in forming the canyons of the desert, such as a contact zone between two earthquake faults, and sedimentary layers of metamorphic and igneous rock.

The 1.6-mile round-trip Yaqui Well Nature Trail takes you along a path to a desert water hole where birds and wildlife are abundant. It's also a good place to look for wildflowers in spring. At the trailhead across from Tamarisk Campground you can pick up a brochure describing what can be seen along the trail.

Traversing a boulder-strewn trail is the easy, mostly flat Pictograph/Smuggler's Canyon Trail. At the end is a collection of rocks covered with muted red and yellow pictographs painted within the last hundred years or so by Native Americans. Walk about ½ mile beyond the pictures to reach Smuggler's Canyon, where an overlook provides views of the Vallecito Valley. The hike, from 2 to 3 miles round-trip, begins in Blair Valley, 6 miles southeast of Highway 78, off Highway S2, at the Scissors Crossing intersection.

Just a few steps off the paved road, **Carrizo Badlands Overlook** offers a view of eroded and twisted sedimentary rock that obscures the fossils of the mastodons, saber-tooths, zebras, and camels that roamed this region a million years ago. The route to the overlook through Earthquake Valley and Blair Valley parallels the Southern Emigrant Trail. It's off Highway S2, 40 miles south of Scissors Crossing.

Geology students from all over the world visit the Fish Creek area of Anza-Borrego to explore the canyon through Split Mountain. The narrow gorge with 600-foot walls was formed by an ancient stream. Fossils in this area indicate that a sea once covered the desert floor. From Highway 78 at Ocotillo Wells, take Split Mountain Road south 9 miles. ✉ *Visitor Center, 200 Palm Canyon Dr., Hwy. S22* ☎ *760/767–4205, 760/767–4684 wildflower hotline* 🌐 *www.parks.ca.gov* 🎟 *Free; day-use parking in campground areas $10* ☞ *Make a campground reservation at: reservecalifornia.com.*

★ Galleta Meadows

PUBLIC ART | FAMILY | At Galleta Meadows, camels, llamas, saber-toothed tigers, tortoises, and monumental gomphotherium (a sort of ancient elephant) appear to roam the earth again. These life-size bronze figures are of prehistoric animals whose fossils can be found in the Borrego Badlands. The collection of more than 130 sculptures created by Ricardo Breceda was commissioned by the late Dennis Avery, who installed the works of art on property he owned for the entertainment of locals and visitors. Maps are available from Borrego Springs Chamber of Commerce. ✉ *Borrego Springs Rd., from Christmas Circle to Henderson Canyon* ☎ *760/767–5555* 🎟 *Free.*

🍴 Restaurants

The Arches

$$$ | MODERN AMERICAN | On the edge of the Borrego Springs Resort, Golf Club & Spa's golf course, set beneath a canopy of grapefruit trees, The Arches is a pleasant place to eat. For breakfast you'll find burritos alongside French toast, omelets, and eggs Benedict; or for lunch (best enjoyed on the patio) or dinner, the options include sandwiches, salads, and hearty pasta, seafood, grilled meats, and fish entrées. **Known for:** light fare; nightly specials; popular happy hour. [$] *Average main: $24* ✉ *1112 Tilting T Dr.* ☎ *760/767–5700* 🌐 *www.borregospringsresort.com/dining.asp* 🕒 *Summer hrs vary; call ahead.*

Carlee's Place

$$$ | AMERICAN | Sooner or later most visitors to Borrego Springs wind up at Carlee's Place for a drink and a bite to eat, drawn by the extra-large menu with everything from burgers, salads, seafood, sandwiches, and prime rib. It's an all-American type of establishment, where your server might call you "honey" while setting a huge steak in front of you, and diners play pool and dance to jukebox music. **Known for:** all-American down-home setting; martinis and classic cocktails; everything made from scratch. [$] *Average main: $25* ✉ *660 Palm Canyon Dr.* ☎ *760/767–3262* 🌐 *www.carleesplace.com.*

Carmelita's Mexican Grill and Cantina

$ | MEXICAN | A friendly, family-run eatery tucked into a back corner of what is called "The Mall," Carmelita's draws locals and visitors all day, whether it's for a hearty breakfast, a cooked-to-order enchilada or burrito, or to tip back a brew or margarita at the bar. The menu lists typical combination plates (enchiladas, burritos, tamales, and tacos). **Known for:** dog-friendly outdoor patio; house-made masa dough and salsas;

full bar with sports TVs. $ *Average main: $15* ✉ *575 Palm Canyon Dr.* ☎ *760/767–5666.*

Coyote Steakhouse

$$$ | **MODERN AMERICAN** | The upscale Coyote Steakhouse at the Palms at Indian Head hotel caters to those who want a fancy dinner, particularly hunks of filet mignon or rack of lamb served at candlelit tables with white tablecloths overlooking the pool. Pet owners will appreciate the canine menu, whose treats include house-made peanut-butter dog cookies. **Known for:** romantic candlelit dining room; pork tenderloin and prime rib; classic mid-century setting. $ *Average main: $30* ✉ *2220 Hoberg Rd.* ☎ *760/767–7788* ⊕ *www. thepalmsatindianhead.com* ⊗ *No breakfast or lunch.*

Los Jilberto's Taco Shop

$ | **MEXICAN** | A casual local favorite for affordable Mexican dishes, Jilberto's serves up big burritos and meaty enchiladas. **Known for:** authentic Mexican dishes cooked to order; all-day breakfast menu; reasonable prices. $ *Average main: $10* ✉ *655 Palm Canyon Dr.* ☎ *760/767–1008* ⊕ *www.losjilbertostacoshop.com* ▭ *No credit cards.*

🛏 Hotels

Borrego Springs Resort, Golf Club & Spa

$$$ | **RESORT** | The large rooms at this quiet resort set around a swimming pool and with golf, tennis, and golf options come with either a shaded balcony or a patio with desert views. **Pros:** golf, tennis, and bikes available; good desert views from most rooms; close to sculpture gardens. **Cons:** rooms slightly dated; average service; breakfast not included. $ *Rooms from: $182* ✉ *1112 Tilting T Dr.* ☎ *760/767–5700, 888/826–7734* ⊕ *www.borregospringsresort.com* ⇴ *100 rooms* 🍴 *No meals.*

★ Borrego Valley Inn

$$$$ | **B&B/INN** | Those looking for desert landscapes and some stargazing—guests must be 21 or older—may enjoy the adobe Southwestern-style buildings here that house spacious rooms, which boasts plenty of natural light, original art, pine beds, and corner fireplaces. **Pros:** swim under the stars in the clothing-optional pool; exquisite desert gardens; breakfast included. **Cons:** no kids and no pets; rooms could use sprucing up; service inconsistent. $ *Rooms from: $285* ✉ *405 Palm Canyon Dr.* ☎ *760/767–0311, 800/333–5810* ⊕ *www.borregovalleyinn. com* ⇴ *15 rooms* 🍴 *Free Breakfast.*

★ La Casa Del Zorro

$$$ | **RESORT** | **FAMILY** | The draws at this desert hideaway a short drive from Anza Borrego State Park include three guest-only pools, a hot tub, five night-lit tennis courts and two pickle ball courts, a yoga studio, a spa, a restaurant, and the lively Fox Den Bar. The 42-acre property pays tribute to its surroundings with a cactus garden, a fire pit, and two tall, welded-metal animal sculptures by local artist Ricardo Breceda. **Pros:** private pool or hot tub in many casitas; 26 pools and 14 water features; on-site spa, bar, and restaurant. **Cons:** service can be spotty; casitas need updating; occasional strong desert winds sweep sand across the property. $ *Rooms from: $189* ✉ *3845 Yaqui Pass Rd.* ☎ *760/767–0100* ⊕ *www. lacasadelzorro.com* ⇴ *44 rooms, 19 casitas* 🍴 *No meals.*

🏃 Activities

GOLF

Borrego Springs Resort, Golf Club & Spa
GOLF | The two 9-hole courses here, Mesquite and Desert Willow, are generally played as an 18-hole round by most golfers, starting with Mesquite. Both courses have natural desert landscaping and mature date palms. ✉ *1112 Tilting T Dr.* ☎ *760/767–3330* ⊕ *www.*

borregospringsresort.com ✉ *From $45* ⛳ *18 holes, 6760 yards, par 71* ↻ *Closed June–Sept.*

Roadrunner Golf and Country Club
GOLF | Adjacent to the Springs at Borrego course and with some shared facilities, this club has an 18-hole par-3 golf course. Though the course has views of the Santa Rosa, San Ysidro, and Vallecito mountains and Indian Head Mountain, the terrain is relatively flat. Another bonus: there's rarely a wait for a tee time. ✉ *1010 Palm Canyon Dr.* ☎ *760/767–5374* ⊕ *www. roadrunnerclub.com* ✉ *$40* ⛳ *18 holes, 2445 yards, par 3.*

🛍 Shopping

Anza-Borrego State Park Store
SPECIALTY STORES | The Anza-Borrego Foundation, a land conservation group, runs this store that sells guidebooks, maps, clothing, desert art, and gifts for kids. Its enthusiastic staffers also assist with trip planning. Foundation guides organize hikes, naturalist talks, classes, research programs, and nature walks. ✉ *587 Palm Canyon Dr., No. 110* ☎ *760/767–0446* ⊕ *www.theabf.org* ⊗ *Closed weekends June–Sept., and Wed. and Thurs. Oct.–May.*

Borrego Outfitters
CONVENIENCE/GENERAL STORES | This contemporary general store stocks high-end outdoor gear, hiking essentials, personal care items from Burt's Bees, footwear from Teva and Thymes, swimsuits, and tabletop items. You can browse through racks of clothing and piles of hats, all suited to the desert climate. ✉ *579 Palm Canyon Dr.* ☎ *760/767–3502* ⊕ *www.borregooutfitters.com.*

Salton Sea

30 miles southeast of Indio, 29 miles east of Borrego Springs.

The Salton Sea, one of the largest inland seas on Earth, is the product of both natural and artificial forces. The sea occupies the Salton Basin, a remnant of prehistoric Lake Cahuilla. Over the centuries the Colorado River flooded the basin and the water drained into the Gulf of California. In 1905 a flood once again filled the Salton Basin, but the exit to the gulf was blocked by sediment. The floodwaters remained in the basin, creating a saline lake 228 feet below sea level, about 35 miles long and 15 miles wide, with a surface area of nearly 380 square miles. The sea, which lies along the Pacific Flyway, supports 400 species of birds. Fishing for tilapia, boating, camping, and bird-watching are popular activities year-round.

GETTING HERE AND AROUND
Salton Sea State Recreation Area includes about 14 miles of coastline on the northeastern shore of the sea, about 30 miles south of Indio via Highway 111. The Sonny Bono Salton Sea National Wildlife Refuge fills the southernmost tip of the sea's shore. To reach it from the recreation area, continue south about 60 miles to Niland; continue south to Sinclair Road, and turn west following the road to the Refuge Headquarters.

👁 Sights

Salton Sea State Recreation Area
NATIONAL/STATE PARK | FAMILY | This huge recreation area on the sea's north shore draws thousands each year to its playgrounds, hiking trails, fishing spots, and boat launches. Ranger-guided bird walks take place on Saturday; you'll see migrating and native birds including Canada geese, pelicans, and shorebirds. ✉ *100–225 State Park Rd., North Shore* ☎ *760/393–3059, 760/393–3810 visitor center* ⊕ *www.parks.ca.gov* ✉ *$7.*

Sonny Bono Salton Sea National Wildlife Refuge

NATURE PRESERVE | The 2,200-acre wildlife refuge here, on the Pacific Flyway, is a wonderful spot for viewing migratory birds. There's an observation deck where you can watch Canada geese, and along the trails you might view eared grebes, burrowing owls, great blue herons, ospreys, and yellow-footed gulls. ⚠ Though the scenery is beautiful, the waters here give off an unpleasant odor, and the New River, which empties into the sea, is quite toxic. ✉ *906 W. Sinclair Rd., Calipatria* ☏ *760/348–5278* ⊕ *www.fws.gov/ refuge/sonny_bono_salton_sea/* ✉ *Free* ☉ *Closed weekends Mar.–Oct.*

Chapter 6

ORANGE COUNTY AND CATALINA ISLAND

Updated by
Kathy A. McDonald

⊙ Sights	🍴 Restaurants	🛏 Hotels	🛍 Shopping	🍸 Nightlife
★★★★★	★★★★☆	★★★★★	★☆☆☆☆	★☆☆☆☆

WELCOME TO ORANGE COUNTY AND CATALINA ISLAND

TOP REASONS TO GO

★ **Disney Magic:** Walking down Main Street, U.S.A., with Sleeping Beauty Castle straight ahead, you really will feel like you're in one of the happiest places on Earth.

★ **Beautiful Beaches:** Surf, swim, paddleboard, or just relax on one of the state's most breathtaking stretches of coastline. Keep in mind the water may be colder and rougher than you expect.

★ **Island Getaway:** Just a short high-speed catamaran ride from the shore, Catalina Island feels 1,000 miles away from the mainland. Wander around charming Avalon, dive or snorkel through the state's first underwater park, or explore the unspoiled beauty of the island's wild interior.

★ **The Fine Life:** Some of the state's wealthiest communities are in coastal Orange County, so spend at least part of your stay here experiencing how the other half lives.

★ **Family Fun:** Ride roller coasters, eat ice cream, bike on oceanfront paths, fish off ocean piers, or try bodysurfing.

1 Disneyland Resort. Once a humble vision of Walt Disney's, Southern California's top family and tourist destination has grown to become a megaresort, with more attractions spilling over into Disney's California Adventure. There's plenty here to entertain kids and adults alike.

2 Knott's Berry Farm. Amusement park lovers should check out this Buena Park attraction, with thrill rides, the *Peanuts* gang, and lots of fried chicken and boysenberry pie.

3 The Coast. The O.C.'s beach communities may not be quite as glamorous as they appear on TV, but coastal spots like Newport Harbor and Laguna Beach are perfect for chilling out in an oceanfront hotel.

4 Catalina Island. This unspoiled island paradise—with its pocket-size town, Avalon, and large nature preserve—is just off the Orange County coast.

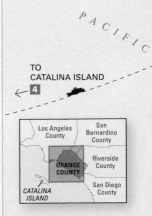

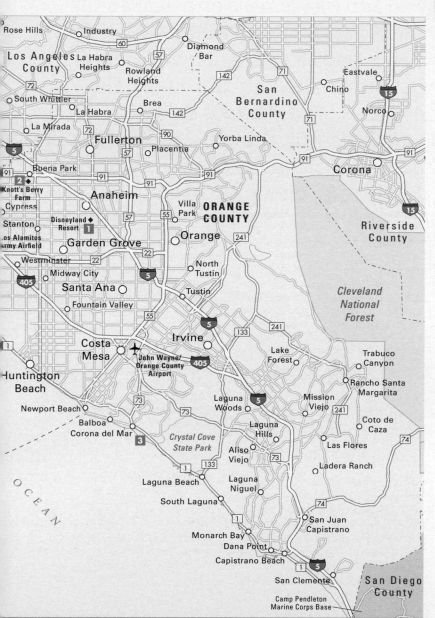

With its tropical flowers and palm trees, the stretch of coast between Seal Beach and San Clemente is often called the California Riviera. Exclusive Newport Beach and artsy Laguna are the stars, but lesser-known gems on the glistening coast—such as Corona del Mar—are also worth visiting. Offshore, meanwhile, lies gorgeous Catalina Island, a terrific spot for boating, diving, snorkeling, and hiking.

Few of the citrus groves that gave Orange County its name remain. This region south and east of Los Angeles is now ruled by tourism and high-tech business rather than agriculture. Despite a building boom that began in the 1990s, the area is still a place to find wilderness trails, canyons, greenbelts, and natural environs. Just offshore is a deep-water wilderness that's possible to explore via daily whale-watching excursions.

Planning

Getting Here and Around

AIR TRAVEL
Orange County's main facility is John Wayne Airport Orange County (SNA), which is served by six major domestic airlines and one commuter line. Long Beach Airport (LGB) is served by four airlines, including its major player, Jet-Blue. It's roughly 20 to 30 minutes by car from Anaheim.

Super Shuttle and Prime Time Airport Shuttle provide transportation from John Wayne and LAX to the Disneyland area of Anaheim. Round-trip fares average about $28 per person from John Wayne and $34 to $80 from LAX.

BUS TRAVEL
The Orange County Transportation Authority will take you virtually anywhere in the county, but it will take time; OCTA buses go from Knott's Berry Farm and Disneyland to Newport Beach. Bus 1 travels along the coast; Buses 701 and 721 provide express service to Los Angeles. Anaheim offers Anaheim Resort Transportation (ART) service that connects hotels to Disneyland Resort, downtown Anaheim, Buena Park, and the Metrolink train center. Rides are $3 each way.

INFORMATION Anaheim Resort Transportation. ☎ 714/563–5287 ⊕ rideart.org. **Orange County Transportation Authority.** ☎ 714/636–7433 ⊕ www.octa.net.

CAR TRAVEL

The San Diego Freeway (Interstate 405), the coastal route, and the Santa Ana Freeway (Interstate 5), the inland route, run north–south through Orange County. South of Laguna, Interstate 405 merges into Interstate 5 (called the San Diego Freeway south from this point). A toll road, Highway 73, runs 15 miles from Newport Beach to San Juan Capistrano; it costs $6.22–$8.48 (lower rates are for weekends and off-peak hours) and is usually less jammed than the regular freeways. Do your best to avoid all Orange County freeways during rush hours (6–9 am and 3:30–6:30 pm). Highway 55 leads to Newport Beach. The Pacific Coast Highway (Highway 1) allows easy access to beach communities and is the most scenic route but expect it to be crowded, especially on summer weekends and holidays.

FERRY TRAVEL

There are two ferries that service Catalina Island; Catalina Express runs from Long Beach (about 90 minutes) and from Newport Beach (about 75 minutes). Reservations are strongly advised for summers and weekends. During the winter months, ferry crossings are not as frequent as in the summer high season.

TRAIN TRAVEL

Amtrak makes daily stops in Orange County at all major towns. Metrolink is a weekday commuter train that runs to and from Los Angeles and Orange County.

INFORMATION Amtrak. ☎ 800/872–7245 ⊕ www.amtrak.com. **Metrolink.** ☎ 800/371–5465 ⊕ www.metrolink-trains.com.

Restaurants

Much like in L.A., restaurants in Orange County are generally casual, and you'll rarely see suits and ties. However, at top resort hotel dining rooms, many guests choose to dress up.

Of course, there's also a swath of casual places along the beachfronts—seafood takeout, taquerias, burger joints—that won't mind if you wear flip-flops. Reservations are recommended for the nicest restaurants.

Many places don't serve past 11 pm, and locals tend to eat early. Remember that according to California law, smoking is prohibited in all enclosed areas.

Hotels

Along the coast there are remarkable luxury resorts; if you can't afford a stay, pop in for the view at Laguna Beach's Montage or the always welcoming Ritz-Carlton at Dana Point. For a taste of the O.C. glam life, have lunch overlooking the yachts of Newport Bay at the Balboa Bay Resort.

As a rule, lodging prices tend to rise the closer the hotels are to the beach. If you're looking for value, consider a hotel that's inland along the Interstate 405 freeway corridor.

In most cases, you can take advantage of some of the facilities of the high-end resorts, such as restaurants and spas, even if you aren't an overnight guest.

Restaurant and hotel reviews have been shortened. For full information, visit Fodors.com.

WHAT IT COSTS

	$	$$	$$$	$$$$
RESTAURANTS				
	under $20	$20–$30	$30–$40	over $40
HOTELS				
	under $200	$200–$300	$301–$400	over $400

Visitor Information

Visit Anaheim is an excellent resource for both leisure and business travelers and can provide materials on many area attractions. Kiosks at the Anaheim Convention Center act as a digital concierge and allow visitors to plan itineraries and buy tickets to area attractions.

The Orange County Visitors Association's website is also a useful source of information.

INFORMATION Orange County Visitors Association. ⊕ www.visittheoc.com. **Visit Anaheim.** ✉ Anaheim Convention Center, 800 W. Katella Ave., Anaheim ☎ 714/765–2800 ⊕ www.visitanaheim.org.

Disneyland Resort

26 miles southeast of Los Angeles, via I–5.

The snowcapped Matterhorn, the centerpiece of Disneyland, punctuates the skyline of Anaheim. Since 1955, when Walt Disney chose this once-quiet farming community for the site of his first amusement park, Disneyland has attracted more than 650 million visitors and tens of thousands of workers, and Anaheim has been their host.

The resort is a sprawling complex that includes Disney's two amusement parks; three hotels; and Downtown Disney, a shopping, dining, and entertainment promenade. Anaheim's tourist center includes Angel Stadium of Anaheim, home of baseball's 2002 World Series Champion, Los Angeles Angels of Anaheim; the Honda Center (formerly the Arrowhead Pond), which hosts concerts and the Anaheim Ducks hockey team; and the enormous Anaheim Convention Center.

GETTING THERE

Disney is about a 30-mile drive from either LAX or Downtown. From LAX, follow Sepulveda Boulevard south to the Interstate 105 freeway and drive east 16 miles to the Interstate 605 north exit. Exit at the Santa Ana Freeway (Interstate 5) and continue south for 12 miles to the Disneyland Drive exit. Follow signs to the resort. From Downtown, follow Interstate 5 south 28 miles and exit at Disneyland Drive. **Disneyland Resort Express** (☎ 800/828–6699 ⊕ dre.coachusa.com) offers daily nonstop bus service between LAX, John Wayne Airport, and Anaheim. Reservations are not required. The cost is $30 one-way from LAX, and $20 from John Wayne Airport.

SAVING TIME AND MONEY

If you plan to visit for more than a day, you can save money by buying two-three-, four-, and five-day Park Hopper tickets that grant same-day "hopping" privileges between Disneyland and Disney's California Adventure. You get a discount on the multiple-day passes if you buy online through the Disneyland website.

Single-day admission prices vary by date. A one-day Park Hopper pass costs $147–$185 for anyone 10 or older, $141–$177 for kids ages three to nine depending on what day you go. Admission to either park (but not both) is $97–$135 or $91–$127 for kids three to nine; kids two and under are free.

In addition to tickets, parking is $20–$35 (unless your hotel has a shuttle or is within walking distance), and meals in the parks and at Downtown Disney range from $10 to $60 per person.

Disneyland

★ Disneyland
AMUSEMENT PARK/WATER PARK | FAMILY |
An imaginative original, Disneyland was an unproven concept when it opened in 1955. But Walt Disney himself could never have predicted the park's success and its beloved place in the hearts of Southern Californians. It is the only one of the parks to have been overseen by Walt himself, has a genuine historic feel, and occupies a unique place in the Disney legend. Expertly run, perfectly maintained, with polite and helpful staff ("cast members" in the Disney lexicon), the park has plenty that you won't find anywhere else—such as the Indiana Jones Adventure ride and Storybook Land, with its miniature replicas of animated Disney scenes from classics such as *Frozen* and *Alice in Wonderland*. Characters appear for autographs and photos throughout the day; times and places are posted at the entrances. Live shows, parades, strolling musicians, fireworks on weekends, and endless snack choices add to the carnival atmosphere. You can also meet some of the animated icons at one of the character meals served at the three Disney hotels (open to the public). Belongings can be stored in lockers just off Main Street; stroller rentals at the entrance gate are a convenient option for families with small tykes. The park's popularity means there are crowds year-round, even on the rare Southern California rainy days. ⊠ *1313 S. Disneyland Dr., between Ball Rd. and Katella Ave., Anaheim* ☎ *714/781–4636 guest information* ⊕ *www.disneyland. com* From $97; parking $20.

PARK NEIGHBORHOODS
Neighborhoods for Disneyland are arranged in geographic order.

MAIN STREET, U.S.A.
Walt's hometown of Marceline, Missouri, was the inspiration behind this romanticized image of small-town America, circa 1900. The sidewalks are lined with a penny arcade and shops that sell everything from tradeable pins to Disney-themed clothing, an endless supply of sugar confections, and a photo shop that offers souvenirs created via Disney's PhotoPass (on-site photographers capture memorable moments digitally—you can access them in person or online via the Disneyland app). Main Street opens half an hour before the rest of the park, so it's a good place to explore if you're getting an early start to beat the crowds (it's also open an hour after the other attractions close, so you may want to save your shopping for the end of the day). **Main Street Cinema** offers a cool respite from the crowds and six classic Disney animated shorts, including *Steamboat Willie.* There's rarely a wait to enter. Grab a cappuccino and fresh-made pastry at the Jolly Holiday bakery to jump-start your visit. Board the **Disneyland Railroad** here to save on walking; it tours all the lands and offers unique views of Splash Mountain, the Grand Canyon, and Primeval World dioramas.

NEW ORLEANS SQUARE
This mini–French Quarter, with narrow streets, hidden courtyards, and live street performances, is home to two iconic attractions and the Cajun-inspired Blue Bayou restaurant. **Pirates of the Caribbean** now features Jack Sparrow and the cursed Captain Barbossa of the blockbuster series, plus enhanced special effects and battle scenes (complete with cannonball explosions). Nearby **Haunted Mansion** continues to spook guests with its stretching room and "doombuggy" rides (there's now an expanded storyline for the beating-heart bride). The *Nightmare Before Christmas* holiday overlay is an annual tradition. This is a good area to get a casual bite to eat; the clam chowder in sourdough bread bowls, sold at the French Market Restaurant and Royal Street Veranda, is a popular choice. Food carts offer everything from just-popped popcorn to churros and even fresh fruit.

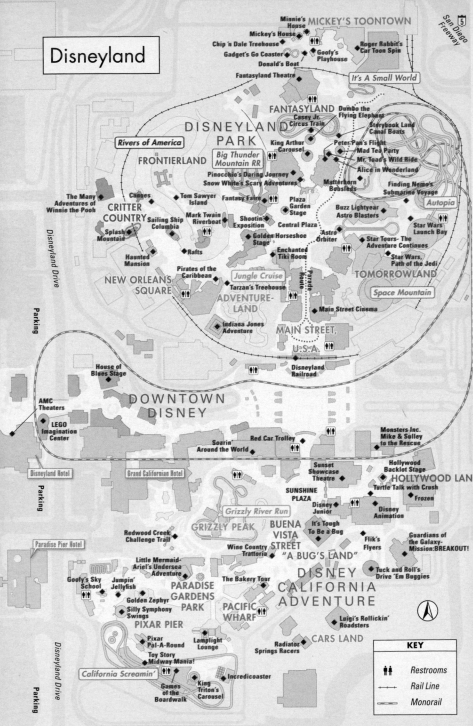

Disneyland

MICKEY'S TOONTOWN

Minnie's House
Mickey's House
Chip 'n Dale Treehouse
Gadget's Go Coaster
Donald's Boat
Fantasyland Theatre
Goofy's Playhouse
Roger Rabbit's Car Toon Spin

San Diego Freeway

It's a Small World

FANTASYLAND

Dumbo the Flying Elephant

Casey Jr. Circus Train
Storybook Land Canal Boats

DISNEYLAND PARK

King Arthur Carousel
Peter Pan's Flight
Mad Tea Party
Mr. Toad's Wild Ride
Alice in Wonderland

Rivers of America

FRONTIERLAND

Big Thunder Mountain RR

Pinocchio's Daring Journey
Snow White's Scary Adventures

Matterhorn Bobsleds

Finding Nemo's Submarine Voyage

Autopia

The Many Adventures of Winnie the Pooh

Canoes
Tom Sawyer Island

Fantasy Faire
Plaza Garden Stage

Buzz Lightyear Astro Blasters

Star Wars Launch Bay

CRITTER COUNTRY

Sailing Ship Columbia
Mark Twain Riverboat

Shootin' Exposition

Central Plaza

Astro Orbiter

Star Tours- The Adventure Continues

Splash Mountain

Rafts

Golden Horseshoe Stage

Star Wars, Path of the Jedi

Haunted Mansion

Enchanted Tiki Room

TOMORROWLAND

Pirates of the Caribbean

Tarzan's Treehouse

Jungle Cruise

Space Mountain

NEW ORLEANS SQUARE

ADVENTURE-LAND

Parade Route

Main Street Cinema

Indiana Jones Adventure

MAIN STREET, U.S.A.

Disneyland Railroad

House of Blues Stage

DOWNTOWN DISNEY

AMC Theaters

LEGO Imagination Center

Red Car Trolley

Monsters Inc. Mike & Sulley to the Rescue

Soarin' Around the World

Disneyland Drive

Parking

Disneyland Hotel

Grand Californian Hotel

Sunset Showcase Theatre

Hollywood Backlot Stage

HOLLYWOOD LAN

SUNSHINE PLAZA

Turtle Talk with Crush
Frozen

Disney Junior
Disney Animation

Grizzly River Run

GRIZZLY PEAK

BUENA VISTA STREET

It's Tough To Be a Bug

Paradise Pier Hotel

Redwood Creek Challenge Trail

Wine Country Trattoria

"A BUG'S LAND"

Flik's Flyers

Guardians of the Galaxy-Mission: BREAKOUT!

Little Mermaid- Ariel's Undersea Adventure

Goofy's Sky School

Jumpin' Jellyfish

The Bakery Tour

DISNEY CALIFORNIA ADVENTURE

Tuck and Roll's Drive 'Em Buggies

PARADISE GARDENS PARK

Golden Zephyr

Silly Symphony Swings

PACIFIC WHARF

Luigi's Rollickin' Roadsters

PIXAR PIER

Pixar Pal-A-Round

Lamplight Lounge

CARS LAND

Radiator Springs Racers

California Screamin'

Toy Story Midway Mania!

Games of the Boardwalk

King Triton's Carousel

Incredicoaster

Disneyland Drive

Parking

Katella Avenue

KEY

🚻	*Restrooms*
┼─┼	*Rail Line*
═══	*Monorail*

FRONTIERLAND

Between Adventureland and Fantasyland, Frontierland transports you to the wild, wild West with its rustic buildings, shooting gallery, mountain range, and foot-stompin' dance hall. The marquee attraction, **Big Thunder Mountain Railroad,** is a relatively tame roller coaster ride (no steep descents) that takes the form of a runaway mine car as it rumbles past desert canyons and an old mining town. Tour the Rivers of America on the **Mark Twain Riverboat** in the company of a grizzled old river pilot or circumnavigate the globe on the **Sailing Ship Columbia,** though its operating hours are usually limited to weekends. From here, you can raft over to Pirate's Lair on **Tom Sawyer Island,** which now features pirate-themed caves, treasure hunts, and music, along with plenty of caves and hills to climb and explore. If you don't mind tight seating, have a snack at the Golden Horseshoe saloon, where Walt himself used to hang out.

CRITTER COUNTRY

Down-home country is the theme in this shaded corner of the park, where Winnie the Pooh and Davy Crockett make their homes. Here you can find **Splash Mountain,** a classic flume ride with music, and appearances by Brer Rabbit and other *Song of the South* characters. Don't forget to check out your photo (the camera snaps close-ups of each car just before it plunges into the water) on the way out. The patio of the popular Hungry Bear Restaurant has great views of Tom Sawyer's Island and Davy Crockett's Explorer Canoes, which ply the waters on weekends only.

ADVENTURELAND

Modeled after the lands of Africa, Polynesia, and Arabia, this tiny tropical paradise is worth braving the crowds that flock here for the ambience and better-than-average food. Sing along with the animatronic birds and tiki gods in the **Enchanted Tiki Room,** sail the rivers of the world with

Disney's Top Attractions

- **Indiana Jones:** You're at the wheel for this thrilling ride through a cursed temple.

- **Haunted Mansion:** A "doombuggy" takes you through a spooky old plantation mansion.

- **Matterhorn Bobsleds:** At the center of the Magic Kingdom, this roller coaster simulates bobsleds.

- **Pirates of the Caribbean:** Watch buccaneers wreak havoc as you float along in a rowboat.

- **Space Mountain:** This scary-but-thrilling roller coaster is indoors—and mostly in the dark.

joke-cracking skippers on **Jungle Cruise,** and climb the *Disneyodendron semperflorens* (the always-blooming Disney tree) to **Tarzan's Treehouse,** where you can walk through scenes, some interactive, from the 1999 animated film. Cap off the visit with a wild jeep ride at **Indiana Jones Adventure,** where the special effects and decipherable hieroglyphics distract you while you're waiting in line. There's a single-rider option for a quicker ride. The skewers (some vegetarian options available) at Bengal Barbecue and pineapple whip at Tiki Juice Bar are some of the best fast-food options in the park.

FANTASYLAND

Sleeping Beauty Castle marks the entrance to Fantasyland, a visual wonderland of princesses, spinning teacups, flying elephants, and other classic storybook characters. Rides, and shops such as the princess-themed Bibbidi Bobbidi Boutique, take precedence over restaurants in this area of the park, but outdoor carts sell everything from churros to turkey legs. Tots love the **King**

Best Tips for Disneyland

■TIP→ **As of 2017, all visitors must pass through metal detectors, and bags are searched before entering the Disneyland Resort. Allot 10–15 extra minutes for passing through the security line.**

Download the Disneyland app. The app provides access to FASTPASS tickets via the digital MAXPASS, shows attraction wait times in real time, lists entertainment and parade times, and can guide you through the park.

Buy entry tickets in advance. Nearby hotels sell park admission tickets; you can also buy them through Disney's website and the Disneyland app. With package deals, like those offered through AAA, tickets are included.

Lines at ticket booths can take more than an hour on busy days. Save time by buying in advance.

Come midweek. Weekends, especially in summer, are a mob scene. Holidays are crowded, too. A rainy winter weekday is often the least crowded time to visit.

Plan your times to hit the most popular rides. Get to the park as early as possible, even before the gates open, and make a beeline for the top rides before the crowds reach a critical mass. Late evening is when the hordes thin out, and you can catch a special show or parade. Save the quieter attractions for mid-afternoon.

Use FASTPASS. These passes allow you to reserve your place in line at some of the most crowded attractions (only one at a time). Distribution machines are posted near the entrances of each attraction. Feed in your park admission ticket, and you'll receive a pass with a printed time frame (generally up to 1–1½ hours later) during which you can return to wait in a much shorter line.

Avoid peak mealtime crowds. Start the day with a big breakfast so you won't be too hungry at noon, when restaurants and vendors get slammed. Wait to have lunch until after 1 pm.

If you want to eat at the **Blue Bayou** in New Orleans Square, you can make a reservation up to six months in advance online. Another (cheaper) option is to bring your own snacks. It's always a good idea to bring water.

Check the daily events schedule online or at the park entrance. During parades, fireworks, and other special events, sections of the parks are filled with crowds. This can work in your favor or against you: an event could make it difficult to get around a park—but if you plan ahead, you can take advantage of the distraction to hit popular rides.

Send the teens next door. Disneyland's newer sister park, California Adventure, features more intense rides suitable for older kids (Park Hopper passes include admission to both parks).

Arthur Carousel, Casey Jr. Circus Train, and Storybook Land Canal Boats. This is also home to Mr. Toad's Wild Ride, Peter Pan's Flight, and Pinocchio's Daring Journey, all classic movie-theater-dark rides that immerse riders in Disney fairy tales. The Abominable Snowman pops up on the Matterhorn Bobsleds, a roller coaster that twists and turns up and around on a made-to-scale model of the real Swiss mountain. Anchoring the east end of Fantasyland is It's a Small World, a smorgasbord of dancing animatronic dolls, cuckoo clock–covered walls, and variations of the song everyone knows, or soon *will* know, by heart. Beloved Disney characters like Ariel from *The Little Mermaid* are also part of the mix. Fantasy Faire is a fairy tale–style village that collects all the Disney princesses together. Each has her own reception nook in the Royal Hall. Condensed retellings of *Tangled* and *Beauty and the Beast* take place at the Royal Theatre.

MICKEY'S TOONTOWN

Geared toward small fries, this lopsided cartoonlike downtown, complete with cars and trolleys that invite exploring, is where Mickey, Donald, Goofy, and other classic Disney characters hang their hats. One of the most popular attractions is Roger Rabbit's Car Toon Spin, a twisting, turning cab ride through the Toontown of *Who Framed Roger Rabbit?* You can also walk through Mickey's House to meet and be photographed with the famous mouse, take a low-key ride on Gadget's Go Coaster, or bounce around the fenced-in playground in front of Goofy's Playhouse.

TOMORROWLAND

This popular section of the park continues to tinker with its future, adding and enhancing rides regularly. *Star Wars*–themed attractions can't be missed, like the immersive, 3-D Star Tours – The Adventures Continue, where you can join the Rebellion in a galaxy far, far away. Finding Nemo's Submarine Voyage updates the old Submarine Voyage ride with the

exploits of Nemo, Dory, Marlin, and other characters from the Disney-Pixar film. Try to visit this popular ride early in the day if you can, and be prepared for a wait. The interactive Buzz Lightyear Astro Blasters lets you zap your neighbors with laser beams and compete for the highest score. Hurtle through the cosmos on Space Mountain or check out mainstays like the futuristic Astro Orbiter rockets, Star Wars Launch Bay, which showcases costumes, models, and props from the franchise, and Star Wars, Path of the Jedi, which catches viewers up on all the movies with a quick 12-minute film. Disneyland Monorail and Disneyland Railroad both have stations here. There's also a video arcade and dancing water fountain that makes a perfect playground for kids on hot summer days. The Jedi Training Academy spotlights future Luke Skywalkers in the crowd.

Besides the eight lands, the daily live-action shows and parades are always crowd pleasers. Among these is Fantasmic!, a musical, fireworks, and laser show in which Mickey and friends wage a spellbinding battle against Disneyland's darker characters. ■TIP→ Arrive early to secure a good view; if there are two shows scheduled for the day, the second one tends to be less crowded. A fireworks display lights up weekends and most summer evenings. Brochures with maps, available at the entrance, list show and parade times.

Disney California Adventure

★ Disney California Adventure
AMUSEMENT PARK/WATER PARK | FAMILY | The sprawling Disney California Adventure, adjacent to Disneyland (their entrances face each other), pays tribute to the Golden State with seven theme areas that re-create vintage architectural styles and embrace several hit Pixar films via engaging attractions. Visitors enter through the art deco–style Buena Vista Street, past shops and a

Did You Know?

The plain purple teacup in Disneyland's Mad Tea Party ride spins the fastest—though no one knows why.

helpful information booth that advises wait times on attractions. The 12-acre Cars Land features Radiator Springs Racers, a speedy trip in six-passenger speedsters through scenes featured in the blockbuster hit. (FASTPASS tickets for the ride run out early most days.) Other popular attractions include the free-falling Guardians of the Galaxy–Mission: BREAKOUT!; World of Color, a nighttime water-effects show; and Toy Story Midway Mania!, an interactive adventure ride hosted by Woody and Buzz Lightyear. At night the park takes on neon hues as glowing signs light up Route 66 in Cars Land and Pixar Pal-A-Round, a giant Ferris wheel on the Pixar Pier. Cocktails, beer, and wine are available; craft beers and premium wines from California are poured. Live nightly entertainment also features a 1930s jazz troupe that arrives in a vintage jalopy. Some rides have a minimum height limit of 40 inches. ✉ *1313 S. Disneyland Dr., between Ball Rd. and Katella Ave., Anaheim* ☎ *714/781–4636* ⊕ *www.disneyland.com* 🎫 *From $97; parking $20.*

PARK NEIGHBORHOODS
BUENA VISTA STREET
California Adventure's grand entryway re-creates the lost 1920s Los Angeles that Walt Disney encountered when he moved to the Golden State. There's a **Red Car trolley** (modeled after Los Angeles's bygone streetcar line); hop on for the brief ride to Hollywood Land. Buena Vista Street is also home to a Starbucks outlet—within the Fiddler, Fifer and Practical Café—and the upscale Carthay Circle Restaurant and Lounge, which serves modern craft cocktails and beer. The comfy booths of the Carthay Circle restaurant on the second floor feel like a relaxing world away from the theme park outside.

GRIZZLY PEAK
This woodsy land celebrates the great outdoors. Test your skills on the **Redwood Creek Challenge Trail,** a challenging

trek across net ladders and suspension bridges. **Grizzly River Run** mimics the river rapids of the Sierra Nevadas; be prepared to get soaked.

Soarin' Around the World is a spectacular simulated hang-gliding ride over internationally known landmarks like Switzerland's Matterhorn and India's Taj Mahal.

HOLLYWOOD LAND
With a main street modeled after Hollywood Boulevard, a fake sky backdrop, and real sound stages, this area celebrates California's film industry. **Disney Animation** gives you an insider's look at how animators create characters. **Turtle Talk with Crush** lets kids have an unscripted chat with a computer-animated Crush, the sea turtle from *Finding Nemo.* The Hyperion Theater hosts **Frozen,** a 45-minute live performance from a Broadway-size cast with terrific visual effects. ■TIP➔ **Plan on getting in line about half an hour in advance; the show is worth the wait.** On the film-inspired ride **Monsters, Inc. Mike & Sulley to the Rescue,** visitors climb into taxis and travel the streets of Monstropolis on a mission to safely return Boo to her bedroom. **Guardians of the Galaxy – Mission: BREAKOUT!,** which opened in summer 2017, replaced the now-closed Twilight Zone Tower of Terror.

CARS LAND
Amble down Route 66, the main thoroughfare of Cars Land, and discover a pitch-perfect re-creation of the vintage highway. Quick eats are found at the Cozy Cone Motel (in a teepee-shape motor court) while Flo's V8 café serves hearty comfort food. Start your day at Radiator Springs Racers, the park's most popular attraction, where waits can be two hours or longer. Strap into a nifty sports car and meet the characters of Pixar's *Cars*; the ride ends in a speedy auto race through the red rocks and desert of Radiator Springs. ■TIP➔ **To bypass the line, there's a single-rider option for Radiator Springs Racers.**

PACIFIC WHARF

In the midst of the California Adventure you'll find 10 different dining options, from light snacks to full-service restaurants. The Wine Country Trattoria is a great place for Italian specialties; relax outside on the restaurant's terrace for a casual bite while sipping a California-made craft beer or wine. Mexican cuisine and potent margaritas are available at the Cocina Cucamonga Mexican Grill and Rita's Baja Blenders, and Lucky Fortune Cookery serves Chinese stir-fry dishes.

PARADISE GARDENS PARK

The far corner of California Adventure is a mix of floating, zigzagging, and flying rides: soar via the **Silly Symphony Swings**; **Goofy's Sky School** rollicks and rolls through a cartoon-inspired landscape; and the sleek retro-styled gondolas of the **Golden Zephyr** mimic 1920s movies and their sci-fi adventures. Journey through Ariel's colorful world on **The Little Mermaid—Ariel's Undersea Adventure.** The best views of the nighttime music, water, and light show, **World of Color,** are from the paths along Paradise Bay. FASTPASS tickets are available. Or for a guaranteed spot, book dinner at the Wine Country Trattoria that includes a ticket to a viewing area to catch all the show's stunning visuals.

PIXAR PIER

This section re-creates the glory days of California's seaside piers, themed with Pixar film characters. If you're looking for thrills, join The Incredibles family on the **Incredicoaster** as the fast moving roller coaster takes its riders from 0 to 55 mph in about four seconds and proceeds through scream tunnels, steeply angled drops, and a 360-degree loop. **Pixar Pal-A-Round,** a giant Ferris wheel, provides a good view of the grounds, though some cars spin and sway for more kicks. There are also carnival games, an aquatic-themed carousel, and **Toy Story Midway Mania!,** an interactive ride where you can

take aim at a series of cartoon targets. Soft-serve ice cream, turkey legs, hot dogs, and churros are readily available for quick snacking. At the **Lamplight Lounge** adults can chill out and overlook the action while sipping on craft cocktails.

OTHER ATTRACTIONS

Downtown Disney District

AMUSEMENT PARK/WATER PARK | FAMILY |
The Downtown Disney District is a 20-acre promenade of dining, shopping, and entertainment that connects the resort's hotels and theme parks. **The Void** provides an immersive virtual reality experience with special effects and more; the current game, **Star Wars: Secrets of the Empire**, transforms visitors into participants in an intergalactic battle. Refresh afterward at the bar or dining room at Splitsville, a mid-century modern–style bowling alley serving American comfort food. At **Ralph Brennan's Jazz Kitchen** you can dig into New Orleans–style food and music. Save room for sweets: **Salt and Straw** has gourmet ice cream while **Sprinkles** offers ultrarich cupcakes. Disney merchandise and artwork is showcased at the brightly lit **World of Disney** store. At the megasize **Lego Store** there are hands-on demonstrations and space to play with the latest Lego creations. **Anna and Elsa's Boutique** speedily makes over kids into their favorite character from the hit film *Frozen*. All visitors must pass through a security checkpoint and metal detectors before entering. With a minimum purchase of $20, parking is free for the first three hours. ⊠ *1580 Disneyland Dr., Anaheim* ☎ *714/300–7800* ⊕ *disneyland.disney. go.com/downtown-disney* ⌂ *Free.*

🍴 Restaurants

Anaheim White House

$$$ | ITALIAN | Although a massive fire gutted the Anaheim White House in 2017, owner Bruno Serato rebuilt and expanded the local landmark known for its specialty pastas. The 1909-built original mansion

was the inspiration for the complete renovation. $ *Average main: $38* ✉ *887 S. Anaheim Blvd., Anaheim* ☎ *714/772–1381* ⊕ *www.anaheimwhitehouse.com* ⊙ *No lunch.*

Catal Restaurant and Uva Bar
$$$ | MEDITERRANEAN | Famed chef Joachim Splichal guides his staff to take a relaxed approach at this bi-level Mediterranean spot, where more than 30 wines by the glass, craft beers, and craft cocktails pair well with his Spanish-influenced dishes. Upstairs, Catal's menu has tapas, a variety of flavorful paellas, and charcuterie. **Known for:** people-watching; gourmet burgers; happy hour. $ *Average main: $30* ✉ *Downtown Disney District, 1580 S. Disneyland Dr., Suite 103, Anaheim* ☎ *714/781–3463* ⊕ *www.patinagroup.com.*

Napa Rose
$$$$ | AMERICAN | Done up in a handsome Craftsman style, Napa Rose's rich seasonal cuisine is matched with an extensive wine list, with 1,500 labels and 80 available by the glass. For a look into the open kitchen, sit at the counter and watch the chefs as they whip up such signature dishes as grilled diver scallops and chanterelles, and lamb pot roast topped with a pomegranate mint glaze. **Known for:** excellent wine list; kid-friendly options; gorgeous dining room. $ *Average main: $48* ✉ *Disney's Grand Californian Hotel, 1600 S. Disneyland Dr., Anaheim* ☎ *714/300–7170, 714/781–3463 reservations* ⊕ *disneyland.disney.go.com/grand-californian-hotel/napa-rose.*

🛏 Hotels

Candy Cane Inn
$ | HOTEL | FAMILY | One of the Disneyland area's first hotels, the Candy Cane is one of Anaheim's most relaxing properties, with spacious and understated rooms and an inviting palm-fringed pool. **Pros:** proximity to everything Disney; friendly service; free breakfast. **Cons:** dated decor; all rooms face parking lot; no elevator. $ *Rooms from: $179* ✉ *1747 S. Harbor Blvd., Anaheim* ☎ *714/774–5284, 800/345–7057* ⊕ *www.candycaneinn.net* ⇥ *171 rooms* ⦿ *Breakfast.*

★ Disney's Grand Californian Hotel and Spa
$$$$ | RESORT | FAMILY | The most opulent of Disneyland's three hotels, the Craftsman-style Grand Californian offers views of Disney California Adventure and Downtown Disney. **Pros:** gorgeous lobby; family friendly; direct access to California Adventure. **Cons:** the $20 self-parking lot is across the street; standard rooms are on the small side; $30 valet parking. $ *Rooms from: $625* ✉ *1600 S. Disneyland Dr., Anaheim* ☎ *714/635–2300* ⊕ *disneyland.disney.go.com/grand-californian-hotel* ⇥ *1019 rooms* ⦿ *No meals.*

Doubletree Suites by Hilton Hotel Anaheim Resort-Convention Center
$ | HOTEL | This busy hotel near the Anaheim Convention Center and a 20-minute walk from Disneyland caters to business travelers and vacationers alike. **Pros:** huge suites; walking distance to a variety of restaurants; chocolate chip cookies at check-in. **Cons:** a bit far from Disneyland; pool area is small; $21 daily parking fee. $ *Rooms from: $153* ✉ *2085 S. Harbor Blvd., Anaheim* ☎ *714/750–3000, 800/215–7316* ⊕ *doubletreeanaheim.com* ⇥ *252 rooms* ⦿ *No meals.*

Hilton Anaheim
$ | HOTEL | FAMILY | Next to the Anaheim Convention Center, this busy Hilton is the third-largest hotel in Southern California, with a restaurant and food court, hopping lobby lounge with communal tables, a full-service gym, and its own Starbucks. **Pros:** efficient service; fast-casual dining options; some rooms have views of the park fireworks. **Cons:** huge size can be daunting; fee to use health club; megasize parking lot. $ *Rooms from: $159* ✉ *777 Convention Way, Anaheim* ☎ *714/750–4321, 800/445–8667* ⊕ *www.hiltonanaheimhotel.com* ⇥ *1572 rooms* ⦿ *No meals.*

Park Vue Inn

$ | **HOTEL** | **FAMILY** | Watch the frequent fireworks from the rooftop sundeck at this bougainvillea-covered Spanish-style inn, one of the closest lodgings to the Disneyland Resort main gate. **Pros:** easy walk to Disneyland, Downtown Disney, and Disney California Adventure; free parking until midnight on checkout day; some rooms have bunk beds. **Cons:** all rooms face the parking lot; rooms near the breakfast room can be noisy; inefficient room air conditioners. $ *Rooms from: $159* ✉ *1570 S. Harbor Blvd., Anaheim* ☎ *714/772–3691, 800/334–7021* ⊕ *www.parkvueinn.com* ⇆ *86 rooms* ⦿ *Breakfast.*

Knott's Berry Farm

25 miles south of Los Angeles, via I–5, in Buena Park.

Knott's Berry Farm

AMUSEMENT PARK/WATER PARK | **FAMILY** | The land where the boysenberry was invented (by crossing raspberry, blackberry, and loganberry bushes) is now occupied by Knott's Berry Farm. In 1934 Cordelia Knott began serving chicken dinners on her wedding china to supplement her family's income. The dinners and her boysenberry pies proved more profitable than husband Walter's farm, so the two moved first into the restaurant business and then into the entertainment business. The park is now a 160-acre complex with close to 40 rides, dozens of restaurants and shops, arcade games, live shows, a brick-by-brick replica of Philadelphia's Independence Hall, and loads of Americana. Although it has plenty to keep small children occupied, the park is best known for its awesome thrill rides. The boardwalk area is home to several coasters, including the zooming HangTime that pauses dramatically then drops nearly 15 stories, plus water features to cool things off on hot days, and a lighted promenade. And, yes, you can still get that boysenberry pie (and jam, juice—you name it). Buy adult tickets online for a major discount; FastLane wristbands—for quicker access to the most popular rides—cost $70 online. ✉ *8039 Beach Blvd., Buena Park* ✛ *Between La Palma Ave. and Crescent St., 2 blocks south of Hwy. 91* ☎ *714/220–5200* ⊕ *www.knotts.com* ✉ *$82.*

Park Neighborhoods

THE BOARDWALK

Not-for-the-squeamish thrill rides and skill-based games dominate the scene at the **boardwalk.** Roller coasters—Coast Rider, Surfside Glider, and Pacific Scrambler—surround a pond that keeps things cooler on hot days. **HangTime** towers 150 feet above the boardwalk as coaster cars hang, invert and drop the equivalent of 15 stories. The boardwalk is also home to a string of test-your-skill games that are fun to watch whether you're playing or not, and Johnny Rockets, the park's all-American diner.

CAMP SNOOPY

It can be gridlock on weekends, but kids love this miniature High Sierra wonderland where the *Peanuts* gang hangs out. Tykes can push and pump their own mini-mining cars on **Huff and Puff,** soar around via **Charlie Brown's Kite Flyer,** and hop aboard **Woodstock's Airmail,** a kids' version of the park's Supreme Scream ride. Most of the rides here are geared toward kids only, leaving parents to cheer them on from the sidelines. **Sierra Sidewinder,** a roller coaster near the entrance of Camp Snoopy, is aimed at older children, with spinning saucer-type vehicles that go a maximum speed of 37 mph.

FIESTA VILLAGE

Over in **Fiesta Village** are two more musts for adrenaline junkies: **Montezooma's Revenge,** a roller coaster that goes from 0 to 55 mph in less than five seconds, and **Jaguar!,** which simulates the motions of a cat stalking its prey, twisting, spiraling, and speeding up and slowing down as it takes you on its stomach-dropping course. There's also **Hat Dance,** a version of the spinning teacups but with sombreros, and a 100-year-old **Dentzel carousel,** complete with an antique organ and menagerie of hand-carved animals. In a nod to history, there are restored scale models of the California Missions at Fiesta Village's southern entrance.

GHOST TOWN

Clusters of authentic old buildings relocated from their original mining-town sites mark this section of the park. You can stroll down the street, stop and chat with a blacksmith, pan for gold (for a fee), crack open a geode, check out the chalkboard of a circa-1875 schoolhouse, and ride an original Butterfield stagecoach. Looming over it all is **GhostRider,** Orange County's first wooden roller coaster. Traveling up to 56 mph and reaching 118 feet at its highest point, the park's biggest attraction is riddled with sudden dips and curves, subjecting riders to forces up to three times that of gravity. On the Western-theme **Silver Bullet,** riders are sent to a height of 146 feet and then back down 109 feet. Riders spiral, corkscrew, fly into a cobra roll, and experience overbanked curves. The **Calico Mine** ride descends into a replica of a working gold mine complete with 50 animatronic figures. The **Timber Mountain Log Ride** is a visitor favorite: the flume ride tours through pioneer scenes before splashing down. Also found here is the **Pony Express,** a roller coaster that lets riders saddle up on packs of "horses" tethered to platforms that take off on a series of hairpin turns and travel up to 38 mph. Take a step inside the **Western Trails Museum,** a dusty old gem full of Old West memorabilia and rural Americana, plus menus from the original chicken restaurant and an impressive antique button collection. **Calico Railroad** departs regularly from Ghost Town station for a round-trip tour of the park (bandit holdups notwithstanding).

This section is also home to **Big Foot Rapids,** a splash-fest of white-water river rafting over towering cliffs, cascading waterfalls, and wild rapids. Don't miss the visually stunning show at **Mystery Lodge,** which tells the story of Native Americans in the Pacific Northwest with lights, music, and special effects.

INDIAN TRAILS

Celebrate Native American traditions through interactive exhibits like tepees and daily dance and storytelling performances.

Knott's Soak City Waterpark is directly across from the main park on 13 acres next to Independence Hall. It has a dozen major water rides; **Pacific Spin** is an oversize waterslide that drops riders 75 feet into a catch pool. There's also a children's pool, a 750,000-gallon wave pool, and a fun house. Soak City's season runs mid-May to mid-September. It's open daily after Memorial Day, weekends only after Labor Day, and then closes for the season.

🍴 Restaurants

Mrs. Knott's Chicken Dinner Restaurant
$$ | **AMERICAN** | **FAMILY** | Cordelia Knott's fried chicken and boysenberry pies drew crowds so big that Knott's Berry Farm was built to keep the hungry customers occupied while they waited. The restaurant's current incarnation (outside the park's entrance) still serves crispy fried chicken, along with fluffy handmade biscuits, mashed potatoes, and Mrs. Knott's signature chilled cherry-rhubarb compote. **Known for:** fried chicken; family friendliness; outdoor dining. *[$] Average main: $22 ✉ Knott's Berry Farm Marketplace, 8039 Beach Blvd., Buena Park ☎ 714/220–5200 🌐 www.knotts.com/california-marketplace/mrs-knott-s-chicken-dinner-restaurant.*

A mural at Huntington Beach

🛏 Hotels

Knott's Berry Farm Hotel

$ | **RESORT** | **FAMILY** | This convenient high-rise hotel is run by the park and sits right on park grounds surrounded by graceful palm trees. **Pros:** easy access to Knott's Berry Farm; plenty of family activities; extra-large swimming pool. **Cons:** lobby and hallways can be noisy; public areas show significant wear and tear; dated room decor. [$] *Rooms from: $129* ✉ *7675 Crescent Ave., Buena Park* ☎ *714/995–1111, 866/752–2444* 🌐 *www.knottshotel.com* 🛏 *320 rooms* 🍴 *No meals.*

The Coast

Running along the Orange County coastline is scenic Pacific Coast Highway (Highway 1, known locally as the PCH). Older beachfront settlements, with their modest bungalow-style homes, are joined by posh gated communities. The pricey land between Newport Beach and Laguna Beach is where ex-Laker Kobe Bryant, novelist Dean Koontz, those infamous Real Housewives of Bravo, and a slew of finance moguls live.

Though the coastline is rapidly being filled in, there are still a few stretches of beautiful, protected open land. And at many places along the way you can catch an idealized glimpse of the Southern California lifestyle: surfers hitting the beach, boards under their arms.

Long Beach

About 25 miles southeast of Los Angeles, via I–110 south.

👁 Sights

★ **Aquarium of the Pacific**

ZOO | **FAMILY** | Sea lions, zebra sharks, and penguins, oh my!—this aquarium focuses on creatures of the Pacific Ocean and is home to more than 11,000 animals. The main exhibits include large tanks of sharks, stingrays, and ethereal sea dragons, which the aquarium has successfully bred in captivity. The Ocean Theater features the multimedia attraction *Penguins 4D,* a panoramic film that captures the world of this endangered species. Be sure to say hello to Betty, a rescue at the engaging sea otter exhibit. For a non-aquatic experience, head to Lorikeet Forest, a walk-in aviary full of the friendliest parrots from Australia. Buy a cup of nectar and smile as you become a human bird perch. If you're a true animal lover, book an up-close-and-personal Animal Encounters Tour ($109) to learn about and assist in the care and feeding of sharks, penguins, and other aquarium residents; or find out how the aquarium functions with the extensive Behind the Scenes Tour ($19 for adults, not including admission). Certified divers can book a supervised dive in the aquarium's Tropical Reef Habitat ($299). Twice daily whale-watching trips on Harbor Breeze Cruises depart from the dock adjacent to the aquarium; summer sightings of blue whales are an unforgettable thrill. ✉ *100 Aquarium Way, Long Beach* ☎ *562/590–3100* 🌐 *www.aquariumofpacific.org* 🎟 *$30.*

Queen Mary

LIGHTHOUSE | **FAMILY** | The *Queen Mary,* though berthed, is an impressive example of 20th-century cruise ship opulence and sadly the last of its kind. The beautifully preserved art deco–style ocean liner was launched in 1936 and made 1,001 transatlantic crossings before finally berthing in Long Beach in 1967. Today there are multiple diversions on board from ongoing theatrical performances by illusionist Aiden Sinclair, *Illusions of the Passed: Legends of the Queen Mary*, a wine tasting room, and a daily British-style high tea.

Also on board you can take one of three daily or five weekend tours, such as the informative Glory Days Historical walk or the downright spooky Haunted Encounters tour. (Spirits have reportedly been spotted in the pool and engine room.) You could stay for dinner at one of the ship's restaurants, listen to live jazz in the original first-class lounge, or even spend the night in one of the 347 wood-panel cabins. The ship's neighbor, a geodesic dome originally built to house Howard Hughes's *Spruce Goose* aircraft, now serves as a terminal for Carnival Cruise Lines, making the *Queen Mary* the perfect pit stop before or after a cruise. Anchored next to the *Queen* is the *Scorpion,* a Russian submarine you can tour for a look at Cold War history. ✉ *1126 Queens Hwy., Long Beach* ☎ *877/342–0738* 🌐 *www.queenmary.com* 🎟 *Tours from $16.*

Hotels

Queen Mary Hotel

$ | **HOTEL** | **FAMILY** | Experience the golden age of transatlantic travel without the seasickness: a 1936 art deco–style reigns on the *Queen Mary,* from the ship's mahogany paneling to its nickel-plated doors to the majestic Grand Salon. **Pros:** a walkable historic Promenade deck; views from Long Beach out to the Pacific; art deco details. **Cons:** spotty service; vintage soundproofing makes for a challenging night's sleep; mandatory facility fee. [$] *Rooms from: $129* ✉ *1126 Queens Hwy., Long Beach* ☎ *562/435–3511, 877/342–0742* 🌐 *www.queenmary.com* 🛏 *347 staterooms* 🍴 *No meals.*

The Varden

$ | **B&B/INN** | Constructed in 1929 to house Bixby Knolls Sr.'s mistress, Dolly Varden, this small, historic, European-style hotel, on the metro line in downtown Long Beach, now caters to worldly budget travelers. Compact rooms are mostly white and blend modern touches like flat-screen TVs and geometric silver fixtures with period details like exposed beams, Dakota Jackson periwinkle chairs, and round penny-tile baths. **Pros:** great value for downtown location; discount passes to Gold's Gym across the street; complimentary continental

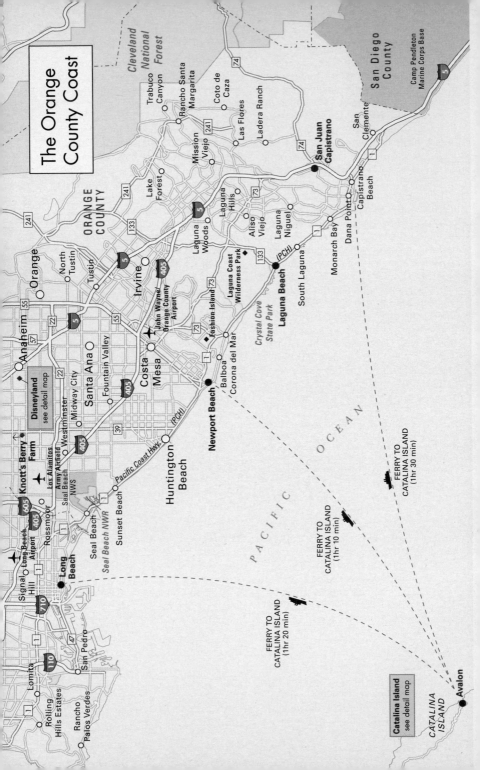

breakfast. **Cons:** no resort services; small rooms; no elevator. $ *Rooms from: $129 ⊠ 335 Pacific Ave., Long Beach ☎ 562/432–8950 ⊕ www.thevardenhotel. com ⇆ 35 rooms* ⑩ *Free Breakfast.*

Newport Beach

6 miles south of Huntington Beach via the Pacific Coast Hwy.

Newport Beach has evolved from a simple seaside village to an icon of chic coastal living. Its ritzy reputation comes from mega-yachts bobbing in the harbor, boutiques that rival those in Beverly Hills, and spectacular homes overlooking the ocean.

The city boasts some of the cleanest beaches in Southern California; inland Newport Beach's concentration of high-rise office buildings, shopping centers, and luxury hotels drives the economy. But on the city's Balboa Peninsula, you can still catch a glimpse of a more humble, down-to-earth town scattered with taco spots, tackle shops, and sailor bars.

ESSENTIALS
VISITOR AND TOUR INFORMATION
Visit Newport Beach Concierge. ⊠ *Atrium Court at Fashion Island, 401 Newport Center Dr.* ☎ *855/563–9767* ⊕ *www. visitnewportbeach.com.*

⊙ Sights

Balboa Island
COMMERCIAL CENTER | FAMILY | This sliver of terra firma in Newport Harbor boasts quaint streets tightly packed with impossibly charming multimillion-dollar cottages. The island's main drag, Marine Avenue, is lined with equally picturesque cafés and shops. A car-free bike path and boardwalk encircles much of the island for an easy and scenic ramble.

Balboa Peninsula
BEACH—SIGHT | FAMILY | Newport's best beaches are on Balboa Peninsula, where many jetties pave the way to ideal swimming areas. The most intense spot for bodysurfing in Orange County, and arguably on the West Coast, known as the **Wedge,** is at the south end of the peninsula. It was created by accident in the 1930s when the Federal Works Progress Administration built a jetty to protect Newport Harbor. ■**TIP➜ Rip currents and punishing waves mean it's strictly for the pros—but it sure is fun to watch an experienced local ride it.** ⊠ *2172 E. Ocean Front* ⊕ *www.visitnewportbeach.com/ beaches-and-parks/the-wedge.*

Discovery Cube's Ocean Quest
MUSEUM | FAMILY | This family-friendly destination has exhibits on the history of the harbor, ocean explorers, and scientific aspects of the Pacific Ocean. Other fun features include a touch tank holding local sea creatures and a lab for kids that encourages innovation. ⊠ *600 E. Bay Ave.* ☎ *949/675–8915* ⊕ *www.oceanquestoc.org* ⊠ *$5* ⊙ *Closed weekdays.*

Newport Harbor
BODY OF WATER | FAMILY | Sheltering nearly 16,000 small boats, Newport Harbor may seduce even those who don't own a yacht. Spend an afternoon exploring the charming avenues and surrounding alleys; take California's longest-running auto ferry across to Balboa Island. The fare is $2 for car and driver for the scenic crossing. Several grassy areas on the primarily residential Lido Isle have views of the water. To truly experience the harbor, rent an electric boat for a pleasant day cruise or try stand-up paddleboarding in the sheltered waters. ⊠ *Pacific Coast Hwy.* ⊕ *www.balboaislandferry.com.*

Newport Pier
MARINA | FAMILY | Jutting out into the ocean near 20th Street, Newport Pier is a popular fishing spot. Street parking is difficult, so grab the first space you find and be prepared to walk. Early on

Wednesday–Sunday mornings you're likely to encounter dory fishermen hawking their predawn catches, as they've done for generations. On weekends the area is alive with kids of all ages on in-line skates, skateboards, and bikes dodging pedestrians and whizzing past fast-food joints and classic dive bars. ✉ *72 McFadden Pl.*

🍴 Restaurants

Basilic
$$$ | **BRASSERIE** | This intimate French-Swiss bistro adds a touch of old-world elegance to the island with its white linen and flower-topped tables. Chef Bernard Althaus grows the herbs used in his classic French dishes. **Known for:** French classics; fine wine; old-school ambience. [$] *Average main: $32* ✉ *217 Marine Ave., Balboa Island* ☎ *949/673–0570* 🌐 *www.basilicrestaurant.com* 🕑 *Closed Sun.*

Bear Flag Fish Co.
$ | **SEAFOOD** | **FAMILY** | Expect long lines in summer at this indoor/outdoor dining spot serving up the freshest local fish (swordfish, sea bass, halibut, and tuna) and a wide range of creative seafood dishes (the Hawaiian-style *poke* salad with ahi tuna is a local favorite). Order at the counter, which doubles as a seafood market, and sit inside the airy dining room or outside on a grand patio. **Known for:** freshest seafood; fish tacos; craft beers. [$] *Average main: $12* ✉ *Newport Peninsula, 3421 Via Lido* ☎ *949/673–3474* 🌐 *www.bearflagfishco.com.*

The Cannery
$$$ | **SEAFOOD** | This 1920s cannery building still teems with fish, but now they go into dishes on the eclectic Pacific Rim menu rather than being packed into crates. Settle in at the sushi bar, in the dining room, or on the patio before choosing between sashimi, freshly shucked oysters, or cilantro-marinated fish tacos. **Known for:** waterfront views; seafood specialties; craft cocktails. [$] *Average main: $35* ✉ *3010 Lafayette Rd.* ☎ *949/566–0060* 🌐 *www.cannerynewport.com* 🕑 *No lunch Mon.*

Gulfstream
$$$ | **SEAFOOD** | **FAMILY** | This on-trend restaurant has an open kitchen, comfortable booths, and outdoor seating. The patio is a fantastic place to hang out. **Known for:** oysters on the half shell; local hangout; outdoor patio. [$] *Average main: $33* ✉ *850 Avocado Ave.* ☎ *949/718–0188* 🌐 *www.gulfstreamrestaurant.com.*

3-Thirty-3
$$ | **AMERICAN** | This stylish eatery attracts a convivial crowd—both young and old—for midday, sunset, and late-night dining. A long list of small, shareable plates heightens the camaraderie. **Known for:** happy hour; brunch burritos; generous portions. [$] *Average main: $26* ✉ *333 Bayside Dr.* ☎ *949/673–8464* 🌐 *www.3thirty3nb.com.*

🛏 Hotels

Balboa Bay Resort
$$$ | **RESORT** | **FAMILY** | Sharing the same frontage as the private Balboa Bay Club that long ago hosted Humphrey Bogart, Lauren Bacall, and the Reagans, this waterfront resort has one of the best bay views around. **Pros:** exquisite bayfront views; comfortable beds; a raked beach for guests. **Cons:** not much within walking distance; $34 nightly hospitality fee; some rooms have courtyard-only views. [$] *Rooms from: $339* ✉ *1221 W. Coast Hwy.* ☎ *949/645–5000* 🌐 *www.balboabayresort.com* 🛏 *159 rooms* 🍽 *No meals.*

Fashion Island Hotel
$$ | **HOTEL** | **FAMILY** | Across a palm tree–lined boulevard from stylish Fashion Island, this 20-story tower caters to business types during the week and luxury seekers on weekends. **Pros:** lively lounge scene; large heated pool; great location. **Cons:** steep valet parking prices; some rooms have views of

Riding the waves at Newport Beach

mall parking; destination fee add-on. [$] *Rooms from: $295* ✉ *690 Newport Center Dr.* ☎ *949/759–0808, 877/591–9145* 🌐 *www.fashionislandhotel.com* 🛏 *295 rooms* 🍴 *No meals.*

★ Lido House, Autograph Collection
$$ | RESORT | FAMILY | Close to the Balboa Peninsula, the Lido House is modeled after a New England–style beach cottage, one grand enough to welcome you and all your family and friends. **Pros:** large hot tub and pool deck; lively hotel bar; free bikes to cruise the nearby beach boardwalk. **Cons:** pricey restaurant; $33 resort fee add-on; $40 valet parking. [$] *Rooms from: $300* ✉ *3300 Newport Blvd., Balboa Island* ☎ *949/524–8500* 🛏 *130 rooms* 🍴 *No meals.*

Newport Beach Marriott Hotel and Spa
$$ | RESORT | Here you'll be smack in the busy part of town: across from Fashion Island, next to a country club, and with a view toward Newport Harbor. **Pros:** four concierge floors offer enhanced amenities; large spa; across from Fashion Island. **Cons:** sprawling floor plan; small bathrooms; car is essential for exploring beyond Fashion Island. [$] *Rooms from: $229* ✉ *900 Newport Center Dr.* ☎ *949/640–4000* 🌐 *www.marriott.com* 🛏 *532 rooms.*

Activities

BOAT RENTALS

Balboa Boat Rentals
BOATING | FAMILY | You can tour the waterways surrounding Lido and Balboa isles with kayaks ($18 an hour), stand-up paddleboards ($25 for two hours), small motorboats ($75 an hour), and electric boats ($80 to $105 an hour) at Balboa Boat Rentals. ✉ *510 E. Edgewater Ave., Balboa Island* ☎ *855/690–0794* 🌐 *www.boats4rent.com.*

BOAT TOURS

Catalina Flyer
TOUR—SPORTS | FAMILY | At Balboa Pavilion, the *Catalina Flyer* operates a 90-minute daily round-trip passage to Catalina Island for $70 in season. Reservations are required; check the schedule,

A whimbrel hunts for mussels at Crystal Cove State Park.

as crossings may be canceled due to annual maintenance. ✉ *400 Main St., Balboa Island* ☎ *949/673–5245* ⊕ *www. catalinainfo.com.*

Hornblower Cruises and Events

TOUR—SPORTS | This operator books three-hour weekend dinner cruises with dancing for $95. The two-hour Sunday brunch cruise starts at $75. Cruises traverse the mostly placid and scenic waters of Newport Harbor. ✉ *2431 W. Coast Hwy.* ☎ *888/467–6256* ⊕ *www. hornblower.com.*

FISHING
Davey's Locker

FISHING | FAMILY | In addition to a complete tackle shop, Davey's Locker offers half-day sportfishing trips starting at $41.50. Whale-watching excursions begin at $26 for weekdays. ✉ *Balboa Pavilion, 400 Main St., Balboa Island* ☎ *949/673–1434* ⊕ *www.daveyslocker.com.*

🛍 Shopping

★ **Fashion Island**

STORE/MALL | Shake the sand out of your shoes to head inland to the ritzy Fashion Island outdoor mall, a cluster of arcades and courtyards complete with koi pond, fountains, and a family-friendly trolley—plus some awesome ocean views. It has the luxe department stores Neiman Marcus and Bloomingdale's, plus expensive spots like Jonathan Adler, Kate Spade, and Michael Stars. ✉ *401 Newport Center Dr., between Jamboree and MacArthur Blvds., off PCH* ☎ *949/721–2000, 855/658–8527* ⊕ *www. shopfashionisland.com.*

Laguna Beach

10 miles south of Newport Beach on PCH, 60 miles south of Los Angeles, I–5 south to Hwy. 133, which turns into Laguna Canyon Rd.

Driving in along Laguna Canyon Road from the Interstate 405 freeway gives you the chance to cruise through a gorgeous coastal canyon, large stretches of which remain undeveloped, before arriving at a glistening wedge of ocean. There are 30 coves and beaches to visit, all with some of the cleanest water in Southern California. There's a convenient and free trolley service through town; service is extended on weekends and holidays.

Laguna's welcome mat is legendary. On the corner of Forest and Park avenues is a gate proclaiming, "This gate hangs well and hinders none, refresh and rest, then travel on." A gay community has long been established here; art galleries dot the village streets, and there's usually someone daubing up in Heisler Park. Along the Pacific Coast Highway you'll find dozens of clothing boutiques, jewelry stores, and cafés.

ESSENTIALS
VISITOR AND TOUR INFORMATION
Visit Laguna Beach Visitors Center. ⊠ *381 Forest Ave.* ☎ *949/497–9229, 800/877–1115* ⊕ *www.visitlagunabeach.com.*

Sights

Laguna Art Museum
MUSEUM | This museum displays American art, with an emphasis on California artists from all periods. Special exhibits change quarterly. ⊠ *307 Cliff Dr.* ☎ *949/494–8971* ⊕ *www.lagunaartmuseum.org* ⧉ *$7* ⊗ *Closed Wed.*

Laguna Coast Wilderness Park
HIKING/WALKING | **FAMILY** | The Laguna Coast Wilderness Park is spread over 7,000 acres of fragile coastal territory, including the canyon. The 40 miles of trails are great for hiking and mountain biking, and are open daily, weather permitting. Docent-led hikes are given most weekends. No dogs are allowed in the park. ⊠ *18751 Laguna Canyon Rd.* ☎ *949/923–2235* ⊕ *www.ocparks.com/parks/lagunac* ⧉ *$3 parking.*

⊘ Beaches

★ Main Beach Park
BEACH—SIGHT | **FAMILY** | A stocky 1920s lifeguard tower marks Main Beach Park, where a wooden boardwalk separates the sand from a strip of lawn. Walk along this soft-sand beach, or grab a bench and watch people bodysurfing, playing volleyball, or scrambling around two half-basketball courts. The beach also has children's play equipment. Most of Laguna's hotels are within a short (but hilly) walk. **Amenities:** lifeguards; toilets; showers. **Best for:** sunset; swimming; walking. ⊠ *Broadway at S. Coast Hwy.* ⊕ *www.visitlagunabeach.com.*

1,000 Steps Beach
BEACH—SIGHT | **FAMILY** | Off South Coast Highway at 9th Street, 1,000 Steps Beach is a hard-to-find spot tucked away in a neighborhood with great waves and hard-packed, white sand. There aren't really 1,000 steps down (but when you hike back up, it'll certainly feel like it). Sea caves and tide pools enhance this already beautiful natural spot. The beach is a rare dog-friendly spot. **Amenities:** showers. **Best for:** snorkeling; surfing; swimming. ⊠ *S. Coast Hwy., at 9th St.*

Wood's Cove
BEACH—SIGHT | **FAMILY** | Off South Coast Highway, Wood's Cove is especially quiet during the week. Big rock formations hide lurking crabs. This is a prime scuba-diving spot, and at high tide much of the beach is underwater. Climbing the steps to leave, you can see a Tudor-style mansion that was once home to Bette Davis. Street parking is limited. **Amenities:** none. **Best for:** snorkeling; scuba diving; sunset. ⊠ *Diamond St. and Ocean Way* ⊕ *www.visitlagunabeach.com.*

Looking for shells on Laguna Beach, one of the nicest stretches of sand in Southern California

🍴 Restaurants

Ocean at Main

$$$ | **AMERICAN** | Set in a handsomely renovated former bank from the 1940s, Ocean at Main's dishes are artfully presented and feature the best of California produce. Owned by the O.C.'s favorite chef, Craig Strong (who guided Studio at Montage for almost a decade), there's an expected emphasis on service but without pretension. **Known for:** handsome dining room; local ingredients; California-focused wine list. $ *Average main: $38* ✉ *222 Ocean Ave.* ☎ *949/715–3870* ⊕ *www.oceanatmain.com.*

Sapphire Laguna

$$ | **INTERNATIONAL** | **FAMILY** | This Laguna Beach establishment set in a historic Craftsman is part gourmet pantry (a must-stop for your every picnic need) and part global dining adventure. Iranian-born chef Azmin Ghahreman takes you on a journey through Europe and Asia with dishes ranging from coconut macaroon pancakes to Malaysian black pepper shrimp. **Known for:** fried chicken sandwich; weekend brunch; pet-friendly patio. $ *Average main: $27* ✉ *The Old Pottery Place, 1200 S. Coast Hwy.* ☎ *949/715–9888* ⊕ *www.sapphirelaguna.com.*

★ Studio

$$$$ | **MODERN AMERICAN** | In a nod to Laguna's art history, Studio has housemade specialties that entice the eye as well as the palate. The restaurant occupies its own Craftsman-style bungalow, atop a 50-foot bluff overlooking the Pacific. **Known for:** attentive service; chef's tasting menu; being great for special occasions. $ *Average main: $60* ✉ *Montage Laguna Beach, 30801 S. Coast Hwy.* ☎ *949/715–6420* ⊕ *www. studiolagunabeach.com* ⊗ *Closed Mon. No lunch.*

Taco Loco

$ | **MEXICAN** | **FAMILY** | This may look like a fast-food taco stand, and the hemp brownies on the menu may make you think the kitchen's *really* laid-back, but the quality of the food here equals that in many higher-price restaurants. Some

Mexican standards get a Louisiana twist, like Cajun-spiced seafood tacos. **Known for:** vegetarian tacos; sidewalk seating; surfer clientele. $ *Average main: $12* ⊠ *640 S. Coast Hwy.* ☎ *949/497–1635* ⊕ *www.tacoloco.net.*

Zinc Café and Market
$ | VEGETARIAN | FAMILY | Families flock to this small Laguna Beach institution for reasonably priced breakfast and lunch options. Try the signature quiches or poached egg dishes in the morning, or swing by later in the day for healthy salads, house-made soups, quesadillas, or pizzettes. **Known for:** gourmet goodies; avocado toast; busy outdoor patio. $ *Average main: $15* ⊠ *350 Ocean Ave.* ☎ *949/494–6302* ⊕ *www.zinccafe.com* ⊗ *No dinner Nov.–Apr.*

🛏 Hotels

Inn at Laguna Beach
$$$ | HOTEL | FAMILY | This bright yellow local landmark is stacked neatly at the north end of Laguna's Main Beach and it's one of the few hotels in SoCal set almost on the sand. **Pros:** rooftop bar; beach essentials provided; beachfront location. **Cons:** ocean-view rooms are pricey; small hot tub; limited breakfast menu. $ *Rooms from: $379* ⊠ *211 N. Coast Hwy.* ☎ *949/497–9722, 800/544–4479* ⊕ *www.innatlagunabeach.com* ⇥ *70 rooms.*

La Casa del Camino
$$ | HOTEL | The look is Old California at the 1929-built La Casa del Camino, with dark woods, arched doors, and wrought iron in the lobby. **Pros:** breathtaking views from rooftop lounge; personable service; close to beach. **Cons:** some rooms face the highway; frequent events can make hotel noisy; some rooms are very small. $ *Rooms from: $229* ⊠ *1289 S. Coast Hwy.* ☎ *949/497–2446, 855/634–5736* ⊕ *www.lacasadelcamino.com* ⇥ *36 rooms* ⦿ *No meals.*

★ Montage Laguna Beach
$$$$ | RESORT | FAMILY | Laguna's connection to the Californian plein-air artists is mined for inspiration at this head-turning, lavish hotel. **Pros:** top-notch, enthusiastic service; idyllic coastal location; numerous sporty pursuits available offshore. **Cons:** rates can be more than $1,100 per night for holidays or summer weekends; $50 valet parking; $42 daily resort fee. $ *Rooms from: $695* ⊠ *30801 S. Coast Hwy.* ☎ *949/715–6000, 866/271-6953* ⊕ *www.montagehotels.com/lagunabeach* ⇥ *250 rooms* ⦿ *No meals.*

Surf and Sand Resort
$$$$ | RESORT | FAMILY | One mile south of downtown, on an exquisite stretch of beach with thundering waves and gorgeous rocks, this is a getaway for those who want a boutique hotel experience without all the formalities. **Pros:** easy beach access; intimate property; slightly removed from Main Street crowds. **Cons:** pricey valet parking; surf can be quite loud; no air conditioning. $ *Rooms from: $575* ⊠ *1555 S. Coast Hwy.* ☎ *949/497–4477, 877/741–5908* ⊕ *www.surfandsandresort.com* ⇥ *167 rooms* ⦿ *No meals.*

🛍 Shopping

Coast Highway, Forest and Ocean avenues, and Glenneyre Street are full of art galleries, fine jewelry stores, souvenir shops, and clothing boutiques.

Adam Neeley Fine Art Jewelry
JEWELRY/ACCESSORIES | Be prepared to be dazzled at Adam Neeley Fine Art Jewelry, where artisan proprietor Adam Neeley creates one-of-a-kind modern pieces. ⊠ *352 N. Coast Hwy.* ☎ *949/715–0953* ⊕ *www.adamneeley.com* ⊗ *Closed Sun. and Mon.*

Art for the Soul
CRAFTS | A riot of color, Art for the Soul has hand-painted furniture, crafts, and unusual gifts. ⊠ *272 Forest Ave.* ☎ *949/675–1791* ⊕ *www.art4thesoul.com.*

Mission San Juan Capistrano

Candy Baron
FOOD/CANDY | FAMILY | Get your sugar fix at the time-warped Candy Baron, filled with old-fashioned goodies like gum-drops, bull's-eyes, and more than 50 flavors of saltwater taffy. ✉ *231 Forest Ave.* ☎ *949/497–7508* ⊕ *www.thecandy-baron.com.*

Fetneh Blake
CLOTHING | Hit Fetneh Blake for pricey, Euro-chic clothes. The emerging design-ers found here lure Angelenos to make the trek south. ✉ *427 N. Coast Hwy.* ☎ *949/494–3787* ⊕ *www.fetnehblake.com.*

La Rue du Chocolat
FOOD/CANDY | This shop dispenses chocolate-covered strawberries and handcrafted chocolates in seasonal flavors. ✉ *Peppertree La., 448 S. Coast Hwy., Suite B* ☎ *949/494–2372* ⊕ *www.larueduchocolat.com.*

San Juan Capistrano

5 miles north of Dana Point, Hwy. 74, 60 miles north of San Diego, I–5.

San Juan Capistrano is best known for its historic mission, where the swallows traditionally return each year, migrating from their winter haven in Argentina, but these days they are more likely to choose other local sites for nesting. St. Joseph's Day, March 19, launches a week of fowl festivities. Charming antiques stores, which range from pricey to cheap, line Camino Capistrano.

GETTING HERE AND AROUND
If you arrive by train, which is far more romantic and restful than battling freeway traffic, you'll be dropped off across from the mission at the San Juan Capistrano depot. With its appealing brick café and preserved Santa Fe cars, the depot retains much of the magic of early American railroads. If driving, park near Ortega and Camino Capistrano, the city's main streets.

Sights

★ Mission San Juan Capistrano

ARCHAEOLOGICAL SITE | FAMILY | Founded in 1776 by Father Junípero Serra (consecrated as St. Serra), Mission San Juan Capistrano was one of two Roman Catholic outposts between Los Angeles and San Diego. The Great Stone Church, begun in 1797, is the largest structure created by the Spanish in California. After extensive retrofitting, the golden-hued interiors are open to visitors who may feel they are touring among ruins in Italy rather than the O.C. Many of the mission's adobe buildings have been restored to illustrate mission life, with exhibits of an olive millstone, tallow ovens, tanning vats, metalworking furnaces, and the padres' living quarters. The gardens, with their fountains and koi pond, are a lovely spot in which to wander. The bougainvillea-covered Serra Chapel is believed to be the oldest church still standing in California and is the only building remaining in which St. Serra actually led Mass. Mass takes place weekdays at 7 am in the chapel. Enter via a small gift shop in the gatehouse. ✉ *26801 Ortega Hwy.* ☎ *949/234–1300* 🌐 *www.missionsjc.com* 🎫 *$10.*

San Juan Capistrano Library

LIBRARY | FAMILY | Near Mission San Juan Capistrano is the San Juan Capistrano Library, a postmodern structure built in 1983. Architect Michael Graves combined classical and Mission styles to striking effect. Its courtyard has secluded places for reading. ✉ *31495 El Camino Real* ☎ *949/493–1752* 🌐 *ocpl.org/libloc/sjc* 🕒 *Closed Fri.*

Restaurants

Cedar Creek Inn

$$$ | AMERICAN | FAMILY | Just across the street from Mission San Juan Capistrano, this restaurant has a patio that's perfect for a late lunch or a romantic dinner. The menu is fairly straightforward, dishes are tasty, and portions are substantial—try the Cobb salad or a burger at lunch, or splurge on the prime rib for dinner. **Known for:** brunch; rich desserts; comfortable seating. [$] *Average main: $30* ✉ *26860 Ortega Hwy.* ☎ *949/240–2229* 🌐 *www.cedarcreekinn.com.*

L'Hirondelle

$$$ | FRENCH | Locals have romanced at cozy tables for decades at this delightful restaurant. Such classic dishes as beef bourguignonne and a New York strip in a black-peppercorn-and-brandy sauce are the hallmark of this French and Belgian restaurant, whose name means "the little swallow." The extensive wine list is matched by an impressive selection of Belgian beers. **Known for:** Sunday brunch; traditional French cuisine; composed salads. [$] *Average main: $35* ✉ *31631 Camino Capistrano* ☎ *949/661–0425* 🌐 *www.lhirondellesjc.com* 🕒 *Closed Mon.*

The Ramos House Cafe

$$ | AMERICAN | It may be worth hopping the Amtrak to San Juan Capistrano just for the chance to have breakfast or lunch at one of Orange County's most beloved restaurants, located in a historic board-and-batten home dating back to 1881. This café sits practically on the railroad tracks across from the depot—nab a table on the patio and dig into a hearty breakfast featuring seasonal items, such as the smoked bacon scramble with wilted rocket. **Known for:** southern specialties; weekend brunch; historic setting. [$] *Average main: $20* ✉ *31752 Los Rios St.* ☎ *949/443–1342* 🌐 *www.ramoshouse.com* 🕒 *Closed Mon. No dinner.*

Nightlife

Swallow's Inn

BARS/PUBS | Across the way from Mission San Juan Capistrano you may spot a line of Harleys in front of the down-home and downright funky Swallow's Inn. Despite a somewhat tough look, it attracts all kinds—bikers, surfers, modern-day cowboys, grandparents—for a drink, a casual bite, karaoke nights, and some rowdy live country music. ⊠ *31786 Camino Capistrano* ☎ *949/493–3188* ⊕ *www.swallowsinn.com.*

Catalina Island

Just 22 miles out from the L.A. coastline, across from Newport Beach and Long Beach, Catalina has virtually unspoiled mountains, canyons, coves, and beaches; best of all, it gives you a glimpse of what undeveloped Southern California once looked like.

Water sports are a big draw, as divers and snorkelers come for the exceptionally clear water surrounding the island. Kayakers are attracted to the calm cove waters and thrill seekers book the eco-themed zipline that traverses a wooded canyon. The main town, Avalon, is a charming, old-fashioned beach community, where yachts and pleasure boats bob in the crescent bay. Wander beyond the main drag and find brightly painted little bungalows fronting the sidewalks; golf carts are the preferred mode of transport.

In 1919, William Wrigley Jr., the chewing-gum magnate, purchased a controlling interest in the company developing Catalina Island, whose most famous landmark, the Casino, was built in 1929 under his orders. Because he owned the Chicago Cubs baseball team, Wrigley made Catalina the team's spring training site, an arrangement that lasted until 1951.

In 1975, the Catalina Island Conservancy, a nonprofit foundation, acquired about 88% of the island to help preserve the area's natural flora and fauna, including the bald eagle and the Catalina Island fox. These days the conservancy is restoring the rugged interior country with plantings of native grasses and trees. The organization helps oversee the interior's 50 miles of bike trails and 165 miles of hiking trails and helps protect the island's 60 endemic species. Along the coast you might spot oddities like electric perch, saltwater goldfish, and flying fish.

GETTING HERE AND AROUND
FERRY TRAVEL
Two companies offer ferry service to Catalina Island. The boats have both indoor and outdoor seating and snack bars. Excessive baggage is not allowed, and there are extra fees for bicycles and surfboards. The waters around Catalina can get rough, so if you're prone to seasickness, come prepared. Winter, holiday, and weekend schedules vary, so reservations are strongly recommended.

Catalina Express makes an hour-long run from Long Beach or San Pedro to Avalon and a 90-minute run from Dana Point to Avalon with some stops at Two Harbors. Round-trip fares begin at $73.50, with discounts for seniors and kids. On busy days, a $15 upgrade to the Commodore Lounge, when available, is worth it. Service from Newport Beach to Avalon is available through the *Catalina Flyer.* The boat leaves from Balboa Pavilion at 9 am (in season), takes 75 minutes to reach the island, and costs $70 round-trip. The return boat leaves Catalina at 4:30 pm. Reservations are required for the *Catalina Flyer* and recommended for all weekend and summer trips. ■TIP→ **Keep an eye out for dolphins, which sometimes swim alongside the ferries.**

FERRY CONTACTS **Catalina Flyer.**
☎ *949/673–5245* ⊕ *www.catalinainfo.com.*

GOLF CARTS
Golf carts constitute the island's main form of transportation for sightseeing in the area; however, some parts of town are off-limits, as is the island's interior. Drivers 21 and over with valid driver's license can rent them along Avalon's Crescent Avenue and Pebbly Beach Road for about $45 per hour with a $45 deposit, payable via cash only.

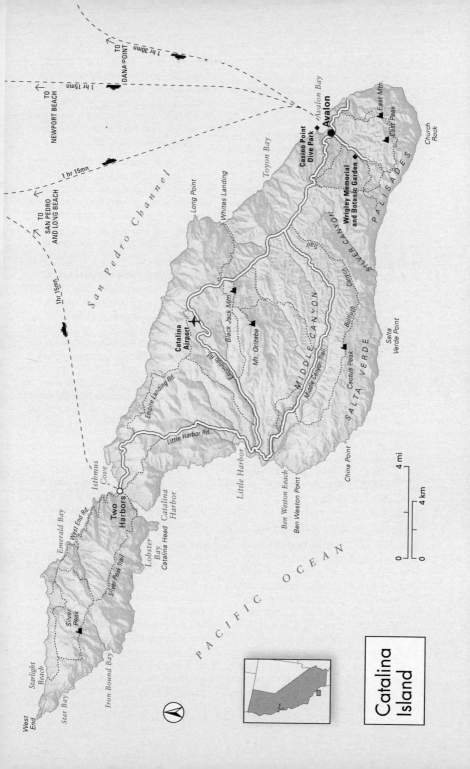

Catalina Island

GOLF CART RENTALS Island Rentals.
✉ *125 Pebbly Beach Rd., Avalon*
☎ *310/510–1456* ⊕ *www.catalinagolfcart-rentals.com.*

HELICOPTER TRAVEL
Island Express helicopters depart from San Pedro (Friday, Saturday, and Sunday only), John Wayne Airport, Burbank Airport, and Long Beach next to the *Queen Mary* (8 am–dusk). The trip from Long Beach takes about 15 minutes and costs $135 one way, $270 round-trip. Reservations a week in advance are recommended; some flights require a minimum passenger load.

TIMING
Although Catalina can be seen in one very hectic day, several inviting hotels make it worth extending your stay for one or more nights. A short itinerary might include breakfast on the pier, a tour of the interior, a snorkeling excursion at Casino Point, or beach day at the Descanso Beach Club and a romantic waterfront dinner in Avalon.

After late October, rooms are much easier to find on short notice, rates drop dramatically, and many hotels offer packages that include transportation from the mainland and/or sightseeing tours. January to March you have a good chance of spotting migrating gray whales on the ferry crossing.

TOURS
Santa Catalina Island Company runs nine land tours and six ocean tours, including the *Flying Fish* boat trip (summer evenings only); a comprehensive inland motor tour; a tour of Skyline Drive; several Casino tours; a scenic tour of Avalon; a glass-bottom-boat tour; an undersea tour on a semisubmersible vessel; an eco-themed zipline tour that traverses a scenic canyon; a speedy Ocean Runner expedition that searches for all manner of sea creatures and a fast Cyclone boat tour that takes you to the less populated center of the island, Two Harbors. Reservations are highly recommended for

the inland tours. Tours cost $14 to $129. There are ticket booths on the Green Pleasure Pier, at the Casino, in the plaza, and at the boat landing. Catalina Adventure Tours, which has booths at the boat landing and on the pier, also arranges excursions at comparable prices.

The Catalina Island Conservancy organizes custom ecotours and hikes of the interior. Naturalist guides drive open jeeps through some gorgeously untrammeled parts of the island. Tours start at $70 per person for a two-hour trip (two-person minimum). The tours run year-round.

ESSENTIALS
VISITOR AND TOUR INFORMATION
Catalina Adventure Tours. ☎ *877/510–2888* ⊕ *www.catalinaadventuretours.com.*
Catalina Island Chamber of Commerce and Visitors Bureau. ✉ *1 Green Pleasure Pier, Avalon* ☎ *310/510–1520* ⊕ *www.catalinachamber.com.* **Catalina Island Conservancy.** ✉ *125 Claressa Ave., Avalon* ☎ *310/510–2595* ⊕ *www.catalinaconservancy.org.* **Santa Catalina Island Company.** ☎ *877/778–8322* ⊕ *www.visitcatalinaisland.com.*

Avalon

A 1- to 2-hour ferry ride from Long Beach, Newport Beach, or San Pedro; a 15-minute helicopter ride from Long Beach or San Pedro, slightly longer from Santa Ana.

Avalon, Catalina's only real town, extends from the shore of its natural harbor to the surrounding hillsides. Its resident population is about 3,800, but it swells with tourists on summer weekends. Most of the city's activity, however, is centered on the pedestrian mall on Crescent Avenue, and most sights are easily reached on foot. Private cars are restricted and rental cars aren't allowed, but taxis, trams, and shuttles can take you anywhere you need to go. Bicycles, electric bikes, and golf carts can be rented from shops along Crescent Avenue.

Did You Know?

You can take a tour of Avalon's Scenic Drive for seven-and-a-half miles of panoramic views and a lesson in Catalina Island folklore.

⊙ Sights

★ Casino

BUILDING | This circular white structure is one of the finest examples of art deco architecture anywhere. Its Spanish-inspired floors and murals gleam with brilliant blue and green Catalina tiles. In this case, *casino*, the Italian word for "gathering place," has nothing to do with gambling. First-run movies are screened nightly at the Avalon Theatre, noteworthy for its classic 1929 theater pipe organ and art deco wall murals. The circular ballroom once famously hosted 1940s big bands and is still used for gala events.

The Santa Catalina Island Company leads three tours of the Casino—the 30-minute basic tour ($14), the 90-minute behind-the-scenes tour ($28), which leads visitors through the green room and into the Wrigleys' private lounge, and a weekend nights evening tour ($45), where guests enjoy wine on the scenic terrace after touring the historic building. ⊠ *1 Casino Way* ☎ *310/510–0179 theater* ⊕ *www.visit-catalinaisland.com.*

Casino Point Dive Park

BEACH—SIGHT | FAMILY | In front of the Casino are the crystal-clear waters of the Casino Point Dive Park, a protected marine preserve where moray eels, bat rays, spiny lobsters, harbor seals, and other sea creatures cruise around kelp forests and along the sandy bottom. No need to don a wet suit: the brilliantly orange garibaldi, California's state marine fish, can sometimes be viewed from the seawall. It's a terrific site for scuba diving, with some shallow areas suitable for snorkeling. Equipment can be rented on and near the pier. The shallow waters of Lover's Cove, east of the boat landing, are also good for snorkeling. ⊠ *Avalon.*

Where the Buffalo Roam ⊙

Zane Grey, the writer who put the Western novel on the map, spent a lot of time on Catalina, and his influence is still evident in a peculiar way. As the story goes, when the movie version of Grey's book *The Vanishing American* was filmed here in 1924, American bison were ferried across from the mainland to give the land that Western plains look. After the crew packed up and left, the buffalo stayed, and a small herd of about 150 still remains, grazing the interior and reinforcing the island's image as the last refuge from SoCal's urban sprawl.

Catalina Island Museum

LOCAL INTEREST | FAMILY | The exterior of the Catalina Island Museum is a nod to Catalina Island's developer William Wrigley Jr.—it's modeled after Wrigley Field in Chicago. Inside, the museum traces the island's history from it's precontact days and native Chumash to its role in Hollywood history and beyond. Two galleries host traveling exhibitions. The view from the outside terrace takes in lovely Avalon and its picturesque harbor. A small gift shop offers reproductions of the island's signature colorful Catalina pottery tiles. ⊠ *217 Metropole Ave.* ☎ *310/510–2414* ⊕ *www.catalinamuseum.org* ⊠ *$17.*

Green Pleasure Pier

LOCAL INTEREST | FAMILY | Head to the Green Pleasure Pier for a good vantage point of Avalon. On the pier you can find the visitor information, snack stands, and scads of squawking sea gulls. It's also the landing where visiting cruise-ship passengers catch tenders back out to their ship. ⊠ *End of Catalina Ave.*

Wrigley Memorial and Botanic Garden
GARDEN | Two miles south of the bay is Wrigley Memorial and Botanic Garden, home to plants native to Southern California. Several grow only on Catalina Island—Catalina ironwood, wild tomato, and rare Catalina mahogany. The Wrigley family commissioned the garden as well as the monument, which has a grand staircase and a Spanish-style mausoleum inlaid with colorful Catalina tile. Wrigley Jr. was once buried here but his remains were moved to Pasadena during World War II. ✉ *Avalon Canyon Rd.* ☎ *310/510–2897* 🌐 *www.catalina-conservancy.org* 🎟 *$8.*

🍴 Restaurants

Bluewater Grill
$$ | **SEAFOOD** | **FAMILY** | Overlooking the ferry landing and the entire harbor, the open-to-the-salt-air Bluewater Grill offers freshly caught fish, savory chowders, and all manner of shellfish. If they're on the menu, don't miss the swordfish steak or the sand dabs. **Known for:** fresh local fish; happy hour (October–May); harbor views. [$] *Average main: $27* ✉ *306 Crescent Ave.* ☎ *310/510–3474* 🌐 *www.bluewatergrill.com.*

Descanso Beach Club
$ | **AMERICAN** | **FAMILY** | Set on an expansive deck overlooking the water, Descanso Beach Club serves a wide range of favorites: buffalo wings, hamburgers, salads, nachos, and tacos are all part of the selection. Watch the harbor seals frolic just offshore while sipping the island's super-sweet signature cocktail, the Buffalo Milk, a mix of fruit liqueurs, vodka, and whipped cream. **Known for:** tropical beach vibe; scenic views; chic cabana rentals. [$] *Average main: $15* ✉ *Descanso Beach, 1 Descanso Ave.* ☎ *310/510–7410.*

The Lobster Trap
$$ | **SEAFOOD** | Seafood rules at the Lobster Trap—the restaurant's owner has his own boat and fishes for the catch of the day and, in season, spiny lobster. Ceviche is a great starter, always fresh and brightly flavored. **Known for:** locally caught seafood; convivial atmosphere; locals' hangout. [$] *Average main: $26* ✉ *128 Catalina St.* ☎ *310/510–8585* 🌐 *catalinalobstertrap.com.*

🛏 Hotels

Aurora Hotel
$$ | **HOTEL** | In a town dominated by historic properties, the Aurora is refreshingly contemporary, with a hip attitude and sleek furnishings. **Pros:** trendy design; quiet location off main drag; close to restaurants. **Cons:** standard rooms are small, even by Catalina standards; no elevator; small bathrooms. [$] *Rooms from: $270* ✉ *137 Marilla Ave.* ☎ *310/510–0454* 🌐 *www.auroracatalina.com* 🔑 *18 rooms* 🍴 *Breakfast.*

Hotel Vista del Mar
$$ | **HOTEL** | **FAMILY** | On the bay-facing Crescent Avenue, this third-floor property is steps from the beach, where complimentary towels, chairs, and umbrellas await guests. **Pros:** comfortable beds; central location; in-room fireplace. **Cons:** no restaurant or spa facilities; few rooms with ocean views; no elevator. [$] *Rooms from: $235* ✉ *417 Crescent Ave.* ☎ *310/510–1452, 800/601–3836* 🌐 *www.hotel-vistadelmar.com* 🔑 *14 rooms* 🍴 *Breakfast.*

Mt. Ada
$$$$ | **B&B/INN** | If you stay in the mansion where Wrigley Jr. once lived, you can enjoy all the comforts of a millionaire's home—at a millionaire's prices. **Pros:** timeless charm; shuttle from heliport and dock; incredible views. **Cons:** smallish rooms and bathrooms; expensive; queen-size beds only. [$] *Rooms from: $480* ✉ *398 Wrigley Rd.* ☎ *310/510–2030, 877/778–8322* ⏲ *Closed mid-Jan.–early Feb.* 🔑 *6 rooms* 🍴 *Some meals.*

Pavilion Hotel

$$ | **HOTEL** | **FAMILY** | This mid-century modern–style hotel is Avalon's most citified spot, though just a few steps from the sand. **Pros:** centrally located, steps from the beach and harbor; friendly staff; plush bedding. **Cons:** no pool; rooms near stairs can be noisy; some rooms fully shaded. $ *Rooms from: $265* ✉ *513 Crescent Ave.* ☎ *310/510–1788, 877/778–8322* ⊕ *www.visitcatalinaisland.com* ⇥ *71 rooms* ❍ *Breakfast.*

Portofino Hotel

$$ | **HOTEL** | **FAMILY** | Steps from the Green Pleasure Pier, this European-style hotel creates an intimate feel with brick courtyards and walkways and suites named after Italian cities. **Pros:** romantic; close to beach; incredible sundeck. **Cons:** ground-floor rooms can be noisy; some rooms are on small side; no elevator. $ *Rooms from: $209* ✉ *111 Crescent Ave.* ☎ *310/510–0555, 888/510–0555* ⊕ *www.hotelvillaportofino.com* ⇥ *35 rooms* ❍ *Breakfast.*

 ## Activities

BICYCLING
Brown's Bikes

BICYCLING | **FAMILY** | Look for rentals on Crescent Avenue and Pebbly Beach Road, where Brown's Bikes is located. Beach cruisers start at $25 per day, mountain bikes are $30 per day, and electric bikes are $50 for a day rental and a good choice for Catalina's hills. ✉ *107 Pebbly Beach Rd.* ☎ *310/510–0986* ⊕ *www.catalinabiking.com.*

DIVING AND SNORKELING

The Casino Point Underwater Park, with its handful of wrecks and ample sea life, is best suited for diving. Lover's Cove is better for snorkeling (but you'll share the area with glass-bottom boats). Both are protected marine preserves.

Catalina Divers Supply

SCUBA DIVING | Head to Catalina Divers Supply to rent equipment, sign up for guided scuba and snorkel tours, and attend certification classes. It also has an outpost at the Dive Park at Casino Point that offers gear rental and tank air fills. ✉ *7 Green Pleasure Pier* ☎ *310/510–0330* ⊕ *www.catalinadiverssupply.com.*

Chapter 7

LOS ANGELES

Updated by
Paul Feinstein,
Michelle Rae Uy,
and Candice Yacono

⊙ Sights	🍴 Restaurants	🛏 Hotels	🛍 Shopping	🍸 Nightlife
★★★★★	★★★★★	★★★★★	★★★★★	★★★★☆

WELCOME TO LOS ANGELES

TOP REASONS TO GO

★ **Stargazing:** Both through the telescope atop Griffith Park and among the residents of Beverly Hills.

★ **Eating:** From food trucks to fine dining, an unparalleled meal awaits your palate.

★ **Beaches and Boardwalks:** The dream of '80s Venice is alive in California.

★ **Shopping:** Peruse eclectic boutiques or window-shop on Rodeo Drive.

★ **Architecture:** Art-deco wonders to Frank Gehry masterpieces abound.

★ **Scenic Drives:** You haven't seen the sunset until you've seen it from a winding L.A. road.

1 **Santa Monica and the Beaches.** In Santa Monica, a lively beach scene plays out daily. Venice is a more raffish mix of artists, beach punks, and yuppies. Drive up the Pacific Coast Highway to Malibu, where the rich and famous reside.

2 **Beverly Hills, West Hollywood, and the Westside.** Rodeo Drive is particularly good for a look at wretched or ravishing excess. West Hollywood is an area for urban indulgences—shopping, restaurants, nightlife—rather than sightseeing.

3 **Hollywood and the Studios.** Glitzy and tarnished, good and bad—Hollywood is just like the entertainment business itself. The Walk of Fame, Chinese Theatre, and the Hollywood Bowl keep the romantic past alive. Universal Studios Hollywood is in the Valley.

4 **Mid-Wilshire and Koreatown.** In Mid-Wilshire is a glorious hodgepodge of manicured lawns and art-deco highrises. Here you can peruse art along Museum Row. Just east is Koreatown, which boasts some of the best bars and restaurants in the city.

5 **Downtown Los Angeles.** DTLA shows off spectacular modern architecture, especially the Walt Disney Concert Hall. The MOCA and the Broad anchor a world-class art scene, while El Pueblo de Los Angeles, Chinatown, and Little Tokyo reflect the city's diversity.

6 **Pasadena.** It's a quiet, genteel area, with outstanding Arts and Crafts homes and a pair of exceptional museums: the Norton Simon Museum and the Huntington Library.

7 **Los Feliz and the Eastside.** This is a land of good eats and better booze. Dine in Los Feliz and Silver Lake and go drinking in Echo Park and Highland Park.

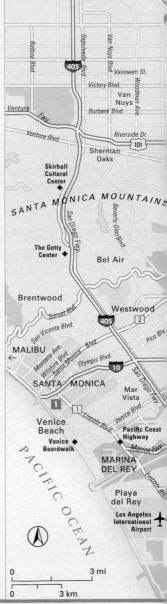

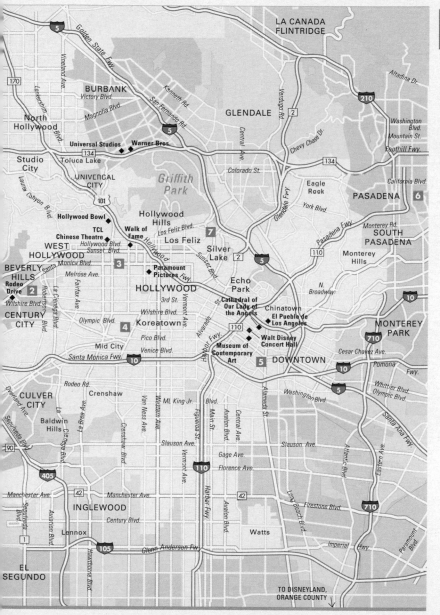

LA CANADA
FLINTRIDGE

BURBANK
Victory Blvd.
GLENDALE
North
Hollywood
Magnolia Blvd.
Studio
City
Universal Studios
Warner Bros.
Toluca Lake
UNIVERSAL
CITY
Griffith
Park
PASADENA
Eagle
Rock
SOUTH
PASADENA
Hollywood Bowl
Hollywood
Hills
Los Feliz
Silver
Lake
WEST
HOLLYWOOD
TCL
Chinese Theatre
Walk of
Fame
Monterey
Hills
BEVERLY
HILLS
Rodeo
Drive
Melrose Ave.
Paramount
Pictures
HOLLYWOOD
Echo
Park
N.
Broadway
MONTEREY
PARK
CENTURY
CITY
Wilshire Blvd.
Koreatown
Cathedral of
Our Lady of
the Angels
Chinatown
El Pueblo de
Los Angeles
Mid City
Museum of
Contemporary
Art
Walt Disney
Concert Hall
DOWNTOWN
CULVER
CITY
Baldwin
Hills
Crenshaw
INGLEWOOD
Lennox
Watts
EL
SEGUNDO
TO DISNEYLAND,
ORANGE COUNTY

SOUTH-OF-THE-BORDER FLAVOR

From Cal-Mex burritos to Mexico City–style tacos, Southern California is a top stateside destination for experiencing Mexico's myriad culinary styles.

Many Americans are surprised to learn that the Mexican menu goes far beyond Tex-Mex (or Cal-Mex) favorites like burritos, chimichangas, enchiladas, fajitas, and nachos—many of which were created or popularized stateside. Indeed, Mexico has rich, regional food styles, like the complex *mole* sauces of Puebla and Oaxaca and the fresh *ceviches* of Veracruz, as well as the trademark snack of Mexico City: tacos.

In Southern California tacos are an obsession, with numerous blogs and websites dedicated to the quest for the perfect taco. They're everywhere—in ramshackle taco stands, roving trucks, and strip-mall taquerias. Whether you're looking for a cheap snack or a lunch on-the-go, SoCal's taco selection can't be beat. But be forewarned: there may not be an English menu. Here we've noted unfamiliar taco terms, along with other potentially new-to-you items from the Mexican menu.

THIRST QUENCHERS

Spanish for "fresh water," *agua fresca* is made from fruit, rice, or seeds that are blended with sugar and water. Lemon, lime, and watermelon are common flavors. Other varieties include *agua de Jamaica*, flavored with red hibiscus petals; *agua de horchata*, a cinnamon-scented rice milk; and *agua de tamarindo*, a bittersweet variety flavored with tamarind. For a little more kick, try a *Michelada*, a beer spiked with lime juice and chili sauce, served in a salt-rimmed glass with ice.

Decoding the Menu

Ceviche—Citrus-marinated raw seafood appetizer from the Gulf shores of Veracruz. Often eaten with tortilla chips.

Chile relleno—Roasted poblano pepper stuffed with ground meat or cheese, then dipped in egg batter, fried, and served in tomato sauce.

Fish taco—A specialty in Southern California, the fish taco is a soft corn tortilla stuffed with grilled or fried white fish (mahimahi, tilapia, or wahoo), pico de gallo, *crema*, and shredded cabbage.

Gordita—"Little fat one" in Spanish, this dish is like a taco, but the cornmeal shell is thicker, similar to pita bread.

Mole—A complex sauce with Aztec roots made from more than 20 ingredients, including chilies, cinnamon, cumin, anise, sesame seeds, and Mexican chocolate. There are many variations, but the most common is *mole poblano* from the Puebla region.

Quesadilla—A snack made from a fresh tortilla that is folded over and stuffed with simple fillings, then toasted on a griddle. Elevated versions of the quesadilla may be stuffed with sautéed *flor de calabaza* (squash blossoms) or *huitlacoche* (corn mushrooms).

Tamales

Salsa—A cooked or raw sauce. Popular salsas include *pico de gallo,* a fresh sauce made from chopped tomatoes, onions, chilies, cilantro, and lime; *salsa verde,* made with tomatillos; and *salsa roja,* a cooked sauce made with chilies, tomatoes, onion, garlic, and cilantro.

Sope—A small, fried corn cake topped with ingredients like refried beans, shredded chicken, and salsa.

Taco—Tacos are made from soft, palm-sized corn tortillas folded over and filled with meat, chopped onion, cilantro, and salsa with meats like *al pastor* (spiced pork), *barbacoa* (braised beef), *carnitas* (roasted pork), *cecina* (chili-coated pork), *carne asada* (roasted, chopped beef), *chorizo* (spicy sausage), *lengua* (beef tongue), *sesos* (cow brain), and *tasajo* (spiced, grilled beef).

Tamales—Sweet or savory corn cakes that are steamed, and may be filled with cheese, roasted chilies, shredded meat, or other fillings.

Torta—A Mexican sandwich served on a crusty sandwich roll. Fillings often include meat, refried beans, and cheese.

Tacos

Los Angeles is a polarizing place, but those who hate it just haven't found their niche—there's truly a corner of the city for everyone. Drive for miles between towering palm trees, bodega-lined streets, and Downtown's skyscrapers, and you'll still never discover all of L.A.'s hidden gems.

Yes, you'll encounter traffic-clogged freeways, but there are also walkable pockets like Venice's Abbot Kinney. You'll drive past Beverly Hills mansions and spy palaces perched atop hills, but you'll also see the roots of mid-century modern architecture in Silver Lake. You'll soak up the sun in Santa Monica and then find yourself barhopping in the city's revitalized Downtown while enjoying scrumptious fish tacos along the way.

You might think that you'll have to spend most of your visit in a car, but that's not the case. In fact, exploring by foot is the only way to really get to know the various fringe neighborhoods and mini-cities that make up the vast L.A. area. But no single locale—whether it's Malibu, Downtown, Beverly Hills, or Burbank—fully embodies Los Angeles. It's in the mix that you'll discover the city's character.

Planning

When to Go

Almost any time of the year is the right time to go to Los Angeles; the climate is mild and pleasant year-round. Winter brings crisp, sunny, unusually smogless days from about November to May (expect brief rains from December to April). Los Angeles summers, which are virtually rainless, can lead to air-quality alerts. Prices skyrocket and reservations are a must when tourism peaks from July through early October.

Getting Here and Around

AIR TRAVEL

It's generally easier to navigate the secondary airports than to get through sprawling LAX, the city's major gateway. Bob Hope Airport in Burbank is closest to Downtown, and domestic flights to it can be cheaper than those to LAX—it's definitely worth checking out. From Long Beach Airport it's equally convenient to go north to central Los Angeles or south to Orange County. Flights to Orange County's John Wayne Airport are often more expensive than those to the other secondary airports. Parking at the smaller airports is cheaper than at LAX.

At LAX, SuperShuttle allows walk-on shuttle passengers without prior reservations. FlyAway buses travel between LAX and Van Nuys, Westwood, La Brea, and Union Station in Downtown.

AIRPORTS Hollywood Burbank Airport (*BUR*). ⊠ *2627 N. Hollywood Way, near I–5 and U.S. 101, Burbank* ☎ *818/840–8840* ⊕ *www.hollywoodburbankairport. com.* **John Wayne Airport** (*SNA*). ⊠ *18601 Airport Way, Santa Ana* ☎ *949/252–5200* ⊕ *www.ocair.com.* **L.A./Ontario International Airport** (*ONT*). ⊠ *E. Airport Dr., off I–10, Ontario* ☎ *909/544–5300* ⊕ *www. flyontario.com.* **Long Beach Airport** (*LGB*). ⊠ *4100 Donald Douglas Dr., Long Beach* ☎ *562/570–2600* ⊕ *www.lgb.org.* **Los Angeles International Airport** (*LAX*). ⊠ *1 World Way, off Hwy. 1* ☎ *855/463–5252* ⊕ *www.flylax.com.*

SHUTTLES FlyAway. ☎ *866/435–9529* ⊕ *www.flylax.com/en/flyaway-bus.* **SuperShuttle.** ☎ *323/775–6600, 800/258–3826* ⊕ *www.supershuttle.com.*

BUS TRAVEL

Inadequate public transportation has plagued L.A. for decades. That said, many local trips can be made, with time and patience, by buses run by the Los Angeles County Metropolitan Transit Authority. In certain cases—visiting the Getty Center, for instance, or Universal Studios—buses may be your best option. There's a special Dodger Stadium Express that shuttles passengers between Union Station and the world-famous ballpark for home games. It's free if you have a ticket in hand and saves you parking-related stress.

Metro buses cost $1.75, plus 50¢ for each transfer to another bus or to the subway. A one-day pass costs $7, and a weekly pass is $25 for unlimited travel on all buses and trains. Passes are valid from Sunday through Saturday. For the fastest service, look for the red-and-white Metro Rapid buses; these stop less frequently. There are 25 Metro Rapid routes, including along Wilshire and Vermont boulevards.

Other bus services make it possible to explore the entire metropolitan area. DASH minibuses cover six different circular routes in Hollywood, Mid-Wilshire, and Downtown. You pay 50¢ every time you get on. The Santa Monica Municipal Bus Line, also known as the Big Blue Bus, is a pleasant and inexpensive way to move around the Westside. Trips cost $1.25. An express bus to and from Downtown L.A., run by Culver CityBus, costs $2.50. Transfers to Metro or Metro Rail are 50¢.

You can pay your fare in cash on MTA, Santa Monica, and Culver City buses, but you must have exact change. You can buy MTA TAP cards at Metro Rail stations, customer centers throughout the city, and some convenience and grocery stores.

BUS INFORMATION Culver CityBus.
☎ *310/253–0510* ⊕ *www.culvercity.org.* **DASH.** ☎ *310/808–2273* ⊕ *www.ladottransit.com.* **Los Angeles County Metropolitan Transit Authority.** ☎ *323/466–3876* ⊕ *www. metro.net.* **Santa Monica Municipal Bus Line.** ☎ *310/451–5444* ⊕ *www.bigbluebus.com.*

CAR TRAVEL

If you're used to urban driving, you shouldn't have too much trouble navigating the streets of Los Angeles. If not, L.A. can be unnerving. However, the city has evolved with drivers in mind. Streets are wide and parking garages abound, so it's more car friendly than many older big cities.

Remember that most freeways are known by a name and a number; for example, the San Diego Freeway is Interstate 405 (or just The 405), the Hollywood Freeway is U.S. 101, the Ventura Freeway is a different stretch of U.S. 101, the Santa Monica Freeway is Interstate 10, and the Harbor Freeway is Interstate 110. It helps, too, to know which direction you're traveling; say, west toward Santa Monica or east toward Downtown Los Angeles. Distance in miles doesn't mean much, depending on the time of day

7

Los Angeles PLANNING

you're traveling: the short 10-mile drive between the San Fernando Valley and Downtown Los Angeles might take an hour to travel during rush hour but only 20 minutes at other times.

There are plenty of identical or similarly named streets in L.A. (Beverly Boulevard and Beverly Drive, for example), so be as specific as you can when asking directions. Expect sudden changes in addresses as streets pass through neighborhoods, then incorporated cities, then back into neighborhoods. This can be most bewildering on Robertson Boulevard, an otherwise useful north–south artery that, by crossing through L.A., West Hollywood, and Beverly Hills, dips in and out of several such numbering shifts in a matter of miles.

INFORMATION Caltrans Current Highway Conditions. ☎ *800/427–7623 for road conditions ⊕ www.dot.ca.gov.*

EMERGENCY SERVICES Metro Freeway Service Patrol. ☎ *511 for breakdowns ⊕ www.go511.com.*

METRO RAIL TRAVEL

Metro Rail covers only a small part of L.A.'s vast expanse, but it's convenient, frequent, and inexpensive. Most popular with visitors is the underground Red Line, which runs from Downtown's Union Station through Mid-Wilshire, Hollywood, and Universal City on its way to North Hollywood, stopping at the most popular tourist destinations along the way.

The light-rail Green Line stretches from Redondo Beach to Norwalk, while the partially underground Blue Line travels from Downtown to the South Bay. The monorail-like Gold Line extends from Union Station to Pasadena and out to the deep San Gabriel Valley and Azusa. The Orange Line, a 14-mile bus corridor, connects the North Hollywood subway station with the western San Fernando Valley.

Most recently extended was the Expo Line, which connects Downtown to the Westside, and terminates in Santa Monica, two blocks from the Pacific Ocean.

Daily service is offered from about 4:30 am to 12:30 am, with departures every 5 to 15 minutes. On weekends trains run until 2 am. Buy tickets from station vending machines; fares are $1.75, or $7 for an all-day pass. Bicycles are allowed on Metro Rail trains at all times.

METRO RAIL INFORMATION Los Angeles County Metropolitan Transit Authority. ☎ *213/922–6235 ⊕ www.metro.net.*

RIDE-SHARING AND TAXI TRAVEL

Request a ride using apps like Lyft, and a driver will usually arrive within minutes. Fares increase during busy times, but it's often the most affordable option, especially for the convenience.

Instead of trying to hail a taxi on the street, phone one of the many taxi companies. The Curb Taxi app allows for online hailing of L.A. taxis. The metered rate is $2.70 per mile, plus a $2.85 per-fare charge. Taxi rides from LAX have an additional $4 surcharge. Be aware that distances are greater than they might appear on the map so fares add up quickly.

TAXI COMPANIES Beverly Hills Cab Co. ☎ *800/273–6611 ⊕ www.beverlyhillscabco.com.* **Independent Cab Co.** ☎ *800/521–8294 ⊕ www.taxi4u.com.* **LA Checker Cab.** ☎ *800/300–5007 ⊕ www.ineedtaxi.com.* **United Independent Taxi.** ☎ *800/822–8294, 323/207–8294 text to order taxi ⊕ www.unitedtaxi.com.* **Yellow Cab Los Angeles.** ☎ *424/222–2222 ⊕ www.layellowcab.com.*

TRAIN TRAVEL

Downtown's Union Station is one of the great American railroad terminals. The interior includes comfortable seating, a restaurant, and several snack bars. As the city's rail hub, it's the place to catch an Amtrak, Metrolink commuter train, or the Red, Gold, or Purple lines. Among

Amtrak's Southern California routes are 11 daily trips to San Diego and 6 to Santa Barbara. Amtrak's luxury *Coast Starlight* travels along the spectacular coastline from Seattle to Los Angeles in just a day and a half (though it's often a little late). The *Sunset Limited* arrives from New Orleans, and the *Southwest Chief* comes from Chicago.

INFORMATION Amtrak. ☎ *800/872–7245* ⊕ *www.amtrak.com.* **Metrolink.** ☎ *800/371–5465* ⊕ *www.metrolinktrains. com.* **Union Station.** ✉ *800 N. Alameda St.* ☎ *213/683–6979* ⊕ *www.unionstationla. com.*

Restaurants

Los Angeles may be known for its beach living and celebrity-infused backdrop, but it was once a farm town. The hillsides were covered in citrus orchards and dairy farms, and agriculture was a major industry. Today, even as L.A. is urbanized, the city's culinary landscape has reembraced a local, sustainable, and seasonal philosophy at many levels—from fine dining to street snacks.

With a growing interest in farm-to-fork, the city's farmers' market scene has exploded, becoming popular at big-name restaurants and small eateries alike. In Hollywood and Santa Monica you can often find high-profile chefs scouring farm stands for fresh produce.

The status of the celebrity chef carries weight around this town. People follow the culinary zeitgeist with the same fervor as celebrity gossip. You can queue up with the hungry hordes at Nancy Silverton's **Mozza,** or try and snag a reservation to Ludo Lefebvre's ever-popular **Trois Mec** or David Chang's L.A. outpost, **Majordomo.**

Global eats continue to be a backbone of the L.A. dining scene. People head to Koreatown for epic Korean cooking and late-night coffeehouses and to West L.A. for phenomenal sushi. Latin food is

well represented in the city, making it tough to choose between Guatemalan eateries, Peruvian restaurants, nouveau Mexican bistros, and Tijuana-style taco trucks. With so many dining options, sometimes the best strategy is simply to drive and explore.

What It Costs			
$	$$	$$$	$$$$
RESTAURANTS			
under $14	$14–$22	$23–$31	over $31

Hotels

When it comes to finding a place to stay, travelers have never been more spoiled for choice than in today's Los Angeles. From luxurious digs in Beverly Hills and along the coast to budget boutiques in Hollywood, hotels are stepping up service, upgrading amenities, and trying all-new concepts, like upscale hostels and retro-chic motels. Hotels in Los Angeles today are more than just a place to rest your head; they're a key part of the experience.

What It Costs			
$	$$	$$$	$$$$
HOTELS			
under $200	$200–$300	$301–$400	over $400

Nightlife

Los Angeles is not the city that never sleeps—instead it parties until 2 am (save for the secret after-hours parties at private clubs or warehouses) and wakes up to imbibe green juices and breakfast burritos as hangover cures or to sweat it out in a yoga class. Whether you plan to test your limit at historic establishments

Downtown or take advantage of a cheap happy hour at a Hollywood dive, this city's nightlife has something for you.

A night out in Los Angeles can simultaneously surprise and impress. Seeing an unscheduled set by an A-list comedian at the stand-up comedy club, being talked into singing karaoke at the diviest place you've ever seen, dancing at a bar with no dance floor because, well, the DJ is just too good at his job—going out isn't always what you expect, but it certainly is never boring.

The focus of nightlife once centered on the Sunset Strip, with its multitude of bars, rock clubs, and dance spots, but more neighborhoods are competing with each other and forcing the nightlife scene to evolve. Although the Strip can be a worthwhile trip, other areas of the city are catching people's attention. Downtown Los Angeles, for instance, is a destination in its own right. Other areas foster more of a neighborhood vibe. Silver Lake and Los Feliz have both cultivated a relaxed environment.

So if you find yourself disappointed with a rude bouncer, or drinks that are too watery, or a cover charge that just isn't worth it, try again. Eventually you'll find that perfect place where each time is the best time. If not, at least you'll walk away with a good story.

Performing Arts

The art scene in Los Angeles extends beyond the screen and onto the stage. A place of artistic innovation and history, one can discover new and challenging theatrical works across L.A. stages, while the city still maintains a respect for tradition with its restored theaters and classic plays. See live music at impeccably designed amphitheaters like the Hollywood Bowl or listen in on captivating lectures by authors and directors at various intimate spaces. In homage to the city's roots as a filmmaking mecca, there are also retrospectives and rare screenings in movie theaters all over the city, often followed by Q&As with the cast.

Visitor Information

Discover Los Angeles, the official tourism site, has an annually updated general information packet that includes suggestions for entertainment, lodging, and dining and a list of special events. There are two visitor information centers, both accessible to Metro stops: the Hollywood & Highland Center and Union Station.

CONTACTS Discover Los Angeles.
☎ 213/624–7300, 800/228–2452
⊕ www.discoverlosangeles.com.

Santa Monica and the Beaches

Hugging the Santa Monica Bay in an arch, the desirable communities of Malibu, Santa Monica, and Venice move from ultrarich and ultracasual Malibu to bohemian, borderline-seedy Venice. What they have in common is cleaner air, mild temperatures, heavy traffic, and an emphasis on beach culture.

Santa Monica

👁 Sights

Santa Monica Pier
AMUSEMENT PARK/WATER PARK | FAMILY | Souvenir shops, carnival games, arcades, eateries, an outdoor trapeze school, a small amusement park, and an aquarium all contribute to the festive atmosphere of this truncated pier at the foot of Colorado Boulevard below Palisades Park. The pier's trademark 46-horse Looff Carousel, built in 1922, has appeared in several films, including *The Sting*. The

Santa Monica Pier's West Coaster and Pacific Wheel provide incredible ocean views.

Soda Jerks ice cream fountain (named for the motion the attendant makes when pulling the machine's arm) inside the carousel building is a pier staple. Free concerts are held on the pier in the summer. ⊠ *Colorado Ave. and the ocean, Santa Monica* ☎ *310/458–8901* ⊕ *www. santamonicapier.org.*

Santa Monica State Beach

BEACH—SIGHT | The first beach you'll hit after the Santa Monica Freeway (Interstate 10) runs into the Pacific Coast Highway, wide and sandy Santa Monica is *the* place for sunning and socializing. Be prepared for a mob scene on summer weekends, when parking becomes an expensive ordeal. Swimming is fine (with the usual post-storm-pollution caveat); for surfing, go elsewhere. For a memorable view, climb up the stairway over PCH to Palisades Park, at the top of the bluffs. Free summer concerts are held on the pier on Thursday evening.
Amenities: parking; lifeguards; toilets; food and drink; showers; water sports.
Best for: partiers; sunset; surfing; swimming; walking. ⊠ *1642 Promenade, PCH at California Incline, Santa Monica* ☎ *310/458–8573* ⊕ *www.smgov.net/ portals/beach* 🅿 *Parking from $6.*

Third Street Promenade and Santa Monica Place

COMMERCIAL CENTER | Stretch your legs along this pedestrian-only, three-block stretch of 3rd Street, close to the Pacific, lined with jacaranda trees, ivy-topiary dinosaur fountains, strings of lights, and branches of nearly every major U.S. retail chain. Outdoor cafés, street vendors, movie theaters, and a rich nightlife make this a main gathering spot for locals, visitors, street musicians, and performance artists. Plan a night just to take it all in or take an afternoon for a long people-watching stroll. There's plenty of parking in city structures on the streets flanking the promenade. **Santa Monica Place,** at the south end of the promenade, is a sleek outdoor mall and foodie haven. Its three stories are home to Nordstrom, Louis Vuitton, Coach, and other upscale retailers. Don't miss

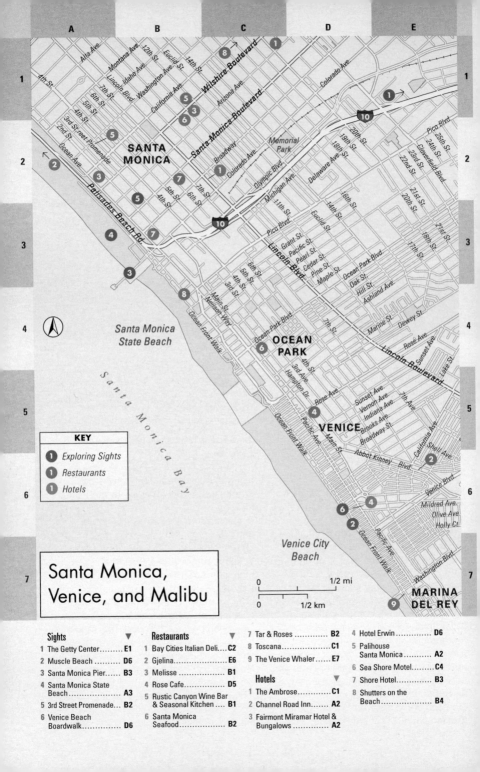

Santa Monica, Venice, and Malibu

KEY

- ① Exploring Sights
- ① Restaurants
- ① Hotels

the ocean views from the rooftop food court. ✉ *3rd St., between Colorado and Wilshire Blvds., Santa Monica* 🌐 *www.downtownsm.com.*

🍴 Restaurants

Bay Cities Italian Deli

$ | **DELI** | Part deli, part market, Bay Cities has been home to incredible Italian subs since 1925. This renowned counter-service spot is always crowded (best to order ahead), but monster subs run the gamut from the mighty meatball to the signature Godmother, made with prosciutto, ham, capicola, mortadella, Genoa salami, and provolone. **Known for:** market with rare imports; excellent service. [$] *Average main: $10* ✉ *1517 Lincoln Blvd., Santa Monica* ☎ *310/395–8279* 🌐 *www.baycitiesitaliandeli.com* 🕒 *Closed Mon.*

★ Mélisse

$$$$ | **FRENCH** | Chef-owner Josiah Citrin enhances his modern French cooking with seasonal California produce at this Santa Monica institution. The tasting menu might feature egg caviar with smoked lemon crème fraiche, wild Scottish red partridge with chocolate persimmons, or Kagoshima Wagyu beef rib eye. **Known for:** domestic and European cheese cart; contemporary/elegant decor. [$] *Average main: $145* ✉ *1104 Wilshire Blvd., Santa Monica* ☎ *310/395–0881* 🌐 *www.melisse.com* 🕒 *Closed Sun. and Mon. No lunch.*

★ Rustic Canyon Wine Bar and Seasonal Kitchen

$$$ | **MODERN AMERICAN** | A Santa Monica mainstay, the seasonally changing menu at this farm-to-table restaurant consistently upends norms. The homey, minimalist space offers sweeping views of Wilshire Boulevard, and on any given night the menu of California cuisine may include Channel Island rockfish with shelling beans and Sun Gold tomatoes, or buttered ricotta dumplings with golden chanterelles and Coolea cheese. **Known for:** never-ending wine list; knowledgeable staff. [$] *Average main: $35* ✉ *1119 Wilshire Blvd., Santa Monica* ☎ *310/393–7050* 🌐 *www.rusticcanyonwinebar.com.*

Santa Monica Seafood

$$ | **SEAFOOD** | **FAMILY** | A Southern California favorite, this Italian seafood haven has been serving up fresh fish since 1939. This freshness comes from its pedigree as the largest seafood distributor in the Southwest. **Known for:** deliciously seasoned rainbow trout; oyster bar; kids' meals. [$] *Average main: $20* ✉ *1000 Wilshire Blvd., Santa Monica* ☎ *310/393–5244* 🌐 *www.santamonicaseafood.com.*

Tar and Roses

$$$ | **MODERN AMERICAN** | This small and dimly lit romantic spot in Santa Monica is full of adventurous options, like octopus skewers and venison loin. The new American cuisine also features standouts like braised lamb belly with minted apple chutney and drool-worthy strawberry ricotta crostata with honeycomb ice cream for dessert. **Known for:** phenomenal oxtail dumplings; delicious hanger steak. [$] *Average main: $30* ✉ *602 Santa Monica Blvd., Santa Monica* ☎ *310/587–0700* 🌐 *www.tarandroses.com.*

🛏 Hotels

The Ambrose

$$$ | **HOTEL** | Tranquility pervades the airy, California Craftsman–style, four-story Ambrose, which blends right into its mostly residential Santa Monica neighborhood. **Pros:** "green" practices like nontoxic cleaners and recycling bins; partial ocean view. **Cons:** quiet, residential area of Santa Monica; parking fee ($27); not walking distance to beach. [$] *Rooms from: $359* ✉ *1255 20th St., Santa Monica* ☎ *310/315–1555, 877/262–7673* 🌐 *www.ambrosehotel.com* 🛏 *77 rooms* 🍴 *Breakfast.*

★ Channel Road Inn

$$ | **B&B/INN** | A quaint surprise in Southern California, the Channel Road Inn is every bit the country retreat bed-and-breakfast lovers adore, with four-poster beds, fluffy duvets, and a cozy living room with a fireplace. **Pros:** free wine and hors d'oeuvres every evening; home-cooked breakfast included; meditative rose garden on-site. **Cons:** no pool; need a car to get around. [$] *Rooms from: $225* ✉ *219 W. Channel Rd., Santa Monica* ☎ *310/459–1920* 🌐 *www.channelroadinn.com* 🛏 *15 rooms* 🍴 *Breakfast.*

Fairmont Miramar Hotel and Bungalows Santa Monica

$$$$ | **HOTEL** | A mammoth Moreton Bay fig tree dwarfs the main entrance of the 5-acre, beach-adjacent Santa Monica wellness retreat and lends its name to the inviting on-site Mediterranean-inspired restaurant, FIG, which focuses on local ingredients and frequently refreshes its menu. **Pros:** guests can play games on the heated patio; swanky open-air cocktail spot, the Bungalow, on-site; stay in retrofitted '20s and '40s bungalows. **Cons:** all this luxury comes at a big price. [$] *Rooms from: $599* ✉ *101 Wilshire Blvd., Santa Monica* ☎ *310/576–7777, 866/540–4470* 🌐 *www.fairmont.com/santamonica* 🛏 *334 rooms* 🍴 *No meals.*

Palihouse Santa Monica

$$$ | **HOTEL** | Tucked in a posh residential area three blocks from the sea and lively Third Street Promenade, Palihouse Santa Monica caters to design-minded world travelers, with spacious rooms and suites decked out in whimsical antiques. **Pros:** Apple TV in rooms; walking distance to Santa Monica attractions; fully equipped kitchens. **Cons:** no pool; decor might not appeal to more traditional travelers; parking fee ($45). [$] *Rooms from: $355* ✉ *1001 3rd St., Santa Monica* ☎ *310/394–1279* 🌐 *www.palihousesantamonica.com* 🛏 *38 rooms* 🍴 *No meals.*

Sea Shore Motel

$ | **HOTEL** | On Santa Monica's busy Main Street, the Sea Shore is a charming throwback to Route 66 and to '60s-style, family-run roadside motels and is surrounded by an ultratrendy neighborhood. **Pros:** close to beach and restaurants; free Wi-Fi, parking, and use of beach equipment; popular rooftop deck and on-site restaurant, Amelia's. **Cons:** street noise; motel-style decor and beds. [$] *Rooms from: $159* ✉ *2637 Main St., Santa Monica* ☎ *310/392–2787* 🌐 *www.seashoremotel.com* 🛏 *25 rooms* 🍴 *No meals.*

★ Shore Hotel

$$$$ | **HOTEL** | With views of the Santa Monica Pier, this hotel with a friendly staff offers eco-minded travelers stylish rooms with a modern design, just steps from the sand and sea. **Pros:** near beach and Third Street Promenade; rainfall showerheads; solar-heated pool and hot tub. **Cons:** expensive rooms and parking fees; fronting busy Ocean Avenue; some sharing a room may be wary of the see-through shower. [$] *Rooms from: $432* ✉ *1515 Ocean Ave., Santa Monica* ☎ *310/458–1515* 🌐 *shorehotel.com* 🛏 *164 rooms* 🍴 *No meals.*

★ Shutters on the Beach

$$$$ | **HOTEL** | **FAMILY** | Set right on the sand, this inn has become synonymous with staycations. **Pros:** built-in cabinets filled with art books and curios; rooms designed by Michael Smith; rooms come with whirlpool tub. **Cons:** have to pay for extras like beach chairs; very expensive. [$] *Rooms from: $675* ✉ *1 Pico Blvd., Santa Monica* ☎ *310/458–0030, 800/334–9000* 🌐 *www.shuttersonthebeach.com* 🛏 *198 rooms* 🍴 *No meals.*

LOS ANGELES INTERNATIONAL AIRPORT

Custom Hotel

$ | **HOTEL** | Close enough to LAX to see the runways, the Custom Hotel is a playful and practical redo of a 12-story, mid-century modern tower by famed L.A. architect Welton Becket (of

Hollywood's Capitol Records building and the Dorothy Chandler Pavilion). **Pros:** shuttle to LAX; close to beach and airport; socializing at poolside restaurant/lounge, Deck 33. **Cons:** at the desolate end of Lincoln Boulevard; thin walls; in need of updating. $ *Rooms from: $183* ✉ *8639 Lincoln Blvd., Los Angeles International Airport* ☎ *310/645–0400, 877/287–8601* ⊕ *www.customhotel.com* ⇥ *250 rooms* ○ *No meals.*

Nightlife

★ Chez Jay
BARS/PUBS | Around since 1959, this dive bar continues to be a well-loved place in Santa Monica. Everyone from the young to the old (including families) frequents this historical landmark. It's a charming place, from the well-worn booths with their red checkered tablecloths to the ship's wheel near the door. Be on the lookout for ongoing *Goliath* filmings, and consider the patio for private parties. ✉ *1657 Ocean Ave., Santa Monica* ☎ *310/395–1741* ⊕ *www.chezjays.com.*

The Galley
BARS/PUBS | Santa Monica's oldest restaurant and bar, the Galley has a consistent nautical theme inside and out: the boatlike exterior features wavy blue neon lights and porthole windows; inside, fishing nets and anchors adorn the walls, and the whole place is aglow with colorful string lights. Most patrons tend to crowd the center bar, with the more dinner-oriented folks frequenting the booths. Prices are a good deal during "most hours" and a steal during "happy hours." ✉ *2442 Main St., Santa Monica* ☎ *310/452–1934.*

UnUrban Coffee House
CAFES—NIGHTLIFE | Looking for a real neighborhood experience, with mismatched furniture and undiscovered talent? This is the place to enjoy a laidback evening of entertainment by local performers (and good espresso drinks

and organic pastries). The music and poetry open-mic nights attract interesting and talented folks, and the musical showcase draws a random mix of musicians. There's no cover to get in, but it typically costs $5 to participate in the open mics. ✉ *3301 Pico Blvd., at Urban Ave., Santa Monica* ☎ *310/315–0056* ⊕ *www.unurban.com.*

⬤ Shopping

Lady Chocolatt
FOOD/CANDY | This is the shop where chocolate dreams are made. The purveyor of the finest Belgian chocolate in all of Los Angeles, Lady Chocolatt is the perfect answer to the age-old question "What should we buy for our loved one's birthday, anniversary, baby shower, celebration, etc.?" The ornate display case is filled with dark chocolate truffles, hazelnut pralines, Grand Marnier ganaches, and so much more. Post up for a late-afternoon espresso and let your chocolate dreams wander. ✉ *12008 Wilshire Blvd., Santa Monica* ☎ *310/442–2245* ⊕ *www.chocolatt.com.*

Planet Blue
CLOTHING | The beachy bohemian style is the focus at this small local chain, with an abundance of jeans, breezy dresses, turquoise jewelry, bikinis, and other SoCal staples. ✉ *800 14th St., Santa Monica* ☎ *310/394–0135* ⊕ *www.shopplanetblue.com.*

Third Street Promenade
SHOPPING CENTERS/MALLS | There is no shortage of spots to shop everything from sporting goods to trendy fashions on this pedestrian-friendly strip. Outposts here are mainly of the chain variety, and in between splurging on books, clothing, sneakers, and more, shoppers can pop into one of the many eateries to stay satiated or even catch a movie at one of the theaters. Additionally, the chef-approved Farmers Market takes over twice a week, and with the beach

just a few steps away, the destination is a quintessential California stop. ✉ *3rd St., between Broadway and Wilshire Blvd., Santa Monica.*

Wasteland

CLOTHING | This vintage emporium, a block from the Third Street Promenade, sells gently used items for both women and men. You'll find everything from wide-lapel polyester shirts to last year's Michael Kors bag. There is also a location on Ventura Boulevard. ✉ *1330 4th St., between Arizona Ave. and Santa Monica Blvd., Santa Monica* ☎ *310/395–2620* 🌐 *www.shopwasteland.com.*

Venice

Sights

Muscle Beach

LOCAL INTEREST | Bronzed young men bench-pressing five girls at once, weight lifters doing tricks on the sand—the Muscle Beach facility fired up the country's imagination from the get-go. There are actually two spots known as Muscle Beach. The original Muscle Beach, just south of the Santa Monica Pier, is where bodybuilders Jack LaLanne and Vic and Armand Tanny used to work out in the 1950s. When it was closed in 1959, the bodybuilders moved south along the beach to Venice, to a city-run facility known as "the Pen," and the Venice Beach spot inherited the Muscle Beach moniker. The spot is probably best known now as a place where a young Arnold Schwarzenegger first came to flex his muscles in the late '60s and began his rise to fame. The area now hosts a variety of sports and gymnastics events and the occasional "beach babe" beauty contests that always draw a crowd. But stop by any time during daylight for an eye-popping array of beefcakes (and would-be beefcakes). ✉ *1800 Ocean Front Walk, Venice* 🌐 *www.musclebeach.net.*

Venice Beach Boardwalk

MARINA | The surf and sand of Venice are fine, but the main attraction here is the boardwalk scene, which is a cosmos all its own. Go on weekend afternoons for the best people-watching experience. You can also swim, fish, surf, and skateboard, or play racquetball, handball, shuffleboard, and basketball (the boardwalk is the site of hotly contested pickup games). You can rent a bike or in-line skates and hit the Strand bike path, then pull up a seat at a sidewalk café and watch the action unfold. ✉ *1800 Ocean Front Walk, west of Pacific Ave., Venice* ☎ *310/392–4687* 🌐 *www.venicebeach.com.*

Restaurants

Gjelina

$$ | **AMERICAN** | Gjelina comes alive the minute you walk through the rustic wooden door and into a softly lit dining room with long communal tables. The menu is seasonal, with outstanding small plates, charcuterie, pastas, and pizza. **Known for:** lively crowd on the patio; late-night menu; inventive pizzas and salads. [$] *Average main: $20* ✉ *1429 Abbot Kinney Blvd., Venice* ☎ *310/450–1429* 🌐 *www.gjelina.com.*

Rose Cafe

$$ | **MODERN AMERICAN** | **FAMILY** | This indoor-outdoor restaurant has served Venice for decades but constantly reinvents itself, serving mouthwatering California cuisines with multiple patios, a full bar, and a bakery. Creative types loiter for the Wi-Fi and sip espressos, while young families gather out back to nibble on yellowtail crudo and crispy brussels sprouts. **Known for:** sophisticated but unpretentious vibe; location in the heart of Venice; being L.A. in a nutshell. [$] *Average main: $25* ✉ *220 Rose Ave., Venice* ☎ *310/399–0711* 🌐 *www.rosecafevenice.com.*

Venice Whaler

$$ | **AMERICAN** | This beachfront bar that's been the local watering hole for musicians like the Doors and the Beach Boys since

1944 boasts an amazing view and serves tasty California pub food like fish tacos, pulled pork sliders, and avocado toast with a basic selection of beers. Be prepared for rowdy crowds of sports fans and beachgoers at happy hour and on weekends. **Known for:** rock-n-roll history; pub food; brunch. Ⓢ *Average main: $15* ⊠ *10 W. Washington Blvd., Venice* ☎ *310/821– 8737* ⊕ *www.venicewhaler.com.*

🛏 Hotels

Hotel Erwin
$$$ | HOTEL | A boutique hotel a block off the Venice Beach Boardwalk, the newly renovated Erwin will make you feel like a hipper version of yourself. **Pros:** dining emphasizes fresh ingredients; playful design in guest rooms; free Wi-Fi. **Cons:** some rooms face a noisy alley; no pool. Ⓢ *Rooms from: $369* ⊠ *1697 Pacific Ave., Venice* ☎ *310/452–1111, 800/786–7789* ⊕ *www.hotelerwin.com* ⤳ *119 rooms* ⏦*⃝ No meals.*

★ The Kinney
$$ | HOTEL | Walking distance to Venice Beach and Abbot Kinney's artsy commercial strip, this playful new hotel announces itself boldly with wall murals by Melissa Scrivner before you even enter the lobby. **Pros:** affordable, artistic rooms; Ping-Pong area; Jacuzzi bar. **Cons:** valet parking is a must ($15). Ⓢ *Rooms from: $239* ⊠ *737 Washington Blvd., Venice* ☎ *310/821–4455* ⊕ *www.thekinneyvenicebeach.com* ⤳ *68 rooms* ⏦*⃝ No meals.*

▽ Nightlife

The Brig
BARS/PUBS | This charming bar has its pluses (interesting drinks, talented DJs) and minuses (ugh, parking) but is worth a look if you're in the area. There's always a food truck around, and the bar's fine with you bringing in outside food. ⊠ *1515 Abbot Kinney Blvd., Venice* ☎ *310/399– 7537* ⊕ *www.thebrig.com.*

🛍 Shopping

General Store
GIFTS/SOUVENIRS | Right at home in the beachy, bohemian neighborhood, this well-curated shop is a decidedly contemporary take on the concept of general stores. The very definition of "California cool," General Store offers beauty and bath products loaded with organic natural ingredients, handmade ceramics, linen tea towels, and a spot on selection of art books. Featuring an impressive number of local makers and designers, the boutique also sells modern, minimal clothing and has a kids' section that will wow even the hippest moms and dads. ⊠ *1801 Lincoln Blvd., Venice* ☎ *310/751– 6393* ⊕ *www.shop-generalstore.com.*

Heist
CLOTHING | Owner Nilou Ghodsi has admitted that she stocks her Westside shop like an extension of her own closet, which in her case means keeping the focus on modern-yet-classic pieces as opposed to trendy ones. The airy boutique offers elegantly edgy separates from American designers like Nili Lotan and Ulla Johnson, as well as from hard-to-find French and Italian designers. ⊠ *1100 Abbot Kinney Blvd., Venice* ☎ *310/450–6531* ⊕ *www.shopheist.com.*

Strange Invisible Perfumes
PERFUME/COSMETICS | Finding your signature fragrance at this sleek Abbot Kinney boutique won't come cheap, but perfumer Alexandra Balahoutis takes creating her scents as seriously as a seasoned winemaker—and they're just as nuanced as a well-balanced glass of vino. Essences for the perfumes are organic, wild crafted, biodynamic, and bottled locally. Highlights from SI's core collection include the cacao-spiked Dimanche and leathery Black Rosette. ⊠ *1138 Abbot Kinney Blvd., Venice* ☎ *310/314–1505* ⊕ *www.siperfumes.com.*

Malibu

◉ Sights

★ Getty Villa Malibu

HOUSE | Feeding off the cultures of ancient Rome, Greece, and Etruria, the villa exhibits astounding antiquities, though on a first visit even they take a backseat to their environment. This megamansion sits on some of the most valuable coastal property in the world. Modeled after the Villa dei Papiri in Herculaneum, a Roman estate owned by Julius Caesar's father-in-law that was covered in ash when Mt. Vesuvius erupted, the Getty Villa includes beautifully manicured gardens, reflecting pools, and statuary. The structures blend thoughtfully into the rolling terrain and significantly improve the public spaces, such as the new outdoor amphitheater, gift store, café, and entry arcade. Talks, concerts, and educational programs are offered at an indoor theater. ■TIP→ **An advance timed entry ticket is required for admission. Tickets are free and may be ordered from the museum's website or by phone.** ⊠ *17985 Pacific Coast Hwy., Pacific Palisades* 🕾 *310/440–7300* ⊕ *www.getty. edu* 🕾 *Free, tickets required; parking $15* ⊗ *Closed Tues.*

⊕ Beaches

Malibu Lagoon State Beach

BEACH—SIGHT | Bird-watchers, take note: in this 5-acre marshy area near Malibu Beach Inn you can spot egrets, blue herons, avocets, and gulls. (You need to stay on the boardwalks so as not to disturb their habitats.) The path leads out to a rocky stretch of Surfrider Beach and makes for a pleasant stroll. The sand is soft, clean, and white, and you're also likely to spot a variety of marine life. Look for the signs to help identify these sometimes exotic-looking creatures. The lagoon is particularly enjoyable in the early morning and at sunset—and even

more so now, thanks to a restoration effort that improved the lagoon's scent. The parking lot has limited hours, but street-side parking is usually available at off-peak times. Close by are shops and a theater. **Amenities:** parking (fee); lifeguards; toilets; showers. **Best for:** sunset; walking. ⊠ *23200 Pacific Coast Hwy., Malibu* 🕾 *310/457–8143* ⊕ *www.parks. ca.gov* 🕾 *Parking $12.*

Westward Beach–Point Dume

BEACH—SIGHT | Go tide pooling, fishing, snorkeling, or bird-watching (prime time is late winter to early spring). Hike to the top of the sandstone cliffs at Point Dume to whale-watch—their migrations can be seen between December and April—and take in dramatic coastal views. Westward is a favorite surfing beach, but the steep surf isn't for novices. The Sunset restaurant is between Westward and Point Dume (at 6800 Westward Beach Road). Bring your own food, since the nearest concession is a long hike away. **Amenities:** parking (fee); lifeguards; toilets; food and drink; showers. **Best for:** surfing; walking. ⊠ *71030 Westward Beach Rd., Malibu* 🕾 *310/305–9503* 🕾 *Parking $14.*

Zuma Beach Park

BEACH—SIGHT | This 2-mile stretch of white sand, usually dotted with tanning teenagers, has it all, from fishing and kitesurfing to swings and volleyball courts. Beachgoers looking for quiet or privacy should head elsewhere. Stay alert in the water: the surf is rough and inconsistent. **Amenities:** parking; lifeguards; toilets; food and drink; showers. **Best for:** partiers; sunset; swimming; walking. ⊠ *30000 Pacific Coast Hwy., Malibu* 🕾 *310/305–9522* ⊕ *www.zuma-beach. com* 🕾 *Parking $10.*

ⓘ Restaurants

Nobu Malibu

$$$$ | JAPANESE | At famous chef-restaurateur Nobu Matsuhisa's coastal outpost, super-chic clientele sails in for morsels of

the world's finest fish. It's hard not to be seduced by the oceanfront property, and stellar sushi and ingenious specialties match the upscale setting. **Known for:** exotic fish; toro with truffle teriyaki; bento box Valrhona chocolate soufflé. $ *Average main: $35* ⊠ *22706 Pacific Coast Hwy., Malibu* ☎ *310/317–9140* ⊕ *www.noburestaurants.com.*

Reel Inn
$$ | SEAFOOD | FAMILY | Long wooden tables and booths are often filled with fish-loving families chowing down on mahimahi sandwiches and freshly caught swordfish. Get in line and choose your fish and sides, then nab a table. **Known for:** easy-to-miss spot on PCH; fresh catches. $ *Average main: $17* ⊠ *18661 Pacific Coast Hwy., Malibu* ☎ *310/456-8221* ⊕ *www.reelinnmalibu.com.*

🛏 Hotels

Malibu Beach Inn
$$$$ | B&B/INN | Set right on exclusive Carbon Beach, Malibu's hideaway for the super-rich remains the room to nab along the coast, with an ultrachic new look thanks to designer Waldo Fernandez, and an upscale restaurant and wine bar perched over the Pacific. **Pros:** see the ocean from your private balcony; wine list curated by sommelier Laurie Sutton; world-class chocolate chip cookies at reception. **Cons:** billionaire's travel budget required; some in-room noise from PCH; no pool, gym, or hot tub. $ *Rooms from: $749* ⊠ *22878 Pacific Coast Hwy., Malibu* ☎ *310/456-6444* ⊕ *www.malibubeachinn.com* ⤳ *47 rooms* ⵔ *No meals.*

ⓨ Nightlife

Duke's Barefoot Bar
BARS/PUBS | FAMILY | With a clear view of the horizon from almost everywhere, a sunset drink at Duke's Barefoot Bar is how many beachgoers like to end their day. The entertainment is in keeping with the bar's theme, with Hawaiian dancers as well as live music on Friday night by Hawaiian artists. The menu features island favorites like *poke* tacos, macadamia-crusted fish, and kalua pork and a Sunday brunch buffet from 10 to 2. Just don't expect beach-bum prices, unless you stop by the happy hour weekday events like Taco Tuesday ($3 fish, kalua pork, or grilled chicken tacos, along with $3 beer). ⊠ *21150 Pacific Coast Hwy., Malibu* ☎ *310/317-0777* ⊕ *www.dukesmalibu.com.*

Moonshadows
BARS/PUBS | This newly renovated outdoor lounge attracts customers with its modern look and views of the ocean. Think dark woods, cabana-style draperies, and ambient lighting in the Blue Lounge. DJs are constantly spinning lounge music in the background, and there's never a cover charge. Try the new lobster roll and dessert lineup. This restaurant maintains some amount of notoriety as the establishment frequented by Mel Gibson just before his infamous 2006 arrest. ⊠ *20356 Pacific Coast Hwy., Malibu* ☎ *310/456-3010* ⊕ *www.moonshadowsmalibu.com.*

🛍 Shopping

Malibu Country Mart
SHOPPING CENTERS/MALLS | Have the quintessential beachside shopping experience complete with browsing designer clothing (Morgane le Fay, Ron Herman, or Madison) and eclectic California housewares and gifts (Burro), picking up body-boosting wellness goodies at Sunlife Organics, and finishing the day off with dinner at iconic eatery Mr. Chow. If you can squeeze in a workout, there's a Pure Barre and 5 Point Yoga to choose from, plus tarot readings at metaphysical outpost Malibu Shaman, and Eastern medicine treatments at Malibu Acupuncture. Then reward yourself for your good health habits by stopping at fan-favorite Italian gelateria Grom's Malibu outpost for out-of-this-world

fresh pistachio or *gianduia* (chocolate hazelnut) gelato. ✉ *3835 Cross Creek Rd., Malibu* ☎ *310/456–7300* ⊕ *www.malibucountrymart.com.*

Malibu Lumber Yard

SHOPPING CENTERS/MALLS | Emblematic Malibu lifestyle stores in this shopping complex include James Perse, Maxfield, and too-chic Intermix. The playground and alfresco dining area make this an ideal weekend destination for families. ✉ *3939 Cross Creek Rd., Malibu* ⊕ *www.themalibulumberyard.com.*

Brentwood

⊙ Sights

★ The Getty Center

MUSEUM | **FAMILY** | With its curving walls and isolated hilltop perch, the Getty Center resembles a pristine fortified city of its own. You may have been lured there by the beautiful views of Los Angeles—on a clear day stretching all the way to the Pacific Ocean—but the amazing architecture, uncommon gardens, and fascinating art collections will be more than enough to capture and hold your attention. When the sun is out, the complex's rough-cut travertine marble skin seems to soak up the light.

Getting to the center involves a bit of anticipatory lead-up. At the base of the hill, a pavilion disguises the underground parking structure. From there you either walk or take a smooth, computer-driven tram up the steep slope, checking out the Bel Air estates across the humming 405 freeway. The five pavilions that house the museum surround a central courtyard and are bridged by walkways. From the courtyard, plazas, and walkways, you can survey the city from the San Gabriel Mountains to the ocean.

In a ravine separating the museum and the Getty Research Institute, conceptual artist Robert Irwin created the playful Central Garden in stark contrast to Richard Meier's mathematical architectural geometry. The garden's design is what Hollywood feuds are made of: Meier couldn't control Irwin's vision, and the two men sniped at each other during construction, with Irwin stirring the pot with every loose twist his garden path took. The result is a refreshing garden walk whose focal point is an azalea maze (some insist the Mickey Mouse shape is on purpose) in a reflecting pool.

Inside the pavilions are the galleries for the permanent collections of European paintings, drawings, sculpture, illuminated manuscripts, and decorative arts, as well as world-class temporary exhibitions and photographs gathered internationally. The Getty's collection of French furniture and decorative arts, especially from the early years of Louis XIV (1643–1715) to the end of the reign of Louis XVI (1774–92), is renowned for its quality and condition; you can even see a pair of completely reconstructed salons. In the paintings galleries, a computerized system of louvered skylights allows natural light to filter in, creating a closer approximation of the conditions in which the artists painted. Notable among the paintings are Rembrandt's *The Abduction of Europa,* Van Gogh's *Irises,* Monet's *Wheatstack, Snow Effects,* and *Morning,* and James Ensor's *Christ's Entry into Brussels.*

If you want to start with a quick overview, pick up the brochure in the entrance hall that guides you to collection highlights. There's also an instructive audio tour (free, but you have to leave your ID) with commentaries by art historians and other experts. Art information rooms with multimedia computer stations contain more details about the collections. The Getty also presents lectures, films, concerts, art workshops, and special programs for kids, families, and all-around culture lovers. The complex includes an upscale restaurant and downstairs cafeteria with panoramic window views. There are also outdoor coffee carts. ■TIP→ On-site parking is subject to availability and can fill up by midday on holidays and in the summer, so try to come early in the day or after lunch. A tram takes you from the street-level entrance to the top of the hill. Public buses (Metro Rapid Line 734) also serve the center and link to the Expo Rail extension. ⊠ 1200 Getty Center Dr., Brentwood ☎ 310/440–7300 ⊕ www.getty.edu ⊠ Free; parking $15 ⊗ Closed Mon.

🍽 Restaurants

Toscana
$$$$ | ITALIAN | This rustic trattoria along San Vicente is a favorite celebrity haunt. Expect elevated sensory offerings, from its cozy atmosphere to its mouthwatering Tuscan fare and excellent wine list. **Known for:** excellent wine list; white truffles; celeb-spotting. $ Average main: $35 ⊠ 11633 San Vicente Blvd., Brentwood ☎ 310/820–2448 ⊕ www.toscana-brentwood.com.

Beverly Hills, West Hollywood, and the Westside

The rumors are true: Beverly Hills delivers on a dramatic, cinematic scale of wealth and excess. A known celebrity haunt, come here to daydream or to live like the rich and famous for a day. Window-shop or splurge at tony stores, and keep an eye out for filming locales; just walking around here will make you feel like you're on a movie set.

West Hollywood is not a place to see things (like museums or movie studios) as much as it is a place to do things— like go to a nightclub, eat at a world-famous restaurant, or attend an art gallery

opening. Since the end of Prohibition, the **Sunset Strip** has been Hollywood's nighttime playground, where stars headed to such glamorous nightclubs as the Trocadero, the Mocambo, and Ciro's. It's still going strong, with crowds still filing into well-established spots like Whisky A Go Go and paparazzi staking out the members-only Soho House. But hedonism isn't all that drives West Hollywood. Also thriving is an important interior design and art gallery trade exemplified by the Cesar Pelli–designed **Pacific Design Center.** The three-block stretch of Wilshire Boulevard known as Museum Row, east of Fairfax Avenue, features intriguing museums and a prehistoric tar pit. Wilshire Boulevard itself is something of a cultural monument—it begins its grand 16-mile sweep to the sea in Downtown L.A.

West Hollywood has emerged as one of the most progressive cities in Southern California. It's also one of the most gay-friendly cities anywhere, with a large LGBTQ community. Its annual Gay Pride Parade is one of the largest in the nation, drawing tens of thousands of participants each June.

The historic **Farmers Market** and **The Grove** shopping mall are both great places to people-watch over breakfast.

Beverly Hills

👁 Sights

Museum of Tolerance
MUSEUM | FAMILY | This museum unflinchingly confronts bigotry and racism. One of the most affecting sections covers the Holocaust, with film footage of deportations and concentration camps. Upon entering, you are issued a "passport" bearing the name of a child whose life was dramatically changed by the Nazis; as you go through the exhibit, you learn the fate of that child. An exhibit called *Anne: The Life and Legacy of Anne Frank*

A	**B**	**C**	**D**	**E**

1 Santa Monica Mountains Nat'l Rec Area

Greystone Park

Doheny Rd.

2

Cynthia St
Vista Grande
Dicks St
Norma Pl.

W Sunset Blvd

3

West Hollywood Park

Rangely Ave.
Dorrington Ave.
Ashcroft Ave.
Rosewood Ave.
Beverly Blvd.

4 Will Rogers Memorial Park

Alden Dr.

5 BEVERLY HILLS

W 3rd St.

Beverly Gardens Park

Burton Way

Dayton Way

6

Clifton Way

Wilshire Boulevard

Charleville Blvd.

7

Santa Monica Boulevard

Sights ▼

1 Museum of Tolerance C7
2 Pierce Brothers Westwood Village Memorial Park and Mortuary A7
3 Rodeo Drive B7
4 Santa Monica Boulevard F2
5 Spadena House A6
6 Sunset Boulevard E2
7 West Hollywood Design District E4

Restaurants ▼

1 Angelini Osteria J5
2 Animal H4
3 A.O.C E5
4 The Bazaar by José Andrés F6
5 Canter's H4
6 Craig's E4
7 Crustacean B6
8 Dan Tana's D4
9 El Coyote Mexican Food J5
10 Greenblatt's Deli H1
11 Maude C7

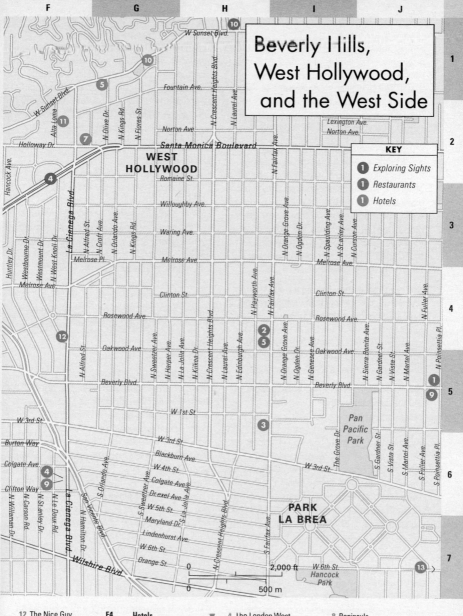

Beverly Hills, West Hollywood, and the West Side

KEY

- 1 Exploring Sights
- 1 Restaurants
- 1 Hotels

WEST HOLLYWOOD

Pan Pacific Park

PARK LA BREA

Hancock Park

2,000 ft

500 m

brings her story to life through immersive environments, multimedia presentations, and interesting artifacts. Simon Wiesenthal's Vienna office is set exactly as the famous "Nazi hunter" had it while conducting his research that brought more than 1,000 war criminals to justice.

Interactive exhibits include the Millennium Machine, which engages visitors in finding solutions to human rights abuses around the world; Globalhate.com, which examines hate on the Internet by exposing problematic sites via touch-screen computer terminals; and the Point of View Diner, a re-creation of a 1950s diner that "serves" a menu of controversial topics on video jukeboxes.

■ TIP→ Plan to spend at least three hours touring the museum; making a reservation is especially recommended for Friday, Sunday, and holiday visits. ✉ *9786 W. Pico Blvd., south of Beverly Hills* ☎ *310/772–2505 for reservations* 🌐 *www.museumoftolerance.com* 🎟 *From $16* 🕓 *Closed Sat.*

Pierce Brothers Westwood Village Memorial Park and Mortuary

CEMETERY | The who's who of the dearly departed can all be found at this peaceful, though unremarkable, cemetery. Notable residents include Marilyn Monroe and Joe DiMaggio; authors Truman Capote, Ray Bradbury, and Jackie Collins; actors Natalie Wood, Rodney Dangerfield, Farrah Fawcett, Jack Lemmon, and Dean Martin; and directors Billy Wilder and John Cassavetes. ✉ *1218 Glendon Ave., Westwood.*

Rodeo Drive

NEIGHBORHOOD | The ultimate shopping indulgence, Rodeo Drive is one of L.A.'s bona fide tourist attractions. The art of window-shopping (and reenacting your *Pretty Woman* fantasies) is prime among the retail elite: Tiffany & Co., Gucci, Jimmy Choo, Valentino, Harry Winston, Prada—you get the picture. Near the southern end of Rodeo Drive is Via Rodeo, a curvy cobblestone street designed to resemble a European shopping area and the perfect backdrop to pose for your Instagram feed. To give your feet a rest, free trolley tours depart from the southeast corner of Rodeo Drive and Dayton Way from 11:30 to 4:30. They're a terrific way to get an overview of the neighborhood. ✉ *Rodeo Dr., Beverly Hills* 🌐 *www.rodeodrive-bh.com.*

Spadena House

BUILDING | Otherwise known as the Witch's House in Beverly Hills, the Spadena House has an interesting history. First built on the Willat Studios lot in 1920, the house was physically moved to its current ritzy location in 1924. The house is not open for tourists, but the fairy-tale-like appearance is viewable from the street for onlookers to snap pics. Movie buffs will also recognize it from a background shot in the film *Clueless.* ✉ *516 Walden Dr., Beverly Hills.*

🍴 Restaurants

The Bazaar by José Andrés

$$$$ | SPANISH | Spanish celebrity chef José Andrés has conquered L.A. with this colorful and opulent Beverly Hills spot, which features a bar stocked with liquid nitrogen and a super-flashy patisserie. Pore over a menu of items like Spanish tapas (with a twist) and "liquid" olives (created using a technique called spherification). **Known for:** molecular gastronomy; foie gras cotton candy. [$] *Average main: $65* ✉ *SLS Hotel at Beverly Hills, 465 S. La Cienega Blvd., Beverly Hills* ☎ *310/246–5555* 🌐 *slshotels.com/beverlyhills/bazaar* 🕓 *No lunch.*

Crustacean

$$$$ | VIETNAMESE | Crustacean, the Euro-Vietnamese fusion gem in the heart of Beverly Hills, received a $10 million makeover in 2018. You can still walk on water above exotic fish, but now you can see the kitchen preparing your perfect garlic noodles through a glass window. **Known for:** sake-simmered dishes; colossal tiger prawns; no-grease garlic noodles. $ *Average main: $16* ⌨ *168 N. Bedford Dr., Beverly Hills* ☎ *310/205–8990* ⊕ *crustaceanbh.com* ⊘ *Closed Mon. No lunch weekends.*

Maude

$$$$ | **INTERNATIONAL** | Maude is a much-needed addition to the Beverly Hills dining scene as it bucks a traditional tried-and-true menu for a tasting explosion that changes four times a year (we'd say seasonally, but it's L.A.). Helmed by celeb chef Curtis Stone, the cuisine ranges from Spanish and Italian influences to French and coastal Californian. **Known for:** titillating tasting menus; intimate dining. $ *Average main: $185* ⌨ *212 S. Beverly Dr., Beverly Hills* ☎ *310/859–3418* ⊕ *www.mauderestaurant.com* ⊘ *Closed Sun. and Mon.*

★ **Spago Beverly Hills**

$$$$ | **MODERN AMERICAN** | Wolfgang Puck's flagship restaurant is a modern L.A. classic. Spago centers on a buzzing redbrick outdoor courtyard (with retractable roof) shaded by 100-year-old olive trees, and a daily-changing menu that offers dishes like smoked salmon pizza or off-menu schnitzel. **Known for:** great people-watching; off-menu schnitzel; sizzling smoked salmon pizza. $ *Average main: $35* ⌨ *176 N. Canon Dr., Beverly Hills* ☎ *310/385–0880* ⊕ *www.wolfgangpuck.com* ⊘ *No lunch Sun. or Mon.*

🛏 Hotels

Beverly Wilshire, a Four Seasons Hotel

$$$$ | **HOTEL** | Built in 1928, this Rodeo Drive–adjacent hotel is part Italian Renaissance (with elegant details like crystal chandeliers) and part contemporary. **Pros:** complimentary car service; Wolfgang Puck restaurant on-site; first-rate spa. **Cons:** small lobby; valet parking is expensive. $ *Rooms from: $545* ⌨ *9500 Wilshire Blvd., Beverly Hills* ☎ *310/275–5200, 800/427–4354* ⊕ *www.fourseasons.com/beverlywilshire* ⤢ *395 rooms* ⏹ *No meals.*

★ **The Crescent Beverly Hills**

$$ | **HOTEL** | Built in 1927 as a dorm for silent-film actors, the Crescent is now a fanciful boutique hotel with a great location—within the Beverly Hills shopping triangle—and with an even better price (for the area). **Pros:** indoor/outdoor fireplace; lively on-site restaurant, Crescent Bar and Terrace; economic room available for $148. **Cons:** resort fee is $30 and not optional; no elevator. $ *Rooms from: $245* ⌨ *403 N. Crescent Dr., Beverly Hills* ☎ *310/247–0505* ⊕ *www.crescentbh.com* ⤢ *35 rooms* ⏹ *Free Breakfast.*

★ **Montage Beverly Hills**

$$$$ | **HOTEL** | **FAMILY** | The nine-story, Mediterranean-style palazzo is dedicated to welcoming those who relish luxury, providing classic style and exemplary service. **Pros:** secret whiskey bar tucked upstairs; Gornick and Drucker barbershop on-site; obliging, highly trained staff; lots of activities and amenities for kids. **Cons:** the hefty tab for all this finery. $ *Rooms from: $550* ⌨ *225 N. Canon Dr., Beverly Hills* ☎ *310/860–7800, 855/691–1162* ⊕ *www.montagebeverlyhills.com/beverlyhills* ⤢ *201 rooms* ⏹ *No meals.*

★ **Peninsula Beverly Hills**

$$$$ | **HOTEL** | This French Riviera–style palace overflowing with antiques and art is a favorite of boldface names, but visitors consistently describe a stay here as near perfect. **Pros:** 24-hour check-in/check-out policy; sunny pool area with cabanas; complimentary Rolls-Royce takes you to nearby Beverly Hills. **Cons:** very expensive; room decor might feel too ornate for some. $ *Rooms from: $600* ⌨ *9882 S. Santa Monica Blvd., Beverly Hills* ☎ *310/551–2888, 800/462–7899* ⊕ *www.peninsula.com/en/beverly-hills/5-star-luxury-hotel-beverly-hills* ⤢ *195 rooms* ⏹ *No meals.*

SLS Hotel Beverly Hills

$$$ | **HOTEL** | From the sleek, Philippe Starck–designed lobby and lounge with fireplaces, hidden nooks, and a communal table, to poolside cabanas with DVD

players, this hotel offers a cushy, dream-like stay. **Pros:** on-property cuisine mas-terminded by José Andrés; free shuttle to nearby Beverly Hills; dreamy Ciel spa. **Cons:** standard rooms are compact; pricey dining and parking; on a busy intersection outside of Beverly Hills. $ *Rooms from: $365 465 S. La Cienega Blvd., Beverly Hills 310/247–0400 slshotels.com/beverlyhills 297 rooms No meals.*

★ **Viceroy L'Ermitage Beverly Hills**
$$$$ | **HOTEL** | This all-suite hotel is the picture of luxury: French doors open to a mini balcony with views of the Holly-wood sign; inside rooms you'll find soak-ing tubs and oversize bath towels, and they even have fully curated packages for your pet. **Pros:** traditional French cuisine at Avec Nous on-site; free shuttle service with 2-mile radius; all suite rooms. **Cons:** small spa and pool; very expensive; a bit of a trek to the Beverly Hills shopping. $ *Rooms from: $495 9291 Burton Way, Beverly Hills 310/278–3344 www.viceroyhotelsandresorts.com/en/beverlyhills 116 rooms No meals.*

🛍 Shopping

Barneys New York
DEPARTMENT STORES | This is truly an impressive one-stop shop for high fashion. Deal hunters will appreciate the co-op section, which introduces indie designers before they make it big. Shop for beauty products, shoes, and accesso-ries on the first floor, then wind your way up the staircase for couture. Keep your eyes peeled for fabulous and/or famous folks spearing salads at Fred's on the top floor. *9570 Wilshire Blvd., Beverly Hills 310/276–4400 www.barneys.com.*

Cartier
JEWELRY/ACCESSORIES | Cartier has a bridal collection to sigh for in its chandeliered and respectfully hushed showroom, along with more playful pieces (chunky, diamond-encrusted panther cocktail rings, for example), watches, and

accessories. The stop itself feels like the ultimate playground for A-list clientele, complete with a red-carpeted spiral stair-case. *370 N. Rodeo Dr., Beverly Hills 310/275–4272 www.cartier.com.*

Céline
CLOTHING | Under designer Hedi Slimane's creative direction, the Parisian brand has entered a new chapter. At the Beverly Hills brick-and-mortar, fashion lovers looking for French Cool Girl clothing will love the selection of the label's leather handbags, heels, and chic ready-to-wear clothing. *319 N. Rodeo Dr., Beverly Hills 310/888–0120 www.celine.com.*

Gearys of Beverly Hills
GIFTS/SOUVENIRS | Since 1930, this has been the ultimate destination for those seeking the most exquisite fine china, crystal, silver, and jewelry, mostly from classic sources like Christofle, Baccarat, and Waterford. No wonder it's a favorite for registries of the rich and famous. *351 N. Beverly Dr., Beverly Hills 310/273–4741 www.gearys.com.*

Neiman Marcus
DEPARTMENT STORES | Luxury shopping at its finest, this couture salon frequently trots out designer trunk shows, and most locals go right for the shoe department, which features high-end footwear favorites like Giuseppe Zanotti and Chris-tian Louboutin. A café on the third floor keeps your blood sugar high during mul-tiple wardrobe changes, while a bar on the fourth is for celebrating those perfect finds with a glass of champagne. *9700 Wilshire Blvd., Beverly Hills 310/550–5900 www.neimanmarcus.com.*

Taschen
BOOKS/STATIONERY | Philippe Starck designed the Taschen space to evoke a cool 1920s Parisian salon—a perfect showcase for the publisher's design-for-ward coffee-table books about architec-ture, travel, culture, and photography. A suspended glass cube gallery in back hosts art exhibits and features

From celebrity mansions to rock 'n' roll lore, Sunset Boulevard is a drive through Hollywood history.

limited-edition books. ⊠ *354 N. Beverly Dr., Beverly Hills* ☎ *310/274–4300* ⊕ *www.taschen.com.*

Tory Burch

CLOTHING | Preppy, stylish, and colorful clothes appropriate for a road trip to Palm Springs or a flight to Palm Beach fill this flagship boutique. ⊠ *142 S. Robertson Blvd., Beverly Hills* ☎ *310/248–2612* ⊕ *www.toryburch.com.*

West Hollywood

◉ Sights

Santa Monica Boulevard

NEIGHBORHOOD | From La Cienega Boulevard in the east to Doheny Drive in the west, Santa Monica Boulevard is the commercial core of West Hollywood's gay community, with restaurants and cafés, bars and clubs, bookstores and galleries, and other establishments catering largely to the LGBTQ scene. Twice a year—during June's L.A. Pride and on Halloween—the boulevard becomes an open-air festival. ⊠ *Santa Monica Blvd., between La Cienega Blvd. and Doheny Dr., West Hollywood* ⊕ *weho.org.*

Sunset Boulevard

NEIGHBORHOOD | One of the most fabled avenues in the world, Sunset Boulevard began humbly enough in the 18th century as a route from El Pueblo de Los Angeles to the Pacific Ocean. Today, as it passes through West Hollywood, it becomes the sexy and seductive Sunset Strip, where rock and roll had its heyday and cocktail bars charge a premium for the views. It slips quietly into the tony environs of Beverly Hills and Bel Air, twisting and winding past gated estates and undulating vistas. ⊠ *Sunset Blvd., West Hollywood* ⊕ *www.weho.org.*

West Hollywood Design District

STORE/MALL | More than 200 businesses—art galleries, antiques shops, fashion outlets (including Rag & Bone and Christian Louboutin), and interior design stores—are found in the design district. There are also about

30 restaurants, including the famous paparazzi magnet, the Ivy. All are clustered within walking distance of each other—rare for L.A. ✉ *Melrose Ave. and Robertson and Beverly Blvds., West Hollywood* ☎ *310/289–2534* 🌐 *westhollywooddesigndistrict.com.*

🍴 Restaurants

★ Angelini Osteria

$$$$ | ITALIAN | Despite its modest, rather congested dining room, this is one of L.A.'s most celebrated Italian restaurants. The keys are chef-owner Gino Angelini's consistently impressive dishes, like whole branzino, *tagliolini al limone,* veal chop *alla* Milanese, as well as lasagna oozing with *besciamella* (Italian béchamel sauce). **Known for:** large Italian wine selection; bold flavors; savory pastas. [$] *Average main: $40* ✉ *7313 Beverly Blvd., West Hollywood* ☎ *323/297–0070* 🌐 *www.angeliniosteria.com* 🕒 *No lunch weekends.*

Animal

$$$ | AMERICAN | Owned by Jon Shook and Vinny Dotolo of *Iron Chef* fame, this oft-packed James Beard Award–winning restaurant offers shareable plates with a focus on meat. Highlights include barbecue pork belly sandwiches, poutine with oxtail gravy, and foie gras *loco moco* (a hamburger topped with foie gras, quail egg, and Spam). **Known for:** bacon-chocolate crunch bar; reputation as a must for foodies; being carnivore heaven. [$] *Average main: $30* ✉ *435 N. Fairfax Ave., Fairfax District* ☎ *323/782–9225* 🌐 *www.animalrestaurant.com* 🕒 *No lunch.*

A.O.C.

$$$ | MEDITERRANEAN | An acronym for Appellation d'Origine Contrôlée, the regulatory system that ensures the quality of local wines and cheeses in France, A.O.C. upholds this standard of excellence from shared plates to perfect wine pairings in its stunning exposed-brick and vine-laden courtyard. Try the Spanish fried chicken; wood-oven brioche with prosciutto, Gruyère, and egg; or *arroz negro* (black rice) with squid. **Known for:** amazing cocktail hour; quaint outdoor courtyard; fireplaces indoors. [$] *Average main: $25* ✉ *8700 W. 3rd St., West Hollywood* ☎ *310/859–9859* 🌐 *www.aocwinebar.com.*

Canter's

$ | DELI | FAMILY | This granddaddy of L.A. delicatessens (it opened in 1931) cures its own corned beef and pastrami and features delectable desserts from the in-house bakery. It's not the best (or friendliest) deli in town, but it's a classic. **Known for:** location adjacent to Kibitz Room bar; plenty of seating and short wait times. [$] *Average main: $12* ✉ *419 N. Fairfax Ave., Fairfax District* ☎ *323/651–2030* 🌐 *www.cantersdeli.com.*

Craig's

$$$$ | AMERICAN | Behind the unremarkable facade is an uber-trendy—yet decidedly old-school—den of American cuisine that doubles as a safe haven for the movie industry's most important names and well-known faces. We're not going to lie: this joint is always busy so you might not even get a table and reservations are hard to come by. **Known for:** celebrities; chick Parm; strong drinks. [$] *Average main: $32* ✉ *8826 Melrose Ave, West Hollywood* ☎ *310/276–1900* 🌐 *craigs.la.*

Dan Tana's

$$$$ | ITALIAN | If you're looking for an Italian vibe straight out of *Goodfellas,* your search ends here. Checkered tablecloths cover the tightly packed tables as Hollywood players dine on the city's best chicken and veal Parm, and down Scotches by the finger. **Known for:** elbow-room-only bar; lively atmosphere; celeb spotting. [$] *Average main: $35* ✉ *9071 Santa Monica Blvd., West Hollywood* ☎ *310/275–9444* 🌐 *www.dantanasrestaurant.com.*

★ El Coyote Mexican Food

$$ | **MEXICAN** | **FAMILY** | Open since 1931, this landmark spot is perfect for those on a budget or anyone after an authentic Mexican meal. The traditional fare is decadent and delicious; the margaritas are sweetened to perfection. **Known for:** affordable, quality cuisine; festive atmosphere; being an L.A. staple. $ *Average main: $14* ✉ *7312 Beverly Blvd., Fairfax* ☎ *323/939–2255* ⊕ *www.elcoyotecafe.com.*

Greenblatt's Deli

$$ | **DELI** | In 1926, Herman Greenblatt opened his eponymous deli which serves Jewish deli food, wine, and spirits. The restaurant claims to have the rarest roast beef in town—and they're probably right. **Known for:** matzo ball soup; pastrami sandwiches; old-school vibe. $ *Average main: $18* ✉ *8017 Sunset Blvd., West Hollywood* ☎ *323/656–0606* ⊕ *www.greenblattsdeli.com.*

The Nice Guy

$$$ | **ITALIAN** | This dark and brooding Italian restaurant sits discretely on La Cienega Boulevard and hides one of the cooler scenes in L.A. A favorite among privacy-minded celebs (there's a no-photo policy), the Nice Guy is known for its cavatelli *alla* vodka and mouthwatering chicken Parm. **Known for:** mouthwatering pastas; see-and-be-seen crowd. $ *Average main: $25* ✉ *401 N. La Cienega Blvd., West Hollywood* ☎ *310/360–9500* ⊕ *www.theniceguyla.com.*

★ Republique

$$$$ | **FRENCH** | **FAMILY** | This stunning expansive space, originally built for Charlie Chaplin back in the 1920s, serves French delicacies for breakfast, lunch, and dinner every day of the week. The scent of homemade croissants wafts through the building in the morning; steak frites can be enjoyed at night. **Known for:** classics like escargot; unbeatable pastries. $ *Average main: $35* ✉ *624 S. La Brea Ave., West Hollywood* ☎ *310/362–6115* ⊕ *www.republiquela.com.*

🛏 Hotels

★ Farmer's Daughter Hotel

$$ | **HOTEL** | A favorite of *Price Is Right* and *Dancing with the Stars* hopefuls (both TV shows tape at the CBS studios nearby), this hotel has a tongue-in-cheek country style with a hopping Sunday brunch and a little pool accented by giant rubber duckies and a living wall. **Pros:** bikes for rent; daily yoga; book lending library. **Cons:** shaded pool; no bathtubs; restaurant is just okay. $ *Rooms from: $200* ✉ *115 S. Fairfax Ave., Fairfax District* ☎ *323/937–3930, 800/334–1658* ⊕ *www.farmersdaughterhotel.com* ⇗ *65 rooms* ⦿ *No meals.*

The London West Hollywood at Beverly Hills

$$$ | **HOTEL** | Cosmopolitan and chic, especially after the recent multimillion-dollar renovation, the London West Hollywood is known for its large suites, rooftop pool with citywide views, and luxury touches throughout. **Pros:** state-of-the-art fitness center; chef Anthony Keene oversees dining program; 110-seat screening room. **Cons:** too refined for kids to be comfortable; lower floors have mundane views. $ *Rooms from: $350* ✉ *1020 N. San Vicente Blvd., West Hollywood* ☎ *310/854–1111* ⊕ *www.thelondonwesthollywood.com* ⇗ *226 suites* ⦿ *No meals.*

Mondrian Los Angeles

$$ | **HOTEL** | The Mondrian has a city club feel; socializing begins in the lobby bar and lounge and extends from the Ivory on Sunset restaurant to the scenic patio and pool, where you can listen to music underwater, and the lively Skybar. **Pros:** acclaimed Skybar on property; Benjamin Noriega-Ortiz guest room design; double-paned windows keep out noise. **Cons:** pricy valet parking only ($44); late-night party scene; no free Wi-Fi. $ *Rooms from: $300* ✉ *8440 Sunset Blvd., West Hollywood* ☎ *323/650–8999, 800/606–6090* ⊕ *www.mondrianhotel.com* ⇗ *237 rooms* ⦿ *No meals.*

Palihouse West Hollywood

$$ | HOTEL | Inside an unassuming condo complex just off West Hollywood's main drag, you'll find DJs spinning tunes on the ground floor and a gorgeous collection of assorted suites with fully equipped kitchens upstairs. **Pros:** fun scene at lobby bar; eclectic design; kitchens in all rooms. **Cons:** lobby can be loud in the evenings; no pool. $ *Rooms from: $280* ⊠ *8465 Holloway Dr., West Hollywood* ☎ *323/656–4100* ⊕ *www.palihousewesthollywood.com* ⇆ *36 suites* ¡O¡ *No meals.*

The Standard

$$ | HOTEL | Hotelier André Balazs created this kitschy Sunset Strip hotel out of a former retirement home, and a '70s aesthetic abounds with pop art, shag carpets, and suede sectionals in the lobby, and beanbag chairs, surfboard tables, and Warhol poppy-print curtains in the rooms. **Pros:** late-night dining on-site; choose-your-own checkout time; secret nightclub, mmhmmm. **Cons:** for partying more than for resting; staff can be aloof. $ *Rooms from: $250* ⊠ *8300 Sunset Blvd., West Hollywood* ☎ *323/650–9090* ⊕ *www.standardhotels.com* ⇆ *139 rooms* ¡O¡ *No meals.*

★ Sunset Marquis Hotel and Villas

$$$ | HOTEL | If you're in town to cut your new hit single, you'll appreciate this near-the-Strip hidden retreat in the heart of WeHo, with two on-site recording studios. **Pros:** favorite among rock stars; 53 villas with lavish extras; exclusive Bar 1200. **Cons:** rooms can feel dark; small balconies. $ *Rooms from: $365* ⊠ *1200 N. Alta Loma Rd., West Hollywood* ☎ *310/657–1333, 800/858–9758* ⊕ *www.sunsetmarquis.com* ⇆ *154 rooms* ¡O¡ *No meals.*

Nightlife

The Abbey

BARS/PUBS | The Abbey in West Hollywood is one of the most famous gay bars in the world. And rightfully so. Seven days a week, a mixed and very good-looking crowd comes to eat, drink, dance, and flirt. Creative cocktails are whipped up by buff bartenders with a bevy of themed nights and parties each day. A generous happy hour runs 4–7 pm on weekdays and until 9 on Friday with $8 apps and $6 cocktails. ⊠ *692 N. Robertson Blvd., West Hollywood* ☎ *310/289–8410* ⊕ *www.theabbeyweho.com.*

Comedy Store

COMEDY CLUBS | Three stages give seasoned and unseasoned comedians a place to perform and try out new material, with big-name performers dropping by just for fun. The front bar along Sunset Boulevard is a popular hangout after or between shows, oftentimes with that night's comedians mingling with fans. ⊠ *8433 Sunset Blvd., West Hollywood* ☎ *323/650–6268* ⊕ *www.thecomedystore.com.*

Delilah

THEMED ENTERTAINMENT | Reservations are definitely required for this swanky, New York–style space in West Hollywood. Waiters in white coats serve a mix of upscale American cuisine, but the true reason to come happens a little later when live jazz and burlesque dancers turn the night into a sultry singles scene that's visited by the who's who of Hollywood celebrity royalty. ⊠ *7969 Santa Monica Blvd., West Hollywood* ☎ *323/745–0600* ⊕ *www.delilahla.com.*

Employees Only

BARS/PUBS | If you're looking for the best cocktail program in L.A., you'll find it at Employees Only. This very chic spot is a sister of the New York original and is consistently awarded worldwide for its delicious drinks. At this iteration, there are various themed nights with burlesque on Saturday and sporadic live music. In the back is a speakeasy called Harry's, which is a more intimate space where you can get up close and personal with the master barkeeps to tailor you the perfect drink. ⊠ *7953 Santa Monica Blvd., West Hollywood* ☎ *323/536–9045* ⊕ *www.employeesonlyla.com.*

Jones

BARS/PUBS | Italian food and serious cocktails are the mainstays at Jones. Whiskey is a popular choice for the classic cocktails, but the bartenders also do up martinis properly (read: strong). The Beggar's Banquet is their version of happy hour (10 pm to 2 am, Sunday through Thursday), with specials on drinks and pizza. ✉ 7205 Santa Monica Blvd., West Hollywood ☎ 323/850–1726 ⊕ www. joneshollywood.com.

Laugh Factory

COMEDY CLUBS | Top stand-up comics appear at this Sunset Boulevard mainstay, often working out the kinks in new material in advance of national tours. Stars such as Whitney Cummings and Tim Allen sometimes drop by unannounced, and themed nights like Midnight Madness and Chocolate Sundaes are extremely popular, with comics performing more daring sets. ✉ 8001 W. Sunset Blvd., West Hollywood ☎ 323/656–1336 ⊕ www.laughfactory. com ➤ $17.

Rage

DANCE CLUBS | The various events at this gay bar and dance club draw different crowds—show queens for Broadway musical sing-alongs on Mondays, drag queens (and more show queens) on themed nights, half-nude chiseled-bodied men most nights, as well as Latin Saturdays and Starboy Sundays. There's lots of eye candy, even more so on weekends. ✉ 8911 Santa Monica Blvd., West Hollywood ☎ 310/652–7055 ⊕ www. ragenightclub.com.

Rainbow Bar and Grill

BARS/PUBS | Its location next door to a long-running music venue, the Roxy, helped cement this bar and restaurant's status as a legendary watering hole for musicians (as well as their entourages and groupies). The Who, Guns N' Roses, Poison, Kiss, and many others have all passed through the doors. Expect a $5–$10 cover, but you'll get the money back in drink tickets or a food discount. ✉ 9015 W. Sunset Blvd., West Hollywood ☎ 310/278–4232 ⊕ www.rainbowbarandgrill.com.

The Troubadour

MUSIC CLUBS | The intimate vibe of the Troubadour helps make this club a favorite with music fans. Around since 1957, this venue has a storied past where legends like Elton John and James Taylor have graced the stage. These days, the eclectic lineup is still attracting crowds, with the focus mostly on rock, indie, and folk music. Those looking for drinks can imbibe to their heart's content at the adjacent bar. ✉ 9081 Santa Monica Blvd., West Hollywood ⊕ www.troubadour.com.

Whisky A Go Go

MUSIC CLUBS | The hard-core metal and rock scene is alive and well at the legendary Whisky A Go Go (the full name includes the prefix "World Famous"), where Janis Joplin, Led Zeppelin, Alice Cooper, Van Halen, the Doors (they were the house band for a short stint), and Frank Zappa have all played. On the Strip for more than five decades, the club books both underground acts and huge names in rock. ✉ 8901 Sunset Blvd., West Hollywood ☎ 310/652–4202 ⊕ www.whiskyagogo.com.

👜 Shopping

★ American Rag Cie

CLOTHING | Half the store features new clothing from established and emerging labels, while the other side is stocked with well-preserved vintage clothing organized by color and style. You'll also find plenty of shoes and accessories being picked over by the hippest of Angelenos. ✉ 150 S. La Brea Ave., West Hollywood ☎ 323/935–3154 ⊕ americanrag.com.

Beverly Center

SHOPPING CENTERS/MALLS | Having gone through a massive renovation in 2018, this eight-level shopping center is home to luxury retailers like Bloomingdale's,

Henri Bendel, and Dolce & Gabbana but also offers plenty of outposts for more affordable brands including Aldo, H&M, and Uniqlo. The refurb also introduced a bevy of great dining options like Farmhouse, a seed-to-table spot with amazing pizzas; Eggslut, an extraordinarily popular breakfast joint; and Yardbird, a fried-chicken lovers' favorite, plus many, many more. ⊠ *8500 Beverly Blvd., West Hollywood* ☏ *310/854–0070* ⊕ *www. beverlycenter.com.*

★ Fred Segal

CLOTHING | One of the most well-known boutiques in all of Los Angeles, Fred Segal is a fashion design mecca that has been clothing the rich, famous, and their acolytes since the 1960s. Since moving from its original location on Melrose, the new flagship store sits atop Sunset Boulevard with more than 21,000 square feet of space that showcases innovative brands and high-end threads. Inside is also Tesse Café and Bakery, which offers fashionistas some fast casual fare as they peruse the merchandise. ⊠ *8500 Sunset Blvd., West Hollywood* ☏ *310/432-0560* ⊕ *www. fredsegal.com.*

The Grove

OUTDOOR/FLEA/GREEN MARKETS | Come to this popular outdoor mall for familiar names like Apple, Nike, and Nordstrom; stay for the central fountain with "dancing" water and light shows, people-watching from the trolley, and, during the holiday season, artificial snowfall and a winter wonderland. Feel-good pop blasting over the loudspeakers aims to boost your mood while you spend, and a giant cineplex gives shoppers a needed break with the latest box office blockbusters. The adjacent Farmers Market offers dozens of freshly farmed food stalls and tons of great restaurants. ⊠ *189 The Grove Dr., West Hollywood* ☏ *323/900–8080* ⊕ *www.thegrovela.com.*

★ Maxfield

CLOTHING | This modern concrete structure is one of L.A.'s most desirable destinations for ultimate high fashion. The space is stocked with sleek offerings from Givenchy, Saint Laurent, Valentino, and Rick Owens, plus occasional pop-ups by fashion's labels-of-the-moment. For serious shoppers (or gawkers) only. ⊠ *8825 Melrose Ave., West Hollywood* ☏ *310/274–8800* ⊕ *www.maxfieldla.com.*

Paul Smith

CLOTHING | You can't miss the massive, minimalist pink box that houses Paul Smith's fantastical collection of clothing, boots, hats, luggage, and objets d'art (seriously, there will be hordes of Instagrammers shooting selfies in front of the bright facade). Photos and art line the walls above shelves of books on pop culture, art, and Hollywood. As for the clothing here, expect the British brand's signature playfully preppy style, with vibrant colors and whimsical patterns mixed in with well-tailored closet staples. ⊠ *8221 Melrose Ave., West Hollywood* ☏ *323/951–4800* ⊕ *www. paulsmith.com/uk.*

Reformation

CLOTHING | Local trendsetters flock here for the sexy, easy-to-wear silhouettes of Reformation's dresses (including a totally affordable bridal line), jumpsuits, and separates—it's a welcome bonus that the pieces here are sustainably manufactured using recycled materials. ⊠ *8000 Melrose Ave., West Hollywood* ☏ *323/852–0005* ⊕ *www.thereformation.com.*

The Way We Wore

CLOTHING | Beyond the over-the-top vintage store furnishings, you'll find one of the city's best selections of well-cared-for and one-of-a-kind items, with a focus on sequins and beads. Upstairs, couture from Halston, Dior, and Chanel can cost up to $20,000. ⊠ *334 S. La Brea Ave., West Hollywood* ☏ *323/937–0878* ⊕ *www.thewaywewore.com.*

Hollywood and the Studios

The Tinseltown mythology of Los Angeles was born in Hollywood, still one of the city's largest and most vibrant neighborhoods. In the Hollywood Hills to the north of Franklin Avenue sit some of the most marvelous mansions the moguls ever built; in the flats below Sunset and Santa Monica boulevards are the classic Hollywood bungalows where studio workers once resided. Reputation aside, though, it's mostly a workaday neighborhood without the glitz and glamour of places like Beverly Hills. The only major studio still located in Hollywood is Paramount; Warner Bros., Disney, and Universal Studios Hollywood are to the north in Burbank and Universal City.

Of course, the notion of Hollywood as a center of the entertainment industry can be expanded to include more than one neighborhood: to the north is Studio City, a thriving strip at the base of the Hollywood Hills, which is home to many smaller film companies; Universal City, where you'll find Universal Studios Hollywood; and Burbank, home to several major studios. North Hollywood, a suburban enclave that's actually in the San Fernando Valley, has its own thriving arts district.

Hollywood

 Sights

Dolby Theatre

ARTS VENUE | More than just a prominent fixture on Hollywood Boulevard, the Dolby Theatre has a few accolades under its belt as well, most notably as home to the Academy Awards. The theater is the blend of the traditional and the modern, where an exquisite classical design inspired by the grand opera houses of Europe meets a state-of-the-art sound and technical system for an immersive, theatrical experience. Watch a concert or a show here to experience it fully, but before you do, take a tour for an informative, behind-the-scenes look and to step into the VIP lounge where celebrities rub elbows on the big night. ⊠ *6801 Hollywood Blvd., Hollywood* ☎ *323/308–6300* ⊕ *www.dolbytheatre.com* ⊠ *Tour $22.*

★ Hollywood Museum

MUSEUM | Don't let its kitschy facade turn you off. The Hollywood Museum, nestled at the busy intersection of Hollywood and Highland, is worth it, especially for film aficionados. A museum deserving of its name, it boasts an impressive collection of exhibits from the moviemaking world, spanning several film genres and eras. Start in its pink, art-deco lobby where the Max Factor exhibit pays tribute to the cosmetics company's pivotal role in Hollywood, make your way to the dark basement, where the industry's penchant for the macabre is on full display, and wrap up your visit by admiring Hollywood's most famous costumes and set props on the top floor. ⊠ *1660 N. Highland Ave., at Hollywood Blvd., Hollywood* ☎ *323/464–7776* ⊕ *www.thehollywoodmuseum.com* ⊠ *$15* ⊙ *Closed Mon. and Tues.*

Hollywood Sign

MEMORIAL | With letters 50 feet tall, Hollywood's trademark sign can be spotted from miles away. The icon, which originally read "Hollywoodland," was erected in the Hollywood Hills in 1923 to advertise a segregated housing development and was outfitted with 4,000 light bulbs. In 1949 the "land" portion of the sign was taken down. By 1973 the sign had earned landmark status, but because the letters were made of wood, its longevity came into question. A makeover project was launched and the letters were auctioned off (rocker Alice Cooper bought an "O" and singing cowboy Gene Autry sponsored an "L") to make way for a new sign made of sheet metal. Inevitably, the sign has drawn pranksters who have altered it over the years, albeit temporarily, to spell

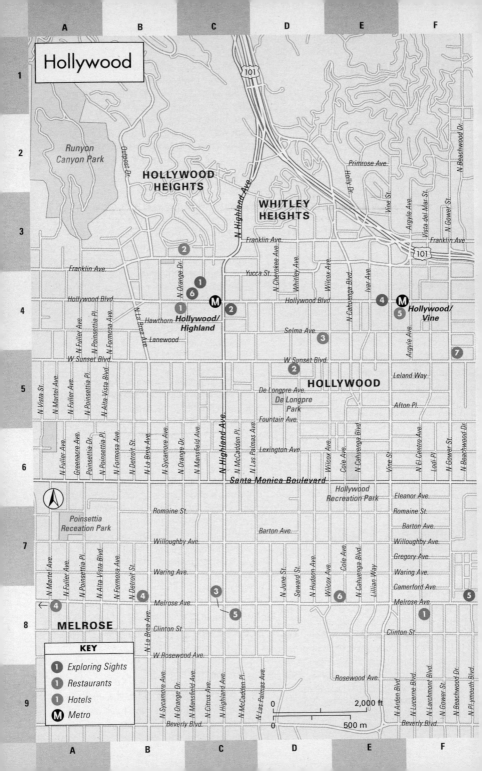

out "Hollyweed" (in the 1970s, to push for more lenient marijuana laws), "Go Navy" (before a Rose Bowl game), and "Perotwood" (during businessman Ross Perot's 1992 presidential bid). A fence and surveillance equipment have since been installed to deter intruders, but another vandal managed to pull the "Hollyweed" prank once again in 2017 after Californians voted to make recreational use of marijuana legal statewide. ⚠ **Use caution if driving up to the sign on residential streets; many cars speed around the blind corners.** ⊠ *Griffith Park, Mt. Lee Dr., Hollywood* ⊕ *www.hollywoodsign.org.*

Hollywood Walk of Fame

ARTS VENUE | Along Hollywood Boulevard (and part of Vine Street) runs a trail of affirmations for entertainment-industry overachievers. On this mile-long stretch of sidewalk, inspired by the concrete handprints in front of TCL Chinese Theatre, names are embossed in brass, each at the center of a pink star embedded in dark gray terrazzo. They're not all screen deities; many stars commemorate people who worked in a technical field, such as sound or lighting. The first eight stars were unveiled in 1960 at the northwest corner of Highland Avenue and Hollywood Boulevard: Olive Borden, Ronald Colman, Louise Fazenda, Preston Foster, Burt Lancaster, Edward Sedgwick, Ernest Torrence, and Joanne Woodward (some of these names have stood the test of time better than others). Since then, more than 2,000 others have been immortalized, though that honor doesn't come cheap—upon selection by a special committee, the personality in question (or more likely his or her movie studio or record company) pays about $30,000 for the privilege. To aid you in spotting celebrities you're looking for, stars are identified by one of five icons: a motion-picture camera, a radio microphone, a television set, a record, or a theatrical mask. ⊠ *Hollywood Blvd. and Vine St., Hollywood* ☎ *323/469–8311* ⊕ *www.walkoffame.com.*

★ Paramount Pictures

FILM STUDIO | With a history dating to the early 1920s, the Paramount lot was home to some of Hollywood's most luminous stars, including Mary Pickford, Rudolph Valentino, Mae West, Marlene Dietrich, and Bing Crosby. Director Cecil B. DeMille's base of operations for decades, Paramount offers probably the most authentic studio tour, giving you a real sense of the film industry's history. This is the only major studio from film's golden age left in Hollywood—all the others are in Burbank, Universal City, or Culver City.

Memorable movies and TV shows with scenes shot here include *Sunset Boulevard, Forrest Gump,* and *Titanic.* Many of the *Star Trek* movies and TV series were shot entirely or in part here, and several seasons of *I Love Lucy* were shot on the portion of the lot Paramount acquired in 1967 from Lucille Ball. You can take a 2-hour studio tour or a 4½-hour VIP tour, led by guides who walk and trolley you around the back lots. As well as gleaning some gossipy history, you'll spot the sets of TV and film shoots in progress. Reserve ahead for tours, which are for those ages 10 and up. ■TIP➔ **You can be part of the audience for live TV tapings (tickets are free), but you must book ahead.** ⊠ *5515 Melrose Ave., Hollywood* ☎ *323/956–1777* ⊕ *www.paramountstudiotour.com* 🎟 *From $58.*

TCL Chinese Theatre

ARTS VENUE | The stylized Chinese pagodas and temples of the former Grauman's Chinese Theatre have become a shrine both to stardom and the combination of glamour and flamboyance that inspire the phrase "only in Hollywood." Although you have to buy a movie ticket to appreciate the interior trappings, the courtyard is open to the public. The main theater itself is worth visiting, if only to see a film in the same setting as hundreds of celebrities who have attended big premieres here.

A concert at the Hollywood Bowl is a summertime tradition for Angelenos.

And then, of course, outside in front are the oh-so-famous cement hand- and footprints. This tradition is said to have begun at the theater's opening in 1927, with the premiere of Cecil B. DeMille's *King of Kings,* when actress Norma Talmadge just happened to step in wet cement. Now more than 160 celebrities have contributed imprints for posterity, including some oddball specimens, such as casts of Whoopi Goldberg's dreadlocks. ✉ *6925 Hollywood Blvd., Hollywood* ☎ *323/461–3331* ⊕ *www. tclchinesetheatres.com* 🎫 *Tour $18.*

🍴 Restaurants

Café Gratitude

$$ | VEGETARIAN | FAMILY | Of L.A.'s long list of vegan restaurants, this is among the best, with luscious dishes that are also social media worthy. But it's more than just gourmet, plant-based dining—Café Gratitude is also about leading a sustainable lifestyle full of positivity and (obviously) gratitude. **Known for:** vegan fare; the Mucho Mexican Bowl; pressed juices.

Ⓢ *Average main: $16* ✉ *639 N. Larchmont Blvd., Hollywood* ☎ *323/580–6383* ⊕ *www.cafegratitude.com.*

★ Gwen

$$$$ | STEAKHOUSE | Upscale carnivores: this is your heaven. A fine-dining restaurant that serves impossibly exquisite dishes in a copper-and-marble setting. **Known for:** steak; duck fat potatoes; house-cured meats. Ⓢ *Average main: $50* ✉ *6600 Sunset Blvd., Hollywood* ☎ *323/946–7513* ⊕ *www.gwenla.com/ butcher-shop-about.html.*

★ Osteria Mozza

$$$ | ITALIAN | How close do you think you can get to divinity? At chef Nancy Silverton's passion project–slash–culinary masterpiece, you'll come pretty damn close after sampling a few of its celestial dishes. **Known for:** ricotta-and-egg ravioli; all-Italian wine; artisanal spirits. Ⓢ *Average main: $30* ✉ *6602 Melrose Ave., Hollywood* ☎ *323/297–0100* ⊕ *osteriamozza.com.*

★ Pink's Hot Dogs

$ | **HOT DOG** | **FAMILY** | Since 1939, Angelenos and tourists alike have been lining up at this roadside hot dog stand. But Pink's is more than just an institution, it's a beloved family-run joint that serves a damn good hot dog. **Known for:** the Brando Dog; late-night dining; chili fries. [$] *Average main: $6* ✉ *709 N. La Brea Ave., Hollywood* ☎ *323/931–4223* 🌐 *www.pinkshollywood.com.*

Pizzeria Mozza

$$ | **ITALIAN** | Chef Nancy Silverton, of Osteria Mozza, owns this upscale pizza and antipasto eatery. The pies—thin-crusted delights with golden, blistered edges—are more Campania than California and are served piping hot daily. **Known for:** late-night eats; goat cheese, leek, scallion, garlic, and bacon pizza; family friendliness. [$] *Average main: $20* ✉ *641 N. Highland Ave., Hollywood* ☎ *323/297–0101* 🌐 *www.pizzeriamozza.com.*

★ Providence

$$$$ | **SEAFOOD** | This is widely considered one of the best seafood restaurants in the country, and chef-owner Michael Cimarusti elevates sustainably driven fine dining to an art form. The elegant space is the perfect spot to sample exquisite seafood with the chef's signature application of French technique, traditional American themes, and Asian accents. **Known for:** seafood; immaculate presentation; excellent wine list. [$] *Average main: $120* ✉ *5955 Melrose Ave., Hollywood* ☎ *323/460–4170* 🌐 *www.providencela.com* ⏲ *No lunch Mon.–Thurs. and weekends.*

Roscoe's House of Chicken and Waffles

$$ | **SOUTHERN** | **FAMILY** | Roscoe's is *the* place for down-home Southern cooking in Southern California. Just ask the patrons who drive from all over L.A. for bargain-priced fried chicken and waffles. The name of this casual eatery honors a late-night combo popularized in Harlem jazz clubs. **Known for:** chicken and waffles; soul food; eggs with cheese and onions. [$] *Average main: $15* ✉ *1514 N. Gower St., Hollywood* ☎ *323/466–7453* 🌐 *www.roscoeschickenandwaffles.com.*

Sqirl

$ | **CAFÉ** | Sitting on the fringe of East Hollywood where L.A.'s most touristy neighborhood transitions into the city's hippest zip code, it's hardly a surprise that Sqirl is every bit as trendy as Silver Lake—from the beautiful twenty- and thirtysomethings that frequent it to the vegan and gluten-free options the café has on hand. But don't let that tidbit turn you off—its worldly breakfast menu is just the ticket to sustain you for a busy day ahead. **Known for:** crispy rice salad; breakfast all day; sorrel-pesto rice. [$] *Average main: $12* ✉ *720 N. Virgil Ave. Suite 4, Hollywood* ☎ *323/284–8147* 🌐 *www.sqirlla.com.*

Hotels

★ Hollywood Roosevelt Hotel

$$$$ | **HOTEL** | Poolside cabana rooms are adorned with cow-skin rugs and marble bathrooms, while rooms in the main building accentuate the property's history at this party-centric hotel in the heart of Hollywood. **Pros:** Spare Room bowling alley on-site; pool is a popular weekend hangout; great burgers at the on-site 25 Degrees restaurant. **Cons:** reports of noise and staff attitude; stiff parking fees ($42). [$] *Rooms from: $419* ✉ *7000 Hollywood Blvd., Hollywood* ☎ *323/466–7000, 800/950–7667* 🌐 *www.hollywoodroosevelt.com* 🔑 *353 rooms* 🍴 *No meals.*

★ Magic Castle Hotel

$ | **HOTEL** | **FAMILY** | Guests at the hotel can secure advance dinner reservations and attend magic shows at the Magic Castle, a private club in a 1908 mansion next door for magicians and their admirers. **Pros:** heated pool; near Hollywood & Highland; lush patio. **Cons:** strict dress code; no elevator; highly trafficked street. [$] *Rooms from: $199* ✉ *7025 Franklin*

Ave., Hollywood ☎ *323/851–0800, 800/741–4915* 🌐 *magiccastlehotel.com* 🛏 *43 rooms* 🍴 *Breakfast.*

★ Mama Shelter

$ | **HOTEL** | Even locals are just catching on to Hollywood's sexiest new property, complete with a rooftop bar populated with beautiful people lounging on love seats, simple affordable rooms with quirky amenities like Bert and Ernie masks, and a down-home lobby restaurant that serves a mean Korean-style burrito. **Pros:** delicious food and cocktails on the property; affordable rooms don't skimp on style; foosball in lobby. **Cons:** spare and small rooms; creaky elevators. [$] *Rooms from: $159* ✉ *6500 Selma Ave., Hollywood* ☎ *323/785–6666* 🌐 *www.mamashelter.com/en/los-angeles* 🛏 *70 rooms* 🍴 *No meals.*

★ Palihotel

$ | **HOTEL** | Catering to young and hip budget travelers who crave style over space, this design-centric boutique property on Melrose Avenue is in the heart of Hollywood's best shopping and dining, including hot spot Hart and the Hunter. **Pros:** funky aesthetic; sweet-corn hush puppies at the Hart and the Hunter restaurant are delish; fantastic location in a walkable neighborhood. **Cons:** small rooms; congested lobby; decor might not appeal to everyone. [$] *Rooms from: $190* ✉ *7950 Melrose Ave., Hollywood* ☎ *323/272–4588* 🌐 *www.pali-hotel.com* 🛏 *33 rooms* 🍴 *No meals.*

W Hollywood

$$$$ | **HOTEL** | This centrally located, ultra-modernly lit location is outfitted for the wired traveler and features a rooftop pool deck and popular on-site bars, like the Station Hollywood and the mod Living Room lobby bar. **Pros:** Metro stop outside the front door; comes with in-room party necessities, from ice to cocktail glasses; comfy beds with petal-soft duvets. **Cons:** small pool; pricey dining and valet parking; in noisy part of Hollywood. [$] *Rooms from: $659* ✉ *6250 Hollywood Blvd., Hollywood* ☎ *323/798–1300, 888/625–4955* 🌐 *www.whotels.com/hollywood* 🛏 *305 rooms* 🍴 *No meals.*

Activities

Bronson Canyon

HIKING/WALKING | Bronson Canyon—or more popularly, Bronson Caves—is one of L.A.'s most famous filming locations, especially for western and sci-fi flicks. This section of Griffith Park, easily accessible through a trail that's less than half a mile, is a great place to visit whether you're a film buff or an exercise junkie. ✉ *3200 Canyon Dr., Hollywood.*

Runyon Canyon Trail and Park

HIKING/WALKING | Is Runyon Canyon the city's most famous trail? To the world, it just might be, what with so many A-listers frequenting it. Many folks visiting L.A. take the trail specifically for celebrity spotting. But, if that's not something you're into, this accessible trail right in the middle of Hollywood is also a good place to hike, run, see the Hollywood sign, photograph the city skyline, or simply get a bit of fresh air. If you just happen to run into a famous face, well that's just the cherry on the cake. ✉ *2000 N. Fuller Ave., Hollywood* ☎ *805/370–2301* 🌐 *www.nps.gov/samo/planyourvisit/runyoncanyon.htm.*

Nightlife

Birds

BARS/PUBS | They call it your neighborhood bar, because even if you don't live in the neighborhood you'll feel at home at this Alfred Hitchcock–themed eatery. Located in Franklin Village, a block-long stretch of bars, cafés, and bookstores, come here for pub food or a cheap poultry-centric dinner. Weekend nights mean cheap beer and well drinks, crowds spilling onto the streets, and a few rounds of oversized Jenga. Right next to the UCB Theatre, you're likely to see a few comedians grabbing a drink here after their shows. ✉ *5925 Franklin Ave., Hollywood* ☎ *323/465–0175* ⊕ *www.birdshollywood.com.*

Burgundy Room

BARS/PUBS | Around since 1919, Burgundy Room attracts a fiercely loyal crowd of locals, as well as the occasional wandering tourists. The bar is supposedly haunted (check out the Ouija boards toward the back), but that just adds to its charm. Its rock-and-roll vibe, strong drinks, and people-watching opportunities make this a worthy detour on any night out on the town. ✉ *1621 N. Cahuenga Blvd., Hollywood* ☎ *323/465–7530.*

★ Dirty Laundry

BARS/PUBS | Tucked away in a basement on the quiet Hudson Avenue, Dirty Laundry is a former speakeasy turned proper cocktail bar with live music and DJs spinning both fresh and throwback music, not to mention jazz-inspired details. There's beer on hand, but here, cocktails are king. ✉ *1725 Hudson Ave., Hollywood* ☎ *323/462–6531.*

★ Good Times at Davey Wayne's

BARS/PUBS | It's a fridge; it's a door; it's the entrance to Davey Wayne's, a bar and lounge that pulls out all the stops to transport you back in time to the '70s. The interior is your living room; the outside is an ongoing backyard barbecue with all of your friends. Except, wait, I don't recognize anyone … who invited all these drunk people to my house?! Come early to beat the crowds or be prepared to get up close and personal with your neighbors. ✉ *1611 N. El Centro Ave., Hollywood* ☎ *323/962–3804* ⊕ *www.goodtimesatdaveywaynes.com.*

Hotel Cafe

MUSIC CLUBS | This intimate venue caters to fans of folk, indie rock, and music on the softer side. With red velvet backdrops, hardwood furnishings, and the occasional celebrity surprise performance—notably John Mayer—musicophiles will not only be very happy but will receive a respite from the ordinary Hollywood experience. ✉ *1623½ N. Cahuenga Blvd., Hollywood* ☎ *323/461–2040* ⊕ *www.hotelcafe.com.*

★ Musso and Frank Grill

BARS/PUBS | FAMILY | The prim and proper vibe of this old-school steak house won't appeal to those looking for a raucous night out; instead, its appeal lies in its history and sturdy drinks. Established a century ago, its dark wood decor, red tuxedo–clad waiters, and highly skilled bartenders can easily shuttle you back to its Hollywood heyday when Marilyn Monroe, F. Scott Fitzgerald, and Greta Garbo once hung around and sipped martinis. ✉ *6667 Hollywood Blvd., Hollywood* ☎ *323/467–7788* ⊕ *www.mussoandfrank.com.*

No Vacancy

BARS/PUBS | Though at first glance, No Vacancy might boast an air of exclusivity and pretentiousness, its relaxed interiors and welcoming staff will almost instantly make you feel like you're at a house party. You know, the kind with burlesque shows, tightrope performances, a speakeasy secret entrance, and mixologists who can pretty much whip up any drink your heart desires. ✉ *1727 N. Hudson Ave., Hollywood* ☎ *323/465–1902* ⊕ *www.novacancyla.com.*

Sassafras Saloon

BARS/PUBS | Put on your dancing shoes (or your cowboy boots) and step back in time. The Sassafras boasts not only an oddly cozy, Western atmosphere but plenty of opportunities to strut your moves on the dance floor. Indulge in exquisite craft mezcal, whiskey, and tequila cocktails for some liquid courage before you salsa the night away. ✉ *1233 N. Vine St., Hollywood* ☎ *323/467–2800* ⊕ *www.sassafrassaloon.com.*

Three Clubs

BARS/PUBS | Cocktail bars are a dime a dozen in Hollywood, but there's something about this Vine Street joint that makes patrons keep coming back for more. Maybe it's the down-to-earth attitude, delicious no-frills cocktails, and the fact that a taco stand serving greasy grub is right next door. Come to see one of the burlesque or comedy shows for a full experience. ✉ *1123 Vine St., Hollywood* ☎ *323/462–6441* ⊕ *www. threeclubs.com.*

★ Upright Citizens Brigade
COMEDY CLUBS | The L.A. offshoot of New York's famous troupe continues its tradition of sketch comedy and improv with weekly shows like "Facebook," where the audience's online profiles are mined for material, and "ASSSSCAT," an improv show with rotating comedians including Zach Woods (*Silicon Valley*) and Matt Walsh (*Veep*). Arrive early as space is limited. A second theater on Sunset Boulevard opened in 2014. ✉ *5919 Franklin Ave., Hollywood* ☎ *323/908–8702* ⊕ *ucbtheatre.com.*

🎭 Performing Arts

★ ArcLight
FILM | This big multiplex includes the historic Cinerama Dome, that impossible-to-miss golf ball–looking structure on Sunset Boulevard, which was built in 1963. Like many L.A. theaters, the ArcLight has assigned seating (you will be asked to select seats when purchasing tickets). The complex is a one-stop shop with a parking garage, shopping area, restaurant, and in-house bar. The events calendar is worth paying attention to, as directors and actors often drop by to chat with audiences. Amy Adams and Samuel L. Jackson, for example, have both made time for postscreening Q&As. Movies here can be pricey, but the theater shows just about every new release. ■TIP→ **Evening shows on the weekend feature "21+" shows, during which moviegoers can bring alcoholic beverages into the screening rooms.** ✉ *6360 Sunset Blvd., Hollywood* ☎ *323/615–2550* ⊕ *www. arclightcinemas.com.*

★ Hollywood Bowl
CONCERTS | For those seeking a quintessential Los Angeles experience, a concert on a summer night at the Bowl, the city's iconic outdoor venue, is unsurpassed. The Bowl has presented world-class performers since it opened in 1920. The L.A. Philharmonic plays here from June to September; its performances and other events draw large crowds. Parking is limited near the venue, but there are additional remote parking locations serviced by shuttles. You can bring food and drink to any event, which Angelenos often do, though you can only bring alcohol when the L.A. Phil is performing. (Bars sell alcohol at all events, and there are dining options.) It's wise to bring a jacket even if daytime temperatures have been warm—the Bowl can get quite chilly at night. ■TIP→ **Visitors can sometimes watch the L.A. Phil practice for free, usually on a weekday; call ahead for times.** ✉ *2301 Highland Ave., Hollywood* ☎ *323/850–2000* ⊕ *www.hollywoodbowl.com.*

Pantages Theatre
THEATER | For the grand-scale theatrics of a Broadway show, such as *Hamilton* and *The Book of Mormon,* the 2,703-seat Pantages Theatre (the last theater built by Greek American vaudeville producer Alexander Pantages) lights up Hollywood Boulevard on show nights, when lines of excited patrons extend down the block. ✉ *6233 Hollywood Blvd., Hollywood* ☎ *323/468–1770* ⊕ *www. hollywoodpantages.com.*

🛍 Shopping

★ Amoeba Records
MUSIC STORES | Touted as the "World's Largest Independent Record Store," Amoeba is a playground for music lovers, with a knowledgeable staff and a focus on local artists. Catch free in-store appearances and signings by artists and bands that play sold-out shows at venues down the road. There's a massive and

eclectic collection of vinyl records, CDs, and cassette tapes, not to mention VHS tapes, DVDs, and Blu-Ray discs. It's a paradise for both music and movie lovers. ✉ *6400 W. Sunset Blvd., at Cahuenga Blvd., Hollywood* ☎ *323/245–6400* 🌐 *www.amoeba.com.*

Hollywood & Highland Center
SHOPPING CENTERS/MALLS | If you're on the hunt for unique boutiques, look elsewhere. However, if you prefer the biggest mall retail chains America has to offer, Hollywood & Highland is a great spot for a shopping spree. The design of the complex pays tribute to the city's film legacy, with a grand staircase leading up to a pair of three-story-tall stucco elephants, a nod to the 1916 movie *Intolerance*. Pause at the entrance arch, called Babylon Court, which frames a picture-perfect view of the Hollywood sign. This place is a huge tourist magnet, so don't expect to mingle with the locals. ✉ *6801 Hollywood Blvd., at Highland Ave., Hollywood* ☎ *323/467–6412* 🌐 *www.hollywoodandhighland.com.*

Larry Edmunds Bookshop
BOOKS/STATIONERY | Cinephiles have long descended upon this iconic 70-plus-year-old shop that in addition to stocking tons of texts about motion picture history offers film fans the opportunity to pick up scripts, posters, and photographs from Hollywood's Golden Era to the present. ✉ *6644 Hollywood Blvd., Hollywood* ☎ *323/463–3273* 🌐 *www.larryedmunds.com.*

The Record Parlour
MUSIC STORES | Vinyl records and music memorabilia abound in this hip yet modest record store–slash–music lover magnet that also touts vintage audio gear and retro jukeboxes. A visit here is usually a multihour affair, one that involves more than just browsing through display cases, digging through wooden carts of used vinyls, and playing your picks at the listening station. ✉ *6408 Selma Ave., Hollywood* ☎ *323/464–7757* 🌐 *therecordparlour.com.*

Studio City

🍴 Restaurants

Good Neighbor Restaurant
$ | **DINER** | Its walls may be heavy with framed photographs of film and TV stars, and folks from the biz might regularly grace its tables, but this Studio City diner is every bit as down-to-earth as your next-door neighbor, even after 40-some years. It gets pretty busy from the Universal City crowd, but a plateful of that home cooking is worth the wait; or if you're in a mad dash, grab a caffeine or fruit smoothie fix from the Neighbarista. **Known for:** omelet; cottage fries; breakfast food. [$] *Average main: $13* ✉ *3701 Cahuenga Blvd., Studio City* ☎ *818/457–6050* 🌐 *goodneighborrestaurant.com.*

Hot Stone Slow Food from Korea
$ | **KOREAN FUSION** | **FAMILY** | Hot Stone Slow Food might sound more like the title of an indie band rather than a legitimate restaurant, but trust that this spot on Ventura is indeed the perfect place to partake in L.A.'s massive Korean gastronomy scene. There'll be no cooking your own meats over a hot grill here; but you may be creating your own bibimbap. **Known for:** Hot Stone bibimbap or dupbap; Hot Stone BBQ; dak kang jung. [$] *Average main: $8* ✉ *12265 Ventura Blvd., Suite 102, Studio City* ☎ *818/358–4223* 🌐 *hotstone.net* 🕒 *Closed Mon.*

🛏 Hotels

Sportsmen's Lodge
$$ | **HOTEL** | **FAMILY** | This sprawling five-story hotel, a San Fernando Valley landmark just a short jaunt over the Hollywood Hills, has an updated contemporary look highlighted by the Olympic-size pool and summer patio with an outdoor bar. **Pros:** close to Ventura Boulevard restaurants; free shuttle to Universal Hollywood; quiet garden-view rooms worth asking for. **Cons:** pricey daily self-parking fee ($18);

a distance from the city. $ Rooms from: $249 ⊠ 12825 Ventura Blvd., Studio City ☎ 818/769–4700, 800/821–8511 ⊕ www. sportsmenslodge.com ⇋ 190 rooms ☉ No meals.

⛾ Nightlife

Baked Potato

MUSIC CLUBS | Baked Potato might be a strange name to give a world-famous jazz club that's been holding performances of well-known acts (Allan Holdsworth and Michael Landau) under its roof since the '70s, but it only takes a quick peek at the menu to understand. Twenty-four different types of baked potatoes dominate its otherwise short menu, each of which come with sour cream, butter, and salad to offset all that carb intake. ⊠ 3787 Cahuenga Blvd., Studio City ☎ 818/980–1615 ⊕ www.thebakedpotato.com.

Pinz Bowling Alley

BOWLING | "Bowl. Eat. Drink. Repeat" might be this bowling alley's motto, but thanks to its neon-slash-backlit lanes— each fully equipped with a touch-screen food and drink ordering system—and its very own arcade, Pinz is more than just your typical bowling experience. A few A-list names are among its loyal clientele, but you don't visit for celebrity sightings; all bells and whistles aside, it's a proper bowling alley and you come here to bowl. ⊠ 12655 Ventura Blvd., Studio City ☎ 818/769–7600 ⊕ pinzla.com.

Universal City

◉ Sights

Universal Studios Hollywood

AMUSEMENT PARK/WATER PARK | FAMILY | A theme park with classic attractions like roller coasters and thrill rides, Universal Studios also provides a tour of some beloved television and movie sets. A favorite attraction is the tram tour, during which you can duck from King Kong; see the airplane wreckage of War of the Worlds; ride along with the cast of the Fast and the Furious; and get chills looking at the house from Psycho. ■ TIP→ The tram ride is usually the best place to begin your visit, because the lines become longer as the day goes on.

Most attractions are designed to give you a thrill in one form or another, including the thrilling Revenge of the Mummy and immersive rides like the 4D Simpsons Ride, where you can actually smell Maggie Simpson's baby powder. The Wizarding World of Harry Potter, however, is the crown jewel of the park, featuring magical rides, pints of frozen butterbeer, and enough merchandise to drain you wallet faster than you can shout "Expecto Patronum." If you're in town in October, stop by for Halloween Horror Nights, featuring mazes full of monsters, murderers, and jump scares.

Geared more toward adults, CityWalk is a separate venue run by Universal Studios, where you'll find shops, restaurants, nightclubs, and movie theaters. ⊠ 100 Universal City Plaza, Universal City ☎ 800/864–8377 ⊕ www.universalstudioshollywood.com ⊠ $99.

⛾ Restaurants

Café Sierra

$$$ | SEAFOOD | FAMILY | Don't let the fact that this airy Californian and pan-Asian spot is located inside a Hilton Hotel scare you; Café Sierra has a drool-worthy seafood and prime rib buffet. Lunching here can be a splurge, but it's worth every penny. Known for: champagne brunch; Alaskan king crab; live jazz music. $ Average main: $30 ⊠ 555 Universal Hollywood Dr., Universal City ☎ 818/824–4237 ⊕ www.cafesierrahilton.com.

Dongpo

$$ | SICHUAN | FAMILY | Upmarket regional Chinese cuisine chain Meizhou Dongpo tries its hand at bringing its modern take on authentic Sichuanese cuisine with

Dongpo Kitchen, and it's exactly what the CityWalk needed to up its dining game. This bright, contemporary-meets-traditional Chinese restaurant serves delightful, affordable fare right in the middle of a sea of tourists. **Known for:** Dongpo roast duck; Sichuan dumplings; kung pao chicken. [$] *Average main: $19* ✉ *1000 Universal Studios Blvd. V103, Universal City* ☎ *818/358–3272* 🌐 *www.citywalkhollywood.com.*

Hotels

Sheraton Universal
$$ | **HOTEL** | **FAMILY** | With large meeting spaces and a knowledgeable staff, this Sheraton buzzes year-round with business travelers and families, providing easy access to the free shuttle that takes guests to adjacent Universal Studios and CityWalk. **Pros:** pool area with cabanas and bar; oversize desks and office chairs in room. **Cons:** average in-house restaurant; touristy. [$] *Rooms from: $299* ✉ *333 Universal Hollywood Dr., Universal City* ☎ *818/980–1212, 888/627–7184* 🌐 *www.sheratonuniversal.com* 🛏 *457 rooms* 🍴 *No meals.*

Burbank

Sights

Warner Bros. Studios
FILM STUDIO | You don't need to be a big film nerd to appreciate a visit to the Warner Bros. Studios, where you can pretend to be your favorite TV or movie characters, whether at a working replica of Central Perk from *Friends* or at a sorting ceremony from Harry Potter. You'll also visit backlots and sound stages to see how the magic is made.

If you're looking for an authentic behind-the-scenes look at how films and TV shows are made, head to this major studio center, one of the world's busiest. After a short film on the studio's movies and TV shows, hop aboard a tram for a ride through the sets and sound stages of such favorites as *Casablanca* and *Rebel Without a Cause*. You'll see the bungalows where Marlon Brando, Bette Davis, and other icons relaxed between shots, and the current production offices for Clint Eastwood and George Clooney. You might even spot a celeb or see a shoot in action—tours change from day to day depending on the productions taking place on the lot. ✉ *3400 W. Riverside Dr., Burbank* ☎ *818/977–8687* 🌐 *www.wbstudiotour.com* 🎟 *From $65.*

Restaurants

Bea Bea's
$ | **DINER** | Just because Bea Bea's is a no-nonsense kind of place, it doesn't mean the food isn't special. This diner serves breakfast food that is about as close to extraordinary as the most important meal of the day can be. **Known for:** large selection of pancakes and French toast; Happy Mornings; friendly staff. [$] *Average main: $12* ✉ *353 N. Pass Ave., Burbank* ☎ *818/846–2327* 🌐 *www.beabeas.com.*

Centanni Trattoria
$$ | **ITALIAN** | In a city full of adventurous restaurants touting new takes on traditional dishes and swanking about with bells and whistles and stunning interiors, a run-of-the-mill-looking place like Centanni Tratorria might never make it onto the radar. But what this authentic Italian spot lacks in swagger, it more than makes up for in delicious home cooking. **Known for:** homemade pasta; panini; seafood. [$] *Average main: $20* ✉ *117 N. Victory Blvd., Burbank* ☎ *818/561–4643* 🌐 *www.centannivenice.com.*

Los Amigos
$$ | **MEXICAN** | **FAMILY** | If you're in the mood for good old-fashioned fun coupled with hearty Mexican fare and delicious margaritas, then you'll want to consider Los Amigos, whose legendary fruity

margaritas alone are worth the drive. Pair those with something from the Platillos Mexicanos menu on karaoke night, and you're guaranteed a good time until the wee hours of the night. **Known for:** molcajete; guacamole; signature cocktails. $ *Average main: $18* ⊠ *2825 W. Olive Ave., Burbank* ☎ *818/842–3700* ⊕ *www. losamigosbarandgrill.com.*

Porto's Bakery

$ | CUBAN | FAMILY | Waiting in line at Porto's is as much a part of the experience as is indulging in a roasted pork sandwich or a chocolate-dipped croissant. This Cuban bakery and café has been an L.A. staple for more than 50 years, often bustling during lunch. **Known for:** counter service; potato balls; roasted pork sandwiches. $ *Average main: $8* ⊠ *3614 W. Magnolia Blvd., Burbank* ☎ *818/846–9100* ⊕ *www.portosbakery.com.*

Hotels

Hotel Amarano Burbank

$$ | HOTEL | Close to Burbank's TV and movie studios, the smartly designed Amarano feels like a Beverly Hills boutique hotel, complete with 24-hour room service, a homey on-site restaurant and lounge, and spiffy rooms. **Pros:** fireplace, cocktails, and tapas in lobby; penthouse with private gym; saltwater pool. **Cons:** street noise. $ *Rooms from: $269* ⊠ *322 N. Pass Ave., Burbank* ☎ *818/842–8887, 888/956–1900* ⊕ *www.hotelamarano. com* ⌂ *98 rooms, 34 suites* ✚ *No meals.*

Nightlife

Flappers Comedy Club

COMEDY CLUBS | Even though this live comedy club doesn't exactly have as long a history as others in town (it opened in 2010), it's attracted an impressive list of big names like Jerry Seinfeld, Maria Bamford, and Adam Sandler thanks to its Celebrity Drop-In Tuesdays. The food and drinks are good though not great, but you're here for the laughs not the grub. ⊠ *102 E. Magnolia Blvd., Burbank* ☎ *818/845–9721* ⊕ *www. flapperscomedy.com.*

The Snug

BARS/PUBS | If you think that Magnolia Boulevard's the Snug is your typical Irish pub, think again. This neighborhood watering hole, which has a wide selection of whiskey, 28 draft and bottled beers, and cocktails, plays host to a number of events throughout the year, from holiday parties to chili cook-offs and trivia nights, not to mention a $3 happy hour on weekdays. ⊠ *4108 W. Magnolia Blvd., Burbank* ☎ *818/557–0018* ⊕ *www. thesnugburbank.com.*

🛍 Shopping

Magnolia Park Vintage

SHOPPING NEIGHBORHOODS | Melrose Avenue might be Los Angeles's most well-known vintage shopping destination, but to many locals, especially those on the Eastside, Burbank's Magnolia Park is, in many ways, better. Spanning several blocks around Magnolia Avenue, this revitalized section blends convenience, plenty of vintage, thrift, and antiques shopping opportunities and has that laid-back small-town vibe that Melrose lacks. Great dining spots and excellent coffee shops abound, as well as foot and nail spas for a bit of pampering. ⊠ *W. Magnolia Blvd., between N. Niagara and N. Avon St., Burbank* ⊕ *www.visitmagnoliapark.com.*

North Hollywood

⊙ Sights

NoHo Arts District

NEIGHBORHOOD | In only a few years, North Hollywood's performance arts hub has grown from the residential home of aspiring actors who frequent a few small theaters and several chain restaurants to a completely revitalized district that boasts its own, albeit small, collection of new coffee shops and restaurants, bars serving up craft beer, and colorful street art. ✉ *Lankershim and Magnolia Blvds., North Hollywood* 🌐 *www.nohoartsdistrict.com.*

🍴 Restaurants

Mofongo's

$$ | PUERTO RICAN | Mofongo's small storefront represents one of the best and only venues to get authentic Puerto Rican food in L.A. Stop by and try the namesake dish (a delectable mash of fried plantains), but stay for the *pasteles* (cakes) and *rellenos de papa* (stuffed potatoes). **Known for:** mofongo de lechon (fried plantains with pork); Puerto Rican food; flan de queso (cream cheese flan). [$] *Average main: $20* ✉ *5757 Lankershim Blvd., North Hollywood* ☎ *818/754–1051* 🌐 *www.mofongosrestaurant.com.*

Rodini Park

$ | MEDITERRANEAN | Nestled in the heart of the NoHo Arts District amid newly minted high-rises, Rodini Park's "build your own" concept and highly rated house-made pastries make it the place to go for a quick, fresh, and delicious take on Greek cuisine. Between the multiple protein, topping, and sauce offerings, it offers something for all palates. **Known for:** chicken shawarma; baklava cheesecake; Mount Olympus sauce. [$] *Average main: $10* ✉ *11049 Magnolia Blvd., North Hollywood* ☎ *818/358–4802* 🌐 *www.rodinipark.com.*

TeaPop

$ | CAFÉ | At first glance, TeaPop may seem to be doing too many things at once, but this tea-centric café, with its art gallery–slash–industrial modern interior and picturesque patio, is a perfect spot to not only study or take a breather, but also to catch pop-up events like comedy nights and workshops. Don't let the hipster vibes turn you off—the service is fantastic and the drinks delicious. **Known for:** vintage milk tea; bubble tea; loose-leaf tea. [$] *Average main: $4* ✉ *5050 Vineland Ave., North Hollywood* ☎ *323/927–0330* 🌐 *teapopla.com.*

🍸 Nightlife

California Institute of Abnormal Arts

MUSIC CLUBS | What do a mummified clown, an alley full of Chinese red lanterns, and a collection of sideshow memorabilia have in common? They can all be found in the California Institute of Abnormal Arts, or CIA for short. This is a bar that proudly showcases the freak side of L.A., from the wonderfully bonkers decor to the utterly bizarre performances that often frequent its stage. ✉ *11334 Burbank Ave., North Hollywood* ☎ *818/221–8065.*

Catcher in the Rye

PIANO BARS/LOUNGES | Catcher in the Rye's theme is not specific to Holden Caulfield but rather to literature. Other odes to fictional greats can be found name-checked on the menu, including Huck Finn and Jay Gatsby. Should you have forgotten your book at home, check one out from the bar's bookshelf, or if reading's not your thing (you're in the wrong bar, pal), you can grab a board game instead. ✉ *10550 Riverside Dr., North Hollywood* ☎ *818/853–7835* 🌐 *www.catcherbar.com.*

The Other Door

BARS/PUBS | The Other Door occupies a strange space, somewhere between a steampunk-themed bar, a dive bar, and a music venue with a varied calendar featuring live music, karaoke, and silent disco. It also has a pool table and a vintage photo booth on hand, in case all these diversions aren't enough to distract you. ✉ *10437 Burbank Blvd., North Hollywood* ☎ *818/508–7008* 🌐 *theotherdoorbar.com.*

🛍 Shopping

Blastoff Comics

BOOKS/STATIONERY | Blastoff rises above L.A.'s collection of fantastic comic book stores. This is a wonderland for the serious collector, especially those looking to dive deep into vintage and rare comics. New comics are also on offer and a friendly, knowledgeable staff makes this a must-visit for any comic fan. ✉ *5118 Lankershim Blvd., North Hollywood* ☎ *323/980-2665* ⊕ *www. blastoffcomics.com.*

The Iliad Book Shop

BOOKS/STATIONERY | For 30 years, Iliad not only has been selling used books but has been a set piece on a number of TV shows and movies, including *Lethal Weapon 3*. But with a collection of 125,000 books of all genres, including a solid selection of graphic novels, it's worth a visit just to peruse the aisles and find that next favorite novel. ✉ *5400 Cahuenga Blvd., North Hollywood* ☎ *818/509-2665* ⊕ *www.iliadbooks.com.*

Mid-Wilshire and Koreatown

While they're two distinctly different neighborhoods, Mid-Wilshire and Koreatown sit side by side and offer Angelenos some of the most interesting sights, sounds, and bites in the city. Mid-Wilshire is broadly known for its wide variety of museums, but there's also a strip called Little Ethiopia, where you can find incredible cuisine. Koreatown, meanwhile, is a haven for Seoul food (pun intended) but also an area with multiethnic dining nuggets that hit the top of many restaurant lists. Once your stomach is sated, check out a Korean spa, where scrubbing and pampering can close out a perfectly long day.

Sandwiched between some of L.A.'s coolest neighborhoods, Culver City has spent the past few years forming its own identity. A place for adventurous eaters, here you can find cuisines spanning the globe.

Mid-Wilshire

◉ Sights

★ Los Angeles County Museum of Art (LACMA)

MUSEUM | Los Angeles has a truly fabulous museum culture and everything that it stands for can be epitomized by the massive, eclectic, and ever-changing Los Angeles County Museum of Art. Opened at its current location in 1965, today the museum boasts the largest collection of art in the western United States with more than 135,000 pieces from 6,000 years of history across multiple buildings atop over 20 acres. Highlights include the *Urban Light* sculpture by Chris Burden (an Instagram favorite), *Levitated Mass* by Michael Heizer, and prominent works by Frida Kahlo, Wassily Kandinsky, Henri Matisse, and Claude Monet. With an illustrative permanent collection to go along with an ever-rotating array of temporary exhibits, film screenings, educational programs, and more, the museum is a beacon of culture that stands alone in the middle of the city.

■TIP→ **Temporary exhibitions sometimes require tickets purchased in advance.** ✉ *5905 Wilshire Blvd., Miracle Mile* ☎ *323/857-6000* ⊕ *www.lacma.org* 🎟 *$20* ⊙ *Closed Wed.*

Petersen Automotive Museum

MUSEUM | FAMILY | L.A. is a mecca for car lovers, which explains the popularity of this museum with a collection of more than 300 automobiles and other motorized vehicles. But you don't have to be a gearhead to appreciate the Petersen; there's plenty of fascinating history here for all to enjoy. Learn how Los Angeles grew up around its freeways, how cars evolve from the design phase to the production line, and how automobiles have influenced film and television. To see how the vehicles, many of them quite rare, are preserved and maintained, take the 90-minute tour of the basement-level

Vault (young kids aren't permitted in the Vault, but they'll find plenty to keep them occupied throughout the museum). ✉ *6060 Wilshire Blvd., Mid-Wilshire* ☎ *323/964–6331* ⊕ *www.petersen.org* ➦ *From $16.*

 Restaurants

★ Meals by Genet

$$ | ETHIOPIAN | In a tucked-away stretch along Fairfax Avenue is Little Ethiopia, where Angelenos of all stripes flock for the African country's signatures like *tibs*, *wat*, and *kitfo*. And while there is a plethora of Ethiopian options, no one does the cuisine justice quite like Meals by Genet. **Known for:** authentic Ethiopian cuisine; jovial atmosphere; unreal tibs. Ⓢ *Average main: $20* ✉ *1053 S. Fairfax Ave., Mid-Wilshire* ☎ *323/938–9304* ⊕ *www.mealsbygenetla.com* ⊗ *Closed Mon.–Wed.*

Sky's Gourmet Tacos

$ | MEXICAN | If you're searching for some of the spiciest and most succulent tacos in L.A., look no further than Sky's. This quaint taco joint offers up beef, chicken, turkey, seafood, and vegan options that will leave your mouth on fire and your belly full in all the best ways possible. **Known for:** tacos; spices; jovial atmosphere. Ⓢ *Average main: $10* ✉ *5303 Pico Blvd., Mid-Wilshire* ☎ *323/932–6253* ⊕ *www.skysgourmettacos.com.*

Koreatown

Restaurants

The Boiling Crab

$$ | SEAFOOD | FAMILY | Put on your bib and prepare to get messy, because this crab shack is not for stodgy eaters. Choices of blue, Dungeness, snow, king, and southern king, are brought out in plastic bags where you can rip, tear, twist, and yank the meaty goodness out of their shells. **Known for:** giant crab legs; unfussy environment; long lines. Ⓢ *Average main:*

$20 ✉ *3377 Wilshire Blvd., Suite 115, Koreatown* ☎ *213/389–2722* ⊕ *www.theboilingcrab.com* ⊗ *Lunch on weekends only* Ⓜ *Wilshire/Normandie Station.*

Guelaguetza

$$ | MEXICAN | FAMILY | A classic L.A. Mexican eatery, Guelaguetza serves the complex but not overpoweringly spicy cooking of Oaxaca, one of Mexico's most renowned culinary capitals. Inside, you'll find a largely Spanish-speaking clientele bobbing their heads to nightly jazz and marimba while wolfing down the restaurant's specialty: the moles. **Known for:** salsa-covered chorizo; chili-marinated pork; family-owned restaurant. Ⓢ *Average main: $15* ✉ *3014 W. Olympic Blvd., Koreatown* ☎ *213/427–0608* ⊕ *www.ilovemole.com.*

★ Here's Looking At You

$$$ | ECLECTIC | Hawaiian and Asian-inspired dishes can be found on this menu featuring veggie, meat, poultry, and seafood. The environment is eclectic, as is the food, with signature dishes like blood cake with duck egg and pork belly with *nam jim.* **Known for:** pie; exceptional cocktails; inventive dishes. Ⓢ *Average main: $25* ✉ *3901 W. 6th St., Koreatown* ☎ *213/568–3573* ⊕ *www.hereslookingatyoula.com.*

Kobawoo House

$$ | KOREAN | FAMILY | Nestled into a dingy strip mall, this Korean powerhouse is given away by the lines of locals waiting outside. Once inside, scents of grilled meats and kimchi immediately fill your nostrils. **Known for:** kalbi beef; long lines; cheap eats. Ⓢ *Average main: $17* ✉ *698 S. Vermont Ave., Koreatown* ☎ *213/389–7300* ⊕ *www.kobawoola.com* Ⓜ *Wilshire/Vermont.*

Hotels

Hotel Normandie

$ | HOTEL | Originally built in 1926, this Renaissance Revival gem has been renovated to today's standards and is now a hip and not-so-pricey spot to post up in the ever-booming center of Koreatown.

Pros: free wine happy hour; complimentary breakfast; cheap prices. **Cons:** feels dated; tiny bathrooms. $ *Rooms from: $190* ⊠ *605 Normandie Ave., Koreatown* ☎ *213/388-8138* ⊕ *www.hotelnormandiela.com* ⟿ *92 rooms.*

The Line

$$ | HOTEL | This boutique hotel pays homage to its Koreatown address with dynamic dining concepts and a hidden karaoke speakeasy. **Pros:** on-site bikes to explore the area; cheery staff; houses the Houston Brothers' '80s-themed bar. **Cons:** expensive parking; lobby club crowds public spaces; far from parts of the city you may want to explore. $ *Rooms from: $250* ⊠ *3515 Wilshire Blvd., Koreatown* ☎ *213/381-7411* ⊕ *www.thelinehotel. com* ⟿ *384 rooms* ⃒○⃒ *No meals* Ⓜ *Wilshire/Normandie Station.*

▼ Nightlife

Dan Sung Sa

BARS/PUBS | Step through the curtained entrance and back in time to 1970s Korea at Dan Sung Sa, which gained wider popularity after Anthony Bourdain paid a visit. At this quirky time-capsule bar, woodblock menus feature roughly 100 small eats. You'll see much that looks familiar, but fortune favors the bold. Take a chance on corn cheese, or try the *makgeolli*: a boozy Korean rice drink you sip from a bowl. It pairs perfectly with good conversation and snacking all night long. ⊠ *3317 W. 6th St., Koreatown* ☎ *213/487-9100* Ⓜ *Wilshire/Vermont Station.*

★ HMS Bounty

BARS/PUBS | This super-kitschy nautical-themed bar in the heart of Koreatown offers drink specials and food at prices that will make you swoon. Make sure you speak to the grandmotherly Korean bartender—introduce yourself once and she'll never forget your name and order. ⊠ *3357 Wilshire Blvd., Koreatown* ☎ *213/385-7275* ⊕ *www.thehmsbounty. com* Ⓜ *Wilshire/Normandy Station.*

The Prince

BARS/PUBS | *Mad Men* and *New Girl* both had multiple scenes filmed in this Old Hollywood relic, which dates back to the early 1900s. The Prince is trimmed with vintage fabric wallpaper and bedecked with a stately mahogany bar; the grand piano waits in the wings. Squire lamps punctuate red leather booths where you can enjoy Korean fare and standard cocktails, wine, and beer. Whatever you do, get the deep-fried chicken. ⊠ *3198 W. 7th St., Koreatown* ☎ *213/389-1586* Ⓜ *Wilshire/Vermont Station.*

⊙ Shopping

Aroma Spa

SPA/BEAUTY | It's not difficult to find amazing spa experiences throughout Koreatown. Most places will offer up standard scrubs, hot and cold baths, dry and wet saunas, and more. Aroma takes things to another level as the spa is just the centerpiece of an entire entertainment complex. Spa services include all the traditional treatments, but when you're done getting pampered, the rest of the facility includes a gym, a swimming pool, restaurants, and a state-of-the-art golf driving range. ⊠ *3680 Wilshire Blvd., Koreatown* ☎ *213/387-2111* ⊕ *www. aromaresort.com.*

Wi Spa

SPA/BEAUTY | Koreatown is filled with endless spa experiences, but there are a few that rise above the rest. Wi Spa is a 24/7 wonderland of treatments that includes hot and cold baths, unique sauna rooms, and floors for men, women, or co-ed family spa fun. Signature sauna rooms vary from intense 231-degree thermotherapy to salt-enriched stations and specialty clay imported from Korea. Just remember, Korean spas are not for the shy at heart—you will be nude, you will get scrubbed, and you will feel like a million bucks after. ⊠ *2700 Wilshire Blvd., Koreatown* ☎ *213/487-2700* ⊕ *www. wispausa.com.*

Culver City

🍴 Restaurants

★ n/naka

$$$$ | JAPANESE | *Chef's Table* star Niki Nakayama helms this *omakase* (chef-selected) fine-dining establishment. Small and intimate, any given night will feature sashimi with *kanpachi*, sea bass with *uni* butter, or Myazaki Wagyu beef. **Known for:** three-hour meals; excellent sake pairings. [$] *Average main: $185* ✉ *3455 Overland Ave., Culver City* ☎ *310/836–6252* 🌐 *www.n-naka.com* 🕒 *Closed Sun. and Mon.*

Vespertine

$$$$ | AMERICAN | Vespertine isn't a restaurant. It's a multisensory event. **Known for:** elaborate tasting menu; modern design; unique everything. [$] *Average main: $250* ✉ *3599 Hayden Ave., Culver City* ☎ *323/320–4023* 🌐 *vespertine.la* 🕒 *Closed Sun. and Mon.*

Downtown

If there's one thing Angelenos love, it's a makeover, and city planners have put the wheels in motion for a dramatic revitalization. Downtown is both glamorous and gritty and is an example of Los Angeles's complexity as a whole. There's a dizzying variety of experiences not to be missed here if you're curious about the artistic, historic, ethnic, or sports-loving sides of L.A.

Downtown Los Angeles isn't just one neighborhood: it's a cluster of pedestrian-friendly enclaves where you can sample an eclectic mix of flavors, wander through world-class museums, and enjoy great live performances or sports events.

👁 Sights

★ Angels Flight Railway

HISTORIC SITE | The turn-of-the-20th-century funicular, dubbed "the shortest railway in the world," operated between 1901 and 1969, when it was dismantled to make room for an urban renewal project. Almost 30 years later, Angels Flight returned with its original orange-and-black wooden cable cars hauling travelers up a 298-foot incline from Hill Street to the fountain-filled Watercourt at California Plaza. Your reward is a stellar view of the neighborhood. Tickets are $1 each way, but you can buy a souvenir round-trip ticket for $2 if you want something to take home with you. ✉ *351 S. Hill St., between 3rd and 4th Sts., Downtown* ☎ *213/626–1901* 🌐 *www.angelsflight.org.*

Bradbury Building

BUILDING | Stunning wrought-iron railings, ornate plaster moldings, pink marble staircases, a birdcage elevator, and a skylighted atrium that rises almost 50 feet—it's easy to see why the Bradbury Building leaves visitors awestruck. Designed in 1893 by a novice architect who drew his inspiration from a science-fiction story and a conversation with his dead brother via Ouija board, the office building was originally the site of turn-of-the-20th-century sweatshops, but now it houses a variety of businesses. Scenes from *Blade Runner* and *Chinatown* were filmed here, which means there's often a barrage of tourists snapping photos. Visits are limited to the lobby and the first-floor landing. **■ TIP→ Historic Downtown walking tours hosted by the L.A. Conservancy cost $15 and include the Bradbury Building.** ✉ *304 S. Broadway, Downtown* ☎ *213/626–1893* 🌐 *www.laconservancy.org/locations/bradbury-building* [M] *Pershing Square Station.*

★ The Broad Museum

MUSEUM | The talk of Los Angeles's art world when it opened in 2015, this museum in an intriguing, honeycomb-looking building was created by philanthropists Eli and Edythe Broad (rhymes with "road") to showcase their stunning private collection of contemporary art, amassed over five decades and still growing. With upward of 2,000 pieces by more than 200 artists, the collection has in-depth representations of the work of such prominent names as Jean Michel Basquiat, Jeff Koons, Ed Ruscha, Cindy Sherman, Cy Twombly, Kara Walker, and Christopher Wool. The "veil and vault" design of the main building integrates gallery space and storage space (visitors can glimpse the latter through a window in the stairwell): the veil refers to the fiberglass, concrete, and steel exterior; the vault is the concrete base. Temporary exhibits and works from the permanent collection are arranged in the small first-floor rooms and in the more expansive third floor of the museum, so you can explore everything in a few hours. Next door to the Broad is a small plaza with olive trees and seating, as well as the museum restaurant, Otium. Admission to the museum is free, but book timed tickets in advance to guarantee entry. ⊠ 221 S. Grand Ave., Downtown ☎ 213/232–6200 ⊕ www.thebroad.org 🎫 Free ⊗ Closed Mon.

California African American Museum

MUSEUM | With more than 4,500 historical artifacts, this museum showcases contemporary art of the African diaspora. Artists represented here include Betye Saar, Charles Haywood, and June Edmonds. The museum has a research library with more than 6,000 books available for public use. ■TIP→ If possible, visit on a Sunday, when there's almost always a diverse lineup of speakers and performances. ⊠ 600 State Dr., Exposition Park ☎ 213/744–2084 ⊕ www.caamuseum.org 🎫 Free; parking $12 ⊗ Closed Mon. Ⓜ Expo/Vermont Station.

California Science Center

MUSEUM | FAMILY | You're bound to see excited kids running up to the dozens of interactive exhibits here that illustrate the prevalence of science in everyday life.

Clustered in different "worlds," the center keeps young guests busy for hours. They can design their own buildings and learn how to make them earthquake-proof; watch Tess, the dramatic 50-foot animatronic star of the exhibit Body Works, demonstrate how the body's organs work together; and ride a bike across a trapeze wire three stories high in the air. One of the exhibits in the Air and Space section shows how astronauts Pete Conrad and Dick Gordon made it to outer space in the Gemini 11 capsule in 1966; also here is NASA's massive space shuttle Endeavor, located in the Samuel Oschin Pavilion, for which a timed ticket is needed to visit. The IMAX theater screens science-related large-format films. ⊠ 700 Exposition Park Dr., Exposition Park ☎ 323/724–3623 ⊕ www.californiasciencecenter.org 🎫 Permanent exhibits free; fees for some attractions, special exhibits, and IMAX screenings vary.

Cathedral of Our Lady of the Angels

RELIGIOUS SITE | A half block from Frank Gehry's curvaceous Walt Disney Concert Hall sits the austere Cathedral of Our Lady of the Angels—a spiritual draw as well as an architectural attraction. Controversy surrounded Spanish architect José Rafael Moneo's unconventional design for the seat of the Archdiocese of Los Angeles. But judging from the swarms of visitors and the standing-room-only holiday masses, the church has carved out a niche for itself in Downtown L.A.

The plaza in front is glaringly bright on sunny days, though a children's play garden with bronze animals mitigates the starkness somewhat. Head underground to wander the mausoleum's mazelike white-marble corridors. Free guided tours start at the entrance fountain at 1 pm on weekdays. ■TIP→ There's plenty of underground visitors parking; the vehicle entrance is on Hill Street. ⊠ 555 W. Temple St., Downtown ☎ 213/680–5200 ⊕ www.olacathedral.org 🎫 Free Ⓜ Civic Center/Grand Park.

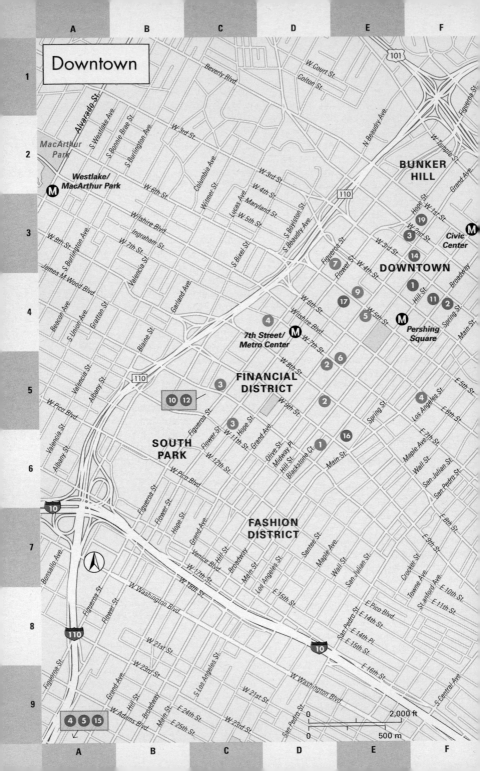

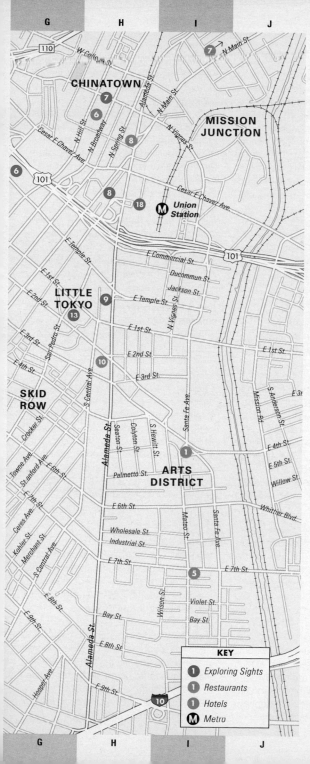

KEY

1 *Exploring Sights*
1 *Restaurants*
1 *Hotels*
M *Metro*

Chinatown

NEIGHBORHOOD | Smaller than San Francisco's Chinatown, this neighborhood near Union Station still represents a slice of East Asian life. Sidewalks are usually jammed with tourists, locals, and residents hustling from shop to shop picking up goods, spices, and trinkets from small shops and miniplazas that line the street. Although some longtime establishments have closed in recent years, the area still pulses with its founding culture. During Chinese New Year, giant dragons snake down the street. And, of course, there are the many restaurants and quick-bite cafés specializing in Chinese feasts. In recent years, a slew of hip eateries like Howlin' Ray's and Majordomo have injected the area with vibrancy.

An influx of local artists has added a spark to the neighborhood by taking up empty spaces and opening galleries along Chung King Road, a faded pedestrian passage behind the West Plaza shopping center between Hill and Yale. Also look for galleries along a little side street called Gin Ling Way on the east side of Broadway. Chinatown has its main action on North Broadway. There are several garages available for parking here that range from $5 to $10 per day. ⊠ Bordered by the 110, 101, and 5 freeways, Downtown ⊕ chinatownla.com Ⓜ Union Station.

El Pueblo de Los Angeles

NEIGHBORHOOD | The oldest section of the city, known as El Pueblo de Los Angeles, represents the rich Mexican heritage of L.A. It had a close shave with disintegration in the early 20th century, but key buildings were preserved, and eventually **Olvera Street,** the district's heart, was transformed into a Mexican American marketplace. Today vendors still sell puppets, leather goods, sandals, and woolen shawls from stalls lining the narrow street. You can find everything from salt and pepper shakers shaped like donkeys to gorgeous glassware and pottery.

At the beginning of Olvera Street is the Plaza, a Mexican-style park with plenty of benches and walkways shaded by a huge Moreton Bay fig tree. On weekends, mariachi bands and folkloric dance groups perform. Nearby places worth investigating include the historic Avila Adobe, the Chinese American Museum, the Plaza Firehouse Museum, and the America Tropical Interpretive Center. Exhibits at the Italian American Museum of Los Angeles chronicle the area's formerly heavy Italian presence. ⊠ Avila Adobe/Olvera Street Visitors Center, 125 Paseo De La Plaza, Downtown ☎ 213/628–1274 ⊕ www.elpueblo.lacity. org ⌚ Free for Olvera St. and guided tours; fees at some museums.

Geffen Contemporary at MOCA

MUSEUM | The Geffen Contemporary is one of architect Frank Gehry's boldest creations. The largest of the three MOCA branches, with 40,000 square feet of exhibition space, it was once used as a police car warehouse. Works from the museum's permanent collection on display here include the artists Willem de Kooning, Franz Kline, Jackson Pollock, Mark Rothko, and Cindy Sherman. ■ TIP→ Present your TAP metro card to get two-for-one admission. ⊠ 152 N. Central Ave., Downtown ☎ 213/626–6222 ⊕ www.moca.org/exhibitions ⌚ $12; free Thurs. 5–8 and weekends through Mar. 25 ⊗ Closed Tues.

GRAMMY Museum

MUSEUM | The GRAMMY Museum brings the music industry to life. Throughout four floors and 30,000 square feet of space, the museum showcases rare footage of GRAMMY performances, plus rotating and interactive exhibits on award-winning musicians and the history of music. A 200-seat theater is great for live events that include screenings, lectures, interviews, and intimate music performances. ⊠ 800 W. Olympic Blvd., Downtown ☎ 213/765–6800 ⊕ www.grammymuseum.org ⌚ $15 ⊗ Closed Tues.

★ Grand Central Market

MARKET | Handmade white-corn tamales, warm olive bread, dried figs, Mexican fruit drinks. Hungry yet? This mouthwatering gathering place is the city's largest and most active food market. Treated to a makeover in 2013, Grand Central Market is now the home to various artisanal food vendors. The spot bustles nonstop with locals and visitors surveying the butcher shop's display of everything from lambs' heads to pigs' tails. Produce stalls are piled high with locally grown avocados and heirloom tomatoes. Stop by **Chiles Secos** at stall C-12 for a remarkable selection of rare chilies and spices; **Ramen Hood** at C-2, for sumptuous vegan noodles and broth; or **Sticky Rice** at stall C-5, for fantastic Thai-style chicken. Even if you don't plan on buying anything, it's a great place to browse and people-watch. ✉ *317 S. Broadway, Downtown* ☎ *213/624–2378* ⊕ *www.grandcentralmarket.com* ✉ *Free.*

L.A. Live

ARTS VENUE | The mammoth L.A. Live entertainment complex was opened in 2007 when there was little to do or see in this section of Downtown. Since its inception, this once creepy ghost town has become a major hub for sports, concerts, award shows, and more. The first things you'll notice as you emerge from the parking lot are the giant LED screens and sparkling lights, and the buzz of crowds as they head out to dinner before or after a Lakers game, movie, or live show at the Microsoft Theater. There are dozens of restaurants and eateries here, including Los Angeles favorite Katsuya, the spot for sizzling Kobe beef platters and excellent sushi (the crab rolls are not to be missed). ■TIP→ **Park for free on weekdays from 11 am to 2 pm if you eat at one of the dozen or so restaurants here.** ✉ *800 W. Olympic Blvd., Downtown* ☎ *213/763–5483* ⊕ *www.lalive.com.*

Little Tokyo

NEIGHBORHOOD | One of three official Japantowns in the country—all of which are in California—Little Tokyo is blossoming again thanks to the next generation of Japanese Americans setting up small businesses. Besides dozens of sushi bars, tempura restaurants, and karaoke bars, there's a lovely garden at the Japanese American Cultural and Community Center and a renovated 1925 Buddhist temple with an ornate entrance at the Japanese American National Museum.

On 1st Street you'll find a strip of buildings from the early 1900s. Look down when you get near San Pedro Street to see the art installation called *Omoide no Shotokyo* ("Remembering Old Little Tokyo"). Embedded in the sidewalk are brass inscriptions naming the original businesses, quoted reminiscences from residents, and steel time lines of Japanese American history up to World War II. Nisei Week (a *nisei* is a second-generation Japanese American) is celebrated every August with traditional drums, dancing, a carnival, and a huge parade. ■TIP→ **Docent-led walking tours are available the last Saturday of every month starting at 10:15 am. The cost is $15 and includes entry to the Japanese American National Museum.** ✉ *Bounded by 1st and 3rd Sts., the 101 and 110 freeways, and LA River, Downtown* ⊕ *www.visitlittletokyo.com* Ⓜ *Civic Center/Grand Park Station.*

MOCA Grand Avenue

MUSEUM | The main branch of the Museum of Contemporary Art, designed by Arata Isozaki, contains underground galleries and presents elegant exhibitions. A huge Nancy Rubins sculpture fashioned from used airplane parts graces the museum's front plaza. The museum gift shop offers apothecary items, modernist ceramics, and even toys and games for children to appease any art lover. ■TIP→ **Take advantage of the free audio tour.** ✉ *250 S. Grand Ave.,*

Downtown ☎ *213/626–6222* ⊕ *www. moca.org* 🎫 *$15; free Thurs. 5–8* ⊘ *Closed Tues.*

Natural History Museum of Los Angeles County

MUSEUM | FAMILY | The hot ticket at this Beaux Arts–style museum completed in 1913 is the Dinosaur Hall, whose more than 300 fossils include adult, juvenile, and baby skeletons of the fearsome *Tyrannosaurus rex.* The Discovery Center lets kids and curious grown-ups touch real animal pelts, and the Insect Zoo gets everyone up close and personal with the white-eyed assassin bug and other creepy crawlers. A massive hall displays dioramas of animals in their natural habitats. Also look for pre-Columbian artifacts and crafts from the South Pacific, or priceless stones in the Gem and Mineral Hall. Outdoors, the 3½-acre Nature Gardens shelter native plant and insect species and contain an expansive edible garden. ■TIP→ Don't miss out on the Dino lab, where you can watch paleontologists unearth and clean real fossils. ✉ *900 W. Exposition Blvd., Exposition Park* ☎ *213/763–3466* ⊕ *www.nhm.org* 🎫 *$15.*

Orpheum Theatre

ARTS VENUE | Opened in 1926, the opulent Orpheum Theatre played host to live attractions including classic comedians, burlesque dancers, jazz greats like Lena Horne, Ella Fitzgerald, and Duke Ellington, and later on rock-and-roll performers such as Little Richard. After extensive restorations, the Orpheum once again revealed a stunning white-marble lobby, majestic auditorium with fleur-de-lis panels, and two dazzling chandeliers. A thick red velvet and gold-trimmed curtain opens at showtime, and a white Wurlitzer pipe organ (one of the last remaining organs of its kind from the silent movie era) is at the ready. The original 1926 rooftop neon sign again shines brightly, signaling a new era for this theater. Today the theater plays host

to live concerts, comedy shows, and movie screenings. ✉ *842 S. Broadway, Downtown* ☎ *877/677–4386* ⊕ *www. laorpheum.com.*

Richard J. Riordan Central Library

LIBRARY | The nation's third-largest public library, the handsome Richard J. Riordan Central Library was designed in 1926 by Bertram Goodhue. Restored to their pristine condition, a pyramid tower and a torch symbolizing the "light of learning" crown the building. The Cook rotunda on the second floor features murals by Dean Cornwell depicting the history of California, and the Tom Bradley Wing, named for another mayor, has a soaring eight-story atrium.

The library offers frequent special exhibits, plus a small café where you can refuel. Don't ignore the gift shop, which is loaded with unique items for readers and writers. Free docent walking tours are offered Monday through Friday at 12:30, Saturday at 11 and 2, and Sunday at 2. An Art-in-the-Garden tour is on Saturdays at 12:30 pm. A self-guided tour map is also available on the library's website. ✉ *630 W. 5th St., Downtown* ☎ *213/228–7000* ⊕ *www.lapl.org* 🎫 *Free.*

★ Walt Disney Concert Hall

CONCERTS | One of the architectural wonders of Los Angeles, the 2,265-seat hall is a sculptural monument of gleaming, curved steel designed by Frank Gehry. It's part of a complex that includes a public park, gardens, shops, and two outdoor amphitheaters, one of them atop the concert hall. The acoustically superlative venue is the home of the city's premier orchestra, the Los Angeles Philharmonic, whose music director, Gustavo Dudamel, is an international celebrity in his own right. The orchestra's season runs from late September to early June, before it heads to the Hollywood Bowl for the summer. Attached to the hall is Patina, an exquisite fine-dining French restaurant that's the perfect date-night spot for predinner shows. ■TIP→ Free 60-minute

guided tours are offered on most days, and there are self-guided audio tours. ✉ *111 S. Grand Ave., Downtown* ☎ *323/850–2000* 🌐 *www.laphil.org* 🎫 *Tours free.*

Union Station

HISTORIC SITE | Even if you don't plan on traveling by train anywhere, head here to soak up the ambience of a great rail station. Envisioned by John and Donald Parkinson, the architects who also designed the grand City Hall, the 1939 masterpiece combines Spanish Colonial Revival and art-deco elements that have retained their classic warmth and quality. The waiting hall's commanding scale and enormous chandeliers have provided the backdrop for countless scenes in films, TV shows, and music videos. Recently added to the majesty are the Imperial Western Beer Company and the Streamliner, two bars that pay homage to the station's original architecture while serving homemade brews and inventive classic cocktails. **■TIP→ Walking tours of Union Station are on Saturday at 10 and cost $15.** ✉ *800 N. Alameda St., Downtown* 🌐 *www.unionstationla.com.*

🍴 Restaurants

★ Bavel

$$$$ | **MIDDLE EASTERN** | Fans of Bestia have been lining up for stellar Mediterranean cuisine at this Arts District hot spot, which is owned by the same restaurateurs. Rose gold stools give way to marble tabletops as the open kitchen bangs out hummus and baba ghanoush spreads, along with flatbreads and lamb neck shawarma. **Known for:** Mediterranean cuisine; sceney atmosphere; great vibe. [$] *Average main: $40* ✉ *500 Mateo St., Downtown* ☎ *213/232–4966* 🌐 *baveldtla.com.*

Bottega Louie

$$$ | **ITALIAN** | A Downtown dining staple, this lively Italian restaurant and gourmet market features open spaces, stark white walls, and majestic floor-to-ceiling windows. If the wait is too long at this no-reservations eatery, you can sip on Prosecco and nibble on pastries at the bar. **Known for:** mouthwatering chicken Parm; one-of-a-kind portobello fries. [$] *Average main: $25* ✉ *700 S. Grand Ave., Downtown* ☎ *213/802–1470* 🌐 *www.bottegalouie.com.*

★ Broken Spanish

$$$$ | **MEXICAN FUSION** | Prepare for a taste explosion at this modern Mexican restaurant. Every dish on the menu is packed with flavor in ways you wouldn't think are possible. **Known for:** modern Mexican; taste explosions; super-friendly staff. [$] *Average main: $35* ✉ *1050 S. Flower St., Downtown* ☎ *213/749–1460* 🌐 *brokenspanish.com.*

★ Cole's French Dip

$ | **AMERICAN** | There's a fight in Los Angeles over who created the French dip sandwich. The first contender is Cole's, whose sign on the door says it's the originator of the salty, juicy, melt-in-your-mouth meats. [$] *Average main: $10* ✉ *118 E. 6th St., Downtown* ☎ *213/622–4090* 🌐 *www.213hospitality.com/coles.*

Guerrilla Tacos

$ | **MEXICAN FUSION** | What started as a food truck serving gourmet tacos has turned into a brick-and-mortar that also has an excellent (and cheap) bar. East L.A. native chef Wes Avila fires up some of the most inventive tacos in the city—sweet potato with almond chili and feta or the Baja fried cod with chipotle crema. **Known for:** gourmet tacos; cheap drinks; long lines. [$] *Average main: $11* ✉ *2000 E. 7th St., Downtown* ☎ *213/375–3300* 🌐 *www.guerrillatacos.com.*

★ Howlin' Ray's

$$ | **SOUTHERN** | **FAMILY** | Don't let the hour-long waits deter you—if you want the best Nashville fried chicken in L.A., Howlin' Ray's is worth the effort. Right in the middle of Chinatown, this tiny chicken joint consists of a few bar seats, a few side tables, and a kitchen that sizzles as staff yell out "yes, chef" with each incoming order. **Known for:** spicy fried chicken; classic Southern sides. [$] *Average main: $15* ✉ *727 N. Broadway, Suite 128, Downtown* ☎ *213/935–8399* 🌐 *www.howlinrays.com* 🕒 *Closed Mon.*

★ Majordomo

$$$$ | **ECLECTIC** | You would never just stumble upon this out-of-the-way spot in Chinatown, but world-famous celeb chef David Chang likes it that way. This is a dining destination, and it's worth the trip. **Known for:** minimal design; chuck short rib with raclette; rice-based drinks. [$] *Average main: $40* ✉ *1725 Naud St., Downtown* ☎ *323/545–4880* 🌐 *www.majordomo.la.*

★ Philippe the Original

$ | **AMERICAN** | **FAMILY** | First opened in 1908, Philippe's is one of L.A.'s oldest restaurants and claims to be the originator of the French dip sandwich. While the debate continues around the city, one thing is certain: the dips made with beef, pork, ham, lamb, or turkey on a freshly baked roll stand the test of time. **Known for:** 50¢ coffee; communal tables; post–Dodgers game eats. [$] *Average main: $8* ✉ *1001 N. Alameda St., Downtown* ☎ *213/628–3781* 🌐 *www.philippes.com.*

71Above

$$$$ | **ECLECTIC** | As its name suggests, this sky-high dining den sits on the 71st floor, 950 feet above ground level. With that elevation come the most stunning views of any restaurant in L.A., and the food comes close to matching it. **Known for:** sky-high views; fine dining. [$] *Average main: $39* ✉ *633 W. 5th St., 71st fl., Downtown* ☎ *213/712–2683* 🌐 *www.71above.com* [M] *Pershing Square Station.*

Sushi Gen

$$ | **JAPANESE** | Consistently rated one of the top sushi spots in L.A., Sushi Gen continues to dole out the freshest and tastiest fish in town. Sit at the elongated bar and get to know the sushi masters while they prepare your lunch. **Known for:** chef recommendations; limited seating; great lunch specials. [$] *Average main: $20* ✉ *422 E. 2nd St., Downtown* ☎ *213/617–0552* 🌐 *www.sushigen-dtla.com* 🕒 *Closed Sun. and Mon. No lunch Sat.*

Hotels

Ace Hotel Downtown Los Angeles

$$ | **HOTEL** | The L.A. edition of this bohemian-chic hipster haven is at once a hotel, theater, bar, and poolside lounge, housed in the gorgeous Spanish Gothic–style United Artists building in the heart of Downtown. **Pros:** lively rooftop lounge/pool area, aptly named Upstairs; gorgeous building and views; heart of Downtown. **Cons:** expensive parking rates compared to nightly rates ($36); some kinks in the service; compact rooms. [$] *Rooms from: $239* ✉ *929 S. Broadway, Downtown* ☎ *213/623–3233* 🌐 *www.acehotel.com/losangeles* 🛏 *183 rooms* 🍴 *No meals.*

★ Freehand Los Angeles

$ | **HOTEL** | Part hotel, part hostel, the Freehand is one of the newest hotels in Downtown Los Angeles and also one of the coolest. **Pros:** range of rooms from lofts to bunk beds; active social scene; great rooftop pool and bar. **Cons:** sketchy area at night around the hotel; free lobby Wi-Fi attracts dubious crowds at times. [$] *Rooms from: $100* ✉ *416 W. 8th St., Downtown* ☎ *213/612–0021* 🌐 *freehandhotels.com/los-angeles* 🛏 *59 shared rooms, 167 private rooms* 🍴 *No meals* [M] *Pershing Square.*

Hotel Figueroa

$$ | **HOTEL** | After years of renovation, the Hotel Figueroa has finally made its return to the Downtown hospitality scene, and it was well worth the wait. **Pros:** a short walk to Nokia Theatre, L.A. Live, and the convention center; great poolside bar; in-room iPads and complimentary minibar snacks. **Cons:** the area can be sketchy

at night; expensive parking ($45/night). $ *Rooms from: $200 ⊠ 939 S. Figueroa St., Downtown ☎ 866/734–6018 ⊕ www. hotelfigueroa.com ⇌ 268 rooms ⵏ⌾⵾ No meals* Ⓜ *Olympic/Figueroa.*

InterContinental Los Angeles Downtown

$$ | HOTEL | This five-star addition to the Downtown L.A. scene impresses with views, an enormous gym, dining, and an outdoor pool. **Pros:** best views; incredible F&B outlets; top-rate service. **Cons:** too big and impersonal; busy and tricky intersection. $ *Rooms from: $300 ⊠ 900 Wilshire Blvd., Downtown ☎ 213/688–7777 ⊕ dtla.intercontinental. com ⇌ 889 rooms ⵏ⌾⵾ No meals* Ⓜ *7th Street/Metro Center.*

Millennium Biltmore Hotel

$$ | HOTEL | As the local headquarters of John F. Kennedy's 1960 presidential campaign and the location of some of the earliest Academy Awards ceremonies, this Downtown treasure, with its gilded 1923 Beaux Arts design, exudes ambience and history. **Pros:** 24-hour business center; tiled indoor pool and steam room; multimillion-dollar refurbishment in 2017. **Cons:** pricey valet parking ($45); standard rooms are compact. $ *Rooms from: $200 ⊠ 506 S. Grand Ave., Downtown ☎ 213/624–1011, 866/866–8086 ⊕ www. millenniumhotels.com ⇌ 683 rooms* ⵏ⌾⵾ *No meals* Ⓜ *Pershing Square.*

The NoMad Hotel

$$ | HOTEL | This stunningly refurbished property used to house the Bank of Italy and touches of the old bank can still be seen throughout—most notably in the lobby bathrooms that are cut out of the original vault. **Pros:** freestanding tubs; smart TVs in rooms; 24-hour gym. **Cons:** sketchy area at night, expensive parking ($48/night). $ *Rooms from: $250 ⊠ 649 S. Olive St., Downtown ☎ 213/358–0000 ⊕ www.thenomadhotel.com/los-angeles ⇌ 241 rooms* ⵏ⌾⵾ *No meals* Ⓜ *7th Street/ Metro Center.*

Westin Bonaventure Hotel and Suites

$$ | HOTEL | FAMILY | Step inside the futuristic lobby of L.A.'s largest hotel to be greeted by fountains, an indoor lake and track, and 12 glass elevators leading up to the historic rooms of this 35-story property. Color-coded hotel floors help newcomers navigate the hotel, which takes up an entire city block. **Pros:** spa with shiatsu massage; revolving rooftop lounge; many on-site restaurants. **Cons:** massive hotel might feel too corporate; mazelike lobby and public areas. $ *Rooms from: $250 ⊠ 404 S. Figueroa St., Downtown ☎ 213/624–1000 ⊕ westin.marriott. com ⇌ 1493 rooms* ⵏ⌾⵾ *No meals.*

 ## Nightlife

Blue Whale

MUSIC CLUBS | This unassuming jazz club in Little Tokyo caters to a serious crowd, bringing progressive and modern jazz to the stage. Although the venue is focused on the music (yes, you may get shushed for talking—that's how small it is), there is a kitchen and bar for snacks and drinks. The club is on the third floor of Weller Court, and the cover runs around $10 to $20. ⊠ *Weller Court Plaza, 123 Astronaut E. S. Onizuka St., Suite 301, Downtown ☎ 213/620–0908 ⊕ www. bluewhalemusic.com.*

Broadway Bar

BARS/PUBS | This watering-hole-meets-dive sits in a flourishing section of Broadway (neighbors include the swank Ace Hotel). Bartenders mix creative cocktails while DJs spin tunes nightly. The two-story space includes a smoking balcony overlooking the street. The crowd is often dressed to impress. ⊠ *830 S. Broadway, Downtown ☎ 213/614–9909 ⊕ 213hospitality.com/broadwaybar.*

★ Golden Gopher

BARS/PUBS | Craft cocktails, beers on tap, an outdoor smoking patio, and retro video games—this bar in the heart of Downtown is not to be missed. With one of the oldest liquor licenses in Los Angeles (issued in 1905), the Golden Gopher is the only bar in Los Angeles with an on-site liquor store for to-go orders—just in case you want to buy another bottle before you head home. ✉ 417 W. 8th St., Downtown ☎ 213/614–8001 ⊕ 213hospitality.com/project/goldengopher.

La Cita

DANCE CLUBS | This dive bar may not look like much, but it more than makes up for it with an interesting mix of barflies, urban hipsters, and reasonable drink prices. Friday and Saturday nights, DJs mix Top 40 hits and a tiny dance floor packs in the crowd. For those more interested in drinking and socializing, head to the back patio where a TV plays local sports. Every day has a differently themed happy hour—hip-hop happy hour on Wednesday or rockabilly happy hour on Thursday. Specials vary from $3 Tecates to free pizza. ✉ 336 S. Hill St., Downtown ☎ 213/687–7111 ⊕ www.lacitabar.com Ⓜ Pershing Square Station.

Love Song Bar

BARS/PUBS | Lovers of T. S. Eliot and vinyl will find themselves instantly at home inside this cozy establishment named after Eliot's "The Love Song of J. Alfred Prufrock." When not pouring drinks, bartenders often act as DJs, playing records (the best of the '60s through the '80s) in their entirety. As it's housed inside the Regent Theater, the cozy nature of the place can be disrupted when there's a concert scheduled. For those with an appetite, fantastic food can be ordered from the pizza parlor next door—naturally, it's called Prufrock's. ✉ 446 S. Main St., Downtown ☎ 323/284–5661.

Redwood Bar & Grill

BARS/PUBS | If you're looking for a place with potent drinks and a good burger, this kitschy bar fits the bill perfectly. Known today as the "pirate bar" because of its nautical decor, the place dates back to the 1940s, when it was rumored to attract mobsters, politicians, and journalists due to its proximity to City Hall, the Hall of Justice, and the original location of the Los Angeles Times. There's nightly music from local rock bands, though it comes with a cover charge. ✉ 316 W. 2nd St., Downtown ☎ 213/680–2600 ⊕ www.theredwoodbar.com.

★ Resident

MUSIC CLUBS | Catch a lineup of indie tastemakers inside this converted industrial space, or hang outdoors in the beer garden while trying bites from on-site food truck KTCHN (on cooler evenings you can congregate around the fire pits). A wide variety of draft beers and a specially curated cocktail program are available inside at the bar or at the trailer bar outside. ✉ 428 S. Hewitt St., Downtown ☎ 213/628–7503 ⊕ www.residentdtla.com.

Seven Grand

BARS/PUBS | The hunting lodge vibe makes you feel like you need a whiskey in hand—luckily, this Downtown establishment stocks more than 700 of them. Attracting whiskey novices and connoisseurs, the bartenders here are more than willing to help you make a selection. Live jazz and blues bands play every night, so even if you're not a big drinker there's still some appeal (although you're definitely missing out). For a more intimate setting, try the on-site **Bar Jackalope,** a bar within a bar, which has a "whiskey tasting library" specializing in Japanese varieties and seats only 18. ✉ 515 W. 7th St., 2nd fl., Downtown ☎ 213/614–0737 ⊕ www.sevengrandbars.com Ⓜ 7th Street/Metro Center.

★ The Varnish

BARS/PUBS | Beeline through the dining room of Cole's to find an unassuming door that leads to this small, dimly lit bar within a bar. Wooden booths line the walls, candles flicker, and live jazz is performed Sunday through Wednesday. The bartenders take their calling to heart and shake and stir some of the finest cocktails in the city. Those who don't have a drink of choice can list their wants ("gin-based and sweet," "strong whiskey and herbaceous") and be served a custom cocktail. Be warned: patrons requiring quick drinks will want to go elsewhere—perfection takes time. ☒ *118 E. 6th St., Downtown* ☎ *213/265–7089* ⊕ *213hospitality.com/the-varnish.*

🎭 Performing Arts

Ahmanson Theatre

THEATER | The largest of L.A.'s Center Group's three theaters, the 2,100-seat Ahmanson Theatre presents larger-scale classic revivals, dramas, musicals, and comedies like *Into the Woods,* which are either going to or coming from Broadway and the West End. The ambience is a theater lover's delight. ☒ *135 N. Grand Ave., Downtown* ☎ *213/628–2772* ⊕ *www.centertheatregroup.org* Ⓜ *Civic Center/Grand Park Station.*

★ Dorothy Chandler Pavilion

CONCERTS | Though half a century old, this theater maintains the glamour of its early years, richly decorated with crystal chandeliers, classical theatrical drapes, and a 24-karat gold dome. Part of the Los Angeles Music Center, this pavilion is home to the L.A. Opera though a large portion of programming is made up of dance and ballet performances as well. Ticket holders can attend free talks that take place an hour before opera performances. ■TIP→ **Reservations for the talks aren't required, but it's wise to arrive early as space is limited.** ☒ *135 N. Grand Ave., Downtown* ☎ *213/972–0711* ⊕ *www. musiccenter.org or www.dorothychandlerpavilion.net.*

Microsoft Theater

CONCERTS | The Microsoft Theater is host to a variety of concerts and big-name awards shows—the Emmys, American Music Awards, BET Awards, and the ESPYs. This theater and the surrounding L.A. Live complex are a draw for those looking for a fun night out. The building's emphasis on acoustics and versatile seating arrangements means that all 7,100 seats are good, whether you're at an intimate Neil Young concert or the People's Choice Awards. Outside, the L.A. Live complex hosts restaurants and attractions, including the GRAMMY Museum, to keep patrons entertained before and after shows (though it's open whether or not there's a performance). ☒ *777 Chick Hearn Ct., Downtown* ☎ *213/763–6030* ⊕ *www.microsofttheater.com.*

The REDCAT (Roy and Edna Disney/Cal Arts Theater)

DANCE | Located inside the Walt Disney Concert Hall, this 288-seat theater serves as a space for innovative performance and visual art in addition to film screenings and literary events. The gallery features changing art installations. Tickets are reasonably priced at $25 and under for most events. ☒ *631 W. 2nd St., Downtown* ☎ *213/237–2800* ⊕ *www. redcat.org.*

Shrine Auditorium

CONCERTS | Since opening in 1926, the auditorium has hosted nearly every major awards show at one point or another, including the Emmys and the GRAMMYs. Today, the venue and adjacent Expo Hall hosts concerts, film premieres, award shows, pageants, and special events. The Shrine's Moorish Revival–style architecture is a spectacle all its own. ☒ *665 W. Jefferson Blvd., Downtown* ☎ *213/748–5116* ⊕ *www.shrineauditorium.com.*

🛍 Shopping

Alchemy Works

CLOTHING | This beautifully curated shop specializes in goods by local brands including hats by Janessa Leone, jewelry by Gabriela Artigas, and bags by Clare V., much of which is decidedly contemporary and minimal. There's also an in-store Warby Parker Glass House, where shoppers can try on different styles by the affordable eyewear brand. Besides wearables, Alchemy Works also offers housewares, apothecary items, books and magazines, and more must-haves for modern design lovers. ⊠ *826 E. 3rd St., Downtown* ☎ *323/487–1497* ⊕ *www. alchemyworks.us.*

★ **The Last Bookstore**
BOOKS/STATIONERY | California's largest used and new book and record shop is a favorite for both book lovers and fans of a good photo op, thanks to elements like an archway created from curving towers of books, a peephole carved into the stacks, and an in-store vault devoted to horror texts. Aside from the awesome aesthetics, shoppers will love to get lost in the store's collection of affordable books, art, and music. ⊠ *453 S. Spring St., ground fl., Downtown* ☎ *213/488–0599* ⊕ *www.lastbookstorela. com* Ⓜ *Pershing Square Station.*

Pasadena Area

Although seemingly absorbed into the general Los Angeles sprawl, Pasadena is a separate and distinct city. It's best known for the Tournament of Roses, or more commonly, the Rose Bowl, seen around the world every New Year's Day. But the city has sites worth seeing year-round—from gorgeous Craftsman homes to exceptional museums, particularly the Norton Simon and the Huntington Library, Art Collections, and Botanical Gardens. Note that the Huntington and the Old Mill reside in San Marino, a wealthy, 4-square-mile residential area just over the Pasadena line.

◉ Sights

The Gamble House
HOUSE | Built by Charles and Henry Greene in 1908, this American Arts and Crafts bungalow illustrates the incredible craftsmanship that went into early L.A. architecture. The term "bungalow" can be misleading, since the Gamble House is a huge three-story home. To wealthy Easterners such as the Gambles (as in Procter & Gamble), this type of vacation home seemed informal compared with their mansions back home. Admirers swoon over the teak staircase and cabinetry, the Greene and Greene–designed furniture, and an Emil Lange glass door. The dark exterior has broad eaves, with sleeping porches on the second floor. An hour-long, docent-led tour of the Gamble's interior will draw your eye to the exquisite details. For those who want to see more of the Greene and Greene homes, there are guided walks around the historic Arroyo Terrace neighborhood. Advance tickets are highly recommended. ■TIP➔ **Film buffs might recognize this as Doc Brown's house from Back to the Future.** ⊠ *4 Westmoreland Pl., Pasadena* ☎ *626/793–3334* ⊕ *www.gamblehouse. org* ⊠ *$15* ☉ *Closed Mon.*

★ Huntington Library, Art Collections, and Botanical Gardens
GARDEN | If you have time for just one stop in the Pasadena area, be sure to see this sprawling estate built for railroad tycoon Henry E. Huntington in the early 1900s. Henry and his wife, Arabella (who was also his aunt by marriage), voraciously collected rare books and manuscripts, botanical specimens, and 18th-century British art. The institution they established became one of the most extraordinary cultural complexes in the world.

The library contains more than 700,000 books and 4 million manuscripts, including one of the world's biggest history of science collections.

Don't resist being lured outside into the Botanical Gardens, which extend out from the main building. The 10-acre Desert Garden has one of the world's largest groups of mature cacti and other succulents (visit on a cool morning or late afternoon). The Shakespeare Garden, meanwhile, blooms with plants mentioned in Shakespeare's works. The

Japanese Garden features an authentic ceremonial teahouse built in Kyoto in the 1960s. A waterfall flows from the teahouse to the ponds below. In the Rose Garden Tea Room, afternoon tea is served (reserve in advance). The Chinese Garden, which is among the largest outside of China, sinews around waveless pools.

The Bing Children's Garden lets tiny tots explore the ancient elements of water, fire, air, and earth. A 1¼-hour guided tour of the Botanical Gardens is led by docents at posted times, and a free brochure with a map and property highlights is available in the entrance pavilion. ⊠ 1151 Oxford Rd., San Marino ☎ 626/405-2100 ⊕ www.huntington.org ⌨ From $25; free admission 1st Thurs. of every month ⊗ Closed Tues.

★ **Norton Simon Museum**
MUSEUM | As seen in the New Year's Day Tournament of Roses Parade, this low-profile brown building is one of the finest midsize museums anywhere, with a collection that spans more than 2,000 years of Western and Asian art. It all began in the 1950s when Norton Simon (Hunt-Wesson Foods, McCalls Corporation, and Canada Dry) started collecting works by Degas, Renoir, Gauguin, and Cézanne. His collection grew to include works by Old Masters and impressionists, modern works from Europe, and Indian and Southeast Asian art.

Today the Norton Simon Museum is richest in works by Rembrandt, Picasso, and, most of all, Degas.

Head down to the bottom floor to see temporary exhibits and phenomenal Southeast Asian and Indian sculptures and artifacts, where pieces like a Ban Chiang black ware vessel date back to well before 1000 BC. Don't miss a living-artwork outdoors: the garden, conceived by noted Southern California landscape designer Nancy Goslee Power. The tranquil pond was inspired by Monet's gardens at Giverny. ⊠ 411 W. Colorado Blvd., Pasadena ☎ 626/449-6840 ⊕ www.nortonsimon.org ⌨ $15; free 1st Fri. of month 5-8 ⊗ Closed Tues.

The Old Mill (El Molino Viejo)
BUILDING | Built in 1816 as a gristmill for the San Gabriel Mission, the mill is one of the last remaining examples in Southern California of Spanish Mission architecture. The thick adobe walls and textured ceiling rafters give the interior a sense of quiet strength. Be sure to step into the back room, now a gallery with rotating quarterly exhibits. Outside, a chipped section of the mill's exterior reveals the layers of brick, ground seashell paste, and ox blood used to hold the structure together. The surrounding gardens are reason enough to visit, with a flower-decked arbor and old sycamores and oaks. In summer the Capitol Ensemble performs in the garden. ⊠ 1120 Old Mill Rd., San Marino ☎ 626/449-5458 ⊕ www.old-mill.org ⌨ Free ⊗ Closed Mon.

Old Town Pasadena
NEIGHBORHOOD | This 22-block historic district contains a vibrant mix of restored 19th-century brick buildings interspersed with contemporary architecture. Chain stores have muscled in, but there are still some homegrown shops, plenty of tempting cafés and restaurants, and a bustling beer scene. In recent years, a vibrant Asian food scene has popped up in the vicinity as well. In the evening and on weekends, the streets are packed with people. Old Town's main action takes place on Colorado Boulevard between Pasadena Avenue and Arroyo Parkway. ⊠ Pasadena ☎ 626/356-9725 ⊕ www.oldpasadena.org.

🍴 **Restaurants**

Lincoln
$$ | CAFÉ | This adorable little café should be a go-to for any and all light breakfast and lunch needs. Healthy breakfast bowls get your body moving, while pesto

Pasadena and Environs

PASADENA

SOUTH PASADENA

SAN MARINO

KEY

- ① Exploring Sights
- ① Restaurants

Sights ▼

1 The Gamble House **A3**
2 Huntington Library,
Art Collections, and
Botanical Gardens....... **E5**
3 Norton Simon
Museum **A3**
4 The Old Mill
(El Molino Viejo)......... **D6**
5 Old Town Pasadena **B4**

Restaurants ▼

1 Lincoln **A1**
2 Pie'n Burger............. **D4**
3 The Raymond 1886...... **B6**

turkey sandwiches fill you up just right. **Known for:** light bites; great patio; strong coffee. $ *Average main: $15* ✉ *1992 Lincoln Ave., Pasadena* ☎ *626/765-6746* ⊕ *lincolnpasadena.com.*

Pie 'n Burger

$ | **DINER** | Since 1963, this small and charming diner has done two things really well—pie and burgers. Most seats are counter-style, with a griddle searing up patties. **Known for:** simple burgers; enormous pie slices; retro style. $ *Average main: $13* ✉ *913 E. California Blvd., Pasadena* ☎ *626/795-1123* ⊕ *pienburger.com.*

The Raymond 1886

$$$ | **MODERN AMERICAN** | The Raymond 1886 is the coolest kid on the Pasadena block. Carved out of an old cottage, the bar and restaurant has an expansive patio with long wooden tables and hanging lights. **Known for:** solid happy hour; great bar food; expansive patio. $ *Average main: $30* ✉ *1250 S. Fair Oaks Ave., Pasadena* ☎ *626/441-3136* ⊕ *theraymond. com* ☾ *Closed Mon.*

🛍 Shopping

★ Rose Bowl Flea Market

OUTDOOR/FLEA/GREEN MARKETS | This massively popular flea market, which happens the second Sunday of each month (rain or shine), deservedly draws crowds that come for deals on goods including mid-century furniture, vintage clothing, pop culture collectibles, books, and music. Food and drink options are on hand to keep shoppers satiated, and general admission is just $9, but VIP/early-bird options are available for a little extra dough. Bring cash to avoid an inevitable line at the ATM, and feel free to try your hand at haggling. ✉ *1001 Rose Bowl Dr., Pasadena* ☎ *323/560-7469* ⊕ *www. rgcshows.com.*

Vroman's Bookstore

BOOKS/STATIONERY | Southern California's oldest and largest independent bookseller is justly famous for its great service.

A newsstand, café, and stationery store add to the appeal. A regular rotation of events including trivia night, kids' story time, author meet-and-greets, crafting sessions, discussions, and more get the community actively involved. ✉ *695 E. Colorado Blvd., Pasadena* ☎ *626/449-5320* ⊕ *www.vromansbookstore.com.*

Los Feliz and the Eastside

The neighborhoods in L.A.'s Eastside are talked about with the same oh-my-god-it's-so-cool reverence by Angelenos as Brooklyn is by New Yorkers. These streets are dripping with trendiness—which will delight some and enrage others. Almost 20 years ago, Los Feliz was the first of these rediscovered, reinvented neighborhoods, then came Silver Lake, then Echo Park. As each one became more expensive, the cool kids relocated, leaving behind their style and influence. Now Highland Park is the center of the oh-so-hip universe. But, the epicenter is constantly shifting. No doubt, by the next edition of this guide, it'll be someplace else.

Los Feliz

👁 Sights

Barnsdall Art Park

HOUSE | FAMILY | The panoramic view of Hollywood alone is worth a trip to this hilltop cultural center. On the grounds you'll find the 1921 **Hollyhock House,** a masterpiece of modern design by architect Frank Lloyd Wright. It was commissioned by philanthropist Aline Barnsdall to be the centerpiece of an arts community. While Barnsdall's project didn't turn out the way she planned, the park now hosts the L.A. Municipal Art Gallery and Theatre, which provides exhibition space for visual and performance artists.

Wright dubbed this style "California Romanza" (*romanza* is a musical term meaning "to make one's own form"). Stylized depictions of Barnsdall's favorite flower, the hollyhock, appear throughout the house in its cement columns, roof line, and furnishings. The leaded-glass windows are expertly placed to make the most of both the surrounding gardens and the city views. On summer weekends, there are wildly popular wine tastings and outdoor movie screenings. Self-guided tours are available Thursday through Sunday from 11 to 4. ✉ *4800 Hollywood Blvd., Los Feliz* ☎ *323/644–6296* 🌐 *www.barnsdall.org* 🎫 *Free; house tours $7* 🕒 *House closed Mon.*

★ Griffith Observatory

OBSERVATORY | Most visitors barely skim the surface of this gorgeous spot in the Santa Monica Mountains, but those in the know will tell you there's more to the Griffith Observatory than its sweeping views and stunning Greek Revival architecture. To start, this free-to-the-public mountaintop observatory is home to the Samuel Oschin Planetarium, a state-of-the-art theater with an aluminum dome and a Zeiss star projector that plays a number of ticketed shows. Those spectacular shows are complemented by a couple of space-related exhibits, and several telescopes (naturally), as well as theater programs and events at the Leonard Nimoy Event Horizon Theater. For visitors who are looking to get up close and personal with the cosmos, monthly star-viewing parties with local amateur astronomers are also on hand. **■ TIP→ For a fantastic view, come at sunset to watch the sky turn fiery shades of red with the city's skyline silhouetted.** ✉ *2800 E. Observatory Ave., Los Feliz* ☎ *213/473–0800* 🌐 *www.griffithobservatory.org* 🕒 *Closed Mon.* ☞ *Observatory grounds and parking are open daily.*

Griffith Park

CITY PARK | FAMILY | The country's largest municipal park, the 4,310-acre Griffith Park is a must for nature lovers, the perfect spot for respite from the hustle and bustle of the surrounding urban areas. Plants and animals native to Southern California can be found within the park's borders, including deer, coyotes, and even a reclusive mountain lion. Bronson Canyon (where the Batcave from the 1960s *Batman* TV series is located) and Crystal Springs are favorite picnic spots.

The park is named after Colonel Griffith J. Griffith, a mining tycoon who donated 3,000 acres to the city in 1896. As you might expect, the park has been used as a film and television location for at least a century. Here you'll find the Griffith Observatory, the Los Angeles Zoo, the Greek Theater, two golf courses, hiking and bridle trails, a swimming pool, a merry-go-round, and an outdoor train museum. ✉ *4730 Crystal Springs Dr., Los Feliz* ☎ *323/913–4688* 🌐 *www.laparks.org/dos/parks/griffithpk* 🎫 *Free; attractions inside park have separate admission fees.*

🍴 Restaurants

The Best Fish Taco in Ensenada

$ | MEXICAN | FAMILY | In mirroring the taco stands of Ensenada, Mexico—simple, cheap, unceremonious, with a selection of spicy house-made salsas—this little local treasure has achieved what many restaurants serving Baja tacos haven't: an authentic (and delicious) experience. **Known for:** fish-and-shrimp tacos; mango salsa; horchata. [$] *Average main: $6* ✉ *1650 Hillhurst Ave., Los Feliz* ☎ *323/466–5552* 🌐 *www.bestfishtacoinensenada.com.*

Kismet

$$ | MEDITERRANEAN | You may feel like you're about to walk into a sauna rather than a restaurant because of its minimalist light-color wood on white paint interior, but Kismet's colorful gorgeous Middle

Eastern dishes tell a different story. This James Beard nominee perfectly blends comforting Middle Eastern and Israeli cuisine with Californian flavors and plant-based flair, all served in a modern space. **Known for:** freekeh fritters; jeweled crispy rice with egg yolk; dessert. [$] *Average main: $18* ✉ *4648 Hollywood Blvd., Los Feliz* ☎ *323/409–0404* 🌐 *www.kismet-losangeles.com.*

Little Dom's

$$ | **ITALIAN** | With a vintage bar and dapper barkeep who mixes up seasonally inspired retro cocktails, an attached Italian deli where you can pick up a pork-cheek sub, and an $18 Monday-night supper, it's not surprising that Little Dom's is a neighborhood gem. Cozy and inviting, with big leather booths you can sink into for the night, the restaurant puts a modern spin on classic Italian dishes such as *burrata* agnolotti and meatballs. **Known for:** ricotta cheese and fresh blueberry pancakes; pizza with sunny-side up egg; breakfast. [$] *Average main: $20* ✉ *2128 Hillhurst Ave., Los Feliz* ☎ *323/661–0055* 🌐 *www.littledoms.com.*

Nightlife

Covell

WINE BARS—NIGHTLIFE | Covell is the embodiment of what every unpretentious wine drinker wishes a wine bar should be—laid back. It's thankfully lacking in servers who might turn up their noses should you—for shame!—forget to swirl the glass. But what else would you expect from a spot with shabby furnishings and a vintage motorcycle mounted to the wall? ✉ *4628 Hollywood Blvd., Los Feliz* ☎ *323/660–4400* 🌐 *www.barcovell.com.*

Dresden Room

PIANO BARS/LOUNGES | This bar's 1940s lounge decor makes it a favorite with folks in Los Angeles. The long-running house band, Marty and Elayne, has entertained patrons for more than three decades. (They found a new generation of fans, thanks to the film *Swingers*.) Other than the entertainment, perhaps the best reason to wander in is to sip on a Blood and Sand cocktail, self-proclaimed to be "the world's most tantalizing drink." ✉ *1760 N. Vermont Ave., Los Feliz* ☎ *323/665–4294* 🌐 *www.thedresden.com.*

Performing Arts

Greek Theatre

CONCERTS | With a robust lineup from May through November, acts such as Bruce Springsteen, John Legend, and Aretha Franklin (RIP) have all graced the stage at this scenic outdoor venue. The 5,900-capacity amphitheater is at the base of Griffith Park, and you may want to make a day of it by hiking or stargazing beforehand. There is usually slow, preshow traffic on concert nights, but it'll give you a chance to take in the beautiful park foliage and homes in the Hollywood Hills. Paid lots are available for parking, but wear comfortable shoes and expect to walk, as some lots are fairly far from the theater. Or, park and enjoy cocktails in the trendy and chic Los Feliz neighborhood below before a show, then walk up to the venue. ✉ *2700 N. Vermont Ave., Los Feliz* ☎ *844/524–7335* 🌐 *www.greektheatrela.com.*

Rockwell Table and Stage

THEATER | Great comfort food, decent cocktails, and a boisterous night of fun await at one of L.A.'s most idiosyncratic nighttime diversions. At the Rockwell Table and Stage performance venue, it's the shows and their hilarious cast that are the main attractions, whether they're doing an unofficial parody of a famous TV show or movie or putting on a political cabaret. ✉ *1714 N. Vermont Ave., Los Feliz* ☎ *323/669–1550* 🌐 *rockwell-la.com.*

Shopping

Skylight Books

BOOKS/STATIONERY | A neighborhood bookstore through and through, Skylight has excellent sections devoted to kids, fiction, travel, food, and it even has a live-in cat. Be sure to browse the Staff Picks section, as the well-informed employees have the inside scoop on new or under-the-radar must-reads. The space also hosts book discussion groups, panels, and author readings with hip literati. Art lovers can peruse texts on design and photography, graphic novels, and indie magazines at Skylight's annex a few doors down. ✉ *1818 N. Vermont Ave., Los Feliz* ☎ *323/660–1175* 🌐 *www.skylightbooks.com.*

Soap Plant/Wacko

GIFTS/SOUVENIRS | This pop-culture supermarket offers a wide range of items, including rows of books on art and design. But it's the novelty stock that makes the biggest impression, with ant farms, X-ray specs, and anime figurines. An adjacent gallery space, La Luz de Jesus, focuses on underground art. ✉ *4633 Hollywood Blvd., Los Feliz* ☎ *323/663–0122* 🌐 *www.soapplant.com.*

Vamp Shoes

CLOTHING | From well-known designers to up-and-comers and handcrafters who make their shoes in small batches, boutique store Vamp Shoes has a solid collection of footwear for women who appreciate and are not afraid to invest in gorgeous, excellent-quality soles. Inventory here also includes cool bags, hosiery, jewelry, and handcrafted ceramics. ✉ *1951 Hillhurst Ave., Los Feliz* ☎ *323/662–1150* 🌐 *www.vampshoeshop.com.*

Silver Lake

Restaurants

★ **Alimento**

$$$ | **ITALIAN** | There's little surprise that Chef Zach Pollack's soulful Italian masterpiece in Silver Lake features a lot of influences and inspirations; the true Angelenos, after all, grew up in a melting pot. Alimento's dishes are modern takes on traditional Italian cuisine, using locally sourced ingredients and varying in influences—from your classic American to Chinese and Mexican. **Known for:** yellowtail-collar affumicato; chicken liver crostone; dinner only. [$] *Average main: $25* ✉ *1710 Silver Lake Blvd., Silver Lake* ☎ *323/928–2888* 🌐 *www.alimentola.com* ⏲ *Closed Mon. No lunch.*

Cafe Stella

$$$$ | **FRENCH** | This strange den of eclectic decor and peeling paint feels undoubtedly French. Come for the aperitifs (Kir Royal, perhaps?), but stick around for the food for an exquisite blend of French and American bistro cuisine, prepared for lunch and dinner using traditional French techniques. **Known for:** brunch; Moroccan eggs; eggs Benedict. [$] *Average main: $34* ✉ *3932 Sunset Blvd., Silver Lake* ☎ *323/666–0265* 🌐 *www.cafestella.com* ⏲ *No brunch Mon.*

Daw Yee Myanmar Corner

$ | **BURMESE** | Burmese food is hard to find in Los Angeles so it's a good thing that tucked away in a Silver Lake strip mall sits the unassuming Daw Yee Myanmar Corner, a restaurant that's as good as it is rare. The food is an explosion of flavors and textures (there's a lot of roasted peanuts and toasted sesame). **Known for:** tea leaf salad; Burmese cuisine; mohinga. [$] *Average main: $12* ✉ *2837 Sunset Blvd., Silver Lake* ☎ *213/413–0568* 🌐 *www.dawyeesilverlake.com* ⏲ *Closed Tues.*

LaMill Coffee

$$ | **CAFÉ** | These folks take their coffee seriously, sourcing estate-grown beans that are prepared in a variety of ways (French press or Clover, to name but two) and offering an inventive list of espresso-based drinks. To go along with the requisite coffee fix is a menu put together by renowned chef Michael Cimarusti of Providence fame, as well as a serious tea list. **Known for:** blanco y negro; orange-infused cappucino; extensive tea list. [$] *Average main: $14* ✉ *1636 Silver Lake Blvd., Silver Lake* ☎ *323/663–4441* 🌐 *www.lamillcoffee.com.*

Pine and Crane

$ | **TAIWANESE** | **FAMILY** | This is not the typical Chinese restaurant one might expect; it's a fast casual, often locally sourced Taiwanese restaurant housed in a modern setting. The menu changes based on season, the wine and beer list updates constantly, and the tea menu is carefully curated. **Known for:** dan dan noodles; beef rolls; Taiwanese food. [$] *Average main: $12* ✉ *1521 Griffith Park Blvd., Silver Lake* ☎ *323/668–1128* 🌐 *www.pineandcrane.com* 🕓 *Closed Tues.*

Sawyer

$$$ | **SEAFOOD** | Simply put, Sawyer is a stunner with its restored brick wall, beautiful hardwood floor, and tiled patio, flourished with mid-century modern furniture; it's exactly the kind of bright and airy place you'd want to start off your day in. Yet most patrons come here less for the ambience and more for the food, with a menu that might lean on the healthy side but isn't afraid to indulge in the hearty stuff, touting an assortment of traditional and modern American fare. **Known for:** seafood boil; oysters; fries. [$] *Average main: $23* ✉ *3709 Sunset Blvd., Silver Lake* ☎ *323/641–3709* 🌐 *www.sawyerlosangeles.com* 🕓 *No brunch weekdays.*

Nightlife

Akbar

BARS/PUBS | This bar's welcoming feel is one of the reasons many people consider it their neighborhood bar, even if they don't live in the neighborhood. The crowd is friendly and inviting, and theme nights attract all sorts of folks, gay or straight. The comedy nights are favorites, as are weekends, when DJs get everyone on the dance floor. ✉ *4356 W. Sunset Blvd., Silver Lake* ☎ *323/665–6810* 🌐 *www.akbarsilverlake.com.*

Cha Cha Lounge

BARS/PUBS | If chaos and the assortment of ill-matched furnishings and decor is something you can forgive—or revel in—then this import from Seattle is a Silver Lake staple you should be partaking in, as there's never a dull moment. Grab your (cheap) poison then meander through the Mexican fiesta-themed bar. Foosball tables, a photo booth, and a vending machine will give you plenty to occupy your time … that is, if you're not already having a swell time. ✉ *2375 Glendale Blvd., Silver Lake* ☎ *323/660–7595* 🌐 *www.chachalounge.com.*

★ 4100

BARS/PUBS | With swaths of fabric draped from the ceiling, this low-lit bar with a bohemian vibe makes it perfect for dates. Groups of locals also come through for the night, making the crowd a plentiful mix of people. The bartenders know how to pour drinks that are both tasty and potent. There's plenty of seating at the tables and stools along the central bar, which gets crowded on the weekends. ✉ *1087 Manzanita St., Silver Lake* ☎ *323/666–4460* 🌐 *213hospitality.com/project/4100bar.*

★ The Satellite

MUSIC CLUBS | Once known as Spaceland, the Satellite holds nightly shows filled with underground musicians, both touring and local, all trying to make a dent. Many of them play indie rock, punk, or something else outside the mainstream, so it's a must-stop for music fans who abhor the Billboard Top 100. If you're around, make sure to take advantage of the free residencies where bands get to take center stage every Monday for an entire month. ⊠ *1717 Silver Lake Blvd., Silver Lake* ☎ *323/661–4380* ⊕ *www. thesatellitela.com.*

Silverlake Lounge

MUSIC CLUBS | Rock bands, burlesque, comedy, and even open-mic nights all have a home at the cross section of Sunset and Silver Lake at a little dive bar called the Silverlake Lounge. This small club with the yellow awning is a neighborhood spot—cash only, by the way—in the best way possible, with cheap drinks and local talent deserving of their time in the limelight. ⊠ *2906 W. Sunset Blvd., Silver Lake* ☎ *323/663–9636* ⊕ *www. thesilverlakelounge.com.*

Thirsty Crow

BARS/PUBS | This whiskey bar serves up seasonal cocktails in a fun, rustic environment. Though small, it manages to find space for live musicians and an open-mic night on Saturday. Part of the same hospitality group as Bigfoot Lodge and Highland Park Bowl, this watering hole has a locals-only feel. As local L.A. musician Father John Misty once said, "nothing good ever happens at the goddamn Thirsty Crow," but we think you should go and see for yourself. ⊠ *2939 W. Sunset Blvd., Silver Lake* ☎ *323/661–6007* ⊕ *www.thirstycrowbar.com.*

🛍 Shopping

Mohawk General Store

CLOTHING | Filled with a brilliant marriage of indie and established designers, this upscale boutique is a mainstay for the modern minimalist. Pick up the wares of local favorites Black Crane and Jesse Kamm, as well as internationally loved labels like Commes des Garcons, Issey Miyake, and Levi's Vintage Clothing. The Sunset Boulevard store stocks goods for men and women, as well as children, plus accessories and some home goods. ⊠ *4011 W. Sunset Blvd., Silver Lake* ☎ *323/522–6459* ⊕ *www.mohawkgeneralstore.com.*

Secret Headquarters

BOOKS/STATIONERY | This could be the coolest comic-book store on the planet, with a selection to satisfy both the geekiest of collectors and those more interested in artistic and literary finds. Rich wood floors and a leather chair near the front window of this intimate space mark the sophisticated setting, which features wall displays neatly organized with new comics and filing cabinets marked DC and Marvel. ⊠ *3817 W. Sunset Blvd., Silver Lake* ☎ *323/666–2228* ⊕ *www.thesecretheadquarters.com.*

Silver Lake Wine

WINE/SPIRITS | Boutique wineries from around the world provide this shop with the vintages that fill the floor-to-ceiling racks. Looking unassuming in jeans and T-shirts, the knowledgeable staff can steer you to the right wine or spirits for any occasion. You can wet your whistle at tastings on Monday and Thursday. ⊠ *2395 Glendale Blvd., Silver Lake* ☎ *323/662–9024* ⊕ *www.silverlakewine.com.*

Echo Park

👁 Sights

Dodger Stadium

SPORTS VENUE | FAMILY | Home of the Dodgers since 1962, it's the third-oldest baseball stadium still in use and has had quite the history in baseball, including Sandy Koufax's perfect game in 1965 and Kirk Gibson's 1988 World Series home run. Not only has it played host to the Dodgers' ups and downs and World Series runs, it's also has been the venue for some of the biggest performers in the world, including the Beatles, Madonna, and Beyonce. The stadium can be tough to get into on game day so consider getting dropped off in the park and walking up. Alternately, arrive early as locals tend not to roll up until the third inning. If you have the opportunity to take in a Friday night game, make sure to stick around for the fireworks show that follows—if you're patient, you can even wait in line and watch it from the field. ✉ *1000 Vin Scully Ave., Echo Park* ☎ *866/363–4377* 🌐 *dodgers.mlb.com/la/ballpark* 🕒 *Check schedule.*

Echo Park Lake

BODY OF WATER | FAMILY | If this charming little park and its lake of swan boats looks a little familiar to you, it's most likely because you've seen it in one L.A.-shot movie or another (*Chinatown*, for instance). After a major overhaul, the park has blossomed into a beautiful urban landscape, set against the backdrop of the Downtown skyline. Weekends are always bustling, as are mornings when joggers and early risers take laps around the lake. There's a tiny breakfast-slash-lunch spot that serves healthy nosh and good coffee. ✉ *751 Echo Park Ave., Echo Park* 🌐 *www.laparks.org/aquatic/lake/echo-park-lake.*

🍴 Restaurants

Dinette

$ | CAFÉ | Coffee shops may be a dime a dozen, but Dinette stands out. First of all, this is a walk-up-window-only establishment, which gives it a nice vintage-diner feel. **Known for:** coffee; avocado toast; waffle with bacon and poached egg. [$] *Average main: $11* ✉ *1608½ Sunset Blvd., Echo Park* ☎ *213/278–0301* 🌐 *dinettela.com* 🕒 *Closed Mon.*

Masa of Echo Park

$$ | PIZZA | FAMILY | While Masa of Echo Park does do excellent "bistro pizzas," as the restaurant calls them, it's mostly known for their delectable deep-dish pies that may just be the best you'll find this side of Chicago. Be prepared though—it can take a while to get seated and up to 45 minutes to get that deep dish you ordered, so it might be best to call ahead. **Known for:** vegan menu; family-style dining; Italian classics. [$] *Average main: $20* ✉ *1800 W. Sunset Blvd., Echo Park* ☎ *213/989–1558* 🌐 *www.masaofechopark.com.*

Taix

$$ | FRENCH | FAMILY | Serving French cuisine since 1927—and at its current location since 1962—Taix is the opportunity to peek at a time in L.A. that's mostly disappeared. Dark, wooden tables, intimate booths, low lighting, and portrait-adorned walls all help to set the scene. **Known for:** steak frites; being a local institution; French onion soup. [$] *Average main: $21* ✉ *1911 W. Sunset Blvd., Echo Park* ☎ *213/484–1265* 🌐 *taixfrench.com.*

🍸 Nightlife

Button Mash

BARS/PUBS | FAMILY | Button Mash hits all the right buttons (sorry), with a wide selection of rotating arcade games, most of which are from the golden age, not to mention a fantastically curated wine and beer list, and a menu put together by the old Starry Kitchen pop-up team that specializes in Asian fusion bar food. Before 9, this bar-cade is all ages, so everyone can be the next pinball wizard between bites of double-fried chicken wings. ✉ *1391 Sunset Blvd., Echo Park* ☎ *213/250–9903* 🌐 *www.buttonmashla.com.*

★ The Echo and Echoplex

MUSIC CLUBS | These two venues, one sitting on top of the other, are the heart of live music in Echo Park. Both offer a full bar and the ability to order pizza from Two Boots next door as well as recurring themed nights like Part-Time Punks. While they both host cutting-edge music, the Echo usually has up-and-coming local and touring acts whereas more well-known bands play downstairs. ✉ *1822 Sunset Blvd., Echoplex entrance at 1154 Glendale Blvd, Echo Park* ☎ *213/413–8200* 🌐 *www.theecho.com.*

★ **Mohawk Bend**

BARS/PUBS | There are so many reasons to stop by Mohawk Bend: 72 craft beers on tap, a wide range of California-only liquor, a vegetarian and vegan-friendly menu that includes tailored-to-your-wants pizza, and a buffalo cauliflower that—rumor has it—started the whole trend. There might be a long line to get into this 100-year-old former theater in the evenings, but it's worth it. ✉ *2141 Sunset Blvd., Echo Park* ☎ *213/483–2337* 🌐 *mohawk.la.*

★ **1642 Beer and Wine**

BARS/PUBS | This romantically lit hole-in-the-wall is easy to miss. Perfect for first dates, come here to experiment with craft beers or to warm up with wine. On the first Thursday of every month, get a free tamale with your drink, and hear some live old-time fiddle tunes. ✉ *1642 W. Temple St., Echo Park* ☎ *213/989–6836.*

Shopping

Esqueleto

JEWELRY/ACCESSORIES | There's a bit of the macabre on display at Esqueleto, but what do you expect from a jewelry boutique with a name meaning "skeleton" in Spanish? But that doesn't mean the light, airy, contemporary shop is stereotypically Goth in style; both its design and the inventory it stocks are perfectly polished and selected with a discerningly artistic eye. With a mix of excellent vintage finds and emerging designers (Melissa Joy Manning, Lauren Wolf, and Satomi Kawakita are favorites here), the shop has become a go-to destination for alternative brides' engagement rings and wedding bands. ✉ *1928 W. Sunset Blvd., Echo Park* ☎ *213/947–3508* 🌐 *www.shopesqueleto.com.*

Stories Books and Café

BOOKS/STATIONERY | With an off-the-beaten path collection of new and used literature, a café catering to freelancers and free thinkers, and a back patio that showcases singer-songwriters, Stories Books and Café is an authentic reflection of Echo Park. Readings, signings, and other events are a regular occurrence. ✉ *1716 Sunset Blvd., Echo Park* ☎ *213/413–3733* 🌐 *www.storiesla.com.*

Time Travel Mart

SPECIALTY STORES | **FAMILY** | You probably won't find anything useful in the Time Travel Mart and that's exactly the point. From dinosaur eggs to robot milk, this is a store that touts the ridiculous—all of which should bring back memories of your childhood and maybe a little bit of joy. But that's because the store holds a secret: it's really a fundraiser for the nonprofit 826LA, which tutors neighborhood kids in the back section. So, know when you're buying that totally unnecessary, but absolutely wonderful, samurai umbrella, the proceeds are going to a good cause. ✉ *1714 W. Sunset Blvd., Echo Park* ☎ *213/413–3388* 🌐 *826la.org/store.*

Atwater Village

Restaurants

Dune

$ | **MEDITERRANEAN** | **FAMILY** | Simple, small, and understated, it's easy to miss the best falafel spot in town. Hearty Middle Eastern falafel and chicken shawarma are piled on house-made flatbread. **Known for:** organic green-herb falafel sandwich; fried chicken shawarma sandwich; lunch and dinner. [$] *Average main: $12* ✉ *3143 Glendale Blvd., Atwater Village* ☎ *323/486–7073* 🌐 *www.dune.kitchen.*

★ **Good Measure**

$$ | **CONTEMPORARY** | Good Measure's proprietors decided to mix their love of travel with their passion for wine and start their own space offering a by-the-glass selection that spans the globe. The result is this romantic restaurant with an eclectic and excellent wine menu, not to mention an incredible dining menu with a quarterly On Tour section, which explores the food and

wines of various regions. **Known for:** crispy chicken confit; chickpea fries; desserts. $ *Average main: $18* ✉ *3224 Glendale Blvd., Atwater Village* 📞 *323/426–9461* ⊕ *www.goodmeasurela.com.*

Link N Hops

$ | **HOT DOG** | Link N Hops is your typical sports bar, almost. There are a couple things that elevate it: excellent hot dog sandwiches and 24 craft beers on tap. **Known for:** Atwater knackwurst; smoked Portuguese Hawaiian; happy hour specials. $ *Average main: $10* ✉ *3111 Glendale Blvd., Atwater Village* 📞 *323/426–9049* ⊕ *linknhops.com.*

Sepan Chicken

$ | **MIDDLE EASTERN** | Don't knock it until you've tried it. Despite appearances (it looks like a fast-food chicken shack), Sepan Chicken serves one of the best rotisserie chickens in town, or at least this side of Hollywood. **Known for:** Middle Eastern dishes; chicken kebabs; hummus. $ *Average main: $10* ✉ *3324 Glendale Blvd., Atwater Village* 📞 *323/669–0616* ⊕ *sepan-chicken.com.*

Tacos Villa Corona

$ | **MEXICAN** | You likely won't notice this cramped little spot on Glendale Boulevard unless there's a line or you're a fan of the late, great Anthony Bourdain, who was a big fan. About that line—it's almost always there, especially weekend mornings, when Tacos Villa Corona caters to the hangover crowd. **Known for:** chorizo and potato burrito; tacos. $ *Average main: $4* ✉ *3185 Glendale Blvd., Atwater Village* 📞 *323/661–3458.*

Tam O'Shanter

$$$$ | **IRISH** | It's a bit of a specific recognition, but Tam O'Shanter is the oldest restaurant run by the same family in the same location in Los Angeles, operating for more than 90 years in its Tudor-style spot—that alone makes this place a worthy addition to any Atwater Village visit. Then there's their delicious food whose $30 prices are completely worth it, not to

mention the fact that, once upon a time, it was Walt Disney's favorite restaurant. **Known for:** steak; toad-in-the-hole; Scottish decor. $ *Average main: $32* ✉ *2980 Los Feliz Blvd., Atwater Village* 📞 *323/664–0228* ⊕ *www.lawrysonline. com/tam-oshanter.*

🍸 Nightlife

★ Bigfoot Lodge

BARS/PUBS | Don't be turned off by the glaring log cabin theme (which is intensified by signature cocktails called Scout's Honor and Roasted Marshmallow). Bigfoot Lodge is beloved by Eastside denizens, and despite appearances, it's every bit a low-key, unpretentious neighborhood bar that specializes in shots and beer and welcomes the occasional tourist that happens to stumble inside. ✉ *3172 Los Feliz Blvd., Atwater Village* 📞 *323/662–9227* ⊕ *www.bigfootlodge.com.*

Moonlight Rollerway Skating Rink

SPORTS VENUE | It seems like every night there's a hubbub at Moonlight Rollerway, whether it's skating to *Purple Rain* for a Prince tribute night, a tricky mannequin challenge, or a Harry Potter–themed skate night. If you're looking for a quick throwback to your childhood or a simple break from life, this is just the ticket. This vintage roller rink also offers affordable lessons, in case you're rusty and need a crash course. ✉ *5110 San Fernando Rd., Atwater Village* 📞 *818/241–3630* ⊕ *moonlightrollerway.com.*

Verdugo Bar

BARS/PUBS | It's hard to decide whether the best thing about this place is its selection of 22 craft beers on tap and menu of "to-go" beer or the large beer garden furnished with picnic tables. It's probably a tie. But be warned, this place can get crowded, but it's worth it, especially on a hot sunny day (so pretty much every day). ✉ *3408 Verdugo Rd., Atwater Village* 📞 *323/257–3408* ⊕ *www. verdugobar.com.*

Shopping

Potted

FLOWERS | There's something comforting about Potted, like you've just walked into your parents' sunroom or a woodland fairy's home. This is a garden full of colors, nooks and crannies to tuck yourself into, and treasures of the botanic kind waiting to be discovered. It's every plant lover's paradise, but even those who wouldn't consider themselves to be plant fiends will be tempted to spend a fortune here. ✉ *3158 Los Feliz Blvd., Atwater Village* ☎ *323/665–3801* 🌐 *pottedstore.com.*

Treehaus

CLOTHING | The beauty of Treehaus isn't that it's an independent boutique—Los Angeles has plenty of those—but that it carries a great assortment of retail pieces, from women's and children's clothing to accessories and home goods, all in a cozy rectangular space. ✉ *3153 Glendale Blvd., Atwater Village* ☎ *323/230–6776* 🌐 *www.treehaus.biz.*

Highland Park

Sights

Heritage Square Museum

MUSEUM | Looking like a prop street set up by a film studio, Heritage Square resembles a row of bright dollhouses in the modest Highland Park neighborhood. Five 19th-century residences, a train station, a church, a carriage barn, and a 1909 boxcar that was originally part of the Southern Pacific Railroad, all built between the Civil War and World War I, were moved to this small park from various locations in Southern California to save them from the wrecking ball. The latest addition, a re-creation of a World War I–era drugstore, has a vintage soda fountain and traditional products. Docents dressed in period costume lead visitors through the lavish homes, giving an informative picture of Los Angeles in the early 1900s. Don't miss the unique 1893 Octagon House, one of just a handful of its kind built in California. ✉ *3800 Homer St., Highland Park* ☎ *323/225–2700* 🌐 *www.heritagesquare.org* 🎟 *$10* 🕒 *Closed Tues.–Thurs. and federal holiday Mon.* ☞ *Tour included with admission price.*

Restaurants

Cafe Birdie

$$ | **MEDITERRANEAN** | Though it only opened in 2016, this spacious 1920s spot along this quickly revitalizing stretch of Figueroa has already established itself as a neighborhood bistro frequented by Highland Park residents, as well as folks from nearby neighborhoods. The eclectic menu skillfully blends elements of European, Southern, and Japanese cuisines, tying them together with a fresh California flair and a gorgeous interior inspired by a fictional meeting-of-two-souls narrative. **Known for:** Mediterranean dishes; cocktails; great ambience. [$] *Average main: $19* ✉ *5631 N. Figueroa St., Highland Park* ☎ *323/739–6928* 🌐 *www.cafebirdiela.com.*

★ **Dave's Chillin'-n-Grillin'**

$ | **AMERICAN** | **FAMILY** | Dave's Chillin'-n-Grillin' has been making the kind of sandwiches people dream about for more than 10 years. On a couple of griddles, Dave himself often turns out no-nonsense wonders. **Known for:** Rosemary's Turkey; the Pilgrim; the Surf and Turf. [$] *Average main: $12* ✉ *5715 N. Figueroa St., Highland Park* ☎ *323/490–0988* 🕒 *Closed Sun.*

★ **Donut Friend**

$ | **BAKERY** | When this music-influenced donut shop first opened on York Boulevard in the early days of Highland Park's renaissance, there wasn't much there, and its arrival helped shape the now bustling strip and its vegan inclinations. Donut Friend had evolved into a destination in its own right, touting both a signature and limited menu of purely vegan donuts—which also happen to be inspired by the pop punk and emo music scene—that taste better than Dunkin'. **Known for:** Green Teagan and Sara; Jets to Basil; make-your-own donut. [$] *Average main: $4* ✉ *5107 York Blvd., Highland Park* ☎ *213/995–6191* 🌐 *www.donutfriend.com.*

El Huarache Azteca

$ | MEXICAN | FAMILY | While you definitely should try the flat shoe-shaped dish El Huarache Azteca is named after—think somewhere between a flatbread and a tostada—you cannot go wrong with any of the other options at this family restaurant that's been a fixture in the area for the last couple decades. Just be aware there's often a wait for the food to come out. **Known for:** huarache; agua fresca; barbacoa de barrego. [$] *Average main: $10* ✉ *5225 York Blvd., Highland Park* ☎ *323/478–9572* 🌐 *elhuaracheaztecalive.com* 💳 *No credit cards.*

★ Knowrealitypie

$ | BAKERY | The award-winning Knowrealitypie, hidden in a shop the size of a large walk-in closet, serves homemade pies every Friday through Saturday and only stays open until it sells out, which it often does. So hurry on down to partake in a rotating menu of seasonal savory and sweet pies, turnovers, and other pastries while supplies last. **Known for:** triple cherry Cabernet pie; caramel mango passion pie; minipies. [$] *Average main: $6* ✉ *5106 Townsend Ave., Highland Park* ☎ *323/610–2244* 🌐 *www.knowrealitypie.com* ⏲ *Closed Mon.–Thurs.*

Polka Polish Cuisine

$$ | POLISH | There's a coziness in Polka Polish Cuisine that can only be matched by a grandmother's living room. The food here, traditional Polish fare, also has that same comfort. **Known for:** royal platter; pierogi; stuffed cabbage. [$] *Average main: $20* ✉ *4112 Verdugo Rd., Highland Park* ☎ *323/255–7887* 🌐 *www.polkarestaurant.com* ⏲ *Closed Mon. and Tues.*

🍸 Nightlife

The Hermosillo

BARS/PUBS | The Hermosillo is the kind of laid-back pub every neighborhood should have, with an excellent selection of locally focused draft beer on tap, rotating wine list, and mouthwatering food. To add to its allure, award-winning Highland Park Brewery got its start in the pub's back storage room and is still featured prominently on the menu. ✉ *5125 York Blvd., Highland Park* ☎ *323/739–6459* 🌐 *thehermosillo.com.*

The Hi Hat

MUSIC CLUBS | The only thing left from its previous life as a pool hall are the two tables that greet customers as they enter. Now, it's the epicenter of live music in Highland Park and part of the revitalization of York Boulevard. Its exposed brick walls and pop-up kitchen are the cherry on top of the real treat—the local, underground bands performing here. ✉ *5043 York Blvd., Highland Park* 🌐 *hihat.la.*

Highland Park Bowl

BARS/PUBS | FAMILY | Highland Park Bowl was an ambitious restoration project and is now a massive throwback to its Prohibition Era roots as an alcohol-prescribing doctor's office and drugstore with its own bowling alley. That bowling alley remains, complete with the original pin machine. The hooch-pushing doctor and druggist, however, are long gone. But now there's an Italian restaurant that serves excellent pizza made from scratch using a mother dough brought all the way from Italy. ✉ *5621 N. Figueroa St., Highland Park* ☎ *323/257–2695* 🌐 *www.highlandparkbowl.com.*

★ The Old Chalet

BARS/PUBS | This ski lodge–inspired neighborhood bar may have changed ownership and management, but that doesn't mean that it's gotten a major and pretentious overhaul. In fact, besides its beefed-up whiskey and agave spirit lists (which desperately needed to be updated), new seasonal cocktails, and a new wave of eclectic clientele, it's still pretty much the same neighborhood bar the local residents have come to know and love. Plus, it's got a karaoke night that can't be beat. ⊠ *1630 Colorado Blvd., Highland Park* ☎ *323/508–5058* ⊕ *www.theoldchalet.com.*

The York

BARS/PUBS | Since 2007, before Highland Park became trendy, the York has been holding its own as the neighborhood bar. It's not just that the aesthetic gives off that neighborhood vibe (think exposed brick and chalkboard menus), but the craft beers on tap are great, and the pub food is delicious—the cheddar burger and the fish-and-chips are favorites. ⊠ *5018 York Blvd., Highland Park* ☎ *323/255–9675* ⊕ *theyorkonyork.wordpress.com.*

💼 Shopping

Galco's Soda Pop Stop

FOOD/CANDY | **FAMILY** | Galco's, a local fixture in Highland Park for decades, is in some ways a trip down memory lane, carrying more than 600 sodas—most of which harken back to the days when soda was a regional affair—and options from all over the world. They also have a collection of retro candies, a soda creation station with more than 100 syrups to choose from, and a selection of alcohol that would put most liquor stores to shame. ⊠ *5702 York Blvd., Highland Park* ☎ *323/255–7115* ⊕ *sodapopstop.com.*

Permanent Records

MUSIC STORES | Permanent Records has been a part of the vinyl resurgence since 2013, stocking new and used vinyl for every musical taste and doing it without any snobbery. The record store, which often has in-store performances, also runs its own label that focuses on local bands, limited-edition runs, and reissues. ⊠ *5116 York Blvd., Highland Park* ☎ *323/739–6141* ⊕ *www.permanentrecordsla.com.*

Chapter 8

JOSHUA TREE NATIONAL PARK

8

Updated by
Sarah Amandolare

◉ Sights	🍴 Restaurants	🛏 Hotels	🛍 Shopping	🍸 Nightlife
★★★★★	★★★★☆	★★★★★	★☆☆☆☆	★☆☆☆☆

WELCOME TO JOSHUA TREE NATIONAL PARK

TOP REASONS TO GO

★ **Rock climbing:** Joshua Tree is a world-class site with challenges for climbers of just about every skill level.

★ **Peace and quiet:** Roughly two hours from Los Angeles, this great wilderness is the ultimate escape from technology.

★ **Stargazing:** You'll be mesmerized by the Milky Way flowing across the summer sky. For spectacular natural fireworks, visit in mid-August during the Perseid meteor shower and watch shooting stars streak overhead.

★ **Wildflowers:** In spring, the hillsides explode in a patchwork of yellow, blue, pink, and white.

★ **Sunsets:** Twilight is a magical time here, especially during the winter, when the setting sun casts a golden glow on the mountains.

1 Keys View. This is the most dramatic overlook in the park—on clear days you can see Signal Mountain in Mexico.

2 Hidden Valley. Crawl between the big rocks and you'll understand why this boulder-strewn area was once a cattle rustlers' hideout.

3 Cholla Cactus Garden. Come here in the late afternoon, when the spiky stalks of the bigelow (jumping) cholla cactus are backlit against an intense blue sky.

4 Oasis of Mara. Walk the nature trail around this desert oasis, which the first settlers, the Serrano, dubbed "the place of little springs and much grass."

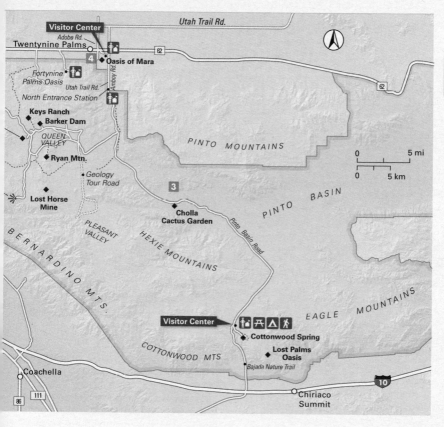

Joshua Tree National Park teems with fascinating landscapes and life-forms. It attracts around 1.5 million visitors each year, yet is mysteriously quiet at dawn and dusk. The landscape shifts abruptly from the arid stubble of the low Sonoran Desert to vast stands of the park's namesake Joshua trees in the higher, wetter Mojave Desert.

Planning

When to Go

October through May, when the desert is cooler, is when most visitors arrive. Daytime temperatures range from the mid-70s in December and January to mid-90s in October and May. Lows can dip to near freezing in midwinter, and you may even encounter snow at the higher elevations. Summers can be torrid, with daytime temperatures reaching 110°F.

Festivals and Events

Pioneer Days

FESTIVAL | FAMILY | Outhouse races, live music, and arm wrestling mark this celebration held annually, during the third full October weekend, in Twentynine Palms. The event also features a parade, carnival, chili dinner, and an old timers' gathering. ✉ *Twentynine Palms* ☎ *760/367-3445* ⊕ *www.visit29.org.*

Riverside County Fair & National Date Festival

FESTIVAL | FAMILY | Head to Indio for camel and ostrich races. ✉ *Riverside County Fairgrounds, 82–503 Hwy. 111, Indio* ☎ *800/811–3247* ⊕ *www.datefest.org.*

Planning Your Time

JOSHUA TREE IN ONE DAY

After stocking up on water, snacks, and lunch in Yucca Valley or Joshua Tree (you won't find any supplies inside the park), begin your visit at the **Joshua Tree Visitor Center,** where you can pick up maps and peruse exhibits to get acquainted with what awaits you. Enter the park itself at the nearby **West Entrance Station** and continue driving along the highly scenic and well-maintained **Park Boulevard.** Stop first at **Hidden Valley,** where you can relax at the picnic area or hike the easy 1-mile loop trail. After a few more miles turn left onto the spur road that takes you to the trailhead for the **Barker Dam Nature Trail.** Walk the easy 1.1-mile loop to view a water tank ranchers built to quench their cattle's thirst; along the way you'll spot birds and a handful of cactus

AVERAGE HIGH/LOW TEMPERATURES					
JAN.	FEB.	MAR.	APR.	MAY	JUNE
62/32	65/37	72/40	80/50	90/55	100/65
JULY	AUG.	SEPT.	OCT.	NOV.	DEC.
105/70	101/78	96/62	85/55	72/40	62/31

varieties. Return to Park Boulevard and head south; you'll soon leave the main road again for the drive to **Keys View.** The easy loop trail here is only 0.25 mile, but the views extend for miles in every direction—look for the San Andreas Fault, the Salton Sea, and nearby mountains. Return to Park Boulevard, where you'll find **Cap Rock,** another short loop trail winding amid rock formations and Joshua trees.

Continuing along Park Boulevard, the start of the 18-mile self-guided **Geology Tour Road** will soon appear on your right. A brochure outlining its 16 stops is available at visitor centers; note that the round-trip will take about two hours, and high-clearance, four-wheel-drive vehicles are recommended after stop 9. ■TIP➔ **Do not attempt if it has recently rained.** Back on Park Boulevard, you'll soon arrive at the aptly named **Skull Rock.** This downright spooky formation is next to the parking lot; a nearby trailhead marks the beginning of a 1.7-mile nature trail. End your day with a stop at the **isitor Center** in Twentynine Palms, where you can stroll through the historic **Oasis of Mara,** popular with area settlers.

Getting Here and Around

AIR TRAVEL
Palm Springs International Airport is the closest major airport to Joshua Tree National Park. It's about 45 miles from the park. The drive from Los Angeles International Airport to Joshua Tree takes about two to three hours.

CAR TRAVEL
An isolated island of pristine wilderness—a rarity these days—Joshua Tree National Park is within a short drive of 11 million Southern California residents. Most visitors, in fact, make the two- to three-hour drive from the Los Angeles area to enjoy a weekend of solitude in 792,726 acres of untouched desert. The urban sprawl of Palm Springs (home to the nearest airport) is 45 miles away, but gateway towns Joshua Tree, Yucca Valley, and Twentynine Palms are just north of the park. If you're staying in the Palm Springs area, you can enjoy the highlights of the park in one day, including a stop for a picnic at a scenic spot.

■TIP➔ **If you'd prefer not to drive, most Palm Springs area hotels can arrange a half- or full-day tour that hits the highlights of Joshua Tree National Park.** But you'll need to spend two or three days camping here to truly experience the quiet beauty of the desert.

Park Essentials

ACCESSIBILITY
Black Rock Canyon and Jumbo Rocks campgrounds have one accessible campsite each. Nature trails at Oasis of Mara, Bajada, Keys View, and Cap Rock are accessible. Some trails at roadside viewpoints can be negotiated by those with limited mobility.

PARK FEES AND PERMITS
Park admission is $30 per car, $15 per person on foot, bicycle, or horse, and $25 per person by motorcycle. The Joshua Tree Pass, good for one year, is $55.

PARK HOURS

The park is open every day, around the clock, but visitor centers are staffed from approximately 8 am to 5 pm. The park is in the Pacific time zone.

CELL PHONE RECEPTION

Cell phones don't work in most areas of the park. There are no telephones in the interior of the park.

Educational Offerings

LECTURES

The Desert Institute at Joshua Tree National Park

COLLEGE | The nonprofit educational partner of the park offers a full schedule of lectures, classes, and hikes. Class topics include basket making, painting, and photography, while field trips include workshops on cultural history, natural science, and how to survive in the desert. ⊠ *74485 National Park Dr., Twentynine Palms* ☎ *760/367–5525* ⊕ *www.joshuatree.org.*

Stargazing

COLLEGE | At Joshua Tree National Park you can tour the Milky Way on summer evenings using binoculars. Rangers also offer programs on some evenings when the moon isn't visible. Browse the schedule online. ⊠ *Cottonwood Campground Amphitheater and Oasis Visitor Center* ⊕ *www.nps.gov/jotr/planyourvisit/calendar.htm.*

RANGER PROGRAMS

Evening Programs

TOUR—SIGHT | Rangers present 45-minute-long programs, often on Friday or Saturday evening, at Cottonwood Amphitheater, Indian Cove Amphitheater, and Jumbo Rocks Campground. Topics range from natural history to local lore. The schedule is posted online. ⊠ *Joshua Tree National Park* ☎ *Free.*

★ Keys Ranch Tour

HOUSE | A guide takes you through the former home of a family that homesteaded here for 60 years. In addition to the ranch, a workshop, store, and schoolhouse are still standing, and the grounds are strewn with vehicles and mining equipment. The 90-minute tour, which begins at the Keys Ranch gate, tells the history of the family that built the ranch. Tickets are $10, and reservations are required. ⊠ *Keys Ranch gate* ☎ *760/367–5522* ⊕ *www.nps.gov/jotr.*

Restaurants

Dining options in the gateway towns around Joshua Tree National Park are extremely limited—you'll mostly find fast-food outlets and a few casual cafés in Yucca Valley and Twentynine Palms. The exception is the restaurant at 29 Palms Inn, which has an interesting California-cuisine menu that features lots of veggies. Still, you'll have to travel to the Palm Springs desert resort area for a fine-dining experience.

Hotels

Lodging choices in the Joshua Tree National Park area are limited to a few motels, chain hotels, and a luxury bed-and-breakfast establishment in the gateway towns. In general, most offer few amenities and are modestly priced. Book ahead for the spring wildflower season—reservations may be difficult to obtain then.

For a more extensive range of lodging options, you'll need to head to Palm Springs and the surrounding desert resort communities. *Hotel reviews have been shortened. For full information, visit Fodors.com.*

What It Costs

	$	$$	$$$	$$$$
RESTAURANTS				
	under $12	$12–$20	$21–$30	over $30
HOTELS				
	under $100	$100–$150	$151–$200	over $200

Tours

Big Wheel Tours

TOUR—SIGHT | Based in Palm Desert, Big Wheel Tours offers van excursions, jeep tours, and hiking trips through the park. Bicycle tours (road and mountain bike) are available outside the park boundary. Pickups are available at Palm Springs area hotels. ⊠ *42160 State St., Palm Desert* ☎ *760/779–1837* ⊕ *www.bwbtours.com* ✉ *From $119.*

Trail Discovery

TOUR—SIGHT | You can get a full day of exploring Joshua Tree with Trail Discovery, along with information on the park's plants, animals, geography, and history. Sunrise treks are offered in hot, summer months. Park admission, bottled water, hip packs, snacks, and fruit are included. Transportation is not provided. ☎ *760/413–1575* ⊕ *www.palmspringshiking.com* ✉ *From $125.*

Visitor Information

PARK CONTACT INFORMATION Joshua Tree National Park. ⊠ *74485 National Park Dr., Twentynine Palms* ☎ *760/367–5522* ⊕ *www.nps.gov/jotr.*

VISITOR CENTERS

Cottonwood Visitor Center

INFO CENTER | The south entrance is the closest to Interstate 10, the east–west highway from Los Angeles to Phoenix. Exhibits in this small center, staffed by rangers and volunteers, illustrate the

Plants and Wildlife in Joshua Tree

Joshua Tree will shatter your notions of the desert as a wasteland. Life flourishes here, as flora and fauna have adapted to heat and drought. In most areas you'll be walking among native Joshua trees, ocotillos, and yuccas. One of the best spring desert wildflower displays in Southern California blooms here. You'll see plenty of animals—reptiles such as nocturnal sidewinders, birds like golden eagles or burrowing owls, and occasionally mammals like coyotes and bobcats.

region's natural history. The center also has restrooms with flush toilets. ⊠ *Cottonwood Spring, Pinto Basin Rd.* ⊕ *www.nps.gov/jotr.*

Joshua Tree Visitor Center

INFO CENTER | This visitor center has maps and interesting exhibits illustrating park geology, cultural and historic sites, and hiking and rock-climbing activities. There's also a small bookstore and café. Restrooms with flush toilets are on the premises. ⊠ *6554 Park Blvd., Joshua Tree* ☎ *760/366–1855* ⊕ *www.nps.gov/jotr.*

Oasis Visitor Center

INFO CENTER | Exhibits here illustrate how Joshua Tree was formed, reveal the differences between the park's two types of desert, and demonstrate how plants and animals eke out an existence in this arid climate. Take the ½-mile nature walk through the nearby Oasis of Mara, which is alive with cottonwood trees, palm trees, and mesquite shrubs. Facilities include picnic tables, restrooms, and a bookstore. ⊠ *74485 National Park Dr., Twentynine Palms* ☎ *760/367–5500* ⊕ *www.nps.gov/jotr.*

👁 Sights

You can experience Joshua Tree National Park on several levels. Even on a short excursion along Park Boulevard between the Joshua Tree entrance station and Oasis of Mara, you'll see the essence of North American desert scenery—including a staggering abundance of flora visible along a dozen self-guided nature trails. You'll also see remnants of homesteads from a century ago, now mostly abandoned and wind-worn. If rock climbing is your passion, this is the place for you; boulder-strewn mountaintops and slopes beckon. But in the end, Joshua Tree National Park is a pristine wilderness where you can enjoy a solitary stroll along an animal trail and commune with nature. Be sure to take some time to explore on your own and enjoy the peace and quiet.

SCENIC DRIVES

Geology Tour Road

SCENIC DRIVE | Some of the park's most fascinating landscapes can be observed from this 18-mile dirt road. Parts of the journey are rough; a 4X4 vehicle is required after mile marker 9. Sights to see include a 100-year-old stone dam called Squaw Tank, defunct mines, and a large plain with an abundance of Joshua trees. There are 16 stops along the way, so give yourself about two hours to complete the round-trip trek. ⊠ *South of Park Blvd., west of Jumbo Rocks.*

Park Boulevard

SCENIC DRIVE | If you have time only for a short visit, driving Park Boulevard is your best choice. Traversing the most scenic portions of Joshua Tree, this well-paved road connects the north and west entrances in the park's high desert section. Along with some sweeping desert views, you'll see jumbles of splendid boulder formations, stands of Joshua trees, and Hidden Valley and Barker Dam, remnants of the area's wild and woolly past. From the Oasis Visitor Center, drive south. After about 5 miles, the road forks; turn right and head west toward Jumbo Rocks (clearly marked with a road sign). ⊠ *Joshua Tree National Park.*

Pinto Basin Road

SCENIC DRIVE | This paved road takes you from high Mojave desert to low Colorado desert. A long, slow drive, the route runs from the main part of the park to Interstate 10; it can add as much as an hour to and from Palm Springs (round-trip), but the views and roadside exhibits make it worth the extra time. From the Oasis Visitor Center, drive south. After about 5 miles, the road forks; take a left and continue another 9 miles to the Cholla Cactus Garden, where the sun fills the cactus needles with light. Past that is the Ocotillo Patch, filled with spindly plants bearing razor-sharp thorns and, after a rain, bright green leaves and brilliant red flowers. Side trips from this route require a 4X4. ⊠ *Joshua Tree National Park.*

HISTORIC SITES

Hidden Valley

NATURE SITE | FAMILY | This legendary cattle-rustlers' hideout is set among big boulders along a 1-mile loop trail. Kids love to scramble on and around the rocks. There are shaded picnic tables here. ⊠ *Park Blvd.* ✛ *14 miles south of west entrance.*

★ Keys Ranch

TOUR—SIGHT | This 150-acre ranch, which once belonged to William and Frances Keys and is now on the National Historic Register, illustrates one of the area's most successful attempts at homesteading. The couple raised five children under extreme desert conditions. Most of the original buildings, including the house, school, store, and workshop, have been restored to the way they were when William died in 1969. The only way to see the ranch is on one of the 90-minute walking tours usually offered Friday–Sunday, October–May, and weekends in summer; advance reservations required. ⊠ Joshua Tree National Park ✛ 2 miles north of Barker Dam Rd. ☎ 760/367–5522 ⊕ www.nps. gov/jotr/planyourvisit/ranchtour.htm ⊠ $10, available at Oasis Visitor Center or reserve by phone.

Lost Horse Mine

MINE | This historic mine, which produced 10,000 ounces of gold and 16,000 ounces of silver between 1894 and 1931, was among Southern California's most productive mines. The 10-stamp mill is considered one of the best preserved of its type in the park system. The site is accessed via a fairly strenuous 4-mile round-trip hike. Mind the park warnings and don't enter any mine in Joshua Tree. ⊠ Keys View Rd. ✛ About 15 miles south of west entrance.

SCENIC STOPS

Barker Dam

DAM | Built around 1900 by ranchers and miners to hold water for cattle and mining operations, the dam now collects rainwater and is a good place to spot wildlife such as the elusive bighorn sheep. ⊠ Barker Dam Rd. ✛ Off Park Blvd., 10 miles south of west entrance.

Cholla Cactus Garden

GARDEN | This stand of bigelow cholla (sometimes called jumping cholla, because its hooked spines seem to jump at you) is best seen and photographed in late afternoon, when the backlit spiky stalks stand out against a colorful sky. ⊠ Pinto Basin Rd. ✛ 20 miles north of Cottonwood Visitor Center.

Cottonwood Spring

NATIVE SITE | Home to the native Cahuilla people for centuries, this spring provided water for travelers and early prospectors. The area, which supports a large stand of fan palms and cottonwood trees, is one of the best stops for bird-watching, as migrating birds (and bighorn sheep) rely on the water as well. A number of gold mines were

located here, and the area still has some remains, including concrete pillars. ⊠ Cottonwood Visitor Center.

Fortynine Palms Oasis

NATIVE SITE | A short drive off Highway 62, this site is a bit of a preview of what the park's interior has to offer: stands of fan palms, interesting petroglyphs, and evidence of fires built by early Native Americans. Because animals frequent this area, you may spot a coyote, bobcat, or roadrunner. ⊠ End of Canyon Rd. ✛ 4 miles west of Twentynine Palms.

★ Keys View

VIEWPOINT | At 5,185 feet, this point affords a sweeping view of the Santa Rosa Mountains and Coachella Valley, the San Andreas Fault, the peak of 11,500-foot Mt. San Gorgonio, the shimmering surface of Salton Sea, and—on a rare clear day—Signal Mountain in Mexico. Sunrise and sunset are magical times, when the light throws rocks and trees into high relief before bathing the hills in brilliant shades of red, orange, and gold. ⊠ Keys View Rd. ✛ 16 miles south of park's west entrance.

Lost Palms Oasis

TRAIL | More than 100 fan palms comprise the largest group of the exotic plants in the park. A spring bubbles from between the rocks, but disappears into the sandy, boulder-strewn canyon. The 7.5-mile round-trip hike is not for everyone, and not recommended during summer months. Bring plenty of water! ⊠ Cottonwood Visitor Center.

Ocotillo Patch

GARDEN | Stop here for a roadside exhibit on the dramatic display made by the red-tipped succulent after even the shortest rain shower. ⊠ Pinto Basin Rd. ✛ About 3 miles east of Cholla Cactus Gardens.

🏃 Activities

BICYCLING

Mountain biking is a great way to see Joshua Tree. Bikers are restricted to roads that are used by motorized vehicles, including the main park roads and a few four-wheel-drive trails. Bicycling on dirt roads is not recommended during the summer. Most scenic stops and picnic areas, and the Wall Street Mill trailhead, have bike racks.

Black Eagle Mine Road

BICYCLING | This 9-mile dead-end road is peppered with defunct mines, the entrances of which should be avoided. It runs along the edge of a former lake bed, then crosses a number of dry washes before navigating several of Eagle Mountain's canyons. ✉ *Joshua Tree National Park ✛ Trailhead: off Pinto Basin Rd., 6½ miles north of Cottonwood Visitor Center.*

Covington Flats

BICYCLING | This 4-mile route takes you past impressive Joshua trees as well as pinyon pines, junipers, and areas of lush desert vegetation. It's tough going toward the end, but once you reach 5,518-foot Eureka Peak you'll have great views of Palm Springs, the Morongo Basin, and the surrounding mountains. ✉ *Joshua Tree National Park ✛ Trailhead: at Covington Flats picnic area, La Contenta Rd., 10 miles south of Rte. 62.*

Pinkham Canyon and Thermal Canyon Roads

BICYCLING | This challenging 20-mile route begins at the Cottonwood Visitor Center and loops through the Cottonwood Mountains. The unpaved trail follows Smoke Tree Wash through Pinkham Canyon, rounds Thermal Canyon, and loops back to the beginning. Rough and narrow in places, the road travels through soft sand and rocky floodplains. ✉ *Joshua Tree National Park ✛ Trailhead: at Cottonwood Visitor Center.*

Queen Valley

BICYCLING | This 13.4-mile network of mostly level roads winds through one of the park's most impressive groves of Joshua trees. You can also leave your bike at one of the racks placed in the area and explore on foot. ✉ *Joshua Tree National Park ✛ Trailhead: at Hidden Valley Campground, and accessible opposite Geology Tour Rd. at Big Horn Pass.*

BIRD-WATCHING

Joshua Tree, located on the inland portion of the Pacific Flyway, hosts about 240 species of birds, and the park is a popular seasonal location for bird-watching. During the fall migration, which runs mid-September through mid-October, there are several reliable sighting areas. At Barker Dam you might spot white-throated swifts, several types of swallows, or red-tailed hawks. Lucy's warbler, flycatchers, and Anna's hummingbirds cruise around Cottonwood Spring, a serene palm-shaded setting; occasional ducks, herons, and egrets, as well as migrating rufous and calliope hummingbirds, wintering prairie falcons, and a resident barn owl could show up. Black Rock Canyon sees pinyon jays, while Covington Flats reliably gets mountain quail, and you may see La Conte's thrashers, ruby-crowned kinglets, and warbling vireos at either locale. Rufous hummingbirds, Pacific slope flycatchers, and various warblers are frequent visitors to Indian Cove. Lists of birds found in the park, as well as information on recent sightings, are available at visitor centers.

HIKING

There are more than 190 miles of hiking trails in Joshua Tree, ranging from quarter-mile nature trails to 35-mile treks. Some connect with each other, so you can design your own desert maze. Remember that drinking water is hard to come by—you won't find water in the park except at the entrances. Bring along at least a gallon per person for all but the shortest hikes, more if the weather is hot.

Did You Know?

Found only in Arizona,
California, Nevada,
and Utah, the Joshua
tree (*Yucca brevifolia*)
is actually a member
of the agave family.
Native Americans used
the Joshua tree's hearty
foliage like leather,
forming it into everyday
items like baskets and
shoes. Later, early settlers
used its core and limbs for
building fences to contain
their livestock.

Bajada All Access

HIKING/WALKING | Learn all about what plants do to survive in the desert on this wheelchair-accessible ¼-mile loop. *Easy.* ☒ *Joshua Tree National Park* ✥ *Trailhead: south of Cottonwood Visitor Center, ½ mile from park entrance.*

Boy Scout Trail

HIKING/WALKING | The moderately strenuous 8-mile trail, suitable for backpackers, extends from Indian Cove to Park Boulevard. It runs through the westernmost edge of the Wonderland of Rocks (where you're likely to see climbers on the outcroppings), passing through a forest of Joshua trees, past granite towers, and around willow-lined pools. Completing the round-trip journey may require camping along the way, so you may want to hike only part of the trail or have a car waiting at the other end. *Difficult.* ☒ *Joshua Tree National Park* ✥ *Trailhead: between Quail Springs Picnic Area and Indian Cove Campground.*

California Riding and Hiking Trail

HIKING/WALKING | You'll need a backcountry camping pass to traverse this 35-mile route between the Black Rock Canyon entrance and the north entrance. You can access the trail for a short or long hike at several points. The visitor centers have trail maps. *Difficult.* ☒ *Joshua Tree National Park* ✥ *Trailheads: at Upper Covington Flats, Ryan Campground, Twin Tanks, south of north park entrance, and Black Rock Campground.*

Cap Rock

HIKING/WALKING | This ½-mile wheelchair-accessible loop—named after a boulder that sits atop a huge rock formation like a cap—winds through fascinating rock formations and has signs that explain the geology of the Mojave Desert. *Easy.* ☒ *Joshua Tree National Park* ✥ *Trailhead: Keys View Rd. near junction with Park Blvd.*

Fortynine Palms Oasis Trail

HIKING/WALKING | Allow three hours for this moderately strenuous 3-mile trek. There's no shade, and the trail makes a steep climb in both directions, eventually dropping down into a canyon where you'll find an oasis lined with fan palms, which can be viewed from boulders above, but not accessed. If you look carefully, you'll find evidence of Native Americans in this area, from traces of cooking fires to rocks carved with petroglyphs. *Difficult.* ☒ *Joshua Tree National Park* ✥ *Trailhead: at end of Canyon Rd., 4 miles west of Twentynine Palms.*

Hidden Valley

HIKING/WALKING | **FAMILY** | Crawl through the rocks surrounding Hidden Valley to see where cattle rustlers supposedly hung out on this 1-mile loop. *Easy.* ☒ *Joshua Tree National Park* ✥ *Trailhead: at Hidden Valley Picnic Area.*

Hi-View Nature Trail

HIKING/WALKING | This 1.3-mile loop climbs nearly to the top of 4,500-foot Summit Peak. The views of nearby Mt. San Gorgonio (snowcapped in winter) make the moderately steep journey worth the effort. You can pick up a pamphlet describing the vegetation you'll see along the way at any visitor center. *Moderate.* ☒ *Joshua Tree National Park* ✥ *Trailhead: ½ mile west of Black Rock Canyon Campground.*

Indian Cove Trail

HIKING/WALKING | Look for lizards and roadrunners along this ½-mile loop that follows a desert wash. A walk along this well-signed trail reveals signs of Indian habitation, animals, and flora such as desert willow and yucca. *Easy.* ☒ *Joshua Tree National Park* ✥ *Trailhead: at west end of Indian Cove Campground.*

Lost Horse Mine Trail

HIKING/WALKING | This fairly strenuous 4-mile round-trip hike follows a former mining road to a well-preserved mill that was used in the 1890s to crush gold-encrusted rock mined from the nearby mountain. The operation was one of the area's most successful, and the mine's cyanide settling tanks and stone buildings are the area's best-preserved structures. From the mill area, a short but steep 10-minute side trip takes you to the top of a 5,278-foot peak with great views of the valley. *Difficult.* ⊠ *Joshua Tree National Park* ✛ *Trailhead: 1¼ miles east of Keys View Rd.*

Lost Palms Oasis Trail

HIKING/WALKING | Allow four to six hours for the moderately strenuous, 7¼-mile round-trip, which leads to the most impressive oasis in the park. It's uphill on the way back to the trailhead. You'll find more than 100 fan palms and an abundance of wildflowers here. *Difficult.* ⊠ *Joshua Tree National Park* ✛ *Trailhead: at Cottonwood Spring Oasis.*

Mastodon Peak Trail

HIKING/WALKING | Some boulder scrambling is optional on this 3-mile hike that loops up to the 3,371-foot Mastodon Peak, and the journey rewards you with stunning views of the Salton Sea. The trail passes through a region where gold was mined from 1919 to 1932, so be on the lookout for open mines. The peak draws its name from a large rock formation that early miners believed looked like the head of a prehistoric behemoth. *Moderate.* ⊠ *Joshua Tree National Park* ✛ *Trailhead: at Cottonwood Spring Oasis.*

Oasis of Mara

HIKING/WALKING | A stroll along this short, wheelchair-accessible trail, located just outside the visitor center, reveals how early settlers took advantage of this oasis, which was first settled by the Serrano tribe. *Mara* means "place of little springs and much grass" in their language. The Serrano, who farmed the oasis until the mid-1850s, planted one palm tree for each male baby born during the first year of the settlement. *Easy.* ⊠ *Joshua Tree National Park* ✛ *Trailhead: at Oasis Visitor Center.*

★ Ryan Mountain Trail

HIKING/WALKING | The payoff for hiking to the top of 5,461-foot Ryan Mountain is one of the best panoramic views of Joshua Tree. From here you can see Mt. San Jacinto, Mt. San Gorgonio, Lost Horse Valley, and the Pinto Basin. You'll need two to three hours to complete the 3-mile round-trip with 1,000-plus feet of elevation gain. *Moderate.* ⊠ *Joshua Tree National Park* ✛ *Trailhead: at Ryan Mountain parking area, 13 miles southeast of park's west entrance, or Sheep Pass, 16 miles southwest of Oasis Visitor Center.*

Skull Rock Trail

HIKING/WALKING | The 1.7-mile loop guides hikers through boulder piles, desert washes, and a rocky alley. It's named for what is perhaps the park's most famous rock formation, which resembles the eye sockets and nasal cavity of a human skull. Access the trail from within Jumbo Rocks Campground or from a small parking area on the highway just east of the campground. *Easy.* ⊠ *Joshua Tree National Park* ✛ *Trailhead: at Jumbo Rocks Campground.*

ROCK CLIMBING

With an abundance of weathered igneous boulder outcroppings, Joshua Tree is one of the nation's top winter-climbing destinations. There are more than 4,500 established routes offering a full menu of climbing experiences—from bouldering for beginners in the Wonderland of Rocks to multiple-pitch climbs at Echo Rock and Saddle Rock. The best-known climb in the park is Hidden Valley's Sports Challenge Rock. A map inside the *Joshua Tree Guide* shows locations of selected wilderness and nonwilderness climbs.

Joshua Tree Rock Climbing School

CLIMBING/MOUNTAINEERING | The school offers several programs, from one-day introductory classes to multiday programs for experienced climbers, and provides all needed equipment. Beginning classes, offered year-round on most weekends, are limited to six people age eight or older. ⊠ *Joshua Tree National Park* ☎ *760/366–4745* ⊕ *www.joshuatreerockclimbing.com* 🖅 *From $195.*

Vertical Adventures Rock Climbing School
CLIMBING/MOUNTAINEERING | About 1,000 climbers each year learn the sport in Joshua Tree National Park through this school. Classes, offered September–May, meet at a designated location in the park, and all equipment is provided. ⊠ *Joshua Tree National Park* ☎ *800/514–8785* ⊕ *www.verticaladventures.com* 🖅 *From $155.*

Nearby Towns

About 9 miles north of Palm Springs and closer to the park is **Desert Hot Springs,** which has more than 1,000 natural hot mineral pools and 40 health spas ranging from low-key to luxurious. **Yucca Valley** is the largest and fastest growing of the communities straddling the park's northern border. The town boasts a handful of motels, supermarkets, and a Walmart. Tiny **Joshua Tree,** the closest community to the park's west entrance, is where the serious rock climbers make their headquarters. **Twentynine Palms,** known as "two-nine" by locals, is sandwiched between the Marine Corps Air Ground Task Force Center to the north and Joshua Tree National Park to the south. Here you'll find a smattering of coffeehouses, antiques shops, and cafés.

VISITOR INFORMATION California Welcome Center Yucca Valley. ⊠ *56711 Twentynine Palms Hwy., Yucca Valley* ☎ *760/365–5464* ⊕ *www.californiawelcomecenter.com.* **Joshua Tree Chamber of Commerce.** ⊠ *6448 Hallee Rd., Joshua Tree* ☎ *760/366–3723* ⊕ *www.joshuatreechamber.org.* **Palm Springs Visitor Center.** ⊠ *2109 N. Palm Canyon Dr., Palm Springs* ☎ *760/778–8415, 800/348–7746* ⊕ *www.visitpalmsprings.com.* **Twentynine Palms Chamber of Commerce.** ⊠ *73484 Twentynine Palms Hwy., Twentynine Palms* ☎ *760/367–3445* ⊕ *www.29chamber.org.* **Yucca Valley Chamber of Commerce.** ⊠ *56711 Twentynine Palms Hwy., Yucca Valley* ☎ *760/365–6323* ⊕ *www.yuccavalley.org.*

👁 Sights

Hi-Desert Nature Museum
MUSEUM | FAMILY | Natural and cultural history of the Morongo Basis and High Desert are the focus here. A small live-animal display includes scorpions, snakes, lizards, and small mammals. You'll also find gems and minerals, fossils from the Paleozoic era, taxidermy, and Native American artifacts. There's also a children's area and art exhibits. ⊠ *Yucca Valley Community Center, 57090 Twentynine Palms Hwy., Yucca Valley* ☎ *760/369–7212* ⊕ *hidesertnaturemuseum.org* 🖅 *Free* ⊘ *Closed Sun.–Tues.*

Oasis of Murals
PUBLIC ART | Twenty-six murals painted on the sides of buildings depict the history, wildlife, and landscape of Twentynine Palms. If you drive around town you can't miss the murals, but you can also pick up a free map from the visitor center. ⊠ *Twentynine Palms* ⊕ *www.action-29palmsmurals.com.*

Pioneertown
TOWN | In 1946 Roy Rogers, Gene Autry, the Sons of the Pioneers (the music group for whom the town is named), and Russ Hayden built Pioneertown, an 1880s-style Wild West movie set complete with hitching posts, saloon, and an OK Corral. You can stroll past wooden and adobe storefronts and feel like you're back in the Old West. Pappy & Harriet's Pioneertown Palace, now the town's top draw, has evolved into a hip venue for indie and mainstream performers such as Dengue Fever, Neko Case, and Robert Plant. ⊠ *53688 Pioneertown Rd., Pioneertown* ✛ *4 miles north of Yucca Valley* ⊕ *pappyandharriets.com.*

Did You Know?

Joshua Tree is one of the world's most popular rock-climbing and bouldering destinations, with more than 400 climbing formations (including Frigid Tower, pictured here) and 4,500 routes.

Learn about the park's flora and fauna by attending the ranger programs.

🍴 Restaurants

IN THE PARK
PICNIC AREAS
Black Rock Canyon

CANYON | Set among Joshua trees, pinyon pines, and junipers, this popular picnic area has barbecue grills and drinking water. It's one of the few with flush toilets. ⊠ *Joshua Tree National Park* ✛ *End of Joshua La. at Black Rock Canyon Campground.*

Covington Flats

RESTAURANT—SIGHT | This is a great place to get away from crowds. There's just one table, and it's surrounded by flat, open desert dotted here and there by Joshua trees. ⊠ *La Contenta Rd.* ✛ *10 miles from Rte. 62.*

Hidden Valley

RESTAURANT—SIGHT | Set among huge rock formations, with picnic tables shaded by dense trees, this is one of the most pleasant places in the park to stop for lunch. ⊠ *Park Blvd.* ✛ *14 miles south of the west entrance.*

OUTSIDE THE PARK
C&S Coffee Shop

$ | AMERICAN | If you're yearning for pork chops and gravy for breakfast or eggs over easy for dinner, head to this tidy diner, which has been a local hangout since 1946. The typical diner menu also features soups, salads, and sandwiches, all cooked to order and presented in heaping portions. **Known for:** perfectly cooked fries; prompt service. Ⓢ *Average main: $8* ⊠ *55795 Twentynine Palms Hwy., Yucca Valley* ☎ *760/365–9946.*

Edchada's

$$ | MEXICAN | Rock climbers who spend their days in Joshua Tree swear by the margaritas at this Mexican eatery. Specialties include prodigious portions of fajitas, carnitas, seafood enchiladas, and fish tacos. **Known for:** margaritas; large portions. Ⓢ *Average main: $12* ⊠ *73502 Twentynine Palms Hwy., Twentynine Palms* ☎ *760/367–2131.*

Best Campgrounds in Joshua Tree

Camping is the best way to experience the stark, exquisite beauty of Joshua Tree. You'll also have a rare opportunity to sleep outside in a semi-wilderness setting. The campgrounds, set at elevations from 3,000 to 4,500 feet, have only primitive facilities; few have drinking water. Black Rock, Indian Cove, Jumbo Rocks, and Cottonwood campgrounds accept reservations up to six months in advance, and only for October through Memorial Day. Campsites elsewhere are on a first-come, first-served basis. Belle and White Tank campgrounds, and parts of Black Rock Canyon, Cottonwood, and Indian Cove campgrounds, are closed from the day after Memorial Day to September.

Belle Campground. This small campground is popular with families, as there are a number of boulders kids can scramble over and around. ✉ *9 miles south of Oasis of Mara* ☎ *760/367–5500* 🌐 *www.nps.gov/jotr.*

Black Rock Canyon Campground. Set among juniper bushes, cholla cacti, and other desert shrubs, Black Rock Canyon is one of the prettiest campgrounds in Joshua Tree. ✉ *Joshua La., south of Hwy. 62 and Hwy. 247* ☎ *877/444–6777* 🌐 *www.recreation.gov.*

Cottonwood Campground. In spring this campground, the southernmost one in the park (and therefore often the last to fill up), is surrounded by some of the desert's finest wildflowers and is a great spot to watch the night sky. ✉ *Pinto Basin Rd., 32 miles south of North Entrance Station* ☎ *877/444–6777* 🌐 *www.nps.gov/jotr.*

Hidden Valley Campground. This campground is a favorite with rock climbers, who make their way up valley formations that have names like the Blob, Old Woman, and Chimney Rock. ✉ *Off Park Blvd., 20 miles southwest of Oasis of Mara* ☎ *760/367–5500* 🌐 *www.nps.gov/jotr.*

Indian Cove Campground. This is a sought-after spot for rock climbers, primarily because it lies among the 50 square miles of rugged terrain at the Wonderland of Rocks. ✉ *Indian Cove Rd., south of Hwy. 62* ☎ *877/444–6777* 🌐 *www.nps.gov/jotr.*

Jumbo Rocks. Each campsite at this well-regarded campground tucked among giant boulders has a bit of privacy. It's a good home base for visiting many of Joshua Tree's attractions. ✉ *Park Blvd., 11 miles from Oasis of Mara* ☎ *877/444–6777* 🌐 *www.nps.gov/jotr.*

White Tank. This small, quiet campground is popular with families because a nearby trail leads to a natural arch. ✉ *Pinto Basin Rd., 11 miles south of Oasis of Mara* ☎ *760/367–5500* 🌐 *www.nps.gov/jotr.*

Park Rock Café

$ | **CAFÉ** | If you're on your way to the national park on Highway 62, stop in the town of Joshua Tree to grab a hearty breakfast bagel sandwich and order a box lunch to take with you. The café creates some tasty sandwiches, including a healthy option with avocado and pesto mayo. **Known for:** takeout; outdoor dining; lentil barley soup. [$] *Average main: $9* ✉ *6554 Park Blvd., Joshua Tree* ☎ *760/366–8200* 🌐 *jtparkrockcafe.com* 🕓 *No dinner.*

Hotels

OUTSIDE THE PARK

★ 29 Palms Inn

$$$ | **B&B/INN** | **FAMILY** | The closest lodging to the entrance to Joshua Tree National Park, the funky 29 Palms Inn scatters a collection of adobe and wood-frame cottages, some dating back to the 1920s and 1930s, over 70 acres of grounds that include the ancient Oasis of Mara, a popular destination for birds and bird-watchers year-round. **Pros:** gracious hospitality; exceptional bird-watching; art gallery, pool, and on-site restaurant. **Cons:** rustic accommodations; limited amenities. [$] *Rooms from: $165* ✉ *73950 Inn Ave., Twentynine Palms* ☎ *760/367–3505* 🌐 *www.29palmsinn.com* 🛏 *20 rooms, 4 guesthouses* 🍴 *Breakfast.*

Chapter 9

MOJAVE DESERT

Updated by
Cheryl Crabtree

⊙ Sights	🍴 Restaurants	🛏 Hotels	🛍 Shopping	🍸 Nightlife
★★★★★	★★★★☆	★★★★★	★☆☆☆☆	★☆☆☆☆

WELCOME TO MOJAVE DESERT

TOP REASONS TO GO

★ **Nostalgia:** Old neon signs, historic motels, and restored (or neglected but still striking) rail stations abound across this desert landscape. Don't miss the classic eateries along the way, including Emma Jean's Holland Burger Cafe in Victorville.

★ **Death Valley wonders:** Visit this distinctive landscape to tour some of the most varied desert terrain in the world.

★ **Great ghost towns:** California's gold rush brought miners to the Mojave, and the towns they left behind have their own unique charms.

★ **Desert flora and fauna:** Explore the Mojave National Preserve to view Joshua trees, volcanic cinder cones, huge sand dunes, desert tortoises, and other natural wonders.

★ **Explore ancient history:** The Mojave Desert is replete with rare petroglyphs, some dating back almost 16,000 years.

The Mojave Desert, once part of an ancient inland sea, is one of the largest swaths of open land in Southern California. Its boundaries include the San Gabriel and San Bernardino mountain ranges to the south; Palmdale and Ridgecrest to the west; Death Valley to the north; and Needles and Lake Havasu in Arizona to the east. The area is distinguishable by its wide-open sandy spaces, peppered with creosote bushes, Joshua trees, cacti, and abandoned homesteads. Access the Mojave via Interstates 40 and 15, Highways 14 and 95, and U.S. 395.

1 **Lancaster.**

2 **Red Rock Canyon State Park.**

3 **Ridgecrest.**

4 **Randsburg.**

5 **Victorville.**

6 **Barstow.**

7 **Mojave National Preserve.**

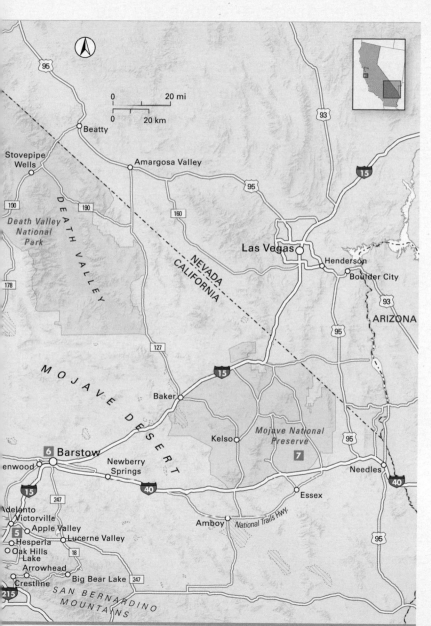

95

20 mi
0
20 km
0

Beatty

Stovepipe
Wells

Amargosa Valley

95

93

15

190

190

160

D E A T H   V A L L E Y

Death Valley
National
Park

178

NEVADA
CALIFORNIA

Las Vegas

Henderson

Boulder City

93

ARIZONA

95

127

15

M O J A V E   D E S E R T

Baker

Kelso

Mojave National
Preserve

7

95

6 Barstow

enwood

Newberry
Springs

Needles

40

40

15

Essex

247

Adelanto
Victorville

Amboy   National Trails Hwy.

5

Apple Valley

Hesperia

Lucerne Valley

95

Oak Hills
Lake

Arrowhead

Big Bear Lake   247

Crestline

215

S A N   B E R N A R D I N O
M O U N T A I N S

18

Dust and desolation, tumbleweeds and rattlesnakes, barren landscapes and failed dreams—these are the bleak images that come to mind when most people hear the word desert. Yet the remote regions east of the Sierra Nevada possess a singular beauty, the vast open spaces populated with spiky Joshua trees, undulating sand dunes, faulted mountains, and dramatic rock formations. With a few exceptions the area is not heavily peopled, providing expanses in which visitors can both lose and find themselves.

The topography is extreme; while Death Valley drops to almost 300 feet below sea level and contains the lowest (and hottest) spot in North America, the Mojave Desert, which lies to the south, has elevations ranging from 3,000 to 5,000 feet.

Planning

When to Go

Spring and fall are the best seasons to tour the desert. Winters are generally mild, but summers can be cruel. If you're on a budget, be aware that room rates drop as the temperatures rise.

Getting Here and Around

AIR TRAVEL

McCarran International Airport in Las Vegas is the nearest airport to many eastern Mojave destinations. Needles Airport and Inyokern Airport serve small, private planes.

CONTACTS Inyokern Airport. ⊠ *1669 Airport Rd., off Hwy. 178, 9 miles west of Ridgecrest, Inyokern* ☎ *760/377–5844* ⊕ *www.inyokernairport.com.* **McCarran International Airport.** ⊠ *5757 Wayne Newton Blvd., Las Vegas* ☎ *702/261–5211* ⊕ *www.mccarran.com.* **Needles Airport.** ⊠ *711 Airport Rd., Needles* ☎ *760/247–2371* ⊕ *cms.sbcounty.gov/airports.*

BUS TRAVEL

Greyhound provides bus service to Barstow, Victorville, and Palmdale; check with the chambers of commerce about local bus service, which is generally more useful to residents than to tourists.

CONTACTS Greyhound. ☎ *800/231–2222, 214/849–8100 international* ⊕ *www. greyhound.com.*

CAR TRAVEL

The major north–south route through the western Mojave is U.S. 395, which intersects with Interstate 15 between Cajon Pass and Victorville. Farther west, Highway 14 runs north–south between Inyokern (near Ridgecrest) and Palmdale. Two major east–west routes travel through the Mojave: to the north, Interstate 15 to Las Vegas, Nevada; to the south, Interstate 40 to Needles. At the intersection of the two interstates, in Barstow, Interstate 15 veers south toward Victorville and Los Angeles, and Interstate 40 gives way to Highway 58 west toward Bakersfield.

■TIP➜ **For the latest Mojave traffic and weather, tune in to the Highway Stations (98.1 FM near Barstow, 98.9 FM near Essex, and 99.7 FM near Baker).** Traffic can be especially troublesome Friday through Sunday, when thousands of Angelenos head to Las Vegas for a bit of R&R.

CONTACTS Caltrans Current Highway Conditions. ☎ *800/427–7623* ⊕ *www.dot. ca.gov.*

TRAIN TRAVEL

Amtrak trains traveling east and west stop in Victorville, Barstow, and Needles, but the stations aren't staffed, so you'll have to purchase tickets in advance and handle your own baggage. The Barstow station is served daily by Amtrak California motor coaches that stop in Los Angeles, Bakersfield, Las Vegas, and elsewhere. Metrolink's Antelope Valley line travels from Los Angeles Union Station north to Burbank Airport, Palmdale, and Lancaster.

CONTACTS Amtrak. ☎ *800/872–7245, 215/856–7924 international* ⊕ *www. amtrak.com.* **Metrolink.** ☎ *800/371–5465* ⊕ *metrolinktrains.com.*

Health and Safety

Let someone know your trip route, destination, and estimated time of return. Before setting out, make sure your vehicle is in good condition. Carry water, a jack, tools, and towrope or chain. Keep an eye on your gas gauge and try to keep the needle above half. Stay on main roads, and watch out for wildlife, horses, and cattle.

Drink at least a gallon of water a day (more if you're hiking or otherwise exerting yourself). Dress in layered clothing and wear comfortable, sturdy shoes and a hat. Keep snacks, sunscreen, and a first-aid kit on hand. If you have a headache or feel dizzy or nauseous, you could be suffering from dehydration. Get out of the sun immediately and drink plenty of water. Dampen your clothing to lower your body temperature. Do not enter abandoned mine tunnels or shafts of which there are hundreds in the Mojave Desert. The structures may be unstable, and there may be hidden dangers such as pockets of bad air. Avoid canyons during rainstorms. Floodwaters can quickly fill up dry riverbeds and cover or wash away roads. Never place your hands or feet where you can't see them: rattlesnakes, scorpions, and black widow spiders may be hiding there.

CONTACTS Barstow Community Hospital. ✉ *820 E. Mountain View St., Barstow* ☎ *760/256–1761* ⊕ *www.harstowhospital.com.* **BLM Rangers.** ☎ *916/978–4400* ⊕ *www.blm.gov/california.* **San Bernardino County Sheriff.** ☎ *760/256–4838 in Barstow, 760/326–9200 in Needles* ⊕ *wp. sbcounty.gov/sheriff/.*

Hours of Operation

Early morning is the best time to visit sights and avoid crowds, but some museums and visitor centers don't open until 10. If you schedule your town arrivals for the late afternoon, you can drop by the visitor centers just before closing hours to line up an itinerary for the next day.

Restaurants

Throughout the desert, dining is a fairly simple affair. There are chain establishments in Ridgecrest, Victorville, and Barstow, as well as some ethnic eateries. *Restaurant reviews have been shortened. For full information, visit Fodors.com.*

Hotels

Chain hotel properties and roadside motels are the desert's primary lodging options. The tourist season runs from late May through September. Reservations are rarely a problem, but it's still wise to make them. *Hotel reviews have been shortened. For full information, please visit Fodors.com.*

What it Costs

	$	$$	$$$	$$$$
RESTAURANTS				
	under $16	$16–$22	$23–$30	over $30
HOTELS				
	under $120	$120–$175	$176–$250	over $250

Tours

Sierra Club
SPECIAL-INTEREST | The San Gorgonio Chapter of the Sierra Club and the chapter's Mojave Group conduct interesting field trips and desert excursions. Activities are often volunteer-run and free, but participants are sometimes required to cover parking and other expenses. ☎ 951/684–6203 ⊕ sangorgonio2.sierraclub.org ✉ Some free; fee tour prices vary.

Visitor Information

CONTACTS Bureau of Land Management. ✉ California Desert District Office, 22835 Calle San Juan De Los Lagos, Moreno Valley ☎ 951/697–5200 ⊕ www.blm. gov/office/california-desert-district-office. **California Welcome Center Barstow.** ✉ 2796 Tanger Way, Barstow ☎ 760/253–4782 ⊕ www.visitcalifornia.com/attraction/ california-welcome-center-barstow. **Death Valley Chamber of Commerce.** ☎ 888/600– 1844 ⊕ www.deathvalleychamber.org.

Lancaster

8 miles north of Palmdale.

Points of interest around Lancaster include a state poppy reserve that bursts to life in the spring and Edwards Air Force Base, which offers a fascinating tour of historical military aircraft. Lancaster was founded in 1876, when the Southern Pacific Railroad arrived. Before that, several Native American tribes, some of whose descendants still live in the surrounding mountains, inhabited it.

GETTING HERE AND AROUND
From the Los Angeles basin, take Highway 14, which proceeds north to Mojave and Highway 58, a link between Bakersfield and Barstow. Regional Metrolink trains serve Lancaster from the Los Angeles area. Local transit exists, but a car is the best way to experience this area.

ESSENTIALS
VISITOR INFORMATION Destination Lancaster. ✉ 554 W. Lancaster Blvd. ☎ 661/948–4518 ⊕ www.destinationlancasterca.org.

Sights

Air Force Flight Test Museum at Edwards Air Force Base

MILITARY SITE | This museum, at what many consider to be the birthplace of supersonic flight, chronicles the rich history of flight testing. Numerous airplanes are on exhibit, from the first F-16B to the only remaining YF-22. While those with approved base entry have access to regular museum hours, a general-public tour takes place once a month. The 3½-hour tour includes indoor museum exhibits and driving tours of the base. The tour requires a reservation and you have to provide basic information for a background check at least two weeks in advance (a month for non-U.S. residents), but be aware that slots fill up fast. On the base's website, click Tours for details. ✉ *Edwards Air Force Base Visitor Control Center, 405 S. Rosamond Blvd., Edwards* ☎ *661/277–8050, 661/277–3510* ⊕ *www.afftcmuseum.org* ⌦ *Free.*

Antelope Valley California Poppy Reserve

NATIONAL/STATE PARK | The California poppy, the state flower, can be spotted throughout the state, but this quiet park holds the densest concentration. Eight miles of trails wind through 1,745 acres of hills carpeted with poppies and other wildflowers, including a paved section that allows wheelchair access. Keep in mind that poppy flowers will curl up their petals if it's too windy or cold, so plan accordingly. ⚠ Heed the rules and stay on the official trails when taking photos. ■TIP→ **Blooming season is usually March through May.** On a clear day at any time of year, you'll be treated to sweeping views of Antelope Valley. Visit the website or call the wildflower hotline for the current bloom status. ✉ *15101 Lancaster Rd., west off Hwy. 14, Ave. I Exit* ☎ *661/724–1180 wildflower hotline, 661/946–6092 administration* ⊕ *www.parks.ca.gov/poppyreserve* ⌦ *$10 per vehicle* ⊙ *Visitor center closed mid-May–Feb.*

Antelope Valley Indian Museum

MUSEUM | FAMILY | This museum got its start as a private collection of American Indian antiquities gathered in the 1920s by artist and amateur naturalist Howard Arden Edwards. Today, his Swiss chalet–style home is a state museum known for one-of-a-kind artifacts from California, Southwest, and Great Basin native cultures, including ancient tools, artwork, basketry, and rugs. To get here, exit north off Highway 138 at 165th Street East and follow the signs, or take the Avenue K exit off Highway 14. ✉ *15701 E. Ave. M* ☎ *661/946–3055* ⊕ *www.avim.parks.ca.gov* ⌦ *$3* ⊙ *Closed weekdays.*

Antelope Valley Winery/Donato Family Vineyard

STORE/MALL | Cyndee and Frank Donato purchased the Los Angeles–based McLester Winery in 1990 and moved it to Lancaster, where the high-desert sun and nighttime chill work their magic on wine grapes such as Merlot, Zinfandel, and Sangiovese. In addition to tastings, the winery hosts a Saturday farmers' market (from May through November between 9 and noon) and sells grass-fed buffalo and other game and exotic meats such as venison, pheasant, and wild boar. ✉ *42041 20th St. W, at Ave. M* ☎ *661/722–0145, 888/282–8332* ⊕ *www.avwinery. com* ⌦ *Winery free, tastings from $8* ⊙ *Closed Mon. and Tues.*

The BLVD

ARTS VENUE | Lancaster's downtown arts and culture district and social hub, The BLVD, stretches for nine blocks along West Lancaster Boulevard from 10th Street West to Sierra Highway. Boeing Plaza anchors the east end and marks the start of the Aerospace Walk of Honor—a series of murals and monuments lauding 100 legendary figures, including Neil Armstrong and Chuck Yeager. The district is also home to the Lancaster Performing Arts Center, the

Lancaster Museum of Art & History, galleries, restaurants, boutiques, coffee and tea shops, craft breweries, and entertainment venues. ⊠ *W. Lancaster Blvd.* ✚ *10th St. W to Sierra Hwy. and Jackman to Milling Sts.* ☏ *661/723–6074* ⊕ *www.theblvdlancaster.com.*

Devil's Punchbowl Natural Area

NATURE SITE | A mile from the San Andreas Fault, the namesake of this attraction is a natural bowl-shape depression in the earth, framed by 300-foot rock walls. At the bottom is a stream, which you can reach via a moderately strenuous 1-mile hike. You also can detour on a short nature trail; at the top an interpretive center has displays of native flora and fauna, including live animals such as snakes, lizards, and birds of prey. ⊠ *28000 Devil's Punchbowl Rd., south of Hwy. 138, Pearblossom* ☏ *661/944–2743* ⊕ *parks.lacounty.gov/ devils-punchbowl-natural-area-and-na-ture-center/* 🎫 *Free.*

Exotic Feline Breeding Compound's Feline Conservation Center

ZOO | About two dozen species of wild cats, from the unusual, weasel-size jaguarundi to leopards, tigers, and jaguars, inhabit this small, orderly facility. You can see the cats up close (behind barrier fences) in the parklike public zoo and research center, and docents are available to answer questions. ⊠ *Rhyolite Ave. off Mojave-Tropico Rd., Rosamond* ☏ *661/256–3793* ⊕ *www.wildcatzoo.org* 🎫 *$10* ⊘ *Closed Wed.*

St. Andrew's Abbeys

RELIGIOUS SITE | Nestled in the foothills of the Antelope Valley, this peaceful enclave is both Benedictine monastery and restful retreat for those wanting to get away from the bustle of everyday life. Day visitors can walk the lush tree-lined grounds, including a large, shaded pond teeming with ducks and red-eared turtles, or browse the well-stocked gift shop for religious keepsakes. An extensive collection of ceramic tiles

in the image of saints and angels by Father Maur van Doorslaer, a Belgian monk whose work U.S. and Canadian collectors favor, are among the items sold here to help sustain the monastery and its good works. ⊠ *31001 N. Valyermo Rd., south of Hwy. 138, Valyermo* ☏ *888/454–5411, 661/944–2178 ceramics studio* ⊕ *www.saintandrewsabbey. com* 🎫 *Free.*

Red Rock Canyon State Park

48 miles north of Lancaster.

On the stretch of Highway 14 that slices through Red Rock Canyon State Park, it's easy to become caught up in the momentum of rushing to your "real" destination. But it would be a shame not to stop for this deeply beautiful canyon, with its rich, layered colors and Native American heritage.

GETTING HERE AND AROUND
The only practical way to get here is by car, taking Highway 14 north from the Palmdale-Lancaster area or south from Ridgecrest.

⊙ Sights

Red Rock Canyon State Park

NATIONAL/STATE PARK | A geological feast for the eyes with its layers of pink, white, red, and brown rock, this remote canyon is also a region of fascinating biological diversity—the ecosystems of the Sierra Nevada, the Mojave Desert, and the Basin Range all converge here. Native Americans known as the Kawaiisu lived here some 20,000 years ago; later, Mojave Indians roamed the land for centuries. You can still see remains of gold mining operations in the park, and movies such as *Jurassic Park* have been shot here. For a quiet nature trail a little off the beaten path try

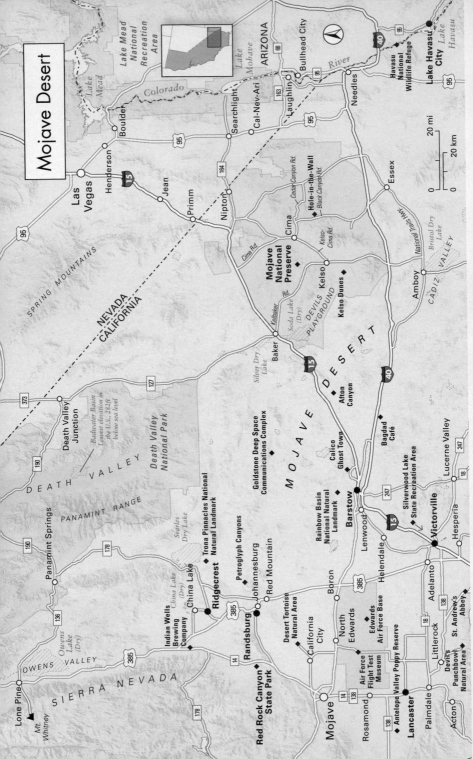

the 0.75-mile loop at Red Cliffs Natural Preserve on Highway 14, across from the entrance to the Ricardo Campground. ⊠ *Visitor Center, 37749 Abbott Dr., off Hwy. 14, Cantil* ☎ *661/946–6092* ⊕ *www.parks.ca.gov* ⊠ *$6 per vehicle.*

Ridgecrest

28 miles northeast of Red Rock Canyon State Park, 77 miles south of Lone Pine.

A military town that serves the U.S. Naval Weapons Center to its north, Ridgecrest has scores of stores, restaurants, and hotels. With about 29,000 residents, it's the last city of any significant size you'll encounter as you head northeast toward Death Valley National Park. It's a good base for visiting regional attractions such as the Trona Pinnacles and Petroglyph Canyons.

GETTING HERE AND AROUND
Arrive here by car via U.S. 395 or, from the Los Angeles area, Highway 14. The local bus service is of limited use to tourists.

ESSENTIALS
TRANSPORTATION CONTACTS Ridgerunner Transit. ☎ *760/499–5040* ⊕ *ridgecrest-ca.gov/transit/transit.*

VISITOR INFORMATION Ridgecrest Area Convention and Visitors Bureau. ⊠ *643 N. China Lake Blvd., Suite C* ☎ *760/375–8202, 800/847–4830* ⊕ *www.racvb.com.*

⊙ Sights

Indian Wells Brewing Company
WINERY/DISTILLERY | After driving through the hot desert, you'll surely appreciate a cold one at Indian Wells Brewing Company, where master brewer Rick Lovett lovingly crafts his Lobotomy Bock, Amnesia I.P.A., and Lunatic Lemonade, among others. If you have the kids along, grab a six-pack of his specialty root beer, black cherry, orange, or cream

soda. ⊠ *2565 N. Hwy. 14, 2 miles west of U.S. 395, Inyokern* ☎ *760/377–5989* ⊕ *www.mojavered.com.*

Maturango Museum
CANYON | FAMILY | The museum contains interesting exhibits that survey the Upper Mojave Desert area's art, history, and geology, and sponsors tours of the amazing rock drawings in Petroglyph Canyons. ⊠ *100 E. Las Flores Ave., at Hwy. 178* ☎ *760/375–6900* ⊕ *www.maturango.org* ⊠ *$5.*

★ Petroglyph Canyons
CANYON | FAMILY | Thousands of well-preserved images of animals and humans are scratched or pecked into dark basaltic rocks at Big Petroglyph and Little Petroglyph canyons in the Coso Mountain range, the largest concentration of ancient rock art in the Northern Hemisphere. The canyons lie within the million-acre U.S. Naval Weapons Center at China Lake. Only the drawings of Little Petroglyph can be visited, and only on a guided tour arranged in advance through the Maturango Museum. Tour participants must be U.S. citizens over 10 years of age, and fill out an online application to obtain security clearance. Detailed information about the spring and fall tours, which fill up fast, is provided on the museum's website. ⊠ *100 E. Las Flores Ave.* ☎ *760/375–6900* ⊕ *www.maturango.org* ⊠ *$60* ⊗ *Closed Dec.–Feb. and June–mid-Sept.*

Trona Pinnacles National Natural Landmark
ARCHAEOLOGICAL SITE | Fantastic-looking formations of calcium carbonate, known as tufa, were formed underwater along fault lines in the bed of what is now Searles Dry Lake. Some of the more than 500 spires stand as tall as 140 feet, creating a landscape so surreal that it doubled for outer-space terrain in the film *Star Trek V.*

An easy-to-walk ½-mile trail allows you to see the tufa up close, but wear sturdy shoes—tufa cuts like coral. The

Did You Know?

Movies like *Jurassic Park* have been shot in Red Rock Canyon State Park in the Mojave Desert.

best road to the area can be impassable after a rainstorm. ✉ *Pinnacle Rd.* ↕ *5 miles south of Hwy. 178, 18 miles east of Ridgecrest* ☎ *760/384–5400 Ridgecrest BLM office* 🌐 *www.blm.gov/visit/trona-pinnacles.*

Hotels

Hampton Inn & Suites Ridgecrest

$$ | HOTEL | Clean and reliable, the Hampton has a well-equipped exercise room, pool, spotless Internet service, and complimentary breakfast. **Pros:** attentive, friendly service; good breakfast; big rooms. **Cons:** a rather strong chain vibe; thin walls; basic breakfast. [$] *Rooms from: $159* ✉ *104 E. Sydnor Ave.* ☎ *760/446–1968* 🌐 *hamptoninn3.hilton.com* 🛏 *93 rooms* 🍴 *Breakfast.*

SpringHill Suites Ridgecrest

$$ | HOTEL | The spacious rooms and contemporary feel of this all-suites Marriott brand hotel make this a welcome choice after a long drive in the desert. **Pros:** spacious rooms; good breakfast; helpful staff. **Cons:** small fitness room; basic bathrooms; property needs updating. [$] *Rooms from: $159* ✉ *113 E. Sydnor Ave.* ☎ *888/236–2427, 760/446–1630* 🌐 *www.marriott.com/hotels/travel/iyksh-springhill-suites-ridgecrest* 🛏 *93 studio suites* 🍴 *Breakfast.*

Randsburg

21 miles south of Ridgecrest, 26 miles east of Red Rock Canyon State Park.

Randsburg and nearby Red Mountain and Johannesburg make up the Rand Mining District, which first boomed with the discovery of gold in the Rand Mountains in 1895. Rich tungsten ore, used in World War I to make steel alloy, was discovered in 1907, and silver was found in 1919. The boom has gone bust, but the area still has some residents, a few antiques shops, and plenty of character. Butte Avenue is the main drag in Randsburg, whose tiny city jail, just off Butte, is among the original buildings still standing. An archetypal Old West cemetery perched on a hillside looms over Johannesburg.

GETTING HERE AND AROUND

Arriving by car is the best transportation option. From Red Rock Canyon, drive east on Redrock Randsburg Road. From Ridgecrest, drive south on South China Lake Road and U.S. 395.

Sights

Desert Tortoise Natural Area

NATURE PRESERVE | It may not always be easy to spot the elusive desert tortoise in this peaceful protected habitat but the approximately 40-square-mile area often blazes with wildflowers in the spring and early summer. It is also a great spot to see desert kit fox, red-tailed hawks, cactus wrens, and Mojave rattlesnakes; walking paths and a small interpretive center are part of the experience. ✉ *8 miles northeast of California City via Randsburg Mojave Rd.* ☎ *951/683–3872* 🌐 *www.tortoise-tracks.org* 🎟 *Free.*

General Store

RESTAURANT—SIGHT | Built as Randsburg's Drug Store in 1896, the General Store is one of the area's few surviving ghost-town buildings with an original tin ceiling, light fixtures, and 1904-era marble-and-stained-glass soda fountain. You can still enjoy a phosphate soda from that same fountain, or a lunch of burgers, hot dogs, and chili. ✉ *35 Butte Ave.* ☎ *760/374–2143* 🌐 *www.randsburggeneralstore.com* 🕐 *Closed Tues. and Wed.*

Rand Desert Museum

MUSEUM | The colorful history of the Rand Mining District during its heyday is celebrated in this small museum, including historical mining photographs, documents, and artifacts. ✉ *161 Butte Ave.* ☎ *760/371–0965* 🌐 *www.randdesertmuseum.com* 🎟 *Free* 🕐 *Closed weekdays.*

White House Saloon

BUILDING | This still-surviving saloon served miners and cowboys when it was first established way back in 1897; nowadays tourists and bikers sidle up to the bar for a burger, ice-cold brew, and a giant dose of Old West nostalgia. ⊠ *168 Butte Ave.* ☎ *760/374–2464* ⊘ *Closed Mon.–Thurs.*

Victorville

87 miles south of Ridgecrest.

At the southwest corner of the Mojave is the sprawling town of Victorville, a town with a rich Route 66 heritage and a museum dedicated to the Mother Road. Victorville was named for Santa Fe Railroad pioneer Jacob Nash Victor, who drove the first locomotive through the Cajon Pass here in 1885. Once home to Native Americans, the town later became a rest stop for Mormons and missionaries. In 1941 George Air Force Base, now an airport and storage area, brought scores of military families to the area, many of which have stayed on to raise families of their own.

GETTING HERE AND AROUND

Drive here on Interstate 15 from Los Angeles or Las Vegas, or from the north via U.S. 395. Amtrak and Greyhound also serve the town. There are local buses, but touring by car is more practical.

ESSENTIALS

TRANSPORTATION INFORMATION Victor Valley Transit Authority. ☎ *760/948–3030* ⊕ *www.vvta.org.*

VISITOR INFORMATION Victor Valley Chamber of Commerce. ⊠ *14174 Green Tree Blvd., at St. Andrews Dr.* ☎ *760/245–6506* ⊕ *www.vvchamber.com.*

⊙ Sights

California Route 66 Museum

MUSEUM | Visitors from around the world still think of Historic Route 66 as one of the best ways to see the real America and this 4,500-square-foot museum is chock-full of memorabilia such as maps and postcards, photographs, paintings, and nostalgic displays that bring the iconic highway's history to life. Friendly museum volunteers are more than happy to answer questions and take your picture inside the flower-painted VW Love Bus. ⊠ *16825 S. D St., between 5th and 6th Sts.* ☎ *760/951–0436* ⊕ *califrt66museum.org* ⊠ *Free* ⊘ *Closed Tues. and Wed.*

Mojave Narrows Regional Park

CITY PARK | FAMILY | This 840-acre park is one of the few spots where the Mojave River flows aboveground and the result is open pastures, wetlands, and two lakes surrounded by cottonwoods and cattails. Amenities include camping, fishing, equestrian/walking trails, and a large playground with water park. ⊠ *18000 Yates Rd., north on Ridgecrest Rd. off Bear Valley Rd.* ☎ *760/245–2226* ⊕ *cms.sbcounty.gov/parks* ⊠ *From $8* ⊘ *Closed Tues. and Wed.*

Silverwood Lake State Recreation Area

NATIONAL/STATE PARK | One of the desert's most popular boating and fishing areas, 1,000-acre Silverwood Lake also has campgrounds and a beach with a lifeguard. You can rent boats; fish for trout, largemouth bass, crappie, and catfish; and hike and bike the trails. In winter, bald eagles nest in the tall Jeffrey pines by the shore. ⊠ *14651 Cedar Cir., at Cleghorn Rd., off Hwy. 138, Hesperia* ☎ *760/389–2281* ⊕ *www.parks.ca.gov* ⊠ *$10 per car, $10 per boat.*

Restaurants

Emma Jean's Holland Burger Cafe

$ | **DINER** | The short-order cook and his grill are literally center stage in this tiny, family-owned restaurant along Historic Route 66, which has changed little since it first opened in 1947. It's the peach cobbler, Brian burger, and fried chicken that keep locals lining up at the door, but anyone wanting a glimpse of 20th-century Americana can get their kicks here, too. **Known for:** Route 66 memorabilia; historical diner; hearty breakfasts. *$ Average main: $9 ✉ 17143 N. D St., at Water Power Housing Dr. ☎ 760/243–9938 🌐 www.hollandburger.com ▭ No credit cards ⏲ Closed Sun. No dinner.*

Molly Brown's Country Cafe

$ | **AMERICAN** | **FAMILY** | There's no mystery why this place is a locals' favorite—the cozy eatery offers a mouthwatering breakfast menu that includes everything from chicken fried steak to a sizzling garden skillet brimming with fresh vegetables. Lunch includes sandwiches, salads, and hot plates such as meat loaf with potatoes, veggies, and corn bread. **Known for:** hearty breakfasts; locals' favorite; homemade breads. *$ Average main: $10 ✉ 15775 Mojave Dr. ☎ 760/241–4900 🌐 www.mollybrownscountrycafe.com.*

Hotels

Courtyard Marriott Victorville Hesperia

$$ | **HOTEL** | **FAMILY** | Rooms are spacious and contemporary, and there is both an indoor pool and large outdoor patio and pool area ideal for large groups. **Pros:** convenient location off Interstate 15; some rooms with desert views; two pools. **Cons:** breakfast only with certain room rates; bistro menu options limited; some rooms close to freeway noise. *$ Rooms from: $136 ✉ 9619 Mariposa Rd., Hesperia ☎ 760/956–3876 🌐 www.marriott.com ⇆ 131 rooms.*

La Quinta Inn and Suites Victorville

$ | **HOTEL** | **FAMILY** | This small hotel offers a touch more than your typical chain, with contemporary decor in cozy earth tones and spacious rooms. **Pros:** near shopping mall; helpful staff; outdoor pool and Jacuzzi. **Cons:** some freeway noise; aging building; fronts a busy street. *$ Rooms from: $109 ✉ 12000 Mariposa Rd., Hesperia ☎ 760/949–9900 🌐 www.lq.com ⇆ 75 rooms 🍴 Breakfast.*

Barstow

32 miles northeast of Victorville.

Barstow was born in 1886, when a subsidiary of the Atchison, Topeka, and Santa Fe Railway began construction of a Harvey House depot and hotel here. The depot has been restored and includes two free museums, the family-friendly Calico Ghost Town is just north of town, and there are well-known chain motels and restaurants right off Interstate 15 if you need a rest and refuel before the next stop.

GETTING HERE AND AROUND

Driving here on Interstate 15 from Los Angeles or Las Vegas is the best option, although you can reach Barstow via Amtrak or Greyhound. The local bus service is helpful for sights downtown.

ESSENTIALS

TRANSPORTATION INFORMATION **Barstow Area Transit/Victor Valley Transit.** *☎ 760/948–3030 🌐 vvta.org.*

VISITOR INFORMATION **Barstow Area Chamber of Commerce and Visitors Bureau.** *✉ 229 E. Main St. ☎ 760/256–8617 🌐 www.barstowchamber.com.* **California Welcome Center.** *✉ 2796 Tanger Way, Suite 100, off Lenwood Rd. ☎ 760/253–4782 🌐 www.visitcalifornia.com/attraction/california-welcome-center-barstow.* **Mojave National Preserve Headquarters.** *✉ 2701 Barstow Rd. ☎ 760/252–6100 🌐 www.nps.gov/moja/planyourvisit/visitorcenters.htm.*

Many of the buildings in the popular Calico Ghost Town are authentic.

⊙ Sights

Afton Canyon

CANYON | Because of its colorful, steep walls, Afton Canyon is often called the Grand Canyon of the Mojave. It was carved over thousands of years by the rushing waters of the Mojave River, which makes one of its few aboveground appearances here. The dirt road that leads to the canyon is ungraded in spots, so it is best to explore it in an all-terrain vehicle. ⊠ *Off Afton Rd., 36 miles northeast of Barstow via I–15* ⊕ *www.recreation.gov.*

Bagdad Café

RESTAURANT—SIGHT | Tourists from all over the world flock to this Route 66 eatery where the 1987 film of the same name was shot. Built in the 1940s, the divey Bagdad Café's walls are crammed with memorabilia donated by visitors famous and otherwise. The very limited bill of fare includes the Bagdad omelet and a buffalo burger with fries, but this place is really about soaking up the Route

66-Americana vibe. ⊠ *46548 National Trails Hwy., at Nopal La., Newberry Springs* ☎ *760/257–3101.*

★ Calico Ghost Town

GHOST TOWN | **FAMILY** | This former silver-mining boom town was started in 1881 and within a few years boasted 500 mines and 22 saloons. Its reconstruction by Walter Knott of Knott's Berry Farm makes it more about G-rated family entertainment than the town's gritty past, but that doesn't seem to take away from the fun of panning for (fool's) gold, touring the original tunnels of Maggie Mine, or taking a leisurely ride on the Calico Odessa Railroad. Five of the original buildings are still standing, such as the impressive Lane's General Store, and its setting among the stark beauty of the Calico Hills can make a stroll along this once-bustling Main Street downright peaceful. ■ **TIP→ Calico also has ghost tours and regular events such as the yearly bluegrass festival on Mother's Day weekend.** ⊠ *36600 Ghost Town Rd., off I–15,*

Yermo ☎ 760/254–2122 ⊕ cms.sbcounty.
gov/parks/Parks/CalicoGhostTown.aspx
🖙 $8.

Casa Del Desierto Harvey House

HISTORIC SITE | This historic train depot
was built around 1911 (the original 1885
structure was destroyed by fire) and was
one of the original Harvey Houses, providing dining and lodging for weary travelers along the rail lines. Waitresses at the
depots were popularized in movies such
as *The Harvey Girls* with Judy Garland. It
now houses offices and two museums:
the Western American Railroad and
Route 66 Mother Road, but you can still
walk along the porticos of the impressive
Spanish Renaissance Classical building,
or stroll into the restored lobby where
you'll find the original staircase, terrazzo
floor, and copper chandeliers. ⊠ 681 N.
1st Ave., near Riverside Dr. ☎ 760/818–
4400 ⊕ www.barstowharveyhouse.com
🖙 Free ⊗ Closed Sun.

Desert Discovery Center

MUSEUM | **FAMILY** | The center's main
attraction is Old Woman Meteorite, the
second-largest such celestial object
ever found in the United States. It was
discovered in 1976 about 50 miles from
Barstow. The center also has exhibits
of fossils, plants, and local animals.
Environmental education, history, and the
arts are among the topics of workshops
and presentations the center hosts.
Follow the outdoor desert nature trail
with interpretive signs on desert plants
and early man's relationship with native
plants for shelter, medicine, clothing,
food, and weaponry. ■TIP→ Reserve a
spot in advance for the Stone Age to Space
Age tour, offered the first Saturday of the
month at 10 am (about 1½ hours, donations
appreciated). It begins with a Route 66
history presentation at the Desert Discovery
Center, followed by visits to the Main Street
Murals and the NASA Goldstone Visitor
Center. ⊠ 831 Barstow Rd. ☎ 760/252–
6060 ⊕ www.desertdiscoverycenter.com
🖙 Free ⊗ Closed Sun. and Mon.

★ Goldstone Deep Space Communications Complex

MUSEUM | **FAMILY** | Friendly and enthu-
siastic staffers conduct guided tours
of this 53-square-mile complex at Fort
Irwin Military Base, 35 miles north of
Barstow. Tours start at the Goldstone
Museum, where exhibits detail past and
present space missions and Deep Space
Network history. From there, you'll drive
out to see the massive concave anten-
nas, starting with those used for early
manned space flights and culminating
with the 24-story-tall "listening" device.
This is one of only three complexes in
the world that make up the Deep Space
Network, tracking and communicating
with spacecraft throughout our solar
system. Appointments are required;
contact the complex to reserve a slot.
■TIP→ No time to tour? Stop by the NASA
Goldstone Visitor Center in the Casa del
Desierto Harvey House in Barstow to view
exhibits and learn about the Deep Space
Network and space missions. ⊠ NASA
Goldstone Visitor Center, 681 N. 1st
Ave. ☎ 760/255–8688 ⊕ www.gdscc.
nasa.gov 🖙 Free ⊗ Closed Sun.

Inscription Canyon

CANYON | Located 42 miles northwest of
Barstow in the remote Black Mountains,
Inscription has one of the world's largest
collections of Native American petroglyphs and pictographs, but it is not
an easy trek. Visitors need four-wheel-
drive, high-clearance vehicles that are
meant to go off road; portions of the
journey include pockets of deep sand.
It's also best to avoid in the hot summer
months, but no matter the season, fill
the gas tank and bring plenty of water.
⊠ Barstow ☎ 760/252–6000 ⊕ www.
recreation.gov.

Main Street Murals

PUBLIC ART | **FAMILY** | A series of
hand-painted murals (a total of 30
when all are completed) in downtown
Barstow depicts the town's history, from
prehistoric times and early explorers

to pioneer caravans, mining eras, and Route 66. Walking tour guides are available at the Barstow Chamber of Commerce and the public library. Contact the Desert Discovery Center for more details on the murals and monthly guided tours. ✉ *E. Main St.* ✣ *Between 1st and 7th Sts.* ☎ *760/252–6060* 🌐 *www.mainstreetmurals.com.*

Mojave River Valley Museum
MUSEUM | **FAMILY** | The floor-to-ceiling collection of local history, both quirky and conventional, includes Ice Age fossils such as a giant mammoth tusk dug up in 2006, Native American artifacts, 19th-century handmade quilts, and displays on early settlers. Entrance is free and there's a little gift shop with a nice collection of books about the area. **■ TIP→ The story about Possum Trot and its population of folk-art dolls is not to be missed.** ✉ *270 E. Virginia Way, at Barstow Rd.* ☎ *760/256–5452* 🌐 *www.mojaverivervalleymuseum.org* 🎫 *Free.*

Rainbow Basin National Natural Landmark
NATIONAL/STATE PARK | Many science-fiction movies set on Mars have been filmed at this landmark 8 miles north of Barstow. Huge slabs of red, orange, white, and green stone tilt at crazy angles like ships about to capsize and traces of ancient beasts such as mastodons and bear-dogs, which roamed the basin up to 16 million years ago have been discovered in its fossil beds. The dirt road around the basin is narrow and bumpy so vehicles with higher clearance are recommended and rain can quickly turn the road to mud; at times, only four-wheel-drive vehicles are permitted. ✉ *Fossil Bed Rd., 3 miles west of Fort Irwin Rd. (head north from I–15)* ☎ *760/252–6000* 🌐 *www.recreation.gov.*

Skyline Drive-In Theatre
ARTS VENUE | Check out a bit of surviving Americana at this dusty drive-in, where you can watch the latest Hollywood flicks among the Joshua trees and starry night sky. Keep in mind the old-time speakers are no more; sound is tuned in via car radio. ✉ *31175 Old Hwy. 58* ☎ *760/256–3333* 🎫 *$9 per person* 🕓 *Closed early Dec.–early Mar.*

Western America Railroad Museum
MUSEUM | **FAMILY** | You can almost hear the murmur of passengers and rhythmic, metal-on-metal clatter as you stroll past the old cabooses, railcars and engines, such as Sante Fe number 95, that are on display outside the historic Barstow station where this museum is located. The next stop is the indoor portion of the collection, including a train simulator, rail equipment, model railroad display, and other memorabilia. A handful of artifacts from the depot's Harvey House days are on display, as well as period dining-car china from railways around the country. ✉ *Casa Del Desierto, 685 N. 1st Ave., near Riverside Dr.* ☎ *760/256–9276* 🌐 *www.barstowrailmuseum.org* 🎫 *Free* 🕓 *Closed Mon.–Thurs.*

🍴 Restaurants

Idle Spurs Steakhouse
$$$ | **STEAKHOUSE** | This spacious steak-and-seafood restaurant, with its Western-style memorabilia and cheerful white fairy lights, has been a favorite among locals for decades. The menu is very basic no-frills steak-house fare, but the service is friendly and it's a bit of cozy, mid-century charm in the middle of the Mojave. **Known for:** locals' favorite; family run; dated but cozy. [$] *Average main: $28* ✉ *690 Old Hwy. 58, at Camarillo Ave.* ☎ *760/256–8888* 🌐 *www.theidlespurs.com* 🕓 *Closed Mon. No lunch.*

Peggy Sue's 50s Diner
$ | **AMERICAN** | **FAMILY** | Checkerboard floors and life-size versions of Elvis and Marilyn Monroe greet you at this funky '50s coffee shop and pizza parlor in the middle of the Mojave. The fare is basic American—fries, onion rings, burgers, pork chops—with some fun surprises

such as pineapple pie and deep-fried dill pickles. **Known for:** movie, TV memorabilia, over-the-top '50s vibe; gift shop, jukebox, soda fountain, duck pond. $ *Average main: $11* ✉ *35654 W. Yermo Rd., at Daggett-Yermo Rd., Yermo* ☏ *760/254–3370* ⊕ *www.peggysuesdiner.com.*

Hotels

Ayres Hotel Barstow

$$ | **HOTEL** | **FAMILY** | In a sea of chain hotels this one has a few homespun touches up its sleeves, such as fresh-baked cookies in the cozy lobby lounge every evening. **Pros:** clean rooms, engaged management; entirely non-smoking; Tesla charging stations. **Cons:** pricey for Barstow; near freeway; shared parking lot with other businesses. $ *Rooms from: $139* ✉ *2812 Lenwood Rd.* ☏ *760/307–3121* ⊕ *www.ayreshotels.com/ayres-hotel-barstow* ⌇ *92 rooms* ⦿ *Breakfast.*

Mojave National Preserve

Visitor center 118 miles east of Barstow, 58 miles west of Needles.

The 1.6 million acres of the Mojave National Preserve hold a surprising abundance of plant and animal life—especially considering their elevation (nearly 8,000 feet in some areas). There are traces of human history here as well, including abandoned army posts and vestiges of mining and ranching towns. The Cinder Cone Lava Beds area holds 75 inactive volcanoes; the youngest is 11,500 years old. North Cima Road passes the world's largest Joshua tree forest. Mojave National Preserve rangers also oversee the adjacent 20,920-acre Castle Mountains National Monument, created in 2016.

GETTING HERE AND AROUND

A car is the best way to access the preserve, which lies between Interstates 15 and 40. Kelbaker Road bisects the park from north to south; northbound from Interstate 40, Essex Road gets you to Hole-in-the-Wall on pavement but is graveled beyond there.

⊙ Sights

Hole-in-the-Wall

NATURE SITE | Created millions of years ago by volcanic activity, Hole-in-the-Wall formed when gases were trapped between layers of deposited ash, rock, and lava; the gas bubbles left holes in the solidified material. You will encounter one of California's most distinctive hiking experiences here. Proceeding clockwise from a small visitor center, you walk gently down and around a craggy hill, past cacti and fading petroglyphs to Banshee Canyon, whose pockmarked walls resemble Swiss cheese. From there you head back out of the canyon, supporting yourself with widely spaced iron rings (some of which wiggle precariously from their rock moorings) as you ascend a 50-foot incline that deposits you back near the visitor center. The one-hour adventure can be challenging but wholly entertaining. ■TIP➜ **There are no services (gas or food) nearby; be sure to fill your tank and pack some snacks before heading out here.** ✉ *Mojave National Preserve* ☏ *760/252–6104* ⊕ *www.nps.gov/moja* ⌂ *Free.*

★ Kelso Dunes

NATURE SITE | As you enter the preserve from the south, you'll pass miles of open scrub brush, Joshua trees, and beautiful red-black cinder cones before encountering the Kelso Dunes. These golden, fine-sand slopes cover 70 square miles, reaching heights of 600 feet. You can reach them via a short walk from the main parking area, but be prepared for a serious workout. When you reach the top of a dune, kick a little bit of sand down the lee side and listen to the sand "sing." North of the dunes, in the town of Kelso, is the Mission revival–style **Kelso Depot Visitor Center.** The striking building, which dates to 1923, contains several rooms of desert- and train-theme exhibits. ⊠ *For Kelso Depot Visitor Center, take Kelbaker Rd. exit from I–15 (head south 34 miles) or I–40 (head north 22 miles)* ☎ *760/252–6100, 760/252–6108* ⊕ *www.nps.gov/moja* ✉ *Free* ⊙ *Kelso Depot visitor center closed Tues. and Wed.*

Chapter 10

SEQUOIA AND KINGS CANYON NATIONAL PARKS

Updated by
Cheryl Crabtree

⊙ **Sights**
★★★★★

🍴 **Restaurants**
★★★★☆

🛏 **Hotels**
★★★★★

🛍 **Shopping**
★☆☆☆☆

🍸 **Nightlife**
★☆☆☆☆

WELCOME TO SEQUOIA AND KINGS CANYON NATIONAL PARKS

TOP REASONS TO GO

★ **Gentle giants:** You'll feel small—in a good way—walking among some of the world's largest living things in Sequoia's Giant Forest and Kings Canyon's Grant Grove.

★ **Because it's there:** You can't even glimpse it from the main part of Sequoia, but the sight of majestic Mt. Whitney is worth the trip to the eastern face of the High Sierra.

★ **Underground exploration:** Far older even than the giant sequoias, the gleaming limestone formations in Crystal Cave will draw you along dark, marble passages.

★ **A grander-than-Grand Canyon:** Drive the twisting Kings Canyon Scenic Byway down into the jagged, granite Kings River canyon, deeper in parts than the Grand Canyon.

★ **Regal solitude:** To spend a day or two hiking in a subalpine world of your own, pick one of the many trailheads at Mineral King.

The two parks comprise 865,964 acres (1,353 square miles), mostly on the western flank of the Sierra. A map of the adjacent parks looks vaguely like a mitten, with the palm of Sequoia National Park south of the north-pointing, skinny thumb and long fingers of Kings Canyon National Park. Between the western thumb and eastern fingers, north of Sequoia, lies part of Sequoia National Forest, which includes Giant Sequoia National Monument.

1 Giant Forest–Lodgepole Village. One of the most heavily visited areas of Sequoia contains major sights such as Giant Forest, General Sherman Tree, Crystal Cave, and Moro Rock.

2 Grant Grove Village–Redwood Canyon. The "thumb" of Kings Canyon National Park is its busiest section, where Grant Grove, General Grant Tree, Panoramic Point, and Big Stump are the main attractions.

3 Cedar Grove. The drive through the high-country portion of Kings Canyon National Park to Cedar Grove Village, on the canyon floor, reveals magnificent granite formations of varied hues.

Rock meets river in breathtaking fashion at Zumwalt Meadow.

4 Mineral King. In the southeast section of Sequoia, the highest road-accessible part of the park is a good place to hike, camp, and soak up the unspoiled grandeur of the Sierra Nevada.

5 Mount Whitney. The highest peak in the Lower 48 stands on the eastern edge of Sequoia; to get there from Giant Forest you must either backpack eight days through the mountains or drive nearly 400 miles around the park to its other side.

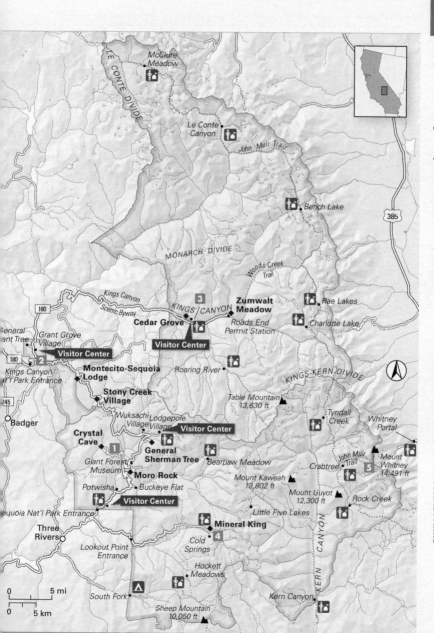

McClure Meadow

LE CONTE DIVIDE

Le Conte Canyon

John Muir Trail

Bench Lake

385

MONARCH DIVIDE

Woods Creek Trail

Kings Canyon
Scenic Byway

180

KINGS CANYON

3

Zumwalt Meadow

Cedar Grove

Rae Lakes

Charlotte Lake

Roads End Permit Station

Visitor Center

General Grant Tree

Grant Grove Village

180

2

Kings Canyon Nat'l Park Entrance

Montecito-Sequoia Lodge

Roaring River

KINGS-KERN DIVIDE

245

Badger

Stony Creek Village

Wuksachi Village   Lodgepole Village

Table Mountain 13,630 ft

Tyndall Creek

Whitney Portal

Crystal Cave

1

Visitor Center

Giant Forest Museum

General Sherman Tree

Bearpaw Meadow

John Muir Trail

Crabtree

5

Mount Whitney 14,491 ft

Moro Rock

Buckeye Flat

Mount Kaweah 13,802 ft

Mount Guyot 12,300 ft

Rock Creek

Potwisha

Sequoia Nat'l Park Entrance

Visitor Center

Little Five Lakes

KERN CANYON

Three Rivers

Mineral King

4

Lookout Point Entrance

Cold Springs

Hockett Meadows

Kern Canyon

0   5 mi
0   5 km

South Fork

Sheep Mountain 10,050 ft

The monstrously thick trunks and branches, remarkably shallow root systems, and neck-craning heights of the sequoias are almost impossible to believe, as is the fact they can live for more than 2,500 years. Many of these towering marvels are in the Giant Forest stretch of Generals Highway, which connects Sequoia and Kings Canyon national parks.

Next to or a few miles off the 46-mile Generals Highway are most of Sequoia National Park's main attractions and Grant Grove Village, the orientation hub for Kings Canyon National Park. The two parks share a boundary that runs from the Central Valley in the west, where the Sierra Nevada foothills begin, to the range's dramatic eastern ridges. Kings Canyon has two portions: the smaller is shaped like a bent finger and encompasses Grant Grove Village and Redwood Mountain Grove (two of the parks' largest concentration of sequoias), and the larger is home to stunning Kings River Canyon, whose vast, unspoiled peaks and valleys are a backpacker's dream. Sequoia is in one piece and includes Mt. Whitney, the highest point in the lower 48 states (although it is impossible to see from the western part of the park and is a chore to ascend from either side).

Planning

When to Go

The best times to visit are spring and fall, when temperatures are moderate and crowds thin. Summertime can draw hordes of tourists to see the giant sequoias, and the few, narrow roads mean congestion at peak holiday times. If you must visit in summer, go during the week. By contrast, in wintertime you may feel as though you have the parks all to yourself. But because of heavy snows, sections of the main park roads can be closed without warning, and low-hanging clouds can move in and obscure mountains and valleys for days. From early October to late April, check road and weather conditions before venturing out.
■TIP➜ Even in summer, you can escape hordes of people just walking ¼ to ½ mile off the beaten path on a less-used trail.

Festivals and Events

Annual Trek to the Tree
FESTIVAL | On the second Sunday of December, thousands of carolers gather at the base of General Grant Tree, the nation's official Christmas tree. ☎ 559/565–3341.

Big Fresno Fair
FESTIVAL | Over 12 days in October, agricultural, home-arts, and other competitions, plus horse racing and a carnival make for a lively county fair. ✉ Fresno ☎ 559/650–3247 ⊕ www.fresnofair.com.

Blossom Days Festival
FESTIVAL | On the first Saturday of March, communities along Fresno County's Blossom Trail celebrate the flowering of the area's orchards, citrus groves, and vineyards. ☎ 559/981–5500 ⊕ www.goblossomtrail.com.

Jazzaffair
FESTIVAL | On the second weekend of April, a festival of mostly traditional jazz takes place at several venues just south of the parks. ⊕ sierratraditionaljazzclub.com.

Woodlake Rodeo
FESTIVAL | The local Lions Club sponsors this rousing rodeo that draws large crowds to Woodlake on Mother's Day weekend. ☎ 559/564–8555 ⊕ www.woodlakelionsclub.com.

Planning Your Time

SEQUOIA NATIONAL PARK IN ONE DAY
After spending the night in Visalia or Three Rivers—and provided your vehicle's length does not exceed 22 feet—take off early on Route 198 to the **Sequoia National Park entrance.** Pull over at the **Hospital Rock** picnic area to gaze up at the imposing granite formation of Moro Rock, which you later will climb. Heed signs that advise "10 mph" around tight turns as you climb 3,500 feet on **Generals Highway** to the **Giant Forest Museum.** Spend a half hour here, then examine trees firsthand by circling the lovely **Round Meadow** on the **Big Trees Trail,** to which you must walk from the museum or from its parking lot across the road.

Get back in your car and continue a few miles north on Generals Highway to see the jaw-dropping **General Sherman Tree.** Then set off on the **Congress Trail** so that you can be further awed by the Senate and House big-tree clusters. Buy lunch at the **Lodgepole** complex, 2 miles to the north, and eat at the nearby **Pinewood** picnic area. Now you're ready for the day's big exercise, climbing **Moro Rock.**

You can drive there or, if it is summer, park at the museum lot and take the free shuttle. Count on spending at least an hour for the 350-step ascent and descent, with a pause on top to appreciate the 360-degree view. Get back in the car, or on the shuttle, and proceed past the **Tunnel Log** to **Crescent Meadow.** Spend a relaxing hour or two strolling on the trails that pass by, among other things, **Tharp's Log.** By now you've probably renewed your appetite; head to **Lodgepole Grill & Market** or the restaurant at **Wuksachi Lodge.**

KINGS CANYON NATIONAL PARK IN ONE DAY
Enter the park via the **Kings Canyon Scenic Byway** (Route 180), having spent the night in Fresno or Visalia. Better yet, wake up already in **Grant Grove Village,** perhaps in the **John Muir Lodge.** Stock up for a picnic with takeout food from the **Grant Grove Restaurant,** or purchase prepackaged food from the nearby market. Drive east a mile to see the **General Grant Tree** and compact **Grant Grove's** other sequoias. If it's no later than mid-morning, walk up the short trail at **Panoramic Point,** for a great view of Hume Lake and the High Sierra. Either way, return to Route 180 and continue east. Stop at Junction View to

AVERAGE HIGH/LOW TEMPERATURES					
JAN.	FEB.	MAR.	APR.	MAY	JUNE
42/24	44/25	46/26	51/30	58/36	68/44
JULY	AUG.	SEPT.	OCT.	NOV.	DEC.
76/51	76/50	71/45	61/38	50/31	44/27

take in several noteworthy peaks that tower over Kings Canyon. From here, visit **Boyden Cavern** or continue to **Cedar Grove Village,** pausing along the way for a gander at **Grizzly Falls.** Eat at a table by the **South Fork of the Kings River,** or on the deck off the Cedar Grove Snack Bar. Now you are ready for the day's highlight, strolling **Zumwalt Meadow,** which lies a few miles past the village.

After you have enjoyed that short trail and the views it offers of **Grand Sentinel** and **North Dome,** you might as well go the extra mile to **Roads End,** where backpackers embark for the High Sierra wilderness. Make the return trip—with a quick stop at **Roaring River Falls**—past Grant Grove and briefly onto southbound **Generals Highway.** Pull over at the **Redwood Mountain Overlook** and use binoculars to look down upon the world's largest sequoia grove, then drive another couple of miles to the **Kings Canyon Overlook,** where you can survey some of what you have done today. Make reservations for a late dinner at **Wuksachi Lodge.**

Getting Here and Around

AIR TRAVEL
The closest airport to Sequoia and Kings Canyon national parks is Fresno Yosemite International Airport (FAT).

AIRPORT CONTACTS Fresno Yosemite International Airport (*FAT*). ✉ *5175 E. Clinton Way, Fresno* ☎ *800/244–2359 automated info, 559/454–2052 terminal info desk* ⊕ *www.flyfresno.com.*

CAR TRAVEL
Sequoia is 36 miles east of Visalia on Route 198; Grant Grove Village in Kings Canyon is 56 miles east of Fresno on Route 180. There is no automobile entrance on the eastern side of the Sierra. Routes 180 and 198 are connected by Generals Highway, a paved two-lane road that sometimes sees delays at peak times due to ongoing improvements. The road is extremely narrow and steep from Route 198 to Giant Forest, so keep an eye on your engine temperature gauge, as the incline and congestion can cause vehicles to overheat; to avoid overheated brakes, use low gears on downgrades.

If you are traveling in an RV or with a trailer, study the restrictions on these vehicles. Do not travel beyond Potwisha Campground on Route 198 with an RV longer than 22 feet; take straighter, easier Route 180 instead. Maximum vehicle length on Generals Highway is 40 feet, or 50 feet combined length for vehicles with trailers.

Generals Highway between Lodgepole and Grant Grove is sometimes closed by snow. The Mineral King Road from Route 198 into southern Sequoia National Park is closed 2 miles below Atwell Mill either on November 1 or after the first heavy snow. The Buckeye Flat–Middle Fork Trailhead road is closed from mid-October to mid-April when the Buckeye Flat Campground closes. The lower Crystal Cave Road is closed when the cave closes (typically in November). Its upper 2 miles, as well as the Panoramic Point and Moro Rock–Crescent Meadow roads, close with the first heavy snow.

Because of the danger of rockfall, the portion of Kings Canyon Scenic Byway east of Grant Grove closes in winter. For current road and weather conditions, call ☎ 559/565-3341 or visit the park website: ⊕ www.nps.gov/seki.

■ TIP→ Snowstorms are common from late October through April. Unless you have a four-wheel-drive vehicle with snow tires, you should carry chains and know how to install them.

Park Essentials

ACCESSIBILITY

All the visitor centers, the Giant Forest Museum, and Big Trees Trail are wheelchair accessible, as are some short ranger-led walks and talks. General Sherman Tree can be reached via a paved, level trail near a parking area. None of the caves is accessible, and wilderness areas must be reached by horseback or on foot. Some picnic tables are extended to accommodate wheelchairs. Many of the major sites are in the 6,000-foot range and thin air at high elevations can cause respiratory distress for people with breathing difficulties. Carry oxygen if necessary. Contact the park's main number for more information.

PARK FEES AND PERMITS

The admission fee is $35 per vehicle, $30 per motorcycle, and $20 per person for those who enter by bus, on foot, bicycle, horse, or any other mode of transportation; it is valid for seven days in both parks. U.S. residents over the age of 62 pay $80 for a lifetime pass, and permanently disabled U.S. residents are admitted free.

If you plan to camp in the backcountry, you need a permit, which costs $15 for hikers or $30 for stock users (e.g., horseback riders). One permit covers the group. Availability of permits depends upon trailhead quotas. Reservations are accepted by mail or email for a $15

processing fee, beginning March 1, and must be made at least 14 days in advance (☎ 559/565-3766). Without a reservation, you may still get a permit on a first-come, first-served basis starting at 1 pm the day before you plan to hike. For more information on backcountry camping or travel with pack animals (horses, mules, burros, or llamas), contact the Wilderness Permit Office (☎ 530/565-3766).

PARK HOURS

The parks are open 24/7 year-round. They are in the Pacific time zone.

CELL PHONE RECEPTION

Cell phone reception is poor to nonexistent in the higher elevations and spotty even on portions of Generals Highway, where you can (on rare clear days) see the Central Valley. Public telephones may be found at the visitor centers, ranger stations, some trailheads, and at all restaurants and lodging facilities in the park.

Educational Offerings

Educational programs at the parks include museum-style exhibits, ranger- and naturalist-led talks and walks, film and other programs, and sightseeing tours, most of them conducted by either the park service or the nonprofit Sequoia Parks Conservancy. Exhibits at the visitor centers and the Giant Forest Museum focus on different aspects of the park: its history, wildlife, geology, climate, and vegetation—most notably the giant sequoias. Weekly notices about programs are posted at the visitor centers and elsewhere.

Grant Grove Visitor Center at Kings Canyon National Park has maps of self-guided park tours. Ranger-led walks and programs take place throughout the year in Grant Grove. Cedar Grove and Forest Service campgrounds have activities from Memorial Day to Labor Day. Check bulletin boards or visitor centers for schedules.

328

EXHIBITS

Giant Forest Museum

MUSEUM | Well-imagined and interactive displays at this worthwhile stop provide the basics about sequoias, of which there are 2,161 with diameters exceeding 10 feet in the approximately 2,000-acre Giant Forest. ⊠ *Sequoia National Park ⊹ Generals Hwy., 4 miles south of Lodgepole Visitor Center* ☎ *559/565–4436* ⚏ *Free* ⚏ *Shuttle: Giant Forest or Moro Rock–Crescent Meadow.*

PROGRAMS AND SEMINARS

Evening Programs

TOUR—SIGHT | The Sequoia Parks Conservancy presents films, hikes, and evening lectures during the summer and winter. From May through October the popular Wonders of the Night Sky programs celebrate the often stunning views of the heavens experienced at both parks. ⊠ *Sequoia National Park* ☎ *559/565–4251* ⊕ *www.sequoiaparksconservancy.org.*

Free Nature Programs

TOUR—SIGHT | Almost any summer day, ½-hour to 1½-hour ranger talks and walks explore subjects such as the life of the sequoia, the geology of the park, and the habits of bears. Giant Forest, Lodgepole Visitor Center, and Wuksachi Village are frequent starting points. Look for less frequent tours in the winter from Grant Grove. Check bulletin boards throughout the park for the week's offerings. ⊕ *www.sequoiaparksconservancy.org.*

Junior Ranger Program

TOUR—SIGHT | FAMILY | Children over age five can earn a patch upon completion of a fun set of age-appropriate tasks outlined in the Junior Ranger booklet. Pick one up at any visitor center. ☎ *559/565–3341.*

Seminars

TOUR—SIGHT | Expert naturalists lead seminars on a range of topics, including birds, wildflowers, geology, botany, photography, park history, backpacking, and pathfinding. Reservations are required. Information about times and prices is available at the visitor centers or through the Sequoia Parks Conservancy. ⊠ *Sequoia National Park* ☎ *559/565–4251* ⊕ *www.sequoiaparksconservancy.org.*

TOURS

★ Sequoia Parks Conservancy Field Institute

TOUR—SIGHT | The Sequoia Parks Conservancy's highly regarded educational division conducts half-day, single-day, and multiday tours that include backpacking hikes, natural-history walks, cross-country skiing, kayaking excursions, and motor-coach tours. ⊠ *47050 Generals Hwy., Unit 10, Three Rivers* ☎ *559/565–4251* ⊕ *www.sequoiaparksconservancy.org* ⚏ *From $40 for ½-day guided tour.*

Sequoia Sightseeing Tours

TOUR—SIGHT | This locally owned operator's friendly, knowledgeable guides conduct daily interpretive sightseeing tours in Sequoia and Kings Canyon. Reservations are essential. The company also offers private tours. ⊠ *Three Rivers* ☎ *559/561–4189* ⊕ *www.sequoiatours.com* ⚏ *From $79 tour of Sequoia; from $139 tour of Kings Canyon.*

Restaurants

In Sequoia and Kings Canyon national parks, you can treat yourself (and the family) to a high-quality meal in a wonderful setting in the Peaks restaurant at Wuksachi Lodge, but otherwise you should keep your expectations modest. You can grab bread, spreads, drinks, and fresh produce at one of several small grocery stores for a picnic, or get takeout food from the Grant Grove Restaurant, the Cedar Grove snack bar, or one of the two small Lodgepole eateries. Between the parks and just off Generals Highway, the Montecito Sequoia Lodge has a year-round buffet. *Restaurant reviews have been shortened. For full information, visit Fodors.com.*

Hotels

Hotel accommodations in Sequoia and Kings Canyon are limited, and—although they are clean and comfortable—tend to lack much in-room character. Keep in mind, however, that the extra money you spend on lodging here is offset by the time you'll save by being inside the parks. You won't be faced with a 60- to 90-minute commute from the less-expensive motels in Three Rivers (by far the most charming option), Visalia, and Fresno. Reserve as far in advance as you can, especially for summertime stays. *Hotel reviews have been shortened. For full information, visit Fodors.com.*

What It Costs			
$	$$	$$$	$$$$
RESTAURANTS			
under $12	$12–$20	$21–$30	over $30
HOTELS			
under $100	$100–$150	$151–$200	over $200

Visitor Information

NATIONAL PARK SERVICE Sequoia and Kings Canyon National Parks. ⊠ *47050 Generals Hwy. (Rte. 198), Three Rivers* ☎ *559/565–3341* ⊕ *nps.gov/seki.*

SEQUOIA VISITOR CENTERS
Foothills Visitor Center
INFO CENTER | Exhibits here focus on the foothills and resource issues facing the parks. You can pick up books, maps, and a list of ranger-led walks, and get wilderness permits. ⊠ *47050 Generals Hwy., Rte. 198, 1 mile north of Ash Mountain entrance, Sequoia National Park* ☎ *559/565–3341.*

Lodgepole Visitor Center
INFO CENTER | Along with exhibits on the area's history, geology, and wildlife, the center screens an outstanding 22-minute film about bears. You can buy books, maps, and tickets to cave tours here. ⊠ *Sequoia National Park ✛ Generals Hwy. (Rte. 198), 21 miles north of Ash Mountain entrance* ☎ *559/565–3341* ⊗ *Closed Oct.–Apr.* ⌖ *Shuttle: Giant Forest or Wuksachi-Lodgepole-Dorst.*

KINGS CANYON VISITOR CENTERS
Cedar Grove Visitor Center
INFO CENTER | Off the main road and behind the Sentinel Campground, this small ranger station has books and maps, plus information about hikes and other activities. ⊠ *Kings Canyon National Park ✛ Kings Canyon Scenic Byway, 30 miles east of Rte. 180/198 junction* ☎ *559/565–3341* ⊗ *Closed mid-Sept.–mid-May.*

Kings Canyon Park Visitor Center
INFO CENTER | The center's 15-minute film and various exhibits provide an overview of the park's canyon, sequoias, and human history. Books, maps, and weather advice are dispensed here, as are (if available) free wilderness permits. ⊠ *Kings Canyon National Park ✛ Grant Grove Village, Generals Hwy. (Rte. 198), 3 miles northeast of Rte. 180, Big Stump entrance* ☎ *559/565–3341.*

Sequoia National Park

⊙ Sights

SCENIC DRIVES
★ Generals Highway
SCENIC DRIVE | One of California's most scenic drives, this 46-mile road is the main asphalt artery between Sequoia and Kings Canyon national parks. Some portions are also signed as Route 180, others as Route 198. Named after the landmark Grant and Sherman trees that leave so many visitors awestruck,

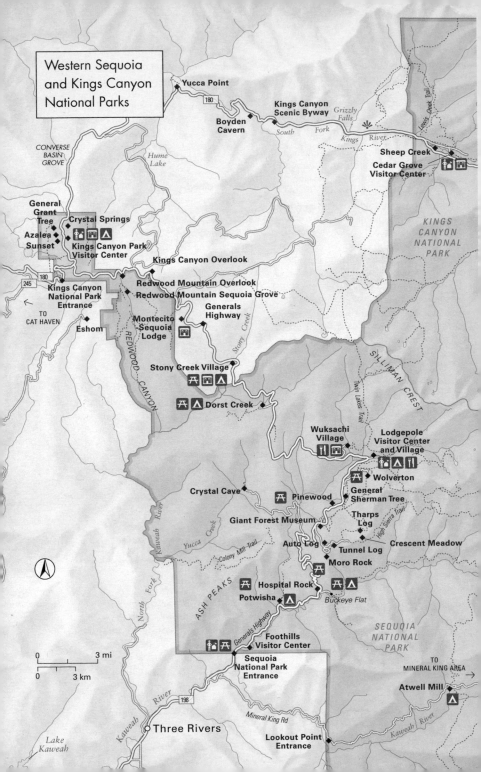

Western Sequoia and Kings Canyon National Parks

Yucca Point

180

Kings Canyon Scenic Byway

Boyden Cavern

Grizzly Falls

South Fork Kings River

Lewis Creek Trail

Sheep Creek

Cedar Grove Visitor Center

CONVERSE BASIN GROVE

Hume Lake

KINGS CANYON NATIONAL PARK

General Grant Tree

Crystal Springs

Azalea

Sunset

Kings Canyon Park Visitor Center

Kings Canyon Overlook

Redwood Mountain Overlook

Redwood Mountain Sequoia Grove

180

245

Kings Canyon National Park Entrance

TO CAT HAVEN

Eshom

REDWOOD CANYON

Montecito Sequoia Lodge

Generals Highway

Stony Creek

SILLIMAN CREST

Stony Creek Village

Dorst Creek

Wuksachi Village

Twin Lakes Trail

Lodgepole Visitor Center and Village

Wolverton

Crystal Cave

Pinewood

General Sherman Tree

Kaweah River

Giant Forest Museum

Tharps Log

High Sierra Trail

Crescent Meadow

Yucca Creek

Colony Mill Trail

Auto Log

Tunnel Log

Moro Rock

ASH PEAKS

Hospital Rock

Potwisha

Buckeye Flat

North Fork Kaweah River

SEQUOIA NATIONAL PARK

Generals Highway

Foothills Visitor Center

Sequoia National Park Entrance

TO MINERAL KING AREA

Atwell Mill

0   3 mi

0   3 km

198

Mineral King Rd

Three Rivers

Lake Kaweah

Kaweah River

Lookout Point Entrance

Generals Highway runs from Sequoia's Foothills Visitor Center north to Kings Canyon's Grant Grove Village. Along the way, it passes the turnoff to Crystal Cave, the Giant Forest Museum, Lodgepole Village, and other popular attractions. The lower portion, from Hospital Rock to the Giant Forest, is especially steep and winding. If your vehicle is 22 feet or longer, avoid that stretch by entering the parks via Route 180 (from Fresno) rather than Route 198 (from Visalia or Three Rivers). Take your time on this road—there's a lot to see, and wildlife can scamper across at any time. ⊠ *Sequoia National Park.*

Mineral King Road

SCENIC DRIVE | Vehicles longer than 22 feet are prohibited on this side road into southern Sequoia National Park, and for good reason: it contains 589 twists and turns. Anticipating an average speed of 20 mph is optimistic. The scenery is splendid as you climb nearly 6,000 feet from Three Rivers to the Mineral King Area. In addition to maneuvering the blind curves and narrow stretches, you might find yourself sharing the pavement with bears, rattlesnakes, and even softball-size spiders. Allow 90 minutes each way. ⊠ *Sequoia National Forest* ✛ *East off Sierra Dr. (Rte. 198), 3.5 miles northeast of Three Rivers* ⊗ *Road typically closed Nov.–late May.*

SCENIC STOPS

Sequoia National Park is all about the trees, and to understand the scale of these giants you must walk among them. If you do nothing else, get out of the car for a short stroll through one of the groves. But there is much more to the park than the trees. Try to access one of the vista points that provide a panoramic view over the forested mountains. Generals Highway (on Routes 198 and 180) will be your route to most of the park's sights. A few short spur roads lead from the highway to some sights, and Mineral King Road branches off

Route 198 to enter the park at Lookout Point, winding east from there to the park's southernmost section.

Auto Log

FOREST | Before its wood showed signs of severe rot, cars drove right on top of this giant fallen sequoia. Now it's a great place to pose for pictures or shoot a video. ⊠ *Sequoia National Park* ✛ *Moro Rock–Crescent Meadow Rd., 1 mile south of Giant Forest.*

Crescent Meadow

TRAIL | A sea of ferns signals your arrival at what John Muir called the "gem of the Sierra." Walk around for an hour or two and you might decide that the Scotland-born naturalist was exaggerating a bit, but the verdant meadow is quite pleasant and you just might see a bear. Wildflowers bloom here throughout the summer. ⊠ *Sequoia National Park* ✛ *End of Moro Rock–Crescent Meadow Rd., 2.6 miles east off Generals Hwy.* ☞ *Shuttle: Moro Rock–Crescent Meadow.*

★ Crystal Cave

CAVE | One of more than 200 caves in Sequoia and Kings Canyon, Crystal Cave is composed largely of marble, the result of limestone being hardened under heat and pressure. It contains several eye-popping formations. There used to be more, but some were damaged or obliterated by early-20th-century dynamite blasting. You can only see the cave on a tour. The Daily Tour ($16), a great overview, takes about 50 minutes. To immerse yourself in the cave experience—at times you'll be crawling on your belly—book the exhilarating Wild Cave Tour ($135). Availability is limited—reserve tickets at least 48 hours in advance at ⊕ *www.recreation.gov* or stop by either the Foothills or Lodgepole visitor center first thing in the morning to try to nab a same-day ticket; they're not sold at the cave itself. ⊠ *Crystal Cave Rd., off Generals Hwy.* ☎ *877/444–6777* ⊕ *www.sequoiaparksconservancy.org/crystalcave.html* ⊠ *$16* ⊗ *Closed Oct.–late May.*

★ General Sherman Tree

LOCAL INTEREST | The 274.9-foot-tall General Sherman is one of the world's tallest and oldest sequoias, and it ranks No. 1 in volume, adding the equivalent of a 60-foot-tall tree every year to its approximately 52,500 cubic feet of mass. The tree doesn't grow taller, though—it's dead at the top. A short, wheelchair-accessible trail leads to the tree from Generals Highway, but the main trail (½ mile) winds down from a parking lot off Wolverton Road. The walk back up the main trail is steep, but benches along the way provide rest for the short of breath. ⊠ *Sequoia National Park* ✛ *Main trail Wolverton Rd. off Generals Hwy. (Rte. 198)* ☞ *Shuttle: Giant Forest or Wolverton–Sherman Tree.*

Mineral King Area

NATURE PRESERVE | A subalpine valley of fir, pine, and sequoia trees, Mineral King sits at 7,500 feet at the end of a steep, winding road. This is the highest point to which you can drive in the park. It is open only from Memorial Day through late October. ⊠ *Sequoia National Park* ✛ *Mineral King Rd., 25 miles east of Generals Hwy. (Rte. 198)* ☉ *Closed late Oct.–May.*

★ Moro Rock

NATURE SITE | This sight offers panoramic views to those fit and determined enough to mount its 350 or so steps. In a case where the journey rivals the destination, Moro's stone stairway is so impressive in its twisty inventiveness that it's on the National Register of Historic Places. The rock's 6,725-foot summit overlooks the Middle Fork Canyon, sculpted by the Kaweah River and approaching the depth of Arizona's Grand Canyon, although smoggy, hazy air often compromises the view. ⊠ *Sequoia National Park* ✛ *Moro Rock–Crescent Meadow Rd., 2 miles east off Generals Hwy. (Rte. 198) to parking area* ☞ *Shuttle: Moro Rock–Crescent Meadow.*

Tunnel Log

LOCAL INTEREST | This 275-foot tree fell in 1937, and soon a 17-foot-wide, 8-foot-high hole was cut through it for vehicular passage (not to mention the irresistible photograph) that continues today. Large vehicles take the nearby bypass. ⊠ *Sequoia National Park* ✛ *Moro Rock–Crescent Meadow Rd., 2 miles east of Generals Hwy. (Rte. 198)* ☞ *Shuttle: Moro Rock–Crescent Meadow.*

🏃 Activities

The best way to see Sequoia is to take a hike. Unless you do so, you'll miss out on the up-close grandeur of mist wafting between deeply scored, red-orange tree trunks bigger than you've ever seen. If it's winter, put on some snowshoes or cross-country skis and plunge into the snow-swaddled woodland. There are not too many other outdoor options: no off-road driving is allowed in the parks, and no special provisions have been made for bicycles. Boating, rafting, and snowmobiling are also prohibited.

BICYCLING

Steep, winding roads and shoulders that are either narrow or nonexistent make bicycling here more of a danger than a pleasure. Outside of campgrounds, you are not allowed to pedal on unpaved roads.

BIRD-WATCHING

More than 200 species of birds inhabit Sequoia and Kings Canyon national parks. Not seen in most parts of the United States, the white-headed woodpecker and the pileated woodpecker are common in most mid-elevation areas here. There are also many hawks and owls, including the renowned spotted owl. Species are diverse in both parks due to the changes in elevation, and range from warblers, kingbirds, thrushes, and sparrows in the foothills to goshawk, blue grouse, red-breasted nuthatch, and brown creeper at the highest elevations. The Sequoia Parks Conservancy (☎ 559/565–4251 ⊕ www.sequoiaparksconservancy.org) has information about bird-watching in the southern Sierra.

CROSS-COUNTRY SKIING

For a one-of-a-kind experience, cut through the groves of mammoth sequoias in Giant Forest. Some of the Crescent Meadow trails are suitable for skiing as well; none of the trails is groomed. You can park at Giant Forest. Note that roads can be precarious in bad weather. Some advanced trails begin at Wolverton.

Alta Market and Ski Shop

SKIING/SNOWBOARDING | Rent cross-country skis and snowshoes here. Depending on snowfall amounts, instruction may also be available. Reservations are recommended. Marked trails cut through Giant Forest, about 5 miles south of Wuksachi Lodge. ⊠ Sequoia National Park ✛ At Lodgepole, off Generals Hwy. (Rte. 198) ☎ 559/565–3301 ⚲ Shuttle: Wuksachi-Lodgepole-Dorst.

FISHING

There's limited trout fishing in the creeks and rivers from late April to mid-November. The Kaweah River is a popular spot; check at visitor centers for open and closed waters. Some of the park's secluded backcountry lakes have good fishing. A California fishing license, required for persons 16 and older, costs about $16 for one day, $24 for two days, and $48 for 10 days (discounts are available for state residents and others). For park regulations, closures, and restrictions, call the parks at ☎ 559/565–3341 or stop at a visitor center. Licenses and fishing tackle are usually available at Hume Lake.

California Department of Fish and Game

FISHING | The department supplies fishing licenses and provides a full listing of regulations. ☎ 916/928–5805 ⊕ www.wildlife.ca.gov.

HIKING

The best way to see the park is to hike it. The grandeur and majesty of the Sierra is best seen up close. Carry a hiking map and plenty of water. Visitor center gift shops sell maps and trail books and pamphlets. Check with rangers for current trail conditions, and be aware of rapidly changing weather. As a rule of thumb, plan on covering about a mile per hour.

★ Big Trees Trail

HIKING/WALKING | This hike is a must, as it does not take long and the setting is spectacular: beautiful Round Meadow surrounded by many mature sequoias, with well-thought-out interpretive signs along the path that explain the ecology on display. The 0.7-mile Big Trees Trail is wheelchair accessible. Parking at the trailhead lot off Generals Highway is for cars with handicap placards only. The round-trip loop from the Giant Forest Museum is about a mile long. Easy. ⊠ Sequoia National Park ✛ Trailhead: off Generals Hwy. (Rte. 198), near the Giant Forest Museum ⚲ Shuttle: Giant Forest.

★ Congress Trail

HIKING/WALKING | This 2-mile trail, arguably the best hike in the parks in terms of natural beauty, is a paved loop that begins near General Sherman Tree. You'll get close-up views of more big trees here than on any other Sequoia hike. Watch for the clusters known as the House and Senate. The President Tree, also on the trail, supplanted the General Grant Tree in 2012 as the world's second largest in volume (behind the General Sherman). An offshoot of the Congress Trail leads to Crescent Meadow, where in summer you can catch a free shuttle back to the Sherman parking lot. Easy. ⊠ Sequoia National Park ✛ Trailhead: off Generals Hwy. (Rte. 198), 2 miles north of Giant Forest ⚲ Shuttle: Giant Forest.

Crescent Meadow Trails

HIKING/WALKING | A 1-mile trail loops around lush Crescent Meadow to Tharp's Log, a cabin built from a fire-hollowed sequoia. From there you can embark on a 60-mile trek to Mt. Whitney, if you're prepared and have the time. Brilliant wildflowers bloom here in midsummer. *Easy.* ⊠ *Sequoia National Park* ✛ *Trailhead: the end of Moro Rock–Crescent Meadow Rd., 2.6 miles east off Generals Hwy. (Rte. 198)* ☞ *Shuttle: Moro Rock–Crescent Meadow.*

Little Baldy Trail

HIKING/WALKING | Climbing 700 vertical feet in 1.75 miles of switchbacking, this trail ends at a granite dome with a great view of the peaks of the Mineral King area and the Great Western Divide. The walk to the summit and back takes about four hours. *Moderate.* ⊠ *Sequoia National Park* ✛ *Trailhead: Little Baldy Saddle, Generals Hwy. (Rte. 198), 9 miles north of General Sherman Tree* ☞ *Shuttle: Lodgepole-Wuksachi-Dorst.*

Marble Falls Trail

HIKING/WALKING | The 3.7-mile trail to Marble Falls crosses through the rugged foothills before reaching the cascading water. Plan on three to four hours one-way. *Moderate.* ⊠ *Sequoia National Park* ✛ *Trailhead: off dirt road across from concrete ditch near site 17 at Potwisha Campground, off Generals Hwy. (Rte. 198).*

Mineral King Trails

HIKING/WALKING | Many trails to the high country begin at Mineral King. Two popular day hikes are Eagle Lake (6.8 miles round-trip) and Timber Gap (4.4 miles round-trip). At the Mineral King Ranger Station (☎ *559/565–3768*) you can pick up maps and check about conditions from late May to late September. *Difficult.* ⊠ *Sequoia National Park* ✛ *Trailheads: at end of Mineral King Rd., 25 miles east of Generals Hwy. (Rte. 198).*

Muir Grove Trail

HIKING/WALKING | You will attain solitude and possibly see a bear or two on this unheralded gem of a hike, a 4-mile round-trip from the Dorst Creek Campground. The remote grove is small but lovely, its sound track provided solely by nature. The trailhead is subtly marked. In summer, park in the amphitheater lot and walk down toward the group campsite area. *Easy.* ⊠ *Sequoia National Park* ✛ *Trailhead: Dorst Creek Campground, Generals Hwy. (Rte. 198), 8 miles north of Lodgepole Visitor Center* ☞ *Shuttle: Lodgepole-Wuksachi-Dorst.*

Tokopah Falls Trail

HIKING/WALKING | This trail with a 500-foot elevation gain follows the Marble Fork of the Kaweah River for 1.75 miles one-way and dead-ends below the impressive granite cliffs and cascading waterfall of Tokopah Canyon. The trail passes through a mixed-conifer forest. It takes 2½ to 4 hours to make the round-trip journey. *Moderate.* ⊠ *Sequoia National Park* ✛ *Trailhead: off Generals Hwy. (Rte. 198), ¼ mile north of Lodgepole Campground* ☞ *Shuttle: Lodgepole-Wuksachi-Dorst.*

HORSEBACK RIDING

Trips take you through forests and flowering meadows and up mountain slopes.

Grant Grove Stables

HORSEBACK RIDING | Grant Grove Stables isn't too far from parts of Sequoia National Park, and is perfect for short rides from June to September. Reservations are recommended. ☎ *559/335–9292 summer* ⊕ *www.nps.gov/seki/planyourvisit/horseride.htm* ☞ *From $40.*

Horse Corral Packers

HORSEBACK RIDING | One- and two-hour trips through Sequoia are available for beginning and advanced riders. ⊠ *Big Meadow Rd., 12 miles east of Generals Hwy. (Rte. 198) between Sequoia and Kings Canyon national parks* ☎ *559/565–3404 summer, 559/565–6429 off-season,* ⊕ *hcpacker.com* ☞ *From $45.*

Did You Know?

Sequoias once grew throughout the North-ern Hemisphere, until they were almost wiped out by glaciers. Some of the fossils in Arizona's Petrified Forest National Park are extinct sequoia species.

SLEDDING AND SNOWSHOEING

The Wolverton area, on Route 198 near Giant Forest, is a popular sledding spot, where sleds, inner tubes, and platters are allowed. You can buy sleds and saucers, with prices starting at $15, at the Alta Market and Ski Shop (☎ 559/565–3301), at the Lodgepole Visitor Center.

You can rent snowshoes for $18–$24 at the Alta Market and Ski Shop, at the Lodgepole Visitor Center. Naturalists lead snowshoe walks around Giant Forest and Wuksachi Lodge, conditions permitting, on Saturday and holidays. Make reservations and check schedules at Giant Forest Museum (☎ 559/565–3341) or Wuksachi Lodge.

SWIMMING

Drowning is the number-one cause of death in both Sequoia and Kings Canyon parks. Though it is sometimes safe to swim in the parks' rivers in the late summer and early fall, it is extremely dangerous to do so in the spring and early summer, when the snowmelt from the high country causes swift currents and icy temperatures. Stand clear of the water when the rivers are running, and stay off wet rocks to avoid falling in. Check with rangers for safety information.

Kings Canyon National Park

 Sights

SCENIC DRIVES

★ Kings Canyon Scenic Byway

SCENIC DRIVE | The 30-mile stretch of Route 180 between Grant Grove Village and Zumwalt Meadow delivers eye-popping scenery—granite cliffs, a roaring river, waterfalls, and Kings River canyon itself—much of which you can experience at vista points or on easy walks. The canyon comes into view about 10 miles east of the village at **Junction View.** Five miles beyond, at **Yucca Point,** the canyon is thousands of feet deeper than the more famous Grand Canyon. **Canyon View,** a special spot 1 mile east of the Cedar Grove Village turnoff, showcases evidence of the area's glacial history. Here, perhaps more than anywhere else, you'll understand why John Muir compared Kings Canyon vistas with those in Yosemite. Driving the byway takes about an hour each way without stops. ✉ *Kings Canyon National Park* ✛ *Rte. 180 north and east of Grant Grove village.*

HISTORIC SITES

Fallen Monarch

TOUR—SIGHT | This toppled sequoia's hollow base was used in the second half of the 19th century as a home for settlers, a saloon, and even to stable U.S. Cavalry horses. As you walk through it (assuming entry is permitted, which is not always possible), notice how little the wood has decayed, and imagine yourself tucked safely inside, sheltered from a storm or protected from the searing heat. ✉ *Kings Canyon National Park* ✛ *Grant Grove Trail, 1 mile north of Kings Canyon Park Visitor Center.*

Gamlin Cabin

BUILDING | Despite being listed on the National Register of Historic Places, this replica of a modest 1872 pioneer cabin is only borderline historical. The structure, which was moved and rebuilt several times over the years, once served as U.S. Cavalry storage space and, in the early 20th century, a ranger station. ✉ *Grant Grove Trail.*

SCENIC STOPS

Kings Canyon National Park consists of two sections that adjoin the northern boundary of Sequoia National Park. The western portion, covered with sequoia and pine forest, contains the park's most visited sights, such as Grant Grove. The vast eastern portion is remote high country, slashed across half its southern

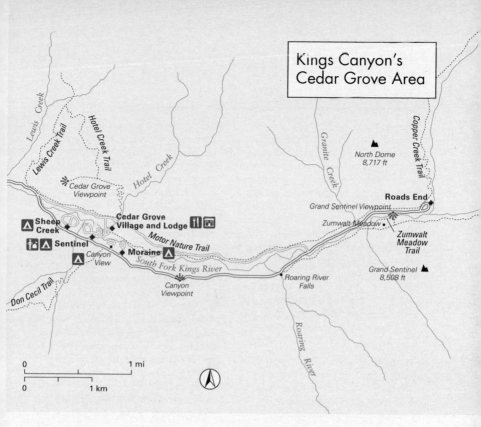

Kings Canyon's Cedar Grove Area

Lewis Creek
Lewis Creek Trail
Hotel Creek Trail
Hotel Creek
Cedar Grove Viewpoint
Granite Creek
Copper Creek Trail
North Dome 8,717 ft
Roads End
Grand Sentinel Viewpoint
Sheep Creek
Cedar Grove Village and Lodge
Zumwalt Meadow
Sentinel
Motor Nature Trail
Zumwalt Meadow Trail
Canyon View
Moraine
South Fork Kings River
Don Cecil Trail
Canyon Viewpoint
Roaring River Falls
Grand Sentinel 8,508 ft
Roaring River

0   1 mi
0   1 km

breadth by the deep, rugged Kings River canyon. Separating the two is Sequoia National Forest, which encompasses Giant Sequoia National Monument. The Kings Canyon Scenic Byway (Route 180) links the major sights within and between the park's two sections.

General Grant Tree

LOCAL INTEREST | President Coolidge proclaimed this to be the "nation's Christmas tree," and 30 years later President Eisenhower designated it as a living shrine to all Americans who have died in wars. Bigger at its base than the General Sherman Tree, it tapers more quickly. It's estimated to be the world's third-largest sequoia by volume. A spur trail winds behind the tree, where scars from a long-ago fire remain visible. ⊠ *Kings Canyon National Park* ✛ *Trailhead: 1 mile north of Grant Grove Visitor Center.*

Redwood Mountain Sequoia Grove

FOREST | One of the world's largest sequoia groves, Redwood contains within its 2,078 acres nearly 2,200 sequoias whose diameters exceed 10 feet. You can view the grove from afar at an overlook or hike 6 to 10 miles down into the richest regions, which include 2 of the world's 25 heaviest trees. ⊠ *Kings Canyon National Park* ✛ *Drive 6 miles south of Grant Grove on Generals Hwy. (Rte. 198), then turn right at Quail Flat; follow it 2 miles to the Redwood Canyon trailhead.*

🏃 Activities

The siren song of beauty, challenge, and relative solitude (by national parks standards) draws hard-core outdoors enthusiasts to the Kings River canyon and the backcountry of the

Plants and Wildlife in Sequoia and Kings Canyon

The parks can be divided into three distinct zones. In the west (1,500–4,500 feet) are the rolling, lower-elevation foothills, covered with shrubby chaparral vegetation or golden grasslands dotted with oaks. Chamise, red-barked manzanita, and the occasional yucca plant grow here. Fields of white popcorn flower cover the hillsides in spring, and the yellow fiddleneck flourishes. In summer, intense heat and absence of rain cause the hills to turn golden brown. Wildlife includes the California ground squirrel, noisy blue-and-gray scrub jay, black bears, coyotes, skunks, and gray fox.

At middle elevation (5,000–9,000 feet), where the giant sequoia belt resides, rock formations mix with meadows and huge stands of evergreens—red and white fir, incense cedar, and ponderosa pines, to name a few. Wildflowers like yellow blazing star and red Indian paintbrush bloom in spring and summer. Mule deer, golden-mantled ground squirrels, Steller's jays, and black bears (most active in fall) inhabit the area, as does the chickaree.

The high alpine section of the parks is extremely rugged, with a string of rocky peaks reaching above 13,000 feet to Mt. Whitney's 14,494 feet. Fierce weather and scarcity of soil make vegetation and wildlife sparse. Foxtail and whitebark pines have gnarled and twisted trunks, the result of high wind, heavy snowfall, and freezing temperatures. In summer you can see yellow-bellied marmots, pikas, weasels, mountain chickadees, and Clark's nutcrackers.

park's eastern section. Backpacking, rock-climbing, and extreme-kayaking opportunities abound, but the park also has day hikes for all ability levels. Winter brings sledding, skiing, and snowshoeing fun. No off-road driving or bicycling is allowed in the park, and snowmobiling is also prohibited.

BICYCLING

Bicycles are allowed only on the paved roads in Kings Canyon. Cyclists should be extremely cautious along the steep highways and narrow shoulders.

CROSS-COUNTRY SKIING

Roads to Grant Grove are accessible even during heavy snowfall, making the trails here a good choice over Sequoia's Giant Forest when harsh weather hits.

FISHING

There is limited trout fishing in the park from late April to mid-November, and catches are minor. Still, Kings River is a popular spot. Some of the park's secluded backcountry lakes have good fishing. Licenses are available, along with fishing tackle, in Grant Grove and Cedar Grove. *See Activities, in Sequoia National Park, above, for more information about licenses.*

HIKING

You can enjoy many of Kings Canyon's sights from your car, but the giant gorge of the Kings River canyon and the sweeping vistas of some of the highest mountains in the United States are best seen on foot. Carry a hiking map—available at any visitor center—and plenty of water. Check with rangers for current trail conditions, and be aware of rapidly changing weather. Except for one trail to Mt. Whitney, permits are not required for day hikes.

Big Baldy

HIKING/WALKING | This hike climbs 600 feet and 2 miles up to the 8,209-foot summit of Big Baldy. Your reward is the view of Redwood Canyon. Round-trip the hike is 4 miles. *Moderate.* ⊠ *Kings Canyon National Park* ✥ *Trailhead: 8 miles south of Grant Grove on Generals Hwy. (Rte. 198).*

Big Stump Trail

HIKING/WALKING | From 1883 until 1890, logging was done here, complete with a mill. The 1-mile loop trail, whose unmarked beginning is a few yards west of the Big Stump entrance, passes by many enormous stumps. *Easy.* ⊠ *Kings Canyon National Park* ✥ *Trailhead: near Big Stump Entrance, Generals Hwy. (Rte. 180).*

Buena Vista Peak

HIKING/WALKING | For a 360-degree view of Redwood Canyon and the High Sierra, make the 2-mile ascent to Buena Vista. *Difficult.* ⊠ *Kings Canyon National Park* ✥ *Trailhead: off Generals Hwy. (Rte. 198), south of Kings Canyon Overlook, 7 miles southeast of Grant Grove.*

★ Grant Grove Trail

HIKING/WALKING | Grant Grove is only 128 acres, but it's a big deal. More than 120 sequoias here have a base diameter that exceeds 10 feet, and the **General Grant Tree** is the world's third-largest sequoia by volume. Nearby, the Confederacy is represented by the **Robert E. Lee Tree,** recognized as the world's 11th-largest sequoia. Also along the easy-to-walk trail are the **Fallen Monarch** and the **Gamlin Cabin,** built by 19th-century pioneers. *Easy.* ⊠ *Kings Canyon National Park* ✥ *Trailhead: off Generals Hwy. (Rte. 180), 1 mile north of Kings Canyon Park Visitor Center.*

Hotel Creek Trail

HIKING/WALKING | For gorgeous canyon views, take this trail from Cedar Grove up a series of switchbacks until it splits. Follow the route left through chaparral to the forested ridge and rocky outcrop known as Cedar Grove Overlook, where you can see the Kings River canyon stretching below. This strenuous 5-mile round-trip hike gains 1,200 feet and takes three to four hours to complete. *Difficult.* ⊠ *Kings Canyon National Park* ✥ *Trailhead: at Cedar Grove Pack Station, 1 mile east of Cedar Grove Village.*

Mist Falls Trail

TRAIL | This sandy trail follows the glaciated South Fork Canyon through forest and chaparral, past several rapids and cascades, to one of the largest waterfalls in the two parks. Nine miles round-trip, the hike is relatively flat, but climbs 600 feet in the last 2 miles. It takes from four to five hours to complete. *Moderate.* ⊠ *Kings Canyon National Park* ✥ *Trailhead: at end of Kings Canyon Scenic Byway, 5½ miles east of Cedar Grove Village.*

Panoramic Point Trail

HIKING/WALKING | You'll get a nice view of whale-shape Hume Lake from the top of this Grant Grove path, which is paved and only 300 feet long. It's fairly steep—strollers might work here, but not wheelchairs. Trailers and RVs are not permitted on the steep and narrow road that leads to the trailhead parking lot. *Moderate.* ⊠ *Kings Canyon National Park* ✥ *Trailhead: at end of Panoramic Point Rd., 2.3 miles from Grant Grove Village.*

Redwood Canyon Trails

HIKING/WALKING | Two main trails lead into Redwood Canyon grove, the world's largest sequoia grove. The 6.5-mile **Hart Tree and Fallen Goliath Loop** passes by a 19th-century logging site, pristine Hart Meadow, and the hollowed-out Tunnel Tree before accessing a side trail to the grove's largest sequoia, the 277.9-foot-tall Hart Tree.

Mount Whitney

At 14,494 feet, Mt. Whitney is the highest point in the contiguous United States and the crown jewel of Sequoia National Park's wild eastern side. The peak looms high above the tiny, high-mountain desert community of Lone Pine, where numerous Hollywood Westerns have been filmed. The high mountain ranges, arid landscape, and scrubby brush of the eastern Sierra are beautiful in their vastness and austerity.

Despite the mountain's scale, you can't see it from the more traveled west side of the park because it is hidden behind the Great Western Divide. The only way to access Mt. Whitney from the main part of the park is to circumnavigate the Sierra Nevada via a 10-hour, nearly 400-mile drive outside the park. No road ascends the peak; the best vantage point from which to catch a glimpse of the mountain is at the end of Whitney Portal Road. The 13 miles of winding road leads from U.S. 395 at Lone Pine to the trailhead for the hiking route to the top of the mountain. Whitney Portal Road is closed in winter.

Mt. Whitney Trail. The most popular route to the summit, the Mt. Whitney Trail can be conquered by very fit and experienced hikers. If there's snow on the mountain, this is a challenge for expert mountaineers only. All overnighters must have a permit, as must day hikers on the trail beyond Lone Pine Lake, about 2½ miles from the trailhead. From May through October, permits are distributed via a lottery run each February by ⊕ recreation.gov. The Eastern Sierra Interagency Visitor Center (☎ 760/876–6200), on Route 136 at U.S. 395 about a mile south of Lone Pine, is a good resource for information about permits and hiking. ⊠ Kings Canyon National Park ☎ 760/873–2483 trail reservations ⊕ www.fs.usda.gov/inyo.

The 6.4-mile **Sugar Bowl Loop** provides views of Redwood Mountain and Big Baldy before winding down into its namesake, a thick grove of mature and young sequoias. Moderate. ⊠ Kings Canyon National Park ⊹ Trailhead: off Quail Flat. Drive 5 miles south of Grant Grove on Generals Hwy. (Rte. 198), turn right at Quail Flat and proceed 1½ miles to trailhead.

Roads End Permit Station

HIKING/WALKING | You can obtain wilderness permits, maps, and information about the backcountry at this station, where bear canisters, a must for campers, can be rented or purchased. When the station is closed (typically October–mid-May), complete a self-service permit form. ⊠ Kings Canyon National Park ⊹ Eastern end of Kings Canyon Scenic Byway, 6 miles east of Cedar Grove Visitor Center.

Roaring River Falls Walk

HIKING/WALKING | Take a shady five-minute walk to this forceful waterfall that rushes through a narrow granite chute. The trail is paved and mostly accessible. Easy. ⊠ Kings Canyon National Park ⊹ Trailhead: 3 miles east of Cedar Grove Village turnoff from Kings Canyon Scenic Byway.

★ Zumwalt Meadow Trail

HIKING/WALKING | Rangers say this is the best (and most popular) day hike in the Cedar Grove area. Just 1.5 miles long, it offers three visual treats: the South Fork of the Kings River, the lush meadow, and the high granite walls above, including those of Grand Sentinel and North Dome. *Easy.* ⊠ *Kings Canyon National Park* ✛ *Trailhead: 4½ miles east of Cedar Grove Village turnoff from Kings Canyon Scenic Byway.*

HORSEBACK RIDING

One-day destinations by horseback out of Cedar Grove include Mist Falls and Upper Bubb's Creek. In the backcountry, many equestrians head for Volcanic Lakes or Granite Basin, ascending trails that reach elevations of 10,000 feet. Costs per person range from $40 for a one-hour guided ride to around $300 per day for fully guided trips for which the packers do all the cooking and camp chores.

Cedar Grove Pack Station

HORSEBACK RIDING | Take a day ride or plan a multiday adventure along the Kings River canyon with Cedar Grove Pack Station. Popular routes include the Rae Lakes Loop and Monarch Divide. Closed early September–late May. ⊠ *Kings Canyon National Park* ✛ *Kings Canyon Scenic Byway, 1 mile east of Cedar Grove Village* ☎ *559/565–3464 summer, 559/337–2413 off-season* ⊕ *www.nps.gov/seki/plan-yourvisit/horseride.htm* ⛵ *From $40 per hr or $100 per day.*

Grant Grove Stables

HORSEBACK RIDING | A one- or two-hour trip through Grant Grove leaving from the stables provides a taste of horseback riding in Kings Canyon. Closed October–early June. ⊠ *Kings Canyon National Park* ✛ *Rte. 180, ½ mile north of Grant Grove Visitor Center* ☎ *559/335–9292* ⊕ *www.nps.gov/seki/planyourvisit/horseride.htm* ⛵ *From $40.*

SLEDDING AND SNOWSHOEING

In winter, Kings Canyon has a few great places to play in the snow. Sleds, inner tubes, and platters are allowed at both the Azalea Campground area on Grant Tree Road, ¼ mile north of Grant Grove Visitor Center, and at the Big Stump picnic area, 2 miles north of the lower Route 180 entrance to the park.

Snowshoeing is good around Grant Grove, where you can take occasional naturalist-guided snowshoe walks from mid-December through mid-March as conditions permit. Grant Grove Market rents sleds and snowshoes.

Nearby Towns

Numerous towns and cities tout themselves as "gateways" to the parks, with some more deserving of the title than others. One that certainly merits the name is frisky **Three Rivers,** a Sierra foothills hamlet (population 2,200) along the Kaweah River. Close to Sequoia's Ash Mountain and Lookout Point entrances, Three Rivers is a good spot to find a room when park lodgings are full. Either because Three Rivers residents appreciate their idyllic setting or because they know that tourists are their bread and butter, you'll find them almost uniformly pleasant and eager to share tips about the best spots for "Sierra surfing" the Kaweah's smooth, moss-covered rocks or where to find the best cell phone reception.

Visalia, a Central Valley city of about 128,000 people, lies 58 miles southwest of Sequoia's Wuksachi Village and 56 miles southwest of the Kings Canyon Park Visitor Center. Its vibrant downtown contains several good restaurants. If you're into Victorian and other old houses, drop by the visitor center and pick up a free map of them. A clear day's view of the Sierra from Main Street is spectacular, and even Sunday night can find the streets bustling with pedestrians. Visalia provides easy access to grand Sequoia National Park and the serene Kaweah Oaks Preserve.

Closest to Kings Canyon's Big Stump entrance, **Fresno,** the main gateway to the southern Sierra region, is about 55 miles west of Kings Canyon and about 85 miles northwest of Wuksachi

Village. This Central Valley city of nearly a half-million people is sprawling and unglamorous, but it has all the cultural and other amenities you'd expect of a major crossroads.

GETTING HERE AND AROUND

Sequoia Shuttle

In summer the Sequoia Shuttle connects Three Rivers to Visalia and Sequoia National Park. ☎ 877/287–4453 ⊕ www.sequoiashuttle.com 🖃 $15 round-trip.

VISITOR INFORMATION

Fresno/Clovis Convention & Visitors Bureau. ✉ 1550 E. Shaw Ave., Suite 101, Fresno ☎ 559/981–5500, 800/788–0836 ⊕ www.playfresno.org. **Sequoia Foothills Chamber of Commerce.** ✉ 42268 Sierra Dr., Three Rivers ☎ 559/561–3300. **Visalia Convention & Visitors Bureau.** ✉ Kiosk, 303 E. Acequia Ave., at S. Bridge St., Visalia ☎ 559/334–0141, 800/524–0303 ⊕ www.visitvisalia.org.

◉ Sights

★ Colonel Allensworth State Historic Park

HISTORIC SITE | It's worth the slight detour off Highway 99 to learn about and pay homage to the dream of Allen Allensworth and other black pioneers who in 1908 founded Allensworth, the only California town settled, governed, and financed by African Americans. At its height, the town prospered as a key railroad transfer point, but after cars and trucks reduced railroad traffic and water was diverted for Central Valley agriculture, the town declined and was eventually deserted. Today the restored and rebuilt schoolhouse, library, and other structures commemorate Allensworth's heyday, as do festivities that take place each October. ✉ 4129 Palmer Ave., off Hwy. 43; from Hwy. 99 at Delano, take Garces Hwy. west to Hwy. 43 north; from Earlimart, take County Rd. J22 west to Hwy. 43 south, Allensworth ☎ 661/849–3433 ⊕ www.parks.ca.gov 🖃 $6 per car.

Exeter Murals

PUBLIC ART | More than two dozen murals in the Central Valley city of Exeter's cute-as-a-button downtown make it worth a quick detour if you're traveling on Route 198. Several of the murals, which depict the area's agricultural and social history, are quite good. All adorn buildings within a few blocks of the intersection of Pine and E streets. If you're hungry, the **Wildflower Cafe,** at 121 South E Street, serves inventive salads and sandwiches. Shortly after entering Exeter head west on Pine Street (it's just before the water tower) to reach downtown. ✉ Exeter ⊕ Rte. 65, 2 miles south of Rte. 198, about 11 miles east of Visalia ⊕ cityofexeter.com/galleries/exeter-murals.

★ Forestiere Underground Gardens

GARDEN | FAMILY | Sicilian immigrant Baldassare Forestiere spent four decades (1906–46) carving out an odd, subterranean realm of rooms, tunnels, grottoes, alcoves, and arched passageways that once extended for more than 10 acres between Highway 99 and busy, mall-pocked Shaw Avenue. Though not an engineer, Forestiere called on his memories of the ancient Roman structures he saw as a youth and on techniques he learned digging subways in New York and Boston. Only a fraction of his prodigious output is on view, but you can tour his underground living quarters, including bedrooms (one with a fireplace), the kitchen, living room, and bath, as well as a fishpond and auto tunnel. Skylights allow exotic full-grown fruit trees to flourish more than 20 feet belowground. ✉ 5021 W. Shaw Ave., 2 blocks east of Hwy. 99, Fresno ☎ 559/271–0734 ⊕ www.undergroundgardens.com 🖃 $17 ⊘ Closed Dec.–Mar.

Kaweah Oaks Preserve

NATURE PRESERVE | Trails at this 344-acre wildlife sanctuary off the main road to Sequoia National Park lead past majestic valley oak, sycamore, cottonwood, and willow trees. Among the 134 bird species you might spot are hawks, hummingbirds, and great blue herons. Bobcats, lizards, coyotes, and cottontails also live here. The Sycamore Trail has digital signage with QR codes you can scan with your smartphone to access plant and animal information. ⊠ *Follow Hwy. 198 for 7 miles east of Visalia, turn north on Rd. 182, and proceed ½ mile to gate on left side, Visalia* ☎ *559/738–0211* ⊕ *www.sequoiariverlands.org* ⊠ *Free.*

Project Survival's Cat Haven

ZOO | Take the rare opportunity to glimpse a Siberian lynx, a clouded leopard, a Bengal tiger, and other endangered wild cats at this conservation facility that shelters more than 30 big cats. A guided hour-long tour along a quarter mile of walkway leads to fenced habitat areas shaded by trees and overlooking the Central Valley. ⊠ *38257 E. Kings Canyon Rd. (Rte. 180), 15 miles west of Kings Canyon National Park, Dunlap* ☎ *559/338–3216* ⊕ *www. cathaven.com* ⊠ *$15.*

Sequoia National Forest and Giant Sequoia National Monument

FOREST | Delicate spring wildflowers, cool summer campgrounds, and varied winter-sports opportunities—not to mention more than half of the world's giant sequoia groves—draw outdoorsy types year-round to this sprawling district surrounding the national parks. Together, the forest and monument cover nearly 1,700 square miles, south from the Kings River and east from the foothills along the San Joaquin Valley. The monument's groves are both north and south of Sequoia National Park. One of the most popular is the **Converse Basin Grove**, home of the Boole Tree, the forest's largest sequoia. The grove is accessible by car on an unpaved road.

The Hume Lake Forest Service District Office, at 35860 Kings Canyon Scenic Byway (Route 180), has information about the groves, along with details about recreational activities. In springtime, diversions include hiking among the wildflowers that brighten the foothills. The floral display rises with the heat as the mountain elevations warm up in summer, when hikers, campers, and picnickers become more plentiful. The abundant trout supply attracts anglers to area waters, including 87-acre **Hume Lake,** which is also ideal for swimming and nonmotorized boating. By fall the turning leaves provide the visual delights, particularly in the Western Divide, Indian Basin, and the Kern Plateau. Winter activities include downhill and cross-country skiing, snowshoeing, and snowmobiling. ⊠ *Sequoia National Park ✚ Northern Entrances: Generals Hwy. (Rte. 198), 7 miles southeast of Grant Grove; Hume Lake Rd. between Generals Hwy. (Rte. 198) and Kings Canyon Scenic Byway (Rte. 180); Kings Canyon Scenic Byway (Rte. 180) between Grant Grove and Cedar Grove. Southern Entrances: Rte. 190 east of Springville; Rte. 178 east of Bakersfield* ☎ *559/784–1500 forest and monument, 559/338–2251 Hume Lake* ⊕ *www. fs.usda.gov/sequoia.*

Activities

BOATING AND RAFTING
Hume Lake

BODY OF WATER | This reservoir, built by loggers in the early 1900s, is now the site of several church-affiliated camps, a gas station, and a public campground. Outside Kings Canyon's borders, Hume Lake offers intimate views of the mountains. Summer lodge room rentals start at $160. ⊠ *Hume Lake Rd., off Kings Canyon Hwy., 8 miles northeast of Grant Grove, 64144 Hume Lake Rd., Hume* ☎ *559/305–7770* ⊕ *www.humelake.org, visitsequoia.com.*

Kaweah White Water Adventures

BOATING | Kaweah's trips include a two-hour excursion (good for families) through Class III rapids, a longer paddle through Class IV rapids, and an extended trip (typically Class IV and V rapids). ✉ *40443 Sierra Dr., Three Rivers* ☎ *559/740–8251* 🌐 *www.kaweah-whitewater.com* 🎫 *From $50 per person.*

Kings River Expeditions
TOUR—SPORTS | This outfit arranges one- and two-day white-water rafting trips on the Kings River. The office is in Clovis, but all trips depart from Twin Pines Camp, 60 miles east of Fresno. ✉ *Twin Pines Camp, Clovis* ☎ *559/233–4881, 800/846–3674* 🌐 *www.kingsriver.com* 🎫 *From $145.*

HORSEBACK RIDING

Wood 'n' Horse Training Stables
HORSEBACK RIDING | For hourly horseback rides, riding lessons, or trail rides in the foothills, contact this outfit. From $45 for lessons; from $65 for trail rides. ✉ *42846 N. Fork Dr., Three Rivers* ☎ *559/561–4268* 🌐 *www.wdnhorse.com.*

🎫 Performing Arts

Fresno Philharmonic Orchestra
CONCERTS | The orchestra performs classical concerts from September through June. ✉ *Saroyan Theatre, 730 M St., near Inyo St., Fresno* ☎ *559/261–0600* 🌐 *fresnophil.org.*

Roger Rocka's Dinner Theater
THEATER | This Tower District venue stages Broadway-style musicals. ✉ *1226 N. Wishon Ave., at E. Olive Ave., Fresno* ☎ *559/266–9494* 🌐 *www.rogerrockas.com.*

🛍 Shopping

Cedar Grove Gift Shop and Market
GIFTS/SOUVENIRS | This place is small, but it's stocked with the essentials for RV and auto travelers. ✉ *Cedar Grove Village, Kings Canyon National Park* ☎ *559/565–3096* ⏲ *Closed late Oct.–mid-May.*

Grant Grove Gift Shop
GIFTS/SOUVENIRS | This shop sells park-related gifts and souvenirs. ✉ *Grant Grove Village, Kings Canyon National Park* ☎ *559/335–5500.*

Lodgepole Market Center
GIFTS/SOUVENIRS | You'll find gifts, toys, books, souvenirs, and outdoor equipment in Sequoia National Park's largest store. Its grocery department has a fairly wide selection of items, some of them organic, including grab-and-go items for hikes and picnics. Across the hall is a café with various dishes for breakfast, lunch, and dinner. ✉ *63204 Lodgepole Rd., next to Lodgepole Visitor Center, Sequoia National Park* ☎ *559/565–3301* 🌐 *www.visitsequoia.com.*

Wuksachi Gift Shop
GIFTS/SOUVENIRS | Souvenir clothing, Native American crafts, postcards, and snacks are for sale at this tasteful shop off the Wuksachi Lodge lobby. ✉ *Wuksachi Village* ☎ *559/625–7700.*

🍴 Restaurants

IN THE PARKS

SEQUOIA

Lodgepole Market and Grill
$$ | **CAFÉ** | The choices here run the gamut from simple to very simple, with several counters only a few strides apart in a central eating complex. The café also sells fresh and prepackaged salads, sandwiches, and wraps. **Known for:** quick and convenient dining; many healthful options; grab-and-go items for picnics. [$] *Average main: $12* ✉ *Next to Lodgepole Visitor Center, Sequoia National Park* ☎ *559/565–3301.*

The Peaks
$$$ | **MODERN AMERICAN** | Huge windows run the length of the Wuksachi Lodge's high-ceilinged dining room, and a large fireplace on the far wall warms both body and soul. The diverse dinner menu—by far the best at both parks—reflects a commitment to

locally sourced and sustainable products. **Known for:** seasonal menus with fresh local ingredients; great views of sequoia grove; box lunches. [$] *Average main: $28* ✉ *Wuksachi Lodge, 64740 Wuksachi Way, Wuksachi Village* ☎ *559/625–7700* 🌐 *www.visitsequoia.com/dine/the-peaks-restaurant.*

PICNIC AREAS

Take care to dispose of your food scraps properly (the bears might not appreciate this short-term, but the practice helps ensure their long-term survival).

Crescent Meadow

RESTAURANT—SIGHT | A mile or so past Moro Rock, this comparatively remote picnic area has meadow views and is close to a lovely hiking trail. Tables are under the giant sequoias, off the parking area. There are restrooms and drinking water. Fires are not allowed. ✉ *Sequoia National Park* ✥ *End of Moro Rock–Crescent Rd., 2.6 miles east off Generals Hwy. (Rte. 198).*

Foothills Picnic Area

RESTAURANT—SIGHT | Near the parking lot at the southern entrance of the park, this area has tables, drinking water, and restrooms. ✉ *Sequoia National Park* ✥ *Across Generals Hwy. from Foothills Visitor Center.*

Hospital Rock

RESTAURANT—SIGHT | Native Americans once ground acorns into meal at this site; outdoor exhibits tell the story. The picnic area's name, however, stems from a hunter/trapper who was treated for a leg wound here in 1873. Look up, and you'll see Moro Rock. Grills, drinking water, and restrooms are available. ✉ *Sequoia National Park* ✥ *Generals Hwy. (Rte. 198), 6 miles north of Ash Mountain entrance.*

Pinewood Picnic Area

RESTAURANT—SIGHT | Picnic in Giant Forest, in the vicinity of sequoias if not actually under them. Drinking water, restrooms, grills, and wheelchair-accessible spots are provided in this expansive setting near Sequoia National Park's most popular attractions. ✉ *Sequoia National Park* ✥ *Generals Hwy. (Rte. 198), 2 miles north of Giant Forest Museum, halfway between Giant Forest Museum and General Sherman Tree.*

Wolverton Meadow

RESTAURANT—SIGHT | At a major trailhead to the backcountry, this is a great place to stop for lunch before a hike. The area sits in a mixed-conifer forest adjacent to parking. Drinking water, grills, and restrooms are available. ✉ *Sequoia National Park* ✥ *Wolverton Rd., 1½ miles northeast off Generals Hwy. (Rte. 198).*

KINGS CANYON

Cedar Grove Snack Bar

$$ | **AMERICAN** | The menu here is surprisingly extensive, with dinner entrées such as pasta, pork chops, trout, and steak. For breakfast, try the egg burrito, French toast, or pancakes; sandwiches, wraps, burgers (including vegetarian patties) and hot dogs dominate the lunch and dinner choices. **Known for:** scenic river views; extensive options; alfresco dining on balcony overlooking the Kings River. [$] *Average main: $16* ✉ *Cedar Grove Village, Kings Canyon National Park* ☎ *559/565–3096* 🌐 *www.visitsequoia.com/dine/cedar-grove-snack-bar* ⏲ *Closed Oct.–May.*

Grant Grove Restaurant

$$ | **AMERICAN** | Gaze at giant sequoias and a verdant meadow while dining in this eco-friendly restaurant's spacious dining room with fireplace, or outdoors on the expansive deck. The menu centers around locally sourced natural and organic ingredients and offers standard American fare. **Known for:** takeout service year-round; walk-up window for pizza, sandwiches, coffee, ice cream; picnic tables on outdoor deck. [$] *Average main: $16* ✉ *Grant Grove Village, Kings Canyon National Park* ☎ *559/335–5500.*

PICNIC AREAS

Big Stump

RESTAURANT—SIGHT | Some trees still stand at this site at the edge of a logged sequoia grove. Near the park's entrance, the area is paved and next to the road. It's the only picnic area in either park that is plowed in the wintertime. Restrooms (portable toilets), grills, and drinking water are available, and the area is entirely accessible. ✉ *Kings Canyon National Park* ✣ *Generals Hwy. (Rte. 180), just inside Big Stump entrance.*

Grizzly Falls

RESTAURANT—SIGHT | This little gem is worth a pull-over, if not a picnic at the roadside tables. A less-than-a-minute trek from the parking lot delivers you to the base of the delightful, 100-foot-plus falls. On a hot day, nothing feels better than dipping your feet in the cool water. An outhouse is on-site, but grills are not, and water is not available. ✉ *Kings Canyon National Park* ✣ *Off Rte. 180, 2½ miles west of Cedar Grove entrance.*

OUTSIDE THE PARKS

Antoinette's Coffee and Goodies

$ | **CAFÉ** | For smoothies, well-crafted espresso drinks, breakfast bowls, and pumpkin chocolate-chip muffins and other homemade baked goods, stop for a spell at this convivial coffee shop. Antoinette's is known as the town's hub for vegan and gluten-free items. **Known for:** plentiful vegan and gluten-free items; Wi-Fi on-site; all organic, locally roasted coffee. [$] *Average main: $7* ✉ *41727 Sierra Dr., Three Rivers* ☎ *559/561–2253* 🌐 *www.antoinettescoffeeandgoodies.com* 🕘 *Closed Tues. No dinner.*

Buckaroo Diner

$$ | **AMERICAN** | Set on a bluff overlooking the Kaweah River, the boho-chic Buckaroo serves fresh, house-made dishes made with seasonal organic ingredients. The restaurant's main dining room occupies a building that housed the original restaurant ('Ol Buckaroo) for decades; you can also sit in the cozy sun room or outdoor terrace overlooking the river. **Known for:** weekend beer garden; smoked foods; daily specials. [$] *Average main: $18* ✉ *41695 Sierra Dr., Three Rivers* ☎ *559/465–5088* 🌐 *theolbuckaroo.com* 🕘 *Closed Tues. and Wed. No lunch weekdays.*

Café 225

$$$ | **MODERN AMERICAN** | High ceilings and contemporary decor contribute to the relaxed and sophisticated atmosphere at this popular downtown restaurant. Meats and fish grilled on a wood-fired rotisserie figure prominently on the menu, which also includes pastas and unusual treats such as artichoke fritters and goat cheese and roast lamb pizza. **Known for:** wood-fired rotisserie menu items; fresh local ingredients; sophisticated vibe. [$] *Average main: $22* ✉ *225 W. Main St., Visalia* ☎ *559/733–2967* 🌐 *www.cafe225.com* 🕘 *Closed Sun.*

Gateway Restaurant and Lodge

$$$ | **AMERICAN** | The view's the draw at this roadhouse that overlooks the Kaweah River as it plunges out of the high country. The Gateway serves everything from osso buco and steaks to shrimp in Thai chili sauce; dinner reservations are essential on summer weekends. **Known for:** scenic riverside setting; fine dining in otherwise casual town; popular bar. [$] *Average main: $30* ✉ *45978 Sierra Dr., Three Rivers* ☎ *559/561–4133* 🌐 *www.gateway-sequoia.com.*

School House Restaurant & Tavern

$$$ | **MODERN AMERICAN** | A Wine Country–style establishment that sources ingredients from the on-site gardens and surrounding farms and orchards, this popular restaurant occupies a redbrick 1921 schoolhouse in the town of Sanger. Chef Ryan Jackson, who grew up on local fruit farms, creates seasonal menus from the bounty of familiar backyards, mostly filled with classic American dishes with a contemporary twist. **Known for:** fresh ingredients from neighboring farms and orchards; historic country setting; convenient stop between Kings Canyon and Fresno. $ *Average main: $29* ✉ *1018 S. Frankwood Ave., at Hwy. 180 (King's Canyon Rd.), 20 miles east of Fresno, Sanger* ☎ *559/787–3271* ⊕ *schoolhousesanger. com* ⊗ *Closed Mon. and Tues.*

Sierra Subs and Salads

$ | AMERICAN | This well-run sandwich joint satisfies carnivores and vegetarians alike with crispy-fresh ingredients prepared with panache. Depending on your preference, the centerpiece of the Bull's Eye sandwich, for instance, will be roast beef or a portobello mushroom, but whichever you choose, the accompanying flavors—of ciabatta bread, horseradish-and-garlic mayonnaise, roasted red peppers, Havarti cheese, and spinach—will delight your palate. **Known for:** many vegetarian, vegan, and gluten-free options; weekly specials; Wi-Fi. $ *Average main: $9* ✉ *41717 Sierra Dr., Three Rivers* ☎ *559/561–4810* ⊕ *www.sierrasubsandsalads.com* ⊗ *Closed Mon. No dinner.*

★ **The Vintage Press**

$$$$ | EUROPEAN | Built in 1966, this is one of the best restaurants in the Central Valley. The California–Continental cuisine includes dishes such as crispy veal sweetbreads with a port-wine sauce and filet mignon with a cognac-mustard sauce. **Known for:** wine list with more than 900 selections; chocolate Grand Marnier cake and other homemade desserts; sophisticated vibe. $ *Average main: $32* ✉ *216 N. Willis St., Visalia* ☎ *559/733–3033* ⊕ *www.thevintage-press.com.*

 Hotels

IN THE PARKS
SEQUOIA
Silver City Mountain Resort

$$$ | RESORT | High on Mineral King Road, this privately owned resort has rustic

cabins and deluxe chalets—all with a stove, refrigerator, and sink—plus three hotel rooms with private baths. **Pros:** rustic setting; friendly staff; great location for hikers. **Cons:** long, winding road is not for everybody; not much entertainment except hiking; some units have shared baths. $ *Rooms from: $165* ✉ *Sequoia National Park* ✛ *Mineral King Rd., 21 miles southeast of Rte. 198* ☎ *559/561–3223* ⊕ *www.silvercityresort.com* ⊗ *Closed Nov.–late May* ⚲ *13 cabins, 3 hotel rooms* ⑩ *No meals.*

★ **Wuksachi Lodge**

$$$$ | HOTEL | The striking cedar-and-stone main building is a fine example of how a structure can blend effectively with lovely mountain scenery. **Pros:** best place to stay in the parks; lots of wildlife; easy access to hiking and snowshoe/ski trails. **Cons:** rooms can be small; main lodge is a few-minutes' walk from guest rooms; slow Wi-Fi. $ *Rooms from: $229* ✉ *64740 Wuksachi Way, Wuksachi Village* ☎ *559/625–7700, 888/252–5757 reservations* ⊕ *www.visitsequoia.com/lodging/wuksachi-lodge* ⚲ *102 rooms* ⑩ *No meals.*

KINGS CANYON
Cedar Grove Lodge

$$ | HOTEL | Backpackers like to stay here on the eve of long treks into the High Sierra wilderness, so bedtimes tend to be early. **Pros:** a definite step up from camping in terms of comfort; great base camp for outdoor adventures; on-site snack bar. **Cons:** impersonal; not everybody agrees it's clean enough; remote location. $ *Rooms from: $147* ✉ *Kings Canyon Scenic Byway, Kings Canyon National Park* ☎ *866/807–3598* ⊕ *www.visitsequoia com/lodging/cedar-grove-lodge* ⊗ *Closed mid-Oct.–mid-May* ⚲ *21 rooms* ⑩ *No meals.*

Grant Grove Cabins

$$ | HOTEL | Some of the wood-panel cabins here have heaters, electric lights, and private baths, but most have wood-stoves, battery lamps, and shared baths.

Pros: warm, woodsy feel; clean; walk to Grant Grove Restaurant. **Cons:** can be difficult to walk up to if you're not in decent physical shape; costly for what you get; only basic amenities. $ *Rooms from: $135* ✉ *Kings Canyon Scenic Byway in Grant Grove Village, Kings Canyon National Park* ☎ *866/807–3598* ⊕ *www.visitsequoia.com/Grant-Grove-Cabins.aspx* ⇘ *33 cabins, 9 with bath; 17 tent cabins* ❢◯❢ *No meals.*

John Muir Lodge

$$$$ | HOTEL | In a wooded area in the hills above Grant Grove Village, this modern, timber-sided lodge has rooms and suites with queen- or king-size beds and private baths. **Pros:** open year-round; common room stays warm; quiet. **Cons:** check-in is down in the village; spotty Wi-Fi; remote location. $ *Rooms from: $210* ✉ *Kings Canyon Scenic Byway, ¼ mile north of Grant Grove Village, 86728 Hwy. 180, Kings Canyon National Park* ☎ *866/807–3598* ⊕ *www.visitsequoia. com/john-muir-lodge.aspx* ⇘ *36 rooms* ❢◯❢ *No meals.*

OUTSIDE THE PARKS

The only lodging immediately outside the parks is in Three Rivers. Options include inns, chain and mom-and-pop motels, and riverside cabins. Numerous chain properties operate in Visalia or Fresno (your favorite is likely represented in one or both cities), about an hour from the south and north entrances, respectively.

Montecito-Sequoia Lodge

$$$$ | HOTEL | FAMILY | Outdoor activities are what this year-round family resort is all about, including many that are geared toward teenagers and small children. **Pros:** friendly staff; great for kids; lots of fresh air and planned activities. **Cons:** can be noisy with all the activity; no TVs or phones in rooms; not within national park. $ *Rooms from: $229* ✉ *63410 Generals Hwy., 11 miles south of Grant Grove, Sequoia National Forest* ☎ *559/565–3388, 800/227–9900* ⊕ *www.mslodge.com* ⊘ *Closed 1st 2 wks of Dec.* ⇘ *52 rooms* ❢◯❢ *All meals.*

★ Rio Sierra Riverhouse

$$$ | B&B/INN | Guests at Rio Sierra come for the river views, the sandy beach, and the proximity to Sequoia National Park (6 miles away), but invariably end up raving equally about the warm, laid-back hospitality of proprietress Mars Roberts. **Pros:** seductive beach; add-on breakfast option; river views from all rooms; contemporary ambience. **Cons:** books up quickly in summer; some road noise audible in rooms; long walk or drive to restaurants. $ *Rooms from: $200* ✉ *41997 Sierra Dr., Hwy. 198, Three Rivers* ☎ *559/561–4720* ⊕ *www.rio-sierra. com* ⇘ *5 rooms* ❢◯❢ *No meals* ⌇ *2-night min stay on summer weekends. Closed Jan.–mid-Feb.*

Chapter 11

THE CENTRAL COAST

11

Updated by
Cheryl Crabtree

⊙ Sights	🍴 Restaurants	🛏 Hotels	💼 Shopping	🍸 Nightlife
★★★★★	★★★★☆	★★★★★	★☆☆☆☆	★☆☆☆☆

WELCOME TO
THE CENTRAL COAST

TOP REASONS TO GO

★ **Incredible nature:**
The wild and wonderful
Central Coast is home to
Channel Islands National
Park, two national marine
sanctuaries, state parks
and beaches, and the
rugged Los Padres
National Forest.

★ **Edible bounty:** Land
and sea provide enough
fresh regional foods to
satisfy the most sophis-
ticated foodies. Get
your fill at countless
farmers' markets, winer-
ies, and restaurants.

★ **Outdoor activities:**
Kick back and revel in
the California lifestyle.
Surf, golf, kayak, hike,
play tennis—or just
hang out and enjoy the
gorgeous scenery.

★ **Small-town charm, big-
city culture:** With all the
amazing cultural opportunities—museums, theater,
music, and festivals—you
might start thinking you're
in L.A. or San Francisco.

★ **Wine tasting:** Central
Coast wines earn high
critical praise. Sample
them in urban tasting
rooms, dusty crossroads
towns, and at high- and
low-tech rural wineries.

1 Ventura.

2 Channel Islands
National Park.

3 Ojai.

4 Santa Barbara.

5 Santa Ynez.

6 Los Olivos.

7 Solvang.

8 Buellton.

9 Lompoc.

10 Pismo Beach.

11 Avila Beach.

12 San Luis Obispo.

13 Morro Bay.

14 Paso Robles.

15 Cambria.

16 San Simeon.

17 Southern Big Sur.

18 Central Big Sur.

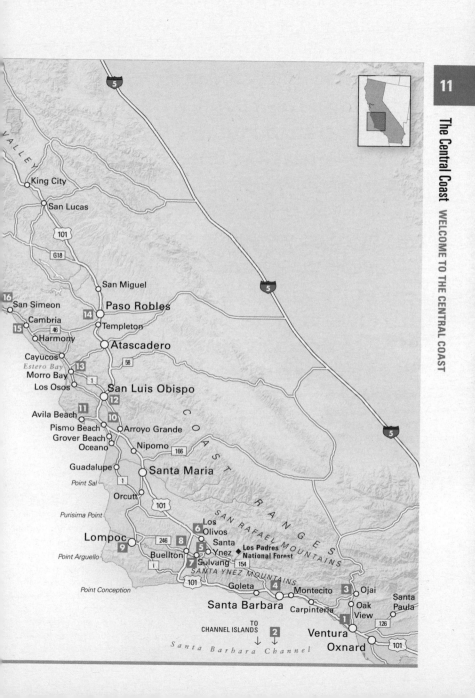

King City
San Lucas
101
G18
San Miguel
Paso Robles 14
Templeton
Atascadero
16 San Simeon
Cambria
15 46
Harmony
Cayucos
Estero Bay 13
Morro Bay 1
Los Osos
San Luis Obispo 12
Avila Beach 11
Pismo Beach 10
Grover Beach
Oceano
Nipomo 166
Guadalupe
Point Sal 1
Santa Maria
Orcutt
101
Purisima Point
Los 6
Olivos
Lompoc 246 8 Santa 5
9 Ynez
Buellton 7 Los Padres
Point Arguello 1 Solvang 154 National Forest
SANTA YNEZ MOUNTAINS
101
Goleta 4
Point Conception Montecito 3 Ojai
Santa Barbara Carpinteria Santa
Oak Paula
View
1
TO 126
CHANNEL ISLANDS 2 Ventura
Santa Barbara Channel Oxnard 101

5
5
5
58
COAST RANGES
SAN RAFAEL MOUNTAINS
VALLEY

Balmy weather, glorious beaches, crystal-clear air, and serene landscapes have lured people to the Central Coast since prehistoric times. Today it's also known for its farm-fresh bounty, from grapes vintners crafted into world-class wines, to strawberries and other produce incorporated by chefs into distinctive cuisine. The scenic variety along the Pacific coast is equally impressive—you'll see everything from dramatic cliffs and grass-tufted bluffs to wildlife estuaries and miles of dunes. It's an ideal place to relax, slow down, and appreciate the abundant natural beauty.

Offshore, a pristine national park and a vast marine sanctuary protect the wild, wonderful underwater resources of this incredible corner of the planet. But not all of the Central Coast's top attractions are natural: Ventura, Santa Barbara, and San Luis Obispo are filled with sparkling examples of Spanish-Mediterranean architecture, bustling shopping districts, and first-rate restaurants showcasing regional foods and wines.

Planning

When to Go

The Central Coast climate is mild year-round. If you like to swim in warmer (if still nippy) ocean waters, July and August are the best months to visit. Be aware that this is also high season. Fog often rolls in along the coastal areas in early summer; you'll need a jacket, especially after sunset, close to the shore. It usually rains from December through March. From April to early June and early fall the weather is almost as fine as in high season, and the pace is less hectic.

Getting Here and Around

AIR TRAVEL

Alaska Air, American, Contour, Delta, Frontier, and United fly to Santa Barbara Airport (SBA), 9 miles from downtown. United, Alaska, and American provide service to San Luis Obispo County Regional Airport (SBP), 3 miles from downtown San Luis Obispo.

Santa Barbara Airbus shuttles travelers between Santa Barbara and Los Angeles for $55 one-way and $100 round-trip. The Santa Barbara Metropolitan Transit District Bus 11 ($1.75) runs every 30 minutes from the airport to the downtown transit center. A taxi between the airport and the hotel districts costs between $22 and $40.

AIRPORT CONTACTS San Luis Obispo County Regional Airport. ⊠ *901 Airport Dr., off Hwy. 227, San Luis Obispo* ☎ *805/781–5205* ⊕ *sloairport.com.* **Santa Barbara Airbus.** ☎ *805/964–7759, 800/423–1618* ⊕ *www.sbairbus.com.* **Santa Barbara Airport.** ⊠ *500 Fowler Rd., off U.S. 101 Exit 104B, Santa Barbara* ☎ *805/683–4011* ⊕ *flysba.com.* **Santa Barbara Metropolitan Transit District.** ☎ *805/963–3366* ⊕ *sbmtd.gov.*

BUS TRAVEL

Greyhound provides service from Los Angeles and San Francisco to San Luis Obispo, Ventura, and Santa Barbara. Local transit companies serve these three cities and several smaller towns. Buses can be useful for visiting some urban sights, particularly in Santa Barbara; they're less so for rural ones.

BUS CONTACTS Greyhound. ☎ *800/231–2222* ⊕ *www.greyhound.com.*

CAR TRAVEL

Driving is the easiest way to experience the Central Coast. U.S. 101 and Highway 1, which run north–south, are the main routes to and through the Central Coast from Los Angeles and San Francisco. Highly scenic Highway 1 hugs the coast, and U.S. 101 runs inland. Between Ventura County and northern Santa Barbara County, the two highways are the same road. Highway 1 again separates from U.S. 101 north of Gaviota, then rejoins the highway at Pismo Beach. Along any stretch where these two highways are separate, U.S. 101 is the quicker route.

The most dramatic section of the Central Coast is the 70 miles between San Simeon and Big Sur. The road is narrow and twisting, with a single lane in each direction. In fog or rain the drive can be downright nerve-racking; in wet seasons mudslides can close portions of the road.

Other routes into the Central Coast include Highway 46 and Highway 33, which head, respectively, west and south from Interstate 5 near Bakersfield.

ROAD CONDITIONS Caltrans. ☎ *800/427–7623, 888/836–0866 Hwy. 1 visitor hotline (Cambria north to Carmel)* ⊕ *www.dot.ca.gov.*

TRAIN TRAVEL

The Amtrak *Coast Starlight*, which runs between Los Angeles and Seattle via Oakland, stops in Paso Robles, San Luis Obispo, Santa Barbara, and Oxnard. Amtrak runs several *Pacific Surfliner* trains and buses daily between San Luis Obispo, Santa Barbara, Los Angeles, and San Diego. Metrolink Regional Rail Service trains connect Ventura and Oxnard with Los Angeles and points between.

TRAIN CONTACTS Amtrak. ☎ *800/872–7245* ⊕ *www.amtrak.com.* **Metrolink.** ☎ *800/371–5465* ⊕ *metrolinktrains.com.*

Restaurants

The cuisine in Ventura and Santa Barbara is every bit as eclectic as it is in California's bigger cities; fresh seafood is a standout. A foodie renaissance has overtaken the entire region from Ventura to Paso Robles, spawning dozens of restaurants touting locavore cuisine made with fresh organic produce and meats. Dining attire on the Central Coast is generally casual, though slightly dressy casual wear is the custom at pricier restaurants. *Restaurant reviews have been shortened. For full information, visit Fodors.com.*

Hotels

Expect to pay top dollar for rooms along the shore, especially in summer. Moderately priced hotels and motels do exist—most just a short drive inland from their higher-price counterparts. Make your reservations as early as possible, and take advantage of midweek specials to get the best rates. It's common for lodgings to require two-day minimum stays on holidays and some weekends, especially in summer, and to double rates during festivals and other events. *Hotel reviews have been shortened. For full information, visit Fodors.com.*

WHAT IT COSTS

	$	$$	$$$	$$$$
RESTAURANTS				
	under $16	$16–$22	$23–$30	over $30
HOTELS				
	under $120	$120–$175	$176–$250	over $250

Tours

Many tour companies will pick you up at your hotel or central locations; ask about this when booking.

Central Coast Food Tours

SPECIAL-INTEREST | Food and wine destinations are the focus of this outfit's walking tours of shops, restaurants, wineries, and other spots in San Luis Obispo, Paso Robles, and elsewhere. Some tours combine wine tasting with an ocean sail or a zip-line adventure. ☎ 844/337–1686 ⊕ *centralcoastfoodtours.com* ✉ *From $78.*

Cloud Climbers Jeep and Wine Tours

SPECIAL-INTEREST | This outfit conducts trips in open-air, six-passenger jeeps to the Santa Barbara/Santa Ynez mountains and Wine Country. Tour options include wine tasting, mountain, sunset, and a discovery adventure for families. The company also offers a four-hour All Around Ojai Tour and arranges horseback riding and trap-shooting tours. ☎ 805/646–3200 ⊕ *ccjeeps.com* ✉ *From $89.*

Grapeline Wine Tours

SPECIAL-INTEREST | Wine and vineyard picnic tours in Paso Robles and the Santa Ynez Valley are Grapeline's specialty. ☎ 951/693–5755 ⊕ *gogrape.com* ✉ *From $129.*

Santa Barbara Wine Country Cycling Tours

BICYCLE TOURS | The company leads half- and full-day tours of the Santa Ynez wine region, conducts hiking and cycling tours, and rents out bicycles. ☎ 888/557–8687, 805/686–9490 ⊕ *winecountrycycling.com* ✉ *From $110.*

Stagecoach Co. Wine Tours

SPECIAL-INTEREST | Locally owned and operated, Stagecoach runs daily wine-tasting excursions through the Santa Ynez Valley in vans, minicoaches, and SUVs. ✉ Solvang ☎ 805/686–8347 ⊕ *winetourssantaynez.com* ✉ *From $171.*

Sustainable Vine Wine Tours

SPECIAL-INTEREST | This green-minded company specializes in eco-friendly Santa Ynez Valley wine tours in luxury vans and Tesla SUVs. Trips include tastings at limited-production wineries committed to sustainable practices. An organic picnic lunch is served. ☎ 805/698–3911 ⊕ *sustainablevine.com* ✉ *$150.*

TOAST Tours

SPECIAL-INTEREST | Owned and operated by a sommelier couple with extensive guiding experience in Europe, Napa and Sonoma before relocating to Paso Robles, TOAST leads small-group tours to Central Coast wineries tasting rooms, and Hearst Castle. They also offer three-day tours from either Los Angeles or San Francisco to Central Coast wineries and Hearst Castle, and private tours, charters, and transportation. ☎ 805/400–3141 ⊕ www.toasttours.com ✉ From $119.

Wine Edventures

SPECIAL-INTEREST | This learning-oriented company conducts Santa Ynez Valley wine and craft beer tours in vans, minicoaches, and other vehicles. ⊠ Santa Barbara ☎ 805/965–9463 ⊕ welovewines. com ✉ From $135.

Visitor Information

CONTACTS Central Coast Tourism Council. ⊕ centralcoast-tourism.com.

Ventura

60 miles north of Los Angeles.

Like Los Angeles, the city of Ventura enjoys gorgeous weather and sun-kissed beaches—but without the smog and congestion. The miles of beautiful beaches attract athletes—body-surfers and boogie boarders, runners and bikers—and those who'd rather doze beneath an umbrella all day. Ventura Harbor is home to myriad fishing boats, restaurants, and water-activity centers where you can rent boats and take harbor cruises. Foodies can get their fix all over Ventura—dozens of upscale cafés and wine and tapas bars have opened in recent years. Arts and antiques buffs have long trekked downtown to browse the galleries and shops here. One of the greatest perks of Ventura is its walkability. If you drive here, park your car in one of the free 24-hour parking lots sprinkled around the city and hoof it on foot, or board a free trolley that cruises from downtown along the waterfront (Thursday–Sunday noon–9 pm).

GETTING HERE AND AROUND

Amtrak and Metrolink trains serve the area from Los Angeles. Greyhound buses stop in Ventura; Gold Coast Transit serves the city and the rest of Ventura County.

U.S. 101 is the north–south main route into town, but for a scenic drive, take Highway 1 north from Santa Monica. The highway merges with U.S. 101 just south of Ventura. ■TIP→ Traveling north to Ventura from Los Angeles on weekdays, it's best to depart before 6 am, between 10 and 2, or after 7 pm, or you'll get caught in the extended rush-hour traffic. Coming south from Santa Barbara, depart before 1 or after 6 pm. On weekends, traffic is generally fine except southbound on U.S. 101 between Santa Barbara and Ventura on Sunday late afternoon and early evening.

ESSENTIALS

BUS CONTACT Gold Coast Transit. ☎ 805/487–4222 ⊕ www.goldcoasttransit.org.

VISITOR INFORMATION Ventura Visitors and Convention Bureau. ⊠ Downtown Visitor Center, 101 S. California St. ☎ 805/648–2075 ⊕ visitventuraca.com.

⊙ Sights

Albinger Archaeological Museum

MUSEUM | More than three millennia of human history in the Ventura region is charted in the archaeological exhibits at the small Albinger Archaeological Museum. Some of the relics on display date back to 1600 BC. ⊠ 113 E. Main St. ☎ 805/658–4728 ⊕ www.cityofventura.ca.gov/639/Albinger-Archaeological-Museum ✉ Free ⊙ Closed early Sept.–mid-June. Closed weekdays.

Lake Casitas Recreation Area

AMUSEMENT PARK/WATER PARK | FAMILY |
Lunker largemouth bass, rainbow trout, crappie, redears, and channel catfish live in the waters at this park, one of the country's best bass-fishing areas. Nestled below the Santa Ynez Mountains' Laguna Ridge, Lake Casitas is also a beautiful spot for pitching a tent or having a picnic. The Casitas Water Adventure, which has two water playgrounds and a lazy river for tubing and floating, provides kids with endless diversions in summer. ⊠ *11311 Santa Ana Rd., off Hwy. 33, 13 miles northwest of Ventura* ☎ *805/649–2233, 805/649–1122 campground and water park reservations* ⊕ *www.lakecasitas.info* ⌛ *From $10 per vehicle, $13 per boat; Water Adventure $12 ($6, 5–7 pm).*

Mission San Buenaventura

HISTORIC SITE | The ninth of the 21 California missions, Mission San Buenaventura was established in 1782 and the current church was rebuilt and rededicated in 1809. A self-guided tour takes you through a small museum, a quiet courtyard, and a chapel with 250-year-old paintings. ⊠ *211 E. Main St., at Figueroa St.* ☎ *805/648–4496 gift shop* ⊕ *www. sanbuenaventuramission.org* ⌛ *$5.*

Museum of Ventura County

MUSEUM | Exhibits in a contemporary complex of galleries and a sunny courtyard plaza tell the story of Ventura County from prehistoric times to the present. A highlight is the gallery that contains Ojai artist George Stuart's historical figures, dressed in exceptionally detailed, custom-made clothing reflecting their particular eras. In the courtyard, eight panels made with 45,000 pieces of cut glass form a history time line. ⊠ *100 E. Main St., at S. Ventura Ave.* ☎ *805/653–0323* ⊕ *www. venturamuseum.org* ⌛ *$5, free 1st Sun. of month* ☾ *Closed Mon.*

★ Ventura Oceanfront

PROMENADE | Four miles of gorgeous coastline stretch from the county fairgrounds at the northern border of the city of San Buenaventura, through San Buenaventura State Beach, down to Ventura Harbor in the south. The main attraction here is the San Buenaventura City Pier, a landmark built in 1872 and restored in 1993. Surfers rip the waves just north of the pier, and sunbathers relax on white-sand beaches on either side. The mile-long promenade and the Omer Rains Bike Trail north of the pier attract scores of joggers, surrey cyclers, and bikers throughout the year. ⊠ *California St., at ocean's edge.*

🍴 Restaurants

Brophy Bros.

$$$ | SEAFOOD | The Ventura outpost of the wildly popular Santa Barbara restaurant provides the same fresh seafood-oriented meals in a spacious second-story setting overlooking the harbor. Feast on everything from fish-and-chips and crab cakes to chowder and delectable fish— often straight from the boats moored below. **Known for:** lively atmosphere; harbor views; killer clam bar. ⌛ *Average main: $26* ⊠ *1559 Spinnaker Dr., in Ventura Harbor Village* ☎ *805/639–0865* ⊕ *brophybros.com.*

★ Café Zack

$$$ | AMERICAN | A local favorite for anniversaries and other celebrations, Zack's serves classic European dishes in an intimate, two-room 1930s cottage adorned with local art. Entrées of note include seafood specials (depending on the local catch), slow-roasted boar shank and filet mignon, the latter typically crusted in peppercorns or topped with porcini mushrooms. **Known for:** personal service; house-made desserts; excellent California wines. ⌛ *Average main: $30* ⊠ *1095 E. Thompson Blvd., at S. Ann St.* ☎ *805/643–9445* ⊕ *cafezack.com* ☾ *Closed Sun. No lunch Sat.*

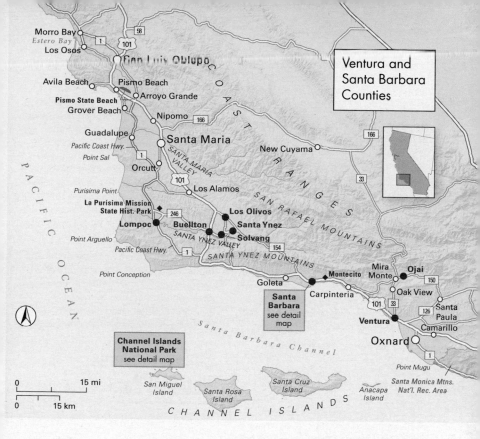

Lure Fish House

$$$ | SEAFOOD | Fresh, sustainably caught seafood charbroiled over a mesquite grill, a well-stocked oyster bar, specialty cocktails, and a wine list heavy on local vintages lure diners into this slick, nautical-theme space downtown. The menu centers on the mostly local catch and organic vegetables, and includes tacos, sandwiches, and salads. **Known for:** shrimp-and-chips; cioppino; citrus crab-cake salad. $ *Average main: $24* ⊠ *60 S. California St.* ☎ *805/567–4400* ⊕ *lurefishhouse.com.*

Rumfish y Vino

$$$ | CARIBBEAN | The sibling of a popular namesake restaurant in Placencia, Belize, Rumfish y Vino serves up zesty Caribbean fare with a California Wine Country twist in a courtyard venue just off Main Street near the mission. Dine in the beach-chic dining room or in the heated patio with a roaring fireplace, where live music plays several nights a week. The seafood-heavy menu changes depending on the local catch. **Known for:** delectable fish tacos and flatbreads; happy hour and creative cocktails; Caribbean fish stew. $ *Average main: $26* ⊠ *434 N. Palm St.* ☎ *805/667–9288* ⊕ *www.rumfishyvinoventura.com.*

🛏 Hotels

Crowne Plaza Ventura Beach

$$$ | HOTEL | A 12-story hotel with an enviable location on the beach and next to a historic pier, the Crowne Plaza is within walking distance of downtown restaurants and nightlife. **Pros:** on the beach; near downtown; steps from waterfront. **Cons:** early-morning train noise; waterfront crowded in summer; self parking is in an adjacent public lot. $ *Rooms from: $200* ⊠ *450 E. Harbor Blvd.* ☎ *800/842–0800, 805/648–2100* ⊕ *cpventura.com* ↩ *235 rooms* ❍❙ *No meals.*

Four Points by Sheraton Ventura Harbor Resort

$$$ | RESORT | An on-site restaurant, spacious rooms, and a slew of amenities make this 17-acre property—which includes sister hotel Holiday Inn Express—a popular and practical choice for Channel Islands visitors. **Pros:** close to island transportation; quiet location; short drive to historic downtown. **Cons:** not in the heart of downtown; noisy seagulls sometimes congregate nearby; service can be spotty. $ *Rooms from: $199* ⊠ *1050 Schooner Dr.* ☎ *805/658–1212, 800/368–7764* ⊕ *fourpoints.com/ventura* ↩ *106 rooms* ❍❙ *No meals.*

Holiday Inn Express Ventura Harbor

$$$ | HOTEL | A favorite among Channel Islands visitors, this quiet, comfortable, lodge-inspired property sits right at the Ventura Harbor entrance. **Pros:** quiet at night; easy access to harbor restaurants and activities; five-minute drive to downtown. **Cons:** busy area on weekends; complaints of erratic service; fee for parking. $ *Rooms from: $189* ⊠ *1080 Navigator Dr.* ☎ *805/856–9533, 888/233–9450* ⊕ *hiexpress.com* ↩ *69 rooms* ❍❙ *Breakfast.*

Ventura Beach Marriott

$$$ | HOTEL | Spacious, contemporary rooms, a peaceful location just steps from San Buenaventura State Beach, and easy access to downtown arts and culture make the Marriott a popular choice. **Pros:** walk to beach and biking/jogging trails; a block from historic pier; great value for location. **Cons:** close to highway; near busy intersection; special event noise some evenings. $ *Rooms from: $239* ⊠ *2055 E. Harbor Blvd.* ☎ *805/643–6000, 888/236–2427* ⊕ *marriottventurabeach.com* ↩ *285 rooms* ❍❙ *No meals.*

🏃 Activities

The most popular outdoor activities in Ventura are beach-going and whale-watching. California gray whales migrate offshore through the Santa Barbara Channel from late December through March; giant blue and humpback whales feed here from mid-June through September. The channel teems with marine life year-round, so tours, which depart from Ventura Harbor, include more than just whale sightings.

Island Packers Cruises

TOUR—SPORTS | A cruise through the Santa Barbara Channel with Island Packers will give you the chance to spot dolphins, seals, and sometimes even whales. ⊠ *Ventura Harbor, 1691 Spinnaker Dr.* ☎ *805/642–1393* ⊕ *islandpackers.com.*

Channel Islands National Park

11 miles southwest of Ventura Harbor via boat.

On crystal-clear days the craggy peaks of the Channel Islands are easy to see from the mainland, jutting from the Pacific in such sharp detail it seems you could reach out and touch them. The islands are not too far away—a high-speed boat will whisk you to the closest ones in less than an hour—yet very few people ever visit them. Those who do venture out to the islands will experience one of the most splendid land-and-sea wilderness areas on the planet. Camping is your only lodging choice on the islands, but it's a fantastic way to experience the natural beauty and isolation of the park. Campsites are primitive, with no water (except on Santa Rosa and Santa Cruz) or electricity. Campsites are $15 per night; you must arrange your transportation before you reserve your site (☎ *877/444–6777*) or online (⊕ *www.recreation.gov*) up to five months in advance.

Channel Islands National Park includes five of the eight Channel Islands and the one nautical mile of ocean that surrounds them. Six nautical miles of surrounding channel waters are designated a National Marine Sanctuary, and are teeming with life, including giant kelp forests, 345 fish species, dolphins, whales, seals, sea lions, and seabirds. To maintain the integrity of their habitats, pets are not allowed in the park.

GETTING HERE AND AROUND

Most visitors access the Channel Islands via an Island Packers boat from Ventura Harbor. To reach the harbor by car, exit U.S. 101 in Ventura at Seaward Boulevard or Victoria Avenue and follow the signs to Ventura Harbor/Spinnaker Drive. An Island Packers boat heads to Anacapa Island from Oxnard's Channel Islands Harbor, which you can reach from Ventura Harbor by following Harbor Boulevard south about 6 miles and continuing south on Victoria Avenue. Private vehicles are not permitted on the islands.

BOAT TOURS

Island Packers

Sailing on high-speed catamarans from Ventura or a mono-hull vessel from Oxnard, Island Packers goes to Santa Cruz Island daily most of the year, weather permitting. The boats also go to Anacapa several days a week, and to the outer islands from April through November. They also cruise along Anacapa's north shore on three-hour wildlife tours (no disembarking) several times a week. ⊠ *3550 Harbor Blvd., Oxnard* ☎ *805/642–1393* ⊕ *islandpackers.com* ⊠ *$38.*

 Sights

Anacapa Island

ISLAND | Most people think of Anacapa as an island, but it's actually comprised of three narrow islets. Although the tips of these volcanic formations nearly touch, the islets are inaccessible from one another except by boat. All three

have towering cliffs, isolated sea caves, and natural bridges; Arch Rock, on East Anacapa, is one of the best-known symbols of Channel Islands National Park.

Wildlife viewing is the main activity on East Anacapa, particularly in summer when seagull chicks are newly hatched and sea lions and seals lounge on the beaches. Exhibits at East Anacapa's compact **museum** include the original lead-crystal Fresnel lens from the 1932 lighthouse.

On West Anacapa, depending on the season and the number of desirable species lurking about here, boats travel to **Frenchy's Cove.** On a voyage here you might see anemones, limpets, barnacles, mussel beds, and colorful marine algae in the pristine tide pools. The rest of West Anacapa is closed to protect nesting brown pelicans. ⊠ *Channel Islands National Park.*

Channel Islands National Park Visitor Center

INFO CENTER | The park's Robert J. Lagomarsino Visitor Center has a museum, a bookstore, and a three-story observation tower with telescopes. The museum's exhibits and a 24-minute film, *Treasure in the Sea,* provide an engaging overview of the islands. In the marine life exhibit, sea stars cling to rocks, and a brilliant orange Garibaldi darts around. Also on display are full-size reproductions of a male northern elephant seal and the pygmy mammoth skeleton unearthed on Santa Rosa Island in 1994.

On weekends and holidays at 11 am and 3 pm, rangers lead various free public programs describing park resources, and from Wednesday through Saturday in summer the center screens live ranger broadcasts of hikes and dives on Anacapa Island. Webcam images of bald eagles and other land and sea creatures are shown at the center and on the park's website. ⊠ *1901 Spinnaker Dr., Ventura* ☎ *805/658–5730* ⊕ *www.nps.gov/chis.*

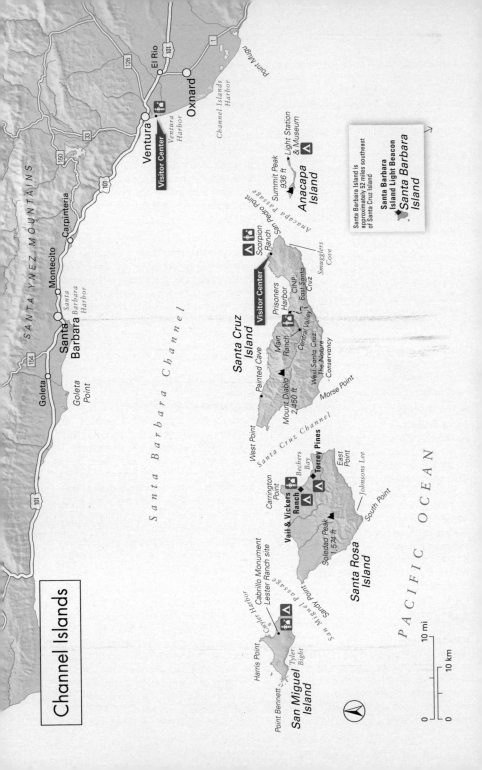

Channel Islands

SANTA YNEZ MOUNTAINS

El Rio
Oxnard
Ventura
Visitor Center
Ventura Harbor
Point Mugu
Channel Islands Harbor

Carpinteria
Montecito
Santa Barbara
Santa Barbara Harbor
Goleta
Goleta Point

Santa Barbara Channel

Santa Barbara Island is approximately 52 miles southeast of Santa Cruz Island

Santa Barbara Island Light Beacon
Santa Barbara Island

Light Station & Museum
Summit Peak 936 ft
Anacapa Island
Anacapa Passage

San Pedro Point
Scorpion Ranch
Visitor Center
Prisoners Harbor
Main Ranch
Painted Cave
West Point
CINP, East Santa Cruz
Central Valley
West Santa Cruz: The Nature Conservancy
Morse Point
Smugglers Cove
Mount Diablo 2,450 ft
Santa Cruz Island

Santa Cruz Channel

Carrington Point
Bechers Bay
Torrey Pines
Vail & Vickers Ranch
East Point
Johnsons Lee
South Point
Soledad Peak 1,574 ft
Santa Rosa Island

Harris Point
Cuyler Harbor
Cabrillo Monument Lester Ranch site
Point Bennett
Tyler Bight
Sandy Point
San Miguel Passage
San Miguel Island

PACIFIC OCEAN

Santa Barbara Channel

10 mi
0
10 km
0

San Miguel Island

ISLAND | The westernmost of the Channel Islands, San Miguel Island is frequently battered by storms sweeping across the North Pacific. The 15-square-mile island's wild windswept landscape is lush with vegetation. Point Bennett, at the western tip, offers one of the world's most spectacular wildlife displays when more than 30,000 pinnipeds hit its beach. Explorer Juan Rodríguez Cabrillo was the first European to visit this island; he claimed it for Spain in 1542. Legend holds that Cabrillo died on one of the Channel Islands—no one knows where he's buried, but there's a memorial to him on a bluff above Cuyler Harbor. ⊠ *Channel Islands National Park.*

Santa Barbara Island

ISLAND | At about 1 square mile, Santa Barbara Island is the smallest of the Channel Islands and nearly 35 miles south of the others. Triangular in shape, Santa Barbara's steep cliffs—which offer a perfect nesting spot for the Scripps's murrelet, a rare seabird—are topped by twin peaks. In spring you can enjoy a brilliant display of yellow coreopsis. Learn about the wildlife on and around the islands at the island's small museum. ⊠ *Channel Islands National Park.*

★ Santa Cruz Island

ISLAND | Five miles west of Anacapa, 96-square-mile Santa Cruz Island is the largest of the Channel Islands. The National Park Service manages the easternmost 24% of the island; the rest is owned by the Nature Conservancy, which requires a permit to land. When your boat drops you off on a portion of the 70 miles of craggy coastline, you see two rugged mountain ranges with peaks soaring to 2,500 feet and deep canyons traversed by streams. This landscape is the habitat of a remarkable variety of flora and fauna—more than 600 types of plants, 140 kinds of land birds, 11 mammal species, five varieties of reptiles, and three amphibian species live here. Bird-watchers may want to look for the endemic island scrub jay, which is found nowhere else in the world.

One of the largest and deepest sea caves in the world, **Painted Cave** lies along the northwest coast of Santa Cruz. Named for the colorful lichen and algae that cover its walls, Painted Cave is nearly ¼ mile long and 100 feet wide. In spring a waterfall cascades over the entrance. Kayakers may encounter seals or sea lions cruising alongside their boats inside the cave. The Channel Islands hold some of the richest archaeological resources in North America; all artifacts are protected within the park. Remnants of a dozen Chumash villages can be seen on the island. The largest of these villages, at the eastern end, occupied the area now called **Scorpion Ranch.** The Chumash mined extensive chert deposits on the island for tools to produce shell-bead money, which they traded with people on the mainland. You can learn about Chumash history and view artifacts, tools, and exhibits on native plant and wildlife at the interpretive visitor center near the landing dock. Visitors can also explore remnants of the early-1900s ranching era in the restored historic adobe and outbuildings. ⊠ *Channel Islands National Park.*

Santa Rosa Island

ISLAND | Between Santa Cruz and San Miguel, Santa Rosa is the second largest of the Channel Islands. The terrain along the coast varies from broad, sandy beaches to sheer cliffs—a central mountain range, rising to 1,589 feet, breaks the island's relatively low profile. Santa Rosa is home to about 500 species of plants, including the rare Torrey pine, and three unusual mammals, the island fox, the spotted skunk, and the deer mouse. They hardly compare, though, to their predecessors: a nearly complete skeleton of a 6-foot-tall pygmy mammoth was unearthed in 1994.

From 1901 to 1998, cattle were raised at the island's **Vail & Vickers Ranch.** The route from Santa Rosa's landing dock to the campground passes by the historic ranch buildings, barns, equipment, and the wooden pier where cattle were brought onto the island. ⊠ *Channel Islands National Park.*

🏃 Activities

Channel Islands Adventure Company (owned and operated by Santa Barbara Adventure Company) arranges paddling, kayaking, and other Channel Islands excursions out of Ventura, and various concessionaires at Ventura Harbor Village (☎ *805/477–0470* ⊕ *www.venturaharborvillage.com*) arrange diving, kayaking, and other rentals and tours. Island Packers conducts whale-watching cruises.

DIVING

Some of the best snorkeling and diving in the world can be found in the cool waters surrounding the Channel Islands. In the relatively warm water around Anacapa and eastern Santa Cruz, photographers can get great shots of rarely seen giant black bass swimming among the kelp forests. Here you also find a reef covered with red brittle starfish. If you're an experienced diver, you might swim among five species of seals and sea lions, or try your hand at spearing rockfish or halibut near San Miguel and Santa Rosa. The best time to scuba dive is in summer and fall, when the water is often clear up to a 100-foot depth.

KAYAKING

The most remote parts of the Channel Islands are accessible only by a sea kayak. Some of the best kayaking in the park can be found on Anacapa, Santa Barbara, and the eastern tip of Santa Cruz. It's too far to kayak from the mainland out to the islands, but outfitters have tours that take you to the islands. Tours are offered year-round, but high seas may cause trip cancellations between December and March. ⚠ **Channel waters can be unpredictable and challenging. Guided trips are highly recommended.**

WHALE-WATCHING

About a third of the world's cetacean species (27 to be exact) can be seen in the Santa Barbara Channel. In July and August, humpback and blue whales feed off the north shore of Santa Rosa. From late December through March, up to 10,000 gray whales pass through the Santa Barbara Channel on their way from Alaska to Mexico and back again; if you go on a whale-watching trip during this time frame you're likely to spot one or more of them. Other types of whales, but fewer in number, swim the channel from June through August.

Ojai

15 miles north of Ventura.

The Ojai Valley, which director Frank Capra used as a backdrop for his 1936 film *Lost Horizon,* sizzles in the summer when temperatures routinely reach 90°F. The acres of orange and avocado groves here evoke postcard images of long-ago agricultural Southern California. Many artists and celebrities have sought refuge from life in the fast lane in lush Ojai.

GETTING HERE AND AROUND

From northern Ventura, Highway 33 veers east from U.S. 101 and climbs inland to Ojai. From Santa Barbara, exit U.S. 101 at Highway 150 in Carpinteria, then travel east 20 miles on a twisting, two-lane road that is not recommended at night or during poor weather. You can also access Ojai by heading west from Interstate 5 on Highway 126. Exit at Santa Paula and follow Highway 150 north for 16 miles to Ojai. Gold Coast Transit provides service to Ojai from Ventura.

Ojai can be easily explored on foot; you can also hop on the Ojai Trolley ($1.50, or $2 day pass), which until about 5 pm follows two routes around Ojai and neighboring Miramonte on weekdays and one route on weekends. Tell the driver you're visiting and you'll get an informal guided tour.

ESSENTIALS

BUS CONTACTS Gold Coast Transit. ☎ *805/487–4222* 🌐 *goldcoasttransit.org.* **Ojai Trolley.** ☎ *805/646–5581* 🌐 *ojaitrolley.com.*

VISITOR INFORMATION Ojai Visitors Bureau. 🌐 *ojaivisitors.com.*

👁 Sights

Ojai Art Center
ARTS VENUE | California's oldest nonprofit, multipurpose arts center exhibits visual art from various disciplines and presents theater, dance, and other performances. ✉ *113 S. Montgomery St., near E. Ojai Ave.* ☎ *805/646–0117* 🌐 *www.ojaiart-center.org* 🕒 *Closed Mon.*

Ojai Avenue
NEIGHBORHOOD | The work of local artists is displayed in the Spanish-style shopping arcade along the avenue downtown. On Sunday between 9 and 1, organic and specialty growers sell their produce at the outdoor market behind the arcade.

Ojai Valley Museum
MUSEUM | **FAMILY** | The museum collects, preserves, and presents exhibits about the art, history, and culture of Ojai and Ojai Valley. Walking tours of Ojai depart from here. ✉ *130 W. Ojai Ave.* ☎ *805/640–1390* 🌐 *ojaivalleymuseum.org* 🎟 *Museum $5, walking tours from $7* 🕒 *Closed Mon.*

Ojai Valley Trail
TRAIL | The 18-mile trail is open to pedestrians, joggers, equestrians, bikers, and others on nonmotorized vehicles. You can access it anywhere along its route. ✉ *Parallel to Hwy. 33 from Soule Park in Ojai to ocean in Ventura* ☎ *888/652–4669* 🌐 *ojaivisitors.com.*

🍴 Restaurants

Azu
$$$ | **MEDITERRANEAN** | Slick furnishings, piped-in jazz, craft cocktails, and local beers and wines draw diners to this artsy Mediterranean bistro known for tapas made from organic ingredients. You can also order soups, salads, and bistro fare such as steak frites and paella. **Known for:** many vegan and gluten-free options; amazing homemade gelato; more than 30 wines by the glass. [$] *Average main: $25* ✉ *457 E. Ojai Ave.* ☎ *805/640–7987* 🌐 *azuojai.com.*

Boccali's
$ | **ITALIAN** | Edging a ranch, citrus groves, and a seasonal garden that provides produce for menu items, the modest but cheery Boccali's attracts many loyal fans. When it's warm, you can dine alfresco in the oak-shaded patio and lawn area and sometimes listen to live music. **Known for:** family-run operation; hand-rolled pizzas and home-style pastas; seasonal strawberry shortcake. [$] *Average main: $15* ✉ *3277 Ojai Ave., about 2 miles east of downtown* ☎ *805/646–6116* 🌐 *boccalis.com* 🕒 *No lunch Mon. and Tues.*

Farmer and the Cook
$ | **AMERICAN** | An organic farmer and his chef-wife run this funky café/bakery/market in Meiners Oaks, just a few miles west of downtown Ojai. Fill up at the soup and salad bar, order a wood-fired pizza, bento box, sandwich, or a daily special, then grab a table indoors or out on the patio. **Known for:** many veggie, vegan, and gluten-free options; grab-and-go meals; Mexican-focused menu. [$] *Average main: $14* ✉ *339 W. El Roblar* ☎ *805/640–9608* 🌐 *www.farmer-andcook.com.*

★ **Nocciola**
$$$ | **ITALIAN** | Authentic northern Italian dishes with a California twist, a cozy fireplace dining room in a century-old Craftsman-style house, and a covered

patio amid the oaks draw locals and visitors alike to this popular eatery, owned by an Italian chef and his American wife (the family lives upstairs). The menu changes seasonally, but regular stars include seared sea scallops with Parmesan fondue and truffle shavings, homemade pastas made with organic egg yolks, and *pappardelle* with slow-roasted wild boar. **Known for:** great wild fish and game; Moment Pink signature cocktail; five-course tasting menu. $ *Average main: $30* ⊠ *314 El Paseo Rd.* ☎ *805/640–1648* ⊕ *nocciolaojai.com* ⊘ *No lunch.*

Hotels

The Iguana Inns of Ojai

$$ | B&B/INN | Artists own and operate these two bohemian-chic inns: The Blue Iguana, a cozy Southwestern-style hotel about 2 miles west of downtown, and the Emerald Iguana, which has art nouveau rooms, suites, and cottages in a secluded residential setting near downtown Ojai. **Pros:** colorful art everywhere; secluded; pet-friendly (Blue Iguana). **Cons:** 2 miles from downtown; on a highway; no pets or children under 14 at Emerald Iguana. $ *Rooms from: $159* ⊠ *11794 N. Ventura Ave.* ☎ *805/646–5277* ⊕ *iguanainnsofojai.com* ⋤ *12 rooms, 8 cottages* ⦿ *Breakfast.*

Ojai Rancho Inn

$$ | HOTEL | A collection of one-story buildings and cottages tucked between Ojai Avenue and the bike trail, this ranch-style motel attracts hipsters and those who appreciate a rustic getaway with modern comforts and a laid-back vintage vibe. **Pros:** free loaner cruiser bikes; small on-site bar; nice pool area with lounge chairs. **Cons:** not fancy or luxurious; rooms could use soundproofing; some road noise in rooms close to the road. $ *Rooms from: $159* ⊠ *615 W. Ojai Ave.* ☎ *805/646–1434* ⊕ *ojairanchoinn.com* ⋤ *17 rooms* ⦿ *No meals.*

★ Ojai Valley Inn & Spa

$$$$ | RESORT | This outdoorsy, golf-oriented resort and spa is set on beautifully landscaped grounds, with hillside views in nearly all directions. **Pros:** Spanish-colonial architecture; exceptional outdoor activities; seven on-site restaurants serving regional cuisine. **Cons:** expensive; areas near restaurants can be noisy. $ *Rooms from: $349* ⊠ *905 Country Club Rd.* ☎ *805/646–1111, 855/697–8780* ⊕ *ojairesort.com* ⋤ *303 rooms* ⦿ *No meals.*

Su Nido Inn

$$$ | B&B/INN | A short walk from downtown Ojai sights and restaurants, this posh Mission Revival–style inn sits in a quiet neighborhood a few blocks from Libbey Park. **Pros:** walking distance from downtown; homey feel; soaking tubs and private patios or balconies in some rooms. **Cons:** no pool; can get hot during summer; too quiet for some. $ *Rooms from: $199* ⊠ *301 N. Montgomery St.* ☎ *805/646–7080, 866/646–7080* ⊕ *www.sunidoinn.com* ⋤ *12 rooms* ⦿ *No meals* ⌇ *2-night minimum stay on weekends.*

Santa Barbara

27 miles northwest of Ventura and 29 miles west of Ojai.

Santa Barbara has long been an oasis for Los Angelenos seeking respite from big-city life. The attractions begin at the ocean and end in the foothills of the Santa Ynez Mountains. A few miles up the coast east and west—but still very much a part of Santa Barbara—are the exclusive residential districts of Montecito and Hope Ranch. Santa Barbara is on a jog in the coastline, so the ocean is actually to the south, instead of the west. "Up" the coast toward San Francisco is west, "down" toward Los Angeles is east, and the mountains are north.

GETTING HERE AND AROUND

U.S. 101 is the main route into Santa Barbara. If you're staying in town, a car is handy but not essential; the beaches and downtown are easily explored by bicycle or on foot. Visit the Santa Barbara Car Free website for bike-route and walking-tour maps, suggestions for car-free vacations, and transportation discounts.

Santa Barbara Metropolitan Transit District's Line 22 bus serves major tourist sights. Several bus lines connect with the very convenient electric shuttles that cruise the downtown and waterfront every 10 to 15 minutes (50¢ each way, $1 day pass).

Santa Barbara Trolley Co. operates a motorized San Francisco–style cable car that loops past major hotels, shopping areas, and attractions from 10 am to 4 pm. Get off whenever you like, and pick up another trolley (they come every hour) when you're ready to move on. The fare is $25 for the day.

TOURS

Land and Sea Tours

SPECIAL-INTEREST | This outfit conducts 90-minute narrated tours in an amphibious 49-passenger vehicle nicknamed the Land Shark. The adventure begins with a drive through the city, followed by a plunge into the harbor for a cruise along the coast. ⊠ 10 E. Cabrillo Blvd., at Stearns Wharf ☎ 805/683–7600 ⊕ out-2seesb.com ⌨ From $30.

Segway Tours of Santa Barbara

SPECIAL-INTEREST | After a brief training session, a guide leads you around town on electric-powered personal balancing transporters. Tour options include the waterfront (1¼ hours), Butterfly Beach and Montecito (2 hours), historic downtown Santa Barbara (2½ hours), and through town to the mission (3 hours). ⊠ 122 Gray Ave., at E. Mason St. ☎ 805/963–7672 ⊕ segwayofsb.com ⌨ $75–$115.

ESSENTIALS

TRANSPORTATION CONTACTS Santa Barbara Car Free. ☎ 805/696–1100 ⊕ santabarbaracarfree.org. Santa Barbara Metropolitan Transit District. ☎ 805/963–3366 ⊕ sbmtd.gov. Santa Barbara Trolley Co. ☎ 805/965–0353 ⊕ www.sbtrolley.com.

VISITOR INFORMATION Santa Barbara Visitor Center. ⊠ 1 Garden St., at Cabrillo Blvd. ☎ 805/965–3021 ⊕ www.sbchamber.org. Visit Santa Barbara. ⊠ 500 E. Montecito St. ☎ 805/966–9222 ⊕ santabarbaraca.com.

⊙ Sights

Santa Barbara's waterfront is beautiful, with palm-studded promenades and plenty of sand. In the few miles between the beaches and the hills are downtown, Mission Santa Barbara, and the Santa Barbara Botanic Garden.

Andree Clark Bird Refuge

NATURE PRESERVE | This peaceful lagoon and its gardens sit north of East Beach. Bike trails and footpaths, punctuated by signs identifying native and migratory birds, skirt the lagoon. ⊠ 1400 E. Cabrillo Blvd., near the zoo ⌨ Free.

Carriage and Western Art Museum

MUSEUM | FAMILY | The country's largest collection of old horse-drawn vehicles—painstakingly restored—is exhibited here, everything from polished hearses to police buggies to old stagecoaches and circus vehicles. In August the Old Spanish Days Fiesta borrows many of the vehicles for a jaunt around town. Docents lead free tours from 1 to 4 pm the third Sunday of the month. ⊠ Pershing Park, 129 Castillo St. ☎ 805/962–2353 ⊕ carriagemuseum.org ⌨ Free ⊙ Closed weekends.

El Presidio State Historic Park

MILITARY SITE | Founded in 1782, El Presidio was one of four military strongholds established by the Spanish along the coast of California. The park

Be sure to visit Santa Barbara's beautiful—and usually uncrowded—beaches.

encompasses much of the original site in the heart of downtown. El Cuartel, the adobe guardhouse, is the oldest building in Santa Barbara and the second oldest in California. ■TIP→ **Admission is free for children 16 and under.** ⊠ *123 E. Canon Perdido St., at Anacapa St.* ☎ *805/965–0093* ⊕ *www.sbthp.org* ⊠ *$5.*

Funk Zone
NEIGHBORHOOD | A formerly run-down industrial neighborhood near the waterfront and train station, the Funk Zone has evolved into a hip hangout filled with wine-tasting rooms, arts-and-crafts studios, murals, breweries, distilleries, restaurants, and small shops. It's fun to poke around the three-square-block district. ■TIP→ **Street parking is limited, so leave your car in a nearby city lot and cruise up and down the alleys on foot.** ⊠ *Between State and Garden Sts. and Cabrillo Blvd. and U.S. 101* ⊕ *funkzone.net.*

Karpeles Manuscript Library
LIBRARY | Ancient political tracts and old Disney cartoons are among the holdings at this facility, which also houses one of the world's largest privately owned collections of rare manuscripts. Fifty display cases contain a sampling of the archive's million-plus documents. ⊠ *21 W. Anapamu St., near Chapala St.* ☎ *805/962–5322* ⊕ *www.rain. org/~karpeles* ⊠ *Free* ⊗ *Closed Mon. and Tues.*

★ Lotusland
GARDEN | **FAMILY** | The 37-acre estate called Lotusland—often ranked among the world's 10 best gardens—once belonged to the Polish opera singer Ganna Walska, who purchased it in 1941 and lived here until her death in 1984. Many of the exotic trees and other subtropical flora were planted in 1882 by horticulturist R. Kinton Stevens. On the two-hour guided tour—the only option for visiting unless you're a member (reserve well ahead in summer)—you'll see an outdoor theater, a topiary garden,

a lotus pond, and a huge collection of rare cycads, an unusual plant genus that has been around since the time of the dinosaurs. ■TIP→ **Child-friendly family tours are available for groups with children under the age of 10; contact Lotusland for scheduling.** ⊠ *695 Ashley Rd., off Sycamore Canyon Rd. (Hwy. 192), Montecito ✛ Visitor entrance gate is on Cold Spring Rd., at Sycamore Canyon Rd.* ☎ *805/969–9990* ⊕ *lotusland.org* ⊠ *$50* ⊘ *Closed mid-Nov.–mid-Feb. No tours Sun.–Tues.*

Montecito

TOWN | Since the late 1800s the tree-studded hills and valleys of this town have attracted the rich and famous: Hollywood icons, business tycoons, tech moguls, and old-money families who installed themselves years ago. Shady roads wind through the community, which consists mostly of gated estates. Swank boutiques line **Coast Village Road,** where well-heeled residents such as Oprah Winfrey sometimes browse for truffle oil, picture frames, and designer jeans. Residents also hang out in the Upper Village, a chic shopping area with restaurants and cafés at the intersection of San Ysidro and East Valley roads.

★ Mission Santa Barbara

RELIGIOUS SITE | Widely referred to as the "Queen of Missions," this is one of the most beautiful and frequently photographed buildings in coastal California. Dating to 1786, the architecture evolved from adobe-brick buildings with thatch roofs to more permanent edifices as the mission's population burgeoned. An earthquake in 1812 destroyed the third church built on the site. Its replacement, the present structure, is still a functioning Catholic church. Mission Santa Barbara has a splendid Spanish/Mexican colonial art collection, as well as Chumash sculptures and the only Native American–made altar and tabernacle left in the California missions. Docents lead

Best Views 👁

Drive along Alameda Padre Serra, a hillside road that begins near the mission and continues to Montecito, to feast your eyes on spectacular views of the city and the Santa Barbara Channel.

60-minute tours ($13 adult) weekdays at 11 am, Saturday at 10:30 am, and Sunday at 12:30 pm. ⊠ *2201 Laguna St., at E. Los Olivos St.* ☎ *805/682–4149 gift shop, 805/682–4713 tours* ⊕ *www.santabarbaramission.org* ⊠ *$9 self-guided tour.*

★ MOXI–The Wolf Museum of Exploration and Innovation

MUSEUM | **FAMILY** | It took more than two decades of unrelenting community advocacy to plan and build this exceptional science hub, which opened in early 2017 in a gorgeous three-story Spanish-Mediterranean building next to the train station and a block from Stearns Wharf and the beach. MOXI ignites learning through interactive activities in science and creativity for curious minds of all ages, from pre-K to gray. The 70-plus interactive exhibits—devoted to science, technology, engineering, arts, and mathematics (STEAM)—are integrated so visitors can explore seven themed areas (called tracks) in concert with one another and discover connections between them, for example, the relationship between music and electricity. In the Speed and Motion track you can build a model car and challenge two others to a race on a test track—then use the collected data to reconfigure your car for improved performance. In the Fantastic Forces space, build a contraption to send on a test flight in a wind column. Other sections include Light and Color, The

California's Missions

California history changed forever in the 18th century when Spanish explorers founded a series of missions along the Pacific coast. Believing they were following God's will, they wanted to spread the gospel and convert as many natives as possible. The process produced a collision between the Hispanic and California Indian cultures, resulting in one of the most striking legacies of Old California: the Spanish mission churches. Rising like mirages in the middle of desert plains and rolling hills, these historic sites transport you back to the days of the Spanish colonial period.

assumed control of the territory, and California became part of the United States. Today, all 21 of these missions stand as extraordinary monuments to their colorful past. Many are found on or near the "King's Road"—El Camino Real—which linked these mission outposts. At the height of the mission system the trail was approximately 600 miles long, eventually extending from San Diego to Sonoma. Today the road is commemorated on portions of Routes 101 and 82 in the form of roadside bell markers erected by CalTrans every 1 to 2 miles between San Diego and San Francisco.

Father of the Missions
Father Junípero Serra is an icon of the Spanish colonial period. At the behest of the Spanish government, the diminutive padre—then well into his fifties, and despite a chronic leg infection—started out on foot from Baja California to search for suitable mission sites, with a goal of reaching Monterey. In 1769 he helped establish Alta California's first mission in San Diego and continued his travels until his death in 1784, by which time he had founded eight more missions.

El Camino Real
The system ended about a decade after the Mexican government took control of Alta California in the early 1820s and began to secularize the missions. In 1848, the Americans

Mission Architecture
Mission architecture reflects a gorgeous blend of European and New World influences. While naves followed the simple forms of Franciscan Gothic, cloisters (with beautiful arcades) adopted aspects of the Romanesque style, and ornamental touches of the Spanish Renaissance—including red-tiled roofs and wrought-iron grilles—added even more elegance. In the 20th century, the Mission Revival Style had a huge impact on architecture and design in California, as seen in examples ranging from San Diego's Union Station to Stanford University's main quadrangle. For information on California's missions, see ⊕ *california-missionsfoundation.org*.

Tech Track, Innovation Workshop, Sound Track, and interactive media spaces. Up on the rooftop Sky Garden, which has some of the best panoramic views in downtown, you can listen to an orchestra of wind and solar-powered instruments and peer down through glass floor-windows to view the happy faces of explorers on the floors below. ✉ *125 State St.* ☎ *805/770–5000* ⊕ *moxi.org* ✉ *$15*.

Santa Barbara Botanic Garden

GARDEN | Five miles of scenic trails meander through the garden's 78 acres of native plants. The Mission Dam, built in 1806, stands just beyond the redwood grove and above the restored aqueduct that once carried water to Mission Santa Barbara. More than a thousand plant species thrive in various themed sections, including mountains, deserts, meadows, redwoods, and Channel Islands. ■TIP→ A conservation center dedicated to rare and endangered plant species opened in 2016 and presents rotating exhibitions. ⊠ 1212 Mission Canyon Rd., north of Foothill Rd. (Hwy. 192) ☎ 805/682-4726 ⊕ www.sbbg.org ⊑ $14.

★ Santa Barbara County Courthouse

GOVERNMENT BUILDING | Hand-painted tiles and a spiral staircase infuse the courthouse, a national historic landmark, with the grandeur of a Moorish palace. This magnificent building was completed in 1929. An elevator rises to an arched observation area in the tower that provides a panoramic view of the city. Before or after you take in the view, you can (if it's open) visit an engaging gallery devoted to the workings of the tower's original, still operational Seth Thomas clock. The murals in the ceremonial chambers on the courthouse's second floor were painted by an artist who did backdrops for some of Cecil B. DeMille's films. ■TIP→ Join a free guided tour weekdays at 10:30, daily at 2. ⊠ 1100 Anacapa St., at E. Anapamu St. ☎ 805/962-6464 ⊕ sbcourthouse.org.

Santa Barbara Historical Museum

MUSEUM | The historical society's museum exhibits decorative and fine arts, furniture, costumes, and documents from the town's past. Adjacent to it is the Gledhill Library, a collection of books, photographs, maps, and manuscripts. Tours are by appointment only. Admission is free for anyone under 18. ⊠ 136 E. De La Guerra St., at Santa Barbara St.

☎ 805/966-1601 ⊕ www.sbhistorical.org ⊑ Museum $7; library from $2 per hr for research ⊘ Closed Mon.

Santa Barbara Maritime Museum

MUSEUM | FAMILY | California's seafaring history is the focus here. High-tech, hands-on exhibits, such as a virtual sportfishing activity that lets participants haul in a "big one" and a local surfing history retrospective, make this a fun stop for families. In 2018, the museum introduced a fascinating History of Oil in the Santa Barbara Channel exhibit that traces the Chumash Indians' use of natural seeps to the infamous 1969 oil spill that spawned the modern environmental movement. The museum's shining star is a rare, 17-foot-tall Fresnel lens from the historic Point Conception Lighthouse. Ride the elevator to the fourth-floor observation area for great harbor views. ⊠ 113 Harbor Way, off Shoreline Dr. ☎ 805/962-8404 ⊕ sbmm. org ⊑ $8 ⊘ Closed Wed.

Santa Barbara Museum of Art

MUSEUM | The highlights of this museum's permanent collection include ancient sculpture, Asian art, impressionist paintings, contemporary art, photography, and American works in several mediums. ⊠ 1130 State St., at E. Anapamu St. ☎ 805/963-4364 ⊕ sbma.net ⊑ $10, free Thurs. 5–8 ⊘ Closed Mon.

Santa Barbara Museum of Natural History

MUSEUM | FAMILY | The gigantic blue whale skeleton greets you at the entrance to this 17-acre complex whose major draws include its planetarium, paleo and marine life, and gem and mineral display. Startlingly alive-looking stuffed specimens in Mammal and Bird Halls include a smiling grizzly bear and nesting California condors. A room of dioramas illustrates Chumash Indian history and culture while a Santa Barbara Gallery showcases the region's unique biodiversity. Outdoors, nature trails wind through the serene oak woodlands and a summer butterfly pavilion.

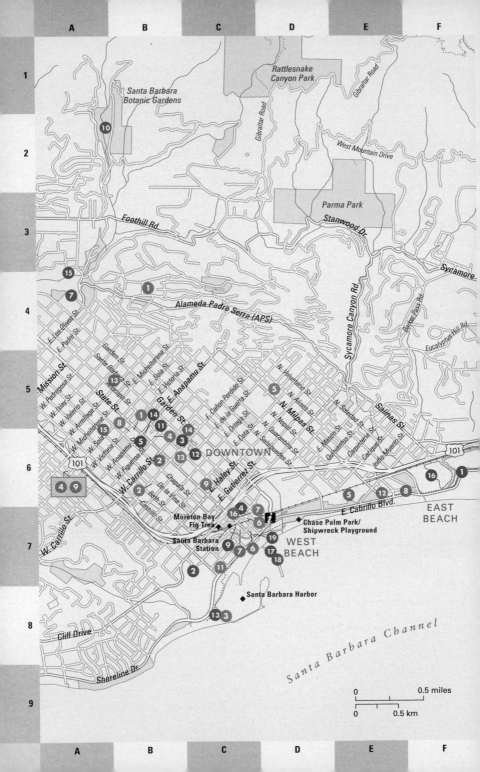

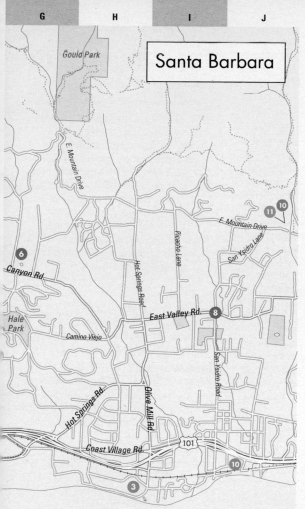

Santa Barbara

Sights ▼

1 Andree Clark Bird Refuge F6
2 Carriage and Western Art Museum C7
3 El Presidio State Historic Park ...B6
4 Funk Zone.............................C7
5 Karpeles Manuscript Library.....B6
6 Lotusland G3
7 Mission Santa Barbara A4
8 Montecito............................I4
9 MOXI–The Wolf Museum of Exploration and Innovation........C7
10 Santa Barbara Botanic Garden.. A2
11 Santa Barbara County Courthouse B6
12 Santa Barbara Historical Museum C6
13 Santa Barbara Maritime Museum C8
14 Santa Barbara Museum Of Art... B6
15 Santa Barbara Museum of Natural History.....................A3
16 Santa Barbara Zoo F6
17 Sea Center............................D7
18 Stearns Wharf D7
19 Urban Wine Trail...................C7

Restaurants ▼

1 Arigato Sushi........................B6
2 Barbareño B6
3 Brophy Bros. C8
4 Jeannine's B6
5 La Super-Rica D5
6 The Lark C7
7 Loquita C7
8 Olio e Limone B6
9 Palace Grill C6
10 The Stonehouse J3
11 Toma C7
12 Wine Cask B6

Hotels ▼

1 Belmond El Encanto...............B4
2 Canary Hotel B6
3 Four Seasons Resort The Biltmore Santa Barbara H6
4 The Goodland A6
5 Hilton Santa Barbara Beachfront Resort................E6
6 Hotel Californian C7
7 Hotel Indigo C7
8 Hyatt Santa Barbara F6
9 The Ritz-Carlton Bacara, Santa Barbara A6
10 Rosewood Miramar Beach.......J6
11 San Ysidro Ranch...................J3
12 Santa Barbara Inn...................E6
13 Simpson House Inn................B5
14 Spanish Garden Inn C5
15 The Upham B6
16 The Wayfarer C7

KEY

🅵 Exploring Sights
🅵 Restaurants
🅵 Hotels
ℹ️ Tourist information

✉ *2559 Puesta del Sol Rd., off Mission Canyon Rd.* ☎ *805/682–4711* ⊕ *sbnature. org* 💲 *$15; free one Sun. of month Sept.–Apr.*

Santa Barbara Zoo

ZOO | FAMILY | This compact zoo's gorgeous grounds shelter elephants, gorillas, exotic birds, and big cats, and has many exhibits that educate visitors on conservation efforts to save endangered species like the California condor and the red-legged frog. For small children, there's a scenic railroad and barnyard area where they can feed domestic sheep. Three high-tech dinosaurs and an 8-foot-tall grizzly bear puppet perform in live stage shows (free with admission), daily in summer and on weekends the rest of the year. Kids especially love feeding the giraffes from a view deck overlooking the beach. ■TIP→ **The palm-studded lawns on a hilltop overlooking the beach are perfect spots for family picnics.** ✉ *500 Niños Dr., off El Cabrillo Blvd.* ☎ *805/962–5339 main line* ⊕ *santabarbarazoo.org* 💲 *Zoo $18, parking $11.*

Sea Center

ZOO | FAMILY | A branch of the Santa Barbara Museum of Natural History, the center specializes in Santa Barbara Channel marine life and conservation. Though small compared to aquariums in Monterey and Long Beach, this is a fascinating, hands-on marine science laboratory that lets you participate in experiments, projects, and exhibits, including touch pools. The two-story glass walls here open to stunning ocean, mountain, and city views. ✉ *211 Stearns Wharf* ☎ *805/962–2526* ⊕ *sbnature.org* 💲 *$9.*

Stearns Wharf

MARINA | Built in 1872, Stearns Wharf is Santa Barbara's most visited landmark. Expansive views of the mountains, cityscape, and harbor unfold from every vantage point on the three-block-long pier. Although it's a nice walk from the Cabrillo Boulevard parking areas, you can also park on the pier and then

Santa Barbara Style ◉

After a 1925 earthquake demolished many buildings, the city seized a golden opportunity to assume a Spanish-Mediterranean style. It established an architectural board of review, which, along with city commissions, created strict building codes for the downtown district: red-tile roofs, earth-tone facades, arches, wrought-iron embellishments, and height restrictions (about four stories).

wander through the shops or stop for a meal at one of the wharf's restaurants. ✉ *Cabrillo Blvd. and State St.* ⊕ *stearnswharf.org.*

Urban Wine Trail

WINERY/DISTILLERY | Nearly 30 winery tasting rooms form the Urban Wine Trail; most are within walking distance of the waterfront and the lower State Street shopping and restaurant district. **Santa Barbara Winery,** at 202 Anacapa Street, and **Au Bon Climat,** at 813 Anacapa Street, are good places to start your oenological trek. ✉ *Santa Barbara* ⊕ *urbanwinetrailsb.com.*

⊙ Beaches

Arroyo Burro Beach

BEACH—SIGHT | FAMILY | The beach's usually gentle surf makes it ideal for families with young children. It's a local favorite because you can walk for miles in both directions when tides are low. Leashed dogs are allowed on the main stretch of beach and westward; they are allowed to romp off-leash east of the slough at the beach entrance. The parking lots fill early on weekends and throughout the summer, but the park is relatively quiet at other times. Walk along the beach just a few hundreds yards away from the main steps at the entrance to escape crowds on warm-weather days. Surfers, swimmers, stand-up paddlers, and boogie boarders regularly ply the waves, and photographers come often to catch the vivid sunsets. **Amenities:** food and drink; lifeguard in summer; parking; showers, toilets. **Best for:** sunset; surfing; swimming; walking. ⊠ *Cliff Dr. and Las Positas Rd.* ⊕ *countyofsb. org/parks.*

★ **East Beach**

BEACH—SIGHT | FAMILY | The wide swath of sand at the east end of Cabrillo Boulevard is a great spot for people-watching. East Beach has sand volleyball courts, summertime lifeguard and sports competitions, and arts-and-crafts shows on Sundays and holidays. You can use showers, a weight room, and lockers (bring your own towel) and rent umbrellas and boogie boards at the Cabrillo Bathhouse. Next door, there's an elaborate jungle-gym play area for kids. Hotels line the boulevard across from the beach. **Amenities:** food and drink; lifeguards in summer; parking (fee); showers; toilets; water sports. **Best for:** walking; swimming; surfing. ⊠ *1118 Cabrillo Blvd., at Ninos Dr.* ☎ *805/897–2680.*

🍴 Restaurants

Arigato Sushi

$$$ | JAPANESE | You might have to wait for a table at this two-story restaurant and sushi bar—locals line up early for the wildly creative combination rolls and other delectables (first come, first served). Fans of authentic Japanese food sometimes disagree about the quality of the seafood, but all dishes are fresh and artfully presented. **Known for:** innovative creations; lively atmosphere; patio and second-floor balcony seating. $ *Average main: $30* ⊠ *1225 State St., near W. Victoria St.* ☎ *805/965–6074* ⊕ *www. arigatosb.com* ⊗ *No lunch.*

Barbareño

$$$ | MODERN AMERICAN | Determined to push the boundaries of farm-to-table, college friends who worked at the same Los Angeles eatery banded together in 2014 to launch Barbareño. They churn their own butter, bake their own breads, make condiments from scratch, and forage mushrooms, eucalyptus leaves, and other ingredients from the wild. **Known for:** youthful, sophisticated vibe; chef's sampler plate; monthly seasonal menu. $ *Average main: $24* ⊠ *205 W. Canon Perdido St., at De La Vina St.* ☎ *805/963–9591* ⊕ *barbareno.com* ⊗ *Closed Tues. No lunch.*

Brophy Bros.

$$$ | SEAFOOD | The outdoor tables at this casual harborside restaurant have perfect views of the marina and mountains. Staffers serve enormous, exceptionally fresh fish dishes and provide guests with a pager so you can stroll along the waterfront until the beep lets you know your table is ready. **Known for:** seafood salad and chowder; stellar clam bar; long wait times. $ *Average main: $26* ⊠ *119 Harbor Way, off Shoreline Dr.* ☎ *805/966–4418* ⊕ *brophybros.com.*

Jeannine's

$ | AMERICAN | Take a break from State Street shopping at Jeannine's, revered locally for its wholesome sandwiches, salads, and baked goods, made from scratch with organic and natural ingredients. Dine in the expansive dining room or patio, or pick up a turkey cranberry or chicken pesto sandwich to go, and picnic in the courthouse gardens a block away. **Known for:** fantastic pastries; hearty, healthful breakfasts; turkey roasted or smoked in house. $ *Average main: $15* ⊠ *La Arcada, 15 E. Figueroa St., at State St.* ☎ *805/966–1717* ⊕ *jeannines.com/restaurants.*

La Super-Rica

$ | MEXICAN | This food stand on the east side of town serves some of the spiciest and most authentic Mexican dishes between Los Angeles and San Francisco. Fans (the late chef Julia Child was one) fill up on the soft tacos served with yummy spicy or mild sauces and legendary beans; portions are on the small side; order several dishes and share. **Known for:** house-made tortillas; daily specials such as chilaquiles; vegetarian and gluten-free dishes. Ⓢ *Average main: $14 ⊠ 622 N. Milpas St., at Alphonse St. ☎ 805/963–4940 ▭ No credit cards ⊗ Closed Tues. and Wed.*

★ The Lark

$$$ | **MODERN AMERICAN** | Shared dining—small plates and larger—and a seasonal menu showcasing local ingredients are the focus at this urban-chic restaurant named for an overnight all-Pullman train that chugged into the nearby railroad station for six decades. Sit at the 24-seat communal table set atop vintage radiators, or at tables and booths crafted from antique Spanish church pews and other repurposed or recycled materials. **Known for:** social environment; wines curated by a master sommelier; handcrafted locavore cocktails. Ⓢ *Average main: $30 ⊠ 131 Anacapa St., at E. Yanonali St. ☎ 805/284–0370 ⊕ www.thelarksb.com ⊗ Closed Mon. No lunch.*

Loquita

$$$ | **SPANISH** | In a cozy space in a prime corner at the gateway to the Funk Zone near Stearns Wharf, Loquita honors Santa Barbara's Spanish heritage by serving up authentic Spanish dishes, wines, and cocktails made with fresh, sustainably sourced local ingredients. The menu covers all bases, from tapas, to wood-fired seafood, and grilled meats, to Spanish wines, vermouth, gin and tonics, and sangria. **Known for:** multiple types of paella; counter and takeaway items; great gin and tonic. Ⓢ *Average main: $29 ⊠ 202 State St. ☎ 805/880–3380 ⊕ www.loquitasb.com.*

Take the Kids 👁

Two fun playgrounds provide welcome interludes for the young set. Children love tooling around **Kids' World** (⊠ *Garden and Micheltorena Sts.*), a public playground with a castle-shaped maze of climbing structures, slides, and tunnels. At **Shipwreck Playground** (⊠ *Chase Palm Park, E. Cabrillo Blvd., east of Garden St.*), parents take as much pleasure in the waterfront views as the kids do in the nautical-theme diversions.

Olio e Limone

$$$$ | **ITALIAN** | Sophisticated Italian cuisine with an emphasis on Sicily is served at this restaurant near the Arlington. The juicy veal chop is popular, but surprises abound here; be sure to try unusual dishes such as ribbon pasta with quail and sausage in a mushroom ragout, or the duck ravioli. **Known for:** grilled veal and lamb chops; cozy white-tablecloth dining room; adjacent raw bar and casual pizzeria. Ⓢ *Average main: $32 ⊠ 17 W. Victoria St., at State St. ☎ 805/899–2699 ⊕ www.olioelimone.com ⊗ No lunch Sun.*

Palace Grill

$$$ | **SOUTHERN** | Mardi Gras energy, team-style service, lively music, and great Cajun, creole, and Caribbean food have made the Palace a Santa Barbara icon. Be prepared to wait for a table on Friday and Saturday nights (when reservations are taken for a 5:30 seating only), though the live entertainment and free appetizers, sent out front when the line is long, will whet your appetite for the feast to come. **Known for:** blackened fish and meats; Louisiana bread pudding soufflé; Cajun martini served in a mason jar. Ⓢ *Average main: $30 ⊠ 8 E. Cota St., at State St. ☎ 805/963–5000 ⊕ palacegrill.com.*

★ The Stonehouse

$$$$ | AMERICAN | The elegant Stonehouse—consistently lauded as one of the nation's top restaurants—is inside a century-old granite former farmhouse at the San Ysidro Ranch resort. The menu changes constantly, but might include pan-seared abalone or classic steak Diane flambéed table-side. **Known for:** ingredients from on-site garden; heated ocean-view deck with fireplace; elegant dining room. $ *Average main: $49* ✉ *900 San Ysidro La., off San Ysidro Rd., Montecito* ☎ *805/565–1700* ⊕ *www.sanysidroranch.com.*

★ Toma

$$$ | ITALIAN | Seasonal, locally sourced ingredients and softly lit muted-yellow walls evoke the flavors and charms of Tuscany and the Mediterranean at this rustic-romantic restaurant across from the harbor and West Beach. Ahi sashimi tucked in a crisp sesame cone is a popular appetizer, after which you can proceed to a house-made pasta dish or rock shrimp gnocchi. **Known for:** house-made pastas and gnocchi; wines from Italy and California's Central Coast; romantic waterfront setting. $ *Average main: $30* ✉ *324 W. Cabrillo Blvd., near Castillo St.* ☎ *805/962–0777* ⊕ *www.tomarestaurant.com* ☾ *No lunch.*

Wine Cask

$$$$ | AMERICAN | The Wine Cask serves bistro-style meals in a comfortable and classy dining room with a huge fireplace and wood-beam ceiling decorated with gold leaf. The more casual bar-café, Intermezzo, across the courtyard, serves pizzas, salads, small plates, wines, and cocktails and is open late. **Known for:** extensive wine list and pairing suggestions; historic courtyard patio; late hours. $ *Average main: $31* ✉ *El Paseo, 813 Anacapa St., at E. De La Guerra St.* ☎ *805/966–9463* ⊕ *winecask.com* ☾ *Closed Sun. and Mon.*

🛏 Hotels

★ Belmond El Encanto

$$$$ | HOTEL | Built in 1915 and following more than a $100 million of extensive renovations a century later, this Santa Barbara icon lives on to thrill a new generation of guests with its relaxed-luxe bungalow rooms, lush gardens, and personalized service. **Pros:** dining terrace with panoramic city and ocean views; stellar spa facility; infinity pool with ocean views. **Cons:** long walk to downtown; pricey; guests staying for more than a few days may find the restaurant menus limited. $ *Rooms from: $404* ✉ *800 Alvarado Pl.* ☎ *805/845–5800, 800/393–5315* ⊕ *www.belmond.com/elencanto* ⤳ *92 rooms* ⚏ *No meals.*

Canary Hotel

$$$$ | HOTEL | A full-service hotel in the heart of downtown, this Kimpton property blends a casual, beach-getaway feel with contemporary California style. **Pros:** upscale local cuisine at on-site Finch & Fork restaurant; rooms come with candles, yoga mats, and binoculars (for touring); adjacent fitness center. **Cons:** across from transit center; a mile from the beach; some rooms on the small side. $ *Rooms from: $415* ✉ *31 W. Carrillo St.* ☎ *805/884–0300, 866/999–5401* ⊕ *www.canarysantabarbara.com* ⤳ *97 rooms* ⚏ *No meals.*

★ Four Seasons Resort The Biltmore Santa Barbara

$$$$ | RESORT | Surrounded by lush, perfectly manicured gardens and across from the beach, Santa Barbara's grande dame has long been a favorite for quiet, California-style luxury. **Pros:** spa with 11 treatment rooms; access to members-only clubs and restaurant on-site; steps from the beach. **Cons:** back rooms are close to train tracks; expensive; several miles from downtown hub. $ *Rooms from: $795* ✉ *1260 Channel Dr.* ☎ *805/969–2261, 805/565–8299 for reservations only* ⊕ *www.fourseasons.com/santabarbara* ⤳ *206 rooms* ⚏ *No meals.*

The Goodland

$$$$ | HOTEL | A vintage Woody car, a silver Airstream trailer, and a lobby record shop are among the elements that bring 1960s California surf culture to life at this Kimpton hotel in Goleta. **Pros:** cool and casual vibe; live music or DJs several evenings a week; complimentary wine-and-beer social hour and s'mores by the fireside. **Cons:** not close to downtown Santa Barbara; some rooms on the small side; thin walls allow for noise transfer from neighboring rooms. $ *Rooms from: $284* ✉ *5650 Calle Real, Goleta* ☎ *877/480–1465, 805/964–6241* ⊕ *www.thegoodland.com* �){ *158 rooms* ¦O¦ *No meals.*

Hilton Santa Barbara Beachfront Resort

$$$$ | RESORT | A full-scale resort with seven buildings spread over 24 landscaped acres across from East Beach, the hotel was founded by the late TV actor Fess Parker, best known for playing Davy Crockett and Daniel Boone. **Pros:** numerous amenities; right across from the beach; free shuttle to train station and airport. **Cons:** train noise filters into some rooms; too spread out for some; pricey. $ *Rooms from: $475* ✉ *633 E. Cabrillo Blvd.* ☎ *800/879–2929, 805/564–4333* ⊕ *www.hiltonsantabarbarabeachfrontresort.com* ➵ *360 rooms* ¦O¦ *No meals.*

★ Hotel Californian

$$$$ | HOTEL | A sprawling collection of Spanish-Moorish buildings that opened in summer 2017 at the site of the historic 1925 Hotel Californian, this sophisticated hotel with a hip youthful vibe occupies nearly three full blocks on State Street just steps from Stearns Wharf, MOXI, the Funk Zone, beaches, and the harbor. **Pros:** steps from the waterfront, Funk Zone, and beaches; resort-style amenities; on-site parking. **Cons:** pricey; must walk or ride the shuttle to downtown attractions; train whistle noise in rooms close to station. $ *Rooms from: $550* ✉ *36 State St.* ☎ *805/882–0100* ⊕ *www.thehotelcalifornian.com* ➵ *121 rooms.*

Hotel Indigo

$$$ | HOTEL | The closest hotel to the train station and across the street from the Funk Zone, artsy Hotel Indigo is a fine choice for travelers who appreciate contemporary art and want easy access to dining, nightlife, and the beach. **Pros:** multilingual staff; a block from Stearns Wharf; great value for location. **Cons:** showers only (no bathtubs); train whistles early morning; rooms on small side. $ *Rooms from: $249* ✉ *121 State St.* ☎ *805/966–6586* ⊕ *www.indigosantabarbara.com* ➵ *41 rooms* ¦O¦ *No meals.*

Hyatt Santa Barbara

$$$$ | HOTEL | A complex of four buildings on 3 landscaped acres, the Hyatt provides an appealing lodging option in a prime location right across from East Beach. **Pros:** steps from the beach; many room types and rates; walk to the zoo and waterfront shuttle. **Cons:** motel feel; busy area in summer. $ *Rooms from: $289* ✉ *1111 E. Cabrillo Blvd.* ☎ *805/882–1234, 800/643–1994* ⊕ *santabarbara.centric.hyatt.com* ➵ *174 rooms* ¦O¦ *No meals.*

★ The Ritz-Carlton Bacara, Santa Barbara

$$$$ | RESORT | A luxury resort with four restaurants and a 42,000-square-foot spa and fitness center with 36 treatment rooms, the Ritz-Carlton Bacara provides a gorgeous setting for relaxing retreats. **Pros:** many diversions including hiking and stargazing; three zero-edge pools; three golf courses nearby. **Cons:** pricey; not close to downtown; sand on beach not pristine enough for some. $ *Rooms from: $475* ✉ *8301 Hollister Ave., Goleta* ☎ *805/968–0100* ⊕ *www.ritzcarlton.com/santabarbara* ➵ *358 rooms* ¦O¦ *No meals.*

★ Rosewood Miramar Beach

$$$$ | RESORT | This luxury resort, opened in 2019, sprawls across 16 lush acres on one of the area's most scenic and exclusive beaches. **Pros:** two cabana-lined pools; six restaurants and bars; steps to the beach. **Cons:** too exclusive

for some. $ Rooms from: $680 ✉ 1759 S. Jameson La., Montecito ☎ 214/880–4292 ⊕ www.rosewoodhotels.com/en/miramar-beach-montecito ⇥ 161 rooms ⦿ No meals.

★ San Ysidro Ranch
$$$$ | RESORT | At this romantic hideaway on a historic property in the Montecito foothills—where John and Jackie Kennedy spent their honeymoon and Oprah sends her out-of-town visitors—guest cottages are scattered among groves of orange trees and flower beds. **Pros:** rooms come with private outdoor spas; 17 miles of hiking trails nearby; Plow & Angel Bistro and Stonehouse restaurants on-site are Santa Barbara institutions. **Cons:** very expensive; too remote for some. $ Rooms from: $845 ✉ 900 San Ysidro La., Montecito ☎ 805/565–1700, 800/368–6788 ⊕ www.sanysidroranch.com ⇥ 41 rooms and cottages ⦿ No meals ⚑ 2-day minimum stay on weekends, 3 days on holiday weekends.

★ Santa Barbara Inn
$$$$ | HOTEL | This full-service, Spanish-Mediterranean, family-owned hotel occupies a prime waterfront corner across from East Beach. **Pros:** more than half the rooms have ocean views; suites come with whirlpool tubs; delicious on-site restaurant Convivo. **Cons:** on a busy boulevard; limited street parking; not withing easy walking distance of downtown. $ Rooms from: $350 ✉ 901 E. Cabrillo Blvd. ⚓ At Milpas St. ☎ 805/966–3636 ⊕ www.santabarbarainn.com ⇥ 70 rooms ⦿ Breakfast.

★ Simpson House Inn
$$$$ | B&B/INN | If you're a fan of traditional bed-and-breakfast inns, this property, with its beautifully appointed Victorian main house and acre of lush gardens, is for you. **Pros:** elegant furnishings; impeccable landscaping; within walking distance of downtown. **Cons:** some rooms in main building are small; two-night minimum stay on weekends May–October; no pets allowed. $ Rooms from:

$339 ✉ 121 E. Arrellaga St. ☎ 805/963–7067 ⊕ www.simpsonhouseinn.com ⇥ 15 rooms ⦿ Breakfast.

Spanish Garden Inn
$$$$ | B&B/INN | A half block from the Presidio in the heart of downtown, this Spanish-Mediterranean retreat celebrates Santa Barbara style, from the tile floors, wrought-iron balconies, and exotic plants to the original art by local plein-air artists. **Pros:** walking distance from downtown; classic Spanish-Mediterranean style; free parking. **Cons:** no restaurant; tiny fitness room; no hot tub. $ Rooms from: $339 ✉ 915 Garden St. ☎ 805/564–4700 ⊕ www.spanishgardeninn.com ⇥ 24 rooms ⦿ Breakfast.

The Upham
$$$$ | B&B/INN | Built in 1871, this downtown Victorian in the arts and culture district has been restored as a full-service hotel. **Pros:** 1-acre garden; easy walk to theaters; excellent on-site restaurant. **Cons:** some rooms are small; not near beach or waterfront; no in-room safes. $ Rooms from: $285 ✉ 1404 De la Vina St. ☎ 805/962–0058 ⊕ www.uphamhotel.com ⇥ 50 rooms ⦿ Breakfast ⚑ 2-night minimum stay on weekends.

The Wayfarer
$$$ | HOTEL | The hip and stylish Wayfarer occupies a prime Funk Zone location, three blocks from Stearns Wharf and the beach, and across the street from the train station. **Pros:** outdoor heated pool; breakfast included; free parking. **Cons:** some rooms on the small side; freeway and train noise bothers some guests; pricey during high season. $ Rooms from: $239 ✉ 12 E. Montecito St. ☎ 805/845–1000 ⊕ wayfarersb.com ⇥ 31 rooms ⦿ Breakfast.

▼ Nightlife

The bar, club, and live music scene centers on lower State Street, between the 300 and 800 blocks.

Dargan's

BARS/PUBS | Lively Dargan's pub has pool tables, great draft beers and Irish whiskies, and serves a full menu of traditional Irish dishes. ⊠ 18 E. Ortega St., at Anacapa St. ☎ 805/568–0702 ⊕ darganssb.com.

The Good Lion

BARS/PUBS | The cocktail menu at this intimate neighborhood bar near The Granada Theatre changes weekly, depending on the fresh organic bounty available at the markets. All juices are organic and squeezed fresh daily, and all syrups are made in house with organic produce and sweeteners. ⊠ 1212 State St. ☎ 805/845–8754 ⊕ www.goodlion-cocktails.com.

James Joyce

BARS/PUBS | A good place to have a few beers and while away an evening; the James Joyce hosts rock, blues, jazz, and other performers six nights a week. ⊠ 513 State St., at W. Haley St. ☎ 805/962–2688 ⊕ sbjamesjoyce.com.

Joe's Cafe

BARS/PUBS | Steins of beer and stiff cocktails accompany hearty bar food at Joe's. It's a fun, if occasionally rowdy, collegiate scene. ⊠ 536 State St., at E. Cota St. ☎ 805/966–4638 ⊕ joescafesb.com.

Les Marchands

WINE BARS—NIGHTLIFE | A world-class team of sommeliers operates this European-styled wine bar, store, and eatery in the Funk Zone. ⊠ 131 Anacapa St., at Yananoli St. ☎ 805/284–0380 ⊕ www.lesmarchandswine.com.

Lucky's

BARS/PUBS | A slick sports bar attached to an upscale steak house owned by the maker of Lucky Brand dungarees, this place attracts hip patrons hoping to see and be seen. ⊠ 1279 Coast Village Rd., near Olive Mill Rd., Montecito ☎ 805/565–7540 ⊕ luckys-steakhouse.com.

Milk & Honey

BARS/PUBS | Artfully prepared tapas, mango mojitos, and exotic cocktails lure trendy crowds to swank M&H, despite high prices and a reputation for inattentive service. ⊠ 30 W. Anapamu St., at State St. ☎ 805/275–4232 ⊕ www.milknhoneytapas.com.

SOhO

MUSIC CLUBS | A lively restaurant, bar, and music venue, SOhO books all kinds of musical acts, from jazz to blues to rock. ⊠ 1221 State St., at W. Victoria St. ☎ 805/962–7776 ⊕ www.sohosb.com.

▣ Performing Arts

The arts district, with theaters, restaurants, and cafés, starts around the 900 block of State and continues north to the 1300 block. To see what's scheduled around town, pick up the free weekly Santa Barbara Independent newspaper or visit its website, ⊕ www.independent.com.

Arlington Theatre

ARTS CENTERS | This Moorish-style auditorium presents touring performers and films throughout the year. ⊠ 1317 State St., at Arlington Ave. ☎ 805/963–4408 ⊕ thearlingtontheatre.com.

Center Stage Theatre

ARTS CENTERS | This venue hosts plays, music, dance, and readings. ⊠ Paseo Nuevo Center, Chapala and De la Guerra Sts., 2nd fl. ☎ 805/963–0408 ⊕ www.centerstagetheater.org.

Ensemble Theatre Company (ETC)

THEATER | The company stages classic and contemporary comedies, musicals, and dramas. ⊠ 33 W. Victoria St., at Chapala St. ☎ 805/965–5400 ⊕ www.etcsb.org.

The Granada Theatre

THEATER | A restored, modernized landmark that dates from 1924, the Granada hosts Broadway touring shows and dance, music, and other cultural events. ⌧ *1214 State St., at E. Anapamu St.* ☎ *805/899–2222* ⊕ *granadasb.org.*

I Madonnari

ARTS FESTIVALS | Artists of all ages create 150 large-scale pastel drawings on the pavement near the Old Mission steps during an Italian street painting festival held Memorial Day weekend. ⌧ *Santa Barbara* ⊕ *imadonnarifestival.com.*

Lobero Theatre

THEATER | A state landmark, the Lobero hosts community theater groups and touring professionals. ⌧ *33 E. Canon Perdido St., at Anacapa St.* ☎ *805/963–0761* ⊕ *www.lobero.com.*

Music Academy of the West

MUSIC | The academy presents orchestral, chamber, and operatic works every summer. ⌧ *1070 Fairway Rd., off Channel Dr.* ☎ *805/969–4726, 805/969–8787 box office* ⊕ *www.musicacademy.org.*

★ Old Spanish Days Fiesta

CULTURAL FESTIVALS | The city celebrates its Spanish, Mexican, and Chumash heritage in early August with events that include music, dancing, an all-equestrian parade, a carnival, and a rodeo. ⌧ *Santa Barbara* ⊕ *oldspanishdays-fiesta.org.*

★ Santa Barbara International Film Festival

FESTIVALS | The 12-day festival in late January and early February attracts film enthusiasts and major stars to downtown venues for screenings, panels, and tributes. ⌧ *Santa Barbara* ⊕ *www.sbiff.org.*

Summer Solstice Celebration

ARTS FESTIVALS | More than 100,000 revelers celebrate the arts at this mid-June event whose highlight is a huge parade of costumed participants who dance, drum, and ride people-powered floats up State Street. ⌧ *Santa Barbara* ☎ *805/965–3396* ⊕ *www.solsticeparade.com.*

Earth Day 👁

In 1969, 200,000 gallons of crude oil spilled into the Santa Barbara Channel, causing an immediate outcry from residents. The day after the spill, Get Oil Out (GOO) was established; the group helped lead the successful fight for legislation to limit and regulate offshore drilling in California. The Santa Barbara spill also spawned Earth Day, which is still celebrated across the nation today.

🏃 Activities

BIKING

Cabrillo Bike Lane

BICYCLING | The level, two-lane, 3-mile Cabrillo Bike Lane passes the Santa Barbara Zoo, the Andree Clark Bird Refuge, beaches, and the harbor. Stop for a meal at one of the restaurants along the way, or for a picnic along the palm-lined path looking out on the Pacific.

Wheel Fun Rentals

BICYCLING | You can rent bikes, quadricycles, and skates here. ⌧ *24 E. Mason St,* ☎ *805/966–2282* ⊕ *wheelfunrentalssb.com.*

BOATS AND CHARTERS

★ Condor Express

BOATING | From SEA Landing, the *Condor Express,* a 75-foot high-speed catamaran, whisks up to 149 passengers toward the Channel Islands on whale-watching excursions and sunset and dinner cruises. ⌧ *301 W. Cabrillo Blvd.* ☎ *805/882–0088, 888/779–4253* ⊕ *condorexpress.com.*

Paddle Sports Center

WATER SPORTS | A full-service paddle-sports center in the harbor, this outfit rents kayaks, stand-up paddleboards, surfboards, boogie boards, and water-sports gear. ⌧ *117 B Harbor Way, off*

Shoreline Dr. ☎ 805/617–3425 rentals ⊕ www.paddlesportsca.com.

Santa Barbara Sailing Center

BOATING | The center offers sailing instruction, rents and charters sailboats, kayaks, and stand-up paddleboards, and organizes dinner and sunset champagne cruises, island excursions, and whale-watching trips. ⊠ Santa Barbara Harbor launching ramp ☎ 805/962–2826 ⊕ sbsail.com.

Santa Barbara Water Taxi

BOATING | FAMILY | Children beg to ride Lil' Toot, a cheery yellow water taxi that cruises from the harbor to Stearns Wharf and back again. The fare for kids is $2 each way. ⊠ Santa Barbara Harbor and Stearns Wharf ☎ 805/465–6676 ⊕ www.celebrationsantabarbara.com/ ⚓ $5 one-way.

SEA Landing

BOATING | This outfit operates surface and deep-sea fishing charters year-round. ⊠ Cabrillo Blvd., at Bath St., and breakwater in Santa Barbara Harbor ☎ 805/963–3564 ⊕ sealanding.net.

Truth Aquatics

SCUBA DIVING | Truth runs kayaking, paddleboarding, hiking, snorkeling, and scuba excursions to the National Marine Sanctuary and Channel Islands National Park. ⊠ Departures from SEA Landing, Santa Barbara Harbor ☎ 805/962–1127 ⊕ truthaquatics.com ⚓ From $130.

🛍 Shopping

CLOTHING

Channel Islands Surfboards

CLOTHING | Come here for top-of-the-line surfboards and the latest in California beachwear, sandals, and accessories. ⊠ 36 Anacapa St., at E. Mason St. ☎ 805/966–7213 ⊕ www.cisurfboards.com.

DIANI

CLOTHING | This upscale, European-style women's boutique dresses clients in designer clothing from around the world. Sibling shoe and home-and-garden shops are nearby. ⊠ 1324 State St., at Arlington Ave. ☎ 805/966–3114, 805/966–7175 shoe shop ⊕ dianiboutique.com.

Surf N Wear's Beach House

CLOTHING | This shop carries surf clothing, gear, and collectibles; it's also the home of Santa Barbara Surf Shop and the exclusive local dealer of Surfboards by Yater. ⊠ 10 State St., at Cabrillo Blvd. ☎ 805/963–1281 ⊕ www.surfnwear.com.

Wendy Foster

CLOTHING | This store sells casual-chic women's fashions. ⊠ 833 State St., at W. Canon Perdido St. ☎ 805/966–2276 ⊕ wendyfoster.com.

FOOD AND WINE

Santa Barbara Public Market

FOOD/CANDY | A dozen food and beverage vendors occupy this spacious arts district galleria. Stock up on olive oils, vinegars, and other gourmet goodies; sip on hand-crafted wines and beers while watching sports events; and nosh on noodle bowls, sushi and baked goods. ⊠ 38 W. Victoria St., at Chapala St. ☎ 805/770–7702 ⊕ sbpublicmarket.com.

SHOPPING AREAS

★ El Paseo

SHOPPING NEIGHBORHOODS | Wine-tasting rooms, shops, art galleries, and studios share the courtyard and gardens of this historic arcade. ⊠ Canon Perdido St., between State and Anacapa Sts.

★ State Street

SHOPPING NEIGHBORHOODS | Between Cabrillo Boulevard and Sola Street, State Street is a shopper's paradise. Chic malls, quirky storefronts, antiques emporia, elegant boutiques, and funky thrift shops abound. You can shop on foot or ride a battery-powered trolley (50¢ or $1 day pass) that runs between the waterfront and the 1300 block. Nordstrom and Macy's anchor **Paseo Nuevo,** an open-air mall in the 700 block. Shops, restaurants, galleries, and fountains line the tiled walkways of **La Arcada,** a small complex of landscaped courtyards in the 1100 block designed by architect Myron Hunt in 1926.

Summerland

SHOPPING NEIGHBORHOODS | Serious antiques hunters head southeast of Santa Barbara to Summerland, which is full of shops and markets. Several good ones are along Lillie Avenue and Ortega Hill Road. ⊠ *Summerland.*

Santa Ynez

31 miles north of Goleta.

Founded in 1882, the tiny town of Santa Ynez still has many of its original frontier buildings. You can walk through the three-block downtown area in a few minutes, shop for antiques, and hang around the old-time saloon. At some of the Santa Ynez Valley's best restaurants, you just might bump into one of the celebrities who own nearby ranches.

GETTING HERE AND AROUND

Take Highway 154 over San Marcos Pass or U.S. 101 north 43 miles to Buellton, then 7 miles east.

⊙ Sights

Chumash Casino Resort

CASINO—SIGHT | Just south of Santa Ynez on the Chumash Indian Reservation lies this Las Vegas–style casino with 2,300 slot machines, three restaurants and a food court, a spa, and a 12-story upscale hotel with a rooftop pool. ⊠ *3400 E. Hwy. 246* ☎ *800/248–6274* ⊕ *www. chumashcasino.com* 🖭 *Free.*

Gainey Vineyard

WINERY/DISTILLERY | The 1,800-acre Gainey Ranch, straddling the banks of the Santa Ynez River, includes about 100 acres of organic vineyards: Sauvignon Blanc, Merlot, Cabernet Sauvignon, and Cabernet Franc. The winery also makes

wines from Chardonnay, Pinot Noir, and Syrah grapes from the Santa Rita Hills. You can taste the latest releases—the estate Pinot Noir is especially good—in a Spanish-style hacienda overlooking the ranch. Barrel tasting on weekdays and jeep tours and tasting in the historic barn on weekends are also available (except in winter). ⊠ *3950 E. Hwy. 246* ☎ *805/688–0558* ⊕ *www.gaineyvineyard.com* 🖭 *Tastings from $15, jeep tour and barn tasting $25.*

🍴 Restaurants

Santa Ynez Kitchen

$$$ | **ITALIAN** | The owners of Toscana, a popular eatery in L.A.'s Brentwood neighborhood, run this rustic-chic restaurant with an Italy–meets–California Wine Country vibe. Chef and co-owner Luca Crestanelli, a native of Verona, Italy, typically offers about 10 seasonal daily specials. **Known for:** wood-fired pizzas and oak-grilled entrées; creative craft cocktails; gelatos and "not-so-classic" tiramisu. Ⓢ *Average main: $28* ⊠ *1110 Faraday St., at Sagunto St.* ☎ *805/691–9794* ⊕ *www.sykitchen.com.*

Trattoria Grappolo

$$$ | **ITALIAN** | Authentic Italian fare, an open kitchen, and festive, family-style seating make this trattoria equally popular with celebrities from Hollywood and ranchers from the Santa Ynez Valley. The noise level tends to rise in the evening, so this isn't the best spot for a romantic getaway. **Known for:** thin-crust wood-fired pizzas; risottos and homemade pastas; carpaccio. Ⓢ *Average main: $28* ⊠ *3687–C Sagunto St.* ☎ *805/688–6899* ⊕ *trattoriagrappolo.com* ⊙ *No lunch Mon.*

🛏 Hotels

ForFriends Inn

$$$$ | **B&B/INN** | Close friends own and operate this luxury bed-and-breakfast, designed as a social place where friends gather to enjoy good wine, food, and music in a casual backyard setting. **Pros:** three-course breakfast, evening wine and appetizers included; friendly innkeepers; "Friendship Pass" provides perks and savings at restaurants and wineries. **Cons:** not suitable for children; no pets allowed; must climb stairs to second-floor rooms. [$] *Rooms from: $295* ✉ *1121 Edison St.* ☎ *805/693–0303* 🌐 *www.forfriendsinn.com* 🛏 *5 rooms, 2 cottages* 🍴 *Breakfast.*

Santa Ynez Inn

$$$$ | **B&B/INN** | This posh two-story Victorian inn in downtown Santa Ynez was built from scratch in 2002, and the owners have furnished all the rooms with authentic historical pieces. **Pros:** near restaurants; unusual antiques; spacious rooms. **Cons:** high price for location; building not historic. [$] *Rooms from: $349* ✉ *3627 Sagunto St.* ☎ *805/688–5588* 🌐 *www.santaynezinn.com* 🛏 *20 rooms* 🍴 *Breakfast.*

Activities

Cloud Nine Glider Rides

FLYING/SKYDIVING/SOARING | The outfit's scenic glider rides last from 10 to 50 minutes. Tour options include the Santa Ynez Valley, coastal mountains and the Channel Islands, and celebrity homes. ✉ *Santa Ynez Airport, 900 Airport Rd.* ☎ *805/602–6620* 🌐 *cloud9gliderrides.com* 🎟 *From $185.*

Los Olivos

4 miles north of Santa Ynez.

This pretty village was once on Spanish-built El Camino Real (Royal Road) and later a stop on major stagecoach and rail routes. Tasting rooms, art galleries, antiques stores, and country markets line Grand Avenue and intersecting streets for several blocks.

GETTING HERE AND AROUND

From U.S. 101 north or south, exit at Highway 154 and drive east about 8 miles. From Santa Barbara, travel 30 miles northwest on Highway 154.

Sights

Blair Fox Cellars

WINERY/DISTILLERY | Blair Fox, a Santa Barbara native, crafts small-lot Rhône-style wines made from organic grapes. The bar in his rustic Los Olivos tasting room, where you can sample exceptional vineyard-designated Syrahs and other wines, was hewn from Australian white oak reclaimed from an old Tasmanian schoolhouse. ✉ *2902–B San Marcos Ave.* ☎ *805/691–1678* 🌐 *www.blairfoxcellars.com* 🎟 *Tastings $15* ⏲ *Closed Tues. and Wed.*

Coquelicot Estate Vineyard

WINERY/DISTILLERY | Named for the vivid red poppy flowers that blanket the French countryside and appear on all its labels, this limited-production winery focuses on handcrafted Bordeaux wines made from grapes at its certified organic 58-acre Santa Ynez Valley vineyard. Don't miss samples of the flagship wines: Sixer (a Syrah and Viogner blend), Mon Amour (a Bordeaux blend), and the estate Sauvignon Blanc and Rosé. ✉ *2884 Grand Ave.* ☎ *805/688–1500* 🌐 *www.coquelicotwines.com* 🎟 *Tastings from $15.*

Firestone Vineyard

WINERY/DISTILLERY | Heirs to the Firestone tire fortune developed (but no longer own) this winery known for Chardonnay, Gewürztraminer, Cabernet Sauvignon, and Syrah—and for the fantastic valley views from its tasting room and picnic area. The walking tour here (daily at 11:15 and 1:15) is highly informative. ✉ *5017 Zaca Station Rd., off U.S. 101* ☎ *805/688–3940* 🌐 *www.firestonewine.com* 🎟 *Tastings from $10, tour $25.*

🍴 Restaurants

Los Olivos Wine Merchant Cafe
$$$ | AMERICAN | Part wine store and part social hub, this café focuses on wine-friendly fish, pasta, and meat dishes, plus salads, pizzas, and burgers. Don't miss the homemade muffuletta and olive tapenade spreads, or the homemade focaccia bread. **Known for:** nearly everything made in-house; ingredients from own organic café farm; wines from own estate winery. *[$] Average main: $23 ✉ 2879 Grand Ave. ☎ 805/688–7265 🌐 www.winemerchant-cafe.com ⏲ No breakfast.*

Sides Hardware & Shoes: A Brothers Restaurant
$$$ | AMERICAN | Inside a historic storefront they renovated, brothers Matt and Jeff Nichols serve comfort food prepared with panache. The Kobe-style burgers, especially the one with bacon and white cheddar, make a great lunch, and the dinner favorites include Scottish salmon and lamb sirloin. **Known for:** in-house cured and smoked bacon; juicy burgers; jalapeño margaritas. *[$] Average main: $30 ✉ 2375 Alamo Pintado Ave. ☎ 805/688–4820 🌐 sides-restaurant.com.*

🛏 Hotels

★ Ballard Inn & The Gathering Table
$$$$ | B&B/INN | Set among orchards and vineyards in the tiny town of Ballard, 2 miles south of Los Olivos, this inn makes an elegant Wine Country escape. **Pros:** exceptional food; attentive staff; secluded setting. **Cons:** some baths could use updating; restaurant noise sometimes travels upstairs; no in-room phones or TVs. *[$] Rooms from: $299 ✉ 2436 Baseline Ave., Ballard ☎ 805/688–7770, 800/638–2466 🌐 ballardinn.com 🛏 15 rooms 🍴 Breakfast.*

Fess Parker's Wine Country Inn
$$$$ | B&B/INN | This luxury inn includes an elegant, tree-shaded French country–style main building and an equally attractive annex across the street with a pool and day spa. **Pros:** convenient wine-touring base; walking distance from restaurants and galleries; rate includes full breakfast at The Bear and Star on-site. **Cons:** pricey; not pet-friendly; thin walls between some rooms. *[$] Rooms from: $395 ✉ 2860 Grand Ave. ☎ 805/688–7788, 800/446–2455 🌐 www.fessparker-inn.com 🛏 19 rooms 🍴 Breakfast.*

Solvang

5 miles south of Los Olivos.

You'll know you've reached the town of Solvang when the architecture suddenly changes to half-timber buildings and windmills. Danish educators settled the town in 1911—the flatlands and rolling green hills reminded them of home. Solvang has attracted tourists for decades, but it's lately become more sophisticated, with smorgasbords giving way to galleries, upscale restaurants, and wine-tasting rooms by day and wine bars by night. The visitor center on Copenhagen Drive has walking-tour maps (also available online). The Sweet Treats tour covers the town's Danish bakeries, confectionary stores, and ice-cream parlors. The Olsen's and Solvang bakeries and Ingeborg's Danish Chocolates are worth investigating.

GETTING HERE AND AROUND

Highway 246 West (Mission Drive) traverses Solvang, connecting with U.S. 101 to the west and Highway 154 to the east. Alamo Pintado Road connects Solvang with Ballard and Los Olivos to the north. Park your car in one of the free public lots and stroll the town. Or take the bus: Santa Ynez Valley Transit shuttles run between Solvang and nearby towns.

ESSENTIALS

VISITOR INFORMATION Solvang Conference & Visitors Bureau. ✉ *1639 Copenhagen Dr., at 2nd St.* ☎ *805/688–6144* 🌐 *www.solvangusa.com.*

Sights

Mission Santa Inés

RELIGIOUS SITE | The mission holds an impressive collection of paintings, statuary, vestments, and Chumash and Spanish artifacts in a serene bluff-top setting. You can tour the museum, sanctuary, and gardens. ✉ *1760 Mission Dr., at Alisal Rd.* ☎ *805/688–4815* 🌐 *missionsantaines.org* 🎟 *$5.*

Rideau Vineyard

WINERY/DISTILLERY | This winery celebrates its locale's rich history—the King of Spain himself once owned this land, and the tasting room occupies a former guest ranch inn—but fully embraces the area's wine-making present. Wines made from the Rhône varietals Mourvèdre, Roussanne, Syrah, and Viognier are the specialty here. Winery and vineyard tours (free with tasting) are offered twice daily on weekdays (1:30 and 3) and thrice on weekends (12:30, 2, and 3:30). ✉ *1562 Alamo Pintado Rd., 2 miles north of Hwy. 246* ☎ *805/688–0717* 🌐 *rideauvineyard.com* 🎟 *Tastings from $15.*

Sevtap

WINERY/DISTILLERY | Winemaker Art Sevtap, an Istanbul native, is often on hand to pour samples of his limited-production wines—mostly from Bordeaux varietals—in this artsy wine bar that's decked out with Tibetan prayer flags and chalkboard walls and has a stage where guests can pick up a guitar and strum away. ✉ *1622 Copenhagen Dr., at 2nd St.* ☎ *805/693–9200* 🌐 *www.sevtapwinery.com* 🎟 *Tastings $15.*

Restaurants

★ First & Oak

$$$$ | **AMERICAN** | Create your own custom tasting menu by choosing among five different groups of eclectic California-French dishes paired with local wines at this elegant farm-to-table restaurant inside the Mirabelle Inn. The seasonal menu changes constantly, but regulars include smoked sweet-and-spicy duck wings, truffle-roasted cauliflower, local spot prawns, short rib bourguignonne, and pears poached in red wine from the sommelier-owner's organic Coceliquot Estate Vineyard. **Known for:** intimate fine-dining setting; sommelier-owner selected wine list; complex dishes and presentation. [$] *Average main: $36* ✉ *409 1st St.* ✣ *At Oak St.* ☎ *805/688–1703* 🌐 *www.firstandoak.com.*

★ Root 246

$$$$ | **AMERICAN** | This chic restaurant's chefs tap local purveyors and shop for organic ingredients at farmers' markets before deciding on the day's menu. Depending on the season, you might feast on organic chicken liver pâté, grilled shrimp with peanut mole, butter-basted local fish, pork osso bucco with preserved lemon, lamb or Wagyu beef burger in a potato roll, or braised ribs with a slab of house-made cornbread. **Known for:** gorgeous contemporary Native American–influenced design; responsibly sourced meats, seafood, fruits, and veggies; popular happy hour with craft cocktails. [$] *Average main: $34* ✉ *Hotel Corque, 420 Alisal Rd., at Molle Way* ☎ *805/686–8681* 🌐 *www.root-246.com* 🕒 *Closed Mon. No lunch. No brunch weekdays.*

Succulent Café

$$$ | **AMERICAN** | Locals flock to this cozy café for its comfort cuisine and regional wines and craft beers. Order at the counter, and staffers will deliver your meal to the interior dining areas

or the sunny outdoor patio. **Known for:** artisanal charcuterie plates; pet-friendly patio; homemade biscuits and gravy, house-roasted turkey. $ *Average main: $26* ✉ *1555 Mission Dr., at 4th Pl.* ☎ *805/691–9444* 🌐 *succulentcafe.com* 🕒 *Closed Tues.*

Hotels

★ Alisal Guest Ranch and Resort
$$$$ | RESORT | Since 1946 celebrities and plain folk alike have come to this 10,000-acre ranch to join in a slew of activities, including horseback riding, tennis, golf, and archery, boating, and fishing You can also just lounge by the pool or book a treatment at the day spa. **Pros:** Old West atmosphere; breakfast and dinner included in the rate; free Wi-Fi. **Cons:** no in-room phones or TVs; not close to downtown; jacket required for dinner. $ *Rooms from: $600* ✉ *1054 Alisal Rd.* ☎ *805/688–6411, 800/425–4725* 🌐 *alisal.com* 🛏 *73 rooms* 🍴 *Some meals.*

★ Hotel Corque
$$$ | HOTEL | Owned by the Santa Ynez Band of Chumash Indians, the stunning three-story "Corque" provides a full slate of upscale amenities. **Pros:** friendly, professional staff; short walk to shops, tasting rooms and restaurants; free Wi-Fi. **Cons:** no kitchenettes or laundry facilities; some rooms need updating; not pet-friendly. $ *Rooms from: $239* ✉ *400 Alisal Rd.* ☎ *805/688–8000* 🌐 *hotelcorque.com* 🛏 *132 rooms* 🍴 *No meals.*

The Landsby
$$$ | B&B/INN | New owners remodeled the former old-world-style Petersen Village Inn and transformed it into a cozy, contemporary Scandinavian retreat that feels like a residence in downtown Copenhagen. **Pros:** in the heart of Solvang; easy parking; courtyard with fire pits. **Cons:** on highway; unusual hallway configuration can be confusing; thin walls in some rooms. $ *Rooms from: $195* ✉ *1576 Mission Dr.* ☎ *805/688–3121* 🌐 *thelandsby.com* 🛏 *50 rooms* 🍴 *No meals.*

★ Mirabelle Inn
$$$ | B&B/INN | French, Danish, and American flags at the entrance and crystal chandeliers, soaring ceilings, and skylights in the lobby set the tone from the get-go in this elegant four-story inn a few blocks from the main tourist hub. **Pros:** excellent farm-to-table restaurant (dinner only); full cook-to-order breakfast included; away from noisy crowds. **Cons:** some rooms on the small side; not in the heart of town; restaurant noise travels to nearby rooms. $ *Rooms from: $250* ✉ *409 1st St.* ✥ *At Oak St.* ☎ *805/688–1703, 800/786–7925* 🌐 *mirabelleinn.com* 🛏 *12 rooms* 🍴 *Breakfast.*

Performing Arts

Solvang Festival Theater
THEATER | Pacific Conservatory of the Performing Arts presents crowd-pleasing musicals like *A Gentleman's Guide to Love and Murder* and *Million Dollar Quartet*, as well as Oscar Wilde's *The Importance of Being Earnest*, and contemporary plays at this 700-seat outdoor amphitheater. ✉ *420 2nd St., at Molle Way* ☎ *805/922–8313* 🌐 *pcpa.org* ☞ *Performances June–Oct.*

Buellton

3 miles west of Solvang.

A crossroads town at the intersection of U.S. 101 and Highway 246, Buellton has evolved from a sleepy gas and coffee stop into an enclave of wine-tasting rooms, beer gardens, and restaurants. It's also a gateway to Lompoc and the Santa Rita Hills Wine Trail to the west, and to Solvang, Santa Ynez, and Los Olivos to the east.

GETTING HERE AND AROUND

Driving is the easiest way to get to Buellton. From Santa Barbara, follow U.S. 101 north to the Highway 246 exit. Santa Ynez Valley Transit serves Buellton with shuttle buses from Solvang and nearby towns.

ESSENTIALS

VISITOR INFORMATION Discover Buellton. ✉ *597 Ave. of the Flags, No. 101* ☎ *805/688–7829* 🌐 *visitbuellton.com.*
Santa Rita Hills Wine Trail. 🌐 *santaritahills-winetrail.com.*

👁 Sights

Alma Rosa Winery
WINERY/DISTILLERY | Winemaker Richard Sanford helped put Santa Barbara County on the international wine map with a 1989 Pinot Noir. For Alma Rosa, started in 2005, he crafts wines from grapes grown on 100-plus acres of certified organic vineyards in the Santa Rita Hills. The Pinot Noirs and Chardonnays are exceptional. Vineyard tours and tastings are available by appointment, ✉ *181 C Industrial Way, off Hwy. 246, west of U.S. 101* ☎ *805/688–9090* 🌐 *almarosawinery.com* 🎟 *Tastings $20.*

Industrial Way
NEIGHBORHOOD | A half mile west of U.S. 101, head south from Highway 246 on Industrial Way to explore a hip and happening collection of food and drink destinations. Top stops include **Industrial Eats** (a craft butcher shop and restaurant), **Figueroa Mountain Brewing Co.,** the **Alma Rosa Winery** tasting room, **Margerum Wine Company, Tesora Sweets,** and the **Ascendant Spirits Distillery.** ✉ *Industrial Way, off Hwy. 246* 🌐 *www.industrialwaysbc.com.*

Lafond Winery and Vineyards
WINERY/DISTILLERY | A rich, concentrated Pinot Noir is the main attention-getter at this winery that also produces noteworthy Chardonnays and Syrahs. Bottles with Lafond's SRH (Santa Rita Hills) label are an especially good value. The winery also has a tasting room at 111 East Yanonali Street in Santa Barbara's Funk Zone. ✉ *6855 Santa Rosa Rd., west off U.S. 101 Exit 139* ☎ *805/688–7921* 🌐 *lafondwinery.com* 🎟 *Tastings $15 (includes logo glass).*

🍴 Restaurants

The Hitching Post II
$$$$ | **AMERICAN** | You'll find everything from grilled artichokes to quail at this casual eatery, but most people come for the smoky Santa Maria–style barbecue. Be sure to try a glass of owner-chef-winemaker Frank Ostini's signature Highliner Pinot Noir, a star in the film *Sideways.* **Known for:** entrées grilled over local red oak; chef-owner makes his own wines; classic cocktails. [$] *Average main: $32* ✉ *406 E. Hwy. 246, off U.S. 101* ☎ *805/688–0676* 🌐 *www.hitchingpost2.com* ⏲ *No lunch.*

Lompoc

20 miles west of Solvang.

Known as the flower-seed capital of the world, Lompoc is blanketed with vast fields of brightly colored flowers that bloom from May through August. Also home to a starkly beautiful mission, Lompoc has emerged as a major Pinot Noir and Chardonnay grape-growing region. Overlapping the Santa Rita Hills Wine Trail in parts, the Lompoc Wine Trail includes wineries in the Wine Ghetto, a downtown industrial park, and along Highway 246 and (to the south) Santa Rosa Road, which form a loop between Lompoc and Buellton.

GETTING HERE AND AROUND

Driving is the easiest way to get to Lompoc. From Santa Barbara, follow U.S. 101 north to Highway 1 exit off Gaviota Pass, or Highway 246 west at Buellton.

ESSENTIALS
VISITOR INFORMATION Lompoc Valley Chamber of Commerce & Visitors Bureau. ✉ *111 S. I St., at Hwy. 246* ☎ *805/736–4567* ⊕ *lompoc.com.*

Sights

La Purísima Mission State Historic Park
RELIGIOUS SITE | FAMILY | The state's most fully restored mission, founded in 1787, stands in a stark and still remote location that powerfully evokes the lives and isolation of California's Spanish settlers. Docents lead afternoon tours Wednesday–Sunday (daily June–August), and vivid displays illustrate the secular and religious activities that formed mission life. ✉ *2295 Purisima Rd., off Hwy. 246* ☎ *805/733–3713* ⊕ *www.lapurisimamission.org* 🎫 *$6 per vehicle* ⊗ *No tour Mon. and Tues. afternoon June.*

Lompoc Valley Flower Festival
FESTIVAL | Around the last weekend of June, Lompoc celebrates its floral heritage with a parade, a carnival, and a crafts show. ⊕ *explorelompoc.com.*

Lompoc Wine Ghetto
WINERY/DISTILLERY | Laid-back tasting rooms can be found in a downtown industrial park. Taste of Sta. Rita Hills and Flying Goat are two rooms worth checking out here. ✉ *200 N. 9th St.* ⊕ *lompoctrail.com* 🎫 *Tasting fees vary, some free* ⊗ *Many tasting rooms closed Mon.–Wed.*

Pismo Beach

40 miles north of Lompoc.

About 20 miles of sandy shoreline—nicknamed the Bakersfield Riviera for the throngs of vacationers who come here from the Central Valley—begins at the town of Pismo Beach. The southern end of town runs along sand dunes, some of which are open to cars and off-road vehicles. Sheltered by the dunes,

Volcanoes? ◉

Those eye-catching sawed-off peaks along the drive from Pismo Beach to Morro Bay are called the Nine Sisters—a series of ancient volcanic plugs. Morro Rock, the northernmost sibling and a state historic monument, is the most famous and photographed of the clan.

a grove of eucalyptus trees attracts thousands of migrating monarch butterflies from November through February. A long, broad beach fronts the center of town, where a municipal pier extends into the sea at the foot of shop-lined Pomeroy Street. To the north, hotels and homes perch atop chalky oceanfront cliffs. Fewer than 10,000 people live in this quintessential surfer haven, but Pismo Beach has a slew of hotels and restaurants with great views of the Pacific Ocean.

GETTING HERE AND AROUND
Pismo Beach straddles both sides of U.S. 101. If you're coming from the south and have time for a scenic drive, exit U.S. 101 in Santa Maria and take Highway 166 west for 8 miles to Guadalupe and follow Highway 1 north 16 miles to Pismo Beach. South County Area Transit (SCAT; ⊕ *www.slorta.org*) buses run throughout San Luis Obispo and connect the city with nearby towns. On summer weekends, the free Avila Trolley extends service to Pismo Beach.

ESSENTIALS
VISITOR INFORMATION California Welcome Center. ✉ *333 5 Cities Dr.* ☎ *805/773–7924.* **Pismo Beach Visitor Information Center.** ✉ *Dolliver St./Hwy. 1, at Hinds Ave.* ☎ *800/443–7778, 805/556–7397* ⊕ *classiccalifornia.com.*

San Luis Obispo County and Big Sur Coast

Pacific Grove
Salinas
Monterey
Carmel
Carmel Highlands
Pinnacles National Park
Gonzales
Bixby Creek Bridge
Point Sur State Historic Park
Big Sur
Soledad
Pfeiffer Beach
Pfeiffer Big Sur State Park
Central Big Sur
Greenfield
Julia Pfeiffer Burns State Park
Southern Big Sur
Highway 1
Lucia
King City
Lopez Point
San Lucas
Jade Cove
Gorda
Jolon
Ragged Point
Lake San Antonio
Lake Nacimiento
San Miguel
Piedras Blancas Light Station
Point Piedras Blancas
Piedras Blancas Elephant Seal Rookery
William Randolph Hearst Memorial Beach
Hearst Castle
San Simeon
Paso Robles
Sensorio
Shandon
Cambria
Harmony
Templeton
Atascadero
Cayucos
Santa Margarita
Morro Bay
Estero Bay
Los Osos
California Valley
Point San Luis Lighthouse
San Luis Obispo
TO SANTA BARBARA
Avila Beach
Pismo Beach
Arroyo Grande

PACIFIC OCEAN

0   15 mi
0   15 km

🏖 Beaches

★ Oceano Dunes State Vehicular Recreation Area

BEACH—SIGHT | Part of the spectacular Guadalupe-Nipomo Dunes, this 3,600-acre coastal playground is one of the few places in California where you can drive or ride off-highway vehicles on the beach and sand dunes. Hike, ride horses, kiteboard, join a Hummer tour, or rent an ATV or a dune buggy and cruise up the white-sand peaks for spectacular views. At **Oso Flaco Lake Nature Area**—3 miles west of Highway 1 on Oso Flaco Road—a 1½-mile boardwalk over the lake leads to a platform with views up and down the coast. Leashed dogs are allowed in much of the park except Oso Flaco and Pismo Dunes Natural Reserve. **Amenities:** food and drink; lifeguards (seasonal); parking (fee); showers; toilets; water sports. **Best for:** sunset; surfing; swimming; walking. ✉ *West end of Pier Ave., off Hwy. 1, Oceano* ☎ *805/473–7220* ⊕ *www.parks. ca.gov* 🅿 *$5 per vehicle.*

Pismo State Beach

BEACH—SIGHT | Hike, surf, ride horses, swim, fish in a lagoon or off the pier, and dig for Pismo clams at this busy state beach. One of the day-use parking areas is off Highway 1 near the **Monarch Butterfly Grove,** where from November through February monarch butterflies nest in eucalyptus and Monterey pines. The other parking area is about 1½ miles south at Pier Avenue. **Amenities:** food and drink; lifeguards (seasonal); parking (fee); showers; toilets; water sports. **Best for:** sunset; surfing; swimming; walking. ✉ *555 Pier Ave., off Hwy. 1, 3 miles south of downtown Pismo Beach,*

Oceano ☎ 805/473-7220 ⊕ www.parks.
ca.gov 🚗 Day-use $10 per vehicle if
parking at beach.

🍴 Restaurants

Cracked Crab

$$$ | SEAFOOD | This traditional New England–style crab shack imports fresh seafood daily from Australia, Alaska, and the East Coast. Fish is line-caught, much of the produce is organic, and everything is made from scratch. **Known for:** shellfish meals in a bucket, dumped on the table; casual setting; menu changes daily. Ⓢ *Average main: $30* ✉ *751 Price St., near Main St.* ☎ *805/773-2722* ⊕ *www. crackedcrab.com.*

Doc Burnstein's Ice Cream Lab

$ | AMERICAN | FAMILY | The delectable ice creams are churned on-site at this beloved old-fashioned parlor east of Pismo Beach. Top-selling flavors include the Elvis Special (banana and peanut butter) and Motor Oil, a blend of dark chocolate and Kahlua with a fudge swirl. **Known for:** antique model train that chugs along a circular ceiling track; different featured flavors every month along with the classics; Wednesday afternoon creamery tours. Ⓢ *Average main: $7* ✉ *114 W. Branch St., at Nevada St., east off U.S. 101, Arroyo Grande* ☎ *805/474-4688* ⊕ *docburnsteins.com.*

★ Ember

$$$ | MODERN AMERICAN | A barn-style restaurant with high ceilings and an open kitchen, Ember enjoys a red-hot reputation for Italian-inflected dishes prepared in an authentic Tuscan fireplace or a wood-burning oven. Chef-owner Brian Collins, a native of Arroyo Grande, the town bordering Pismo Beach, honed his culinary skills at Berkeley's legendary Chez Panisse Restaurant. **Known for:** seasonal menu changes monthly; wood-fired flatbread pizzas; long lines during prime time (no reservations). Ⓢ *Average main: $26* ✉ *1200 E. Grand Ave., at Brisco Rd.,* Arroyo Grande ☎ *805/474-7700* ⊕ *www. emberwoodfire.com* ⊗ *Closed Mon. and Tues. No lunch.*

Giuseppe's Cucina Italiana

$$$ | ITALIAN | The classic flavors of southern Italy are highlighted at this lively downtown spot. Most recipes originate from Bari, a seaport on the Adriatic; the menu includes breads and pizzas baked in the wood-burning oven, hearty dishes such as dry-aged steak and rack of lamb, and homemade pastas. **Known for:** lively family-style atmosphere; daily specials; most fruits and veggies come from owner's 12-acre farm. Ⓢ *Average main: $27* ✉ *891 Price St., at Pismo Ave.* ☎ *805/773-2870* ⊕ *giuseppesrestaurant.com* ⊗ *No lunch weekdays.*

Splash Café

$ | SEAFOOD | Folks stand in line down the block for clam chowder served in a sourdough bread bowl at this wildly popular seafood stand. You can also order beach food such as fresh steamed clams, burgers, and fried calamari at the counter (no table service) here and at Splash's second location in San Luis Obispo, which has an on-site bakery and additional menu items. **Known for:** famous clam chowder; sourdough bread bowls baked in house; cheery hole-in-the-wall. Ⓢ *Average main: $10* ✉ *197 Pomeroy St., at Cypress St.* ☎ *805/773-4653* ⊕ *splashcafe.com.*

The Spoon Trade

$$$ | AMERICAN | A silver spoon display at the entrance reflects this casual eatery's mission to "spoon food and trade stories" with diners who indulge in traditional American comfort food with a modern twist. Perennial menu faves include tri-tip tartare, deviled eggs, meat loaf Stroganoff, and fried chicken with sourdough waffles; save room for a root beer float or brown sugar pot de creme for dessert. **Known for:** pet-friendly patio; house-made pastas; lively dining room with open kitchen.

$ *Average main: $25* ✉ *295 W Grand Ave.* ☎ *805/904–6773* 🌐 *www.thespoontrade.com* 🕓 *No lunch weekdays.*

Ventana Grill

$$$ | **FUSION** | Perched on a bluff at the northern edge of Pismo Beach, Ventana Grill offers ocean views from nearly every table, unusual seafood-centered Latin American–California fusion dishes, and more than 50 tequilas plus craft cocktails at the bar. Reservations are essential—this place is almost always packed, especially during the weekday happy hour. **Known for:** happy hour with sunset views; salsas and sauces made from scratch; more than 50 tequila selections. $ *Average main: $27* ✉ *2575 Price St.* ☎ *805/773–0000* 🌐 *ventanagrill.com.*

Hotels

The Cliffs Hotel & Spa

$$$ | **RESORT** | Lawns and palm trees surround this full-service resort that perches dramatically on an oceanfront cliff. **Pros:** beach access via short downhill path; oceanfront restaurant and lounge; bluff-top walking trail. **Cons:** not close to downtown; rooms near service areas and elevator can be noisy; resort fee. $ *Rooms from: $209* ✉ *2757 Shell Beach Rd.* ☎ *805/773–5000, 800/826–7827* 🌐 *www.cliffsresort.com* 🛏 *160 rooms* 🍴 *No meals.*

Dolphin Bay Resort & Spa

$$$$ | **RESORT** | On grass-covered bluffs overlooking Shell Beach, this luxury resort looks and feels like an exclusive community of villas; choose among sprawling one- or two-bedroom suites, each with a gourmet kitchen, laundry room with washer and dryer, and contemporary furnishings. **Pros:** lavish apartment units; Lido farm-to-table restaurant; many suites have ocean views. **Cons:** hefty price tag; vibe too upper-crust for some; not close to downtown. $ *Rooms from: $489* ✉ *2727 Shell Beach Rd.* ☎ *805/773–4300, 800/516–0112 reservations, 805/773–8900 restaurant* 🌐 *www.thedolphinbay.com* 🛏 *60 suites* 🍴 *No meals.*

Hilton Garden Inn

$$$ | **HOTEL** | A slew of on-site amenities, easy access to the freeway and state beaches, and reasonable rates for the location make this chain hotel a good choice at the southern edge of Pismo Beach. **Pros:** newly renovated rooms with adjustable beds; on-site restaurant, bar and lounge; free parking and Wi-Fi. **Cons:** chain hotel; some rooms overlook freeway; not pet-friendly. $ *Rooms from: $199* ✉ *601 James Way* ☎ *805/773–6020* 🌐 *www.sanluisobispopismobeach.hgi.com* 🛏 *120 rooms* 🍴 *Breakfast.*

Inn at the Pier

$$$$ | **HOTEL** | The luxe Inn at the Pier opened in winter 2017, covering a prime city block just steps from the sand and across from the pier. **Pros:** walk to downtown restaurants, sights, shops; fitness center and cruiser bike rentals; new building. **Cons:** daily resort fee; valet parking only; bar noise travels to some rooms. $ *Rooms from: $269* ✉ *601 Cypress St.* ☎ *805/295–5565* 🌐 *www.theinnatthepier.com* 🛏 *104 rooms* 🍴 *No meals.*

Pismo Lighthouse Suites

$$$$ | **HOTEL** | Each of the well-appointed two-room, two-bath suites at this oceanfront resort has a private balcony or patio. **Pros:** sport court features life-size chess game; nautical-style furnishings; nice pool area. **Cons:** not easy to walk to main attractions; some units are next to busy road; first-floor units can hear footsteps from suites above. $ *Rooms from: $259* ✉ *2411 Price St.* ☎ *805/773–2411, 800/245–2411* 🌐 *www.pismolighthousesuites.com* 🛏 *70 suites* 🍴 *Breakfast.*

SeaVenture Beach Hotel & Restaurant
$$$ | **HOTEL** | The bright, homey rooms at this hotel all have fireplaces and featherbeds; most have balconies with private hot tubs, and some have beautiful ocean views. **Pros:** on the beach; excellent food; romantic rooms. **Cons:** touristy area; some rooms and facilities dated; dark hallways. [$] *Rooms from: $249* ✉ *100 Ocean View Ave.* ☎ *805/773–4994* 🌐 *www.seaventure.com* 🛏 *50 rooms* 🍴 *No meals.*

Avila Beach

4 miles north of Pismo Beach.

Because the village of Avila Beach and the sandy, cove-front shoreline for which it's named face south into the Pacific Ocean, they get more sun and less fog than any other stretch of coast in the area. With its fortuitous climate and protected waters, Avila's public beach draws sunbathers and families; summer weekends are very busy. Downtown Avila Beach has a lively seaside promenade and some shops and hotels, but for real local color, head to the far end of the cove and watch the commercial fishers offload their catch on the old Port San Luis wharf. On Friday from mid-April through mid-September, a fish and farmers' market livens up the beach area with music, fresh local produce and seafood, and children's activities.

GETTING HERE AND AROUND

Exit U.S. 101 at Avila Beach Drive and head 3 miles west to reach the beach. The free Avila Trolley operates weekends year-round, plus Friday afternoon and evening from April to September. The minibuses connect Avila Beach and Port San Luis to Shell Beach, with multiple stops along the way. Service extends to Pismo Beach in summer.

ESSENTIALS

VISITOR INFORMATION Avila Beach Tourism Alliance. 🌐 *visitavilabeach.com.*

Sights

Avila Valley Barn
RESTAURANT—SIGHT | **FAMILY** | An old-fashioned, family-friendly country store jam-packed with local fruits and vegetables, prepared foods, and gifts, Avila Valley Barn also gives visitors a chance to experience rural American traditions. You can pet farm animals and savor homemade ice cream and pies daily, and on weekends ride a hay wagon out to the fields to pick your own produce. ✉ *560 Avila Beach Dr., San Luis Obispo* ☎ *805/595–2816* 🌐 *www.avilavalleybarn.com* 🕒 *Closed Tues. and Wed. Jan.–Mar.*

Central Coast Aquarium
MUSEUM | You'll learn all about local marine plants and animals from the hands-on exhibits at this science center next to the main beach. ✉ *50 San Juan St., at 1st St., off Avila Beach Dr.* ☎ *805/595–7280* 🌐 *www.centralcoastaquarium.com* 🎟 *$8* 🕒 *Closed Mon.*

Point San Luis Lighthouse
LIGHTHOUSE | **FAMILY** | Docents lead hikes along scenic Pecho Coast Trail (3½ miles round-trip) to see the historic 1890 lighthouse and its rare Fresnel lens. **■ TIP→ If you'd prefer a lift out to the lighthouse, join a trolley tour. Hikes and tours require reservations.** ✉ *Point San Luis, 1¾ miles west of Harford Pier, Port San Luis* ☎ *805/540–5771, 805/528–8758 hikes reservations* 🌐 *www.pointsanluislighthouse.org* 🎟 *Trolley tours $22; hikes free ($5 to enter lighthouse).*

Beaches

Avila City Beach
BEACH—SIGHT | **FAMILY** | At the edge of a sunny cove next to downtown shops and restaurants, Avila's ½-mile stretch of white sand is especially family-friendly, with a playground, barbecue and picnic tables, volleyball and basketball courts, and lifeguards on watch in summer and on many holiday weekends. The

free beachfront parking fills up fast, but there's a nearby pay lot ($6 for the day, $2 after 4 pm). Dogs aren't allowed on the beach from 10 to 5. **Amenities:** food and drink; lifeguards (seasonal); parking; showers; toilets; water sports. **Best for:** sunset; surfing; swimming; walking. ✉ *Avila Beach Dr., at 1st St.* 🌐 *www.visitavilabeach.com* 🎫 *Free.*

🍴 Restaurants

Mersea's
$ | **SEAFOOD** | Walk down the pier to this casual crab shack where you can order at the counter, grab a drink at the bar, and find a seat on the deck or in the casual indoor dining area to gaze at spectacular Avila Bay views while you dine. The menu includes chowder bowls, burgers, sandwiches, seafood, and salads, plus bowls of fish, shrimp, or chicken served over rice pilaf and veggies. **Known for:** clam chowder in sourdough bread bowls; fish tacos; fresh local ingredients. [$] *Average main: $14* ✉ *3985 Port San Luis Pier* ⊕ *At Port San Luis* ☎ *805/548–2290* 🌐 *www.merseas.com.*

Ocean Grill
$$$ | **SEAFOOD** | Across from the promenade, beach, and pier, Ocean Grill serves up fresh seafood to diners who typically arrive before sunset to enjoy the views. Boats anchored in the bay provide much of the seafood, which pairs well with the mostly regional wines on the list. **Known for:** fantastic ocean views; wood-fired pizzas; gluten-free and vegetarian options. [$] *Average main: $29* ✉ *268 Front St.* ☎ *805/595–4050* 🌐 *www.oceangrillavila.com* ⏲ *No lunch Mon.–Thurs.*

🛏 Hotels

Avila La Fonda
$$$$ | **HOTEL** | Modeled after a village in early California's Mexican period, Avila La Fonda surrounds guests with rich jewel tones, fountains, and upscale comfort; its facade replicates eight different casitas, including several famous historic homes in Mexico. **Pros:** one-of-a-kind theme and artwork; flexible room combinations; a block from the beach. **Cons:** pricey for the area; most rooms don't have an ocean view; spotty Wi-Fi. [$] *Rooms from: $329* ✉ *101 San Miguel St.* ☎ *805/595–1700* 🌐 *www.avilalafondahotel.com* 🛏 *28 rooms* 🍽 *No meals.*

Avila Lighthouse Suites
$$$$ | **HOTEL** | Families, honeymooners, and business travelers all find respite at this two-story, all-suites luxury hotel. **Pros:** directly across from beach; easy walk to restaurants and shops; free underground parking. **Cons:** noise from passersby can be heard in room; some ocean-view rooms have limited vistas; basic breakfast. [$] *Rooms from: $359* ✉ *550 Front St.* ☎ *805/627–1900, 800/372–8452* 🌐 *www.avilalighthousesuites.com* 🛏 *54 suites* 🍽 *Breakfast.*

Avila Village Inn
$$$ | **HOTEL** | This intimate hotel embraces Craftsman style in its wood-and-stone architecture and in custom furnishings such as faux-Tiffany lampshades. **Pros:** in a residential community; access to great fitness center with pool; gorgeous lobby. **Cons:** some rooms are small and dark; several miles from the beach; spotty Wi-Fi. [$] *Rooms from: $200* ✉ *6655 Bay Laurel Dr.* ☎ *800/454–0840, 805/627–1810* 🌐 *www.avilavillageinn.com* 🛏 *30 rooms* 🍽 *No meals.*

Sycamore Mineral Springs Resort & Spa
$$$ | **RESORT** | This wellness resort's hot mineral springs bubble up into private outdoor tubs on an oak-and-sycamore-forest hillside. **Pros:** great place to rejuvenate; nice hiking nearby; incredible spa with yoga classes, integrative healing arts, and many treatments. **Cons:** rooms vary in quality; 2½ miles from the beach; road noise can travel to certain areas of property. [$] *Rooms from: $185* ✉ *1215 Avila Beach Dr., San*

Luis Obispo ☎ *805/595-7302* ⊕ *www. sycamoresprings.com* ➾ *72 rooms* †⊙| *No meals.*

San Luis Obispo

8 miles north of Avila Beach.

About halfway between San Francisco and Los Angeles, San Luis Obispo spreads out below gentle hills and rocky extinct volcanoes. Its main appeal lies in its architecturally diverse, pedestrian-friendly downtown, which bustles with shoppers, restaurant goers, and students from California Polytechnic State University, known as Cal Poly. On Thursday evening from 6 to 9 the city's famed farmers' market fills Higuera Street with local produce, entertainment, and food stalls.

GETTING HERE AND AROUND

U.S. 101/Highway 1 traverses the city for several miles. From the north, Highway 1 merges with U.S. 101 when it reaches the city limits. The wineries of the Edna Valley and Arroyo Grande Valley wine regions lie south of town off Highway 227, the parallel (to the east) Orcutt Road, and connecting roads.

SLO City Transit buses operate daily; Regional Transit Authority (SLORTA) buses connect with north county towns. The Downtown Trolley provides evening service to the city's hub every Thursday, on Friday from June to early September, and Saturday from April through October.

ESSENTIALS

VISITOR INFORMATION San Luis Obispo Chamber of Commerce. ⊠ *895 Monterey St.* ☎ *805/781-2777* ⊕ *www.visitslo.com.* **San Luis Obispo City Visitor Information.** ☎ *877/756-8698* ⊕ *www.sanluisobispovacations.com.*

◉ Sights

Biddle Ranch Vineyard

WINERY/DISTILLERY | Glass doors and walls in a converted dairy barn fill the Biddle Ranch Vineyard tasting room with light and sweeping valley, mountain, and vineyard views. The small-production winery focuses on estate Chardonnay (the adjacent 17-acre vineyard is planted exclusively to the grape), plus Pinot Noir and sparkling wines. The winery also crafts Sangiovese and Cabernet and Syrah blends. ⊠ *2050 Biddle Ranch Rd.* ⊹ *At Hwy. 227* ☎ *805/543-2399* ⊕ *www. biddleranch.com* ▨ *Tastings $15.*

Claiborne & Churchill

WINERY/DISTILLERY | An eco-friendly winery built from straw bales, C&C makes small lots of aromatic Alsatian-style wines such as dry Riesling and Gewürztraminer, plus Pinot Noir blends, Syrah, and Chardonnay. ⊠ *2649 Carpenter Canyon Rd., at Price Canyon Rd.* ☎ *805/544-4066* ⊕ *www.claibornechurchill.com* ▨ *Tastings $18.*

Edna Valley Vineyard

WINERY/DISTILLERY | For sweeping valley views and crisp Sauvignon Blancs and Chardonnays, head to the modern tasting bar here. ■TIP➔ **The 18 Barrel Flight tasting ($35) that showcases five exclusive, limited production wines, is the best option.** ⊠ *2585 Biddle Ranch Rd., off Edna Rd.* ☎ *805/544-5855* ⊕ *www.ednavalleyvineyard.com* ▨ *Tastings from $20.*

History Center of San Luis Obispo County

MUSEUM | FAMILY | Across the street from the old Spanish mission, the center presents exhibits that explore topics such as Native American life in the county, the California ranchos, and the impact of railroads. On the center's website are links to free downloadable video-podcast walking tours of historic San Luis Obispo. ⊠ *696 Monterey St., at Broad St.* ☎ *805/543-0638* ⊕ *www.historycenterslo.org* ▨ *Free* ⊙ *Closed Tues.*

Mission San Luis Obispo de Tolosa

RELIGIOUS SITE | Sun-dappled Mission Plaza fronts the fifth mission established in 1772 by Franciscan friars. A small museum exhibits artifacts of the Chumash Indians and early Spanish settlers. ⊠ *751 Palm St., at Chorro St.* ☎ *805/543–6850* ⊕ *www.missionsanluisobispo.org* ✉ *$3.*

Niven Family Wine Estates

WINERY/DISTILLERY | A refurbished 1909 schoolhouse serves as tasting room for four Niven Family wineries: Baileyana, Tangent, True Myth, and Zocker. The winemaker for all these labels is Christian Roguenant, whose Cadre Pinot Noirs are worth checking out. ⊠ *5828 Orcutt Rd., at Righetti Rd.* ☎ *805/269–8200* ⊕ *www.nivenfamilywines.com* ✉ *Tastings from $15.*

Old Edna

TOWN | This peaceful, 2-acre site once *was* the town of Edna. Nowadays you can peek at the vintage 1897 and 1908 farmhouse cottages, taste Sextant wines, pick up sandwiches at the gourmet deli, and stroll along Old Edna Lane. ⊠ *1655 Old Price Canyon Rd., at Hwy. 227* ☎ *805/710–3701 Old Edna Townsite, 805/542–0133 tasting room and deli* ⊕ *oldedna.com.*

Parks and Recreation Department

INFO CENTER | Hilly greenbelts with extensive hiking trails surround San Luis Obispo. For information about trailheads, call the parks department or download a trail map on its website. ☎ *877/756–8696* ⊕ *www.slocity.org/parksandrecreation.*

San Luis Obispo Children's Museum

MUSEUM | FAMILY | Activities at this facility geared to kids under age 10 include an "imagination-powered" elevator that transports visitors to a series of underground caverns. Elsewhere, simulated lava and steam sputter from an active volcano. Kids can pick rubber fruit at a farmers' market and race in a fire engine to fight a fire. ⊠ *1010 Nipomo St., at Monterey St.* ☎ *805/544–5437* ⊕ *www.*

slocm.org ✉ *$8* ⊘ *Closed nonholiday Mon. Sept.–Apr.*

San Luis Obispo Museum of Art

MUSEUM | The permanent collection here focuses on the artistic legacy of the Central Coast. Temporary exhibits include traditional and cutting-edge arts and crafts by Central Coast, national, and international artists. ⊠ *Mission Plaza, 1010 Broad St., at Monterey St.* ☎ *805/543–8562* ⊕ *www.sloma.org* ⊘ *Closed Tues. early July–early Sept.*

★ Talley Vineyards

WINERY/DISTILLERY | Acres of Chardonnay and Pinot Noir, plus smaller parcels of Sauvignon Blanc, Syrah, and other varietals blanket Talley's mountain-ringed dell in the Arroyo Grande Valley. The estate tour ($45), worth a splurge, includes wine and cheese, a visit to an 1860s adobe, and barrel-room tastings of upcoming releases. ⊠ *3031 Lopez Dr., off Orcutt Rd., Arroyo Grande* ☎ *805/489–0446* ⊕ *www.talleyvineyards.com* ✉ *Tastings from $15; tours from $25.*

Wolff Vineyards

WINERY/DISTILLERY | Syrah, Petite Sirah, and Riesling join the expected Pinot Noir and Chardonnay as the stars at this family-run winery 6 miles south of downtown. The pourers are friendly, and you'll often meet one of the owners or their children in the tasting room. With its hillside views, the outdoor patio is a great place to enjoy an afternoon picnic.

✉ 6200 Orcutt Rd., near Biddle Ranch Rd. ☎ 805/781–0448 🌐 www.wolffvineyards.com 🎫 Tastings $12.

🍴 Restaurants

Big Sky Café

$$ | **ECLECTIC** | Family-friendly Big Sky turns local and organically grown ingredients into global dishes, starting with breakfast. Just pick your continent: braised Argentinian lamb shanks, Southeast Asian noodle bowls, Middle Eastern lamb burger, Maryland crab cakes. **Known for:** artsy, creative vibe; ample choices for vegetarians; locavore pioneer. [$] *Average main: $21* ✉ *1121 Broad St., at Higuera St.* ☎ *805/545–5401* 🌐 *bigskycafe.com.*

Buona Tavola

$$$ | **ITALIAN** | Northern Italian dishes are this casual spot's specialty. You might find homemade pumpkin-stuffed tortellini in a creamy mascarpone sauce on the menu, or porcini-mushroom risotto with river shrimp. **Known for:** daily fresh fish and salad specials; impressive wine list; gluten-free menus. [$] *Average main: $25* ✉ *1037 Monterey St., near Osos St.* ☎ *805/545–8000* 🌐 *btslo.com* ⏲ *No lunch weekends.*

Café Roma

$$$ | **NORTHERN ITALIAN** | At this Railroad Square restaurant you can dine on authentic northern Italian cuisine in the warmly lit dining room or out on the covered patio. Menu favorites include ricotta-filled squash blossoms, and beef tenderloin glistening with porcini butter and a Pinot Noir reduction. **Known for:** classic Italian dining room and bar; well-selected international wine list with more than 200 choices; attentive service. [$] *Average main: $26* ✉ *1020 Railroad Ave., at Osos St.* ☎ *805/541–6800* 🌐 *www.caferomaslo.com* ⏲ *No lunch weekends.*

★ **Giuseppe's Cucina Rustica**

$$$ | **ITALIAN** | The younger sibling of the hugely popular Guiseppe's restaurant in Pismo Beach, this lively downtown eatery serves up authentic southern Italian fare in the historic Sinsheimer Bros. building, originally constructed in 1884. Dine in the spacious main restaurant amid high ceilings, fireplaces, and bar, or in the creekside courtyard beneath strings of twinkling lights. **Known for:** bread, sauce, pasta, gelato and other desserts made in-house; organic ingredients from the owner's 12-acre farm or sourced from local purveyors; historic ambience. [$] *Average main: $27* ✉ *849 Monterey St.* ☎ *805/541–9922* 🌐 *www.giuseppesrestaurant.com.*

Luna Red

$$$ | **INTERNATIONAL** | A spacious, contemporary space with a festive outdoor patio, this restaurant near Mission Plaza serves creative tapas and cocktails. The small plates include birria braised beef tacos, avocado-tuna ceviche, and empanadas stuffed with squash and goat cheese. **Known for:** excellent traditional Valencian paellas; craft cocktails; lively music scene. [$] *Average main: $27* ✉ *1023 Chorro St., at Monterey St.* ☎ *805/540–5243* 🌐 *www.lunaredslo.com.*

Mo's Smokehouse BBQ

$ | **SOUTHERN** | Barbecue joints abound on the Central Coast, but this one excels. Various Southern-style sauces season tender hickory-smoked ribs and shredded-meat sandwiches, and sides such as baked beans, coleslaw, homemade potato chips, and garlic bread extend the pleasure. **Known for:** barbecue sampler with ribs, pork, and chicken; barbecue chicken and other fresh salads; house-made potato chips, garlic fries, and other sides. [$] *Average main: $15* ✉ *1005 Monterey St., at Osos St.* ☎ *805/544–6193* 🌐 *smokinmosbbq.com.*

Novo Restaurant & Lounge

$$$ | ECLECTIC | In the colorful dining room or on the large creek-side deck, this animated downtown eatery will take you on a culinary world tour. The salads, small plates, and entrées come from nearly every continent. **Known for:** value-laden happy hour from 3 to 6; savory curry and noodle dishes; local farmers' market ingredients. [$] *Average main: $25* ✉ *726 Higuera St., at Broad St.* ☎ *805/543–3986* 🌐 *www.novorestaurant.com.*

SLO Provisions

$ | AMERICAN | Stop at this casual café/market in the Upper Monterey neighborhood for a sit-down or take-away meal all day. Apart from full meals, order specialty sandwiches, farm-fresh salads, and baked goods, or hang out and taste wine or beer at the casual tasting bar. **Known for:** house-roasted rotisserie meats; family-style dinners; daily specials. [$] *Average main: $14* ✉ *1255 Monterey St.* ☎ *805/439–4298* 🌐 *www.sloprovisions.com* 🕒 *Closed Sun.*

Vegetable Butcher

$$ | AMERICAN | Vegans, vegetarians, pescatarians, and carnivores alike can indulge in their preferred dietary choices in this casual downtown eatery in a spacious industrial-chic building, where organic and sustainably sourced Central Coast ingredients take center stage. Most menu choices (shared plates or larger mains, salads and rice bowls) begin with a plant-sourced foundation—add your preferred protein, or not. **Known for:** locally sourced premium meats and seafood; global flavors; happy hour weekdays. [$] *Average main: $21* ✉ *712 Marsh St.* ☎ *805/439–4801* 🌐 *www.vegetablebutcherslo.com* 🕒 *Closed Sun. No lunch Mon.*

🛏 Hotels

Apple Farm

$$$ | HOTEL | Decorated to the hilt with floral bedspreads and watercolors by local artists, this Wine Country–theme hotel is highly popular. **Pros:** flowers everywhere; convenient to Cal Poly and U.S. 101; creek-side setting. **Cons:** hordes of tourists during the day; some rooms too floral for some people's tastes; spotty Wi-Fi in some rooms. [$] *Rooms from: $219* ✉ *2015 Monterey St.* ☎ *800/255–2040, 805/544–2040* 🌐 *www.applefarm.com* 🛏 *106 rooms* 🍴 *No meals.*

Garden Street Inn

$$$ | B&B/INN | From this restored 1887 Italianate Queen Anne downtown, you can walk to many restaurants and attractions; uniquely decorated rooms, each with private bath, are filled with antiques, and some rooms have stained-glass windows, fireplaces, and decks. **Pros:** lavish homemade breakfast; convenient location; complementary wine-and-cheese reception. **Cons:** city noise filters into some rooms; not great for families; no elevator. [$] *Rooms from: $199* ✉ *1212 Garden St.* ☎ *805/545–9802, 800/488–2045* 🌐 *www.gardenstreetinn.com* 🛏 *13 rooms* 🍴 *Breakfast.*

Granada Hotel & Bistro

$$$$ | HOTEL | Built in 1922 in the heart of downtown and sparkling again after renovations completed in 2012, the two-story Granada is a vintage-style retreat with hardwood floors, redbrick walls, and antique rugs. **Pros:** one of a few full-service hotels in the heart of downtown; easy walk to restaurants, shops, and sights; farm-to-table Granada Bistro, Nightcap cocktail bar, and Nourish restaurant on-site. **Cons:** some rooms are tiny; sometimes noisy near restaurant kitchen; late-night bar noise travels to some rooms. [$] *Rooms from: $279* ✉ *1126 Morro St.* ☎ *805/544–9100* 🌐 *www.granadahotelandbistro.com* 🛏 *17 rooms* 🍴 *No meals.*

★ Hotel Cerro

$$$$ | HOTEL | San Luis Obispo's Chumash, mission, and 19th-century industrial eras blend with urban sophistication in thio eco-friendly, four-story complex, which opened in summer 2019. **Pros:** on-site restaurant, café, and lobby lounge; tree-lined outdoor terrace; designed and built to meet LEED Silver status. **Cons:** in the heart of the downtown bar scene. [$] *Rooms from: $275* ✉ *1125 Garden St.* ☎ *805/548–1000* 🌐 *www.hotelcerro.com* 🛏 *65 rooms* 🍴 *No meals.*

Hotel San Luis Obispo
$$$$ | **HOTEL** | Completed in 2019, the sleek, three-story Hotel San Luis Obispo offers a full range of services and upscale amenities, just a block from the mission and steps from restaurants, shops, and nightlife. **Pros:** in the heart of the downtown historic district; park the car and walk to most attractions; new building. **Cons:** valet parking only. [$] *Rooms from: $375* ✉ *877 Palm St.* ☎ *805/235–0700* 🌐 *hotel-slo.com* 🛏 *78 rooms* 🍴 *No meals.*

The Kinney San Luis Obispo
$$ | **HOTEL** | Redesigned and renamed in 2018, The Kinney celebrates nearby Cal Poly's culture and history in fun, hipster fashion, with local photos, college sports equipment displays, and hanging wicker swings and vintage games and books in the lobby lounge. **Pros:** close to Cal Poly campus; heated pool and sundeck; free parking and Wi-Fi. **Cons:** air-conditioning less than adequate in some rooms; tiny fitness center; motel vibe. [$] *Rooms from: $168* ✉ *1800 Monterey St.* ☎ *805/544–8600* 🌐 *www.thekinneyslo.com* 🛏 *100 rooms* 🍴 *Free Breakfast.*

★ **Madonna Inn**
$$$ | **HOTEL** | From its rococo bathrooms to its pink-on-pink froufrou steak house, the Madonna Inn is fabulous or tacky, depending on your taste. **Pros:** fun, one-of-a-kind experience; infinity pool, exercise room, and day spa; each room has its own distinct identity, for example, Safari Room. **Cons:** rooms vary widely; must appreciate kitsch; no elevator. [$] *Rooms from: $209* ✉ *100 Madonna Rd.* ☎ *805/543–3000, 800/543–9666* 🌐 *www.madonnainn.com* 🛏 *110 rooms* 🍴 *No meals.*

Petit Soleil
$$$ | **B&B/INN** | A cobblestone courtyard, country-French custom furnishings, and Gallic music piped through the halls evoke a Provençal mood at this cheery inn. **Pros:** includes wine and appetizers at cocktail hour; includes scrumptious breakfasts; cozy rooms with luxury touches. **Cons:** sits on a busy avenue; cramped parking; some rooms are tiny. [$] *Rooms from: $179* ✉ *1473 Monterey St.* ☎ *805/549–0321, 800/676–1588* 🌐 *www.psslo.com* 🛏 *16 rooms* 🍴 *Breakfast.*

SLO Brew Lofts
$$$$ | **HOTEL** | If you want to be in the heart of the downtown nightlife action, you can't get much closer than this contemporary collection of apartment-stye rooms on the second floor of the historic brick SLO Brew building. **Pros:** in the heart of downtown; upscale amenities; residential vibe. **Cons:** live music plays on the first floor Thursday–Monday; no on-site desk staff after business hours; parking is in a city lot several blocks away. [$] *Rooms from: $350* ✉ *738 Higuera St,* ☎ *805/543–1843* 🌐 *www.slobrew.com/the-lofts* 🛏 *5 suites* 🍴 *No meals.*

🍸 Nightlife

SLO's club scene is centered on Higuera Street, off Monterey Street.

Koberl at Blue
BARS/PUBS | A trendy crowd hangs out at this upscale restaurant's slick bar to sip on exotic martinis and the many local and imported beers and wines. ✉ *998 Monterey St., at Osos St.* ☎ *805/783–1135* 🌐 *www.epkoberl.com.*

The Libertine Brewing Company

BREWPUBS/BEER GARDENS | Come to Libertine to savor 76 craft beers and wines on tap, house-made brews of kombucha and cold brew coffee, and pub food infused with the brewery's own wild ales. ⊠ *1234 Broad St.* ☎ *805/548–2337* ⊕ *www.libertinebrewing.com/san-luis-obispo.*

Linnaea's

BARS/PUBS | A mellow java joint, Linnaea's hosts poetry readings, as well as blues, jazz, and folk music performances. ⊠ *1110 Garden St., at Higuera St.* ☎ *805/541–5888* ⊕ *linnaeas.com* ☞ *No events Mon.*

MoTav

BARS/PUBS | Chicago-style MoTav draws crowds with good pub food and live entertainment in a turn-of-the-20th-century setting, complete with antique U.S. flags and a wall-mounted moose head. ⊠ *725 Higuera St., at Broad St.* ☎ *805/541–8733* ⊕ *motherstavern.com.*

Nightcap

BARS/PUBS | Indulge in craft and vintage cocktails at the Granada Hotel's artsy cocktail lounge, decked out in pink- and rose-colored velvet, mirrored ceilings, and marble tables and countertops. ⊠ *1130 Morro St.* ☎ *805/544–9100.*

SLO Brew

BARS/PUBS | Handcrafted microbrews and live music most nights make for a winning combination at this downtown watering hole and restaurant in a restored historic brick building. In 2017 SLO Brew opened The Rock, a satellite brewing and tasting facility near the airport with a beer garden, restaurant, and regular live music performances. ⊠ *736 Higuera St.* ☎ *805/543–1843* ⊕ *www.slobrew.com.*

🎭 Performing Arts

Festival Mozaic

FESTIVALS | The festival celebrates five centuries of classical music during popular concert series held intermittently from mid-summer to early spring. ☎ *805/781–3009, 877/881–8899* ⊕ *www.festivalmozaic.com.*

Performing Arts Center, San Luis Obispo

ARTS CENTERS | A truly great performance space, the center hosts live theater, dance, and music. ⊠ *Cal Poly, 1 Grand Ave., off U.S. 101* ☎ *805/756–4849* ⊕ *www.calpolyarts.org.*

San Luis Obispo Repertory Theatre

THEATER | SLO County's only nonprofit, fully professional theater group presents dramas, musicals, readings, and other performances year-round. ⊠ *888 Morro St.* ☎ *805/786–2440 box office* ⊕ *www.slolittletheatre.org.*

🛍 Shopping

Higuera Street

SHOPPING NEIGHBORHOODS | Many of San Luis Obispo's locally owned and operated shops cluster around downtown's Higuera Street in the blocks east of the mission. Also head up Monterey Street just north of the mission to find additional one-of-a-kind treasures at junkgirls, Taste of SLO, and other small storefronts. ⊠ *San Luis Obispo.*

Morro Bay

14 miles north of San Luis Obispo.

Commercial fishermen slog around Morro Bay in galoshes, and beat-up fishing boats bob in the bay's protected waters. Nature-oriented activities take center stage here: kayaking, hiking, biking, fishing, and wildlife-watching around the bay and national marine estuary and along the state beach.

GETTING HERE AND AROUND
From U.S. 101 south or north, exit at Highway 1 in San Luis Obispo and head west. Scenic Highway 1 passes through the eastern edge of town. From Atascadero, two-lane Highway 41 West treks

over the mountains to Morro Bay. San Luis Obispo RTA Route 12 buses travel year-round between Morro Bay, San Luis Obispo, Cayucos, Cambria, San Simeon, and Hearst Castle. The Morro Bay Shuttle picks up riders throughout the town from Friday through Monday in summer ($1.25 one-way, $3 day pass).

ESSENTIALS

VISITOR INFORMATION Morro Bay Visitors Center. ⊠ *695 Harbor St., at Napa Ave.* ☎ *805/225–1633, 800/231–0592* ⊕ *www. morrobay.org.*

Sights

Embarcadero

NEIGHBORHOOD | The center of Morro Bay action on land is the Embarcadero, where vacationers pour in and out of souvenir shops and seafood restaurants and stroll or bike along the scenic half-mile Harborwalk to Morro Rock. From here, you can get out on the bay in a kayak or tour boat. ⊠ *On waterfront from Beach St. to Tidelands Park.*

Montaña de Oro State Park

NATIONAL/STATE PARK | West of San Luis Obispo, Los Osos Valley Road winds past farms and ranches to this state park whose miles of nature trails traverse rocky shoreline, wild beaches, and hills overlooking dramatic scenery. Check out the tide pools, watch the waves roll into the bluffs, and picnic in the eucalyptus groves. From Montaña de Oro you can reach Morro Bay by following the coastline along South Bay Boulevard 8 miles through the quaint residential villages of Los Osos and Baywood Park. ⊠ *West about 13 miles from downtown San Luis Obispo on Madonna Rd., to Los Osos Valley Rd., to Pecho Valley Rd.; to continue on to Morro Bay, backtrack east to Los Osos Valley Rd., then head north on S. Bay Blvd., and west on State Park Rd., San Luis Obispo* ☎ *805/528–0513, 805/772–7434* ⊕ *www. parks.ca.gov.*

Morro Bay Maritime Museum

MUSEUM | At this tiny but fascinating museum in a parking lot across from the harbor you can learn about Morro Bay's colorful maritime history, dating back thousands of years to the native tribes that fished along the coast. Displays include a tule boat constructed by Salinan tribal members, explorers and traders, commercial fishing, abalone diving, and recreational sailing and boating. If the museum is closed, you can still check out the outdoor exhibits, including a tugboat that rescued sailors from a sinking oil tanker torpedoed by the Japanese during World War II. ⊠ *1210 Embarcadero* ☎ *805/225–5044* ⊕ *morrobaymaritime.org* ☜ *Free* ☉ *Closed Sun.–Fri.*

Morro Bay State Park Museum of Natural History

MUSEUM | FAMILY | The museum's entertaining interactive exhibits explain the natural environment and how to preserve it—in the bay and estuary and on the rest of the planet. ■TIP→ **Kids age 16 and under are admitted free.** ⊠ *20 State Park Rd., south of downtown* ☎ *805/772–2694* ⊕ *centralcoastparks.org* ☜ *$3.*

Morro Rock

NATURE PRESERVE | At the mouth of Morro Bay stands 576-foot-high Morro Rock, one of nine small volcanic peaks, or morros, in the area. A short walk leads to a breakwater, with the harbor on one side and crashing ocean waves on the other. You may not climb the rock, where endangered falcons and other birds nest. Sea lions and otters often play in the water below the rock. ⊠ *Northern end of Embarcadero.*

Restaurants

Dorn's Original Breakers Cafe

$$ | SEAFOOD | This restaurant overlooking the harbor has satisfied local appetites since 1942. In addition to straightahead dishes such as cod or shrimp fish-and-chips or calamari tubes sautéed in butter and wine, Dorn's serves breakfast. **Known for:** sweeping views of Morro Rock and the bay; fresh local seafood; friendly, efficient service. $ *Average main: $22 ⊠ 801 Market Ave., at Morro Bay Blvd. ☎ 805/772–4415 ⊕ www. dornscafe.com.*

Taco Temple

$ | **SOUTHWESTERN** | This family-run diner serves some of the freshest food around. The seafood-heavy menu includes salmon burritos, superb fish tacos with mango salsa, and other dishes hailing from somewhere between California and Mexico. **Known for:** fresh seafood and salsa bar; hefty portions; daily specials. $ *Average main: $15 ⊠ 2680 Main St., at Elena St., just north of Hwy. 1/Hwy. 41 junction ☎ 805/772–4965 ⊕ tacotemple.com.*

★ Tognazzini's Dockside

$$ | **SEAFOOD** | Captain Mark Tognazzini catches seasonal seafood and delivers the bounty to his family's collection of down-home, no-frills enterprises in the harbor: a fish market with patio dining and up-close views of Morro Rock (Dockside Too), and the original Dockside restaurant. Local musicians play live music nearly every day at the outdoor patio at Dockside Too. **Known for:** fresh-as-it-gets local seafood; live music nearly every day year-round; front-row seats to Morro Rock views. $ *Average main: $20 ⊠ 1245 Embarcadero ☎ 805/772–8100 restaurant, 805/772–8120 fish market and patio dining.*

Windows on the Water

$$$$ | **SEAFOOD** | Diners at this second-floor restaurant view the sunset through giant picture windows. Meanwhile, fresh fish and other dishes based on local ingredients emerge from the wood-fired oven in the open kitchen, and oysters on the half shell beckon from the raw bar. **Known for:** sustainably sourced seafood; 20-plus wines by the glass; menu changes nightly. $ *Average main: $37 ⊠ 699 Embarcadero, at Pacific St. ☎ 805/772–0677 ⊕ www. windowsmb.com ⊗ No lunch.*

🛏 Hotels

★ Anderson Inn

$$$$ | **B&B/INN** | Friendly, personalized service and an oceanfront setting keep loyal patrons returning to this Embarcadero inn, which was built from scratch in 2008, and features well-appointed rooms with state-of-the-art tiled bathrooms and cozy comforters atop queen beds. **Pros:** walk to restaurants and sights; spacious rooms; oceanfront rooms have fireplaces and private balconies. **Cons:** not low-budget; waterfront area can get crowded; need to book well in advance—fills quickly. $ *Rooms from: $269 ⊠ 897 Embarcadero ☎ 805/772–3434, 866/950–3434 toll-free reservations ⊕ andersoninnmorrobay. com ⟳ 8 rooms ❍I No meals.*

Cass House

$$$$ | **B&B/INN** | In tiny Cayucos, 4 miles north of Morro Bay, a shipping pioneer's 1867 home is now a luxurious bed-and-breakfast surrounded by rose and other gardens. **Pros:** historic property; some ocean views; delicious lobster roll at The Grill. **Cons:** away from nightlife and attractions; not good for families; no elevator. $ *Rooms from: $265 ⊠ 222 N. Ocean Ave., Cayucos ☎ 805/995–3669 ⊕ casshousecayucos.com ⟳ 5 rooms ❍I Breakfast.*

456 Embarcadero Inn & Suites

$$$ | **HOTEL** | The rooms at this waterfront hotel are cheery and welcoming, and many have fireplaces. **Pros:** across from waterfront; free parking; in-room refrigerators and microwaves. **Cons:** tiny lobby; no pool; basic breakfast. $ *Rooms from: $189 ⊠ 456 Embarcadero ☎ 805/772–2700, 800/292–7625 ⊕ www.embarcaderoinn.com ⟳ 33 rooms ❍I Breakfast.*

The Inn at Morro Bay
$$$ | **RESORT** | Surrounded by eucalyptus trees, this inn abuts a heron rookery and Morro Bay State Park. **Pros:** great for wildlife lovers; stellar views from restaurant and some rooms; nearby golf course, wellness center on-site. **Cons:** some rooms on the small side; birds and seals can wake you early; some rooms need updating. $ *Rooms from: $189* ✉ *60 State Park Rd.* ☎ *805/772–5651* 🌐 *innatmorrobay.com* 🛏 *98 rooms* 🍴 *No meals.*

Activities

Kayak Horizons
KAYAKING | This outfit rents kayaks and paddleboards and gives lessons and guided tours. ✉ *551 Embarcadero, near Marina St.* ☎ *805/772–6444* 🌐 *kayakhorizons.com.*

The Paddleboard Co
WATER SPORTS | Come to this waterfront shop to rent stand-up paddleboards and to take paddleboard lessons and yoga and fitness classes (for all ages and skill levels), and stock up on outdoor wear and paddling gear. You can sign up for classes online as well. ✉ *575 Embarcadero* ☎ *805/225–5555* 🌐 *www.thepaddleboardcompany.com* 🎫 *Board rentals from $25 per hr, lessons from $85.*

Sub-Sea Tours & Kayaks
BOATING | You can view sea life aboard this outfit's glass-bottom boat, watch whales from its catamaran, or rent a kayak, canoe, or stand-up paddleboard. ✉ *699 Embarcadero* ☎ *805/772–9463* 🌐 *subseatours.com.*

Virg's Landing
FISHING | Virg's conducts deep-sea-fishing and whale-watching trips. ✉ *1169 Market Ave.* ☎ *805/772–1222* 🌐 *virgslanding.com.*

Paso Robles

30 miles north of San Luis Obispo, 25 miles northwest of Morro Bay.

In the 1860s, tourists began flocking to this ranching outpost to "take the cure" in a bathhouse fed by underground mineral hot springs. An Old West town emerged, and grand Victorian homes went up, followed in the 20th century by Craftsman bungalows. These days, the wooded hills of Paso Robles west of U.S. 101 and the flatter, more open land to the freeway's east hold more than 250 wineries, many with tasting rooms. Hot summer days, cool nights, and varied soils and microclimates allow growers to cultivate an impressive array of Bordeaux, Rhône, and other grape types. Cabernet Sauvignon grows well in the Paso Robles AVA—40,000 of its 600,000-plus acres are planted to grapes—as do Petit Verdot, Grenache, Syrah, Viognier, and Zinfandel. In recognition of the diverse growing conditions, the AVA was divided into 11 subappellations in 2014. Pick up a wine-touring map at lodgings, wineries, and attractions around town. The fee at most tasting rooms is between $10 and $25; many lodgings pass out discount coupons.

Upmarket restaurants, bars, antiques stores, and little shops fill the streets around oak-shaded City Park, where special events of all kinds—custom car shows, an olive festival, Friday-night summer concerts—take place on many weekends. Despite its increasing sophistication, Paso (as the locals call it) retains a small-town vibe. The city celebrates its cowboy roots in late July and early August with the two-week California Mid-State Fair, complete with livestock auctions, carnival rides, and corn dogs.

GETTING HERE AND AROUND

U.S. 101 runs north–south through Paso Robles. Highway 46 West links Paso Robles to Highway 1 and Cambria on the coast. Highway 46 East connects Paso Robles with Interstate 5 and the San Joaquin Valley. Public transit is not convenient for wine touring and sightseeing.

VISITOR INFORMATION Paso Robles CAB Collective. ☎ 805/543–2288 ⊕ pasoroblescab.com. **Paso Robles Wine Country Alliance.** ☎ 805/239–8463 ⊕ pasowine. com. **Paso Robles Visitor Center.** ✉ 1225 Park St., near 12th St. ☎ 805/238–0506 ⊕ travelpaso.com. **Rhone Rangers/Paso Robles.** ⊕ www.rhonerangers.org.

👁 Sights

★ Calcareous Vineyard

WINERY/DISTILLERY | Elegant wines, a stylish tasting room, and knockout hilltop views make for a winning experience at this winery along winding Peachy Canyon Road. Cabernet Sauvignon, Syrah, and Zinfandel grapes thrive in the summer heat and limestone soils of the two vineyards near the tasting room; and a third vineyard on cooler York Mountain produces Pinot Noir, Chardonnay, and a Cabernet with a completely different character from the Peachy Canyon edition. ∎TIP→ The picnic area's expansive eastward views invite lingering. ✉ 3430 Peachy Canyon Rd. ☎ 805/239–0289 ⊕ calcareous.com ☜ Tastings $15; tour and tasting (reservations required) from $35.

Carnegie Historic Library

LIBRARY | Philanthropist and steel magnate Andrew Carnegie funded this sturdy and splendid structure, erected in 1908. The jewel of City Park, it hosts thoughtful exhibits on local history, many of which include quirky products and advertisements from days gone by. ✉ 800 12th St., at Park St. ☎ 805/238–4996 ⊕ www. pasorobleshistoricalsociety.org ⊙ Closed Mon., Wed., and holidays.

Eberle Winery

WINERY/DISTILLERY | Even if you don't drink wine, stop here for a tour of the huge wine caves beneath the vineyards (departs every half hour all day). Eberle produces wines from Bordeaux, Rhône, and Italian varietals and makes intriguing blends including Grenache Blanc–Viognier and Cabernet Sauvignon–Syrah. ✉ 3810 Hwy. 46 E, 3½ miles east of U.S. 101 ☎ 805/238–9607 ⊕ www.eberlewinery. com ☜ Basic tasting and tour free, private tour and tasting $35 by appointment.

Estrella Warbirds Museum

MUSEUM | FAMILY | An entertaining homage to fighter planes, flyboys, and flygirls, this museum maintains indoor exhibits about wartime aviation and displays retired aircraft outdoors and in repair shops. Bonus attraction: a huge building with spruced-up autos, drag racers, and "funny cars." ✉ 4251 Dry Creek Rd., off Airport Rd., north off Hwy. 46E ☎ 805/238–9317 ⊕ ewarbirds.org ☜ $10 ⊙ Closed Mon.– Wed. except legal holidays.

Firestone Walker Brewing Company

WINERY/DISTILLERY | At this working craft brewery you can sample medal-winners such as the Double Barrel Ale and learn about the beer-making process on 30-minute guided tours of the brew house and cellar. ✉ 1400 Ramada Dr., east side of U.S. 101; exit at Hwy. 46 W/ Cambria, but head east ☎ 805/225–5911 ⊕ www.firestonebeer.com ☜ Tastings from $2 per sample, tour $10 (includes 4 samples).

Halter Ranch Vineyard

WINERY/DISTILLERY | A good place to learn about contemporary Paso Robles wine making, this ultramodern operation produces high-quality wines from estate-grown Bordeaux and Rhône grapes grown in sustainably farmed vineyards. The gravity-flow winery, which you can view on tours, is a marvel of efficiency. Ancestor, the flagship wine, a potent Bordeaux-style blend of Cabernet Sauvignon, Petit Verdot, and Malbec, is named for the ranch's huge centuries-old coast oak tree. ⊠ *8910 Adelaida Rd., at Vineyard Dr.* ☎ *888/367–9977* ⊕ *www.halterranch. com* ⊠ *Tastings $20.*

★ **HammerSky Vineyards**
WINERY/DISTILLERY | Owner Doug Hauck handcrafts Bordeaux-centric wines on a 50-acre estate on the far western slopes of Paso Robles. Set amid rolling hills of vineyards punctuated by a huge oak, HammerSky's bright-white contemporary structure houses both the tasting and barrel-aging rooms; an outdoor patio has views of the estate vines. ⊠ *7725 Vineyard Dr., at Jensen Rd.* ☎ *805/239–0930* ⊕ *www.hammersky.com* ⊠ *Tastings $15.*

★ **Jada Vineyard & Winery**
WINERY/DISTILLERY | Jada biodynamically farms 65 acres of estate vineyards in the Templeton Gap/Willow Creek district, and uses the flavorful fruit to craft its nuanced, highly structured wines. Two worth checking out are Jack of Hearts, starring Petit Verdot, and Passing By, a Cabernet-heavy blend. Galzignato also shines with Tannat and with Rhône-style wines, particularly Grenache. ⊠ *5620 Vineyard Dr., north of Hwy. 46 W* ☎ *805/226–4200* ⊕ *jadavineyard.com* ⊠ *Tastings $15.*

JUSTIN Vineyards & Winery
WINERY/DISTILLERY | This suave winery built its reputation on Isosceles, a hearty Bordeaux blend, usually of Cabernet Sauvignon, Cabernet Franc, and Merlot. JUSTIN's Cabernet Sauvignon is also well regarded, as is the Right Angle blend of Cab and three other varietals. Tastings here take place in an expansive room whose equally expansive windows provide views of the hillside vineyards. ⊠ *11680 Chimney Rock Rd., 15 miles west of U.S. 101's Hwy 46 E exit; take 24th St. west and follow road (name changes along the way) to Chimney Rock Rd.* ☎ *805/238–6932* ⊕ *justinwine. com* ⊠ *Tastings $25, tour and tasting $30* ☞ *Tours 10 and 2:30 (reservations recommended).*

Paso Robles Pioneer Museum
MUSEUM | The delightful museum's one-room schoolhouse and its displays of ranching paraphernalia, horse-drawn vehicles, hot-springs artifacts, and photos evoke Paso's rural heritage. ⊠ *2010 Riverside Ave., at 21st St.* ☎ *805/239–4556* ⊕ *www.pasoroblespioneermuseum.org* ⊠ *Free* ⊗ *Closed Mon.–Wed.*

Paso Robles Wine Festival
FESTIVAL | Most local wineries pour at this mid-May outdoor festival that has live bands and diverse food vendors. Winery open houses and winemaker dinners round out the weekend. ⊠ *City Park, Spring St., between 10th and 12th Sts.* ☎ *805/239–8463* ⊕ *www.pasowine. com* ⊠ *$80 basic admission, designated driver $25.*

★ **Pasolivo**
WINERY/DISTILLERY | While touring the idyllic west side of Paso Robles, take a break from wine tasting by stopping at Pasolivo. Find out how the artisans here make their Tuscan-style olive oils on a high-tech Italian press, and test the acclaimed results. ⊠ *8530 Vineyard Dr., west off U.S. 101 (Exit 224) or Hwy. 46 W (Exit 228)* ☎ *805/227–0186* ⊕ *www. pasolivo.com* ⊠ *Tastings $5.*

Pomar Junction Vineyard & Winery
WINERY/DISTILLERY | **FAMILY** | A vintage railroad boxcar and a caboose provide a visual change of pace at Pomar Junction. Its flagship wine, Train Wreck, is a daring but usually winning blend of Cabernet Sauvignon, Zinfandel, Mourvèdre, Syrah, and Petite Sirah. With sparkling wine, a Grenache Blanc, Pinot Noir, a smooth Merlot, and several white and red blends, there's something for pretty much everyone here. ■TIP→ Picnic areas shaded by elms, oaks, and other trees—not to mention old farm equipment and those train cars—make this a popular stop for wine tasters with kids. ⊠ *5036 S. El Pomar Rd., at El Pomar Dr.* ☎ *805/238–9940* ⊕ *pomarjunction.com* ⊠ *Tastings from $10.*

Re:Find Handcrafted Spirits

WINERY/DISTILLERY | The owners of Villacana Winery in west Paso Robles launched the first local distillery in 2011, aiming to repurpose the saignee (free-run juice) that's typically tossed out during the wine-making process. They ferment and distill the leftover high-quality juices into premium spirits, thus reclaiming about 60 acres of premium wine grapes. Taste vodka, gin, whiskey, bourbon, limoncello, and kumquat liqueurs in the tiny tasting space in the barrel room. ⊠ *2725 Adelaida Rd.* ☎ *805/239–9456* ⊕ *refinddistillery.com.*

River Oaks Hot Springs & Spa

SPA—SIGHT | The lakeside spa, on 240 hilly acres near the intersection of U.S. 101 and Highway 46 East, is a great place to relax after wine tasting or festival-going. Soak in a private indoor or outdoor hot tub fed by natural mineral springs, or indulge in a massage or facial. ⊠ *800 Clubhouse Dr., off River Oaks Dr., just north of River Oaks Golf Course* ☎ *805/238–4600* ⊕ *riveroakshotsprings. com* 🖭 *From $15 per hr.*

Robert Hall Winery

WINERY/DISTILLERY | The late Robert Hall's winery made its reputation on a well-made, reasonably priced Cabernet Sauvignon from Paso Robles AVA grapes, but at the high-ceilinged tasting room you can sample less widely distributed wines. These include a reserve Cabernet, a Merlot, a Malbec, a Bordeaux-style Meritage blend, and a Port made from Portuguese grapes. Whites of note include Roussanne, Sauvignon Blanc, and Viognier. ■TIP→ **Ask for a 30-minute tour if you'd like to see the production facilities.** ⊠ *3443 Mill Rd., at Hwy. 46E, 3 miles east of U.S. 101* ☎ *805/239–1616* ⊕ *roberthallwinery.com* 🖭 *Tastings $15; tour free.*

Sensorio

This 386-acre interactive garden engages the senses, honors the natural topography, and offers a wide range of amusing,

SIP Certification

Many wineries in Paso Robles take pride in being SIP (Sustainability in Practice) Certified, for which they undergo a rigorous third-party audit of their entire operations. Water and energy conservation practices are reviewed, along with pest management and other aspects of farming. Also considered are the wages, benefits, and working conditions of the employees, and the steps taken to mitigate the impact of grape growing and wine production on area habitats.

mystical, and kinetic experiences. It launches with an interactive light installation by Bruce Munro. ⊠ *Paso Robles.*

Studios on the Park

MUSEUM | A 1951 Hudson Hornet (a nod to the building's automotive past) greets visitors at the entrance to this nonprofit open studios art center on the east side of the downtown City Park. Interact with professional artists as they work on their latest pieces, browse the four galleries and gift shop, and on the first Saturday evening of the month, sip wine and listen to music while viewing the center's latest art exhibit. ⊠ *1130 Pine St.* ☎ *805/238–9800* ⊕ *www.studiosonthepark.org.*

SummerWood Winery

WINERY/DISTILLERY | Rhône varietals do well in the Paso Robles AVA, where many wineries, including this one, produce "GSM" (Grenache, Syrah, Mourvèdre) red blends, along with whites such as Viognier, Marsanne, and Grenache Blanc. Winemaker Mauricio Marchant displays a subtle touch with Rhône whites and reds, as well as Sentio, a Petit Verdot–heavy Bordeaux red blend. Tastings here are relaxed and informal, and there's a patio from which you can enjoy the vineyard views. ✉ 2175 Arbor Rd., off Hwy. 46W ☎ 805/227–1365 ⊕ summerwoodwine. com 🍷 Tastings $15.

Tablas Creek Vineyard

WINERY/DISTILLERY | Tucked in the western hills of Paso Robles, Tablas Creek is known for its blends of certified biodynamically grown, hand-harvested Rhône varietals. Roussanne and Viognier are the standout whites; the Mourvèdre-heavy blend called Panoplie (it also includes Grenache and Syrah) has received high praise in recent years. ■TIP→ There's a fine picnic area here. ✉ 9339 Adelaida Rd., west of Vineyard Dr. ☎ 805/237–1231 ⊕ www.tablascreek.com 🍷 Tastings from $15 (reserve $40 by appointment), tour free.

★ Tin City

WINERY/DISTILLERY | This industrial park on the southern border of Paso Robles houses a collection of wineries, craft breweries, distilleries, and specialty shops where you can pick up sheep's milk ice cream, fresh pasta, and other local wares. Good places to start your explorations include Giornata Winery, Levo Winery, Barrel House Brewery, and TinCity Cider House. Dine casually at Tin Canteen restaurant or upscale (dinner only) at Six Test Kitchen. ✉ Limestone Way ✛ East of Ramada Dr. via Marquita Ave. ⊕ www.tincitypaso.com.

Villa San-Juliette Vineyard & Winery

WINERY/DISTILLERY | Nigel Lithgoe (co-creator of So You Think You Can Dance is one of his many titles), and Ken Warwick (executive producer of American Idol, among other programs) established this winery northeast of Paso Robles. With a cast that includes Petit Verdot, a fine Grenache, and a perky Albariño (a Spanish white varietal), their stylish operation is no flash in the pan. From 11 to 4 you can order snacks, panini, pizzas, soup and salad, and cheese and charcuterie

plates to enjoy with your wine in the tasting room or on the view-filled outdoor terrace. ✉ 6385 Cross Canyons Rd., at Ranchita Canyon Rd., San Miguel ☎ 805/467–0014 ⊕ www.villasanjuliette. com 🍷 Tastings $15 ⊗ Closed Tues. and Wed. except by appointment.

Vina Robles

WINERY/DISTILLERY | "European inspiration, California character" is the motto of this winery whose owners hail from Switzerland. The flagship Suendero wine is a lush blend of Cabernet Sauvignon and Petit Verdot. You can enjoy it along with some winery-only whites and reds at the large hospitality center. ■TIP→ In good weather the patio out back, outfitted with a fountain and a fire pit and shaded by a large oak tree, is a nice relaxing space to hang out. ✉ 3700 Mill Rd., at Hwy. 46E, 3 miles east of U.S. 101 ☎ 805/227–4812 ⊕ vinarobles.com 🍷 Tastings $15, wine and cheese pairing $35, wine and food pairing $70 by appointment.

🍴 Restaurants

BL Brasserie

$$$$ | FRENCH | Owner-chef Laurent Grangien's handsome, welcoming French bistro occupies an 1890s brick building across from City Park. He focuses on traditional dishes such as duck confit, rack of lamb, and onion soup, but always prepares a few au courant daily specials as well. Known for: classic French dishes made with local ingredients; good selection of local and international wines; four- or five-course tasting menus. $ Average main: $32 ✉ 1202 Pine St., at 12th St. ☎ 805/226–8191 ⊕ www.bistrolaurent. com ⊗ Closed Sun. and Mon.

The Hatch

$$ | AMERICAN | A wood-fired rotisserie in an open kitchen, simple but tasty comfort foods and a lively bar scene attract locals and visitors alike to this cozy, casual space in an historic brick building a block north from the main square. Fuel

up body and soul with menu favorites like meat loaf, shrimp and grits, bacon burgers, donuts, cakes, and sundaes. **Known for:** house-made sauces, house-pickled fruits and veggies, house-cured ham; craft cocktails and small-batch whiskies; daily rotisserie specials: chicken, ribs, lamb, tri-tip. $ *Average main: $22* ⊠ *835 13th St.* ☎ *805/221–5727* ⊕ *hatchpaso-robles.com* ⊘ *No lunch.*

★ Il Cortile
$$$$ | MODERN ITALIAN | One of two Paso establishments owned by chef Santos MacDonal and his wife, Carole, this Italian restaurant entices diners with complex flavors and a contemporary space with art-deco overtones. Consistent crowd-pleasers often on the menu include beef carpaccio with white truffle cream sauce and shaved black truffles and pappardelle with wild boar ragu. **Known for:** house-made pastas; excellent wine pairings; ingredients from chef's garden. $ *Average main: $38* ⊠ *608 12th St., near Spring St.* ☎ *805/226–0300* ⊕ *www.ilcortileristorante.com* ⊘ *Closed Tues. No lunch.*

Jeffry's Wine Country BBQ
$ | AMERICAN | Award-winning local chef Jeff Wiesinger and his wife Kathleen opened this casual eatery, tucked in a hidden courtyard a block from downtown City Park. Feast indoors or out on made-to-order sandwiches, hearty mac-and-cheese bowls, house-made potato chips, fresh salads, craft beer, and local wines while listening to throwback sound tracks from the '60s and '70s. **Known for:** delectable mac-and-cheese dishes; smoked tri-tip and other meats; savory paella. $ *Average main: $15* ⊠ *819 12th St., Suite B* ✥ *In alley between 12th and 13th Sts.* ☎ *805/369–2132* ⊕ *jeffryswinecountrybbq.com* ⊘ *Closed Wed.*

La Cosecha
$$$ | SOUTH AMERICAN | At barlike, tin-ceilinged La Cosecha (Spanish for "the harvest"), Honduran-born chef

Santos MacDonal faithfully re-creates dishes from Spain and South America. Noteworthy starters include *pastelitos catracho*, Honduran-style empanadas in a light tomato sauce served with *queso fresco* (fresh cheese) and micro cilantro. **Known for:** fusion of Latin spices and fresh local fare; daily paella special; artisanal cocktails. $ *Average main: $29* ⊠ *835 12th St., near Pine St.* ☎ *805/237–0019* ⊕ *www.lacosechabr. com* ⊘ *Closed Mon. Closed Tues. Jan. and Feb.*

McPhee's Grill
$$$$ | AMERICAN | Just south of Paso Robles in tiny Templeton, this casual chophouse in an 1860s wood-frame storefront serves sophisticated, contemporary versions of traditional Western fare such as oak-grilled filet mignon and fresh seafood tostadas. The house-label wines, made especially for the restaurant, are quite good. **Known for:** meats grilled over red oak; local seasonal menu; excellent wine selections. $ *Average main: $34* ⊠ *416 S. Main St., at 5th St., Templeton* ☎ *805/434–3204* ⊕ *mcpheesgrill.com* ⊘ *No lunch Sun.*

Tin Canteen
$ | AMERICAN | Decorated in industrial-chic style befitting its Tin City location, this lively eatery with an open kitchen and wood-fired oven showcases local and regional ingredients. The menu changes frequently depending on what's in season, but usually includes faves like garlic fries, burgers, and farm-to-table appetizers and salads. **Known for:** fresh pastas from the neighboring shop; lively local vibe; close to tasting rooms, distilleries, breweries, and shops. $ *Average main: $15* ⊠ *3070 Limestone Way* ✥ *in Tin City* ☎ *805/369–2787* ⊕ *www.tincanteenpaso. net* ⊘ *Closed Mon. and Tues. No dinner Wed. and Sun.*

Hotels

★ Allegretto

$$$$ | RESORT | This swank, 20-acre Tuscan-style resort amid estate vineyards is also a private museum where owner Douglas Ayres displays hundreds of artworks and artifacts collected on his world travels: ancient Indian river stones and statues; a massive cross section from a giant sequoia; Russian and California impressionist paintings; mandalas; and more (nonguests are welcome to walk around). **Pros:** yoga in medieval abbey; full-service restaurant Cello and spa; bocce ball, fire pit, and other diversions. **Cons:** not close to downtown square; pricey; some rooms close to courtyard music. [$] *Rooms from: $349* ✉ *2700 Buena Vista Dr.* ☎ *805/369–2500* 🌐 *www.allegrettoresort.com* ➪ *171 rooms.*

★ Hotel Cheval

$$$$ | HOTEL | Equestrian themes surface throughout this intimate European-style boutique hotel a half block from the main square and near some of Paso's best restaurants. **Pros:** most rooms have fireplaces; sip wine and champagne at the on-site Pony Club and zinc bar; extremely personalized service. **Cons:** views aren't great; no pool or hot tub; no elevator. [$] *Rooms from: $380* ✉ *1021 Pine St.* ☎ *805/226–9995, 866/522–6999* 🌐 *www.hotelcheval.com* ➪ *16 rooms* 🍴 *Breakfast.*

JUST Inn

$$$$ | B&B/INN | Fine wines, a destination restaurant, and a vineyard's-edge setting make a stay at Justin winery's on site inn an exercise in sophisticated seclusion. **Pros:** amazing night skies; vineyard views; destination restaurant. **Cons:** half-hour drive to town; location may be too secluded for some; spotty cell service. [$] *Rooms from: $475* ✉ *11680 Chimney Rock Rd.* ☎ *805/238–6932, 800/726–0049* 🌐 *www.justinwine.com* ➪ *4 suites* 🍴 *Breakfast.*

La Bellasera Hotel & Suites

$$$ | HOTEL | A full-service hotel just off Highway 101 at the Highway 46 exit, La Bellasera caters to those looking for high-tech amenities and easy access to major Central Coast roadways. **Pros:** oversize rooms; Romanesque architectural features; close to freeways. **Cons:** far from downtown; at a major intersection; freeway noise heard in some rooms. [$] *Rooms from: $199* ✉ *206 Alexa Ct.* ☎ *805/238–2834, 866/782–9669* 🌐 *labellasera.com* ➪ *60 rooms* 🍴 *No meals.*

La Quinta Inn & Suites

$$$ | HOTEL | A good value for Paso Robles, this three-story chain property attracts heavy repeat business with its upbeat staff and slew of perks. **Pros:** apartment-style suites in separate building; free happy hour with local wines and appetizers; good for leisure or business travelers. **Cons:** conventional decor; not downtown; basic breakfast. [$] *Rooms from: $189* ✉ *2615 Buena Vista Dr.* ☎ *805/239–3004, 800/753–3757* 🌐 *www.laquintapasorobles.com* ➪ *101 rooms* 🍴 *Breakfast.*

Paso Robles Inn

$$ | HOTEL | On the site of an old spa hotel of the same name, the various buildings at this historic inn cluster around a lush, shaded garden with a pool. **Pros:** private hot tubs in many rooms; special touches like unique photography in each room; across from town square. **Cons:** fronts a busy street; rooms vary in size and amenities. [$] *Rooms from: $149* ✉ *1103 Spring St.* ☎ *805/238–2660, 800/676–1713* 🌐 *www.pasoroblesinn.com* ➪ *122 rooms* 🍴 *No meals.*

★ SummerWood Inn

$$$$ | B&B/INN | Easygoing hospitality, vineyard-view rooms, and elaborate breakfasts make this inn a mile west of U.S. 101 worth seeking out. **Pros:** convenient wine-touring base; elaborate breakfasts; complimentary tastings at associated winery. **Cons:** some noise from nearby highway during the day;

no elevator; not close to downtown restaurants. $ *Rooms from: $300* ⊠ *2130 Arbor Rd., 1 mile west of U.S. 101, at Hwy. 46W* ☎ *805/227–1111* ⊕ *www. summerwoodwine.com/inn* ⚲ *9 rooms* ⧖ *Breakfast.*

▽ Nightlife

1122 Speakeasy

BARS/PUBS | Press the doorbell and request permission to enter this elegant, 1930s-era cocktail lounge and speakeasy on the back patio of Pappy McGregor's Pub on the main square. It has just 28 seats, so be prepared to wait in line on weekend nights. ⊠ *1122 Pine St.* ⚑ *Entrance on Railroad St. or walk through pub* ☎ *805/805–8055* ⊕ *www.eleven-twentytwo.com* ⚲ *Closed Mon.*

⊕ Performing Arts

Vina Robles Amphitheatre

CONCERTS | At this 3,300-seat, Mission-style venue with good food, wine, and sight lines, you can enjoy acclaimed musicians in concert. ⊠ *Vina Robles winery, 3800 Mill Rd., off Hwy. 46* ☎ *805/286–3680* ⊕ *www.vinarobles-amphitheatre.com* ⚲ *Performances Apr.–Nov.*

Cambria

28 miles west of Paso Robles, 20 miles north of Morro Bay.

Cambria, set on piney hills above the sea, was settled by Welsh miners in the 1890s. In the 1970s the isolated setting attracted artists and other independent types; the town now caters to tourists, but it still bears the imprint of its bohemian past. Both of Cambria's downtowns, the original East Village and the newer West Village, are packed with art and crafts galleries, antiques shops, cafés, restaurants, and bed-and-breakfasts.

Two diverting detours lie between Morro Bay and Cambria. In the laid-back beach town of **Cayucos,** 4 miles north of Morro Bay, you can stroll the long pier, feast on chowder (at Duckie's), and sample the namesake delicacies of the Brown Butter Cookie Co. Over in **Harmony,** a quaint former dairy town 7 miles south of Cambria (population 18), you can take in the glassworks, pottery, and other artsy enterprises.

GETTING HERE AND AROUND
Highway 1 leads to Cambria from the north and south. Highway 246 West curves from U.S. 101 through the mountains to Cambria. San Luis Obispo RTA Route 12 buses stop in Cambria (and Hearst Castle).

ESSENTIALS
VISITOR INFORMATION Cambria Chamber of Commerce. ⊠ *767 Main St.* ☎ *805/927–3624* ⊕ *www.cambriachamber.org.*

⊙ Sights

Covells California Clydesdales

NATURE PRESERVE | Come to the vast 2,000-acre Covells Ranch to see one of the world's largest private stands of endangered Monterey pines and witness herds of gentle Clydesdales roaming the range. Much of the ranch is in a conservation easement that will never be developed. The two-hour guided tours include a 3-mile ride that takes you through an historic picnic grove amid the pines to the barn. The ranch also offers trail rides and Saturday-night barbecue dinners at the barn, where you can take a hayride on a custom-built "people mover" wagon. ⊠ *5694 Bridge St.* ☎ *805/975–7332* ⊕ *www.covellscaliforniaclydesdales. com* ⧖ *Tours $100 per person, Sat.-night barbecues $100 per person* ⊙ *Tours, trail rides, and barbecues by appointment only.*

Fiscalini Ranch Preserve

NATURE PRESERVE | Walk down a mile-long coastal bluff trail to spot migrating whales, otters, and shorebirds at this

450-acre public space. Miles of additional scenic trails crisscross the protected habitats of rare and endangered species of flora and fauna, including a Monterey pine forest, western pond turtles, monarch butterflies, and burrowing owls. Dogs are permitted on-leash everywhere and off-leash on all trails except the bluff. ⊠ *Hwy. 1, between Cambria Rd. and Main St. to the north, and Burton Dr. and Warren Rd. to the south; access either end of bluff trail off Windsor Blvd.* ☎ *805/927–2856* ⊕ *www.ffrpcambria.org.*

Leffingwell Landing

CITY PARK | A state picnic ground, the landing is a good place for examining tidal pools and watching otters as they frolic in the surf. ⊠ *North end of Moonstone Beach Dr.* ☎ *805/927–2070.*

Moonstone Beach Drive

SCENIC DRIVE | The drive runs along a bluff above the ocean, paralleled by a 3-mile boardwalk that winds along the beach. On this photogenic walk you might glimpse sea lions and sea otters, and perhaps a gray whale during winter and spring. Year-round, birds fly about, and tiny creatures scurry amid the tidepools. ⊠ *Off Hwy. 1.*

Nit Wit Ridge

HOUSE | Arthur Beal (aka Captain Nit Wit, Der Tinkerpaw) spent 51 years building a home above Cambria's West Village out of collected junk: beer cans, rocks, abalone shells, car parts, TV antennas—you name it. The site, sometimes signed as Nitt Witt Ridge, is a state landmark. ■TIP→ **You can drive by and peek in—from the 700 block of Main Street, head southeast on Cornwall Street and east on Hillcrest Drive. Or, schedule a guided tour.** ⊠ *881 Hillcrest Dr.* ☎ *805/927–2690* ⊕ *visitcambriaca.com* ⌦ *$10.*

★ Stolo Family Vineyards

WINERY/DISTILLERY | Just 3 miles from the ocean and a short drive from Cambria's East Village, the 52-acre Stolo estate produces about 5,000 cases of premium wine each year. The estate Syrahs consistently win top awards; sample these and other estate wines, including Pinot Noir, dry Gewurztraminer, Sauvignon Blanc, and Chardonnays, in the hilltop tasting room on the site of a former dairy farm. If the weather's nice, sit out on the sprawling lawn near a 1920s barn and 1895 farmhouse. ⊠ *3776 Santa Rosa Creek Rd.* ☎ *805/924–3131* ⊕ *stolofamilyvineyards.com.*

🍴 Restaurants

Centrally Grown at Off the Grid

$$ | MODERN AMERICAN | A collection of sustainably conscious spaces fashioned from repurposed materials, Centrally Grown encompasses a coffee shop, wine tasting, exotic gardens, and a second-floor restaurant with fantastic views of San Simeon Bay and the Big Sur Coast. The restaurant, decorated in a "planet-friendly chic" style that includes a driftwood archway, serves classic California cuisine with global influences. **Known for:** all-day dining; great place to stop before or after driving the Big Sur Coast; exotic gardens with meandering paths. $ *Average main: $22* ⊠ *7432 Exotic Garden Dr., off Hwy. 1* ☎ *800/927–3563* ⊕ *www.centrallygrown.com.*

Linn's Restaurant

$$$ | AMERICAN | FAMILY | Homemade olallieberry pies, soups, potpies, and other farmhouse comfort foods share the menu at this spacious East Village restaurant with fancier farm-to-table dishes such as organic, free-range chicken topped with raspberry-orange-cranberry sauce. Also on-site are a bakery, a café serving more casual fare (take-out available), and a gift shop that sells gourmet foods. **Known for:** olallieberry pie; numerous gluten-free and vegan options; family-owned-and-operated for decades. $ *Average main: $25* ⊠ *2277 Main St., at Wall St.* ☎ *805/927–0371* ⊕ *www.linnsfruitbin.com.*

★ Madeline's

$$$$ | FRENCH FUSION | Dine on stellar French-American delights at a romantic, candlit table in this tiny restaurant within a tasting room and wineshop in Cambria's West Village. The menu changes seasonally, but you might start with crab and lobster cakes or lamb empanadas, then move on to Louisiana seafood gumbo or Long Island duck breast, and bananas foster or crème brûlée for dessert. **Known for:** unusual entrées like venison chops and rabbit; excellent selection of local wines; five-course chef's tasting menu ($55). $ *Average main: $33 ⊠ 788 Main St. ☎ 805/927–4175 ⊙ No lunch.*

Robin's

$$$ | ECLECTIC | An international, vegetarian-friendly dining experience awaits you at this cozy East Village cottage. Dinner choices include wild prawn enchiladas, grilled Skuna Bay salmon, lamb curry, and short ribs. **Known for:** savory curries; top-notch salmon bisque; secluded (heated) garden patio. $ *Average main: $28 ⊠ 4095 Burton Dr., at Center St. ☎ 805/927–5007 ⊕ robinsrestaurant.com.*

★ Sea Chest Oyster Bar and Restaurant

$$$$ | SEAFOOD | Cambria's best place for seafood fills up soon after it opens at 5:30 (no reservations taken). Those in the know grab seats at the oyster bar and take in spectacular sunsets while watching the chefs broil fresh halibut, steam garlicky clams, and fry crispy calamari steaks; if you arrive to a wait, play cribbage or checkers in the game room. **Known for:** New England chowder house vibe; savory cioppino; waiting areas in wine bar, game room, and patio with fire pit. $ *Average main: $32 ⊠ 6216 Moonstone Beach Dr., near Weymouth St. ☎ 805/927–4514 ⊕ www.seachestrestaurant.com ▭ No credit cards ⊙ Closed Tues. mid-Sept.–May. No lunch.*

🛏 Hotels

Bluebird Inn

$$ | HOTEL | This sweet motel in Cambria's East Village sits amid beautiful gardens along Santa Rosa Creek. **Pros:** excellent value; well-kept gardens; friendly staff. **Cons:** few frills; basic rooms; not on beach. $ *Rooms from: $125 ⊠ 1880 Main St. ☎ 805/927–4634, 800/552–5434 ⊕ www.bluebirdinncambria.com/ ➷ 37 rooms ⊙ No meals.*

Cambria Pines Lodge

$$ | RESORT | This 25-acre retreat up the hill from the East Village is a good choice for families; accommodations range from basic fireplace cabins to motel-style standard rooms to large fireplace suites and deluxe suites with spa tubs. **Pros:** short walk from downtown; live music nightly in the lounge; verdant gardens. **Cons:** service and housekeeping not always top-quality; some units need updating; thin walls in some units. $ *Rooms from: $149 ⊠ 2905 Burton Dr. ☎ 805/927–4200, 800/966–6490 ⊕ www.cambriapineslodge.com ➷ 152 rooms ⊙ Breakfast.*

Fog Catcher Inn

$$$ | B&B/INN | The landscaped gardens and 10 faux-thatched and timbered buildings here evoke an English-country village. **Pros:** romantic rooms; across from Moonstone Beach; updated furnishings. **Cons:** breakfast quality varies; pricey rates. $ *Rooms from: $209 ⊠ 6400 Moonstone Beach Dr. ☎ 805/927–1400, 800/425–4121 ⊕ www.fogcatcherinn.com ➷ 60 rooms ⊙ Breakfast.*

J. Patrick House

$$$ | B&B/INN | Monterey pines and flower gardens surround this Irish-theme inn, which sits on a hilltop above Cambria's East Village. **Pros:** fantastic breakfasts; friendly innkeepers; quiet neighborhood. **Cons:** few rooms; fills up quickly; not pet- or kid-friendly. $ *Rooms from: $195 ⊠ 2990 Burton Dr. ☎ 805/927–3812 ⊕ jpatrickhouse.com ➷ 7 rooms ⊙ Breakfast.*

Moonstone Landing

$$$ | HOTEL | This up-to-date motel's amenities, reasonable rates, and accommodating staff make it a Moonstone Beach winner. **Pros:** sleek furnishings; across from the beach; cheery lounge. **Cons:** narrow property; some rooms overlook a parking lot. $ *Rooms from: $189 ⊠ 6240 Moonstone Beach Dr.* ☎ *805/927–0012, 800/830–4540* ⊕ *www.moonstonelanding.com* ⇨ *29 rooms* ❑ *Breakfast.*

★ Olallieberry Inn

$$$ | B&B/INN | The second-oldest home in Cambria (built in 1875) and a national historic monument, this painstakingly restored bed-and-breakfast inn offers luxurious creature comforts in a pristine English garden setting on the banks of Santa Rosa Creek. **Pros:** gourmet three-course breakfast; wine hour with homemade appetizers; walk to East Village restaurants and shops. **Cons:** no elevator; no children under 12; some rooms front busy road. $ *Rooms from: $225 ⊠ 2476 Main St.* ☎ *805/927–3222* ⊕ *www.olallieberry.com* ⇨ *9 rooms* ❑ *Free Breakfast.*

San Simeon

9 miles north of Cambria, 65 miles south of Big Sur.

Whalers founded San Simeon in the 1850s, but had virtually abandoned it by 1865, when Senator George Hearst began purchasing most of the surrounding ranch land. Hearst turned San Simeon into a bustling port, and his son, William Randolph Hearst, further developed the area while erecting Hearst Castle (one of the many remarkable stops you'll encounter when driving along Highway 1). Today San Simeon is basically a strip of unremarkable gift shops and so-so motels that straddle Highway 1 about 4 miles south of the castle's entrance, but **Old San Simeon,** right across from the entrance, is worth a peek. Julia Morgan, William Randolph Hearst's architect, designed some of the village's Mission Revival–style buildings.

GETTING HERE AND AROUND

Highway 1 is the only way to reach San Simeon. Connect with the highway off U.S. 101 directly or via rural routes such as Highway 41 West (Atascadero to Morro Bay) and Highway 46 West (Paso Robles to Cambria).

San Simeon Chamber of Commerce Visitor Center
⊠ *250 San Simeon Ave.* ☎ *805/927–3500* ⊕ *www.visitsansimeonca.com.*

◉ Sights

★ Hearst Castle

CASTLE/PALACE | Officially known as "Hearst San Simeon State Historical Monument," Hearst Castle sits in solitary splendor atop La Cuesta Encantada (the Enchanted Hill). Its buildings and gardens spread over 127 acres that were the heart of newspaper magnate William Randolph Hearst's 250,000-acre ranch. Hearst commissioned renowned California architect Julia Morgan to design the estate, but he was very much involved with the final product, a blend of Italian, Spanish, and Moorish styles. The 115-room main structure and three huge "cottages" are connected by terraces and staircases and surrounded by pools, gardens, and statuary. In its heyday the castle, whose buildings hold about 22,000 works of fine and decorative art, was a playground for Hearst and his guests—Hollywood celebrities, political leaders, scientists, and other well-known figures. Construction began in 1919 and was never officially completed. Work was halted in 1947 when Hearst had to leave San Simeon because of failing health. The Hearst Corporation donated the property to the State of California in 1958, and it is now part of the state park system.

Access to the castle is through the visitor center at the foot of the hill, where you can view educational exhibits and a 40-minute film about Hearst's life and the castle's construction. Buses from the center zigzag up to the hilltop estate, where guides conduct four daytime tours, each with a different focus: Grand Rooms, Upstairs Suites, Designing the Dream, and Cottages and Kitchen. These tours take about three hours and include a movie screening, and time at the end to explore the castle's exterior and gardens. In spring and fall, docents in period costume portray Hearst's guests and staff for the Evening Tour, which begins around sunset. Reservations are recommended for all tours, which include a ½-mile walk and between 150 and 400 stairs. ⊠ *San Simeon State Park, 750 Hearst Castle Rd.* ☎ *800/444–4445, 518/218–5078 international reservations* ⊕ *www.hearstcastle.org* ⚑ *Daytime tours from $25, evening tours $36.*

Hearst Ranch Winery
WINERY/DISTILLERY | Old whaling equipment and Hearst Ranch and Hearst Castle memorabilia decorate this winery's casual Old San Simeon outpost. The tasting room occupies part of Sebastian's, a former whaling store built in 1852 and moved by oxen to its present location in 1878. The flagship wines include a Bordeaux-style red blend with Petite Sirah added to round out the flavor, and Rhône-style white and red blends. Malbec and Tempranillo are two other strong suits. ■TIP→ **Templeton chef Ian McPhee serves burgers and other lunch items at the adjacent deli, whose outdoor patio is a delight in good weather.** ⊠ *442 SLO San Simeon Rd., off Hwy. 1* ☎ *805/927–4100* ⊕ *www.hearstranchwinery.com* ⚑ *Tastings from $10.*

Piedras Blancas Elephant Seal Rookery
NATURE PRESERVE | **FAMILY** | A large colony of elephant seals (at last count 25,000) gathers every year at Piedras Blancas Elephant Seal Rookery, on the beaches near Piedras Blancas Lighthouse. The huge males with their pendulous, trunklike noses typically start appearing on shore in late November, and the females begin to arrive in December to give birth—most babies are born in the last two weeks of January. The newborn pups spend about four weeks nursing before their mothers head out to sea, leaving them on their own; the "weaners" leave the rookery when they are about 3½ months old. The seals return in the spring and summer months to molt or rest, but not en masse as in winter. You can watch them from a boardwalk along the bluffs just a few feet above the beach; do not attempt to approach them as they are wild animals. The nonprofit Friends of the Elephant Seal runs a small visitor center and gift shop (*250 San Simeon Ave.*) in San Simeon. ⊠ *Off Hwy. 1, 4½ miles north of Hearst Castle, just south of Piedras Blancas Lighthouse* ☎ *805/924–1628* ⊕ *www.elephantseal.org.*

Piedras Blancas Light Station
TOUR—SIGHT | If you think traversing craggy, twisting Highway 1 is tough, imagine trying to navigate a boat up the rocky coastline (*piedras blancas* means "white rocks" in Spanish) near San Simeon before lighthouses were built. Captains must have cheered wildly when the beam began to shine here in 1875. Try to time a visit to include a morning tour (reservations not required). Tours are at 9:45 am on Tuesday, Thursday, and Saturday year-round (except for on major holidays). ■TIP→ **Do not meet your guide at the gate to the lighthouse—you'll miss the tour. Meet instead at the former Piedras Blancas Motel, 1½ miles north of the light station.** ⊠ *San Simeon* ☎ *805/927–7361* ⊕ *www.piedrasblancas.org* ⚑ *$10* ☞ *No pets allowed.*

Did You Know?

McWay Cove at Julia Pfeiffer Burns State Park is one of the most famous spots on the Big Sur Coast.

Beaches

William Randolph Hearst Memorial Beach
BEACH—SIGHT | This wide, sandy beach edges a protected cove on both sides of San Simeon Pier. Fish from the pier or from a charter boat, picnic and barbecue on the bluffs, or boogie board or bodysurf the relatively gentle waves. In summer you can rent a kayak and paddle out into the bay for close encounters with marine life and sea caves. The NOAA Coastal Discovery Center, next to the parking lot, has interactive exhibits and hosts educational activities and events. **Amenities:** food and drink; parking; toilets; water sports. **Best for:** sunset; swimming; walking. ✉ *750 Hearst Castle Rd., off Hwy. 1, west of Hearst Castle entrance* ☎ *805/927–2020, 805/927–6575 Coastal Discovery Center* 🌐 *www.parks.ca.gov/?page_id=589* 🎟 *Free.*

Hotels

Cavalier Oceanfront Resort
$$$ | **HOTEL** | Reasonable rates, an oceanfront location, evening bonfires, and well-equipped rooms—some with wood-burning fireplaces and private patios—make this motel a great choice. **Pros:** on the bluffs; fantastic views; close to Hearst Castle. **Cons:** room amenities and sizes vary; pools are small and sometimes crowded; some rooms need updating. [$] *Rooms from: $229* ✉ *9415 Hearst Dr.* ☎ *805/927–4688, 800/826–8168* 🌐 *www.cavalierresort.com* 🛏 *90 rooms* 🍴 *No meals.*

The Morgan San Simeon
$$ | **HOTEL** | On Highway 1's ocean side, the Morgan offers motel-style rooming options in two buildings designed to reflect the life and style of Hearst Castle architect, Julia Morgan. **Pros:** fascinating artwork; easy access to Hearst Castle; some ocean views. **Cons:** not right on beach; no fitness room or laundry facilities. [$] *Rooms from: $149* ✉ *9135 Hearst Dr.* ☎ *805/927–3878, 800/451–9900* 🌐 *www.hotel-morgan.com* 🛏 *55 rooms* 🍴 *Breakfast.*

Southern Big Sur

Hwy. 1 from San Simeon to Julia Pfeiffer Burns State Park.

This especially rugged stretch of oceanfront is a rocky world of mountains, cliffs, and beaches.

GETTING HERE AND AROUND

Highway 1 is the only major access route from north or south. From the south, access Highway 1 from U.S. 101 in San Luis Obispo. From the north, take rural route Highway 46 West (Paso Robles to Cambria) or Highway 41 West (Atascadero to Morro Bay). Nacimiento-Fergusson Road snakes through mountains and forest from U.S. 101 at Jolon about 25 miles to Highway 1 at Kirk Creek, about 4 miles south of Lucia; this curving, at times precipitous road is a motorcyclist favorite, not recommended for the faint of heart or during inclement weather.

Sights

★ Highway 1
SCENIC DRIVE | One of California's most spectacular drives, Highway 1 snakes up the coast north of San Simeon. Numerous pullouts along the way offer tremendous views and photo ops. On some of the beaches huge elephant seals lounge nonchalantly, seemingly oblivious to the attention of rubberneckers. Heavy rain sometimes causes mudslides that block the highway north and south of Big Sur. ⚠ **Sections of Highway 1 are sometimes closed for general maintenance or to repair damage from natural incidents such as mudslides. It's wise to visit bigsurcalifornia.org and click on the Highway 1 Conditions and Information link for the latest news before you travel.** 🌐 *www.dot.ca.gov.*

Jade Cove

NATURE SITE | In Los Padres National Forest just north of the town of Gorda is Jade Cove, a well-known jade-hunting spot. Rock hunting is allowed on the beach, but you may not remove anything from the walls of the cliffs. ✉ *Hwy. 1, 34 miles north of San Simeon.*

Julia Pfeiffer Burns State Park

NATIONAL/STATE PARK | The park provides fine hiking, from an easy ½-mile stroll with marvelous coastal views to a strenuous 6-mile trek through redwoods. The big draw here, an 80-foot waterfall that drops into the ocean, gets crowded in summer; still, it's an astounding place to contemplate nature. Migrating whales, harbor seals, and sea lions can sometimes be spotted just offshore. ✉ *Hwy. 1, 15 miles north of Lucia* ☎ *831/667–2315* 🌐 *www.parks.ca.gov* 🎟 *$10.*

Hotels

Ragged Point Inn

$$$ | **HOTEL** | At this cliff-top resort—the only inn and restaurant for miles around—glass walls in most rooms open to awesome ocean views. **Pros:** on the cliffs; good burgers and locally made ice cream; idyllic views. **Cons:** busy road stop during the day; often booked for weekend weddings; spotty cell phone service. [$] *Rooms from: $219* ✉ *19019 Hwy. 1, 20 miles north of San Simeon, Ragged Point* ☎ *805/927–4502, 805/927–5708 restaurant, 888/584–6374* 🌐 *www.raggedpointinn.com* 🔑 *39 rooms* 🍴 *No meals.*

Treebones Resort

$$$$ | **RESORT** | Perched on a hilltop surrounded by national forest and stunning, unobstructed ocean views, this yurt resort provides a stellar back-to-nature experience along with creature comforts. **Pros:** luxury yurts with cozy beds; lodge with fireplace and games; local food at Wild Coast Restaurant and decked sushi bar. **Cons:** steep paths; no private bathrooms; not good for families with young children. [$] *Rooms from: $370* ✉ *71895 Hwy. 1, Willow Creek Rd., 32 miles north of San Simeon, 1 mile north of Gorda* ☎ *805/927–2390, 877/424–4787* 🌐 *www.treebonesresort.com* 🔑 *16 yurts, 1 autonomous tent, 5 campsites, 1 human nest w/campsite* 🍴 *Breakfast* ☞ *2-night minimum.*

Central Big Sur

Hwy. 1, from Partington Cove to Bixby Bridge.

The countercultural spirit of Big Sur—which instead of a conventional town is a loose string of coast-hugging properties along Highway 1—is alive and well today. Its few residents include the very wealthy, the enthusiastically outdoorsy, and the thoroughly evolved: since the 1960s the Esalen Institute, a center for alternative education and East–West philosophical study, has attracted seekers of higher consciousness and devotees of the property's hot springs. Today posh and rustic resorts hidden among the redwoods cater to visitors drawn from near and far by the extraordinary scenery and serene isolation.

GETTING HERE AND AROUND

From the north, follow Highway 1 south from Carmel. From the south, continue the drive north from Julia Pfeiffer Burns State Park on Highway 1. Monterey-Salinas Transit operates the Line 22 Big Sur bus from Monterey and Carmel to Central Big Sur (the last stop is Nepenthe), daily from late May to early September and weekends only the rest of the year.

BUS CONTACT Monterey-Salinas Transit. ☎ *888/678–2871* 🌐 *www.mst.org.*

👁 Sights

Bixby Creek Bridge

BRIDGE/TUNNEL | The graceful arc of Bixby Creek Bridge is a photographer's dream. Built in 1932, the bridge spans a deep canyon, more than 100 feet wide at the bottom. From the north-side parking area you can admire the view or walk the 550-foot structure. ⊠ *Hwy. 1, 6 miles north of Point Sur State Historic Park, 13 miles south of Carmel, Big Sur.*

Pfeiffer Big Sur State Park

NATIONAL/STATE PARK | Among the many hiking trails at Pfeiffer Big Sur, a short route through a redwood-filled valley leads to a waterfall. You can double back or continue on the more difficult trail along the valley wall for views over miles of treetops to the sea. ⊠ *47231 Hwy. 1, Big Sur* ☎ *831/667–2315* ⊕ *www.parks. ca.gov* ⌦ *$10 per vehicle.*

★ Pfeiffer Canyon Bridge

BRIDGE/TUNNEL | In February 2017, heavy winter rains caused an old concrete bridge built in 1968 to crack and slip downhill at Pfeiffer Canyon, in the heart of Big Sur. Engineers deemed the old bridge irreparable, and auto and pedestrian access to Highway 1 south of the bridge was cut off indefinitely. CalTrans quickly made plans to construct a new, $24-million bridge to span the deep canyon. Normally, such a massive project would take at least seven years, but CalTrans accelerated the project and completed it in less than a year. The new bridge—a 21st-century engineering marvel—stretches 310 feet across the ravine without the need for column support. It's made of 15 steel girders, each weighing 62 tons and connected by steel plates holding 14,000 bolts. ⊠ *Hwy. 1, Big Sur* ✛ *0.7 mile south of Big Sur Station.*

Point Sur State Historic Park

NATIONAL/STATE PARK | An 1889 lighthouse at this state park still stands watch from atop a large volcanic rock. Four lighthouse keepers lived here with their families until 1974, when the light station became automated. Their homes and working spaces are open to the public only on 2½- to 3-hour ranger-led tours. Considerable walking, including up two stairways, is involved. Strollers are not allowed. ⊠ *Hwy. 1, 7 miles north of Pfeiffer Big Sur State Park, Big Sur* ☎ *831/625–4419* ⊕ *www.pointsur.org* ⌦ *$15* ☞ *Call or visit website for current tour schedule.*

🏖 Beaches

Pfeiffer Beach

BEACH—SIGHT | Through a hole in one of the gigantic boulders at secluded Pfeiffer Beach, you can watch the waves break first on the seaside and then on the beach side. Keep a sharp eye out for the unsigned, nongated road to the beach: it branches west of Highway 1 between the post office and Pfeiffer Big Sur State Park. The 2-mile, one-lane road descends sharply. **Amenities:** parking (fee); toilets. **Best for:** solitude; sunset. ⊠ *Off Hwy. 1, 1 mile south of Pfeiffer Big Sur State Park, Big Sur* ⌦ *$10 per vehicle.*

🍴 Restaurants

★ Deetjen's Big Sur Inn

$$$ | **AMERICAN** | The candle-lighted, creaky-floor restaurant in the main house at the historic inn of the same name is a Big Sur institution. It serves spicy seafood paella, grass-fed filet mignon, and rack of lamb for dinner and flavorful eggs Benedict for breakfast. **Known for:** rustic, romantic setting; ingredients from sustainable purveyors; stellar weekend breakfast. Ⓢ *Average main: $30* ⊠ *Hwy. 1, 3½ miles south of Pfeiffer Big Sur State Park, Big Sur* ☎ *831/667–2378* ⊕ *www.deetjens.com* ☺ *No lunch.*

★ Nepenthe

$$$$ | **AMERICAN** | It may be that no other restaurant between San Francisco and Los Angeles has a better coastal view than Nepenthe, named for an opiate mentioned in Greek literature that would induce a state of "no sorrow." For the real show, settle on the terraced deck in the late afternoon, order a glass from the extensive wine list, and watch the sun slip into the Pacific Ocean. **Known for:** ambrosia burger, fresh fish, hormone-free steaks; multiple view decks; brunch and lunch at casual outdoor Café Kevah. $ *Average main: $32 ⊠ 48510 Hwy. 1, 2½ miles south of Big Sur Station, Big Sur ☎ 831/667–2345 ⊕ nepenthebigsur.com.*

★ **Sierra Mar**

$$$$ | AMERICAN | At cliff's edge 1,200 feet above the Pacific at the ultrachic Post Ranch Inn, Sierra Mar serves cutting-edge American cuisine made from mostly organic, seasonal ingredients, some from the on-site chef's garden. The four-course prix-fixe option always shines, and the six-course tasting menu centers on ingredients grown or foraged on the property or sourced locally. **Known for:** stunning panoramic ocean views; one of the nation's most extensive wine lists; iconic Big Sur farm-to-table experience. $ *Average main: $125 ⊠ Hwy. 1, 1½ miles south of Pfeiffer Big Sur State Park, Big Sur ☎ 831/667–2800 ⊕ www.postranchinn.com/dining.*

★ **The Sur House**

$$$$ | AMERICAN | The Ventana Inn's restaurant sits high on a ridge, and magnificent terraces offer stunning ocean views and a full-service outdoor bar. Regional and international wines on a comprehensive list pair well with the California-inspired dishes, many of whose ingredients are sourced from local purveyors, and the bar serves seasonal specialty cocktails and California craft beers. **Known for:** stunning views; Pacific-sourced seafood and free-range meats and produce from local purveyors; excellent wine list. $ *Average main: $40 ⊠ 48123 Hwy. 1, 1½ miles south of Pfeiffer Big Sur State Park, Big Sur ☎ 831/667–2331 ⊕ www.ventanainn.com.*

🛏 Hotels

Big Sur Lodge

$$$$ | HOTEL | The lodge's modern, motel-style cottages with Mission-style furnishings and vaulted ceilings sit in a meadow surrounded by redwood trees and flowering shrubbery. **Pros:** secluded setting near trailheads; good camping alternative; rates include state parks pass. **Cons:** basic rooms; walk to main lodge; thin common walls in some units. $ *Rooms from: $279 ⊠ Pfeiffer Big Sur State Park, 47225 Hwy. 1, Big Sur ☎ 831/667–3100, 855/238–6950 reservations ⊕ www.bigsurlodge.com ⤳ 62 rooms ⊚ No meals.*

Big Sur River Inn

$$$$ | B&B/INN | During summer at this rustic property you can sip drinks beside—or in—the Big Sur River fronted by the inn's wooded grounds; if you're here on a Sunday afternoon between May and September you can enjoy live music on the restaurant's deck. **Pros:** riverside setting; next to a restaurant and small market, outdoor pool; recently renovated baths. **Cons:** standard motel rooms across the road; no phone in rooms; fronts busy road. $ *Rooms from: $275 ⊠ Hwy. 1, 2 miles north of Pfeiffer Big Sur State Park, Big Sur ☎ 831/667–2700, 831/667–2743, 800/548–3610 ⊕ www.bigsurriverinn.com ⤳ 22 rooms ⊚ No meals.*

Deetjen's Big Sur Inn

$$ | B&B/INN | This historic 1930s Norwegian-style property is endearingly rustic, with its village of cabins nestled in the redwoods; many of the very individual rooms have their own fireplaces. **Pros:** tons of character; wooded grounds; excellent food and wine in on-site restaurant. **Cons:** thin walls; some rooms don't have private baths; no TVs or Wi-Fi, limited cell service. $ *Rooms from: $170 ⊠ Hwy. 1, 3½ miles south of Pfeiffer Big Sur State Park, Big Sur ☎ 831/667–2377 ⊕ www.deetjens.com ⤳ 20 rooms, 15 with bath ⊚ No meals ☞ 2-night minimum stay on weekends.*

Glen Oaks Big Sur

$$$$ | **HOTEL** | At this rustic-modern cluster of adobe-and-redwood buildings, you can choose between motel-style rooms, cabins, and cottages in the woods. **Pros:** in the heart of town; natural river-rock radiant-heated tiles; gas fireplaces in each room. **Cons:** near busy road and parking lot; no TVs; some cabins tiny. [$] *Rooms from: $300* ✉ *Hwy. 1, 1 mile north of Pfeiffer Big Sur State Park, Big Sur* ☎ *831/667–2105* 🌐 *www.glenoaksbigsur.com* 🛏 *16 rooms, 2 cottages, 10 cabins, 1 house* 🍴 *No meals.*

★ Post Ranch Inn

$$$$ | **RESORT** | This luxurious retreat is perfect for getaways; the redwood guesthouses, all of which have views of the sea or the mountains, blend almost invisibly into a wooded cliff 1,200 feet above the ocean. **Pros:** units come with fireplaces and private decks; on-site activities like yoga and stargazing; gorgeous property with hiking trails and spectacular views. **Cons:** expensive; austere design; not a good choice if you're afraid of heights. [$] *Rooms from: $995* ✉ *Hwy. 1, 1½ miles south of Pfeiffer Big Sur State Park, Big Sur* ☎ *831/667–2200, 800/527–2200* 🌐 *www.postranchinn.com* 🛏 *39 rooms, 2 houses* 🍴 *Breakfast.*

★ Ventana

$$$$ | **HOTEL** | Hundreds of celebrities, from Oprah Winfrey to Sir Anthony Hopkins, have escaped to Ventana, a romantic resort on 160 tranquil acres 1,200 feet above the Pacific. **Pros:** secluded; nature trails everywhere; rates include daily guided hike, yoga, wine and cheese hour. **Cons:** expensive; some rooms lack an ocean view; not family-friendly. [$] *Rooms from: $750* ✉ *Hwy. 1, almost 1 mile south of Pfeiffer Big Sur State Park, Big Sur* ☎ *831/667–2331, 800/628–6500* 🌐 *www.ventanainn.com* 🛏 *59 rooms, 15 tent cabins* 🍴 *No meals.*

Chapter 12

MONTEREY BAY AREA

12

Updated by
Cheryl Crabtree

👁 Sights	🍽 Restaurants	🛏 Hotels	🛍 Shopping	🍸 Nightlife
★★★★★	★★★★☆	★★★★★	★☆☆☆☆	★☆☆☆☆

WELCOME TO MONTEREY BAY AREA

TOP REASONS TO GO

★ **Marine life:** Monterey Bay is the location of the world's third-largest marine sanctuary, home to whales, otters, and other underwater creatures.

★ **Getaway central:** For more than a century, urbanites have come to the Monterey Bay area to unwind, relax, and have fun. It's a great place to browse unique shops and galleries, ride a giant roller coaster, or play a round of golf on a world-class course.

★ **Nature preserves:** More than the sea is protected here: the region boasts nearly 30 state parks, beaches, and preserves—fantastic places for walking, jogging, hiking, and biking.

★ **Wine and dine:** The area's rich agricultural bounty translates into abundant fresh produce, great wines, and fabulous dining. It's no wonder more than 300 culinary events take place here every year.

★ **Small-town vibes:** Even the cities here are friendly, walkable places where you'll feel like a local.

North of Big Sur the coastline softens into lower bluffs, windswept dunes, pristine estuaries, and long, sandy beaches, bordering one of the world's most amazing marine environments—Monterey Bay. On the Monterey Peninsula, at the southern end of the bay, are Carmel-by-the-Sea, Pacific Grove, and Monterey; Santa Cruz sits at the northern tip of the crescent. In between, Highway 1 cruises along the coastline, passing windswept beaches piled high with sand dunes. Along the route are wetlands and artichoke and strawberry fields.

1 **Carmel-by-the-Sea.**

2 **Carmel Valley.**

3 **Pebble Beach.**

4 **Pacific Grove.**

5 **Monterey.**

6 **Salinas.**

7 **Pinnacles National Park.**

8 **San Juan Bautista.**

9 **Moss Landing.**

10 **Aptos.**

11 **Capitola and Soquel.**

12 **Santa Cruz.**

0		5 mi
0		5 km

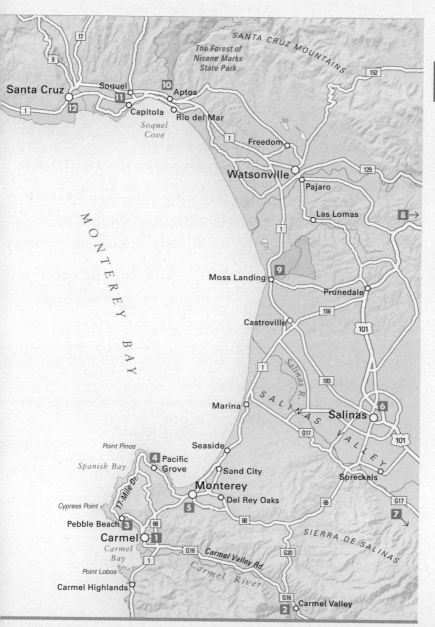

SANTA CRUZ MOUNTAINS

The Forest of
Nisene Marks
State Park

17

9

152

Santa Cruz

Soquel

10 Aptos

11

12

Capitola

Rio del Mar

1

Soquel
Cove

Freedom

Watsonville

129

Pajaro

Las Lomas

8

M O N T E R E Y

Moss Landing 9

Prunedale

156

Castroville

101

B A Y

1

Salinas R.

183

S A L I N A S

Marina

Salinas 6

G17

V A L L E Y

101

Point Pinos

4 Pacific
Grove

Seaside

Sand City

Spreckels

Spanish Bay

17-Mile Dr.

Monterey

G17

Cypress Point

Del Rey Oaks

7

Pebble Beach 3

68

68

68

SIERRA DE SALINAS

Carmel 1

5

Carmel Valley Rd.

G16

G20

Point Lobos

Carmel
Bay

1

Carmel River

Carmel Highlands

G16

2 Carmel Valley

Natural beauty is at the heart of the Monterey Bay area's enormous appeal—it's everywhere, from the redwood-studded hillsides to the pristine shoreline with miles of walking paths and bluff-top vistas. Nature even takes center stage indoors at the world-famous Monterey Bay Aquarium, but history also draws visitors, most notably to Monterey's well-preserved waterfront district. Quaint, walkable towns and villages such as Carmel-by-the-Sea and Carmel Valley Village lure with smart restaurants and galleries, while sunny Aptos, Capitola, Soquel, and Santa Cruz, with miles of sand and surf, attract surfers and beach lovers.

Monterey Bay life centers on the ocean. The bay itself is protected by the Monterey Bay National Marine Sanctuary, the nation's largest undersea canyon—bigger and deeper than the Grand Canyon. On-the-water activities abound, from whale-watching and kayaking to sailing and surfing. Bay cruises from Monterey and Moss Landing almost always encounter other enchanting sea creatures, among them sea otters, sea lions, and porpoises.

Land-based activities include hiking, zip-lining in the redwood canopy, and wine tasting along urban and rural trails. Golf has been an integral part of the Monterey Peninsula's social and recreational scene since the Del Monte Golf Course opened in 1897. Pebble Beach's championship courses host prestigious tournaments, and though the greens fees at these courses can run up to $500, elsewhere on the peninsula you'll find less expensive options. And, of course, whatever activity you pursue, natural splendor appears at every turn.

Planning

When to Go

Summer is peak season; mild weather brings in big crowds. In this coastal region a cool breeze generally blows and fog often rolls in from offshore; you will frequently need a sweater or windbreaker. Off-season, from November through April, fewer people visit and the mood is mellower. Rainfall is heaviest in January and February. Fall and spring days are often clearer than those in summer.

Getting Here and Around

AIR TRAVEL

Monterey Regional Airport, 3 miles east of downtown Monterey off Highway 68, is served by Alaska, Allegiant, American, and United. Taxi service costs from $14 to $16 to downtown, and from $23 to $25 to Carmel. Monterey Airbus service between the region and the San Jose and San Francisco airports starts at $42; the Early Bird Airport Shuttle costs from $100 to $235 ($250 from Oakland).

AIRPORT CONTACTS Monterey Regional Airport *(MRY).* ⊠ *200 Fred Kane Dr., at Olmsted Rd., off Hwy. 68, Monterey* ☎ *831/648–7000* ⊕ *www.montereyairport.com.*

GROUND TRANSPORTATION Central Coast Cab Company. ☎ *831/626–3333* ⊕ *www.centralcoastcab.com.* **Early Bird Airport Shuttle.** ☎ *831/462–3933* ⊕ *www.earlybirdairportshuttle.com.* **Monterey Airbus.** ☎ *831/373–7777* ⊕ *www.montereyairbus.com.* **Yellow Cab.** ☎ *831/333–1234.*

BUS TRAVEL

Greyhound serves Santa Cruz and Salinas from San Francisco and San Jose. The trips take about 3 and 4½ hours, respectively. Monterey-Salinas Transit (MST) provides frequent service in Monterey County (from $1.75 to $3.50; day pass $10), and Santa Cruz METRO ($2; day pass from $6 to $14) buses operate throughout Santa Cruz County. You can switch between the lines in Watsonville.

BUS CONTACTS Greyhound. ☎ *800/231–2222* ⊕ *www.greyhound.com.* **Monterey-Salinas Transit.** ☎ *888/678–2871* ⊕ *mst.org.* **Santa Cruz METRO.** ☎ *831/425–8600* ⊕ *scmtd.com.*

CAR TRAVEL

Highway 1 runs south–north along the coast, linking the towns of Carmel-by-the-Sea, Monterey, and Santa Cruz; some sections have only two lanes. The freeway, U.S. 101, lies to the east, roughly parallel to Highway 1. The two roads are connected by Highway 68 from Pacific Grove to Salinas; Highway 156 from Castroville to Prunedale; Highway 152 from Watsonville to Gilroy; and Highway 17 from Santa Cruz to San Jose. ■TIP→ **Traffic near Santa Cruz can crawl to a standstill during commuter hours. In the morning, avoid traveling between 7 and 9; in the afternoon, avoid traveling between 4 and 7.**

The drive south from San Francisco to Monterey can be made comfortably in three hours or less. The most scenic way is to follow Highway 1 down the coast. A generally faster route is Interstate 280 south to Highway 85 to Highway 17 to Highway 1. The drive from the Los Angeles area takes five or six hours. Take U.S. 101 to Salinas and head west on Highway 68. You can also follow Highway 1 up the coast.

TRAIN TRAVEL

Amtrak's *Coast Starlight* runs between Los Angeles, Oakland, and Seattle. You can also take the *Pacific Surfliner* to San Luis Obispo and connect to Amtrak buses to Salinas or San Jose. From the train station in Salinas you can connect with buses serving Carmel and Monterey, and from the train station in San Jose with buses to Santa Cruz.

TRAIN CONTACTS Amtrak. ☎ *800/872–7245* ⊕ *amtrak.com.*

Restaurants

The Monterey Bay area is a culinary paradise. The surrounding waters are full of fish, wild game roams the foothills, and the inland valleys are some of the most fertile in the country—local chefs draw on this bounty for their fresh, truly Californian cuisine. Except at beachside stands and inexpensive eateries, where anything goes, casual but neat dress is the norm. *Restaurant reviews have been shortened. For full information, visit Fodors.com.*

Hotels

Accommodations in the Monterey area range from no-frills motels to luxurious hotels. Pacific Grove, amply endowed with ornate Victorian houses, is the region's bed-and-breakfast capital; Carmel also has charming inns. Lavish resorts cluster in exclusive Pebble Beach and pastoral Carmel Valley.

High season runs from May through October. Rates in winter, especially at the larger hotels, may drop by 50% or more, and smaller inns often offer midweek specials. Whatever the month, some properties require a two-night stay on weekends. *Hotel reviews have been shortened. For full information, visit Fodors.com.* ■TIP→ **Many of the fancier accommodations aren't suitable for children; if you're traveling with kids, ask before you book.**

WHAT IT COSTS

	$	$$	$$$	$$$$
RESTAURANTS				
	under $16	$16–$22	$23–$30	over $30
HOTELS				
	under $120	$120–$175	$176–$250	over $250

Tour Options

Ag Venture Tours & Consulting

GUIDED TOURS | Crowd-pleasing half- and full-day wine tasting, sightseeing, and agricultural tours are Ag Venture's specialty. Tastings are at Monterey and Santa Cruz Mountains wineries; sightseeing opportunities include the Monterey Peninsula, Big Sur, and Santa Cruz; and the agricultural forays take in the Salinas and Pajaro valleys. Customized itineraries can be arranged. ☎ 831/761–8463 ⊕ agventuretours.com ✉ From $105 (day).

California Pacific Excursions

BUS TOURS | This outfit operates motorcoach tours from San Francisco that include one or two days in Monterey and Carmel. The company's three-day San Francisco–Los Angeles tours include stops in Monterey and Carmel. ☎ 415/228–9865 ⊕ www.californiaparlorcar.com ✉ From $95 (day) and $300 (overnight).

Monterey Guided Wine Tours

SPECIAL-INTEREST | The company's guides lead customized wine tours in Monterey, Carmel, and Carmel Valley, along with the Santa Lucia Highlands, the Santa Cruz Mountains, and the Paso Robles area. Tours, which typically last from four to six hours, take place in a town car, a stretch limo, or a party bus. ☎ 831/920–2792 ⊕ montereyguidedwinetours.com ✉ From $125.

Visitor Information

CONTACTS **Monterey County Convention & Visitors Bureau.** ☎ 888/221–1010 ⊕ www.seemonterey.com. **Monterey Wine Country.** ☎ 831/375–9400 ⊕ www.montereywines.org. **Santa Cruz Mountains Winegrowers Association.** ✉ 335 spreckels Dr., #B, Aptos ☎ 831/685–8463 ⊕ www.scmwa.com. **Visit Santa Cruz County.** ✉ 303 Water St., No. 100, Santa Cruz ☎ 831/425–1234, 800/833–3494 ⊕ visitsantacruz.org.

Carmel-by-the-Sea

26 miles north of Big Sur.

Even when its population quadruples with tourists on weekends and in summer, Carmel-by-the-Sea, commonly referred to as Carmel, retains its identity as a quaint village. Self-consciously charming, the town is populated by many celebrities, major and minor, and has its share of quirky ordinances. For instance, women wearing high heels do not have the right to pursue legal action if they trip and fall on the cobblestone streets, and drivers who hit a tree and leave the scene are charged with hit-and-run.

Buildings have no street numbers—street names are written on discreet white posts—and consequently no mail delivery. One way to commune with the locals: head to the post office. Artists started this community, and their legacy is evident in the numerous galleries.

GETTING HERE AND AROUND
From north or south follow Highway 1 to Carmel. Head west at Ocean Avenue to reach the main village hub.

TOURS
Carmel Food Tours
WALKING TOURS | Taste your way through Carmel-by-the-Sea culinary delights on this guided walking tour to restaurants and shops serving small portions of standout offerings, from empanadas and ribs to honey and chocolate. Along the way, the guide shares colorful tales about local culture, history, and architecture. The Classic Tour includes seven tasting stops and lasts three hours. Tickets must be purchased in advance. Tours depart from the Sunset Cultural Center at 9th Avenue and San Carlos Street. ⊠ *Sunset Cultural Center, 9th Ave. at San Carlos St., Carmel* ☎ *831/256–3007* ⊕ *www.carmelfood-tour.com* ⊠ *From $94.*

Carmel Walks
WALKING TOURS | For insight into Carmel's history and culture, join one of these guided two-hour ambles through hidden courtyards, gardens, and pathways. Tours depart from the Pine Inn courtyard, on Lincoln Street. Call to reserve a spot. ⊠ *Lincoln St. at 6th Ave., Carmel* ☎ *831/223–4399* ⊕ *carmelwalks.com* ⊠ *From $30.*

ESSENTIALS
VISITOR INFORMATION Carmel Chamber of Commerce. ⊠ *Visitor Center, in Carmel Plaza, Ocean Ave. between Junipero and Mission Sts., Carmel* ☎ *831/624–2522, 800/550–4333* ⊕ *carmelchamber.org.*

⊙ Sights

Carmel Mission
RELIGIOUS SITE | Long before it became a shopping and browsing destination, Carmel was an important religious center during the establishment of Spanish California. That heritage is preserved in the Mission San Carlos Borroméo del Rio Carmelo, more commonly known as the Carmel Mission. Founded in 1771, it served as headquarters for the mission system in California under Father Junípero Serra. Adjoining the stone church is a tranquil garden planted with California poppies. Museum rooms at the mission include an early kitchen, Serra's spartan sleeping quarters and burial shrine, and the first college library in California. ⊠ *3080 Rio Rd., at Lasuen Dr., Carmel* ☎ *831/624–1271* ⊕ *carmel-mission.org* ⊠ *$10.*

Carmel Wine Walk By-the-Sea
TOUR—SIGHT | If you purchase a Wine Walk Passport, you can park the car and sample local wines at any 10 of 13 tasting rooms, all within a few blocks of each other in downtown Carmel. Individual passports can be used by two or more people at the same tasting room, and they entitle holders to free corkage at some local restaurants. ⊠ *Carmel*

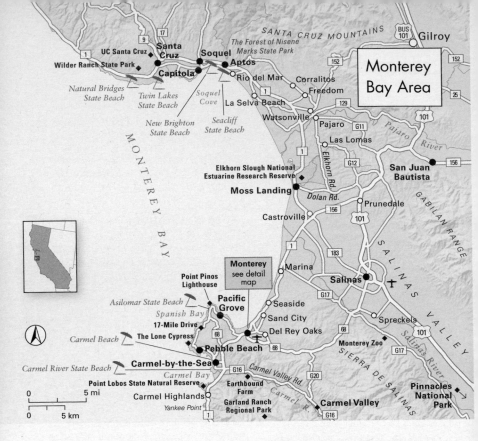

Chamber of Commerce Visitor Center, San Carlos St., between 5th and 6th Aves., Carmel ☎ 831/624–2522, 800/550–4333 ⊕ winewalkcarmel.com ☜ $100.

Dawson Cole Fine Art

MUSEUM | Amazing images of dancers, athletes, and other humans in motion come to life in this gallery that is devoted to the artworks of Monterey Bay resident Richard MacDonald, one of the most famed figurative sculptors of our time. ⊠ Lincoln St., at 6th Ave., Carmel ☎ 800/972–5528 ⊕ dawsoncolefineart.com ☜ Free.

★ Ocean Avenue

NEIGHBORHOOD | Downtown Carmel's chief lure is shopping, especially along its main street, Ocean Avenue, between Junipero Avenue and Camino Real. The architecture here is a mishmash of ersatz Tudor, Mediterranean, and other styles. ⊠ Carmel.

★ Point Lobos State Natural Reserve

NATIONAL/STATE PARK | A 350-acre headland harboring a wealth of marine life, the reserve lies a few miles south of Carmel. The best way to explore here is to walk along one of the many trails. The Cypress Grove Trail leads through a forest of Monterey cypress (one of only two natural groves remaining) that clings to the rocks above an emerald-green cove. Sea Lion Point Trail is a good place to view sea lions. From those and other trails, you might also spot otters, harbor seals, and (in winter and spring) migrating whales. An additional 750 acres of the reserve is an undersea marine park open to qualified scuba divers. No pets are allowed.

■ TIP→ Arrive early (or in late afternoon) to avoid crowds; the parking lots fill up. ⊠ Hwy. 1, Carmel ☎ 831/624–4909, 831/624–8413 water sports reservations ⊕ www. pointlobos.org ☜ $10 per vehicle.

Tor House

HOUSE | Scattered throughout the pines of Carmel-by-the-Sea are houses and cottages originally built for the writers, artists, and photographers who discovered the area decades ago. Among the most impressive dwellings is Tor House, a stone cottage built in 1919 by poet Robinson Jeffers on a craggy knoll overlooking the sea. Portraits, books, and unusual art objects fill the low-ceilinged rooms. The highlight of the small estate is Hawk Tower, a detached edifice set with stones from the Carmel coastline—as well as one from the Great Wall of China. The docents who lead tours (six people maximum) are well informed about the poet's work and life. Reservations are required. Call the reservation line or click on the reservation link on the website. ✉ 26304 Ocean View Ave., Carmel ☎ 831/624–1813 direct docent office line, Fri. and Sat. only ⊕ www.torhouse.org ✎ $12 ⌕ No children under 12.

Beaches

Carmel Beach

BEACH—SIGHT | Carmel-by-the-Sea's greatest attraction is its rugged coastline, with pine and cypress forests and countless inlets. Carmel Beach, an easy walk from downtown shops, has sparkling white sands and magnificent sunsets. ■TIP➔ Dogs are allowed to romp off-leash here. Amenities: parking (no fee); toilets. Best for: sunset; surfing; walking. ✉ End of Ocean Ave., Carmel.

Carmel River State Beach

NATURE PRESERVE | This sugar-white beach, stretching 106 acres along Carmel Bay, is adjacent to a bird sanctuary, where you might spot pelicans, kingfishers, hawks, and sandpipers. Dogs are allowed on leash. Amenities: parking (no fee); toilets. Best for: sunrise; sunset; walking. ✉ Off Scenic Rd., south of Carmel Beach, Carmel ☎ 831/649–2836 ⊕ www.parks.ca.gov ✎ Free.

🍴 Restaurants

Anton and Michel

$$$$ | AMERICAN | Carefully prepared California cuisine is the draw at this airy restaurant. The rack of lamb is carved at the table, the grilled halloumi cheese and tomatoes are meticulously stacked and served with basil and Kalamata olive tapenade, and the desserts are set aflame before your eyes. Known for: romantic courtyard with fountain; elegant interior with fireplace lounge; flambé desserts. Ⓢ Average main: $32 ✉ Mission St. and 7th Ave., Carmel ☎ 831/624–2406 ⊕ antonandmichel.com.

★ Aubergine

$$$$ | AMERICAN | To eat and sleep at luxe L'Auberge Carmel is an experience in itself, but even those staying elsewhere can splurge at the inn's intimate restaurant. Chef Justin Cogley's nine-course prix-fixe tasting menu (your only option at dinner, $185 per person) is a gastronomical experience unrivaled in the region. Known for: exceptional chef's choice tasting menu; expert wine pairings; intimate nine-table dining room. Ⓢ Average main: $185 ✉ Monte Verde at 7th Ave., Carmel ☎ 831/624–8578 ⊕ auberginecarmel.com ⊘ No lunch.

★ Basil

$$$ | MODERN AMERICAN | Eco-friendly Basil was Monterey County's first restaurant to achieve a green dining certification, recognition of chef-owner Soerke Peters's commitment to using organic, sustainably cultivated ingredients in his cuisine. Peters grows many of his own herbs, which find their way into creative dishes such as black squid linguine with sea urchin sauce, charred octopus, and smoked venison and other house-made charcuterie. Known for: organic ingredients; creative cocktails; year-round patio dining. Ⓢ Average main: $25 ✉ Paseo Square, San Carlos St., between Ocean Ave. and 7th Ave., Carmel ☎ 831/626–8226 ⊕ basilcarmel.com.

Point Lobos State Natural Reserve offers stunning vistas of sea and sky.

Casanova

$$$$ | MEDITERRANEAN | This restaurant inspires European-style celebration and romance in an intimate French Country setting and serves authentic dishes from southern France and northern Italy—think beef tartare and veal sweetbreads. Private dining and a special tasting menu are offered at Van Gogh's Table, a relic from France's Auberge Ravoux, the artist's final residence. **Known for:** house-made pastas and gnocchi; private dining at antique Van Gogh's table; romantic candlelight dining room and outdoor patio. $ *Average main: $32 ⊠ 5th Ave., between San Carlos and Mission Sts., Carmel* ☎ *831/625–0501* ⊕ *www.casanovarestaurant.com.*

The Cottage Restaurant

$ | AMERICAN | This family-friendly spot serves sandwiches, pizzas, and homemade soups at lunch, but the best meal is breakfast (good thing it's served all day). The menu offers six variations on eggs Benedict, and all kinds of sweet and savory crepes. **Known for:** artichoke soup; eggs Benedict and crepes; daily specials. $ *Average main: $15 ⊠ Lincoln St. between Ocean and 7th Aves., Carmel* ☎ *831/625–6260* ⊕ *cottagerestaurant.com* ⊗ *No dinner.*

Flying Fish Grill

$$$ | SEAFOOD | Simple in appearance yet bold with its flavors, this Japanese–California seafood restaurant is one of Carmel's most inventive eateries. The warm, wood-lined dining room is broken up into very private booths. **Known for:** almond-crusted sea bass served with Chinese cabbage and rock shrimp stir-fry; clay pot dinners for two cooked at the table; authentic Asian decor. $ *Average main: $30 ⊠ Carmel Plaza, Mission St. between Ocean and 7th Aves., Carmel* ☎ *831/625–1962* ⊕ *flyingfishgrill. com* ⊗ *No lunch.*

Grasing's Coastal Cuisine

$$$$ | AMERICAN | Chef Kurt Grasing draws from fresh Carmel Coast and Central Valley ingredients to whip up contemporary adaptations of European-provincial and American cooking. Longtime menu favorites include artichoke lasagna in a roasted tomato sauce, duck with fresh cherries in a red wine sauce, a savory paella, and grilled steaks and chops. **Known for:** artichoke heart lasagna; grilled steaks; bar, patio lounge, and rooftop deck. [$] *Average main: $39* ✉ *6th Ave. and Mission St., Carmel* ☎ *831/624–6562* 🌐 *grasings.com.*

L'Escargot

$$$$ | **FRENCH** | Chef-owner Kericos Loutas personally sees to each plate of food served at this romantic, unpretentious French restaurant. Order the pan-roasted duck breast or the veal medallions with wild mushrooms or white wine sauce; or, if you can't decide, choose the three-course prix-fixe dinner. **Known for:** authentic French Country dishes; prix-fixe dinner option; locally sourced ingredients. [$] *Average main: $35* ✉ *Mission and 4th Ave., Carmel* ☎ *831/620–1942* 🌐 *escargot-carmel.com* 🕘 *No lunch.*

Lugano Swiss Bistro

$$$ | **SWISS** | Fondue is the centerpiece here—the house specialty is a version made with Gruyère, Emmentaler, and Appenzeller. Rotisserie-broiled meats are also popular, and include rosemary chicken, plum-basted duck, and fennel pork loin. **Known for:** schnitzel, fondue, and other Swiss specialties; alpine-style heated patio; back room with a hand-painted street scene of Lugano. [$] *Average main: $29* ✉ *Barnyard Shopping Center, Hwy. 1 and Carmel Valley Rd., Carmel* ☎ *831/626–3779* 🌐 *www.swissbistro.com* 🕘 *Closed Mon.*

Tuck Box

$ | **AMERICAN** | This bright little restaurant is in a cottage right out of a fairy tale, complete with stone fireplace. Handmade scones, good for breakfast or afternoon tea, are the specialty. **Known for:** traditional English afternoon tea; fairy-tale atmosphere; handmade scones. [$] *Average main: $14* ✉ *Dolores St., between Ocean and 7th Aves., Carmel* ☎ *831/624–6365* 🌐 *tuckbox.com* 💳 *No credit cards* 🕘 *No dinner.*

Vesuvio

$$$ | **ITALIAN** | Chef and restaurateur Rich Pèpe heats up the night with this lively trattoria downstairs and swinging rooftop terrace, the Starlight Lounge 65°. Pèpe's elegant take on traditional Italian cuisine yields dishes such as wild-boar Bolognese pappardelle, lobster ravioli, and velvety limoncello mousse cake. **Known for:** traditional cuisine of Campania, Italy; two bars with pizzas and small plates; live music on rooftop terrace in summer. [$] *Average main: $30* ✉ *6th and Junipero Aves., Carmel* ☎ *831/625–1766* 🌐 *vesuviocarmel.com* 🕘 *No lunch.*

Hotels

Cypress Inn

$$$$ | **B&B/INN** | This luxurious inn has a fresh Mediterranean ambience with Moroccan touches. **Pros:** luxury without snobbery; popular lounge and restaurant; British-style afternoon tea on Saturdays. **Cons:** not for the pet-phobic; some rooms and baths are tiny; basic amenities. [$] *Rooms from: $279* ✉ *Lincoln St. and 7th Ave., Carmel* ☎ *831/624–3871, 800/443–7443* 🌐 *cypress-inn.com* 🛏 *44 rooms* 🍴 *Breakfast.*

The Hideaway

$$$$ | **HOTEL** | On a quiet street with a residential vibe, The Hideaway is a peaceful haven for those seeking stylish comfort in the heart of town. **Pros:** easy walk to shops, restaurants, galleries; short walk to Carmel Beach; pet-friendly amenities. **Cons:** street parking only; no pool or hot tub; some rooms are tiny. [$] *Rooms from: $295* ✉ *Junipero St. at 8th Ave., Carmel* ☎ *831/625–5222* 🌐 *hideawaycarmel.com* 🛏 *24 rooms* 🍴 *Breakfast.*

Hyatt Carmel Highlands

$$$$ | **HOTEL** | High on a hill overlooking the Pacific, this place has superb views; accommodations include king rooms

with fireplaces, suites with personal Jacuzzis, and full town houses with many perks. **Pros:** killer views; romantic getaway; great food. **Cons:** thin walls; must drive to the center of town; some rooms and buildings need update. $ *Rooms from: $399* ⊠ *120 Highlands Dr., Carmel* ☎ *831/620–1234, 800/233–1234* ⊕ *www. hyatt.com* ⤴ *48 rooms.*

★ L'Auberge Carmel

$$$$ | B&B/INN | Stepping through the doors of this elegant inn is like being transported to a little European village. **Pros:** in town but off the main drag; four blocks from the beach; full-service luxury. **Cons:** touristy area; not a good choice for families; no air-conditioning. $ *Rooms from: $465* ⊠ *Monte Verde at 7th Ave., Carmel* ☎ *831/624–8578* ⊕ *www.laubergecarmel.com* ⤴ *20 rooms* ⦿ *Breakfast.*

La Playa Carmel

$$$$ | HOTEL | A historic complex of lush gardens and Mediterranean-style buildings, La Playa has light and airy interiors done in Carmel Bay beach-cottage style. **Pros:** residential neighborhood; manicured gardens; two blocks from the beach. **Cons:** four stories (no elevator); busy lobby; some rooms are on the small side. $ *Rooms from: $449* ⊠ *Camino Real at 8th Ave., Carmel* ☎ *831/293– 6100, 800/582–8900* ⊕ *laplayahotel.com* ⤴ *75 rooms* ⦿ *Breakfast.*

Mission Ranch

$$ | HOTEL | Movie star Clint Eastwood owns this sprawling property whose accommodations include rooms in a converted barn, and several cottages, some with fireplaces. **Pros:** farm setting; pastoral views; great for tennis buffs. **Cons:** busy parking lot; must drive to the heart of town; old buildings. $ *Rooms from: $175* ⊠ *26270 Dolores St., Carmel* ☎ *831/624–6436, 800/538–8221, 831/625–9040 restaurant* ⊕ *www. missionranchcarmel.com* ⤴ *31 rooms* ⦿ *Breakfast.*

Pine Inn

$$$ | HOTEL | A favorite with generations of visitors, the Pine Inn is four blocks from the beach and has Victorian-style furnishings, complete with grandfather clock, padded fabric wall panels, antique tapestries, and marble tabletops. **Pros:** elegant; close to shopping and dining; full breakfast included weekdays. **Cons:** on the town's busiest street; public areas a bit dark; limited parking. $ *Rooms from: $189* ⊠ *Ocean Ave. and Monte Verde St., Carmel* ☎ *831/624–3851, 800/228–3851* ⊕ *pineinn.com* ⤴ *49 rooms* ⦿ *Breakfast.*

Tally Ho Inn

$$$ | B&B/INN | This inn is nearly all suites, many of which have fireplaces and floor-to-ceiling glass walls that open onto ocean-view patios. **Pros:** within walking distance of shops, restaurants, beach; free parking; spacious rooms. **Cons:** small property; busy area; basic breakfast. $ *Rooms from: $229* ⊠ *Monte Verde St. and 6th Ave., Carmel* ☎ *831/624–2232, 800/652–2632* ⊕ *tallyho-inn.com* ⤴ *12 rooms* ⦿ *Breakfast.*

Tickle Pink Inn

$$$$ | B&B/INN | Atop a towering cliff, this inn has views of the Big Sur coastline, which you can contemplate from your private balcony. **Pros:** close to great hiking; intimate; dramatic views. **Cons:** close to a big hotel; lots of traffic during the day; basic breakfast. $ *Rooms from: $329* ⊠ *155 Highland Dr., Carmel* ☎ *831/624– 1244, 800/635–4774* ⊕ *ticklepink.com* ⤴ *33 rooms, 1 cottage* ⦿ *Breakfast.*

Tradewinds Carmel

$$$ | B&B/INN | This converted motel with sleek decor inspired by the South Seas encircles a courtyard with waterfalls, a meditation garden, and a fire pit. **Pros:** serene; within walking distance of restaurants; friendly service. **Cons:** no pool; long walk to the beach; thin walls. $ *Rooms from: $250* ⊠ *Mission St. at 3rd Ave., Carmel* ☎ *831/624–2776* ⊕ *tradewindscarmel.com* ⤴ *28 rooms* ⦿ *Breakfast.*

ⓨ Nightlife

BARS AND PUBS

Barmel

BARS/PUBS | Al Capone and other Prohibition-era legends once sidled up to this hip nightspot's carved wooden bar. Rock to DJ music and sit indoors, or head out to the pet-friendly patio. Some menu items pay homage to California's early days, and you can order Baja-style dishes from the adjacent Pescadero restaurant, which is under the same ownership. ⊠ San Carlos St., between Ocean and 7th Aves., Carmel ☎ 831/626–2095.

Mulligan Public House

BARS/PUBS | A sports bar with seven TV screens, 12 beers on tap, and extensive menu packed with hearty American pub food, Mulligan usually stays open until midnight. ⊠ 5 Dolores St., at Ocean ☎ 831/250–5910 ⊕ mulliganspublichouse.com.

ⓔ Shopping

ART GALLERIES

Carmel Art Association

ART GALLERIES | Carmel's oldest gallery, established in 1927, exhibits original paintings and sculptures by local artists. ⊠ Dolores St., between 5th and 6th Aves., Carmel ☎ 831/624–6176 ⊕ carmelart.org.

Galerie Plein Aire

ART GALLERIES | The gallery showcases the oil paintings of a group of local artists. ⊠ Dolores St., between Ocean and 6th Aves., Carmel ☎ 831/250–5698, 831/277–6165 after hrs ⊕ galeriepleinaire.com ⓒ Closed Tues.

Gallery Sur

ART GALLERIES | Fine art photography of the Big Sur Coast and the Monterey Peninsula, including scenic shots and golf images, is the focus here. ⊠ 6th Ave., between Dolores and Lincoln Sts., Carmel ☎ 831/626–2615 ⊕ gallerysur.com.

★ Weston Gallery

ART GALLERIES | Run by the family of the late Edward Weston, this is hands down the best photography gallery around, with contemporary color photography and classic black-and-whites. ⊠ 6th Ave., between Dolores and Lincoln Sts., Carmel ☎ 831/624–4453 ⊕ westongallery.com ⓒ Closed Mon.

MALLS

Carmel Plaza

SHOPPING CENTERS/MALLS | Tiffany & Co. and J. Crew are among the name brands doing business at this mall on Carmel's east side, but what makes it worth a stop are homegrown enterprises such as Carmel Honey Company, for local honey harvested and packaged by a high school student and his family; Madrigal for women's fashion; and J. Lawrence Khaki's for debonair menswear. Flying Fish Grill and several other restaurants are here, along with the Wrath Wines tasting room (Chardonnay and Pinot Noir). The Carmel Chamber of Commerce Visitor Center (open daily) is on the second floor. ⊠ Ocean Ave. and Mission St., Carmel ☎ 831/624–1385 ⊕ carmelplaza.com.

SPECIALTY SHOPS

Bittner

SPECIALTY STORES | The shop carries collectible and vintage pens from around the world. ⊠ Ocean Ave., between Mission and San Carlos Sts., Carmel ☎ 831/626–8828 ⊕ bittner.com.

elizabethW

GIFTS/SOUVENIRS | Named after the designer and owner's pioneering great-grandmother, elizabethW handcrafts fragrances, essential oils, candles, silk eye pillows, and other soul-soothing goods for bath, body, and home. ⊠ Ocean Ave., between Monte Verde and Lincoln, Carmel ☎ 831/626–3892 ⊕ elizabethw.com.

Foxy Couture

CLOTHING | Shop for one-of-a-kind treasures at this curated collection of gently used luxury couture and vintage clothes and accessories—think Chanel, Hermes, and Gucci—without paying a hefty price tag. ⊠ *San Carlos St., in Vanervort Court, between Ocean and 7th Aves., Carmel* ☎ *831/625–9995* ⊕ *foxycouturecarmel.com.*

Intima

SPECIALTY STORES | The European lingerie ranges from lacy to racy. ⊠ *San Carlos St., between Ocean and 6th Aves., Carmel* ☎ *831/625–0599* ⊕ *www.intimacarmel.com.*

Jan de Luz

SPECIALTY STORES | This shop monograms and embroiders fine linens (including bathrobes) while you wait. ⊠ *Dolores St., between Ocean and 7th Aves., Carmel* ☎ *831/622–7621* ⊕ *jandeluzlinens.com.*

Carmel Valley

10 miles east of Carmel.

Carmel Valley Road, which heads inland from Highway 1 south of Carmel, is the main thoroughfare through this valley, a secluded enclave of horse ranchers and other well-heeled residents who prefer the area's sunny climate to coastal fog and wind. Once thick with dairy farms, the valley has evolved into an esteemed wine appellation. Carmel Valley Village has crafts shops, art galleries, and the tasting rooms of numerous local wineries.

GETTING HERE AND AROUND

From U.S. 101 north or south, exit at Highway 68 and head west toward the coast. Scenic, two-lane Laureles Grade winds west over the mountains to Carmel Valley Road north of the village.

TOURS

Carmel Valley Grapevine Express

BUS TOURS | An incredible bargain, the express—aka MST's Bus 24—travels between downtown Monterey and Carmel Valley Village, with stops near wineries, restaurants, and shopping centers. ☎ *888/678–2871* ⊕ *mst.org* ⊠ *$10 all-day pass.*

Sights

Bernardus Tasting Room

WINERY/DISTILLERY | At the tasting room of Bernardus, known for its Bordeaux-style red blend, called Marinus, and Chardonnays, you can sample current releases and library and reserve wines. ⊠ *5 W. Carmel Valley Rd., at El Caminito Rd.* ☎ *831/298–8021, 800/223–2533* ⊕ *bernardus.com* ⊠ *Tastings from $12.*

Cowgirl Winery

WINERY/DISTILLERY | Cowgirl chic prevails in the main tasting building here, and it's just plain rustic at the outdoor tables, set amid chickens, a tractor, and a flatbed truck. The wines include Chardonnay, Cabernet Sauvignon, Malbec, Pinot Noir, Rosé, and some blends. You can order a wood-fired pizza from sister business Corkscrew Café, and play boccie ball, horseshoes, or corn hole until your food arrives. ⊠ *25 Pilot Rd., off W. Carmel Valley Rd.* ☎ *831/298–7030* ⊕ *cowgirlwinery.com* ⊠ *Tastings from $15.*

Earthbound Farm

FARM/RANCH | **FAMILY** | Pick up fresh vegetables, ready-to-eat meals, gourmet groceries, flowers, and gifts at Earthbound Farm, the world's largest grower of organic produce. You can also take a romp in the kids' garden, cut your own herbs, and stroll through the chamomile aromatherapy labyrinth. Special events, on Saturday from April through December, include bug walks and garlic-braiding workshops. ⊠ *7250 Carmel Valley Rd., Carmel* ☎ *831/625–6219* ⊕ *www.ebfarm.com* ⊠ *Free.*

★ Folktale Winery & Vineyards
WINERY/DISTILLERY | The expansive winery on a 15-acre estate (formerly Chateau Julienne) offers daily tastings, live music on weekends (plus Friday in summer and fall), and special events and programs such as Saturday yoga in the vineyard. Best-known wines include the estate Pinot Noir, Sparkling Rosé, and Le Mistral Joseph's Blend. Chefs in the on-site restaurant cook up small plates with wine pairing suggestions. Tours of the winery and organically farmed vineyards are available by appointment. ✉ *8940 Carmel Valley Rd.* ✥ *At Schetter Rd.* ☎ *831/293–7500* 🌐 *folktalewinery.com* 🎫 *Tastings from $20; tours $40 (includes tasting).*

Garland Ranch Regional Park
NATIONAL/STATE PARK | Hiking trails stretch across much of this park's 4,500 acres of meadows, forested hillsides, and creeks. ✉ *700 W. Carmel Valley Rd., 9 miles east of Carmel-by-the-Sea* ☎ *831/372–3196* 🌐 *www.mprpd.org.*

🍴 Restaurants

Café Rustica
$$$ | **EUROPEAN** | European country cooking is the focus at this lively roadhouse, where specialties include roasted meats, seafood, pastas, and thin-crust pizzas from the wood-fired oven. It can get noisy inside; for a quieter meal, request a table outside. **Known for:** Tuscan-flavored dishes from Alsace; open kitchen with wood-fired oven; outdoor patio seating. [$] *Average main: $25* ✉ *10 Delfino Pl., at Pilot Rd., off Carmel Valley Rd.* ☎ *831/659–4444* 🌐 *caferusticavillage.com* 🕒 *Closed Mon.*

Corkscrew Café
$$$ | **MODERN AMERICAN** | Farm-fresh food is the specialty of this casual, Old Monterey–style bistro. Herbs and seasonal produce come from the Corkscrew's own organic gardens; the catch of the day comes from local waters; and the meats are hormone-free. **Known for:** wood-fired pizzas; fish tacos and chicken salad; garden patio. [$] *Average main: $24* ✉ *55 W. Carmel Valley Rd., at Pilot Rd.* ☎ *831/659–8888* 🌐 *corkscrewcafe.com* 🕒 *Closed Jan. Closed Tues. and Wed.*

Wagon Wheel Coffee Shop
$ | **AMERICAN** | This local hangout decorated with wagon wheels, cowboy hats, and lassos serves terrific hearty breakfasts, including oatmeal and banana pancakes, eggs Benedict, and biscuits and gravy. The lunch menu includes a dozen different burgers and other sandwiches. **Known for:** traditional American breakfast; cowboy-theme setting; lively local clientele. [$] *Average main: $15* ✉ *Valley Hill Center, 7156 Carmel Valley Rd., next to Quail Lodge, Carmel* ☎ *831/624–8878* 💳 *No credit cards* 🕒 *No dinner.*

🛏 Hotels

★ Bernardus Lodge & Spa
$$$$ | **RESORT** | The spacious guest rooms at this luxury spa resort have vaulted ceilings, French oak floors, featherbeds, fireplaces, patios, and bathrooms with heated-tile floors and soaking tubs for two. **Pros:** exceptional personal service; outstanding food and wine; huge suites. **Cons:** hefty rates; some guests can seem snooty; resort fee. [$] *Rooms from: $475* ✉ *415 W. Carmel Valley Rd.* ☎ *831/658–3400* 🌐 *bernarduslodge.com* 🛏 *73 rooms and villas.*

★ Carmel Valley Ranch
$$$$ | **RESORT** | The activity options at this luxury ranch are so varied that the resort provides a program director to guide you through them. **Pros:** stunning natural setting; tons of activities; River Ranch center with a pool, splash zone, bocce courts, and fitness center. **Cons:** must drive several miles to shops and nightlife; high rates. [$] *Rooms from: $400* ✉ *1 Old Ranch Rd., Carmel* ☎ *831/625–9500, 855/687–7262 toll-free reservations* 🌐 *carmelvalleyranch.com* 🛏 *181 suites* 🍽 *No meals.*

Quail Lodge & Golf Club
$$$ | **HOTEL** | **FAMILY** | A sprawling collection of ranch-style buildings on 850 acres of meadows, fairways, and lakes, Quail Lodge offers luxury rooms and outdoor activities at surprisingly affordable rates. **Pros:** on the golf course; on-site restaurant; spacious rooms. **Cons:** service sometimes spotty; 5 miles from the beach and Carmel Valley Village; basic amenities. [$] *Rooms from: $225* ✉ *8205 Valley Greens Dr., Carmel* ☎ *866/675–1101 reservations, 831/624–2888* 🌐 *www.quaillodge.com* 🛏 *93 rooms* 🍴 *No meals.*

★ Stonepine Estate
$$$$ | **RESORT** | Set on 330 pastoral acres, the former estate of the Crocker banking family has been converted to a luxurious inn. **Pros:** supremely exclusive; close to Carmel Valley Village; attentive, personalized service. **Cons:** difficult to get a reservation; far from the coast; expensive rates. [$] *Rooms from: $500* ✉ *150 E. Carmel Valley Rd.* ☎ *831/659–2245* 🌐 *www.stonepineestate.com* 🛏 *12 rooms, 3 cottages.*

Activities

GOLF

Quail Lodge & Golf Club
GOLF | Robert Muir Graves designed this championship semiprivate 18-hole course next to Quail Lodge that provides challenging play for golfers of all skill levels. The scenic course, which incorporates five lakes and edges the Carmel River, was completely renovated in 2015 by golf architect Todd Eckenrode to add extra challenge to the golf experience, white sand bunkers, and other enhancements. For the most part flat, the walkable course is well maintained, with stunning views, lush fairways, and ultrasmooth greens. ✉ *8000 Valley Greens Dr., Carmel* ☎ *831/620–8808 golf shop, 831/620–8866 club concierge* 🌐 *www.quaillodge.com* 🎟 *$185* 🏌 *18 holes, 6500 yards, par 71.*

Shopping

★ Refuge
SPA/BEAUTY | At this co-ed, European-style center on 2 serene acres you can recharge without breaking the bank. Heat up in the eucalyptus steam room or cedar sauna, plunge into cold pools, and relax indoors in zero-gravity chairs or outdoors in Adirondack chairs around fire pits. Repeat the cycle a few times, then lounge around the thermal waterfall pools. Talk is not allowed, and bathing suits are required. ✉ *27300 Rancho San Carlos Rd., south off Carmel Valley Rd., Carmel* ☎ *831/620–7360* 🌐 *refuge.com* 🎟 *$44* ☞ *$52 admission; $125 50-min massage (includes Refuge admission), $12 robe rental, hot tubs (outdoor), sauna, steam room. Services: aromatherapy, hydrotherapy, massage.*

Pebble Beach

Off North San Antonio Ave. in Carmel-by-the-Sea or off Sunset Dr. in Pacific Grove.

In 1919 the Pacific Improvement Company acquired 18,000 acres of prime land on the Monterey Peninsula, including the entire Pebble Beach coastal region and much of Pacific Grove. Pebble Beach Golf Links and The Lodge at Pebble Beach opened the same year, and the private enclave evolved into a world-class golf destination with three posh lodges, five golf courses, hiking and riding trails, and some of the West Coast's ritziest homes. Pebble Beach has hosted major international golf tournaments, including the U.S. Open in 2019. The annual Pebble Beach Food & Wine, a four-day event in late April with 100 celebrity chefs, is one of the West Coast's premier culinary festivals.

GETTING HERE AND AROUND

If you drive south from Monterey on Highway 1, exit at 17-Mile Drive/Sunset Drive in Pacific Grove to find the northern entrance gate. Coming from Carmel, exit at Ocean Avenue and follow the road almost to the beach; turn right on North San Antonio Avenue to the Carmel Gate. You can also enter through the Highway 1 Gate off Highway 68. Monterey–Salinas Transit buses provide regular service in and around Pebble Beach.

Sights

★ The Lone Cypress

FOREST | The most-photographed tree along 17-Mile Drive is the weather-sculpted Lone Cypress, which grows out of a precipitous outcropping above the waves about 1½ miles up the road from Pebble Beach Golf Links. You can't walk out to the tree, but you can stop for a view of it at a small parking area off the road.

★ 17-Mile Drive

SCENIC DRIVE | Primordial nature resides in quiet harmony with palatial, mostly Spanish Mission–style estates along 17-Mile Drive, which winds through an 8,400-acre microcosm of the Pebble Beach coastal landscape. Dotting the drive are rare Monterey cypresses, trees so gnarled and twisted that Robert Louis Stevenson described them as "ghosts fleeing before the wind." The most famous of these is the **Lone Cypress**. Other highlights include **Bird Rock** and **Seal Rock,** home to harbor seals, sea lions, cormorants, and pelicans and other sea creatures and birds, and the **Crocker Marble Palace,** inspired by a Byzantine castle and easily identifiable by its dozens of marble arches.

Enter 17-Mile Drive at the Highway 1 Gate, at Highway 68; the Carmel Gate, off North San Antonio Avenue; the Pacific Grove Gate, off Sunset Drive; S.F.B. Morse Gate, Morse Drive off Highway 68; and Country Club Gate, at Congress Avenue and Forest Lodge Road. ■ TIP→ If you spend $35 or more on dining in Pebble Beach and show a receipt upon exiting, you'll receive a refund off the drive's $10.25 per car fee. ⊠ Hwy. 1 Gate, 17-Mile Dr., west of Hwy. 1 and Hwy. 68 intersection ☎ $11 per car, free for bicyclists.

Hotels

★ Casa Palmero

$$$$ | RESORT | This exclusive boutique hotel evokes a stately Mediterranean villa. **Pros:** ultimate in pampering; sumptuous decor; more private than sister resorts. **Cons:** rates out of reach for most visitors; not the best views compared to sister lodges too posh for some; some showers on the small side. $ Rooms from: $1100 ⊠ 1518 Cypress Dr. ☎ 831/622–6650, 800/877–0597 reservations ⊕ www.pebblebeach.com ⤶ 24 rooms ⏐⊚⏐ Breakfast.

The Inn at Spanish Bay

$$$$ | RESORT | This resort sprawls across a breathtaking stretch of shoreline, and has lush, 600-square-foot rooms. **Pros:** attentive service; many amenities; spectacular views. **Cons:** huge hotel; 4 miles from other Pebble Beach Resorts facilities; atmosphere too snobbish for some. $ Rooms from: $820 ⊠ 2700 17-Mile Dr. ☎ 831/647–7500, 800/877–0597 ⊕ www.pebblebeach.com ⤶ 269 rooms.

The Lodge at Pebble Beach

$$$$ | RESORT | Most rooms have wood-burning fireplaces and many have wonderful ocean views at this circa-1919 resort, which expanded to include Fairway One, an additional 38-room complex, in 2017. **Pros:** world-class golf; borders the ocean and fairways; fabulous facilities. **Cons:** some rooms are on the small side; very pricey; not many activities if you don't golf. $ Rooms from: $940 ⊠ 1700 17-Mile Dr. ☎ 831/624–3811, 800/877–0597 ⊕ www.pebblebeach.com ⤶ 199 rooms ⏐⊚⏐ No meals.

Did You Know?

The Lone Cypress has stood on this rock for more than 250 years. The tree is the official symbol of the Pebble Beach Company.

✿ Activities

GOLF

Links at Spanish Bay

GOLF | This course, which hugs a choice stretch of shoreline, was designed by Robert Trent Jones Jr., Tom Watson, and Sandy Tatum in the rugged manner of traditional Scottish links, with sand dunes and coastal marshes interspersed among the greens. A bagpiper signals the course's closing each day. ■TIP➜ **Nonguests of the Pebble Beach Resorts can reserve tee times up to two months in advance.** ⊠ *17-Mile Dr., north end* ☎ *800/877–0597* ⊕ *www.pebble-beach.com* ✉ *$290* ⚑ *18 holes, 6821 yards, par 72.*

★ Pebble Beach Golf Links

GOLF | Each February, show-business celebrities and golf pros team up at this course, the main site of the glamorous AT&T Pebble Beach National Pro-Am tournament. On most days the rest of the year, tee times are available to guests of the Pebble Beach Resorts who book a minimum two-night stay. Nonguests can reserve a tee time only one day in advance on a space-available basis; resort guests can reserve up to 18 months in advance. ⊠ *17-Mile Dr., near The Lodge at Pebble Beach* ☎ *800/877–0597* ⊕ *www.pebblebeach.com* ✉ *$550* ⚑ *18 holes, 6828 yards, par 72.*

Peter Hay

GOLF | The only 9-hole, par-3 course on the Monterey Peninsula open to the public, Peter Hay attracts golfers of all skill levels. It's an ideal place for warm-ups, practicing short games, and for those who don't have time to play 18 holes. ⊠ *17-Mile Dr. and Portola Rd.* ☎ *800/877–0597* ⊕ *www.pebblebeach.com* ✉ *$30* ⚑ *9 holes, 725 yards, par 27.*

Poppy Hills

GOLF | An 18-hole course designed in 1986 by Robert Trent Jones Jr., Poppy Hills reopened in 2014 after a yearlong renovation that Jones supervised. Each hole has been restored to its natural elevation along the forest floor, and all 18 greens have been rebuilt with bent grass. Individuals may reserve up to a month in advance. ■TIP➜ **Poppy Hills, owned by a golfing nonprofit, represents good value for this area.** ⊠ *3200 Lopez Rd., at 17-Mile Dr.* ☎ *831/250–1819* ⊕ *poppyhillsgolf.com* ✉ *$250* ⚑ *18 holes, 7002 yards, par 73.5.*

Spyglass Hill

GOLF | With three holes rated among the toughest on the PGA tour, Spyglass Hill, designed by Robert Trent Jones Sr. and Jr., challenges golfers with its varied terrain but rewards them with glorious views. The first 5 holes border the Pacific, and the other 13 reach deep into the Del Monte Forest. Reservations are essential and may be made up to one month in advance (18 months for resort guests). ⊠ *Stevenson Dr. and Spyglass Hill Rd.* ☎ *800/877–0597* ⊕ *www.pebblebeach.com* ✉ *$395* ⚑ *18 holes, 6960 yards, par 72.*

Pacific Grove

3 miles north of Carmel-by-the-Sea.

This picturesque town, which began as a summer retreat for church groups more than a century ago, recalls its prim and proper Victorian heritage in its host of tiny board-and-batten cottages and stately mansions. However, long before the church groups flocked here the area received thousands of annual pilgrims—in the form of bright orange-and-black monarch butterflies. They still come, migrating south from Canada and the Pacific Northwest to take residence in pine and eucalyptus groves from October through March. In Butterfly Town USA, as Pacific Grove is known, the sight of a mass of butterflies hanging from the branches like a long, fluttering veil is unforgettable.

A prime way to enjoy Pacific Grove is to walk or bicycle the 3 miles of city-owned shoreline along Ocean View Boulevard, a cliff-top area landscaped with native plants and dotted with benches meant for sitting and gazing at the sea. You can spot many types of birds here, including the web-footed cormorants that crowd the massive rocks rising out of the surf. Two Victorians of note along Ocean View are the Queen Anne–style Green Gables, at No. 301—erected in 1888, it's now an inn—and the 1909 Pryor House, at No. 429, a massive, shingled, private residence with a leaded- and beveled-glass doorway.

GETTING HERE AND AROUND
Reach Pacific Grove via Highway 68 off Highway 1, just south of Monterey. From Cannery Row in Monterey, head north until the road merges with Ocean Boulevard and follow it along the coast. MST buses travel within Pacific Grove and surrounding towns.

◉ Sights

Lovers Point Park
CITY PARK | FAMILY | The coastal views are gorgeous from this waterfront park whose sheltered beach has a children's pool and a picnic area. The main lawn has a volleyball court and a snack bar. ⊠ *Ocean View Blvd. northwest of Forest Ave.* ⊕ *www.cityofpacificgrove.org/ living/recreation/parks/lovers-point-park.*

Monarch Grove Sanctuary
NATURE PRESERVE | FAMILY | The sanctuary is a reliable spot for viewing monarch butterflies between November and February. ■TIP→ **The best time to visit is between noon and 3 pm.** ⊠ *250 Ridge Rd., off Lighthouse Ave.* ⊕ *www.pgmuseum. org/monarch-viewing.*

Pacific Grove Museum of Natural History
MUSEUM | The museum, a good source for the latest information about monarch butterflies, has permanent exhibitions about the butterflies, birds of Monterey County, biodiversity, and plants. There's a native plant garden, and a display documents life in Pacific Grove's 19th-century Chinese fishing village. ⊠ *165 Forest Ave., at Central Ave.* ☎ *831/648–5716* ⊕ *pgmuseum.org* ⌸ *$9* ⊘ *Closed Mon.*

Point Pinos Lighthouse
LIGHTHOUSE | FAMILY | At this 1855 structure, the West Coast's oldest continuously operating lighthouse, you can learn about the lighting and foghorn operations and wander through a small museum containing U.S. Coast Guard memorabilia. ⊠ *Asilomar Ave., between Lighthouse Ave. and Del Monte Blvd.* ☎ *831/648–3176* ⊕ *pointpinoslighthouse. org* ⌸ *$2* ⊘ *Closed Tues. and Wed.*

⚓ Beaches

Asilomar State Beach
BEACH—SIGHT | A beautiful coastal area, Asilomar State Beach stretches between Point Pinos and the Del Monte Forest. The 100 acres of dunes, tidal pools, and pocket-size beaches form one of the region's richest areas for marine life—including surfers, who migrate here most winter mornings. Leashed dogs are allowed on the beach. **Amenities:** none. **Best for:** sunrise; sunset; surfing; walking. ⊠ *Sunset Dr. and Asilomar Ave.* ☎ *831/646–6440* ⊕ *www. parks.ca.gov.*

🍴 Restaurants

Beach House
$$$ | MODERN AMERICAN | Patrons of this bluff-top perch sip classic cocktails, sample California fare, and watch the otters frolic on Lovers Point Beach below. The sunset discounts between 4 and 6 (reservations recommended) are a great value. **Known for:** sweeping bluff-top views; sunset discounts; seafood and organic pastas. Ⓢ *Average main: $24* ⊠ *620 Ocean View Blvd.* ☎ *831/375–2345* ⊕ *beachhousepg.com* ⊘ *No lunch.*

★ **Fandango**

$$$$ | **MEDITERRANEAN** | The menu here is mostly Mediterranean and southern French, with such dishes as osso buco and paella. The decor follows suit: stone walls and country furniture lend the restaurant the earthy feel of a European farmhouse. **Known for:** wood-fire-grilled rack of lamb, seafood, and beef; convivial residential vibe; traditional European flavors. [$] *Average main: $34* ✉ *223 17th St., south of Lighthouse Ave.* ☎ *831/372–3456* 🌐 *fandangorestaurant.com.*

Fishwife

$$ | **SEAFOOD** | Fresh fish with a Latin accent makes this a favorite of locals for lunch or a casual dinner. Standards are the sea garden salads topped with your choice of fish and the fried seafood plates. **Known for:** fisherman's bowls with fresh local seafood; house-made desserts; crab cakes and New Zealand mussels. [$] *Average main: $22* ✉ *1996½ Sunset Dr., at Asilomar Blvd.* ☎ *831/375–7107* 🌐 *fishwife.com.*

Jennini Kitchen + Wine Bar

$$$ | **MEDITERRANEAN** | Sommelier Thamin Saleh named his lively restaurant and wine bar after his hometown in Palestine, and designed a menu that showcases his favorite dishes from the region, especially southern Spain and the eastern Mediterranean and the islands. The menu (small plates and entrées) changes seasonally, but usually includes faves like chicken and merguez tagine, crispy lamb shanks, hummus and baba ghanoush, and filone bread with goat butter. **Known for:** daily happy hour 4 to 6; eclectic, value-driven wine list with 180 selections; creative twists on classic dishes. [$] *Average main: $25* ✉ *542 Lighthouse Ave.* ☎ *831/920–2662* 🌐 *www.jeninni.com* ⏲ *Closed Wed. No lunch.*

La Mia Cucina

$$$ | **ITALIAN** | Pasta, fish, steaks, and veal dishes are the specialties at this modern trattoria, the best in town for Italian food. The look is spare and clean, with colorful antique wine posters decorating the white walls. **Known for:** house-made gnocchi, ravioli, and sausage; festive dining room; menu centers around Italian family recipes. [$] *Average main: $27* ✉ *208 17th St., at Lighthouse Ave.* ☎ *831/373–2416* 🌐 *lamiacucinaristorante.com* ⏲ *Closed Mon. and Tues. No lunch.*

★ **Passionfish**

$$$ | **MODERN AMERICAN** | South American artwork and artifacts decorate Passionfish, and Latin and Asian flavors infuse the dishes. The chef shops at local farmers' markets several times a week to find the best produce, fish, and meat available, then pairs it with creative sauces like a caper, raisin, and walnut relish. **Known for:** sustainably sourced seafood and organic ingredients; reasonably priced wine list that supports small producers; slow-cooked meats. [$] *Average main: $26* ✉ *701 Lighthouse Ave., at Congress Ave.* ☎ *831/655–3311* 🌐 *passionfish.net* ⏲ *No lunch.*

Peppers Mexicali Cafe

$$ | **MEXICAN** | This cheerful white-walled storefront serves traditional dishes from Mexico and Latin America, with an emphasis on fresh seafood. Excellent red and green salsas are made throughout the day, and there's a large selection of beers, along with fresh lime margaritas. **Known for:** traditional Latin American dishes; fresh lime margaritas; daily specials. [$] *Average main: $18* ✉ *170 Forest Ave., between Lighthouse and Central Aves.* ☎ *831/373–6892* 🌐 *peppersmexicalicafe.com* ⏲ *Closed Tues. No lunch Sun.*

Red House Café

$$ | **AMERICAN** | When it's nice out, sun pours through the big windows of this cozy restaurant and across tables on the porch; when fog rolls in, the fireplace is lit. The American menu changes with the seasons but grilled lamb chops atop mashed potatoes are often on offer for dinner, and a grilled calamari steak

might be served for lunch, either in a salad or as part of a sandwich. **Known for:** cozy homelike dining areas; comfort food; stellar breakfast and brunch. [$] *Average main: $21* ✉ *662 Lighthouse Ave., at 19th St.* ☎ *831/643–1060* 🌐 *redhousecafe.com* 🕓 *No dinner Mon.*

Taste Café and Bistro
$$ | **AMERICAN** | **FAMILY** | Grilled marinated rabbit, roasted half chicken, filet mignon, and other meats are the focus at Taste, which serves hearty European-inspired food in a casual, open-kitchen setting. **Known for:** grilled meats; house-made desserts; kids' menu. [$] *Average main: $22* ✉ *1199 Forest Ave., at Prescott La.* ☎ *831/655–0324* 🌐 *tastecafebistro.com* 🕓 *Closed Sun. and Mon.*

Hotels

Asilomar Conference Grounds
$$$ | **RESORT** | On 107 acres in a state park, Asilomar stands among evergreen woods on the edge of a wild beach. **Pros:** general public can book individual rooms up to six months in advance; tasteful and modern rooms; many activities. **Cons:** basic amenities and furnishings; some rooms aging and need updating; service sometimes disorganized. [$] *Rooms from: $225* ✉ *800 Asilomar Ave.* ☎ *831/372–8016, 888/635–5310* 🌐 *visitasilomar.com* 🛏 *312 rooms.*

Gosby House Inn
$$ | **B&B/INN** | Though in the town center, this turreted butter-yellow Queen Anne Victorian has an informal feel. **Pros:** peaceful; homey; within walking distance of shops and restaurants. **Cons:** too frilly for some; area is busy during the day; limited parking. [$] *Rooms from: $155* ✉ *643 Lighthouse Ave.* ☎ *831/375–1287* 🌐 *gosbyhouseinn.com* 🛏 *22 rooms, 21 with bath* 🍴 *Breakfast.*

★ **Green Gables Inn**
$$ | **B&B/INN** | Stained-glass windows and ornate interior details compete with spectacular ocean views at this Queen Anne–style mansion. **Pros:** exceptional views; impeccable attention to historic detail; afternoon wine and cheese served in the parlor. **Cons:** some rooms are small; thin walls; breakfast room can be crowded. [$] *Rooms from: $169* ✉ *301 Ocean View Blvd.* ☎ *831/375–2095* 🌐 *www.greengablesinnpg.com* 🛏 *11 rooms, 8 with bath* 🍴 *Breakfast.*

Martine Inn
$$$ | **B&B/INN** | The glassed-in parlor and many guest rooms at this 1899 Mediterranean-style villa have stunning ocean views. **Pros:** romantic; exquisite antiques; ocean views. **Cons:** not child-friendly; sits on a busy thoroughfare; inconvenient parking. [$] *Rooms from: $229* ✉ *255 Ocean View Blvd.* ☎ *831/373–3388* 🌐 *martineinn.com* 🛏 *25 rooms* 🍴 *Breakfast.*

Monterey

2 miles southeast of Pacific Grove, 2 miles north of Carmel.

Monterey is a scenic city filled with early California history: adobe buildings from the 1700s, Colton Hall, where California's first constitution was drafted in 1849, and Cannery Row, made famous by author John Steinbeck. Thousands of visitors come each year to mingle with otters and other sea creatures at the world-famous Monterey Bay Aquarium and in the protected waters of the national marine sanctuary that hugs the shoreline.

GETTING HERE AND AROUND

From San Jose or San Francisco, take U.S. 101 south to Highway 156 West at Prunedale. Head west about 8 miles to Highway 1 and follow it about 15 miles south. From San Luis Obispo, take U.S. 101 north to Salinas and drive west on Highway 68 about 20 miles.

Many MST bus lines connect at the Monterey Transit Center, at Pearl Street and Munras Avenue. In summer (daily from 10 until at least 7) and on weekends and holidays the rest of the year, the free MST Monterey Trolley travels from downtown Monterey along Cannery Row to the Aquarium and back.

TOURS

Monterey Movie Tours
SPECIAL-INTEREST | Board a customized motor coach and relax while a film-savvy local takes you on a scenic tour of the Monterey Peninsula enhanced by film clips from the more than 200 movies shot in the area. The three-hour adventure travels a 32-mile loop through Monterey, Pacific Grove, and Carmel. ✉ Departs from Monterey Conference Center, 1 Portola Plaza ☎ 831/372–6278, 800/343–6437 ⊕ montereymovietours.com ✉ $55.

Old Monterey Walking Tour
WALKING TOURS | Learn all about Monterey's storied past by joining a guided walking tour through the historic district. Tours begin at the Custom House in Custom House Plaza, across from Fisherman's Wharf and are typically offered Thursday through Sunday at 10:30, 12:30, and 2. ■TIP→ Tours are free for everyone on the last Sunday of the month. ✉ Monterey ⊕ www.parks.ca.gov/?page_id=951 ✉ Tours $10.

The Original Monterey Walking Tours
WALKING TOURS | Learn more about Monterey's past, primarily the Mexican period until California statehood, on a guided tour through downtown Monterey. You can also join a guided walking tour of Cannery Row in the afternoon. Tours last 1½ to 2 hours and are offered Thursday–Sunday at 10 am and 2. Reservations are essential. ✉ Monterey ☎ 831/521–4884 ⊕ www.walkmonterey.com ✉ From $25.

ESSENTIALS
VISITOR INFORMATION Monterey County Convention & Visitors Bureau. ✉ Visitor center, 401 Camino El Estero ☎ 888/221–1010 ⊕ seemonterey.com.

◉ Sights

California's First Theatre
MUSEUM | This adobe began its life in 1846 as a saloon and lodging house for sailors. Four years later stage curtains were fashioned from army blankets, and some U.S. officers staged plays to the light of whale oil lamps. The building is open only for private tours and events, but you can stroll in the garden. ✉ Monterey State Historic Park, Scott and Pacific Sts. ☎ 831/649–2907 ⊕ www.parks.ca.gov/mshp ✉ Free.

Cannery Row
NEIGHBORHOOD | When John Steinbeck published the novel Cannery Row in 1945, he immortalized a place of rough-edged working people. The waterfront street, edging a mile of gorgeous coastline, once was crowded with sardine canneries processing, at their peak, nearly 200,000 tons of the smelly silver fish a year. During the mid-1940s, however, the sardines disappeared from the bay, causing the canneries to close. Through the years the old tin-roof canneries have been converted into restaurants, art galleries, and malls with shops selling T-shirts, fudge, and plastic sea otters. Recent tourist development along the row has been more tasteful, however, and includes stylish inns and hotels, wine tasting rooms, and upscale specialty shops. ✉ Cannery Row, between Reeside and David Aves. ⊕ canneryrow.com.

Casa Soberanes
HOUSE | A classic low-ceiling adobe structure built in 1842, this was once a Custom House guard's residence. Exhibits at the house survey life in Monterey from the era of Mexican rule to the present. The building is open only for private tour requests (call for times and fees), but you can visit the peaceful rear garden and its rose-covered arbor. ✉ Monterey State Historic Park, 336 Pacific St., at Del Monte Ave. ☎ 831/649–2907 ⊕ www.parks.ca.gov/mshp ✉ Free.

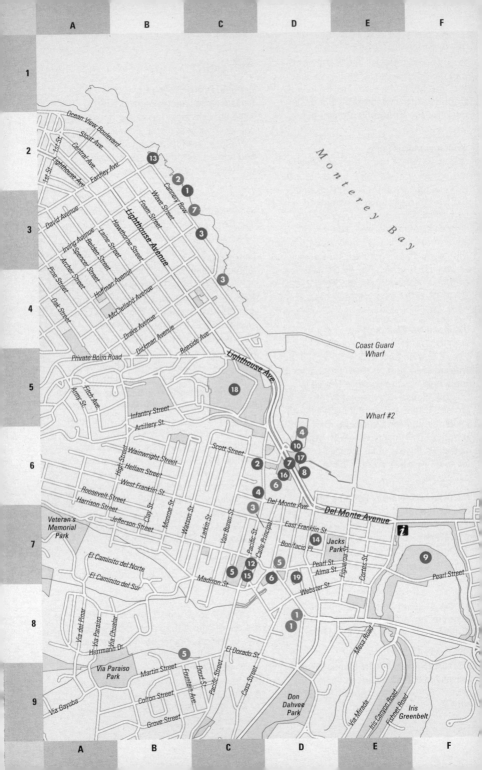

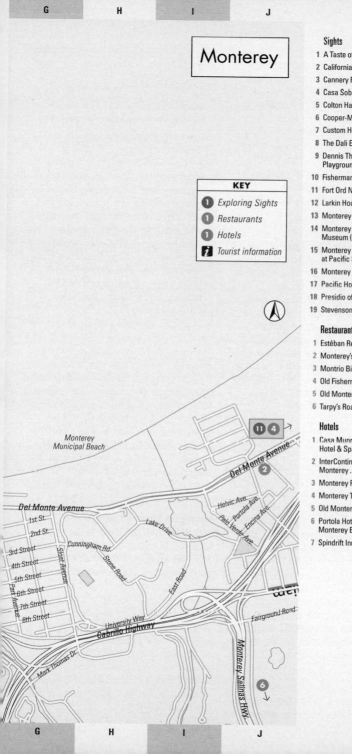

Monterey

KEY

1 Exploring Sights

1 Restaurants

1 Hotels

i Tourist information

Colton Hall

MUSEUM | A convention of delegates met here in 1849 to draft the first state constitution. The stone building, which has served as a school, a courthouse, and the county seat, is a city-run museum furnished as it was during the constitutional convention. The extensive grounds outside the hall surround the Old Monterey Jail. ⊠ *570 Pacific St., between Madison and Jefferson Sts.* ☎ *831/646–5640* ⊕ *www.monterey.org/ museums* ☒ *Free.*

Cooper-Molera Adobe

HOUSE | The restored 2-acre complex includes a house dating from the 1820s, a gift shop, and a large garden enclosed by a high adobe wall. The mostly Victorian-era antiques and memorabilia that fill the house provide a glimpse into the life of a prosperous sea merchant's family. If the house is closed, you can still stop by the Cooper Store and pick up walking-tour maps and stroll the grounds. ⊠ *Monterey State Historic Park, Polk and Munras Sts.* ☎ *831/649–7118* ⊕ *www. parks.ca.gov/mshp* ☒ *$5 tour.*

Custom House

MUSEUM | FAMILY | Built by the Mexican government in 1827 and now California's oldest standing public building, the Custom House was the first stop for sea traders whose goods were subject to duties. In 1846 Commodore John Sloat raised the American flag over this adobe structure and claimed California for the United States. The lower floor displays cargo from a 19th-century trading ship. The Custom House Store sells Monterey-themed items. If the house is closed, you can visit the cactus gardens and stroll the plaza. ⊠ *Monterey State Historic Park, 1 Custom House Plaza, across from Fisherman's Wharf* ☎ *831/649–7111 gift shop* ⊕ *www.parks.ca.gov/mshp.*

The Dali Expo

MUSEUM | Whether you're a fan of surrealist art or not, come to The Dali Expo to gain rare insight into the life and work

John Steinbeck's Cannery Row

"Cannery Row in Monterey in California is a poem, a stink, a grating noise, a quality of light, a tone, a habit, a nostalgia, a dream. Cannery Row is the gathered and scattered, tin and iron and rust and splintered wood, chipped pavement and weedy lots and junk heaps, sardine canneries of corrugated iron, honky tonks, restaurants and whore houses, and little crowded groceries, and laboratories and flophouses." —John Steinbeck, *Cannery Row*

of famed Spanish artist Salvador Dali, who lived in Monterey in the 1940s. The permanent exhibition houses nearly 600 artworks in various media, including 400 Dali originals. The museum's name reflects Dali's ties to nearby 17-Mile Drive, where he lived, worked, and hosted parties that included Andy Warhol, Walt Disney, Bob Hope, and other celebrities. ⊠ *5 Custom House Plaza* ☎ *831/372–2608* ⊕ *www.thedaliexpo. com* ☒ *$20.*

Dennis the Menace Playground

CITY PARK | FAMILY | The late cartoonist Hank Ketcham designed this play area. Its equipment is on a grand scale and made for Dennis-like daredevils: kid favorites include the roller slide, rock-climbing area, and clanking suspension bridge. You can rent a rowboat or a paddleboat for cruising around U-shape Lake El Estero, populated with an assortment of ducks, mud hens, and geese. ⊠ *El Estero Park, Pearl St. and Camino El Estero* ☎ *831/646–3866* ⊕ *www.monterey.org/parks* ☒ *Closed Tues., Sept.–May.*

Fisherman's Wharf

PEDESTRIAN MALL | **FAMILY** | The mournful barking of sea lions provides a steady sound track all along Monterey's waterfront, but the best way to actually view the whiskered marine mammals is to walk along one of the two piers across from Custom House Plaza. Lined with souvenir shops, the wharf is undeniably touristy, but it's lively and entertaining. At Wharf No. 2, a working municipal pier, you can see the day's catch being unloaded from fishing boats on one side and fishermen casting their lines into the water on the other. The pier has a couple of low-key restaurants, from whose seats lucky customers might spot otters and harbor seals. ⊠ *At end of Calle Principal* ⊕ *www.monterey-wharf.com.*

Fort Ord National Monument

NATIONAL/STATE PARK | Scenic beauty, biodiversity, and miles of trails make this former U.S. Army training grounds a haven for nature lovers and outdoor enthusiasts. The 7,200-acre park, which stretches east over the hills between Monterey and Salinas, is also protected habitat for 35 species of rare and endangered plants and animals. There are 86 miles of single-track, dirt, and paved trails for hiking, biking, and horseback riding. The main trailheads are the Creekside, off Creekside Terrace near Portola Road, and Badger Hills, off Highway 68 in Salinas. Maps are available at the various trail-access points and on the park's website. ■ TIP→ **Dogs are permitted on trails, but should be leashed when other people are nearby.** ⊠ *Bordered by Hwy. 68 and Gen. Jim Moore and Reservation Rds.* ☎ *831/582–2200* ⊕ *www.blm.gov/programs/national-conservation-lands/california/fort-ord-national-monument* ▨ *Free.*

Larkin House

HOUSE | A veranda encircles the second floor of this 1835 adobe, whose design bears witness to the Mexican and New England influences on the Monterey style. The building's namesake, Thomas O. Larkin, an early California statesman, brought many of the antiques inside from New Hampshire. Tours are available by special appointment only. If the building is closed, you can peek in the windows and stroll the gardens. ⊠ *Monterey State Historic Park, 464 Calle Principal, between Jefferson and Pacific Sts.* ☎ *831/649–2907* ⊕ *www.parks.ca.gov/mshp.*

★ Monterey Bay Aquarium

ZOO | **FAMILY** | Sea creatures surround you the minute you hand over your ticket at this extraordinary facility: right at the entrance dozens of them swim in a three-story-tall, sunlit kelp-forest tank. All the exhibits here provide a sense of what it's like to be in the water with the animals—sardines swim around your head in a circular tank, and jellyfish drift in and out of view in dramatically lighted spaces that suggest the ocean depths. A petting pool puts you literally in touch with bat rays, and the million-gallon Open Seas tank illustrates the variety of creatures, from sharks to placid-looking turtles, that live in the eastern Pacific. At the Splash Zone, which has 45 interactive bilingual exhibits, kids can commune with African black-footed penguins, potbellied seahorses, and other creatures. The only drawback to the aquarium experience is that it must be shared with the throngs that congregate daily, but most visitors think it's worth it. ⊠ *886 Cannery Row, at David Ave.* ☎ *831/648–4800 info, 866/963–9645 for advance tickets* ⊕ *montereybayaquarium.org* ▨ *$50.*

Monterey County Youth Museum (MY Museum)

MUSEUM | **FAMILY** | Monterey Bay comes to life from a child's perspective in this fun-filled, interactive indoor exploration center. The seven exhibit galleries showcase the science and nature of the Big Sur coast, theater arts, Pebble

California sea lions are intelligent, social animals that live (and sleep) close together in groups.

Beach golf, and beaches. Also here are a live performance theater, a creation station, a hospital emergency room, and an agriculture corner where kids follow artichokes, strawberries, and other fruits and veggies on their evolution from sprout to harvest to farmers' markets. ⊠ *425 Washington St., between E. Franklin St. and Bonifacio Pl.* ☎ *831/649–6444* ⊕ *mymuseum.org* ⌨ *$8* ⊗ *Closed Mon.*

Monterey Museum of Art at Pacific Street
MUSEUM | Photographs by Ansel Adams and Edward Weston and works by other artists who have spent time on the peninsula are on display here, along with international folk art, from Kentucky hearth brooms to Tibetan prayer wheels. ⊠ *559 Pacific St., across from Colton Hall* ☎ *831/372–5477* ⊕ *montereyart.org* ⌨ *$10* ⊗ *Closed Wed.*

★ Monterey State Historic Park
NATIONAL/STATE PARK | You can glimpse Monterey's early history in several well-preserved adobe buildings downtown. Some of the structures have

gardens that are themselves worthy sights, and they're visitable even if the buildings—among them **Casa Soberanes,** the **Larkin House,** and the **Stevenson House**—are closed. ■ **TIP→ If buildings are closed when you visit you can access a cell phone tour 24/7 at 831/998–9458 or download a mobile app.** ⊠ *Pacific House Museum visitor center, 10 Custom House Plaza* ☎ *831/649–7118* ⊕ *www.parks.ca.gov/mshp* ⌨ *Free–$5, 1-hr history walk $10.*

Pacific House Museum
MUSEUM | Once a hotel and saloon, this facility, also a visitor center, commemorates life in pioneer-era California with gold-rush relics and photographs of old Monterey. On the upper floor are Native American artifacts, including gorgeous baskets and pottery. ⊠ *Monterey State Historic Park, 10 Custom House Plaza* ☎ *831/649–2907* ⊕ *www.parks.ca.gov/mshp* ⌨ *Free.*

Presidio of Monterey Museum
MUSEUM | This spot has been significant for centuries. Its first incarnation was as a Native American village for the

Rumsien tribe. The Spanish explorer Sebastián Vizcaíno landed here in 1602, and Father Junípero Serra arrived in 1770. Notable battles fought here include the 1818 skirmish in which the corsair Hipólito Bruchard conquered the Spanish garrison that stood on this site and claimed part of California for Argentina. The indoor museum tells the stories; plaques mark the outdoor sites. ⊠ *Presidio of Monterey, Corporal Ewing Rd., off Lighthouse Ave.* ☎ *831/646–3456* ⊕ *www.monterey.org/museums* ⊠ *Free* ⊗ *Closed Tues. and Wed.*

Former Capital of California ◉

In 1602 Spanish explorer Sebastián Vizcaíno stepped ashore on a remote California peninsula. He named it after the viceroy of New Spain—Count de Monte Rey. Soon the Spanish built a military outpost, and the site was the capital of California until the state came under American rule.

Stevenson House

HOUSE | This house was named in honor of author Robert Louis Stevenson, who boarded here briefly in a tiny upstairs room. Items from his family's estate furnish Stevenson's room; period-decorated chambers elsewhere in the house include a gallery of memorabilia and a children's nursery stocked with Victorian toys and games. Visit the website or call for tour times and fees. If the building is closed, you can stroll around the gardens. ⊠ *Monterey State Historic Park, 530 Houston St., near Pearl St.* ☎ *831/649–2907* ⊕ *www.parks.ca.gov/mshp.*

A Taste of Monterey

WINERY/DISTILLERY | Without driving the back roads, you can taste the wines of nearly 100 area vintners (craft beers, too) while taking in fantastic bay views. Bottles are available for purchase, and food is served from 11:30 until closing. ⊠ *700 Cannery Row, Suite KK* ☎ *831/646–5446* ⊕ *atasteofmonterey. com* ⊠ *Tastings $15.*

🍽 Restaurants

Estéban Restaurant

$$$ | **SPANISH** | In a festive fireplace dining room at Casa Munras hotel, Estéban serves modern and classic versions of Spanish cuisine: empanadas, Moorish chickpea stew, and three types of paella. Midweek specials abound: on Tuesday

nights, feast on a four-course prix-fixe paella dinner ($54 per couple), bottles of wine are half off on Monday, and Wednesday wine flights are just $14 for three tastes. **Known for:** daily tapas happy hour from 4:30 to 6; outdoor patio with fire pit; special menus for kids and pups. ⓢ *Average main: $30* ⊠ *700 Munras Ave.* ☎ *831/375–0176* ⊕ *www.estebanrestaurant.com* ⊗ *No lunch.*

Monterey's Fish House

$$ | **SEAFOOD** | Casual yet stylish and always packed, this seafood restaurant is removed from the hubbub of the wharf. The bartenders and waitstaff will gladly advise you on the perfect wine to go with your poached, blackened, or oak-grilled seafood. **Known for:** seafood, steaks, house-made pasta; festive atmosphere; oyster bar. ⓢ *Average main: $22* ⊠ *2114 Del Monte Ave., at Dela Vina Ave.* ☎ *831/373–4647* ⊕ *montereyfishhouse. com* ⊗ *No lunch weekends.*

★ Montrio Bistro

$$$ | **AMERICAN** | This quirky converted firehouse, with its rawhide walls and iron indoor trellises, has a wonderfully sophisticated menu. Organic produce and meats and sustainably sourced seafood are used in imaginative dishes that reflect the area's agriculture—crispy artichoke hearts with Mediterranean baba ghanoush, for instance, and scallop crudo with avocado-jalapeño panna cotta. **Known for:** green-certified restaurant; extensive international wine list; inventive cocktails. $ *Average main: $30* ✉ *414 Calle Principal, at W. Franklin St.* ☎ *831/648–8880* ⊕ *montrio.com* ☾ *No lunch.*

Old Fisherman's Grotto

$$$ | SEAFOOD | Otters and seals frolic in the water just below this nautical-theme Fisherman's Wharf restaurant famous for its creamy clam chowder. Seafood paella, sand dabs, filet mignon, teriyaki chicken, and several pastas are among the many entrée options. **Known for:** Monterey-style clam chowder and calamari; Monterey Bay views; full bar and carefully curated wine list. $ *Average main: $29* ✉ *39 Fisherman's Wharf* ☎ *831/375–4604* ⊕ *oldfishermansgrotto.com.*

Old Monterey Café

$ | AMERICAN | Breakfast here gets constant local raves—its fame rests on familiar favorites: a dozen kinds of omelets, and pancakes from blueberry to cinnamon-raisin-pecan. For lunch are good soups, salads, and sandwiches. $ *Average main: $15* ✉ *489 Alvarado St., at Munras Ave.* ☎ *831/646–1021* ⊕ *old-montereycafeca.com* ☾ *No dinner.*

Tarpy's Roadhouse

$$$ | AMERICAN | Fun, dressed-up American favorites—a little something for everyone—are served in this renovated early-1900s stone farmhouse several miles east of town. The kitchen cranks out everything from Cajun-spiced prawns to meat loaf with marsala–mushroom gravy to grilled ribs and steaks. **Known for:** American comfort food with a California twist; rustic dining: indoor fireplace or garden courtyard; generous portions. $ *Average main: $29* ✉ *2999 Monterey–Salinas Hwy., Hwy. 68* ☎ *831/647–1444* ⊕ *tarpys.com.*

🛏 Hotels

Casa Munras Garden Hotel & Spa

$$$ | HOTEL | FAMILY | A Spanish-theme cluster of buildings in the heart of downtown, Casa Munras pays homage to Monterey's historic roots and the legacy of Spanish diplomat Don Estéban Munras, who built a residence on the site in 1824. **Pros:** full-service spa, heated swimming pool, hot tub, and fitness room; on-site tapas restaurant; walk to downtown sights and restaurants; excellent on-site tapas restaurant. **Cons:** $15 parking fee; pool area can get noisy; thin walls. $ *Rooms from: $199* ✉ *700 Munras Ave.* ☎ *831/375–2411, 800/222–2446* ⊕ *www.hotelcasamunras.com* ⚲ *163 rooms* ☖ *No meals.*

InterContinental The Clement Monterey

$$$$ | HOTEL | FAMILY | Spectacular bay views, upscale amenities, assiduous service, and a superb location next to the aquarium propelled this luxury hotel to immediate stardom. **Pros:** a block from the aquarium; fantastic waterfront views from some rooms; great for families. **Cons:** a tad formal; not budget; Cannery Row crowds everywhere on busy weekends and holidays. $ *Rooms from: $269* ✉ *750 Cannery Row* ☎ *831/375–4500, 866/781–2406 toll-free* ⊕ *www.ictheclementmonterey.com* ⚲ *208 rooms* ☖ *No meals.*

Monterey Plaza Hotel & Spa

$$$$ | HOTEL | Guests at this waterfront Cannery Row hotel can see frolicking sea otters from its wide outdoor patio and many room balconies. **Pros:** on the ocean; many amenities; attentive service. **Cons:** touristy area; heavy traffic; resort fee. $ *Rooms from: $289* ✉ *400 Cannery Row* ☎ *831/920–6710, 877/862–7552* ⊕ *www.montereyplaza-hotel.com* ⚲ *290 rooms.*

Monterey Tides

$$$ | RESORT | One of the area's best values, this hotel has a great waterfront location—2 miles north of Monterey,

The Monterey Bay National Marine Sanctuary

Although Monterey's coastal landscapes are stunning, their beauty is more than equaled by the wonders that lie offshore. The Monterey Bay National Marine Sanctuary—which stretches 276 miles, from north of San Francisco almost down to Santa Barbara—teems with abundant life, and has topography as diverse as that aboveground.

The preserve's 5,322 square miles include vast submarine canyons, which reach down 10,663 feet at their deepest point. They also encompass dense forests of giant kelp—a kind of seaweed that can grow more than a hundred feet from its roots on the ocean floor. These kelp forests are especially robust off Monterey.

The sanctuary was established in 1992 to protect the habitat of the many species that thrive in the bay. Some animals can be seen quite easily from land. In summer and winter you might glimpse the offshore spray of gray whales as they migrate between their summer feeding grounds in Alaska and their breeding grounds in Baja. Clouds of marine birds—including white-faced ibis, three types of albatross, and more than 15 types of gull—skim the waves, or roost in the rock islands along 17-Mile Drive. Sea otters dart and gambol in the calmer waters of the bay; and of course, you can watch the sea lions—and hear their round-the-clock barking—on the wharves in Santa Cruz and Monterey.

The sanctuary supports many other creatures, however, that remain unseen by most on-land visitors. Some of these are enormous, such as the giant blue whales that arrive to feed on plankton in summer; others, like the more than 22 species of red algae in these waters, are microscopic. So whether you choose to visit the Monterey Bay Aquarium, take a whale-watch trip, or look out to sea with your binoculars, remember you're seeing just a small part of a vibrant underwater kingdom.

with views of the bay and the city skyline—and offers a surprising array of amenities. **Pros:** on the beach; great value; family-friendly. **Cons:** several miles from major attractions; big-box mall neighborhood; most rooms on the small side. $ *Rooms from: $206* ⊠ *2600 Sand Dunes Dr.* ☎ *831/394–3321, 800/242–8627* ⊕ *montereytides.com* ⚲ *196 rooms* ❌ *No meals.*

★ Old Monterey Inn
$$$$ | B&B/INN | This three-story manor house was the home of Monterey's first mayor, and today it remains a private enclave within walking distance of downtown, set off by lush gardens shaded by huge old trees and bordered by a creek. **Pros:** gorgeous gardens; spa room with treatments by the fireplace; extensive breakfast served in the dining room or in the rooms. **Cons:** must drive to attractions and sights; fills quickly; no pool or hot tub. $ *Rooms from: $379* ⊠ *500 Martin St.* ☎ *831/652–8999* ⊕ *www.old-montereyinn.com* ⚲ *9 rooms, 1 cottage* ❌ *Breakfast.*

Portola Hotel & Spa at Monterey Bay
$$$$ | HOTEL | One of Monterey's largest hotels and locally owned and operated for more than 40 years, the nautical-theme Portola anchors a prime city block between Custom House Plaza

and the Monterey Conference Center. **Pros:** walk to Fisherman's Wharf, Custom House Plaza, and downtown restaurants and shops; three on-site restaurants and coffee shop; pet- and family-friendly. **Cons:** crowded when conferences convene; no air-conditioning; parking fee. $ *Rooms from: $269* ⊠ *2 Portola Plaza* ☎ *831/649–4511, 888/222–5851* ⌁ *379 rooms* ⏐⊙⏐ *No meals.*

Spindrift Inn

$$$ | **HOTEL** | This boutique hotel on Cannery Row has beach access and a rooftop garden that overlooks the water. **Pros:** close to aquarium; steps from the beach; friendly staff. **Cons:** throngs of visitors outside; can be noisy; not good for families. $ *Rooms from: $216* ⊠ *652 Cannery Row* ☎ *831/646–8900, 800/841–1879* ⊕ *spindriftinn.com* ⌁ *45 rooms* ⏐⊙⏐ *Breakfast.*

⛾ Nightlife

BARS

Alvarado Street Brewery & Grill

BREWPUBS/BEER GARDENS | Housed in an historic Beaux Arts building that dates back to 1916, this craft brewery lures locals and visitors alike with a full bar and 20 craft beers on tap, decent gastropub menu, beer garden, and shaded sidewalk patio. ⊠ *426 Alvarado St.* ☎ *831/655–2337* ⊕ *www.alvaradostreetbrewery.com.*

Cibo

MUSIC CLUBS | An Italian restaurant and event venue with a big bar area, Cibo brings live jazz and other music to downtown from Tuesday through Sunday. ⊠ *301 Alvarado St., at Del Monte Ave.* ☎ *831/649–8151* ⊕ *cibo.com.*

Crown & Anchor

BARS/PUBS | An authentic British pub, downtown Crown & Anchor has 20 beers on tap, classic cocktails, and a full menu, including 18 daily specials available in the restaurant and heated patio until midnight. ⊠ *150 W. Franklin St.* ☎ *831/649–6496* ⊕ *crownandanchor.net.*

Peter B's Brewpub

BREWPUBS/BEER GARDENS | House-made beers, 18 HDTVs, a decent pub menu, and a pet-friendly patio ensure lively crowds at this craft brewery in back of the Portola Plaza Hotel. ⊠ *2 Portola Plaza* ☎ *831/649–2699* ⊕ *www.petersbrewpub.com.*

Turn 12 Bar & Grill

BARS/PUBS | The motorcycles and vintage photographs at this downtown watering hole pay homage to nearby 11-turn Laguna Seca Raceway. The large-screen TVs, heated outdoor patio, happy-hour specials, and live entertainment keep the place jumpin' into the wee hours. ⊠ *400 Tyler St., at E. Franklin St.* ☎ *831/372–8876* ⊕ *turn12barandgrill.com.*

MUSIC FESTIVALS

Jazz Bash by the Bay

FESTIVALS | Traditional jazz bands play early jazz, big band, swing, ragtime, blues, zydeco, and gypsy jazz at waterfront venues during this festival, held on the first full weekend of March. ☎ *888/349–6879, 831/754–8786* ⊕ *jazzbashmonterey.com.*

Monterey International Blues Festival

FESTIVALS | Blues fans flock to the Monterey Fairgrounds for this festival, held the last weekend in June. ⊕ *montereyinternationalbluesfestival.com.*

Monterey Jazz Festival

FESTIVALS | The world's oldest jazz festival attracts top-name performers to the Monterey Fairgrounds on the third full weekend of September. ☎ *888/248–6499 ticket office, 831/373–3366* ⊕ *montereyjazzfestival.org.*

⛾ Activities

Monterey Bay waters never warm to the temperatures of their Southern California counterparts—the warmest they get is the low 60s. That's one reason why the marine life here is so diverse, which in turn brings out the fishers, kayakers, and whale-watchers. During the rainy winter, the waves grow larger, and surfers flock to the water. On land pretty much year-round, bikers find opportunities to ride, and walkers have plenty of waterfront to stroll.

BIKING

Adventures by the Sea

BICYCLING | You can rent surreys plus tandem, standard, and electric bicycles from this outfit that also conducts bike and kayak tours, and rents kayaks and stand-up paddleboards. There are multiple locations along Cannery Row and Custom House Plaza as well as branches at Lovers Point in Pacific Grove and 17-Mile Drive in Pebble Beach. ⊠ *299 Cannery Row* ☎ *831/372–1807, 800/979–3370 reservations* ⊕ *adventuresbythesea.com.*

FISHING

J&M Sport Fishing

FISHING | This outfit takes beginning and experienced fishers out to sea to catch rock cod, ling cod, sand dabs, mackerel, halibut, salmon (in season), albacore, squid, Dungeness crab, and other species. ⊠ *66 Fisherman's Wharf* ☎ *831/372–7440* ⊕ *jmsportfishing.com.*

KAYAKING

★ Monterey Bay Kayaks

KAYAKING | For many visitors the best way to see the bay is by kayak. This company rents equipment and conducts classes and natural-history tours. ⊠ *693 Del Monte Ave.* ☎ *831/373–5357* ⊕ *www. montereybaykayaks.com.*

WALKING

Monterey Bay Coastal Recreation Trail

HIKING/WALKING | From Custom House Plaza, you can walk along the coast in either direction on this 29-mile-long trail and take in spectacular views of the sea. The trail runs from north of Monterey in Castroville south to Pacific Grove, with sections continuing around Pebble Beach. Much of the path follows an old Southern Pacific Railroad route. ☎ *888/221–1010* ⊕ *seemonterey.com/ things-to-do/parks/coastal-trail/.*

WHALE-WATCHING

Thousands of gray whales pass close by the Monterey Coast on their annual migration between the Bering Sea and Baja California, and a whale-watching cruise is the best way to see these magnificent mammals close up. The migration south takes place from December through March; January is prime viewing time. The whales migrate north from March through June. Blue whales and humpbacks also pass the coast; they're most easily spotted in late summer and early fall.

Fast Raft Ocean Safaris

TOUR—SPORTS | Naturalists lead whale-watching and sightseeing tours of Monterey Bay aboard the 33-foot *Ranger,* a six-passenger, rigid-hull inflatable boat. The speedy craft slips into coves inaccessible to larger vessels; its quiet engines enable intimate marine experiences without disturbing wildlife. Children ages eight and older are welcome to participate. ⊠ *32 Cannery Row, Suite F2* ☎ *408/659–3900* ⊕ *www.fastraft.com* ⌫ *From $165.*

Monterey Bay Whale Watch

WHALE-WATCHING | The marine biologists here lead three- to five-hour whale-watching tours. ⊠ *84 Fisherman's Wharf* ☎ *831/375–4658* ⊕ *montereybaywhalewatch.com.*

Princess Monterey Whale Watching

WHALE-WATCHING | Tours are offered daily on a 100-passenger high-speed cruiser and a large 100-foot boat. ⊠ *96 Fisherman's Wharf* ☎ *831/372–2203* ⊕ *montereywhalewatching.com.*

⬤ Shopping

Alvarado and nearby downtown streets are good places to start a Monterey shopping spree, especially if you're interested in antiques and collectibles.

Boston Store

ANTIQUES/COLLECTIBLES | Antiques and reproductions of 1850s merchandise—linens, crockery, preserves, soaps, and so forth—are available here. ⊠ *Monterey State Historic Park, 1 Custom House Plaza, across from Fisherman's Wharf* ☎ *831/277–0343* ⊕ *www.historicgarden-league.org.*

Cannery Row Antique Mall

ANTIQUES/COLLECTIBLES | Bargain hunters can sometimes find little treasures at the mall, which houses more than 100 local vendors under one roof. ⊠ *471 Wave St.* ☎ *831/655–0264* ⊕ *canneryrowantique-mall.com.*

The Custom House Gift Shop

SPECIALTY STORES | This store sells 1800s-theme items such as toys, as well as books related to Monterey and California heritage. ⊠ *Custom House Plaza, in the Custom House bldg.* ☎ *831/649–7111.*

Old Monterey Book Co.

BOOKS/STATIONERY | Antiquarian books and prints are this shop's specialties. ⊠ *136 Bonifacio Pl., off Alvarado St.* ☎ *831/372–3111* ⊗ *Closed Mon.*

Salinas

17 miles east of Monterey on Hwy. 68.

Salinas, a hardworking city surrounded by vineyards and fruit and vegetable fields, honors the memory and literary legacy of John Steinbeck, its most famous native, with the National Steinbeck Center. The facility is in Old Town Salinas, where renovated turn-of-the-20th-century stone buildings house shops and restaurants.

ESSENTIALS

TRAIN INFORMATION **Salinas Amtrak Station.** ⊠ *11 Station Pl., at W. Market St.* ☎ *800/872–7245* ⊕ *www.amtrak.com.*

VISITOR INFORMATION **California Welcome Center.** ⊠ *1213 N. Davis Rd., west of U.S. 101, exit 330* ☎ *831/757–8687* ⊕ *visitcalifornia.com/attraction/california-welcome-center-salinas.*

⊙ Sights

Monterey Zoo

ZOO | FAMILY | Exotic animals, many of them retired from film, television, and live production work or rescued from less than ideal environments, find sanctuary here. The zoo offers daily tours (1 pm and 3 pm June–August, 1 pm September–May), but for an in-depth experience, stay in a safari bungalow on-site at Vision Quest Safari B&B, where guests can join the elephants in their enclosures for breakfast. The inn's room rate includes a complimentary zoo tour. ⊠ *400 River Rd., off Hwy. 68* ☎ *831/455–1901* ⊕ *www.montereyzoo.com* ⊠ *From $20.*

National Steinbeck Center

MUSEUM | The center's exhibits document the life of Pulitzer- and Nobel-prize winner John Steinbeck and the history of the nearby communities that inspired novels such as *East of Eden*. Highlights include reproductions of the green pickup-camper from *Travels with Charley* and the bunk room from *Of Mice and Men*. **Steinbeck House,** the author's Victorian birthplace, at 132 Central Avenue, is two blocks from the center. Now a decent restaurant (only open for lunch) and gift shop with docent-led tours, it displays memorabilia. ⊠ *1 Main St., at Central Ave.* ☎ *831/775–4721* ⊕ *steinbeck.org* ⊠ *$13.*

Pinnacles National Park

38 miles southeast of Salinas.

Pinnacles may be the nation's newest national park, but Teddy Roosevelt recognized the uniqueness of this ancient volcano—its jagged spires and monoliths thrusting upward from chaparral-covered mountains—when he made it a national monument in 1908. Though only about two hours from the bustling Bay Area, the outside world seems to recede even before you reach the park's gates.

GETTING HERE AND AROUND

One of the first things you need to decide when visiting Pinnacles is which entrance—east or west—you'll use, because there's no road connecting the two rugged peaks separating them. Entering from Highway 25 on the east is straightforward. The gate is only a mile or so from the turnoff. From the west, once you head east out of Soledad on Highway 146, the road quickly becomes narrow and hilly, with many blind curves. Drive slowly and cautiously along the 10 miles or so before you reach the west entrance.

ESSENTIALS

Pinnacles Visitor Center

At the park's main visitor center, located at the eastern entrance, you can purchase admission passes, get maps, browse books, and buy gifts. The adjacent campground store sells snacks and drinks. ✉ *Hwy. 146, 2 miles west of Hwy. 25, Paicines* ☎ *831/389–4485* ⊕ *www.nps.gov/pinn.*

West Pinnacles Visitor Contact Station

This station is just past the park's western entrance, about 10 miles east of Soledad. Here you can get maps and information, watch a 13-minute film about Pinnacles, and view some displays. Food and drink aren't available here. ✉ *Hwy. 146, off U.S. 101, Soledad* ☎ *831/389–4427* ⊕ *www.nps.gov/pinn.*

◉ Sights

Pinnacles National Park

NATIONAL/STATE PARK | FAMILY | The many attractions at Pinnacles include talus caves, 30 miles of hiking trails, and hundreds of rock-climbing routes. A mosaic of diverse habitats supports an amazing variety of wildlife species: 185 birds, 49

mammals, 70 butterflies, and nearly 400 bees. The park is also home to some of the world's remaining few hundred condors in captivity and release areas. Fourteen of California's 25 bat species live in caves and other habitats in the park. President Theodore Roosevelt declared this remarkable 26,000-acre geologic and wildlife preserve a national monument in 1908. President Barack Obama officially designated it a national park in 2013.

The pinnacles are believed to have been created when two major tectonic plates collided and pushed a smaller plate down beneath the earth's crust, spawning volcanoes in what's now called the Gabilan Mountains, southeast of Salinas and Monterey. After the eruptions ceased, the San Andreas Fault split the volcanic field in two, carrying part of it northward to what is now Pinnacles National Park. Millions of years of erosion left a rugged landscape of rocky spires and crags, or pinnacles. Boulders fell into canyons and valleys, creating talus caves and a paradise for modern-day rock climbers. Spring is the most popular time to visit, when colorful wildflowers blanket the meadows; the light and scenery can be striking in fall and winter; the summer heat is often brutal. The park has two entrances—east and west—but they are not connected. The Pinnacles Visitor Center, Bear Gulch Nature Center, Park Headquarters, the Pinnacles Campground, and the Bear Gulch Cave and Reservoir are on the east side. The Chaparral Parking Area is on the west side, where you can feast on fantastic views of the Pinnacles High Peaks from the parking area. Dogs are not allowed on hiking trails. ■TIP→ The east entrance is 32 miles southeast of Hollister via Highway 25. The west entrance is about 12 miles east of Soledad via Highway 146. ✉ *5000 Hwy. 146, Paicines* ☎ *831/389–4486, 831/389–4427 Westside* ⊕ *www.nps. gov/pinn* 🎟 *$10 per vehicle, $5 per visitor if biking or walking.*

🏃 Activities

HIKING

Hiking is the most popular activity at Pinnacles, with more than 30 miles of trails for every interest and level of fitness. Because there isn't a road through the park, hiking is also the only way to experience its interior, including the High Peaks, the talus caves, and the reservoir.

Balconies Cliffs-Cave Loop

HIKING/WALKING | Grab your flashlight before heading out from the Chaparral Trailhead parking lot for this 2.4-mile loop that takes you through the Balconies Caves. This trail is especially beautiful in spring, when wildflowers carpet the canyon floor. About 0.6 mile from the start of the trail, turn left to begin ascending the Balconies Cliffs Trail, where you'll be rewarded with close-up views of Machete Ridge and other steep, vertical formations; you may run across rock climbers testing their skills before rounding the loop and descending back through the cave. *Easy.* ⊠ *West side of park* ⊹ *Trailhead: from West Pinnacles Visitor Contact Station, drive about 2 miles to Chaparral Trailhead parking lot. Trail picks up on west side of lot.*

Moses Spring-Rim Trail Loop

HIKING/WALKING | FAMILY | Perhaps the most popular hike at Pinnacles, this relatively short (2.2 miles) trail is fun for kids and adults. It leads to the Bear Gulch cave system, and if your timing is right, you'll pass by several seasonal waterfalls inside the caves (flashlights are required). If it has been raining, check with a ranger, as the caves could be flooded. The upper side of the cave is usually closed in spring and early summer to protect the Townsend's big-ear bats and their pups. *Easy.* ⊠ *East side of park* ⊹ *Trailhead: just past Bear Gulch Nature Center, on south side of overflow parking lot.*

San Juan Bautista

20 miles northeast of Salinas.

Much of the small town that grew up around Mission San Juan Bautista, still a working church, has been protected from development since 1933, when a state park was established here. Small antiques shops and restaurants occupy the Old West and art-deco buildings that line 3rd Street.

GETTING HERE AND AROUND

From Highway 1 north or south, exit east onto Highway 156. MST buses do not serve San Juan Bautista.

👁 Sights

San Juan Bautista State Historic Park

HISTORIC SITE | With the low-slung, colonnaded **Mission San Juan Bautista** as its drawing card, this park 20 miles northeast of Salinas is about as close to early-19th-century California as you can get. Historic buildings ring the wide green plaza, among them an adobe home furnished with Spanish-colonial antiques, a hotel frozen in the 1860s, a blacksmith shop, a pioneer cabin, and a jailhouse. The mission's cemetery contains the unmarked graves of more than 4,300 Native American converts. ■ TIP→ On the first Saturday of the month, costumed volunteers engage in quilting bees, tortilla making, and other frontier activities; and sarsaparilla and other non-alcoholic drinks are served in the saloon. ⊠ *19 Franklin St., off Hwy. 156, east of U.S. 101* ☎ *831/623–4881* ⊕ *www.parks.ca.gov* ⊠ *$3 park, $4 mission.*

Moss Landing

17 miles north of Monterey, 12 miles north of Salinas.

Moss Landing is not much more than a couple of blocks of cafés and restaurants, art galleries, and studios, plus a busy fishing port, but therein lies its charm. It's a fine place to overnight or stop for a meal and get a dose of nature.

GETTING HERE AND AROUND
From Highway 1 north or south, exit at Moss Landing Road on the ocean side. MST buses serve Moss Landing.

TOURS
Elkhorn Slough Safari Nature Boat Tours
This outfit's naturalists lead two-hour tours of Elkhorn Sough aboard a 27-foot pontoon boat. Reservations are required. ⊠ *Moss Landing Harbor* ☎ *831/633–5555* ⊕ *elkhornslough.com* ⊠ *$39.*

ESSENTIALS
VISITOR INFORMATION Moss Landing Chamber of Commerce. ☎ *831/633–4501* ⊕ *mosslandingchamber.com.*

◉ Sights

Elkhorn Slough National Estuarine Research Reserve
NATURE PRESERVE | The reserve's 1,700 acres of tidal flats and salt marshes form a complex environment that supports some 300 species of birds. A walk along the meandering waterways and wetlands can reveal hawks, white-tailed kites, owls, herons, and egrets. Also living or visiting here are sea otters, sharks, rays, and many other animals. ■TIP→ On weekends, guided walks from the visitor center begin at 10 and 1. On the first Saturday of the month, an early-bird tour departs at 8:30. ⊠ *1700 Elkhorn Rd., Watsonville* ☎ *831/728–2822* ⊕ *elkhornslough. org* ⊠ *$4 day-use fee (credit card only)* ⊗ *Closed Mon. and Tues.*

 Restaurants

Haute Enchilada
$$$ | **SOUTH AMERICAN** | Part of a complex that includes art galleries and an events venue, the Haute adds bohemian character to the seafaring village of Moss Landing. The inventive Latin American–inspired dishes include shrimp and black corn enchiladas topped with a citrus cilantro cream sauce, and roasted *pasilla* chilies stuffed with mashed plantains and caramelized onions. **Known for:** extensive cocktail and wine list; many vegan and gluten-free options; artsy atmosphere. Ⓢ *Average main: $25* ⊠ *7902 Moss Landing Rd.* ☎ *831/633–5843* ⊕ *hauteenchilada.com.*

Phil's Fish Market & Eatery
$$ | **SEAFOOD** | Exquisitely fresh, simply prepared seafood (try the cioppino) is on the menu at this warehouselike restaurant on the harbor; all kinds of glistening fish are for sale at the market in the front. **Known for:** cioppino; clam chowder; myriad artichoke dishes. Ⓢ *Average main: $22* ⊠ *7600 Sandholdt Rd.* ☎ *831/633–2152* ⊕ *philsfishmarket.com.*

Hotels

Captain's Inn
$$$ | **B&B/INN** | Commune with nature and pamper yourself with upscale creature comforts at this green-certified complex in the heart of town. **Pros:** walk to restaurants and shops; tranquil natural setting; free Wi-Fi and parking. **Cons:** rooms in historic building don't have water views; far from urban amenities; not appropriate for young children. Ⓢ *Rooms from: $197* ⊠ *8122 Moss Landing Rd.* ☎ *831/633–5550* ⊕ *www.captainsinn.com* ⇥ *10 rooms* ⧫ *Breakfast.*

🏃 Activities

KAYAKING
Monterey Bay Kayaks
KAYAKING | Rent a kayak to paddle out into Elkhorn Slough for up-close wildlife encounters. ⊠ *2390 Hwy. 1, at North Harbor* ☎ *831/373–5357* ⊕ *monterey-baykayaks.com.*

Aptos

17 miles north of Moss Landing.

Backed by a redwood forest and facing the sea, downtown Aptos—known as Aptos Village—is a place of wooden walkways and false-fronted shops. Antiques dealers cluster along Trout Gulch Road, off Soquel Drive east of Highway 1.

GETTING HERE AND AROUND

Use Highway 1 to reach Aptos from Santa Cruz or Monterey. Exit at State Park Drive to reach the main shopping hub and Aptos Village. You can also exit at Freedom Boulevard or Rio del Mar. Soquel Drive is the main artery through town.

ESSENTIALS

VISITOR INFORMATION Aptos Chamber of Commerce. ✉ *7605–A Old Dominion Ct.* ☎ *831/688–1467* 🌐 *aptoschamber.com.*

Beaches

★ Seacliff State Beach

BEACH—SIGHT | FAMILY | Sandstone bluffs tower above popular Seacliff State Beach. The 1.5-mile walk north to adjacent New Brighton State Beach in Capitola is one of the nicest on the bay. Leashed dogs are allowed on the beach. **Amenities:** food and drink; lifeguards; parking (fee); showers; toilets. **Best for:** sunset; swimming; walking. ✉ *201 State Park Dr., off Hwy. 1* ☎ *831/685–6500* 🌐 *www.parks.ca.gov* 🎫 *$10 per vehicle.*

Restaurants

Bittersweet Bistro

$$$ | MEDITERRANEAN | A large old tavern with cathedral ceilings houses this popular bistro, where the Mediterranean-California menu changes seasonally, but regular highlights include paella, seafood puttanesca, and pepper-crusted rib-eye steak with Cabernet demi-glace. Breakfast and lunch are available in the casual Bittersweet Café. **Known for:** value-laden happy hour; seafood specials; house-made desserts. [$] *Average main: $29* ✉ *787 Rio Del Mar Blvd., off Hwy. 1* ☎ *831/662–9799* 🌐 *www.bittersweetbistro.com* 🕒 *Closed Mon. and Tues.*

Hotels

Best Western Seacliff Inn

$$$ | HOTEL | FAMILY | Families and business travelers like this 6-acre property near Seacliff State Beach that's more resort than hotel. **Pros:** walking distance to the beach; family-friendly; hot breakfast buffet. **Cons:** close to freeway; occasional nighttime bar noise; no elevator. [$] *Rooms from: $230* ✉ *7500 Old Dominion Ct.* ☎ *831/688–7300, 800/367–2003* 🌐 *seacliffinn.com* 🛏 *158 rooms* 🍴 *Breakfast.*

Rio Sands Hotel

$$$ | HOTEL | A property-wide makeover completed in 2015 has made this casual two-building complex near the beach an even more exceptional value. **Pros:** two-minute walk to Rio Del Mar Beach (Seacliff State Beach is also nearby); free parking and Wi-Fi; close to a deli and restaurants. **Cons:** some rooms and suites are small; neighborhood becomes congested in summer. [$] *Rooms from: $179* ✉ *116 Aptos Beach Dr.* ☎ *831/688–3207, 800/826–2077* 🌐 *riosands.com* 🛏 *50 rooms* 🍴 *Breakfast.*

Seascape Beach Resort

$$$$ | RESORT | FAMILY | It's easy to unwind at this full-fledged resort on a bluff overlooking Monterey Bay. The spacious suites sleep from two to eight people. **Pros:** time share–style apartments; access to miles of beachfront; superb views. **Cons:** far from city life; most bathrooms are small; some rooms need updating. [$] *Rooms from: $387* ✉ *1 Seascape Resort Dr.* ☎ *831/662–7171, 866/867–0976* 🌐 *seascaperesort.com* 🛏 *285 suites* 🍴 *No meals.*

Capitola and Soquel

4 miles northwest of Aptos.

On the National Register of Historic places as California's first seaside resort town, the village of Capitola has been in a holiday mood since the late 1800s. Casual eateries, surf shops, and ice cream parlors pack its walkable downtown. Inland, across Highway 1, antiques shops line Soquel Drive in the town of Soquel. Wineries dot the Santa Cruz Mountains beyond.

GETTING HERE AND AROUND

From Santa Cruz or Monterey, follow Highway 1 to the Capitola/Soquel (Bay Avenue) exit about 7 miles south of Santa Cruz and head west to reach Capitola and east to access Soquel Village. On summer weekends, park for free in the lot behind the Crossroads Center, a block west of the freeway, and hop aboard the free Capitola Shuttle to the village.

ESSENTIALS

VISITOR INFORMATION Capitola-Soquel Chamber of Commerce. ✉ *716-G Capitola Ave., Capitola* ☎ *831/475–6522* 🌐 *capitolachamber.com.*

Beaches

★ New Brighton State Beach

BEACH—SIGHT | FAMILY | Once the site of a Chinese fishing village, New Brighton is now a popular surfing and camping spot. Its Pacific Migrations Visitor Center traces the history of the Chinese and other peoples who settled around Monterey Bay. It also documents the migratory patterns of the area's wildlife, such as monarch butterflies and gray whales. Leashed dogs are allowed in the park. New Brighton connects with Seacliff Beach, and at low tide you can walk or run along this scenic stretch of sand for nearly 16 miles south (though you might have to wade through a few creeks). ■ **TIP→ The 1½-mile stroll from New Brighton to Seacliff's concrete ship is a local favorite. Amenities:** parking (fee); showers; toilets. **Best for:** sunset; swimming; walking. ✉ *1500 State Park Dr., off Hwy. 1, Capitola* ☎ *831/464–6329* 🌐 *www.parks.ca.gov* 🎫 *$10 per vehicle.*

Restaurants

Carpo's

$ | **SEAFOOD** | **FAMILY** | Locals love this casual counter where seafood predominates, but you can also order burgers, salads, and steaks. Baskets of battered snapper are among the favorites, along with calamari, prawns, seafood kebabs, fish and chips, and homemade olallieberry pie. **Known for:** large portions of healthy comfort food; lots of options under $10; soup and salad bar. [$] *Average main: $14* ✉ *2400 Porter St., at Hwy. 1, Soquel* ☎ *831/476–6260* 🌐 *carposrestaurant.com.*

Gayle's Bakery & Rosticceria

$$ | **CAFÉ** | **FAMILY** | Whether you're in the mood for an orange-olallieberry muffin, a wild rice and chicken salad, or tri-tip on garlic toast, this bakery-deli's varied menu is likely to satisfy. Munch on your lemon meringue tartlet or chocolate brownie on the shady patio, or dig into the daily blue-plate dinner—teriyaki grilled skirt steak with edamame-shiitake sticky rice, perhaps, or roast turkey breast with Chardonnay gravy—amid the whirl of activity inside. **Known for:** prepared meals to go; on-site bakery and rosticceria; deli and espresso bar. [$] *Average main: $17* ✉ *504 Bay Ave., at Capitola Ave., Capitola* ☎ *831/462–1200* 🌐 *gaylesbakery.com.*

Michael's on Main

$$$ | **AMERICAN** | Creative variations on classic comfort food and live music five nights a week draw lively crowds to this upscale but casual creek-side eatery. For a quiet conversation spot, ask for a table on the romantic patio overlooking the creek. **Known for:** locally sourced,

Did You Know?

Soquel Cove in Santa Cruz is surrounded by New Brighton State Beach, and Seacliff State Beach, where a WWI concrete ship sits partially submerged in the water.

usually within 50 miles; excellent wine list; romantic patio overlooking Soquel Creek. $ *Average main: $29* ✉ *2591 Main St., at Porter St., Soquel* ☎ *831/479–9777* ⊕ *michaelsonmain.net* ⊘ *Closed Mon.*

Shadowbrook

$$$$ | EUROPEAN | To get to this romantic spot overlooking Soquel Creek, you can take a cable car or walk the stairs down a steep, fern-lined bank beside a running waterfall. Dining room options include the rooftop Redwood Room, the wood-paneled Wine Cellar, the creek-side, glass-enclosed Greenhouse, the Fireplace Room, and the airy Garden Room. **Known for:** romantic creek-side setting; prime rib and grilled seafood; local special-occasion favorite for nearly 70 years. $ *Average main: $34* ✉ *1750 Wharf Rd., at Lincoln Ave., Capitola* ☎ *831/475–1511* ⊕ *www.shadowbrook-capitola.com* ⊘ *No lunch.*

🛏 Hotels

Inn at Depot Hill

$$$$ | B&B/INN | This inventively designed bed-and-breakfast in a former rail depot views itself as a link to the era of luxury train travel. **Pros:** short walk to beach and village; historic charm; excellent service. **Cons:** fills quickly; hot-tub conversation audible in some rooms; rooms need updating. $ *Rooms from: $309* ✉ *250 Monterey Ave., Capitola* ☎ *831/462–3376, 800/572–2632* ⊕ *www.innatdepothill.com* ⤳ *12 rooms* ❍ *Breakfast.*

Santa Cruz

5 miles west of Capitola, 48 miles north of Monterey.

The big city on this stretch of the California coast, Santa Cruz (pop. 63,364) is less manicured than Carmel or Monterey. Long known for its surfing and its amusement-filled beach boardwalk,

California's Oldest Resort Town 👁

As far as anyone knows for certain, Capitola is the oldest seaside resort town on the Pacific Coast. In 1856 a pioneer acquired Soquel Landing, the picturesque lagoon and beach where Soquel Creek empties into the bay, and built a wharf. Another man opened a campground along the shore, and his daughter named it Capitola after a heroine in a novel series. After the train came to town in the 1870s, thousands of vacationers began arriving to bask in the sun on the glorious beach.

12

Monterey Bay Area SANTA CRUZ

the town is a mix of grand Victorian-era homes and rinky-dink motels. The opening of the University of California campus in the 1960s swung the town sharply to the left politically, and the counterculture more or less lives on here. At the same time, the revitalized downtown and an insane real-estate market reflect the city's proximity to Silicon Valley and to a growing Wine Country in the surrounding mountains. Amble around the downtown Santa Cruz Farmers' Market (Wednesday afternoons year-round) to experience the local culture, which derives much of its character from close connections to food and farming. The market covers a city block and includes not just the expected organic produce, but also live music and booths with local crafts and prepared food.

GETTING HERE AND AROUND

From the San Francisco Bay area, take Highway 17 south over the mountains to Santa Cruz, where it merges with Highway 1. Use Highway 1 to get around the area. The Santa Cruz Transit Center is at

920 Pacific Avenue, at Front Street, a short walk from the wharf and boardwalk, with connections to public transit throughout the Monterey Bay and San Francisco Bay areas. You can purchase day passes for Santa Cruz METRO buses (see Bus Travel, in Planner) here.

ESSENTIALS
VISITOR INFORMATION Visit Santa Cruz County. ⊠ 303 Water St., No. 100 ☎ 831/425–1234, 800/833–3494 ⊕ visitsantacruz.org.

⊙ Sights

Monterey Bay National Marine Sanctuary Exploration Center
INFO CENTER | FAMILY | The interactive and multimedia exhibits at this fascinating interpretive center reveal and explain the treasures of the nation's largest marine sanctuary. The two-story building, across from the main beach and municipal wharf, has films and exhibits about migratory species, watersheds, underwater canyons, kelp forests, and intertidal zones. The second-floor deck has stellar ocean views and an interactive station that provides real-time weather, surf, and buoy reports. ⊠ 35 Pacific Ave., near Beach St. ☎ 831/421–9993 ⊕ montereybay.noaa.gov/vc/sec ⊠ Free ⊙ Closed Mon. and Tues.

Mystery Spot
LOCAL INTEREST | Hokey tourist trap or genuine scientific enigma? Since 1940, curious throngs baffled by the Mystery Spot have made it one of the most visited attractions in Santa Cruz. The laws of gravity and physics don't appear to apply in this tiny patch of redwood forest, where balls roll uphill and people stand on a slant. ■TIP→ **On weekends and holidays, it's wise to purchase tickets online in advance.** ⊠ 465 Mystery Spot Rd., off Branciforte Dr. (north off Hwy. 1) ☎ 831/423–8897 ⊕ mysteryspot.com ⊠ $8, parking $5.

Pacific Avenue
NEIGHBORHOOD | When you've had your fill of the city's beaches and waters, take a stroll in downtown Santa Cruz, especially on Pacific Avenue between Laurel and Water streets. Vintage boutiques and mountain-sports stores, sushi bars, and Mexican restaurants, day spas, and nightclubs keep the main drag and the surrounding streets hopping from midmorning until late evening.

★ Santa Cruz Beach Boardwalk
CAROUSEL | FAMILY | Santa Cruz has been a seaside resort since the mid-19th century. Along one end of the broad, south-facing beach, the boardwalk has entertained holidaymakers for more than a century. Its Looff carousel and classic wooden Giant Dipper roller coaster, both dating from the early 1900s, are surrounded by high-tech thrill rides and easygoing kiddie rides with ocean views. Video and arcade games, a minigolf course, and a laser-tag arena pack one gigantic building, which is open daily even if the rides aren't running. You have to pay to play, but you can wander the entire boardwalk for free while sampling carnival fare such as corn dogs and garlic fries. ⊠ Along Beach St. ☎ 831/423–5590 info line ⊕ beachboardwalk.com ⊠ $40 day pass for unlimited rides, or pay per ride ⊙ Some rides closed Sept.–May.

Santa Cruz Mission State Historic Park
HISTORIC SITE | On the northern fringes of downtown is the site of California's 12th Spanish mission, built in the 1790s and destroyed by an earthquake in 1857. A museum in a restored 1791 adobe and a half-scale replica of the mission church are part of the complex. ⊠ 144 School St., at Adobe St. ☎ 831/425–5849 ⊕ www.parks.ca.gov ⊠ Free ⊙ Closed Tues. and Wed.

Santa Cruz Municipal Wharf
MARINA | FAMILY | Jutting half a mile into the ocean near one end of the boardwalk, the century-old Municipal Wharf

is lined with seafood restaurants, a wine bar, souvenir shops, and outfitters offering bay cruises, fishing trips, and boat rentals. A salty sound track drifts up from under the wharf, where barking sea lions lounge in heaps on the crossbeams. Docents from the Seymour Marine Discovery Center lead free 30-minute tours on spring and summer weekends at 1 and 3; meet at the stage on the west side of the wharf between Olitas Cantina and Marini's Candies. ✉ *Beach St. and Pacific Ave.* ☎ *831/459–3800 tour information.*

Santa Cruz Surfing Museum

MUSEUM | This museum inside the Mark Abbott Memorial Lighthouse chronicles local surfing history. Photographs show old-time surfers, and a display of boards includes rarities such as a heavy redwood plank predating the fiberglass era and the remains of a modern board chomped by a great white shark. Surfer docents reminisce about the good old days. ✉ *Lighthouse Point Park, 701 W. Cliff Dr. near Pelton Ave.* ☎ *831/420–6289* ▤ *$2 suggested donation* ⊘ *Closed Tues. and Wed. except open Tues. July–early Sept.*

Seymour Marine Discovery Center

ZOO | FAMILY | Part of the Long Marine Laboratory at the University of California Santa Cruz's Institute of Marine Sciences, the center looks more like a research facility than a slick aquarium. Interactive exhibits demonstrate how scientists study the ocean, and the aquarium displays creatures of interest to marine biologists. The 87-foot blue whale skeleton is one of the world's largest. ■TIP➔ **General tours take place in the afternoon, and there's an abbreviated tour at 11 am for families with small children.** ✉ *100 Shaffer Rd., end of Delaware Ave., west of Natural Bridges State Beach* ☎ *831/459–3800* ⊕ *seymourcenter.ucsc. edu* ▤ *$9* ⊘ *Closed Mon.*

Surf City Vintners

WINERY/DISTILLERY | A dozen tasting rooms of limited-production wineries occupy renovated warehouse spaces west of the beach. MJA, Sones Cellars, Santa Cruz Mountain Vineyard, and Equinox are good places to start. Also here are the Santa Cruz Mountain Brewing Company and El Salchichero, popular for its homemade sausages, jams, and pickled and candied vegetables. ✉ *Swift Street Courtyard, 334 Ingalls St., at Swift St., off Hwy. 1 (Mission St.)* ⊕ *surfcityvintners.com.*

UC Santa Cruz

COLLEGE | The 2,000-acre University of California Santa Cruz campus nestles in the forested hills above town. Its sylvan setting, ocean vistas, and redwood architecture make the university worth a visit, as does its **arboretum** ($5, open daily from 9 to 5), whose walking path leads through areas dedicated to the plants of California, Australia, New Zealand, and South Africa. ■TIP➔ **Free shuttles help students and visitors get around campus, and you can join a guided tour (online reservation required).** ✉ *Main entrance at Bay and High Sts. (turn left on High for arboretum)* ☎ *831/459–0111* ⊕ *www. ucsc.edu/visit.*

★ West Cliff Drive

SCENIC DRIVE | The road that winds along an oceanfront bluff from the municipal wharf to Natural Bridges State Beach makes for a spectacular drive, but it's even more fun to walk or bike the paved path that parallels the road. Surfers bob and swoosh in Monterey Bay at several points near the foot of the bluff, especially at a break known as **Steamer Lane.** Named for a surfer who died here in 1965, the nearby Mark Abbott Memorial Lighthouse stands at Point Santa Cruz, the cliff's major promontory. From here you can watch pinnipeds hang out, sunbathe, and frolic on Seal Rock. ✉ *Santa Cruz.*

Wilder Ranch State Park

NATIONAL/STATE PARK | In this park's Cultural Preserve you can visit the homes, barns, workshops, and bunkhouse of a 19th-century dairy farm. Nature has reclaimed most of the ranch land, and native plants and wildlife have returned to the 7,000 acres of forest, grassland, canyons, estuaries, and beaches. Hike, bike, or ride horseback on miles of ocean-view trails. Dogs aren't allowed at Wilder Ranch. ✉ *Hwy. 1, 1 mile north of Santa Cruz* ☎ *831/426–0505 Interpretive Center, 831/423–9703 trail information* 🌐 *www.parks.ca.gov* 🎟 *$10 per car* 🕒 *Interpretive center closed Mon.–Wed.*

Beaches

Natural Bridges State Beach

BEACH—SIGHT | **FAMILY** | At the end of West Cliff Drive lies this stretch of soft sand edged with tide pools and sea-sculpted rock bridges. **■TIP→ From September to early January a colony of monarch butterflies roosts in the eucalyptus grove. Amenities:** lifeguards; parking (fee); toilets. **Best for:** sunrise; sunset; surfing; swimming. ✉ *2531 W. Cliff Dr.* ☎ *831/423–4609* 🌐 *www.parks.ca.gov* 🎟 *Beach free, parking $10.*

Twin Lakes State Beach

BEACH—SIGHT | **FAMILY** | Stretching a half mile along the coast on both sides of the small-craft jetties, Twin Lakes is one of Monterey Bay's sunniest beaches. It encompasses Seabright State Beach (with access in a residential neighborhood on the upcoast side) and Black's Beach on the downcoast side. Families often come here to sunbathe, picnic, and hike the nature trail around adjacent Schwann Lake. Parking is tricky from May through September—you need to pay for an $8 day-use permit at a kiosk and the lot fills quickly—but you can park all day in the harbor pay lot and walk here. Leashed dogs are allowed. **Amenities:** food and drink; lifeguards (seasonal); parking; showers; toilets; water sports (seasonal). **Best for:** sunset; surfing; swimming; walking. ✉ *7th Ave., at East Cliff Dr.* ☎ *831/427–4868* 🌐 *www.parks.ca.gov.*

Restaurants

Crow's Nest

$$$ | **SEAFOOD** | **FAMILY** | A classic California beachside restaurant, the Crow's Nest sits right on the water in Santa Cruz Harbor–vintage surfboards and local surf photography line the walls in the main dining room, and nearly every table overlooks sand and surf. For sweeping ocean views and fish tacos, burgers, and other casual fare, head upstairs to the Breakwater Bar & Grill. **Known for:** house-smoked salmon and calamari apps; crab-cake eggs Benedict and olallieberry pancakes; on-site market with pizzas, sandwiches, soups, and salads. [$] *Average main: $24* ✉ *2218 E. Cliff Dr., west of 7th Ave.* ☎ *831/476–4560* 🌐 *crowsnest-santacruz.com.*

Gabriella Café

$$$ | **ITALIAN** | The work of local artists hangs on the walls of this petite, romantic café in a tile-roof cottage. Featuring organic produce from area farms, the seasonal Italian menu has included wild-mushroom risotto; bouillabaisse; marinated chicken with apricots, currants, and olives; and roasted beet salad with wild arugula, goat cheese, and pistachios. **Known for:** nearly all produce comes from local organic farmers; romantic interior with Moorish arches; weekend brunch. [$] *Average main: $26* ✉ *910 Cedar St., at Church St.* ☎ *831/457–1677* 🌐 *www.gabriellacafe.com.*

★ **Laili Restaurant**

$$ | **MEDITERRANEAN** | Exotic Mediterranean flavors with an Afghan twist take center stage at this artsy, stylish space with soaring ceilings. Evenings are especially lively, when locals come to relax over wine and soft jazz at the blue-concrete bar, the heated patio with twinkly lights, or at a communal table near the open kitchen. **Known for:** house-made pastas and numerous vegetarian and vegan options; fresh naan, chutneys and dips with every meal; traditional dishes like pomegranate eggplant and maush-awa soup. $ *Average main: $22* ✉ *101–B Cooper St., near Pacific Ave.* ☎ *831/423–4545* ⊕ *lailirestaurant.com* ✆ *Closed Mon.*

La Posta

$$$ | ITALIAN | Authentic Italian fare made with fresh local produce lures diners into cozy, modern-rustic La Posta. Nearly everything is made in-house, from the pizzas and breads baked in the brick oven to the pasta and the vanilla-bean gelato. **Known for:** seasonal wild-nettle lasagna; braised lamb shank; in the heart of the Seabright neighborhood. $ *Average main: $24* ✉ *538 Seabright Ave., at Logan St.* ☎ *831/457–2782* ⊕ *lapostarestaurant.com* ✆ *Closed Mon. No lunch.*

Oswald

$$$$ | EUROPEAN | Sophisticated yet unpretentious European-inspired California cooking is the order of the day at this intimate and stylish bistro with a seasonal menu, which might include such items as seafood risotto or crispy duck breast in a pomegranate reduction sauce. The creative concoctions poured at the slick marble bar include whiskey mixed with apple and lemon juice, and tequila with celery juice and lime. **Known for:** house-made pork sausage; craft cocktails; local art displays that changes monthly. $ *Average main: $32* ✉ *121 Soquel Ave., at Front St.* ☎ *831/423–7427* ⊕ *oswaldrestaurant.com* ✆ *Closed Mon. No lunch Sun. and Tues.*

★ Soif

$$$ | MEDITERRANEAN | Wine reigns at this sleek bistro and wineshop that takes its name from the French word for thirst— the selections come from near and far, and you can order many of them by the taste or glass. Mediterranean-inspired small plates and entrées are served at the copper-top bar, the big communal table, and private tables. **Known for:** Mediterranean-style dishes; well-stocked wineshop; jazz combo or solo pianist plays on some evenings. $ *Average main: $28* ✉ *105 Walnut Ave., at Pacific Ave.* ☎ *831/423–2020* ⊕ *soifwine. com* ✆ *Closed Sun. No lunch.*

Zachary's

$ | AMERICAN | This noisy café filled with students and families defines the funky essence of Santa Cruz. It also dishes up great breakfasts: stay simple with sourdough pancakes, or go for Mike's Mess—eggs scrambled with bacon, mushrooms, and home fries, then topped with sour cream, melted cheese, and fresh tomatoes. **Known for:** nearly everything made in house; "Mike's Mess" egg dishes; local organic ingredients. $ *Average main: $14* ✉ *819 Pacific Ave.* ☎ *831/427–0646* ⊕ *www. zacharyssantacruz.com* ✆ *Closed Mon. No dinner.*

🛏 Hotels

Babbling Brook Inn

$$$$ | B&B/INN | Though it's in the middle of Santa Cruz, this bed-and-breakfast has lush gardens, a running stream, and tall trees that make you feel like you're in a secluded wood. **Pros:** close to UCSC; within walking distance of downtown shops; woodsy feel. **Cons:** near a high school; some rooms close to a busy street; many stairs and no elevator. $ *Rooms from: $280* ✉ *1025 Laurel St.* ☎ *831/427–2437, 800/866–1131* ⊕ *babblingbrookinn.com* ⇥ *13 rooms* ⚫ *Breakfast.*

Carousel Beach Inn

$$ | HOTEL | This basic but comfy motel, decorated in bold, retro seaside style and across the street from the boardwalk, is ideal for travelers who want easy access to the sand and the amusement

park rides without spending a fortune. **Pros:** steps from Santa Cruz Main Beach; affordable lodging rates and ride packages; free parking and Wi-Fi. **Cons:** no pool or spa; no exercise room; not pet-friendly. [$] *Rooms from: $159* ✉ *110 Riverside Ave.* ☎ *831/425–7090* 🌐 *santacruzmotels.com/carousel.html* 🛏 *34 rooms* 🍴 *Breakfast.*

Chaminade Resort & Spa

$$$$ | **RESORT** | Secluded on 300 hilltop acres of redwood and eucalyptus forest with hiking trails, this Mission-style complex commands expansive views of Monterey Bay. Guest rooms are furnished in an eclectic, bohemian style that pays homage to the artsy local community and the city's industrial past, while incorporating vintage game elements throughout. **Pros:** far from city life; spectacular property; ideal spot for romance and rejuvenation. **Cons:** must drive to attractions and sights; near a major hospital; resort fee. [$] *Rooms from: $280* ✉ *1 Chaminade La.* ☎ *800/283–6569 reservations, 831/475–5600* 🌐 *www.chaminade.com* 🛏 *156 rooms* 🍴 *No meals.*

★ **Dream Inn Santa Cruz**

$$$$ | **HOTEL** | A short stroll from the boardwalk and wharf, this full-service luxury hotel is the only lodging in Santa Cruz directly on the beach. **Pros:** on-site restaurant with sweeping south-facing views of Monterey Bay; easy parking; walk to boardwalk and downtown. **Cons:** expensive; area gets congested on summer weekends; pool area and hallways can be noisy. [$] *Rooms from: $369* ✉ *175 W. Cliff Dr.* ☎ *831/740–8141, 844/510–1746* 🌐 *dreaminnsantacruz.com* 🛏 *165 rooms* 🍴 *No meals.*

Hotel Paradox

$$$$ | **HOTEL** | About a mile from the ocean and two blocks from Pacific Avenue, this stylish, forest-theme complex (part of the Marriott Autograph Collection) is among the few full-service hotels in town. **Pros:** close to downtown and main beach; spacious pool area with cabanas, fire pits, hot tub, and dining and cocktail service; on-site farm-to-table restaurant. **Cons:** pool area can get crowded on warm-weather days; some rooms on the small side; thin walls. [$] *Rooms from: $279* ✉ *611 Ocean St.* ☎ *831/425–7100, 855/425–7200* 🌐 *hotelparadox.com* 🛏 *172 rooms* 🍴 *No meals.*

Hyatt Place Santa Cruz

$$$ | **HOTEL** | Displays of vintage surfboards and local art grace the walls of the spacious ocean-theme lobby at this new downtown hotel, which opened in 2018. **Pros:** close to downtown restaurants and shops; outdoor pool and hot tub and 24-hour fitness center; on-site restaurant and bar. **Cons:** not on the beach; valet parking only; fronts busy road. [$] *Rooms from: $219* ✉ *407 Broadway* ☎ *831/226–2304* 🌐 *hyattplace.com* 🛏 *106 rooms* 🍴 *No meals.*

Pacific Blue Inn

$$$ | **B&B/INN** | Green themes predominate in this three-story, eco-friendly bed-and-breakfast, on a sliver of prime downtown property. **Pros:** free parking; free bicycles; downtown location. **Cons:** tiny property; not suitable for children; parking lot is a block away. [$] *Rooms from: $189* ✉ *636 Pacific Ave.* ☎ *831/600–8880* 🌐 *pacificblueinn.com* 🛏 *9 rooms* 🍴 *No meals.*

Sea & Sand Inn

$$$ | **HOTEL** | Location is the main appeal of this motel atop a waterfront bluff where all rooms have an ocean view and the boardwalk is just down the street. **Pros:** beach is steps away; friendly staff; tidy landscaping. **Cons:** tight parking lot; fronts a busy road; can be noisy. [$] *Rooms from: $229* ✉ *201 W. Cliff Dr.* ☎ *831/427–3400* 🌐 *santacruzmotels.com* 🛏 *20 rooms, 2 cottages* 🍴 *Breakfast.*

★ **West Cliff Inn**

$$$$ | **B&B/INN** | With views of the boardwalk and Monterey Bay, the West Cliff perches on the bluffs across from

O'Neill: A Santa Cruz Icon

O'Neill wet suits and beachwear weren't exactly born in Santa Cruz, but as far as most of the world is concerned, the O'Neill brand is synonymous with Santa Cruz and surfing legend.

The O'Neill wet-suit story began in 1952, when Jack O'Neill and his brother Robert opened their first Surf Shop in a garage across from San Francisco's Ocean Beach. While shaping balsa surfboards and selling accessories, the O'Neills experimented with solutions to a common surfer problem: frigid waters. Tired of being forced back to shore, blue-lipped and shivering, after just 20 or 30 minutes riding the waves, they played with various materials and eventually designed a neoprene vest.

In 1959 Jack moved his Surf Shop 90 miles south to Cowell's Beach in Santa Cruz. It quickly became a popular surf hangout, and O'Neill's new wet suits began to sell like hotcakes. In the early 1960s, the company opened a warehouse for manufacturing on a larger scale. Santa Cruz soon became a major surf city, attracting wave riders to prime breaks at Steamer Lane, Pleasure Point, and the Hook. In 1965 O'Neill pioneered the first wet-suit boots, and in 1971 Jack's son invented the surf leash. By 1980, O'Neill stood at the top of the world wet-suit market. On June 2, 2017, Jack O'Neill passed away at the age of 94, in his longtime Pleasure Point residence overlooking the surf.

Cowell Beach. **Pros:** killer views; walking distance of the beach; close to downtown. **Cons:** boardwalk noise; street traffic. $ *Rooms from: $279* ✉ *174 West Cliff Dr.* ☎ *831/457–2200* 🌐 *www.westcliffinn.com* 🛏 *9 rooms, 1 cottage* 🍴 *Breakfast.*

Nightlife

Catalyst

DANCE CLUBS | This huge, grimy, and fun club books rock, indie rock, punk, death-metal, reggae, and other acts. ✉ *1011 Pacific Ave.* ☎ *877/987–6487* 🌐 *catalystclub.com.*

Kuumbwa Jazz Center

MUSIC CLUBS | The center draws top performers such as the Lee Ritenour and Dave Grusin, Chris Potter, and the Dave Holland Trio; the café serves meals an hour before most shows. ✉ *320–2 Cedar St.* ☎ *831/427–2227* 🌐 *kuumbwajazz.org.*

Moe's Alley

MUSIC CLUBS | Blues, salsa, reggae, funk: delightfully casual Moe's presents it all (and more). ✉ *1535 Commercial Way* ☎ *831/479–1854* 🌐 *moesalley.com* ⏲ *Closed Mon.*

Performing Arts

Tannery Arts Center

ARTS CENTERS | The former Salz Tannery now contains nearly 30 studios and live-work spaces for artists whose disciplines range from ceramics and glass to film and digital media; most have public hours of business. The social center is the **Bistro One Twelve,** which in the late afternoons and evenings hosts poets, all types of performers, and live music. Performances also take place at the on-site Colligan Theater. The center also hosts assorted arts events on weekends and occasionally on weekdays. ✉ *1060 River St., at intersection of Hwys. 1 and 9* 🌐 *tanneryartscenter.org/.*

⚙ Activities

ADVENTURE TOURS

Mount Hermon Adventures

TOUR—SPORTS | Zip-line through the redwoods at this adventure center in the Santa Cruz Mountains. On some summer weekends there's an aerial adventure course with obstacles and challenges in the redwoods. ■ **TIP→ To join a tour (reservations essential), you must be at least 10 years old and at least 54 inches tall, and weigh between 75 and 250 pounds.** ⊠ *17 Conference Dr., 9 miles north of downtown Santa Cruz near Felton, Mount Hermon* ☎ *831/430–4357* ⊕ *mounthermonadventures.com* ✉ *From $65.*

BICYCLING

Another Bike Shop

BICYCLING | Mountain bikers should head here for tips on the best area trails and to browse cutting-edge gear made and tested locally. ⊠ *2361 Mission St., at King St.* ☎ *831/427–2232* ⊕ *www. anotherbikeshop.com.*

BOATS AND CHARTERS

Chardonnay II Sailing Charters

BOATING | The 70-foot *Chardonnay II* departs year-round from Santa Cruz yacht harbor on whale-watching, sunset, and other cruises around Monterey Bay. Most regularly scheduled excursions cost $68; food and drink are served on many of them. Reservations are essential. ⊠ *Santa Cruz West Harbor, 790 Mariner Park Way* ☎ *831/423–1213* ⊕ *chardonnay.com.*

Stagnaro Sport Fishing, Charters & Whale Watching Cruises

BOATING | Stagnaro operates salmon, albacore, and rock-cod fishing expeditions; the fees include bait. The company (aka Santa Cruz Whale Watching) also runs whale-watching, dolphin, and sea-life cruises year-round. ⊠ *1718 Brommer St., near Santa Cruz Harbor* ☎ *831/427–0230* ⊕ *stagnaros.com* ✉ *From $52.*

GOLF

DeLaveaga Golf Course

GOLF | Woodsy DeLaveaga, a public course set in a hilly park, overlooks Santa Cruz and the bay. With its canyons, tree-lined fairways, and notoriously difficult par-5, dogleg 10th hole, the course challenges novices and seasoned golfers. ⊠ *401 Upper Park Rd.* ☎ *831/423–7214* ⊕ *www.delaveagagolf. com* ✉ *$49 weekdays, $64 weekends/ holidays* ⛳. *18 holes, 5700 yards, par 70.*

Pasatiempo Golf Club

GOLF | Designed by famed golf architect Dr. Alister MacKenzie in 1929, this semiprivate course, set amid undulating hills just above the city, is among the nation's top championship courses. Golfers rave about the spectacular views and challenging terrain. According to the club, MacKenzie, who designed Pebble Beach's exclusive Cypress Point course and Augusta National in Georgia, the home of the Masters Golf Tournament, declared this his favorite layout. ⊠ *20 Clubhouse Rd.* ☎ *831/459–9155* ⊕ *www. pasatiempo.com* ✉ *From $260* ⛳. *18 holes, 6125 yards, par 72.*

KAYAKING

Kayak Connection

KAYAKING | From March through May, participants in this outfit's tours mingle with gray whales and their calves on their northward journey to Alaska. Throughout the year, the company rents kayaks and paddleboards and conducts tours of Natural Bridges State Beach, Capitola, and Elkhorn Slough. ⊠ *Santa Cruz Harbor, 413 Lake Ave., No. 3* ☎ *831/479–1121* ⊕ *kayakconnection.com* ✉ *From $60 for scheduled tours.*

Venture Quest Kayaking

KAYAKING | Explore hidden coves and kelp forests on guided two-hour kayak tours that depart from Santa Cruz Wharf. The tours include a kayaking lesson. Venture Quest also rents kayaks (and wet suits and gear), and arranges tours at other Monterey Bay destinations, including Elkhorn Slough. ⊠ *2 Santa Cruz Wharf* ☎ *831/427–2267 kayak hotline, 831/425–8445 rental office* ⊕ *kayaksantacruz.com* 🖅 *From $35 for rentals, $60 for tours.*

SURFING
EQUIPMENT AND LESSONS
Club-Ed Surf School and Camps
SURFING | Find out what all the fun is about at Club-Ed. Your first private or group lesson ($100 and up) includes all equipment. ⊠ *Cowell's Beach, at Dream Inn Santa Cruz* ☎ *831/464–0177* ⊕ *club-ed.com.*

Cowell's Beach Surf Shop
SURFING | This shop sells gear, clothing, and swimwear; rents surfboards, stand-up paddle boards, and wet suits; and offers lessons. ⊠ *30 Front St.* ☎ *831/427–2355* ⊕ *cowellssurfshop.com.*

Richard Schmidt Surf School
SURFING | Since 1978 Richard Schmidt has shared the stoke of surfing and the importance of ocean awareness and conservation with legions of students of all ages. Today the outfit offers surfing and stand-up paddleboard lessons (equipment provided) and marine adventure tours in Santa Cruz and elsewhere on the bay. Locations depend on where the waves are breaking or the wind's a'blowing, but typically convene at Cowell's Beach or Pleasure Point. ⊠ *Santa Cruz* ☎ *831/423–0928* ⊕ *www.richardschmidt.com* 🖅 *From $90.*

🛍 Shopping

Bookshop Santa Cruz
BOOKS/STATIONERY | In 2016 the town's best and most beloved independent bookstore celebrated its 50th anniversary of selling new, used, and remaindered titles. The children's section is especially comprehensive, and the shop's special events calendar is packed with readings, social mixers, book signings, and discussions. ⊠ *1520 Pacific Ave.* ☎ *831/423–0900* ⊕ *bookshopsantacruz.com.*

O'Neill Surf Shop
SPORTING GOODS | Local surfers get their wetties (wet suits) and other gear at this O'Neill store or the one in Capitola, at 1115 41st Avenue. There's also a satellite shop on the Santa Cruz Boardwalk. ⊠ *110 Cooper St.* ☎ *831/469–4377* ⊕ *www.oneill.com.*

Santa Cruz Downtown Farmers' Market
OUTDOOR/FLEA/GREEN MARKETS | FAMILY | Santa Cruz is famous for its long tradition of organic growing and sustainable living, and its downtown market (one of five countywide) especially reflects the incredible diversity and quality of local agriculture and synergistic daily life of community-minded residents. The busy market, which always has live music, happens every Wednesday from 1:30 to 5:30 (6:30 in summer), rain or shine. The stalls cover much of an entire city block near Pacific Avenue and include fresh produce plus everything from oysters, beer, bread, and charcuterie, to arts and crafts and hot prepared foods made from ingredients sourced from on-site vendors. ⊠ *Cedar St. at Lincoln St.* ☎ *831/454–0566* ⊕ *www.santacruzfarmersmarket.org.*

The True Olive Connection
FOOD/CANDY | Taste your way through boutique extra-virgin olive oils and balsamic vinegars from around the world at this family-run shop. You can also pick up gourmet food products and olive oil–based gift items. There's another location in Aptos, at 7960 Soquel Drive. ⊠ *106 Lincoln St., at. Pacific Ave.* ☎ *831/458–6457* ⊕ *trueoliveconnection.com.*

Chapter 13

DEATH VALLEY NATIONAL PARK

13

Updated by
Deb Hopewell

⊙ Sights	🍴 Restaurants	🛏 Hotels	🛍 Shopping	🍸 Nightlife
★★★★★	★★★★☆	★★★★★	★☆☆☆☆	★☆☆☆☆

WELCOME TO
DEATH VALLEY NATIONAL PARK

TOP REASONS TO GO

★ **Roving rocks:** Death Valley's Racetrack is home to moving boulders, an unexplained phenomenon that has scientists baffled.

★ **Lowest spot on the continent:** Stand on the lowest spot on the continent at Badwater, 282 feet below sea level.

★ **Wildflower explosion:** During the spring, this desert landscape is ablaze with greenery and colorful flowers, especially between Badwater and Ashford Mill.

★ **Ghost towns:** Death Valley is renowned for its Wild West heritage and is home to dozens of crumbling settlements including Ballarat, Cerro Gordo, Chloride City, Greenwater, Harrisburg, Keeler, Leadfield, Panamint City, Rhyolite, and Skidoo.

★ **Naturally amazing:** From canyons to sand dunes to salt flats and dry lake beds, Death Valley serves up plenty of geological treasures.

1 Central Death Valley. Furnace Creek sits in the heart of Death Valley—if you have only a short time in the park, head here. You can visit gorgeous Golden Canyon, Zabriskie Point, the Salt Creek Interpretive Trail, and Artist's Drive, among other popular points of interest.

2 Northern Death Valley. This region is uphill from Furnace Creek, which means marginally cooler temperatures. Be sure to stop by Rhyolite Ghost Town on Highway 374 before entering the park and exploring colorful Titus Canyon, and jaw-dropping Ubehebe Crater.

3 Southern Death Valley. This is a desolate area, but there are plenty of sights that help convey Death Valley's rich history. Don't miss the Dublin Gulch Caves.

4 Western Death Valley. Panamint Springs Resort is a nice place to grab a meal and get your bearings before moving on to quaint Darwin Falls, smooth rolling sand dunes, beehive-shaped Wildrose Charcoal Kilns, and historic Stovepipe Wells Village.

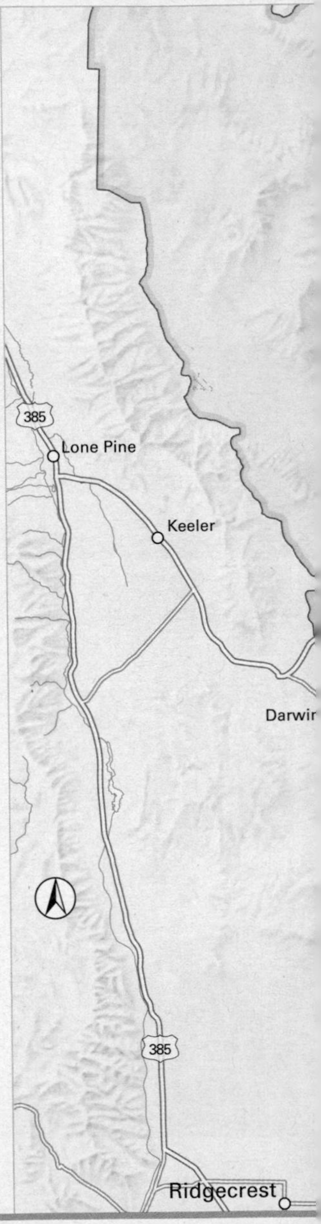

Lone Pine

Keeler

Darwin

385

385

Ridgecrest

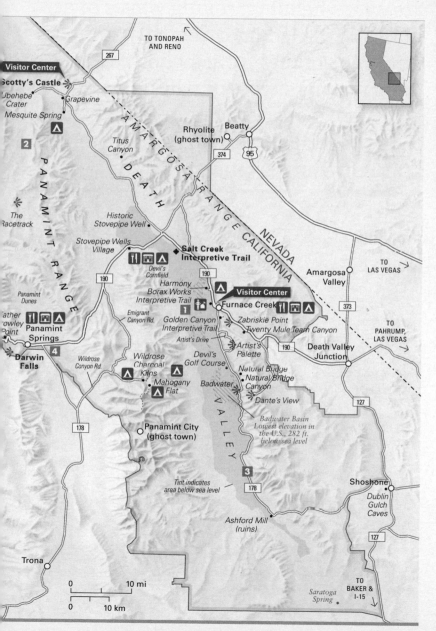

TO TONOPAH
AND RENO

267

Visitor Center
Scotty's Castle

Ubehebe
Crater

Mesquite Spring

2

Grapevine

Titus
Canyon

Rhyolite
(ghost town)

Beatty

374

95

TO
LAS VEGAS

The
Racetrack

Historic
Stovepipe Well

Stovepipe Wells
Village

Salt Creek
Interpretive Trail

Devil's
Cornfield

190

Harmony
Borax Works
Interpretive Trail

Visitor Center

Amargosa
Valley

373

TO
PAHRUMP,
LAS VEGAS

Panamint
Dunes

Father
Crowley
Point

Panamint
Springs

4

Darwin
Falls

Emigrant
Canyon Rd.

Golden Canyon
Interpretive Trail

Furnace Creek

Zabriskie Point

Twenty Mule Team Canyon

190

Death Valley
Junction

190

Artist's Drive

Artist's
Palette

Devil's
Golf Course

Wildrose
Canyon Rd.

Wildrose
Charcoal
Kilns

Mahogany
Flat

Natural Bridge

Natural Bridge
Canyon

Badwater

Dante's View

127

178

Panamint City
(ghost town)

*Badwater Basin
Lowest elevation in
the U.S., 282 ft.
below sea level*

3

*Tint indicates
area below sea level*

178

Shoshone

Dublin
Gulch
Caves

Ashford Mill
(ruins)

127

Trona

0   10 mi

0   10 km

TO
BAKER &
I-15

Saratoga
Spring

AMARGOSA RANGE

DEATH

PANAMINT RANGE

NEVADA

CALIFORNIA

VALLEY

The natural riches of Death Valley—the largest national park outside Alaska—are overwhelming: rolling waves of sand dunes, black cinder cones thrusting up hundreds of feet from a blistered desert floor, riotous sheets of wildflowers, bizarrely shaped Joshua trees basking in the orange glow of a sunset, tiny pupfish, and a dramatic silence.

Planning

When to Go

Most of the park's one million annual visitors come between late fall and early spring, taking advantage of moderate temperatures and the lack of rainfall. During these cooler months you will need to book a room in advance, but don't worry: the park never feels crowded. If you visit in summer, believe everything you've ever heard about desert heat—it can be brutal, with temperatures often topping 120°F. The dry air wicks moisture from the body without causing a sweat, so drink plenty of water. Bring sunglasses, a hat, and sufficient clothing to block the sun's rays and the wind. Flash floods are fairly common; sections of roadway can be flooded or washed away, as they were after a major flood in 2015. The wettest month is February, when the park receives an average of 0.3 inches of rain.

Festivals and Events

Bishop Mule Days
FESTIVAL | Entertainment at this five-day festival over the Memorial Day weekend includes top country-music stars, an arts-and-crafts fair, barbecues, country dances, the longest-running nonmotorized parade in the United States, and more than 700 mules competing in 181 events. Admission is free. ⊠ 1141 N. Main St., Bishop ☎ 760/872–4263 ⊕ www.muledays.org.

Death Valley Chamber of Commerce Art Show
FESTIVAL | Admission is free for this arts-and-crafts show and sale weekend, held on the lawn of The Ranch at Death Valley (formerly Ranch at Furnace Creek). ⊠ The Ranch at Death Valley, Greenland Ranch Rd., Death Valley ☎ 760/852–4420 ⊕ www.deathvalleychamber.org.

Death Valley 49er Encampment Days
FESTIVAL | FAMILY | Originally a centennial celebration held in 1949 to honor the area's first European visitors, this five-day event draws thousands of people from around the world to the Ranch at Death

AVERAGE HIGH/LOW TEMPERATURES

JAN.	FEB.	MAR.	APR.	MAY	JUNE
65/39	72/46	80/53	90/62	99/71	109/80
JULY	AUG.	SEPT.	OCT.	NOV.	DEC.
115/88	113/85	106/75	92/62	76/48	65/39

Valley for art shows, a wagon train, live music, artisan booths, dancing, and even a poker tournament. ⊠ *Ranch at Death Valley, Greenland Ranch Rd., Death Valley* ⊕ *www.deathvalley49ers.org.*

Lone Pine Film Festival
FESTIVAL | Every Columbus Day weekend, this town pays tribute to its Hollywood history with three days of tours, films, lectures, and celebrity panels. ⊠ *701 S. Main St., Lone Pine* ☎ *760/876–9103* ⊕ *www.lonepinefilmfestival.org.*

Shoshone Old West Days
FESTIVAL | Just outside of Death Valley, this annual three-day festival celebrates Wild West heritage with live performances, arts-and-crafts, and deep-pit barbecue. ⊠ *Shoshone* ☎ *760/852–4335* ⊕ *www.shoshonevillage.com.*

Planning Your Time

DEATH VALLEY IN ONE DAY
If you begin the day in Furnace Creek, you can see several sights without doing much driving. Bring plenty of water with you, and some food, too. Get up early and drive the 20 miles on Badwater Road to **Badwater,** which looks out on the lowest point in the Western Hemisphere and is a dramatic place to watch the sunrise. Returning north, stop at **Natural Bridge,** a medium-size conglomerate rock formation that has been hollowed at its base to form a span across the canyon, and then at the **Devil's Golf Course,** so named because of the large pinnacles of salt present here. Detour to the right onto **Artist's Drive,** a 9-mile one-way, northbound route that passes **Artist's Palette.** The reds, yellows, oranges, and

greens come from minerals in the rocks and the earth. Four miles north of Artist's Drive you will come to the **Golden Canyon Interpretive Trail,** a 2-mile round-trip that winds through a canyon with colorful rock walls. Just before Furnace Creek, take Highway 190 3 miles east to **Zabriskie Point,** overlooking dramatic, furrowed red-brown hills and the **Twenty Mule Team Canyon.** Return to Furnace Creek, where you can grab a meal and visit the museum at the Furnace Creek Visitor Center. Heading north from Furnace Creek, pull off the highway and take a look at the **Harmony Borax Works.**

Getting Here and Around

AIR TRAVEL
The closest airport to the park with commercial service, Las Vegas McCarren International Airport, is 130 miles away, so you'll still need to drive a couple of hours to reach the park. Roughly 160 miles to the west, Burbank's Bob Hope Airport is the second-closest airport.

CAR TRAVEL
It can take more than three hours to cross from one side of the park to another, so it's important to choose an entrance point that makes sense for what you want to see. If you're driving from Los Angeles, enter through the western portion along Highway 395; if you're coming from Las Vegas, enter from the north at Beatty, Nevada, or via the central entrance at Death Valley Junction. Travelers from Orange County, San Diego, and the Inland Empire should access the park via Interstate 15 North at Baker.

Distances can be deceiving within the park: what seems close can be very far away. Much of the park can be viewed on regularly scheduled bus tours, but these often don't allow time for hikes to sites not seen from the road, such as Salt Creek, Golden Canyon, and Natural Bridge. The best option is to drive to a number of the sites, get out of the car, and walk.

When driving in Death Valley, reliable maps are important, as signage is often limited or, in a few places, nonexistent. Bring a phone but don't rely on cell coverage exclusively in every remote area, and pack plenty of food and water (3 gallons per person per day is recommended). Cars, especially in summer, should be prepared for the hot, dry weather, too. Some of the park's most spectacular canyons are only accessible via four-wheel-drive vehicles but if this is the way you want to travel, make sure the trip is well planned and use a backcountry map. Be aware of possible winter closures or driving restrictions because of snow. The National Park Service's website (⊕ nps.gov/deva) stays up-to-date on road closures during the wet (and popular) months. ⚠ One of the park's signature landmarks, Scotty's Castle, and the 8-mile road connecting it to the park border may be closed until 2020 due to damage from a 2015 flood.

DRIVING INFORMATION California Highway Patrol. ☎ 800/427–7623 recorded info from CalTrans, 760/872–5900 live dispatcher at Bishop Communications Center ⊕ www.chp.ca.gov. **California State Department of Transportation Hotline.** ☎ 800/427–7623 ⊕ www.dot.ca.gov

Park Essentials

ACCESSIBILITY
All of Death Valley's visitor centers, contact stations, and museums are accessible to all visitors. The campgrounds at Furnace Creek, Sunset, and Stovepipe Wells have wheelchair-accessible sites. Highway 190, Badwater Road, and paved roads to Dante's View and Wildrose provide access to the major scenic viewpoints and historic points of interest.

PARK FEES AND PERMITS
The entrance fee is $30 per vehicle, $25 for motorcycles, and $15 for those entering on foot or bike. The payment, valid for seven consecutive days, is collected at the park's ranger stations, self-serve fee stations, and the visitor center at Furnace Creek. Annual park passes, valid only at Death Valley, are $55.

A permit is not required for groups of 14 or fewer, but if you're planning an overnight visit to the backcountry, complete a registration form at the Furnace Creek Visitor Center. Backcountry camping is allowed in areas that are at least 2 miles from maintained campgrounds and the main paved or unpaved roads and ¼ mile from water sources. Most abandoned mining areas are restricted to day use.

PARK HOURS
The park is open year-round, and can be visited day or night. Most facilities within the park remain open year-round, daily 8–6.

CELL PHONE RECEPTION
Results vary, but in general you should be able to get fairly good cell phone reception on the valley floor. In the surrounding mountains, however, don't count on it.

Educational Offerings

RANGER PROGRAMS
Junior Ranger Program
TOUR—SIGHT | FAMILY | Children can join this program at the Furnace Creek Visitor Center, where they can pick up a workbook and complete activities to earn a souvenir badge. ✉ Death Valley National Park.

Restaurants

Inside the park, if you're looking for a special evening out in Death Valley, head to the Inn at Death Valley Dining Room, where you'll be spoiled with fine wines and juicy steaks. It's also a great spot to start the day with a hearty gourmet breakfast. Most other eateries within the park are mom-and-pop-type places with basic American fare. Outside the park, dining choices are much the same, with little cafés and homey diners serving up coffee shop–style burgers, chicken, and steaks. If you're vegetarian or vegan, BYOB (bring your own beans). *Restaurant reviews have been shortened. For full information, visit Fodors.com.*

Hotels

It's difficult to find lodging anywhere in Death Valley that doesn't have breathtaking views of the park and surrounding mountains. Most accommodations, aside from the Inn at Death Valley, are homey and rustic. Rooms fill up quickly during the fall and spring seasons, and reservations are required about three months in advance for the prime weekends.

Outside the park, head to Beatty or Amargosa Valley in Nevada for a bit of nightlife and casino action. The western side of Death Valley, along the eastern Sierra Nevada, is a gorgeous setting, though it's quite a distance from Furnace Creek. Here, you can stay in the historic Dow Villa Motel, where John Wayne spent many a night, or head farther south to the ghost towns of Randsburg or Cerro Gordo for a true Wild West experience. *Hotel reviews have been shortened. For full information, visit Fodors.com.*

What It Costs

	$	$$	$$$	$$$$
RESTAURANTS				
	under $12	$12–$20	$21–$30	over $30
HOTELS				
	under $100	$100–$150	$151–$200	over $200

Tours

Death Valley Adventure Tour (*Adventure Motorcycle [AdMo] Tours*)
TOUR—SIGHT | Motorcycle enthusiasts can sign up for a guided Death Valley Adventure Tour that starts and ends in Las Vegas. The five-day tour through Death Valley covers 800 miles. The tours, which run October through May, include hotel accommodations, gasoline, breakfasts, two dinners, snacks, a support vehicle, and a professional guide. To join, you'll need a motorcycle driver's license and experience with off-road and all-terrain riding. ⊠ *Death Valley* ☎ *760/249–1105* ⊕ *www.admotours.com* ⟟ *From $3568.*

Furnace Creek Visitor Center programs
GUIDED TOURS | This center has many programs, including ranger-led hikes that explore natural wonders such as Golden Canyon, nighttime stargazing parties with telescopes, and evening ranger talks. Visit the website for a complete list. ⊠ *Furnace Creek Visitor Center, Rte. 190, 30 miles northwest of Death Valley Junction, Death Valley* ☎ *760/786–2331* ⊕ *www.nps.gov/deva/planyourvisit/tours.htm* ⟟ *Free.*

Pink Jeep Tours Las Vegas
GUIDED TOURS | A 10-passenger luxury vehicle with oversized viewing windows will pick you up at most Strip hotels for visits to landmarks such as Dante's View, Furnace Creek, Devil's Golf Course, Badwater Basin, and Artist's Palette. The tours run from about 7 am to 4 pm from September through May,

are professionally narrated, and include lunch and bottled water. ⊠ *3629 W. Hacienda Ave., Las Vegas* ☎ *888/900–4480* ⊕ *pinkjeeptourslasvegas.com* ⌫ *From $275.*

Visitor Information

MAPS AND INFO

The Death Valley Natural History Association sells a variety of books on the area and publishes a pamphlet outlining a self-guided tour of Golden Canyon, which is available from the association or the bookstore at the visitor center. The association also sells a waterproof, tear-proof topographical map of the entire park. Additional topo maps covering select areas are available at the visitor center or from the **Death Valley Natural History Association** (☎ *760/786–2146 or 800/478–8564* ⊕ *www.dvnha.org*).

PARK CONTACT INFORMATION Death Valley National Park. ☎ *760/786–3200* ⊕ *www.nps.gov/deva.*

VISITOR CENTERS

⚠ **The popular visitor center at Scotty's Castle is closed until at least 2020 as a result of a major flash flood in 2015 that damaged the structure and destroyed the access road.**

Furnace Creek Visitor Center and Museum
INFO CENTER | The exhibits and artifacts here provide a broad overview of how Death Valley formed; you can pick up maps at the bookstore run by the Death Valley Natural History Association. This is also the place to sign up for ranger-led walks (available November through April) or check out a live presentation about the valley's cultural and natural history. The helpful center offers regular showings of a 20-minute film about the park and children can get their free Junior Ranger booklet here, packed with games and information about the park and its critters. ⊠ *Hwy. 190, Death Valley* ✛ *30 miles northwest of Death Valley Junction* ☎ *760/786–3200* ⊕ *www.nps.gov/deva.*

◉ Sights

SCENIC DRIVE
Artist's Drive
SCENIC DRIVE | This 9-mile, one-way route skirts the foothills of the Black Mountains and provides intimate views of the changing landscape. Once inside the palette, the huge expanses of the valley are replaced by the small-scale natural beauty of pigments created by volcanic deposits or sedimentary layers. It's a quiet, lonely drive, and shouldn't be rushed. Reach Artist's Palette by heading south on Badwater Road from its intersection with Route 190. ⊠ *Death Valley National Park.*

HISTORIC SITES
Charcoal Kilns
MINE | Ten well-preserved stone kilns, each 25 feet high and 30 feet wide, stand as if on parade. The kilns, built by Chinese laborers for a mining company in 1877, were used to burn wood from pinyon pines to turn it into charcoal. The charcoal was then transported over the mountains into Death Valley, where it was used to extract lead and silver from the ore mined there. If you hike nearby Wildrose Peak, you will be rewarded with terrific views of the kilns. ⊠ *Wildrose Canyon Rd., Death Valley* ✛ *37 miles south of Stovepipe Wells.*

Harmony Borax Works
HISTORIC SITE | Death Valley's mule teams hauled borax from here to the railroad town of Mojave, 165 miles away. The teams plied the route until 1889, when the railroad finally arrived in Zabriskie. Constructed in 1883, one of the oldest buildings in Death Valley houses the Borax Museum, 2 miles south of the borax works at the Ranch at Death Valley (between the restaurants and the post office). Originally a miners' bunkhouse, the building once stood in Twenty Mule Team Canyon. Now it displays mining machinery and historical exhibits. The adjacent structure is the original

Plants and Wildlife in Death Valley 👁

There's a general misconception that Death Valley National Park consists of mile upon endless mile of flat desert sands, scattered cacti, and an occasional cow skull. Many people don't realize that across the valley floor from Badwater—the lowest point in the Western Hemisphere—Telescope Peak towers at 11,049 feet above sea level. The extreme topography of Death Valley is a lesson in geology. Two hundred million years ago seas covered the area, depositing layers of sediment and fossils. Between 3.5 million and 5 million years ago faults in the Earth's crust and volcanic activity pushed and folded the ground, causing mountain ranges to rise and the valley floor to drop. The valley was then filled periodically by lakes, which eroded the surrounding rocks into fantastic formations and deposited the salts that now cover the floor of the basin.

Most animal life in Death Valley (51 mammal, 36 reptile, 307 bird, and 3 amphibian species) is found near the limited sources of water. The bighorn sheep spend most of their time in the secluded upper reaches of the park's rugged canyons and ridges. Coyotes often can be seen lazing in the shade next to the golf course and have been known to run onto the fairways to steal a golf ball. The only native fish in the park is the pupfish, which grows to slightly longer than one inch. In winter, when the water is cold, the fish lie dormant in the bottom mud, becoming active again in spring. Because they are wary of large moving shapes, you must stand quietly over a pool at Salt Creek to see them.

Botanists say there are more than 1,000 species of plants here (21 exist nowhere else in the world), though many annual plants lie dormant as seeds for all but a few months in spring, when rains trigger a bloom. The rest congregate around the few water sources. Most of the low-elevation vegetation grows around the oases at Furnace Creek and Scotty's Castle, where oleanders, palms, and salt cedar grow. At higher elevations you will find pinyon, juniper, and bristlecone pine.

---

mule-team barn. ⊠ *Harmony Borax Works Rd., west of Hwy. 190 at Ranch at Death Valley* ⊕ *www.nps.gov/deva/historyculture/harmony.htm.*

SCENIC STOPS
Artist's Palette
NATURE SITE | So called for the contrasting colors of its volcanic deposits and sedimentary layers, this is one of the signature sights of Death Valley. Artist's Drive, the approach to the area, is one-way heading north off Badwater Road, so if you're visiting Badwater from Furnace Creek, come here on the way back. The drive winds through foothills of sedimentary and volcanic rocks. About 4 miles into the drive, a short side road veers right to a parking lot that's a few hundred feet before the "palette," whose natural colors include shades of green, gold, and pink. ⊠ *Off Badwater Rd., Death Valley* ✛ *11 miles south of Furnace Creek.*

Badwater
SCENIC DRIVE | At 282 feet below sea level, Badwater is the lowest spot of land in North America—and also one of the hottest. Stairs and wheelchair ramps descend from the parking lot to a wooden platform that overlooks a sodium

chloride pool, a small but remarkably persistent reminder that the valley floor used to contain a lake. You can continue past the platform on a broad, white path that peters out after a half mile or so. Badwater is one of the most popular and easily accessible sites within the park. From this lowest point, be sure to look across to Telescope Peak, which towers more than 2 miles above the valley floor. ⊠ *Badwater Rd., Death Valley* ✛ *19 miles south of Furnace Creek.*

★ Dante's View

VIEWPOINT | This lookout is 5,450 feet above sea level in the Black Mountains. In the dry desert air you can see across most of 160-mile-long Death Valley. The view is astounding. Take a 10-minute, mildly strenuous walk from the parking lot toward a series of rocky overlooks, where with binoculars you can spot some of Death Valley's signature sites. A few interpretive signs point out the highlights below in the valley and across, in the Sierra. Getting here from Furnace Creek takes about an hour—time well invested. ⊠ *Dante's View Rd., Death Valley* ✛ *Off Hwy. 190, 35 miles from Badwater, 20 miles south of Twenty Mule Team Canyon.*

Devil's Golf Course

NATURE SITE | Thousands of miniature salt pinnacles carved into surreal shapes by the desert wind dot this wildly varied landscape. The salt was pushed up to the earth's surface by pressure created as underground salt- and water-bearing gravel crystallized. Get out of your vehicle and take a closer look; you'll see perfectly round holes descending into the ground. ⊠ *Badwater Rd., Death Valley* ✛ *13 miles south of Furnace Creek. Turn right onto dirt road and drive 1 mile.*

Golden Canyon

NATURE SITE | Just south of Furnace Creek, these glimmering mountains are perhaps best known for their role in the original *Star Wars*. The canyon is also a fine hiking spot, with gorgeous views

of the Panamint Mountains, ancient dry lake beds, and alluvial fans. ⊠ *Hwy. 178, Death Valley* ✛ *From Furnace Creek Visitor Center, drive 2 miles south on Hwy. 190, then 2 miles south on Hwy. 178 to parking area; the lot has kiosk with trail guides.*

Racetrack

NATURE SITE | Getting here involves a 28-mile journey over a washboard dirt road, but the reward is well worth the trip. Where else in the world do rocks move on their own? This phenomenon has baffled scientists for years and is perhaps one of the last great natural mysteries. The best research on the rocks shows the movement requires a rare confluence of conditions: rain and then cold to create a layer of ice that becomes a sail for gusty winds that push the rocks along—sometimes for several hundred yards. When the mud dries, a telltale trail remains. The trek to the Racetrack can be made in a sedan, but beware—sharp rocks can slash tires; a truck or SUV with thick tires, high clearance, and a spare tire are suggested. ⊠ *Death Valley* ✛ *27 miles west of Ubehebe Crater via rough dirt road.*

Sand Dunes at Mesquite Flat

NATURE SITE | These dunes, made up of minute pieces of quartz and other rock, are ever-changing products of the wind-rippled hills, with curving crests and a sun-bleached hue. The dunes are the most photographed destination in the park, and you can see them at their best at sunrise and sunset. Keep your eyes open for animal tracks—you may even spot a coyote or fox. Bring plenty of water, and note where you parked your car: It's easy to become disoriented in this ocean of sand. If you lose your bearings, climb to the top of a dune and scan the horizon for the parking lot. ⊠ *Death Valley* ✛ *19 miles north of Hwy. 190, northeast of Stovepipe Wells Village.*

The Mesquite Flat Sand Dunes.

Stovepipe Wells Village

TOWN | This tiny 1926 town, the first resort in Death Valley, takes its name from the stovepipe that an early prospector left to indicate where he found water. The area contains a motel, restaurant, convenience store, gas station, RV hookups, swimming pool, and landing strip, though first-time park visitors are better off staying in Furnace Creek, which is more central. Off Highway 190, on a 3-mile gravel road immediately southwest, are the multicolor walls of Mosaic Canyon. ⊠ *Hwy. 190, Death Valley* ✛ *2 miles from Sand Dunes, 77 miles east of Lone Pine* ☎ *760/786–2387* ⊕ *www.deathvalleyhotels.com.*

Titus Canyon

SCENIC DRIVE | This popular one-way, 27-mile drive starts at Nevada Highway 374 (Daylight Pass Road), 2 miles from the park's boundary. Along the way you'll see Leadville Ghost Town and finally the spectacular limestone and dolomite narrows. Toward the end, a two-way section of gravel road leads you into the mouth of the canyon from Scotty's Castle Road. This drive is steep, bumpy, and narrow. High-clearance vehicles are strongly recommended. ⊠ *Death Valley National Park* ✛ *Access road off Nevada Hwy. 374, 6 miles west of Beatty, NV.*

Twenty Mule Team Canyon

CANYON | This canyon was named in honor of the 20-mule teams that, between 1883 and 1889, carried 10-ton loads of borax through the burning desert (though they didn't actually pass through this canyon). Along the 2.7-mile, one-way loop road off Highway 190, you'll find the soft rock walls reach high on both sides, making it seem like you're on an amusement-park ride. Remains of prospectors' tunnels are visible here, along with some brilliant rock formations. ⊠ *20 Mule Team Rd.* ✛ *Off Hwy. 190, 4 miles south of Furnace Creek, 20 miles west of Death Valley Junction.*

Ubehebe Crater

VOLCANO | At 500 feet deep and ½ mile across, this crater resulted from underground steam and gas explosions about

3,000 years ago. Volcanic ash spreads out over most of the area, and the cinders lie as deep as 150 feet, near the crater's rim. Trek down to the crater's floor or walk around it on a fairly level path. Either way, you need about an hour and will be treated to fantastic views. The hike from the floor can be strenuous. ⊠ *N. Death Valley Hwy., Death Valley* ✛ *8 miles northwest of Scotty's Castle.*

Zabriskie Point

VIEWPOINT | Although only about 710 feet in elevation, this is one of Death Valley National Park's most scenic spots, overlooking a striking panorama of wrinkled, multicolor hills. It's a great place to watch the sunrise, but it can be bustling any time of day. Pair it with a drive out to magnificent Dante's View. ⊠ *Hwy. 190, Death Valley* ✛ *5 miles south of Furnace Creek.*

🏃 Activities

BICYCLING

Mountain biking is permitted on any of the back roads and roadways open to the public (bikes aren't permitted on hiking trails). Visit ⊕ *www.nps.gov/deva/planyourvisit/bikingandmtbiking.htm* for a list of suggested routes for all levels of ability. Bicycle Path, a 4-mile round-trip trek from the visitor center to Mustard Canyon, is a good place to start. Bike rentals are available at the Oasis at Death Valley, by the hour or by the day.

Escape Adventures (*Escape Adventures*)

BICYCLING | Ride into the heart of Death Valley on the Death Valley & Red Rock Mountain Bike Tour, a five-day trip through the national park. The customizable two-day journey (on single-track trails and jeep roads) includes accommodations (both camping and inns). Bikes, tents, sleeping bags, helmets, and other gear may be rented for an additional price. Tours are available February–April and October only. ⊠ *Death Valley National Park* ☎ *800/596–2953, 702/596–2953* ⊕ *www.escapeadventures.com* 🖻 *From $1720.*

BIRD-WATCHING

Approximately 350 bird species have been identified in Death Valley. The best place to see the park's birds is along the Salt Creek Interpretive Trail, where you can spot ravens, common snipes, killdeer, spotted sandpipers, and great blue herons. Along the fairways at Furnace Creek Golf Course, you can see kingfishers, peregrine falcons, hawks, Canada geese, yellow warblers, and the occasional golden eagle. Scotty's Castle, closed until at least 2020, draws wintering birds from around the globe that are attracted to its running water, shady trees, and shrubs. Other good spots to find birds are at Saratoga Springs, Mesquite Springs, Travertine Springs, and Grimshaw Lake near Tecopa.

You can download a complete park bird checklist, divided by season, at ⊕ *www.nps.gov/deva/learn/nature/upload/death-valley-bird-checklist.pdf.* Rangers at Furnace Creek Visitor Center often lead birding walks through various locations between November and March.

FOUR-WHEELING

Maps and SUV guidebooks for four-wheel-drive and other backcountry roads (including the popular Cottonwood/Marble canyons, Racetrack, Eureka Dunes, Saratoga Springs, and Warm Springs Canyon) are offered at the Furnace Creek Visitor Center. Remember: never travel alone and be sure to pack plenty of water and snacks. The park recommends checking ⊕ *www.nps.gov/deva/planyourvisit/backcountryroads.htm* for back-road conditions before setting out. Driving off established roads is strictly prohibited in the park.

Butte Valley

TOUR—SPORTS | This 21-mile road in the southwest part of the park climbs from 200 feet below sea level to an elevation of 4,700 feet. The geological formations along the drive reveal the development of Death Valley. High-clearance and four-wheel-drive required. If you have a

Sunset over Furnace Creek in Death Valley.

four-wheel-drive high-clearance vehicle and nerves of steel, this route takes you past Warm Springs talc mine and through Butte Valley to Geologist's Cabin, a charming and cheery little cabin where you can spend the night, if nobody else beats you to it. The park suggests checking their website or asking a ranger to check current conditions on all backcountry roads. The cabin, which sits under a cottonwood tree, has a fireplace, table and chairs, and a sink. Farther up the road, Stella's Cabin and Russell Camp are also open for public use. Keep the historic cabins clean and restock any items that you use. The road is even rougher if you continue over Mengel Pass. ⊠ *Trailhead on Warm Spring Canyon Rd., Death Valley* ✛ *50 miles south of Furnace Creek Visitor Center.*

GOLF
Furnace Creek Golf Course at the Oasis at Death Valley
GOLF | Golfers rave about how their drives carry at altitude, so what happens on the lowest golf course in the world (214 feet below sea level)? Its improbably green fairways are lined with date palms and tamarisk trees, and its level of difficulty is rated surprisingly high. You can rent clubs and carts, and there are golf packages available for The Oasis at Death Valley guests. In winter, reservations are essential. ⊠ *Hwy. 190, Furnace Creek* ☎ *760/786–2301* ⊕ *www.oasisatdeathvalley.com* ⊠ *From $35* ⚑. *18 holes, 6215 yards, par 70.*

HIKING
Plan to hike before or after midday in the spring, summer, or fall, unless you're in the mood for a masochistic baking. Carry plenty of water, wear protective clothing, and keep an eye out for black widows, scorpions, snakes, and other potentially dangerous creatures. Some of the best trails are unmarked; if the opportunity arises, ask for directions.

★ Darwin Falls
HIKING/WALKING | FAMILY | This lovely 2-mile round-trip hike rewards you with a refreshing year-round waterfall surrounded by thick vegetation and a rocky gorge.

No swimming or bathing is allowed, but it's a beautiful place for a picnic. Adventurous hikers can scramble higher toward more rewarding views of the falls. *Easy.* ⊠ *Death Valley National Park* ✛ *Trailhead: access the 2-mile graded dirt road and parking area off Hwy. 190, 1 mile west of Panamint Springs Resort.*

Fall Canyon

HIKING/WALKING | This is a 3-mile, one-way hike from the Titus canyon parking area. First, walk ½ mile north along the base of the mountains to a large wash, then go 2½ miles up the canyon to a 35-foot dry fall. You can continue by climbing around to the falls on the south side. *Moderate.* ⊠ *Death Valley National Park* ✛ *Trailhead: access road off Scotty's Castle Rd., 33 miles northwest of Furnace Creek.*

Keane Wonder Mine

HIKING/WALKING | This fascinating relic of Death Valley's gold-mining past, built in 1907, reopened in November 2017 after nine years of repair work. Its most unique feature is the mile-long tramway that descends 1,000 vertical feet, which once carried gold ore and still has the original cables attached. From here, a network of trails leads to other old mines. A climb to the uppermost tramway terminal is rewarded by expansive views of the valley. ⊠ *Access road off Beatty Cutoff Rd., 17½ miles north of Furnace Creek, Death Valley.*

Mosaic Canyon

HIKING/WALKING | **FAMILY** | A gradual uphill trail (4 miles round-trip) winds through the smoothly polished, marbleized limestone walls of this narrow canyon. There are dry falls to climb at the upper end. *Moderate.* ⊠ *Death Valley* ✛ *Trailhead: access road off Hwy. 190, ½ mile west of Stovepipe Wells Village.*

Natural Bridge Canyon

HIKING/WALKING | A rough 2-mile access road from Badwater Road leads to a trailhead. From there, set off to see interesting geological features in addition to the bridge, which is a half mile away. The one-way trail continues for a few hundred yards, but scenic returns diminish quickly and eventually you're confronted with climbing boulders. *Easy.* ⊠ *Death Valley* ✛ *Trailhead: access road off Badwater Rd., 15 miles south of Furnace Creek.*

Salt Creek Interpretive Trail

HIKING/WALKING | **FAMILY** | This trail, a ½-mile boardwalk circuit, loops through a spring-fed wash. The nearby hills are brown and gray, but the floor of the wash is alive with aquatic plants such as pickleweed and salt grass. The stream and ponds here are among the few places in the park to see the rare pupfish, the only native fish species in Death Valley. The pupfish are most easily observed during their spawning season in February and March. Animals such as bobcats, fox, coyotes, and snakes visit the spring, and you may also see ravens, common snipes, killdeer, and great blue herons. *Easy.* ⊠ *Death Valley* ✛ *Trailhead: off Hwy. 190, 14 miles north of Furnace Creek.*

★ Telescope Peak Trail

HIKING/WALKING | The 14-mile round-trip (with 3,000 feet of elevation gain) begins at Mahogany Flat Campground, which is accessible by a rough dirt road. The steep and at some points treacherous trail winds through pinyon, juniper, and bristlecone pines, with excellent views of Death Valley and Panamint Valley. Ice axes and crampons may be necessary in winter—check at the Furnace Creek Visitor Center. It takes a minimum of six grueling hours to hike to the top of the 11,049-foot peak and then return. Getting to the peak is a strenuous endeavor; take plenty of water and only attempt it in fall unless you're an experienced hiker. *Difficult.* ⊠ *Death Valley* ✛ *Trailhead: off Wildrose Rd., south of Charcoal Kilns.*

HORSEBACK AND CARRIAGE RIDES

Furnace Creek Stables

HORSEBACK RIDING | FAMILY | Set off on a one- or two-hour guided horseback, carriage, or hay wagon ride from Furnace Creek Stables. The rides traverse trails with views of the surrounding mountains, where multicolor volcanic rock and alluvial fans form a background for date palms and other vegetation. Evening carriage rides take passengers around the golf course and The Ranch at Death Valley. The stables are open October–May only. ✉ *Hwy. 190, Furnace Creek* ☎ *760/614–1018* 🌐 *www.furnacecreek-stables.net* 🎟 *From $55.*

Shopping

Experienced desert travelers carry a cooler stocked with food and beverages. You're best off replenishing your food stash in Ridgecrest, Barstow, or Pahrump, larger towns that have a better selection and nontourist prices.

Ranch General Store

CONVENIENCE/GENERAL STORES | This convenience store carries groceries, souvenirs, camping supplies, and other basics. ✉ *Hwy. 190, Furnace Creek* ☎ *760/786–2345* 🌐 *www.oasisatdeathvalley.com.*

Restaurants

IN THE PARK

★ Inn at Death Valley Dining Room

$$$$ | AMERICAN | Fireplaces, beamed ceilings, and spectacular views provide a visual feast to match this fine-dining restaurant's ambitious menu. Dinner entrées include fare such as salmon, free-range chicken, and filet mignon, and there's a seasonal menu of vegetarian dishes. **Known for:** views of surrounding desert; old-school charm; can be pricey. [$] *Average main: $38* ✉ *Inn at Death Valley, Hwy. 190, Furnace Creek* ☎ *760/786–3385* 🌐 *www.oasisatdeathvalley.com.*

19th Hole

$ | AMERICAN | Next to the clubhouse of the world's lowest golf course, this open-air spot serves hamburgers, hot dogs, chicken, and sandwiches. The full-service bar has a drive-through service for golfers in carts. **Known for:** kielbasa dog; breakfast burrito; golf cart drive-through. [$] *Average main: $8* ✉ *Furnace Creek Golf Course, Hwy. 190, Furnace Creek* ☎ *760/786–2345* 🌐 *www.oasisatdeathvalley.com/dining/* ⏲ *Closed mid-May–mid-Oct. No dinner.*

Panamint Springs Resort Restaurant

$$ | AMERICAN | This is a great place for steak and a beer—choose from more than 150 different beers and ales—or pasta and a salad. In summer, evening meals are served outdoors on the porch, which has spectacular views of Panamint Valley. **Known for:** good burgers; extensive beer selection. [$] *Average main: $15* ✉ *Hwy. 190, Death Valley* ✥ *31 miles west of Stovepipe Wells* ☎ *775/482–7680* 🌐 *www.panamintsprings.com/services/dining-bar.*

OUTSIDE THE PARK

Crowbar Café and Saloon

$$ | AMERICAN | FAMILY | In an old wooden building where antique photos adorn the walls and mining equipment stands in the corners, the Crowbar serves enormous helpings of regional dishes such as steak and taco salads. Home-baked fruit pies make fine desserts, and frosty beers are surefire thirst quenchers. **Known for:** home-baked fruit pies; rattlesnake chili; great breakfast spot. [$] *Average main: $15* ✉ *Rte. 127, Shoshone* ☎ *760/852–4123* 🌐 *www.shoshonevillage.com/shoshone-crowbar-cafe-saloon.html.*

Mt. Whitney Restaurant

$ | AMERICAN | A boisterous family-friendly restaurant with four flat-screen televisions, this place serves the best burgers in town. In addition to the usual beef variety, you can choose from ostrich, elk, venison, and buffalo burgers. **Known**

Best Campgrounds in Death Valley

You'll need a high-clearance or 4X4 vehicle to reach these locations. To find out where you can camp in the backcountry, pick up a copy of the backcountry map at the visitor center, or check the website 🌐 *www.nps.gov/deva/planyourvisit/camping.htm.*

You can only build fires in the metal fire grates that are available at most campgrounds, though fires may be restricted in summer (check with rangers about current conditions). Wood gathering is prohibited at all campgrounds. A limited supply of firewood is available at general stores in Furnace Creek and Stovepipe Wells, but because prices are high and supplies limited, you're better off bringing your own if you intend to have a campfire. Camping is prohibited in the historic Inyo, Los Burro, and Ubehebe Crater areas, as well as all day-use spots, including Aguerberry Point Road, Cottonwood Canyon Road, Racetrack Road, Skidoo Road, Titus Canyon Road, Wildrose Road, and West Side Road.

Furnace Creek. This campground, 196 feet below sea level, has some shaded tent sites and is open all year. ✉ *Hwy. 190, Furnace Creek* ☎ *760/786–2441.*

Mahogany Flat. If you have a four-wheel-drive vehicle and want to scale Telescope Peak, the park's highest mountain, you might want to sleep at one of the few shaded spots in Death Valley, at a cool 8,133 feet. ✉ *Off Wildrose Rd., south of Charcoal Kilns* ☎ *No phone.*

Panamint Springs Resort. Part of a complex that includes a motel and cabin, this campground is surrounded by cottonwoods. The daily fee includes use of the showers and restrooms. ✉ *Hwy. 190, 28 miles west of Stovepipe Wells* ☎ *775/482–7680.*

Sunset Campground. This first-come, first-served campground is a gravel-and-asphalt RV city. Closed mid-April to mid-October. ✉ *Sunset Campground Rd., 1 mile north of Furnace Creek* ☎ *800/365–2267.*

Texas Spring. This campsite south of the Furnace Creek Visitor Center has good views and facilities and is a few dollars cheaper than Furnace Creek. Closed mid-May to mid-October. ✉ *Off Badwater Rd., south of Furnace Creek Visitor Center* ☎ *800/365–2267.*

for: burgers; John Wayne memorabilia. [$] *Average main: $10* ✉ *227 S. Main St., Lone Pine* ☎ *760/876–5751.*

Randsburg General Store

$ | **AMERICAN** | **FAMILY** | Built as Randsburg's Drug Store in 1896, this popular biker and family spot is one of the area's few surviving ghost-town buildings with original furnishings intact, such as a tin ceiling, light fixtures, and a 1904 marble-and-stained-glass soda fountain. You can still enjoy a phosphate soda from that same fountain, or lunch on slow-roasted barbecue sandwiches and blueberry milk shakes along with chili, hamburgers, and breakfast. **Known for:** friendly service; located in a ghost town. [$] *Average main: $10* ✉ *35 Butte Ave., Randsburg* ☎ *760/374–2143* 🌐 *www.randsburggeneralstore.com* 🕒 *Closed Mon.–Thurs.; for extended opening during holiday wks, call ahead.*

Hotels

IN THE PARK

For the busy season (November–March) you should make reservations for lodgings within the park several months in advance.

★ **The Inn at Death Valley**

$$$$ | **HOTEL** | Built in 1927, this adobe-brick-and-stone lodge in one of the park's greenest oases reopened in 2018 after an extensive renovation, offering Death Valley's most luxurious accommodations, including 22 brand-new one- and two-bedroom casitas. **Pros:** refined; comfortable; great views. **Cons:** services reduced during low season (July and August); expensive; resort fee. [$] *Rooms from: $499* ✉ *Furnace Creek Village, near intersection of Hwy. 190 and Badwater Rd., Death Valley* ☎ *760/786–2345* 🌐 *www.oasisatdeathvalley.com* 🛏 *88 rooms* 🍴 *No meals.*

Panamint Springs Resort

$ | **B&B/INN** | Ten miles inside the west entrance of the park, this low-key resort overlooks the sand dunes and peculiar geological formations of the Panamint Valley. **Pros:** slow-paced; friendly; peaceful and quiet after sundown. **Cons:** far from the park's main attractions; Internet very limited; most rooms don't have TV. [$] *Rooms from: $94* ✉ *Hwy. 190, Death Valley* ✣ *28 miles west of Stovepipe Wells* ☎ *775/482–7680* 🌐 *www.panamintsprings.com* 🛏 *15 rooms, 8 cabins* 🍴 *No meals.*

The Ranch at Death Valley

$$$$ | **RESORT** | **FAMILY** | Originally the crew headquarters for the Pacific Coast Borax Company, the four buildings here have motel-style rooms that are a great option for families. **Pros:** good family atmosphere; central location. **Cons:** rooms can get hot despite air-conditioning; parking near your room can be problematic. [$] *Rooms from: $279* ✉ *Hwy. 190, Furnace Creek* ☎ *760/786–2345, 800/236–7916* 🌐 *www.oasisatdeathvalley.com* 🛏 *224 rooms* 🍴 *No meals.*

Stovepipe Wells Village

$$ | **HOTEL** | If you prefer quiet nights and an unfettered view of the night sky and nearby Mesquite Flat Sand Dunes and Mosaic Canyon, this property is for you. **Pros:** intimate, relaxed; no big-time partying; authentic desert-community ambience. **Cons:** isolated; cheapest patio rooms very small; limited Wi-Fi access. [$] *Rooms from: $140* ✉ *Hwy. 190, Stovepipe Wells* ☎ *760/786–2387* 🌐 *www.escapetodeathvalley.com* 🛏 *83 rooms* 🍴 *No meals.*

Chapter 14

YOSEMITE NATIONAL PARK

Updated by
Cheryl Crabtree

👁 Sights	🍴 Restaurants	🛏 Hotels	🛍 Shopping	🍸 Nightlife
★★★★★	★★★★☆	★★★★★	★☆☆☆☆	★☆☆☆☆

WELCOME TO YOSEMITE NATIONAL PARK

TOP REASONS TO GO

★ **Scenic falls:** An easy stroll brings you to the base of Lower Yosemite Fall, where roaring springtime waters make for misty lens caps and lasting memories.

★ **Tunnel vision:** Approaching Yosemite Valley, Wawona Road passes through a mountainside and emerges before one of the park's most heart-stopping vistas.

★ **Inhale the beauty:** Pause to take in the light, pristine air as you travel about the High Sierra's Tioga Pass and Tuolumne Meadows, where 10,000-foot granite peaks just might take your breath away.

★ **Walk away:** Leave the crowds behind—but do bring along a buddy—and take a hike somewhere along Yosemite's 800 miles of trails.

★ **Winter wonder:** Observe the snowflakes and stillness of winter in the park.

1 Yosemite Valley. At an elevation of 4,000 feet, in roughly the center of the park, beats Yosemite's heart. This is where you'll find the park's most famous sights and biggest crowds.

2 Wawona and Mariposa Grove. The park's southern tip holds Wawona, with its grand old hotel and pioneer history center, and the Mariposa Grove of Giant Sequoias. These are closest to the south entrance, 35 miles (a one-hour drive) south of Yosemite Village.

3 Tuolumne Meadows. The highlight of east-central Yosemite is this wildflower-strewn valley with hiking trails, nestled among sharp, rocky peaks. It's a 1½-hour drive northeast of Yosemite Valley along Tioga Road (closed mid-October–late May).

4 Hetch Hetchy. The most remote, least visited part of Yosemite accessible by automobile, this glacial valley is dominated by a reservoir and veined with wilderness trails. It's near the park's western boundary, about a half-hour drive north of the Big Oak Flat entrance.

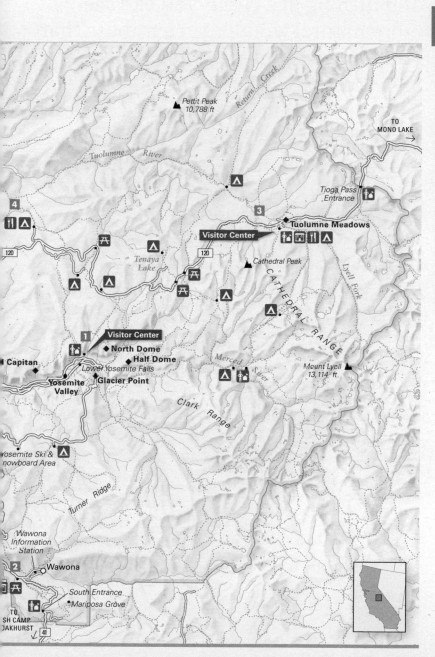

Pettit Peak
10,788 ft

TO
MONO LAKE

Tuolumne River

Return Creek

Tioga Pass
Entrance

3

Tuolumne Meadows

Visitor Center

4

120

Tenaya
Lake

120

Cathedral Peak

CATHEDRAL RANGE

Lyell Fork

1

Visitor Center

North Dome

Half Dome

Merced River

Mount Lyell
13,114 ft

Capitan

Lower Yosemite Falls

Yosemite
Valley

Glacier Point

Clark Range

Yosemite Ski &
Snowboard Area

Turner Ridge

Wawona
Information
Station

2

Wawona

South Entrance

Mariposa Grove

TO
SH CAMP
OAKHURST

41

By merely standing in Yosemite Valley and turning in a circle, you can see more natural wonders in a minute than you could in a full day pretty much anywhere else. Half Dome, Yosemite Falls, El Capitan, Bridalveil Fall, Sentinel Dome, the Merced River, white-flowering dogwood trees, maybe even bears ripping into the bark of fallen trees or sticking their snouts into beehives—it's all in Yosemite Valley.

In the mid-1800s, when tourists were arriving to the area, the valley's special geologic qualities and the giant sequoias of Mariposa Grove 30 miles to the south so impressed a group of influential Californians that they persuaded President Abraham Lincoln to grant those two areas to the state for protection on June 30, 1864. On October 1, 1890—thanks largely to lobbying efforts by naturalist John Muir and Robert Underwood Johnson, the editor of *Century Magazine*—Congress set aside an additional 1,500 square miles for Yosemite National Park; the valley and Mariposa Grove remained under state control until 1906, when they merged with the national park.

Planning

When to Go

During extremely busy periods—such as weekends and holidays throughout the year—you will experience delays at the entrance gates. For smaller crowds, visit midweek. Or come January through March, when the park is a bit less busy and the days usually are sunny and clear.

Summer rainfall is rare. In winter, heavy snows occasionally cause road closures, and tire chains or four-wheel drive may be required on the roads that remain open. The road to Glacier Point beyond the turnoff for Yosemite Ski & Snowboard Area is closed after the first major snowfall; Tioga Road is closed from late October through May or mid-June. Mariposa Grove Road is typically closed for a shorter period in winter.

Festivals and Events

Bluesapalooza
FESTIVAL | The first weekend of every August, Mammoth Lakes hosts a blues and beer festival—with an emphasis on the beer tasting. ⊠ *Mammoth Lakes* ☎ *888/992–7397* ⊕ *www.mammoth-bluesbrewsfest.com.*

The Bracebridge Dinner at Yosemite
FESTIVAL | Held at The Majestic Yosemite Hotel (formerly The Ahwahnee) in Yosemite Village every Christmas since 1928, this 17th-century-theme madrigal dinner is so popular that most seats are booked months in advance. Dinner costs $380; lodging packages start at $1,019, or $1,219 if you want to stay at The Majestic Yosemite Hotel. ⊠ *The Majestic Yosemite Hotel, 1 Ahwahnee Dr., Yosemite Village* ☎ *888/413–8869, 602/278–8888 international* ⊕ *www.travelyosemite.com.*

Fireman's Muster
FESTIVAL | North of Sonora in the old mining town of Columbia, history springs to life at this festival of antique fire engines, with hose-spraying contests and a parade of the old pumpers. ⊠ *Columbia* ☎ *209/533–4420, 800/446–1333.*

The Grand Grape Celebration
FESTIVAL | Some of California's most prestigious vintners hold two- and three-day midweek seminars in the Great Room of The Majestic Yosemite Hotel (formerly The Ahwahnee) in Yosemite Village. They culminate with an elegant—albeit pricey—banquet dinner. Arrive early for seats; book early for dinner ($208) and lodging and dining packages (from $317). ⊠ *Yosemite Village* ☎ *888/413–8869, 602/278–8888 international* ⊕ *www.travelyosemite.com.*

Mammoth Jazzfest
FESTIVAL | This weekend festival funded by the town of Mammoth Lakes features free jazz performances at The Village at Mammoth. ⊠ *Mammoth Lakes* ☎ *760/934–2712, 888/466–2666* ⊕ *www.mammothjazzfest.org.*

Mother Lode Roundup Parade and Rodeo
FESTIVAL | On Mother's Day weekend, the town of Sonora celebrates its gold-mining, agricultural, and lumbering heritage with a parade, rodeo, entertainment, and food. ⊠ *Sonora* ☎ *209/533–4420, 800/446–1333* ⊕ *www.motherloderoundup.com.*

Sierra Art Trails
FESTIVAL | The work of more than 100 artists is on display in studios and galleries throughout eastern Madera and Mariposa counties. Purchase the catalog of locations and hours at area shops. ☎ *559/658–8844* ⊕ *www.sierraarttrails.org.*

A Taste of Yosemite
FESTIVAL | Celebrated chefs present cooking demonstrations and multicourse meals at The Majestic Yosemite Hotel in Yosemite Village from mid-January to early February. Dinner-only costs $208. Two-night packages start at $297 per person; three- and four-night packages are also available. Space is limited. ⊠ *Yosemite Village* ☎ *888/413–8869, 602/278–8888 international* ⊕ *www.travelyosemite.com.*

Planning Your Time

YOSEMITE IN ONE DAY
Begin at the **Valley Visitor Center,** where you can watch the documentary *Spirit of Yosemite.* A minute's stroll from there is the **Native American village of the Ahwahnee,** which recalls Native American life circa 1870. Take another 20 minutes to see the **Yosemite Museum.** Then, hop aboard the free shuttle to Yosemite Falls and hike the **Lower Yosemite Fall Trail** to the base of the falls. Have lunch at **Yosemite Valley Lodge,** which you can access by shuttle or walk to from the falls in 20 minutes.

AVERAGE HIGH/LOW TEMPERATURES					
JAN.	FEB.	MAR.	APR.	MAY	JUNE
48/29	53/30	55/32	61/36	69/43	78/49
JULY	AUG.	SEPT.	OCT.	NOV.	DEC.
85/55	84/55	79/49	70/42	56/34	47/29

You can either leisurely explore **Half Dome Village (formerly Curry Village)**—by swimming or ice-skating, shopping, renting a bike, or having a beer on the deck; check out family-friendly **Happy Isles Art and Nature Center** and the adjacent nature trail; or hike up the **Mist Trail** to the Vernal Fall footbridge to admire the view.

Hop back on the shuttle, then disembark at **The Majestic Yosemite Hotel (formerly The Ahwahnee).** The Great Lounge here has a magnificent fireplace and Native American artwork; have a meal in the Dining Room if you're up for a splurge. Or, take the shuttle to **Yosemite Village** where you can grab some fixings, then drive to **El Capitan picnic area** and enjoy an outdoor evening meal. At this time of day, "El Cap" should be sun-splashed. (You will have also gotten several good looks at world-famous **Half Dome** throughout the day.) If the sun hasn't set yet, drive to the base of **Bridalveil Fall** to take a short hike.

Getting Here and Around

AIR TRAVEL

The closest airport to the south and west entrances is Fresno Yosemite International Airport (FAT). Mammoth Yosemite Airport (MMH) is closest to the east entrance. Sacramento International Airport (SMF) is also close to the north and west entrances.

BUS AND TRAIN TRAVEL

Amtrak's daily San Joaquin train stops in Merced and connects with YARTS buses that travel to Yosemite Valley along Highway 140 from Merced. Seasonal YARTS buses (typically mid-May to late September) also travel along Highway 41

from Fresno, Highway 120 from Sonora, and Highway 395 and Tioga Road from Mammoth Lakes with scheduled stops at towns along the way. Once you're in Yosemite Valley you can take advantage of the free shuttle buses, which operate on low emissions, have 21 stops, and run from 7 am to 10 pm year-round. Buses run about every 10 minutes in summer, a bit less frequently in winter. A separate (but also free) summer-only shuttle runs out to El Capitan. Also in summer, you can pay to take the "hikers' bus" from Yosemite Valley to Tuolumne or to ride a tour bus up to Glacier Point. During the snow season, buses run regularly between Yosemite Valley and Yosemite Ski & Snowboard Area.

CAR TRAVEL

Roughly 200 miles from San Francisco, 300 miles from Los Angeles, and 500 miles from Las Vegas, Yosemite takes a while to reach—and its many sites and attractions merit much more time than what rangers say is the average visit: four hours.

Of the park's four entrances, Arch Rock is the closest to Yosemite Valley. The road that goes through it, Route 140 from Merced and Mariposa, is a scenic western approach that snakes alongside the boulder-packed Merced River. Route 41, through Wawona, is the way to come from Los Angeles (or Fresno, if you've flown in and rented a car). Route 120, through Crane Flat, is the most direct route from San Francisco. The only way in from the east is Tioga Road, which may be the best route in terms of scenery—though due to snow accumulation it's open for a frustratingly short amount of time each year (typically early June through mid-October). Once you enter Yosemite Valley, park your car in one of the two main day parking areas, at Yosemite Village and Yosemite Falls, then visit the sights via the free shuttle bus system. Or walk or bike along the valley's 12 miles of paved paths.

There are few gas stations within Yosemite (Crane Flat and Wawona; none in the valley), so fuel up before you reach the park. From late fall until early spring, the weather is especially unpredictable, and driving can be treacherous. You should carry chains during this period as they are required when roads are icy and when it snows.

Park Essentials

ACCESSIBILITY

Yosemite's facilities are continually being upgraded to make them more accessible. Many of the valley floor trails—particularly at Lower Yosemite Fall, Bridalveil Fall, and Mirror Lake—are wheelchair accessible, though some assistance may be required. The Valley Visitor Center is fully accessible, as are the park shuttle buses. A sign-language interpreter is available for ranger programs. Visitors with respiratory difficulties should take note of the park's high elevations—the valley floor is approximately 4,000 feet above sea level, but Tuolumne Meadows and parts of the high country hover around 10,000 feet.

PARK FEES AND PERMITS

The admission fee, valid for seven days, is $35 per vehicle, $30 per motorcycle, or $20 per individual.

If you plan to camp in the backcountry or climb Half Dome, you must have a wilderness permit. Availability of permits depends upon trailhead quotas. It's best to make a reservation, especially if you will be visiting May through September. You can reserve two days to 24 weeks in advance by phone, mail, or fax (preferred method) (✉ Box 545, Yosemite, CA ☎ 209/372–0740 🖷 209/372–0739); you'll pay $5 per person plus $5 per reservation if and when your reservations are confirmed. You can download the reservation forms from ⊕ www.nps.gov/yose/planyourvisit/upload/wildpermitform.pdf. Without a reservation, you may still get a free permit on a first-come, first-served basis at wilderness permit offices at Big Oak Flat, Hetch Hetchy, Tuolumne Meadows, Wawona, the Wilderness Center in Yosemite Village, and Yosemite Valley in summer. From fall to spring, visit the Valley Visitor Center.

PARK HOURS

The park is open 24/7 year-round. All entrances are open at all hours, except for Hetch Hetchy entrance, which is open roughly dawn to dusk. Yosemite is in the Pacific time zone.

CELL PHONE RECEPTION

Cell phone reception depends on the service provider and can be hit or miss everywhere in the park. There are public telephones at park entrance stations, visitor centers, all restaurants and lodging facilities in the park, gas stations, and in Yosemite Village.

Educational Offerings

CLASSES AND SEMINARS
Art Classes

ARTS VENUE | Professional artists conduct workshops in watercolor, etching, drawing, and other mediums. Bring your own materials or purchase the basics at the Happy Isles Art and Nature Center. Children under 12 must be accompanied by an adult. The center also offers beginner art workshops and children's art and family craft programs ($5–$20 per person). ✉ Happy Isles Art and Nature Center ☎ 209/372–1442 ⊕ www.yosemiteconservancy.org 🎫 $20 ⊗ No classes Sun. Closed Dec.–Feb.

Yosemite Outdoor Adventures

TOUR—SIGHT | Naturalists, scientists, and park rangers lead multihour to multiday educational outings on topics from woodpeckers to fire management to pastel painting. Most sessions take place spring through fall, but a few focus on winter phenomena. ⊠ *Yosemite National Park* ☎ *209/379–2317* ⊕ *www.yosemiteconservancy.org* ⊒ *From $99.*

MUSEUMS

Happy Isles Art and Nature Center

MUSEUM | FAMILY | This family-focused center has a rotating selection of hands-on, kid-friendly exhibits that teach tykes and their parents about the park's ecosystem. Books, toys, T-shirts, and water bottles are stocked in the small gift shop. ⊠ *Yosemite National Park* ✛ *Off Southside Dr., about ¾ mile east of Half Dome Village* ☎ *209/372–0631* ⊒ *Free* ☾ *Closed Oct.–Apr.*

Yosemite Museum

MUSEUM | This small museum consists of a permanent exhibit that focuses on the history of the area and the people who once lived here. An adjacent gallery promotes contemporary and historic Yosemite art in revolving gallery exhibits. A docent demonstrates traditional Native American basket-weaving techniques a few days a week. ⊠ *Yosemite Village* ☎ *209/372–0299* ⊒ *Free.*

RANGER PROGRAMS

Junior Ranger Program

TOUR—SIGHT | FAMILY | Children ages seven and up can participate in the informal, self-guided Junior Ranger program. A park activity handbook is available at the Valley Visitor Center, the Happy Isles Art and Nature Center, and the Wawona Visitor Center. Once kids complete the book, rangers present them with a badge and, in some cases, a certificate. ⊠ *Valley Visitor Center or the Happy Isles Art & Nature Center* ☎ *209/372–0299.*

Ranger-Led Programs

TOUR—SIGHT | Rangers lead entertaining walks and give informative talks several times a day from spring to fall. The schedule is more limited in winter, but most days you can find a program somewhere in the park. In the evenings at Yosemite Valley Lodge and Half Dome Village, lectures, slide shows, and documentary films present unique perspectives on Yosemite. On summer weekends, campgrounds at Half Dome Village and Tuolumne Meadows host sing-along campfire programs. Schedules and locations are posted on bulletin boards throughout the park as well as in the indispensable *Yosemite Guide,* which is distributed to visitors as they arrive at the park. ⊠ *Yosemite National Park* ⊕ *nps.gov/yose.*

Restaurants

Yosemite National Park has a couple of moderately priced restaurants in lovely (which almost goes without saying) settings: the Mountain Room at Yosemite Valley Lodge and Big Trees Lodge's dining room. The Majestic Yosemite Hotel (formerly The Ahwahnee) provides one of the finest dining experiences in the country.

Otherwise, food service is geared toward satisfying the masses as efficiently as possible. Yosemite Valley Lodge's Base Camp Eatery is the valley's best lower-cost, hot-food option, with Italian, classic American, and world flavor counter options; Half Dome Village Pavilion's offerings are overpriced and usually fairly bland, but you can get decent pizzas on the adjacent outdoor deck. In Yosemite Valley Village, the Village Grill whips up burgers and fries, Degnan's Kitchen has made-to-order sandwiches, and The Loft at Degnan's has a chalet-like open dining area in which you can enjoy pizza, salads, rice bowls, and desserts.

The White Wolf Lodge and Tuolumne Meadows Lodge—both off Tioga Road and therefore guaranteed open only from early June through September—have small restaurants where meals are competently prepared. Tuolumne Meadows also has a grill, and the gift shop at Glacier Point sells premade sandwiches, snacks, and hot dogs. During the ski season you'll also find one at Yosemite Ski & Snowboard Area, off Glacier Point Road.

Hotels

Indoor lodging options inside the park appear more expensive than initially seems warranted, but that premium pays off big-time in terms of the time you'll save—unless you are bunking within a few miles of a Yosemite entrance, you will face long commutes to the park when you stay outside its borders (though the Yosemite View Lodge, on Route 140, is within a reasonable half-hour's drive of Yosemite Valley).

Because of Yosemite National Park's immense popularity—not just with tourists from around the world but with Northern Californians who make weekend trips here—reservations are all but mandatory. Book up to one year ahead. ■TIP→ If you're not set on a specific hotel or camp but just want to stay somewhere inside the park, call the main reservation number to check for availability and reserve (888/413–8869 or 602/278–8888 international). Park lodgings have a seven-day cancellation policy, so you may be able to snag last-minute reservations.

⚠ A trademark dispute with the former park concessioner, Delaware North, has resulted in Yosemite National Park changing the names of several historic park lodges and properties, including the iconic Ahwahnee. This guide uses the new names: Yosemite Lodge at the Falls is now Yosemite Valley Lodge; The Ahwahnee is now The Majestic Yosemite Hotel; Curry Village is now Half Dome Village; Wawona Hotel is now Big

Trees Lodge; and Badger Pass Ski Area is now Yosemite Ski & Snowboard Area. For the latest information visit the Yosemite National Park website.

Hotel reviews have been shortened. For full information, visit Fodors.com.

What It Costs			
$	$$	$$$	$$$$
RESTAURANTS			
under $12	$12–$20	$21–$30	over $30
HOTELS			
under $100	$100–$150	$151–$200	over $200

Tours

★ **Ansel Adams Camera Walks**
SPECIAL-INTEREST | Photography enthusiasts shouldn't miss these 90-minute guided camera walks offered four mornings (Monday, Tuesday, Thursday, and Saturday) each week by professional photographers. All are free, but participation is limited to 15 people. Meeting points vary, and advance reservations are essential. ✉ *Yosemite National Park* ☎ *209/372–4413* ⊕ *www.anseladams. com* ⌫ *Free.*

Discover Yosemite
GUIDED TOURS | This outfit operates daily tours to Yosemite Valley, Mariposa Grove, and Glacier Point in 14- and 29-passenger vehicles. The tour travels along Highway 41 with stops in Bass Lake, Oakhurst, and Fish Camp; rates include lunch. Sunset tours to Sentinel Dome are additional summer options. ☎ *559/642–4400* ⊕ *www.discoveryo-semite.com* ⌫ *From $152.*

Glacier Point Tour
GUIDED TOURS | This four-hour trip takes you from Yosemite Valley to the Glacier Point vista, 3,214 feet above the valley floor. Some people buy a $26 one-way

ticket and hike down. Shuttles depart from the Yosemite Valley Lodge three times a day. ✉ *Yosemite National Park* ☎ *888/413–8869* ⊕ *www.travelyosemite. com* ✉ *From $52* ⊙ *Closed Nov.–late May* ⚹ *Reservations essential.*

Grand Tour

TOUR—SIGHT | For a full-day tour of Yosemite Valley, the Mariposa Grove of Giant Sequoias and Glacier Point, try the Grand Tour, which departs from the Yosemite Valley Lodge in the valley. The tour stops for a picnic lunch (included) at the historic Big Trees Lodge. ✉ *Yosemite National Park* ☎ *209/372–1240* ⊕ *www. yosemitepark.com* ✉ *$102* ⚹ *Reservations essential.*

Moonlight Tour

TOUR—SIGHT | This after-dark version of the Valley Floor Tour takes place on moonlit nights from June through September, depending on weather conditions. ✉ *Yosemite National Park* ☎ *209/372–4386* ⊕ *www.travelyosemite.com* ✉ *$37.*

Tuolumne Meadows Hikers Bus

BUS TOURS | For a full day's outing to the high country, opt for this ride up Tioga Road to Tuolumne Meadows. You'll stop at several overlooks, and you can connect with another shuttle at Tuolumne Lodge. This service is mostly for hikers and backpackers who want to reach high-country trailheads, but everyone is welcome. ✉ *Yosemite National Park* ☎ *209/372– 1240* ⊕ *www.travelyosemite.com* ✉ *$15 one-way, $23 round-trip* ⊙ *Closed Labor Day–mid-June* ⚹ *Reservations essential.*

Valley Floor Tour

GUIDED TOURS | Take a two-hour tour of Yosemite Valley's highlights, complete with narration on the area's history, geology, and flora and fauna. Tours are either in trams or enclosed motor coaches, depending on weather conditions. Tours run year-round. ✉ *Yosemite National Park* ☎ *209/372–1240, 888/413–8869 reservations* ⊕ *www.travelyosemite.com* ✉ *From $37.*

Wee Wild Ones

TOUR—SIGHT | **FAMILY** | Designed for kids under 10, this 45-minute program includes naturalist-led games, songs, stories, and crafts about Yosemite wildlife, plants, and geology. The event is held outdoors before the regular Yosemite Valley Lodge evening programs in summer and fall. All children must be accompanied by an adult. ✉ *Yosemite National Park* ☎ *209/372–1153* ⊕ *www. travelyosemite.com* ✉ *Free.*

Visitor Information

PARK CONTACT INFORMATION Yosemite National Park. ☎ *209/372–0200* ⊕ *www. nps.gov/yose.*

VISITOR CENTERS

Valley Visitor Center

INFO CENTER | Learn about Yosemite Valley's geology, vegetation, and human inhabitants at this visitor center, which is also staffed with helpful rangers and contains a bookstore with a wide selection of books and maps. Two films, including one by Ken Burns, alternate on the half hour in the theater behind the visitor center. ✉ *Yosemite Village* ☎ *209/372–0200* ⊕ *www.nps.gov/yose.*

Yosemite Conservation Heritage Center

INFO CENTER | This small but striking National Historic Landmark (formerly Le Conte Memorial Lodge), with its granite walls and steeply pitched shingle roof, is Yosemite's first permanent public information center. Step inside to see the cathedral-like interior, which contains a library and environmental exhibits. To find out about evening programs, check the kiosk out front. ✉ *Southside Dr., about ½ mile west of Half Dome Village* ⊕ *sierraclub.org/yosemite-heritage-center* ⊙ *Closed Mon., Tues., and Oct.–Apr.*

Did You Know?

A "firefall" appears once a year in February at Horsetail Falls when the sun illuminates the water at the perfect angle.

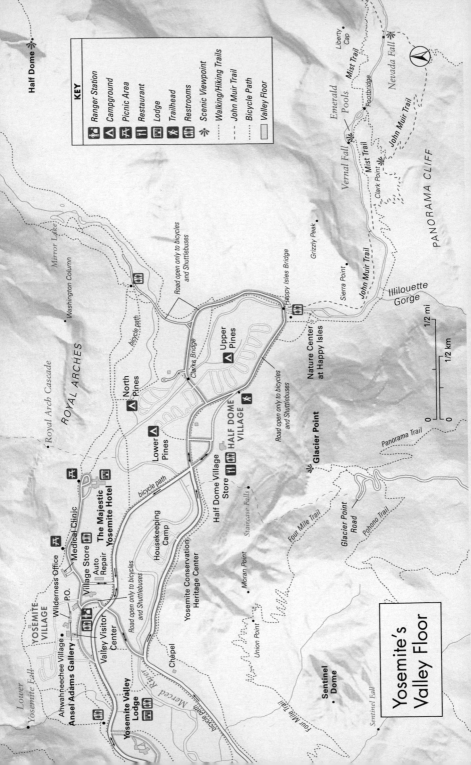

Yosemite's Valley Floor

KEY

- ▲ Ranger Station
- ◢ Campground
- ⋔ Picnic Area
- ¶ Restaurant
- ⌂ Lodge
- ⚑ Trailhead
- ⚑ Restrooms
- ✳ Scenic Viewpoint
- ⋯⋯ Walking/Hiking Trails
- – – – John Muir Trail
- ····· Bicycle Path
- ▭ Valley Floor

Half Dome

Liberty Cap

Nevada Fall

Mist Trail

Emerald Pools

Vernal Fall

Mist Trail

Footbridge

Clark Point

John Muir Trail

Sierra Point

PANORAMA CLIFF

Ililouette Gorge

Grizzly Peak

Happy Isles Bridge

Nature Center at Happy Isles

Road open only to bicycles and Shuttlebuses

Upper Pines

North Pines

Clarks Bridge

bicycle path

Royal Arch Cascade

ROYAL ARCHES

Washington Column

Mirror Lake

Lower Pines

HALF DOME VILLAGE

Half Dome Village Store

Housekeeping Camp

Yosemite Conservation Heritage Center

Staircase Falls

Glacier Point

Four Mile Trail

Glacier Point Road

Pohono Trail

Panorama Trail

Moran Point

Union Point

Sentinel Dome

Sentinel Fall

Four Mile Trail

bicycle path

Merced River

Chapel

Yosemite Valley Lodge

Ansel Adams Gallery

Ahwahneechee Village

YOSEMITE VILLAGE

Wilderness Office

P.O.

Medical Clinic

The Majestic Yosemite Hotel

Village Store

Auto Repair

Valley Visitor Center

Road open only to bicycles and Shuttlebuses

Lower Yosemite Fall

1/2 mi

1/2 km

0

0

☺ Sights

SCENIC DRIVE

Tioga Road

SCENIC DRIVE | Few mountain drives can compare with this 59-mile road, especially its eastern half between Lee Vining and Olmstead Point. As you climb 3,200 feet to the 9,945-foot summit of Tioga Pass (Yosemite's sole eastern entrance for cars), you'll encounter broad vistas of the granite-splotched High Sierra and its craggy but hearty trees and shrubs. Past the bustling scene at Tuolumne Meadows, you'll see picturesque Tenaya Lake and then Olmstead Point, where you'll get your first peek at Half Dome. Driving Tioga Road one way takes approximately 1½ hours. Wildflowers bloom here in July and August. By November, the high-altitude road closes for the winter; it sometimes doesn't reopen until early June. ⊠ *Yosemite National Park.*

HISTORIC SITES

Big Trees Lodge

HOTEL—SIGHT | Imagine a white-bearded Mark Twain relaxing in a rocking chair on one of the broad verandas of one of the park's first lodges (formerly the Wawona Hotel), a whitewashed series of two-story buildings from the Victorian era. Plop down in one of the dozens of white Adirondack chairs on the sprawling lawn and look across the road at the area's only golf course, one of the few links in the world that does not employ fertilizers or other chemicals. ⊠ *Rte. 41, Wawona* ☎ *209/375–1425* ⊕ *www.travelyosemite. com/lodging/big-trees-lodge/* ⊘ *Closed Dec.–Mar. except 2 wks around Christmas and New Year's.*

Half Dome Village

HOTEL—SIGHT | A couple of schoolteachers from Indiana founded Camp Curry in 1899 as a low-cost option for staying in the valley, which it remains today. Half Dome Village's 400-plus lodging options (formerly Curry Village), many of them tent cabins, are spread over a large chunk of the valley's southeastern side. This is one family-friendly place, but it's more functional than attractive. ⊠ *Southside Dr., about ½ mile east of Yosemite Village.*

Indian Village of Ahwahnee

MUSEUM VILLAGE | This solemn smattering of structures, accessed by a short loop trail behind the Yosemite Valley Visitor Center, is a look at what Native American life might have been like in the 1870s. One interpretive sign points out that the Miwok people referred to the 19th-century newcomers as "Yohemite" or "Yohometuk," which have been translated as meaning "some of them are killers." ⊠ *Northside Dr., Yosemite Village* ⌗ *Free.*

The Majestic Yosemite Hotel

HOTEL—SIGHT | Gilbert Stanley Underwood, architect of the Grand Canyon Lodge, also designed The Majestic Yosemite Hotel (formerly The Ahwahnee hotel). Opened in 1927, it is generally considered his best work. You can stay here (for about $500 a night), or simply explore the first-floor shops and perhaps have breakfast or lunch in the bustling and beautiful Dining Room or more casual bar. The Great Lounge, 77 feet long with magnificent 24-foot-high ceilings and all manner of artwork on display, beckons with big, comfortable chairs and relative calm. ⊠ *Ahwahnee Rd., about ¾ mile east of Yosemite Valley Visitor Center, Yosemite Village* ☎ *209/372–1489* ⊕ *www.travelyosemite.com/lodging/ the-majestic-yosemite-hotel/.*

Pioneer Yosemite History Center

MUSEUM | FAMILY | These historic buildings reflect different eras of Yosemite's history, starting in the 1850s through the early 1900s. They were moved to Wawona (the largest stage stop in Yosemite in the late 1800s) from various areas of Yosemite in the '50s and '60s. There is a self-guided-tour pamphlet available for 50¢. Weekends and some weekdays in the summer, costumed docents conduct free blacksmithing and "wet-plate" photography demonstrations, and for a

Plants and Wildlife in Yosemite

Dense stands of incense cedar and Douglas fir—as well as ponderosa, Jeffrey, lodgepole, and sugar pines—cover much of the park, but the stellar standout, quite literally, is the *Sequoiadendron giganteum*, the giant sequoia. Sequoias grow only along the west slope of the Sierra Nevada between 4,500 and 7,000 feet in elevation. Starting from a seed the size of a rolled-oat flake, each of these ancient monuments assumes remarkable proportions in adulthood; you can see them in the Mariposa Grove of Giant Sequoias. In late May the valley's dogwood trees bloom with white, starlike flowers. Wildflowers, such as black-eyed Susan, bull thistle, cow parsnip, lupine, and meadow goldenrod, peak in June in the valley and in July at higher elevations.

The most visible animals in the park—aside from the omnipresent western gray squirrels, which fearlessly attempt to steal your food at every campground and picnic site—are the mule deer. Though sightings of bighorn sheep are infrequent in the park itself, you can sometimes see them on the eastern side of the Sierra Crest, just off Route 120 in Lee Vining Canyon. You may also see the American black bear, which often has a brown, cinnamon, or blond coat. The Sierra Nevada is home to thousands of bears, and you should take all necessary precautions to keep yourself—and the bears—safe. Bears that acquire a taste for human food can become very aggressive and destructive and often must be destroyed by rangers, so store all your food and even scented toiletries in the bear lockers located at many campgrounds and trailheads, or use bear-resistant canisters if you'll be hiking in the backcountry.

Watch for the blue Steller's jay along trails, near public buildings, and in campgrounds, and look for golden eagles soaring over Tioga Road.

small fee you can take a stagecoach ride. ✉ *Rte. 41, Wawona* ☎ *209/375–9531* ⊕ *www.nps.gov/yose/planyourvisit/waw. htm* 🎟 *Free* ⊘ *Closed Mon., Tues., and mid-Sept.–early June.*

SCENIC STOPS

El Capitan

NATURE SITE | Rising 3,593 feet—more than 350 stories—above the valley, El Capitan is the largest exposed-granite monolith in the world. Since 1958, people have been climbing its entire face, including the famous "nose." You can spot adventurers with your binoculars by scanning the smooth and nearly vertical cliff for specks of color. ✉ *Yosemite National Park* ✚ *Off Northside Dr., about 4 miles west of Valley Visitor Center.*

★ Glacier Point

VIEWPOINT | If you lack the time, desire, or stamina to hike more than 3,200 feet up to Glacier Point from the Yosemite Valley floor, you can drive here—or take a bus from the valley—for a bird's-eye view. You are likely to encounter a lot of day-trippers on the short, paved trail that leads from the parking lot to the main overlook. Take a moment to veer off a few yards to the Geology Hut, which succinctly explains and illustrates what the valley looked like 10 million, 3 million, and 20,000 years ago. ✉ *Yosemite National Park* ✚ *Glacier Point Rd., 16 miles northeast of Rte. 41* ☎ *209/372–0200* ⊘ *Closed late Oct.–mid-May.*

★ Half Dome

NATURE SITE | Visitors' eyes are continually drawn to this remarkable granite formation that tops out at more than 4,700 feet above the valley floor. Despite its name, the dome is actually about three-quarters intact. You can hike to the top of Half Dome on an 8.5-mile (one-way) trail whose last 400 feet must be ascended while holding onto a steel cable. Permits are required (and checked on the trail), and available only by lottery. Call ☎ 877/444–6777 or visit ⊕ www. recreation.gov well in advance of your trip for details. Back down in the valley, see Half Dome reflected in the Merced River by heading to Sentinel Bridge just before sundown. The brilliant orange light on Half Dome is a stunning sight. ⊠ Yosemite National Park ⊕ www.nps.gov/yose/planyourvisit/halfdome.htm.

Hetch Hetchy Reservoir

BODY OF WATER | When Congress approved the O'Shaughnessy Dam in 1913, pragmatism triumphed over aestheticism. Some 2.5 million residents of the San Francisco Bay Area continue to get their water from this 117-billion-gallon reservoir. Although spirited efforts are being made to restore the Hetch Hetchy Valley to its former, pristine glory, three-quarters of San Francisco voters in 2012 ultimately opposed a measure to even consider draining the reservoir. Eight miles long, the reservoir is Yosemite's largest body of water, and one that can be seen up close from several trails. ⊠ Hetch Hetchy Rd., about 15 miles north of Big Oak Flat entrance station.

High Country

NATURE PRESERVE | The above-tree-line, high-alpine region east of the valley—a land of alpenglow and top-of-the-world vistas—is often missed by crowds who come to gawk at the more publicized splendors. Summer wildflowers, which usually pop up mid-July through August, carpet the meadows and mountainsides with pink, purple, blue, red, yellow, and orange. On foot or on horseback are the only ways to get here. For information on trails and backcountry permits, check with the visitor center. ⊠ Yosemite National Park.

Mariposa Grove of Giant Sequoias

FOREST | Of Yosemite's three sequoia groves—the others being Merced and Tuolumne, both near Crane Flat well to the north—Mariposa is by far the largest and easiest to walk around. Grizzly Giant, whose base measures 96 feet around, has been estimated to be one of the largest in the world. Perhaps more astoundingly, it's about 1,800 years old. Park at the grove's welcome plaza and ride the free shuttle (required most of the year). Summer weekends are usually crowded here. ⊠ Yosemite National Park ✛ Rte. 41, 2 miles north of south entrance station ⊕ www.nps.gov/yose/planyourvisit/mg.htm.

Sentinel Dome

VIEWPOINT | The view from here is similar to that from Glacier Point, except you can't see the valley floor. A moderately steep 1.1-mile path climbs to the viewpoint from the parking lot. Topping out at an elevation of 8,122 feet, Sentinel is more than 900 feet higher than Glacier Point. ⊠ Glacier Point Rd., off Rte. 41.

Tuolumne Meadows

MOUNTAIN—SIGHT | The largest subalpine meadow in the Sierra (at 8,600 feet) is a popular way station for backpack trips along the Pacific Crest and John Muir trails. The setting is not as dramatic as Yosemite Valley, 56 miles away, but the almost perfectly flat basin, about 2½ miles long, is intriguing, and in July it's resplendent with wildflowers. The most popular day hike is up Lembert Dome, atop which you'll have breathtaking views of the basin below. Keep in mind that Tioga Road rarely opens before June and usually closes by mid-October. ⊠ Tioga Rd. (Rte. 120), about 8 miles west of Tioga Pass entrance station.

WATERFALLS

Yosemite's waterfalls are at their most spectacular in May and June. When the snow starts to melt (usually peaking in May), streaming snowmelt spills down to meet the Merced River. By summer's end, some falls, including the mighty Yosemite Falls, trickle or dry up. Their flow increases in late fall, and in winter they may be hung dramatically with ice. Even in drier months, the waterfalls can be breathtaking. If you choose to hike any of the trails to or up the falls, be sure to wear shoes with no-slip soles; the rocks can be extremely slick. Stay on trails at all times.

■TIP→ **Visit the park during a full moon and you can stroll without a flashlight and still make out the ribbons of falling water, as well as silhouettes of the giant granite monoliths.**

Bridalveil Fall

BODY OF WATER | This 620-foot waterfall is often diverted dozens of feet one way or the other by the breeze. It is the first marvelous site you will see up close when you drive into Yosemite Valley. ⊠ *Yosemite Valley, access from parking area off Wawona Rd.*

Nevada Fall

BODY OF WATER | Climb Mist Trail from Happy Isles for an up-close view of this 594-foot cascading beauty. If you don't want to hike (the trail's final approach is quite taxing), you can see it—albeit distantly—from Glacier Point. Stay safely on the trail, as there have been fatalities in recent years after visitors have fallen and been swept away by the water. ⊠ *Yosemite Valley, access via Mist Trail from Nature Center at Happy Isles.*

Ribbon Fall

BODY OF WATER | At 1,612 feet, this is the highest single fall in North America. It's also the first waterfall to dry up in summer; the rainwater and melted snow that create the slender fall evaporate quickly at this height. Look just west of El Capitan for the best view of the fall from the base of Bridalveil Fall. ⊠ *Yosemite Valley, west of El Capitan Meadow.*

Vernal Fall

BODY OF WATER | Fern-covered black rocks frame this 317-foot fall, and rainbows play in the spray at its base. You can get a distant view from Glacier Point, or hike to see it close up. You'll get wet, but the view is worth it. ⊠ *Yosemite Valley, access via Mist Trail from Nature Center at Happy Isles.*

★ Yosemite Falls

BODY OF WATER | Actually three falls, they together constitute the highest combined waterfall in North America and the fifth highest in the world. The water from the top descends a total of 2,425 feet, and when the falls run hard, you can hear them thunder across the valley. If they dry up—that sometimes happens in late summer—the valley seems naked without the wavering tower of spray. If you hike the mile-long loop trail (partially paved) to the base of the Lower Fall in spring, prepare to get wet. You can get a good full-length view of the falls from the lawn of Yosemite Chapel, off Southside Drive. ⊠ *Yosemite Valley, access from Yosemite Valley Lodge or trail parking area.*

🏃 Activities

BIKING

One enjoyable way to see Yosemite Valley is to ride a bike beneath its lofty granite monoliths. The eastern valley has 12 miles of paved, flat bicycle paths across meadows and through woods, with bike racks at convenient stopping points. For a greater challenge but at no small risk, you can ride on 196 miles of paved park roads—but bicycles are not allowed on hiking trails or in the backcountry. Kids under 18 must wear a helmet.

Yosemite bike rentals

BICYCLING | You can arrange for rentals from Yosemite Valley Lodge and Half Dome Village bike stands. Bikes with

Half Dome at sunset.

child trailers, baby-jogger strollers, and wheelchairs are also available. The cost for bikes is $12 per hour, or $33.50 a day. ⊠ *Yosemite Valley Lodge or Half Dome Village* ☎ *209/372–4386* ⊕ *www. travelyosemite.com.*

BIRD-WATCHING

More than 250 bird species have been spotted in the park, including the sage sparrow, pygmy owl, blue grouse, and mountain bluebird. Park rangers lead free bird-watching walks in Yosemite Valley a few days each week in summer; check at a visitor center or information station for times and locations. Binoculars sometimes are available for loan.

Birding seminars

BIRD WATCHING | The Yosemite Conservancy organizes day- and weekend-long seminars for beginner and intermediate birders, as well as bird walks a few times a week. They can also arrange private naturalist-led walks any time of year. ⊠ *Yosemite National Park* ☎ *209/379–2321* ⊕ *www.yosemitecon-servancy.org* ⊠ *From $99.*

FISHING

The waters in Yosemite are not stocked; trout, mostly brown and rainbow, live here but are not plentiful. Yosemite's fishing season begins on the last Saturday in April and ends on November 15. Some waterways are off-limits at certain times; be sure to inquire at the visitor center about regulations.

A California fishing license is required; licenses cost around $16 for one day, $24 for two days, and $48 for 10 days. Full-season licenses cost $48 for state residents and $130 for nonresidents (costs fluctuate year to year). Buy your license in season at **Yosemite Mountain Shop in Half Dome Village** (☎ *209/372–1286*) or at the **Big Trees General Store** (☎ *209/375–6574*).

HIKING

Wilderness Center

HIKING/WALKING | This facility provides free wilderness permits, which are required for overnight camping (advance reservations are available for $5 per person plus $5 per reservation and are highly recommended for popular trailheads in summer and on weekends). The staff here also provides maps and advice to hikers heading into the backcountry, and rents and sells bear-resistant canisters, which are required if you don't have your own. ⊠ *Between Ansel Adams Gallery and post office, Yosemite Village* ☎ *209/372–0308.*

Yosemite Mountaineering School and Guide Service

HIKING/WALKING | From April to November, you can learn to climb, hire a guide, or join a two-hour to full-day trek with Yosemite Mountaineering School. They also rent gear and lead backpacking and overnight excursions. Reservations are recommended. In winter, cross-country ski programs are available at Yosemite Ski & Snowboard Area. ⊠ *Yosemite Mountain Shop, Half Dome Village* ☎ *209/372–8344* ⊕ *yosemitemountaineering.com.*

Cook's Meadow Loop

HIKING/WALKING | FAMILY | Take this 1-mile, wheelchair-accessible, looped path around Cook's Meadow to see and learn the basics about Yosemite Valley's past, present, and future. A self-guiding trail guide (available at a kiosk just outside the entrance) explains how to tell oaks, cedars, and pines apart; how fires help keep the forest floor healthy; and how pollution poses significant challenges to the park's inhabitants. *Easy.* ⊠ *Yosemite National Park* ⊹ *Trailhead: across from Valley Visitor Center.*

Chilnualna Falls Trail

HIKING/WALKING | This Wawona-area trail runs 4 miles one way to the top of the falls, then leads into the backcountry, connecting with miles of other trails. This is one of the park's most inspiring and secluded—albeit strenuous—trails. Past the tumbling cascade, and up through forests, you'll emerge before a panoramic vista at the top. *Difficult.* ⊠ *Wawona* ⊹ *Trailhead: at Chilnualna Falls Rd., off Rte. 41.*

★ John Muir Trail to Half Dome

HIKING/WALKING | Ardent and courageous trekkers continue on from Nevada Fall to the top of Half Dome. Some hikers attempt this entire 10- to 12-hour, 16¾-mile round-trip trek in one day; if you're planning to do this, remember that the 4,800-foot elevation gain and the 8,842-foot altitude will cause shortness of breath. Another option is to hike to a campground in Little Yosemite Valley near the top of Nevada Fall the first day, then climb to the top of Half Dome and hike out the next day. Get your wilderness permit (required for a one-day hike to Half Dome, too) at least a month in advance. Be sure to wear hiking boots and bring gloves. The last pitch up the back of Half Dome is very steep—the only way to climb this sheer rock face is to pull yourself up using the steel cable handrails, which are in place only from late spring to early fall. Those who brave the ascent will be rewarded with an unbeatable view of Yosemite Valley below and the high country beyond. Only 300 hikers per day are allowed atop Half Dome, and they all must have permits, which are distributed by lottery, one in the spring before the season starts and another two days before the climb. Contact ⊕ *www.recreation.gov* for details. *Difficult.* ⊠ *Yosemite National Park* ⊹ *Trailhead: at Happy Isles* ⊕ *www.nps.gov/yose/planyourvisit/halfdome.htm.*

Mist Trail

HIKING/WALKING | Except for Lower Yosemite Fall, more visitors take this trail (or portions of it) than any other in the park. The trek up to and back from Vernal Fall is 3 miles. Add another 4 miles total by continuing up to 594-foot Nevada Fall; the trail becomes quite steep and slippery in its final stages. The elevation gain to Vernal Fall is 1,000 feet, and to Nevada Fall an additional 1,000 feet. The Merced River tumbles down both falls on its way to a tranquil flow through the valley. *Moderate.* ⊠ *Yosemite National Park* ⊹ *Trailhead: at Happy Isles.*

Ansel Adams's Black-and-White Yosemite 👁

What John Muir did for Yosemite with words, Ansel Adams did with photographs. His photographs have inspired millions of people to visit Yosemite, and his persistent activism helped to ensure the park's conservation.

Born in 1902, Adams first came to the valley when he was 14, photographing it with a Box Brownie camera. He later said his first visit "was a culmination of experience so intense as to be almost painful. From that day in 1916 my life has been colored and modulated by the great earth gesture of the Sierra." By 1919 he was working in the valley, as custodian of LeConte Memorial Lodge (now called Yosemite Conservation Heritage Center), the Sierra Club headquarters in Yosemite National Park.

Adams had harbored dreams of a career as a concert pianist, but the park sealed his fate as a photographer in 1928, the day he shot *Monolith: The Face of Half Dome*, which remains one of his most famous works. Adams also married Virginia Best in 1928, in her father's studio in the valley (now the Ansel Adams Gallery).

As Adams's photographic career took off, Yosemite began to sear itself into the American consciousness. David Brower, first executive director of the Sierra Club, later said of Adams's impact, "That Ansel Adams came to be recognized as one of the great photographers of this century is a tribute to the places that informed him."

In 1934 Adams was elected to the Sierra Club's board of directors; he would serve until 1971. As a representative of the conservation group, he combined his work with the club's mission, showing his photographs of the Sierra to influential officials such as Secretary of the Interior Harold L. Ickes, who showed them to President Franklin Delano Roosevelt. The images were a key factor in the establishment of Kings Canyon National Park.

In 1968, the Department of the Interior granted Adams its highest honor, the Conservation Service Award, and in 1980 he received the Presidential Medal of Freedom in recognition of his conservation work. Until his death in 1984, Adams continued not only to record Yosemite's majesty on film but to urge the federal government and park managers to do right by the park.

In one of his many public pleas on behalf of Yosemite, Adams said, "Yosemite Valley itself is one of the great shrines of the world and— belonging to all our people—must be both protected and appropriately accessible." As an artist and an activist, Adams never gave up on his dream of keeping Yosemite wild yet within reach of every visitor who wants to experience that wildness.

Did You Know?

Yosemite's Merced River formed roughly 10 million years ago as the surrounding Sierra Nevada Mountain range rose up.

★ Panorama Trail

HIKING/WALKING | Few hikes come with the visual punch that this 8½-mile trail provides. It starts from Glacier Point and descends to Yosemite Valley. The star attraction is Half Dome, visible from many intriguing angles, but you also see three waterfalls up close and walk through a manzanita grove. *Moderate.* ⊠ *Yosemite National Park* ✚ *Trailhead: at Glacier Point.*

★ Yosemite Falls Trail

HIKING/WALKING | Yosemite Falls is the highest waterfall in North America. The upper fall (1,430 feet), the middle cascades (675 feet), and the lower fall (320 feet) combine for a total of 2,425 feet, and when viewed from the valley appear as a single waterfall. The ¼-mile trail leads from the parking lot to the base of the falls. Upper Yosemite Fall Trail, a strenuous 7.2-mile round-trip climb rising 2,700 feet, takes you above the top of the falls. Lower trail: *Easy.* Upper trail: *Difficult.* ⊠ *Yosemite National Park* ✚ *Trailhead: off Camp 4, north of Northside Dr.*

HORSEBACK RIDING

Reservations for guided trail rides must be made in advance at the hotel tour desks or by phone. Scenic trail rides range from two hours to a half day; four- and six-day High Sierra saddle trips are also available.

Big Trees Stable

HORSEBACK RIDING | Two-hour rides at these stables start at $67, and a challenging full-day ride to the Mariposa Grove of Giant Sequoias (for experienced riders in good physical condition only) costs $140. Reservations are recommended. ⊠ *Rte. 41, Wawona* ☎ *209/375–6502* ⊕ *www. travelyosemite.com/things-to-do/horseback-mule-riding/* ⊞ *From $67.*

RAFTING

Rafting is permitted only on designated areas of the Middle and South forks of the Merced River. Check with the Valley Visitor Center for closures and other restrictions.

Half Dome Village Recreation Center

WHITE-WATER RAFTING | The per-person rental fee ($33) at Half Dome Village Recreation Center covers the four- to six-person raft, two paddles, and life jackets, plus a return shuttle at the end of your trip. ⊠ *South side of Southside Dr., Half Dome Village* ☎ *209/372–4386* ⊕ *www.travelyosemite.com/things-to-do/rafting/* ⊞ *From $33.*

ROCK CLIMBING

The granite canyon walls of Yosemite Valley are world renowned for rock climbing. El Capitan, with its 3,593-foot vertical face, is the most famous, but there are many other options here for all skill levels.

Yosemite Mountaineering School & Guide Service

CLIMBING/MOUNTAINEERING | The one-day basic lesson at Yosemite Mountaineering School and Guide Service includes some bouldering and rappelling, and three or four 60-foot climbs. Climbers must be at least 10 years old and in reasonably good physical condition. Intermediate and advanced classes include instruction in first aid, anchor building, multipitch climbing, summer snow climbing, and big-wall climbing. There's a Nordic program in the winter. ⊠ *Yosemite Mountain Shop, Half Dome Village* ☎ *209/372–8444* ⊕ *www.travelyosemite.com* ⊞ *From $172.*

SWIMMING

The pools at **Half Dome Village** (☎ *209/372–8324* ⊕ *www.travelyosemite.com*) and **Yosemite Valley Lodge** (☎ *209/372–1250* ⊕ *www.travelyosemite. com*) are open to nonguests for $5, late May through early or mid-September. Additionally, several swimming holes with small sandy beaches can be found in midsummer along the Merced River at the eastern end of Yosemite Valley. Find gentle waters to swim; currents are often stronger than they appear, and temperatures are chilling. To conserve riparian habitats, step into the river at sandy beaches and other obvious entry points. ■TIP→ **Do not attempt to swim above or near waterfalls or rapids; people have died trying.**

WINTER ACTIVITIES

The beauty of Yosemite under a blanket of snow has long inspired poets and artists, as well as ordinary folks. Skiing and snowshoeing activities in the park center on Yosemite Ski & Snowboard Area, California's oldest snow-sports resort, which is about 40 minutes away from the valley on Glacier Point Road. Here you can rent equipment, take a lesson, have lunch, join a guided excursion, and take the free shuttle back to the valley after a drink in the lounge.

ICE-SKATING
Half Dome Village Ice Rink

ICE SKATING | Winter visitors have skated at this outdoor rink for decades, and there's no mystery why: it's a kick to glide across the ice while soaking up views of Half Dome and Glacier Point. ⊠ *South side of Southside Dr., Half Dome Village* ☎ *209/372–8319* ⊕ *www. travelyosemite.com* ➤ *$10 per session, $4 skate rental.*

SKIING AND SNOWSHOEING
Yosemite Ski & Snowboard Area

SKIING/SNOWBOARDING | California's first ski resort has five lifts and 10 downhill runs, as well as 90 miles of groomed cross-country trails. Free shuttle buses from Yosemite Valley operate between December and the end of March, weather permitting. Lessons, backcountry guiding, and cross-country and snowshoeing tours are also available. You can rent downhill, telemark, and cross-country skis, plus snowshoes and snowboards. **Facilities:** 10 trails; 90 acres; 800-foot vertical drop; 5 lifts. ⊠ *Yosemite National Park ⊹ Badger Pass Rd., off Glacier Point Rd., 18 miles from Yosemite Valley* ☎ *209/372–8430* ⊕ *www.travelyosemite. com/winter/yosemite-ski-snowboard-area/* ➤ *Lift ticket: from $55.*

Yosemite Cross-Country Ski School

SKIING/SNOWBOARDING | The highlight of Yosemite's cross-country skiing center is a 21-mile loop from Yosemite Ski & Snowboard Area to Glacier Point. You can rent cross-country skis for $28 per day at the Cross-Country Ski School, which also rents snowshoes ($23 per day) and telemarking equipment ($28). ☎ *209/372–8444* ⊕ *www.travelyosemite.com.*

Yosemite Mountaineering School

SKIING/SNOWBOARDING | This branch of the Yosemite Mountaineering School, open at the Yosemite Ski & Snowboard Area during ski season only, conducts snowshoeing, cross-country skiing, telemarking, and skate-skiing classes starting at $44. ⊠ *Yosemite Ski & Snowboard Area* ☎ *209/372–8444* ⊕ *www.travelyosemite.com.*

Yosemite Ski & Snowboard Area School

SKIING/SNOWBOARDING | The gentle slopes of Yosemite Ski & Snowboard Area make the ski school an ideal spot for children and beginners to learn downhill skiing or snowboarding for as little as $75 for a group lesson. ☎ *209/372–8430* ⊕ *www. travelyosemite.com.*

ⓨ Nightlife

Vintage Music of Yosemite

MUSIC CLUBS | A pianist-singer performs four hours of live old-time music at the Big Trees Lodge (formerly Wawona Hotel); call for schedule of performances. ⊠ *Big Trees Lodge, Rte. 41, Wawona* ☎ *209/375–6556* ➤ *Free.*

ⓟ Performing Arts

Yosemite Theatre

THEATER | Various theater and music programs are held throughout the year, and one of the best loved is Lee Stetson's portrayal of John Muir in *Conversation with a Tramp* and other Muir-theme shows. Purchase tickets in advance at the Conservancy Store at the Valley Visitor Center or the Tour and Activity Desk at Yosemite Valley Lodge. Unsold seats are available at the door at performance time, 7 pm. ⊠ *Valley Visitor Center, Yosemite Village* ☎ *209/372–0299* ✆ *$10.*

🛍 Shopping

Ansel Adams Gallery

ART GALLERIES | Framed prints of the famed nature photographer's best works are on sale here, as are affordable posters. New works by contemporary artists are available, along with Native American jewelry and handicrafts. The gallery's elegant camera shop conducts photography workshops, from free camera walks a few mornings a week to five-day workshops. ⊠ *Northside Dr., Yosemite Village* ☎ *209/372–4413* ⊕ *anseladams.com/ansel-adams-gallery-in-yosemite/.*

Majestic Hotel Gift Shop

GIFTS/SOUVENIRS | This shop sells more upscale items, such as Native American crafts, photographic prints, handmade ceramics, and elegant jewelry. For less expensive gift items, browse the small book selection, which includes writings by John Muir. ⊠ *The Majestic Yosemite Hotel, Ahwahnee Rd.* ☎ *209/372–1409.*

Yosemite Mountain Shop

SPECIALTY STORES | A comprehensive selection of camping, hiking, backpacking, and climbing equipment, along with experts who can answer all your questions, make this store a valuable resource for outdoors enthusiasts. This is the best place to ask about climbing conditions and restrictions around the park, as well as purchase almost any kind of climbing gear. ⊠ *Half Dome Village* ☎ *209/372–8436.*

Nearby Towns

Marking the southern end of the Sierra's gold-bearing mother lode, **Mariposa** is the last town before you enter Yosemite on Route 140 to the west of the park. In addition to a fine mining museum, Mariposa has numerous shops, restaurants, and service stations.

Motels and restaurants dot both sides of Route 41 as it cuts through the town of **Oakhurst,** a boomtown during the gold rush that is now an important regional refueling station in every sense of the word, including organic foods and a full range of lodging options. Oakhurst has a population of about 3,000 and sits 15 miles south of the park.

Almost surrounded by the Sierra National Forest, **Bass Lake** is a warm-water reservoir whose waters can reach 80 degrees F in summer. Created by a dam on a tributary of the San Joaquin River, the lake is owned by Pacific Gas and Electric Company and is used to generate electricity as well as for recreation.

As you climb in elevation along Highway 41 northbound, you see nothing but trees until you get to **Fish Camp,** where there's a post office and general store, but no gasoline. (For gas, head 7 miles north to Wawona, in Yosemite, or 14 miles south to Oakhurst.)

Near the park's eastern entrance, the tiny town of **Lee Vining** is home to the eerily beautiful, salty Mono Lake, where millions of migratory birds nest. Visit **Mammoth Lakes,** about 40 miles southeast of Yosemite's Tioga Pass entrance, for excellent skiing and snowboarding in winter, with fishing, mountain biking, hiking, and horseback riding in summer. Nine deep-blue lakes form the Mammoth Lakes Basin, and another hundred dot the surrounding countryside. Devils Postpile National Monument sits at the base of Mammoth Mountain.

VISITOR INFORMATION Mammoth Lakes Tourism. ⊠ *2510 Main St., Mammoth Lakes* ☎ *760/934–2712, 888/466–2666* ⊕ *www.visitmammoth.com.* **Mono Lake Information Center and Bookstore.** ☎ *760/647–6595* ⊕ *www.leevining.com.* **Tuolumne County Visitors Bureau.** ⊠ *193 S. Washington St., Sonora* ☎ *209/533–4420, 800/446–1333* ⊕ *www.visittuolumne. com.* **Visit Yosemite/Madera County.** ⊠ *40343 Hwy. 41, Oakhurst* ☎ *559/683– 4636* ⊕ *www.yosemitethisyear.com.* **Yosemite Mariposa County Tourism Bureau.** ⊠ *5158 Hwy. 140, Suite E, Mariposa* ☎ *209/742–4567, 866/425–3366 visitor center toll-free, 209/966–7081 visitor center* ⊕ *www.yosemite.com.*

◉ Sights

California State Mining and Mineral Museum

MUSEUM | FAMILY | A California state park, the museum has displays on gold-rush history including a replica hard-rock mine shaft to walk through, a miniature stamp mill, and a 13-pound chunk of crystallized gold. ⊠ *5005 Fairground Rd., off Hwy. 49, Mariposa* ☎ *209/742–7625* ⊕ *www.parks.ca.gov/miningandmineral-museum* ⌦ *$4* ⊙ *Closed Mon.–Wed.*

★ Devils Postpile National Monument

NATURE SITE | Volcanic and glacial forces sculpted this formation of smooth, vertical basalt columns. For a bird's-eye view, take the short, steep trail to the top of a 60-foot cliff. To see the monument's second scenic wonder, **Rainbow Falls,** hike 2 miles past Devils Postpile. A branch of the San Joaquin River plunges more than 100 feet over a lava ledge here. When the water hits the pool below, sunlight turns the resulting mist into a spray of color. From mid-June to early September, day-use visitors must ride the shuttle bus from the Mammoth Mountain Ski Area to the monument. ⊠ *Mammoth Lakes* ⊹ *13 miles south-west of Mammoth Lakes off Minaret Rd. (Hwy. 203)* ☎ *760/934–2289,*

760/872–1901 shuttle ⊕ *www.nps.gov/ depo* ⌦ *$10 per vehicle (allowed when the shuttle isn't running, usually early Sept.–mid-Oct.), $8 per person shuttle.*

Hot Creek Geologic Site

NATURE SITE | Forged by an ancient volcanic eruption, the Hot Creek Geologic Site is a landscape of boiling hot springs, fumaroles, and geysers about 10 miles southeast of the town of Mammoth Lakes. You can stroll along boardwalks through the canyon to view the steaming volcanic features. Fly-fishing for trout is popular upstream from the springs. ⊠ *Hot Creek Hatchery Rd. east of U.S. 395, Mammoth Lakes* ☎ *760/873–2400* ⊕ *www.fs.usda.gov/recarea/inyo/ recarea/?recid=20414* ⌦ *Free.*

Yosemite Mountain Sugar Pine Railroad

TRANSPORTATION SITE (AIRPORT/BUS/FERRY/ TRAIN) | FAMILY | Travel back to a time when powerful steam locomotives hauled massive log trains through the Sierra. This 4-mile, narrow-gauge railroad excursion takes you near Yosemite's south gate. There's a moonlight special ($58), with dinner and entertainment, and you can pan for gold ($10) and visit the free museum. ⊠ *56001 Hwy. 41, 8 miles south of Yosemite, Fish Camp* ☎ *559/683–7273* ⊕ *www.ymsprr.com* ⌦ *$24* ⊙ *Closed Nov.–Mar. Closed some weekdays Apr. and Oct.*

◉ Activities

RAFTING

Zephyr Whitewater Expeditions

BOATING | This outfitter conducts half-day to three-day white-water trips on the Tuolumne, Merced, and American rivers for paddlers of all experience levels. ☎ *800/431–3636 reservations, 209/532– 6249* ⊕ *www.zrafting.com* ⌦ *From $112.*

SKIING

★ Mammoth Mountain Ski Area

SKIING/SNOWBOARDING | One of the West's largest and best ski areas, Mammoth has more than 3,500 acres of skiable terrain and a 3,100-foot vertical drop. The views from the 11,053-foot summit are some of the most stunning in the Sierra. Below, you'll find a 6½-mile-wide swath of groomed boulevards and canyons, as well as pockets of tree-skiing and a dozen vast bowls. Snowboarders are everywhere on the slopes; there are seven outstanding freestyle terrain parks of varying difficulty, with jumps, rails, tabletops, and giant super pipes—this is the location of several international snowboarding competitions, and, in summer, mountain-bike meets. Mammoth's season begins in November and often lingers into July. Lessons and equipment are available, and there's a children's ski and snowboard school. Mammoth runs free shuttle-bus routes around town and to the ski area, and the Village Gondola runs from the Village complex to Canyon Lodge. However, only overnight guests are allowed to park at the Village for more than a few hours. **Facilities:** 155 trails; 3,500 acres; 3,100-foot vertical drop; 25 lifts. ✉ *Minaret Rd., west of Mammoth Lakes, Rte. 203, off U.S. 395, Mammoth Lakes* ☎ *760/934–2571, 800/626–6684, 760/934–0687 shuttle* 🌐 *www.mammothmountain.com* 🎫 *From $99.*

🍴 Restaurants

IN THE PARK

In addition to the dining options listed here, you'll find fast-food grills and cafeterias, plus temporary snack bars, hamburger stands, and pizza joints lining park roads in summer. Many dining facilities in the park are open summer only.

Base Camp Eatery

$$ | **AMERICAN** | The design of this modern food court, open for breakfast, lunch, and dinner, honors the history of rock climbing in Yosemite. Choose from a wide range of menu options, from hamburgers, salads, and pizzas, to rice and noodle bowls. **Known for:** grab-and-go selections; best casual dining venue in the park; automated ordering kiosks to speed up service. [$] *Average main: $12* ✉ *Yosemite Valley Lodge, about ¾ mile west of visitor center, Yosemite Village* ☎ *209/372–1265* 🌐 *www.travelyosemite.com.*

Big Trees Lodge Dining Room

$$$ | **AMERICAN** | Watch deer graze on the meadow while you dine in the romantic, candlelit dining room of the whitewashed Big Trees Lodge (formerly the Wawona Hotel), which dates from the late 1800s. The American-style cuisine favors fresh ingredients and flavors; trout and flatiron steaks are menu staples. **Known for:** Saturday-night barbecues on the lawn; historic ambience; Mother's Day and other Sunday holiday brunches. [$] *Average main: $28* ✉ *8308 Wawona Rd., Wawona* ☎ *209/375–1425* 🕒 *Closed most of Dec., Jan., Feb., and Mar.*

Half Dome Village Pavilion

$$ | **AMERICAN** | Formerly Curry Village Pavilion, this cafeteria-style eatery serves everything from roasted meats and salads to pastas, burritos, and beyond. Alternatively, order a pizza from the stand on the deck, and take in the views of the valley's granite walls. **Known for:** convenient eats; Saturday evening chuck wagon barbecues mid-June–August; additional venues: Meadow Grill, Pizza Patio, Coffee Corner and Village Bar. [$] *Average main: $18* ✉ *Half Dome Village* ☎ *209/372–8303* 🕒 *Closed mid-Oct.–mid-Apr. No lunch.*

★ The Majestic Yosemite Hotel Dining Room

$$$$ | **EUROPEAN** | Formerly The Ahwahnee Hotel Dining Room, rave reviews about the dining room's appearance are fully justified—it features towering windows, a 34-foot-high ceiling with interlaced sugar-pine beams, and massive chandeliers. Reservations are always advised, and the attire is "resort casual." **Known for:** lavish $56 Sunday brunch; finest dining in the park; bar menu with lighter lunch and dinner fare at more affordable prices.

Did You Know?

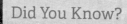

In the Sierra's mixed-conifer forests, telling the many types of pines apart can be difficult if you don't know the trick: sizing up the cones and examining the branches to count how many needles are in discrete clusters. If the needles are paired, you're likely looking at a lodgepole pine. If the needles are long and come in threes, chances are you've come upon a ponderosa pine.

$ *Average main: $39* ✉ *The Majestic Yosemite Hotel, Ahwahnee Rd., about ¾ mile east of Yosemite Valley Visitor Center, Yosemite Village* ☎ *209/372–1489* 🌐 *www.travelyosemite.com.*

★ **Mountain Room**

$$$ | AMERICAN | Gaze at Yosemite Falls through this dining room's wall of windows—almost every table has a view—as you nosh on steaks, seafood, and classic California salads and desserts. The Mountain Room Lounge, a few steps away in the Yosemite Lodge complex, has about 10 beers on tap. **Known for:** locally sourced, organic ingredients; usually there is a wait for a table (no reservations); vegetarian and vegan options. $ *Average main: $29* ✉ *Yosemite Valley Lodge, Northside Dr., about ¾ mile west of visitor center, Yosemite Village* ☎ *209/372–1403* 🌐 *www.travelyosemite.com* 🕒 *No lunch except Sun. brunch.*

Tuolumne Meadows Grill

$ | FAST FOOD | Serving continuously throughout the day until 5 or 6 pm, this fast-food eatery cooks up basic breakfast, lunch, and snacks. It's possible that ice cream tastes better at this altitude. **Known for:** soft serve ice cream; crowds; fresh local ingredients. $ *Average main: $8* ✉ *Tioga Rd. (Rte. 120), 1½ miles east of Tuolumne Meadows Visitor Center* ☎ *209/372–8426* 🌐 *www.travelyosemite.com* 🕒 *Closed Oct.–Memorial Day. No dinner.*

Tuolumne Meadows Lodge

$$$ | AMERICAN | In a central dining tent beside the Tuolumne River, this restaurant serves a menu of hearty American fare at breakfast and dinner. The red-and-white-checkered tablecloths and a handful of communal tables give it the feeling of an old-fashioned summer camp. **Known for:** box lunches; communal tables; small menu. $ *Average main: $24* ✉ *Tioga Rd. (Rte. 120)* ☎ *209/372–8413* 🌐 *www.travelyosemite.com* 🕒 *Closed late Sept.–mid-June. No lunch.*

Village Grill Deck

$$ | FAST FOOD | If a burger joint is what you've been missing, head to this bustling eatery in Yosemite Village that serves veggie, salmon, and a few other burger varieties in addition to the usual beef patties. Order at the counter, then take your tray out to the deck and enjoy your meal under the trees. **Known for:** burgers, sandwiches, and hot dogs; crowds; outdoor seating on expansive deck. $ *Average main: $12* ✉ *Yosemite Village* ✥ *100 yards east of Yosemite Valley Visitor Center* ☎ *209/372–1207* 🌐 *www.travelyosemite.com* 🕒 *Closed Oct.–May. No dinner.*

PICNIC AREAS

Considering how large the park is and how many visitors come here—some 5 million people every year, most of them just for the day—it is somewhat surprising that Yosemite has few formal picnic areas, though in many places you can find a smooth rock to sit on and enjoy breathtaking views along with your lunch. The convenience stores all sell picnic supplies, and prepackaged sandwiches and salads are widely available. Those options can come in especially handy during the middle of the day, when you might not want to spend precious daylight hours in such a spectacular setting sitting in a restaurant for a formal meal. *None of the below options has drinking water available; most have some type of toilet.*

Cathedral Beach. You may have some solitude picnicking here, as this spot usually has fewer people than picnic areas at the eastern end of the valley. *Southside Dr. underneath spirelike Cathedral Rocks.*

Church Bowl. Tucked behind The Majestic Yosemite Hotel, this picnic area nearly abuts the granite walls below the Royal Arches. If you're walking from the village with your supplies, this is the shortest trek to a picnic area. *Behind The Majestic Yosemite Hotel, Yosemite Valley.*

El Capitan. Come here for great views that look straight up the giant granite wall above. *Northside Dr., at western end of valley.*

Sentinel Beach. Usually crowded in season, this area is right alongside a running creek and the Merced River. *Southside Dr., just south of Swinging Bridge.*

Swinging Bridge. This picnic area is just before the little wooden footbridge that crosses the Merced River, which babbles pleasantly by. *Southside Dr., east of Sentinel Beach.*

OUTSIDE THE PARK
Ducey's on the Lake/Ducey's Bar & Grill
$$$$ | **AMERICAN** | With elaborate chandeliers sculpted from deer antlers, the lodge-style restaurant at Ducey's attracts boaters, locals, and tourists with its lake views and standard lamb, beef, seafood, and pasta dishes. It's also open for breakfast: try the Bass Lake seafood omelet, huevos rancheros, or the Rice Krispies–crusted French toast. **Known for:** steaks and fresh fish; lake views; upstairs bar and grill with more affordable eats. $ *Average main: $32* ⊠ *Pines Resort, 54432 Rd. 432, Bass Lake* ☎ *559/642–3131* ⊕ *www.basslake.com.*

★ Erna's Elderberry House
$$$$ | **EUROPEAN** | Erna Kubin-Clanin, the grande dame of Château du Sureau, created this culinary oasis, stunning for its understated elegance, gorgeous setting, and impeccable service. Earth-tone walls and wood beams accent the dining room's high ceilings, and arched windows reflect the glow of candles. **Known for:** elite waitstaff; romantic setting; seasonal prix-fixe and à la carte menus. $ *Average main: $48* ⊠ *Château du Sureau, 48688 Victoria La., off Hwy. 41, Oakhurst* ☎ *559/683–6800* ⊕ *www.elderberryhouse.com* ⊗ *No lunch Mon.–Sat.*

★ South Gate Brewing Company
$$ | **AMERICAN** | Locals pack this family-friendly, industrial-chic restaurant to socialize and savor small-lot beers, crafted on-site, along with tasty meals. The creative pub fare runs a wide gamut, from thin-crust brick-oven pizzas to fish tacos, fish-and-chips, and vegan black-bean burgers. **Known for:** craft beer; homemade desserts; live-music calendar. $ *Average main: $16* ⊠ *40233 Enterprise Dr., off Hwy. 49, north of Von's shopping center, Oakhurst* ☎ *559/692–2739* ⊕ *southgatebrewco.com.*

Hotels

At this writing, a still-ongoing trademark dispute with a former park concessioner resulted in Yosemite National Park changing the names of several historic park lodges and properties, including the iconic Ahwahnee. This guide has changed the historic names, with some references to the former. The changes include: Yosemite Lodge at the Falls is Yosemite Valley Lodge, The Ahwahnee is The Majestic Yosemite Hotel, Curry Village is Half Dome Village, Wawona Hotel is Big Trees Lodge, and Badger Pass Ski Area is Yosemite Ski & Snowboard Area.

IN THE PARK
Big Trees Lodge
$$ | **HOTEL** | This 1879 National Historic Landmark at Yosemite's southern end (formerly Wawona Hotel) is a Victorian-era mountain resort, with whitewashed buildings, wraparound verandas, and pleasant, no-frills rooms decorated with period pieces. **Pros:** lovely building; peaceful atmosphere; historic photos in public areas. **Cons:** few modern amenities, such as phones and TVs; an hour's drive from Yosemite Valley; shared bathrooms in half the rooms. $ *Rooms from: $148* ⊠ *8308 Wawona Rd., Wawona* ☎ *888/413–8869* ⊕ *www.travelyosemite.com* ⊗ *Closed Dec.–Mar., except mid-Dec.–Jan. 2* ⇥ *104 rooms, 50 with bath* ⚭ *Breakfast.*

Half Dome Village

$$ | HOTEL | Opened in 1899 as a place for budget-conscious travelers, Half Dome Village (formerly Curry Village) has plain accommodations: standard motel rooms, simple cabins with either private or shared baths, and tent cabins with shared baths. **Pros:** close to many activities; family-friendly atmosphere; surrounded by iconic valley views. **Cons:** community bathrooms need updating; can be crowded; sometimes a bit noisy. $ *Rooms from: $143* ⊠ *South side of Southside Dr.* ☎ *888/413–8869, 602/278–8888 international* ⊕ *www. travelyosemite.com* ⇥ *583 rooms and cabins* ⏉ *No meals.*

★ The Majestic Yosemite Hotel

$$$$ | HOTEL | Formerly The Ahwahnee, this National Historic Landmark is constructed of sugar-pine logs and features Native American design motifs; public spaces are enlivened with art-deco flourishes, Persian rugs, and elaborate iron- and woodwork. **Pros:** best lodge in Yosemite; helpful concierge; in the historic heart of the valley. **Cons:** expensive rates; some reports that service has slipped in recent years. $ *Rooms from: $581* ⊠ *Ahwahnee Rd., about ¾ mile east of Yosemite Valley Visitor Center, Yosemite Village* ☎ *801/559–4884* ⊕ *www.travelyosemite.com* ⇥ *125 rooms and suites* ⏉ *No meals.*

Redwoods in Yosemite

$$$$ | RENTAL | This collection of more than 125 homes in the Wawona area is a great alternative to the overcrowded valley. **Pros:** sense of privacy; peaceful setting; full kitchens. **Cons:** 45-minute drive from the valley; some have no air-conditioning; cell phone service can be spotty. $ *Rooms from: $260* ⊠ *8038 Chilnualna Falls Rd., off Rte. 41, Wawona* ☎ *209/375–6666 international, 888/225–6666* ⊕ *www.redwoodsinyosemite.com* ⇥ *125 units* ⏉ *No meals.*

White Wolf Lodge

$$ | HOTEL | Set in a subalpine meadow, the rustic accommodations at White Wolf Lodge make it an excellent base camp for hiking the backcountry. **Pros:** quiet location; near some of Yosemite's most beautiful, less crowded hikes; good restaurant. **Cons:** far from the valley; tent cabins share bathhouse; remote setting. $ *Rooms from: $138* ⊠ *Yosemite National al Park* ⊹ *Off Tioga Rd. (Rte. 120), 25 miles west of Tuolumne Meadows and 15 miles east of Crane Flat* ☎ *801/559–4884* ⊘ *Closed mid-Sept.–mid-June* ⇥ *28 cabins* ⏉ *No meals.*

Yosemite Valley Lodge

$$$$ | HOTEL | This 1915 lodge near Yosemite Falls (formerly Yosemite Lodge at the Falls) is a collection of numerous two-story, glass-and-wood structures tucked beneath the trees. **Pros:** centrally located; dependably clean rooms; lots of tours leave from out front. **Cons:** can feel impersonal; high prices; no in-room air-conditioning. $ *Rooms from: $260* ⊠ *9006 Yosemite Valley Lodge Dr., Yosemite Village* ☎ *888/413–8869* ⊕ *www.travelyosemite.com* ⇥ *245 rooms* ⏉ *No meals.*

OUTSIDE THE PARK

Best Western Plus Yosemite Gateway Inn

$$$$ | HOTEL | FAMILY | Perched on 11 hillside acres, Oakhurst's best motel has carefully tended landscaping and rooms with stylish contemporary furnishings and hand-painted murals of Yosemite. **Pros:** close to park's southern entrance; on-site restaurant; indoor and outdoor swimming pools; frequent deer and wildlife sightings. **Cons:** some rooms on the small side; Internet connection can be slow; some rooms need updating. $ *Rooms from: $249* ⊠ *40530 Hwy. 41, Oakhurst* ☎ *559/683–2378* ⊕ *www. yosemitegatewayinn.com* ⇥ *149 rooms* ⏉ *No meals.*

Camping in Bear Country

The national parks' campgrounds and some campgrounds outside the parks provide food-storage boxes that can keep bears from pilfering your edibles (portable canisters for backpackers can be rented in most park stores). It's imperative that you move all food, coolers, and items with a scent (including toiletries, toothpaste, chewing gum, and air fresheners) from your car (including the trunk) to the storage box at your campsite; day-trippers should lock food in bear boxes provided at parking lots.

If you don't, a bear may break into your car by literally peeling off the door or ripping open the trunk, or ransack your tent. The familiar tactic of hanging your food from high tree limbs is not an effective deterrent, as bears easily can scale trees. In the southern Sierra, bear canisters are the only effective and proven method for preventing bears from getting human food. Details on bears and food storage are posted on the park website, ⊕ www.nps.gov/yose/plany-ourvisit/bears.htm.

★ Château du Sureau

$$$$ | RESORT | The inn here is straight out of a children's book: every room is impeccably styled with European antiques, sumptuous fabrics, fresh-cut flowers, and oversize soaking tubs. Pros: luxurious; great views; sumptuous spa facility. Cons: expensive; cost might not seem worth it to guests not spa-oriented; can seem pretentious to some. $ Rooms from: $420 ⊠ 48688 Victoria La., Oakhurst ☎ 559/683–6860 ⊕ www.chateausureau. com ⇋ 11 rooms |◎| Breakfast.

Evergreen Lodge at Yosemite

$$$$ | RESORT | FAMILY | Amid the trees near Yosemite National Park's Hetch Hetchy entrance, this sprawling property is perfect for families. Pros: cabin complex includes amphitheater, pool, and more; guided tours available; great roadhouse-style restaurant. Cons: no TVs; long, winding access road; spotty cell service. $ Rooms from: $280 ⊠ 33160 Evergreen Rd., 30 miles east of town of Groveland, Groveland ☎ 209/379–2606 ⊕ www.evergreen-lodge.com ⇋ 88 cabins.

Homestead Cottages

$$$ | B&B/INN | Set on 160 acres of rolling hills that once held a Miwok village, these cottages (the largest sleeps six) have gas fireplaces, fully equipped kitchens, and queen-size beds. Pros: remote location; quiet setting; friendly owners. Cons: might be too quiet for some; breakfasts on the simple side; 7 miles from center of Oakhurst. $ Rooms from: $189 ⊠ 41110 Rd. 600, 2½ miles off Hwy. 49, Ahwahnee ☎ 559/683–0495 ⊕ www. homesteadcottages.com ⇋ 7 cottages |◎| Breakfast.

Narrow Gauge Inn

$$$$ | HOTEL | The well-tended rooms at this family-owned property have balconies with views of the surrounding woods and mountains. Pros: close to Yosemite's south entrance; nicely appointed rooms; wonderful balconies. Cons: rooms can be a bit dark; dining options are limited, especially for vegetarians; housekeeping service can be spotty. $ Rooms from: $229 ⊠ 48571 Hwy. 41, Fish Camp ☎ 559/683–7720, 888/644–9050 ⊕ www.narrowgaugeinn. com ⇋ 27 rooms |◎| No meals.

Best Campgrounds in Yosemite

If you are going to concentrate solely on valley sites and activities, you should endeavor to stay in one of the "Pines" campgrounds, which are clustered near Half Dome Village and within an easy stroll from that busy complex's many facilities. For a more primitive and quiet experience, and to be near many backcountry hikes, try one of the Tioga Road campgrounds.

National Park Service Reservations Office. Reservations are required at many of Yosemite's campgrounds. You can book a site up to five months in advance, starting on the 15th of the month. Unless otherwise noted, book your site through the central National Park Service Reservations Office. If you don't have reservations when you arrive, many sites, especially those outside Yosemite Valley, are available on a first-come, first-served basis. ☎ 877/444–6777 reservations, 518/885–3639 international, 888/448–1474 customer service ⊕ www.recreation.gov.

Bridalveil Creek. This campground sits among lodgepole pines at 7,200 feet, above the valley on Glacier Point Road. From here, you can easily drive to Glacier Point's magnificent valley views. ⊠ From Rte. 41 in Wawona, go north to Glacier Point Rd. and turn right; entrance to campground is 25 miles ahead on right side.

Camp 4. Formerly known as Sunnyside Walk-In, and extremely popular with rock climbers, who don't mind that a total of six are assigned to each campsite; no matter how many are in your group, this is the only valley campground available on a first-come, first-served basis. ⊠ Base of Yosemite Falls Trail, just west of Yosemite Valley Lodge on Northside Dr., Yosemite Village.

Housekeeping Camp. Composed of three concrete walls and covered with two layers of canvas, each unit has an open-ended fourth side that can be closed off with a heavy white canvas curtain. You can rent "bedpacks," consisting of blankets, sheets, and other comforts. ⊠ Southside Dr., ½ mile west of Half Dome Village.

Porcupine Flat. Sixteen miles west of Tuolumne Meadows, this campground sits at 8,100 feet. If you want to be in the high country, this is a good bet. ⊠ Rte. 120, 16 miles west of Tuolumne Meadows.

Tuolumne Meadows. In a wooded area at 8,600 feet, just south of its namesake meadow, this is one of the most spectacular and sought-after campgrounds in Yosemite. ⊠ Rte. 120, 46 miles east of Big Oak Flat entrance station.

Upper Pines. This is one of the valley's largest campgrounds and the closest one to the trailheads. Expect large crowds in the summer—and little privacy. ⊠ At east end of valley, near Half Dome Village.

Wawona. Near the Mariposa Grove, just downstream from a popular fishing spot, this year-round campground has larger, less densely packed sites than campgrounds in the valley. ⊠ Rte. 41, 1 mile north of Wawona.

White Wolf. Set in the beautiful high country at 8,000 feet, this is a prime spot for hikers from early July to mid-September. ⊠ Tioga Rd., 15 miles east of Big Oak Flat entrance.

★ Rush Creek Lodge

$$$$ | RESORT | FAMILY | This sleek, nature-inspired complex occupies 20 acres on a wooded hillside and includes a saltwater pool and hot tubs, a restaurant and tavern with indoor/outdoor seating, a guided recreation program, massage studios and wellness program, and a general store. **Pros:** close to Yosemite's Big Oak Flat entrance; YARTS bus stops here and connects with Yosemite Valley and Sonora spring; year-round evening s'mores. **Cons:** no TVs; pricey in high season; spotty cell service. [$] *Rooms from: $410* ✉ *34001 Hwy. 120, Groveland* ✣ *25 miles east of Groveland, 23 miles north of Yosemite Valley* ☎ *209/379–2373* 🌐 *www.rushcreeklodge.com* 🛏 *143 rooms and suites* 🍴 *No meals.*

Sierra Sky Ranch

$$$$ | HOTEL | Off Highway 41 just 10 miles south of the Yosemite National Park, this 19th-century cattle ranch near a hidden grove of giant sequoia trees provides a restful, rustic retreat. **Pros:** peaceful setting; historic property; short drive to giant sequoias. **Cons:** some rooms on the small side; not in town; basic breakfast. [$] *Rooms from: $249* ✉ *50552 Rd. 632, Oakhurst* ☎ *559/683–8040* 🌐 *www.sierraskyranch.com* 🛏 *26 rooms* 🍴 *Breakfast.*

Tamarack Lodge Resort

$$$ | RESORT | Tucked away on the edge of the John Muir Wilderness Area, where cross-country ski trails loop through the woods, this 1924 lodge looks like something out of a snow globe. **Pros:** rustic but not run-down; tons of nearby outdoor activities; excellent wine list in restaurant. **Cons:** thin walls; some shared bathrooms; some cabins are tiny. [$] *Rooms from: $169* ✉ *Lake Mary Rd., off Rte. 203, Mammoth Lakes* ☎ *760/934–2442, 800/237–6879* 🌐 *www.tamaracklodge.com* 🛏 *45 rooms and cabins* 🍴 *Free Breakfast.*

★ Tenaya Lodge

$$$$ | RESORT | FAMILY | One of the region's largest hotels, Tenaya Lodge is ideal for people who enjoy wilderness treks by day but prefer creature comforts at night. **Pros:** close to Yosemite and Mariposa Grove of Giant Sequoias; exceptional spa and exercise facility, 36 miles of mountain bike trails; activities for all ages. **Cons:** so big it can seem impersonal; pricey during summer; daily resort fee. [$] *Rooms from: $379* ✉ *1122 Hwy. 41, Fish Camp* ☎ *559/683–6555, 888/514–2167* 🌐 *www.tenayalodge.com* 🛏 *352 rooms* 🍴 *No meals.*

Yosemite View Lodge

$$$$ | HOTEL | Two miles outside Yosemite's Arch Rock entrance, this modern property is the most convenient place to spend the night if you are unable to secure lodgings in the valley. **Pros:** great location; good views; lots of on-site amenities. **Cons:** somewhat pricey; it can be a challenge to get the dates you want; rooms could use an update. [$] *Rooms from: $239* ✉ *11136 Hwy. 140, El Portal* ☎ *209/379–2681, 888/742–4371* 🌐 *www.stayyosemiteviewlodge.com* 🛏 *335 rooms* 🍴 *No meals.*

Chapter 15

EASTERN SIERRA

Updated by
Cheryl Crabtree

⊙ Sights	🍽 Restaurants	🛏 Hotels	🛍 Shopping	🍸 Nightlife
★★★★★	★★★★☆	★★★★★	★☆☆☆☆	★☆☆☆☆

WELCOME TO EASTERN SIERRA

TOP REASONS TO GO

★ **Hiking:** Whether you walk the paved loops in the national parks or head off the beaten path into the backcountry, a hike through groves and meadows or alongside streams and waterfalls will allow you to see, smell, and feel nature up close.

★ **Winter fun:** Famous for its incredible snowpack— some of the deepest in the North American continent—the Sierra Nevada has something for every winter-sports fan.

★ **Live it up:** Mammoth Lakes is eastern California's most exciting resort area.

★ **Road trip heaven:** Legendary Highway 395 is one of California's most scenic byways, and stops in Independence, Lone Pine, Bishop, and Bodie Ghost Town give you a glimpse of Old West history.

★ **Go with the flow:** Fish, float, raft, and row in the abundant lakes, hot springs, creeks, and rivers.

The transition between Los Angeles and the Mojave Desert and the rugged Eastern Sierra may be the most dramatic in California sightseeing. U.S. 395 is the main north–south road on the eastern side of the Sierra Nevada, at the western edge of the Great Basin, and a gateway to Death Valley National Park. It's one of California's most beautiful highways. The 395 is generally open year-round.

1 Lone Pine. Mount Whitney and the Alabama Hills in Lone Pine have provided authentic backdrops for hundreds of films and TV shows for nearly a century, as evidenced in the town's Museum of Western Film History.

2 Independence. The moving Manzanar National Historic Site, where 11,000 Japanese-Americans were interned during World War II, lies 6 miles south of Independence, a tiny Old West town.

3 Bishop. One of the largest towns along Highway 395, Bishop is an excellent road stop and base camp for exploration in the surrounding mountains.

4 Mammoth Lakes. Easy access to year-round outdoor adventures has made Mammoth Lakes one of the Sierra Nevada's most popular destinations. The bustling town's many attractions include sprawling Mammoth Mountain Ski and Bike Area and nearby Mammoth Lakes Basin and Devil's Postpile National Monument.

5 Lee Vining. The eastern gateway to Yosemite National Park via Tioga Road (open seasonally), tiny Lee Vining sits at the western shores of vast Mono Lake.

6 Bodie State Historic Park. The town of Bridgeport is the main portal to Bodie State Historic Park and the well-preserved Bodie Ghost Town.

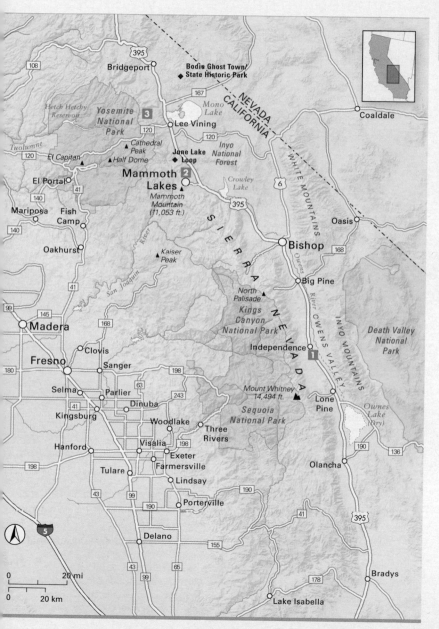

The Eastern Sierra's granite peaks and ancient pines bedazzle heart and soul so completely that for many visitors the experience surpasses that at more famous urban attractions. Most of the Sierra's wonders lie within national parks, but outside them deep-blue Mono Lake and its tufa towers never cease to astound. The megaresort Mammoth Lakes, meanwhile, lures skiers and snowboarders in winter and hikers and mountain bikers in summer.

The Eastern Sierra is accessed most easily via Highway 395, which travels the length of the region from the Mojave Desert in the south to Bridgeport in the north. Main towns along the route include Lone Pine, Independence, Bishop, Mammoth Lakes, June Lake, and Lee Vining, a small town at the eastern endpoint of Tioga Road from Yosemite National Park. Pristine lakes and rolling hills outside the parks offer year-round opportunities for rest and relaxation. Or not. In winter the thrill of the slopes—and their relative isolation compared to busy Lake Tahoe—draws a hearty breed of outdoor enthusiasts. In summer a hike through groves and meadows or alongside streams and waterfalls allows you to see, smell, and feel nature up close.

Planning

Getting Here and Around

AIR TRAVEL

Three main airports provide access to the Eastern Sierra: Fresno Yosemite International (FAT), on the western side, and, on the eastern side, Mammoth–Yosemite (MMH), 6 miles east of Mammoth Lakes, and Reno–Tahoe (RNO), 130 miles north of Mammoth Lakes via U.S. 395. Alaska, Allegiant, American, Delta, Frontier, United, and a few other carriers serve Fresno and Reno. United and JetSuiteX serve Mammoth Lakes.

AIRPORTS Fresno Yosemite International Airport (FAT). ✉ 5175 E. Clinton Ave., Fresno ☎ 800/244–2359 automated information, 559/454–2052 terminal info desk ⊕ www.flyfresno.com. **Mammoth–Yosemite Airport.** ✉ 1200 Airport

Rd., Mammoth Lakes ☎ 760/934–2712, 888/466–2666 ⊕ www.visitmammoth. com/getting-mammoth-lakes. **Reno–Tahoe International Airport.** ✉ 2001 E. Plumb La., Reno ☎ 775/328–6400 ⊕ www.renoair-port.com.

BUS TRAVEL

Eastern Sierra Transit Authority buses serve Mammoth Lakes, Bishop, and other Eastern Sierra towns along Highway 395, from Reno in the north to Lancaster in the south. In summer YARTS (Yosemite Area Regional Transportation System) connects Yosemite National Park with Mammoth Lakes, June Lake, and Lee Vining in the Eastern Sierra, and Central Valley cities and towns in the west, including Fresno and Merced. This is a good option during summer, when parking in Yosemite Valley and elsewhere in the park can be difficult.

BUS CONTACTS Eastern Sierra Transit Authority. ☎ 760/872–1901 general, 800/922–3190 toll-free, 760/924–3184 Mammoth Lakes ⊕ www.estransit. com. **YARTS.** ☎ 877/989–2787 ⊕ www. yarts.com.

CAR TRAVEL

Interstate 5 and Highway 99 travel north–south along the western side of the Sierra Nevada. U.S. 395 follows a roughly parallel route on the eastern side. In summer, Tioga Pass Road in Yosemite National Park opens to car and bus travel, intersecting with U.S. 395 at Lee Vining.

From San Francisco: Head east on Interstate 80 to Sacramento, then continue on Interstate 80 to U.S. 395, east of Lake Tahoe's north shore, or take U.S. 50 to Lake Tahoe's south shore and continue on 207E to U.S. 395, then head south.

From Los Angeles: Head north on Interstate 5, exiting and continuing north onto Highway 14 and later onto U.S. 395.

■ TIP→ **Gas stations are few and far between in the Sierra, so fill your tank when you can.** Between October and May heavy snow may cover mountain roads. Always check road conditions before driving. Carry tire chains, and know how to install them. On Interstate 80 and U.S. 50, and at the Mammoth Lakes exit off U.S. 395 chain installers assist travelers (for $40), but elsewhere you're on your own.

TRAVEL REPORTS Caltrans Current Highway Conditions. ☎ 800/427–7623 ⊕ www. dot.ca.gov.

TRAIN TRAVEL

Amtrak's daily San Joaquin train stops in Fresno and Merced, where you can connect to YARTS for travel to Yosemite National Park and in summer to smaller gateway towns, including Mammoth Lakes, June Lake, and Lee Vining.

TRAIN CONTACT Amtrak. ☎ 800/872–7245, 215/856–7924 international ⊕ www.amtrak.com.

Restaurants

Most small towns in the Sierra Nevada have at least one restaurant. Standard American fare is the norm, but you'll also find sophisticated cuisine. With few exceptions, dress is casual. Local grocery stores and delis stock picnic fixings, good to have on hand should the opportunity for an impromptu meal under giant trees emerge. Restaurant reviews have been shortened. For full information, visit Fodors.com.

Hotels

The lodgings in Mammoth Lakes and nearest Yosemite National Park generally fill up the quickest; book hotels everywhere in the Eastern Sierra well in advance in summer. Hotel reviews have been shortened. For full information, visit Fodors.com.

What It Costs

	$	$$	$$$	$$$$
RESTAURANTS				
	under $16	$16–$22	$23–$30	over $30
HOTELS				
	under $120	$120–$175	$176–$250	over $250

Tours

MAWS Transportation

BUS TOURS | This outfit (aka Mammoth All Weather Shuttle) operates summer tours from Mammoth Lakes to Yosemite; north to June Lake, Mono Lake, and Bodie Ghost Town; and around the lakes region. The company also transfers passengers from the Mammoth–Yosemite Airport into town, drops off and picks up hikers at trailheads, and runs charters to Bishop, Los Angeles, Reno, and Las Vegas airports—useful when inclement weather causes flight cancellations at Mammoth's airport. ⊠ *Mammoth Lakes* ☎ *760/709–2927* ⊕ *www.mawshuttle. com* 🖭 *From $60.*

Visitor Information

Eastern Sierra Visitor Center

Pull off the 395 at this one-stop, interagency center for visitor, wilderness, and highway information, plus views of Mt. Whitney. You can also pick up wilderness permits, rent or buy bear-resistant food containers, and picnic on the grounds. It's open year-round from 9 to 5 (8 to 5 May–October). ✛ *2 miles south of Lone Pine, at junctions of U.S. Hwy. 395 and CA Hwy. 136* ☎ *760/876–6200, 760/876–6222* ⊕ *www.fs.usda.gov/recarea/inyo/ recarea/?recid=20698.*

Mammoth Lakes Tourism

⊠ *Mammoth Lakes* ☎ *760/934–2712, 888/466–2666* ⊕ *www.visitmammoth. com.*

Mono County Tourism
⊠ *Mammoth Lakes* ☎ *800/845–7922* ⊕ *monocounty.org.*

Lone Pine

30 miles west of Panamint Valley.

Mt. Whitney towers majestically over this tiny community, which supplied nearby gold- and silver-mining outposts in the 1860s, and for the past century the town has been touched by Hollywood glamour: several hundred movies, TV episodes, and commercials have been filmed here.

GETTING HERE AND AROUND

Arrive by car via U.S. 395 from the north or south, or Highway 190 or Highway 138 from Death Valley National Park. Eastern Sierra Transit buses connect Lone Pine to Reno in the north and Lancaster in the south.

ESSENTIALS

VISITOR INFORMATION Lone Pine Chamber of Commerce. ⊠ *120 S. Main St., at Whitney Portal Rd.* ☎ *760/876–4444* ⊕ *www.lonepinechamber.org.*

◉ Sights

Alabama Hills

MOUNTAIN—SIGHT | Drop by the Lone Pine Visitor Center for a map of the Alabama Hills and take a drive up Whitney Portal Road (turn west at the light) to this wonderland of granite boulders. Erosion has worn the rocks smooth; some have been chiseled to leave arches and other formations. The hills have become a popular location for rock climbing. Tuttle Creek Campground sits among the rocks, with a nearby stream for fishing. The area has served as a scenic backdrop for hundreds of films; ask about the self-guided tour of the various movie locations at the Museum of Western Film History. ⊠ *Whitney Portal Rd., 4½ miles west of Lone Pine.*

Mt. Whitney

MOUNTAIN—SIGHT | Straddling the border of Sequoia National Park and Inyo National Forest–John Muir Wilderness, Mt. Whitney (14,496 feet) is the highest mountain in the contiguous United States. A favorite game for travelers passing through Lone Pine is trying to guess which peak is Mt. Whitney. Almost no one gets it right, because Mt. Whitney is hidden behind other mountains. There is no road that ascends the peak, but you can catch a glimpse of the mountain by driving curvy Whitney Portal Road west from Lone Pine into the mountains. The pavement ends at the trailhead to the top of the mountain, which is also the start of the 211-mile John Muir Trail from Mt. Whitney to Yosemite National Park. Day and overnight permits are required to ascend Mt. Whitney. The highly competitive lottery for these permits opens on February 1st. At the portal, a restaurant (known for its pancakes) and a small store cater to hikers and campers staying at Whitney Portal Campground. You can see a waterfall from the parking lot and go fishing in a small trout pond. The portal area is closed from mid-October to early May; the road closes when snow conditions require. ✉ *Whitney Portal Rd., west of Lone Pine* 🌐 *www.fs.usda.gov/attmain/inyo.*

Museum of Western Film History

MUSEUM | Hopalong Cassidy, Barbara Stanwyck, Roy Rogers, John Wayne—even Robert Downey Jr.—are among the stars who have starred in Westerns and other films shot in the Alabama Hills and surrounding dusty terrain. The marquee-embellished museum relates this Hollywood-in-the-desert tale via exhibits and a rollicking 20-minute documentary. ✉ *701 S. Main St., U.S. 395* ☎ *760/876–9909* 🌐 *www.museumofwesternfilmhistory.org* 🎟 *$5.*

🍴 Restaurants

Alabama Hills Café & Bakery

$ | **AMERICAN** | The extensive breakfast and lunch menus at this eatery just off the main drag include many vegetarian items. Sandwiches are served on homemade bread; choose from up to six varieties baked fresh daily, and get a homemade pie, cake, or loaf to go. **Known for:** house-roasted turkey and beef; huge portions; on-site bakery. [$] *Average main: $13* ✉ *111 W. Post St., at S. Main St.* ☎ *760/876–4675.*

The Grill

$$ | **AMERICAN** | **FAMILY** | Open for three meals a day, this small restaurant next to the Dow Villa Motel is a convenient place to stop for a break while driving along Highway 395. The extensive menu includes an array of options, from omelets and French toast for breakfast and sandwiches and burgers for lunch, to grilled steaks and fish for dinner. **Known for:** hearty meals with large portions; friendly service; house-made desserts. [$] *Average main: $21* ✉ *446 S. Main St.* ☎ *760/876–4240.*

Seasons Restaurant

$$$ | **AMERICAN** | **FAMILY** | This inviting, country-style diner serves all kinds of traditional American fare. For a special treat, try the medallions of Cervena elk, smothered in port wine, dried cranberries, and toasted walnuts; finish with the Baileys Irish Cream cheesecake or the Grand Marnier crème brûlée for dessert. **Known for:** high-end dining in remote area; steaks and wild game; children's menu. [$] *Average main: $27* ✉ *206 S. Main St.* ☎ *760/876–8927* 🌐 *www.seasonslonepine.com* 🕒 *Closed Mon. Nov.–Mar. No lunch.*

Hotels

Dow Villa Motel and Dow Hotel
$$ | **HOTEL** | Built in 1923 to cater to the film industry, the Dow Villa Motel and the historic Dow Hotel sit in the center of Lone Pine. **Pros:** clean rooms; great mountain views; in-room whirlpool tubs in some motel rooms. **Cons:** some rooms in hotel share bathrooms; sinks in some rooms are in the bedroom, not the bath; on busy highway. [$] *Rooms from: $119* ✉ *310 S. Main St.* ☎ *760/876–5521, 800/824–9317* 🌐 *www.dowvillamotel.com* 🛏 *92 rooms* 🍴 *No meals.*

Independence

17 miles north of Lone Pine.

Named for a military outpost that was established near here in 1862, sleepy Independence has some wonderful historic buildings and is worth a stop for two other reasons. The Eastern California Museum provides a marvelous overview of regional history, and 6 miles south of the small downtown lies the Manzanar National Historic Site, one of 10 camps in the West where people of Japanese descent were confined during the Second World War.

GETTING HERE AND AROUND

Eastern Sierra Transit buses pass through town, but most travelers arrive by car on U.S. 395.

Sights

Ancient Bristlecone Pine Forest
FOREST | **FAMILY** | About an hour's drive from Independence or Bishop you can view some of the oldest living trees on Earth, some of which date back more than 40 centuries. The world's largest bristlecone pine can be found in Patriarch Grove, while the world's oldest known living tree is along Methusula Trail in Schulman Grove. Getting to Patriarch Grove is slow going along the narrow dirt road, especially for sedans with low clearance, but once there you'll find picnic tables, restrooms, and self-guided interpretive trails. ✉ *Schulman Grove Visitor Center, White Mountain Rd., Bishop* ✥ *From U.S. 395, turn east onto Hwy. 168 and follow signs for 23 miles* 🌐 *www.fs.usda.gov/main/inyo/home* 🎟 *$3.*

Eastern California Museum
MUSEUM | **FAMILY** | The highlights of this museum dedicated to Inyo County and the Eastern Sierra's history include photos and artifacts from the Manzanar War Relocation Center, Paiute and Shoshone baskets, and exhibits on the Los Angeles Aqueduct and mountaineer Norman Clyde. ✉ *155 N. Grant St., at W. Center St.* ☎ *760/878–0258* 🌐 *www.inyocounty.us/ecmsite* 🎟 *Free.*

★ **Manzanar National Historic Site**
HISTORIC SITE | A reminder of an ugly episode in U.S. history, the former Manzanar War Relocation Center is where more than 11,000 Japanese-Americans were confined behind barbed-wire fences between 1942 and 1945. A visit here is both deeply moving and inspiring—the former because it's hard to comprehend that the United States was capable of confining its citizens in such a way, the latter because those imprisoned here showed great pluck and perseverance in making the best of a bad situation. Most of the buildings from the 1940s are gone, but two sentry posts, the auditorium, and numerous Japanese rock gardens remain. One of eight guard towers, two barracks, and a women's latrine have been reconstructed, and a mess hall has been restored. Interactive exhibits inside the barracks include audio and video clips from people who were incarcerated in Manzanar during WWII. You can drive the one-way road on a self-guided tour past various ruins to a small cemetery, where a monument stands. Signs mark where the barracks, a hospital, a school, and the

fire station once stood. An outstanding 8,000-square-foot interpretive center has exhibits and documentary photographs and screens a short film. ⊠ *Independence* ✦ *West side of U.S. 395 between Independence and Lone Pine* ☎ *760/878–2194* ⊕ *www.nps.gov/manz* 🖾 *Free.*

Mt. Whitney Fish Hatchery

FISH HATCHERY | FAMILY | A delightful place for a family picnic, the hatchery was one of California's first trout farms. The Tudor Revival–style structure, completed in 1917, is an architectural stunner, its walls nearly 3 feet thick with locally quarried granite. Fish production ceased in 2007 after a fire and subsequent mudslide, but dedicated volunteers staff the facility and raise trout for display purposes in a large pond out front. Bring change for the fish-food machines. ⊠ *1 Golden Trout Circle, 2 miles north of town* ☎ *760/279–1592* ⊕ *www.mtwhitneyfishhatchery.org* 🖾 *Free (donations welcome)* ⊙ *Closed mid-Dec.–mid-Apr. Closed Tues. and Wed.*

Bishop

43 miles north of Independence.

One of the biggest towns along U.S. 395, bustling Bishop has views of the Sierra Nevada and the White and Inyo mountains. First settled by the Northern Paiute Indians, the area was named in 1861 for cattle rancher Samuel Bishop, who established a camp here. Paiute and Shoshone people reside on four reservations in the area. Bishop kicks off the summer season with its Mule Days Celebration. Held over Memorial Day weekend, the five-day event includes mule races, a rodeo, an arts-and-crafts show, and country-music concerts.

GETTING HERE AND AROUND

To fully enjoy the many surrounding attractions, you should get here by car. Arrive and depart via U.S. 395 or, from Nevada, U.S. 6. Local transit provides limited service to nearby tourist sites.

ESSENTIALS

BUS INFORMATION Eastern Sierra Transit Authority. ☎ *760/872–1901* ⊕ *www.estransit.com.*

VISITOR INFORMATION Bishop Chamber of Commerce. ⊠ *690 N. Main St., at Park St.* ☎ *760/873–8405, 888/395–3952* ⊕ *www.bishopvisitor.com.*

👁 Sights

Laws Railroad Museum

MUSEUM | FAMILY | The laid-back and wholly nostalgic railroad museum celebrates the Carson and Colorado Railroad Company, which set up a narrow-gauge railroad yard here in 1883. Among the exhibits are a self-propelled car from the Death Valley Railroad, a stamp mill from an area mine, and a full village of rescued buildings, including a post office, the original 1883 train depot, and a restored 1900 ranch house. Many of the buildings are full of "modern amenities" of days gone by. ⊠ *200 Silver Canyon Rd., off U.S. 6, 4.5 miles north of town* ☎ *760/873–5950* ⊕ *www.lawsmuseum.org* 🖾 *$5 suggested donation.*

Mule Days Celebration

FESTIVAL | For five days around Memorial Day weekend more than 30,000 tourists and locals pack into Bishop to celebrate the humble mule. Activities include what organizers bill as the longest nonmotorized parade in the world, a rodeo, and good old-fashioned country-and-western concerts. ⊠ *1141 N. Main St.* ☎ *760/872–4263* ⊕ *www.muledays.org.*

🍴 Restaurants

Erick Schat's Bakkerÿ

$ | BAKERY | A bustling stop for motorists traveling to and from Mammoth Lakes, this shop is crammed with delicious pastries, cookies, rolls, and other baked goods. The biggest draw, though, is the sheepherder bread, a hand-shaped and stone hearth–baked sourdough that was introduced during the gold rush by immigrant Basque sheepherders in 1907. **Known for:** sheepherder bread and pastries; convenient place to stock up; hefty sandwiches. $ *Average main: $10* ✉ *763 N. Main St., near Park St.* ☎ *760/873–7156* ⊕ *www.erickschatsbakery.com.*

Great Basin Bakery

$ | **AMERICAN** | Stop at this small, old-world-style community bakery for fresh and healthy salads, sandwiches (made all day), bagels, artisan breads, cookies, pies, and pastries. Savor your goodies indoors and listen to local banter (it's a favorite gathering spot), or take them along to eat at a picnic spot while adventuring nearby. **Known for:** sandwiches on fresh-baked, house-made bread; all items made and packaged by hand; stellar pies and other desserts. $ *Average main: $13* ✉ *275 S. Main St.* ☎ *760/873–9828* ⊕ *greatbasinbakerybishop.com.*

🛏 Hotels

Bishop Creekside Inn

$$ | **B&B/INN** | The nicest spot to stay in Bishop, this clean and comfortable mountain-style hotel is a good base from which to explore the town or go skiing and trout fishing nearby. **Pros:** nice pool; spacious and modern rooms; on-site restaurant. **Cons:** pets not allowed; hotel fronts busy road; basic breakfast. $ *Rooms from: $170* ✉ *725 N. Main St.* ☎ *760/872–3044, 800/273–3550* ⊕ *www.bishopcreeksideinn.com* ⤳ *89 rooms* ⚟ *Breakfast.*

🏃 Activities

The Owens Valley is trout country; its glistening alpine lakes and streams are brimming with feisty rainbow, brown, brook, and golden trout. Good spots include Owens River, the Owens River gorge, and Pleasant Valley Reservoir. Although you can fish year-round here, some fishing is catch-and-release. Bishop is the site of fishing derbies throughout the year, including the Blake Jones Blind Bogey Trout Derby in March. Rock-climbing, mountain biking, and hiking are also popular Owens Valley outdoor activities.

FISHING
Reagan's Sporting Goods

FISHING | Stop at Reagan's to pick up bait, tackle, and fishing licenses and to find out where the fish are biting. They can also recommend guides. ✉ *963 N. Main St.* ☎ *760/872–3000* ⊕ *www.reaganssportinggoods.com.*

TOURS
Sierra Mountain Center

TOUR—SPORTS | The guided experiences Sierra Mountain offers include hiking, skiing, snowshoeing, rock-climbing, and mountain-biking trips for all levels of expertise. ✉ *200 S. Main St.* ☎ *760/873–8526* ⊕ *www.sierramountaincenter.com* ⚟ *From $140.*

Sierra Mountain Guides

TOUR—SPORTS | Join expert guides on custom and scheduled alpine adventures, from backcountry skiing and mountaineering to backpacking and mountain running. Programs range from half-day forays to treks that last several weeks. ✉ *312 N. Main St.* ☎ *760/648–1122* ⊕ *www.sierramtnguides.com* ⚟ *From $150.*

Mammoth Lakes

30 miles south of the eastern edge of Yosemite National Park.

International real-estate developers joined forces with Mammoth Mountain Ski Area to transform the once sleepy town of Mammoth Lakes (elevation 7,800 feet) into an upscale ski destination. Relatively sophisticated dining and lodging options can be found at the Village at Mammoth complex, and multimillion-dollar renovations to tired motels and restaurants have revived

Twin Lakes, in the Mammoth Lakes region, is a great place to unwind.

the "downtown" area of Old Mammoth Road. Also here is the hoppin' Mammoth Rock 'n' Bowl, a two-story activity, dining, and entertainment complex. Winter is high season at Mammoth; in summer, the room rates drop.

GETTING HERE AND AROUND

The best way to get to Mammoth Lakes is by car. The town is about 2 miles west of U.S. 395 on Highway 203, signed as Main Street in Mammoth Lakes and Minaret Road west of town. In summer and early fall (until the first big snow) you can drive to Mammoth Lakes east through Yosemite National Park on scenic Tioga Pass Road; signed as Highway 120 outside the park, the road connects to U.S. 395 north of Mammoth. In summer YARTS provides once-a-day public-transit service between Mammoth Lakes and Yosemite Valley. The shuttle buses of Eastern Sierra Transit Authority serve Mammoth Lakes and nearby tourist sites.

ESSENTIALS

VISITOR INFORMATION Mammoth Lakes Visitor Center. ⊠ *Welcome Center, 2510 Main St., near Sawmill Cutoff Rd.* ☎ *760/934–2712, 888/466–2666* ⊕ *www. visitmammoth.com.*

HOTEL CONTACTS Mammoth Reservations. ☎ *800/223–3032* ⊕ *www.mammothres-ervations.com.*

◉ Sights

★ Devils Postpile National Monument

NATURE SITE | Volcanic and glacial forces sculpted this formation of smooth, vertical basalt columns. For a bird's-eye view, take the short, steep trail to the top of a 60-foot cliff. To see the monument's second scenic wonder, **Rainbow Falls,** hike 2 miles past Devils Postpile. A branch of the San Joaquin River plunges more than 100 feet over a lava ledge here. When the water hits the pool below, sunlight turns the resulting mist into a spray of color. From mid-June to early September, day-use visitors must ride the shuttle bus from the Mammoth Mountain Ski Area to the monument. ⊠ *Mammoth Lakes* ✛ *13 miles southwest of Mammoth Lakes off Minaret Rd. (Hwy. 203)* ☎ *760/934–2289, 760/872–1901 shuttle* ⊕ *www.nps.gov/ depo* ⌦ *$10 per vehicle (allowed when the shuttle isn't running, usually early Sept.–mid-Oct.), $8 per person shuttle.*

Hot Creek Geological Site
NATURE SITE | Forged by an ancient volcanic eruption, the geological site is a landscape of boiling hot springs, fumaroles, and occasional geysers. Swimming is prohibited—the water can go from warm to boiling in a short time—but you can look down from the parking area into the canyon to view the steaming volcanic features, a very cool sight indeed. You can also hike the foot path along the creek shores. Fly-fishing for trout is popular upstream from the springs. ⊠ *Hot Creek Hatchery Rd., off U.S. 395 (airport exit), about 10 miles southeast of Mammoth Lakes* ☎ *760/924–5501* ⊕ *www. fs.usda.gov/inyo* ⌦ *Free.*

Hot Creek Trout Hatchery
FISH HATCHERY | FAMILY | This outdoor fish hatchery has the breeding ponds for many of the fish—typically from 3 to 5 million annually—with which the state stocks Eastern Sierra lakes and rivers. In recent years budget cuts have reduced these numbers, but locals have formed foundations to keep the hatchery going. For more details, take the worthwhile self-guided tour. ■TIP➔ **Kids enjoy feeding the fish here.** ⊠ *121 Hot Creek Hatchery Rd., off U.S. 395 (airport exit), about 10 miles southeast of Mammoth Lakes* ☎ *760/934–2664* ⌦ *Free.*

June Lake Loop
SCENIC DRIVE | Heading south from Lee Vining, U.S. 395 intersects the June Lake Loop. This gorgeous 17-mile drive follows an old glacial canyon past Grant, June, Gull, and Silver lakes before reconnecting with U.S. 395 on its way to Mammoth Lakes. ■TIP➔ **The loop is especially colorful in fall.** ⊠ *Hwy. 158 W, Lee Vining.*

★ Mammoth Lakes Basin
BODY OF WATER | Mammoth's seven main lakes are popular for fishing and boating in summer, and a network of multiuse paths connects them to the North Village. First comes Twin Lakes, at the far end of which is Twin Falls, where water cascades 300 feet over a shelf of volcanic rock. Also popular are Lake Mary, the largest lake in the basin; Lake Mamie; and Lake George. ■TIP➔ **Horseshoe Lake is the only lake in which you can swim.** ⊠ *Lake Mary Rd., off Hwy. 203, southwest of town.*

Mammoth Rock 'n' Bowl
RESTAURANT—SIGHT | FAMILY | A sprawling complex with sweeping views of the Sherwin Mountains, Mammoth Rock 'n' Bowl supplies one-stop recreation, entertainment, and dining. Downstairs are 12 bowling lanes, lounge areas, Ping-Pong and foosball tables, dartboards, and a casual bar-restaurant ($$) serving burgers, pizzas, and small plates. The upstairs floor has three golf simulators, a pro shop, and Mammoth Rock Brasserie ($$$), an upscale dining room and lounge. ■TIP➔ **If the weather's nice, sit on the outdoor patio or the upstairs deck and enjoy the unobstructed vistas.** ⊠ *3029 Chateau Rd., off Old Mammoth Rd.* ☎ *760/934–4200* ⊕ *mammothrocknbowl. com* ⌦ *Bowling: from $16.*

Minaret Vista
NATURE SITE | The glacier-carved sawtooth spires of the Minarets, the remains of an ancient lava flow, are best viewed from the Minaret Vista. Pull off the road, park your car in the visitors' viewing area, and walk along the path, which has interpretive signs explaining the spectacular peaks, ridges, and valleys beyond. ⊠ *Off Hwy. 203, 1¼ mile west of Mammoth Mountain Ski Area.*

★ Panorama Gondola
MOUNTAIN—SIGHT | FAMILY | Even if you don't ski, ride the gondola to see Mammoth Mountain, the aptly named dormant volcano that gives Mammoth

Lakes its name. Gondolas serve skiers in winter and mountain bikers and sightseers in summer. The high-speed, eight-passenger gondolas whisk you from the chalet to the summit, where you can learn about the area's volcanic history in the interpretive center, have lunch in the café, and take in top-of-the-world views. Standing high above the tree line, you can look west 150 miles across the state to the Coastal Range; to the east are the highest peaks of Nevada and the Great Basin beyond. You won't find a better view of the Sierra High Country without climbing. ⚠ **The air is thin at the 11,053-foot summit; carry water, and don't overexert yourself.** ✉ *Boarding area at Main Lodge, off Minaret Rd. (Hwy. 203), west of village center* ☎ *760/934–0745, 800/626–6684* 🌐 *www.mammothmountain.com* 🎫 *From $34.*

Village at Mammoth

TOWN | This huge complex of shops, restaurants, and luxury accommodations is the town's tourist center, and the venue for many special events—check the website for the weekly schedule. The complex is also the transfer hub for the free public transit system, with fixed routes throughout the Mammoth Lakes area. The free village gondola starts here and travels up the mountain to Canyon Lodge and back. ■ **TIP→ Unless you're staying in the village and have access to the on-site lots, parking can be very difficult here.** ✉ *100 Canyon Blvd.* 🌐 *villageatmammoth.com.*

🍴 Restaurants

Black Velvet

$$ | **CAFÉ** | Start your day the way scores of locals do—with a stop at the slick Black Velvet espresso bar for Belgian waffles, baked treats, and coffee drinks made from small batches of beans roasted on-site. Then return in the afternoon or evening to hang out with friends in the upstairs wine bar (open 4 to 9). **Known for:** small-batch coffee roasting; small-lot wines by the glass; Belgian waffles. [$] *Average main: $16* ✉ *3343 Main St., Suite F* ☎ 🌐 *www.blackvelvetcoffee.com.*

Bleu Handcrafted Foods

$$ | **WINE BAR** | Handcrafted artisanal cheeses and meats, wine and beer tastings, bread baked on-site, and specialty meats and seafood draw patrons to Bleu, a combination market, restaurant (lunch and dinner), and wine bar. Bleu also cooks up savory pub fare at The Eatery at Mammoth Brewing Company. **Known for:** organic, locally sourced ingredients; bar and lounge with wine and craft beer tastings; on-site deli, butchery, bakery, and market. [$] *Average main: $20* ✉ *106 Old Mammoth Rd.* ☎ *760/914–2538* 🌐 *www.bleufoods.com.*

Burgers

$ | **AMERICAN** | Don't even think about coming to this bustling restaurant unless you're hungry. Burgers is known, appropriately enough, for its burgers and sandwiches, and everything comes in mountainous portions. **Known for:** great service; hefty portions; burgers and seasoned fries. [$] *Average main: $15* ✉ *6118 Minaret Rd., across from the Village* ☎ *760/934–6622* 🌐 *www.burgersrestaurant.com* 🕒 *Closed 2 wks in May and 4–6 wks in Oct. and Nov.*

Mammoth Brewing Company

$$ | **AMERICAN** | Steps from the Village gondola and main bus transfer hub, this brewery lures hungry patrons with about a dozen craft beers on tap, tasty grub from the on-site restaurant, tasting flights, a contemporary vibe at two spacious bar areas, and a beer garden. The dining menu changes constantly, but reflects a locals' twist on pub food, for example, wild game sausages, fig-and-house-made-ricotta flatbread, or house-made "hopped tots." **Known for:** craft beer made on-site; upscale pub food; popular après-ski hangout. [$] *Average main: $16* ✉ *18 Lake Mary Rd.* ✣ *At intersection of Main St. and Minaret Rd.* ☎ *760/934–7141* 🌐 *mammothbrewingco.com.*

The Mogul

$$$ | STEAKHOUSE | FAMILY | Come here for straightforward steaks—top sirloin, New York, filet mignon, and T-bone. The only catch is that the waiters cook them, and the results vary depending on their skill level; but generally things go well, and kids love the experience. **Known for:** traditional alpine atmosphere; servers custom-grill your order; all-you-can-eat salad bar. $ *Average main: $30* ✉ *1528 Tavern Rd., off Old Mammoth Rd.* ☎ *760/934–3039* ⊕ *www.themogul.com* ⊗ *No lunch.*

Petra's Bistro & Wine Bar

$$$ | AMERICAN | The ambience at Petra's—quiet, dark, and warm (there's a great fireplace)—complements its seductive meat and seafood entrées and smart selection of wines from California and around the world. With its pub grub, whiskies, and craft beers and ales, the downstairs Clocktower Cellar bar provides a lively, if sometimes rowdy, alternative. **Known for:** romantic atmosphere; top-notch service; lively downstairs bar. $ *Average main: $30* ✉ *Alpenhof Lodge, 6080 Minaret Rd.* ☎ *760/934–3500* ⊕ *www.petrasbistro.com* ⊗ *Closed Mon. No lunch.*

★ Restaurant at Convict Lake

$$$$ | AMERICAN | The lake is one of the most spectacular spots in the Eastern Sierra, and the food here lives up to the view. The woodsy room has a vaulted knotty-pine ceiling and a copper-chimney fireplace; natural light abounds in the daytime, but if it's summer, opt for a table outdoors under the white-barked aspens. **Known for:** beef wellington, rack of lamb, and pan-seared local trout; exceptional service; extensive wine list with reasonably priced European and California bottlings. $ *Average main: $36* ✉ *Convict Lake Rd. off U.S. 395, 4 miles south of Mammoth Lakes* ☎ *760/934–3800* ⊕ *www.convictlake.com* ⊗ *No lunch early Sept.–mid-June.*

Toomey's

$$ | MODERN AMERICAN | FAMILY | A passionate baseball fan, chef Matt Toomey designed this casual space near the Village Gondola to resemble a dugout, and decorated it with baseball memorabilia. Fill up on coconut mascarpone pancakes or a smoked trout bagel in the morning before heading outdoors; relax later over buffalo meat loaf, seafood jambalaya, or a New Zealand elk rack chop. **Known for:** lobster taquitos and fish tacos; curbside take-out delivery to your car; homemade organic and gluten-free desserts. $ *Average main: $20* ✉ *6085 Minaret Rd., at the Village* ☎ *760/924–4408* ⊕ *toomeysmammoth.com.*

★ The Warming Hut

$ | AMERICAN | FAMILY | Warm up by a crackling fire in the stone fireplace while fueling up on healthy, made-from-scratch breakfast and lunch dishes at this ski-lodge-style eatery. The flexible menu allows for lots of choice, including a DIY breakfast with more than 20 mix-and-match items, five types of hash, keto selections, grab-and-go sandwiches, salads, burgers, and soups. **Known for:** nearly everything made in-house, including ketchup; build-your-own pancake stack (batters, mix-ins, toppings); family-owned and operated. $ *Average main: $15* ✉ *343 Old Mammoth Rd.* ☎ *760/965–0549* ⊗ *No dinner.*

🛏 Hotels

Alpenhof Lodge

$ | HOTEL | Across from the Village at Mammoth, this mom-and-pop motel offers basic comforts and a few niceties such as the attractive pine furniture. **Pros:** convenient for skiers; reasonable rates; excellent dinner at on-site restaurant, Petra's. **Cons:** some bathrooms are small; rooms above pub can be noisy; no elevator. $ *Rooms from: $159* ✉ *6080 Minaret Rd., Box 1157* ☎ *760/934–6330, 800/828–0371* ⊕ *www.alpenhof-lodge. com* ⤶ *54 rooms, 3 cabins* ‖◯‖ *Breakfast.*

★ Convict Lake Resort

$$$ | RESORT | The cabins at this resort a 10-minute drive south from Mammoth Lakes range from rustic to modern and come with fully equipped kitchens, including coffeemakers and premium coffee. **Pros:** great views; tranquil atmosphere; wildlife galore. **Cons:** the smallest quarters feel cramped; spotty Wi-Fi and cell service; too remote for some. $ *Rooms from: $189* ⌂ *Convict Rd., 2 miles off U.S. 395* ☎ *760/934–3800, 800/992–2260* ⊕ *www.convictlake.com* ⇋ *28 cabins, 3 houses* ⌾ *No meals.*

★ Double Eagle Resort and Spa

$$$ | RESORT | Lofty pines tower over this very fine spa retreat on the June Lake Loop. **Pros:** pretty setting; spectacular indoor pool; 1½ miles from June Mountain Ski Area. **Cons:** expensive; remote; no in-room air-conditioning. $ *Rooms from: $249* ⌂ *5587 Hwy. 158, Box 736, June Lake* ☎ *760/648–7004* ⊕ *www.doubleeagle.com* ⇋ *17 2-bedroom cabins, 16 rooms, 1 3-bedroom house* ⌾ *No meals.*

Holiday Haus

$$ | HOTEL | A short walk from the Village, Holiday Haus is a collection of contemporary mountain-activity-theme rooms and suites—many with full kitchens—at relatively affordable prices. **Pros:** free parking and Wi-Fi; good option for groups and families; walk to the Village. **Cons:** showers, no tubs in most rooms; no 24-hour desk; basic breakfast. $ *Rooms from: $149* ⌂ *3905 Main St.* ☎ *760/934–2414* ⊕ *holidayhausmotelandhostel.com* ⇋ *23 rooms, 1 cabin, 1 26-bed hostel.*

Juniper Springs Resort

$$$ | RESORT | Tops for slope-side comfort, these condominium-style units have full kitchens and ski-in ski-out access to the mountain. **Pros:** bargain during summer; direct access to the slopes in winter; free shuttle to town in winter. **Cons:** no nightlife within walking distance; no air-conditioning; property needs updating. $ *Rooms from: $199* ⌂ *4000 Meridian Blvd.* ☎ *760/924–1102, 800/626–6684* ⊕ *www.mammothmountain.com* ⇋ *184 studios and apartments* ⌾ *No meals.*

Mammoth Mountain Inn

$$$ | RESORT | If you want to be within walking distance of the Mammoth Mountain Main Lodge, this is the place. **Pros:** great location; big rooms; a traditional place to stay. **Cons:** can be crowded in ski season; needs updating; not in the heart of town. $ *Rooms from: $179* ⌂ *1 Minaret Rd.* ☎ *760/934–2581, 800/626–6684* ⊕ *www.mammothmountain.com* ⇋ *216 rooms, 50 condos.*

Sierra Nevada Resort & Spa

$$$ | RESORT | A full-service resort in the heart of Old Mammoth, the Sierra Nevada has it all: Old Mammoth rustic elegance, three restaurants, four bars, a dedicated spa facility, on-site ski and snowboard rentals, a seasonal pool and Jacuzzi, seasonal miniature golf, and room and suite options in three buildings. **Pros:** kids' club on weekends from 4 to 9; walk to restaurants on property or downtown; complimentary shuttle service. **Cons:** must drive or ride a bus or shuttle to the slopes; thin walls in older rooms; resort fee. $ *Rooms from: $199* ⌂ *164 Old Mammoth Rd.* ☎ *760/934–2515, 800/824–5132* ⊕ *the-sierranevadaresort.com* ⇋ *143 rooms, 6 townhomes* ⌾ *No meals.*

★ Tamarack Lodge Resort & Lakefront Restaurant

$$$ | RESORT | On the edge of the John Muir Wilderness Area, where cross-country ski trails lace the woods, this 1924 lodge looks like something out of a snow globe. **Pros:** rustic; eco-sensitive; many nearby outdoor activities. **Cons:** high price tag; shared bathrooms for some main lodge rooms; spartan furnishings in lodge rooms. $ *Rooms from: $239* ⌂ *Lake Mary Rd., off Hwy. 203* ☎ *760/934–2442, 800/626–6684* ⊕ *www.tamaracklodge.com* ⇋ *46 rooms and cabins* ⌾ *No meals.*

The Village Lodge

$$$ | **RESORT** | With their exposed timbers and peaked roofs, these four-story condo buildings at the epicenter of Mammoth's dining and nightlife scene pay homage to Alpine style. **Pros:** central location; big rooms; good restaurants nearby. **Cons:** pricey; can be noisy outside; somewhat sterile decor. [$] *Rooms from: $239* ✉ *1111 Forest Trail* ☎ *760/934–1982, 800/626–6684* 🌐 *www.mammothmountain.com* 🛏 *277 units* 🍴 *No meals.*

★ Westin Monache Resort

$$$$ | **RESORT** | On a hill just steps from the Village at Mammoth, the Westin provides full-service comfort and amenities close to restaurants, entertainment, and free public transportation. **Pros:** full bar, pool, 24-fitness center; prime location; free gondola to the slopes is across the street. **Cons:** long, steep stairway down to village; added resort fee. [$] *Rooms from: $359* ✉ *50 Hillside Dr.* ☎ *760/934–0400, 888/627–8154 reservations, 760/934–4686* 🌐 *www.marriott.com/mmhwi* 🛏 *230 rooms and suites* 🍴 *No meals.*

Activities

Mammoth Mega Zip

ZIP LINING | In summer 2019, Mammoth Mountain opened a zip-line tour with the tallest vertical drop (2,100 feet) in North America. Ride the Panoramic Gondola up to the summit of Mammoth Mountain, then descend side by side on parallel cables that run more than a mile back down to the base, at speeds of up to 60 mph (minimum weight 75 lbs). ✉ *Mammoth Adventure Center, 10001 Minaret Rd.* ☎ *800/626–6684* 🌐 *www.mammothmountain.com.*

Via Ferrata

CLIMBING/MOUNTAINEERING | In Europe, a Via Ferrata is a protected climbing network that allows people to experience the thrills of rock climbing and mountaineering without as much risk. Mammoth's version has six different routes of varying ability, with steel cables, iron rungs, and a suspended bridge, all permanently affixed to the rock. The fully guided tour begins with a gondola ride up the mountain. Clip yourself into a cable and climb securely to sweeping views of the Sierra Nevada range. If time and group ability allow, you can follow multiple routes during a session. No climbing experience is required. ✉ *Mammoth Mountain, 10001 Minaret Rd.* ☎ *800/626–6684* 🌐 *www.mammothmountain.com* 🎟 *From $359.*

BIKING

★ Mammoth Bike Park

BICYCLING | The park opens when the snow melts, usually by July, and has 80 miles of single-track trails—from mellow to super-challenging. Chairlifts and shuttles provide trail access, and rentals are available. ✉ *Mammoth Mountain Ski Area* ☎ *760/934–0677, 800/626-6684* 🌐 *www.mammothmountain.com* 🎟 *$55 day pass.*

FISHING

The main fishing season runs from the last Saturday in April until November 15; there are opportunities for catch-and-release fishing in winter. Crowley Lake is the top trout-fishing spot in the area; Convict Lake, June Lake, and the lakes of the Mammoth Basin are other prime spots. One of the best trout rivers is the super-scenic Upper Owens River, near the east side of Crowley Lake. Hot Creek, a designated Wild Trout Stream, is renowned for fly-fishing (catch-and-release only).

Kittredge Sports

FISHING | This outfit rents rods and reels and conducts guided trips. ✉ *3218 Main St., at Forest Trail* ☎ *760/934–7566* 🌐 *kittredgesports.com.*

Sierra Drifters Guide Service

FISHING | To maximize your time on the water, get tips from local anglers, or

Camping in the Eastern Sierra

Camping in the Sierra Nevada means gazing up at awe-inspiring constellations and awakening to the sights of nearby meadows and streams and the unforgettable landscape of giant granite. More than a hundred campgrounds, from remote, tents-only areas to full-service facilities with RV hookups close to the main attractions, operate in the Eastern Sierra. Be aware that Yosemite National Park's most accessible campgrounds can be jam-packed and claustrophobic in the summer. Luckily, there are many options to the east, including calm and beautiful sites such as Lake Mary Campground in the Mammoth Lakes area. The following campsites are recommended. Reserve sites at ⊕ *www.recreation.gov.*

Convict Lake Campground. A 10-minute drive south of Mammoth, this campground near the Convict Lake Resort is run by the U.S. Forest Service. ⊠ *Convict Lake Rd., 2 miles off U.S. 395* ☎ *760/924–5500* ⇱ *88 campsites.*

Lake Mary Campground. There are few sites as beautiful as this lakeside campground at 8,900 feet, open from June to September. ⊠ *Lake Mary Loop Dr., off Hwy. 203* ☎ *760/924–5500* ➡ *No credit cards* ⇱ *48 sites (tent or RV)* ⑩ *No meals.*

better yet, book a guided fishing trip, contact Sierra Drifters. ⊠ *Mammoth Lakes* ☎ *760/935–4250* ⊕ *www.sierra-drifters.com.*

HIKING

Hiking in Mammoth is stellar, especially along the trails that wind through alpine scenery around the Lakes Basin. Carry lots of water; and remember, the air is thin at 8,000-plus feet.

Visit the Mammoth Lakes Trail System website (⊕ *www.mammothtrails.org*) for descriptions of more than 300 miles of trails, maps, and a wealth of information on recreation in Mammoth Lakes and the Inyo National Forest in all seasons.

Mammoth Lakes Welcome Center
HIKING/WALKING | Stop at the Mammoth Lakes Welcome Center, just east of the town of Mammoth Lakes, for an area trail map and permits for backpacking in wilderness areas. ⊠ *2510 Main St., Hwy. 203* ☎ *760/924–5501* ⊕ *www.visitmammoth.com.*

EASY
Convict Lake Loop
HIKING/WALKING | This 2.8-mile trail loops gently around deep blue Convict Lake, a popular site for anglers. Feast your eyes on stunning views of tall peaks, glistening water, and aspen and cottonwood groves while you hike. *Easy.* ⊠ *Trailhead: at Convict Lake, 9 miles south of Mammoth Lakes.*

Minaret Falls
HIKING/WALKING | **FAMILY** | Hike along portions of both the Pacific Crest and John Muir trails on this scenic trail (3 miles round-trip) that leads to Devil's Postpile, Minaret Falls, and natural volcanic springs. This is a good family hike, especially in late summer when the water has receded a bit and kids can climb boulders and splash around. *Easy.* ⊠ *Trailhead: At Devil's Postpile National Monument.*

MODERATE
Emerald Lake and Sky Meadows
HIKING/WALKING | The first part of this trail travels through shady pine forest along Coldwater Creek to bright-green Emerald

Lake (1.8 miles round-trip). Extend the hike by climbing up a trail along an inlet stream up to Gentian Meadow and Sky Meadows (4 miles round-trip), especially beautiful in July and August when various alpine wildflowers, fed by snowmelt, are at their peak splendor. *Moderate.* ⊠ *Trailhead: Coldwater Campground, Mammoth Lakes.*

DIFFICULT
Duck Lake

HIKING/WALKING | This popular and busy trail (11 miles round-trip) heads up Coldwater Canyon along Mammoth Creek, past a series of spectacular lakes and wildflower meadows over 10,797-foot Duck Pass to dramatic Duck Lake, which eventually links up with the John Muir Trail. *Difficult.* ⊠ *Trailhead: Coldwater Campground.*

HORSEBACK RIDING

Stables around Mammoth are typically open from June through September.

Mammoth Lakes Pack Outfit

HORSEBACK RIDING | This company runs day and overnight horseback and mule trips and will shuttle you to the high country. ⊠ *Lake Mary Rd., between Twin Lakes and Lake Mary* ☎ *888/475–8747, 760/934–2434* ⊕ *www.mammothpack.com.*

McGee Creek Pack Station

HORSEBACK RIDING | These folks customize pack trips or will shuttle you to camp alone. ⊠ *2990 McGee Creek Rd., Crowley Lake* ☎ *760/935–4324 summer, 760/878–2207, 800/854–7407* ⊕ *www.mcgeecreekpackstation.com.*

SKIING

In winter, check the On the Snow website or call the Snow Report for information about Mammoth weather conditions.

June Mountain Ski Area

SKIING/SNOWBOARDING | FAMILY | Snowboarders especially dig June Mountain, a compact, low-key resort north of Mammoth Mountain. Three beginner-to-intermediate terrain areas—the Surprise Fun Zone, and Mambo Playground—are for both skiers and boarders. There's rarely a line for the lifts here: if you must ski on a weekend and want to avoid the crowds, this is the place to come, and in a storm it's better protected from wind and blowing snow than Mammoth is. (If it starts to storm, you can use your Mammoth ticket at June.) The services include a rental-and-repair shop, a ski school, and a sports shop. There's food, but the options are better at Mammoth. ■TIP→ Kids 12 and under ski and ride free. ⊠ *3819 Hwy. 158/June Lake Loop, off U.S. 395, 22 miles northwest of Mammoth, June Lake* ☎ *760/648–7733, 888/586–3686* ⊕ *www.junemountain.com* ☜ *From $99* ☞ *35 trails on 1,400 acres, rated 35% beginner, 45% intermediate, 20% advanced. Longest run 2 miles, base 7,545 feet, summit 10,190 feet. Lifts: 7.*

★ Mammoth Mountain Ski Area

SKIING/SNOWBOARDING | One of the West's largest and best ski areas, Mammoth has more than 3,500 acres of skiable terrain and a 3,100-foot vertical drop. The views from the 11,053-foot summit are some of the most stunning in the Sierra. Below, you'll find a 6½-mile-wide swath of groomed boulevards and canyons, as well as pockets of tree-skiing and a dozen vast bowls. Snowboarders are everywhere on the slopes; there are seven outstanding freestyle terrain parks of varying difficulty, with jumps, rails, tabletops, and giant super pipes—this is the location of several international snowboarding competitions, and, in summer, mountain-bike meets. Mammoth's season begins in November and often lingers into July. Lessons and equipment are available, and there's a children's ski and snowboard school. Mammoth runs free shuttle-bus routes around town and to the ski area, and the Village Gondola runs from the Village complex to Canyon Lodge. However, only overnight guests are allowed to

Why Is There So Much Snow?

The Sierra Nevada receives some of the deepest snow anywhere in North America. In winter, houses literally get buried, and homeowners have to build tunnels to their front doors (though many install enclosed wooden walkways). In the high country, it's not uncommon for a single big storm to bring 10 feet of snow and for 30 feet of snow to accumulate at the height of the season. In the enormous bowls of Mammoth Mountain, you might ski past a tiny pine that looks like a miniature Christmas tree—until you remember that more than 30 feet of tree is under the snow.

To understand the weather, you have to understand the terrain. The Sierra Nevada are marked by a gentle western rise from sea level to the Sierra crest, which tops out at a whopping 14,494 feet at Sequoia National Park's Mt. Whitney, the highest point in the continental United States. On the eastern side of the crest, at the escarpment, the mountains drop sharply—as much as 5,000 feet—giving way to the Great Basin and the high-mountain deserts of Nevada and Utah.

When winter storms blow in off the Pacific, carrying vast stores of water with them, they race across the relatively flat, 100-mile-wide Central Valley. As they ascend the wall of mountains, though, the decrease in temperature and the increase in pressure on the clouds force them to release their water. Between October and April, that means snow—lots of it. Storms can get hung up on the peaks for days, dumping foot after foot of the stuff. By the time they finally cross over the range and into the Great Basin, there isn't much moisture left for the lower elevations on the eastern side. This is why, if you cross the Sierra eastward on your way to U.S. 395, you'll notice that brightly colored wildflowers and forest-green trees give way to pale-green sagebrush and brown sand as you drop out of the mountains.

The coastal cities and farmlands of the rest of the state depend heavily on the water from the Sierra snowpack. Most of the spring and summer runoff from the melting snows is caught in reservoirs in the foothills and routed to farmlands and cities throughout the state via a complex system of levees and aqueducts, which you'll no doubt see in the foothills and Central Valley, to the west of the range. But much of the water remains in the mountains, forming lakes, most notably giant Lake Tahoe to the north, Mono Lake to the east, and the thousands of little lakes along the Sierra Crest. The lakes are an essential part of the ecosystem, providing water for birds, fish, and plant life.

park at the Village for more than a few hours. **Facilities:** 155 trails; 3,500 acres; 3,100-foot vertical drop; 25 lifts. ✉ Minaret Rd., west of Mammoth Lakes, Rte. 203, off U.S. 395 ☎ 760/934–2571, 800/626–6684, 760/934–0687 shuttle ⊕ www.mammothmountain.com ⛷ From $99.

Tamarack Cross Country Ski Center
SKIING/SNOWBOARDING | Trails at the center, adjacent to Tamarack Lodge, meander around several lakes. Rentals are available. ✉ Lake Mary Rd., off Hwy. 203 ☎ 760/934–5293, 760/934–2442 ⊕ tamaracklodge.com ⛷ $58 all-inclusive day rate.

SKI RENTALS AND RESOURCES

★ Black Tie Ski Rentals

SKIING/SNOWBOARDING | Skiers and snowboarders love this rental outfit whose staffers will deliver and custom-fit equipment for free. They also offer slope-side assistance. ✉ 501 Old Mammoth Rd. ☎ 760/934–7009 ⊕ mammothskis.com.

Footloose

SKIING/SNOWBOARDING | When the U.S. Ski Team visits Mammoth and needs boot adjustments, everyone heads to Footloose, the best place in town—and possibly all California—for ski-boot rentals and sales, as well as custom insoles. ✉ 3043 Main St., at Mammoth Rd. ☎ 760/934–2400 ⊕ www.footloosesports.com.

Kittredge Sports

SKIING/SNOWBOARDING | Advanced skiers should consider this outfit, which has been around since the 1960s. ✉ 3218 Main St. ☎ 760/934–7566 ⊕ kittredgesports.com.

Snow Report

SKIING/SNOWBOARDING | For information on winter conditions around Mammoth, call the Snow Report. ✉ Mammoth Lakes ☎ 760/934–7669, 888/766–9778 ⊕ www.mammothmountain.com/winter/mountain-information.

Woolly's Tube Park & Snow Play

SNOW SPORTS | FAMILY | Ride a lift to the top of the hill and whoosh down in a high-speed snow tube as often as you like during a 1¼-hour session. The park has six lanes, a heated deck, and snack shop. Discounts available for a second session if you're not ready to stop riding. Little ones can hang out in the snow play area with sleds and saucers. ✉ 9000 Minaret Rd. ☎ 800/626–6684 reservations, 760/934–7533 direct line ⊕ www.mammothmountain.com ⛷ From $39, play area $20.

SNOWMOBILING

Mammoth Snowmobile Adventures

SNOW SPORTS | Mammoth Snowmobile Adventures conducts guided tours along wooded trails. ✉ Mammoth Mountain Main Lodge ☎ 760/934–9645, 800/626–6684 ⊕ www.mammothmountain.com ⛷ From $119.

Lee Vining

20 miles east of Tuolumne Meadows, 30 miles north of Mammoth Lakes.

Tiny Lee Vining is known primarily as the eastern gateway to Yosemite National Park (summer only) and the location of vast and desolate Mono Lake. Pick up supplies at the general store year-round, or stop here for lunch or dinner before or after a drive through the high country. In winter the town is all but deserted, except for the ice climbers who come to scale frozen waterfalls.

GETTING HERE AND AROUND

Lee Vining is on U.S. 395, north of the road's intersection with Highway 120 and on the south side of Mono Lake. In summer YARTS public transit (⊕ yarts.com) can get you here from Yosemite Valley, but you'll need a car to explore the area.

ESSENTIALS

VISITOR INFORMATION Lee Vining Chamber of Commerce. ☎ 760/647–6629 ⊕ www.leevining.com. **Mono Basin National Forest Scenic Area Visitor Center.** ✉ Visitor Center Dr., off U.S. 395, 1 mile north of Hwy. 120 ☎ 760/647–3044 ⊕ www.monolake.org/visit/vc.

◉ Sights

June Lake Loop

SCENIC DRIVE | Heading south from Lee Vining, U.S. 395 intersects the June Lake Loop. This gorgeous 17-mile drive follows an old glacial canyon past Grant, June, Gull, and Silver lakes before reconnecting with U.S. 395 on its way to Mammoth Lakes. ■TIP→ The loop is especially colorful in fall. ✉ Hwy. 158 W.

Did You Know?

These "tufa" towers on the shores Mono Lake are essentially made of limestone and form over decades. Some can be as tall as 30 feet.

Did You Know?

The town of Bodie offers ghost tours of its abandoned village at night.

★ **Mono Lake**

BODY OF WATER | Since the 1940s Los Angeles has diverted water from this lake, exposing striking towers of tufa, or calcium carbonate. Court victories by environmentalists have meant fewer diversions, and the lake is rising again. Although to see the lake from U.S. 395 is stunning, make time to visit South Tufa, whose parking lot is 5 miles east of U.S. 395 off Highway 120. There in summer you can join the naturalist-guided **South Tufa Walk,** which lasts about 90 minutes. The **Scenic Area Visitor Center,** off U.S. 395, is a sensational stop for its interactive exhibits and sweeping Mono Lake views (closed in winter). In town at U.S. 395 and 3rd Street, the **Mono Lake Committee Information Center & Bookstore**, open from 9 to 5 daily (extended hours in summer), has more information about this beautiful area. ✉ *Hwy. 120, east of Lee Vining* ☎ *760/647–3044 visitor center, 760/647–6595 info center* 🌐 *www.monolake.org* 🎫 *Free.*

🍴 Restaurants

Epic Cafe

$ | **AMERICAN** | **FAMILY** | Hungry travelers and locals feast on fresh, healthy, cooked-to-order comfort food at this casual café at Lakeview Lodge, near the Tioga Road and Highway 395 junction. The menu changes daily, but you can count on items like waffles and fritattas for breakfast; paninis, sandwiches, salads, rice bowls, and soups for lunch; and three special dinner entrées, perhaps locally caught fish, chicken potpie, or braised short ribs. **Known for:** local and organic food sources; cozy indoor dining room and garden patio; fresh-baked scones, muffins, desserts, and other goodies. [$] *Average main: $15* ✉ *349 Lee Vining Ave.* ☎ *760/965–6282* 🌐 *epiccafesierra.com* 🕓 *Closed Nov.–early May. Closed Sun.*

Mono Cone

$ | **AMERICAN** | Get soft-serve ice cream, burgers, and fries at this hopping shack in the middle of Lee Vining, but be prepared to do what's rare in these uncrowded parts: wait in line. There's some indoor seating, but unless the clouds are leaking, take your food to nearby (and quiet) Hess Park, whose views of Mono Lake make it one of the best picnic spots in eastern California. [$] *Average main: $9* ✉ *51508 U.S. 395* ☎ *760/647–6606* 💳 *No credit cards* 🕓 *Closed in winter.*

Tioga Gas Mart & Whoa Nelli Deli

$$ | **AMERICAN** | This might be the only gas station in the United States serving craft beers and lobster taquitos, but its appeal goes beyond novelty. Order at the counter and grab a seat inside, or sit at one of the picnic tables on the lawn outside and take in the distant view of Mono Lake. **Known for:** fish tacos and barbecued ribs; regular live music; convenient location. [$] *Average main: $16* ✉ *Hwy. 120 and U.S. 395* ☎ *760/647–1088* 🌐 *www.whoanelliedeli.com* 🕓 *Closed early Nov.–late Apr.*

🛏 Hotels

Lake View Lodge

$$ | **B&B/INN** | Enormous rooms and landscaping that includes several shaded sitting areas set this motel apart from its competitors in town. **Pros:** convenient access to Yosemite, Mono Lake, Bodie State Historic Park; peaceful setting; on-site restaurant. **Cons:** could use updating; slow Wi-Fi in some areas; no views from some rooms. [$] *Rooms from: $143* ✉ *51285 U.S. 395* ☎ *760/647–6543, 800/990–6614* 🌐 *www.lakeviewlodgeyosemite.com* 🛏 *76 rooms, 12 cottages.*

Bodie State Historic Park

31 miles northeast of Lee Vining.

Bodie State Historic Park's scenery is spectacular, with craggy, snowcapped peaks looming over vast prairies. The town of Bridgeport is the gateway to the park, and the only supply center for miles around. Bridgeport's claims to fame include an historic courthouse that's been in continuous use since 1880 and the excellent fishing—the California state record brown trout, at 26 pounds 12 ounces, was caught in Bridgeport's Twin Lakes. In winter, much of Bridgeport shuts down.

GETTING HERE AND AROUND

A car is the best way to reach this area. Bodie is on Highway 270 about 13 miles east of U.S. 395.

Sights

★ Bodie Ghost Town

GHOST TOWN | The mining village of Rattlesnake Gulch, abandoned mine shafts, and the remains of a small Chinatown are among the sights at this fascinating ghost town. The town boomed from about 1878 to 1881, but by the late 1940s all its residents had departed. A state park was established here in 1962, with a mandate to preserve everything in a state of "arrested decay." Evidence of Bodie's wild past survives at an excellent museum, and you can tour an old stamp mill where ore was crushed into fine powder to extract gold and silver. Bodie lies 13 miles east of U.S. 395 off Highway 270. The last 3 miles are unpaved, and snow may close the highway from late fall through early spring. No food, drink, or lodging is available in Bodie. ⊠ *Bodie Rd., off Hwy. 270, Bodie* ☎ *760/616–5040* ⊕ *www.parks.ca.gov/bodie* ⊠ *$8.*

Chapter 16

SAN FRANCISCO

Updated by
Rebecca Flint
Marx, Denise Leto,
Andrea Powell, and
Trevor Felch

◉ Sights	🍴 Restaurants	🛏 Hotels	🛍 Shopping	🍸 Nightlife
★★★★★	★★★★☆	★★★★★	★☆☆☆☆	★☆☆☆☆

WELCOME TO SAN FRANCISCO

TOP REASONS TO GO

★ **The bay:** It's hard not to gasp as you catch sight of sunlight dancing on the water when you crest a hill, or watch the Golden Gate Bridge vanish and reemerge in the summer fog.

★ **The food:** San Franciscans are serious about what they eat, and with good reason. Home to some of the nation's best chefs, top restaurants, and finest local produce, it's hard not to eat well here.

★ **The shopping:** Shopaholics visiting the city will not be disappointed—San Francisco is packed with browsing destinations, everything from quirky boutiques to massive malls.

★ **The good life:** A laid-back atmosphere, beautiful surroundings, and oodles of cultural, culinary, and aesthetic pleasures … if you spend too much time here, you might not leave.

★ **The great outdoors:** From Golden Gate Park to sidewalk cafés in North Beach, San Franciscans relish their outdoor spaces.

San Francisco is a compact city; just 46.7 square miles. Essentially a tightly packed cluster of extremely diverse neighborhoods, the city dearly rewards walking. The areas that most visitors cover are easy (and safe) to reach on foot, but many have steep—make that steep—hills.

1 **Union Square.**

2 **Chinatown.**

3 **Financial District.**

4 **SoMa.**

5 **Civic Center.**

6 **Hayes Valley.**

7 **Nob Hill.**

8 **Polk Gulch.**

9 **Russian Hill.**

10 **North Beach.**

11 **Fisherman's Wharf.**

12 **Embarcadero.**

13 **The Marina.**

14 **Cow Hollow.**

15 **Presidio.**

16 **Golden Gate Park.**

17 **The Richmond.**

18 **The Sunset.**

19 **The Haight.**

20 **The Castro.**

21 **Noe Valley.**

22 **Mission District.**

23 **Pacific Heights.**

24 **Japantown.**

25 **Western Addition.**

26 **The Tenderloin.**

27 **Potrero Hill.**

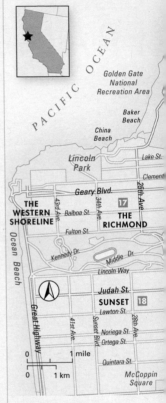

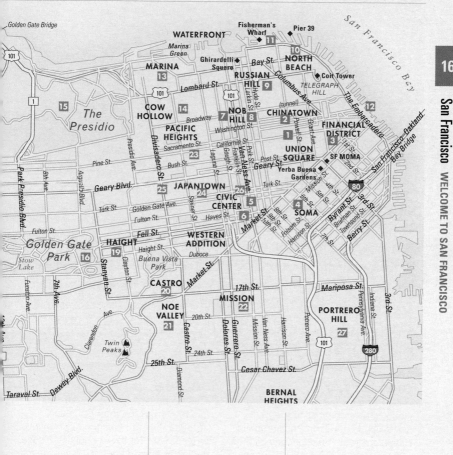

Golden Gate Bridge

101

1

15

The Presidio

WATERFRONT

Marina Green

MARINA
13

Fisherman's Wharf

Pier 39

11

Bay St.
Ghirardelli Square

101

Lombard St.

101

COW HOLLOW
14

Broadway

PACIFIC HEIGHTS

Presidio Ave.

Divisadero St.

Sacramento St.

23

Pine St.

Bush St.

RUSSIAN HILL
9

Hyde St.
Larkin St.

NOB HILL
7   8

Washington St.

California St.

Van Ness Ave.

Park St.

Gough St.

Laguna St.

Steiner St.

10

NORTH BEACH

Columbus Ave.

Coit Tower

TELEGRAPH HILL

(tunnel)

CHINATOWN
2

Powell St.

Grant Ave.

The Embarcadero

12

Stockton St.

FINANCIAL DISTRICT
3

1st St.

UNION SQUARE
1

Post St.

Geary St.

SF MOMA

2nd St.

San Francisco–Oakland Bay Bridge

San Francisco Bay

Aguallo Blvd.

Geary Blvd.

Turk St.

25

JAPANTOWN

24

Golden Gate Ave.

Fulton St.

CIVIC CENTER

26

5

6

Hayes St.

Turk St.

Yerba Buena Gardens

3rd St.

4th St.

5th St.

6th St.

Mission St.

80

4

SOMA

Folsom St.

Harrison St.

7th St.

8th St.

9th St.

Bryant St.

Brannan St.

Townsend St.

Berry St.

3rd St.

Park Presidio Blvd.

8th Ave.

Fulton St.

Golden Gate Park

Stow Lake

16

7th Ave.

Funston Ave.

Stanyan St.

HAIGHT
19

Haight St.

Fell St.

Clayton St.

Buena Vista Park

WESTERN ADDITION

Duboce

Market St.

Market St.

CASTRO
20

17th St.

MISSION
22

Castro St.

NOE VALLEY
21

20th St.

24th St.

Guerrero St.

Dolores St.

Mission St.

Van Ness Ave.

Harrison St.

Potrero Ave.

Mariposa St.

PORTRERO HILL
27

Indiana St.

Pennsylvania Ave.

3rd St.

101

280

Clarendon Ave.

Twin Peaks

Diamond St.

25th St.

Cesar Chavez St.

Taraval St.

Dewey Blvd.

BERNAL HEIGHTS

HOW TO EAT LIKE A LOCAL

Several farmers' markets occupy the Ferry Building

San Francisco may well be the most piping-red-hot dining scene in the nation now. After all, with a booming tech industry, there are mouths to feed. Freedom to do what you want. Innovation. Eccentricity. These words define the culture, the food, and the cuisine of the city by the bay. Get in on what locals know by enjoying their favorite foods.

FOOD TRUCKS

This is where experimentation begins, where the overhead is low, and risk-taking is fun. From these mobile kitchens careers are launched. A food meet-up called "Off the Grid" happens in season at Fort Mason where you can have a progressive dinner among the 25 or so trucks. Year-round the convoy roams to different locations, selling things like Korean poutine, Indian burritos, and Vietnamese burgers. Each dish seems to reflect a refusal to follow the norm.

DIM SUM

The tradition of dim sum took hold in San Francisco when Chinese immigrants from Guangdong Province arrived with Cantonese cuisine. These earlier settlers eventually established teahouses and bakeries that sold dim sum, like the steamed dumplings stuffed with shrimp (*har gow*) or pork (*shao mai*). Now carts roll from table to table in Chinatown restaurants—and other parts of the city. Try the grilled and fried bite-size savories but also the sweets like *dan tat,* an egg custard tart.

BARBECUE

Whaaa? San Francisco barbecue? And what would that be? You can bet it's meat from top purveyors nearby. The city is surrounded by grazing lands, where the animals and their minders, the ranchers, are king. Until now, meats came simply plated. Now it's messy, with smokiness, charred crusts, and gorgeous marbling. But you may never hear of a San-Fran-style barbecue because, in the words of one chef, we're "nondenominational." You'll see it all: Memphis, Texas, Carolina, and Kansas City.

The food truck

ICE CREAM

How ice cream became so popular in a place that spends many of its 365 days below the 75 degree mark is a mystery. But the lines attest to the popularity of the frozen dessert that gets its own San Francisco twist. This is the vanilla-bean vanilla and Tcho chocolate crowd. Bourbon and cornflakes? Reposado tequila? Cheers to that. Diversity and local produce is blended into flavors like ube (purple yam), yuzu, and Thai latte.

BURRITOS

This stuffed tortilla got its Bay Area start in the 1960s in the Mission District. Because the size and fillings distinguish it from other styles, it became

Dim sum

known as the Mission burrito. Look for rice (Southern Californians are cringing), beans, salsa, and enough meat in the burrito for two meals. The aluminum foil keeps the interior neat, in theory. Popular choices are *carne asada* (beef) and *carnitas* (pork). But then there's *lengua* (beef tongue) and *birria* (goat). This is a hands-on meal.

COFFEE

Coffee roasters here are like sports teams in other cities. You pick one of the big five or six to be loyal to, and defend it tirelessly. San Francisco favorites source impeccably and blend different beans as if they were wine making. In addition, a few of the big names—Four Barrel, Sightglass, Ritual, Blue Bottle—roast their own to control what they grind and pour at their outlets across the city—and now nationally and internationally.

FARMERS' MARKETS

These are our new grocery stores. They're the places to discover the latest in fruits, vegetables, and dried beans—much of it grown within a 60-mile radius. Cheeses, cured salami, breads, and nuts are sampled. Then there are the local ready-to-eat snacks, like pizza and *huevos rancheros*. The most popular market is the one on Saturday at the Ferry Plaza.

On a 46½-square-mile strip of land between San Francisco Bay and the Pacific Ocean, San Francisco has charms great and small. Residents cherish their city for the same reasons visitors do: the proximity to the bay, rows of Victorian homes clinging precariously to the hillsides, the sun setting behind the Golden Gate Bridge, the world-class cuisine. Locals and visitors alike spend hours exploring downtown, Chinatown, North Beach, the northern and western waterfronts, and Golden Gate Park, along with colorful neighborhoods like the Haight, the Mission murals, and the Castro.

The city's attraction, though, goes much deeper than its alluring physical space, from the diversity of its neighborhoods to its free-spirited tolerance. Take all these things together and you'll understand why many San Franciscans—despite the dizzying cost of living and the chilly summers—can't imagine calling any place else home.

You won't want to miss the City by the Bay's highlights, whether it's a cable car ride over Nob Hill; a walk down the Filbert Street Steps; gazing at the thundering Pacific from the cliffs of Lincoln Park; cheering the San Francisco Giants to *beat* L.A. in lively Oracle Park; or eating freshly shucked oysters at the Ferry Building. San Francisco is a beautiful metropolis packed with diverse wonders that inspire at every turn.

Planning

When to Go

You can visit San Francisco comfortably any time of year. Possibly the best time is September and October, when the city's summerlike weather brings outdoor concerts and festivals. The climate here always feels Mediterranean and moderate, with a foggy, sometimes chilly bite. The temperature rarely drops below 40°F, and anything warmer than 80°F is considered a heat wave. Be prepared for rain in winter, especially December and January. Winds off the ocean can add to the chill factor. That old joke about summer in San Francisco feeling like winter is true at heart, but once you move inland, it gets warmer. (And some locals swear that the thermostat has inched up in recent years.)

Getting Here and Around

AIR TRAVEL
The major gateway to San Francisco is San Francisco International Airport (SFO), 15 miles south of the city. It's off U.S. 101 near Millbrae and San Bruno. Oakland International Airport (OAK) is across the bay, not much farther away from downtown San Francisco (via Interstate 80 east and Interstate 880 south), but rush-hour traffic on the Bay Bridge may lengthen travel times considerably. San Jose International Airport (SJC) is about 40 miles south of San Francisco; travel time depends largely on traffic flow, but plan on an hour and a half with moderate traffic.

AIRPORTS San Francisco International Airport (SFO). ⊠ McDonnell and Links Rds., San Francisco ☎ 800/435–9736, 650/821–8211 ⊕ www.flysfo.com. **Oakland International Airport** (OAK). ⊠ 1 Airport Dr., Oakland ☎ 510/563–3300 ⊕ www.oaklandairport.com. **San Jose International Airport** (SJC). ⊠ 1701 Airport Blvd., San Jose ☎ 408/392–3600 ⊕ www.flysanjose.com.

AIRPORT TRANSFERS Marin Airporter. ☎ 415/461–4222 ⊕ www.marinairporter.com. **Marin Door to Door.** ☎ 415/457–2717 ⊕ www.marindoortodoor.com. **SamTrans.** ☎ 800/660–4287 ⊕ www.samtrans.com.

BART TRAVEL
BART (Bay Area Rapid Transit) trains, which run until midnight, travel under the bay via tunnel to connect San Francisco with Oakland, Berkeley, and other cities and towns beyond. Within San Francisco, stations are limited to downtown, the Mission, and a couple of outlying neighborhoods.

Trains travel frequently from early morning until evening on weekdays. After 8 pm weekdays and on weekends there's often a 20-minute wait between trains on the same line. Trains also travel south from San Francisco as far as Millbrae. BART trains connect downtown San Francisco to San Francisco International Airport; the ride costs $8.95.

Intracity San Francisco fares are $1.95; intercity fares are $3.20 to $11.45. BART bases its ticket prices on miles traveled and doesn't offer price breaks by zone. The easy-to-read maps posted in BART stations list fares based on destination, radiating out from your starting point of the current station.

During morning and evening rush hour, trains within the city are crowded—even standing room can be hard to come by. Cars at the far front and back of the train are less likely to be filled to capacity. Smoking, eating, and drinking are prohibited on trains and in stations.

CONTACTS Bay Area Rapid Transit (BART). ☎ 510/465-2278 ⊕ www.bart.gov.

BOAT TRAVEL
Several ferry lines run out of San Francisco. Blue & Gold Fleet operates a number of routes, including service to Sausalito ($11.50 one-way) and Tiburon ($11.50 one-way). Tickets are sold at Pier 39; boats depart from Pier 41 nearby. Alcatraz Cruises, owned by Hornblower Cruises and Events, operates the ferries to Alcatraz Island ($35.50 including audio tour and National Park Service ranger-led programs) from Pier 33, about a half-mile east of Fisherman's Wharf.

16

San Francisco PLANNING

Boats leave 14 times a day (more in summer), and the journey itself takes 30 minutes. Allow at least 2½ hours for a round-trip jaunt. Golden Gate Ferry runs daily to and from Sausalito and Larkspur ($11.75 and $11 one-way), leaving from Pier 1, behind the San Francisco Ferry Building. The Alameda/Oakland Ferry operates daily between Alameda's Main Street Terminal, Oakland's Jack London Square, and San Francisco's Pier 41 and the Ferry Building ($6.60 one-way); some ferries go only to Pier 41 or the Ferry Building, so ask when you board. Purchase tickets on board.

INFORMATION Alameda/Oakland Ferry. ☎ 877/643–3779 ⊕ sanfranciscobayferry. com. **Alcatraz Cruises.** ☎ 415/981–7625 ⊕ www.alcatrazcruises.com. **Blue & Gold Fleet.** ☎ 415/705–8200 ⊕ www.blueand- goldfleet.com. **Ferry Building Marketplace.** ✉ 1 Ferry Bldg., at foot of Market St. on Embarcadero, San Francisco ☎ 415/983– 8030 ⊕ www.ferrybuildingmarketplace. com. **Golden Gate Ferry.** ☎ 415/923–2000 ⊕ www.goldengateferry.org.

CABLE-CAR TRAVEL

Don't miss the sensation of moving up and down some of San Francisco's steepest hills in a clattering cable car. Jump aboard as it pauses at a designated stop, and wedge yourself into any available space. Then just hold on.

The fare (for one direction) is $7. You can buy tickets on board (exact change isn't required but operators can only make change up to $20) or at the kiosks at the cable-car turnarounds at Hyde and Beach streets and at Powell and Market streets.

The heavily traveled Powell–Mason and Powell–Hyde lines begin at Powell and Market streets near Union Square and terminate at Fisherman's Wharf; lines for these routes can be long, especially in summer. The California Street line runs east and west from Market and California streets to Van Ness Avenue; there's often no wait to board this route.

CAR TRAVEL

Driving in San Francisco can be a challenge because of the one-way streets, snarly traffic, and steep hills. The first two elements can be frustrating enough, but those hills are tough for unfamiliar drivers. ■TIP➔ **Remember to curb your wheels when parking on hills—turn wheels away from the curb when facing uphill, toward the curb when facing downhill. You can get a ticket if you don't do this.**

MUNI TRAVEL

The San Francisco Municipal Railway, or Muni, operates light-rail vehicles, the historic F-line streetcars along Fisherman's Wharf and Market Street, buses, and the world-famous cable cars. Light rail travels along Market Street to the Mission District and Noe Valley (J line), the Ingleside District (K line), and the Sunset District (L, M, and N lines) while also passing through the West Portal, Glen Park, and Castro neighborhoods. The N line continues around the Embarcadero to the Caltrain station at 4th and King streets; the T-line light rail runs from the Castro, down Market Street, around the Embarcadero, and south past Mission Bay and Hunters Point to Sunnydale Avenue and Bayshore Boulevard. Muni provides 24-hour service on select lines to all areas of the city.

On buses and streetcars the fare is $2.50. Exact change is required, and dollar bills are accepted in the fare boxes. For all Muni vehicles other than cable cars, 90-minute transfers are issued free upon request at the time the fare is paid. These are valid for unlimited transfers in any direction until they expire (time is indicated on the ticket). Cable cars cost $7 and include no transfers (see Cable-Car Travel).

One-day ($21), three-day ($32), and seven-day ($42) Passports valid on the entire Muni system can be purchased at several outlets, including the cable-car ticket booth at Powell and Market streets and the visitor information center downstairs in Hallidie Plaza. A monthly ticket is available for $80, and can be used on all Muni lines (including cable cars) and on BART within city limits. The San Francisco CityPass ($86), a discount ticket booklet to several major city attractions, also covers all Muni travel for seven consecutive days.

The San Francisco Municipal Transit and Street Map ($5) is a useful guide to the extensive transportation system. You can buy the map at most bookstores and at the San Francisco Visitor Information Center, on the lower level of Hallidie Plaza at Powell and Market streets.

BUS OPERATORS

Outside the city, AC Transit serves the East Bay, and Golden Gate Transit serves Marin County and a few cities in southern Sonoma County.

BUS AND MUNI INFORMATION San Francisco Municipal Transportation Agency (*Muni*). ☎ *311, 415/701–3000* ⊕ *www. sfmta.com.*

TAXI TRAVEL

Taxi service is notoriously bad in San Francisco, and finding a cab can be frustratingly difficult. Popular nightspots such as the Mission, SoMa, North Beach, and the Castro are the easiest places to hail a cab off the street; hotel taxi stands are also an option. If you're going to the airport, make a reservation or book a shuttle instead. Taxis in San Francisco charge $3.50 for the first 0.5 mile (one of the highest base rates in the United States), 55¢ for each additional 0.2 mile, and 55¢ per minute in stalled traffic; a $4 surcharge is added for trips from the airport. There's no charge for additional passengers; there's no surcharge for luggage. For trips farther than 15 miles outside city limits, multiply the metered rate by 1.5; tolls and tip are extra.

That said, San Francisco's poor taxi service was a direct factor in the creation of ride-sharing services such as Uber and Lyft, which are easy to use and prominent throughout the city and its surrounding areas. San Franciscans generally regard taxis as a thing of the past and use ride-sharing on a day-to-day basis. If you're willing to share a car with strangers, a trip within the city can run as low as $4; rates go up for private rides and during peak demand times. These services are especially economical when going to or from the airport, where a shared ride will run you about $25—half the cost of a cab.

TAXI COMPANIES Flywheel Taxi. ☎ *415/970–1303* ⊕ *flywheeltaxi.com.* **Luxor Cab.** ☎ *415/282–4141* ⊕ *www. luxorcab.com.* **National Veterans Cab.** ☎ *415/321–8294* ⊕ *sfnationalcab. sftaxischool.com/index.html.* **Yellow Cab.** ☎ *415/333–3333* ⊕ *yellowcabsf.com.*

COMPLAINTS San Francisco Police Department Taxi Complaints. ☎ *415/701–4400.*

TRAIN TRAVEL

Amtrak trains travel to the Bay Area from some cities in California and the United States. The *Coast Starlight* travels north from Los Angeles to Seattle, passing the Bay Area along the way, but contrary to its name, the train runs inland through the Central Valley for much of its route through Northern California; the most scenic stretch is in Southern California, between San Luis Obispo and Los Angeles. Amtrak also has several routes between San Jose, Oakland, and Sacramento. The *California Zephyr* travels from Chicago to the Bay Area, and has spectacular alpine vistas as it crosses the Sierra Nevada range. San Francisco doesn't have an Amtrak train station but does have an Amtrak bus stop at the Ferry Building, from which shuttle buses transport passengers to trains in Emeryville, just over the Bay Bridge. Shuttle buses also connect the Emeryville train station with BART and other points in downtown San Francisco. You can buy a California Rail Pass, which gives you 7 days of travel in a 21-day period for $159.

Caltrain connects San Francisco to Palo Alto, San Jose, Santa Clara, and many smaller cities en route. In San Francisco, trains leave from the main depot, at 4th and Townsend streets, and a rail-side stop at 22nd and Pennsylvania streets. One-way fares are $3.75 to $13.75, depending on the number of zones through which you travel; tickets are valid for four hours after purchase time. A ticket is $7.75 from San Francisco to Palo Alto, at least $9.75 to San Jose. You can also buy a day pass ($7.50–$27.50) for unlimited travel in a 24-hour period. It's worth waiting for an express train for trips that last from 1 to 1¾ hours. On weekdays, trains depart three or four times per hour during the morning and evening, only once or twice per hour during daytime non-commute hours and late night. Weekend trains run once per hour, though there are two bullet trains per day, one in late morning and one in early evening. The system shuts down after midnight. There are no onboard ticket sales. You must buy tickets before boarding the train or risk paying up to $250 for fare evasion.

INFORMATION Amtrak. ☎ *800/872–7245* ⊕ *www.amtrak.com.* **Caltrain.** ☎ *800/660–4287* ⊕ *www.caltrain.com.* **San Francisco Caltrain station.** ✉ *700 4th St., near Townsend St., San Francisco* ☎ *800/660–4287.*

Restaurants

Make no mistake, San Francisco is one of America's top food cities. Some of the biggest landmarks are restaurants. In fact, on a Saturday, the Ferry Building—a temple to local eating—may attract more visitors than the Golden Gate Bridge: cheeses, breads, "salty pig parts," homemade delicacies, and sensory-perfect vegetables and fruits attract rabidly dedicated aficionados. You see, San Franciscans are a little loco about their edibles. If you ask

them what their favorite season is, don't be surprised if they respond, "tomato season."

Some renowned restaurants are booked weeks or even months in advance. But you can get lucky at the last minute if you're flexible—and friendly. Most restaurants keep a few tables open for walk-ins and VIPs. Show up for dinner early (5:30 pm) or late (after 9 pm) and politely inquire about any last-minute vacancies or cancellations.

What It Costs

$	$$	$$$	$$$$
RESTAURANTS			
under $16	$16–$22	$23–$30	over $30

Hotels

San Francisco accommodations are diverse, ranging from cozy inns and kitschy motels, to chic little inns and true grande dames, housed in century-old structures and sleek high-rises. While the tech boom has skyrocketed the prices of even some of the most dependable low-cost options, luckily, some Fodor's faves still offer fine accommodations without the jaw-dropping prices to match those steep hills. In fact, the number of reasonably priced accommodations is impressive.

Hotel reviews have been shortened. For full information, visit Fodors.com.

What It Costs

$	$$	$$$	$$$$
HOTELS			
under $150	$150–$249	$250–$350	over $350

Nightlife

After hours, business folk and the working class give way to costume-clad partygoers, hippies and hipsters, downtown divas, frat boys, and those who prefer something a little more clothing-optional.

Entertainment information is printed in the "Datebook" section and the more calendar-based "96 Hours" section of the *San Francisco Chronicle* (⊕ *www. sfgate.com*). Also consult any of the free alternative weeklies, notably the *SF Weekly* (⊕ *www.sfweekly.com*), which blurbs nightclubs and music, and the *San Francisco Bay Guardian* (⊕ *www. sfbg.com*), which lists neighborhood, avant-garde, and budget events. SF Station (⊕ *www.sfstation.com*; online only) has an up-to-date calendar of entertainment goings-on.

You're better off taking public transportation or taxis on weekend nights, unless you're heading downtown (Financial District or Union Square) and are willing to park in a lot. There's only street parking in North Beach, the Mission, Castro, and the Haight, and finding a spot can be practically impossible. Muni stops running between 1 am and 5 am but has its limited Owl Service on a few lines—including the K, N, L, 90, 91, 14, 24, 38, and 22—every 30 minutes. Service cuts have put a dent in frequency; check ⊕ *www.sfmuni.com* for current details. You can sometimes hail a taxi on the street in well-trodden nightlife locations like North Beach or the Mission, but you can also call for one (☎ *415/626–2345 Yellow Cab, 415/648–3181 Arrow*). The best option by far is booking a taxi with a smartphone-based app (⊕ *www.uber. com*, ⊕ *www.lyft.com*). ■TIP→ **Cabs in San Francisco are more expensive than in other areas of the United States; expect to pay at least $15 to get anywhere within the city. Keep in mind that BART service across the bay stops shortly after midnight.**

Performing Arts

Sophisticated, offbeat, and often ahead of the curve, San Francisco's performing arts scene supports world-class opera, ballet, and theater productions, along with alternative-dance events, avant-garde plays, groundbreaking documentaries, and a slew of spoken-word and other literary happenings.

The best guide to the arts is printed in the "Datebook" section and the "96 Hours" section of the *San Francisco Chronicle* (⊕ *www.sfgate.com*). Also check out the city's free alternative weeklies, including *SF Weekly* (⊕ *www. sfweekly.com*) and the *San Francisco Bay Guardian* (⊕ *www.sfbg.com*).

Online, SF Station (⊕ *www.sfstation. com*) has a frequently updated arts and nightlife calendar. *San Francisco Arts Monthly* (⊕ *www.sfarts.org*), which is published at the end of the month, has arts features and events listings, plus a helpful "Visiting San Francisco?" section. For offbeat, emerging-artist performances, consult CounterPULSE (⊕ *www. counterpulse.org*).

Shopping

With its grand department stores and funky secondhand boutiques, San Francisco summons a full range of shopping experiences. From the anarchist bookstore to the mouthwatering specialty-food purveyors at the gleaming Ferry Building, the local shopping opportunities reflect the city's various personalities. Visitors with limited time often focus their energies on the high-density Union Square area, where several major department stores tower over big-name boutiques. But if you're keen to find unique local shops, consider moving beyond the square's radius.

Each neighborhood has its own distinctive finds, whether it's 1960s housewares, cheeky stationery, or vintage Levi's. If shopping in San Francisco has a downside, it's that real bargains can be few and far between. Sure, neighborhoods such as the Lower Haight and the Mission have thrift shops and other inexpensive stores, but you won't find many discount outlets in the city, where rents are sky-high and space is at a premium.

Visitor Information

The San Francisco Convention and Visitors Bureau can mail you brochures, maps, and events listings. Once in town, you can stop by the bureau's info center near Union Square.

CONTACTS San Francisco Visitor Information Center. ⊠ *Hallidie Plaza, lower level, 900 Market St., at Powell St., Union Sq.* ☎ *415/391–2000* ⊕ *www.sftravel.com.*

Union Square

The Union Square area bristles with big-city bravado. The crowds zigzag among international brands, trailing glossy shopping bags.

👁 Sights

Maiden Lane
BUILDING | Known as Morton Street in the raffish Barbary Coast era, this former red-light district reported at least one murder a week during the late 19th century. Things cooled down after the 1906 fire destroyed the brothels, and these days Maiden Lane is a chic, designer-boutique-lined pedestrian mall stretching two blocks, between Stockton and Kearny streets. Wrought-iron gates close the street to traffic most days between 11 and 5, when the lane becomes an alfresco hot spot dotted with a patchwork of umbrella-shaded tables. At **140 Maiden Lane** is the only Frank Lloyd Wright building in San Francisco, fronted by a large brick archway. The graceful, curving ramp and skylights of the interior, which houses exclusive Italian menswear boutique Isaia, are said to have been his model for the Guggenheim Museum in New York. ⊠ *Between Stockton and Kearny Sts., Union Sq.*

Union Square
PLAZA | Ground zero for big-name shopping in the city and within walking distance of many hotels, Union Square is home base for many visitors. The Westin St. Francis Hotel and Macy's line two of the square's sides, and Saks, Neiman-Marcus, and Tiffany & Co. edge the other two. Four globular contemporary lamp sculptures by the artist R. M. Fischer preside over the landscaped, 2½-acre park, which has a café with outdoor seating, an open-air stage, and a visitor-information booth—along with a familiar kaleidoscope of characters: office workers sunning and brown-bagging, street musicians, shoppers taking a rest, kids chasing pigeons, and a fair number of homeless people. The constant clang of cable cars traveling up and down Powell Street helps maintain a festive mood. ⊠ *Bordered by Powell, Stockton, Post, and Geary Sts., Union Sq.*

Westin St. Francis Hotel
HOTEL—SIGHT | Built in 1904 and barely established as the most sumptuous hotel in town before it was ravaged by fire following the 1906 earthquake, this grande-dame hotel designed by Walter Danforth Bliss and William Baker Faville reopened in 1907 with the addition of a luxurious Italian Renaissance–style residence designed to attract loyal clients from among the world's rich and powerful. The hotel's checkered past includes the ill-fated 1921 bash in the suite of the silent-film superstar Fatty Arbuckle, at which a woman became ill and later died. Arbuckle endured three sensational trials for rape and murder before being acquitted, by which time his career was

The epicenter of high-end shopping, Union Square is lined with department stores.

kaput. In 1975, Sara Jane Moore, standing among a crowd outside the hotel, attempted to shoot then-President Gerald Ford. Of course, the grand lobby contains no plaques commemorating these events. ■TIP→ **Some visitors make the St. Francis a stop whenever they're in town, soaking up the lobby ambience or enjoying a cocktail at the Clock Bar or lunch at the Oak Room Restaurant.** ⊠ *335 Powell St., at Geary St., Union Sq.* ☎ *415/397–7000* ⊕ *westinstfrancis.com.*

🍴 Restaurants

★ Liholiho Yacht Club

$$$$ | **MODERN AMERICAN** | Inspired but not defined by the chef's native Hawaii, Ravi Kapur's lively restaurant is known for big hearted, high-spirited cooking, including contemporary riffs on poke and Spam, but also squid served with crispy tripe, and beef ribs with kimchi chili sauce. The dining room and front bar area are perpetually packed, and dominated by an enormous photo of a beaming woman who happens to be none other than the chef's mother. **Known for:** Hawaiian-inspired food; giant mains that serve two to four people; lively buzz. $ *Average main: $40* ⊠ *871 Sutter St., Union Sq.* ☎ *415/440–5446* ⊕ *www.lycsf.com* ⊗ *Closed Sun. No lunch.*

🛏 Hotels

★ Golden Gate Hotel

$$ | **B&B/INN** | **FAMILY** | Budget seekers looking for accommodations around Union Square will enjoy this four-story Edwardian with bay windows, an original birdcage elevator, hallways lined with historical photographs, and rooms decorated with antiques, wicker pieces, and Laura Ashley bedding and curtains. **Pros:** friendly staff; spotless rooms; good location if you're a walker. **Cons:** some rooms share a bath; resident cat and dog, so not good for guests with allergies; some rooms on small side. $ *Rooms from: $185* ⊠ *775 Bush St., Union Sq.* ☎ *415/392–3702, 800/835–1118* ⊕ *www.goldengatehotel.com* ⤳ *23 rooms* ⦿❘ *Breakfast.*

Union Square, Chinatown, and the Financial District

KEY

- ① Exploring Sights
- ① Restaurants
- ① Hotels
- Ⓑ BART station

Hotel Diva

$$ | **HOTEL** | Entering this magnet for urbanites craving modern decor requires stepping over footprints, handprints, and autographs embedded in the sidewalk by visiting stars; in the rooms, designer carpets complement mid-century-modern chairs and brushed-steel headboards whose shape mimics that of ocean waves. **Pros:** contemporary design; in the heart of the theater district; accommodating staff. **Cons:** few frills; tiny bathrooms (but equipped with eco-friendly bath products); many rooms are small. [$] *Rooms from: $209* ✉ *440 Geary St., Union Sq.* ☎ *415/885–0200, 800/553–1900* 🌐 *www.hoteldiva.com* 🛏 *130 rooms* 🍴 *No meals.*

Hotel Emblem

$$$ | **HOTEL** | Inspiration is everywhere at intimate Hotel Emblem, refurbished and rebranded in 2019 with a literary theme that celebrates San Francisco's Beat poets, from its lobby wall of books and poetry-laced carpet to in-room libraries and typewriters. **Pros:** fun, creative vibe; excellent Union Square location; amenities available by request include essential oil diffusers, coloring books, and bath bombs. **Cons:** $25 nightly amenity fee; expensive parking; some rooms on the small side. [$] *Rooms from: $295* ✉ *562 Sutter St., Union Sq.* ☎ *415/433–4434* 🌐 *www.viceroyhotelsandresorts.com/en/emblem* 🛏 *96 rooms* 🍴 *No meals.*

Hotel Triton

$$$ | **HOTEL** | With a fresh top-to-bottom 2018 redesign and a location at the convergence of Chinatown, the Financial District, and Union Square, this boutique anchor attracts a design-conscious crowd. **Pros:** arty environs; good location; room service from next-door Café de la Presse. **Cons:** rooms and baths are on the small side; hallways feel cramped; $25 obligatory fee for fitness center access, Wi-Fi, and lobby beverages. [$] *Rooms from: $279* ✉ *342 Grant Ave., Union Sq.* ☎ *415/394–0500, 877/793–9931* 🌐 *www.hoteltriton.com* 🛏 *140 rooms* 🍴 *No meals.*

Cable Car Terminus

Two of the three cable-car lines begin and end their runs at Powell and Market streets, a couple blocks south of Union Square. These two lines are the most scenic, and both pass near Fisherman's Wharf, so they're usually clogged with first-time sightseers. The wait to board a cable car at this intersection is longer than at any other stop in the system. If you'd rather avoid the mob, board the less-touristy California line at the bottom of Market Street, at Drumm Street.

Westin St. Francis

$$$$ | **HOTEL** | The survivor of two major earthquakes, some headline-grabbing scandals, and even an attempted presidential assassination, this richly appointed and superbly located grande dame dating to 1904 is comprised of the landmark building, renovated in 2018, and a modern 32-story tower whose glass elevators reveal Union Square views from the upper floors. **Pros:** prime Union Square location; great views from some rooms; Chateau Montelena wine-tasting room. **Cons:** rooms in original building can be small; public spaces lack the panache of days gone by; no dinner at on-site Oak Room Restaurant. [$] *Rooms from: $356* ✉ *335 Powell St., Union Sq.* ☎ *415/397–7000, 800/917–7458* 🌐 *www.westinstfrancis.com* 🛏 *1,195 rooms* 🍴 *No meals.*

Nightlife

Harry Denton's Starlight Room

BARS/PUBS | Forget low-key drinks—the only way to experience Harry Denton's is to cough up the cover charge and enjoy the opulent, over-the-top decor. Red velvet booths and romantic lighting help re-create the 1950s high life on the 21st floor of the Sir Francis Drake Hotel. Sunday brunch brings a popular drag show, and the small dance floor is packed on Friday and Saturday nights. Jackets are preferred for men. ✉ *Sir Francis Drake Hotel, 450 Powell St., between Post and Sutter Sts., Union Sq.* ☎ *415/395–8595* ⊕ *starlightroomsf.com.*

Pacific Cocktail Haven

BARS/PUBS | PCH for short, this neighborhood hangout with a convivial aura and industrial-chic decor hits all the right notes. Plus the well-chosen and unique ingredients mean there's a little something for everyone, and the glassware is as dazzling as the elixirs inside. ■TIP→ **The must-try cocktail is the Oh Snap!, a concoction of gin, sugar snap peas, citrus, and absinthe.** ✉ *580 Sutter St., at Mason St., Union Sq.* ☎ *415/398–0195* ⊕ *pacificcocktailsf.com* ⊘ *Closed Sun.*

🎭 Performing Arts

TIX Bay Area

TICKETS | Half-price, same-day tickets for many local and touring shows go on sale (cash only) at the TIX booth in Union Square, which is open daily from 10 to 6. Discount purchases can also be made online. ✉ *350 Powell St., at Geary St., Union Sq.* ☎ *415/433–7827* ⊕ *www.tixbayarea.org.*

THEATER

American Conservatory Theater

THEATER | One of the nation's leading regional theater companies presents about eight plays a year, from classics to contemporary works, often in repertory. The season runs from early fall to late spring. In December ACT stages a beloved version of Charles Dickens's *A Christmas Carol.* ✉ *415 Geary St., Union Sq.* ☎ *415/749–2228* ⊕ *www.act-sf.org.*

🛍 Shopping

ART GALLERIES

★ Berggruen Gallery

ART GALLERIES | Twentieth-century European and American paintings, including Bay Area figurative works, are displayed throughout two airy floors at this well-respected gallery established in 1970. Some recent exhibitions have included the works of Robert Kelly and Isca Greenfield-Sanders. Look for thematic shows here, too; past exhibits have had titles such as Summer Highlights and Four Decades. ✉ *10 Hawthorne St., at Howard St., SoMa* ☎ *415/781–4629* ⊕ *www.berggruen.com.*

CLOTHING: MEN AND WOMEN

★ Margaret O'Leary

CLOTHING | If you can only buy one piece of clothing in San Francisco, make it a hand-loomed cashmere sweater by this Irish-born local legend. The perfect antidote to the city's wind and fog, the sweaters are so beloved by San Franciscans that some of them never wear anything else. Pick up an airplane wrap for your trip home. Another store is in Pacific Heights, at 2400 Fillmore Street. ✉ *1 Claude La., at Sutter St., just west of Kearny St., Union Sq.* ☎ *415/391–1010* ⊕ *www.margaretoleary.com.*

Chinatown

A few blocks uphill from Union Square is the abrupt beginning of dense and insular Chinatown—the oldest such community in the country. When the street signs have Chinese characters, produce stalls crowd pedestrians off the sidewalk, and whole roast ducks hang in deli windows, you'll know you've arrived. (The neighborhood huddles together in the 17 blocks and 41 alleys bordered roughly by Bush, Kearny, and Powell streets and Broadway.) Chinatown has been attracting the curious for more than 100 years, and no other

Continued on page 567

CHINATOWN

Chinatown's streets flood the senses. Incense and cigarette smoke mingle with the scents of briny fish and sweet vanilla. Rooflines flare outward, pagoda-style. Loud Cantonese bargaining and honking car horns rise above the sharp clack of mah-jongg tiles and the eternally humming cables beneath the street.

Most Chinatown visitors march down Grant Avenue, buy a few trinkets, and call it a day. Do yourself a favor and dig deeper. This is one of the largest Chinese communities outside Asia, and there is far more to it than buying a back-scratcher near Chinatown Gate. To get a real feel for the neighborhood, wander off the main drag. Step into a temple or an herb shop and wander down a flag-draped alley. And don't be shy: residents welcome guests warmly, though rarely in English.

Whatever you do, don't leave without eating something. Noodle houses, bakeries, tea houses, and dim sum shops seem to occupy every other storefront. There's a feast for your eyes as well: in the market windows on Stockton and Grant, you'll see hanging whole roast ducks, fish, and shellfish swimming in tanks, and strips of shiny, pink-glazed Chinese-style barbecued pork.

CHINATOWN'S HISTORY

Sam Brannan's 1848 cry of "Gold!" didn't take long to reach across the world to China. Struggling with famine, drought, and political upheaval at home, thousands of Chinese jumped at the chance to try their luck in California. Most came from the Pearl River Delta region, in the Guangdong province, and spoke Cantonese dialects. From the start, Chinese businesses circled around Portsmouth Square, which was conveniently central. Bachelor rooming houses sprang up, since the vast majority of new arrivals were men. By 1853, the area was called Chinatown.

The Street of Gamblers (Ross Alley), 1898 (top). The first Chinese telephone operator in Chinatown (bottom).

COLD WELCOME

The Chinese faced discrimination from the get-go. Harrassment became outright hostility as first the gold rush, then the work on the Transcontinental Railroad petered out. Special taxes were imposed to shoulder aside competing "coolie labor." Laws forbidding the Chinese from moving outside Chinatown kept the residents packed in like sardines, with nowhere to go but up and down—

thus the many basement establishments in the neighborhood. State and federal laws passed in the 1870s deterred Chinese women from immigrating, deeming them prostitutes. In the late 1870s, looting and arson attacks on Chinatown businesses soared.

The coup de grace, though, was the Chinese Exclusion Act, passed by the U.S. Congress in 1882, which slammed the doors to America for "Asiatics." This was

Chinatown's Grant Avenue.

Women and children flooded into the neighborhood after the Great Quake.

the country's first significant restriction on immigration. The law also prevented the existing Chinese residents, including American-born children, from becoming naturalized citizens. With a society of mostly men (forbidden, of course, from marrying white women), San Francisco hoped that Chinatown would simply die out.

OUT OF THE ASHES

When the devastating 1906 earthquake and fire hit, city fathers thought they'd seize the opportunity to kick the Chinese out of Chinatown and get their hands on that desirable piece of downtown real estate. Then Chinatown businessman Look Tin Eli had a brainstorm of Disneyesque proportions.

He proposed that Chinatown be rebuilt, but in a tourist-friendly, stylized, "Oriental" way. Anglo-American architects would design new buildings with pagoda roofs and dragon-covered columns. Chinatown would attract more tourists—the curious had been visiting on the sly for decades—and add more tax money to the city's coffers. Ka-ching: the sales pitch worked.

PAPER SONS

For the Chinese, the 1906 earthquake turned the virtual "no entry" sign into a flashing neon "welcome!" All the city's immigration records went up in smoke, and the Chinese quickly began to apply for passports as U.S. citizens, claiming their old ones were lost in the fire. Not only did thousands of Chinese become legal overnight, but so did their sons in China, or "sons," if they weren't really related. Whole families in Chinatown had passports in names that weren't their own; these "paper sons" were not only a windfall but also an uncomfortable neighborhood conspiracy. The city caught on eventually and set up an immigration center on Angel Island in 1910. Immigrants spent weeks or months being inspected and interrogated while their papers were checked. Roughly 250,000 people made it through. With this influx, including women and children, Chinatown finally became a more complete community.

A GREAT WALK THROUGH CHINATOWN

- Start at the Chinatown Gate and walk ahead on Grant Avenue, entering the souvenir gauntlet. (You'll also pass Old St. Mary's Cathedral.)

- Make a right on Clay Street and walk to Portsmouth Square. Sometimes it feels like the whole neighborhood's here, playing chess and exercising.

- Head up Washington Street to the Old Chinese Telephone Exchange building, now the EastWest Bank. Across Grant, look left for Waverly Place. Here Free Republic of China (Taiwanese) flags flap over some of the neighborhood's most striking buildings, including Tin How Temple.

- At the Sacramento Street end of Waverly Place stands the First Chinese Baptist Church of 1908. Just across the way, the Clarion Music Center is full of unusual instruments, as well as exquisite lion-dance sets.

- Head back to Washington Street and check out the many herb shops.

- Follow the scent of vanilla down Ross Alley (entrance across from Superior Trading Company) to the Golden Gate Fortune Cookie Factory. Then head across the alley to Sam Bo Trading Co., where religious items are stacked in the narrow space. Tell the owners your troubles and they'll prepare a package of joss papers, joss sticks, and candles, and tell you how and when to offer them up.

- Turn left on Jackson Street; ahead is the real Chinatown's main artery, Stockton Street, where most residents do their grocery shopping. Vegetarians will want to avoid Luen Fat Market (No. 1135), with tanks of live frogs, turtles, and lobster as well as chickens and ducks. Look toward the back of stores for Buddhist altars with offerings of oranges and grapefruit. From here you can loop one block east back to Grant.

neighborhood in the city absorbs as many tourists without seeming to forfeit its character. Join the flow and step into another world. Good-luck banners of crimson and gold hang beside drag-on-entwined lampposts and pagoda roofs, while honking cars chime in with shoppers bargaining loudly in Cantonese or Mandarin.

◉ Sights

Chinatown Gate

BUILDING | This is the official entrance to Chinatown. Stone lions flank the base of the pagoda-topped gate; the lions, drag-ons, and fish up top symbolize wealth, prosperity, and other good things. The four Chinese characters immediately beneath the pagoda represent the philosophy of Sun Yat-sen (1866–1925), the leader who unified China in the early 20th century. Sun Yat-sen, who lived in exile in San Francisco for a few years, promoted the notion of friendship and peace among all nations based on equal-ity, justice, and goodwill. The vertical characters under the left pagoda read "peace" and "trust," the ones under the right pagoda "respect" and "love." The whole shebang telegraphs the interna-tionally understood message of "photo op." Immediately beyond the gate, dive into souvenir shopping on Grant Avenue, Chinatown's tourist strip. ⊠ *Grant Ave. at Bush St., Chinatown.*

Golden Gate Fortune Cookie Factory

FACTORY | FAMILY | Follow your nose down Ross Alley to this tiny but fragrant cook-ie factory. Two workers sit at circular motorized griddles and wait for dollops of batter to drop onto a tiny metal plate, which rotates into an oven. A few moments later out comes a cookie that's pliable and ready for folding. It's easy to peek in for a moment, and hard to leave without a few free samples. A bagful of cookies—with mildly racy "adult" fortunes or more benign ones—costs less than $5. ⊠ *56 Ross*

Look Up! ◉

When wandering around China-town, don't forget to look up! Above the chintziest souvenir shop might loom an ornate balcony or a curly pagoda roof. The best examples are on the 900 block of Grant Avenue (at Washington Street) and at Waverly Place.

Alley, between Washington and Jackson Sts., west of Grant Ave., Chinatown ☎ *415/781–3956* 🖙 *Free.*

Portsmouth Square

PLAZA | Chinatown's living room buzzes with activity. The square, with its pagoda-shape structures, is a favorite spot for morning tai chi; by noon dozens of men huddle around Chinese chess tables, engaged in competition. Kids scamper about the square's two grungy playgrounds. Back in the late 19th century this land was near the waterfront. The square is named for the USS *Portsmouth*, the ship helmed by Captain John Montgomery, who in 1846 raised the American flag here and claimed the then-Mexican land for the United States. A couple of years later, Sam Brannan kicked off the gold rush at the square when he waved his loot and proclaimed, "Gold from the American River!" Robert Louis Stevenson, the author of *Treasure Island,* often dropped by, chatting up the sailors who hung out here. Some of the information he gleaned about life at sea found its way into his fiction. A bronze galleon sculp-ture, a tribute to Stevenson, anchors the square's northwest corner. A plaque marks the site of California's first public school, built in 1847. ⊠ *Bordered by Walter Lum Pl. and Kearny, Washington, and Clay Sts., Chinatown.*

★ Tin How Temple

RELIGIOUS SITE | Duck into the inconspicuous doorway, climb three flights of stairs, and be assaulted by the aroma of incense in this tiny, altar-filled room. In 1852, Day Ju, one of the first three Chinese to arrive in San Francisco, dedicated this temple to the Queen of the Heavens and the Goddess of the Seven Seas, and the temple looks largely the same today as it did more than a century ago. In the entryway, elderly ladies can often be seen preparing "money" to be burned as offerings to various Buddhist gods or as funds for ancestors to use in the afterlife. Hundreds of red-and-gold lanterns cover the ceiling; the larger the lamp, the larger its donor's contribution to the temple. Gifts of oranges, dim sum, and money left by the faithful, who kneel mumbling prayers, rest on altars to different gods. Tin How presides over the middle back of the temple, flanked by one red and one green lesser god. Take a good look around, since taking photographs is not allowed. ⊠ *125 Waverly Pl., between Clay and Washington Sts., Chinatown* ⌷ *Free, donations accepted.*

🍴 Restaurants

Mister Jiu's

$$$$ | CHINESE | Brandon Jew's ambitious, graceful restaurant offers the chef's contemporary, farm-to-table interpretation of Chinese cuisine, including options such as hot-and-sour soup garnished with nasturtiums and pot stickers made with Swiss chard and local chicken. The elegant dining room—accented with plants and a chrysanthemum chandelier—provides beautiful views of Chinatown, while the menu breathes new life into it. **Known for:** modern Chinese food; cocktails; one Michelin star. Ⓢ *Average main: $36* ⊠ *28 Waverly Pl., Chinatown* ☎ *415/857–9688* ⊕ *www.misterjius.com* ☾ *Closed Sun. and Mon. No lunch.*

R&G Lounge

$$ | CHINESE | FAMILY | Salt-and-pepper Dungeness crab is a delicious draw at this bright, three-level Cantonese eatery that draws a packed crowd for its crustacean specialties—crab portions are easily splittable by three—and dim sum. A menu with photographs will help you sort through other HK specialties, including Peking duck and shrimp-stuffed bean curd, and much of the seafood is fresh from the tank. **Known for:** fresh-from-the-tank crab; Cantonese specialties; extensive menu. Ⓢ *Average main: $20* ⊠ *631 Kearny St., Chinatown* ☎ *415/982–7877* ⊕ *www.rnglounge.com.*

Financial District

🍴 Restaurants

Cotogna

$$$ | ITALIAN | The draw at this urban trattoria—just as in demand as its fancier big sister, Quince, next door—is chef Michael Tusk's flavorful, rustic, seasonally driven Italian cooking, such as the irresistible raviolo di ricotta, filled with warm house-made ricotta and topped with an egg yolk, and bistecca alla Fiorentina. The look is comfortably chic, with wood tables, quality stemware, and fantastic Italian wines by the bottle and glass. **Known for:** rustic Italian; fantastic wine list; chic space. Ⓢ *Average main: $27* ⊠ *490 Pacific Ave., Financial District* ☎ *415/775–8508* ⊕ *www.cotognasf.com* ☾ *No lunch Sun.*

Perbacco

$$$$ | ITALIAN | From the complimentary basket of skinny, brittle bread sticks to the pappardelle with short rib ragu, Chef Staffan Terje's entire menu is a delectable paean to northern Italy. With a long marble bar and open kitchen, this brick-lined two-story space oozes big-city charm, attracting business types and Italian food aficionados with such standouts as the house-made cured meats (Terje makes some of the city's finest salumi), burrata with seasonal vegetables, and delicate *agnolotti dal plin* (pasta stuffed with meat and cabbage). **Known for:** pasta stuffed with meat and cabbage; house-made cured meats; authentic northern Italian cuisine. $ *Average main: $31* ⊠ *230 California St., Financial District* ☎ *415/955–0663* ⊕ *www.perbaccosf.com* ⊘ *Closed Sun. No lunch Sat.*

Yank Sing
$$ | **CHINESE** | **FAMILY** | This bustling teahouse serves some of San Francisco's best dim sum to office workers on weekdays and boisterous families on weekends, and the take-out counter makes a meal on the run a satisfying compromise when office duties—or touring—won't wait. The several dozen varieties prepared daily include both the classic and the creative; steamed pork buns, shrimp dumplings, scallion-skewered prawns tied with bacon, and basil seafood dumplings are among the many delights, and the Shanghai soup dumplings are perfection. **Known for:** classic dim sum; Shanghai soup dumplings; energetic room. $ *Average main: $18* ⊠ *49 Stevenson St., Financial District* ☎ *415/541–4949* ⊕ *www.yanksing.com* ⊘ *No dinner.*

⚡ Performing Arts

San Francisco Performances
TICKETS | SFP brings an eclectic array of top-flight global music and dance talents to various venues—mostly the Yerba Buena Center for the Arts, Davies Symphony Hall, and Herbst Theatre. Artists have included Yo-Yo Ma, Edgar Meyer, the Paul Taylor Dance Company, and Midori. Tickets can be purchased in person through City Box Office, online, or by phone. ⊠ *500 Sutter St., Suite 710, Financial District* ☎ *415/392–2545* ⊕ *www.sfperformances.org.*

SoMa

SoMa is less a neighborhood than a sprawling area of wide, traffic-heavy boulevards lined with office skyscrapers and ultrachic condo high-rises. Aside from the fact that many of them work in the area, locals are drawn to the cultural offerings, destination restaurants, and concentration of bars and restaurants. In terms of sightseeing, gigantic and impressive SFMOMA tops the list, followed by the specialty museums of the Yerba Buena arts district.

👁 Sights

Contemporary Jewish Museum
MUSEUM | Daniel Libeskind designed the postmodern CJM, whose impossible-to-ignore diagonal blue cube juts out of a painstakingly restored power substation. A physical manifestation of the Hebrew phrase *l'chaim* (to life), the cube may have obscure philosophical origins, but Libeskind created a unique, light-filled space that merits a stroll through the lobby even if current exhibits don't entice you into the galleries. ■TIP➔ **San Francisco's best Jewish deli, Wise Sons, operates a counter in the museum, giving you a chance to sample the company's wildly popular smoked trout or a slice of chocolate babka.** ⊠ *736 Mission St., between 3rd and 4th Sts., SoMa* ☎ *415/655–7800* ⊕ *www.thecjm.org* 🎟 *$14; $5 Thurs. after 5 pm, free 1st Tues. of month* ⊘ *Closed Wed.*

Museum of the African Diaspora (MoAD)
MUSEUM | Dedicated to the influence that people of African descent have had all over the world, MoAD focuses on temporary exhibits in its four galleries over three floors. With floor-to-ceiling windows onto Mission Street, the museum fits perfectly into the cultural scene of Yerba Buena and is well worth a 30-minute foray. Most striking is its front-window exhibit: a three-story mosaic, made

Sights ▼

1 Asian Art Museum................. **D6**
2 City Hall **C6**
3 Contemporary Jewish
  Museum **H4**
4 Museum of the African
  Diaspora (MoAD) **H4**
5 SFJAZZ Center.................... **B7**
6 San Francisco Museum of
  Modern Art........................ **I4**
7 Yerba Buena Center
  for the Arts **H4**
8 Yerba Buena Gardens............. **H4**

Restaurants ▼

1 Benu................................. **I4**
2 In Situ **I4**
3 Marlowe **J7**
4 Nojo Ramen Tavern **B7**
5 Rich Table **B8**
6 Trou Normand...................... **I4**
7 Zuni Café........................... **B8**

Hotels ▼

1 Four Seasons Hotel
  San Francisco..................... **G4**
2 Hotel Zetta San Francisco........ **G5**
3 Metro Hotel........................ **A8**
4 The St. Regis San Francisco **H4**

SoMa, Civic Center, and Hayes Valley

from thousands of photographs, that forms the image of a young girl's face.

■ TIP→ **Walk up the stairs inside the museum to view the photographs up close—Malcolm X is there, Muhammad Ali, too, along with everyday folks—but the best view is from across the street.** ⊠ *685 Mission St., SoMa* ☎ *415/358–7200* ⊕ *www.moadsf. org* ✉ *$10* ☾ *Closed Mon. and Tues.*

★ **San Francisco Museum of Modern Art**
MUSEUM | First opened in 1935, the San Francisco Museum of Modern Art was the first museum on the West Coast dedicated to modern and contemporary art. In 2016, after a major three-year building expansion designed by Snøhetta, SFMOMA emerged as one of the largest modern art museums in the country and the revitalized anchor of the Yerba Buena arts district. Nearly tripling its gallery space over seven floors, the museum displays only a portion of its more than 33,000-work collection, including numerous temporary exhibits. It can be overwhelming—you could easily spend a day taking it all in, but allow at least two hours; three is better. The museum's expanded collection includes a heavy dose of new art from the Doris and Donald Fisher Collection, one of the greatest private collections of modern and contemporary art in the world. Highlights include a deep collection of German abstract expressionist Gerhard Richter, American painter Ellsworth Kelly, and a tranquil gallery of Agnes Martin. Photography has long been one of the museum's strong suits, and the third floor is dedicated to it. Also look for seminal works by Diego Rivera, Alexander Calder, Matisse, and Picasso. Don't miss the new third-floor sculpture terrace with its striking living wall. The first floor is free to the public and contains four large works, as well as the museum's wonderful shop and expensive restaurant. If you don't have hours, save the steep entrance fee and take a spin through here. Ticketing, information, and one gallery are on the second floor; save time and reserve timed tickets online.

Daily guided tours—a quick 20 minutes or 45 minutes—are an excellent way to get a foothold in this expansive space. And if you start to fade, grab a cup of Sightglass coffee at the café on the third floor; another café/restaurant is located by the fifth-floor sculpture garden. ⊠ *151 3rd St., SoMa* ☎ *415/357–4000* ⊕ *www. sfmoma.org* ✉ *$25.*

Yerba Buena Center for the Arts
ARTS VENUE | You never know what's going to be on display at this facility in Yerba Buena Gardens, but whether it's an exhibit of Mexican street art (graffiti to laypeople), innovative modern dance, or a baffling video installation, it's likely to be memorable. The productions here, which lean toward the cutting edge, tend to draw a young, energetic crowd.
■ TIP→ **Present any public library card or public transit ticket to receive a 10% discount.** ⊠ *701 Mission St., SoMa* ☎ *415/978–2787* ⊕ *www.ybca.org* ✉ *Galleries $10, free 1st Tues. of month* ☾ *Closed Mon.*

Yerba Buena Gardens
CONVENTION CENTER | FAMILY | There's not much south of Market Street that encourages lingering outdoors—or indeed walking at all—with this notable exception. These two blocks encompass the Yerba Buena Center for the Arts, the Metreon, and newly renovated Moscone Convention Center, but the gardens themselves are the everyday draw. Office workers escape to the green swath of the East Garden, the focal point of which is the memorial to Martin Luther King Jr. Powerful streams of water surge over large, jagged stone columns, mirroring the enduring force of King's words that are carved on the stone walls and on glass blocks behind the waterfall. Moscone North is behind the memorial, and an overhead walkway leads to Moscone South and its rooftop attractions. ■ TIP→ **The gardens are liveliest during the week and especially during the Yerba Buena Gardens Festival, from May**

through October (www.ybgfestival.org), with free performances of everything from Latin music to Balinese dance.

Atop the Moscone Convention Center perch a few lures for kids. The historic Looff carousel (*$4 for two rides*) twirls daily 10–5. The carousel is attached to the Children's Creativity Museum (☎ *415/820–3320*, 🌐 *creativity.org*), a high-tech, interactive arts-and-technology center (*$13*) geared to children ages 3–12. Just outside, kids adore the excellent slides, including a 25-foot tube slide, at the play circle. Also part of the rooftop complex are gardens, an ice-skating rink, and a bowling alley. ✉ *Bordered by 3rd, 4th, Mission, and Folsom Sts., SoMa* 🌐 *yerbabuenagardens.com* 🎟 *Free.*

🍴 Restaurants

★ Benu

$$$$ | **MODERN AMERICAN** | Chef Corey Lee's three-Michelin-star fine-dining mecca is a must-stop for those who hop from city to city, collecting memorable meals. Each of the tasting menu's courses is impossibly meticulous, a marvel of textures and flavors. **Known for:** high-end dining; tasting menu; good service. [$] *Average main: $310* ✉ *22 Hawthorne St., SoMa* ☎ *415/685–4860* 🌐 *www.benusf.com* 🕓 *Closed Sun. and Mon. No lunch.*

★ In Situ

$$$ | **CONTEMPORARY** | Benu chef Corey Lee's restaurant at SFMOMA is an exhibition of its own, with a rotating menu comprised of dishes from 80 famous chefs around the world. You might taste David Chang's sausage and rice cakes, Rene Redzepi's wood sorrel granita, or Wylie Dufresne's shrimp grits. **Known for:** global influences; originality; museum location. [$] *Average main: $30* ✉ *151 3rd St., SoMa* ☎ *415/941–6050* 🌐 *insitu.sfmoma.org* 🕓 *Closed Tues. and Wed. No dinner Mon.*

Marlowe

$$$ | **AMERICAN** | Hearty American bistro fare and hip design draw crowds to this Anna Weinberg–Jennifer Puccio production. The menu boasts one of the city's best burgers, and the dining room gleams with white penny tile floors and marble countertops. **Known for:** burgers; strong drinks; festive atmosphere. [$] *Average main: $27* ✉ *500 Brannan St., SoMa* ☎ *415/777–1413* 🌐 *www.marlowesf.com.*

★ Trou Normand

$$$ | **MODERN AMERICAN** | Thad Vogler's second endeavor (Bar Agricole was the first) delivers a fun boozy evening in stunning surroundings. Located off the lobby of the art deco–era Pacific Telephone building, it excels at house-cured salami and charcuterie and classic cocktails. **Known for:** house-made charcuterie; cocktails. [$] *Average main: $28* ✉ *140 New Montgomery St., SoMa* ☎ *415/975–0876* 🌐 *www.trounormandsf.com.*

🛏 Hotels

Four Seasons Hotel San Francisco

$$$$ | **HOTEL** | Occupying floors 5 through 17 of a skyscraper, the Four Seasons delivers subdued elegance in rooms with contemporary artwork, fine linens, floor-to-ceiling windows that overlook Yerba Buena Gardens or downtown, and bathrooms with deep soaking tubs and glass-enclosed showers. **Pros:** near museums, galleries, restaurants, shopping, and clubs; terrific fitness facilities; luxurious rooms and amenities. **Cons:** pricey; rooms can feel sterile. [$] *Rooms from: $569* ✉ *757 Market St., SoMa* ☎ *415/633–3000* 🌐 *www.fourseasons.com/sanfrancisco* 🛏 *277 rooms* 🍴 *No meals.*

★ Hotel Zetta San Francisco

$$$ | **HOTEL** | With a playful lobby lounge, the London-style Cavalier brasserie, and slick-yet-homey tech-friendly rooms, this trendy redo behind a stately 1913 neoclassical facade is a leader in the

SoMa hotel scene. **Pros:** tech amenities and arty design; in-room spa services; noteworthy fitness center. **Cons:** lots of hubbub and traffic; no bathtubs; aesthetic too frenetic for some guests. *[$] Rooms from: $315 ✉ 55 5th St., SoMa ☎ 415/543–8555 🌐 hotelzetta.com 🛏 116 rooms 🍴 No meals.*

★ The St. Regis San Francisco

$$$$ | HOTEL | Across from Yerba Buena Gardens and SFMOMA, the luxurious and modern St. Regis is favored by celebrities such as Lady Gaga and Al Gore. **Pros:** excellent views; stunning lap pool; luxe spa. **Cons:** expensive rates; small front-desk area; cramped space for passenger unloading. *[$] Rooms from: $382 ✉ 125 3rd St., SoMa ☎ 415/284–4000 🌐 www.stregis.com/sanfrancisco 🛏 260 rooms 🍴 No meals.*

Nightlife

City Beer Store

BARS/PUBS | Called CBS by locals, this friendly tasting room-cum-liquor mart has a wine bar's sensibility. Perfect for connoisseurs and the merely beer curious, CBS stocks hundreds of different bottled beers, and more than a dozen are on tap. The indecisive can mix and match six-packs to go. *✉ 1148 Mission St., between 7th and 8th Sts., SoMa ☎ 415/503–1033 🌐 www.citybeerstore.com.*

The Stud

BARS/PUBS | Glam trans women, gay bears, tight-teed pretty boys, ladies and their ladies, and a handful of straight onlookers congregate here to dance to live DJ sounds and watch world-class drag performers on the small stage. The entertainment is often campy, pee-your-pants funny, and downright fantastic. Each night's music is different—from funk, soul, and hip-hop to '80s tunes and disco favorites. *✉ 399 9th St, at Harrison St., SoMa ☎ 415/863–6623 🌐 www.studsf.com ⏲ Closed Mon.*

21st Amendment Brewery

BARS/PUBS | This popular brewery is known for its range of beer types, with multiple taps going at all times. In the spring, the Hell or High Watermelon—a wheat beer—gets rave reviews. **■ TIP→ Serious beer drinkers should try the Back in Black, a black IPA-style beer this brewpub helped pioneer.** The space has an upmarket warehouse feel, though exposed wooden ceiling beams, framed photos, whitewashed brick walls, and hardwood floors make it feel cozy. It's a good spot to warm up before a Giants game and an even better place to party after they win. *✉ 563 2nd St., between Bryant and Brannan Sts., SoMa ☎ 415/369–0900 🌐 www.21st-amendment.com.*

Performing Arts

Yerba Buena Center for the Arts

ARTS CENTERS | Across the street from the San Francisco Museum of Modern Art and abutting a lovely urban garden, this performing arts complex schedules interdisciplinary art exhibitions, touring and local dance troupes, music, film programs, and contemporary theater events. You can depend on the quality of the productions at Yerba Buena. Film buffs often come here to check out the San Francisco Cinematheque (🌐 *www.sfcinematheque.org*), which showcases experimental film and digital media. And dance enthusiasts can attend concerts by a roster of city companies that perform here, including Smuin Ballet/SF (🌐 *www.smuinballet.org*), ODC/San Francisco (🌐 *www.odcdance.org*), the Margaret Jenkins Dance Company (🌐 *www.mjdc.org*), and Alonzo King's Lines Ballet (🌐 *www.linesballet.org*). The Lamplighters (🌐 *www.lamplighters.org*), an alternative opera that specializes in Gilbert and Sullivan, also performs here. *✉ 3rd and Mission Sts., SoMa ☎ 415/978–2787 🌐 www.ybca.org.*

🛍 Shopping

BOOKS

★ Chronicle Books

BOOKS/STATIONERY | This local beacon of publishing produces inventively designed fiction, cookbooks, art books, and other titles, as well as diaries, planners, and address books—all of which you can purchase at two different airy and attractive spaces. The other store is located at 680 2nd Street, near Oracle Park. ⌂ *Metreon Westfield Shopping Center, 165 4th St., near Howard St., SoMa* ☎ *415/369–6271* ⊕ *www.chroniclebooks.com.*

FOOD AND DRINK

K&L Wine Merchants

WINE/SPIRITS | More than any other wine store, this one has an ardent cult following around town. The friendly staffers promise not to sell what they don't taste themselves, and weekly events—on Friday from 5 pm to 6:30 pm and Saturday from noon to 3 pm—open the tastings to customers. The best-seller list for varietals and regions for both the under- and over-$30 categories appeals to the wine lover in everyone. ⌂ *855 Harrison St., near 4th St., SoMa* ☎ *415/896–1734* ⊕ *www.klwines.com.*

Civic Center

The eye-catching, gold-domed City Hall presides over this patchy neighborhood bordered roughly by Franklin, McAllister, Hyde, and Grove streets. The optimistic "City Beautiful" movement of the early 20th century produced the Beaux Arts–style complex for which the area is named, including City Hall, the War Memorial Opera House, the Veterans Building, and the old public library, now the home of the Asian Art Museum. The wonderful Main Library on Larkin Street between Fulton and Grove streets is a modern variation on the Civic Center's architectural theme.

👁 Sights

★ Asian Art Museum

MUSEUM | You don't have to be a connoisseur of Asian art to appreciate a visit to this museum whose monumental exterior conceals a light, open, and welcoming space. The fraction of the Asian's collection on display (about 2,500 pieces out of 18,000-plus total) is laid out thematically and by region, making it easy to follow historical developments.

Begin on the third floor, where highlights of Buddhist art in Southeast Asia and early China include a large, jewel-encrusted, exquisitely painted 19th-century Burmese Buddha, and clothed rod puppets from Java. On the second floor you can find later Chinese works, as well as pieces from Korea and Japan. The joy here is all in the details: on a whimsical Korean jar, look for a cobalt tiger jauntily smoking a pipe, or admire the delicacy of the Japanese tea implements. The ground floor is devoted to temporary exhibits and the museum's wonderful gift shop. During spring and summer, visit the museum on Thursday evenings for extended programs and sip drinks while a DJ spins tunes. ⌂ *200 Larkin St., between McAllister and Fulton Sts., Civic Center* ☎ *415/581–3500* ⊕ *www.asianart. org* ⌛ *$25, free 1st Sun. of month; $10 Thurs. 5–9* ⊙ *Closed Mon.*

City Hall

GOVERNMENT BUILDING | This imposing 1915 structure with its massive gold-leaf dome—higher than the U.S. Capitol's—is about as close to a palace as you're going to get in San Francisco. The classic granite-and-marble behemoth was modeled after St. Peter's Basilica in Rome. Architect Arthur Brown Jr., who also designed Coit Tower and the War Memorial Opera House, designed an interior with grand columns and a sweeping central staircase. San Franciscans were thrilled, and probably a bit surprised, when his firm built City Hall in just a few years. The 1899 structure it replaced had taken 27 years to erect, as corrupt builders and politicians lined their pockets with funds earmarked for it. That building collapsed in about 27 seconds during the 1906 earthquake, revealing trash and newspapers mixed into the construction materials.

City Hall was spruced up and seismically retrofitted in the late 1990s, but the sense of history remains palpable. Some noteworthy events that have taken place here include the marriage of Marilyn Monroe and Joe DiMaggio (1954); the hosing—down the central staircase—of civil-rights and freedom-of-speech protesters (1960); the murders of Mayor George Moscone and openly gay supervisor Harvey Milk (1978); the torching of the lobby by angry members of the gay community in response to the light sentence given to the former supervisor who killed both men (1979); and the registrations of scores of gay couples in celebration of the passage of San Francisco's Domestic Partners Act (1991). In 2004, Mayor Gavin Newsom took a stand against then-current state and federal law by issuing marriage licenses to same-sex partners.

On display in the South Light Court are city artifacts including maps, documents, and photographs. That enormous, 700-pound iron head once crowned the *Goddess of Progress* statue, which topped the old City Hall building until it crumbled during the 1906 earthquake.

Across Polk Street from City Hall is **Civic Center Plaza,** with lawns, walkways, seasonal flower beds, a playground, and an underground parking garage. This sprawling space is generally clean but somewhat grim. Many homeless people hang out here, so the plaza can feel dodgy. ⊠ *Bordered by Van Ness Ave. and Polk, Grove, and McAllister Sts., Civic Center* ☎ *415/554–6023 recorded tour info, 415/554–6139 tour reservations* ⊕ *sfgov.org/cityhall/city-hall-tours* ⚑ *Free* ⊘ *Closed weekends.*

🎭 Performing Arts

City Box Office
TICKETS | This charge-by-phone service sells tickets for many performances and lectures. You can also buy tickets online, or in person on weekdays from 9:30 to 5:30. ⊠ *180 Redwood St., Suite 100, off Van Ness Ave., between Golden Gate Ave. and McAllister St., Civic Center* ☎ *415/392–4400* ⊕ *www.cityboxoffice.com.*

DANCE
★ San Francisco Ballet
DANCE | For ballet lovers, the nation's oldest professional company is reason alone to visit the Bay Area. SFB's performances, for the past three decades under the direction of Helgi Tomasson, have won critical raves. The primary season runs from February through May. The repertoire includes full-length ballets such as *Don Quixote* and *Sleeping Beauty*; the December presentation of *The Nutcracker* is truly spectacular. The company also performs bold new dances from star choreographers such as William Forsythe and Mark Morris, alongside modern classics by George Balanchine and Jerome Robbins. Tickets are available at the **War Memorial Opera House.** ⊠ *War Memorial Opera House, 301 Van Ness Ave., at Grove St., Civic Center* ☎ *415/865–2000* ⊕ *www.sfballet.org.*

MUSIC
★ San Francisco Symphony
MUSIC | One of America's top orchestras performs from September through May, with additional summer performances of light classical music and show tunes. The orchestra and its charismatic music director, Michael Tilson Thomas, known for his daring programming of 20th-century American works, often perform with soloists of the caliber of Andre Watts, Gil Shaham, and Renée Fleming. The symphony's adventurous projects include its collaboration with the heavy-metal band Metallica. ■TIP→ Deep discounts on tickets are often available through Travelzoo,

Groupon, and other vendors. ✉ *Davies Symphony Hall, 201 Van Ness Ave., at Grove St., Civic Center* ☎ *415/864–6000* 🌐 *www.sfsymphony.org.*

OPERA

★ San Francisco Opera

OPERA | Founded in 1923, this internationally recognized organization has occupied the War Memorial Opera House since the building's completion in 1932. From September through December and June through July, the company presents a wide range of operas, from *Carmen* to an operatic take on *It's a Wonderful Life*. The opera also frequently collaborates with European companies and presents unconventional, sometimes edgy projects designed to attract younger audiences. Translations are projected above the stage during most non-English productions. ✉ *War Memorial Opera House, 301 Van Ness Ave., at Grove St., Civic Center* ☎ *415/864–3330 tickets* 🌐 *www.sfopera.com* ☞ *Box office open Mon. 10–5, Tues.–Fri. 10–6.*

★ War Memorial Opera House

ARTS CENTERS | With its soaring vaulted ceilings and marble foyer, this elegant 3,146-seat venue, built in 1932, rivals the old-world theaters of Europe. Part of the San Francisco War Memorial and Performing Arts Center, which also includes Davies Symphony Hall and Herbst Theatre, this is the home of the San Francisco Opera and the San Francisco Ballet. ✉ *301 Van Ness Ave., at Grove St., Civic Center* ☎ *415/621–6600* 🌐 *www.sfwmpac.org.*

Hayes Valley

A chic neighborhood due west of Civic Center, Hayes Valley has terrific eateries, cool watering holes, and great browsing in its funky clothing, home-decor, and design boutiques. Locals love this quarter, but without any big-name draws it remains off the radar for many visitors.

👁 Sights

★ SFJAZZ Center

ARTS VENUE | Devoted entirely to jazz, the center hosts performances by jazz greats such as McCoy Tyner, Joshua Redman, Regina Carter, and Chick Corea. Walk by and the street-level glass walls will make you feel as if you're inside; head indoors and the acoustics will knock your socks off. ✉ *201 Franklin St., at Fell St., Hayes Valley* ☎ *866/920–5299* 🌐 *www.sfjazz.org.*

🍴 Restaurants

Nojo Ramen

$$ | **JAPANESE** | For a little bonhomie before the symphony, it's hard to go wrong with this buzzy (and typically crowded) ramen spot. Noodles are the star of the menu, and deservedly so, but you'll also find izakaya-style small plates and comfort food like chicken teriyaki. **Known for:** ramen with chicken-based (paitan) broth; Japanese comfort foods; long lines. [$] *Average main: $17* ✉ *231 Franklin St., Hayes Valley* ☎ *415/896–4587* 🌐 *www.nojosf.com* ⏲ *Closed Mon. No lunch.*

★ Rich Table

$$$$ | **MODERN AMERICAN** | Sardine chips and porcini doughnuts are popular bites at co-chefs Evan and Sarah Rich's lively restaurant—and indicative of its creativity. The mains are also clever stunners: try one of the proteins or pastas, like the sea urchin cacio e pepe. **Known for:** creative food; freshly baked bread; seasonal ingredients. [$] *Average main: $34* ✉ *199 Gough St., Hayes Valley* ☎ *415/355–9085* 🌐 *www.richtablesf.com* ⏲ *No lunch.*

★ Zuni Café

$$$$ | **MEDITERRANEAN** | After one bite of Zuni's succulent brick-oven-roasted whole chicken with Tuscan bread salad, you'll understand why the two-floor café is a perennial star. Its long copper bar is a hub for a disparate mix of patrons

who commune over oysters on the half shell and cocktails and wine. **Known for:** famous roast chicken; classic San Francisco dining; power lunches. $ *Average main: $35* ⊠ *1658 Market St., Hayes Valley* ☎ *415/552–2522* ⊕ *www.zunicafe. com* ⊘ *Closed Mon.*

🛏 Hotels

★ **Metro Hotel**

$ | HOTEL | These tiny rooms, with simple yet modern decor and equipped with private, if small, bathrooms, are within walking distance to the lively Haight, Hayes Valley, Panhandle, NoPa, and Castro neighborhoods. **Pros:** can't beat the price; out-of-downtown location; friendly staffers. **Cons:** small rooms and bathrooms; street noise; no elevator. $ *Rooms from: $107* ⊠ *319 Divisadero St., Hayes Valley* ☎ *415/861–5364* ⊕ *www.metrohotelsf.com* ⏎ *24 rooms* ⦿ *No meals.*

🅨 Nightlife

★ **Smuggler's Cove**

BARS/PUBS | With the decor of a pirate ship and a slew of rum-based cocktails, you half expect Captain Jack Sparrow to sidle up next to you at this offbeat, Disney-esque hangout. But don't let the kitschy ambience fool you. The folks at Smuggler's Cove take rum so seriously they've even had it made for them from distillers around the world, which you can sample along with more than 550 other offerings, some of them vintage and very hard to find. A punch card is provided so you can try the entire menu (featuring 80-plus cocktails) and remember where you left off without getting shipwrecked. The small space fills up quickly, so arrive early. ⊠ *650 Gough St., at McAllister St., Hayes Valley* ☎ *415/869–1900* ⊕ *www. smugglerscovesf.com.*

🎭 Performing Arts

★ **SFJAZZ Center**

MUSIC | Jazz legends Branford Marsalis and Herbie Hancock have performed at the snazzy center, as have Rosanne Cash and world-music favorite Esperanza Spalding. The sight lines and acoustics here impress. Shows often sell out quickly. ⊠ *201 Franklin St., Hayes Valley* ☎ *866/920–5299* ⊕ *www.sfjazz.org.*

🛍 Shopping

FOOD AND DRINK
Arlequin Wine Merchant

WINE/SPIRITS | If you like the wine list at Absinthe Brasserie, you can walk next door and pick up a few bottles from its highly regarded sister establishment. This small, unintimidating shop carries hard-to-find wines from small producers. Why wait to taste? Crack open a bottle on the patio out back. ⊠ *384A Hayes St., near Gough St., Hayes Valley* ☎ *415/863–1104* ⊕ *www.arlequinwinemerchant.com.*

Miette

FOOD/CANDY | There is truly nothing sweeter than a cellophane bag tied with colorful ribbon and filled with malt balls or floral meringues from this Insta-friendly candy and pastry-store. Grab a gingerbread cupcake or a tantalizing macaron or some shortbread. The pastel-color cake stands make even window-shopping a treat. ⊠ *449 Octavia Blvd., between Hayes and Linden Sts., Hayes Valley* ☎ *415/626–6221* ⊕ *www.miette.com.*

Nob Hill

Nob Hill was officially dubbed during the 1870s when "the Big Four"—Charles Crocker, Leland Stanford, Mark Hopkins, and Collis P. Huntington, who were involved in the construction of the transcontinental railroad—built their hilltop estates. The lingo is thick from this era: those on the hilltop were referred to as "nabobs" (originally meaning a provincial governor from India) and "swells," and the hill itself was called Snob Hill, a term that survives to this day. By 1882 so many estates had sprung up on Nob Hill that Robert Louis Stevenson called it "the hill of palaces." But the 1906 earthquake and fire destroyed all the palatial mansions except for portions of the James Flood brownstone. History buffs may choose to linger here, but for most visitors, a casual glimpse from a cable car will be enough.

⊙ Sights

Cable Car Museum

MUSEUM | FAMILY | One of the city's best free offerings, this museum is an absolute must for kids. You can even ride a cable car here—all three lines stop between Russian Hill and Nob Hill. The facility, which is inside the city's last cable-car barn, takes the top off the system to let you see how it all works. Eternally humming and squealing, the massive powerhouse cable wheels steal the show. You can also climb aboard a vintage car and take the grip, let the kids ring a cable-car bell (briefly), and check out vintage gear dating from 1873. ⊠ 1201 Mason St., at Washington St., Nob Hill ☎ 415/474–1887 ⊕ www.cablecarmuseum.org ⊒ Free.

Grace Cathedral

RELIGIOUS SITE | Not many churches can boast an altarpiece by Keith Haring and not one but two labyrinths. The seat of the Episcopal Church in San Francisco, this soaring Gothic-style structure, erected on the site of the 19th-century railroad baron Charles Crocker's mansion, took 14 years to build, beginning in 1927 and eventually wrapping up in 1964. The gilded bronze doors at the east entrance were taken from casts of Lorenzo Ghiberti's incredible Gates of Paradise, which are on the Baptistery in Florence, Italy. A sculpture of St. Francis by Beniamino Bufano greets you as you enter.

The 34-foot-wide limestone labyrinth is a replica of the 13th-century stone maze on the floor of Chartres Cathedral. All are encouraged to walk the 1/8-mile-long labyrinth, a ritual based on the tradition of meditative walking. There's also a granite outdoor labyrinth on the church's northeast side. The AIDS Interfaith Chapel, to the right as you enter Grace, contains a bronze triptych by the late artist Keith Haring and panels from the AIDS Memorial Quilt. ■TIP→ Especially dramatic times to view the cathedral are during Thursday-night evensong (5:15 pm) and during special holiday programs. ⊠ 1100 California St., at Taylor St., Nob Hill ☎ 415/749–6300 ⊕ www.gracecathedral.org ⊒ Free; tours $25.

✦ Restaurants

★ Sons & Daughters

$$$$ | AMERICAN | The nine-course tasting menu that chef-owner Teague Moriarty serves at his elegant Michelin-starred restaurant serves as a primer for how to do highly seasonal cuisine—and tasting menus—the right way. Each course is nuanced and beautifully executed, whether it's tender grilled squid with a fennel-persimmon mole or a sorrel granita with buckwheat shortbread. Known for: changing prix-fixe menu; excellent housemade bread; attentive service. $ Average main: $145 ⊠ 708 Bush St., Nob Hill ☎ 415/391–8311 ⊕ www.sonsanddaughterssf.com ⊗ No lunch.

🛏 Hotels

Fairmont San Francisco

$$$$ | HOTEL | Dominating the top of Nob Hill like a European palace, the Fairmont indulges guests in luxury—rooms in the main building, adorned in sapphire blues with platinum and pewter accents, have high ceilings, decadent beds, and marble bathrooms; rooms in the newer Tower, many with fine views, have a neutral color palette with

bright-silver notes. **Pros:** huge bathrooms; stunning lobby; great location. **Cons:** some older rooms are small; hills can be challenging for those on foot. [$] *Rooms from: $459* ✉ *950 Mason St., Nob Hill* ☎ *415/772–5000, 800/257–7544* 🌐 *www.fairmont.com/san-francisco* 🛏 *606 rooms* 🍴 *No meals.*

★ The Ritz-Carlton, San Francisco

$$$$ | **HOTEL** | A tribute to beauty and attentive, professional service, the Ritz-Carlton emphasizes luxury and elegance, which is evident in the Ionic columns that grace the neoclassical facade and the crystal chandeliers that illuminate marble floors and walls in the lobby. **Pros:** terrific service; beautiful surroundings; Parallel 37 restaurant and Lobby Lounge. **Cons:** expensive; hilly location; no pool. [$] *Rooms from: $538* ✉ *600 Stockton St., at Pine St., Nob Hill* ☎ *415/296–7465, 800/542–8680* 🌐 *www.ritzcarlton.com/sanfrancisco* 🛏 *336 rooms* 🍴 *No meals.*

Polk Gulch

Polk Gulch, the microhood surrounding north–south Polk Street, hugs the western edges of Nob Hill and Russian Hill but is nothing like either. It's actually two microhoods: Upper Polk Gulch, fairly classy in its northern section, runs from about Union Street south to California Street; Lower Polk Gulch, the rougher southern part, continues south from California to Geary or so. Polk Gulch was the Castro before the Castro. It was the city's gay neighborhood into the 1970s, hosting San Francisco's first pride parade in 1972 and several festive Halloween extravaganzas.

Restaurants

★ Acquerello

$$$$ | **ITALIAN** | Chef-co-owner Suzette Gresham has elicited plenty of swoons over the years with her high-end but soulful Italian cooking. Her Parmesan *budino* (pudding) is a star of the menu, which features both classic and cutting-edge dishes. **Known for:** prix-fixe dining; Parmesan budino; extensive Italian wine list. [$] *Average main: $95* ✉ *1722 Sacramento St., Polk Gulch* ☎ *415/567–5432* 🌐 *www.acquerello.com* ⏲ *Closed Sun. and Mon. No lunch.*

★ Lord Stanley

$$$$ | **AMERICAN** | Husband-and-wife team Carrie and Rupert Blease bring European training and a Californian sensibility to their sophisticated but approachable Michelin-starred cooking, pairing refined technique with earthy and inventive charm. You may find kimchi dip accompanying *brandade* (creamed cod) beignets, or tender roast duck served with sweet-and-sour cabbage heart. **Known for:** excellent wine list; new interpretations of California cooking; attentive service. [$] *Average main: $35* ✉ *2065 Polk St., Polk Gulch* ☎ *415/872–5512* 🌐 *lordstanleysf.com* ⏲ *Closed Mon. No lunch.*

★ Swan Oyster Depot

$$ | **SEAFOOD** | Half fish market and half diner, this small, slim, family-run seafood operation, open since 1912, has no tables, just a narrow marble counter with about 18 stools. Most people come in to buy perfectly fresh salmon, halibut, crabs, and other seafood to take home. **Known for:** fresh seafood; long lines; rich history. [$] *Average main: $18* ✉ *1517 Polk St., Polk Gulch* ☎ *415/673–1101* 💳 *No credit cards* ⏲ *Closed Sun. No dinner.*

Russian Hill

Essentially a tony residential neighborhood of spiffy pieds-à-terre, Victorian flats, Edwardian cottages, and boxlike condos, Russian Hill has some of the city's loveliest stairway walks, hidden garden ways, and steepest streets—not to mention those bay views.

Nob Hill, Russian Hill, and Polk Gulch

KEY

- ❶ Exploring Sights
- ❶ Restaurants
- ❶ Hotels
- 🅱️ BART station

0   300 m

0   1,000 ft

⊙ Sights

Lombard Street

NEIGHBORHOOD | The block-long "Crookedest Street in the World" makes eight switchbacks down the east face of Russian Hill between Hyde and Leavenworth streets. Residents bemoan the traffic jam outside their front doors, but the throngs continue. Join the line of cars waiting to drive down the steep hill, or avoid the whole mess and walk down the steps on either side of Lombard. You take in super views of North Beach and Coit Tower whether you walk or drive—though if you're the one behind the wheel, you'd better keep your eye on the road lest you become yet another of the many folks who ram the garden barriers. ■**TIP**➔ **Can't stand the traffic? Thrill seekers of a different stripe may want to head two blocks south of Lombard to Filbert Street. At a gradient of 31.5%, the hair-raising descent between Hyde and Leavenworth streets is one of the city's steepest. Go slowly!** ⊠ *Lombard St. between Hyde and Leavenworth Sts., Russian Hill.*

San Francisco Art Institute

MUSEUM | The number-one reason for a visit is Mexican master Diego Rivera's *The Making of a Fresco Showing the Building of a City* (1931), in the student gallery to your immediate left inside the entrance. Rivera himself is in the fresco—his broad behind is to the viewer—and he's surrounded by his assistants. They in turn are surrounded by a construction scene, laborers, and city notables such as sculptor Robert Stackpole and architect Timothy Pflueger. *Making* is one of three San Francisco murals painted by Rivera. The number-two reason to come here is the café, or more precisely the eye-popping, panoramic view from the café, which serves surprisingly decent food for a song.

The **Walter & McBean Galleries** (*415/749–4563; Tues. 11–7, Wed.–Sat. 11–6*) exhibit the often provocative works of established artists. ⊠ *800 Chestnut St., Russian Hill* ☎ *415/771–7020* ⊕ *www.sfai.edu* ⊠ *Galleries free.*

North Beach

San Francisco novelist Herbert Gold calls North Beach "the longest-running, most glorious, American bohemian operetta outside Greenwich Village." Indeed, to anyone who's spent some time in its eccentric old bars and cafés, North Beach evokes everything from the Barbary Coast days to the no-less-rowdy Beatnik era.

⊙ Sights

★ City Lights Bookstore

STORE/MALL | Take a look at the exterior of the store: the replica of a revolutionary mural destroyed in Chiapas, Mexico, by military forces; the art banners hanging above the windows. This place isn't just doling out best sellers. Designated a city landmark, the hangout of Beat-era writers and independent publishers remains a vital part of San Francisco's literary scene. Browse the three levels of poetry, philosophy, politics, fiction, history, and local zines, to the tune of creaking wood floors.

Back in the day, writers like Ginsberg and Jack Kerouac would read and even receive mail in the basement. Co-founder Lawrence Ferlinghetti cemented City Lights's place in history by publishing Ginsberg's *Howl and Other Poems* in 1956. The small volume was ignored in the mainstream ... until Ferlinghetti and the bookstore manager were arrested for obscenity and corruption of youth. In the landmark First Amendment trial that followed, the judge exonerated both men, declaring that a work that has "redeeming social significance" can't be obscene. *Howl* went on to become a classic.

Continued on page 587

SAN FRANCISCO'S CABLE CARS

The moment it dawns on you that you severely underestimated the steepness of the San Francisco hills will likely be the same moment you look down and realize those tracks aren't just for show—or just for tourists.

VanNess Ave.. California
59
& Market Streets

Sure, locals rarely use the cable cars for commuting these days. (That's partially due to the $7 fare—hear that, Muni?) So you'll likely be packed in with plenty of fellow sightseers. You may even be approaching cable-car fatigue after seeing its image on so many souvenirs. But if you fear the magic is gone, simply climb on board, and those jaded thoughts will dissolve. Grab the pole and gawk at the view as the car clanks down an insanely steep grade toward the bay. Listen to the humming cable, the clang of the bell, and the occasional quip from the gripman. It's an experience you shouldn't pass up, whether on your first trip or your fiftieth.

HOW CABLE CARS WORK

The mechanics are pretty simple: cable cars grab a moving subterranean cable with a "grip" to go. To stop, they release the grip and apply one or more types of brakes. Four cables, totaling 9 miles, power the city's three lines. If the gripman doesn't adjust the grip just right when going up a steep hill, the cable will start to slip and the car will have to back down the hill and try again. This is an extremely rare occurrence—imagine the ribbing the gripman gets back at the cable car barn!

Gripman: Stands in front and operates the grip, brakes, and bell. Favorite joke, especially at the peak of a steep hill: "This is my first day on the job folks . . ."

Conductor: Moves around the car, deals with tickets, alerts the grip about what's coming up, and operates the rear wheel brakes.

❶ Cable: Steel wrapped around flexible sisal core; 2 inches thick; runs at a constant 9½ mph.

❷ Bells: Used for crew communication; alerts other drivers and pedestrians.

❸ Grip: Vice-like lever extends through the center slot in the track to grab or release the cable.

❹ Grip Lever: Left-hand lever; operates grip.

❺ Car: Entire car weighs 8 tons.

❻ Wheel Brake: Steel brake pads on each wheel.

❼ Wheel Brake Lever: Foot pedal; operates wheel brakes.

❽ Rear Wheel Brake Lever: Applied for extra traction on hills.

❾ Track Brake: 2-foot-long sections of Monterey pine push down against the track to help stop the car.

❿ Track Brake Lever: Middle lever; operates track brakes.

⓫ Emergency Brake: 18-inch steel wedge, jams into street slot to bring car to an immediate stop.

⓬ Emergency Brake Lever: Right-hand lever, red; operates emergency brake.

ROUTES

Cars run at least every 15 minutes, from around 6 am to about 1 am.

Powell–Hyde line: Most scenic, with classic Bay views. Begins at Powell and Market streets, then crosses Nob Hill and Russian Hill before a white-knuckle descent down Hyde Street, ending near the Hyde Street Pier.

Powell–Mason line: Also begins at Powell and Market streets, but winds through North Beach to Bay and Taylor streets, a few blocks from Fisherman's Wharf.

California line: Runs from the foot of Market Street, at Drumm Street, up Nob Hill and back. Great views (and aromas and sounds) of Chinatown on the way up. Sit in back to catch glimpses of the Bay. ■TIP→ **Take the California line if it's just the cable-car experience you're after—the lines are shorter, and the grips and conductors say it's friendlier and has a slower pace.**

RULES OF THE RIDE

Tickets. There are ticket booths at all three turnarounds, or you can pay the conductor after you board (they can make change). Try not to grumble about the price—they're embarrassed enough as it is.

■TIP→ **If you're planning to use public transit a few times, or if you'd like to ride back and forth on the cable car without worrying about the price, consider a one-day Muni passport. You can get passports online, at the Powell Street turnaround, the TIX booth on Union Square, or the Fisherman's Wharf cable-car ticket booth at Beach and Hyde streets.**

All Aboard. You can board on either side of the cable car. It's legal to stand on the running boards and hang on to the pole, but keep your ears open for the gripman's warnings. ■TIP→ **Grab a seat on the outside bench for the best views.**

Most people wait (and wait) in line at one of the cable car turnarounds, but you can also hop on along the route. Board wherever you see a white sign showing a figure climbing aboard a brown cable car; wave to the approaching driver, and wait until the car stops.

Riding on the running boards can be part of the thrill.

CABLE CAR HISTORY

HALLIDIE FREES THE HORSES

In the 1850s and '60s, San Francisco's streetcars were drawn by horses. Legend has it that the horrible sight of a car dragging a team of horses downhill to their deaths roused Andrew Smith Hallidie to action. The English immigrant had invented the "Hallidie Ropeway," essentially a cable car for mined ore, and he was convinced that his invention could also move people. In 1873, Hallidie and his intrepid crew prepared to test the first cable car high on Russian Hill. The anxious engineer peered down into the foggy darkness, failed to see the bottom of the hill, and promptly turned the controls over to Hallidie. Needless to say, the thing worked . . . but rides were free for the first two days because people were afraid to get on.

SEE IT FOR YOURSELF

The Cable Car Museum is one of the city's best free offerings and an absolute must for kids. (You can even ride a cable car there, since all three lines stop between Russian Hill and Nob Hill.) The museum, which is inside the city's last cable-car barn, takes the top off the system to let you see how it all works. Eternally humming and squealing, the massive powerhouse cable wheels steal the show. You can also climb aboard a vintage car and take the grip, let the kids ring a cable-car bell (briefly, please!), and check out vintage gear dating from 1873.

■TIP→ The gift shop sells cable car paraphernalia, including an authentic gripman's bell for $600 (it'll sound like Powell Street in your house every day). For significantly less, you can pick up a key chain made from a piece of worn-out cable.

CHAMPION OF THE CABLE CAR BELL

Each September the city's best and brightest come together to crown a bell-ringing champion at Union Square. The crowd cheers gripmen and conductors as they stomp, shake, and riff with the rope. But it's not a popularity contest; the ringers are judged by former bell-ringing champions who take each ping and gong very seriously.

Stroll Kerouac Alley, branching off Columbus Avenue next to City Lights, to read the quotes from Ferlinghetti, Maya Angelou, Confucius, John Steinbeck, and the street's namesake embedded in the pavement. ✉ *261 Columbus Ave., North Beach* ☎ *415/362–8193* ⊕ *www. citylights.com.*

Coit Tower

BUILDING | Among San Francisco's most distinctive skyline sights, this 210-foot tower is often considered a tribute to firefighters because of the donor's special attachment to the local fire company. As the story goes, a young gold rush–era girl, Lillie Hitchcock Coit (known as Miss Lil), was a fervent admirer of her local fire company—so much so that she once deserted a wedding party and chased down the street after her favorite engine, Knickerbocker No. 5, while clad in her bridesmaid finery. She became the Knickerbocker Company's mascot and always signed her name "Lillie Coit 5." When Lillie died in 1929 she left the city $125,000 to "expend in an appropriate manner ... to the beauty of San Francisco." You can ride the elevator to the top of the tower—the only thing you have to pay for here—to enjoy the view of the Bay Bridge and the Golden Gate Bridge; due north is Alcatraz Island. Most visitors saunter right past the 27 fabulous Depression-era murals inside the tower that depict California's economic and political life, but take the time to appreciate the first New Deal art project supported by taxpayer money. ✉ *Telegraph Hill Blvd. at Greenwich St. or Lombard St., North Beach* ☎ *415/362– 0808* ⊕ *sfrecpark.org* 🖅 *Free; elevator to top $9.*

Grant Avenue

NEIGHBORHOOD | Originally called Calle de la Fundación, Grant Avenue is the oldest street in the city, but it's got plenty of young blood. Here dusty bars such as the Saloon and perennial favorites like the Savoy Tivoli mix with hotshot boutiques,

odd curio shops and antique jumbles like the vintage map store Schein & Schein, atmospheric cafés such as the boho haven Caffè Trieste, and authentic Italian delis. While the street runs from Union Square through Chinatown, North Beach, and beyond, the fun stuff in this neighborhood is crowded into the four blocks between Columbus Avenue and Filbert Street. ✉ *North Beach.*

★ Telegraph Hill

NEIGHBORHOOD | Residents here have some of the city's best views, as well as the most difficult ascents to their aeries. The hill rises from the east end of Lombard Street to a height of 284 feet and is capped by Coit Tower. Imagine lugging your groceries up that! If you brave the slope, though, you can be rewarded with a "secret treasure" San Francisco moment. Filbert Street starts up the hill, then becomes the **Filbert Steps** when the going gets too steep. You can cut between the Filbert Steps and another flight, the **Greenwich Steps,** on up to the hilltop. As you climb, you can pass some of the city's oldest houses and be surrounded by beautiful, flowering private gardens. In some places the trees grow over the stairs so it feels like you're walking through a green tunnel; elsewhere, you'll have wide-open views of the bay. The cypress trees that grow on the hill are a favorite roost of local avian celebrities, the wild parrots of Telegraph Hill; you'll hear the cries of the cherry-headed conures if they're nearby. And the telegraphic name? It comes from the hill's status as the first Morse code signal station back in 1853. ✉ *Bordered by Lombard, Filbert, Kearny, and Sansome Sts., North Beach.*

Washington Square

PLAZA | Once the daytime social heart of Little Italy, this grassy patch has changed character numerous times over the years. The Beats hung out here in the 1950s, hippies camped out in the 1960s and early '70s, and nowadays you're more

The Birds

While on Telegraph Hill, you might be startled by a chorus of piercing squawks and a rushing sound of wings. No, you're not about to have a Hitchcock bird-attack moment. These small, vivid green parrots with cherry red heads number in the hundreds; they're descendants of former pets that escaped or were released by their owners. (The birds dislike cages, and they bite if bothered—must've been some disillusioned owners along the way.)

The parrots like to roost high in the aging cypress trees on the hill, chattering and fluttering, sometimes taking wing en masse. They're not popular with some residents, but they did find a champion in local bohemian Mark Bittner, a former street musician. Bittner began chronicling their habits, publishing a book and battling the homeowners who wanted to cut down the cypresses. A documentary, *The Wild Parrots of Telegraph Hill*, made the issue a cause célèbre. In 2007 City Hall, which recognizes a golden goose when it sees one, stepped in and brokered a solution to keep the celebrity birds in town. The city would cover the homeowners' insurance worries and plant new trees for the next generation of wild parrots.

likely to see elderly Asians doing tai chi than Italian folks reminiscing about the old country. You might also see homeless people hanging out on the benches and young locals sunbathing or running their dogs. Lillie Hitchcock Coit, in yet another show of affection for San Francisco's firefighters, donated the statue of two firemen with a child they rescued. ⊠ *Bordered by Columbus Ave. and Stockton, Filbert, and Union Sts., North Beach.*

🍴 Restaurants

Tony's Pizza Napoletana
$$$ | PIZZA | FAMILY | Repeatedly crowned the World Champion Pizza Maker at the World Pizza Cup in Naples, Tony Gemignani is renowned here for his flavorful dough and impressive range. The multiple gas, electric, and wood-burning ovens in his casual, modern pizzeria turn out many different pies—the famed Neapolitan-style Margherita, but also Sicilian, Romana, and Detroit styles—while salads, antipasti, homemade pastas, and calzone round out the menu. **Known for:** World Champion Pizza chef; multiple pizza ovens and pie styles; family dining. $ *Average main: $27* ⊠ *1570 Stockton St., North Beach* ☎ 415/835–9888 ⊕ *www.tonyspizzanapoletana.com* ⊗ *Closed Tues.*

Tosca Cafe
$$$ | ITALIAN | The leather booths and chairs are in high demand at this dark and clubby 1919 boho classic, where celebs and local scenesters dine on food that skews Italian. You can eat at the bar, which is first come, first served, or stop by for a cappuccino with local Dandelion chocolate and a shot of bourbon while a jukebox belts out tunes. **Known for:** Italian-American comfort food; tasty cocktails; signature roast chicken for two. $ *Average main: $24* ⊠ *242 Columbus Ave., North Beach* ☎ 415/986–9651 ⊕ *www.toscacafesf.com* ⊗ *No lunch.*

🛏 Hotels

★ San Remo Hotel
$ | HOTEL | FAMILY | A few blocks from Fisherman's Wharf, this three-story 1906 Italianate Victorian—once home to longshoremen and Beat poets—has a narrow

stairway to the front desk and labyrinthine hallways. **Pros:** inexpensive rates; free Wi-Fi; rooftop penthouse (reserve way ahead) has private bath and deck with Coit Tower views. **Cons:** some rooms are dark; only the penthouse suite has a private bath; parking (discounted fee) is off-site. $ *Rooms from: $144* ✉ *2237 Mason St., North Beach* ☎ *415/776–8688, 800/352–7366* ⊕ *www.sanremohotel.com* ⤳ *64 rooms* ⦿ *No meals.*

Y Nightlife

Bimbo's 365 Club

MUSIC CLUBS | The plush main room and adjacent lounge of this club, here since 1951, retain a retro vibe perfect for the "Cocktail Nation" programming that keeps the crowds entertained. For a taste of the old-school San Francisco nightclub scene, you can't beat it. Indie low-fi and pop bands such as Mustache Harbor and Tainted Love play here. ✉ *1025 Columbus Ave., at Chestnut St., North Beach* ☎ *415/474–0365* ⊕ *www.bimbos365club.com.*

★ Club Fugazi

CABARET | The claim to fame here is *Beach Blanket Babylon,* an ever-changing wacky musical send-up of San Francisco moods and mores that has been going strong since 1974, making it the longest-running musical revue anywhere. Although the choreography is colorful, the singers brassy, and the satirical songs witty, the real stars are the comically exotic costumes and famous ceiling-high "hats"—which are worth the price of admission alone. The revue sells out as early as a month in advance. ✉ *678 Green St., at Powell St., North Beach* ☎ *415/421–4222* ⊕ *www.beachblanketbabylon.com.*

★ Vesuvio Cafe

BARS/PUBS | If you're hitting only one bar in North Beach, it should be this one. The low-ceilinged second floor of this raucous boho hangout, little altered since its 1960s heyday (when Jack Kerouac frequented the place), is a fine vantage point for watching the colorful Broadway and Columbus Avenue intersection. Another part of Vesuvio's appeal is its diverse clientele, from older neighborhood regulars and young couples to Bacchanalian posses. ✉ *255 Columbus Ave., at Broadway, North Beach* ☎ *415/362–3370* ⊕ *www.vesuvio.com.*

SHOPPING

Knitz & Leather

CLOTHING | Local artisans Julia Relinghaus and Katharina Ernst have been producing one-of-a-kind and custom products of extraordinary craftsmanship for 30 years. Ernst's bold knitted sweaters and accessories and Relinghaus's exquisite, high-quality leather jackets for men and women are expensive but made to last. ✉ *1453 Grant Ave., North Beach* ☎ *415/391–3480.*

Fisherman's Wharf

The crack of fresh Dungeness crab, the aroma of sourdough warm from the oven, the cry of the gulls—in some ways you can experience Fisherman's Wharf today as it has been for more than 100 years.

⊙ Sights

F-line

TRANSPORTATION SITE (AIRPORT/BUS/FERRY/TRAIN) | The city's system of vintage electric trolleys, the F-line, gives the cable cars a run for their money as a beloved mode of transportation. The beautifully restored streetcars—some dating from the 19th century—run from the Castro District down Market Street to the Embarcadero, then north to Fisherman's Wharf. Each car is unique, restored to the colors of its city of origin, from New Orleans and Philadelphia to Moscow and Milan. ■TIP→ **Purchase tickets on board; exact change is required.** ✉ *San Francisco* ⊕ *www.streetcar.org* ⛟ *$3.*

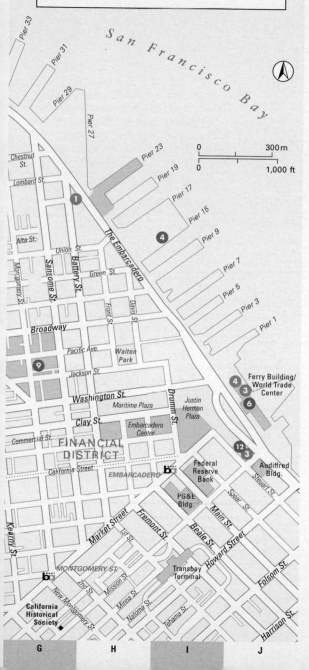

North Beach, Fisherman's Wharf, and Embarcadero

★ Hyde Street Pier

MARINA | FAMILY | If you want to get to the heart of the Wharf, there's no better place to do it than at this pier. Don't pass up the centerpiece collection of historic vessels, part of the **San Francisco Maritime National Historical Park,** almost all of which can be boarded. The *Balclutha*, an 1886 full-rigged three-masted sailing vessel that's more than 250 feet long, sailed around Cape Horn 17 times. Kids especially love the *Eureka*, a side-wheel passenger and car ferry, for her onboard collection of vintage cars. The *Hercules* is a steam-powered tugboat, and the *C.A. Thayer* is a beautifully restored three-masted schooner. Across the street from the pier and a museum in itself is the maritime park's **Visitor Center** (*499 Jefferson St., 415/447–5000, June–Aug., daily 9:30–5:30; Sept.–May, daily 9:30–5*), whose fun, large-scale exhibits make it an engaging stop. See a huge First Order Fresnel lighthouse lens and a shipwrecked boat. Then stroll through time in the exhibit "The Waterfront," where you can touch the timber from a gold rush–era ship recovered from below the Financial District, peek into 19th-century storefronts, and see the sails of an Italian fishing vessel. ⊠ *Hyde and Jefferson Sts., Fisherman's Wharf* ☎ *415/561–7100* ⊕ *www.nps.gov/safr* ⏦ *Ships $15 (ticket good for 7 days).*

Jackson Square Historic District

NEIGHBORHOOD | This was the heart of the Barbary Coast of the Gay '90s—the 1890s, that is. Although most of the red-light district was destroyed in the fire that followed the 1906 earthquake, the remaining old redbrick buildings, many of them now occupied by advertising agencies, law offices, and antiques firms, retain hints of the romance and rowdiness of San Francisco's early days.

With its gentrified gold rush–era buildings, the 700 block of **Montgomery Street** just barely evokes the Barbary Coast

days, but this was a colorful block in the 19th century and on into the 20th. Writers Mark Twain and Bret Harte were among the contributors to the spunky *Golden Era* newspaper, which occupied No. 732 (now part of the building at No. 744).

Restored 19th-century brick buildings line Hotaling Place, which connects Washington and Jackson streets. The lane is named for the **A.P. Hotaling Company whiskey distillery** (*451 Jackson St., at Hotaling Pl.*), the largest liquor repository on the West Coast in its day. The exceptional City Guides (☎ *415/557–4266,* ⊕ *www.sfcityguides.org*) Gold Rush City walking tour covers this area and brings its history to life. ⊠ *Bordered by Columbus Ave., Broadway, and Washington and Sansome Sts., San Francisco.*

★ Musée Mécanique

LOCAL INTEREST | FAMILY | Once a staple at Playland-at-the-Beach, San Francisco's early 20th-century amusement park, the antique mechanical contrivances at this time-warped arcade—including peep shows and nickelodeons—make it one of the most worthwhile attractions at the Wharf. Some favorites are the giant and rather creepy "Laffing Sal," an arm-wrestling machine, the world's only steam-powered motorcycle, and mechanical fortune-telling figures that speak from their curtained boxes. Note the depictions of race that betray the prejudices of the time: stoned Chinese figures in the "Opium-Den" and clown-faced African Americans eating watermelon in the "Mechanical Farm." ■ **TIP→ Admission is free, but you'll need quarters to bring the machines to life.** ⊠ *Pier 45, Shed A, Fisherman's Wharf* ☎ *415/346–2000* ⊕ *museemecaniquesf. com* ⏦ *Free.*

Pier 39

MARINA | FAMILY | The city's most popular waterfront attraction draws millions of visitors each year, who come to browse through its shops and concessions

Thousands of visitors take ferries to Alcatraz each day to walk in the footsteps of the notorious criminals who were held on "The Rock."

hawking every conceivable form of souvenir. The pier can be quite crowded, and the numerous street performers may leave you feeling more harassed than entertained. Arriving early in the morning ensures you a front-row view of the sea lions that bask here, but if you're here to shop—and make no mistake about it, Pier 39 wants your money—be aware that most stores don't open until 9:30 or 10 (later in winter).

Follow the sound of barking to the northwest side of the pier to view the **sea lions** that flop about the floating docks. During the summer, orange-clad naturalists answer questions and offer fascinating facts about the playful pinnipeds—for example, that most of the animals here are males.

At the **Aquarium of the Bay** (☎ *415/623–5300 or 888/732–3483,* 🌐 *www.aquariumofthebay.org, $27.95, hrs vary but at least 10–6 daily*) moving walkways transport you through a space surrounded on three sides by water filled with indigenous San Francisco Bay marine life, from fish and plankton to sharks. ✉ *Beach St. at Embarcadero, Fisherman's Wharf* 🌐 *www.pier39.com.*

🍴 Restaurants

Gary Danko

$$$$ | AMERICAN | This San Francisco classic has earned a legion of fans—and a Michelin star—for its namesake chef's refined and creative seasonal California cooking, displayed in dishes such as pan-seared scallops with parsnip puree, and juniper-crusted venison. The cost of a meal is pegged to the number of courses, from three to five, the wine list is the size of a small-town phone book, and the banquette-lined rooms, with stunning floral arrangements, are as memorable as the food and impeccable service. **Known for:** prix-fixe menu; fine dining; extensive wine list. [$] *Average main: $92* ✉ *800 N. Point St., Fisherman's Wharf* ☎ *415/749–2060* 🌐 *www.garydanko.com* 🕒 *No lunch* 👔 *Jacket required.*

Hotels

★ Argonaut Hotel

$$$ | **HOTEL** | **FAMILY** | The nautically themed Argonaut's spacious guest rooms have exposed-brick walls, wood-beam ceilings, and best of all, windows that open to the sea air and the sounds of the waterfront; many rooms enjoy Alcatraz and Golden Gate Bridge views. **Pros:** bay views; near Hyde Street cable car; toys for the kids. **Cons:** nautical theme isn't for everyone; cramped public areas; far from crosstown attractions. [$] *Rooms from: $269* ✉ *495 Jefferson St., at Hyde St., Fisherman's Wharf* ☎ *415/563–0800, 866/415–0704* 🌐 *www.argonauthotel.com* 🛏 *252 rooms* 🍴 *No meals.*

Hotel Zoe Fisherman's Wharf

$$ | **HOTEL** | A smart-looking boutique hotel with guest-room interiors inspired by luxury Mediterranean yachts, the Zoe aims for subtle contemporary elegance in the form of lightly stained woods and soft-brown and cream fabrics and walls. **Pros:** cozy feeling; steps from Fisherman's Wharf; smart-looking contemporary design. **Cons:** congested touristy area; small rooms; resort fee catches some guests off guard. [$] *Rooms from: $249* ✉ *425 N. Point St., at Mason St., Fisherman's Wharf* ☎ *415/561–1100, 800/648–4626* 🌐 *www.hotelzoesf.com* 🛏 *221 rooms* 🍴 *No meals.*

Nightlife

Buena Vista Café

BARS/PUBS | At the end of the Hyde Street cable-car line, the Buena Vista packs 'em in for its famous Irish coffee—which, according to owners, was the first served stateside (in 1952). The place oozes nostalgia, drawing devoted locals as well as out-of-towners relaxing after a day of sightseeing. It's narrow and can get crowded, but this spot provides a fine alternative to the overpriced tourist joints nearby. ✉ *2765 Hyde St., at Beach St., Fisherman's Wharf* ☎ *415/474–5044* 🌐 *www.thebuenavista.com.*

Embarcadero

Stretching from below the Bay Bridge to Fisherman's Wharf, San Francisco's flat, accessible waterfront invites you to get up close and personal with the bay, the picturesque and constant backdrop to this stunning city. For decades the Embarcadero was obscured by a terrible raised freeway and known best for the giant buildings on its piers that further cut off the city from the bay. With the freeway gone and a few piers restored for public access, the Embarcadero has been given a new lease on life. Millions of visitors may come through the northern waterfront every year, lured by Fisherman's Wharf and Pier 39, but locals tend to stop short of these, opting instead for the gastronomic pleasures of the Ferry Building. Between the two, though, you'll find tourists and San Franciscans alike soaking up the sun, walking out over the water on a long pier to see the sailboats, savoring the excellent restaurants and old-time watering holes, watching the street performers that crowd Embarcadero Plaza on a sunny day—these are the simple joys that make you happy you're in San Francisco, whether for a few days or a lifetime.

Alcatraz

JAIL | **FAMILY** | Thousands of visitors come every day to walk in the footsteps of Alcatraz's notorious criminals. The stories of life and death on "the Rock" may sometimes be exaggerated, but it's almost impossible to resist the chance to wander the cell block that tamed the country's toughest gangsters and saw daring escape attempts of tremendous desperation. Fewer than 2,000 inmates ever did time on the Rock, and though they weren't the worst criminals, they were definitely the worst prisoners, including Al "Scarface" Capone, Robert "The Birdman" Stroud, and George "Machine Gun" Kelly.

Some tips for escaping to Alcatraz: (1) Buy your ticket in advance. Visit the website for Alcatraz Cruises (⊕ www.alcatrazcruises.com) to scout out available departure times for the ferry. Prepay by credit card and keep a receipt record; the ticket price covers the boat ride and the audio tour. Pick up your ticket at the "will call" window at Pier 33 up to an hour before sailing. (2) Dress smart. Bring a jacket to ward off the chill from the boat ride and wear comfortable shoes. (3) Go for the evening tour. You'll get even more out of your Alcatraz experience at night. The evening tour has programs not offered during the day, the bridge-to-bridge view of the city twinkles at night, and your "prison experience" will be amplified as darkness falls. (4) Be mindful of scheduled and limited-capacity talks. Some programs are given only once a day (the schedule is posted in the cell house) and have limited seating, so keep an eye out for a cell-house staffer handing out passes shortly before the start time.

The boat ride to the island is brief (15 minutes), but affords beautiful views of the city, Marin County, and the East Bay. The audio tour, highly recommended, includes observations by guards and prisoners about life in one of America's most notorious penal colonies. Plan your schedule to allow at least three hours for the visit and boat rides combined. Not inspired by the prison? Wander around the lovely native plant gardens and (if the tide is cooperating) the tide pools on the north side of the island. ⊠ Pier 33, Embarcadero ☎ 415/981–7625 ⊕ www.nps.gov/alca ⤳ From $40.

★ Exploratorium
MUSEUM | FAMILY | Walking into this fascinating "museum of science, art, and human perception" is like visiting a mad-scientist's laboratory. Most of the exhibits are supersize, and you can play with everything. Signature experiential exhibits include the Tinkering Studio and a glass Bay Observatory building, where the exhibits inside help visitors better understand what they see outside. Get an Alice-in-Wonderland feeling in the distorted room, where you seem to shrink and grow as you walk across the slanted, checkered floor. In the shadow room, a powerful flash freezes an image of your shadow on the wall; jumping is a favorite pose. More than 650 other exhibits focus on sea and insect life, computers, electricity, patterns and light, language, the weather, and more. One surefire hit is the pitch-black, touchy-feely Tactile Dome ($15 extra; reservations required): crawl through a course of ladders, slides, and tunnels, relying solely on your sense of touch." ⊠ Piers 15–17, Embarcadero ☎ 415/528–4444 general information, 415/528–4407 Tactile Dome reservations ⊕ www.exploratorium.edu ⤳ $30.

★ Ferry Building
MARKET | The jewel of the Embarcadero, erected in 1896, is topped by a 230-foot clock tower modeled after the campanile of the cathedral in Seville, Spain. On the morning of April 18, 1906, the tower's four clock faces stopped at 5:17—the moment the great earthquake struck—and stayed still for 12 months.

Today San Franciscans flock to the street-level marketplace, stocking up on supplies from local favorites such as Acme Bread, Cowgirl Creamery, Blue Bottle Coffee, and Humphry Slocombe ice cream. Slanted Door, the city's beloved high-end Vietnamese restaurant, is here, along with the well-regarded Hog Island Oyster Company. On the plaza side, the outdoor tables at Gott's Roadside offer great people-watching with their famous burgers. On Saturday morning the plazas outside the building buzz with an upscale farmers' market where you can buy exotic sandwiches and other munchables. Extending south from the piers north of the building all the way to the Bay Bridge, the waterfront promenade out front is a favorite among joggers and picnickers, with a front-row view of sailboats plying the bay. True to its name, the Ferry Building still serves actual ferries: from its eastern flank they sail to Sausalito, Larkspur, Tiburon, and the East Bay. ✉ *Embarcadero at foot of Market St., Embarcadero* ☎ *415/983–8030* 🌐 *www.ferrybuildingmarketplace.com.*

San Francisco Railway Museum

MUSEUM | **FAMILY** | A labor of love brought to you by the same vintage-transit enthusiasts responsible for the F-line's revival, this one-room museum and store celebrates the city's streetcars and cable cars with photographs, models, and artifacts. The permanent exhibit includes the replicated end of a streetcar with a working cab—complete with controls and a bell—for kids to explore; the cool, antique Wiley birdcage traffic signal; and models and display cases to view. Right on the F-line track, just across from the Ferry Building, this is a great quick stop. ✉ *77 Steuart St., Embarcadero* ☎ *415/974–1948* 🌐 *www.streetcar.org* 🎫 *Free* ⏲ *Closed Mon.*

🍴 Restaurants

Fog City

$$ | **AMERICAN** | **FAMILY** | All but hidden on a far-flung stretch of the Embarcadero, this 21st-century diner that's well worth the hike is best known for its updated classics, like a short-rib BLT with kimchi mayo and cornbread that emerges hot from the wood-fired oven. An inviting U-shape bar and tables-with-a-view attract a mix of FiDi locals and tourists who've wandered right into a gold mine. **Known for:** updated diner food; excellent cocktails; views of Battery Street and the Embarcadero. [$] *Average main: $22* ✉ *1300 Battery St., Embarcadero* ☎ *415/982–2000* 🌐 *www.fogcitysf.com.*

Hog Island Oyster Company

$$ | **SEAFOOD** | A thriving oyster farm north of San Francisco in Tomales Bay serves up its harvest at this raw bar and restaurant in the Ferry Building, where devotees come for impeccably fresh oysters and clams on the half shell. Other mollusk-centered options include a first-rate seafood stew, baked oysters, clam chowder, and "steamer" dishes, but the bar also turns out one of the city's best grilled-cheese sandwiches, made with three artisanal cheeses on artisanal bread. **Known for:** fresh oysters; first-rate seafood stew; busy raw bar. [$] *Average main: $19* ✉ *Ferry Bldg., Embarcadero at Market St., Embarcadero* ☎ *415/391–7117* 🌐 *www.hogislandoysters.com.*

Slanted Door

$$$$ | **VIETNAMESE** | Celebrated chef-owner Charles Phan has mastered the upmarket, Western-accented Vietnamese menu, showcased in a big space with sleek wooden tables and chairs, a big bar, an enviable bay view, and dedicated clientele. His popular dishes, including green-papaya salad, daikon rice cakes, cellophane crab noodles, chicken clay pot, and shaking beef (tender beef cubes with garlic and onion) don't come cheap, but they're made with quality ingredients. **Known for:** upscale Vietnamese food; some of the city's best cocktails; bustling dining room with great bay views. [$] *Average main: $38* ✉ *Ferry Bldg., Embarcadero at Market St., Embarcadero* ☎ *415/861–8032* 🌐 *www.slanteddoor.com.*

🛏 Hotels

★ Hotel Vitale

$$$$ | **HOTEL** | **FAMILY** | The emphasis on luxury and upscale relaxation at this eight-story bay-front property is apparent: limestone-lined baths stocked with top-of-the-line products; the penthouse-level day spa with soaking tubs set in a rooftop bamboo forest; terraces on the fifth, seventh, and eighth floors with great waterfront views. **Pros:** family-friendly studios; great waterfront views; penthouse spa. **Cons:** some rooms feel cramped; "urban fee" adds further expense to an already pricey property; yet another charge for Wi-Fi beyond basic. $ *Rooms from: $385* ⊠ *8 Mission St., Embarcadero* ☎ *415/278–3700, 888/890–8688* ⊕ *www.hotelvitale.com* ⇘ *200 rooms* ❍| *No meals.*

Nightlife

Hard Water
BARS/PUBS | This waterfront restaurant and bar with stunning bay views pays homage to America's most iconic spirit—bourbon—with a wall of whiskeys and a lineup of specialty cocktails. The menu, crafted by Charles Phan of Slanted Door fame, is an ode to New Orleans cuisine and includes spicy pork-belly cracklings, jambalaya, and other fun snacks. ⊠ *Pier 3, at Embarcadero, Embarcadero* ☎ *415/392–3021* ⊕ *www. hardwaterbar.com.*

Pagan Idol
BARS/PUBS | Giving the Tonga Bar a run for its money as the kitchiest tiki bar in town, Pagan Idol features a secret back room complete with erupting volcano, giant tikis, and a starry night sky. The folks from Bourbon & Branch are behind this faux pirate ship, so even if the cocktails are served in goofy tiki glasses with paper umbrellas—even if they're on fire—rest assured they're top-shelf and on the money. Expect live music Tuesday through Thursday. ⊠ *375 Bush St., near Kearney St., Financial District* ☎ *415/985– 6375* ⊕ *www.paganidol.com.*

Rickhouse
BARS/PUBS | An after-work FiDi crowd fills this brick-walled and dimly lit speakeasy, revered for its extensive whiskey menu and curated list of seasonal cocktails. It's a beautiful space with barrels aplenty, an evening oasis in a neighborhood that traditionally rolls up the sidewalks at sunset. ⊠ *246 Kearney St., near Bush St., Financial District* ☎ *415/398–2827* ⊕ *www.rickhousebar.com.*

🛍 Shopping

FARMERS' MARKETS
★ Ferry Plaza Farmers' Market
OUTDOOR/FLEA/GREEN MARKETS | The partylike Saturday edition of the city's most upscale and expensive farmers' market places baked goods, gourmet cheeses, smoked fish, and fancy pots of jam alongside organic basil, specialty mushrooms, heirloom tomatoes, and juicy-ripe locally grown fruit. Smaller markets also take place on Tuesday and Thursday from April through December. ⊠ *Ferry Plaza, at Market St., Embarcadero* ☎ *415/291–3276* ⊕ *www.ferrybuildingmarketplace.com.*

The Marina

Well-funded postcollegiates and the nouveau riche flooded the Marina after the 1989 Loma Prieta earthquake had sent many residents running for more-solid ground, changing the tenor of this formerly low-key neighborhood. The number of yuppie coffee emporiums skyrocketed, a bank became a Williams-Sonoma store, and the local grocer gave way to a Pottery Barn. On weekends a young, fairly homogeneous, well-to-do crowd floods the cafés and bars.

👁 Sights

★ Palace of Fine Arts
BUILDING | At first glance this stunning, rosy rococo palace seems to be from another world, and indeed, it's the sole survivor of the many tinted-plaster structures (a temporary classical city of sorts) built for the 1915 Panama-Pacific International Exposition, the world's fair that celebrated San Francisco's recovery from the 1906 earthquake and fire. The

expo buildings originally extended about a mile along the shore. Bernard Maybeck designed this faux-Roman classic beauty, which was reconstructed in concrete and reopened in 1967. A victim of the elements, the Palace required a piece-by-piece renovation that was completed in 2008.

The pseudo-Latin language adorning the Palace's exterior urns continues to stump scholars. The massive columns (each topped with four "weeping maidens"), great rotunda, and swan-filled lagoon have been used in countless fashion layouts, films, and wedding photo shoots. After admiring the lagoon, look across the street to the house at 3460 Baker Street. If the maidens out front look familiar, they should—they're original casts of the "garland ladies" you can see in the Palace's colonnade. ✉ *3301 Lyon St., at Beach St., Marina* ☎ *415/563–6504* 🎫 *Free.*

🍴 Restaurants

A16

$$$$ | ITALIAN | Named after a highway that runs through southern Italy, this trattoria specializes in the food from that region, done very, very well. The menu is stocked with pizza and rustic pastas like *maccaronara* with *ragu napoletana* and house-made salted ricotta, as well as entrées like roasted chicken with sage salsa verde. **Known for:** equally noteworthy pastas and pizzas; one of the city's best Italian wine lists; meatball Mondays. [$] *Average main: $36* ✉ *2355 Chestnut St., Marina* ☎ *415/771–2216* 🌐 *www.a16pizza.com* 🕒 *No lunch Mon.–Thurs.*

Bistro Aix

$$$ | BISTRO | In a neighborhood full of trendy minichains, this over-two-decades-old Californian-French spot is the calm elder statesmen for the often rowdy Marina. The food is unfussy (perfect duck leg confit cassoulet; house-smoked salmon and potato galette) and doesn't try to be anything overly ambitious, yet everything is consistently on the mark. **Known for:** honest bistro cooking with quality ingredients; rear courtyard with beautiful olive tree; warm, romantic atmosphere. [$] *Average main: $26* ✉ *3340 Steiner St., Marina* ✣ *Between Chestnut St. and Lombard St.* ☎ *415/202–0100* 🌐 *www.bistroaix.com* 🕒 *Closed Sun.*

Causwells

$$$ | AMERICAN | There are two personalities to Chestnut Street's sleek grown-up diner—the double-stack burger that draws burgerhounds from dozens of miles away and the rest of the honest, spruced-up comfort food menu. Start with homemade ricotta and a bountiful salad, then go straight after the burger and jerk chicken with creamed corn, before concluding with the must-try doughnut bread pudding. **Known for:** the Americana burger; excellent wine list full of lesser known regions; kitchen open until midnight on weekends. [$] *Average main: $25* ✉ *2346 Chestnut St., Marina* ☎ *415/447–6081* 🌐 *www.causwells.com.*

Greens

$$$ | VEGETARIAN | Owned and operated by the San Francisco Zen Center, this legendary vegetarian restaurant gets some of its fresh produce from the center's organic Green Gulch Farm. Despite the lack of meat, hearty dishes from chef Annie Somerville—such as green squash curry and chestnut fettuccine with chanterelle mushrooms—really satisfy. **Known for:** unbeatable views; superb vegetarian food; pizza at lunch. [$] *Average main: $25* ✉ *Bldg. A, Fort Mason, 2 Marina Blvd., Marina* ☎ *415/771–6222* 🌐 *www.greensrestaurant.com* 🕒 *No lunch Mon.*

Nightlife

California Wine Merchant
WINE BARS—NIGHTLIFE | Part cluttered shop, part cozy bar, Chestnut Street's marquee wine destination is a longtime favorite for grabbing a glass or three. Wines featured always come from some of the state's most highly regarded vintners of all sizes and celebrity status. The neighborhood has many wine bars, but this is where the locals go when the focus is on the wine itself. ✉ *2113 Chestnut St., Marina* ☎ *415/567–0646* 🌐 *www.californiawinemerchant.com.*

The Interval at Long Now
BARS/PUBS | Even many locals don't realize that the Fort Mason Center is home to one of the city's most impressive and scene-free cocktail bars. As part of the Long Now Foundation, a nonprofit devoted to long-term thinking, the cocktails reflect that commitment to finding innovative ways to serve tried-and-true libations. The Navy Gimlet with clarified lime juice is a modern day San Francisco classic. ✉ *2 Marina Blvd., Landmark Bldg. A, Marina* ☎ *415/496–9187* 🌐 *www.theinterval.org.*

Cow Hollow

Between old-money Pacific Heights and the well-heeled, postcollegiate Marina lies comfortably upscale Cow Hollow. The neighborhood's name harks back to the 19th-century dairy farms whose owners eked out a living here despite the fact that there was more sand than grass.

Sights

Octagon House
HOUSE | This eight-sided home sits across the street from its original site on Gough Street; it's one of two remaining octagonal houses in the city (the other is on Russian Hill), and the only one open to the public. White quoins accent each of the eight corners of the pretty blue-gray exterior, and a colonial-style garden completes the picture. The house is full of antique American furniture, decorative arts (paintings, silver, rugs), and documents from the 18th and 19th centuries, including the contents of a time capsule left by the original owners in 1861 that was discovered during a 1950s renovation. A deck of Revolutionary-era hand-painted playing cards takes an anti-monarchist position: in place of kings, queens, and jacks, the American upstarts substituted American statesmen, Roman goddesses, and Indian chiefs. Note that the home is only open on the second Sunday, and second and fourth Thursday of each month (closed all January). ✉ *2645 Gough St., near Union St., Cow Hollow* ☎ *415/441–7512* 🌐 *nscda-ca.org/octagon-house/* 🎫 *Free, donations encouraged.*

Restaurants

★ **Atelier Crenn**
$$$$ | MODERN FRENCH | Dinner at the spectacularly inventive flagship of San Francisco's most celebrated chef of the moment, Dominique Crenn, starts with the presentation of a poem. Each course is described by a line in the poem, so the "Hidden beneath the bluffs" might be whole grilled Monterey abalone with a purée of its own liver and a grilled mussel sauce. **Known for:** extraordinary, whimsical tasting menu; stratospheric prices; hip-elegant atmosphere. [$] *Average main: $335* ✉ *3127 Fillmore St., Cow Hollow* ☎ *415/440–0460* 🌐 *www.ateliercrenn.com* 🕒 *Closed Sun. and Mon.*

Bar Crenn
$$$$ | FRENCH | Dominique Crenn's sumptuous salon decked out with fur-draped bar stools, chandeliers, and lush velvet drapes is really a bar only in name. Yes, there's a bar pouring outstanding wines and it's possible to graze on warm gougères and oysters. **Known for:** Versailles-style furnishings; eggshell filled

with bone marrow custard, topped with caviar; fine Champagne. $ *Average main: $36* ⊠ *3131 Fillmore St., Cow Hollow* ☎ *415/440–0460* ⊕ *www.barcrenn.com* ⊘ *Closed Sun. and Mon.*

Kaiyo

$$ | **PERUVIAN** | San Francisco has a handful of Peruvian restaurants, but this uber hip Union Street spot is the first "Nikkei" cuisine (Japanese-Peruvian) restaurant for diners to explore. Skip the pedestrian *pollo a la brasa* and have fun sampling around the *tiraditos* and sushi rolls. **Known for:** creative pisco cocktails; smoked duck and shaved foie gras sushi; street art murals in bathrooms. $ *Average main: $18* ⊠ *1838 Union St., Cow Hollow* ☎ *415/525–4804* ⊕ *www.kaiyosf.com* ⊘ *Closed Mon.*

Rose's Café

$$$ | **ITALIAN** | **FAMILY** | Although it's open morning until night, this cozy café is most synonymous with brunch. Sleepy-headed locals turn up for delights like the smoked ham, fried egg, and Gruyère breakfast sandwich and the French toast bread pudding with caramelized apples. **Known for:** pizzas for the morning and night; house-baked goods; brunch lines. $ *Average main: $28* ⊠ *2298 Union St., Cow Hollow* ☎ *415/775–2200* ⊕ *www.rosescafesf.com.*

🛏 Hotels

⭐ Union Street Inn

$$ | **B&B/INN** | Antiques, unique artwork, and such touches as candles, fresh flowers, wineglasses, and fine linens make rooms in this green-and-cream 1902 Edwardian popular with honeymooners and those looking for a romantic getaway with an English countryside ambience. **Pros:** personal service; excellent full breakfast; beautiful secret garden. **Cons:** parking is pricey; two-night minimum stay on weekends; no elevator. $ *Rooms from: $249* ⊠ *2229 Union St., Cow Hollow* ☎ *415/346–0424* ⊕ *www.unionstreetinn.com* 🛏 *6 rooms* ⭐ *Breakfast.*

🛍 Shopping

The Caviar Company

FOOD/CANDY | "The Caviar Sisters" Petra and Saskia Bergstein created this sustainability-minded brand that developed a cult following among caviar connoisseurs and chefs in the Bay Area. Their chic above-street level boutique on Union Street allows the public to pick out some of the finest caviar products in town—and feel good about it. ⊠ *1954 Union St., Cow Hollow* ☎ *415/300–0299* ⊕ *www.thecaviarco.com* ⊘ *Closed Mon.*

Ginger Elizabeth Chocolates

FOOD/CANDY | **FAMILY** | A Sacramento chocolatier with a nationally known name expanded to San Francisco in 2018. It's already a marquee destination for macarons or a box of chocolate bonbons with atypical flavors like sweet cream chai and buttermilk lime. ⊠ *3108 Fillmore St., Cow Hollow* ☎ *415/671–7113* ⊕ *www.gingerelizabeth.com* ⊘ *Closed Mon. and Tues.*

Wrecking Ball Coffee Roasters

FOOD/CANDY | The Instagram set knows this Wi-Fi-free, almost seating-free Union Street roaster and café as the place with the pineapple wallpaper. Everyone enjoys some of the finest lattes and espresso shots around, usually to-go, but sometimes enjoyed on the low bench in front of that famous wallpaper. ⊠ *2271 Union St., Cow Hollow* ☎ *415/638–9227* ⊕ *www.wreckingballcoffee.com.*

🍸 Nightlife

The Black Horse London Pub

BARS/PUBS | Barely seven stools fit in San Francisco's smallest bar. Plus, there are just as many bottled beers (no taps) as seats and be sure to bring some cash since credit cards aren't accepted. It's as bare-bones as it gets but there's sports on TV, a fun dice game, and most importantly a neighborhood camaraderie that is increasingly hard to find. ⊠ *1514 Union St., Cow Hollow* ⊕ *www.blackhorselondon.com.*

West Coast Wine & Cheese

WINE BARS—NIGHTLIFE | Whether you're in the mood for a Mendocino County rosé or an Oregon Pinot Noir, as the name suggests, you'll find it at this narrow, sleek locals' favorite. The kitchen isn't much more than a stove top, but does some pretty impressive work beyond cheese and charcuterie. Take advantage of the ability to order half pours and sample more wines. ⊠ *2165 Union St., Cow Hollow* ☎ *415/376–9720* ⊕ *www. westcoastsf.com.*

Presidio

At the foot of the Golden Gate Bridge, one of city residents' favorite in-town getaways is the 1,400-plus-acre Presidio, which combines accessible nature-in-the-raw with a window into the past.

👁 Sights

★ Baker Beach

BEACH—SIGHT | FAMILY | West of the Golden Gate Bridge is a mile-long stretch of soft sand beneath steep cliffs, beloved for its spectacular views and laid-back vibe (read: you'll see naked people here on the northernmost end). Its isolated location makes it rarely crowded, but many San Franciscans know that there is no better place to take in the sunset than this beach. Kids love climbing around the old Battery Chamberlin. This is truly one of those places that inspires local pride. ⊠ *Baker Beach, Presidio* ⊹ *Accessed from Bowley St. off Lincoln Blvd.* ⊕ *www.parksconservancy.org/parks-baker-beach.*

Crissy Field

BEACH—SIGHT | FAMILY | One of the most popular places for San Franciscans to get fresh air is a stretch of restored marshland along the sand of the bay. Kids on bikes, folks walking dogs, and joggers share the paved path along the shore, often winding up at the Warming Hut, a combination café and fun gift store at the end of the path, for a hot chocolate in the shadow of the Golden Gate Bridge. Midway along the Golden Gate Promenade that winds along the shore is the Gulf of the Farallones National Marine Sanctuary Visitor Center, where kids can get a close-up view of small sea creatures and learn about the rich ecosystem offshore. Alongside the main green of Crissy Field, there are several renovated airplane hangars and warehouses that are now home to the likes of rock-climbing gyms, an air trampoline park, and a craft brewery. ⊠ *Crissy Field, Presidio* ⊕ *www.presidio.gov/places/crissy-field.*

★ Golden Gate Bridge

BRIDGE/TUNNEL | With its simple but powerful art-deco design, the 1.7-mile suspension span that connects San Francisco and Marin County was built to withstand winds of more than 100 mph. It's also not a bad place to be in an earthquake: designed to sway almost 28 feet, the Golden Gate Bridge (unlike the Bay Bridge) was undamaged by the 1989 Loma Prieta quake. If you're walking on the bridge when it's windy, stand still and you can feel it swaying a bit.

Crossing the Golden Gate Bridge under your own power is exhilarating—a little scary, and definitely chilly. From the bridge's eastern-side walkway, the only side pedestrians are allowed on, you can take in the San Francisco skyline and the bay islands; look west for the wild hills of the Marin Headlands, the curving coast south to Lands End, and the Pacific Ocean. On sunny days, sailboats dot the water, and brave windsurfers test the often-treacherous tides beneath the bridge. A vista point on the Marin County side provides a spectacular city panorama.

A structural engineer, dreamer, and poet named Joseph Strauss worked tirelessly for 20 years to make the bridge a reality, first promoting the idea of it and then

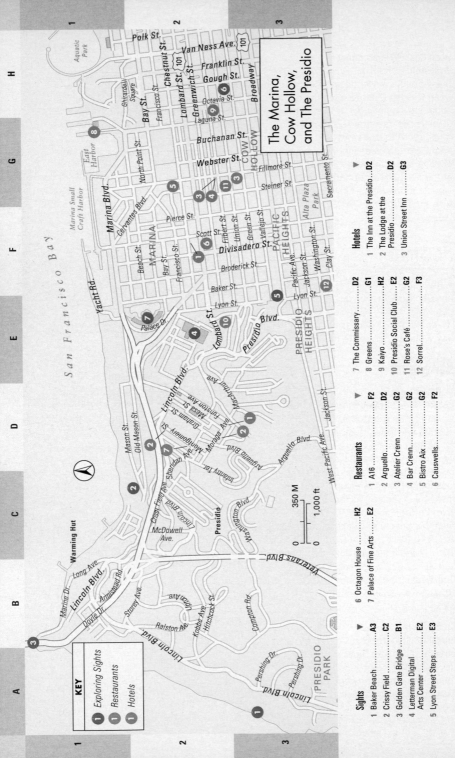

The Marina,
Cow Hollow,
and The Presidio

Sights ▶
1 Baker Beach A3
2 Crissy Field C2
3 Golden Gate Bridge B1
4 Letterman Digital
   Arts Center E2
5 Lyon Street Steps E3
6 Octagon House H2
7 Palace of Fine Arts E2

Restaurants ▶
1 A16 .... F2
2 Arguello D2
3 Atelier Crenn G2
4 Bar Crenn G2
5 Bistro Aix G2
6 Causwells F2
7 The Commissary D2
8 Greens G1
9 Kaiyo H2
10 Presidio Social Club E2
11 Rose's Café G2
12 Sorrel F3

Hotels ▶
1 The Inn at the Presidio ... D2
2 The Lodge at the
   Presidio D2
3 Union Street Inn G3

KEY
1 Exploring Sights
1 Restaurants
1 Hotels

overseeing design and construction. Though the final structure bore little resemblance to his original plan, Strauss guarded his legacy jealously, refusing to recognize the seminal contributions of engineer Charles A. Ellis. In 2007, the Golden Gate Bridge district finally recognized Ellis's role, though Strauss, who died less than a year after opening day in 1937, would doubtless be pleased with the inscription on his statue, which stands sentry in the southern parking lot: "The Man Who Built the Bridge."

You won't see it on a T-shirt, but the bridge is perhaps the world's most publicized suicide platform, with an average of one jumper about every 10 days. Signs on the bridge refer the disconsolate to special telephones, and officers patrol the walkway and watch by security camera to spot potential jumpers. A suicide barrier, an unobtrusive net not unlike the one that saved 19 workers during the bridge's construction, is expected to be completed in 2020.

While at the bridge, you can grab a healthy snack at the art deco–style Bridge Café. The Bridge Pavilion sells attractive, high-quality souvenirs and has a small display of historical artifacts. At the outdoor exhibits, you can see the bridge rise before your eyes on hologram panels, learn about the features that make it art deco, and read about the personalities behind its design and construction. City Guides offers free walking tours of the bridge every Thursday and Sunday at 11 am. ✉ *Lincoln Blvd. near Doyle Dr. and Fort Point, Presidio* ☎ *415/921–5858* 🌐 *www.goldengatebridge.org* 🎟 *Free.*

Letterman Digital Arts Center

BUILDING | **FAMILY** | Bay Area filmmaker George Lucas's 23-acre **Letterman Digital Arts Center,** a digital studio "campus," along the eastern edge of the land, is exquisitely landscaped and largely open to the public. If you have kids in tow or are a *Star Wars* fan yourself, make the pilgrimage to the **Yoda Fountain** (Letterman Drive at Dewitt Road), between two of the arts-center buildings, then take your picture with the life-size Darth Vader statue in the lobby, open to the public on weekdays. ✉ *1 Letterman Dr., Presidio* 🌐 *www.presidio.gov/letterman-digital-arts-center.*

Lyon Street Steps

VIEWPOINT | Get ready for a stairs workout—and a spectacularly rewarding view at the top—when tackling the 332 steps at the eastern edge of the Presidio. There will likely be no shortage of exercise seekers huffing and puffing up the steps, but feel free to conquer the climb slowly. The trimmed hedge landscaping is worthy of its own visit, but there's no doubt that the view of the Presidio forests and the bay are the reason these steps are a top attraction. ✉ *2545 Lyon St., Presidio Heights* ✥ *Between Green St. and Pacific Ave.*

🍴 Restaurants

Arguello

$$$ | **MODERN MEXICAN** | **FAMILY** | Whether enjoying shrimp tacos at lunch on the beautiful, intimate patio or a perfect margarita with a host of small plates at the bar for a casual dinner, celebrated chef Traci Des Jardins's Californian-Mexican restaurant always hits the right notes. Tortillas and salsas are made in-house, and the tequila and mezcal selection is one of the deepest in San Francisco. **Known for:** intimate outdoor patio; superb pozole verde; various lunch tacos. [$] *Average main: $23* ✉ *50 Moraga St., Presidio* ✥ *In Presidio Officers' Club* ☎ *415/561–3650* 🌐 *www.arguellosf.com* ⏲ *Closed Mon. No dinner Tues. and Sun.*

The Commissary

$$$$ | **SPANISH** | Order a Spanish brandy riff on a Negroni and a few tapas, then get ready for one of the city's top Spanish dining experiences right by the Walt Disney Museum. Chef-owner Traci Des Jardins and her team does a fantastic job incorporating local produce and Bay Area spirit to tapas bar classics like patatas bravas and warm cheese fritters. **Known for:** large format steak dishes; excellent, simple desserts; terrific wine and sherry program but ugly stemless wineglasses. $ *Average main: $35* ✉ *101 Montgomery St., Presidio* ☎ *415/561–3600* ⊕ *www.thecommissarysf.com* ☯ *Closed Sun.*

Presidio Social Club

$$$ | AMERICAN | FAMILY | Set in an old barracks building at the eastern edge of the Presidio, American comfort classics meet seasonal California cooking. Like the military base/national park itself, the restaurant has a blend of the nostalgic past and the trendy present (beef liver and onions; ahi tuna poke and crisp eggplant fries). **Known for:** weekend brunch; PSC meat loaf; barrel-aged cocktails. $ *Average main: $24* ✉ *563 Ruger St., Presidio* ☎ *415/885–1888* ⊕ *www.presidiosocialclub.com.*

Sorrel

$$$$ | MODERN AMERICAN | After a long run as one of San Francisco's most important dining pop-ups, Alex Hong's refined Californian-Italian cooking finally found a permanent home in 2018. And, what a gorgeous home it is in swanky Laurel Heights! **Known for:** exemplary pastas; dry-aged duck for two; upscale dinner party vibe. $ *Average main: $33* ✉ *3228 Sacramento St., Presidio Heights* ☎ *415/525–3765* ⊕ *www.sorrelrestaurant.com* ☯ *Closed Sun. and Mon.*

🛏 Hotels

The Inn at the Presidio

$$$ | B&B/INN | FAMILY | Built in 1903 and opened as a hotel in 2012, this two-story, Georgian Revival–style structure once served as officers' quarters but now has 26 guest rooms—most of them suites—complete with gas fireplaces and modern-meets-salvage-store finds such as wrought-iron beds, historic black-and-white photos, and Pendleton blankets. **Pros:** beautifully designed rooms; peaceful, away from the frenetic city feel; Presidio's hiking and biking trails, Disney museum, and other attractions. **Cons:** lack of noise blocking because of old building; no elevator; challenging to get a taxi/ride-share. $ *Rooms from: $310* ✉ *42 Moraga Ave., Presidio* ☎ *415/800–7356* ⊕ *www.innatthepresidio.com* 🛏 *26 rooms* ¶◎¶ *Breakfast.*

★ The Lodge at the Presidio

$$$ | B&B/INN | The Presidio's hotel population doubled in 2018 with the opening of its second boutique accommodation, a slightly more upscale sibling to The Inn at the Presidio. **Pros:** gorgeous and spacious rooms; charming staff; feels like a vacation from the city within the city. **Cons:** traffic noise is fairly loud in rooms facing Golden Gate Bridge; isolated from many attractions; prices are similar to downtown. $ *Rooms from: $275* ✉ *105 Montgomery St., Presidio* ☎ *415/561–1234* ⊕ *www.presidiolodging.com/lodge-at-the-presidio* 🛏 *42 rooms* ¶◎¶ *Free Breakfast.*

🛍 Shopping

Dash Lane

HOUSEHOLD ITEMS/FURNITURE | From longtime landscape designer Katherine Webster, gorgeous outdoor furnishings and accessories are the theme of this beautiful Presidio Heights showroom. While alfresco entertaining is the prominent theme, many of the goods from boutique luxury labels like Janus et Cie and DEDON work just as well indoors. ✉ *3352 B Sacramento St., Presidio Heights* ✥ *Upstairs from street level at orange door* ☎ *415/757–0794* ⊕ *www. dashlanesf.com.*

Armed with only helmets, safety harnesses, and painting equipment, a full-time crew of 38 painters keeps the Golden Gate Bridge clad in International Orange.

Golden Gate Park

Jogging, cycling, skating, picnicking, going to a museum, checking out a concert, dozing in the sunshine … Golden Gate Park is the perfect playground for fast-paced types, laid-back dawdlers, and everyone in between.

👁 Sights

★ California Academy of Sciences

MUSEUM | FAMILY | With its native plant–covered living roof, retractable ceiling, three-story rain forest, gigantic planetarium, living coral reef, and frolicking penguins, the California Academy of Sciences is one of the city's most spectacular treasures. Dramatically designed by Renzo Piano, it's an eco-friendly, energy-efficient adventure in biodiversity and green architecture; the roof's large mounds and hills mirror the local topography. Moving away from a restrictive role as a museum that cataloged natural history, the academy these days is all about sustainability and the future, but the locally beloved dioramas in African Hall remain.

By the time you arrive, hopefully you've decided which shows and programs to attend, looked at the academy's floor plan, and designed a plan to cover it all in the time you have. And if not, here's the quick version: Head left from the entrance to the wooden walkway over otherworldly rays in the Philippine Coral Reef, then continue to the Swamp to see Claude, the famous albino alligator. Swing through African Hall and gander at the penguins, take the elevator up to the living roof, then return to the main floor and get in line to explore the Rain-forests of the World, ducking free-flying butterflies and watching for other live surprises. You'll end up below ground in the Amazonian Flooded Rainforest, where you can explore the academy's other aquarium exhibits. Phew. The academy's popular adult-only NightLife event, held every Thursday evening, includes after-dark access to all exhibits, as well as special programming and a full bar. ■TIP→ **Considering the hefty price of admission here, start out early and take advantage of in-and-out privileges to take a break.** ✉ *55 Music Concourse Dr., Golden Gate Park* ☎ *415/379–8000* ⊕ *www.calacademy.org* ✉ *$36, save $3 if you bike, walk, or take public transit here.*

Conservatory of Flowers

GARDEN | Whatever you do, be sure to at least drive by the Conservatory of Flowers—it's too darn pretty to miss. The gorgeous, white-framed 1878 glass structure is topped with a 14-ton glass dome. Stepping inside the giant greenhouse is like taking a quick trip to the rain forest, with its earthy smell and humid warmth. The undeniable highlight is the Aquatic Plants section, where lily pads float and carnivorous plants dine on bugs to the sounds of rushing water. On the east side of the conservatory (to the right as you face the building), cypress, pine, and redwood trees surround the **Dahlia Garden,** which blooms in summer and fall. Adding to the allure are temporary exhibits such as a past one devoted to prehistoric plants; a recurring holiday-season model-train display punctuated with mini buildings, found objects, and dwarf plants; and a butterfly garden that returns periodically. To the west is the **Rhododendron Dell,** which contains 850 varieties, more than any other garden in the country. It's a favorite local Mother's Day picnic spot. ✉ *John F. Kennedy Dr. at Conservatory Dr., Golden Gate Park* ☎ *415/831–2090* ⊕ *conservatoryofflowers.org* ✉ *$9, free 1st Tues. of month* ↝ *No strollers allowed inside.*

de Young Museum

MUSEUM | It seems that everyone in town has a strong opinion about the de Young Museum: some adore its striking copper facade, while others just hope that the green patina of age will mellow the effect. Most maligned is the 144-foot tower, but the view from its ninth-story observation room, ringed by floor-to-ceiling windows and free to the public, is worth a trip here by itself. The building almost overshadows the de Young's respected collection of American, African, and Oceanic art. The museum also plays host to major international exhibits, such as 100 works from Paris's Musée National Picasso and a collection of the work of Jean Paul Gaultier from the Montreal Museum of Fine Arts; there's often an extra admission charge for these. The annual Bouquets to Art is a fanciful tribute to the museum's collection by notable Bay Area floral designers. On many Friday evenings in the fall, admission is free and the museum hosts fun events, with live music and a wine and beer bar (the café stays open late, too). ✉ *50 Hagiwara Tea Garden Dr., Golden Gate Park* ☎ *415/750–3600* ⊕ *deyoung.famsf.org* ✉ *$15, good for same-day admittance to the Legion of Honor; free 1st Tues. of month* ☾ *Closed Mon.*

The Richmond

In the mid-19th century, the western section of town just north of Golden Gate Park was known as the Outer Lands, covered in sand dunes and seen fit for cemeteries and little else. Today it's the Richmond, comprised of two distinct neighborhoods: the Inner Richmond, from Arguello Boulevard to about 20th Avenue, and the Outer Richmond, from 20th to the ocean.

⊙ Sights

Cliff House

LOCAL INTEREST | Spectacular ocean views have been bringing diners to its several restaurants for more than a century—you can see 30 miles or more on a clear day. Three buildings have occupied this site—today owned by the National Park Service—since 1863, and the current building dates from 1909. Sitting on the observation deck is the **Giant Camera,** a camera obscura with its lens pointing skyward housed in a cute yellow-painted wooden shack. Built in the 1940s and threatened many times with demolition, it's now on the National Register of Historic Places. To the north of the Cliff House lie the ruins of the once grand glass-roof **Sutro Baths.** Adolph Sutro, eccentric onetime San Francisco mayor and Cliff House owner, built the bath complex in 1896, so that everyday folks could enjoy the benefits of swimming. Six enormous baths—freshwater and seawater—more than 500 dressing rooms, and several restaurants covered 3 acres north of the Cliff House and accommodated 25,000 bathers. Likened to Roman baths in a European glass palace, the baths were for decades a favorite destination of San Franciscans. The complex fell into disuse after World War II, was closed in 1952, and burned down (under questionable circumstances) during demolition in 1966. ⊠ *1090 Point Lobos Ave., Richmond* ☎ *415/386–3330* ⊕ *www. cliffhouse.com* ⊒ *Free.*

Legion of Honor
MUSEUM | Built to commemorate Californian soldiers who died in World War I, and set atop cliffs overlooking the ocean, the Golden Gate Bridge, and the Marin Headlands, this beautiful Beaux Arts building in Lincoln Park displays an impressive collection of 4,000 years of ancient and European art. A pyramidal glass skylight in the entrance court illuminates the lower-level galleries, which exhibit prints and drawings, English and European porcelain, and ancient Assyrian, Greek, Roman, and Egyptian art. The 20-plus galleries on the upper level display the permanent collection of European art (paintings, sculpture, decorative arts, and tapestries) from the 14th century to the present day. The noteworthy Auguste Rodin collection includes two galleries devoted to the master and

a third with works by Rodin and other 19th-century sculptors. An original cast of Rodin's *The Thinker* welcomes you as you walk through the courtyard. As fine as the museum is, the setting and view outshine the collection and also make a trip here worthwhile. ⊠ *34th Ave. at Clement St., Richmond* ☎ *415/750–3600* ⊕ *legionofhonor.famsf.org* ⊒ *$15, free 1st Tues. of month* ⊗ *Closed Mon.*

★ Lincoln Park
CITY PARK | Although many of the city's green spaces are gentle and welcoming, Lincoln Park is a wild, 275-acre park in the Outer Richmond with windswept cliffs and panoramic views. The Coastal Trail, the park's most dramatic one, leads out to **Lands End**; pick it up west of the Legion of Honor (at the end of El Camino del Mar) or from the parking lot at Point Lobos and El Camino del Mar. Time your hike to hit Mile Rock at low tide, and you might catch a glimpse of two wrecked ships peeking up from their watery graves. ⚠ **Be careful if you hike here; landslides are frequent, and people have fallen into the sea by standing too close to the edge of a crumbling bluff top.**

Lincoln Park's 18-hole golf course is on land that in the 19th century was the Golden Gate Cemetery. In 1900 the Board of Supervisors voted to ban burials within city limits, and all but two city cemeteries (at Mission Dolores and the Presidio) were moved to Colma, a small town just south of San Francisco. When digging has to be done in the park, bones occasionally surface again. ⊠ *Entrance at 34th Ave. at Clement St., Richmond.*

🍴 Restaurants

Burma Superstar
$ | **ASIAN** | Locals make the trek to the "Avenues" for this perennially crowded spot's flavorful, well-prepared Burmese food, including its extraordinary signature tea leaf salad, a combo of spicy, salty, crunchy, and sour that is mixed

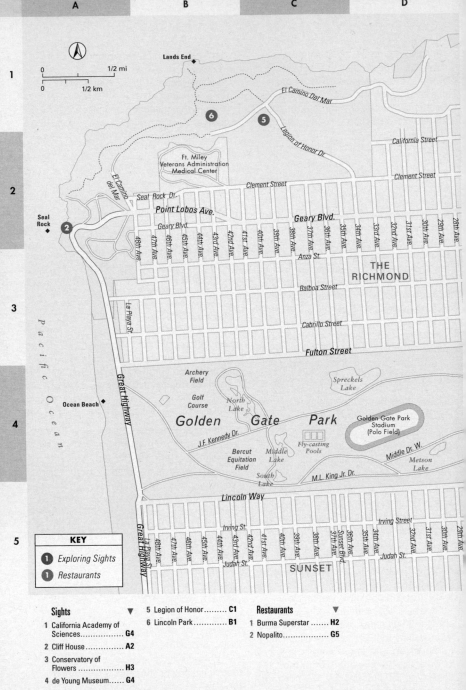

KEY

- **1** Exploring Sights
- **1** Restaurants

Sights ▼

1 California Academy of Sciences **G4**
2 Cliff House **A2**
3 Conservatory of Flowers **H3**
4 de Young Museum **G4**
5 Legion of Honor **C1**
6 Lincoln Park **B1**

Restaurants ▼

1 Burma Superstar **H2**
2 Nopalito **G5**

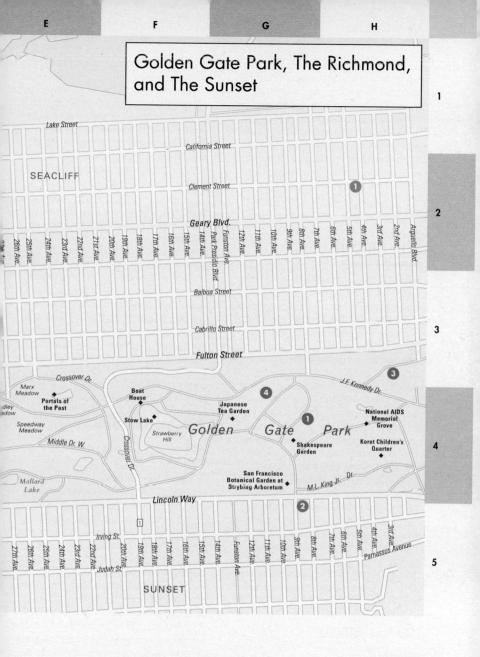

Golden Gate Park, The Richmond, and The Sunset

E   F   G   H

1

2

3

4

5

Lake Street

California Street

SEACLIFF

Clement Street

Geary Blvd.

Balboa Street

Cabrillo Street

Fulton Street

Crossover Dr.

J.F. Kennedy Dr.

Marx Meadow

Portals of the Past

Boat House

Speedway Meadow

Stow Lake

Japanese Tea Garden

National AIDS Memorial Grove

Middle Dr. W

Strawberry Hill

Golden Gate Park

Koret Children's Quarter

Shakespeare Garden

Mallard Lake

San Francisco Botanical Garden at Strybing Arboretum

M.L. King Jr. Dr.

Crossover Dr.

Lincoln Way

Irving St.

SUNSET

Judah St.

Parnassus Avenue

26th Ave. 25th Ave. 24th Ave. 23rd Ave. 22nd Ave. 21st Ave. 20th Ave. 19th Ave. 18th Ave. 17th Ave. 16th Ave. 15th Ave. 14th Ave. Park Presidio Blvd. Funston Ave. 12th Ave. 11th Ave. 10th Ave. 9th Ave. 8th Ave. 7th Ave. 6th Ave. 5th Ave. 4th Ave. 3rd Ave. 2nd Ave. Arguello Blvd.

27th Ave. 26th Ave. 25th Ave. 24th Ave. 23rd Ave. 22nd Ave. 21st Ave. 20th Ave. 19th Ave. 18th Ave. 17th Ave. 16th Ave. 15th Ave. 14th Ave. Funston Ave. 12th Ave. 11th Ave. 10th Ave. 9th Ave. 8th Ave. 7th Ave. 6th Ave. 5th Ave. 4th Ave. 3rd Ave.

table-side. The modestly decorated, no-reservations restaurant is small and lines can be long during peak times, so leave your number and wait for the call or walk a couple blocks east to B-Star, owned by the same people but often less crowded and with a welcoming patio. **Known for:** tea leaf salad; samusa soup; long lines. $ *Average main: $15* ✉ *309 Clement St., Richmond* ☎ *415/387–2147* 🌐 *www.burmasuperstar.com.*

The Sunset

Hugging the southern edge of Golden Gate Park and built atop the sand dunes that covered much of western San Francisco into the 19th century, the Sunset is made up of two distinct neighborhoods— the popular Inner Sunset, from Stanyan Street to 19th Avenue, and the foggy Outer Sunset, from 19th to the beach. The Inner Sunset is perhaps the perfect San Francisco "suburb": not too far from the center of things, reachable by public transit, and home to main streets—Irving Street and 9th Avenue just off Golden Gate Park—packed with excellent dining options, with Asian food particularly well represented. Long the domain of surfers and others who love the laid-back beach vibe and the fog, the slow-paced Outer Sunset finds itself newly on the radar of locals, with high-quality cafés and restaurants and quirky shops springing up along Judah Street between 42nd and 46th avenues. The zoo is the district's main tourist attraction.

🍴 Restaurants

Nopalito

$$ | MEXICAN | An upscale take on Mexican featuring local, sustainable, and fresh ingredients is on the menu at this sleek, popular neighborhood spot just off the park, the second outpost of the Nopa favorite. Highlights include the pozole, anything with mole, and carnitas locals cross the city for, all of which you can enjoy on the front or back patio on sunny days, but be prepared for a wait almost anytime. **Known for:** carnitas worth waiting for; focus on freshness; Mexican beyond the taqueria. $ *Average main: $22* ✉ *1224 9th Ave., Sunset* ☎ *415/233–9966* 🌐 *nopalitosf.com.*

🍸 Nightlife

The Riptide

BARS/PUBS | A cozy cabin bar that's the perfect finale for beachgoers, Riptide is a surfer favorite, but you don't have to own a board to feel at home. You'll find classic beers and good food, all at wallet-friendly prices. There's live music most nights, often country, bluegrass, honky-tonk, and open mike. Many tourists fooled by San Francisco's version of summer end up warming their popsicle toes at the bar's fireplace. Sunday features a bacon Bloody Mary, great for hangovers. ✉ *3639 Taraval St, Sunset* ☎ *415/681–8433* 🌐 *www.riptidesf.com.*

🎟 Performing Arts

★ Stern Grove Festival

FESTIVALS | The nation's oldest continual free summer music festival hosts Sunday-afternoon performances of symphony, opera, jazz, pop music, and dance. The amphitheater is in a beautiful eucalyptus grove, perfect for picnicking before the show. World-music favorites such as Ojos de Brujas, Seu Jorge, and Shuggie Otis get the massive crowds dancing. **■ TIP→ Shows generally start at 2 pm, but arrive hours earlier if you want to see the performances up close—and dress for cool weather, as the fog often rolls in.** ✉ *Sigmund Stern Grove, Sloat Blvd. at 19th Ave., Sunset* ☎ *415/252–6252* 🌐 *www.sterngrove.org.*

The Haight

During the 1960s the siren song of free love, peace, and mind-altering substances lured thousands of young people to the Haight, a neighborhood just east of Golden Gate Park. By 1966 the area had become a hot spot for rock artists, including the Grateful Dead, Jefferson Airplane, and Janis Joplin. Some of the most infamous flower children, including Charles Manson and People's Temple founder Jim Jones, also called the Haight home.

◉ Sights

Haight-Ashbury Intersection
NEIGHBORHOOD | On October 6, 1967, hippies took over the intersection of Haight and Ashbury streets to proclaim the "Death of Hip." If they thought hip was dead then, they'd find absolute confirmation of it today, what with the only tie-dye in sight on the famed corner being Ben & Jerry's storefront. ⊠ *Haight.*

🍽 Restaurants

Parada 22
$$ | PUERTO RICAN | A small, colortul space sandwiched between larger restaurants on either side, Parada 22 serves up heaping plates of Puerto Rican cuisine—think plantains, seafood, and slow-roasted pork. This still being the Haight, there's plenty of vegetarian fare on offer, and the yuca fries will be devoured by everyone. **Known for:** home-style Puerto Rican cuisine; marinated meats and vegetables; lunch specials. $ *Average main: $17* ⊠ *1805 Haight St., near Shrader St., Haight* ☎ *415/750–1111* ⊕ *parada22.com.*

🍸 Nightlife

Magnolia Brewing Company
BREWPUBS/BEER GARDENS | Known for its food as much as its beers, Magnolia is a San Francisco institution, thanks in part to its prime location one block away from the famous Haight-Ashbury intersection. Come for the smoked trout croquettes, falafel salad, and famed burgers, or just grab any one of the over a dozen beers on tap, many made right there in the in-house brewery. ⊠ *1398 Haight St., Haight ✛ At Masonic St.* ☎ *415/864–7468* ⊕ *magnoliabrewing.com.*

🛍 Shopping

MUSIC
★ **Amoeba Music**
MUSIC STORES | With well over a million new and used CDs, DVDs, and records at bargain prices, this warehouselike offshoot of the Berkeley original carries titles you likely can't find on Amazon. No niche is ignored—from electronica and hip-hop to jazz and classical—and the stock changes frequently. ■TIP➔ **Weekly in-store performances attract large crowds.** ⊠ *1855 Haight St., between Stanyan and Shrader Sts., Haight* ☎ *415/831–1200* ⊕ *www.amoeba.com.*

The Castro

The Castro district—the social, political, and cultural center of San Francisco's thriving gay community— stands at the western end of Market Street. This neighborhood is one of the city's liveliest and most welcoming, especially on weekends. Streets teem with folks out shopping, pushing political causes, heading to art films, and lingering in bars and cafés. It's also one of the city's most expensive neighborhoods to live in, with an influx of tech money exacerbating an identity crisis that's been simmering for a couple of decades.

◉ Sights

★ **Castro Theatre**
ARTS VENUE | Here's a classic way to join in a beloved Castro tradition: grab some popcorn and catch a flick at this

A   **B**   **C**   **D**   **E**

Buena Vista Park

Buena Vista Ave. East

Buena Vista Ter.

⑤ ⑧

Castro Street

14th Street

15th Street

Corona Heights Playground

Market Street

Landers St.

Dolores Street

16th Street

THE CASTRO

⑦

⑤

17th Street

17th Street

Market Street

⑥ ②

Noe Street

Ford St.

Sanchez Street

①

Church Street

Guerrero Street

③

Eureka Street

Douglass Street

Diamond Street

Collingwood Street

Castro Street

18th Street

18th Street

18th Street

Hancock St.

Mission Dolores Park

③

19th Street

19th Street

19th Street

20th Street

④

21st Street

NOE VALLEY

22nd Street

23rd Street

②

24th Street

25th Street

26th Street

KEY

① *Exploring Sights*

① *Restaurants*

① *Hotels*

🚇 *BART station*

Sights ▼
1. Balmy Alley murals..... **H6**
2. Castro Theatre **B3**
3. Dolores Park **D4**
4. Golden fire hydrant..... **D4**
5. Haight-Ashbury Intersection **B1**
6. Harvey Milk Plaza **B3**
7. Mission Dolores **E2**
8. Museum of Craft and Design.................. **J7**

Restaurants ▼
1. AL's Place................ **F7**
2. Barney's Gourmet Hamburgers............. **B6**
3. Delfina **E3**
4. flour + water............ **H4**
5. Frances **C2**
6. Lazy Bear **F3**
7. Mission Chinese Food **F3**
8. Parada 22................ **B1**
9. SanJalisco.............. **G4**
10. Tartine Manufactory ... **H3**

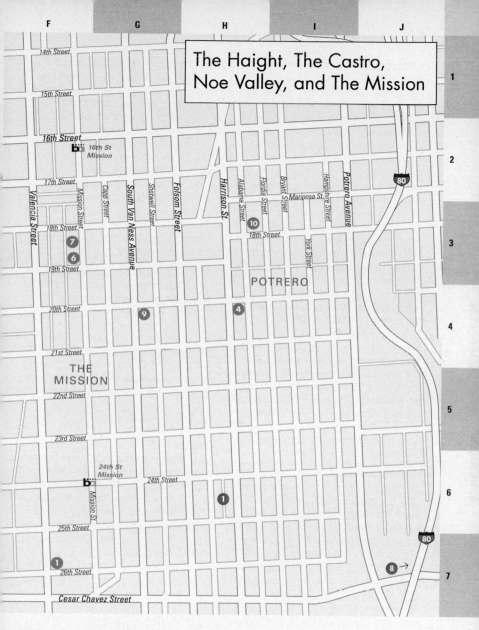

The Haight, The Castro, Noe Valley, and The Mission

F G H I J

1

14th Street
15th Street
16th Street
b 16th St Mission

2

17th Street
Valencia Street
Mission Street
Capp Street
South Van Ness Avenue
Shotwell Street
Folsom Street
Harrison St.
Alabama Street
Florida Street
Bryan Street
Mariposa St.
Hampshire Street
Potrero Avenue
80

18th Street
7
6
18th Street
10
York Street

3

19th Street

POTRERO

20th Street
9
4

4

21st Street
THE MISSION
22nd Street

5

23rd Street

24th St Mission
b
24th Street
1

6

25th Street
Mission St.
80

1
26th Street
8 →

7

Cesar Chavez Street

Hotels ▼

1,500-seat art-deco theater; built in 1922, it's the grandest of San Francisco's few remaining movie palaces. The neon marquee, which stands at the top of the Castro strip, is the neighborhood's great landmark. The Castro was the fitting host of 2008's red-carpet preview of Gus Van Sant's film *Milk*, starring Sean Penn as openly gay San Francisco supervisor Harvey Milk. The theater's elaborate Spanish baroque interior is fairly well preserved. Before many shows the theater's pipe organ rises from the orchestra pit and an organist plays pop and movie tunes, usually ending with the Jeanette McDonald standard "San Francisco" (go ahead, sing along). The crowd can be enthusiastic and vocal, talking back to the screen as loudly as it talks to them. Flicks such as *Who's Afraid of Virginia Woolf?* take on a whole new life, with the assembled beating the actors to the punch and fashioning even snappier comebacks for Elizabeth Taylor. There are often family-friendly sing-alongs to classics like *Mary Poppins*, as well as the occasional niche film festival. ✉ *429 Castro St., Castro* ☎ *415/621–6120* 🌐 *www.castrotheatre.com.*

Harvey Milk Plaza

HISTORIC SITE | An 18-foot-long rainbow flag, the symbol of gay pride, flies above this plaza named for the man who electrified the city in 1977 by being elected to its Board of Supervisors as an openly gay candidate. In the early 1970s Milk had opened a camera store on the block of Castro Street between 18th and 19th streets. The store became the center for his campaign to open San Francisco's social and political life to gays and lesbians.

The liberal Milk hadn't served a full year of his term before he and Mayor George Moscone, also a liberal, were shot in November 1978 at City Hall. The murderer was a conservative ex-supervisor named Dan White, who had recently resigned his post and then became enraged when Moscone wouldn't reinstate him. Milk and White had often been at odds on the board, and White thought Milk had been part of a cabal to keep him from returning to his post. Milk's assassination shocked the gay community, which became infuriated when the infamous "Twinkie defense"—that junk food had led to diminished mental capacity—resulted in a manslaughter verdict for White. During the so-called White Night Riot of May 21, 1979, gays and their allies stormed City Hall, torching its lobby and several police cars.

Milk, who had feared assassination, left behind a tape recording in which he urged the community to continue the work he had begun. His legacy is the high visibility of gay people throughout city government; a bust of him was unveiled at City Hall on his birthday in 2008, and the 2008 film *Milk* gives insight into his life. ✉ *Southwest corner of Castro and Market Sts., Castro.*

🍴 Restaurants

Frances

$$$ | MODERN AMERICAN | Still one of the hottest tickets in town, chef Melissa Perello's simple, sublime restaurant is a consummate date-night destination. Perello's seasonal California-French cooking is its own enduring love affair. **Known for:** seasonal menu; neighborhood gem; tough reservation. [$] *Average main: $34* ✉ *3870 17th St., Castro* ☎ *415/621–3870* 🌐 *www.frances-sf.com* 🕓 *Closed Mon. No lunch.*

🎟 Performing Arts

FILM

★ Castro Theatre

FILM | A large neon sign marks the exterior of this 1,400-plus-seat art-deco movie palace whose exotic interior transports you back to 1922, when the theater first opened. High-profile festivals present

A colorful mosaic mural in the Castro

films here, along with classic revivals and foreign flicks. There are a few cult-themed drag shows every month. ■TIP→ Lines for the Castro's popular sing-along movie musicals often trail down the block. ⊠ *429 Castro St., near Market St., Castro* ☎ *415/621–6120* ⊕ *www. castrotheatre.com.*

Noe Valley

This upscale but relaxed enclave just south of the Castro is among the city's most desirable places to live, with laid-back cafés, kid-friendly restaurants, and comfortable, old-time shops along Church Street and 24th Street, its main thoroughfares. You can also see remnants of Noe Valley's agricultural beginnings: Billy Goat Hill (at Castro and 30th streets), a wild-grass hill often draped in fog and topped by one of the city's best rope-swinging trees, is named for the goats that grazed here right into the 20th century.

◉ Sights

Golden fire hydrant

LOCAL INTEREST | When all the other fire hydrants went dry during the fire that followed the 1906 earthquake, this one kept pumping. Noe Valley and the Mission District were thus spared the devastation wrought elsewhere in the city, which explains the large number of prequake homes here. Every year on April 18 (the anniversary of the quake), folks gather here to share stories about the earthquake, and the famous hydrant gets a fresh coat of gold paint. ⊠ *Church and 20th Sts., southeastern corner, across from Dolores Park, Noe Valley.*

🍴 Restaurants

Barney's Gourmet Hamburgers

$ | AMERICAN | FAMILY | The Noe Valley location of this family-friendly California burger chain offers a cozy indoor-outdoor dining area, the latter really a patio encased in glass windows for watching foot traffic along 24th Street. The menu

Castro and Noe Walk

The Castro and Noe Valley are both neighborhoods that beg to be walked—or ambled through, really, without time pressure or an absolute destination. Hit the Castro first, beginning at **Harvey Milk Plaza** under the gigantic rainbow flag. If you're going on to Noe Valley, first head east down **Market Street** for the cafés, bistros, and shops, then go back to **Castro Street** and head south, past the glorious art-deco **Castro Theatre**, checking out boutiques and cafés along the way (Cliff's Variety, at 479 Castro Street, is a must). To tour Noe Valley, go east down **18th Street** to Church (at Dolores Park), and then either strap on your hiking boots and head south over the hill or hop the J–Church to **24th Street**, the center of this rambling neighborhood.

is loaded with fancier versions of diner classics—think the "gastropub" burger with a fried egg, blackened potato chips, and a pretzel bun, or the "maui waui," with a teriyaki glaze and grilled pineapple. **Known for:** diverse menu selection; vegetarian options; milk shakes. $ *Average main: $14* ✉ *4138 24th St., near Castro St., Noe Valley* ☎ *415/282–7770* ⊕ *www. barneyshamburgers.com.*

Mission District

The Mission has a number of distinct personalities: it's the Latino neighborhood, where working-class folks raise their families and where gangs occasionally clash; it's the hipster hood, where tattooed and pierced twenty- and thirtysomethings hold court in the coolest cafés and bars in town; it's a culinary epicenter, with the strongest concentration of destination restaurants and affordable ethnic cuisine; it's the face of gentrification, where high-tech money prices out longtime commercial and residential renters; and it's the artists' quarter, where murals adorn literally blocks of walls long after the artists have moved to cheaper digs. It's also the city's equivalent of the Sunshine State—this neighborhood's always the last to succumb to fog.

⊙ Sights

Balmy Alley murals
PUBLIC ART | Mission District artists have transformed the walls of their neighborhood with paintings, and Balmy Alley is one of the best-executed examples. Many murals adorn the one-block alley, with newer ones continually filling in the blank spaces. In 1971, artists began teaming with local children to create a space to promote peace in Central America, community spirit, and (later) AIDS awareness; since then dozens of artists have added their vibrant works. ⚠ Be alert here: the 25th Street end of the alley adjoins a somewhat dangerous area. ✉ *24th St. between and parallel to Harrison and Treat Sts., alley runs south to 25th St., Mission District.*

★ Dolores Park
LOCAL INTEREST | A two-square-block microcosm of life in the Mission, Dolores Park is one of San Francisco's liveliest green spaces: dog lovers and

their pampered pups congregate, kids play at the extravagant playground, and hipsters hold court, drinking beer on sunny days. During the summer, the park hosts movie nights; performances by Shakespeare in the Park, the San Francisco Mime Troupe, and the San Francisco Symphony; and any number of pop-up events and impromptu parties. Spend a warm day here—maybe sitting at the top of the park with a view of the city and the Bay Bridge—surrounded by locals and that laid-back San Francisco energy, and you may well find yourself plotting your move to the city. ⊠ *Between 18th and 20th Sts. and Dolores and Church Sts., Mission District.*

Mission Dolores

RELIGIOUS SITE | Two churches stand side by side here, including the small adobe **Mission San Francisco de Asís,** which, along with the Presidio's Officers' Club, is the oldest standing structure in San Francisco. Completed in 1791, it's the sixth of the 21 California missions founded by Franciscan friars in the 18th and early 19th centuries. Its ceiling depicts original Ohlone Indian basket designs, executed in vegetable dyes. The tiny chapel includes frescoes and a hand-painted wooden altar.

There's a hidden treasure here, too, a mural forgotten and rediscovered over more than 200 years. In 2004 an archaeologist and an artist crawled along the ceiling's rafters and opened a trapdoor behind the altar in an attempt to finally document the mission's original mural, painted with natural dyes by Native Americans in 1791. The centuries have taken their toll, so the team photographed the 20-by-22-foot mural and began digitally restoring the photographic version. Among the images is a dagger-pierced Sacred Heart of Jesus.

The small museum here covers the mission's founding and history, and the pretty little cemetery—which appears in Alfred Hitchcock's film *Vertigo*—contains the graves of mid-19th-century European immigrants. The remains of an estimated 5,000 Native Americans who died at the mission lie in unmarked graves. Services are held in both the old mission and next door in the handsome multidome basilica. ⊠ *Dolores and 16th Sts., Mission District* ☎ *415/621–8203* ⊕ *www.missiondolores.org* ✉ *Suggested donation $7.*

Museum of Craft and Design

MUSEUM | Right at home in this once-industrial neighborhood now bursting with creative energy, this small, four-room space—definitely a quick view—mounts temporary art and design exhibitions. The focus might be sculpture, metalwork, furniture, or jewelry—or industrial design, architecture, or other topics. The MakeArt Lab gives kids (and grown-ups) the opportunity to create their own exhibit-inspired work, and the beautifully curated shop sells tempting textiles, housewares, jewelry, and other well-crafted items. ⊠ *2569 3rd St., near 22nd St., Dogpatch* ☎ *415/773–0303* ⊕ *sfmcd.org* ✉ *$8, free 1st Tues. of month* ⊗ *Closed Mon.*

🍽 Restaurants

AL's Place

$$ | MODERN AMERICAN | AL is chef Aaron London, and his place is a sunny, whitewashed corner spot that serves inventive, Michelin-starred vegetable-forward cooking. London's menu changes frequently, but some dishes, like lightly cured trout and grits with seasonal produce, stick around, and the fries have a cult following. **Known for:** seasonal cooking; inventive vegetable-heavy menu; fries with cult following. Ⓢ *Average main: $18* ⊠ *1499 Valencia St., Mission* ☎ *415/416–6136* ⊕ *www.alsplacesf.com* ⊗ *Closed Mon. and Tues. No lunch.*

★ Delfina

$$$ | ITALIAN | Crowds are a constant fixture at Craig and Annie Stoll's cultishly adored northern Italian spot, where aluminum-topped tables are squeezed into an urban interior, with hardwood floors and a tile bar that seems to radiate with happiness. Deceptively simple, exquisitely flavored dishes include the signature spaghetti with plum tomatoes and consistently great roast chicken, and the panna cotta is best in class. **Known for:** signature spaghetti with plum tomatoes; long waits; much-lauded panna cotta. $ *Average main: $24* ✉ *3621 18th St., Mission District* ☎ *415/552–4055* ⊕ *www.delfinasf.com* ☾ *No lunch.*

flour + water

$$$ | ITALIAN | This handsome and boisterous hot spot with slate-gray walls, sturdy wooden tables, and a taxidermy cabinet in the bathroom is synonymous with pasta, though its blistery thin-crust Neapolitan pizzas are also top notch, but the grand experience here is the seven-course pasta-tasting menu (extra for wine pairings). The homemade rutabaga tortelli with candy cap mushrooms is a crowd-pleaser, as is the toasted sourdough rigatoni. **Known for:** difficult-to-get reservations; delicious pizzas and pastas; noisy scene. $ *Average main: $25* ✉ *2401 Harrison St., Mission District* ☎ *415/826–7000* ⊕ *www.flourandwater.com* ☾ *No lunch.*

Lazy Bear

$$$$ | MODERN AMERICAN | There's no end to the buzz around chef David Barzelay's 14-plus-course prix-fixe modern American dinners, which might include sweet pea custard lamb with dates, or charred onion broth with country ham. An ode to the Western lodge, the two-level dining room, which includes a fireplace, charred wood walls, wooden rafters, and tables made of American elm, hosts what is essentially a dinner party for 40, with cocktails and bites enjoyed upstairs and dinner downstairs at two communal tables. **Known for:** hot-ticket often resold; communal dining; dinner party setup. $ *Average main: $185* ✉ *3416 19th St., Mission District* ☎ *415/874–9921* ⊕ *www.lazybearsf.com* ☾ *Closed Sun. and Mon. No lunch.*

Mission Chinese Food

$$ | CHINESE | While the setting is somewhat one-star, the food draws throngs for its bold, cheerfully inauthentic riffs on Chinese cuisine made with quality meats and ingredients, including the fine and super-fiery kung pao pastrami, salt cod fried rice with mackerel confit, and sour chili chicken. Some of the food spikes hot (mapo tofu) while milder dishes (Westlake rice porridge) are homey and satisfying. **Known for:** kung pao pastrami; salt cod fried rice; to-go spot due to long waits. $ *Average main: $16* ✉ *2234 Mission St., Mission District* ☎ *415/863–2800* ⊕ *www.missionchinesefood.com* ☾ *No lunch Tues. and Wed.*

SanJalisco

$ | MEXICAN | FAMILY | This colorful old-time, sun-filled, family-run restaurant has been a neighborhood favorite for more than 30 years, and not only because it serves breakfast all day—though the hearty *chilaquiles* hit the spot. On weekends, adventurous eaters may opt for *birria*, a spicy barbecued goat stew, or *menudo*, a tongue-searing soup made from beef tripe, complemented by beer and sangria. **Known for:** breakfast all day; beef-tripe menudo; delicious sangria. $ *Average main: $13* ✉ *901 S. Van Ness Ave., Mission District* ☎ *415/648–8383.*

Tartine Manufactory

$$$ | MODERN AMERICAN | FAMILY | At this sunny, cathedral-like space in the Heath Ceramics building, you'll find Chad Robertson's bread and Liz Prueitt's pastries, but also breakfast, lunch, and dinner, with seasonal salads front and center, as well as a porchetta sandwich that tends to sell out early. As with the original bakery, you can expect to spend some time

Did You Know?

These pastel Victorian homes in Pacific Heights are closer to the original hues sported back in the 1900s. It wasn't until the 1960s that the bold, electric colors now seen around San Francisco gained popularity. Before that, the most typical house paint color was a standard gray.

in line—and to be rewarded for your troubles. **Known for:** Chad Robertson's bread; Liz Prueitt's pastries; seasonal salads. [$] *Average main: $28* ✉ *595 Alabama St., Mission District* ☎ *415/757–0007* 🌐 *www.tartinemanufactory.com.*

Hotels

★ The Parker Guest House
$$ | B&B/INN | Two yellow 1909 Edwardian houses enchant travelers wanting an authentic San Francisco experience; dark hallways and steep staircases lead to bright earth-toned rooms with private tiled baths (most with tubs), comfortable sitting areas, and cozy linens. **Pros:** handsome affordable rooms; just steps from Dolores Park and the vibrant Castro District on a Muni line; elaborate gardens. **Cons:** stairs can be challenging for those with limited mobility; parking can be difficult if garage is full; standard rooms are a little tight. [$] *Rooms from: $249* ✉ *520 Church St., Mission District* ☎ *415/621–4139* 🌐 *parkerguesthouse.com* 🛏 *21 rooms* 🍴 *Breakfast.*

Nightlife

ABV
BARS/PUBS | One of the city's top cocktail bars offers elevated small plates—think pork belly with peanut mole, burgers, and meat and cheese boards—until 1 am to pair with the excellent cocktail menu, which features such favorites as the Mumbai Mule with saffron vodka. A knowledgeable and friendly staff serves a hipster crowd that knows their drinks in a smart modern setting, with hard surfaces, bar-stool seating, and a giant mural. The sidewalk tables are popular on sunny days. ✉ *3174 16th St., near Guerrero St., Mission District* ☎ *415/400–4748* 🌐 *www.abvsf.com.*

★ El Rio
MUSIC CLUBS | A dive bar in the best sense, El Rio has a calendar chock-full of events, from free bands and films to Salsa Sunday (seasonal), all of which keep Mission kids coming back. Bands play several nights a week, and there are plenty of other events. No matter what day you attend, expect to find a diverse gay-straight crowd. When the weather's warm, the large patio out back is especially popular, and the midday dance parties are *the* place to be. ✉ *3158 Mission St., between César Chavez and Valencia Sts., Mission District* ☎ *415/282–3325* 🌐 *www.elriosf.com.*

Martuni's
BARS/PUBS | A mixed crowd enjoys cocktails in the semi-refined environment of this piano bar where the Castro, the Mission, and Hayes Valley intersect; variations on the martini are a specialty. In the intimate back room a pianist plays nightly, and patrons take turns boisterously singing show tunes. Martuni's often gets busy after symphony and opera performances—Davies Hall and the Opera House are both within walking distance. ■ **TIP→ The Godiva Chocolate Martini is a crowd favorite.** ✉ *4 Valencia St., at Market St., Mission District* ☎ *415/241–0205.*

Zeitgeist
BARS/PUBS | It's a dive but one of the city's best beer bars—there are almost 50 on tap—a great place to relax with a cold one or an ever-popular Bloody Mary in the large "garden" (there's not much greenery) on a sunny day. Burgers and brats are available, and if you own a trucker hat, a pair of Vans, and a Pabst Blue Ribbon T-shirt, you'll fit right in. ✉ *199 Valencia St., at Duboce Ave., Mission District* ☎ *415/255–7505.*

Shopping

FURNITURE, HOUSEWARES, AND GIFTS

★ Paxton Gate
GIFTS/SOUVENIRS | Elevating gardening to an art, this serene shop offers beautiful earthenware pots, amaryllis and

narcissus bulbs, decorative garden items, and coffee-table books such as *An Inordinate Fondness for Beetles.* The collection of taxidermy and preserved bugs provides more unusual gift ideas. A couple of storefronts away is too-cute Paxton Gate Curiosities for Kids, jam-packed with retro toys, books, and other stellar finds. ✉ *824 Valencia St., between 19th and 20th Sts., Mission District* ☎ *415/824–1872* 🌐 *www.paxtongate.com.*

Pacific Heights

Pacific Heights defines San Francisco's most expensive and dramatic real estate. Grand Victorians line the streets, mansions and town houses are priced in the millions, and there are magnificent views from almost any point in the neighborhood. Old money and new, personalities in the limelight and those who prefer absolute media anonymity live here, and few outsiders see anything other than the pleasing facades of Queen Anne charmers, English Tudor imports, and baroque bastions. Nancy Pelosi and Dianne Feinstein, Larry Ellison, and Gordon Getty all own impressive homes here, but not even pockets as deep as those can buy a large garden—space in the city is simply at too much of a premium. Luckily, two of the city's most spectacular parks are located in the area. The boutiques and restaurants along Fillmore Street, which range from glam to funky, are a draw for the whole city as well.

👁 Sights

Haas-Lilienthal House

HOUSE | A small display of photographs on the bottom floor of this elaborate, gray 1886 Queen Anne house makes clear that despite its lofty stature and striking, round third-story tower, the house was modest compared with some of the giants that fell victim to the 1906 earthquake and fire. San Francisco Heritage, a foundation to preserve San Francisco's architectural history, operates the home, whose carefully kept rooms provide a glimpse into late-19th-century life through period furniture, authentic details (antique dishes in the kitchen built-in), and photos of the Haas family who occupied the house for three generations until 1972. ■ **TIP→ You can admire hundreds of gorgeous San Francisco Victorians from the outside, but this is the only one that's open to the public, and it's worth a visit.** Volunteers conduct one-hour house tours three days a week, and informative two-hour walking tours of Pacific Heights on Sunday afternoon (call or check website for schedule). ✉ *2007 Franklin St., between Washington and Jackson Sts., Pacific Heights* ☎ *415/441–3004* 🌐 *www.haaslilienthalhouse.org* 🎟 *Tours $10.*

🍴 Restaurants

True Laurel

$$$ | **MODERN AMERICAN** | A great Plan B for those who didn't book far enough ahead to score a table at Lazy Bear, this excellent cocktail bar and small-plates restaurant by the same people offers intriguing combinations and endless conversation starters in a cool modern setting. Menu standouts include the Dungeness-crab-and-aged-cheddar fondue and fried hen-of-the-woods mushrooms, while don't-misses on the cocktail side include the Top Dawg, a house-fermented sparkling concoction, and aquavit-based A-Dilla. **Known for:** equal focus on food and cocktails; unusual ingredients; innovative combinations. [$] *Average main: $24* ✉ *753 Alabama St., Mission District* ☎ *415/341–0020* 🌐 *truelaurelsf.com* ⏲ *No lunch.*

Hotels

★ Hotel Drisco

$$$$ | HOTEL | Pretend you're a denizen of one of San Francisco's wealthiest residential neighborhoods while you stay at this understated, elegant 1903 Edwardian hotel. **Pros:** terrific recent renovation of rooms and public spaces; great service and many amenities; quiet residential retreat. **Cons:** not an easy walk to nearby restaurants and bars; room prices are as steep as nearby hill; no complimentary chauffeur service in the afternoon or evening. [$] *Rooms from: $499* ✉ *2901 Pacific Ave., Pacific Heights* ☎ *415/346–2880, 800/634–7277* 🌐 *www.hoteldrisco.com* 🛏 *64 rooms* 🍴 *Breakfast.*

Nightlife

The Snug

BARS/PUBS | Open since late 2017, this Lower Pac Heights bar is exactly the welcoming yet refined drinking destination the well-heeled and fun-loving neighborhood needed. It's the rare bar that emphasizes clever cocktails, in-high-demand local craft beer, and smartly selected wine in equal parts. Come hungry, as well, because elevated takes on bar bites like seabream poke and fresh-from-the-tandoor sesame naan with shiitake mushroom hummus are created by a chef formerly at some of the country's gastronomic heavyweights (Benu, Alinea). ✉ *2301 Fillmore St., Lower Pacific Heights* ✥ *Near Clay St.* 🌐 *www.thesnugsf.com.*

Shopping

Browser Books

BOOKS/STATIONERY | FAMILY | One of the city's most beloved independent bookstores resides quietly among the chic fashion boutiques lining Fillmore Street. Opened in 1976, all ages will find ample choices for their next reading material from contemporary fiction to children's books to a large selection of Buddhist Dharma literature. ✉ *2195 Fillmore St., Lower Pacific Heights* ☎ *415/567–8027* 🌐 *www.browserbookstore.com.*

★ Verve Wine

WINE/SPIRITS | Wine nerds will fall in love with this trendy, upscale destination from one of the country's few Master Sommeliers, Dustin Wilson. High-quality, smaller producers from prominent and lesser known regions share wall space in this exceptionally organized boutique. ✉ *Verve Wine, 2358 Fillmore St., Lower Pacific Heights* ✥ *Between Washington St. and Jackson St.* ☎ *415/896–4935* 🌐 *www.vervewine.com/about/san-francisco.*

Japantown

Though still the spiritual center of San Francisco's Japanese American community, Japantown feels somewhat adrift. The Japan Center mall, for instance, comes across as rather sterile, and whereas Chinatown is densely populated and still largely Chinese, Japantown struggles to retain its unique character.

Sights

Japan Center

HISTORIC SITE | FAMILY | Cool and curious trinkets, noodle houses and sushi joints, a destination bookstore, and a peek at Japanese culture high and low await at this 5-acre complex designed in 1968 by noted American architect Minoru Yamasaki. The Japan Center includes the shop- and restaurant-filled Kintetsu and Kinokuniya buildings; the excellent Kabuki Springs & Spa; the Hotel Kabuki; and the AMC Kabuki reserved-seating cinema/restaurant complex.

The Kinokuniya Bookstore, in the Kinokuniya Building, has an extensive selection of Japanese-language books, *manga* (graphic novels), books on design, English-language translations, and books on Japanese topics. Just outside, follow the Japanese teenagers to Pika Pika, where you and your friends can step into a photo booth and then use special effects and stickers to decorate your creation. On the bridge connecting the buildings, check out Shige Antiques for *yukata* (lightweight cotton kimonos) for kids and lovely silk kimonos, and Asakichi and its tiny incense shop for tinkling wind chimes and display-worthy teakettles. Continue into the Kintetsu Building for a selection of Japanese restaurants.

Between the West Mall and the East Mall are the five-tier, 100-foot-tall **Peace Pagoda** and the Peace Plaza, where seasonal festivals are held. The pagoda, which draws on the 1,200-year-old tradition of miniature round pagodas dedicated to eternal peace, was designed in the late 1960s by Yoshiro Taniguchi to convey the "friendship and goodwill" of the Japanese people to the people of the United States. ⊠ *Bordered by Geary Blvd. and Fillmore, Post, and Laguna Sts., Japantown* ⊕ *www.japancentersf.com.*

★ Kabuki Springs & Spa

SPA—SIGHT | This serene spa is one Japantown destination that draws locals from all over town, from hipster to grandma, Japanese American or not. Balinese urns decorate the communal bath area of this house of tranquility.

The extensive service menu includes facials, salt scrubs, and mud and seaweed wraps, in addition to massage. You can take your massage in a private room with a bath or in a curtained-off area.

The communal baths ($30) contain hot and cold tubs, a large Japanese-style bath, a sauna, a steam room, and showers. Bang the gong for quiet if your fellow bathers are speaking too loudly. The clothing-optional baths are open for men only on Monday, Thursday, and Saturday;

women bathe on Wednesday, Friday, and Sunday. Bathing suits are required on Tuesday, when the baths are coed.

Men and women can reserve private rooms daily. ⊠ *1750 Geary Blvd., Japantown* ☎ *415/922–6000* ⊕ *www.kabukisprings.com.*

🍴 Restaurants

Marufuku Ramen

$ | RAMEN | Hakata style *tonkotsu* (pork) or extra intense chicken *paitan* ramen are the specialties of this modern-looking Japan Center restaurant that serves what many San Franciscans consider the city's finest bowl of ramen. As a result, long lines can be daunting, but luckily prospective guests can join an online wait list. **Known for:** rich bowls of ramen; more "al dente" style noodles; lively, contemporary vibe. Ⓢ *Average main: $13* ⊠ *1581 Webster St. #235, Japantown* ✚ *In Kinokuniya Bldg.* ☎ *415/872–9786* ⊕ *www.marufukuramen.com* ⊗ *Closed Mon.*

Mifune Don

$ | JAPANESE | FAMILY | Homemade thin soba and thick udon, served either hot or cold with various toppings, are the stars of this low-key, charming restaurant with a wooden facade that looks like it was imported directly from the countryside. Seating is at wooden tables, where diners of every age can be heard slurping down big bowls of traditional Japanese combinations. **Known for:** bowls of noodles; savory Japanese pancakes (okonomiyaki); bargain lunch deals. Ⓢ *Average main: $12* ⊠ *22 Peace Plaza, Suite 560, Japantown* ✚ *2nd fl. of East Mall* ☎ *415/346 1993* ⊗ *Closed Tues.*

Pacific Heights, Japantown, Western Addition, and The Tenderlion

Shopping

BOOKS

Kinokuniya Bookstore
BOOKS/STATIONERY | The selection of English-language books about Japanese culture—everything from medieval history to origami instructions—is one of the finest in the country. Kinokuniya is the city's biggest seller of Japanese-language books. Dozens of glossy Asian fashion magazines attract the young and trendy; the manga and anime books and magazines are wildly popular, too. ✉ *Kinokuniya Bldg., 1581 Webster St., at Geary Blvd., Japantown* ☎ *415/567–7625* 🌐 *www.kinokuniya.com/us.*

Western Addition

Part of the Western Addition, the Lower Fillmore in its post–World War II heyday was known as the Harlem of the West for its profusion of jazz night spots, where such legends as Billie Holliday, Duke Ellington, and Charlie Parker would play. These days the neighborhood tries to maintain its African American core and its link to that heritage; one success is the annual Fillmore Jazz Festival in June. More live music rings at the Fillmore Auditorium, made famous in the 1960s by Bill Graham and the iconic bands he booked there, and at the blues-centric Boom Boom Room.

Sights

★ Alamo Square Park
CITY PARK | **FAMILY** | Whether you've seen them on postcards or on the old TV show "Full House," the colorful "Painted Ladies" Victorians are some of San Francisco's world-renowned icons. The signature view of them with the downtown skyline in the background is from the east side of this hilly park that reopened in 2017 after an extensive renovation. Tourists love the photo opportunities, but locals also adore the park's tennis courts, dog-playing area, and ample picnic area—with great views, of course. After taking plenty of photos, swing by the park's northwest corner and admire the William Westerfeld House (*1198 Fulton St.*), a splendid five-story late-19th-century Victorian mansion. ✉ *Western Addition* ✥ *Between Steiner St., Hayes St., Fulton St., and Hayes St.*

Cathedral of Saint Mary of the Assumption
RELIGIOUS SITE | Residing at the prominent intersection of two busy thoroughfares (Geary Boulevard and Gough Street), there's no missing this striking cathedral and its sweeping contemporary design. Opened in 1971, Italian architects Pietro Belluschi and Pier Luigi Nervi intended to create a spectacular cathedral that reflects the Catholic faith and modern technology. It was controversial at first, yet now is applauded for its grand, curving roof that rises to a height of 190 feet, meeting to form a cross. Don't miss the ceiling's intricate stained glass work. The cathedral is open daily for visitors other than during Mass times and usually has docents on duty in the late morning hours. ✉ *1111 Gough St., Western Addition* ✥ *At Geary St.* 🌐 *smcsf.org.*

Restaurants

Avery
$$$$ | **MODERN AMERICAN** | With caviar bumps, a cheese course in buckwheat tartlet form, and dazzling crispy shrimp "aebelskivers" (Danish beignet), the solo debut of wunderkind chef Rodney Wages is definitely not your average proper fine dining destination. Then again, with its triple-digit price tags and liberal use of luxe ingredients, it very much fits right into the exclusive San Francisco lavish spectacle dining club. **Known for:** captivating tasting menu with distinct Japanese influences; minimalist elegant decor; strong sake roster. [$] *Average main: $130* ✉ *1552 Fillmore*

St., Western Addition ✛ By Geary St. ☎ 415/817–1187 ⊕ www.averysf.com ⊘ Closed Mon. and Tues.

Che Fico

$$$ | **MODERN ITALIAN** | This red-hot Divisadero spot on the second floor of a revamped auto body shop was San Francisco's biggest restaurant debut of 2018. In a city full of Italian restaurants, it sets itself apart with homemade charcuterie, antipasti, pastas, and pizza that effortlessly blur the line between modern and traditional. **Known for:** pineapple pizza; hard-to-get reservations; Roman Jewish specialties. Ⓢ Average main: $28 ⊠ 838 Divisadero St., Western Addition ☎ 415/416–6959 ⊕ www.chefico.com ⊘ Closed Sun. and Mon.

4505 Burgers & BBQ

$$ | **BARBECUE** | The smoker works overtime from noon to night at this hipster-chic barbecue shack, churning out an array of succulent meats that can be had by the plate, the pound, or as a sandwich. Every plate comes with two sides, and you should certainly make the frankaroni one of them. **Known for:** smoked meats; decadent sides; self-named "Best Damn Cheeseburger". Ⓢ Average main: $17 ⊠ 705 Divisadero St., Western Addition ✛ Between Grove St. and Fulton St. ☎ 415/231–6993 ⊕ www.4505burgersandbbq.com.

Merchant Roots

$ | **CAFÉ** | It's hard to look past the vintage pasta machine by the sidewalk window, cranking out fresh pastas all day. However, the Fillmore café/craft grocer is so much more than pastas with salads, sandwiches, baked goods, and a noteworthy wineshop in the back. **Known for:** chocolate chip cookies; excellent pasta; photogenic chocolate cannolis. Ⓢ Average main: $13 ⊠ 1365 Fillmore St., Western Addition ☎ 530/574–7365 ⊕ www.merchantroots.com ⊘ Closed Sun. and Mon.

★ The Mill

$ | **BAKERY** | "Four-dollar toast" is a phrase used around San Francisco referring to gentrification—and it was inspired by this sun-drenched, Wi-Fi-less café. It's a project between one of the city's leading bakers, Josey Baker (yes, that's really his last name and profession!), and the Mission's Four Barrel Coffee. **Known for:** toast in various forms; stellar loaves of bread; a precious, post-yoga vibe. Ⓢ Average main: $8 ⊠ 736 Divisadero St., Western Addition ☎ 415/345–1953 ⊕ www.themillsf.com.

★ Nopa

$$$ | **AMERICAN** | This is the good-food granddaddy of the hot corridor of the same name (it's hard to tell which came first—Nopa the restaurant or NoPa the North of the Panhandle neighborhood). The Cali-rustic fare here draws dependable crowds regardless of the night. **Known for:** high-quality comforting food with smart twists; actually good food after 11 pm; a constant and diverse crowd. Ⓢ Average main: $27 ⊠ 560 Divisadero St., Western Addition ☎ 415/864–8643 ⊕ www.nopasf.com ⊘ No lunch weekdays.

★ Octavia

$$$$ | **MODERN AMERICAN** | Regardless of the time of year, Melissa Perello's second and more upscale restaurant (Frances) is a perennial favorite for diners seeking out what "California cuisine" really tastes like. The warm, immaculate dining room is a perfect setting for edgier dishes like the popular chilled squid ink noodles starter, along with more comforting produce-driven small plates and entrées. **Known for:** exciting preparations with peak-of-season produce; spicy deviled egg starter; truly professional service. Ⓢ Average main: $32 ⊠ 1701 Octavia St., Lower Pacific Heights ✛ At Bush St. ☎ 415/408–7507 ⊕ www.octavia-sf.com.

★ State Bird Provisions

$$$ | MODERN AMERICAN | It's more or less impossible to score a reservation for a normal dinner hour at husband-and-wife Stuart Brioza and Nicole Krasinski's game-changing restaurant. But once you nab a golden ticket for one of the 80 dining room and chef counter seats, you'll be rewarded with fascinating bites served from roving carts and an à la carte printed menu. **Known for:** dim sum–style dining; long lines at opening time; "State Bird" namesake buttermilk fried quail. Ⓢ *Average main: $23* ✉ *1529 Fillmore St., Western Addition* ☎ *415/795–1272* ⊕ *www.statebirdsf. com* ☾ *No lunch.*

Nightlife

Boom Boom Room

MUSIC CLUBS | One of San Francisco's liveliest music spots is this Fillmore blues favorite, opened in 1997 by the "King of Boogie" John Lee Hooker. The club has a fun blend of blues, funk, and hip-hop shows most nights of the week. ✉ *1601 Fillmore St., Western Addition* ✛ *At Geary Blvd.* ☎ *415/673–8000* ⊕ *www. boomboomroom.com.*

Fat Angel

BARS/PUBS | Part of San Francisco knows this intimate, dimly lit Fillmore spot as the unofficial waiting room for State Bird Provisions. However, its many regulars know this gastropub is one of the finest craft beer bars in the entire city. Belgian beers and hard-to-find West Coast small-batch brews share space on the tap list and bottle roster. On the food front, spicy mac 'n' cheese and SF's best chicken potpie are crowd favorites for soaking up multiple rounds. ✉ *1740 O'Farrell St., Western Addition* ✛ *Near Fillmore St.* ☎ *415/525–3013* ⊕ *www.fatangelsf.com.*

The Fillmore

MUSIC CLUBS | This is *the* club that all the big names, from Coldplay to Clapton, want to play. San Francisco's most famous rock-music hall presents national and local acts: rock, reggae, grunge, jazz, folk, acid house, and more. Go upstairs to view the amazing collection of rock posters lining the walls. At the end of each show, free apples are set near the door, and staffers hand out collectible posters. ■TIP➔ **Avoid steep service charges by purchasing tickets at the club's box office on Sunday from 10 to 4.** ✉ *1805 Geary Blvd., at Fillmore St., Western Addition* ☎ *415/346–6000* ⊕ *www.thefillmore.com.*

Horsefeather

BARS/PUBS | Creative produce-driven cocktails and a chic, low-key vibe make this Divisadero drinking destination a locals' frequent top choice for a fun night out. The always interesting (but never too bizarre) cocktails range from a breezy "California Cooler" with celery juice to the rum-and-whiskey-based "Breakfast Punch" featuring clarified Cinnamon Toast Crunch-infused milk. Weekend brunch is excellent as is the delightfully messy double cheeseburger. As an added bonus, the kitchen stays open until 1 am nightly. ✉ *528 Divisadero St., Western Addition* ☎ *415/817–1939* ⊕ *www.horsefeatherbar.com.*

Indian Paradox

WINE BARS—NIGHTLIFE | This festive, tiny Divisadero spot is hardly your average "wine bar." Cheese and charcuterie plates are swapped out here for Indian street food and chaat. With an eye-catching bar background made of milk crates and murals of the colorful delivery trucks in India, it also certainly doesn't look like your typical wine bar. Most of all, the quirky but beautiful wines work wonders with the exciting small bites offered à la carte or in a very reasonably priced tasting menu. ✉ *258 Divisadero St., Western Addition* ☎ *415/593–5386* ⊕ *www.indian-paradoxsf.com.*

The Tenderloin

Hotels

Phoenix Hotel

$$ | HOTEL | A magnet for the boho crowd, the Phoenix is retro and low-key, with colorful furniture, white bedspreads, and original pieces by local artists, as well as modern amenities like flat-screen TVs. **Pros:** mellow staffers set boho tone; cheeky design; hip restaurant/bar; free parking. **Cons:** somewhat seedy location; no elevators; can be loud in the evening. $ *Rooms from: $230* ⊠ *601 Eddy St., Tenderloin* ☎ *415/776–1380, 800/248–9466* ⊕ *www.phoenixsf. com* ⇰ *44 rooms* ⭘ *No meals.*

☕ Nightlife

★ Bourbon & Branch

BARS/PUBS | Bourbon & Branch reeks of Prohibition-era speakeasy cool. It's not exclusive, though: everyone is granted a password. The place has sex appeal, with tin ceilings, bordello-red silk wallpaper, intimate booths, and low lighting; loud conversations and cell phones are not allowed. The menu of expertly mixed cocktails and quality bourbon and whiskey is substantial, though the servers aren't always authorities. ■TIP→ **Your reservation dictates your exit time, which is strictly enforced.** There's also a speakeasy within the speakeasy called Wilson & Wilson, which is more exclusive, but just as funky. ⊠ *501 Jones St., at O'Farrell St., Tenderloin* ☎ *415/346–1735* ⊕ *www.bourbonand-branch.com.*

Great American Music Hall

MUSIC CLUBS | You can find top-drawer entertainment at this eclectic concert venue. Acts range from the best in blues, folk, and jazz to up-and-coming college-radio and American-roots artists to indie rockers such as OK Go, Mates of State, and Cowboy Junkies. The colorful marble-pillared emporium (built in 1907 as a bordello) also accommodates dancing at some shows. Pub grub is available on most nights. ⊠ *859 O'Farrell St., between Polk and Larkin Sts., Tenderloin* ☎ *415/885–0750* ⊕ *www. slimspresents.com.*

Potrero Hill

☕ Nightlife

Bottom of the Hill

MUSIC CLUBS | This is a great live-music dive—in the best sense of the word—and truly the epicenter of Bay Area indie rock. The club has hosted some great acts over the years, including the Strokes and the Throwing Muses. Rap and hip-hop acts occasionally make it to the stage. ⊠ *1233 17th St., at Texas St., Potrero Hill* ☎ *415/621–4455* ⊕ *www. bottomofthehill.com.*

Chapter 17

THE BAY AREA

Updated by
Monique Peterson

⊙ Sights	🍴 Restaurants	🛏 Hotels	🛍 Shopping	🍸 Nightlife
★★★★☆	★★★★☆	★★☆☆☆	★★☆☆☆	★★★★☆

WELCOME TO THE BAY AREA

TOP REASONS TO GO

★ **Bite into the "Gourmet Ghetto":** Eat your way through this area of North Berkeley, starting with a slice of perfect pizza from Cheese Board Pizza (just look for the line).

★ **Find solitude at Point Reyes National Seashore:** Hike beautifully rugged—and often deserted—beaches at one of the most beautiful places on Earth, period.

★ **Sit on a dock by the bay:** Admire the beauty of the Bay Area from the rocky, picturesque shores of Sausalito or Tiburon.

★ **Go barhopping in Oakland's hippest hood:** Spend an evening swinging through the watering holes of Uptown, Oakland's artsy-hip and fast-rising corner of downtown.

★ **Walk among giants:** Walking into Muir Woods, a mere 12 miles north of the Golden Gate Bridge, is like entering a cathedral built by God.

1 Berkeley. Independent bookstores, coffee spots, and cyclists.

2 Oakland. Lively arts, nightlife, and food scene.

3 The Marin Headlands. From the Golden Gate Bridge to Muir Beach, these headlands offer spectacular views.

4 Sausalito. Stunning views and a bohemian feel.

5 Tiburon. This scenic, quaint town has lots of good dining and hiking.

6 Mill Valley. A superb natural setting with a lively downtown area.

7 Muir Woods National Monument. Home to some of the most majestic redwoods in the world.

8 Mt. Tamalpais State Park. This park offers views of the entire Bay Area and the Pacific Ocean to the west.

9 Muir Beach. A quiet beach has a distinctly local feel.

10 Stinson Beach. Expect a nonchalant surfer vibe.

11 Point Reyes National Seashore. A dramatic rocky coastline with miles of sandy beaches.

0		8 miles
0		1/2 km

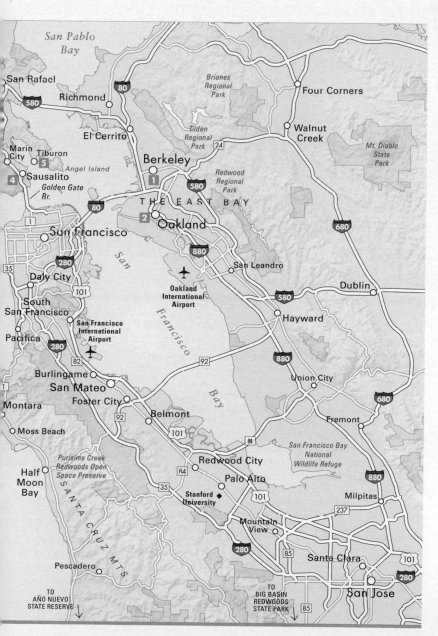

San Pablo Bay

San Rafael
Richmond
580
80
Briones Regional Park
Four Corners
El Cerrito
Walnut Creek
Tilden Regional Park
24
Mt. Diablo State Park
Marin City
Tiburon
5
Angel Island
Berkeley
1
580
Redwood Regional Park
Sausalito
4
Golden Gate Br.
80
THE EAST BAY
2
Oakland
680
San Francisco
280
880
San Leandro
Daly City
35
Oakland International Airport
Dublin
101
580
South San Francisco
Hayward
Pacifica
San Francisco International Airport
280
Francisco
92
880
Union City
82
Burlingame
San Mateo
Foster City
Bay
680
Montara
92
Belmont
101
Fremont
Moss Beach
84
San Francisco Bay National Wildlife Refuge
Purisima Creek Redwoods Open Space Preserve
Redwood City
84
Half Moon Bay
35
Palo Alto
Milpitas
880
Stanford University
101
SANTA CRUZ MTS.
Mountain View
237
280
Pescadero
85
Santa Clara
101
TO AÑO NUEVO STATE RESERVE
TO BIG BASIN REDWOODS STATE PARK
85
San Jose
280

It's rare for a metropolis to compete with its suburbs for visitors, but the view from any of San Francisco's hilltops shows that the Bay Area's temptations extend far beyond the city limits. East of the city are the energetic urban centers of Berkeley and Oakland. Famously radical Berkeley is also comfortably sophisticated, while Oakland has an arts and restaurant scene so hip that it pulls San Franciscans across the bay. To the north is Marin County with its dramatic coastal beauty and chic, affluent villages.

MAJOR REGIONS

The East Bay. The college town of Berkeley has long been known for its liberal ethos, stimulating university community (and perhaps even more stimulating coffee shops), and activist streak. But these days, the lively restaurant and arts scenes are luring even those who wouldn't be caught dead in Birkenstocks. Meanwhile, life in the diverse, harbor-front city of Oakland is strongly defined by a turbulent history. Today, progressive Oakland is an incubator for artisans of all kinds, and the thriving culinary and art scenes are taking off.

Marin County. Marin is considered the prettiest of the Bay Area counties, primarily because of its wealth of open space. Anchored by water on three sides, the county is mostly parkland, including long stretches of undeveloped coastline. The picturesque small towns here—Sausalito, Tiburon, Mill Valley, and Bolinas among them—may sometimes look rustic, but most are in a dizzyingly high tax bracket.

Planning

When to Go

As with San Francisco, you can visit the rest of the Bay Area any time of year, and it's especially nice in late spring and fall. Unlike San Francisco, though, the surrounding areas are reliably sunny in summer—it gets hotter as you head inland. Even the rainy season has its charms, as otherwise golden hills turn a rich green and wildflowers become plentiful. Precipitation is usually the heaviest between November and

March. Berkeley is a university town, so it's easier to navigate the streets and find parking near the university between semesters, but there's also less buzz around town.

Getting Here and Around

Seamless travel from train to ferry to bus with one fare card is possible—and often preferable to driving on congested freeways and over toll bridges. For trips from one city to the next across the bay, take a tip from locals and save time and money with a Clipper card. They work with BART, Muni, buses, and ferries. ■TIP→ **Order a Clipper card before you travel:** ⊕ www.clippercard.com.

BART TRAVEL

Using public transportation to reach Berkeley or Oakland is ideal. The under- and aboveground BART (Bay Area Rapid Transit) trains make stops in both cities as well as other East Bay destinations. Trips to either take about a half hour one-way from the center of San Francisco. BART does not serve Marin County.

CONTACTS BART. ☎ 510/465–2278 ⊕ www.bart.gov.

BOAT AND FERRY TRAVEL

For sheer romance, nothing beats the ferry; there's service from San Francisco to Sausalito, Tiburon, and Larkspur in Marin County, and to Alameda and Oakland in the East Bay.

The Golden Gate Ferry crosses the bay to Larkspur and Sausalito from San Francisco's Ferry Building (✉ Market St. and the Embarcadero). Blue & Gold Fleet ferries depart daily for Sausalito and Tiburon from Pier 41 at Fisherman's Wharf; weekday commuter ferries leave from the Ferry Building for Tiburon. The trip to either Sausalito or Tiburon takes from 25 minutes to an hour. Purchase tickets from terminal vending machines.

The Angel Island–Tiburon Ferry sails to the island daily from April through October and on weekends the rest of the year.

The San Francisco Bay Ferry runs several times daily between San Francisco's Ferry Building or Pier 41 and Oakland's Jack London Square by way of Alameda. The trip lasts from 25 to 45 minutes, and leads to Oakland's waterfront shopping and restaurant district. Purchase tickets on board.

BOAT AND FERRY LINES Angel Island– Tiburon Ferry. ☎ 415/435–2131 ⊕ www. angelislandferry.com. **Blue & Gold Fleet.** ☎ 415/705–8200 ⊕ www.blueandgold-fleet.com. **Golden Gate Ferry.** ☎ 415/921–5858 ⊕ www.goldengateferry.org. **San Francisco Bay Ferry.** ☎ 707/643–3779, 877/643–3779 ⊕ sanfranciscobayferry. com.

BUS TRAVEL

Golden Gate Transit buses travel north to Sausalito, Tiburon, and elsewhere in Marin County from the Transbay Temporary Terminal (located at Howard and Main, two blocks south of Market) and other points in San Francisco. For Mt. Tamalpais State Park and West Marin (Stinson Beach, Bolinas, and Point Reyes Station), take any route to Marin City and then transfer to the West Marin Stagecoach. San Francisco Muni buses primarily serve the city, though the 76X does cross the Golden Gate and end at the Marin Headlands Visitors Center on weekends. ■TIP→ **Several other bus options exist for local and regional travel throughout the Bay Area, including Amtrak, Greyhound, California Shuttle, and more (www.bayareatransit.net/regional).**

Though less speedy than BART, more than 30 AC Transit bus lines provide service to and from the Transbay Temporary Terminal and throughout the East Bay, even after BART shuts down. The F and FS lines will get you to Berkeley, while lines C, P, B, and O take you to Oakland and Piedmont.

BUS LINES **AC Transit.** ☎ *510/891–4777* ⊕ *www.actransit.org.* **Golden Gate Transit.** ☎ *511* ⊕ *www.goldengatetransit.org.* **SamTrans.** ☎ *800/660–4287* ⊕ *www. samtrans.com.* **San Francisco Muni.** ☎ *311* ⊕ *www.sfmta.com.* **West Marin Stagecoach.** ☎ *511* ⊕ *www.marintransit.org.*

CAR TRAVEL

To reach the East Bay from San Francisco, take Interstate 80 East across the San Francisco–Oakland Bay Bridge. For U.C. Berkeley, merge onto Interstate 580 West and take Exit 11 for University Avenue. For Oakland, merge onto Interstate 580 East. To reach downtown, take Interstate 980 West from Interstate 580 East and exit at 14th Street. Travel time varies depending on traffic, but should take about 30 minutes (or more than an hour if it's rush hour).

For all points in Marin, head north on U.S. 101 and cross the Golden Gate Bridge. Sausalito, Tiburon, the Marin Headlands, and Point Reyes National Seashore are all accessed off U.S. 101. The scenic coastal route, Highway 1, also called Shoreline Highway and Panoramic for certain stretches, can be accessed off U.S. 101 as well. Follow this road to Muir Woods, Mt. Tamalpais State Park, Muir Beach, Stinson Beach, and Bolinas. From Bolinas, you can continue north on Highway 1 to Point Reyes.

Restaurants

The Bay Area is home to many popular and innovative restaurants, such as Chez Panisse in Berkeley and Commis in Oakland—for which reservations must be made well in advance. There are also countless casual but equally tasty eateries to test out; expect an emphasis on organic seasonal produce, locally raised meats, craft cocktails, and curated wine menus. Marin's dining scene trends toward the sleepy side, so be sure to check hours ahead of time. *Restaurant*

reviews have been shortened. For full information, visit Fodors.com.

Hotels

With a few exceptions, hotels in Berkeley and Oakland tend to be standard-issue, but many Marin hotels package themselves as cozy retreats. Summer in Marin is often booked well in advance, despite weather that can be downright chilly. Check for special packages during this season. *Hotel reviews have been shortened. For full information, visit Fodors.com.*

WHAT IT COSTS			
$	$$	$$$	$$$$
RESTAURANTS			
under $16	$16–$22	$23–$30	over $30
HOTELS			
under $150	$150–$199	$200–$250	over $250

Tours

★ **Best Bay Area Tours**

SPECIAL-INTEREST | Morning and afternoon tours of Muir Woods and Sausalito include at least 90 minutes in the redwoods before heading on to Sausalito. On returning to the city, tours make a scenic stop in the Marin Headlands to enjoy fantastic views. Knowledgeable guides lead small tours in comfortable vans, and hotel pickup is included, though park entrance is not. Another tour option includes a visit to Muir Woods and Wine Country exploration. ☎ *877/705–8687* ⊕ *bestbayareatours. com* ✉ *From $60.*

Berkeley

2 miles northeast of Bay Bridge.

Berkeley is the birthplace of the Free Speech Movement, the radical hub of the 1960s, the home of arguably the nation's top public university, and a frequent site of protests and political movements. The city of 115,000 is also a culturally diverse breeding ground for social trends, a bastion of the counterculture, and an important center for Bay Area writers, artists, and musicians. Berkeley residents, students, and faculty spend hours nursing coffee concoctions while they read, discuss, and debate at the dozens of cafés that surround campus. It's the quintessential university town, with numerous independent bookstores, countless casual eateries, myriad meetups, and thousands of cyclists.

Oakland may have Berkeley beat when it comes to ethnic diversity and cutting-edge arts, but unless you're accustomed to sipping hemp milk lattes while planning a protest prior to yoga, you'll likely find Berkeley charmingly offbeat.

GETTING HERE AND AROUND
BART is the easiest way to get to Berkeley from San Francisco. Exit at the Downtown Berkeley station, and walk a block up Center Street to get to the western edge of campus. AC Transit buses F and FS lines stop near the university and 4th Street shopping. By car, take Interstate 80 East across the Bay Bridge, merge onto Interstate 580 West, and take the University Avenue exit through downtown Berkeley or take the Ashby Avenue exit and turn left on Telegraph Avenue. Once you arrive, explore on foot. Berkeley is very pedestrian-friendly.

ESSENTIALS
VISITOR INFORMATION Koret Visitor Center. ⊠ *2227 Piedmont Ave., at California Memorial Stadium, Downtown*

A Tasting Tour 👁

For an unforgettable foodie experience, book a **Culinary Walking Tour** with Edible Excursions (☎ *415/806–5970,* ⊕ *www.edible-excursions.net).* Come hungry for knowledge and noshing. Tours ($110) take place on Thursday at 11 and Saturday at 10.

☎ *510/642–5215* ⊕ *visit.berkeley.edu.* **Visit Berkeley.** ⊠ *2030 Addison St., Suite 102, Downtown* ☎ *510/549–7040, 800/847–4823* ⊕ *www.visitberkeley.com.*

👁 Sights

BAMPFA (Berkeley Art Museum and Pacific Film Archive)
MUSEUM | This combined art museum and repertory movie theater and film archive contains more than 19,000 works of art and 16,000 films and videos. Art works span five centuries and include modernist notables Mark Rothko, Jackson Pollock, David Smith, and Hans Hofmann. The Pacific Film Archive specializes in international films and offers regular screenings, programs, and performances. ⊠ *2155 Center St., Downtown* ☎ *510/642–0808* ⊕ *bampfa.org* 🎫 *$13; free 1st Thurs. of month* 🕑 *Closed Mon. and Tues.*

4th Street
NEIGHBORHOOD | Once an industrial area, this walkable stretch of 4th Street north of University Avenue has transformed into the busiest few blocks of refined shopping and eating in Berkeley. For lovers of design, curated taste experiences, artful living, and fashion, the vibrant district boasts more than 70 shops, specialty stores, cafés, and restaurants. See creation and inspiration at Castle in the Air, Builders Booksource, and The Stained Glass Garden, or sip a "live roast" at

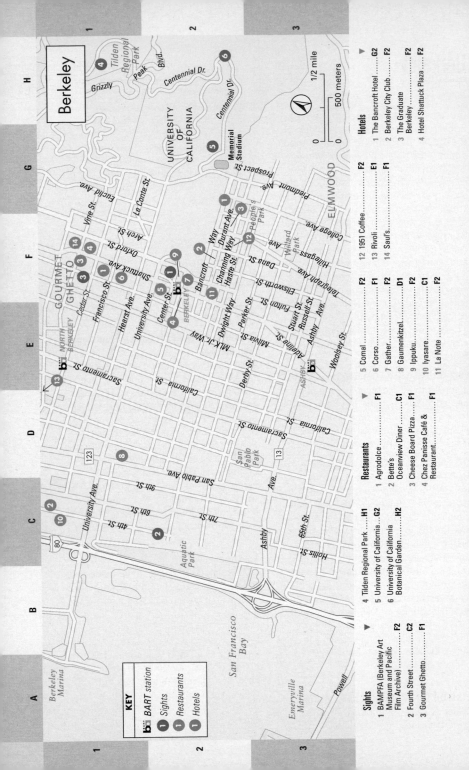

Berkeley

Tilden Regional Park

Grizzly Peak Blvd.

Centennial Dr.

UNIVERSITY OF CALIFORNIA

Centennial Dr.

Memorial Stadium

Prospect St.

ELMWOOD

Piedmont Ave.

College Ave.

Willard Park

Hillegass Ave.

Dana St.

Ellsworth St.

Fulton St.

Adeline St.

Ashby Ave.

Woolsey St.

Russell St.

Stuart St.

Milvia St.

Parker St.

Derby St.

California St.

Sacramento St.

Ashby Ave.

Hollis St.

6th St.

7th St.

9th St.

San Pablo Ave.

Ave.

San Pablo Park

California St.

University Ave.

4th St.

6th St.

Sacramento St.

Aquatic Park

San Francisco Bay

Berkeley Marina

Emeryville Marina

Powell

NORTH BERKELEY

GOURMET GHETTO

Vine St.

Cedar St.

Francisco St.

Hearst Ave.

University Ave.

Center St.

MLK Jr. Way

Dwight Way

BERKELEY

Bancroft Way

Channing Way

Haste St.

Telegraph Ave.

Durant Ave.

People's Park

Way

Le Conte Ave.

Arch St.

Oxford St.

Shattuck Ave.

Euclid Ave.

Peak

0   1/2 mile
0   500 meters

KEY

b BART station
1 Sights
1 Restaurants
1 Hotels

Artis, where you can watch small-batch coffee roasting in progress. ⊠ *4th St. between University Ave. and Virginia St.* ⊕ *www.fourthstreet.com.*

★ **Gourmet Ghetto**

NEIGHBORHOOD | The success of Alice Waters's Chez Panisse defined California cuisine and attracted countless food-related enterprises to a stretch of Shattuck Avenue now known as the Gourmet Ghetto. Foodies will do well here poking around the shops, grabbing a quick bite, or indulging in a feast.

César (*1515 Shattuck*) wine bar provides afternoon tapas and late-night drinks, while the **Epicurious Garden** (*1509–1513 Shattuck*) food stands sell everything from sushi to gelato. A small terraced garden winds up to the **Imperial Tea Court**, a Zen-like teahouse rife with imports and tea ware.

Across Vine, the **Vintage Berkeley** (*2113 Vine*) wineshop offers regular tastings and reasonably priced bottles within the walls of a historic former pump house. Coffee lovers can head to the original **Peet's Coffee & Tea** at the corner of Walnut and Vine (*2124 Vine*).

South of Cedar Street, the **Local Butcher Shop** (*No. 1600*) sells locally sourced meat and hearty sandwiches of the day. For high-end food at takeout prices, try the salads, sandwiches, and signature potato puffs at **Grégoire**, around the corner on Cedar Street (*No. 2109*). **Masse's Pastries** (*No. 1469 Shattuck*) is a museum of edible artwork. We could go on, but you get the idea. ⊠ *Shattuck Ave. between Delaware and Rose Sts., North Berkeley* ⊕ *www.gourmetghetto.org.*

★ **Tilden Regional Park**

NATIONAL/STATE PARK | FAMILY | Stunning bay views, a scaled-down steam train, and a botanic garden that boasts the nation's most complete collection of California plant life are the hallmarks of this 2,000-acre park in the hills just east of the U.C. Berkeley campus. The garden's visitor center offers tours, as well as information about Tilden's other attractions, including its picnic spots, Lake Anza swimming site, golf course, and hiking trails (the paved **Nimitz Way**, at Inspiration Point, is a popular hike with wonderful sunset views). ■TIP→ **Children love Tilden's interactive Little Farm and vintage carousel.** ⊠ *Tilden Regional Park, 2501 Grizzly Peak Blvd., Tilden Park* ☎ *510/544–2747 park office* ⊕ *www. ebparks.org/parks/tilden* ⧉ *Free parking and botanic garden.*

University of California

COLLEGE | Known simply as "Cal," the founding campus of California's university system is one of the leading intellectual centers in the United States and a major site for scientific research. Chartered in 1868, the university sits on 178 oak-covered acres split by Strawberry Creek; it's bound by Bancroft Way to the south, Hearst Avenue to the north, Oxford Street to the west, and Gayley Road to the east. Campus highlights include bustling and historic **Sproul Plaza** (*Bancroft Way and Sather Rd.*), the seven floors and 61-bell carillon of **Sather Tower** (*Campanile Esplanade*), the nearly 3 million artifacts in the **Phoebe A. Hearst Museum of Anthropology** (Kroeber Hall), hands-on **Lawrence Hall of Science** (*1 Centennial Dr.*), the vibrant 34-acre **Botanical Gardens** (*200 Centennial Dr.*), and the historic **Hearst Greek Theatre** (*2001 Gayley Rd.*), the classic outdoor amphitheater designed by John Galen Howard. ⊠ *Downtown* ☎ *510/642–6000* ⊕ *www.berkeley.edu.*

University of California Botanical Garden

GARDEN | FAMILY | Thanks to Berkeley's temperate climate, more than 10,000 types of plants from all corners of the world flourish in the 34-acre University of California Botanical Garden. Free garden tours are given regularly with paid admission. Benches and shady picnic tables make this a relaxing place for a snack with a breathtaking view. ⊠ *200*

The University of California is the epicenter of Berkeley's energy and activism.

Centennial Dr., Downtown ☎ *510/643–2755* 🌐 *botanicalgarden.berkeley.edu* 🎟 *$12* 🕒 *Closed 1st Tues. every month.*

🍴 Restaurants

Dining in Berkeley may be low-key when it comes to dress, but it's top-of-class in quality, even in less-refined spaces. Late diners beware: Berkeley is an "early to bed" kind of town.

Agrodolce
$$ | **ITALIAN** | **FAMILY** | Angelo D'Alo's family brings Sicilian flavors and their love for preparing them freshly to the heart of the Gourmet Ghetto, where black-and-white photos and Italian home decor add to the old-world atmosphere. The menu features local, sustainable, and organic ingredients in such dishes as house-made orecchiette, seafood risotto, and free-range *pollo scarpariello*. **Known for:** braised pork pappardelle; homemade sauces; antipasti specialties. [$] *Average main: $17* ✉ *1730 Shattuck Ave., North Berkeley* ☎ *510/848–8748* 🌐 *www.agrodolceberkeley.com* 🕒 *Closed Tues.*

Bette's Oceanview Diner
$ | **DINER** | **FAMILY** | Checkered floors, vintage burgundy booths, and an old-time jukebox set the scene at this retro-chic diner in the heart of Berkeley's fashionable 4th Street shopping district. The wait for a seat at breakfast can be quite long; luckily Bette's To Go is always an option. **Known for:** soufflé pancakes; poached egg specialties; meat loaf and gravy. [$] *Average main: $13* ✉ *1807 4th St., near Delaware St., 4th Street* ☎ *510/644–3230* 🌐 *www.bettesdiner.com* 🕒 *No dinner.*

★ **Cheese Board Pizza**
$ | **PIZZA** | A jazz combo entertains the line that usually snakes down the block outside Cheese Board Pizza; it's that good. The cooperatively owned takeout spot and restaurant draws devoted customers with the smell of just-baked garlic on the pie of the day. **Known for:** vegetarian pizza by the slice or slab; live music performances; green sauce. [$] *Average*

main: $11 ✉ 1504–1512 Shattuck Ave., at Vine St., North Berkeley ☎ 510/549–3183 🌐 cheeseboardcollective.coop/pizza 🕒 Pizza closed Sun. and Mon., bakery closed Sun.

★ Chez Panisse Café & Restaurant

$$$$ | **MODERN AMERICAN** | Alice Waters's legendary eatery is known for its locally sourced ingredients, formal prix-fixe menus, and personal service, while its upstairs café offers simpler fare in a more casual setting. Both menus change daily and legions of loyal fans insist that Chez Panisse lives up to its reputation. **Known for:** sustainably sourced meats; inventive use of seasonal ingredients; attention to detail. [$] *Average main: $125 ✉ 1517 Shattuck Ave., at Vine St., North Berkeley ☎ 510/548–5525 restaurant, 510/548–5049 café 🌐 www.chezpanisse.com 🕒 Closed Sun. No lunch in restaurant.*

★ Comal

$$ | **MODERN MEXICAN** | Relaxed yet trendy, Comal's cavernous indoor dining space and intimate back patio and fire pit draw a diverse, decidedly casual crowd for creative Oaxacan-inspired fare and well-crafted cocktails. The modern Mexican menu centers on small dishes that lend themselves to sharing and are offered alongside more than 100 tequilas and mezcals. **Known for:** margaritas and mezcal; house-made chicharrones; wood-fired entrées. [$] *Average main: $16 ✉ 2020 Shattuck Ave., near University Ave., Downtown ☎ 510/926–6300 🌐 www.comalberkeley.com 🕒 No lunch.*

Corso

$$$ | **MODERN ITALIAN** | This lively spot serves up a seasonal menu of excellent Tuscan cuisine and Italian wines in a sparse but snazzy space. The open kitchen dominates a room, which includes closely spaced tables and festive flickering candles. **Known for:** handcrafted pastas; house-cured salumi; daily butcher's specials. [$] *Average main: $24 ✉ 1788 Shattuck Ave., at Delaware St., North Berkeley ☎ 510/704–8004 🌐 www.corsoberkeley.com 🕒 No lunch.*

Gather

$$$ | **MODERN AMERICAN** | All things local, organic, seasonal, and sustainable reside harmoniously under one roof at Gather. This haven for vegans, vegetarians, and carnivores alike is a vibrant, well-lit space that boasts funky light fixtures, shiny wood furnishings, and banquettes made of recycled leather belts. **Known for:** heirloom varietals; wood-fired pizzas; house-made liqueurs. [$] *Average main: $24 ✉ 2200 Oxford St., at Allston Way, Downtown ☎ 510/809–0400 🌐 www.gatherrestaurant.com.*

Gaumenkitzel

$$ | **GERMAN** | **FAMILY** | This convivial locale for organic, slow-food German fare is also the spot for the Bay Area's best variety of German beers. With dishes like spätzle and caramelized onions, house-made *brezel* with bratwurst, *jägerschnitzel* with braised red cabbage, and panfried rainbow trout, this kitchen puts a fresh stamp on traditional German favorites. **Known for:** German wine and beer selection; house-made German breads; fresh, sustainable ingredients. [$] *Average main: $20 ✉ 2121 San Pablo Ave., Downtown ☎ 510/647–5016 🌐 www.gaumenkitzel.net 🕒 Closed Mon.*

★ Ippuku

$$$ | **JAPANESE** | More Tokyo street chic than standard sushi house, this *izakaya*—the Japanese equivalent of a bar with appetizers—is decked with bamboo-screen booths. Servers pour an impressive array of sakes and *shōchū* and serve up surprising fare. **Known for:** shōchū selection; charcoal-grilled yakitori skewers; selection of small dishes. [$] *Average main: $28 ✉ 2130 Center St., Downtown ☎ 510/665–1969 🌐 www.ippukuberkeley.com 🕒 Closed Mon. No lunch.*

Famed Berkeley restaurant Chez Panisse focuses on seasonal local ingredients.

Iyasare

$$$ | JAPANESE | Reservations are recommended at this 4th Street hot spot where the outdoor seating is ideal for people-watching and the Japanese country food is uniquely prepared. Locals come back for seasonally changing eclectic dishes made with a blend of local ingredients, such as burdock root tempura and ume-cured sashimi or miso-bell pepper puree with Dungeness crab. **Known for:** Japanese whiskey and specialty sakes; donburi and small plates; cured salads. [$] *Average main: $23* ✉ *1830 4th St., 4th Street* ☎ *510/845–8100* 🌐 *iyasare-berkeley.com.*

★ La Note

$$ | FRENCH | A charming taste of Provence in a 19th-century locale with stone floors, country tables, and a seasonal flowering patio, La Note's rustic French food is as thoughtfully prepared as the space is lovely. Enjoy breakfast and brunch outdoors with fresh crusty breads and pastries, eggs *Lucas* with house-roasted tomatoes, and lemon gingerbread pancakes or romantic dinners with mussels *mouclade,* ratatouille, and homemade fondue. **Known for:** sandwiches; house-made Merguez sausage; brioche pan perdu. [$] *Average main: $18* ✉ *2377 Shattuck Ave., Downtown* ✥ *Between Channing and Durant* ☎ *510/843–1525* 🌐 *www.lanoterestaurant.com* ⏲ *No dinner Sun.–Wed.*

1951 Coffee

$ | CAFÉ | Taking its name from the 1951 Refugee Convention at which the United Nations first set guidelines for refugee protections, 1951 Coffee Company is a nonprofit coffee shop inspired and powered by refugees. In addition to crafting high-caliber coffee drinks and dishing out local pastries and savory bites, this colorful café also serves as an inspiring advocacy space and training center for refugees. Just three blocks south of campus, it's a favorite meet-up spot for locals and students alike. **Known for:** 1951 hand-roasted blends; Third Culture Bakery Mochi doughnuts and muffins; chai latte. [$] *Average main: $7* ✉ *2410*

Channing Way, at Dana St., Downtown ☎ 510/280–6171 ⊕ 1951coffee.com.

Rivoli

$$$$ | MODERN AMERICAN | Italian-inspired dishes using fresh California ingredients star on a menu that changes regularly. Inventive offerings are served in a Zen-like modern dining room with captivating views of the lovely back garden. **Known for:** line-caught fish and sustainably sourced meats; curated wine list; thoughtfully combined ingredients. $ Average main: $32 ⊠ 1539 Solano Ave., at Neilson St., North Berkeley ☎ 510/526–2542 ⊕ www.rivolirestaurant. com ⊗ No lunch.

★ Saul's

$$ | AMERICAN | FAMILY | High ceilings and red-leather booths add to the friendly, retro atmosphere of Saul's deli, a Berkeley institution that is well known for its homemade celery tonic sodas and enormous sandwiches made with Acme bread. Locals swear by the pastrami sandwiches, stuffed-cabbage rolls, and challah French toast. **Known for:** hand-rolled organic bagels; matzo ball soup; Niman Ranch grass-fed beef and Monterey Fish Company seafood. $ Average main: $16 ⊠ 1475 Shattuck Ave., near Vine St., North Berkeley ☎ 510/848–3354 ⊕ www.saulsdeli.com.

🛏 Hotels

For inexpensive lodging, investigate University Avenue, west of campus. The area can be noisy, congested, and somewhat dilapidated, but it does include a few decent motels and chain properties. All Berkeley lodgings are strictly mid-range.

The Bancroft Hotel

$$ | HOTEL | This eco-friendly boutique hotel—across from the U.C. campus—is quaint, charming, and completely green. **Pros:** closest hotel in Berkeley to U.C. campus; friendly staff; many rooms have good views. **Cons:** some rooms are quite small; despite renovation, the building shows its age with thin walls; no elevator. $ Rooms from: $160 ⊠ 2680 Bancroft Way, Downtown ☎ 510/549–1000, 800/549–1002 toll-free ⊕ bancrofthotel. com ⌂ 22 rooms |○| Breakfast.

★ Berkeley City Club

$$$ | HOTEL | Moorish design and Gothic architecture meet modern amenities at this historic locale steps from campus, arts, and eateries. **Pros:** art gallery and courtyard seating; laundry facilities; on-site salon and skin care. **Cons:** no nonservice pets allowed; limited, fee-only parking; no televisions in rooms. $ Rooms from: $245 ⊠ 2315 Durant Ave., Downtown ☎ ⊕ www.berkeleycityclub.com ⌂ 38 rooms |○| Free Breakfast.

The Graduate Berkeley

$$$ | HOTEL | Fresh, colorful design and Bohemian flair set the tone at this historically renovated hotel just steps from campus and downtown eating, shopping, and entertainment. **Pros:** convenient location; pet-friendly; complimentary bikes. **Cons:** rooms can be noisy; rooms can be small; fee parking only. $ Rooms from: $239 ⊠ 2600 Durant Ave., Downtown ☎ 510/845–8981 ⊕ www.graduatehotels.com/berkeley ⌂ 144 rooms |○| No meals.

★ Hotel Shattuck Plaza

$$$ | HOTEL | This historic boutique hotel sits amid Berkeley's downtown arts district, just steps from the U.C. campus and a short walk from the Gourmet Ghetto. **Pros:** central location near public transit; special date night and B&B packages; modern facilities. **Cons:** public and street parking only; limited on-site fitness center; street-facing rooms may be loud. $ Rooms from: $246 ⊠ 2086 Allston Way, at Shattuck Ave., Downtown ☎ 510/845–7300 ⊕ www.hotelshattuck-plaza.com ⌂ 199 rooms |○| No meals.

▼ Nightlife

★ The Freight & Salvage Coffeehouse

MUSIC CLUBS | For more than 50 years, the Freight has been a venue for some of the world's finest practitioners of folk, jazz, gospel, blues, world-beat, bluegrass, and storytelling. The nonprofit organization grew from an 87-seat coffee house to a thriving, 500-seat venue in the heart of Berkeley's Art District. Many tickets cost less than $30. ⊠ *2020 Addison St., between Shattuck Ave. and Milvia St., Downtown* ☎ *510/644–2020* ⊕ *www.thefreight.org.*

★ Tupper & Reed

BARS/PUBS | Housed in the former music shop of John C. Tupper and Lawrence Reed, this music-inspired cocktail haven features a symphony of carefully crafted libations, which are mixed with live music performed by local musicians. The historic 1925 building features a balcony bar, cozy nooks, antique fixtures, a pool table, and romantic fireplaces. ⊠ *2271 Shattuck Ave., at Kitteredge St., Downtown* ☎ *510/859–4472* ⊕ *www.tupperandreed.com.*

▶ Performing Arts

Berkeley Repertory Theatre

THEATER | One of the region's most highly respected and innovative repertory theaters, Berkeley Rep performs the work of classic and contemporary playwrights. Well-known pieces such as *Tartuffe* and *Macbeth* mix with world premieres and edgier fare like Green Day's *American Idiot* and Lemony Snicket's *The Composer Is Dead.* The theater's complex is in the heart of downtown Berkeley's arts district, near BART's Downtown Berkeley station. ⊠ *2025 Addison St., near Shattuck Ave., Downtown* ☎ *510/647–2949* ⊕ *www.berkeleyrep.org.*

Cal Performances

CONCERTS | Based out of U.C. Berkeley, this series runs from September through May. It features a varied bill of internationally acclaimed artists ranging from classical soloists to the latest jazz, world-music, theater, and dance ensembles. Past performers include Alvin Ailey American Dance Theater, the National Ballet of China, and Yo-Yo Ma. ⊠ *101 Zellerbach Hall, Suite 4800, Dana St. and Bancroft Way, Downtown* ☎ *510/642–9988* ⊕ *calperformances.org.*

🛍 Shopping

★ Acci Gallery

ART GALLERIES | The Arts and Crafts Cooperative, Inc., a collective of Berkeley artists and artisans, has been a stalwart gallery and retail store showcasing ceramics, textiles, paintings, photography, jewelry, and various media for more than 60 years. Explore the amazing range of local talent in a well-lit historic space, and find truly one-of-a-kind gems to take home. ⊠ *1652 Shattuck Ave., North Berkeley* ✛ *At Lincoln* ☎ *510/843–2527* ⊕ *www.accigallery.com.*

★ Amoeba Music

MUSIC STORES | Heaven for audiophiles and movie collectors, this legendary Berkeley favorite is *the* place to head for new and used CDs, vinyl, cassettes, VHS tapes, Blu-ray discs, and DVDs. The massive and ever-changing stock includes thousands of titles for all music tastes, as well as plenty of Amoeba merch. There are branches in San Francisco and Hollywood, but this is the original. ⊠ *2455 Telegraph Ave., at Haste St., Downtown* ☎ *510/549–1125* ⊕ *www.amoeba.com.*

Kermit Lynch Wine Merchant

WINE/SPIRITS | Credited with taking American appreciation of old-world wines to a higher level, this small shop is a great place to peruse as you educate your palate. The friendly salespeople will happily direct you to the latest French and Italian bargains. ⊠ *1605 San Pablo Ave., at Cedar St.* ☎ *510/524–1524* ⊕ *www.kermitlynch.com* ☉ *Closed Sun. and Mon.*

Moe's Books

BOOKS/STATIONERY | The spirit of Moe—the creative, cantankerous, cigar-smoking late proprietor—lives on in this world-famous four-story house of new and used books. Students and professors come here to browse the large selection, which includes literary and cultural criticism, art titles, and literature in foreign languages. ⊠ *2476 Telegraph Ave., near Haste St., Downtown* ☎ *510/849–2087* ⊕ *www. moesbooks.com.*

Oakland

East of Bay Bridge.

In contrast to San Francisco's buzz and beauty and Berkeley's storied counterculture, Oakland's allure lies in its amazing diversity. Here you can find a Nigerian clothing store, a Gothic revival skyscraper, a Buddhist meditation center, and a lively salsa club, all within the same block.

Oakland's multifaceted nature reflects its colorful and tumultuous history. Once a cluster of Mediterranean-style homes and gardens that served as a bedroom community for San Francisco, the town had a major rail terminal and port city by the turn of the 20th century. Already a hub of manufacturing, Oakland became a center for shipbuilding and industry when the United States entered World War II. New jobs in the city's shipyards, railroads, and factories attracted thousands of laborers from across the country, including sharecroppers from the Deep South, Mexican Americans from the Southwest, and some of the nation's first female welders. Neighborhoods were imbued with a proud but gritty spirit, along with heightened racial tension. In the wake of the civil rights movement, racial pride gave rise to militant groups like the Black Panther Party, but they were little match for the economic hardships and racial tensions that plagued Oakland. In many neighborhoods the reality was widespread poverty and gang violence—subjects that dominated the songs of such Oakland-bred rappers as the late Tupac Shakur. The highly publicized protests of the Occupy Oakland movement in 2011 and 2012 and the #BlackLivesMatter movement of 2014 and 2015 illustrate just how much Oakland remains a mosaic of its past.

Oakland's affluent reside in the city's hillside homes and wooded enclaves like Claremont, Piedmont, and Montclair, which provide a warmer, more spacious alternative to San Francisco, while a constant flow of newcomers ensures continued diversity, vitality, and growing pains. Many neighborhoods to the west and south of the city center have yet to be touched by gentrification, but a renovated downtown and vibrant arts scene has injected new energy into the city. Even San Franciscans, often loath to cross the Bay Bridge, come to Uptown and Temescal for the nightlife, arts, and restaurants.

Everyday life here revolves around the neighborhood. In some areas, such as Piedmont and Rockridge, you'd swear you were in Berkeley or San Francisco's Noe Valley. Along Telegraph Avenue just south of 51st Street, Temescal is littered with hipsters and pulsing with creative culinary and design energy. These are perfect places for browsing, eating, or relaxing between sightseeing trips to Oakland's architectural gems, rejuvenated waterfront, and numerous green spaces.

GETTING HERE AND AROUND

Driving from San Francisco, take Interstate 80 East across the Bay Bridge, then take Interstate 580 East to the Grand Avenue exit for Lake Merritt. To reach downtown and the waterfront, take Interstate 980 West from Interstate 580 East and exit at 12th Street; exit at 18th Street for Uptown. For Temescal, take Interstate 580 East to Highway 24 and exit at 51st Street.

By BART, use the Lake Merritt Station for the Oakland Museum and southern Lake Merritt; the Oakland City Center–12th Street Station for downtown, Chinatown, and Old Oakland; and the 19th Street Station for Uptown, the Paramount Theatre, and the north side of Lake Merritt.

By bus, take the AC Transit's C and P lines to get to Piedmont in Oakland. The O bus stops at the edge of Chinatown near downtown Oakland.

Oakland's Jack London Square is an easy hop on the ferry from San Francisco. Those without cars can take advantage of the free Broadway Shuttle, which runs from the Jack London Square to 27th Street via downtown on weekdays and Friday and Saturday nights.

Be aware of how quickly neighborhoods can change. Walking is generally safe downtown and in the Piedmont and Rockridge areas, but be mindful when walking west and southeast of downtown, especially at night.

SHUTTLE CONTACT Broadway Shuttle.
⊕ www.oaklandca.gov.

ESSENTIALS
VISITOR INFORMATION Visit Oakland.
✉ 481 Water St., near Broadway, Jack London Square ☎ 510/839–9000 ⊕ www. visitoakland.com.

Sights

Lake Merritt
NATURE PRESERVE | This lagoon with its unique habitat for more than 100 bird species became the nation's first wildlife refuge in 1870. Today the 3.1-mile path around the lake is also a refuge for walkers, bikers, joggers, and nature lovers. **Lakeside Park** has **Children's Fairyland** (699 Bellevue) and the **Rotary Nature Center** (600 Bellevue), where monthly bird walks commence every fourth Wednesday. For views from the water, the **Lake Merritt Boating Center** (568 Bellevue) rents kayaks and rowboats (⊕ www.lakemerritt.

org). Venetian gondolas cruise from the Oakland Boathouse ($60 for 30 mins for 2, ⊕ gondolaservizio.com).

On the lake's south side, the **Camron-Stanford House** (1418 Lakeside Dr.), is the last of the grand Victorians that once dominated the area; it's open Sundays for tours. Nearby bold **Oakland mural art** offers a more modern feast for the eyes (between Madison and Webster Strs. and 7th and 11th Sts.).

The lake's necklace of lights adds allure for dinner-goers to the art-deco **Terrace Room** (1800 Madison St.) or **Lake Chalet** (1520 Lakeside Dr.), as well as to a host of tasty spots along Grand Avenue, from **Enssaro** Ethiopian (357a) and Korean BBQ at **Jong Ga House** (372) to comfort gourmet at **Grand Lake Kitchen** (576). ✉ Lake Merritt.

★ Oakland Museum of California
MUSEUM | FAMILY | This museum, designed by Kevin Roche, is one of the country's quintessential examples of mid-century modern architecture. Explore the robust collection of nearly 2 million objects in three distinct galleries celebrating the state's history, natural sciences, and art. Listen to native species and environmental soundscapes in the Library of Natural Sounds and engage in stories of the state's past and future from Ohlone basket making to emerging technologies and current events. Not to be missed are the photographs from Dorothea Lange's personal archive and a worthy collection of Bay Area figurative painters including David Park and Joan Brown. Take a break at the Blue Oak café for seasonal dishes sourced from local ingredients. ■TIP→ **On Friday evening the museum gets lively, with live music, food trucks, and after-hours gallery access.** ✉ 1000 Oak St., at 10th St., Downtown ☎ 510/318–8400, 888/625–6873 toll-free ⊕ museumca.org ☑ $16, free 1st Sun. of month ☉ Closed Mon. and Tues.

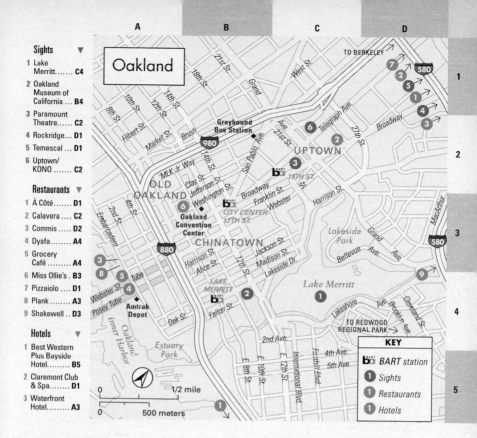

KEY

BART station

Sights

Restaurants

Hotels

★ Paramount Theatre

ARTS VENUE | A glorious art-deco specimen, the Paramount operates as a venue for concerts and performances of all kinds, from the Oakland Symphony to Jerry Seinfeld and Elvis Costello. The popular classic movie nights start off with a 30-minute Wurlitzer concert. ■TIP→ **Docent-led tours, offered the first and third Saturday of the month, are fun and informative.** ✉ *2025 Broadway, at 20th St., Uptown* ☎ *510/465-6400* ⊕ *www. paramounttheatre.com* ✆ *Tour $5.*

★ Rockridge

NEIGHBORHOOD | **FAMILY** | This fashionable upscale neighborhood is one of Oakland's most desirable places to live. Explore the tree-lined streets that radiate out from **College Avenue** just north and south of the Rockridge BART station for a look at California Craftsman bungalows at their finest. By day College Avenue between Broadway and Alcatraz Avenue is crowded with shoppers buying fresh flowers, used books, and clothing; by night the same folks are back for handcrafted meals, artisan wines, and locally brewed ales. With its specialty-food shops and quick bites to go, **Market Hall,** an airy European-style marketplace at Shafter Avenue, is a hub of culinary activity. ✉ *5655 College Ave., between Alcatraz Ave. and Broadway, Rockridge* ⊕ *www. rockridgedistrict.com.*

★ Temescal

NEIGHBORHOOD | Centering on Telegraph Avenue between 40th and 51st streets, Temescal (the Aztec term for "sweat house") is a low-pretension, moneyed-hipster hood with young families and middle-aged folks thrown into the mix. A critical mass of excellent eateries draws folks from around the Bay Area; there's veteran **Doña Tomás** (*5004 Telegraph Ave.*) and favorites **Pizzaiolo** (*5008 Telegraph Ave.*) and **Rose's Taproom** (*4930 Telegraph Ave.*) as well as **Bakesale Betty** (*5098 Telegraph Ave.*), where folks line up for the fried-chicken sandwich. Old-time dive bars and smog-check stations share space with the trendy children's clothing shop **Ruby's Garden** (*5026 Telegraph Ave.*) and the stalwart **East Bay Depot for Creative Reuse** (*4695 Telegraph Ave.*), where you might find a bucket of buttons or 1,000 muffin wrappers among birdcages, furniture, lunch boxes, and ribbon.

Around the corner, **Temescal Alley** (*49th St.*), a tucked-away lane of tiny storefronts, crackles with the creative energy of local makers. Find botanical wonders at **Crimson Horticultural Rarities** (*No. 470*) or an old-fashioned straight-edge shave at **Temescal Alley Barbershop** (*No. 470B*). Don't miss grabbing a sweet scoop at **Curbside Creamery** (*No. 482*). ⊠ *Telegraph Ave., between 40th and 51st Sts., Temescal* ⊕ *www.temescaldistrict.org.*

★ Uptown/KONO

NEIGHBORHOOD | Uptown and KONO (Koreatown-Northgate) is where nightlife and cutting-edge art merge. Dozens of galleries cluster around Telegraph Avenue and north of Grand Avenue into KONO, exhibiting everything from photography and installations to glasswork and fiber arts. The first Friday of each month, upwards of 50,000 descend for **Art Murmur** (⊕ *oaklandartmurmur.org*), a late-night gallery event that has expanded into **First Friday** (⊕ *oaklandfirstfridays.org*), a festival of food trucks, street vendors, and live music along Telegraph Avenue.

Restaurants with a distinctly urban vibe make Uptown/KONO a dining destination every night of the week. Favorites include eclectic Japanese-inspired fare at **Hopscotch** (*1915 San Pablo Ave.*), stylish cuisine at art-deco **Flora** (*1900 Telegraph Ave.*), tasty tapas at trendy **Duende** (*468 19th*), just to name a few.

Toss in the bevy of bars and there's plenty within walking distance to keep you busy all evening: **Bar Three Fifty-Five** (*355 19th St.*), an upscale dive with iconic cocktails; the three-generation **Stork Club Oakland** (*2330 Telegraph Ave.*), a stalwart venue for new music and comedy; **Drake's Dealership** (*2325 Broadway*), with its spacious hipster-friendly beer garden; and **Somar** (*1727 Telegraph Ave.*), a bar, music lounge, and art gallery in one. ⊠ *Oakland* ⊹ *Telegraph Ave. and Broadway from 14th to 27th Sts.*

🍴 Restaurants

À Côté

$$ | MEDITERRANEAN | This Mediterranean hot spot is all about seasonal small plates, cozy tables, family-style eating, and excellent wine. Heavy wooden tables, intimate dining nooks, natural light, and a heated patio make this an ideal destination for couples, families, and the after-work crowd. **Known for:** Pernod mussels; exquisite small plates; global and regional wine list. $ *Average main: $19* ⊠ *5478 College Ave., at Taft Ave., Rockridge* ☎ *510/655–6469* ⊕ *acoterestaurant.com* ⊗ *No lunch.*

Calavera

$$$ | MODERN MEXICAN | This Oaxacan-inspired hot spot offers inventive and elevated plates in an industrial-chic space with lofty ceilings, warm wooden tables, exposed brick walls, and heated outdoor dining. Innovative cocktails like the salt-air margarita come from a beautiful bar with a library of more than 100 agaves. **Known for:** fresh ceviche; wide selection of tequilas and mezcal; carnitas tacos served in nixtamal heirloom corn tortillas. $ *Average main: $24* ⊠ *2337 Broadway, at 24th St., Uptown* ☎ *510/338–3273* ⊕ *calaveraoakland.com* ⊗ *Closed Mon.*

★ Commis

$$$$ | AMERICAN | A slender, unassuming storefront houses the first East Bay restaurant with a Michelin star (two of them, in fact). The room is minimalist and polished: nothing distracts from the artistry of chef James Syhabout, who creates a multicourse dining experience based on the season and his distinctive vision. **Known for:** inventive multicourse tasting menu; Michelin-winning execution; artful precision. [$] *Average main: $165* ✉ *3859 Piedmont Ave., at Rio Vista Ave., Piedmont* ☎ *510/653–3902* 🌐 *commisrestaurant.com* 🕒 *Closed Mon. and Tues. No lunch.*

Dyafa

$$$ | MIDDLE EASTERN | FAMILY | Reem Assil, one of the Bay Area's best chefs, brings Arabic heritage flavors to Jack London Square at Dyafa, where hot and cold *mezze* dishes such as Hummus Kawarma (served warm with lamb and cured lime) and *suhoon* dishes such as Musakhan (sumac-spiced chicken confit) are best shared family-style. Menus pair cocktails and wine flights with seasonally changing dishes for brunch, lunch, and dinner. **Known for:** freshly baked mana'eesh; house-made dips and pickles; Arabic-inspired cocktails. [$] *Average main: $30* ✉ *44 Webster St., Jack London Square* ☎ *510/250–9491* 🌐 *www.dyafaoakland.com.*

Grocery Café

$$ | BURMESE | Home-style Burmese food may be one of the best kept secrets in the Jack London Square area, where the bright, cozy Grocery Café serves up savory street food like *khauk swe thoke* (rainbow noodle salad) alongside traditional favorites like *mohinga* (fish chowder soup) and mango chutney pork stew. Vegan and veggie house special tofu and vegetarian hinga soup are among the locals' favorites on the menu. **Known for:** tea leaf salad; pork belly thoke; coconut rice. [$] *Average main: $19* ✉ *90 Franklin St., Jack London Square.*

Miss Ollie's

$$ | CARIBBEAN | FAMILY | Centrally located in the city's historic district, Miss Ollie's is a colorful Afro-Caribbean gem in Swan's Market that packs in mouthwatering flavors. Daily lunch specialties include juicy, crispy fried chicken and waffles, braised oxtails, and creole doughnuts, while hearty dinner fare offers jerk chicken, island-style slow-cooked pork, split-pea and okra fritters, and exceptional pea and pumpkin soups. **Known for:** fried chicken; sweet plantains; jerk shrimp. [$] *Average main: $17* ✉ *901 Washington St., Old Oakland* ☎ *510/285–6188* 🌐 *www.realmissolliesoakland.com.*

Pizzaiolo

$$$ | ITALIAN | FAMILY | Chez Panisse alum Charlie Hallowell helms the kitchen of this rustic-chic Oakland institution. Diners of all ages perch on wooden chairs with red-leather backs and nosh on farm-to-table Italian fare from a daily changing menu. **Known for:** seasonal wood-fired pizza; daily house-made breads; rustic California-Italian entrées. [$] *Average main: $23* ✉ *5008 Telegraph Ave., at 51st St., Temescal* ☎ *510/652–4888* 🌐 *www.pizzaiolooakland.com* 🕒 *No lunch.*

Plank

$$ | AMERICAN | FAMILY | Plank brings food and entertainment together in an expansive indoor-outdoor space with a waterfront view. Sip from more than 50 handcrafted local beers while playing bocce ball in the beer garden, lunch on Cuban sandwiches and Cajun mahi tacos during a bowling or billiards match, or try your hand at the arcade before biting into baby back ribs. **Known for:** fun outdoor space with fire pits; generous portions; games and activities. [$] *Average main: $17* ✉ *98 Broadway, Jack London Square* ☎ *510/817–0980* 🌐 *www.plankoakland.com.*

★ Shakewell

$$$ | MEDITERRANEAN | Two *Top Chef* vets opened this stylish Lakeshore restaurant, which serves creative and memorable Mediterranean small plates in a lively setting that features an open kitchen, wood-fired oven, communal tables, and snug seating. As the name implies, well-crafted cocktails are shaken (or stirred) and poured with panache. **Known for:** wood-oven paella; Spanish and Mediterranean small plates; unique cocktails. [$] *Average main: $26* ✉ *3407 Lakeshore Ave., near Mandana Blvd., Grand Lake* ☎ *510/251–0329* 🌐 *www.shakewelloakland.com* 🕒 *Closed Mon. No lunch Tues.*

Hotels

Best Western Plus Bayside Hotel
$$ | HOTEL | Sandwiched between the serene Oakland Estuary and an eight-lane freeway, this all-suites property has handsome accommodations with balconies or patios, many overlooking the water. **Pros:** attractive, budget-conscious choice; free parking; free shuttle to and from airport, Jack London Square, and downtown locations. **Cons:** few shops or restaurants in walking distance; freeway-side rooms can be loud; some rooms have no views or patios/balconies. [$] *Rooms from: $189* ✉ *1717 Embarcadero, off I–880, at 16th St. exit* ☎ *510/356–2450* 🌐 *www.baysidehoteloakland.com* 🛏 *81 rooms* 🍴 *Breakfast.*

★ Claremont Club & Spa
$$$$ | HOTEL | FAMILY | Straddling the Oakland–Berkeley border, this amenities-rich Fairmont property—which is more than 100 years old—beckons like a gleaming white castle in the hills. **Pros:** amazing spa; supervised child care; solid business amenities. **Cons:** parking is pricey; mandatory facilities charge; remote from shops or restaurants. [$] *Rooms from: $338* ✉ *41 Tunnel Rd., at Ashby and Domingo Aves.* ☎ *510/843–3000, 800/257–7544 reservations* 🌐 *www.fairmont.com/claremont-berkeley* 🛏 *276 rooms* 🍴 *No meals.*

Waterfront Hotel
$$$ | HOTEL | FAMILY | This thoroughly modern, pleasantly appointed Joie de Vivre property sits among the many high-caliber restaurants of Jack London Square. **Pros:** complimentary wine-and-cheese hour weekdays; lovely views; free shuttle service to downtown. **Cons:** passing trains can be noisy on city side; parking is pricey; limited amenities. [$] *Rooms from: $209* ✉ *10 Washington St., Jack London Square* ☎ *510/836–3800 front desk, 888/842–5333 reservations* 🌐 *www.jdvhotels.com* 🛏 *145 rooms* 🍴 *No meals.*

Nightlife

Back when rent was still relatively cheap, artists flocked to Oakland, giving rise to a cultural scene—visual arts, indie music, spoken word, film—that's still buzzing, especially in Uptown. Trendy new spaces pop up regularly and the beer-garden renaissance is already well established. Whether you're a self-proclaimed beer snob or just someone who enjoys a cold drink on a sunny day, there's something for everyone. Oakland's nightlife scene is less crowded and more intimate than what you'll find in San Francisco. Music is just about everywhere, though the most popular venues are downtown.

BARS

★ Café Van Kleef
BARS/PUBS | Long before Uptown got hot, the late Peter Van Kleef was serving stiff fresh-squeezed greyhounds, telling tales about his collection of pop-culture mementos, and booking live music at Café Van Kleef, a funky café-bar that crackles with creative energy—there's still live music every weekend. This local favorite still serves some of the stiffest drinks in town. ✉ *1621 Telegraph Ave., between 16th and 17th Sts., Uptown* ☎ *510/763–7711* 🌐 *cafevankleef.net.*

★ Heinold's First and Last Chance Saloon
BARS/PUBS | Arguably California's longest continuously active saloon since it opened in 1884, this watering hole, built from the hull of a flat-bottomed stern-wheeler, is the famous place where young Jack London got his start

as a writer. Historic photos, artifacts, and turn-of-the-20th-century curios hang from the crooked walls and ceilings, which have been atilt since the 1906 earthquake. Sit at the slanted bar for beers on tap and bottomless stories of Oakland history or take drinks outside and enjoy the marina view. ✉ 48 Webster St., Jack London Square ☎ 510/839–6761 ⊕ oaklandsaloon.com.

The Layover Music Bar and Lounge
BARS/PUBS | Bright, bold, and unabashedly bohemian, this hangout filled with recycled furniture is constantly evolving because everything is for sale, from the artwork to the pillows, rugs, and lamps. The busy bar serves up signature organic cocktails, and live entertainment includes comedy shows, storytelling, and local DJs. ✉ 1517 Franklin St., near 15th St., Uptown ☎ 510/834–1517 ⊕ www.oaklandlayover.com.

Make Westing
BARS/PUBS | Named for a short story by Oakland native Jack London, this sprawling industrial-chic space is always abuzz with hipsters playing bocce, the postwork crowd sipping old-fashioneds, or pretheater couples passing Mason jars of unexpected delectables like Cajun shrimp boil. The patio's your best bet for a conversation on a busy evening. ✉ 1741 Telegraph Ave., at 18th St., Uptown ☎ 510/251–1400 ⊕ makewesting.com.

BREWPUBS AND BEER GARDENS
Beer Revolution
BREWPUBS/BEER GARDENS | Hard-core beer geeks: with hundreds of bottled beers and 50 taps, this craft beer and bottle shop is for you. When you're done salivating over the extensive beer lists, grab a table on the patio. ✉ 464 3rd St., at Broadway, Jack London Square ☎ 510/452–2337 ⊕ www.beer-revolution.com.

Diving Dog Brewhouse
BARS/PUBS | The brewing scene is alive and hopping in Oakland, and among the dozens of stops on the Oakland Ale Trail, the Diving Dog is one craft locale where folks can brew their own alongside the masters (and bottle it in two-weeks' time). With more than 100 rare and unusual bottled beers and 30 flavors on tap, this modern space is an ideal place to improve your brew IQ and sample what's fresh before a show at the Fox or other Uptown venue. ✉ 1802 Telegraph Ave., Uptown ☎ 510/306–1914 ⊕ www.divingdogbrew.com.

★ Lost & Found
BREWPUBS/BEER GARDENS | FAMILY | The diversions on the spacious, succulent-filled patio include Ping-Pong, cornhole, and communal tables full of chilled-out locals. The beer selection ranges from blue collar to Belgian, and a seasonal menu focuses on internationally inspired small bites. ✉ 2040 Telegraph Ave., at 21st St., Uptown ☎ 510/763–2040 ⊕ www.lostandfound510.com ⏱ Closed Mon.

The Trappist
BREWPUBS/BEER GARDENS | Brick walls, dark wood, soft lighting, and a buzz of conversation set a warm and mellow tone inside this Old Oakland Victorian space that's been renovated to resemble a traditional Belgian pub. The setting (which includes two bars and a back patio) is definitely a draw, but the real stars are the artisan beers—more than 100 Belgian, Dutch, and North American brews. Light fare includes bar snacks and meat and cheese boards. ✉ 460 8th St., near Broadway, Old Oakland ☎ 510/238–8900 ⊕ www.thetrappist.com.

ROCK, POP, HIP-HOP, FOLK, AND BLUES CLUBS
Fox Theater
MUSIC CLUBS | This renovated 1928 theater, Oakland's favorite performance venue, is a remarkable feat of Mediterranean Moorish architecture and has seen the likes of Willie Nelson, Magnetic Fields, Rebelution, and B.B. King, to name a few. The venue boasts good sight lines, a state-of-the-art sound system,

brilliant acoustics, and a restaurant and bar, among other amenities. ⊠ *1807 Telegraph Ave., between 18th and 19th Sts., Uptown* ☎ *510/302–2250* ⊕ *thefox-oakland.com.*

★ Yoshi's

MUSIC CLUBS | Opened in 1972 as a sushi bar, Yoshi's has evolved into one of the area's best jazz and live music venues. The full Yoshi's experience includes traditional Japanese and Asian fusion cuisine in the adjacent restaurant. ⊠ *510 Embarcadero W, between Washington and Clay Sts., Jack London Square* ☎ *510/238–9200* ⊕ *www.yoshis.com.*

🛍 Shopping

Pop-up shops and stylish, locally focused stores are scattered throughout the funky alleys of Old Oakland, Uptown, Rockridge, and Temescal, while the streets around Lake Merritt and Grand Lake offer more modest boutiques.

Maison d'Etre

GIFTS/SOUVENIRS | Close to the Rockridge BART station, this store epitomizes the Rockridge neighborhood's funky-chic shopping scene. Look for high-end housewares and impulse buys like whimsical watches, imported fruit-tea blends, and funky slippers. ⊠ *5640 College Ave., at Keith Ave., Rockridge* ☎ *510/658–2801* ⊕ *maisondetre.com.*

★ Oaklandish

CLOTHING | This is the place for Oaktown swag. What started in 2000 as a public art project of local pride has become a celebrated brand around the bay, and a portion of the proceeds from hip Oaklandish brand T-shirts and accessories supports grassroots nonprofits committed to bettering the local community. It's good-looking stuff for a good cause. ⊠ *1444 Broadway, near 15th St., Uptown* ☎ *510/251–9500* ⊕ *oaklandish.com.*

Viscera

JEWELRY/ACCESSORIES | Urban planning meets fashion in this atypical men's and women's boutique. With 3D printing technology and custom-made items in house, the creators behind this Oakland flagship brand achieve artful, innovative functionality in their American-made clothing, gifts, and accessories. Ask about their in-house DIY workshops. ⊠ *1542 Broadway, Uptown* ☎ *510/500–5376* ⊕ *shopviscera.com* ⊗ *Closed Sun. and Mon. (open by appt. only).*

The Marin Headlands

Due west of the Golden Gate Bridge's northern end.

The term *Golden Gate* has become synonymous with the world-famous bridge, but it was first given to the narrow waterway that connects the Pacific and the San Francisco Bay. To the north of the Golden Gate Strait lies the Marin Headlands, part of the Golden Gate National Recreation Area (GGNRA), which boasts some of the area's most dramatic scenery.

GETTING HERE AND AROUND

Driving from San Francisco, head north on U.S. 101. Just after you cross the Golden Gate Bridge, take Exit 442 for Alexander Avenue. Keep left at the fork and follow signs for "San Francisco/U.S. 101 South", go through the tunnel under the freeway, and turn right up the hill. Muni bus 76X runs hourly from Sutter and Sansome streets to the Marin Headlands Visitor Center on weekends and major holidays only.

◉ Sights

★ Marin Headlands

NATIONAL/STATE PARK | FAMILY | The headlands stretch from the Golden Gate Bridge to Muir Beach. Photographers perch on the southern headlands for spectacular shots of the city and bridge. Equally remarkable are the views north along the coast and out to the ocean, where the Farallon Islands are visible on clear days.

The headlands' strategic position at the mouth of San Francisco Bay made them a logical site for military installations from 1890 through the Cold War. Today you can explore the crumbling concrete batteries where naval guns once protected the area. The headlands' main attractions are centered on Fts. Barry and Cronkhite, which are separated by Rodeo Lagoon and Rodeo Beach, a dark stretch of sand that attracts sand-castle builders and dog owners.

The visitor center is a worthwhile stop for its exhibits on the area's history and ecology, and kids enjoy the "please touch" educational sites and small play area inside. You can pick up guides to historic sites and wildlife, and get information about programming and guided walks. ⊠ Golden Gate National Recreation Area, Visitors Center, Fort Barry Chapel, Ft. Barry, Bldg. 948, Field and Bunker Rds., Fort Baker ☎ 415/331–1540 ⊕ www.nps.gov/goga/marin-headlands. htm ⊙ Closed Tues.

Point Bonita Lighthouse

LIGHTHOUSE | FAMILY | A restored beauty that still guides ships to safety with its original 1855 refractory lens, the lighthouse anchors the southern headlands. Half the fun of a visit is the steep half-mile walk from the parking area through a rock tunnel, across a suspension bridge, and down to the lighthouse. Signposts along the way detail the bravado of surfmen, as the early lifeguards were called, and the tenacity of the "wickies," the first keepers of the light. ■TIP→ Call about 90-minute full-moon tours. ⊠ End of Conzelman Rd., Ft. Barry, Bldg. 948, Sausalito ☎ 415/331–1540 ⊕ www.nps.gov/goga/pobo.htm ⊙ Closed Tues.–Sat.

Sausalito

2 miles north of Golden Gate Bridge.

Bougainvillea-covered hillsides and an expansive yacht harbor give Sausalito the feel of an Adriatic resort. The town sits on the northwestern edge of San Francisco Bay, where it's sheltered from the ocean by the Marin Headlands; the mostly mild weather here is perfect for strolling and outdoor dining. Nevertheless, morning fog and afternoon winds can roll over the hills without warning, funneling through the central part of Sausalito once known as Hurricane Gulch.

South of Bridgeway, which snakes between the bay and the hills, a waterside esplanade is lined with restaurants on piers that lure diners with good seafood and even better views. Stairs along the west side of Bridgeway and throughout town climb into wooded hillside neighborhoods filled with both rustic and opulent homes, while back on the northern portion of the shoreline, harbors shelter a community of more than 400 houseboats. As you amble along Bridgeway past shops and galleries, you'll notice the absence of basic services. Find them and more on Caledonia Street, which runs parallel to Bridgeway and inland a couple of blocks. While ferry-side shops flaunt kitschy souvenirs, smaller side streets and narrow alleyways offer eccentric jewelry and handmade crafts.

■TIP→ The ferry is the best way to get to Sausalito from San Francisco; you get more romance (and less traffic) and disembark in the heart of downtown.

Sausalito developed its bohemian flair in the 1950s and '60s, when creative types, including artist Jean Varda, poet Shel Silverstein, and madam Sally Stanford, established an artists' colony and a houseboat community here (this is Otis Redding's "Dock of the Bay"). Both the spirit of the artists and the neighborhood of floating homes persist. For a

Marin County

0 —— 5 mi

0 —— 5 km

close-up view of the quirky community, head north on Bridgeway, turn right on Gate Six Road, park where it dead-ends, and enter through the unlocked gates.

GETTING HERE AND AROUND

From San Francisco by car or bike, follow U.S. 101 north across the Golden Gate Bridge and take Exit 442 for Alexander Avenue, just past Vista Point; continue down the winding hill to the water to where the road becomes Bridgeway. Golden Gate Transit buses will drop you off in downtown Sausalito, and the ferries dock downtown as well. The center of town is flat, with plenty of sidewalks and bay views. It's a pleasure and a must to explore on foot.

ESSENTIALS

VISITOR INFORMATION Sausalito Chamber of Commerce. ⊠ *1913 Bridgeway* ☎ *415/331–7262* ⊕ *www.sausalito.org.*

◉ Sights

The Marine Mammal Center

COLLEGE | FAMILY | This hospital for distressed, sick, and injured marine animals is a leading center for ocean conservancy in the Bay Area and the largest rehabilitation center of its kind. Dedicated to pioneering education, rehabilitation, and research, the center is free and open daily to the public. Tour the facilities and see how elephant seals, sea lions, and pups are cared for and meet the scientists who care for them. Bonus: you'll see some of the best views of the Marin Headlands and San Francisco Bay along the way. ⊠ *2000 Bunker Rd., Fort Baker* ☎ *415/289–7325* ⊕ *www.marinemammalcenter.org* ⚓ *Guided tours $10.*

Sally Stanford Drinking Fountain

FOUNTAIN | There's an unusual historic landmark on the Sausalito Ferry Pier—a drinking fountain inscribed "Have a drink on Sally" in remembrance of Sally Stanford, the former San Francisco brothel madam who became Sausalito's mayor in the 1970s. Sassy Sally would have appreciated the fountain's eccentric attachment: a knee-level basin with the inscription "Have a drink on Leland," in memory of her beloved dog. ✉ *Sausalito Ferry Pier, Anchor St. at Humboldt St., off southwest corner of Gabrielson Park* 🌐 *www.oursausalito.com/sausalito-ferry-1.html.*

Sausalito Ice House Visitors Center and Museum

INFO CENTER | The local historical society operates this dual educational exhibit and visitor center, where you can get your bearings, learn some history, and find out what's happening in town. The artifacts of indigenous Miwok peoples and photography of turn-of-the-20th-century Sausalito are worth a peek. ✉ *780 Bridgeway, at Bay St.* ☎ *415/332–0505* 🌐 *www.sausalitohistoricalsociety.com* 🕒 *Closed Mon.*

Viña del Mar Plaza and Park

PLAZA | The landmark Plaza Viña del Mar, named for Sausalito's sister city in Chile, marks the center of town. Adjacent to the parking lot and ferry pier, the plaza is flanked by two 14-foot-tall elephant statues, which were created for the San Francisco Panama–Pacific International Exposition in 1915. It also features a picture-perfect fountain that's great for people-watching. ✉ *Bridgeway and El Portal St.* 🌐 *www.oursausalito.com/parks-in-sausalito/vina-del-mar-park.html.*

🍴 Restaurants

Bridgeway Cafe

$ | **CAFÉ** | The view's the thing at this diner-café on the main drag across the road from the bay. People line up on weekends for great traditional breakfast fare and fresh café lunch items. **Known for:** all-day breakfast fare, including eggs Benedict; Mediterranean-inspired hummus and kabobs; generous burgers. [$] *Average main: $14* ✉ *633 Bridgeway, at Princess St.* ☎ *415/332–3426* 🌐 *bridgewaycafe.com* 🕒 *No dinner.*

Fast Food Français

$$ | **BISTRO** | **FAMILY** | F3 puts a French twist on classic American fast food and dishes up some French nibbles, too, in this casual bistro. The same folks who started Le Garage branch out here with quick-bites like French onion burgers with cheddar fondue and double-cream mac and cheese among servings of Brussels sprouts chips, deviled eggs, and ratatouille. **Known for:** fries and frites; spacious locale; brunch. [$] *Average main: $17* ✉ *39 Caledonia St.* ☎ *415/887–9047* 🌐 *www.eatf3.com.*

★ Fish

$$ | **SEAFOOD** | **FAMILY** | Unsurprisingly, fish—specifically, fresh, sustainably caught fish—is the focus at this gleaming dockside fish house a mile north of downtown. Order at the counter—cash only—and then grab a seat by the floor-to-ceiling windows or at a picnic table on the pier, overlooking the yachts and fishing boats. **Known for:** taco plate; barbecued oysters; sustainably caught, fire-grilled entrées. [$] *Average main: $21* ✉ *350 Harbor Dr., at Gate 5 Rd., off Bridgeway* ☎ *415/331–3474* 🌐 *www.331fish.com* 💳 *No credit cards.*

★ Hamburgers Sausalito

$ | **BURGER** | Patrons queue up daily outside this tiny street-side shop for organic Angus beef patties that are made to order on a wheel-shaped grill. Brave the line (it moves fast) and take your food to the esplanade to enjoy fresh air and bayside views. **Known for:** legendary burgers; bay views; local following. [$] *Average main: $9* ✉ *737 Bridgeway, at Anchor St.* ☎ *415/332–9471* 🕒 *No dinner.*

Le Garage

$$$ | FRENCH | Brittany-born Olivier Souvestre serves traditional French bistro fare in a relaxed, bay-side setting that feels more sidewalk café than the converted garage that it is. The restaurant seats only 35 inside and 15 outside, so make reservations or arrive early. **Known for:** PEI mussels and house-cut fries; weekend brunch; balsamic-glazed Brussels sprouts. $ *Average main: $26* ⊠ *85 Liberty Ship Way, Suite 109* ☎ *415/332–5625* ⊕ *www. legaragebistrosausalito.com* ☞ *No reservations for weekend brunch.*

Poggio

$$$ | ITALIAN | A hillside dining destination, Poggio serves modern Tuscan-style comfort food in a handsome, old-world-inspired space whose charm spills onto the sidewalks. An extensive and ever-changing menu, with ingredients sourced from their own garden and local farms, include house-made capellini, grilled fish, and wood-fired pizzas. **Known for:** fresh local ingredients and traditional northern Italian dishes; rotisserie chicken with property-grown organic herbs and vegetables; lobster-roe pasta. $ *Average main: $30* ⊠ *777 Bridgeway, at Bay St.* ☎ *415/332–7771* ⊕ *www.poggiotrattoria.com.*

Sausalito Seahorse

$$$ | ITALIAN | Live music and dancing served alongside Tuscan seafood and pasta specialties make the Seahorse one of Sausalito's most spirited supper clubs. Sample an abundant antipasti menu and homemade focaccia on outdoor patios or enjoy the band inside with traditional seafood stew or lasagna classica. **Known for:** happy hour; Sunday salsa dancing; fun atmosphere. $ *Average main: $24* ⊠ *305 Harbor Dr.* ☎ *415/331–2899* ⊕ *www. sausalitoseahorse.com.*

★ Sushi Ran

$$$ | JAPANESE | Sushi aficionados swear that this tiny, stylish restaurant—in business for more than three decades—is the Bay Area's best option for raw fish, but don't overlook the excellent Pacific Rim fusions, a melding of Japanese ingredients and French cooking techniques. Book in advance or expect a wait, which you can soften by sipping one of the bar's 30 by-the-glass sakes. **Known for:** fish imported from Tokyo's famous Tsukiji market; local miso-glazed black cod; outstanding sake and wine list. $ *Average main: $30* ⊠ *107 Caledonia St., at Pine St.* ☎ *415/332–3620* ⊕ *www.sushiran.com* ☉ *No lunch weekends.*

Taste of Rome

$$ | ITALIAN | FAMILY | From early-morning espresso and frittatas to late-night wine and marsalas, there's something just right at the Taste of Rome any time of day. With spacious indoor and outdoor seating and a bountiful menu of fresh and homemade Italian specialties, it's easy to see why this family-owned café is beloved among locals. **Known for:** coffee drinks; desserts; house-made pasta. $ *Average main: $16* ⊠ *1000 Bridgeway* ☎ *415/332–7660* ⊕ *tasteofrome.co.*

Venice Gourmet Deli & Pizza

$ | ITALIAN | The Italian deli sandwiches, pizzas made daily, and a shop filled with gourmet delectables, wines, kitchenware, and local flavor here have enticed taste buds along picturesque Bridgeway for more than 50 years. Enjoy a meal alfresco at the sidewalk tables, or take a picnic a few steps away to Yee Toch Chee Park for a waterside bite. **Known for:** picnic-perfect sandwiches; service and quality from family owners; plentiful selections. $ *Average main: $13* ⊠ *625 Bridgeway* ☎ *415/332–3544* ⊕ *www. venicegourmet.com.*

 Hotels

Hotel Sausalito

$$$ | HOTEL | Handcrafted furniture and tasteful original art and reproductions give this Mission Revival–style inn the feel of a small European hotel. **Pros:** some rooms have harbor or park views; central location; vouchers to nearby Cafe Tutti provided. **Cons:** no room service; most rooms are small; daily public parking fee. $ *Rooms from: $240* ✉ *16 El Portal, at Bridgeway* ☎ *415/332–0700* ⊕ *www.hotelsausalito.com* ⌁ *16 rooms* ⑩ *No meals.*

The Inn Above Tide

$$$$ | **B&B/INN** | The balconies at the Inn Above Tide literally hang over the water, and each of its rooms has a "perfect 10" view that takes in wild Angel Island as well as the city lights across the bay. **Pros:** generous continental breakfast; free bikes to tour the area; in-room spa services available. **Cons:** costly daily parking; some rooms are on the small side; ferry-side rooms can be noisy. $ *Rooms from: $415* ✉ *30 El Portal* ☎ *415/332–9535, 800/893–8433* ⊕ *www.innabovetide.com* ⌁ *33 rooms* ⑩ *Breakfast.*

🛍 Shopping

Studio 333 Downtown

ART GALLERIES | There's always something new, interesting, and eye-catching on display at this storefront, including curated collections of handcrafted gifts, housewares, jewelry, and accessories by more than 40 Bay Area artisans. Visit the original art gallery and event space on 333 Caledonia for more delightful creations. ✉ *803 Bridgeway* ☎ *415/332–5483* ⊕ *www.studio333downtown.com.*

Tiburon

7 miles north of Sausalito, 11 miles north of Golden Gate Bridge.

On a peninsula that was named Punta de Tiburon (Shark Point) by 18th-century Spanish explorers, this beautiful Marin County community retains the feel of a village—it's more low-key than

Sausalito—despite the encroachment of commercial establishments from the downtown area. The harbor faces Angel Island across Raccoon Strait, and San Francisco is directly south across the bay—which means the views from the decks of harbor restaurants are major attractions. Since 1884, when the San Francisco and North Pacific Railroad relocated their ferry terminal facilities to the harbor town, Tiburon has centered on the waterfront. ■TIP➜ **The ferry is the most relaxing (and fastest) way to get here, and allows you to skip traffic and parking problems.**

GETTING HERE AND AROUND

Blue & Gold Fleet ferries travel between San Francisco and Tiburon daily. By car, head north from San Francisco on U.S. 101 and get off at CA 131/Tiburon Boulevard/East Blithedale Avenue (Exit 447). Turn right onto Tiburon Boulevard and drive just over 4 miles to downtown. Golden Gate Transit serves downtown Tiburon from San Francisco; watch for changes during evening rush hour. Tiburon's Main Street is made for wandering, as are the footpaths that frame the water's edge.

ESSENTIALS

VISITOR INFORMATION Tiburon. ✉ *Town Hall, 1505 Tiburon Blvd.* ☎ *415/435–7373* ⊕ *www.destinationtiburon.org.*

👁 Sights

Angel Island State Park

NATIONAL/STATE PARK | **FAMILY** | One of the bay's best secrets in plain sight, its largest natural island was once a favored camp for Coast Miwok (later for the U.S. Army to protect San Francisco Bay), and is now a natural wildlife habitat and historic park favored by bikers, hikers, and picnickers. Thirteen miles of roads and trails from the perimeter up to Mt. Livermore (788 feet) offer magnificent panoramic views. The 12-minute ferry ride to Angel Island from Tiburon ($15 round-trip) includes the cost of the park. ■ **TIP→ To see the sites by bike, rent on the island (angelisland.com/bicycles) or in Tiburon at Pedego Electric Bikes (10 Main Street).** ✉ *Angel Island* ✥ *Accessible only by public ferry or private boat* ☎ *415/435–1915* 🌐 *www.parks.ca.gov.*

Ark Row

STORE/MALL | FAMILY | The second block of Main Street is known as historic Ark Row and has a tree-shaded walk lined with antiques, restaurants, and specialty stores. The quaint stretch gets its name from the 19th-century ark houseboats that floated in Belvedere Cove before being beached and transformed into stores. ■ **TIP→ If you're curious about architectural history, the Tiburon Heritage & Arts Commission has a self-guided walking-tour map, available online and at local businesses.** ✉ *Ark Row, Main St., south of Juanita La.* 🌐 *tiburonheritageandarts.org.*

Old St. Hilary's Landmark and John Thomas Howell Wildflower Preserve

NATURE PRESERVE | The architectural centerpiece of this attraction is a stark-white 1888 Carpenter Gothic church that overlooks the town and the bay from its hillside perch. Surrounding the church, which was dedicated as a historical monument in 1959, is a wildflower preserve that's spectacular in May and June, when the rare Tiburon paintbrush or black jewelflower blooms. Expect a steep walk uphill to reach the preserve. The Landmarks Society will arrange guided tours by appointment. ■ **TIP→ The hiking trails behind the landmark wind up to a peak that has views of the entire Bay Area.** ✉ *201 Esperanza St., off Mar West St. or Beach Rd.* ☎ *415/435–1853* 🌐 *landmarkssociety.com/landmarks/st-hilarys/* 🕒 *Church closed Mon.–Sat. and Nov.–Mar.*

Railroad and Ferry Depot Museum

HISTORIC SITE | A short waterfront walk from the ferry landing, this free museum in Shoreline Park is a well-preserved time capsule of the city's industrial history, complete with working trains. The landmark building has a detailed scale model of Tiburon and its 43-acre rail yard at the turn of the 20th century when the city served as a major railroad and ferry hub for the San Francisco Bay. The Depot House Museum on the second floor showcases a restoration of the stationmaster's living quarters. ✉ *1920 Paradise Dr.* ☎ *415/435–1853* 🌐 *landmarkssociety.com/landmarks/railroad-ferry-museum* 🕒 *Closed Nov.–Mar; Mon. and Tues.*

🍴 Restaurants

Caffe Acri

$ | CAFÉ | This Italian espresso bar and café at the end of the Tiburon Ferry dock is a sweet spot to enjoy a leisurely breakfast or lunch with a cup of locally roasted coffee while waiting for the ferry. In addition to daily-baked pastries and desserts, the menu ranges from omelets and toasted sandwiches to smoothies and farm-fresh salads. **Known for:** desserts; espresso drinks; soups and paninis. [$] *Average main: $9* ✉ *1 Main St.* ☎ *415/435–8515* 🌐 *www.caffeacri.com.*

Luna Blu

$$$ | SICILIAN | Friendly, informative staff serve Sicilian-inspired seafood in this lively sliver of an Italian restaurant just a stone's throw from the ferry. Take a seat on the heated patio overlooking the bay, or cozy up with friends on one of the high-sided booths near the bar. **Known for:** sustainably caught seafood and local, organic ingredients; homemade pastas; rock crab bisque. [$] *Average main: $26* ✉ *35 Main St.* ☎ *415/789–5844* 🌐 *lunablurestaurant.com* 🕒 *Closed Tues. No lunch weekdays.*

New Morning Cafe

$ | AMERICAN | FAMILY | Omelets, scrambles, and pancakes are served all day long at this homey triangular bay-side café with sunny outdoor seating. If you're past morning treats, this locals' go-to brunch spot offers many soups, salads, and sandwiches, best enjoyed at picnic tables. **Known for:** hearty American breakfast fare; fresh-squeezed orange juice; sour cream waffles. $ *Average main: $14* ⊠ *1696 Tiburon Blvd., near Juanita La.* 🕾 *415/435–4315* ⊗ *No dinner.*

Salt & Pepper

$$ | AMERICAN | FAMILY | This bright and welcoming American bistro on Ark Row is known for its seafood starters and salads (think: oyster poppers, crab stacks, and steamers) as well as shareable dishes and burgers, chops, and ribs. The airy, rustic space has a pleasant café-like atmosphere that makes it easy to stay and consider the organic ice cream sundaes and banana splits for dessert. **Known for:** clam chowder; kabocha squash and vegetable curry; Mongolian pork chops. $ *Average main: $21* ⊠ *38 Main St.* 🕾 *415/435–3594* ⊕ *www. saltandpeppertiburon.com.*

Sam's Anchor Cafe

$$$ | AMERICAN | Open since 1920, this casual dockside restaurant, rife with plastic chairs and blue-checked oilcloths, is the town's most famous eatery. Most people flock to the deck for beers, views, sunsets, and exceptionally tasty seafood. **Known for:** raw bar; pink lemonade and margarita "bowls"; hurricane fries. $ *Average main: $25* ⊠ *27 Main St.* 🕾 *415/435–4527* ⊕ *www. samscafe.com.*

Servino Ristorante

$$ | SOUTHERN ITALIAN | FAMILY | This family-owned eatery specializes in southern Italian recipes including lobster agnolotti, seafood stew, pork sausage fondue, and pizza made with local, sustainable ingredients. With spacious indoor and outdoor seating and waterfront views, the scene is cozy and welcoming even in cooler weather, when there's heated patio dining. **Known for:** alfresco dining; wines from Italy and California; black truffle raviolacci. $ *Average main: $22* ⊠ *9 Main St.* 🕾 *415/435–2676* ⊕ *www. servino.com.*

Waypoint Pizza

$ | PIZZA | FAMILY | A nautical theme and a tasty "between the sheets" pizza-style sandwich are signatures of this creative pizzeria, which is housed in the 19th-century landmark building that was once home to the Pioneer Boat House and is now owned by two sailing aficionados. Booths are brightened with blue-checked tablecloths, and a playful air is added by indoor deck chairs and a picnic table complete with umbrella. **Known for:** pizza-style sandwiches; wild shrimp pesto pizza; soft-serve organic ice cream. $ *Average main: $13* ⊠ *15 Main St.* 🕾 *415/435–3440* ⊕ *www.waypointpizza. com* ⊗ *Closed Tues.*

🛏 Hotels

Waters Edge Hotel

$$$$ | B&B/INN | Checking into this stylish downtown hotel feels like tucking away into an inviting retreat by the water—the views are stunning and the lighting is perfect. **Pros:** complimentary wine and cheese for guests every evening; restaurants/sights are steps away; free bike rentals for guests. **Cons:** downstairs rooms lack privacy and balconies; paid self-parking; fitness center is off-site. $ *Rooms from: $299* ⊠ *25 Main St., off Tiburon Blvd.* 🕾 *415/789–5999, 877/789–5999* ⊕ *www.marinhotels.com* ⤏ *23 rooms* ⦿ *Breakfast.*

Mill Valley

2 miles north of Sausalito, 4 miles north of Golden Gate Bridge.

Chic and woodsy Mill Valley has a dual personality. Here, as elsewhere in the county, the foundation is a superb natural setting. Virtually surrounded by parkland, the town lies at the base of Mt. Tamalpais and contains dense redwood groves traversed by countless creeks. But this is no lumber camp. Smart restaurants and chichi boutiques line streets that have been roamed by more rock stars than one might suspect.

The rustic village flavor isn't a modern conceit, but a holdover from the town's early days as a center for the lumber industry. In 1896, the Mt. Tamalpais Scenic Railroad—dubbed "The Crookedest Railroad in the World" because of its curvy tracks—began transporting visitors from Mill Valley to the top of Mt. Tam and down to Muir Woods, and the town soon became a vacation retreat for city slickers. The trains stopped running in the 1930s, as cars became more popular, but the old railway depot still serves as the center of town: the 1929 building has been transformed into the popular Depot Bookstore & Cafe, at 87 Throckmorton Avenue.

The small downtown area has the constant bustle of a leisure community; even at noon on a Tuesday, people are out shopping for fancy cookware, eco-friendly home furnishings, and boutique clothing.

GETTING HERE AND AROUND
By car from San Francisco, head north on U.S. 101 and get off at CA 131/Tiburon Boulevard/East Blithedale Avenue (Exit 447). Turn left onto East Blithedale Avenue and continue west to Throckmorton Avenue; turn left to reach Depot Plaza, then park. Golden Gate Transit buses serve Mill Valley from San Francisco. Once here, explore the town on foot.

ESSENTIALS
VISITOR INFORMATION Mill Valley Chamber of Commerce and Visitor Center. ⊠ 85 Throckmorton Ave. ☎ 415/388–9700 ⊕ www.millvalley.org.

Sights

Lytton Square
PLAZA | FAMILY | Mill Valley locals congregate on weekends to socialize in the coffeehouses and cafés near the town's central square, but it bustles most of

---

Off the Beaten Path

Marin County Civic Center. A wonder of arches, circles, and skylights just 10 miles north of Mill Valley, the Civic Center was Frank Lloyd Wright's largest public project and has been designated a national and state historic landmark, as well as a UNESCO World Heritage Site. One-hour docent-led tours leave from the café on the second floor Wednesday and Friday morning at 10:30. ⊠ 3501 Civic Center Dr., off N. San Pedro Rd., San Rafael ☎ 415/473–3762 visitor services office ⊕ www.marincounty.org/depts/cu/tours 🎟 Free admission; $10 tour fee.

---

the day. The Mill Valley Book Depot and Cafe at the hub of it all is the place to grab a coffee and sweet treat while reading or playing a game of chess. Shops, restaurants, and cultural venues line the nearby streets. ⊠ Miller and Throckmorton Aves.

★ Mill Valley Lumber Yard
HISTORIC SITE | FAMILY | The Mill Valley Lumber Yard, once a vital center of the region's logging industry, is now a vibrant micro village of craftsfolk, bakers, makers, and their boutiques and restaurants. The preserved brick-red historic structures are hard to miss along Miller Avenue, and with plenty of parking in the area, plus picnic tables and outdoor space, it's well worth a visit. ⊠ 129 Miller Ave. ⊕ millvalleylumberyard.com.

Old Mill Park
CITY PARK | FAMILY | To see one of the numerous outdoor oases that make Mill Valley so appealing, follow Throckmorton Avenue a quarter mile west from Lytton Square to Old Mill Park, a shady patch of redwoods that shelters a playground

and reconstructed sawmill and hosts September's annual Mill Valley Arts Festival. From the park, Cascade Way winds its way past creek-side homes to the trailheads of several forest paths. ⊠ *Throckmorton Ave. and Cascade Dr.* ⊕ *www.millvalleyrecreation.org.*

 **Restaurants**

Avatar's Restaurant
$ | INDIAN | The lines can get long at this hole-in-the-wall kitchen, where Indian curries are served burrito style while you wait (note: it's cash only). Punjabi burritos or rice plates come with savory lamb, chicken, fish, vegetarian, and vegan ingredients flavored with seasonal fruit chutneys, tamarind sauce, and aromatic blends. **Known for:** curried pumpkin; smoked eggplant; lassi drinks. Ⓢ *Average main: $8* ⊠ *15 Madrona St.* ☎ *415/381–8293* ⊕ *avatars-restaurant-mill-valley. sites.tablehero.com* ▭ *No credit cards.*

Boo Koo
$ | ASIAN | Southeast Asian street food with a local flair is fired up in this hip and modern street café, where there's outdoor seating and a 10-tap bar. Summer rolls, satays, and skewers complement pho and wok specialties. **Known for:** green curry noodles; mint salad; Asian brussels sprouts. Ⓢ *Average main: $11* ⊠ *25 Miller Ave.* ☎ *415/888–8303* ⊕ *eatbookoo.com.*

Buckeye Roadhouse
$$$$ | AMERICAN | House-smoked meats and fish, grilled steaks, classic salads, and decadent desserts bring locals and visitors back again and again to this 1937 lodge-style roadhouse. Enjoy a Marin martini at the cozy mahogany bar or sip local wine beside the river-rock fireplace. **Known for:** oysters bingo; chili-lime "brick" chicken; ribs and chops. Ⓢ *Average main: $35* ⊠ *15 Shoreline Hwy., off U.S. 101* ☎ *415/331–2600* ⊕ *www. buckeyeroadhouse.com.*

Bungalow 44
$$$ | AMERICAN | An open, well-lit space with booths and countertop seating from which diners can watch the cooks in action sets the scene at this lively eatery, which serves contemporary Californian cuisine and inventive cocktails. A 2018 remodel revitalized the decor as well as the menu, with its focus on locally sourced veggies and seafood. **Known for:** $1 oyster daily happy hour; tuna carpaccio; kickin' fried chicken. Ⓢ *Average main: $25* ⊠ *44 E. Blithedale Ave., at Sunnyside Ave.* ☎ *415/381–2500* ⊕ *www.bungalow44.com* ⊙ *No lunch.*

The Dipsea Cafe
$$ | AMERICAN | FAMILY | Named after the 7-mile trail that winds from Mill Valley to Stinson Beach, this bustling diner serves hearty breakfast favorites, sandwiches, salads, and Mediterranean-inspired lunch plates. Locals crowd the checkered tables, bright yellow booths, and a shiny wooden counter and stools. **Known for:** weekend brunches; huevos rancheros; Mediterranean gyros, calamari, and souvlaki. Ⓢ *Average main: $18* ⊠ *200 Shoreline Hwy.* ☎ *415/381–0298* ⊕ *www. dipseacafe.com* ⊙ *No dinner.*

Equator Coffees and Teas
$ | CAFÉ | This is the prime spot for a pick-me-up (and people-watching) over a picturesque view of downtown Mill Valley and Mt. Tam. The owners are as serious about coffee as they are about social responsibility, from their fair-chain single-origin beans and organic loose teas down to locally recycled metal decor. **Known for:** espresso and cappuccino drinks; breakfast sandwiches; strawberry and chocolate waffles. Ⓢ *Average main: $9* ⊠ *2 Miller Ave.* ☎ *415/383–1651* ⊕ *www.equatorcoffees.com/pages/ mill-valley-1.*

La Ginestra
$$ | ITALIAN | FAMILY | In business since 1964, La Ginestra—named for the flowers that grow on Mt. Vesuvius, the owners' homeland—is a Mill Valley

institution renowned for its no-pretense, family-style Italian meals and impressive wine list. The Sorrento Bar, off the dining room, serves up a delectable array of bar bites, pizzas, and sweets to enjoy while sipping wines and cocktails inspired by the Aversa's family's homeland. **Known for:** handmade pasta and gnocchi; ravioli; daily fish and small plates. $ *Average main: $19* ⊠ *127 Throckmorton Ave., off Miller Ave.* ☎ *415/388–0224* ⊕ *www.laginestramv.com* ⊗ *Closed Mon. No lunch.*

Piazza D'Angelo

$$ | **ITALIAN | FAMILY** | In the heart of downtown, busy D'Angelo's is known for its authentic and fresh pastas; there even are gluten-free options. Another draw is the scene, especially in the lounge area, which hosts a lively cocktail hour that serves food until 10 or 11 pm—late for Mill Valley. **Known for:** fresh seafood; homemade pasta; tiramisu. $ *Average main: $20* ⊠ *22 Miller Ave., off Throckmorton* ☎ *415/388–2000* ⊕ *www.piazzadangelo.com.*

★ Pizza Molina

$$ | **CONTEMPORARY** | A cozy and clean aesthetic, a convivial vibe, and impeccable pizza from a wood-fired oven are central to this neighborhood spot. Chef Justin Bruckert spent months developing the perfect dough with just the right texture, pliability, and flavor as a base for the freshest seasonal ingredients. **Known for:** wood-fired pizzas; house-made meatballs; local beers on tap. $ *Average main: $16* ⊠ *17 Madrona St., between Lovell and Throckmorton Aves.* ☎ *415/383–4200* ⊕ *www.pizzamolina.com* ⊗ *No lunch.*

Playa

$$ | **MODERN MEXICAN** | Modern Mexican farm-to-table creations and inspired cocktails are the focus of this festive indoor-outdoor space that's popular for its fire pit, made-to-order masa station, and happy hour. An open kitchen serves up locally sourced, organic, and sustainable dishes like ceviche and flautas, grilled octopus tacos, and braised pork tortas. **Known for:** taco Tuesdays; rare tequilas and mezcals; moles and salsas. $ *Average main: $18* ⊠ *41 Throckmorton Ave.* ☎ *415/384–8871* ⊕ *www.playamv.com.*

Vasco

$$ | **ITALIAN** | This lovely corner restaurant, with its wood-fired pizza, wine bar, and live music in the evening, has serious neighborhood charm. Authentic Italian specialties include chicken marsala and calamari steak. **Known for:** great atmosphere; tiramisu; pizzas. $ *Average main: $16* ⊠ *106 Throckmorton Ave.* ☎ *415/381–3343* ⊕ *vascorestaurantmillvalley.com.*

🛏 Hotels

Acqua Hotel

$$$ | **HOTEL** | Astride Richardson Bay, this stylish boutique hotel has modern, elegant rooms decorated in soft Zen-like color schemes. **Pros:** evening wine service; free parking and Wi-Fi; hearty breakfast buffet. **Cons:** next to freeway; traffic audible in rooms facing east; not much within walking distance. $ *Rooms from: $229* ⊠ *555 Redwood Hwy., off U.S. 101* ☎ *415/388–9353* ⊕ *www.marinhotels.com* ⤳ *49 rooms* ⦿ *Breakfast.*

Mill Valley Inn

$$$$ | **B&B/INN** | The only hotel in downtown Mill Valley is comprised of one of the area's first homes, the Creek House, with smart-looking Victorian rooms, and two small cottages tucked in a grove beyond a creek. **Pros:** steps from local shops and restaurants; some rooms have balconies, soaking tubs, and fireplaces; free mountain bikes. **Cons:** limited room service; dark in winter because of surrounding trees; some rooms are not accessible via elevator. $ *Rooms from: $369* ⊠ *165 Throckmorton Ave., near Miller Ave.* ☎ *415/389–6608, 855/334–7946* ⊕ *www.marinhotels.com* ⤳ *25 rooms* ⦿ *Breakfast.*

Did You Know?

The gorgeous old-growth redwood trees in Muir Woods are often enveloped in fog, which provides the moisture to help them survive the dry summers.

Mountain Home Inn

$$$ | **B&B/INN** | Abutting 40,000 acres of state and national parks, this airy wooden inn sits on the skirt of Mt. Tamalpais, where you can follow hiking trails all the way to Stinson Beach. **Pros:** amazing terrace and views; peaceful, remote setting; cooked-to-order breakfast. **Cons:** nearest town is a 12-minute drive away; restaurant can get crowded on sunny weekend days; no on-site fitness option. [$] *Rooms from: $210* ✉ *810 Panoramic Hwy., at Edgewood Ave.* ☎ *415/381–9000* 🌐 *www.mtnhomeinn.com* 🛏 *10 rooms* 🍴 *Breakfast.*

Nightlife

BREWPUS AND BEER GARDENS

Mill Valley Beerworks

BREWPUBS/BEER GARDENS | A great place to rest your feet after shopping or hiking, this neighborhood taproom serves a rotating selection of local and imported drafts and bottles alongside choice house brews on tap. A simple menu of small plates includes locally sourced cheeses and enticing salads. Weekend brunches include fresh recipes like strawberry pepper scones or polenta with roasted beets along with Verve coffee. ✉ *173 Throckmorton Ave.* ☎ *415/888–8218* 🌐 *millvalleybeerworks.com.*

MUSIC VENUES

Sweetwater Music Hall

MUSIC CLUBS | With the help of part-owner Bob Weir of the Grateful Dead, this renowned nightclub and café reopened in a historic Masonic Hall in 2012. Famous as well as up-and-coming bands play on most nights, and local stars such as Bonnie Raitt and Huey Lewis have been known to stop in for a pickup session. ✉ *19 Corte Madera Ave., between Throckmorton and Lovell Aves.* ☎ *415/388–3850, 877/987–6487 tickets* 🌐 *www.sweetwatermusichall.com.*

Performing Arts

★ **Throckmorton Theatre**

ART GALLERIES—ARTS | The restored cinema and vaudeville house in Mill Valley is a vibrant cultural hub in the region and is known for fostering exceptional arts and education. The darling playhouse seats upwards of 260 and features live theater, Tuesday night comedy, and concerts. Two smaller street-side halls, the Tivoli and Crescendo feature free classical concerts on Wednesdays, along with Sunday evening sessions, jazz performances, and new art exhibits every month. ✉ *142 Throckmorton Ave.* ☎ *415/383–9611* 🌐 *throckmortontheatre.org.*

Shopping

Mill Valley Market

FOOD/CANDY | **FAMILY** | This family-owned market has been the go-to stop for specialty foods, grocery, deli, and hot food since 1929. Known for their notable beer and wine selection alongside a variety of local and organic produce and healthy grab-and-go foods, this is an ideal stop to prepare for a picnic or to seek out gourmet gifts like imported chocolates and 100-year-old balsamic vinegars. ✉ *12 Corte Madera Ave.* ☎ *415/388–3222* 🌐 *millvalleymarket.com.*

Muir Woods National Monument

12 miles northwest of the Golden Gate Bridge.

Climbing hundreds of feet into the sky, *Sequoia sempervirens* are the tallest living things on Earth—some are more than 1,800 years old. One of the last remaining old-growth stands of these redwood behemoths, Muir Woods is nature's cathedral: imposing, awe-inspiring, reverence-inducing, and not to be missed.

Though much of California's 2 million acres of redwood forest were lost to the logging industry, this area was saved from destruction by William and Elizabeth Kent, who purchased the land in 1905, and later gifted it to the federal government. Theodore Roosevelt declared the space a national monument in 1908 and Kent named it after naturalist John Muir, whose environmental campaigns helped establish the national park system.

GETTING HERE AND AROUND

If you drive to Muir Woods on a weekend or during peak season, expect to find epic traffic jams around the tiny parking areas and adjacent roads. Do yourself a favor and take a shuttle if you can. Reservations are required for parking, so plan ahead. Marin Transit's Route 66 Muir Woods shuttle ($3 round-trip ⊕ www.marintransit.org) provides weekend and seasonal transport from the Sausalito ferry landing, as well as Marin City, on a seasonal schedule. Private bus tours run year-round. To drive directly from San Francisco by car, take U.S. 101 north across the Golden Gate Bridge to Exit 445B for Mill Valley/Stinson Beach, then follow signs for Highway 1 north and Muir Woods.

⊙ Sights

★ Muir Woods National Monument

NATIONAL/STATE PARK | FAMILY | Nothing gives perspective like walking among old-growth redwoods. The nearly 560 acres of Muir Woods National Monument contain some of the most majestic redwoods in the world—some more than 250 feet tall.

Part of the Golden Gate National Recreation Area, Muir Woods is a pedestrian's park. The popular 2-mile main trail begins at the park headquarters and provides easy access to streams, ferns, azaleas, and redwood groves. Summer weekends can prove busy, so for a

little serenity, consider taking a more challenging route, such as the **Dipsea Trail,** which climbs west from the forest floor to soothing views of the ocean and the Golden Gate Bridge. For a complete list of trails, which vary in difficulty and distance, check with rangers.

Picnicking and camping aren't allowed, and neither are pets. Crowds can be large, especially from May through October, so try to come early in the morning or late in the afternoon. The **Muir Woods Visitor Center** has books and exhibits about redwood trees and the woods' history as well as the latest info on trail conditions; the **Muir Woods Trading Company** serves hot food, organic pastries, and other tasty snacks, and the gift shop offers plenty of souvenirs. ■TIP➔ **Muir Woods has no cell service or Wi-Fi, so plan directions and communication ahead of time.** ✉ 1 Muir Woods Rd., off Panoramic Hwy., Mill Valley ☎ 415/561–2850 park information, 511 Marin transit ⊕ www.nps.gov/muwo ✍ $15; free on government holidays.

Mt. Tamalpais State Park

13 miles northwest of Golden Gate Bridge.

The view of Mt. Tamalpais from all around the bay can be a beauty, but that's nothing compared to the views from the mountain, which range from jaw-dropping to spectacular and take in San Francisco, the East Bay, the coast, and beyond—on a clear day, all the way to the Farallon Islands, 25 miles away.

GETTING HERE AND AROUND

By car, take U.S. 101 north across the Golden Gate Bridge and Exit 445B for Mill Valley/Stinson Beach. Continue north on Highway 1, which will turn into Panoramic Highway. By bus, take Golden Gate Transit to Marin City; in Marin City transfer to the West Marin Stagecoach, Route 61, and get off at

Pantoll Ranger Station (📞 415/226–0855 🌐 www.marintransit.org/stage.html). Once here, the only way to explore is on foot or by bike.

👁 Sights

★ Mt. Tamalpais State Park

NATIONAL/STATE PARK | FAMILY | Although the summit of Mt. Tamalpais is only 2,571 feet high, the mountain rises practically from sea level, dominating the topography of Marin County. Adjacent to Muir Woods National Monument, Mt. Tamalpais State Park affords views of the entire Bay Area and the Pacific Ocean to the west. The name for the sacred mount comes from the Coast Miwok tribe and means "west hill," though some have tied it to a folktale about the "sleeping maiden" in the mountain's profile. For years the 6,300-acre park has been a favorite destination for hikers. There are more than 200 miles of trails, some rugged but many developed for easy walking through meadows, grasslands, and forests and along creeks. Mt. Tam, as it's called by locals, is also the birthplace (in the 1970s) of mountain biking, and today many spandex-clad bikers whiz down the park's winding roads.

The park's major thoroughfare, Panoramic Highway, snakes its way up from U.S. 101 to the **Pantoll Ranger Station** and then drops down to the town of Stinson Beach. Pantoll Road branches off the highway at the station, connecting up with Ridgecrest Boulevard. Along these roads are numerous parking areas, picnic spots, scenic overlooks, and trailheads. Parking is free along the roadside, but there's an $8 fee (cash or check only) to park at the ranger station and additional charges for walk-in campsites and group use.

The **Mountain Theater,** also known as the Cushing Memorial Amphitheatre, is a natural 4,000-seat amphitheater that was reconstructed with stone by the Civilian Conservation Corps in the 1930s. It has showcased summer "Mountain Plays" since 1913.

The **Rock Spring Trail** starts at the Mountain Theater and gently climbs for 1½ miles to the **West Point Inn,** which was once a stop on the Mt. Tam railroad route. Relax at a picnic table and stock up on water before forging ahead, via Old Railroad Grade Fire Road and the Miller Trail, to Mt. Tam's Middle Peak, which is another 1½–2 miles depending on route.

Starting from the Pantoll Ranger Station, the precipitous **Steep Ravine Trail** brings you past stands of coastal redwoods and, in the springtime, small waterfalls. Take the connecting **Dipsea Trail** to reach the town of Stinson Beach and its swath of golden sand. ■ TIP→ If you're too weary to make the 3½-mile trek back up, Marin Transit Bus 61 takes you from Stinson Beach back to the ranger station. ✉ Pantoll Ranger Station, 3801 Panoramic Hwy., at Pantoll Rd. 📞 415/388–2070 🌐 www. parks.ca.gov.

Muir Beach

12 miles northwest of Golden Gate Bridge, 6 miles southwest of Mill Valley.

Except on the sunniest of weekends, Muir Beach is relatively quiet, but the drive here is a scenic adventure.

GETTING HERE AND AROUND
A car is the best way to reach Muir Beach. From Highway 1, follow Pacific Way southwest ¼ mile.

👁 Sights

Green Gulch Farm Zen Center

FARM/RANCH | Giant eucalyptus trees frame the long and winding road that leads to this tranquil Buddhist practice center. Meditation programs, tea instruction, gardening classes, and various other workshops and events take place here; there's also an extensive organic farm. Visitors are welcome to roam the property and walk through the gardens that reach down toward Muir Beach. Public Sunday programs are especially geared toward visitors. ✉ *1601 Shoreline Hwy., at Green Gulch Rd.* ☎ *415/383–3134 welcome center* 🌐 *www.sfzc.org* 🎟 *Free.*

Beaches

Muir Beach

BEACH—SIGHT | FAMILY | Small but scenic, this beach—a rocky patch of shoreline off Highway 1 in the northern Marin Headlands—is a good place to stretch your legs and gaze out at the Pacific. Locals often walk their dogs here; families and cuddling couples come for picnicking and sunbathing. At the northern end of the beach are waterfront homes (and occasional nude sunbathers) and at the other are the bluffs of the Golden Gate National Recreation Area. A land bridge connects directly from the parking lot to the beach, as well as a short trail that leads to a scenic overlook and connects to other coastal paths. There are no lifeguards on duty and the currents can be challenging so swimming is not advised. **Amenities:** parking (free); toilets. **Best for:** solitude; sunsets; hiking. ✉ *100 Pacific Way, off Shoreline Hwy.* 🌐 *www.nps.gov/goga/planyourvisit/muirbeach.htm.*

Hotels

Pelican Inn

$$$ | B&B/INN | From its slate roof to its whitewashed plaster walls, this inn looks so Tudor that it's hard to believe it was built in the 1970s, but the Pelican is English to the core, with its cozy upstairs guest rooms (no elevator), draped half-tester beds, a sun-filled solarium, and bangers and grilled tomatoes for breakfast. **Pros:** five-minute walk to beach; great bar and restaurant; peaceful setting. **Cons:** 20-minute drive to nearby attractions; rooms are quite small and rustic; workout and steam room access not on-site. [$] *Rooms from: $224* ✉ *10 Pacific Way, off Hwy. 1* ☎ *415/383–6000* 🌐 *www.pelicaninn.com* 🛏 *7 rooms* 🍴 *Breakfast.*

Stinson Beach

20 miles northwest of Golden Gate Bridge.

This laid-back hamlet is all about the beach, and folks come from all over the Bay Area to walk its sandy, often windswept shore. Ideal day trip: a morning hike at Mt. Tam followed by lunch at one of Stinson's unassuming eateries and a leisurely beach stroll.

GETTING HERE AND AROUND

If you're driving, take U.S. 101 to the Mill Valley/Stinson Beach/Highway 1 exit and follow the road west and then north. By bus, take Golden Gate Transit to Marin City and then transfer to the West Marin Stagecoach (61) for Bolinas.

Beaches

Stinson Beach

BEACH—SIGHT | FAMILY | When the fog hasn't rolled in, this expansive stretch of sand is about as close as you can get in Marin to the stereotypical feel of a Southern California beach. There are several clothing-optional areas, among them a section south of Stinson Beach called Red Rock Beach. ⚠ **Swimming at Stinson Beach can be dangerous; the undertow is strong, and shark sightings, though infrequent, have occurred; lifeguards are on duty May–September.** On any hot summer weekend, roads to Stinson are packed and the parking lot fills, so factor this into your plans. The town itself—population 600, give or take—has a nonchalant surfer vibe, with a few good eating options and pleasant hippie-craftsy browsing. **Amenities:** food and drink; lifeguards (summer); parking (free); showers; toilets. **Best for:** nudists; sunset; surfing; swimming; walking, windsurfing. ✉ *Hwy. 1, 1 Calle Del Sierra* ☎ *415/868–0942 lifeguard tower* 🌐 *www.stinsonbeachonline.com* ☞ *No pets allowed on national park section of beach.*

🍴 Restaurants

Parkside Cafe

$$$ | **AMERICAN** | **FAMILY** | The Parkside is popular for its 1950s beachfront snack bar, but the adjoining café, coffee bar, marketplace, and bakery shouldn't be missed either. A full menu serves up fresh ingredients, local seafood, wood-fired pizzas, and just-baked breads. **Known for:** espresso and pastry bar; fish-and-chips; rustic house-made breads. [$] *Average main: $27* ✉ *43 Arenal Ave., off Shoreline Hwy.* ☎ *415/868–1272* 🌐 *www.parksidecafe.com.*

🛏 Hotels

Sandpiper Lodging

$$ | **B&B/INN** | **FAMILY** | Recharge, rest, and enjoy the local scenery at this ultrapopular lodging that books up months, even years, in advance. **Pros:** beach chairs, towels, and toys provided; lush gardens with BBQ; minutes from the beach and town. **Cons:** walls are thin; limited amenities; charge for roll-away beds and extra persons. [$] *Rooms from: $185* ✉ *1 Marine Way, off Arenal Ave.* ☎ *415/868–1632* 🌐 *www.sandpiperstinsonbeach.com* 🛏 *11 rooms* 🍽 *No meals.*

Point Reyes National Seashore

Bear Valley Visitor Center is 14 miles north of Stinson Beach.

With sandy beaches stretching for miles, a dramatic rocky coastline, a gem of a lighthouse, and idyllic, century-old dairy farms, Point Reyes National Seashore is one of the most varied and strikingly beautiful corners of the Bay Area.

GETTING HERE AND AROUND

From San Francisco, take U.S. 101 north, head west at Sir Francis Drake Boulevard (Exit 450B) toward San Anselmo, and follow the road just under 20 miles to Bear Valley Road. From Stinson Beach or Bolinas, drive north on Highway 1 and turn left on Bear Valley Road. If you're going by bus, take one of several Golden Gate Transit buses to Marin City; in Marin City transfer to the West Marin Stagecoach (you'll switch buses in Olema). Once at the visitor center, the best way to get around is on foot.

👁 Sights

Bear Valley Visitor Center

INFO CENTER | **FAMILY** | A life-size elephant seal model dominates the center's engaging exhibits about the wildlife, history, and ecology of the Point Reyes National Seashore. The rangers at the barnlike facility are fonts of information about beaches, whale-watching, hiking trails, and camping. Restrooms are available, as well as trailhead parking and a picnic area with barbecue grills. Winter hours may be shorter and summer weekend hours may be longer; call or check the website for details. ✉ *Bear Valley Visitor Center, 1 Bear Valley Visitor Center Access Rd., west of Hwy. 1, off Bear Valley Rd., Point Reyes Station* ☎ *415/464–5100* 🌐 *www.nps.gov/pore/planyourvisit.*

★ **Duxbury Reef**

NATURE PRESERVE | FAMILY | Excellent tide pooling can be had along the 3-mile shoreline of Duxbury Reef; it's the most extensive tide pool area near Point Reyes National Seashore, as well as one of the largest shale intertidal reefs in North America. Look for sea stars, barnacles, sea anemones, purple urchins, limpets, sea mussels, and the occasional abalone. But check a tide table (⊕ tidesandcurrents.noaa.gov) or the local papers if you plan to explore the reef—it's accessible only at low tide. The reef is a 30-minute drive from the Bear Valley Visitor Center. Take Highway 1 south from the center, turn right at Olema–Bolinas Road (keep an eye peeled; the road is easy to miss), left on Horseshoe Hill Road, right on Mesa Road, left on Overlook Drive, and then right on Elm Road, which dead-ends at the Agate Beach County Park parking lot. ✛ At Duxbury Point, 1 mile west of Bolinas ⊕ www.ptreyes.org/activities/tidepools.

Palomarin Field Station & Point Reyes Bird Observatory

NATURE PRESERVE | FAMILY | Birders adore Point Blue Conservation Science, which maintains the Palomarin Field Station and the Point Reyes Bird Observatory (PRBO) that are located in the southernmost part of Point Reyes National Seashore. The Field Station, open daily from sunrise to sunset, has excellent interpretive exhibits, including a comparative display of real birds' talons. The surrounding woods harbor some 200 bird species. As you hike the quiet trails through forest and along ocean cliffs, you're likely to see biologists banding birds to aid in the study of their life cycles. ■TIP➔ Visit Point Blue's website for detailed directions and to find out when banding will occur. ✉ 999 Mesa Rd., Bolinas ☎ 415/868–0655 field station, 707/781–2555 headquarters ⊕ www.pointblue.org.

★ **Point Reyes National Seashore**

NATIONAL/STATE PARK | FAMILY | One of the Bay Area's most spectacular treasures and the only national seashore on the West Coast, the 71,000-acre Point Reyes National Seashore encompasses hiking trails, secluded beaches, and rugged grasslands as well as Point Reyes itself, a triangular peninsula that juts into the Pacific. The town of **Point Reyes Station** is a one-main-drag affair with some good places to eat and gift shops that sell locally made and imported goods.

When explorer Sir Francis Drake sailed along the California coast in 1579, he allegedly missed the Golden Gate and San Francisco Bay, but he did land at what he described as a convenient harbor. In 2012 the federal government conceded a centuries-long debate and officially recognized Drake's Bay, which flanks the point on the east, as that harbor, designating the spot a National Historic Landmark and silencing competing claims in the 433-year-old controversy. Today Point Reyes's hills and dramatic cliffs attract other kinds of explorers: hikers, whale-watchers, and solitude seekers.

The infamous San Andreas Fault runs along the park's eastern edge and up the center of Tomales Bay; take the short **Earthquake Trail** from the visitor center to see the impact near the epicenter of the 1906 earthquake that devastated San Francisco. A half-mile path from the visitor center leads to **Kule Loklo,** a reconstructed Miwok village that sheds light on the daily lives of the region's first inhabitants. From here, trails also lead to the park's hike-in campgrounds (no car camping).

■TIP➔ In late winter and spring, take the short walk at Chimney Rock, just before the lighthouse, to the Elephant Seal Overlook. Even from the cliff, the male seals look enormous as they spar, growling and bloodied, for resident females.

You can experience the diversity of Point Reyes's ecosystems on the scenic **Coast Trail,** which starts at the Palomarin Trailhead, just outside Bolinas. From here, it's a 3-mile trek through eucalyptus groves and pine forests and along seaside cliffs to beautiful and tiny Bass Lake. To reach the Palomarin Trailhead, take Olema–Bolinas Road toward Bolinas, turn right on Mesa Road, follow signs to Point Blue Conservation Science, and then continue until the road dead-ends.

The 4.7-mile-long (one-way) **Tomales Point Trail** follows the spine of the park's northernmost finger of land through a Tule Elk Preserve, providing spectacular ocean views from the high bluffs. Expect to see elk, but keep your distance from the animals. To reach the moderately easy hiking trail, take Sir Francis Drake Boulevard through the town of Inverness; when you come to a fork, veer right to stay on Pierce Point Road and continue until you reach the parking lot at Pierce Point Ranch. ⊠ *Bear Valley Visitor Center, 1 Bear Valley Visitor Center Access Rd., west of Hwy. 1, off Bear Valley Rd., Point Reyes Station* ☎ *415/464–5100* ⊕ *www. nps.gov/pore.*

 Restaurants

Café Reyes

$$ | **PIZZA** | **FAMILY** | Sunny patio seating, hand-tossed pizza, and organic local ingredients are the selling points of this laid-back café. The semi-industrial dining room, which is built around a brick oven, features glazed concrete floors, warm-painted walls, and ceilings high enough to accommodate full-size market umbrellas. **Known for:** wood-fired pizza; Drake's Bay fresh oysters; outdoor patio dining. $ *Average main: $16* ⊠ *11101 Hwy. 1, Point Reyes Station* ☎ *415/663–9493* ⊕ *cafe-reyes.com* ☙ *Closed Mon. and Tues.*

Due West

$$$ | **AMERICAN** | Award-winning chef Jonathan Pfluege brings local, sustainable culinary provisions to this classic Point Reyes tavern, a popular horse-and-wagon stop since the 1860s. The seasonal menu includes American classics from burgers and brick-roasted chicken to seafood specialties like Dungeness crab chowder and oysters fried, grilled, or freshly shucked. **Known for:** artisanal cheese plate; steak frites; regional wine list. $ *Average main: $24* ⊠ *10021 Coastal Hwy. 1, Olema* ☎ *415/663–1264* ⊕ *olemahouse.com/dine.*

★ Hog Island Oyster Co. Marshall Oyster Farm & the Boat Oyster Bar

$$$ | **SEAFOOD** | **FAMILY** | Take a short trek north on Highway 1 to the gritty mecca of Bay Area oysters—the Hog Island Marshall Oyster Farm. For a real culinary adventure, arrange to shuck and barbecue your own oysters on one of the outdoor grills (all tools supplied, reservations required), or for the less adventurous, the Boat Oyster Bar is an informal outdoor café that serves raw and BBQ oysters, local snacks, and tasty beverages. **Known for:** fresh, raw, and BBQ oysters; picnic grills; Hog Shack shellfish to go. $ *Average main: $24* ⊠ *20215 Shoreline Hwy.* ☎ *415/663–9218* ⊕ *hogislandoysters.com/locations/marshall* ☙ *Oyster Bar closed Tues.–Thurs. No dinner.*

★ Osteria Stellina

$$ | **ITALIAN** | Chef-owner Christian Caiazzo's menu of "Point Reyes Italian" cuisine puts an emphasis on showcasing hyperlocal ingredients like Marin-grown kale and Sonoma cheese. Pastas, pizzas, and a handful of entrées are served in a rustic-contemporary space with a raw bar that serves local oysters all day long. **Known for:** locally sourced produce and seafood; fresh oysters; inventive pizzas. $ *Average main: $22* ⊠ *11285 Hwy. 1, at 3rd St., Point Reyes Station* ☎ *415/663–9988* ⊕ *www.osteriastellina.com.*

★ Side Street Kitchen
$$ | AMERICAN | FAMILY | Rotisserie meats and veggies sourced from local farms steal the show at this former mid-century truck stop and diner. It's a go-to for tri-tip and pork belly sandwiches or house-seasoned roasted chicken, best eaten family style with a host of salads, sides, and butterscotch pudding. **Known for:** cold smoked seafood and rotisserie chicken; dog-friendly outdoor patio; apple fritters. $ *Average main: $16* ✉ *60 4th St., Point Reyes Station* ☎ *415/663–0303* ⊕ *sidestreet-prs.com* ⊘ *No dinner.*

Sir and Star at the Olema
$$$$ | AMERICAN | With lovely garden views, creative and cryptically named dishes, and upscale-rustic decor that somehow incorporates taxidermied animals, this historic roadhouse (located within the Olema Inn) elicits both rants and raves, often from diners sharing the same table. The locally focused menu of California cuisine changes seasonally; a special prix fixe is offered by reservation on Saturday evening. **Known for:** great atmosphere; small plates; Saturday Chef's Meal. $ *Average main: $35* ✉ *10000 Sir Francis Drake Blvd., at Hwy. 1, Olema* ☎ *415/663–1034* ⊕ *sirandstar.com* ⊘ *Closed Mon.–Wed. No lunch.*

Station House Cafe
$$ | AMERICAN | In good weather, hikers fresh from the park fill the Station House's lovely outdoor garden as well as its homey indoor tables, banquettes, and bar stools, so prepare for a wait. The community-centric eatery is locally focused and serves a blend of modern and classic California dishes comprised of organic seasonal ingredients, sustainable hormone-free meats, and wild-caught seafood. **Known for:** signature popovers; hearty breakfast items; local fresh seafood. $ *Average main: $22* ✉ *11180 Hwy. 1, at 2nd St., Point Reyes Station* ☎ *415/663–1515* ⊕ *www.stationhousecafe.com* ⊘ *Closed Wed.*

Stinson Beach Breakers Cafe
$$$ | AMERICAN | Hard to miss along the tiny stretch of Main Street, this café is an easy prebeach destination for coffee and griddle specialties or postsurf bar bites and cocktails on the heated patio in the afternoon. Beach cottage hardwood floors and a wood stove add to the warmth of the rustic seaside interior, while a mountain view and fire pit adds to the deck. **Known for:** hearty egg breakfast dishes with a Latin twist; fresh oysters; fish tacos. $ *Average main: $23* ✉ *3465 Hwy. 1, Stinson Beach* ☎ *415/868–2002* ⊕ *stinsonbeachcafe.com* ⊘ *Closed Tues. and Wed., Nov.–Mar.*

Hotels

★ Olema House
$$$$ | B&B/INN | FAMILY | Once a historic 1860s stagecoach stopover, this renovated, luxurious getaway offers just as many reasons to stay on property—with its views of Mt. Wittenberg—as to explore the 71,000 acres of national seashore just steps away. **Pros:** lush garden; convenient parking and horse hitching; friendly and informative staff. **Cons:** steps to some rooms may be steep; street-facing rooms above restaurant may be noisy; Wi-Fi and cell service may be spotty. $ *Rooms from: $300* ✉ *10021 Coastal Hwy. 1, Olema* ☎ *415/663–9000* ⊕ *olemahouse.com* ⤳ *25 rooms* ⦿ *Free Breakfast.*

Shopping

★ Cowgirl Creamery
LOCAL SPECIALTIES | FAMILY | In this former hay barn, a couple of Berkeley foodies (from Chez Panisse and Bette's Oceanview Diner) started their original creamery for artisanal cheeses. In addition to more than 200 specialty cheeses—local, regional, and international—you'll find Tomales Bay Foods offerings featuring West Marin farm

wares. Cowgirl Creamery cheeses harness flavors unique to Point Reyes, such as their award-winning Red Hawk and Mt. Tam made from Straus Family Dairy milk. Sample seasonal cheeses and see how the cheese is made or order a hot mac and cheese at the cantina and stay for a bite at the picnic tables. Abundant deli items, gourmet goodies, and wine selections make it easy to pack a picnic for the beach or a hike here. ⊠ *80 4th St., Point Reyes Station* ☏ *415/663–9335* ⊕ *www.cowgirlcreamery.com/pt-reyes-shop-creamery* ⊗ *Closed Mon. and Tues.*

Gospel Flat Farm Stand
OUTDOOR/FLEA/GREEN MARKETS | FAMILY | This combination art gallery, farm stand, and flower shop captures the true essence of the area, with its dedication to community and bounty of local organic vegetables, fruits, and eggs. A must-see when passing through the Bolinas and Olema area, the self-serve site is open 24 hours. What makes it truly special is that the entire stand operates on the honor system. Weigh and log your produce, and slip your payment (cash or check) in the box. The local art on exhibit adds to the allure of this roadside treasure. ⊠ *140 Olema-Bolinas Rd., Bolinas* ☏ *415/858–4730* ⊕ *gospelflatfarm.com.*

★ Toby's Feed Barn
LOCAL SPECIALTIES | FAMILY | The heart of the community since 1942, this barn has a bounty of local gifts and produce, plus an art gallery, yoga studio, and Toby's Coffee Bar for espresso drinks and sell-out pastries. See and hear what's happening locally, catch a live band, and explore the garden. The internationally renowned all-local, all-organic Point Reyes Farmers' Market is held here on Saturday for 20 weeks during the growing season. ⊠ *11250 Hwy. 1, Point Reyes Station* ☏ *415/663–1223* ⊕ *tobysfeedbarn.com.*

Chapter 18

NAPA AND SONOMA

Updated by
Daniel Mangin

⊙ Sights	🍴 Restaurants	🛏 Hotels	👜 Shopping	🍸 Nightlife
★★★★★	★★★★★	★★★★☆	★★★☆☆	★★★☆☆

WELCOME TO NAPA AND SONOMA

TOP REASONS TO GO

★ **Touring wineries:** Let's face it: this is the reason you're here, and the range of excellent sips to sample would make any oeno- phile (or novice drinker, for that matter) giddy.

★ **Biking:** Gentle hills and vineyard-laced farmland make Napa and Sonoma perfect for combining lei- surely back-roads cycling with winery stops.

★ **Browsing the farmers' markets:** Many towns in Napa and Sonoma have seasonal farmers' markets, each rounding up an amazing variety of local produce.

★ **A meal at The French Laundry:** Chef Thomas Keller's Yountville restau- rant is one of the country's best. The mastery of fla- vors and attention to detail are subtly remarkable.

★ **Viewing the art:** Several wineries, among them the Hess Collection in Napa, The Donum Estate in Sonoma, and Hall St. Helena, display museum- quality artworks indoors and on their grounds.

The Napa and Sonoma valleys run parallel, northwest to southeast, and are separated by the Mayacamas Mountains. Southwest of Sonoma Valley are several other important viticultural areas in Sonoma county, including the Dry Creek, Alexander, and Russian River valleys. The Carneros, which spans southern Sonoma and Napa counties, is just north of San Pablo Bay.

1 **Napa.**

2 **Yountville.**

3 **Oakville.**

4 **Rutherford.**

5 **St. Helena.**

6 **Calistoga.**

7 **Sonoma.**

8 **Glen Ellen.**

9 **Kenwood.**

10 **Healdsburg.**

11 **Geyserville.**

12 **Forestville.**

13 **Guerneville.**

14 **Sebastopol.**

15 **Santa Rosa.**

16 **Pertaluma.**

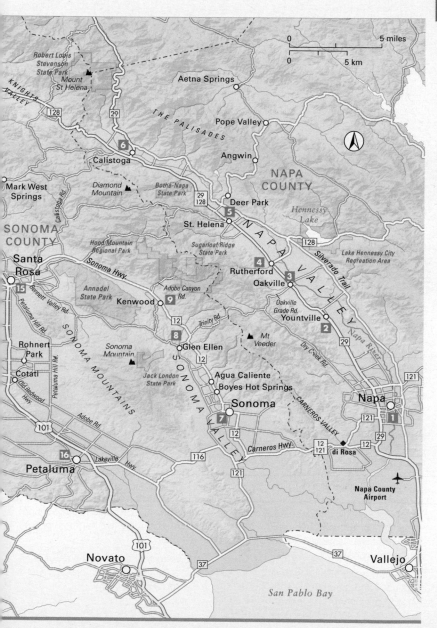

KNIGHTS VALLEY

Robert Louis
Stevenson
State Park

Mount
St Helena

Aetna Springs

128

29

THE PALISADES

Pope Valley

Angwin

6 Calistoga

NAPA
COUNTY

Mark West
Springs

Diamond
Mountain

Bothe-Napa
State Park

29
128

5 Deer Park

Hennessy
Lake

SONOMA
COUNTY

St. Helena

128

Lake Hennessy City
Recreation Area

Santa
Rosa

Hood Mountain
Regional Park

Sugarloaf Ridge
State Park

Silverado Trail

15

Sonoma Hwy

Annadel
State Park

Adobe Canyon
Rd.

4 Rutherford
3 Oakville

Kenwood 9

12

Trinity Rd.

Oakville
Grade Rd.
Yountville

Napa River

Rohnert
Park

8

Glen Ellen

12

Mt
Veeder

2

29

Cotati

Sonoma
Mountain

Jack London
State Park

Agua Caliente
Boyes Hot Springs

Sonoma

7

121

Napa

1

101

Adobe Rd.

12

116

Carneros Hwy.

12
121

di Rosa

12   29

121

16 Petaluma

Lakeville Hwy.

121

Napa County
Airport

Novato

101

37

37

Vallejo

San Pablo Bay

SONOMA MOUNTAINS

SONOMA VALLEY

NAPA VALLEY

CARNEROS VALLEY

Calistoga Rd.

Bennett Valley Rd.

Petaluma Hill Rd.

Old Redwood Hwy.

Dry Creek Rd.

0   5 miles
0   5 km

In California's premier wine region, the pleasures of eating and drinking are celebrated daily. It's easy to join in at famous wineries and rising newcomers off country roads, or at trendy in-town tasting rooms. Chefs transform local ingredients into feasts, and gourmet groceries sell perfect picnic fare. Yountville, Healdsburg, and St. Helena have small-town charm as well as luxurious inns, hotels, and spas, yet the natural setting is equally sublime, whether experienced from a canoe on the Russian River or the deck of a winery overlooking endless rows of vines.

The Wine Country is also rich in history. In Sonoma you can explore California's Spanish and Mexican pasts at the Sonoma Mission, and the origins of modern California wine making at Buena Vista Winery. Some wineries, among them St. Helena's Beringer and Rutherford's Inglenook, have cellars or tasting rooms dating to the late 1800s. Calistoga is a flurry of late-19th-century Steamboat Gothic architecture, though the town's oldest-looking building, the medieval-style Castello di Amorosa, is a 21st-century creation.

Tours at the Napa Valley's Beringer, Mondavi, and Inglenook—and at Buena Vista in the Sonoma Valley—provide an entertaining overview of Wine Country history. The tour at the splashy visitor center at St. Helena's Hall winery will introduce you to 21st-century wine-making technology, and over in Glen Ellen's Benziger Family Winery you can see how its vineyard managers apply biodynamic farming principles to grape growing. At numerous facilities you can play winemaker for a day at seminars in the fine art of blending wines. If that strikes you as too much effort, you can always pamper yourself at a luxury spa.

To delve further into the fine art of Wine Country living, pick up a copy of *Fodor's Napa and Sonoma*.

MAJOR REGIONS

Napa Valley. With more than 500 wineries and many of the biggest brands in the business, the Napa Valley is the Wine Country's star. With a population of about 79,000, Napa, the valley's largest town, lures with its cultural attractions and (relatively) reasonably priced accommodations. A few miles farther north, compact **Yountville** is densely packed with top-notch restaurants and hotels, and **Rutherford** and **Oakville** are renowned for their Cabernet Sauvignon–friendly soils. Beyond them, **St. Helena** teems with elegant boutiques and restaurants, and casual **Calistoga**, known for spas and hot springs, has the feel of an Old West frontier town.

The Sonoma Valley. The birthplace of modern California wine making—Count Aragon Haraszthy opened Buena Vista Winery here in 1857—Sonoma Valley seduces with its unpretentious attitude and pastoral landscape. Tasting rooms, restaurants, and historic sites, among the latter the last mission established in California by Franciscan friars, abound near Sonoma Plaza. Beyond downtown Sonoma, the wineries and attractions are spread out along gently winding roads. Sonoma County's half of the Carneros District lies within Sonoma Valley, whose other towns of note include Glen Ellen and Kenwood. Sonoma Valley tasting rooms are often less crowded than those in Napa or northern Sonoma County, especially midweek, and the vibe here, though sophisticated, is definitely less sceney.

Planning

When to Go

High season extends from April through October. In summer, expect the days to be hot and dry, the roads filled with cars, and traffic heavy at the tasting rooms. Hotel rates are highest during the height of harvest, in September and October. Then and in summer book lodgings well ahead. November, except for Thanksgiving week, and December before Christmas are less busy. The weather in Napa and Sonoma is pleasant nearly year-round. Daytime temperatures average from about 55°F during winter to the 80s in summer, when readings in the 90s and higher are common. April, May, and October are milder but still warm. The rainiest months are usually from December through March.

Getting Here and Around

AIR TRAVEL

Wine Country regulars often bypass San Francisco and Oakland and fly into Santa Rosa's Charles M. Schulz Sonoma County Airport (STS), which receives direct flights from San Diego, Las Vegas, Los Angeles, Phoenix, Portland, and Seattle. The airport is 15 miles from Healdsburg. ■TIP→ **Alaska Airlines allows passengers flying out of STS to check up to one case of wine for free.**

BUS TRAVEL

Bus travel is an inconvenient way to explore the Wine Country, though it is possible. Take Golden Gate Transit from San Francisco to connect with Sonoma County Transit buses. VINE connects with BART commuter trains in the East Bay and the San Francisco Bay Ferry in Vallejo. VINE buses serve the Napa Valley.

CAR TRAVEL

A car is the most convenient way to navigate Napa and Sonoma. If you're flying into the area, it's almost always easiest to pick up a car at the airport. You'll also find rental companies in major Wine Country towns. A few rules to note: Smartphone use for any purpose is prohibited, including mapping applications unless the device is mounted to a car's windshield or dashboard and can be activated with a single swipe or finger tap. A right turn after stopping at a red light is legal unless posted otherwise.

If you base yourself in the Napa Valley towns of Napa, Yountville, or St. Helena, or in Sonoma County's Healdsburg or Sonoma, you can visit numerous tasting rooms and nearby wineries on foot or by bicycle on mostly flat terrain. The free Yountville trolley loops through town, and ride-sharing is viable there and in Napa. Sonoma County sprawls more, but except for far west the public transit and ride-sharing generally work well.

■TIP→ **If you're wine tasting, either select a designated driver or be careful of your wine intake—the police keep an eye out for tipsy drivers.**

From San Francisco to Napa: Cross the Golden Gate Bridge, then go north on U.S. 101. Head east on Highway 37 toward Vallejo, then north on Highway 121, aka the Carneros Highway. Turn left (north) when Highway 121 runs into Highway 29.

From San Francisco to Sonoma: Cross the Golden Gate Bridge, then go north on U.S. 101, east on Highway 37 toward Vallejo, and north on Highway 121. When you reach Highway 12, take it north to the town of Sonoma. For Sonoma County destinations north of Sonoma Valley stay on U.S. 101, which passes through Santa Rosa and Healdsburg.

From Berkeley and Oakland: Take Interstate 80 north to Highway 37 west, then on to Highway 29 north. For the Napa Valley, continue on Highway 29; to reach Sonoma County, head west on Highway 121.

Restaurants

Farm-to-table Modern American cuisine is the prevalent style in the Napa Valley and Sonoma County, but this encompasses both the delicate preparations of Thomas Keller's highly praised The French Laundry and the upscale comfort food served throughout the Wine Country. The quality (and hype) often means high prices, but you can also find

appealing, inexpensive eateries, especially in the towns of Napa, Calistoga, Sonoma, and Santa Rosa, and many high-end delis prepare superb picnic fare. At pricey restaurants you can save money by having lunch instead of dinner. With a few exceptions (noted in individual restaurant listings), dress is informal. *Restaurant reviews have been shortened. For full information, visit Fodors.com.*

Hotels

The fanciest accommodations are concentrated in the Napa Valley towns of Yountville, Rutherford, St. Helena, and Calistoga; Sonoma County's poshest lodgings are in Healdsburg. The spas, amenities, and exclusivity of high-end properties attract travelers with the means and desire for luxury living. The cities of Napa and Santa Rosa are the best bets for budget hotels and inns, but even at a lower price point you'll still find a touch of Wine Country glamour. On weekends, two- or even three-night minimum stays are commonly required at smaller lodgings. Book well ahead for stays at such places during the busy summer or fall season. If your party will include travelers under age 16, inquire about policies regarding younger guests; some smaller lodgings discourage (or discreetly forbid) children. *Hotel reviews have been shortened. For full information, visit Fodors.com.*

What It Costs			
$	$$	$$$	$$$$
RESTAURANTS			
under $16	$16–$22	$23–$30	over $30
HOTELS			
under $200	$200–$300	$301–$400	over $400

Napa

46 miles northeast of San Francisco.

After many years as a blue-collar burg detached from the Wine Country scene, the Napa Valley's largest town (population about 80,000) has evolved into one of its shining stars. Masaharu Morimoto and other chefs of note operate restaurants here, swank hotels and inns can be found downtown and beyond, and the nightlife options include the West Coast edition of the famed Blue Note jazz club. A walkway that follows the Napa River has made downtown more pedestrian-friendly, and the Oxbow Public Market, a complex of high-end food purveyors, is popular with locals and tourists. The nearby CIA at Copia, operated by the Culinary Institute of America, hosts cooking demonstrations and other activities open to the public and has a shop and a restaurant. If you establish your base in Napa, plan on spending at least a half day strolling the downtown district.

GETTING HERE AND AROUND
Downtown Napa lies a mile east of Highway 29—take the 1st Street exit and follow the signs. Ample parking, much of it free for the first three hours and some for the entire day, is available on or near Main Street. Several VINE buses serve downtown and beyond.

◉ Sights

Artesa Vineyards & Winery
WINERY/DISTILLERY | From a distance the modern, minimalist architecture of Artesa blends harmoniously with the surrounding Carneros landscape, but up close its pools, fountains, and large outdoor sculptures make a vivid impression. So, too, do the wines: mostly Chardonnay and Pinot Noir but also Cabernet Sauvignon, sparkling, and limited releases like Albariño and Tempranillo. You can sample wines without a reservation in the Foyer Bar, but one is required for single-vineyard flights and food pairings. The latter can be enjoyed in the light-filled Salon Bar or outside on a terrace with views of estate and neighboring vineyards and, on a clear day, San Francisco. ✉ *1345 Henry Rd., Napa ✛ Off Old Sonoma Rd. and Dealy La.* ☎ *707/224–1668* ⊕ *www.artesawinery.com* ☞ *Tastings from $35, tour $45 (includes tasting).*

★ Ashes & Diamonds
WINERY/DISTILLERY | Barbara Bestor's sleek white design for this appointment-only winery's glass-and-metal tasting space evokes mid-century modern architecture and with it the era and wines before the Napa Valley's rise to prominence. Two much-heralded pros lead the wine-making team assembled by record producer Kashy Khaledi: Steve Matthiasson, known for his classic, restrained style and attention to viticultural detail, and Diana Snowden Seysses, who draws on experiences in Burgundy, Provence, and California. Bordeaux varietals are the focus, most notably Cabernet Sauvignon and Cabernet Franc but also the white blend of Sauvignon Blanc and Sémillon and even the rosé (of Cabernet Franc). With a label designer who was also responsible for a Jay-Z album cover and interiors that recall the *Mad Men* in Palm Springs story arc, the pitch seems unabashedly to millennials, but the wines, low in alcohol and with higher acidity (good for aging), enchant connoisseurs of all stripes. ✉ *4130 Howard La., Napa ✛ Off Hwy. 29* ☎ *707/666–4777* ⊕ *ashesdiamonds.com* ☞ *Tastings from $40.*

★ CIA at Copia
COLLEGE | Full-fledged foodies and the merely curious achieve gastronomical bliss at the Culinary Institute of America's Oxbow District campus, its facade brightened since 2018 by a wraparound mural inspired by the colorful garden that fronts the facility. A restaurant, a

Continued on page 690

WINE TASTING *in* NAPA *and* SONOMA

VISITING WINERIES

Tasting rooms range from the grand to the humble, offering everything from a few sips of wine to in-depth tours of facilities and vineyards. Many are open for drop-in visits, usually daily from around 10 am to 5 pm. Others require guests to make reservations. First-time visitors frequently enjoy the history-oriented tours at Charles Krug and Inglenook, or ones at Mondavi and J Vineyards that highlight the process as well. The environments at some wineries reflect their founders' other interests: art and architecture at Artesa and Hall St. Helena, movie making at Francis Ford Coppola, and medieval history at the Castello di Amorosa.

Many wineries describe their pourers as "wine educators," and indeed some of them have taken online or other classes and have passed an exam to prove basic knowledge of appellations, grape varietals, vineyards, and wine-making techniques. The one constant, however, is a deep, shared pleasure in the experience of wine tasting. To prepare you for winery visits, we've covered the fundamentals: tasting rooms, fees and what to expect, and the types of tours wineries offer.

Fees. In the past few years, tasting fees have skyrocketed. Most Napa wineries charge $25 or $30 to taste a few wines, though $40, $50, or even $75 fees aren't unheard of. Sonoma wineries are often a bit cheaper, in the $15 to $35 range, and you'll still find the occasional freebie.

Some winery tours are free, in which case you're usually required to pay a separate fee if you want to taste the wine. If you've paid a fee for the tour—generally from $20 to $40—your wine tasting is usually included in that price.

Whether you're a serious wine collector making your annual pilgrimage to Nothern California's Wine Country or a newbie who doesn't know the difference between a Merlot and Mourvèdre but is eager to learn, you can have a great time touring Napa and Sonoma wineries. Your gateway to the wine world is the tasting room, where staff members are happy to chat with curious guests.

(opposite page) Carneros vineyards in autumn, Napa Valley. (top) Pinot Gris grapes. (bottom) Bottles from Far Niente winery.

MAKING THE MOST OF YOUR TIME

■ **Call ahead.** Some wineries require reservations to visit or tour. It's wise to check before visiting.

■ **Come on weekdays.** Especially between June and October, try to visit on weekdays to avoid traffic-clogged roads and crowded tasting rooms. For more info on the best times of year to visit, see this chapter's Planner.

■ **Get an early start.** Tasting rooms are often deserted before 11 am or so, when most visitors are still lingering over a second cup of coffee. If you come early, you'll have the staff's undivided attention. You'll usually encounter the largest crowds between 3 and 5 pm.

■ **Schedule strategically.** Visit appointment-only wineries in the morning and ones that allow walk-ins in the afternoon. It'll spare you the stress of being "on time" for later stops.

■ **Hit the Trail.** Beringer, Mondavi, and other high-profile wineries line heavily trafficked Highway 29, but the going is often quicker on the Silverado Trail, which runs parallel to the highway to the east. You'll find famous

(top) Sipping and swirling in the DeLoach tasting room. (bottom) Learning about barrel aging at Robert Mondavi Winery.

names here, too, among them the sparkling wine house Mumm Napa Valley, but the traffic is often lighter and sometimes the crowds as well.

Domaine Carneros.

AT THE BAR

In most tasting rooms, you'll be handed a list of the wines available that day. The wines will be listed in a suggested tasting order, starting with the lightest-bodied whites, progressing to the most intense reds, and ending with dessert wines. If you can't decide which wines to choose, tell the server what types of wines you usually like and ask for a recommendation.

The server will pour you an ounce or so of each wine you select. As you taste it, feel free to take notes or ask questions. Don't be shy—the staff are there to educate you about the wine. If you don't like a wine, or you've simply tasted enough, feel free to pour the rest into one of the dump buckets on the bar.

TOURS

Tours tend to be the most exciting (and the most crowded) in September and October, when the harvest and crushing are underway. Tours typically last from 30 minutes to an hour and give you a brief overview of the winemaking process. At some of the older wineries, the tour guide might focus on the history of the property.

■ **TIP →** If you plan to take any tours, wear comfortable shoes, since you might be walking on wet floors or dirt or gravel pathways or stepping over hoses or other equipment.

MONEY-SAVING TIPS

■ Many hotels and B&Bs distribute coupons for free or discounted tastings to their guests—don't forget to ask.

■ If you and your travel partner don't mind sharing a glass, servers are happy to let you split a tasting.

■ Some wineries will refund all or part of the tasting fee if you buy a bottle. Usually one fee is waived per bottle purchased, though sometimes you must buy two or three.

■ Almost all wineries will also waive the fee if you join their wine club program. However, this typically commits you to buying a certain number of bottles on a regular basis, so be sure you really like the wines before signing up.

Preston of Dry Creek bottles only estate-grown grapes.

TOP 2-DAY ITINERARIES

First-Timer's Napa Tour

Start: Oxbow Public market, Napa. Get underway by browsing the shops selling wines, spices, locally grown produce, and other fine foods, for a taste of what the Wine Country has to offer.

Inglenook, Rutherford. The tour here is a particularly fun way to learn about the history of Napa winemaking—

and you can see the old, atmospheric, ivy-covered château.

Frog's Leap, Rutherford. Friendly, unpretentious, and knowledge-able staff makes this place great for wine newbies. (Make sure you get that reservation lined up.)

Dinner and Overnight: St. Helena. Splurge at Meadowood Napa Valley and you won't need to leave the property for an extravagant din-

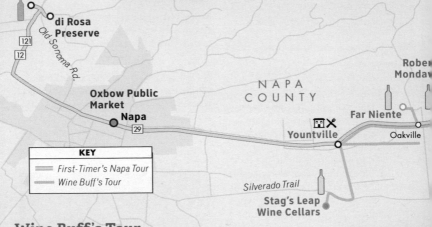

Domaine Carneros

di Rosa Preserve

Old Sonoma Rd.

121

12

Oxbow Public Market

Napa

29

NAPA COUNTY

Rober Monda

Far Niente

Yountville

Oakville

KEY
— First-Timer's Napa Tour
— Wine Buff's Tour

Silverado Trail

Stag's Leap Wine Cellars

Wine Buff's Tour

Start: Stag's Leap Wine Cellars, Yount-ville, Napa. Famed for its Cabernet Sauvignon and Bordeaux blends.

Silver Oak, Oakville. Schedule a tour of this celebrated winery and taste the flagship Cabernet Sauvignon.

Mumm Napa, Rutherford. Come for the bubbly—which is available in a variety of tastings—stay for the photography exhibits.

Dinner and Overnight: Yountville. Have dinner at one of the Thomas Keller restaurants. Splurge at Bardessono; save at

Maison Fleurie.

Next Day: Robert Mondavi, Oakville. Spring for the reserve room tasting so you can sip the top-of-the-line wines, especially the Cabernet Sauvignon. Head across Highway 29 to the Oakville Grocery to pick up a picnic lunch.

ner at its restaurant. Save at El Bonita Motel with dinner at Gott's.

Next Day: Poke around St. Helena's shops, then drive to Yountville for lunch.

di Rosa, Napa. Call ahead to book a one- or two-hour tour of the acres of gardens and galleries, which

are chock-full of thousands of works of art.

Domaine Carneros, Napa. Toast your trip with a glass of outstanding bubbly.

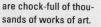

Sonoma Backroads

Far Niente, Oakville. You have to make a reservation and the fee for the tasting and tour is steep, but the payoff is

an especially intimate winery experience. You'll taste excellent Cabernet and Chardonnay, then end your trip on a sweet note with a dessert wine.

Start: Iron Horse Vineyards, Russian River Valley. Soak up a view of vine-covered hills and Mount St. Helena while sipping a sparkling wine or Pinot Noir at this beautifully rustic spot.

Dutton-Goldfield Winery, Russian River Valley. A terrific source for Pinot Noir and Chardonnay, the stars of this valley.

Dinner and Overnight: Forestville. Go all out with a stay at the Farmhouse Inn, whose award-winning restaurant is one of the best in all of Sonoma.

Next Day: Westside Road, Russian River Valley. This scenic route, which follows the river, is crowded with worthwhile wineries like Arista and Rochioli—but it's not crowded with visitors. Pinot fans will find a lot to love. Picnic at either winery and enjoy the view.

Balletto Vineyards, Santa Rosa. End on an especially relaxed note with a walk through the vineyards and a patio tasting.

WINE TASTING 101

TAKE A GOOD LOOK.
Hold your glass by the stem, raise it to the light, and take a close look at the wine. Check for clarity and color. (This is easiest to do if you can hold the glass in front of a white background.) Any tinge of brown usually means that the wine is over the hill or has gone bad.

BREATHE DEEP.
1. Sniff the wine once or twice to see if you can identify any smells.

2. Swirl the wine gently in the glass. Aerating the wine this way releases more of its aromas. (It's called "volatilizing the esters," if you're trying to impress someone.)

3. Take another long sniff. You might notice that experienced wine tasters spend more time sniffing the wine than drinking it. This is because this step is where the magic happens. The number of scents you might detect is almost endless, from berries, apricots, honey, and wildflowers to leather, cedar, or even tar. Does the wine smell good to you? Do you detect any "off" flavors, like wet dog or sulfur?

AT LAST! TAKE A SIP.
1. Swirl the wine around your mouth so that it makes contact with all your taste buds and releases more of its aromas. Think about the way the wine feels in your mouth. Is it watery or rich? Is it crisp or silky? Does it have a bold flavor, or is it subtle? The weight and intensity of a wine are called its body.

2. Hold the wine in your mouth for a few seconds and see if you can identify any developing flavors. More complex wines will reveal many different flavors as you drink them.

SPIT OR SWALLOW.
The pros typically spit, since they want to preserve their palate (and sobriety!) for the wines to come, but you'll find that swallowers far outnumber the spitters in the winery tasting rooms. Whether you spit or swallow, notice the flavor that remains after the wine is gone (the finish).

Swirl

Sniff

Sip

DODGE THE CROWDS

To avoid bumping elbows in the tasting rooms, look for wineries off the main drags of Highway 29 in Napa and Highway 12 in Sonoma. The back roads of the Russian River, Dry Creek, and Alexander valleys, all in Sonoma, are excellent places to explore. In Napa, try the northern end. Also look for wineries that are open by appointment only; they tend to schedule visitors carefully to avoid a big crush at any one time.

HOW WINE IS MADE

1: CRUSHING
Harvested grapes go into a stemmer-crusher, which separates stems from fruit and crushes the grapes to release "free-run" juice.

2. PRESSING
Remaining juice is gently extracted from grapes. Usually done by pressing grapes against the walls of a tank with an inflatable bladder.

3. FERMENTING
Extracted juice (and also grape skins and pulp, when making red wine) goes into stainless-steel tanks or oak barrels to ferment. During fermentation, sugars convert to alcohol.

4. AGING
Wine is stored in stainless-steel or oak casks or barrels, or sometimes in concrete vessels, to develop flavors.

5. RACKING
Wine is transferred to clean barrels; sediment is removed. Wine may be filtered and fined (clarified) to improve its clarity, color, and sometimes flavor.

6. BOTTLING
Wine is bottled either at the winery or at a special facility, then stored again for bottle-aging.

WHAT'S AN APPELLATION?

American Viticultural Area (AVA) or, more commonly, an appellation. What can be confusing is that some appellations encompass smaller subappellations. The Rutherford, Oakville, and Mt. Veeder AVAs, for instance, are among the Napa Valley AVA's 15 subappellations. Wineries often buy grapes from outside their AVA, so their labels might reference different appellations. A winery in the warmer Napa Valley, for instance, might source Pinot Noir grapes from the cooler Russian River Valley, where they grow better. The appellation listed on a label always refers to where a wine's grapes were grown, not to where the wine was made.

By law, if a label bears the name of an appellation, 85% of the grapes must come from it.

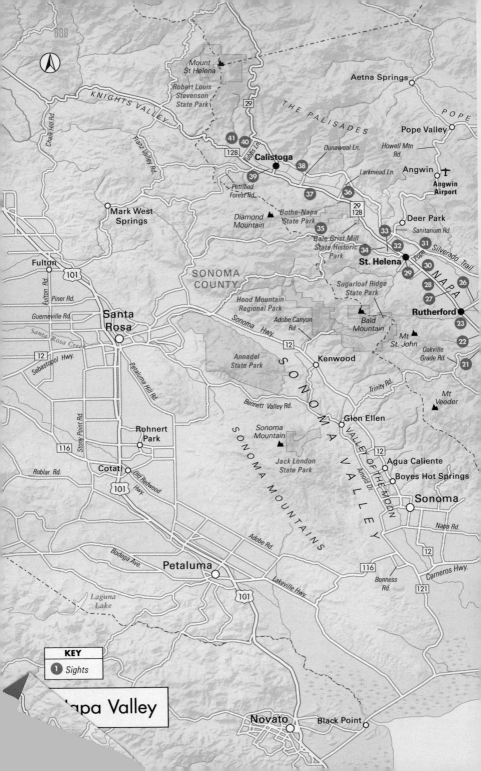

KEY

① Sights

Napa Valley

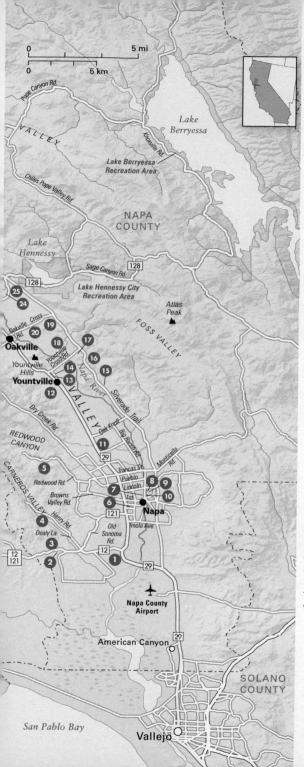

Sights ▼

Wine and contemporary art find a home at di Rosa.

shop, a museum, and the Vintners Hall of Fame—not to mention classes and demonstrations involving food-and-wine pairings, sparkling wines, ancient grains, cheeses, pasta, and sauces—make this a spend-a-half-day-here sort of place. One well-attended class for adults explores the Napa Valley's history through eight glasses of wine, and children join their parents for Family Funday workshops about making mac and cheese and nutritious lunches. Head upstairs to the Chuck Williams Culinary Arts Museum. Named for the founder of the Williams-Sonoma kitchenwares chain, it holds a fascinating collection of cooking, baking, and other food-related tools, tableware, gizmos, and gadgets, some dating back more than a century. ⊠ 500 1st St., Napa ✛ Near McKinstry St. ☎ 707/967–2500 ⊕ www.ciaatcopia. com ⊠ Facility free, demonstrations and classes from $15.

di Rosa Center for Contemporary Art

MUSEUM | The late Rene di Rosa assembled an extensive collection of artworks created by Northern California artists from the 1960s to the present, displaying them on this 217-acre Carneros District property surrounded by Chardonnay and Pinot Noir vineyards. Two galleries at opposite ends of a 35-acre lake show works from the collection and host temporary exhibitions, and the Sculpture Meadow behind the second gallery holds a few dozen large outdoor pieces. As 2019 dawned, di Rosa's residence, previously a highlight of a visit here, remained closed as conservation efforts continued to restore artworks damaged by smoke during the Wine Country's October 2017 wildfires. ■ TIP ➔ **Docent-led tours take place daily at 11 and 1.** ⊠ 5200 Sonoma Hwy./Hwy. 121, Napa ✛ Near Duhig Rd. ☎ 707/226–5991 ⊕ www.dirosaart.org ⊠ $18 ⊘ Closed Mon. and Tues.

★ Domaine Carneros

WINERY/DISTILLERY | A visit to this majestic château is an opulent way to enjoy the Carneros District—especially in fine weather, when the vineyard views are spectacular. The château was modeled after an 18th-century French mansion owned by the Taittinger family. Carved into the hillside beneath the winery, the cellars produce sparkling wines reminiscent of those made by Taittinger, using only Los Carneros AVA grapes. The winery sells flights and glasses of its sparklers, Chardonnay, Pinot Noir, and other wines. Enjoy them all with cheese and charcuterie plates, caviar, or smoked salmon. Seating is in the Louis XV–inspired salon or on the terrace overlooking the vines. The tour covers traditional methods of making sparkling wines. Tours and tastings are by appointment only. ⊠ *1240 Duhig Rd., Napa ✛ At Hwy. 121* ☎ *707/257–0101, 800/716–2788* ⊕ *www.domainecarneros.com* ᐧ *Tastings from $12, tour $50.*

Etude Wines

WINERY/DISTILLERY | You're apt to see or hear hawks, egrets, Canada geese, and other wildlife on the grounds of Etude, known for sophisticated Pinot Noirs. Although the winery and its light-filled tasting room are in Napa County, the grapes for its flagship Carneros Estate Pinot Noir come from the Sonoma portion of Los Carneros, as do those for the rarer Heirloom Carneros Pinot Noir. Hosts pour Chardonnay, Pinot Blanc, Pinot Noir, and other wines daily at the tasting bar and in good weather on the patio. Carneros, Sonoma Coast, Willamette Valley, Santa Barbara County, and New Zealand Pinots, all crafted by winemaker Jon Priest, are compared at Study of Pinot Noir sessions (reservations required). ■TIP➔ **Etude also excels at single-vineyard Napa Valley Cabernets; these can be sampled by appointment at seated tastings overlooking the production facility.** ⊠ *1250 Cuttings Wharf Rd., Napa ✛ 1 mile south of Hwy. 121* ☎ */07/257–5782* ⊕ *www.etudewines.com* ᐧ *Tastings from $25.*

Hess Collection

WINERY/DISTILLERY | About 9 miles northwest of Napa, up a winding road ascending Mt. Veeder, this winery is a delightful discovery. The limestone structure, rustic from the outside but modern and airy within, contains Swiss owner Donald Hess's world-class art collection, including large-scale works by contemporary artists such as Andy Goldsworthy, Anselm Kiefer, and Robert Rauschenberg. Cabernet Sauvignon is a major strength, with Chardonnays, Albariño, and Grüner Veltliner among the whites. Tastings outdoors in the garden and the courtyard take place from spring to fall, with cheese or nuts and other nibbles accompanying the wines. ■TIP➔ **Among the wine-and-food pairings offered year-round, most of which involve a guided tour of the art collection, is a fun one showcasing locally made artisanal chocolates.** ⊠ *4411 Redwood Rd., Napa ✛ West off Hwy. 29 at Trancas St./Redwood Rd. exit* ☎ *707/255–1144* ⊕ *www.hesscollection.com* ᐧ *Tastings from $25, art gallery free.*

Napa Valley Distillery

WINERY/DISTILLERY | Entertaining educators keep the proceedings light and lively at this distillery, which bills itself as Napa's first since Prohibition. NVD makes gin, rum, whiskey, and the flagship grape-based vodka, along with brandies and barrel-aged bottled cocktails that include Manhattans (the top seller), mai tais, and negronis. Visits, always by appointment, begin with a tasting upstairs in the "art-deco speakeasy with a tiki twist" Grand Salon, where lesson number one is how to properly sip spirits (spoiler: don't swirl your glass like you would with wine). Back downstairs in the production facility, you'll learn the basics of alcohol and distilling. ■TIP➔ **If you just want to sample the wares, the distillery operates a tasting bar in the main Oxbow Public Market building.** ⊠ *2485 Stockton St., Napa ✛ Off California Blvd.* ☎ *707/265–6272* ⊕ *www.napadistillery.com* ᐧ *Tastings $30* ☉ *Closed Wed.*

Napa Valley Wine Train

TOUR—SIGHT | Guests on this Napa Valley attraction, a fixture since 1989, ride the same rails along which, from the 1860s to the 1930s, trains transported passengers as far north as Calistoga's spas and hauled wine and other agricultural freight south toward San Francisco. The rolling stock includes restored Pullman railroad cars and a two-story Vista Dome car with a curved glass roof that travel a leisurely, scenic route between Napa and St. Helena. Patrons on the Quattro Vino tour enjoy a four-course lunch and tastings at four wineries, with stops at one or more wineries incorporated into other tours. Some rides involve no winery stops, and themed trips are scheduled throughout the year. ■TIP→ **It's best to make this trip during the day, when you can enjoy the vineyard views.** ⊠ 1275 McKinstry St., Napa ✛ Off 1st St. ☎ 707/253–2111, 800/427–4124 ⊕ www.winetrain.com ☞ From $149.

★ Oxbow Public Market

MARKET | The market's two dozen stands provide an introduction to Northern California's diverse artisanal food products. Swoon over decadent charcuterie at the Fatted Calf (great sandwiches, too), slurp oysters at Hog Island, or chow down on vegetarian, duck, or salmon tacos at C Casa. You can sample wine (and cheese) at the Oxbow Cheese & Wine Merchant, ales at Fieldwork Brewery's taproom, and barrel-aged cocktails at the Napa Valley Distillery. Napa Bookmine is among the few nonfood vendors here. ■TIP→ **If you don't mind eating at the counter, you can select a steak at the Five Dot Ranch meat stand and pay $10 above market price ($14 with two sides) to have it grilled on the spot, a real deal for a quality slab.** ⊠ 610 and 644 1st St., Napa ✛ At McKinstry St. ⊕ www.oxbowpublicmarket.com.

Stags' Leap Winery

WINERY/DISTILLERY | A must for history buffs, this winery was established in 1893 in a bowl-shaped micro valley at the base of the Stags Leap Palisades. Three years earlier its original owners erected the Manor House, which reopened in 2016 after restoration of its castlelike stone facade and redwood-paneled interior. The home, whose open-air porch seems out of a flapper-era movie set, hosts elegant, appointment-only seated tastings of equally refined wines by the Bordeaux-born Christophe Paubert. Estate Cabernet Sauvignons, Merlot, and Petite Sirah, one bottling of the last varietal from vines planted in 1929, are the calling cards. Paubert also makes a blend of these three red grapes, along with Viognier, Chardonnay, and rosé. Some tastings take place on the porch, others inside; all require an appointment and include a tour of the property and tales of its storied past. ⊠ 6150 Silverado Trail, Napa ✛ ¾ mile south of Yountville Cross Rd. ☎ 707/257–5790 ⊕ stagsleap. com ☞ Tastings from $65.

★ St. Clair Brown Winery & Brewery

WINERY/DISTILLERY | Tastings at this women-run "urban winery"—and, since 2017, nanobrewery—a few blocks north of downtown take place in an intimate, light-filled greenhouse or a colorful culinary garden. Winemaker Elaine St. Clair, well regarded for stints at Domaine Carneros and Black Stallion, produces elegant wines—crisp yet complex whites and smooth, French-style reds whose stars include Cabernet Sauvignon and Syrah. While pursuing her wine-making degree, St. Clair also studied brewing; a few of her light-, medium-, and full-bodied brews are always on tap. You can taste the wines or beers by the glass or flight or enjoy them paired with appetizers that might include pork rillette with pickled tomatoes from the garden or addictive almonds roasted with rosemary, lemon zest, and lemon olive oil. Tuesday and Wednesday visits are by appointment only. ⊠ 816 Vallejo St., Napa ✛ Off Soscol Ave. ☎ 707/255–5591 ⊕ www.stclairbrown.com ☞ Tastings from $12 flights, from $4 by the glass.

🍴 Restaurants

★ Compline

$$$ | **MODERN AMERICAN** | The full name of the three-in-one enterprise masterminded by master sommelier Matt Stamp and restaurant wine vet Ryan Stetins is Compline Wine Bar, Restaurant, and Merchant, and indeed you can just sip wine or purchase it here. The place evolved into a hot spot, though, for its youthful vibe and chef Yancy Windsperger's eclectic small and large plates that might include poached egg and polenta or gnocchi vegetable Bolognese. **Known for:** youthful vibe; by-the-glass wines; knowledgeable staff. Ⓢ *Average main: $25* ⊠ *1300 1st St., Suite 312, Napa* ☎ *707/492–8150* ⊕ *complinewine.com* ⊘ *Closed Tues.*

Grace's Table

$$$ | **ECLECTIC** | A dependable, varied, three-squares-a-day menu makes this modest corner restaurant occupying a brick-and-glass storefront many Napans' go-to choice for a simple meal. Iron-skillet corn bread with lavender honey and butter shows up at all hours, with chilaquiles scrambled eggs a breakfast favorite, savory fish tacos a lunchtime staple, and cassoulet and roasted young chicken popular for dinner. **Known for:** congenial staffers; good beers on tap; eclectic menu focusing on France, Italy, and the Americas. Ⓢ *Average main: $24* ⊠ *1400 2nd St., Napa* ⊕ *At Franklin St.* ☎ *707/226–6200* ⊕ *www.gracestable.net.*

Gran Eléctrica

$$ | **MEXICAN** | A neon sign toward the back of Gran Eléctrica translates to "badass bar," but the same goes for the restaurant and its piquant lineup of *botanas* (snacks), tacos, tostadas, quesadillas, entrées, and sides. Ceviche tostadas, fish and carnitas tacos, the chile relleno, and duck-confit mole are among the year-round favorites, with dishes like grilled street-style corn with chipotle mayo appearing in-season. **Known for:** zippy decor; outdoor patio; tequila and mescal flights, specialty cocktails. Ⓢ *Average main: $19* ⊠ *1313 Main St., Napa* ⊕ *Near Clinton St.* ☎ *707/258–1313* ⊕ *www.granelectrica.com/about-napa* ⊘ *No lunch Mon.–Sat.*

★ La Toque

$$$$ | **MODERN AMERICAN** | Chef Ken Frank's La Toque is the complete package: his imaginative French cuisine, served in a formal brown-hued dining space, is complemented by a wine lineup that earned the restaurant a coveted *Wine Spectator* Grand Award. Signature dishes that might appear on the prix-fixe four- or five-course tasting menu include rösti potato with Kaluga caviar, Angus beef tenderloin with grilled king trumpet mushrooms, and New York strip loin with Fiscalini cheddar pearl tapioca and Rutherford red-wine sauce. **Known for:** chef's table menu for entire party; astute wine pairings; vegetarian tasting menu. Ⓢ *Average main: $110* ⊠ *Westin Verasa Napa, 1314 McKinstry St., Napa* ⊕ *Off Soscol Ave.* ☎ *707/257–5157* ⊕ *www.latoque.com* ⊘ *No lunch.*

★ Miminashi

$$$ | **JAPANESE** | Japanese *izakaya*—gastropubs that serve appetizers downed with sake or cocktails—inspired chef Curtis Di Fede's buzz-worthy downtown Napa restaurant, where two peaks in the slatted poplar ceiling echo Shinto and Buddhist temple designs. Ramen, fried rice, and yakitori anchor the menu, whose highlights include wok-fried edamame and the ooh-inspiring *okonomiyaki* pancake with bacon, cabbage, and dried fermented tuna flakes; wines and sakes selected by Jessica Pinzon, formerly of Thomas Keller's Yountville restaurants Bouchon and Ad Hoc, further elevate Di Fede's dishes. **Known for:** distinctive design; wine and sake selection; soft-serve ice cream for dessert and from to-go window. Ⓢ *Average main: $29* ⊠ *821 Coombs St., Napa* ⊕ *Near 3rd St.* ☎ *707/254–9464* ⊕ *miminashi.com* ⊘ *No lunch.*

Morimoto Napa

$$$$ | **JAPANESE** | *Iron Chef* star Masaharu Morimoto is the big name behind this downtown Napa restaurant where everything is delightfully overdone, right down to the desserts. Organic materials such as twisting grapevines above the bar and rough-hewn wooden tables seem simultaneously earthy and modern, creating a fitting setting for the gorgeously plated Japanese fare, from sashimi served with grated fresh wasabi to elaborate concoctions that include sea-urchin carbonara made with Inaniwa udon noodles. **Known for:** elaborate concoctions; gorgeous plating; chef's choice omakase menu (from $130). [$] *Average main: $37* ✉ *610 Main St., Napa* ✣ *At 5th St.* ☎ *707/252–1600* 🌐 *www.morimotonapa.com.*

Oenotri

$$$ | **ITALIAN** | Often spotted at local farmers' markets and his restaurant's gardens, Oenotri's ebullient chef-owner and Napa native Tyler Rodde is ever on the lookout for fresh produce to incorporate into his rustic southern-Italian cuisine. His restaurant, a brick-walled contemporary space with tall windows and wooden tables, is a lively spot to sample house-made salumi and pastas, thin-crust pizzas, and entrées that might include roasted squab, Atlantic salmon, or pork sausage. **Known for:** fresh ingredients; Margherita pizza with San Marzano tomatoes; lively atmosphere. [$] *Average main: $27* ✉ *1425 1st St., Napa* ✣ *At Franklin St.* ☎ *707/252–1022* 🌐 *www.oenotri.com.*

★ Torc

$$$$ | **MODERN AMERICAN** | *Torc* means "wild boar" in an early Celtic dialect, and owner-chef Sean O'Toole, who formerly helmed kitchens at top Manhattan, San Francisco, and Yountville establishments, occasionally incorporates the restaurant's namesake beast into his eclectic offerings. A recent menu featured sea urchin with Persian melon carpaccio, Maine-lobster risotto, and veal sweetbreads with sweet and sour tomatoes, all prepared by O'Toole and his team with style and precision. **Known for:** gracious service; specialty cocktails; Bengali sweet-potato pakora and deviled-egg appetizers. [$] *Average main: $36* ✉ *1140 Main St., Napa* ✣ *At Pearl St.* ☎ *707/252–3292* 🌐 *www.torcnapa.com* ⏲ *Closed Tues. No lunch weekdays.*

★ ZuZu

$$$ | **SPANISH** | At festive ZuZu the focus is on cold and hot tapas, paella, and other Spanish favorites often downed with cava or sangria. Regulars revere the paella, made with Spanish *bomba* rice, and small plates that might include grilled octopus, garlic shrimp, jamón Ibérico, and white anchovies with sliced egg and rémoulade on grilled bread. **Known for:** singular flavors and spicing; Latin jazz on the stereo; sister restaurant La Taberna three doors south for beer, wine, and bar bites. [$] *Average main: $30* ✉ *829 Main St., Napa* ✣ *Near 3rd St.* ☎ *707/224–8555* 🌐 *www.zuzunapa.com* ⏲ *No lunch weekends.*

🛏 Hotels

★ Andaz Napa

$$$ | **HOTEL** | Part of the Hyatt family, this boutique hotel with an urban-hip vibe has spacious, luxurious rooms with flat-screen TVs, laptop-size safes, and white-marble bathrooms stocked with high-quality bath products. **Pros:** proximity to downtown restaurants, theaters, and tasting rooms; access to modern fitness center; complimentary beverage upon arrival; complimentary snacks and nonalcoholic beverages in rooms. **Cons:** parking can be a challenge on weekends; unremarkable views from some rooms; expensive on weekends in high season. [$] *Rooms from: $306* ✉ *1450 1st St., Napa* ☎ *707/687–1234* 🌐 *andaznapa.com* 🛏 *141 rooms* 🍴 *No meals.*

★ Archer Hotel Napa

$$$ | **HOTEL** | A hybrid of New York City and Las Vegas glamour infused downtown Napa with the 2018 completion of this five-story hotel ideal for travelers seeking design pizzazz, a see-and-be-seen atmosphere, and a slate of first-class amenities. **Pros:** restaurants and room service by chef Charlie Palmer; Sky & Vine rooftop bar; views from upper-floor rooms (especially south and west). **Cons:** not particularly rustic; expensive in high season; occasional service, hospitality lapses. $ *Rooms from: $374* ⌧ *1230 1st St., Napa* ☎ *707/690–9800, 855/437–9100* ⊕ *archerhotel.com/napa* ⇗ *183 rooms* ⚞ *No meals.*

★ Carneros Resort & Spa

$$$$ | **RESORT** | Freestanding board-and-batten cottages with rocking chairs on each porch are simultaneously rustic and chic at this luxurious property made even more so by a $6.5 million makeover. **Pros:** cottages have lots of privacy; beautiful views from hilltop pool and hot tub; heaters on private patios. **Cons:** long drive to upvalley destinations; least expensive accommodations pick up highway noise; pricey pretty much year-round. $ *Rooms from: $600* ⌧ *4048 Sonoma Hwy./Hwy. 121, Napa* ☎ *707/299–4900, 888/400–9000* ⊕ *www.carnerosresort.com* ⇗ *100 rooms* ⚞ *No meals.*

★ The Inn on First

$$ | **B&B/INN** | Guests gush over the hospitality at this inn whose painstakingly restored 1905 mansion facing 1st Street contains five rooms, with five additional accommodations, all suites, in a building behind a secluded patio and garden. **Pros:** full gourmet breakfast by hosts-with-the-most owners; gas fireplaces and whirlpool tubs in all rooms; away from downtown but not too far. **Cons:** no TVs; owners "respectfully request no children"; lacks pool, fitness center, and other amenities of larger properties. $ *Rooms from: $220* ⌧ *1938 1st St., Napa* ☎ *707/253–1331*

⊕ *www.theinnonfirst.com* ⇗ *10 rooms* ⚞ *Breakfast.*

★ Inn on Randolph

$$ | **B&B/INN** | A few calm blocks from the downtown action on a nearly 1-acre lot with landscaped gardens, the Inn on Randolph—with a Gothic Revival–style main house and its five guest rooms plus five historic cottages out back—is a sophisticated haven celebrated for its gourmet gluten-free breakfasts and snacks. **Pros:** quiet residential neighborhood; spa tubs in cottages and two main-house rooms; romantic setting. **Cons:** a bit of a walk from downtown; expensive in-season; weekend minimum-stay requirement. $ *Rooms from: $299* ⌧ *411 Randolph St., Napa* ☎ *707/257–2886* ⊕ *www.innonrandolph.com* ⇗ *10 rooms* ⚞ *Breakfast.*

ⓨ Nightlife

Blue Note Napa

MUSIC CLUBS | The famed New York jazz room's West Coast club hosts national headliners such as Brian McKnight, Dee Dee Bridgewater, and Coco Montoya, along with local talents such as Lavay Smith & Her Red Hot Skillet Lickers. There's a full bar, and you can order a meal or small bites from the kitchen. ⌧ *Napa Valley Opera House, 1030 Main St., Napa* ⊹ *At 1st St.* ☎ *707/880–2300* ⊕ *www.bluenotenapa.com.*

Cadet Wine + Beer Bar

WINE BARS—NIGHTLIFE | Cadet plays things urban-style cool with a long bar, high-top tables, an all-vinyl sound track, and a low-lit, generally loungelike feel. When they opened their bar, the two owners described their outlook as "unabashedly pro-California," but their wine-and-beer lineup circles the globe. The crowd here is youngish, the vibe festive. ⌧ *930 Franklin St., Napa* ⊹ *At end of pedestrian alley between 1st and 2nd Sts.* ☎ *707/224–4400* ⊕ *www.cadetbeerandwinebar.com.*

Yountville

9 miles north of the town of Napa.

These days Yountville is something like Disneyland for food lovers. You could stay here for a week and not exhaust all the options—several of them owned by The French Laundry's Thomas Keller—and the tiny town is full of small inns and high-end hotels that cater to those who prefer to walk (not drive) after an extravagant meal. It's also well located for excursions to many big-name Napa wineries, especially those in the Stags Leap District, from which big, bold Cabernet Sauvignons helped make the Napa Valley's wine-making reputation.

GETTING HERE AND AROUND

Downtown Yountville sits just off Highway 29. Approaching from the south take the Yountville exit—from the north take Madison—and proceed to Washington Street, home to the major shops and restaurants. Yountville Cross Road connects downtown to the Silverado Trail, along which many noted wineries do business. The free Yountville Trolley serves the town daily 10 am–7 pm (on-call service until 11 except on Sunday).

◉ Sights

★ Cliff Lede Vineyards

WINERY/DISTILLERY | Inspired by his passion for classic rock, owner and construction magnate Cliff Lede named the blocks in his Stags Leap District vineyard after hits by the Grateful Dead and other bands. The vibe at his efficient, high-tech winery is anything but laid-back, however. Cutting-edge agricultural and enological science informs the vineyard management and wine making here. Architect Howard Backen designed the winery and its tasting room, where Lede's Sauvignon Blanc, Cabernet Sauvignons, and other wines, along with some from sister winery FEL, which produces much-lauded Anderson Valley Pinot Noirs, are poured.

■ TIP → **Walk-ins are welcome at the tasting bar, but appointments are required for the veranda outside and a nearby gallery that displays rock-related art.** ⊠ *1473 Yountville Cross Rd., Yountville* ✛ *Off Silverado Trail* ☎ *707/944–8642* ⊕ *cliffledevineyards.com* ⌂ *Tastings from $35.*

Domaine Chandon

WINERY/DISTILLERY | On a knoll shaded by ancient oak trees, this French-owned maker of sparkling wines claims one of Yountville's prime pieces of real estate. Chandon is best known for bubbles, but the still wines—among them Cabernet Sauvignon, Chardonnay, and Pinot Noir—are also worth a try. You can sip by the flight or by the glass at the bar, or begin there and sit at tables in the lounge and return to the bar as needed; in good weather, tables are set up outside. Bottle service is also available. ⊠ *1 California Dr., Yountville* ✛ *Off Hwy. 29* ☎ *707/204–7530, 888/242–6366* ⊕ *www.chandon. com* ⌂ *Tastings from $10.*

Goosecross Cellars

WINERY/DISTILLERY | When Christi Coors Ficeli purchased this boutique winery in 2013 and commissioned a new barnlike tasting space, she and her architect had one major goal: bring the outside in. Large retractable west-facing windows open up behind the tasting bar to idyllic views of Cabernet vines—in fine weather, guests on the outdoor deck can practically touch them. Goosecross makes Chardonnay and Pinot Noir from Carneros grapes, but the soul of this cordial operation is its 12-acre estate vineyard, its 10 planted acres mostly Cabernet Sauvignon and Merlot with some Cabernet Franc and Petit Verdot. The Cab and Merlot are the stars, along with the Aeros Bordeaux-style blend of the best estate grapes. Aeros isn't usually poured, but a Howell Mountain Petite Sirah with expressive tannins (there's also a Howell Mountain Cabernet) often is. Visits to Goosecross are by appointment only. ⊠ *1119 State La.,*

Yountville ✧ Off Yountville Cross Rd. ☎ 707/944–1986 ⊕ www.goosecross. com ✉ Tastings from $40.

RH Yountville

MUSEUM | Gargantuan crystal chandeliers, century-old olive trees, and strategically placed water features provide visual and aural continuity at Restoration Hardware's quadruple-threat food, wine, art, and design compound. An all-day café fronts two steel, glass, and concrete home-furnishings galleries, with a bluestone walkway connecting them to a reboot of the Ma(i)sonry wine salon. Inside a two-story 1904 manor house constructed from Napa River stone and rechristened The Wine Vault at the Historic Ma(i)sonry Building, it remains an excellent tasting choice. Classic and Connoisseur flights focus on small-lot Napa and Sonoma bottlings; hosts at Collector tastings pour Napa Valley wines by elite winemakers like Heidi Barrett and Philippe Melka. In good weather, some tastings take place in outdoor living rooms where patrons can also enjoy coffee, tea, or wine by the glass or bottle. Walk-ins are welcome, but reservations are recommended (and wise on weekends in-season). ⊠ 6725 Washington St., Yountville ✧ At Pedroni St. ☎ 707/339–4654 ⊕ www.restoration-hardware.com ✉ Tastings from $50.

★ Robert Sinskey Vineyards

WINERY/DISTILLERY | Although the winery produces a well-regarded Stags Leap Cabernet Sauvignon, two Bordeaux-style red blends (Marcien and POV), and white wines, Sinskey is best known for its intense, brambly Carneros District Pinot Noirs. All the grapes are grown in organic, certified biodynamic vineyards. The influence of Robert's wife, Maria Helm Sinskey—a chef and cookbook author and the winery's culinary director—is evident during the tastings, which are accompanied by a few bites of food with each wine. ■TIP→ The Perfect Circle Tour, offered daily, takes in the winery's gardens and ends with a seated pairing of food and wine. Even more elaborate, also by appointment, is the five-course Chef's Table pairing of seasonal dishes with current and older wines. ⊠ 6320 Silverado Trail, Napa ✧ At Yountville Cross Rd. ☎ 707/944–9090 ⊕ www.robertsinskey.com ✉ Tastings from $40, tours (with tastings) from $95.

★ Stewart Cellars

WINERY/DISTILLERY | Three stone structures meant to mimic Scottish ruins coaxed into modernity form this complex that includes public and private tasting spaces, a bright outdoor patio, and a hip, independently run café. The attention to detail in the ensemble's design mirrors that of the wines, whose grapes come from coveted vineyards, most notably all six of the Beckstoffer Heritage Vineyards, among the Napa Valley's most historic sites. Although Cabernet is the focus, winemaker Blair Guthrie, with input from consulting winemaker Paul Hobbs, also makes Sauvignon Blanc, Chardonnay, Pinot Noir, and Merlot. ■TIP→ On sunny days this is a good stop around lunchtime, when you can order a meal from the café and a glass of wine from the tasting room—for permit reasons this must be done separately—and enjoy them on the patio. ⊠ 6752 Washington St., Yountville ✧ Near Pedroni St. ☎ 707/963–9160 ⊕ www.stewartcellars. com ✉ Tastings from $30.

🍴 Restaurants

★ Ad Hoc

$$$$ | MODERN AMERICAN | At this low-key dining room with zinc-top tables and wine served in tumblers, superstar chef Thomas Keller offers a single, fixed-price, nightly menu that might include smoked beef short ribs with creamy herb rice and charred broccolini or sesame chicken with radish kimchi and fried rice. Ad Hoc also serves a small but decadent Sunday brunch, and Keller's Addendum annex, in a separate small building behind the restaurant, sells boxed lunches to go (beyond moist buttermilk fried chicken) from Thursday to Saturday except in winter. **Known for:** casual cuisine at great prices for a Thomas Keller restaurant; don't-miss buttermilk-fried-chicken night; street-side outdoor seating. [$] *Average main: $55* ✉ *6476 Washington St., Yountville* ✣ *At Oak Circle* ☎ *707/944–2487* 🌐 *www.adhocrestaurant.com* ⏲ *No lunch Mon.–Sat.; no dinner Tues. and Wed.* ☞ *Call day ahead to find out next day's menu.*

★ Bistro Jeanty

$$$ | **FRENCH** | Escargots, cassoulet, *daube de boeuf* (beef stewed in red wine), and other French classics are prepared with the utmost precision at this country bistro whose lamb tongue and other obscure delicacies delight daring diners. Regulars often start with the rich tomato soup in a flaky puff pastry before proceeding to sole meunière or coq au vin, completing the French sojourn with a lemon meringue tart or other authentic desserts. **Known for:** traditional preparations; oh-so-French atmosphere; European wines. [$] *Average main: $29* ✉ *6510 Washington St., Yountville* ✣ *At Mulberry St.* ☎ *707/944–0103* 🌐 *www.bistrojeanty.com.*

★ Bouchon Bistro

$$$$ | **FRENCH** | The team that created The French Laundry is also behind this place, where everything—the lively and crowded zinc-topped bar, the elbow-to-elbow seating, the traditional French onion soup—could have come straight from a Parisian bistro. Pan-seared rib eye with béarnaise and mussels steamed with white wine, saffron, and Dijon mustard—both served with crispy, addictive fries—are among the perfectly executed entrées. **Known for:** bistro classics; raw bar; Bouchon Bakery next door. [$] *Average main: $32* ✉ *6534 Washington St., Yountville* ✣ *Near Humboldt St.* ☎ *707/944–8037* 🌐 *www.bouchonbistro.com.*

Ciccio

$$ | **MODERN ITALIAN** | The ranch of Ciccio's owners, Frank and Karen Altamura, supplies some of the vegetables and herbs for the modern Italian cuisine prepared in the open kitchen of this remodeled former grocery store. Seasonal growing cycles dictate the menu, with fried-seafood appetizers (calamari, perhaps, or softshell crabs), a few pasta dishes, bavette steak with red-wine jus, and pancetta pizzas among the frequent offerings. **Known for:** Negroni bar; prix-fixe chef's dinner; mostly Napa Valley wines, some from owners' winery. [$] *Average main: $19* ✉ *6770 Washington St., Yountville* ✣ *At Madison St.* ☎ *707/945–1000* 🌐 *www.ciccionapavalley.com* ⏲ *Closed Mon. and Tues. No lunch* ☞ *No reservations, except for prix-fixe chef's dinner (required; for 2–10 guests).*

★ The French Laundry

$$$$ | **AMERICAN** | An old stone building laced with ivy houses chef Thomas Keller's destination restaurant. Some courses on the two prix-fixe menus, one of which highlights vegetables, rely on luxe ingredients such as *calotte* (cap of the rib eye) while other courses take humble elements like carrots or fava beans and elevate them to art; many courses offer "supplements"—sea urchin, for instance, or black truffles. **Known for:** signature starter "oysters and pearls"; intricate flavors; superior wine list. [$] *Average main: $325* ✉ *6640 Washington St., Yountville* ✣ *At Creek St.* ☎ *707/944–2380* 🌐 *www.frenchlaundry.com* ⏲ *No lunch Mon.–Thurs.* 👔 *Jacket required* ☞ *Reservations essential wks ahead.*

Mustards Grill

$$$ | **AMERICAN** | Cindy Pawlcyn's Mustards Grill fills day and night with fans of her hearty cuisine, equal parts updated renditions of traditional American dishes—what Pawlcyn dubs "deluxe truck stop classics"—and fanciful contemporary fare. Barbecued baby back pork

ribs and a lemon-lime tart piled high with brown-sugar meringue fall squarely in the first category, with sweet corn tamales with tomatillo-avocado salsa and wild mushrooms representing the latter. **Known for:** roadhouse setting; convivial mood; hoppin' bar. $ *Average main: $28* ⊠ *7399 St. Helena Hwy./Hwy. 29, Napa* ✛ *1 mile north of Yountville* ☎ *707/944–2424* ⊕ *www.mustardsgrill.com.*

★ Protéa Restaurant

$$ | LATIN AMERICAN | A meal at Yountville's The French Laundry motivated Puerto Rico–born Anita Cartagena to pursue a career as a chef, which she did for several years at nearby Ciccio and elsewhere before opening this perky storefront serving Latin-inspired multiculti fast-food cuisine. What's in season and the chef's whims determine the order-at-the-counter fare, but Puerto Rican rice bowls (often with pork), empanadas, and sweet-and-sour ramen stir-fries make regular appearances. **Known for:** patio and rooftop seating; beer and wine lineup; eager-to-please staff. $ *Average main: $16* ⊠ *6488 Washington St., Yountville* ✛ *At Oak Circle* ☎ *707/415–5035* ⊕ *www.proteayv.com* ⊗ *Closed Wed.*

Redd Wood

$$ | ITALIAN | Chef Richard Reddington's casual restaurant specializes in thin-crust wood-fired pizzas and contemporary variations on Italian classics. With potato–and–green garlic soup, pizzas such as the sausage with a blend of goat cheese and mozzarella, and the pork chop entrée enlivened in fall by persimmon, Redd Wood does for Italian comfort food what nearby Mustards Grill does for the American version: it spruces it up but retains its innate pleasures. **Known for:** industrial decor; easygoing service; lunch through late-night menu. $ *Average main: $22* ⊠ *North Block Hotel, 6755 Washington St., Yountville* ✛ *At Madison St.* ☎ *707/299–5030* ⊕ *www.redd-wood.com.*

🛏 Hotels

★ Bardessono

$$$$ | RESORT | Tranquillity and luxury with a low carbon footprint are among the goals of this ultragreen wood, steel, and glass resortlike property in downtown Yountville, but there's nothing spartan about its accommodations, arranged around four landscaped courtyards. **Pros:** large rooftop lap pool; in-room spa treatments; smooth service. **Cons:** expensive; limited view from some rooms; a bit of street traffic on hotel's west side. $ *Rooms from: $700* ⊠ *6526 Yount St., Yountville* ☎ *707/204–6000* ⊕ *www.bardessono.com* ⇗ *62 rooms* ⏹ *No meals.*

Maison Fleurie

$$ | B&B/INN | A stay at this comfortable, reasonably priced inn, said to be the oldest hotel in the Napa Valley, places you within walking distance of Yountville's fine restaurants. **Pros:** smallest rooms a bargain; outdoor hot tub and pool; free bike rental. **Cons:** breakfast room can be crowded at peak times; some rooms pick up noise from nearby Bouchon Bakery; hard to book in high season. $ *Rooms from: $229* ⊠ *6529 Yount St., Yountville* ☎ *707/944–2056* ⊕ *www.maisonfleurien-apa.com* ⇗ *13 rooms* ⏹ *Breakfast.*

Napa Valley Lodge

$$ | HOTEL | Clean rooms in a convenient motel-style setting draw travelers willing to pay more than at comparable lodgings in the city of Napa to be within walking distance of Yountville's tasting rooms, restaurants, and shops. **Pros:** clean rooms; filling continental breakfast; large pool area. **Cons:** no elevator; lacks amenities of other Yountville properties; pricey on weekends in high season. $ *Rooms from: $280* ⊠ *2230 Madison St., Yountville* ☎ *707/944–2468, 888/944–3545* ⊕ *www.napavalleylodge.com* ⇗ *55 rooms* ⏹ *Breakfast.*

★ North Block Hotel

$$$$ | HOTEL | A two-story boutique property near downtown Yountville's northern edge, the North Block attracts sophisticated travelers who appreciate its clever but unpretentious style and offhand luxury. **Pros:** extremely comfortable beds; attentive service; room service by Redd Wood restaurant. **Cons:** outdoor areas get some traffic noise; weekend minimum-stay requirement; rates soar on high-season weekends. [$] *Rooms from: $425* ✉ *6757 Washington St., Yountville* ☎ *707/944–8080* 🌐 *northblockhotel.com* 🛏 *20 rooms* 🍴 *No meals.*

Vintage House

$$$ | RESORT | Part of the 22-acre Estate Yountville complex—other sections include sister lodging Hotel Villagio and the shops and restaurants of V Marketplace—this downtown hotel consists of two-story brick buildings along verdant landscaped paths shaded by mature trees. **Pros:** aesthetically pleasing accommodations; private patios and balconies; secluded feeling yet near shops, tasting rooms, and restaurants. **Cons:** highway noise audible in some exterior rooms; very expensive on summer and fall weekends; weekend minimum-stay requirement. [$] *Rooms from: $355* ✉ *6541 Washington St., Yountville* ☎ *707/944–1112* 🌐 *www.vintagehouse.com* 🛏 *80 rooms* 🍴 *Breakfast.*

Activities

BALLOONING

Napa Valley Aloft

BALLOONING | Between 8 and 12 passengers soar over the Napa Valley in balloons that launch from downtown Yountville. Rates include preflight refreshments and a huge breakfast. ✉ *V Marketplace, 6525 Washington St., Yountville* ✥ *Near Mulberry St.* ☎ *707/944–4400, 855/944–4408* 🌐 *www.nvaloft.com* 🎟 *From $200.*

BIKING

Napa Valley Bike Tours

BICYCLING | With dozens of wineries within 5 miles, this shop makes a fine starting point for guided and self-guided vineyard and wine-tasting excursions. The outfit also rents bikes. ✉ *6500 Washington St., Yountville* ✥ *At Mulberry St.* ☎ *707/944–2953* 🌐 *www.napavalleybiketours.com* 🎟 *From $124 (½-day guided tour).*

Shopping

Hunter Gatherer

CLOTHING | A Napa Valley play on the classic general store, Colby Hallen's high-end lifestyle shop sells women's clothing and accessories from designers such as Frēda Salvador and Emerson Fry. She carries some men's items, too, along with everything from ceramic flasks and small gifts and cards to artisanal honey and Vintner's Daughter Active Botanical Serum face oil. ✉ *6795 Washington St., Bldg. B, Yountville* ✥ *At Madison St.* 🌐 *www.huntergathererna-pavalley.com.*

V Marketplace

SHOPPING CENTERS/MALLS | This two-story redbrick market, which once housed a winery, a livery stable, and a brandy distillery, now contains clothing boutiques, art galleries, a chocolatier, and food, wine, and gift shops. Celebrity chef Michael Chiarello operates a restaurant (Bottega), a tasting room for his wines, and Ottimo, with pizza, fresh mozzarella, and other stands plus retail items. Show some love to the shops upstairs, especially Knickers and Pearls (lingerie and loungewear) and Lemondrops (kids' clothing and toys). ✉ *6525 Washington St., Yountville* ✥ *Near Mulberry St.* ☎ *707/944–2451* 🌐 *www.vmarketplace.com.*

SPAS

B Spa Therapy Center

SPA/BEAUTY | Many of this spa's patrons are Bardessono Hotel guests who take their treatments in their rooms' large, customized bathrooms—all of them equipped with concealed massage tables—but the main facility is open to guests and nonguests. An in-room treatment popular with couples starts with massages in front of the fireplace and ends with a tea bath and a split of sparkling wine. The two-hour Yountville Signature treatment, which can be enjoyed in-room or at the spa, begins with a shea-butter-enriched sugar scrub, followed by a Chardonnay grape-seed oil massage and a hydrating hair-and-scalp treatment. The spa engages massage therapists skilled in Swedish, Thai, and several other techniques. In addition to massages, the services include facials and other skin-care treatments. ⊠ Bardessono Hotel, 6526 Yount St., Yountville ✛ At Mulberry St. ☎ 707/204–6050 ⊕ www.bardessono.com/spa ✍ Treatments from $165.

Oakville

2 miles northwest of Yountville.

A large butte that runs east–west just north of Yountville blocks the cooling fogs from the south, facilitating the myriad microclimates of the Oakville AVA, home to several high-profile wineries.

GETTING HERE AND AROUND
Driving along Highway 29, you'll know you've reached Oakville when you see the Oakville Grocery on the east side of the road. You can reach Oakville from the Sonoma County town of Glen Ellen by heading east on Trinity Road from Highway 12. The twisting route, along the mountain range that divides Napa and Sonoma, eventually becomes the Oakville Grade. The views on this drive are breathtaking, though the continual curves make it unsuitable for those who suffer from motion sickness.

◉ Sights

B Cellars
WINERY/DISTILLERY | The chefs take center stage in the open-hearth kitchen of this boutique winery's hospitality house, and with good reason: creating food-friendly wines is B Cellars's raison d'être. Visits to the Oakville facility—all steel beams, corrugated metal, and plate glass yet remarkably cozy—begin with a tour of the winery's culinary garden and in some cases also the caves. Most guests return to the house to sample wines paired with small bites, with some visitors remaining in the caves for exclusive tastings of Cabernet Sauvignons from several historic vineyards of Andy Beckstoffer, a prominent grower. Kirk Venge, whose fruit-forward style well suits the winery's food-oriented approach, crafts these and other wines, among them red and white blends and single-vineyard Cabernets from other noteworthy vineyards. All visits here are strictly by appointment. ⊠ 703 Oakville Cross Rd., Oakville ✛ West of Silverado Trail ☎ 707/709–8787 ⊕ www.bcellars.com ✍ Tastings from $65.

Far Niente
WINERY/DISTILLERY | Hamden McIntyre, a prominent winery architect of his era also responsible for Inglenook and what's now the Culinary Institute of America at Greystone, designed the centerpiece 1885 stone winery here. Abandoned in the wake of Prohibition and only revived beginning in 1979, Far Niente now ranks as one of the Napa Valley's most beautiful properties. Guests participating in the main tour and tasting learn some of this history while strolling the winery and its aging caves. The trip completed, hosts pour the flagship wines, a Chardonnay and a Cabernet Sauvignon blend. The tasting session concludes with Dolce, a late-harvest Sémillon and Sauvignon Blanc wine. Two shorter tastings, one highlighting older vintages, the other showcasing the output of affiliated wineries, dispense with the tour. ■TIP→ Aged

and rare Cabernets from the Far Niente wine library are served at Cave Collection tastings. ⌗ *1350 Acacia Dr., Oakville* ✥ *Off Oakville Grade Rd.* ☎ *707/944–2861* ⊕ *www.farniente.com* ✉ *Tastings from $80; tour and tasting $80.*

Robert Mondavi Winery

WINERY/DISTILLERY | The graceful arch at the center of the winery's Mission-style building frames the lawn and the vineyard behind, inviting a stroll under the arcades. You can head for one of the walk-in tasting rooms, but if you've not toured a winery before, the 75-minute Signature Tour and Tasting is a good way to learn about enology and the late Robert Mondavi's role in California wine making. Those new to tasting should consider the 45-minute Wine Tasting Basics experience. Serious wine lovers can opt for the Exclusive Cellar tasting, during which a server pours and explains limited-production, reserve, and older vintages. The three-course Harvest of Joy Lunch and wine pairing starts with a tour. All visits except walk-in tastings require reservations. ■TIP➔ **Well-attended concerts take place in summer on the lawn.** ⌗ *7801 St. Helena Hwy./Hwy. 29, Oakville* ☎ *888/766–6328* ⊕ *www.robertmondaviwinery.com* ✉ *Tastings and tours from $25.*

★ Silver Oak

WINERY/DISTILLERY | The first review of this winery's Napa Valley Cabernet Sauvignon declared the debut 1972 vintage not all that good and, at $6 a bottle, overpriced. Oops. The celebrated Bordeaux-style Cabernet blend, still the only Napa Valley wine bearing its winery's label each year, evolved into a cult favorite, and Silver Oak founders Ray Duncan and Justin Meyer received worldwide recognition for their signature use of exclusively American oak to age the wines. At the Oakville tasting room, constructed out of reclaimed stone and other materials from a 19th-century Kansas flour mill, you can sip the current Napa Valley vintage, its

counterpart from Silver Oak's Alexander Valley operation, and a library wine without an appointment. One is required for tours, private tastings, and food–wine pairings. ⌗ *915 Oakville Cross Rd., Oakville* ✥ *Off Hwy. 29* ☎ *707/942–7022* ⊕ *www.silveroak.com* ✉ *Tastings from $30, tours from $40 (includes tasting).*

Rutherford

2 miles northwest of Oakville.

With its singular microclimate and soil, Rutherford is an important viticultural center, with more big-name wineries than you can shake a corkscrew at. Cabernet Sauvignon is king here. The well-drained, loamy soil is ideal for those vines, and since this part of the valley gets plenty of sun, the grapes develop exceptionally intense flavors.

GETTING HERE AND AROUND

Wineries around Rutherford are dotted along Highway 29 and the parallel Silverado Trail north and south of Rutherford Road/Conn Creek Road, on which wineries can also be found.

⊙ Sights

★ Frog's Leap

WINERY/DISTILLERY | **FAMILY** | If you're a novice, the tour at Frog's Leap is a fun way to begin your education. You'll taste wines that might include Zinfandel, Merlot, Chardonnay, Sauvignon Blanc, and an estate-grown Cabernet Sauvignon. The winery includes a barn built in 1884, 5 acres of organic gardens, an eco-friendly visitor center, and a frog pond topped with lily pads. Reservations are required for all visits here. ■TIP➔ **The tour is recommended, but you can also just sample wines either inside or on a porch overlooking the garden.** ⌗ *8815 Conn Creek Rd., Rutherford* ☎ *707/963–4704, 800/959–4704* ⊕ *www.frogsleap.com* ✉ *Tastings from $25, tour $35.*

Honig Vineyard & Winery

WINERY/DISTILLERY | **FAMILY** | Sustainable farming is the big story at this family-run winery. The Eco Tour, offered seasonally, focuses on the Honig family's environmentally friendly farming and production methods, which include using biodiesel to fuel the tractors, monitoring water use in the vineyard and winery, and generating power for the winery with solar panels. The family produces only Sauvignon Blanc and Cabernet Sauvignon. By appointment, you can taste whites and reds at a standard tasting; the reserve tasting pairs single-vineyard Cabernets with small bites. ✉ *850 Rutherford Rd., Rutherford* ✣ *Near Conn Creek Rd.* ☎ *800/929–2217* 🌐 *www.honigwine.com* 🎟 *Tastings from $30, tour $45.*

★ Inglenook

WINERY/DISTILLERY | Filmmaker Francis Ford Coppola began his wine-making career in 1975, when he bought part of the historic Inglenook estate. Over the decades he reunited the original property acquired by Inglenook founder Gustave Niebaum, remodeled Niebaum's ivy-covered 1880s château, and purchased the rights to the Inglenook name. The Inglenook Experience, an escorted tour of the château, vineyards, and caves, ends with a seated tasting of wines paired with artisanal cheeses. Among the topics discussed are the winery's history and the evolution of Coppola's signature wine, Rubicon, a Cabernet Sauvignon–based blend. The Heritage Tasting, which also includes a Rubicon pour, is held in the opulent Pennino Salon. Reservations are required for some tastings and tours, and are recommended for all. **■ TIP→ Walk-ins can sip wines by the glass or bottle at The Bistro, a wine bar with a picturesque courtyard.** ✉ *1991 St. Helena Hwy./Hwy. 29, Rutherford* ✣ *At Hwy. 128* ☎ *707/968–1100* 🌐 *www.inglenook.com* 🎟 *Tastings from $45, private experiences from $75.*

Mumm Napa

WINERY/DISTILLERY | In Mumm's light-filled tasting room or adjacent outdoor patio you can enjoy bubbly by the flight, but the sophisticated sparkling wines, elegant setting, and vineyard views aren't the only reasons to visit. An excellent gallery displays original Ansel Adams prints and presents temporary exhibitions by premier photographers. Winery tours cover the major steps in making sparklers. For a leisurely tasting of several vintages of the top-of-the-line DVX wines, book an Oak Terrace tasting. Reservations are required for this tasting and the tour; they're recommended for tastings inside or on the patio. ✉ *8445 Silverado Trail, Rutherford* ✣ *1 mile south of Rutherford Cross Rd.* ☎ *707/967–7700, 800/783–5826* 🌐 *www.mummnapa.com* 🎟 *Tastings from $25, tour $40 (includes tasting).*

🍴 Restaurants

★ Restaurant at Auberge du Soleil

$$$$ | **MODERN AMERICAN** | Possibly the most romantic roost for dinner in all the Wine Country is a terrace seat at the Auberge du Soleil resort's illustrious restaurant, and the Mediterranean-inflected cuisine more than matches the dramatic vineyard views. The prix-fixe dinner menu, which relies mainly on local produce, might include crispy veal sweetbreads and chanterelles or prime beef pavé with hearts of palm, arugula pesto, and tomato confit. **Known for:** polished service; comprehensive wine list; over-the-top weekend brunch. [$] *Average main: $120* ✉ *Auberge du Soleil, 180 Rutherford Hill Rd., Rutherford* ✣ *Off Silverado Trail* ☎ *707/963–1211, 800/348–5406* 🌐 *www.aubergedusoleil.com.*

★ Rutherford Grill

$$$ | **AMERICAN** | Dark-wood walls, subdued lighting, and red-leather banquettes make for a perpetually clubby mood at this Rutherford hangout whose patio, popular for its bar, fireplace, and rocking

Frog's Leap's picturesque country charm extends all the way to the white picket fence.

chairs, is open for full meal service or drinks and appetizers when the weather's right. Many entrées—steaks, burgers, fish, rotisserie chicken, and barbecued pork ribs—emerge from an oak-fired grill operated by master technicians. **Known for:** signature French dip sandwich and grilled jumbo artichokes; reasonably priced wine list with rarities; patio's bar, fireplace, and rocking chairs. [$] *Average main: $30* ✉ *1180 Rutherford Rd., Rutherford* ✣ *At Hwy. 29* ☎ *707/963–1792* 🌐 *www.rutherfordgrill.com.*

Hotels

★ Auberge du Soleil

$$$$ | **RESORT** | Taking a cue from the olive-tree-studded landscape, this hotel with a renowned restaurant and spa cultivates a luxurious look that blends French and California style. **Pros:** stunning views over the valley; spectacular pool and spa areas; the most expensive suites are fit for a superstar. **Cons:** stratospheric prices; least expensive rooms get some noise from the bar and restaurant; weekend minimum-stay requirement. [$] *Rooms from: $950* ✉ *180 Rutherford Hill Rd., Rutherford* ☎ *707/963–1211, 800/348–5406* 🌐 *www.aubergedusoleil.com* 🛏 *52 rooms* 🍴 *Breakfast.*

St. Helena

2 miles northwest of Oakville.

Downtown St. Helena is the very picture of good living in the Wine Country: sycamore trees arch over Main Street (Highway 29), where visitors flit between boutiques, cafés, and storefront tasting rooms housed in sun-faded redbrick buildings. The genteel district pulls in rafts of tourists during the day, though like most Wine Country towns St. Helena more or less rolls up the sidewalks after dark.

The Napa Valley floor narrows between the Mayacamas and Vaca mountains around St. Helena. The slopes reflect heat onto the vineyards below, and since there's less fog and wind, things get pretty toasty. This is one of the valley's hottest AVAs, with midsummer temperatures often reaching the mid-90s. Bordeaux varietals are the most popular grapes grown here—especially Cabernet Sauvignon but also Merlot, Cabernet Franc, and Sauvignon Blanc.

GETTING HERE AND AROUND
Downtown stretches along Highway 29, called Main Street here. Many wineries lie north and south of downtown along Highway 29. More can be found off Silverado Trail, and some of the most scenic spots are on Spring Mountain, which rises southwest of town.

◉ Sights

Beringer Vineyards
WINERY/DISTILLERY | Brothers Frederick and Jacob Beringer opened the winery that still bears their name in 1876. One of California's earliest bonded wineries, it is the oldest one in the Napa Valley never to have missed a vintage—no mean feat, given Prohibition. Frederick's grand Rhine House Mansion, built in 1884, serves as the reserve tasting room. Here, surrounded by Belgian art-nouveau hand-carved oak and walnut furniture and stained-glass windows, you can sample wines that include a limited-release Chardonnay, a few big Cabernets, and a Sauterne-style dessert wine. A less expensive tasting takes place in the original stone winery. Reservations are required for some tastings and recommended for tours. ■TIP→ **The one-hour Taste of Beringer tour of the property and sensory gardens surveys the winery's history and wine making and concludes with a seated wine-and-food pairing.** ⊠ *2000 Main St./ Hwy. 29, St. Helena* ✛ *Near Pratt Ave.* ☎ *707/963–8989* ⊕ *www.beringer.com* ⊠ *Tastings from $25, tours from $30.*

Charles Krug Winery
WINERY/DISTILLERY | A historically sensitive renovation of its 1874 Redwood Cellar Building transformed the former production facility of the Napa Valley's oldest winery into an epic hospitality center. Charles Krug, a Prussian immigrant, established the winery in 1861 and ran it until his death in 1892. Italian immigrants Cesare Mondavi and his wife, Rosa, purchased Charles Krug in 1943, and operated it with their sons Peter and Robert (who later opened his own winery). The winery, still run by Peter's family, specializes in small-lot Yountville and Howell Mountain Cabernet Sauvignons and makes Chardonnay, Merlot, Pinot Noir, Sauvignon Blanc, Zinfandel, and a Zinfandel port. The tour is by appointment only. ⊠ *2800 Main St./Hwy. 29, St. Helena* ✛ *Across from Culinary Institute of America* ☎ *707/967–2229* ⊕ *www.charleskrug.com* ⊠ *Tastings $45, tour $75 (includes tasting).*

Culinary Institute of America at Greystone
COLLEGE | The West Coast headquarters of the country's leading school for chefs is in the 1889 Greystone Cellars, an imposing building once the world's largest stone winery. On the ground floor you can check out the quirky Corkscrew Museum and browse the Spice Islands Marketplace store, stocked with gleaming gadgets and many cookbooks. The Bakery Café by illy serves soups, salads, sandwiches, and baked goods. One-day and multiday cooking and beverage classes often take place. Students run the Gatehouse Restaurant, which serves dinner except during semester breaks. ⊠ *2555 Main St./Hwy. 29, St. Helena* ☎ *707/967–1100* ⊕ *www.ciachef.edu/ california* ⊠ *Museum free, tour $10; class prices vary.*

Hall St. Helena
WINERY/DISTILLERY | The Cabernet Sauvignons produced here are works of art and the latest in organic-farming science and wine-making technology. A glass-walled tasting room allows guests to see in action some of the high-tech equipment winemaker Steve Leveque employs to craft wines that also include

Merlot, Cabernet Franc, and Sauvignon Blanc. Westward from the second-floor tasting area, rows of neatly spaced Cabernet vines capture the eye, and beyond them the tree-studded Mayacamas Mountains. The main guided tour takes in the facility, the grounds, and a restored 19th-century winery, passing artworks by John Baldessari, Jaume Plensa, and other contemporary talents. On Friday and weekends, tastings of limited-production Baca label Zinfandels take place. ■TIP→ Hall Rutherford, an appointment-only sister winery, provides an exclusive, elegant wine-and-food pairing atop a Rutherford hillside. ⊠ 401 St. Helena Hwy./Hwy. 29, St. Helena ✛ Near White La. ☎ 707/967–2626 ⊕ www. hallwines.com ⊠ Tastings from $30, tours from $40.

★ Joseph Phelps Vineyards
WINERY/DISTILLERY | An appointment is required for tastings at the winery started by the late Joseph Phelps, but it's well worth the effort—all the more so after an inspired renovation of the main redwood structure, a classic of 1970s Northern California architecture. Known for wines crafted with grace and precision, Phelps does produce fine whites, but the blockbusters are red, particularly the Cabernet Sauvignon and the luscious-yet-subtle Bordeaux-style blend called Insignia. In good weather, one-hour seated tastings take place on a terrace overlooking vineyards and oaks. At 90-minute tastings as thoughtfully conceived as the wines, guests explore such topics as wine-and-cheese pairing, wine blending, and the role oak barrels play in wine making. Participants in the blending seminar mix the various varietals that go into the Insignia blend. ⊠ 200 Taplin Rd., St. Helena ✛ Off Silverado Trail ☎ 707/963–2745, 800/707–5789 ⊕ www.josephphelps.com ⊠ Tastings and seminars from $75.

★ Mad Fritz Brewing Co.
WINERY/DISTILLERY | #Beerpassion reigns at this St. Helena tap room where enthusiastic fans and palate-cleansing wine tourists stop to quaff small-lot lagers and ales crafted with a winemaker's sensibility. The goal of founder and master brewer Nile Zacherle, who, when he's not at the brewery, works at a Pritchard Hill winery, isn't merely to make great beers. He and his wife, Whitney Fisher, succeed at that, but they also create what they call "origin specific beers," with each label listing where the couple sourced every ingredient from hops to barley to water. The beers' label art and names, among them The Wind and the Sun and The Donkey and the Thistle, derive from a centuries-old Aesop's Fables edition. Along with the label's ingredients list is a summary of the bottling's fable and, in boldface, its moral. ⊠ 1282B Vidovich Ave., St. Helena ✛ At Hwy. 29 ☎ 707/968–5097 ⊕ www.madfritz.com ⊠ Tastings from $3 per pour.

Prager Winery & Port Works
WINERY/DISTILLERY | "If door is locked, ring bell," reads a sign outside the weathered-redwood tasting shack at this family-run winery known for red, white, and tawny ports. The sign, the bell, and the thousands of dollar bills tacked to the walls and ceilings inside are your first indications that you're drifting back in time with the old-school Pragers, who have been making regular and fortified wines in St. Helena since the late 1970s. Five members of the second generation, along with two spouses, run this homespun operation founded by Jim and Imogene Prager. In addition to ports the winery makes Petite Sirah and Sweet Claire, a late-harvest Riesling dessert wine. ⊠ 1281 Lewelling La., St. Helena ✛ Off Hwy. 29 ☎ 707/963–7678 ⊕ www.pragerport.com ⊠ Tastings $30 (includes glass).

Pride Mountain Vineyards

WINERY/DISTILLERY | This winery 2,200 feet up Spring Mountain straddles Napa and Sonoma counties, confusing enough for visitors but even more complicated for the wine-making staff: government regulations require separate wineries and paperwork for each side of the property. It's one of several amusing Pride Mountain quirks, but winemaker Sally Johnson's "big red wines," including a Cabernet Sauvignon that earned 100-point scores from a major wine critic two years in a row, are serious business. At tastings and on tours you can learn about the farming and cellar strategies behind Pride's acclaimed Cabs (the winery also produces Syrah, a Cab-like Merlot, Viognier, and Chardonnay among others). The tour, which takes in vineyards and caves, also includes tastings of wine still in barrel. **■ TIP→ The views here are knock-your-socks-off gorgeous.** ✉ *4026 Spring Mountain Rd., St. Helena* ✣ *Off St. Helena Rd. (extension of Spring Mountain Rd. in Sonoma County)* ☎ *707/963–4949* 🌐 *www.pridewines.com* 🎫 *Tastings from $30* 🕒 *Closed Tues.*

The Prisoner Wine Company

WINERY/DISTILLERY | The iconoclastic brand opened an industrial-chic space with interiors by the wildly original Napa-based designer Richard Von Saal to showcase its flagship The Prisoner red blend. "Getting the varietals to play together" is winemaker Chrissy Wittmann's goal with that wine (Zinfandel, Cabernet Sauvignon, Petite Sirah, Syrah, Charbono) and siblings like the Blindfold white (Viognier, Roussanne, Chenin Blanc, Vermentino). Walk-in patrons can sip these and other selections in the Tasting Lounge, more hip hotel bar than traditional tasting room, or outside in the casual open-air The Yard. Southward in The Makery, private appointment-only experiences unfold, some involving boldly flavored plates the winery kitchen turns out. Several alcoves within The Makery contain products for sale inspired by the Wine Country. The Prisoner's tasting space is quite the party, for most of which a reservation is required. ✉ *1178 Galleron Rd., St. Helena* ✣ *At Hwy. 29* ☎ *707/967–3823, 877/283–5934* 🌐 *www.theprisonerwinecompany.com* 🎫 *Tastings from $45.*

🍴 Restaurants

Charter Oak

$$$ | **MODERN AMERICAN** | Executive chef Christopher Kostow prepares ornate swoon-worthy haute cuisine at The Restaurant at Meadowood, but he and chef Katianna Hong take a simpler approach (fewer ingredients chosen for maximum effect) at this high-ceilinged, brown-brick downtown restaurant. On a recent menu the strategy translated into dishes like hearth-roasted ham with horseradish, black cod grilled in corn leaves, and cauliflower with raisins and brown butter. **Known for:** exceedingly fresh produce; patio dining in brick courtyard; new chicken-wings appetizer recipe from high-profile restaurant each month. [$] *Average main: $29* ✉ *1050 Charter Oak Ave., at Hwy. 29, St. Helena* ☎ *707/302–6996* 🌐 *www.thecharteroak.com* 🕒 *No lunch Mon.–Thurs.*

★ Cook St. Helena

$$$ | **ITALIAN** | A curved marble bar spotlit by contemporary art-glass pendants adds a touch of style to this downtown restaurant whose northern Italian cuisine pleases with similarly understated sophistication. Mussels with house-made sausage in a spicy tomato broth, chopped salad with pancetta and pecorino, and the daily changing risotto are among the dishes regulars revere. **Known for:** top-quality ingredients; reasonably priced local and international wines; Cook Tavern two doors down for pizza and small plates. [$] *Average main: $23* ✉ *1310 Main St., St. Helena* ✣ *Near Hunt Ave.* ☎ *707/963–7088* 🌐 *www.cooksthelena.com.*

★ Farmstead at Long Meadow Ranch

$$$ | MODERN AMERICAN | Housed in a high-ceilinged former barn, Farmstead revolves around an open kitchen where executive chef Stephen Barber's team prepares meals with grass-fed beef and lamb, fruits and vegetables, and eggs, olive oil, wine, honey, and other ingredients from Long Meadow Ranch. Entrées might include wood-grilled trout with fennel, mushroom, onion and a bacon-mustard vinaigrette; Yukon potato gnocchi with wild mushrooms; or a wood-grilled heritage pork chop with jalapeño grits and chutney. **Known for:** Tuesday fried-chicken night; house-made charcuterie; seasonal cocktails. [$] *Average main: $29* ✉ *738 Main St., St. Helena* ✥ *At Charter Oak Ave.* ☎ *707/963–4555* 🌐 *www.longmeadow-ranch.com/eat-drink/restaurant.*

Goose & Gander

$$$ | MODERN AMERICAN | The pairing of food and drink at G&G is as likely to involve cool cocktails as wine. Main courses such as koji-poached sea bass, heritage-pork porterhouse, and dry-aged New York steak with black-lime and pink-peppercorn butter work well with starters that might include blistered shishito peppers and grilled Spanish octopus. **Known for:** intimate main dining room with fireplace; alfresco dining on patio in good weather; basement bar among Napa's best drinking spots. [$] *Average main: $26* ✉ *1245 Spring St., St. Helena* ✥ *At Oak St.* ☎ *707/967–8779* 🌐 *www.goosegander.com.*

Gott's Roadside

$ | AMERICAN | A 1950s-style outdoor hamburger stand goes upscale at this spot whose customers brave long lines to order breakfast sandwiches, juicy burgers, root-beer floats, and garlic fries. Choices not available a half century ago include the ahi tuna burger and the Vietnamese chicken salad. **Known for:** tasty (if pricey) 21st-century diner cuisine; shaded picnic tables (arrive early or late for lunch to get one); second branch at Napa's Oxbow Public Market. [$] *Average main: $13* ✉ *933 Main St./Hwy. 29, St. Helena* ☎ *707/963–3486* 🌐 *www.gotts.com* ☞ *Reservations not accepted.*

★ Press

$$$$ | MODERN AMERICAN | Few taste sensations surpass the combination of a sizzling steak and a Napa Valley red, a union the chef and sommeliers at Press celebrate with a reverence bordering on obsession. Grass-fed beef from celebrated California purveyor Bryan Flannery cooked on the cherry-and-almond-wood-fired grill is the star—especially the 38-ounce Porterhouse and the *côte de boeuf* bone-in rib eye, both dry-aged—but the cooks also prepare pork chops, free-range chicken, and fish. **Known for:** extensive wine cellar; impressive cocktails; casual-chic ambience. [$] *Average main: $59* ✉ *587 St. Helena Hwy./Hwy. 29, St. Helena* ✥ *At White La.* ☎ *707/967–0550* 🌐 *www.pressnapavalley.com* ⏲ *Closed Tues. No lunch.*

★ The Restaurant at Meadowood

$$$$ | MODERN AMERICAN | Chef Christopher Kostow has garnered rave reviews—and three Michelin stars for several years running—for creating a unique dining experience. Patrons choosing the Tasting Menu option ($285 per person) enjoy their meals in the dining room, its beautiful finishes aglow with warm lighting, but up to four guests can select the Counter Menu ($500 per person) for the chance to sit in the kitchen and watch Kostow's team prepare the food ("the height of our vacation," said four recent guests). **Known for:** complex cuisine; first-class service; romantic setting. [$] *Average main: $275* ✉ *900 Meadowood La., St. Helena* ✥ *Off Silverado Trail N* ☎ *707/967–1205, 800/458–8080* 🌐 *www.therestaurantatmeadowood.com* ⏲ *Closed Sun. and Mon. No lunch* ☞ *Jacket suggested but not required.*

Hotels

El Bonita Motel

$ | HOTEL | A classic 1950s-style neon sign marks the driveway to this well-run roadside motel that—when it isn't sold out—offers great value to budget-minded travelers. **Pros:** cheerful rooms; hot tub; microwaves and mini-refrigerators. **Cons:** road noise a problem in some rooms; noise in ground-floor rooms from second floor; lacks amenities of fancier properties. $ *Rooms from: $149* ⊠ *195 Main St./Hwy. 29, St. Helena* ☎ *707/963–3216, 800/541–3284* ⊕ *www.elbonita.com* ⤳ *52 rooms* ⦿⧙ *Breakfast.*

Harvest Inn by Charlie Palmer

$$$ | HOTEL | Although this inn sits just off Highway 29, its patrons remain mostly above the fray, strolling 8 acres of gardens, enjoying views of the vineyards adjoining the property, partaking in spa services, and drifting to sleep in beds adorned with fancy linens and down pillows. **Pros:** garden setting; spacious rooms; near choice wineries, dining spots, and shops. **Cons:** some lower-price rooms lack elegance; high weekend rates; occasional service lapses. $ *Rooms from: $354* ⊠ *1 Main St., St. Helena* ☎ *707/963–9463, 800/950–8466* ⊕ *www.harvestinn.com* ⤳ *78 rooms* ⦿⧙ *Breakfast.*

Ink House

$$$$ | B&B/INN | The goal of the Castellucci family, which lavishly refurbished an 1885 Italianate along Highway 29, is to provide "a curated luxury experience" in impeccably styled rooms with 11-foot ceilings and vineyard views out tall windows. **Pros:** panoramic views from the cupola; attention to detail; Elvis Presley slept here (but it wasn't this stylish). **Cons:** extremely pricey; lacks on-site pool, fitness center, spa; two bathrooms have showers only (albeit nice ones). $ *Rooms from: $500* ⊠ *1575 St. Helena Hwy., St. Helena* ☎ *707/968–9686* ⊕ *www.inkhousenapavalley.com/inn* ⤳ *4 rooms* ⦿⧙ *Free Breakfast.*

Inn St. Helena

$$ | B&B/INN | A large room at this spiffed-up downtown St. Helena inn is named for author Ambrose Bierce *(The Devil's Dictionary)*, who lived in the main Victorian structure in the early 1900s, but sensitive hospitality and modern amenities are what make a stay worth writing home about. **Pros:** filling breakfast; outdoor porch and swing; convenient to shops, tasting rooms, restaurants. **Cons:** no pool, gym, room service, or other hotel amenities; two-night minimum on weekends (three with Monday holiday); per website "children 16 and older are welcome". $ *Rooms from: $279* ⊠ *1515 Main St., St. Helena* ☎ *707/963–3003* ⊕ *www.innsthelena.com* ⤳ *8 rooms* ⦿⧙ *Breakfast.*

Las Alcobas Napa Valley

$$$$ | HOTEL | Upscale-casual luxury is the goal of this hillside beauty—part of the Starwood chain's Luxury Collection—next to Beringer Vineyards and six blocks north of Main Street shopping and dining. **Pros:** pool, spa, and fitness center; vineyard views from most rooms; chef Chris Cosentino's Acacia House restaurant. **Cons:** pricey; per website no children under age 17 permitted; no self-parking. $ *Rooms from: $638* ⊠ *1915 Main St., St. Helena* ☎ *707/963–7000* ⊕ *www.lasalcobasnapavalley.com* ⤳ *68 rooms* ⦿⧙ *Breakfast.*

★ **Meadowood Napa Valley**

$$$$ | RESORT | Founded in 1964 as a country club, Meadowood evolved into an elite resort, a gathering place for Napa's wine-making community, and a celebrated dining destination. **Pros:** superb restaurant; all-organic spa; gracious service. **Cons:** very expensive; far from downtown St. Helena; weekend minimum-stay requirement. $ *Rooms from: $650* ⊠ *900 Meadowood La., St. Helena* ☎ *707/963–3646, 800/458–8080* ⊕ *www.meadowood.com* ⤳ *85 rooms* ⦿⧙ *No meals.*

Wine Country Inn

$$$ | **B&B/INN** | Vineyards flank the three buildings, containing 24 rooms, and five cottages of this pastoral retreat, where blue oaks, maytens, and olive trees provide shade, and gardens feature lantana (small butterflies love it) and lavender. **Pros:** staff excels at anticipating guests' needs; good-size swimming pool; vineyard views from most rooms. **Cons:** some rooms let in noise from neighbors; expensive in high season; weekend minimum-stay requirement. [$] *Rooms from: $349* ✉ *1152 Lodi La., St. Helena* ✥ *East of Hwy. 29* ☎ *707/963–7077, 888/465–4608* 🌐 *www.winecountryinn.com* 🛏 *29 rooms* 🍴 *Breakfast.*

Nightlife

The Saint

WINE BARS—NIGHTLIFE | This high-ceilinged downtown wine bar benefits from the grandeur and gravitas of its setting inside a stone-walled late-19th-century former bank. Lit by chandeliers and decked out in contemporary style with plush sofas and chairs and Lucite stools at the bar, it's a classy, loungelike space to expand your enological horizons comparing the many small-lot Napa Valley wines on offer with their counterparts in France and beyond. There's live or DJ music some nights. ✉ *1351 Main St., St. Helena* ✥ *Near Adams St.* ☎ *707/302–5130* 🌐 *www.thesaintnapavalley.com.*

Calistoga

3 miles northwest of St. Helena.

With false-fronted, Old West–style shops and 19th-century inns and hotels lining its main drag, Lincoln Avenue, Calistoga comes across as more down-to-earth than its more polished neighbors. Don't be fooled, though. On its outskirts lie some of the Wine Country's swankest (and priciest) resorts and its most fanciful piece of architecture, the medieval-style Castello di Amorosa winery.

Calistoga was developed as a spa-oriented getaway from the start. Sam Brannan, a gold rush–era entrepreneur, planned to use the area's natural hot springs as the centerpiece of a resort complex. His venture failed, but old-time hotels and bathhouses—along with some glorious new spas—still operate. You can come for an old-school mud bath, or go completely 21st century and experience lavish treatments based on the latest innovations in skin and body care.

GETTING HERE AND AROUND

Highway 29 heads east (turn right) at Calistoga, where in town it is signed as Lincoln Avenue. If arriving via the Silverado Trail, head west at Highway 29/ Lincoln Avenue.

Sights

Ca' Toga Galleria d'Arte

MUSEUM | The boundless wit, whimsy, and creativity of the Venetian-born Carlo Marchiori, this gallery's owner-artist, finds expression in paintings, watercolors, ceramics, sculptures, and other artworks. Marchiori often draws on mythology and folktales for his inspiration. A stop at this magical gallery might inspire you to tour Villa Ca' Toga, the artist's fanciful Palladian home, a tromp-l'oeil tour de force open for tours from May through October on Saturday morning only, by appointment. ✉ *1206 Cedar St., Calistoga* ✥ *Near Lincoln Ave.* ☎ *707/942–3900* 🌐 *www.catoga.com* ⏲ *Closed Tues. and Wed.*

Castello di Amorosa

WINERY/DISTILLERY | An astounding medieval structure complete with drawbridge and moat, chapel, stables, and secret passageways, the Castello commands Diamond Mountain's lower eastern slope. Some of the 107 rooms contain artist Fabio Sanzogni's replicas of

13th-century frescoes (cheekily signed with his website address), and the dungeon has an iron maiden from Nuremberg, Germany. You must pay for a tour to see most of Dario Sattui's extensive eight-level property, though with a basic tasting you'll have access to part of the complex. Bottlings of note include several Italian-style wines, including La Castellana, a robust "super Tuscan" blend of Cabernet Sauvignon, Sangiovese, and Merlot; and Il Barone, a deliberately big Cab primarily of Rutherford grapes. ■TIP➜ The 2½-hour Royal Food & Wine Pairing Tour by sommelier Mary Davidek (by appointment only) is among the Wine Country's best. ⊠ 4045 N. St. Helena Hwy./Hwy. 29, Calistoga ✛ Near Maple La. ☎ 707/967–6272 ⊕ www.castellodiamorosa.com ⊠ Tastings from $30, tours from $40 (include tastings).

Chateau Montelena

WINERY/DISTILLERY | Set amid a bucolic northern Calistoga landscape, this winery helped establish the Napa Valley's reputation for high-quality wine making. At the pivotal Paris tasting of 1976, the Chateau Montelena 1973 Chardonnay took first place, beating out four white Burgundies from France and five other California Chardonnays, an event immortalized in the 2008 movie *Bottle Shock*. A 21st-century Napa Valley Chardonnay is always part of a Current Release Tasting—the winery also makes Sauvignon Blanc, Riesling, a fine estate Zinfandel, and Cabernet Sauvignon—or you can opt for a Limited Release Tasting focusing more on Cabernets. The walking Estate Tour takes in the grounds and covers the history of this stately property whose stone winery building was erected in 1888. Guests board a vehicle for the seasonal Vineyard Tour. Tours and some tastings require a reservation. ⊠ 1429 Tubbs La., Calistoga ✛ Off Hwy. 29 ☎ 707/942–5105 ⊕ www.montelena.com ⊠ Tastings from $30, tours from $50.

Frank Family Vineyards

WINERY/DISTILLERY | As a former Disney film and television executive, Rich Frank knows a thing or two about entertainment, and it shows in the chipper atmosphere that prevails in the winery's bright-yellow Craftsman-style tasting room. The site's wine-making history dates from the 19th century, and portions of an original 1884 structure, reclad in stone in 1906, remain standing today. From 1952 until 1990, Hanns Kornell made sparkling wines on this site. Frank Family makes sparklers itself, but the high-profile wines are the Cabernet Sauvignons, particularly the Rutherford Reserve and the Winston Hill red blend. Tastings are mostly sit-down affairs, indoors, on the popular back veranda, or at picnic tables under 100-year-old elms. Reservations are required from Friday through Sunday; they're wise on other days, too. ⊠ 1091 Larkmead La., Calistoga ✛ Off Hwy. 29 ☎ 707/942–0859 ⊕ www.frankfamilyvineyards.com ⊠ Tastings from $40.

Tamber Bey Vineyards

WINERY/DISTILLERY | Endurance riders Barry and Jennifer Waitte share their passion for horses and wine at their glam-rustic winery north of Calistoga. Their 22-acre Sundance Ranch remains a working equestrian facility, but the site has been revamped to include a state-of-the-art winery with separate fermenting tanks for grapes from Tamber Bey's vineyards in Yountville, Oakville, and elsewhere. The winemakers produce three Chardonnays and a Sauvignon Blanc, but the stars are several subtly powerful reds, including the flagship Oakville Cabernet Sauvignon and a Yountville Merlot. The top-selling wine, Rabicano, is a Cabernet Sauvignon-heavy blend that in a recent vintage contained the four other main Bordeaux red grapes: Malbec, Merlot, Petit Verdot, and Cabernet Franc. Visits here require an appointment. ⊠ 1251 Tubbs La., Calistoga ✛ At Myrtledale Rd. ☎ 707/942–2100 ⊕ www.tamberbey.com ⊠ Tastings from $45.

All it needs is a fair maiden: Castello di Amorosa's re-created castle.

★ Venge Vineyards

WINERY/DISTILLERY | As the son of Nils Venge, the first winemaker to earn a 100-point score from the wine critic Robert Parker, Kirk Venge had a hard act to follow. Now a consultant to exclusive wineries himself, Kirk is an acknowledged master of balanced, fruit-forward Bordeaux-style blends. At his casual ranch-house tasting room you can sip wines that might include the estate Bone Ash Cabernet Sauvignon, an Oakville Merlot, and the Silencieux Cabernet, a blend of grapes from several appellations. With its views of the well-manicured Bone Ash Vineyard and, west across the valley, Diamond Mountain, the ranch house's porch would make for a magical perch even if Venge's wines weren't works of art in themselves. Tastings are by appointment only. ✉ *4708 Silverado Trail, Calistoga* ✣ *1½ miles south of downtown, near Dunaweal La.* ☎ *707/942–9100* 🌐 *www.vengevineyards.com* 🎟 *Tastings $45* ⏲ *Reservations recommended 3–4 wks in advance for weekend visits.*

🍴 Restaurants

★ Evangeline

$$$ | **MODERN AMERICAN** | The gas-lamp-style lighting fixtures, charcoal-black hues, and bistro cuisine at Evangeline evoke old New Orleans with a California twist. Executive chef Gustavo Rios, whose previous stops include Calistoga's Solbar and Yountville's Bouchon Bistro, puts a jaunty spin on dishes that might include shrimp étouffée, duck confit, or steak frites; the elaborate weekend brunch, with everything from avocado toast to buttermilk biscuits and sausage gravy, is an upvalley favorite. **Known for:** outdoor courtyard; palate-cleansing Sazeracs; addictive fried pickles. [$] *Average main: $27* ✉ *1226 Washington St., Calistoga* ✣ *Near Lincoln Ave.* ☎ *707/341–3131* 🌐 *www.evangelinenapa.com* ⏲ *No lunch weekdays.*

Sam's Social Club

$$$ | **MODERN AMERICAN** | Tourists, locals, and spa guests—some of the latter in bathrobes after treatments—assemble at this resort restaurant for breakfast, lunch, bar snacks, or dinner. Lunch options include pizzas, sandwiches, an aged-cheddar burger, and entrées such as chicken paillard, with the burger reappearing for dinner along with pan-seared Alaskan halibut, rib-eye steak frites, and similar fare, perhaps preceded by oysters and other cocktail-friendly starters. **Known for:** casual atmosphere; active patio scene; thin-crust lunch pizzas. ⑤ *Average main: $28* ✉ *Indian Springs Resort and Spa, 1712 Lincoln Ave., Calistoga* ✛ *At Wappo Ave.* ☎ *707/942–4969* ⊕ *www.samssocialclub.com.*

★ **Solbar**

$$$$ | MODERN AMERICAN | As befits a restaurant at a spa resort, the sophisticated menu at Solbar is divided into "healthy, lighter dishes" and "hearty cuisine," with the stellar wine list's many half-bottle selections encouraging moderation, too. On the lighter side, seared black cod served with bok choy, ginger endive, and carrots, with heartier options recently including hibachi-grilled Wagyu rib eye with new potatoes. **Known for:** stylish dining room; festive outdoor patio; Sunday brunch. ⑤ *Average main: $35* ✉ *Solage Calistoga, 755 Silverado Trail, Calistoga* ✛ *At Rosedale Rd.* ☎ *866/942–7442* ⊕ *solage. aubergeresorts.com/dine.*

🛏 **Hotels**

Calistoga Ranch

$$$$ | RESORT | Spacious cedar-shingle lodges throughout this posh wooded Auberge Resorts property have outdoor living areas—even the restaurant, spa, and reception space have outdoor seating and fireplaces. **Pros:** many lodges have private hot tubs on the deck; hiking trails on property; guests have reciprocal facility privileges at Auberge du Soleil and Solage Calistoga. **Cons:** indoor-outdoor concept works better in fine weather than in rain or cold; no self-parking; expensive. ⑤ *Rooms from: $895* ✉ *580*

Lommel Rd., Calistoga ☎ *707/254–2800, 855/942–4220* ⊕ *www.calistogaranch. com* ➹ *52 lodges* ⑩ *No meals.*

★ **Embrace Calistoga**

$$$ | B&B/INN | Extravagant hospitality defines the Napa Valley's luxury properties, but Embrace Calistoga takes the prize in the "small lodging" category. **Pros:** attentive owners; marvelous breakfasts; restaurants, tasting rooms, and shopping within walking distance. **Cons:** light hum of street traffic; no pool or spa; two-night minimum some weekends. ⑤ *Rooms from: $309* ✉ *1139 Lincoln Ave., Calistoga* ☎ *707/942–9797* ⊕ *embracecalistoga.com* ➹ *5 rooms* ⑩ *Breakfast.*

Indian Springs Resort and Spa

$$ | RESORT | Palm-studded Indian Springs—operating as a spa since 1862—ably splits the difference between laid-back and chic in accommodations that include lodge rooms, suites, 14 historic cottages, three stand-alone bungalows, and two houses. **Pros:** palm-studded grounds with outdoor seating areas; on-site Sam's Social Club restaurant; enormous mineral pool. **Cons:** lodge rooms are small; many rooms have showers but no tubs; two-night minimum on weekends (three with Monday holiday). ⑤ *Rooms from: $279* ✉ *1712 Lincoln Ave., Calistoga* ☎ *707/942–4913* ⊕ *www.indianspringscalistoga.com* ➹ *113 rooms* ⑩ *No meals.*

★ **Solage Calistoga**

$$$$ | RESORT | The aesthetic at this 22-acre property, where health and wellness are priorities, is Napa Valley barn meets San Francisco loft: guest rooms have high ceilings, polished concrete floors, recycled walnut furniture, and all-natural fabrics in soothingly muted colors. **Pros:** great service; complimentary bikes; separate pools for kids and adults. **Cons:** vibe might not suit everyone; longish walk from some lodgings to spa and fitness center; expensive in-season. ⑤ *Rooms from: $481* ✉ *755*

Silverado Trail, Calistoga ☎ *866/942–7442, 707/226–0800* ⊕ *www.solagecalistoga. com* ⇆ *89 rooms* ⭐ *No meals.*

🛍 Shopping

Calistoga Pottery

CERAMICS/GLASSWARE | You might recognize the dinnerware and other pottery sold by owners Jeff and Sally Manfredi—their biggest customers are the area's inns, restaurants, and wineries. ⊠ *1001 Foothill Blvd./Hwy. 29, Calistoga* ⚓ *500 feet south of Lincoln Ave.* ☎ *707/942–0216* ⊕ *www.calistogapottery.com* ⊘ *Closed Sun.*

SPAS

Indian Springs Spa

SPA/BEAUTY | Even before Sam Brannan constructed a spa on this site in the 1860s, the Wappo Indians were building sweat lodges over its thermal geysers. Treatments include a Calistoga-classic, pure volcanic-ash mud bath followed by a mineral bath, after which clients are wrapped in a flannel blanket for a 15-minute cool-down session or until called for a massage if they've booked one. Intraceuticals oxygen-infusion facials are another specialty. Spa clients have access to the Olympic-size mineral-water pool, kept at 92°F in summer and a toasty 102°F in winter. ⊠ *1712 Lincoln Ave., Calistoga* ⚓ *At Wappo Ave.* ☎ *707/942–4913* ⊕ *www. indianspringscalistoga.com/spa* ▧ *Treatments from $95.*

⭐ **Spa Solage**

This eco-conscious spa reinvented the traditional Calistoga mud-and-mineral-water regimen with the hour-long "Mudslide." The three-part treatment includes a mud body mask self-applied in a heated lounge, a soak in a thermal bath, and a power nap in a sound-vibration chair. The mud here, less gloppy than at other resorts, is a mix of clay, volcanic ash, and essential oils. Traditional spa services—combination

Shiatsu-Swedish and other massages, full-body exfoliations, facials, and waxes—are available, as are yoga and wellness sessions. ⊠ *755 Silverado Trail, Calistoga* ⚓ *At Rosedale Rd.* ☎ *707/226–0825* ⊕ *solage.aubergeresorts.com/spa* ▧ *Treatments from $110.*

🏃 Activities

Calistoga Bikeshop

BICYCLING | Options here include regular and fancy bikes that rent for $28 and up for two hours, and there's a self-guided Cool Wine Tour ($110) that includes tastings at three or four small wineries. ⊠ *1318 Lincoln Ave., Calistoga* ⚓ *Near Washington St.* ☎ *707/942–9687* ⊕ *www.calistogabikeshop.net.*

Sonoma

14 miles west of Napa, 45 miles northeast of San Francisco.

One of the few towns in the valley with multiple attractions not related to food and wine, Sonoma has plenty to keep you busy for a couple of hours before you head out to tour the wineries. And you needn't leave town to taste wine. There are about three dozen tasting rooms within steps of the tree-filled Sonoma plaza, some of which pour wines from more than one winery. The valley's cultural center, Sonoma was founded in 1835 when California was still part of Mexico.

GETTING HERE AND AROUND

Highway 12 (signed as Broadway near Sonoma Plaza) heads north into Sonoma from Highway 121 and south from Santa Rosa into downtown Sonoma, where (signed as West Spain Street) it travels east to the plaza. Parking is relatively easy to find on or near the plaza, and you can walk to many restaurants, shops, and tasting rooms. Signs point the way to several wineries a mile or more east of the plaza.

👁 Sights

Bedrock Wine Co.

WINERY/DISTILLERY | Wines, notably Zinfandel, celebrating Sonoma County's heritage vineyards are the focus of Bedrock, whose backstory involves several historical figures. Tastings take place in a home just east of Sonoma Plaza owned in the 1850s by General Joseph Hooker. By coincidence, Hooker planted grapes at what's now the estate Bedrock Vineyard a few miles away. General William Tecumseh Sherman was his partner in the vineyard (a spat over it affected their Civil War interactions), which newspaper magnate William Randolph Hearst's father, George, replanted in the late 1880s. Some Hearst vines still produce grapes. Current owner-winemaker Morgan Twain-Peterson learned about Zinfandel from his dad, Joel Peterson, who started Ravenswood Winery. ■TIP➔ **The shaded patio out back faces the circa-1840 Blue Wing Inn, where Hooker often partied.** ✉ *General Joseph Hooker House, 414 1st St. E, Sonoma* ☎ *707/343–1478* ⊕ *www.bedrockwineco.com* 🍷 *Tastings $30* 🕐 *Closed Tues.*

Buena Vista Winery

WINERY/DISTILLERY | The birthplace of modern California wine making has been transformed into an entertaining homage to the accomplishments of the 19th-century wine pioneer Count Agoston Haraszthy. Tours pass through the original aging caves dug deep into the hillside by Chinese laborers, and banners, photos, and artifacts inside and out convey the history made on this site. The rehabilitated former press house (used for pressing grapes into wine), which dates to 1862, hosts the standard tastings. Chardonnay, Pinot Noir, several red blends, and a vibrant Petit Verdot are the strong suits here. ■TIP➔ **The high-tech Historic Wine Tool Museum displays implements, some decidedly low-tech, used to make wine over the years.** ✉ *18000 Old Winery Rd., Sonoma* ✛ *Off E. Napa St.*

☎ *800/926–1266* ⊕ *www.buenavistawinery.com* 🍷 *Tastings from $20; tours from $25.*

★ The Donum Estate

WINERY/DISTILLERY | Anne Moller-Racke, the founder of this prominent Chardonnay and Pinot Noir producer, calls herself a winegrower in the French *vigneron* tradition that emphasizes agriculture—selecting vineyards with the right soils, microclimates, and varietals, then farming with precision—over wine-making wizardry. The Donum Estate, whose white board-and-batten tasting room affords guests hilltop views of Los Carneros, San Pablo Bay, and beyond, farms two vineyards surrounding the structure, along with one in the Russian River Valley and another in Mendocino County's Anderson Valley. All the wines exhibit the "power yet elegance" that sealed the winery's fame in the 2000s. Tastings are by appointment only. ■TIP➔ **Large museum-quality outdoor sculptures by Anselm Kiefer, Lynda Benglis, Ai Weiwei, and three dozen other contemporary talents add a touch of high culture to a visit here.** ✉ *24500 Ramal Rd., Sonoma* ✛ *Off Hwy. 121/12* ☎ *707/732–2200* ⊕ *www.thedonumestate.com* 🍷 *Tastings $80.*

Gloria Ferrer Caves and Vineyards

WINERY/DISTILLERY | A tasting at Gloria Ferrer is an exercise in elegance: at tables inside the Spanish hacienda–style winery or outside on the terrace (no standing at the bar at Gloria Ferrer), you can take in vistas of gently rolling Carneros hills while sipping sparkling and still wines. The Chardonnay and Pinot Noir grapes from the surrounding vineyards are the product of old-world wine-making knowledge—the same family started the sparkling-wine maker Freixenet in 16th-century Spain—and contemporary soil management techniques and clonal research. The daily tour covers *méthode traditionelle* wine making, the Ferrer family's history, and the winery's vineyard sustainability

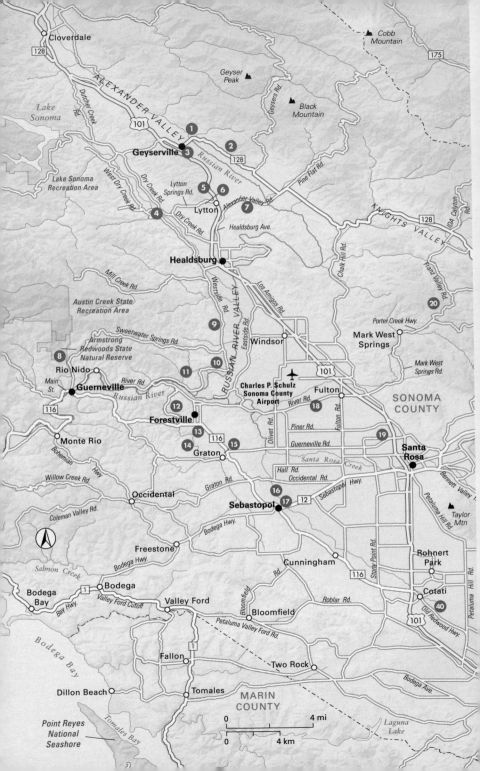

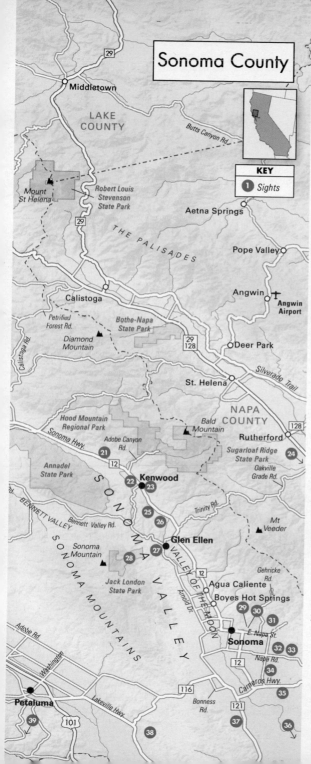

Sonoma County

KEY

1 Sights

practices. ✉ *23555 Carneros Hwy./Hwy. 121, Sonoma* ☎ *707/933–1917* ⊕ *www. gloriaferrer.com* ✆ *Tastings from $9, tour with tasting $25.*

Gundlach Bundschu

WINERY/DISTILLERY | The Bundschu family, which has owned most of this property since 1858, makes reds that include Cabernet Franc, Cabernet Sauvignon, Merlot, and a Bordeaux-style blend of each vintage's best grapes. Gewürztraminer, Chardonnay, and two rosés are also in the mix. Parts of the 1870 stone winery where standard tastings unfold are still used for wine making. For a more comprehensive experience, book a cave tour, a Pinzgauer vehicle vineyard tour, or a Heritage Reserve pairing of limited-release wines with small gourmet bites. Some tastings and all tours are by appointment only. "Gun lock bun shoe" gets you close to pronouncing this winery's name correctly, though everyone here shortens it to Gun Bun. ✉ *2000 Denmark St., Sonoma* ✛ *At Bundschu Rd., off 8th St. E, 3 miles southeast of Sonoma Plaza* ☎ *707/938–5277* ⊕ *www.gunbun. com* ✆ *Tastings from $20, tours $45 (includes tastings).*

Hanson of Sonoma Organic Vodka

WINERY/DISTILLERY | The Hanson family makes grape-based organic vodkas, one of them straightforward and four others infused with cucumbers, ginger, mandarin oranges, and habanero and other chili peppers. To produce these vodkas and a few seasonal offerings, white wine is made from three grape types and then distilled. The family pours its vodkas, which have racked up some impressive awards, in an industrial-looking tasting room heavy on the steel, with wood reclaimed from Deep South smokehouses adding a rustic note. Because you're in a tasting room rather than a bar, there's a limit to the amount poured, but it's sufficient to get to know the product. Book distillery tours through Hanson's website. ■TIP➔ **A popular tasting involves three vodka sips and a well-mixed cocktail.** ✉ *22985 Burndale Rd., Sonoma* ✛ *Off Carneros Hwy. (Hwy. 121)* ☎ *707/343–1805* ⊕ *hansonofsonoma.com* ✆ *Tastings from $15, tours from $25 (includes tasting).*

★ Patz & Hall

WINERY/DISTILLERY | Sophisticated single-vineyard Chardonnays and Pinot Noirs are the trademark of this respected winery whose tastings take place in a fashionable single-story residence 3 miles southeast of Sonoma Plaza. It's a Wine Country adage that great wines are made in the vineyard—the all-star fields represented here include Hyde, Durell, and Gap's Crown—but winemaker James Hall routinely surpasses peers with access to the same fruit, proof that discernment and expertise (Hall is a master at oak aging) play a role, too. You can sample wines at the bar and on some days on the vineyard-view terrace beyond it, but to learn how food-friendly these wines are, consider the Salon Tasting, at which they're paired with gourmet bites. Tastings are by appointment only. ✉ *21200 8th St. E, Sonoma* ✛ *Near Peru Rd.* ☎ *707/265–7700* ⊕ *www.patzhall. com* ✆ *Tastings from $35.*

★ Scribe

WINERY/DISTILLERY | Andrew and Adam Mariani established Scribe in 2007 on land first planted to grapes in 1858 by Emil Dresel, a German immigrant. Dresel's claims to fame include cultivating Sonoma's first Riesling and Sylvaner, an achievement the brothers honor by growing both varietals on land he once farmed. Using natural wine-making techniques, they craft bright, terroir-driven wines from those grapes, along with Chardonnay, Pinot Noir, Syrah, and Cabernet Sauvignon. In restoring their property's 1915 Mission Revival–style hacienda, the brothers preserved various layers of history—original molding and light fixtures, for instance, but also fragments of floral-print wallpaper and 1950s newspapers. Now a tasting space, the hacienda served during Prohibition as a bootleggers' hideout, and its basement harbored a speakeasy. Tastings, which include meze plates whose ingredients come from Scribe's farm, are by appointment only. ✉ *2100 Denmark St., Sonoma* ✣ *Off Napa Rd.* ☎ *707/939–1858* 🌐 *scribewinery.com* 🎟 *Tastings from $60.*

Sonoma Mission

RELIGIOUS SITE | The northernmost of the 21 missions established by Franciscan friars in California, Sonoma Mission was founded in 1823 as Mission San Francisco Solano. These days it serves as the centerpiece of **Sonoma State Historic Park,** which includes several other sites in Sonoma and nearby Petaluma. Some early mission structures were destroyed, but all or part of several remaining buildings date to the era of Mexican rule over California. Worth a look are the **Sonoma Barracks,** a half block west of the mission at 20 East Spain Street, which housed troops under the command of General Mariano Guadalupe Vallejo, who controlled vast tracts of land in the region. **General Vallejo's Home,** a Victorian-era structure, is a few blocks west. ✉ *114 E. Spain St., Sonoma* ✣ *At 1st St. E* ☎ *707/938–9560* 🌐 *www.parks.ca.gov* 🎟 *$3, includes same-day admission to other historic sites.*

🍴 Restaurants

★ Cafe La Haye

$$$ | **AMERICAN** | In a postage-stamp-size open kitchen (the dining room, its white walls adorned with contemporary art, is nearly as compact), chef Jeffrey Lloyd turns out understated, sophisticated fare emphasizing seasonably available local ingredients. Chicken, beef, pasta, and fish get deluxe treatment without fuss or fanfare—the daily risotto special is always good. **Known for:** Napa-Sonoma wine list with French complements; signature butterscotch pudding dessert; owner Saul Gropman on hand to greet diners. [$] *Average main: $24* ✉ *140 E. Napa St., Sonoma* ✣ *Just off Sonoma Plaza* ☎ *707/935–5994* 🌐 *www.cafelahaye.com* ⏲ *Closed Sun. and Mon. No lunch.*

El Dorado Kitchen

$$$ | **MODERN AMERICAN** | This restaurant owes its visual appeal to its clean lines and handsome decor, but the eye inevitably drifts westward to the open kitchen, where the chefs craft dishes full of subtle surprises. The menu might include ahi tuna tartare with wasabi tobiko caviar as a starter, with paella awash with seafood and dry-cured Spanish chorizo sausage among the entrées. **Known for:** subtle tastes and textures; truffle-oil fries with Parmesan; pot de crème and other desserts. [$] *Average main: $27* ✉ *El Dorado Hotel, 405 1st St. W, Sonoma* ✣ *At W. Spain St.* ☎ *707/996–3030* 🌐 *eldoradokitchen.com.*

★ Girl & the Fig

$$$ | **FRENCH** | At this hot spot for inventive French cooking inside the historic Sonoma Hotel bar, you can always find a dish with owner Sondra Bernstein's signature figs on the menu, whether it's a fig-and-arugula salad or an aperitif blending sparkling wine with fig liqueur. Also look for duck confit, a burger with matchstick fries, and wild flounder meunière. **Known for:** Rhône-wines emphasis; artisanal cheese platters; croque monsieur and eggs Benedict at Sunday brunch. [$] *Average main: $28* ✉ *Sonoma Hotel, 110 W. Spain St., Sonoma* ✣ *At 1st St. W* ☎ *707/938–3634* 🌐 *www.thegirlandthefig.com.*

★ Harvest Moon Cafe

$$$ | **AMERICAN** | Everything at this little restaurant with an odd, zigzagging layout is so perfectly executed and the vibe is so genuinely warm that a visit here is deeply satisfying. The ever-changing menu might include homey dishes such as hand-cut tagliatelle with sautéed mushrooms or panfried swordfish with herbed quinoa pilaf. **Known for:** friendly service; patio dining area; husband-and-wife chefs Nick and Jen Demarest. [$] *Average main: $28* ✉ *487 1st St. W, Sonoma* ✣ *At W. Napa St.* ☎ *707/933–8160* 🌐 *www.harvestmooncafesonoma.com* ⏲ *Closed Tues. No lunch.*

Oso Sonoma

$$$ | **MODERN AMERICAN** | Chef David Bush, who achieved national recognition for his food pairings at St. Francis Winery, owns this barlike small-plates restaurant whose menu evolves throughout the day. Lunch might see mole-braised pork-shoulder tacos or an achiote chicken sandwich, with dinner fare perhaps of steamed mussels, miso-glazed salmon, or poutine, all of it served in an 1890s structure, erected as a livery stable, that incorporates materials reclaimed from the building's prior incarnations. **Known for:** bar menu between lunch and dinner; smart beer and wine selections; Sonoma Plaza location. [$] *Average main: $29* ✉ *9 E. Napa St., Sonoma* ✣ *At Broadway* ☎ *707/931–6926* 🌐 *www.ososonoma.com* ⏲ *No lunch Mon.–Wed.*

Sunflower Caffé

$ | **AMERICAN** | Whimsical art and brightly painted walls set a jolly tone at this casual eatery whose assets include sidewalk seating with Sonoma Plaza views and the verdant patio out back. Omelets and waffles are the hits at breakfast, with the smoked duck *banh mi*, served on a toasted baguette with Sriracha aioli, a favorite for lunch. **Known for:** combination café, gallery, and wine bar; local cheeses and hearty soups; free Wi-Fi. [$] *Average main: $14* ✉ *421 1st St. W, Sonoma* ✣ *At W. Spain St.* ☎ *707/996–6645* 🌐 *www.sonomasunflower.com* ⏲ *No dinner.*

🛏 Hotels

Inn at Sonoma

$$ | **B&B/INN** | Little luxuries delight at this well-run inn ¼-mile south of Sonoma Plaza: wine and hors d'oeuvres are served every evening in the lobby, where a jar brims with cookies from noon to 8 pm and free beverages are always available. **Pros:** last-minute specials are a great deal; comfortable beds; good soundproofing blocks out Broadway street noise. **Cons:** on a busy street rather than right on the plaza; pet-friendly rooms book up quickly; some rooms on the small side. [$] *Rooms from: $249* ✉ *630 Broadway, Sonoma* ☎ *707/939–1340* 🌐 *www.innatsonoma.com* 🔑 *27 rooms* 🍴 *Breakfast.*

★ **Ledson Hotel**

$$$ | **B&B/INN** | With just six rooms the Ledson feels intimate, and the furnishings and amenities—down beds, mood lighting, gas fireplaces, whirlpool tubs, and balconies for enjoying breakfast or a glass of wine—stack up well against Wine Country rooms costing more, especially in high season. **Pros:** convenient Sonoma Plaza location; spacious, individually decorated rooms with whirlpool tubs; complimentary tasting at ground-floor Zina Lounge wine bar. **Cons:** maximum occupancy in all rooms is two people; children must be at least 12 years old; front rooms have plaza views but pick up some street noise. [$] *Rooms from: $350* ✉ *480 1st St. E, Sonoma* ☎ *707/996–9779* 🌐 *www.ledsonhotel.com* 🔑 *6 rooms* 🍴 *Free Breakfast.*

★ **MacArthur Place Hotel & Spa**

$$$ | **HOTEL** | Guests at this 7-acre boutique property five blocks south of Sonoma Plaza bask in ritzy seclusion in plush accommodations set amid landscaped gardens. **Pros:** verdant garden setting; tranquil spa; great for a romantic getaway. **Cons:** a bit of a walk from the plaza; some traffic noise audible in street-side rooms; pricey in high season.

$ *Rooms from: $359* ✉ *29 E. MacArthur St., Sonoma* ☎ *707/938–2929, 800/722–1866* 🌐 *www.macarthurplace.com* 🛏 *64 rooms* 🍴 *No meals.*

🍸 Nightlife

Sigh

WINE BARS—NIGHTLIFE | From the oval bar and walls the color of a fine Blanc de Blancs to retro chandeliers that mimic champagne bubbles, everything about this sparkling-wine bar's frothy space screams "have a good time." That owner Jayme Powers and her posse are trained in the fine art of *sabrage* (opening a sparkler with a saber) only adds to the festivity. **■ TIP→ Sigh opens at noon, so it's a good daytime stop, too.** ✉ *120 W. Napa St., Sonoma* ✢ *At 1st St. W* ☎ *707/996–2444* 🌐 *www.sighsonoma.com.*

🛍 Shopping

Sonoma Plaza is a shopping magnet, with tempting boutiques and specialty food purveyors facing the square or within a block or two.

★ **Sonoma Valley Certified Farmers Market**

OUTDOOR/FLEA/GREEN MARKETS | To discover just how bountiful the Sonoma landscape is—and how talented its farmers and food artisans are—head to Depot Park, just north of the Sonoma Plaza, on Friday morning. This market is considered Sonoma County's best. ✉ *Depot Park, 1st St. W, Sonoma* ✢ *At Sonoma Bike Path* ☎ *707/538–7023* 🌐 *www.svcfm.org.*

SPAS

Willow Stream Spa at Fairmont Sonoma Mission Inn & Spa

SPA/BEAUTY | By far the Wine Country's largest spa, the Fairmont resort's 40,000-square-foot facility provides every amenity you could possibly want, including pools and hot tubs fed by local thermal springs. The signature 2½-hour Sonoma Organic Lavender Kur and Facial includes a botanical body wrap, a full-body massage, and a facial. Couples seeking romance often request the treatment room with the two-person copper bathtub. ✉ *100 Boyes Blvd./Hwy. 12, Sonoma* ✢ *2½ miles north of Sonoma Plaza* ☎ *707/938–9000* 🌐 *www.fairmont.com/sonoma/willow-stream* 🎫 *Treatments from $79.*

Glen Ellen

7 miles north of Sonoma.

Unlike its flashier Napa Valley counterparts, Glen Ellen eschews well-groomed sidewalks lined with upscale boutiques and restaurants, preferring instead its crooked streets, some with no sidewalks at all, shaded with stands of old oak trees. Jack London, who represents Glen Ellen's rugged spirit, lived in the area for many years; the town commemorates him with place-names and nostalgic establishments. Hidden among sometimes-ramshackle buildings abutting Sonoma and Calabasas creeks are low-key shops and galleries worth poking through, and several fine dining establishments.

GETTING HERE AND AROUND

Craggy Glen Ellen epitomizes the difference between the Napa and Sonoma valleys. Whereas small Napa towns like St. Helena get their charm from upscale boutiques and restaurants lined up along well-groomed sidewalks, Glen Ellen's crooked streets are shaded with stands of old oak trees and occasionally bisected by the Sonoma and Calabazas creeks. Tucked among the trees of a narrow canyon, where Sonoma Mountain and the Mayacamas pinch in the valley floor, Glen Ellen looks more like a town of the Sierra foothills gold country than a Wine Country village.

● Sights

Benziger Family Winery

WINERY/DISTILLERY | One of the best-known Sonoma County wineries sits on a sprawling estate in a bowl with 360-degree sun exposure, the benefits of which are explored on tram tours that depart several times daily. Guides explain Benziger's biodynamic farming practices and provide a glimpse of the extensive cave system. Choose from a regular tram tour or a more in-depth excursion that concludes with a seated tasting. Known for Chardonnay, Cabernet Sauvignon, Merlot, Pinot Noir, and Sauvignon Blanc, the winery is a beautiful spot for a picnic. ■TIP→ **Reserve a seat on the tram tour through the winery's website or arrive early in the day on summer weekends and during harvest season.** ✉ *1883 London Ranch Rd., Glen Ellen ✛ Off Arnold Dr.* ☎ *888/490–2739* ⊕ *www.benziger.com* 🖅 *Tastings from $20, tours from $30 (includes tastings).*

★ Jack London State Historic Park

NATIONAL/STATE PARK | The pleasures are pastoral and intellectual at author Jack London's beloved Beauty Ranch, where you could easily spend the afternoon hiking some of the 30-plus miles of trails that loop through meadows and stands of oaks, redwoods, and other trees. Manuscripts and personal artifacts depicting London's travels are on view at the House of Happy Walls Museum, which provides an overview of the writer's life, literary passions, humanitarian and conservation efforts, and promotion of organic farming. A short hike away lie the ruins of Wolf House, which burned down just before London was to move in. Also open to visitors are a few outbuildings and the restored wood-framed cottage where London penned many of his later works. He's buried on the property. ■TIP→ **Well-known performers headline the park's Broadway Under the Stars series, a hot ticket in summer.** ✉ *2400 London Ranch Rd., Glen Ellen ✛ Off Arnold Dr.* ☎ *707/938–5216* ⊕ *www. jacklondonpark.com* 🖅 *Parking $10 ($5 walk-in or bike), includes admission to museum; cottage $4.*

★ Lasseter Family Winery

WINERY/DISTILLERY | Immaculately groomed grapevines dazzle the eye at John and Nancy Lasseter's secluded winery, and it's no accident: Phil Coturri, Sonoma Valley's premier organic vineyard manager, tends them. Even the landscaping, which includes an insectary to attract beneficial bugs, is meticulously maintained. Come harvesttime, the wine-making team oversees gentle processes that transform the fruit into wines of purity and grace: a Sémillon–Sauvignon Blanc blend, two rosés, and Bordeaux and Rhône reds. Evocative labels illustrate the tale behind each wine. These stories are well told on tours that precede some tastings of wines, paired with local artisanal cheeses, in an elegant room whose east-facing window frames vineyard and Mayacamas Mountains views. Tastings, by the glass or flight, also take place on the winery's outdoor patio. All visits are by appointment only. ✉ *1 Vintage La., Glen Ellen ✛ Off Dunbar Rd.* ☎ *707/933–2814* ⊕ *www.lasseterfamilywinery.com* 🖅 *Tastings (some including tours) from $30.*

Loxton Cellars

WINERY/DISTILLERY | Back in the day when tasting rooms were low-tech and the winemaker often poured the wines, the winery experience unfolded pretty much the way it does at Loxton Cellars today. The personable Australia-born owner, Chris Loxton, who's on hand many days, crafts Zinfandels, Syrahs, a Pinot Noir, and a Cabernet Sauvignon, all quite good, and some regulars swear by the seductively smooth Syrah Port. You can sample a few current releases without an appointment, but one is needed to taste library- and limited-release wines. ■TIP→ **To learn more about Loxton's**

Hitching a ride on the Benziger Family Winery tram tour

wine-making philosophy and practices, book a Walkabout tour (weekends only) of the vineyard and winery that's followed by a seated tasting. ✉ *11466 Dunbar Rd., Glen Ellen* ✣ *At Hwy. 12* ☎ *707/935–7221* 🌐 *www.loxtonwines.com* 🎟 *Tastings from $15, tour $40.*

🍴 Restaurants

Fig Cafe

$$ | FRENCH | The compact menu at this cheerful bistro focuses on California and French comfort food—pot roast and duck confit, for instance, as well as thin-crust pizza. Steamed mussels are served with crispy fries, which also accompany the Chef's Burger (top sirloin with Gruyère), two of the many dependable dishes that have made this restaurant a downtown Glen Ellen fixture. **Known for:** daily three-course prix-fixe specials; no corkage fee; local winemakers pouring wines on Wednesday evening. [$] *Average main: $19* ✉ *13690 Arnold Dr., Glen Ellen* ✣ *At O'Donnell La.* ☎ *707/938–2130* 🌐 *www.thefigcafe.com* ⏲ *No lunch.*

★ Glen Ellen Star

$$$ | ECLECTIC | Chef Ari Weiswasser honed his craft at The French Laundry, Daniel, and other bastions of culinary finesse, but at his Wine Country outpost he prepares haute-rustic cuisine, much of it emerging from a wood-fired oven that burns a steady 600°F. Crisp-crusted, richly sauced Margherita and other pizzas thrive in the torrid heat, as do tender whole fish entrées and vegetables roasted in small iron skillets. **Known for:** kitchen-view counter for watching chefs cook; prix-fixe Wednesday "neighborhood night" menu with free corkage; Weiswasser's sauces, emulsions, and spices. [$] *Average main: $28* ✉ *13648 Arnold Dr., Glen Ellen* ✣ *At Warm Springs Rd.* ☎ *707/343–1384* 🌐 *glenellenstar.com* ⏲ *No lunch.*

🛏 Hotels

★ Gaige House + Ryokan

$$$ | B&B/INN | There's no other place in Sonoma or Napa quite like the Gaige House + Ryokan, which blends the best elements of a traditional country inn, a boutique hotel, and a longtime expat's classy Asian hideaway. **Pros:** short walk to Glen Ellen restaurants, shops, and tasting rooms; bottomless jar of cookies in the common area; full breakfasts, afternoon wine and appetizers. **Cons:** sound carries in the main house; the least expensive rooms are on the small side; oriented more toward couples than families with children. $ *Rooms from: $358* ✉ *13540 Arnold Dr., Glen Ellen* ☎ *707/935–0237, 800/935–0237* ⊕ *www.gaige.com* ⤴ *23 rooms* ◉ *Breakfast.*

★ Olea Hotel

$$$ | **B&B/INN** | The husband-and-wife team of Ashish and Sia Patel operate this boutique lodging that's at once sophisticated and down-home country casual, and the attention to detail impresses most visitors almost instantly, from the exterior landscaping, pool, and hot tub to the colors and surfaces in the guest rooms and public spaces. **Pros:** beautiful style; complimentary wine; chef-prepared breakfasts. **Cons:** minor road noise in some rooms; fills up quickly on weekends; weekend minimum-stay requirement. $ *Rooms from: $308* ✉ *5131 Warm Springs Rd., Glen Ellen* ✛ *West off Arnold Dr.* ☎ *707/996–5131* ⊕ *www.oleahotel.com* ⤴ *15 rooms* ◉ *Breakfast.*

Kenwood

4 miles north of Glen Ellen.

Tiny Kenwood consists of little more than a few restaurants, shops, tasting rooms, and a historic train depot, now used for private events. But hidden in this pretty landscape of meadows and woods at the north end of Sonoma Valley are several good wineries, most just off the Sonoma Highway. Varietals grown here at the foot of the Sugarloaf Mountains include Sauvignon Blanc, Chardonnay, Zinfandel, and Cabernet Sauvignon.

GETTING HERE AND AROUND

To get to Kenwood from Glen Ellen, head northeast on Arnold Drive and north on Highway 12. Sonoma Transit Bus 30 and Bus 38 serve Kenwood from Glen Ellen and Sonoma.

◉ Sights

B Wise Vineyards Tasting Lounge

WINERY/DISTILLERY | The stylish roadside tasting room (walk-ins welcome) of this producer of small-lot reds sits on the valley floor, but B Wise's winery and vineyards occupy prime acreage high in the Moon Mountain District AVA. The winery made its name crafting big, bold Cabernets, including one from owner Brion Wise's estate, but in recent years has also focused on Pinot Noirs from Sonoma County and Oregon's Willamette Valley. Among the other stars in the uniformly excellent lineup is the Cabernet-heavy blend Trios, whose grapes, all from Wise's estate, include Merlot, Petit Verdot, Syrah, and Tannat. The winery also makes Chardonnay and a rosé of Pinot Noir that quickly sells out. A tasting here may whet your appetite for a visit to the estate, done by appointment only. ✉ *9077 Sonoma Hwy., Kenwood* ✛ *At Shaw Ave.* ☎ *707/282–9169* ⊕ *www.bwisevineyards.com* ✉ *Tastings $20.*

Kunde Estate Winery & Vineyards

WINERY/DISTILLERY | On your way into Kunde you pass a terrace flanked by fountains, virtually coaxing you to stay for a picnic with views over the vineyard. Family owned for more than a century, Kunde prides itself on producing 100% estate wines from its 1,850-acre property, which rises 1,400 feet from the valley floor. Kunde's whites include several Chardonnays and a Sauvignon Blanc, with Cabernet Sauvignon, Merlot, and a Zinfandel from 1880s vines among the reds. ■TIP→ **Make a reservation for the Mountain Top Tasting, a tour by luxury van that ends with a sampling of reserve wines.** ✉ *9825 Sonoma Hwy./Hwy. 12, Kenwood*

☎ *707/833–5501* 🌐 *www.kunde.com* 🎟 *Tastings from $15, grounds and cave tour free.*

St. Francis Winery

WINERY/DISTILLERY | Nestled at the foot of Mt. Hood, St. Francis has earned national acclaim for its wine-and-food pairings. With its red-tile roof and bell tower and views of the Mayacamas Mountains just to the east, the winery's California Mission–style visitor center occupies one of Sonoma County's most scenic locations. The charm of the surroundings is matched by the mostly red wines, including rich, earthy Zinfandels from the Dry Creek, Russian River, and Sonoma valleys. Five-course pairings with small bites and wine—chicken medallions with Chardonnay, for instance, or a grilled lamb chop with Cabernet Franc—are offered from Thursday through Monday; pairings with cheeses and charcuterie are available daily. ✉ *100 Pythian Rd., Kenwood* ✣ *Off Hwy. 12* ☎ *707/538–9463, 888/675–9463* 🌐 *www.stfranciswinery.com* 🎟 *Tastings from $15.*

🍴 Restaurants

★ Salt & Stone

$$$ | **MODERN AMERICAN** | The menu at this upscale roadhouse with a sloping wood-beamed ceiling focuses on seafood (salt) and beef, lamb, chicken, duck, and other meats (stone), with many dishes in both categories grilled. Start with the classics, perhaps a martini and oysters Rockefeller, before moving on to well-plated contemporary entrées that might include crispy-skin salmon or duck breast, fish stew, or grilled rib-eye. **Known for:** suave cocktails including signature New York Sour; mountain-view outdoor seating area; Monday–Wednesday "Bistro Nights" three-course dinners. [$] *Average main: $25* ✉ *9900 Sonoma Hwy., Kenwood* ✣ *At Kunde Winery Rd.* ☎ *707/833–6326* 🌐 *www.saltstonekenwood.com* ⏲ *No lunch Tues. and Wed.*

🛏 Hotels

Kenwood Inn and Spa

$$$$ | **B&B/INN** | Fluffy feather beds, custom Italian furnishings, and French doors in most cases opening onto terraces or balconies lend this inn's uncommonly spacious guest rooms a romantic air. **Pros:** large rooms; lavish furnishings; romantic setting. **Cons:** road or lobby noise in some rooms; expensive in high season; geared more to couples than families with children. [$] *Rooms from: $489* ✉ *10400 Sonoma Hwy./Hwy. 12, Kenwood* ☎ *707/833–1293, 800/353–6966* 🌐 *www.kenwoodinn.com* 🔑 *29 rooms* 🍽 *Breakfast.*

Healdsburg

17 miles north of Santa Rosa.

Easily Sonoma County's ritziest town and the star of many a magazine spread or online feature, Healdsburg is located at the intersection of the Dry Creek Valley, Russian River Valley, and Alexander Valley AVAs. Several dozen wineries bear a Healdsburg address, and around downtown's plaza you'll find fashionable boutiques, spas, hip tasting rooms, and art galleries, and some of the Wine Country's best restaurants. Star chef Kyle Connaughton, who opened SingleThread Farms Restaurant to much fanfare, has motivated his counterparts all over town to up their game.

Especially on weekends, you'll have plenty of company as you tour the downtown area. You could spend a day just exploring the tasting rooms and shops surrounding Healdsburg Plaza, but be sure to allow time to venture into the surrounding countryside. With orderly rows of vines alternating with beautifully overgrown hills, this is the setting you dream about when planning a Wine Country vacation. Many wineries here are barely visible, often tucked behind groves of eucalyptus or hidden high on fog-shrouded hills. Country stores and roadside farm stands alongside relatively untrafficked roads sell just-plucked fruits and vine-ripened tomatoes.

GETTING HERE AND AROUND
Healdsburg sits just off U.S. 101. Heading north, take the Central Healdsburg exit to reach Healdsburg Plaza; heading south, take the Westside Road exit and pass east under the freeway. Sonoma County Transit Bus 60 serves Healdsburg from Santa Rosa.

Sights

★ Arista Winery

WINERY/DISTILLERY | Brothers Mark and Ben McWilliams own this winery specializing in small-lot Pinot Noirs that was founded in 2002 by their parents. The sons have raised the winery's profile in several ways, most notably by hiring winemaker Matt Courtney, who has earned high praise from the *Wine Spectator* and other publications for his balanced, richly textured Pinot Noirs. Courtney shows the same deft touch with Arista's Zinfandels, Chardonnays, and a Gewürztraminer. One tasting focuses on the regions from which Arista sources its grapes, another on small-lot single-vineyard wines. Visits are by appointment only. ■TIP→ **Guests who purchase a bottle are welcome to enjoy it in the picnic area, near a Japanese garden that predates the winery.** ✉ *7015 Westside Rd.* ☎ *707/473–0606* ⊕ *www.aristawinery.com* ☞ *Tastings from $35.*

Dry Creek Vineyard

WINERY/DISTILLERY | Sauvignon Blanc marketed as Fumé Blanc brought instant success to the Dry Creek Valley's first new winery since Prohibition, but this area stalwart established in 1972 receives high marks as well for its Zinfandels, Bordeaux-style red blends, and Cabernet Sauvignons. In the nautical-themed tasting room—Dry Creek has featured sailing vessels on its labels since the 1980s—you can choose an all–Sauvignon Blanc flight, an all-Zinfandel one, or a mix of these and other wines. A vineyard walk and an insectary garden enhance a visit to this historic producer, a fine place for a picnic under the shade of a magnolia and several redwood trees. ■TIP→ **You can reserve a boxed lunch two days ahead through the winery, a time-saver on busy weekends.** ✉ *3770 Lambert Bridge Rd.* ⊕ *Off Dry Creek Rd.* ☎ *707/433–1000, 800/864–9463* ⊕ *www.drycreekvineyard.com* ☞ *Tastings from $15, tour $30.*

Gary Farrell Vineyards & Winery

WINERY/DISTILLERY | Pass through an impressive metal gate and wind your way up a steep hill to reach this winery with knockout Russian River Valley views from the elegant two-tiered tasting room and terrace outside. In 2017 *Wine Enthusiast Magazine* named a Gary Farrell Chardonnay wine of the year, one among many accolades for this winery known for sophisticated single-vineyard Chardonnays and Pinot Noirs. The private Exploration Tour & Tasting, which includes a winery tour and artisanal cheeses, provides a solid introduction. The quicker Elevation Tasting (no tour) takes place inside or on the terrace; the Inspiration Tasting, in a private salon, concentrates on gifted winemaker Theresa Heredia's Pinot Noirs. ■TIP→ **All visits are by appointment, but same-day Elevation reservations are usually possible during the week.** ✉ *10701 Westside Rd.* ☎ *707/473–2909* ⊕ *www.garyfarrellwinery.com* ☞ *Tastings from $35, tour $45.*

★ Jordan Vineyard and Winery

WINERY/DISTILLERY | A visit to this 1,200-acre property revolves around an impressive estate built in the early 1970s to replicate a French château. Founders Tom and Sally Jordan—their son, John, now runs the winery—erected the structure in part to emphasize their goal of producing Sonoma County Chardonnays and Cabernet Sauvignons to rival those in the Napa Valley and France itself. A seated Library Tasting of the current release of each varietal takes place in the château, accompanied by executive chef Todd Knoll's small bites. The tasting concludes with an older vintage Cabernet Sauvignon. The 90-minute Winery Tour & Tasting includes the above, plus a walk through part of the château. All visits are by appointment only. ■TIP➔ For a truly memorable experience, splurge on the three-hour Estate Tour & Tasting, whose pièce de résistance is the Cabernet segment, which unfolds at a 360-degree vista point overlooking vines, olive trees, and countryside. ✉ 1474 Alexander Valley Rd. ✚ 1½ miles east of Healdsburg Ave. ☎ 800/654–1213, 707/431–5250 ⊕ www. jordanwinery.com ✍ Library tasting $30, winery tour and tasting $40, estate tour and tasting $120 ⊘ Closed Sun. Dec.–Mar.

MacRostie Estate House

WINERY/DISTILLERY | A driveway off Westside Road curls through undulating vineyard hills to the steel, wood, and heavy-on-the-glass tasting space of this longtime Chardonnay and Pinot Noir producer. Moments after you've arrived and a host has offered a glass of wine, you'll already feel transported to a genteel, rustic world. Hospitality is clearly a priority here, but so, too, is seeking out top-tier grape sources—30 for the Chardonnays, 15 for the Pinots—among them Dutton Ranch, Bacigalupi, and owner Steve MacRostie's Wildcat. With fruit this renowned, current winemaker Heidi Bridenhagen downplays the oak and other tricks of her trade, letting the vineyard settings, grape clones, and vintage do the talking. Tastings, inside or on balcony terraces with views across the Russian River Valley, are all seated. ■TIP➔ Reservations, required on weekends, are a good idea on weekdays, too. ✉ 4605 Westside Rd. ✚ Near Frost Rd. ☎ 707/473–9303 ⊕ macrostiewinery. com ✍ Tastings from $25.

★ Ridge Vineyards

WINERY/DISTILLERY | Ridge stands tall among local wineries, and not merely because its 1971 Monte Bello Cab placed first in a 30th-anniversary rematch of the famous Judgment of Paris blind tasting of California and French reds. The winery built its reputation on Cabernet Sauvignons, Zinfandels, and Chardonnays of unusual depth and complexity, but you'll also find blends of Rhône varietals. Ridge makes wines using grapes from several California locales—including the Dry Creek Valley, Sonoma Valley, Napa Valley, and Paso Robles—but the focus is on single-vineyard estate wines, such as the Lytton Springs Zinfandel from grapes grown near the tasting room. In good weather you can sit outside, taking in views of rolling vineyard hills while you sip. ■TIP➔ The $25 tasting includes a pour of the top-of-the-line Monte Bello Cabernet Sauvignon from Santa Cruz Mountains grapes. ✉ 650 Lytton Springs Rd. ✚ Off U.S. 101 ☎ 408/867–3233 ⊕ www.ridge-wine.com/visit/lytton-springs ✍ Tastings from $10, tours from $35.

★ Silver Oak

WINERY/DISTILLERY | The views and architecture are as impressive as the wines at the Sonoma County outpost of the same-named Napa Valley winery. In 2018, six years after purchasing a 113-acre parcel with 73 acres planted to grapes, Silver Oak debuted its ultramodern, environmentally sensitive winery and glass-walled tasting pavilion. As in Napa, the Healdsburg facility produces just one wine each year: a robust, well-balanced Alexander Valley Cabernet Sauvignon aged in American rather than French oak barrels. The walk-in tasting includes the current Alexander Valley Cabernet and Napa Valley Bordeaux blend plus an older vintage. Tours, worth taking to experience the high-tech winery, are by appointment. The winery's chef prepares several courses (enough to serve as lunch) paired with library and current Cabernets plus two or more wines of sister operation Twomey Cellars, which produces Sauvignon Blanc, Pinot Noir, and Merlot. ⊠ *7370 Hwy. 128* ☎ *707/942–7082* ⊕ *www.silveroak.com* ☞ *Tastings from $20, tours and tastings from $30.*

🍴 Restaurants

★ Barndiva

$$$$ | AMERICAN | Music plays quietly in the background while servers ferry the inventive seasonal cocktails of this restaurant that abandons the homey vibe of many Wine Country spots for a more urban feel. Make a light meal out of yellowtail tuna crudo or Dungeness crab salad, or settle in for the evening with pan-seared king salmon with caviar and crème fraîche or sautéed rack of lamb with gnocchi. **Known for:** cool cocktails; stylish cuisine; open-air patio. $ *Average main: $34* ⊠ *231 Center St.* ✛ *At Matheson St.* ☎ *707/431–0100* ⊕ *www. barndiva.com* ☾ *Closed Mon. and Tues.*

Bravas Bar de Tapas

$$$ | SPANISH | Spanish-style tapas and an outdoor patio in perpetual party mode make this restaurant, headquartered in a restored 1920s bungalow, a popular downtown perch. Contemporary Spanish mosaics set a perky tone inside, but unless something's amiss with the weather, nearly everyone heads out back for flavorful croquettes, paella, jamón, *pan tomate* (tomato toast), duck egg with chorizo cracklings, grilled octopus, skirt steak, and crispy fried chicken. **Known for:** casual small plates; specialty cocktails, sangrias, and beer; sherry flights. $ *Average main: $27* ⊠ *420 Center St.* ✛ *Near North St.* ☎ *707/433–7700* ⊕ *www.barbravas.com.*

Campo Fina

$$ | ITALIAN | Chef Ari Rosen showcases his contemporary-rustic Italian cuisine at this converted storefront that once housed a bar notorious for boozin' and brawlin'. Sandblasted red brick, satin-smooth walnut tables, and old-school lighting fixtures strike a retro note for a menu built around pizzas and gems such as Rosen's variation on his grandmother's tomato-braised chicken with creamy-soft polenta. **Known for:** outdoor patio and boccie court out of an Italian movie set; lunch sandwiches; wines from California and Italy. $ *Average main: $20* ⊠ *330 Healdsburg Ave.* ✛ *Near North St.* ☎ *707/395–4640* ⊕ *www.campofina.com.*

★ Chalkboard

$$$ | MODERN AMERICAN | Unvarnished oak flooring, wrought-iron accents, and a vaulted white ceiling create a polished yet rustic ambience for executive chef Shane McAnelly's playfully ambitious small-plate cuisine. Starters such as pork-belly biscuits might seem frivolous, but the silky flavor blend—maple glaze, pickled onions, and chipotle mayo playing off feathery biscuit halves—signals a supremely capable tactician at work. **Known for:** festive happy hour; pasta "flights" (choose three or six styles); The Candy Bar dessert. $ *Average main: $30* ⊠ *Hotel Les Mars, 29 North St.* ✛ *West of Healdsburg Ave.* ☎ *707/473–8030* ⊕ *www.chalkboardhealdsburg.com.*

Costeaux French Bakery

$ | FRENCH | Breakfast, served all day at this bright-yellow French-style bakery and café, includes the signature omelet (sun-dried tomatoes, applewood-smoked bacon, spinach, and Brie) and French toast made from thick slabs of cinnamon-walnut bread. French onion soup, salad Niçoise, and smoked-duck, cranberry-turkey, and French dip sandwiches are among the lunch favorites. **Known for:** breads, croissants, and fancy pastries; quiche and omelets; front patio (arrive early on weekends). $ *Average main: $14* ⊠ *417 Healdsburg Ave.* ✛ *At North St.* ☎ *707/433–1913* ⊕ *www.costeaux.com* ☾ *No dinner.*

★ SingleThread Farms Restaurant

$$$$ | ECLECTIC | The seasonally oriented, multicourse Japanese dinners known as *kaiseki* inspired the prix-fixe vegetarian, meat, and seafood menu at the spare, elegant restaurant—redwood walls, walnut tables, mesquite-tile floors, muted-gray yarn-thread panels—of internationally renowned culinary artists Katina and Kyle Connaughton (she farms, he cooks). As Katina describes the endeavor, the 72 microseasons of their farm—5 acres at a nearby vineyard plus SingleThread's rooftop garden of fruit trees and microgreens—dictate Kyle's rarefied fare, prepared in a theatrically lit open kitchen. **Known for:** culinary precision; new online reservation slots released on first of month; impeccable wine pairings. $ *Average main: $275* ⊠ *131 North St.* ⊹ *At Center St.* ☎ *707/723–4646* ⊕ *www.singlethreadfarms.com* ☺ *No lunch weekdays.*

★ Valette

$$$$ | MODERN AMERICAN | Northern Sonoma native Dustin Valette opened this homage to the area's artisanal agricultural bounty with his brother, who runs the high-ceilinged dining room, its playful contemporary lighting tempering the austerity of the exposed concrete walls and butcher-block-thick wooden tables. Charcuterie is an emphasis, but also consider the signature day-boat scallops *en croûte* (in a pastry crust) or dishes that might include Liberty duck breast with blackberry gastrique or Padrón-pepper-crusted Alaskan halibut. **Known for:** intricate cuisine; "Trust me" (the chef) tasting menu; well-chosen mostly Northern California wines. $ *Average main: $34* ⊠ *344 Center St.* ⊹ *At North St.* ☎ *707/473–0946* ⊕ *www.valettehealdsburg.com* ☺ *No lunch.*

🛏 Hotels

★ Harmon Guest House

$$ | HOTEL | A boutique sibling of the h2hotel two doors away, this downtown delight debuted in late 2018 having already earned LEED Gold status for its eco-friendly construction and operating practices. **Pros:** rooftop bar's cocktails, food menu, and views; connecting rooms and suites; convenient to Healdsburg Plaza action. **Cons:** minor room-to-room noise bleed-through; room gadgetry may flummox some guests; minimum-stay requirements some weekends. $ *Rooms from: $264* ⊠ *227 Healdsburg Ave.* ☎ *707/922–5262* ⊕ *harmonguesthouse.com* ⌫ *39 rooms* ⦿ *Free Breakfast.*

★ The Honor Mansion

$$$ | B&B/INN | There's a lot to like about the photogenic Honor Mansion, starting with the main 1883 Italianate Victorian home, the beautiful grounds, the elaborate breakfasts, and the home-away-from-home atmosphere. **Pros:** homemade sweets available at all hours; pool, putting green, and boccie, croquet, tennis, and basketball courts; secluded vineyard suites with indoor soaking tubs, outdoor hot tubs. **Cons:** almost a mile from Healdsburg Plaza; walls can seem thin; weekend minimum-stay requirement includes Thursday. $ *Rooms from: $380* ⊠ *891 Grove St.* ☎ *707/433–4277, 800/554–4667* ⊕ *www.honormansion.com* ☺ *Closed 2 wks at Christmas* ⌫ *13 rooms* ⦿ *Breakfast.*

Hotel Trio Healdsburg

$$ | HOTEL | Named for the three major wine appellations—the Russian River, Dry Creek, and Alexander valleys—whose confluence it's near, this Residence Inn by Marriott a mile and a quarter north of Healdsburg Plaza and its many restaurants and shops caters to families and extended-stay business travelers with spacious rooms equipped with full kitchens. **Pros:** cute robot room service; full kitchens; rooms sleep up to four or six. **Cons:** 30-minute walk to downtown; slightly corporate feel; pricey in high season. $ *Rooms from: $209* ⊠ *110 Dry Creek Rd.* ☎ *707/433–4000* ⊕ *www.hoteltrio.com* ⌫ *122 rooms* ⦿ *Free Breakfast.*

★ River Belle Inn

$$ | B&B/INN | An 1875 Victorian with a storied past and a glorious colonnaded wraparound porch anchors this boutique property along the Russian River. **Pros:** riverfront location near a dozen-plus tasting rooms; cooked-to-order full breakfasts; attention to detail. **Cons:** about a mile from Healdsburg Plaza; minimum-stay requirement on weekends; lacks on-site pool, fitness center, and other amenities. $ *Rooms from: $250* ✉ *68 Front St.* ☎ *707/955–5724* ⊕ *www.riverbelleinn.com* ➟ *12 rooms* ⦿ *Free Breakfast.*

★ SingleThread Farms Inn

$$$$ | B&B/INN | A remarkable Relais & Châteaux property a block north of Healdsburg Plaza, SingleThread is the creation of husband-and-wife team Kyle and Katina Connaughton, who operate the ground-floor destination restaurant and the four guest rooms and a suite above it. **Pros:** multicourse breakfast; in-room amenities from restaurant; rooftop garden. **Cons:** expensive year-round; no pool or fitness center (free passes provided to nearby facility with both); no spa, but in-room massages available. $ *Rooms from: $1000* ✉ *131 North St.* ✛ *At Center St.* ☎ *707/723–4646* ⊕ *www.singlethreadfarms.com* ➟ *5 rooms* ⦿ *Breakfast.*

🛍 Shopping

ART GALLERIES
★ Gallery Lulo

ART GALLERIES | A collaboration between a local artist and jewelry maker and a Danish-born curator, this gallery presents changing exhibits of jewelry, sculpture, and objets d'art. ✉ *303 Center St.* ✛ *At Plaza St.* ☎ *707/433–7533* ⊕ *www. gallerylulo.com.*

CRAFTS
★ One World Fair Trade

CRAFTS | Independent artisans in developing countries create the clothing, household items, jewelry, gifts, and toys sold in this bright, well-designed shop whose owners have a shrewd eye for fine craftsmanship. ✉ *353 Healdsburg Ave.* ✛ *Near North St.* ☎ *707/473–0880* ⊕ *www.oneworldfairtrade.net.*

SPAS
★ Spa Dolce

SPA/BEAUTY | Owner Ines von Majthenyi Scherrer has a good local rep, having run a popular nearby spa before opening this stylish facility just off Healdsburg Plaza. Spa Dolce specializes in skin and body care for men and women, and waxing and facials for women. Curved white walls and fresh-cut floral arrangements set a subdued tone for such treatments as the exfoliating Hauschka body scrub, which combines organic brown sugar with scented oil. There's a romantic room for couples to enjoy massages for two. ■**TIP→ Many guests come just for the European-style facials, which range from a straightforward cleansing to an anti-aging peel.** ✉ *250 Center St.* ✛ *At Matheson St.* ☎ *707/433–0177* ⊕ *www.spadolce.com* ➟ *Treatments from $60.*

🏃 Activities

BICYCLING
★ Wine Country Bikes

BICYCLING | This shop several blocks southeast of Healdsburg Plaza is perfectly located for single or multiday treks into the Dry Creek and Russian River valleys. Bikes, including tandems, rent for $39–$145 per day. One-day tours start at $139. ■**TIP→ The owner and staff can help with bicycling itineraries, including a mostly gentle loop, which takes in Westside Road and Eastside Road wineries and a rusting trestle bridge, as well as a more challenging excursion to Lake Sonoma.** ✉ *61 Front St.* ✛ *At Hudson St.* ☎ *707/473–0610, 866/922–4537* ⊕ *www. winecountrybikes.com.*

Geyserville

8 miles north of Healdsburg.

Several high-profile Alexander Valley AVA wineries, including the splashy Francis Ford Coppola Winery, can be found in the town of Geyserville, a small part of which stretches west of U.S. 101 into northern Dry Creek. Not long ago this was a dusty farm town, and downtown Geyserville retains its rural character, but the restaurants, shops, and tasting rooms along the short main drag hint at Geyserville's growing sophistication.

GETTING HERE AND AROUND
From Healdsburg, the quickest route to downtown Geyserville is north on U.S. 101 to the Highway 128/Geyserville exit. Turn right at the stop sign onto Geyserville Avenue and follow the road north to the small downtown. For a more scenic drive, head north from Healdsburg Plaza along Healdsburg Avenue. About 3 miles north, jog west (left) for a few hundred feet onto Lytton Springs Road, then turn north (right) onto Geyserville Avenue. In town the avenue merges with Highway 128. Sonoma County Transit Bus 60 serves Geyserville from downtown Healdsburg.

◉ Sights

Francis Ford Coppola Winery
WINERY/DISTILLERY | FAMILY | The fun at what the film director calls his "wine wonderland" is all in the excess. You may find it hard to resist having your photo snapped standing next to Don Corleone's desk from *The Godfather* or beside other memorabilia from Coppola films (including some directed by his daughter, Sofia). A bandstand reminiscent of one in *The Godfather Part II* is the centerpiece of a large pool area where you can rent a changing room, complete with shower, and spend the afternoon lounging poolside, perhaps ordering food from the adjacent café. A more elaborate restaurant, Rustic, overlooks the vineyards. As for the wines, the excess continues in the cellar, where several dozen varietal wines and blends are produced. ✉ *300 Via Archimedes ✛ Off U.S. 101* ☏ *707/857–1400 ⊕ www.franciscoppolawinery.com ✉ Tastings free–$25, tours $50, pool pass from $40.*

★ Locals Tasting Room
WINERY/DISTILLERY | If you're serious about wine, Carolyn Lewis's tasting room alone is worth a trek 8 miles north of Healdsburg Plaza to downtown Geyserville. Connoisseurs who appreciate Lewis's ability to spot up-and-comers head here regularly to sample the output of a dozen or so small wineries, most without tasting rooms of their own. There's no fee for tasting—extraordinary for wines of this quality—and the extremely knowledgeable staff are happy to pour you a flight of several wines so you can compare, say, different Cabernet Sauvignons. ✉ *21023A Geyserville Ave. ✛ At Hwy. 128* ☏ *707/857–4900 ⊕ www.tastelocalwines.com ✉ Tastings free.*

★ Robert Young Estate Winery
WINERY/DISTILLERY | Panoramic Alexander Valley views unfold at Scion House, the stylish yet informal knoll-top tasting space this longtime Geyserville grower opened in 2018. The first Youngs began farming this land in the mid-1800s, raising cattle and growing wheat, prunes, and other crops. In the 1960s the late Robert Young, of the third generation, began cultivating grapes, eventually planting two Chardonnay clones now named for him. Grapes from them go into the Area 27 Chardonnay, noteworthy for the quality of its fruit and craftsmanship. The reds—small-lot Cabernet Sauvignons plus individual bottlings of Cabernet Franc, Malbec, Merlot, and Petit Verdot—shine even brighter. Tastings at Scion House, named for the fourth generation, whose members built on Robert Young's legacy and established the winery, are by appointment, but the

winery accommodates walk-ins when possible. ⊠ 5120 Red Winery Rd. ✛ Off Hwy. 128 ☎ 707/431–4811 ⊕ www.ryew.com ⊠ Tastings from $25 ⊗ Closed Tues.

★ **Zialena**

WINERY/DISTILLERY | Sister-and-brother team Lisa and Mark Mazzoni (she runs the business, he makes the wines) debuted their small winery's first vintage in 2014, but their Italian American family's Alexander Valley wine-making heritage stretches back more than a century. Mark—whose on-the-job teachers included the late Mike Lee of Kenwood Vineyards and Philippe Melka, a premier international consultant—specializes in smooth Zinfandel and nuanced Cabernet Sauvignon. Most of the grapes come from the 120-acre estate vineyard farmed by Lisa and Mark's father, Mike, who sells to Jordan and other big-name wineries. Other Zialena wines include a Sauvignon Blanc and Cappella, a Zin-based blend Lisa describes as "Mark's fun wine." Tastings take place in a contemporary stone, wood, and glass tasting room amid the family's vineyards. Tours, one focusing on production, the other on the vineyards, are by appointment only. ⊠ 21112 River Rd. ✛ Off Hwy. 128 ☎ 707/955–5992 ⊕ www.zialena.com ⊠ Tastings from $15, tours $50.

🍴 Restaurants

Diavola Pizzeria & Salumeria

$$ | **ITALIAN** | A dining area with hardwood floors, a pressed-tin ceiling, and exposed-brick walls provides a fitting setting for the rustic cuisine at this Geyserville mainstay. Chef Dino Bugica studied with several artisans in Italy before opening this restaurant that specializes in pizzas pulled from a wood-burning oven and several types of house-cured meats, with a few salads and meaty main courses rounding out the menu. **Known for:** talented chef; smoked pork belly, pancetta, and spicy Calabrese sausage; casual setting.

$ Average main: $20 ⊠ 21021 Geyserville Ave. ✛ At Hwy. 128 ☎ 707/814–0111 ⊕ www.diavolapizzeria.com.

🛏 Hotels

Geyserville Inn

$ | **HOTEL** | Clever travelers give the Healdsburg hubbub and prices the heave-ho but still have easy access to outstanding Dry Creek and Alexander Valley wineries from this modest, motel-like inn. **Pros:** outdoor pool; second-floor rooms in back have vineyard views; picnic area. **Cons:** rooms facing pool or highway can be noisy; not much style; some maintenance issues. $ Rooms from: $179 ⊠ 21714 Geyserville Ave. ☎ 707/857–4343, 877/857–4343 ⊕ www.geyservilleinn.com ⇄ 41 rooms ⦿ No meals.

Forestville

13 miles southwest of Healdsburg.

To experience the Russian River AVA's climate and rusticity, follow the river's westward course to the town of Forestville, home to a highly regarded restaurant and inn and a few wineries producing Pinot Noir from the Russian River Valley and well beyond.

GETTING HERE AND AROUND
To reach Forestville from U.S. 101, drive west from the River Road exit north of Santa Rosa. From Healdsburg, follow Westside Road west to River Road and then continue west. Sonoma County Transit Bus 20 serves Forestville.

⊙ Sights

★ **Hartford Family Winery**
WINERY/DISTILLERY | Pinot Noir lovers appreciate the subtle differences in the wines Hartford's Jeff Stewart crafts from grapes grown in four Sonoma County AVAs, along with fruit from nearby

Russian River Valley AVA

As the Russian River winds its way from Mendocino to the Pacific Ocean, it carves out a valley that's a near-perfect environment for growing certain grape varietals. Because of the low elevation, sea fog pushes far inland to cool the soil, yet in summer it burns off, giving the grapes enough sun to ripen properly. Fog-loving Pinot Noir and Chardonnay grapes are king and queen in the Russian River Valley AVA, which extends from Healdsburg west to the town Guerneville. The namesake river does its part by slowly carving its way downward through many layers of rock, depositing a deep layer of gravel that in parts of the valley measures 60 or 70 feet. This gravel forces the roots of grapevines to go deep in search of water and nutrients. In the process, the plants absorb trace minerals that add complexity to the flavor of the grapes.

Marin and Mendocino counties and Oregon. Stewart also makes highly rated Chardonnays and old-vine Zinfandels. If the weather's good and you've made a reservation, you can enjoy a flight of five or six wines on the patio outside the opulent main winery building. Indoors, at seated private library tastings, guests sip current and older vintages. **■ TIP→ Hartford also has a tasting room in downtown Healdsburg.** ✉ *8075 Martinelli Rd.* ✣ *Off Hwy. 116 or River Rd.* ☎ *707/887–8030, 800/588–0234* 🌐 *www.hartfordwines.com* 🎫 *Tastings from $25.*

Joseph Jewell Wines

WINERY/DISTILLERY | Micah Joseph Wirth and Adrian Jewell Manspeaker founded this winery whose name combines their middle ones. Pinot Noirs from the Russian River Valley and Humboldt County to the north are the strong suit. Wirth, who worked for seven years for vintner Gary Farrell, credits his interactions with Farrell's Russian River growers, among them the owners of Bucher Vineyard and Hallberg Ranch, with easing the winery's access to prestigious fruit. Manspeaker, a Humboldt native, spearheaded the foray into Pinot Noir grown in the coastal redwood country. Joseph Jewell's playfully rustic storefront tasting room in downtown Forestville provides the opportunity to experience what's unique about the varietal's next Northern California frontier. The bonuses: a Zinfandel from 1970s vines and two Chardonnays. ✉ *6542 Front St.* ☎ *707/820–1621* 🌐 *www.josephjewell.com* 🎫 *Tastings from $10, tours from $105 per couple ($500 tour is in a helicopter).*

🍴 Restaurants

Backyard

$$$ | **MODERN AMERICAN** | The folks behind this casually rustic modern American restaurant regard Sonoma County's farms and gardens as their "backyard" and proudly list their purveyors on the menu. Dinner entrées, which change seasonally, might include herb tagliatelle with goat sausage or chicken potpie. **Known for:** buttermilk fried chicken with buttermilk biscuits to stay or go; poplar-shaded outdoor front patio in good weather; Monday locals'-night specials, plus live music. [$] *Average main: $26* ✉ *6566 Front St./Hwy. 116* ✣ *At 1st St.* ☎ *707/820–8445* 🌐 *backyardforestville.com* ⏲ *Closed Tues.–Thurs.*

Hotels

★ The Farmhouse Inn
$$$$ | B&B/INN | With a farmhouse-meets-modern-loft aesthetic, this low-key but upscale getaway with a pale-yellow exterior contains spacious rooms filled with king-size four-poster beds, whirlpool tubs, and hillside-view terraces. **Pros:** fantastic restaurant; luxury bath products; full-service spa. **Cons:** mild road noise audible in rooms closest to the street; two-night minimum on weekends; pricey, especially during high season. [$] *Rooms from: $545* ✉ *7871 River Rd.* ☎ *707/887–3300, 800/464–6642* 🌐 *www.farmhouseinn.com* 🛏 *25 rooms* 🍴 *Breakfast.*

Activities

Burke's Canoe Trips
CANOEING/ROWING/SKULLING | You'll get a real feel for the Russian River's flora and fauna on a leisurely 10-mile paddle downstream from Burke's to Guerneville. A shuttle bus returns you to your car at the end of the journey, which is best taken from late May through mid-October and, in summer, on a weekday—summer weekends can be crowded and raucous. ✉ *8600 River Rd.* ✣ *At Mirabel Rd.* ☎ *707/887–1222* 🌐 *www.burkescanoetrips.com* 🎟 *$78 per canoe.*

Guerneville

7 miles northwest of Forestville, 15 miles southwest of Healdsburg.

Guerneville's tourist demographic has evolved over the years—Bay Area families in the 1950s, lesbians and gays starting in the 1970s, and these days a mix of both groups, plus techies and outdoorsy types—with coast redwoods and the Russian River always central to the town's appeal. The area's most famous winery is Korbel Champagne Cellars, established nearly a century and a half ago. Even older are the stands of trees that except on the coldest winter days make Armstrong Redwoods State Natural Reserve such a perfect respite from wine tasting.

GETTING HERE AND AROUND

To get to Guerneville from Healdsburg, follow Westside Road south to River Road and turn west. From Forestville, head west on Highway 116; alternatively, you can head north on Mirabel Road to River Road and then head west. Sonoma County Transit Bus 20 serves Guerneville.

Sights

★ Armstrong Redwoods State Natural Reserve
NATIONAL/STATE PARK | FAMILY | Here's your best opportunity in the western Wine Country to wander amid *Sequoia sempervirens*, also known as coast redwood trees. The oldest example in this 805-acre state park, the Colonel Armstrong Tree, is thought to be more than 1,400 years old. A half mile from the parking lot, the tree is easily accessible, and you can hike a long way into the forest before things get too hilly. ■ **TIP→ During hot summer days, Armstrong Redwoods's tall trees help the park keep its cool.** ✉ *17000 Armstrong Woods Rd.* ✣ *Off River Rd.* ☎ *707/869–2958 for visitor center, 707/869–2015 for park headquarters* 🌐 *www.parks.ca.gov* 🎟 *$8 per vehicle, free to pedestrians and bicyclists.*

Restaurants

★ boon eat+drink
$$$ | MODERN AMERICAN | A casual storefront restaurant on Guerneville's main drag, boon eat+drink has a menu built around small, "green" (salads and cooked vegetables), and main plates assembled for the most part from locally produced organic ingredients. Like many of chef-owner Crista Luedtke's dishes, the signature polenta lasagna—creamy ricotta salata cheese and polenta served on greens sautéed in garlic, all of it

floating upon a spicy marinara sauce—deviates significantly from the lasagna norm but succeeds on its own merits. **Known for:** adventurous culinary sensibility; all wines from Russian River Valley; local organic ingredients. $ *Average main: $23 ⊠ 16248 Main St. ✛ At Church St. ☎ 707/869–0780 ⊕ eatatboon.com ⊙ Closed Wed.*

Hotels

boon hotel+spa

$ | HOTEL | Redwoods, Douglas firs, and palms supply shade and seclusion at this lushly landscaped resort ¾ mile north of downtown Guerneville. **Pros:** memorable breakfasts; pool area and on-site spa; complimentary bikes. **Cons:** lacks amenities of larger properties; pool rooms too close to the action for some guests; can be pricey in high season. $ *Rooms from: $195 ⊠ 14711 Armstrong Woods Rd. ☎ 707/869–2721 ⊕ boonhotels.com ⇋ 15 rooms ⏐⊙⏐ Breakfast.*

Sebastopol

6 miles east of Occidental, 7 miles southwest of Santa Rosa.

A stroll through downtown Sebastopol—a town formerly known more for Gravenstein apples than for grapes but these days a burgeoning wine hub—reveals glimpses of the distant and recent past and perhaps the future, too. Many hippies settled here in the 1960s and 70s and, as the old Crosby, Stills, Nash & Young song goes, they taught their children well: the town remains steadfastly, if not entirely, countercultural.

GETTING HERE AND AROUND

Sebastopol can be reached from Occidental by taking Graton Road east to Highway 116 and turning south. From Santa Rosa, head west on Highway 12. Sonoma County Transit Buses 20, 22, 24, and 26 serve Sebastopol.

◉ Sights

The Barlow

MARKET | A multibuilding complex on the site of a former apple cannery, The Barlow celebrates Sonoma County's "maker" culture with tenants who produce or sell wine, beer, spirits, crafts, clothing, art, and artisanal food and herbs. Only club members and guests on the allocation waiting list can visit the anchor wine tenant, Kosta Browne, but MacPhail, Pax, and Friedeman have tasting rooms open to the public. Crooked Goat Brewing and Woodfour Brewing Company make and sell ales, and you can have a nip of vodka, gin, sloe gin, or wheat and rye whiskey at Spirit Works Distillery. A locally renowned mixologist teamed up with the duo behind nearby Lowell's and Handline restaurants to open Fern Bar, whose zero-proof (as in nonalcoholic) cocktails entice as much as the traditional ones. ⊠ *6770 McKinley St. ✛ At Morris St., off Hwy. 12 ☎ 707/824–5600 ⊕ www.thebarlow.net ⌲ Complex free; tasting fees at wineries, breweries, distillery.*

★ Dutton-Goldfield Winery

WINERY/DISTILLERY | An avid cyclist whose previous credits include developing the wine-making program at Hartford Court, Dan Goldfield teamed up with fifth-generation farmer Steve Dutton to establish this small operation devoted to cool-climate wines. Goldfield modestly strives to take Dutton's meticulously farmed fruit and "make the winemaker unnoticeable," but what impresses the most about these wines, which include Pinot Blanc, Chardonnay, Pinot Noir, and Zinfandel, is their sheer artistry. Among the ones to seek out are the Angel Camp Pinot Noir, from Anderson Valley (Mendocino County) grapes, and the Morelli Lane Zinfandel, from grapes grown on the remaining 1.8 acres of an 1880s vineyard Goldfield helped revive. Tastings often begin with Pinot Blanc, a white-wine variant of Pinot Noir, proceed through the reds, and end with a palate-cleansing Chardonnay.

736

*3100 Gravenstein Hwy. N/Hwy.
116 ✤ At Graton Rd. ☎ 707/827–3600
⊕ www.duttongoldfield.com ✉ Tastings
from $20.*

★ Iron Horse Vineyards

WINERY/DISTILLERY | A meandering one-lane road leads to this winery known for its sparkling wines and estate Chardonnays and Pinot Noirs. The sparklers have made history: Ronald Reagan served them at his summit meetings with Mikhail Gorbachev; George H. W. Bush took some along to Moscow for treaty talks; and Barack Obama included them at official state dinners. Despite Iron Horse's brushes with fame, a casual rusticity prevails at its outdoor tasting area (large heaters keep things comfortable on chilly days), which gazes out on acres of rolling, vine-covered hills. Regular tours take place on weekdays at 10 am. Tastings and tours are by appointment only. ■TIP→ **When his schedule permits, winemaker David Munksgard leads a private tour by truck at 10 am on Monday.** *✉ 9786 Ross Station Rd. ✤ Off Hwy. 116 ☎ 707/887–1507 ⊕ www.ironhorsevineyards.com ✉ Tastings $30, tours from $50 (includes tasting).*

🍴 Restaurants

Handline Coastal California

$ | **MODERN AMERICAN** | **FAMILY** | Lowell Sheldon and Natalie Goble, who also run a fine-dining establishment (Lowell's) a mile away, converted Sebastopol's former Foster's Freeze location into a 21st-century fast-food palace that won design awards for its rusted-steel frame and translucent panel-like windows. Their menu, a paean to coastal California cuisine, includes oysters raw and grilled, fish tacos, ceviches, tostadas, three burgers (beef, vegetarian, and fish), and, honoring the location's previous incarnation, chocolate and vanilla soft-serve ice cream for dessert. **Known for:** upscale comfort food; outdoor patio; sustainable seafood and other ingredients.

$ Average main: $14 ✉ 935 Gravenstein Hwy. S ✤ Near Hutchins Ave. ☎ 707/827–3744 ⊕ www.handline.com.

★ Ramen Gaijin

$$ | **JAPANESE** | Inside a tall-ceilinged, brick-walled, vaguely industrial-looking space with reclaimed wood from a coastal building backing the bar, the chefs in Ramen Gaijin's turn out richly flavored ramen bowls brimming with crispy pork belly, woodear mushrooms, seaweed, and other well-proportioned ingredients. *Izakaya* (Japanese pub grub) dishes like *donburi* (meat and vegetables over rice) are another specialty, like the ramen made from mostly local proteins and produce. **Known for:** craft cocktails by renowned mixologist Scott Beattie, Japanese whiskeys; gluten-free, vegetarian dishes; pickle, karage (fried-chicken thigh), and other small plates. *$ Average main: $17 ✉ 6948 Sebastopol Ave. ✤ Near Main St. ☎ 707/827–3609 ⊕ www.ramengaijin.com ⊙ Closed Sun. and Mon.*

Santa Rosa

6 miles east of Sebastopol, 55 miles north of San Francisco.

Urban Santa Rosa isn't as popular with tourists as many Wine Country destinations—which isn't surprising, seeing as there are more office parks than wineries within its limits. Nevertheless, this hardworking town is home to a couple of interesting cultural offerings and a few noteworthy restaurants and vineyards. The city's chain motels and hotels can be handy if you're finding that everything else is booked up, especially since Santa Rosa is roughly equidistant from Sonoma, Healdsburg, and the western Russian River Valley, three of Sonoma County's most popular wine-tasting destinations.

GETTING HERE AND AROUND

To get to Santa Rosa from Sebastopol, drive east on Highway 12. From San Francisco, cross the Golden Gate Bridge and continue north on U.S. 101. Santa Rosa's hotels, restaurants, and wineries are spread over a wide area; factor in extra time when driving around the city, especially during morning and evening rush hour. To get here from downtown San Francisco, take Golden Gate Transit Bus 101. Several Sonoma County Transit buses serve the city and surrounding area.

⊙ Sights

Balletto Vineyards

WINERY/DISTILLERY | A few decades ago Balletto was known for quality produce more than for grapes, but the new millennium saw vineyards emerge as the core business. About 90% of the fruit from the family's 650-plus acres goes to other wineries, with the remainder destined for Balletto's estate wines. The house style is light on the oak, high in acidity, and low in alcohol content, a combination that yields exceptionally food-friendly wines. On a hot summer day, sipping a Pinot Gris, rosé of Pinot Noir, or brut rosé sparkler on the outdoor patio can feel transcendent, but the superstars are the Chardonnays and Pinot Noirs. ■TIP→ **Look for the Teresa's unoaked and Cider Ridge Chardonnays and the Burnside Road, Sexton Hill, and Winery Block Pinots, but all the wines are exemplary—and, like the tastings, reasonably priced.** ✉ 5700 Occidental Rd. ⊹ 2½ miles west of Hwy. 12 ☎ 707/568–2455 ⊕ www. ballettovineyards.com ⌚ Tastings $10.

Charles M. Schulz Museum

MUSEUM | FAMILY | Fans of Snoopy and Charlie Brown will love this museum dedicated to the late Charles M. Schulz, who lived his last three decades in Santa Rosa. Permanent installations include a re-creation of the cartoonist's studio, and temporary exhibits often focus on a particular theme in his work.

■TIP→ **Children and adults can take a stab at creating cartoons in the Education Room.** ✉ 2301 Hardies La. ⊹ At W. Steele La. ☎ 707/579–4452 ⊕ www.schulzmuseum. org ⌚ $12 ⊙ Closed Tues. early Sept.– late May.

★ Martinelli Winery

WINERY/DISTILLERY | In a century-old hop barn with the telltale triple towers, Martinelli has the feel of a traditional country store, but the sophisticated wines made here are anything but old-fashioned. The winery's reputation rests on its complex Pinot Noirs, Syrahs, and Zinfandels, including the Jackass Hill Vineyard Zin, made with grapes from 130-year-old vines. Noted winemaker Helen Turley set the Martinelli style—fruit-forward, easy on the oak, reined-in tannins—in the 1990s, and the current team continues this approach. You can sample current releases at a walk-in tasting at the bar or reserve space a couple of days ahead for a seated tasting on the vineyard-view terrace. Rarer and top-rated vintages are poured at appointment-only sessions. ✉ 3360 River Rd., Windsor ⊹ East of Olivet Rd. ☎ 707/525–0570, 800/346–1627 ⊕ www.martinelliwinery.com ⌚ Tastings from $25.

Safari West

NATURE PRESERVE | FAMILY | An unexpected bit of wilderness in the Wine Country, this preserve with African wildlife covers 400 acres. Begin your visit with a stroll around enclosures housing lemurs, cheetahs, giraffes, and rare birds like the brightly colored scarlet ibis. Next, climb with your guide onto open-air vehicles that spend about two hours combing the expansive property, where more than 80 species—including gazelles, cape buffalo, antelope, wildebeests, and zebras—inhabit the hillsides. ■TIP→ **If you'd like to extend your stay, lodging in swank Botswana-made tent cabins is available.** ✉ 3115 Porter Creek Rd. ⊹ Off Mark West Springs Rd. ☎ 707/579–2551, 800/616–2695 ⊕ www. safariwest.com ⌚ From $83.

🍴 Restaurants

★ Bistro 29

$$$ | **FRENCH** | Chef Brian Anderson prepares steak frites, cassoulet, duck confit, and sautéed fish with precision at his perky downtown restaurant—rich-red walls, white tile floors, and butcher paper atop linen tablecloths set the mood—but the mixed-greens salad with Dijon vinaigrette best illustrates his understated approach: its local produce bursts with freshness, and the dressing delicately balances its savory and acidic components. Start with escargots or bay scallops with béchamel, finishing with beignets or orange crème brûlée for dessert. **Known for:** midweek prix-fixe menu; sweet and savory crepes; beer selection, Sonoma County and French wines. [$] *Average main: $27* ✉ *620 5th St.* ✣ *Near Mendocino Ave.* ☎ *707/546–2929* 🌐 *www.bistro29.com* 🕒 *Closed Sun. and Mon. No lunch Sat.*

★ The Spinster Sisters

$$$ | **MODERN AMERICAN** | Modern, well-sourced variations on eggs Benedict and other standards are served at this concrete-and-glass hot spot's weekday breakfast and weekend brunch. Lunch might bring carrot soup, wilted kale salad, or a *banh mi* sandwich, with dinner consisting of shareable bites and small and large plates—think kimchi-and-bacon deviled eggs, vegetable *fritto misto,* and grilled hanger steak. **Known for:** local and international wines; happy hour (Tuesday–Friday 4 pm–6 pm) small bites; horseshoe-shaped bar a good perch for dining single, picking up gossip. [$] *Average main: $26* ✉ *401 S. A St.* ✣ *At Sebastopol Ave.* ☎ *707/528–7100* 🌐 *thespinstersisters.com* 🕒 *No dinner Sun. and Mon.*

🛏 Hotels

Vintners Inn

$$ | **HOTEL** | With a countryside location, a sliver of style, and spacious rooms with comfortable beds, the Vintners Inn further seduces with a slew of amenities and a scenic vineyard landscape. **Pros:** John Ash & Co. restaurant; jogging path through the vineyards; online deals pop up year-round. **Cons:** occasional noise from adjacent events center; trips to downtown Santa Rosa or Healdsburg require a car; pricey on summer and fall weekends. [$] *Rooms from: $295* ✉ *4350 Barnes Rd.* ☎ *707/575–7350, 800/421–2584* 🌐 *www.vintnersinn.com* 🔑 *78 rooms* 🍽 *No meals.*

Petaluma

14 miles west of Sonoma, 39 miles north of San Francisco.

The first thing you should know about Petaluma is that this is a farm town—with more than 60,000 residents, a large one—and the residents are proud of it. Recent years have seen an uptick in the quality of Petaluma cuisine, fueled in part by the proliferation of local organic and artisanal farms and boutique wine production. With the 2018 approval of the Petaluma Gap AVA, the town even has its name on a wine appellation.

Petaluma's agricultural history reaches back to the mid-1800s, when General Mariano Vallejo established Rancho de Petaluma as the headquarters of his vast agrarian empire. From the late 1800s into the 1960s Petaluma marketed itself as the "Egg Capital of the World," and with production totals that peaked at 612 million eggs in 1946, the point was hard to dispute. Although a poultry processor remains Petaluma's second largest employer, the town has diversified. The adobe, an interesting historical stop, was once the area's *only* employer, but these days its visitation figures are dwarfed by Lagunitas Brewing Company, whose free tour is a hoot. At McEvoy Ranch, which started out producing gourmet olive oil and now also makes wine, you can taste both products and tour parts of the farm.

GETTING HERE AND AROUND

Petaluma lies west of Sonoma and southwest of Glen Ellen and Kenwood. From Highway 12 or Arnold Drive, take Watmaugh Road west to Highway 116 west. Sonoma Transit buses (Nos. 30, 40, and 53) serve Petaluma from the Sonoma Valley. From San Francisco take U.S. 101 (or Golden Gate Transit Bus 101) north.

⊙ Sights

Keller Estate

WINERY/DISTILLERY | This boutique winery's guests discover why "wind to wine" is the Petaluma Gap AVA's slogan. The steady Pacific Ocean and San Pablo Bay breezes that mitigate the midday heat give the grapes thick "sailor's skin," heightening their tannins and flavor, says Ana Keller, whose parents planted vineyards three decades ago on former dairy fields. Keller Estate concentrates on Chardonnay, Pinot Noir, and Syrah. In good weather, tastings take place on a stone terrace shaded by umbrellas and flowering pear trees. Book a walking tour to see the property's cave, winery, vineyards, and olive trees, or go farther afield touring in a 1956 Mercedes van. ■TIP➔ **The winery requires reservations for all tastings and tours, but same-day visits are usually possible if you call ahead.** ✉ 5875 Lakeville Hwy. ✛ At Cannon La. ☎ 707/765–2117 ⊕ www.kellerestate.com ✍ Tastings $25, tours (with tastings) from $35 ⊙ Closed Tues. and Wed.

★ Lagunitas Brewing Company

WINERY/DISTILLERY | These days owned by Heineken International, Lagunitas began as a craft brewery in Marin County in 1993 before moving to Petaluma in 1994. In addition to its large facility, the company operates a taproom, the Schwag Shop, and an outdoor beer garden that in good weather bustles even at midday. Guides leading the free weekday Tasting/Walking Tour, which starts with a flight of four beers, provide an irreverent version of the company's rise to international acclaim. An engaging tale involves the state alcohol board's sting operation commemorated by Undercover Investigation Shut-down Ale, one of several small-batch brews made here. ■TIP➔ **The taproom closes on Monday and Tuesday, but tours take place and the gift shop stays open.** ✉ 1280 N. McDowell Blvd. ✛ ½ mile north of Corona Rd. ☎ 707/769–4495 ⊕ lagunitas.com/taproom/petaluma ✍ Tour free ⊙ Taproom closed Mon. and Tues.

★ McEvoy Ranch

WINERY/DISTILLERY | The pastoral retirement project of the late Nan McEvoy after departing as board chair of the San Francisco Chronicle, the ranch produces organic extra virgin olive oil and Pinot Noir and other wines, the estate ones from the Petaluma Gap AVA. Some guests sip a few selections at the bar inside, but far better is to reserve an At Our Table Tasting of wines, oils, seasonal edibles from the organic gardens, and artisanal cheeses. In good weather these relaxing sessions unfold on a pond's-edge flagstone patio with views of alternating rows of Syrah grapes and mature olive trees. Walkabout Ranch Tours of four guests or more take in vineyards, gardens, a Chinese pavilion, and other sites. All visits require an appointment. ✉ 5935 Red Hill Rd. ✛ 6½ miles south of downtown ☎ 866/617–6779 ⊕ www.mcevoyranch.com ✍ Tastings from $20, tour and tasting $95 ⊙ Closed Mon. and Tues. No tour Sun.

🍴 Restaurants

★ Central Market

$$$ | MODERN AMERICAN | A participant in the Slow Food movement, Central Market serves creative, upscale Cal-Mediterranean dishes—many of whose ingredients come from the restaurant's organic farm—in a century-old building with exposed brick walls and an open kitchen. The menu, which changes daily depending on chef Tony Najiola's inspiration and what's ripe and ready, might include tortilla soup or a buttermilk-fried halibut-cheeks starter, a slow-roasted-beets salad, pizzas and stews, and wood-grilled fish and meat. **Known for:** chef's tasting menus; superior wine list; historic setting. [$] *Average main: $25* ✉ *42 Petaluma Blvd. N* ✥ *Near Western Ave.* ☎ *707/778–9900* 🌐 *www.centralmarketpetaluma.com* ⏲ *Closed Wed. No lunch.*

★ Pearl

$$ | MEDITERRANEAN | Regulars of this southern Petaluma "daytime café" with indoor and outdoor seating rave about its eastern Mediterranean–inflected cuisine—then immediately downplay their enthusiasm lest this 2018 arrival become more popular. The menu, divided into "smaller," "bigger," and "sweeter" options, changes often, but mainstays include buckwheat polenta, a lamb burger dripping with tzatziki (pickled fennel and yogurt sauce), and *shakshuka* (tomato-based stew with chickpeas, fava beans, and baked egg). **Known for:** weekend brunch; zippy beverage lineup; menu prices include gratuity. [$] *Average main: $18* ✉ *500 1st St.* ✥ *At G St.* ☎ *707/559–5187* 🌐 *pearlpetaluma.com* ⏲ *Closed Tues. No dinner.*

THE NORTH COAST

19

Updated by
Daniel Mangin

● Sights	🍴 Restaurants	🛏 Hotels	🛍 Shopping	🍸 Nightlife
★★★★★	★★★★☆	★★★★★	★☆☆☆☆	★☆☆☆☆

WELCOME TO THE NORTH COAST

TOP REASONS TO GO

★ **Scenic coastal drives:** There's hardly a road here that isn't scenic.

★ **Wild beaches:** This stretch of California is one of nature's masterpieces. Revel in the unbridled, rugged coastline, without a building in sight.

★ **Dinnertime:** When you're done hiking the beach, refuel with delectable food; you'll find everything from fresh-off-the-boat seafood to haute French cuisine.

★ **Fine wine:** Sip wines at family-owned tasting rooms—cool-climate Pinot Noirs and Chardonnays in the Anderson Valley, then wines from Zinfandel and other heat-loving varietals as you move inland.

★ **Wildlife:** Watch for migrating whales, sun-bathing sea lions, and huge Roosevelt elk with majestic antlers.

It's all but impossible to explore the Northern California coast without a car. Indeed, you wouldn't want to—driving here is half the fun. The main road is Highway 1, two lanes that twist and turn (sometimes 180 degrees) up cliffs and down through valleys in Sonoma and Mendocino counties, with U.S. 101 proceeding parallel inland until the two roads join northward in the Redwood Country of Humboldt County. From south to north, below are a few key towns:

1 **Bodega Bay.**

2 **Jenner.**

3 **Gualala.**

4 **Point Arena.**

5 **Elk.**

6 **Little River.**

7 **Mendocino.**

8 **Ft. Bragg.**

9 **Philo.**

10 **Boonville.**

11 **Hopland.**

12 **Ukiah.**

13 **Weott.**

14 **Ferndale.**

15 **Eureka.**

16 **Trinidad.**

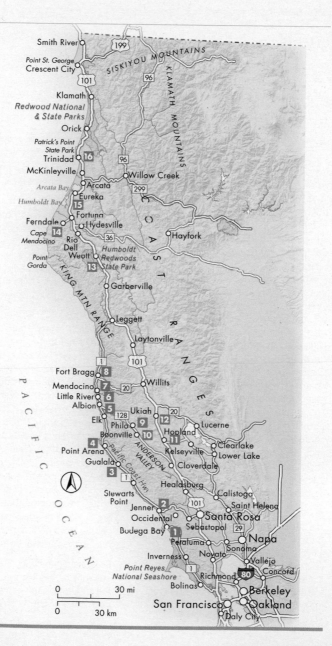

Smith River

Point St. George
Crescent City

199

SISKIYOU MOUNTAINS

101

96

Klamath

Redwood National
& State Parks

KLAMATH MOUNTAINS

Orick

Patrick's Point
State Park
Trinidad 16
McKinleyville

96

Willow Creek

Arcata Bay
Arcata
Eureka 15
Humboldt Bay
Fortuna
Ferndale
Hydesville
14
Cape
Mendocino
Rio
Dell
Weott
Point
Gorda
Humboldt
Redwoods
State Park
13

299

Hayfork

36

C
O
A
S
T

Garberville

Leggett

Laytonville

101

R
A
N
G
E
S

KING MTN RANGE

Fort Bragg 8

Mendocino 7
Little River 6
Albion 5

1

Willits

20

Elk
Boonville
Philo
9
128
Ukiah
12
10
Hopland
11
Kelseyville

20

Lucerne

Clearlake
Lower Lake

Point Arena 4

Gualala

3

ANDERSON
VALLEY

Cloverdale

1

Stewarts
Point

Healdsburg

Calistoga

Pacific Coast Hwy

Jenner
Occidental
2

101

Saint Helena

Santa Rosa

PACIFIC OCEAN

Bodega Bay

1

Petaluma

Sebastopol

29

Napa

Sonoma

Novato

Inverness

Vallejo

80

Concord

Point Reyes
National Seashore

1

Richmond

Bolinas

Berkeley

San Francisco

Oakland

Daly City

0   30 mi

0   30 km

The spectacular coastline between Marin County and the Oregon border defies expectations. The Pacific Ocean defines the landscape, but instead of boardwalks and bikinis there are ragged cliffs and pounding waves—and the sunbathers are mostly sea lions.

Instead of strip malls and freeways, you'll find a two-lane highway that follows a fickle shoreline. Although coastal towns vary from deluxe spa retreat to hippie hideaway, all are reliably sleepy—and that's exactly why many Californians escape here to enjoy nature unspoiled. On a detour inland, you can explore redwoods and taste wines at wineries rarely too crowded or pricey. When you travel the North Coast, turn off your phone; you won't have much of a signal anyway, and this stretch of Highway 1 is made up of numerous little worlds, each different from the last, waiting to be discovered. Everything about life here says slow down. If you don't, you might miss a noble Roosevelt elk grazing in a roadside field or a pod of migrating whales cruising along the shore. ■TIP→ **Don't plan to drive too far in one day. Some drivers stop frequently to appreciate the views, and you can't safely drive faster than 30 or 40 mph on many portions of the highway.**

MAJOR REGIONS

The Sonoma Coast. As you enter Sonoma County from the south on Highway 1, you pass first through gently rolling pastureland. North of Bodega Bay dramatic shoreline scenery takes over. The road snakes up, down, and around sheer cliffs and steep inclines—some without guardrails—where cows seem to cling precariously.

Stunning vistas (or cottony fog) and hairpin turns make for an exhilarating drive.

The Mendocino Coast. The timber industry gave birth to most of the small towns along this stretch of coastline. Although tourism now drives the economy, the region has retained much of its old-fashioned charm. The beauty of the landscape, of course, has not changed. Inland lies the Anderson Valley, whose wineries mostly grow cool-climate grapes.

Redwood Country. There's a different state of mind in Humboldt County. Here, instead of spas, there are old-time hotels. Instead of wineries, there are breweries. The landscape is primarily thick redwood forest; the interior mountains get snow in winter and sizzle in summer while the coast sits covered in fog. Until as late as 1924 there was no road north of Willits; the coastal towns were reachable only by sea. That legacy is apparent in the communities of today: Eureka and Arcata, both former ports, are sizeable, but otherwise towns are tiny and nestled in the woods, and people have an independent spirit that recalls the original homesteaders.

Redwood State Parks. For a pristine encounter with giant redwoods, make the trek to these coastal parks where even casual visitors have easy access to the trees.

Planning

When to Go

The North Coast is a year-round destination, though when you go determines what you will see. The migration of the Pacific gray whales is a wintertime phenomenon, which lasts roughly from mid-December to early April. Wildflowers follow the winter rain, as early as January in southern areas through June and July farther north. Summer is the high season for tourists, but spring, fall, and even winter are arguably better times to visit. The pace is slower, towns are quieter, and lodging is cheaper.

The coastal climate is similar to San Francisco's, although winter nights are colder than in the city. In July and August thick fog can drop temperatures to the high 50s, but fear not: you need only drive inland a few miles to find temperatures that are often 20 degrees higher.

Getting Here and Around

AIR TRAVEL
Arcata/Eureka Airport (ACV), 14 miles north of Eureka in McKinleyville, is served by subsidiaries of United and a few other small airlines. Most arriving passengers rent a car, but you can also taxi ($50–$60), shuttle ($28), or ride share (starting at $22) to Eureka (a little less to Arcata).

AIRPORT CONTACTS Arcata/Eureka Airport. ✉ *3561 Boeing Ave., McKinleyville* 🖀 *707/445–9651* ⊕ *flyhumboldt.org.*

GROUND TRANSPORTATION CONTACTS City Cab. 🖀 *707/442–4551* ⊕ *citycab-humboldt.com.* **Door-to-Door Airporter.** 🖀 *888/338–5497, 707/839–4186* ⊕ *www.doortodoorairporter.com.*

BUS TRAVEL
Greyhound buses travel along U.S. 101 from San Francisco to Garberville, Eureka, and Arcata. Humboldt Transit Authority connects Eureka, Arcata, and Trinidad.

BUS CONTACTS Greyhound. 🖀 *800/231–2222* ⊕ *www.greyhound.com.* **Humboldt Transit Authority.** 🖀 *707/443–0826* ⊕ *www.hta.org.*

CAR TRAVEL
U.S. 101 has excellent services, but long stretches separate towns along Highway 1. ■ TIP→ **If you're running low on fuel and see a gas station, stop for a refill.** Twisting Highway 1 is the scenic route to Mendocino from San Francisco, but the fastest one is U.S. 101 north to Highway 128 west (from Cloverdale) to Highway 1 north. The quickest route to the far North Coast is straight up U.S. 101 past Cloverdale to Hopland and Ukiah and on to Humboldt County.

ROAD CONDITIONS Caltrans. 🖀 *800/427–7623* ⊕ *www.dot.ca.gov.*

Restaurants

Restaurants here, a few with regional reputations but most off the culinary world's radar, entice diners with dishes fashioned from the abundant fresh seafood and locally grown vegetables and herbs. Attire is usually informal, though at pricier establishments dressy casual is the norm. Most kitchens close at 8 or 8:30 pm and few places serve past 9:30 pm. Many restaurants close in January or early February.

Hotels

Restored Victorians, rustic lodges, country inns, and vintage motels are among the accommodations available here. Few have air-conditioning (the ocean breezes make it unnecessary), and many have no phones or TVs in the rooms. Except in Fort Bragg and a few other towns, budget accommodations are rare, but in winter you're likely to find reduced rates and nearly empty lodgings. In summer and on the weekends, though, make bed-and-breakfast reservations as far ahead as possible—rooms at the best inns often sell out months in advance. *Hotel reviews have been shortened. For full information, visit Fodors.com.*

WHAT IT COSTS

	$	$$	$$$	$$$$
RESTAURANTS				
	under $16	$16–$22	$23–$30	over $30
HOTELS				
	under $120	$120–$175	$176–$250	over $250

Visitor Information

CONTACTS **Humboldt Visitors Bureau.** ☎ 707/443–5097, 800/346–3482 ⊕ *www. visitredwoods.com.* **Sonoma County Tourism.** ☎ 707/522–5800, 800/576–6662 ⊕ *www.sonomacounty.com.* **Visit Mendocino County.** ☎ 707/964–9010, 866/466–3636 ⊕ *www.visitmendocino.com.*

Bodega Bay

23 miles west of Santa Rosa.

From this working town's busy harbor west of Highway 1, commercial boats pursue fish and Dungeness crab. In 1962, Alfred Hitchcock shot *The Birds* here. The Tides Wharf complex, an important location, is no longer recognizable, but a few miles inland, in Bodega, you can find Potter Schoolhouse, now a private residence.

GETTING HERE AND AROUND

To reach Bodega Bay, exit U.S. 101 at Santa Rosa and take Highway 12 west (called Bodega Highway west of Sebastopol) 23 miles to the coast. A scenic alternative is to take U.S. 101's East Washington Street/Central Petaluma exit and follow signs west to Bodega Bay; just after you merge onto Highway 1, you'll pass through down-home Valley Ford. Mendocino Transit Authority (⊕ *mendocinotransit.org*) Route 95 buses serve Bodega Bay.

⊙ Sights

Sonoma Coast Vineyards

WINERY/DISTILLERY | This boutique winery with an ocean-view tasting room makes cool-climate Chardonnays and Pinot Noirs from grapes grown close to the Pacific. The Antonio Mountain and Balistreri Family Vineyards Pinot Noirs stand out among wines that also include a mildly oaky Sauvignon Blanc and a well-balanced sparkler. ⊠ *555 Hwy. 1* ☎ *707/921–2860* ⊕ *www.sonomacoast-vineyards.com* ☞ *Tastings from $25.*

⊙ Beaches

★ Sonoma Coast State Park

BEACH—SIGHT | The park's gorgeous sandy coves stretch for 17 miles from Bodega Head to 4 miles north of Jenner. **Bodega Head** is a popular whale-watching perch in winter and early spring, and **Rock Point, Duncan's Landing,** and **Wright's Beach,** at about the halfway mark, have good picnic areas. Rogue waves have swept people off the rocks at Duncan's Landing Overlook, so don't stray past signs warning you away. Calmer **Shell Beach,** about 2 miles north, is known for beachcombing, tidepooling, and fishing. Walk part of the bluff-top **Kortum Trail** or drive about 2½ miles north of Shell Beach to **Blind Beach.** Near the mouth of the Russian River just north of here at **Goat Rock Beach,** you'll find harbor seals; pupping season is from March through August. Bring binoculars and walk north from the parking lot to view the seals. During summer lifeguards are on duty at some beaches, but strong rip currents and heavy surf keep most visitors onshore. **Amenities:** parking (fee); toilets. **Best for:** solitude; sunset; walking. ✉ *Park Headquarters/Salmon Creek Ranger Station, 3095 Hwy. 1* ✣ *2 miles north of Bodega Bay* ☎ *707/875–3483* 🌐 *www.parks.ca.gov* 🎫 *$8 per vehicle.*

🍴 Restaurants

Spud Point Crab Company

$ | **SEAFOOD** | Crab sandwiches, New England or Manhattan clam chowder, and homemade crab cakes with roasted red pepper sauce star on the brief menu of this food stand. Place your order inside, and enjoy your meal to go or at one of the marina-view picnic tables outside. **Known for:** family-run operation; opens at 9 am; seafood cocktails, superb chowder. [$] *Average main: $10* ✉ *1910 Westshore Rd.* ☎ *707/875–9472* 🕒 *No dinner.*

★ Terrapin Creek Cafe & Restaurant

$$$$ | **MODERN AMERICAN** | Intricate but not fussy cuisine based on locally farmed ingredients and *fruits de mer* has made this casual yet sophisticated restaurant with an open kitchen a West County darling. Start with raw Marin Miyagi oysters, rich potato-leek soup, or (in season) Dungeness crabmeat ragout before moving on to halibut or other fish pan-roasted to perfection. **Known for:** intricate cuisine of chefs Liya and Andrew Truong; top Bay Area–foodies' choice; starters and salads. [$] *Average main: $32* ✉ *1580 Eastshore Rd.* ☎ *707/875–2700* 🌐 *www.terrapincreekcafe.com* 🕒 *Closed Tues. and Wed. No lunch.*

🛏 Hotels

Bodega Bay Lodge

$$$ | **HOTEL** | Looking out to the ocean across a wetland, the lodge's shingle-and-river-rock buildings contain Bodega Bay's finest accommodations. **Pros:** ocean views; spacious rooms; fireplaces and patios or balconies in most rooms. **Cons:** pricey in-season; parking lot in foreground of some rooms' views; fairly long drive to other fine dining. [$] *Rooms from: $239* ✉ *103 Coast Hwy. 1* ☎ *707/875–3525* 🌐 *www.bodegabaylodge.com* 🛏 *83 rooms* 🍴 *No meals.*

Bodega Harbor Inn

$ | **HOTEL** | As humble as can be, this is one of the few places on this stretch of the coast with rooms for around $100 a night. **Pros:** budget choice; rooms for larger groups; ocean views from public areas and some rooms. **Cons:** older facility; nondescript rooms; behind a shopping center. [$] *Rooms from: $99* ✉ *1345 Bodega Ave.* ☎ *707/875–3594* 🌐 *www.bodegaharborinn.com* 🛏 *16 rooms* 🍴 *No meals.*

Jenner

10 miles north of Bodega Bay.

The Russian River empties into the Pacific Ocean at Jenner, a wide spot in the road where houses dot a mountainside high above the sea. Facing south, the village looks across the river's mouth to Goat Rock Beach *(see Sonoma Coast State Park, above)*. North of the village, Fort Ross State Historic Park provides a glimpse into Russia's early-19th-century foray into California. South of the fort a winery named for the fort grows Chardonnay and Pinot Noir above the coastal fog line. North of the fort lie more beaches and redwoods to hike and explore.

GETTING HERE AND AROUND

Jenner is north of Bodega Bay on Highway 1; from Guerneville head west on Highway 116 (River Road). Mendocino Transit Authority (🌐 *mendocinotransit.org*) buses serve Jenner from Bodega Bay and other coastal towns.

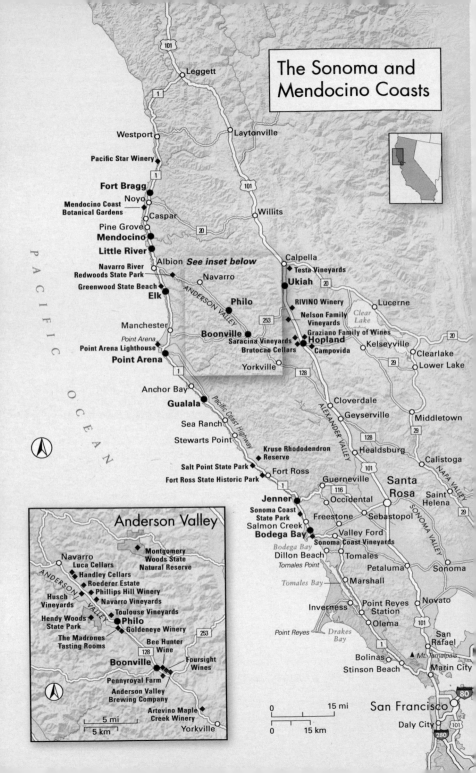

The Sonoma and Mendocino Coasts

101 Leggett

Westport
Laytonville

Pacific Star Winery
Fort Bragg
Noyo
Mendocino Coast
Botanical Gardens
Caspar
Willits
Pine Grove
Mendocino
20
Little River
Albion *See inset below*
Calpella
Navarro River
Redwoods State Park
Navarro
Testa Vineyards
Ukiah
Greenwood State Beach
20
Elk
Philo
RIVINO Winery
Nelson Family
Vineyards
Manchester
253
Graziano Family of Wines
Boonville
Point Arena
Saracina Vineyards
Hopland
Point Arena Lighthouse
Brutocao Cellars
Campovida
Point Arena
Kelseyville
1
Yorkville
128
Clearlake
29
Lower Lake
Anchor Bay
Cloverdale
20
Gualala
Geyserville
Middletown
Sea Ranch
128
29
Stewarts Point
Healdsburg
Calistoga
Kruse Rhododendron
Reserve
Salt Point State Park
101
Fort Ross
Fort Ross State Historic Park
Guerneville
1
**Santa
Rosa**
Saint
Helena
116
Occidental
Jenner
29
Sonoma Coast
State Park
Freestone
Sebastopol
Salmon Creek
Bodega Bay
Valley Ford
Bodega Bay
Sonoma Coast Vineyards
Dillon Beach
Tomales
Petaluma
Tomales Point
Sonoma
Tomales Bay
Marshall
Point Reyes
Inverness
Point Reyes
Station
Novato
*Drakes
Bay*
Olema
101
San
Rafael
Bolinas
1
▲ Mt. Tamalpais
Marin City
Stinson Beach
80
San Francisco
0   15 mi
0   15 km
Daly City
101
280

Clear
Lake
Lucerne

Alexander Valley

Napa Valley

Sonoma Valley

Pacific Coast Highway

Anderson Valley

Anderson Valley

Navarro
Luca Cellars
Montgomery
Woods State
Natural Reserve
Handley Cellars
Roederer Estate
Phillips Hill Winery
Husch
Vineyards
Navarro Vineyards
Hendy Woods
State Park
Toulouse Vineyards
Philo
Goldeneye Winery
253
The Madrones
Tasting Rooms
Bee Hunter
Wine
128
Foursight
Wines
Boonville
Pennyroyal Farm
Anderson Valley
Brewing Company
Artevino Maple
Creek Winery
Yorkville

5 mi
5 km

Sights

Fort Ross State Historic Park

NATIONAL/STATE PARK | **FAMILY** | With its reconstructed Russian Orthodox chapel, stockade, and officials' quarters, Fort Ross looks much the way it did after the Russians made it their major California coastal outpost in 1812. Russian settlers established the fort on land they leased from the native Kashia people. The Russians hoped to gain a foothold in the Pacific coast's warmer regions and to produce crops and other supplies for their Alaskan fur-trading operations. In 1841, with the local marine mammal population depleted and farming having proven unproductive, the Russians sold their holdings to John Sutter, later of gold-rush fame. The land, privately ranched for decades, became a state park in 1909. One original Russian-era structure remains, as does a cemetery. The rest of the compound has been reconstructed to look much as it did during Russian times. An excellent small museum documents the history of the fort, the Kashia people, and the ranch and state-park eras. Note that no dogs are allowed past the parking lot and picnic area. ✉ *19005 Hwy. 1* ✣ *11 miles north of Jenner village* ☎ *707/847–3437* 🌐 *www.fortross.org* 🎫 *$8 per vehicle.*

Salt Point State Park

NATIONAL/STATE PARK | For 5 miles, Highway 1 winds through this park, 6,000 acres of forest, meadows, and rocky shoreline. Heading north, the first park entrance (on the right) leads to forest hiking trails and several campgrounds. The next entrance—the park's main road—winds through meadows and along the wave-splashed coastline. This is also the route to the visitor center and **Gerstle Cove,** a favorite spot for scuba divers and sunbathing seals. Next along the highway is **Stump Beach Cove,** with picnic tables, toilets, and a ¼-mile walk to the sandy beach. The park's final entrance is at **Fisk Mill Cove,** where centuries of wind and rain erosion have carved unusual honeycomb patterns in the sandstone called "tafonis." A five-minute walk uphill from the parking lot leads to a dramatic view of **Sentinel Rock,** an excellent spot for sunsets.

Just up the highway, narrow, unpaved Kruse Ranch Road leads to the **Kruse Rhododendron State Reserve**, where each May thousands of rhododendrons bloom within a quiet forest of redwoods and tan oaks. ✉ *25050 Hwy. 1* ✣ *6 miles north of Fort Ross* ☎ *707/847–3221, 707/865–2391* 🌐 *www.parks.ca.gov* 🎫 *$8 per vehicle.*

Restaurants

Coast Kitchen

$$$ | **MODERN AMERICAN** | On a sunny afternoon or at sunset, glistening ocean views from the Coast Kitchen's outdoor patio and indoor dining space elevate dishes emphasizing seafood and local produce both farmed and foraged. Starters like a baby gem lettuce Caesar and grilled salmon wings precede entrées that may include seared scallops and aged rib eye. **Known for:** ocean-view patio (frequent whale sightings in winter and spring); Sonoma County cheeses, wines, and produce; bar menu 3 pm–5 pm. [$] *Average main: $28* ✉ *Timber Cove, 21780 Hwy. 1* ✣ *3 miles north of Fort Ross State Historic Park* ☎ *707/847–3231* 🌐 *www.coastkitchensonoma.com.*

Hotels

★ Timber Cove Resort

$$$$ | **RESORT** | Restored well beyond its original splendor, this resort anchored to a craggy oceanfront cliff is by far the Sonoma Coast's coolest getaway. **Pros:** dramatic sunsets; grand public spaces, destination restaurant. **Cons:** almost too cool for the laid-back Sonoma Coast; pricey ocean-view rooms; far from nightlife. [$] *Rooms from: $314* ✉ *21780 Hwy. 1* ☎ *707/847–3231* 🌐 *www.timbercoveresort.com* 🔑 *46 rooms* 🍴 *No meals.*

Surfers check out the waves near Bodega Bay on the Sonoma Coast.

Gualala

38 miles north of Jenner, 35 miles south of Mendocino.

This former lumber port on the Gualala River, a good base for exploring the southern Mendocino coast, has all the basic services plus some galleries and gift shops.

GETTING HERE AND AROUND
Gualala is on Highway 1; from U.S. 101 near Santa Rosa, head west on River Road (Exit 494) and turn north at the ocean. Mendocino Transit Authority (⊕ *mendocinotransit.org*) buses serve the area.

 Restaurants

St. Orres
$$$ | AMERICAN | Underneath one of this lodge's two Russian-style onion-dome towers is a romantic atrium dining room where locally farmed and foraged ingredients appear in dishes such as

garlic flan with black chanterelles and rack of wild boar with apple-pear latkes. You can also dine in the bar, where, as with the main room you can choose from the prix-fixe menu (usually about $50) or dine à la carte on wild-mushroom ravioli, baby abalone with seared scallops, and other small plates. **Known for:** elaborate weekend brunch; worthy wine list; lodgings in adjacent hotel and cottages. Ⓢ *Average main: $28* ✉ *36601 S. Hwy. 1, 3 miles north of Gualala* ☎ *707/884–3335* ⊕ *www.saintorres. com* ⊙ *Closed Mon. and Tues. No lunch weekdays. Occasionally closed some weekdays in winter.*

🛏 Hotels

★ Mar Vista Cottages
$$$ | HOTEL | Escape to nature and retro-charm at these refurbished, gadget-free 1930s cottages, four with two bedrooms and eight with one. **Pros:** commune-with-nature solitude; peaceful retreat; walking path to beach. **Cons:** no other businesses within

walking distance; no TVs or phones in rooms; two-night minimum on weekends. $ Rooms from: $190 ⊠ 35101 S. Hwy 1 ⊹ 5 miles north of Gualala ☎ 707/884–3522, 877/855–3522 ⊕ www. marvistamendocino.com ⤳ 12 rooms ⓘⓞⓘ No meals.

Seacliff Motel on the Bluff

$$ | HOTEL | Wedged in back of a small shopping center, this motel is not much to look at, but you'll spend your time here staring at the Pacific panorama because all rooms have ocean views. **Pros:** smart budget choice; Trinks restaurant next door for creative breakfasts (lunch served, too); clean rooms with gas fireplaces, free Wi-Fi, and binoculars. **Cons:** nondescript from highway; standard-issue decor; sometimes foggy in summer. $ Rooms from: $165 ⊠ 39140 S. Hwy. 1 ☎ 707/884–1213, 800/400–5053 ⊕ www.seacliffmotel. com ⤳ 16 rooms ⓘⓞⓘ No meals.

Point Arena

15 miles north of Gualala, 35 miles south of Mendocino.

Occupied by longtime locals and long-haired surfers, this former timber town on Highway 1 is part New Age, part rowdy, and always laid-back. The one road going west out of downtown will lead you to the harbor, where fishing boats unload sea urchins and salmon and someone's nearly always riding the waves.

GETTING HERE AND AROUND

From Gualala follow Highway 1 north; from Mendocino follow it south. Mendocino Transit Authority (⊕ mendocinotransit.org) serves the area.

★ Point Arena Lighthouse

LIGHTHOUSE | For an outstanding view of the ocean and, in winter, migrating whales, take the marked road off Highway 1 north of town to the 115-foot

lighthouse. Climb the 145 steps, and a 360-degree panorama unfolds. It's possible to stay out here in one of four rental units ($$–$$$$), all with full kitchens (weekend minimum-stay requirement). ⊠ 45500 Lighthouse Rd. ⊹ Off Hwy. 1, 4½ miles northwest of town ☎ 707/882–2809, 877/725–4448 ⊕ www.pointarenalighthouse.com ⤳ Tour $8 ($5 if no tour).

🍴 Restaurants

Arena Market and Cafe

$ | CAFÉ | The simple café at this all-organic grocery store serves baked goods for breakfast and has hot soups, sandwiches, and an ample salad bar for lunch and early dinner. The market, which specializes in food from local farms, sells cheese, bread, and other picnic items, and you can sip beer and wine in the café. **Known for:** locally owned co-op; espresso drinks; good soups and salad bar. $ Average main: $9 ⊠ 185 Main St. ☎ 707/882–3663 ⊕ www.arenamarketandcafe.org ⤳ No dinner.

★ Franny's Cup and Saucer

$ | CAFÉ | Aided by her mother Barbara, a former pastry chef at famed Chez Panisse in Berkeley, Franny turns out baked goods that are sophisticated and inventive. Morning favorites include scones and sweet and savory pastries; there are fruit tarts and strawberry-apricot crisps, plus a mouthwatering assortment of cookies, candy, jams, and jellies for indulging anytime. **Known for:** dazzling specialty cakes; delightful ambience; croque monsieurs and frittata of the day. $ Average main: $7 ⊠ 213 Main St. ☎ 707/882–2500 ⊕ www. frannyscupandsaucer.com ▬ No credit cards ☉ Closed Sun.–Tues. No dinner.

Elk

33 miles north of Gualala.

In this quiet town on the cliff above Greenwood Cove, just about every spot has a view of the rocky coastline and stunning Pacific sunsets. A few restaurants and inns do business here, but the main attraction is highly walkable Greenwood State Beach.

GETTING HERE AND AROUND

Elk is along Highway 1, 6 miles south of its intersection with Highway 128. Mendocino Transit Authority (🌐 *mendocinotransit.org*) buses serve the area.

Sights

Greenwood State Beach

BEACH—SIGHT | If you're not staying at one of Elk's cliff-top lodgings, the easiest access to the sandy shore below them is at this state beach whose parking lot sits across Highway 1 from the town's general store. A trail leads from the lot down to the beach, where the waves crashing against the huge offshore rocks are the perfect backdrop. **Amenities:** parking (free). **Good for:** sunset; walking. ✉ *6150 Hwy. 1* ☎ *707/937–5804* 🌐 *www.parks.ca.gov* 🎟 *Free.*

Restaurants

Queenie's Roadhouse Cafe

$ | AMERICAN | If the day's sunny, grab one of the picnic tables in front of this beloved hangout for big breakfasts (served until closing, at 3) and lunches that include blue-cheese burgers topped with onions browned in bourbon and butter. The café's wide windows provide Pacific views to enjoy with your meal. **Known for:** omelets, huevos rancheros, waffles, and pancakes; burgers, salads, and sandwiches; local wines and microbrews. [$] *Average main: $14* ✉ *6061 S. Hwy. 1* ☎ *707/877–3285* 🌐 *www.queeniesroadhousecafe.com* 🕒 *Closed Tues. and Wed. Closed late Dec.–mid-Feb. No dinner.*

Hotels

Elk Cove Inn & Spa

$$ | B&B/INN | Perched on a bluff above pounding surf and a driftwood-strewn beach, this property has stunning views from most of its accommodations, which include seven rooms, five suites, and four cottages. **Pros:** gorgeous views; filling breakfast; steps to the beach. **Cons:** rooms in main house are smallish; not suitable for young children; spa's massage calendar often full. [$] *Rooms from: $175* ✉ *6300 S. Hwy. 1* ☎ *707/877–3321, 800/275–2967* 🌐 *www.elkcoveinn.com* 🛏 *16 rooms* 🍴 *Free Breakfast.*

★ **Harbor House Inn**

$$$$ | B&B/INN | Prepare to be bowled over by every aspect of this showcase property that reopened in 2018 after a five-year multimillion-dollar makeover: its rugged Pacific-cliff setting, destination restaurant, sterling hospitality, and luxurious accommodations in a 1916 redwood Craftsman-style house and a few newer cottages. **Pros:** romantic, ocean-view setting; luxurious base for wine tasting and outdoor activities; destination restaurant. **Cons:** not ideal for kids; 16 miles from Mendocino; best accommodations expensive for the area. [$] *Rooms from: $379* ✉ *5600 S. Hwy. 1* ☎ *707/877–3203, 800/720–7474* 🌐 *www.theharborhouseinn.com* 🛏 *10 rooms* 🍴 *Free Breakfast.*

Little River

13½ miles north of Elk.

The town of Little River is not much more than a post office and a convenience store; Albion, its neighbor to the south, is even smaller. Along this winding portion of Highway 1 you'll find numerous inns and restaurants, all of them quiet and situated to take advantage of the breathtaking ocean views.

GETTING HERE AND AROUND

Little River is along Highway 1, 7 miles north of its junction with Highway 128. Mendocino Transit Authority (🌐 *mendocinotransit.org*) buses serve the area.

Sights

Navarro River Redwoods State Park

NATIONAL/STATE PARK | **FAMILY** | Described by locals as the "11-mile-long redwood tunnel to the sea," this park that straddles Highway 128 is great for walks amid second-growth redwoods and for summer swimming in the gentle Navarro River. In late winter and spring, when the river is higher, you also can fish, canoe, and kayak. ✉ *Hwy. 128, Albion* ✣ *2 miles east of Hwy. 1* ☎ *707/937–5804* 🌐 *www.parks.ca.gov.*

Van Damme State Park

NATIONAL/STATE PARK | Best known for its quiet beach, a prime diving spot, this park is also popular with day hikers. A ¼-mile stroll on a boardwalk leads to the bizarre **Pygmy Forest,** where acidic soil and poor drainage have produced mature cypress and pine trees that are no taller than a person. For more of a challenge, hike the moderate 4¼-mile Pygmy Forest and Fern Canyon Loop past the forest and sword ferns that grow as tall as 4 feet. The visitor center has displays on ocean life and the historical significance of the redwood lumber industry along the coast. ✉ *Little River Park Rd., off Hwy. 1* ☎ *707/937–5804* 🌐 *www.parks.ca.gov* 🎟 *$8 per vehicle, walk-ins free (park at beach).*

Restaurants

Ledford House

$$$ | **FRENCH** | The only thing separating this bluff-top wood-and-glass restaurant from the Pacific Ocean is a great view. Entrées evoke the flavors of southern France and include hearty bistro dishes—stews, cassoulet, and pastas—and large portions of grilled meats and freshly caught fish (though the restaurant also is vegetarian friendly). **Known for:** Mendocino-centric wine list; live jazz nightly; three-course bistro special. [$] *Average main: $27* ✉ *3000 N. Hwy. 1, Albion* ☎ *707/937–0282* 🌐 *www.ledfordhouse.com* ⏲ *Closed Mon. and Tues. and late-Feb.–early Mar. and mid-Oct.–early Nov. No lunch.*

Hotels

Albion River Inn

$$$ | **B&B/INN** | Contemporary New England–style cottages at this inn overlook the dramatic bridge and seascape where the Albion River empties into the Pacific. **Pros:** ocean views; great bathtubs; meat and fresh seafood dishes at romantic glassed-in restaurant. **Cons:** often foggy in summer; no TV in rooms; could use style update. [$] *Rooms from: $195* ✉ *3790 N. Hwy. 1, Albion* ☎ *707/937–1919, 800/479–7944* 🌐 *albionriverinn.com* 🛏 *22 rooms* 🍴 *Free Breakfast.*

Mendocino

3 miles north of Little River.

A flourishing logging town in the late-19th century, Mendocino seduces 21st-century travelers with windswept cliffs, phenomenal Pacific Ocean views, and boomtown-era New England–style architecture. Following the timber industry's mid-20th-century decline, artists and craftspeople began flocking here, and so did Hollywood: Elia Kazan chose Mendocino as a backdrop for his 1955 film adaptation of John Steinbeck's *East of Eden,* starring James Dean, and the town stood in for fictional Cabot Cove, Maine, in the long-running TV series *Murder, She Wrote.* As the arts community thrived, restaurants, cafés, and inns sprang up. Today, the small downtown area consists almost entirely of places to eat and shop.

GETTING HERE AND AROUND

Main Street is off Highway 1 about 10 miles north of its junction with Highway 128. Mendocino Transit Authority (⊕ mendocinotransit.org) buses serve the area.

👁 Sights

Ford House Visitor Center & Museum

HOUSE | The restored Ford House, built in 1854, serves as the visitor center for Mendocino Headlands State Park and the town. The house has a scale model of Mendocino as it looked in 1890, when it had 34 water towers and a 12-seat public outhouse. From the museum, you can head out on a 3-mile trail across the spectacular seaside cliffs that border the town. ⌂ 45035 Main St., west of Lansing St. ☎ 707/937–5397 ⊕ mendoparks.org/visitor-centers 🖭 Museum $2, visitor center free.

Kelley House Museum

MUSEUM | An 1861 structure holds this museum whose artifacts include Victorian-era furniture and historical photographs of Mendocino coast's logging days. Two-hour walking tours of Mendocino depart from the museum at 11 am on weekends and some weekday holidays. ⌂ 45007 Albion St. ☎ 707/937–5791 ⊕ www.kelleyhousemuseum.org 🖭 Museum $5, walking tours $10 ⊘ Closed Tues.–Thurs.

🍴 Restaurants

Cafe Beaujolais

$$$$ | AMERICAN | A garden of heirloom and exotic plantings surrounds this popular restaurant inside a yellow Victorian cottage. Local ingredients find their way into starters such as a silky-creamy wild-foraged-chanterelle soup or a salad of burrata and Brussels sprouts and entrées like duck breast à l'orange and local black cod with a truffle emulsion. **Known for:** breads from a wood-fired brick oven; Mendocino

wines on international list; salads, burgers, sandwiches, pastas, and (some days) pizza for lunch. $ Average main: $33 ⌂ 961 Ukiah St. ☎ 707/937–5614 ⊕ www.cafebeaujolais.com ⊘ No lunch Mon. and Tues.

Trillium Cafe & Inn

$$$ | AMERICAN | The term "light rustic" applies equally well to this comely cafe's decor—plank flooring, wood-top tables, gas fireplace with brick hearth—and its cuisine, which emphasizes local produce and seafood. The menu changes seasonally, with the homemade rosemary bread, peppered-albacore appetizer, Point Reyes blue cheese salad, and grilled organic pork chop among the year-round crowd-pleasers. **Known for:** outdoor patio area with garden and ocean views; wine list favoring Northern California wines, particularly Mendocino; three upstairs rooms (two sharing a bathroom) a good deal in summer. $ Average main: $29 ⌂ 10390 Kasten St. ☎ 707/937–3200 ⊕ www.trillium-mendocino.com.

🛏 Hotels

Blue Door Group Inns of Mendocino

$$$ | B&B/INN | Each inn has its own appeal—Blue Door Inn for its garden, Packard House for its serene setting, JD House for its ocean views (and garden, too)—with all three worth consideration for their proximity to restaurants, shops, and the Mendocino Headlands. **Pros:** historic properties with modern decor; service-oriented staff; wide range of prices and room types. **Cons:** some rooms are on the small side; lacks personal touch of on-site owner-innkeeper; best rooms are pricey. $ Rooms from: $179 ⌂ 10481 Howard St. ☎ 707/937–4892, 888/453–2677 ⊕ www.bluedoorgroup.com ⇗ 19 rooms ⏹ Free Breakfast.

★ **Brewery Gulch Inn**
$$$$ | **B&B/INN** | The feel is modern yet tasteful at this smallish inn with redwood and leather furnishings and plush beds; two rooms have whirlpool tubs with views. **Pros:** luxury in tune with nature; peaceful ocean views; complimentary wine hour and light buffet. **Cons:** must drive to town; expensive in-season; two-night minimum on weekends. [$] *Rooms from: $385* ✉ *9401 N. Hwy. 1, 1 mile south of Mendocino* ☎ *707/937–4752, 800/578–4454* 🌐 *www.brewerygulchinn.com* 🛏 *11 rooms* 🍴 *Free Breakfast.*

Glendeven Inn & Lodge
$$ | **B&B/INN** | If Mendocino is the New England village of the West Coast, then Glendeven—an 1867 farmhouse and several other buildings—is the local country manor, with sea views and 8 acres of gardens, complete with llamas and chickens that provide eggs for three-course breakfasts served in room. **Pros:** romantic setting with acres of gardens; elegant decor; ocean views. **Cons:** not within walking distance of town; some rooms pick up highway noise; weekend minimum-stay requirement. [$] *Rooms from: $170* ✉ *8205 N. Hwy. 1* ☎ *707/937–0083, 800/822–4536* 🌐 *glendeven.com* 🛏 *22 rooms* 🍴 *Free Breakfast.*

MacCallum House
$$$$ | **B&B/INN** | Set on 2 flower-filled acres in the middle of town, this inn is a perfect mix of Victorian charm and modern luxury. **Pros:** excellent breakfast; central location; outstanding restaurant. **Cons:** luxury suites on a separate property are more modern; some rooms in main house lack charm; some guests find the look dated. [$] *Rooms from: $338* ✉ *45020 Albion St.* ☎ *707/937–0289, 800/609–0492* 🌐 *www.maccallumhouse.com* 🛏 *30 rooms* 🍴 *Free Breakfast.*

Stanford Inn by the Sea
$$$$ | **HOTEL** | This woodsy yet luxurious family-run property a few minutes south of town feels like the Northern California version of an old-time summer resort, with an ecologically friendly twist. **Pros:** lovely grounds; wide variety of activities; on-site vegetarian restaurant. **Cons:** New Age feel won't appeal to everyone; carnivores may find menus challenging; least expensive rooms lack ocean views. [$] *Rooms from: $351* ✉ *44850 Comptche Ukiah Rd.* ☎ *707/937–5615, 800/331–8884* 🌐 *www.stanfordinn.com* 🛏 *41 rooms* 🍴 *Free Breakfast.*

Activities

Catch-A-Canoe and Bicycles Too
KAYAKING | Rent kayaks and regular and outrigger canoes here year-round, as well as mountain and suspension bicycles. The outfit's tours explore Big River and its estuary. ✉ *Stanford Inn by the Sea, 1 S. Big River Rd.* ✣ *Off Hwy. 1, 1 mile south of town* ☎ *707/937–0273* 🌐 *www.catchacanoe.com* 🎟 *From $65.*

Fort Bragg

10 miles north of Mendocino.

Fort Bragg is a working-class town that many feel is the most authentic place on the coast. The city maintains a local vibe since most people who work at the area hotels and restaurants also live here, as do many artists and commercial anglers. The pleasures of a visit are mainly outdoors, a stroll through the botanical gardens or along the town's coastal trail, touring by train or boast, tidepooling or fishing at the state park, or tasting wine within steps of the ocean.

GETTING HERE AND AROUND

Highway 20 winds west 33 miles from Willits to Highway 1 just south of Fort Bragg. Mendocino Transit Authority (🌐 *mendocinotransit.org*) buses serve the town.

The North Coast is famous for its locally caught Dungeness crab; be sure to try some during your visit.

👁 Sights

Fort Bragg Coastal Trail
TRAIL | A multiuse path, much of it flat and steps from rocky and highly photogenic shoreline, stretches the length of Fort Bragg. A particularly pleasant section, lined with benches created by local artists, follows the coast north about 2 miles between Noyo Headlands Park in southern Fort Bragg and Glass Beach. From the beach you can continue well into MacKerricher State Park. ■TIP→ **There's free parking at both Noyo Headlands Park and Glass Beach.** ✉ *Fort Bragg* ⊹ *Noyo Headlands Park, W. Cypress St. off S. Main St. (Hwy. 1); Glass Beach, W. Elm St. off N. Main St.*

★ Mendocino Coast Botanical Gardens
GARDEN | Something beautiful is always abloom in these marvelous gardens. Along 3½ miles of trails, including pathways with ocean views and observation points for whale-watching, lie a profusion of flowers. The rhododendrons are at their peak from April through June; the dahlias begin their spectacular show in July and last through September. In winter the heather and camellias add more than a splash of color. The main trails are wheelchair accessible. ✉ *18220 N. Hwy. 1, 2 miles south of Fort Bragg* ☎ *707/964–4352* ⊕ *www.gardenbythesea.org* 🎟 *$15.*

★ Noyo Harbor Tours with Captain Dan
TOUR—SIGHT | The genial Captain Dan owns two commercial fishing boats that hit the high seas, but for his gentle tours of Noyo Harbor from the river up to (but not into) the ocean he ordered a custom-built 18-foot eco-friendly Duffy electric boat. Having been in Fort Bragg for decades he knows everyone and everyone's story, including those of the harbor seals, sea lions, birds, and other wildlife you'll see on his excursion. ✉ *32399 Basin St.* ⊹ *From S. Main St. (Hwy. 1), take Hwy. 20 east ¼ mile, S. Harbor Dr. north ¼ mile, and Basin St. northeast 1 mile* ☎ *707/734–0044* ⊕ *www.noyoharbortours.com* 🎟 *From $35.*

Pacific Star Winery

WINERY/DISTILLERY | When the sun's out and you're sipping wine while viewing whales or other sea creatures swimming offshore, this bluff-top winery's outdoor tasting spaces feel mystical and magical. Equally beguiling on a brooding stormy day, Pacific Star has still more aces up its sleeve: engaging owners, and cheery staffers pouring a lineup of obscure varietals like Charbono and Brunello, a cousin of Sangiovese. The wines, among them a vibrant Mendocino Zin, are good, and they're reasonably priced. ✉ *33000 N. Hwy. 1, 12 miles north of downtown* ☎ *707/964–1155* 🌐 *www.pacificstarwinery.com* 🎟 *Tastings $7* 🕒 *Closed Mon. Dec.–Mar., Tues. and Wed. year-round.*

Skunk Train

TOUR—SIGHT | **FAMILY** | A reproduction train travels a few miles of the route of its 1920s predecessor, a fume-spewing gas-powered motorcar that shuttled passengers along a rail line dating from the 1880s logging days. Nicknamed the Skunk Train, the original traversed redwood forests inaccessible to automobiles. There are also excursions from the town of Willits as well as seasonal and holiday-themed tours. **■ TIP→ For a separate fee you can pedal the same rails as the Skunk Train on two-person side-by-side reclining bikes outfitted for the track, a one-hour ride many patrons find more diverting and a better value than the train trip.** ✉ *100 W. Laurel St., at Main St.* ☎ *707/964–6371* 🌐 *www.skunktrain.com* 🎟 *Train rides $27 Jan.–Mar.; $29, Apr.–May; $42 June–Dec.; rail-bikes $79 for 2 people (no single-rider fee)* 🕒 *No train rides on some weekdays Sept.–May (call or check online calendar); no rail-bike tours Dec.–Feb.*

Triangle Tattoo & Museum

MUSEUM | At the top of a steep staircase, this several-room museum pays homage to Fort Bragg's rough-and-tumble past with memorabilia that includes early-20th-century Burmese tattooing instruments, pictures of astonishing tattoos from around the world, and a small shrine to the late sword-swallowing sideshow king Captain Don Leslie. ✉ *356–B N. Main St.* ☎ *707/964–8814* 🌐 *www.triangletattoo.com* 🎟 *Free.*

Beaches

MacKerricher State Park

NATIONAL/STATE PARK | This park begins at **Glass Beach,** its draw an unfortunately dwindling supply of sea glass (remnants from the city dump once in this area), and stretches north for 9 miles, beginning with rocky headlands that taper into dunes and sandy beaches. The headlands are a good place for whale-watching from December to mid-April. Fishing, canoeing, hiking, tidepooling, jogging, bicycling, beachcombing, camping, and harbor seal watching at Laguna Point are among the popular activities, many of which are accessible to the mobility-impaired. ⚠ **Be vigilant for rogue waves—don't turn your back on the sea. Amenities:** parking; toilets. **Best for:** solitude; sunset; walking. ✉ *24100 MacKerricher Park Rd., off Hwy. 1, 3 miles north of town* ☎ *707/937–5804* 🌐 *www.parks.ca.gov* 🎟 *Free.*

Restaurants

Cowlick's Ice Cream

$ | **AMERICAN** | **FAMILY** | Candy-cap mushroom (tastes like maple syrup) and black raspberry chocolate chunk are among this fun ice-cream shop's top-selling flavors. Chocolate, mocha almond fudge, and ginger appear year-round, supplemented by blackberry-cheesecake, pumpkin, eggnog, and other seasonal offerings; the sorbets might include lemon, pear, or strawberry. **Known for:** handmade ice cream; chai, yellow-cake batter, and other wiggy flavors; sodas, sundaes, and root-beer floats. [$] *Average main: $5* ✉ *250 N. Main St.* ☎ *707/962–9271* 🌐 *www.cowlicksicecream.com.*

North Coast Brewing

$$ | **AMERICAN** | Clam chowder, pork chili, and jumbo chicken wings are among the beer-friendly starters at the brewing company's expansive restaurant—heavy on the oak, especially in the bar—whose headlining entrées include Neapolitan-style pizzas, burgers, pulled-pork sandwiches, and beer-batter fish or jumbo shrimp and chips. The beers, award-winners worldwide, run the gamut from pilsners and the flagship Red Seal amber ale to the Russian-style Rasputin stout and Old Stock Ale, a 12.5%-alcohol (sometimes more) affair. **Known for:** seasonal beers; sampler flights; beer-wise staffers. [$] *Average main: $18* ✉ *444 N. Main St.* ☎ *707/964–3400* 🌐 *northcoastbrewing.com/brewery-taproom.*

Piaci Pub and Pizzeria

$ | **ITALIAN** | The seats are stools and your elbows might bang a neighbor's, but nobody seems to mind at this casual spot for thin-crust pizzas (more than a dozen types), focaccia, and calzones. The food—there are several salads, too—is simple, but everything is carefully prepared and comes out tasty. **Known for:** cash-only; well-chosen beers; dog-friendly outdoor tables. [$] *Average main: $15* ✉ *120 W. Redwood Ave.* ☎ *707/961–1133* 🌐 *www.piacipizza.com* 💳 *No credit cards* 🕒 *No lunch Sun.*

★ **Princess Seafood Market & Deli**

$ | **SEAFOOD** | Captain Heather Sears leads her all-woman crew of "girls gone wild for wild-caught seafood" that heads oceanward on the *Princess* troller, returning with some of the seafood served at this shanty astride the vessel's Noyo Harbor dock. Order chowder (might be clam, crab, or salmon), crab rolls and shrimp po'boys, raw or barbecued oysters, or other sturdy fare at the counter, dining under the all-weather tent kept toasty by heaters and a fire pit when the wind's ablowin'. **Known for:** fresh, sustainable seafood; canned wines and beer; crew members who clearly love their jobs. [$] *Average main: $14* ✉ *32410 N. Harbor Dr., Follow N. Harbor Dr. ½ mile southeast from S. Main St. (Hwy. 1)* ☎ *707/962–3123* 🌐 *fvprincess.com/p/fish-market* 🕒 *Closed Mon.–Wed. No dinner (closes at 6).*

🛏 Hotels

★ **Inn at Newport Ranch**

$$$$ | **B&B/INN** | Attention to detail in both design and hospitality make for an incomparable stay at this 2,000-acre working cattle ranch with 1½ miles of private coastline. **Pros:** over-the-top design; mesmerizing Pacific views; horse riding, ocean-side cocktails by a fire pit, and other diversions. **Cons:** all this design and glamour comes at a price; lengthy drive back from Mendocino and Fort Bragg restaurants at night; coast can be foggy in summer. [$] *Rooms from: $400* ✉ *31502 N. Hwy. 1* ☎ *707/962–4818* 🌐 *theinnatnewportranch.com* 🛏 *11 rooms* 🍴 *Free Breakfast.*

★ **Noyo Harbor Inn**

$$$$ | **HOTEL** | Craftsman touches abound in this luxury inn's lavishly restored 1868 main structure, which overlooks Noyo Harbor, and a nearby newer wing with Pacific Ocean views. **Pros:** landscaped grounds; warm service; restaurant with harbor-view outdoor deck. **Cons:** barking of sea lions in harbor at certain times of year; expensive during high season; some rooms lack water views. [$] *Rooms from: $275* ✉ *500 Casa del Noyo Dr.* ☎ *707/961–4200* 🌐 *noyoharborinn.com* 🛏 *15 rooms* 🍴 *No meals.*

Surf and Sand Lodge

$$ | **HOTEL** | As its name implies, this five-building, two-story property, whose owners run two similar lodgings nearby, sits practically on the beach; pathways lead from the accommodations down to the rock-strewn shore. **Pros:** beach location; gorgeous sunsets from decks and patios of ocean-side rooms; very affordable in the off-season. **Cons:** motel style;

no restaurants close by; least expensive rooms lack view. $ *Rooms from: $159* ✉ *1131 N. Main St.* ☎ *707/964–9383* ⊕ *www.surfsandlodge.com* 🛏 *30 rooms* 🍴 *No meals.*

Weller House Inn
$$ | B&B/INN | It's hard to believe that this 1886 Victorian was abandoned and slated for demolition when it was purchased in 1994 and carefully restored. **Pros:** handcrafted details; radiant heat in the wood floors; colorful and tasteful rooms. **Cons:** some guests find it too old-fashioned; pet cleaning fee; no TVs in rooms. $ *Rooms from: $165* ✉ *524 Stewart St.* ☎ *707/964–4415* ⊕ *www.wellerhouse. com* 🛏 *9 rooms* 🍴 *Free Breakfast.*

🍸 Nightlife

Overtime Brewing
BREWPUBS/BEER GARDENS | Murals depicting logging, fishing, and other local industries adorn the walls of this small-batch brewery two childhood pals opened in 2018. You'll find the expected range of ale types, along with novelties like the Jasmine Green Tea Ale and Overkill Chocolate Raspberry Stout. ✉ *190 E. Elm St* ☎ *707/962–3040* ⊕ *www.overtime-brewing.com.*

Sequoia Room
MUSIC CLUBS | Easily the best jazz venue along the North Coast, this 60-seat room adjoining the North Coast Brewing Company's taproom books name acts like Larry Fuller and Nancy Wright plus talents both established and up-and-coming. Shows take place on Friday and Saturday evenings. ✉ *444 N. Main St.* ☎ *707/964–3400* ⊕ *northcoast-brewing.com/jazz.*

Activities

All Aboard Adventures
FISHING | Captain Tim of All Aboard operates whale-watching trips from late December through April. He also heads out to sea for salmon, crab, rock cod, and other excursions. ✉ *Noyo Harbor, 32410 N. Harbor Dr.* ☎ *707/964–1881* ⊕ *www.allaboardadventures.com* 🛥 *From $40.*

Ricochet Ridge Ranch
HORSEBACK RIDING | Come here for private and group trail rides through the redwood forest and on the beach. ✉ *24201 N. Hwy. 1* ☎ *707/964–7669, 888/873–5777* ⊕ *www.horse-vacation.com* 🛥 *From $60.*

Philo

34 miles southeast of Mendocino, 5 miles west of Boonville.

Many wineries straddle Highway 128 in Philo and nearby Navarro. Tasting rooms here are more low-key than their counterparts in Napa, but the wineries here produce world-class wines, particularly Pinot Noirs and Gewürztraminers, whose grapes thrive in the moderate coastal climate.

GETTING HERE AND AROUND
Highway 128 travels east from coastal Highway 1 south of Mendocino and west from Boonville to Philo. Mendocino Transit Authority (⊕ *mendocinotransit. org*) buses serve the area.

⊙ Sights

Goldeneye Winery
WINERY/DISTILLERY | Established in 1996 by the founders of the Napa Valley's well-respected Duckhorn Wine Company, Goldeneye makes Pinot Noirs from estate and other local grapes, along with a Gewürztraminer, a Pinot Gris, a Chardonnay, and a blush Vin Gris of Pinot Noir. Leisurely tastings, some by appointment only, take place in either a restored farmhouse or on a patio with vineyard views. ✉ *9200 Hwy. 128, Philo* ☎ *800/208–0438, 707/895–3202* ⊕ *www.goldeneyewinery. com* 🛥 *Tastings from $15* 🕐 *Closed. Tues. and Wed. in Jan. and Feb.*

Handley Cellars

WINERY/DISTILLERY | International folk art collected by founding winemaker Milla Handley adorns the tasting room at this Anderson Valley pioneer whose lightly oaked Chardonnays and Pinot Noirs earn high praise from wine critics. The winery, which has an arbored outdoor patio picnic area, also makes Gewürztraminer, Pinot Gris, Riesling, Zinfandel, sparklers, and several other wines. ⊠ *3151 Hwy. 128, Philo* ☎ *707/895–3876, 800/733–3151* ⊕ *www.handleycellars. com* ⌸ *Tasting free.*

Hendy Woods State Park

NATIONAL/STATE PARK | Two groves of ancient redwoods accessible via short trails from the parking lot are the main attractions at this park that's also perfect for a picnic or a summer swim. ⊠ *18599 Philo Greenwood Rd., Philo* ✛ *Entrance ½ mile southwest of Hwy. 128* ☎ *707/937–5804* ⊕ *www.parks.ca.gov* ⌸ *$8 per vehicle.*

Husch Vineyards

WINERY/DISTILLERY | A century-old former pony barn houses the cozy tasting room of the Anderson Valley's oldest winery. Wines of note include Gewürztraminer, Chardonnay, Pinot Noir, and two Zinfandels from old-vine grapes. You can picnic on the deck here or at tables under grape arbors. ⊠ *4400 Hwy. 128, Philo* ☎ *800/554–8724* ⊕ *www.huschvineyards.com* ⌸ *Tasting free.*

Lula Cellars

WINERY/DISTILLERY | Seventeen miles inland from Highway 1, the fun, relaxing, and pet-friendly Lula is among the Anderson Valley wineries closest to the coast. Lula produces Sauvignon Blanc, Gewürztraminer, Zinfandel, and a rosé of Zinfandel and Pinot Noir, but the several Pinot Noirs, each flavorful and with its own personality, are the highlights. ⊠ *2800 Guntly Rd., at Hwy. 128, Philo* ☎ *707/895–3737* ⊕ *www.lulacellars.com* ⌸ *Tastings from $5.*

★ The Madrones Tasting Rooms

WINERY/DISTILLERY | Expand your palate at this 2-acre complex's trio of tasting rooms pouring wines from a dozen varietals. Chardonnay and Pinot Noir are the focus at **Long Meadow Ranch,** where you can also order well-brewed espresso or tea and pick up olive oil, sauces, and similar items from the ranch's Napa Valley operations. Next door, **Drew Family Wines** specializes in Pinot Noir and Syrah beloved by sommeliers. Nearby **Smith Story,** a crowd-funding success story, makes Anderson Valley Pinots plus wines (among them Cabernet Sauvignon) from Sonoma County grapes. Across from Smith Story, Stone and Embers serves gourmet wood-fired pizzas, and the Madrones also includes a spa, a quirky curiosity shop, and lodgings amid landscaped gardens. ■ TIP→ **Days, hours, and fees vary at the tasting rooms; the restaurant (Stone and Embers) opens Thursday–Sunday for lunch and dinner year-round, sometimes other days in summer.** ⊠ *9000 Hwy. 128, Philo* ☎ *707/895–2955* ⊕ *www.themadrones.com/tasting-rooms* ⌸ *Tastings from $10.*

Navarro Vineyards

WINERY/DISTILLERY | A visit to this family-run winery is a classic Anderson Valley experience. Make time if you can for a vineyard tour (call ahead)—the guides draw from years of hands-on experience to explain every aspect of production, from sustainable farming techniques to the choices made in aging and blending. Best known for Alsatian varietals such as Gewürztraminer and Riesling, Navarro also makes Chardonnay, Pinot Noir, and other wines. The tasting room sells cheese and charcuterie for picnickers. ⊠ *5601 Hwy. 128, Philo* ☎ *707/895–3686, 800/537–9463* ⊕ *www.navarrowine.com* ⌸ *Tasting and tour free.*

★ Phillips Hill Winery

WINERY/DISTILLERY | You're apt to meet owner-winemaker Toby Hill on a visit to this winery whose tasting room occupies the upper floor of a weather-worn former apple dryer barn. The several Pinot Noirs here represent a survey of fruit from the Anderson Valley's floor and hillsides, along with some from the Oppenlander Vineyard in nearby Comptche. Hill also makes Chardonnay that finds its way onto local restaurant lists, plus Gewürztraminer and Tempranillo. **■TIP→ Picnic tables on the willow-shaded lawn below the tasting room invite lingering.** ✉ *5101 Hwy. 128, Philo* ☎ *707/895–2209* 🌐 *www.phillipshill.com* 🎫 *Tastings $10* ⏲ *Closed Tues. and Wed. except by appt.*

Roederer Estate

WINERY/DISTILLERY | The Anderson Valley is particularly hospitable to Pinot Noir and Chardonnay grapes, the two varietals used to create Roederer's sparkling wines. The view of vineyards and rolling hills from the patio is splendid. ✉ *4501 Hwy. 128, Philo* ☎ *707/895–2288* 🌐 *www.roedererestate.com* 🎫 *Tastings $10.*

Toulouse Vineyards & Winery

WINERY/DISTILLERY | Especially at sunset the view west across the Anderson Valley from this winery's tasting room and deck is captivating enough to warrant a visit, but the wines here don't disappoint either. Tastings begin with whites that might include Pinot Gris, Riesling, or Gewürztraminer—there's also a rosé of Pinot Noir that sells out quickly each spring—followed by Pinot Noir from estate and sourced fruit and a silky Petite Sirah from inland fruit. Perhaps because the setting is so inspiring, the hosts here are exceptionally chipper. ✉ *8001 Hwy. 128, Philo* ☎ *707/895–2828* 🌐 *www.toulousevineyards.com* 🎫 *Tastings $10.*

🍴 Restaurants

★ Bewildered Pig

$$$$ | **MODERN AMERICAN** | Chef Janelle Weaver cooked for seven years at a prestigious appointment-only Napa Valley winery, perfecting skills that serve her well at the low-key yet polished roadside restaurant. Her Mendo-centric menu might include braised short ribs or extraordinary Peking duck breast from a local provider, with luscious miso deviled eggs and the "Brutus" Caesar salad of petite kale, little gems, garlic crumbs, extra anchovies, and a few daggers of serrano chili. **Known for:** miso deviled eggs starter with sparkling wine; phenomenally fresh salads; Sunday brunch from late May to mid-October. [$] *Average main: $32* ✉ *1810 Hwy. 128, Philo* ☎ *707/895–2088* 🌐 *www.bewilderedpig.com* ⏲ *Closed Jan. and Mon. and Tues. No lunch.*

🛏 Hotels

★ The Madrones Guest Quarters

$$$ | **B&B/INN** | The centerpiece of a 2-acre spread that includes tasting rooms, a gift shop, a spa, and a restaurant, the nine eclectically decorated accommodations here range from apartment-like studios to duplex cottages, some with patios or balconies facing landscaped gardens. **Pros:** location near wineries and Hendy Woods State Park; on-site Stone and Embers restaurant; nearby sister property The Brambles set among redwoods. **Cons:** weekend minimum-stay requirement; pricey on summer weekends; yogurt, cereal, and coffee/tea provided in-room but no breakfast served. [$] *Rooms from: $210* ✉ *9000 Hwy. 128, Philo* ☎ *707/895–2955* 🌐 *www.themadrones.com* 🛏 *9 rooms* 🍴 *No meals.*

The Philo Apple Farm

$$$$ | **HOTEL** | Two founders of the renowned Napa Valley restaurant The French Laundry are among the owners of this farm with three inviting cottages and one guest room set in an organic heirloom apple orchard. **Pros:** rustic-contemporary touches in cottages and room; working farm; relaxing back-to-nature experience. **Cons:** occasionally hot in summer; few "activities"; room service only upon request. $ *Rooms from: $300* ✉ *18501 Greenwood Rd., Philo* ☎ *707/895–2333* ⊕ *www.philoapplefarm.com* ⤴ *4 rooms* ⍾⃝ *Breakfast.*

Boonville

6 miles east of Philo, 28 miles northwest of Hopland.

At first glance Boonville, population a little more than 1,000, looks pretty much as it has for decades, with the 19th-century Boonville Hotel anchoring the few-blocks downtown and sheep farms and fruit orchards fanning out on either side of Highway 128, albeit with more grapevines these days. The founding of the Anderson Valley Brewing Company in the late 1980s and the revitalization of the hotel by its current owners, the Schmitt family, jump-started the transformation of Boonville into a haven of artisanal food, wine, and beer. Despite this, the town retains its old-school character—listen carefully and you may hear fragments of the academically recognized Boontling argot, which dates to the time when this stretch of the valley was even more isolated.

GETTING HERE AND AROUND
Boonville lies along Highway 128 at its junction with Highway 253. Mendocino Transit Authority (⊕ *mendocinotransit. org*) buses serve the area.

⊙ Sights

Anderson Valley Brewing Company
WINERY/DISTILLERY | Brewery tours, tastings in the Tap Room, and 18 holes of disc golf provide a diversified experience at the home of Boont Amber Ale, double and triple Belgian style ales, and other consistent award-winning brews. Local winemakers clear their palates with the Bourbon Barrel Stout, aged in Wild Turkey barrels. ✉ *17700 Hwy. 253, Boonville* ✛ *At Hwy. 128* ☎ *707/895–2337* ⊕ *www. avbc.com* ✉ *Tastings from $10.*

Artevino Maple Creek Winery
WINERY/DISTILLERY | Chardonnay, Pinot Noir, and Zinfandel are the specialties of this winery whose artist owner, Tom Rodrigues, also makes Merlot, two dessert wines, and the Cowboy Red blend of Zinfandel, Merlot, and Carignane. If the art that adorns Maple Creek labels looks familiar, there's a reason: Tom's also responsible for ones at the Napa Valley's Far Niente and other top wineries. ■TIP→ **Picnickers are welcome (wines are sold by the glass).** ✉ *20799 Hwy. 128, Yorkville* ✛ *7½ miles southeast of Boonville* ☎ *707/895–3001* ⊕ *www.maplecreekwine.com* ✉ *Tastings $10.*

Bee Hunter Wine
WINERY/DISTILLERY | Winemaker Andy DuVigneaud of Bee Hunter Wine prefers vineyards close to the ocean because the cool climate requires that grapes stay longer on the vine, preventing them from ripening before their flavors have fully developed. His restrained yet delicious wines, which he pours in a former car repair shop in Boonville, include Sauvignon Blanc, Chardonnay, and a dry and light rosé of Pinot Noir, along with four Pinot Noirs and a Cabernet Sauvignon–Merlot blend. ✉ *14251 Hwy. 128, Boonville* ☎ *707/895–3995* ⊕ *www. beehunterwine.com* ✉ *Tasting free.*

★ Foursight Wines
WINERY/DISTILLERY | Four generations of the Charles family have farmed the land that produces this winery's vegan-friendly all-estate lineup of Sauvignon Blanc, Semillon, and Pinot Noirs. From 11.5 acres of Pinot Noir, winemaker Joe Webb employs various techniques to produce four very different wines, from the light Zero, aged solely in used oak barrels, to the "richer, riper" Paraboll, its flavors heightened by new French oak. ■TIP→ **After a tasting, you can picnic outside the casual wood-frame tasting room, enjoying a glass or bottle.** ✉ *14475 Hwy. 128, Boonville*

☎ *707/895–2889* 🌐 *www.foursight-wines.com* 🎫 *Tastings $10* ⏲ *Closed Tues. and 3rd wk of June.*

★ Pennyroyal Farm

WINERY/DISTILLERY | **FAMILY** | At this Boonville ranch with a contemporary barn tasting room you can sample estate Sauvignon Blanc, one of Mendocino's best rosés, and velvety Pinot Noirs, along with cheeses made on the premises from goat and sheep milk. Tours of the farmstead (reservations required) take place year-round in the morning, with afternoon ones from late spring to early fall. The wines, cheeses, pastoral setting, and adorable goats win most guests' hearts. Chefs prepare a few lunch items you can enjoy on the patio in good weather; cheese boards and other snacks are available throughout the day. ✉ *14930 Hwy. 128, Boonville* ☎ *707/895–2410* 🌐 *www.pennyroyalfarm.com* 🎫 *Tastings from $5, tour $20.*

🍴 Restaurants

Lauren's

$$ | **AMERICAN** | Boonville locals and frequent visitors love Lauren's for its down-home vibe and healthful comfort food—vegetarian and ground-beef burgers, pizzas, pot roast, chicken tostadas, meat loaf, and curry noodle bowls—many of whose ingredients are grown or produced nearby. Chocolate brownie sundaes and (seasonally) apple tarts and honey-baked pears are among the desserts worth a trip on their own. **Known for:** down-home vibe; diverse Mendocino wine selection; trivia nights second and fourth Thursday of the month. [$] *Average main: $16* ✉ *14211 Hwy. 128, Boonville* ☎ *707/895–3869* 🌐 *laurensgoodfood.com* ⏲ *No dinner Sun. (except for occasional pop-ups) and Mon. No lunch Mon.–Wed.*

Mosswood Market Café and Bakery

$ | **AMERICAN** | Pastries for breakfast; wraps, salads, hot soup, and sandwiches for lunch; and espresso drinks all day make this sweet café in downtown Boonville a fine stop for a quick bite. Order at the counter and enjoy your meal—the oven-roasted turkey and chicken mango wraps and Reuben and albacore tuna sandwiches are among the lunchtime choices—at tables inside or out front. **Known for:** empanadas; Danishes and scones; vegan options. [$] *Average main: $12* ✉ *14111 Hwy. 128, Boonville* ☎ *707/895–3635* ⏲ *No dinner.*

★ Table 128

$$$$ | **AMERICAN** | This stylishly funky yet rustic restaurant's chef, Perry Hoffman, got his start (at age five) working in the kitchen of the Napa Valley's The French Laundry, which his grandmother founded and later sold to Thomas Keller. As an adult Hoffman made a name for himself at three Wine Country spots before returning to Boonville in 2019 to prepare prix-fixe California farm-to-table cuisine (including a few original French Laundry dishes) at his family's Table 128. **Known for:** many ingredients grown on-site or nearby; fresh oysters and paella on summer Sundays; alfresco dining on patio April–October. [$] *Average main: $65* ✉ *Boonville Hotel, 14050 Hwy. 128, Boonville* ☎ *707/895–2210* 🌐 *www.boonvillehotel.com* ⏲ *Closed Mon.–Thurs. Nov.–Apr., closed Tues. and Wed. May–Oct. No lunch.*

🛏 Hotels

Boonville Hotel

$$$ | **HOTEL** | From the street this looks like a standard small-town hotel with seven freestanding cottages and a two-room, two-story building out back in the garden, but once you cross the threshold you begin to sense the laid-back sophistication that makes the entire Anderson Valley so appealing. **Pros:** stylish but homey; beautiful gardens and grounds; on-site Table 128 restaurant for prix-fixe meals served family style. **Cons:** minimum-stay requirement most weekends; no TVs or phones, no air-conditioning in some rooms; lacks

You'll find excellent wines and great places to taste them in the laid-back Anderson Valley.

big-hotel amenities. $ *Rooms from: $215* ✉ *14050 Hwy. 128, Boonville* ☎ *707/895–2210* ⊕ *www.boonvillehotel.com* ⇥ *17 rooms* ⧟ *Free Breakfast.*

Hopland

28 miles east of Boonville, 14 miles south of Ukiah, 32 miles north of Healdsburg.

U.S. 101 briefly narrows to one lane in each direction to become Hopland's main drag. For many years a center for the cultivation and drying of beer hops—the source of its name—the small town of Hopland these days is a center of grape growing and wine making and a pleasant stop for a meal or a tasting.

GETTING HERE AND AROUND

Car travelers from Sonoma and Humboldt counties arrive in Hopland via U.S. 101. Highway 253 will get you here from Boonville. Mendocino Transit Authority (⊕ *mendocinotransit.org*) buses serve the area.

VISITOR INFORMATION

Destination Hopland. ☎ *707/564–2582* ⊕ *destinationhopland.com.*

⊙ Sights

Brutocao Cellars

WINERY/DISTILLERY | With 1,250 acres of vineyards mostly in the Hopland area but also the cooler Anderson Valley, family-owned Brutocao produces Sauvignon Blanc, Zinfandel, Merlot, and Cabernet Sauvignon along with Chardonnay and Pinot Noir. Some of these wines plus ones from Italian varietals like Sangiovese and Primitivo are poured in Hopland's 1923 former high school building, whose outdoor areas have picnic tables and regulation bocce courts. ■**TIP**➔ **The winery operates a second tasting room in the Anderson Valley town of Philo.** ✉ *13500 S. U.S. 101, Hopland* ☎ *800/433–3689* ⊕ *www.brutocaocellars.com* ⧟ *Tastings free–$10.*

Campovida
WINERY/DISTILLERY | Wines from Italian and Rhône varietals grown in Mendocino County organic, biodynamic, and sustainable vineyards are the focus of Campovida, on a historic 56-acre property whose previous owners include local railroad magnate A.W. Foster and the Fetzer wine-making clan. The white Tocai Friulano and the red Nero d'Avola are among the wines from grapes rarely seen in California, with Sangiovese among the more familiar offerings.
■TIP→ **After a tasting, you can purchase wine by the glass or bottle to enjoy with a picnic amid the landscaped gardens.**
⊠ 13601 Old River Rd., Hopland ✛ Head east ¾ mile from U.S. 101 on Hwy. 175 ☎ 707/744–8797 ⊕ www.campovida.com ⌷ Tastings $15 ⊙ Closed Tues. and Wed.

Graziano Family of Wines
WINERY/DISTILLERY | A winemaker who never met a grape he didn't want to transform in the cellar, Gregory Graziano creates wines for four separate labels, one devoted to Burgundian grapes like Pinot Noir, two to Italian varietals, and the last to Zinfandel, Rhône, and a few other types. The winery's oldest Mendocino County vineyard was planted just before Prohibition by Gregory's grandfather. The lineup poured in the downtown Hopland tasting space might include Pinot Gris and Arneis whites and Dolcetto and Nebbiolo reds. ⊠ 13275 S. U.S. 101, Hopland ☎ 707/744–8466 ⊕ grazianofamilyofwines.com ⌷ Tasting free.

Saracina Vineyards
WINERY/DISTILLERY | Guests at the contemporary stone and glass tasting room of this boutique winery enjoy views of a landscaped outdoor picnic area and the vineyards beyond. Tastings sometimes begin with a Sauvignon Blanc that helped establish this winery under its original owners, John Fetzer and his wife, Patty Rock. Some of the wine's organic grapes come from California's oldest Sauvignon Blanc vines (1945). The standout reds include Zinfandel, Cabernet Sauvignon, and Malbec.
■TIP→ **Caves are rare in Mendocino, but there's one here you can tour by appointment.** ⊠ 11684 S. U.S. 101, Hopland ☎ 707/670–0199 ⊕ www.saracina.com ⌷ Tastings $10, tour free ⊙ Closed Mon. and Tues.

🍴 Restaurants

★ Golden Pig
$$ | AMERICAN | Grass-fed burgers, pulled-pork and pork-schnitzel sandwiches, and North Coast cod ceviche with house-made tortilla chips are among the popular items this hip-casual restaurant inside a former grocery store serves all day, with bone-in pork chops, rotisserie chicken, and similar plates appearing for dinner. Well-selected breads and buns, crispy fries with the burgers, perfect pickles with the sandwiches, and slivers of fresh ginger in the ceviche elevate the farm-to-table comfort fare, much of it showcasing ingredients from local purveyors. **Known for:** Northern California beers, Mendocino County wines; everything on menu made gluten-free if desired; specialty cocktails. $ Average main: $22 ⊠ 13380 U.S. 101, Hopland ☎ 707/670–6055 ⊕ www.thegoldenpig.com.

🛏 Hotels

Stock Farm Hopland Restaurant & Boutique Inn
$$$ | B&B/INN | Atop the same-named pizzeria and bar, this inn whose owners also operate Campovida winery less than a mile away sits along Hopland's main drag near shops, tasting rooms, and other restaurants. **Pros:** plush rooms with fireplaces, wet bars, whirlpool tubs, refrigerators, and private balconies; two rooms with pullout couches sleep four; pool privileges at adjoining 18-room sister property the 1890s Thatcher Hotel. **Cons:** single-person

whirlpool tubs in two rooms; after check-in (at bar), more self-serve than pampering; weekend minimum-stay requirement. $ *Rooms from: $220* ⊠ *13441 U.S. 101, Hopland* ☎ *707/744–1977* ⊕ *www.stockfarmhopland.com/inn* ⇱ *7 rooms* ⦿⃝ *No meals.*

Ukiah

14 miles north of Hopland, 21 miles northeast of Boonville.

About 16,000 people live in Ukiah, the Mendocino County seat and largest town. Logging and beer hops were two prominent industries starting in the late-19th century and continuing well into the 20th. Grape plantings date to the late 1800s, though many of the head-trained (no trellising) old vines were planted in the early 1900s, when the Italian Swiss Colony expanded from Sonoma County, and during and just after Prohibition. Warmer than the Anderson Valley, the Ukiah area is known for Zinfandel, Cabernet Sauvignon, and other varietals that thrive in high heat. Should you need to cool off, you can repair to the redwoods of Montgomery Woods State Natural Reserve.

GETTING HERE AND AROUND

Ukiah is off U.S. 101; if coming from Boonville, take Highway 253 northeast to U.S. 101 and head north. Mendocino Transit Authority (⊕ *mendocinotransit. org*) buses serve the area.

VISITOR INFORMATION Ukiah Visitor Center. ⊠ *200 S. School St.* ☎ *707/467–5766* ⊕ *www.visitukiah.com.*

⊙ Sights

Montgomery Woods State Natural Reserve

NATIONAL/STATE PARK | Narrow Orr Springs Road winds 13 miles west from Ukiah to this secluded park whose 3-mile loop trail leads to serene old-growth redwood groves. Only the intermittent breezes, rustling of small wildlife, and calls of resident birds punctuate the prehistoric quiet of the most remote one. The reserve (no dogs allowed) is a place like few others in all of California. ◼ TIP→ **From the town of Mendocino you can access the park by taking the Comptche Ukiah Road to Orr Springs Road.** ⊠ *15825 Orr Springs Rd., Ukiah* ⊹ *13 miles west of N. State St.* ☎ *707/937–5804* ⊕ *www. parks.ca.gov* ▨ *Free.*

Nelson Family Vineyards

WINERY/DISTILLERY | The grandparents of the current winemaker and his brother, who manages the estate vineyards, moved to Mendocino County in the early 1950s, establishing a ranch just north of Hopland that now encompasses 2,000 acres. About 10% of the land is devoted to grapes, with olive and pear orchards among the other plantings. Tastings, which take place in the living room of the former family home, usually begin with sparkling wine. ◼ TIP→ **A redwood grove steps from the tasting room has picnic tables.** ⊠ *550 Nelson Ranch Rd., Ukiah* ☎ *707/462–3755* ⊕ *www.nelson-familyvineyards.com* ▨ *Tastings $5.*

Rivino Winery

WINERY/DISTILLERY | The open-air tasting room and outdoor spaces at Rivino are oriented to maximize the views of the 215-acre estate's vineyard and pond. As with the architecture, owner-winemaker Jason McConnell takes a minimalist approach with his wines, all from grapes grown on-site. The Sangiovese and Sedulous blend of Merlot, Cabernet Sauvignon, and a touch of Viognier stand out, as does the Amber Eve rosé, a brisk seller. ◼ TIP→ **Talented local musicians perform on Wednesday and Friday in the late afternoon and early evening from April through October.** ⊠ *4101 Cox Schrader Rd., Ukiah* ⊹ *Exit 545 off U.S. 101* ☎ *707/293–4262* ⊕ *www.rivino.com* ▨ *Tastings from $7.*

★ Testa Vineyards
WINERY/DISTILLERY | This family-owned winery sells most of its grapes—some from vines planted in the 1930s and 1940s—to notable Napa, Sonoma, and Mendocino brands but withholds some of its output for its small label. Winemaker Maria Testa Martinson, whose great-grandparents established Testa Ranch in 1912, makes Charbono, Carignane, Petite Sirah, Zinfandel, Cabernet Sauvignon, and other reds from grapes grown on the estate, with a few whites from outside sources. Tastings take place in a spiffed-up former chicken coop with views of a pond and rolling vineyards. On sunny days you can enjoy at tasting on the patio outside. ✉ *6400 N. State St., Calpella* ☎ *707/485–7051* 🌐 *testaranch.com* 🍷 *Tastings $5* ⏲ *Closed Mon.–Thurs. except by appt.*

🍴 Restaurants

Cultivo
$$ | **AMERICAN** | An oasis of low-key sophistication in downtown Ukiah, Cultivo is known for inventive wood-fired pizzas (try the braised-duck or wild-boar-sausage pie or go meatless with one starring trumpet mushrooms) but also plates up oysters on the half shell, fish tacos, a kale Caesar salad (sourdough croutons make it work), quinoa risotto, and a heritage pork chop. Meals are served on thick wooden tables in the downstairs bar area and in the mezzanine; there's also sidewalk dining out front. **Known for:** something for everyone; California beers on tap; gluten-free options. [$] *Average main: $19* ✉ *108 W. Standley St., Ukiah* ☎ *707/462–7007* 🌐 *cultivorestaurant.com* ⏲ *Closed Sun.*

🛏 Hotels

Vichy Springs Resort
$$$ | **RESORT** | The cottages and multiunit one-story buildings of this historic hot-springs resort—luminaries from Ulysses S. Grant to Nancy Pelosi have unwound here—surround a broad lawn shaded by mature manzanitas and oaks. **Pros:** rural solitude; naturally carbonated hot springs; some accommodations have full kitchens. **Cons:** pool is only heated part of the year; not a pampering-type spa; noise from nearby gun range. [$] *Rooms from: $245* ✉ *2605 Vichy Springs Rd., Ukiah* ☎ *707/462–9515* 🌐 *www.vichysprings.com* 🔑 *26 rooms* 🍴 *Free Breakfast.*

Weott

86 miles northeast of Fort Bragg, 46 miles south of Eureka.

Conservationists banded together a century ago as the Save the Redwoods League and scored a crucial victory when a memorial grove was dedicated in 1921. That grove is now part of Humboldt Redwoods State Park. Headquartered in the town of Weott, the park these days has grown to nearly 53,000 acres, about a third of which are filled with untouched old-growth coast redwoods.

GETTING HERE AND AROUND

Access the park's visitor center off U.S. 101. Southern Humboldt Intercity (🌐 *hta.org*) buses serve the area.

👁 Sights

★ Avenue of the Giants
NATIONAL/STATE PARK | FAMILY | Some of the tallest trees on Earth tower over this magnificent 32-mile stretch of two-lane blacktop, also known as Highway 254, that follows the south fork of the Eel River through Humboldt Redwoods State Park. The highway runs more or less parallel to U.S. 101 from Phillipsville in the south to the town of Pepperwood in the north. A brochure available at either end of the highway or the **visitor center,** 2 miles south of Weott, contains a self-guided tour, with short and

long hikes through various redwood groves. A trail at **Founders Grove** passes by several impressive trees, among them the fallen 362-foot-long Dyerville Giant, whose root base points skyward 35 feet. The tree can be reached via a short trail that begins 4 miles north of the visitor center. About 6 miles north of the center lies **Rockefeller Forest.** The largest remaining old-growth coast redwood forest, it contains more than a third of the 100 tallest trees in the world. ✉ *Humboldt Redwoods State Park Visitor Center, 17119 Ave. of the Giants, Weott* ☎ *707/946–2263* ⊕ *www.parks.ca.gov/humboldtredwoods* ✆ *Free; $8 day-use fee for Williams Grove.*

Briceland Vineyards
WINERY/DISTILLERY | Lean yet flavorful Humboldt County Pinot Noirs are the specialty of this winery set amid the trees. In good weather the delightfully low-key tastings take place in front of the weathered original winery building. Guests sip Gewürztraminer (surprisingly dry), Viognier, or other whites before sampling Pinots and perhaps Syrah or Zinfandel. ■TIP➔ **From late May through August drop-ins are welcome 1–5 on weekends; otherwise tastings are by appointment.** ✉ *5959 Briceland Rd., 10½ miles southwest of Ave. of the Giants southern entrance* ✚ *Take Briceland Rd. 5½ miles west from Redwood Dr. in Redway (from north, U.S. 101 Exit 642; from south, Exit 639B)* ☎ *707/923–2429* ⊕ *bricelandvineyards.com* ✆ *Tastings $15.*

Ferndale

35 miles northwest of Weott, 19 miles south of Eureka.

Ferndale, best known for its colorful Victorian architecture, much of it Stick-Eastlake style, is worth the 5-mile detour off U.S. 101. Many shops carry a self-guided tour map that highlights the most interesting historic buildings. Gift shops and ice-cream stores comprise a fair share of the businesses here, but Ferndale remains a fully functioning small town, and descendants of the Portuguese and Scandinavian dairy farmers who settled here continue to raise dairy cows in the surrounding pastures.

GETTING HERE AND AROUND
To get to Ferndale from U.S. 101, follow Highway 211 southwest 5 miles. Public transit doesn't serve the town.

◉ Sights

Ferndale Historic Cemetery
CEMETERY | The well-worn gravestones at Ferndale's east-side cemetery provide insight into the hard, often short lives of the European immigrants who cultivated this area in the mid-18th century. At the top of the hill, sweeping (and photogenic) vistas unfold of the town, its farms, and the ocean. ✉ *Craig St. and Berding St.* ✆ *Free.*

Ferndale Museum
MUSEUM | The main building of this museum exhibits Victoriana and historical photographs and has a display of an old-style barbershop and another of Wiyot Indian baskets. In the annex are a horse-drawn buggy, a re-created blacksmith's shop, and antique farming, fishing, and dairy equipment. Don't miss the Bosch-Omori seismograph, installed in 1933 in Ferndale; it's still checked daily for recordings of earthquake activity. ✉ *515 Shaw Ave.* ☎ *707/786–4466* ⊕ *www.ferndale-museum.org* ✆ *$2* ⊘ *Closed Mon. and Tues.*

Lost Coast Scenic Drive
SCENIC DRIVE | A loop drive counterclockwise from Ferndale yields amazing ocean views and winds through forests and small towns before heading into Humboldt Redwoods State Park and then back up U.S. 101 toward the starting point. The road has numerous curves and some rugged stretches in need of repair, but driving this

100-or-so-mile stretch is exhilarating. **■TIP→ Allot four hours for this excursion.** *✉ Ferndale ✥ Head southwest from Ferndale on Wildcat Ave., which soon becomes Mattole Rd. Follow Mattole west to the coast, south to Petrolia, and east to Honeydew and the park. At U.S. 101 head north back toward Ferndale. 🌐 visitredwoods.com/listing/lost-coast-scenic-drive/148.*

Hotels

Gingerbread Mansion

$$ | **B&B/INN** | A dazzler that rivals San Francisco's "painted ladies," this Victorian mansion has detailed exterior spindle work, turrets, and gables. **Pros:** elegant decor; relaxing atmosphere; friendly staff. **Cons:** some may find the place gaudy; two-night minimum on weekends; lacks standard hotel amenities. *[$] Rooms from: $165 ✉ 400 Berding St. ☎ 707/786–4000 🌐 www.gingerbread-mansion.com 🛏 11 rooms 🍴 Free Breakfast.*

Shopping

Blacksmith Shop

HOUSEHOLD ITEMS/FURNITURE | With two storefronts in Ferndale, this shop celebrates the survival of traditional blacksmithing arts in the area. The hand-forged works sold here range from flatware to furniture. The rough-handled chef's knives are so sharp there are Band-Aids behind the display, just in case. *✉ 455 and 491 Main St. ☎ 707/786–4216 🌐 www.ferndaleblacksmith.com.*

Eureka

19 miles north of Ferndale.

With a population of 27,200, Eureka is the North Coast's largest city, a good place to fuel up, buy groceries, and learn a little about the region's mining, timber, and fishing pasts. The chamber of commerce visitor center has maps of self-guided driving tours of the town's nearly 100 Victorians, among them the flamboyant 1886 Queen Anne–style **Carson Mansion,** at 143 M Street. The home can only be viewed from outside, but it's worth a look and a photo or two. Art galleries and antiques stores liven up the district from C to I Street between 2nd and 3rd streets, and a walking pier extends into the harbor.

GETTING HERE AND AROUND

U.S. 101 travels through Eureka. Eureka Transit (🌐 *www.eurekatransit.org*) buses serve the town.

VISITOR CENTER

Eureka Chamber of Commerce. *✉ 2112 Broadway ☎ 707/442–3738 🌐 www.eurekachamber.com.*

Sights

Blue Ox Millworks

FACTORY | This wood-shop is among a handful in the country specializing in Victorian-era architecture, but what makes it truly unique is that its craftspeople use antique tools to do the work. Visitors can watch artisans use printing presses, lathes, and other equipment to create gingerbread trim, fence pickets, and other signature Victorian embellishments. The shop is less interesting on Saturday, when most craftspeople take the day off. *✉ 1 X St. ☎ 707/444–3437, 800/248–4259 🌐 www.blueoxmill.com 🎟 $12 🕒 Closed Sat. Dec.–Mar., Sun. yr-round.*

Clarke Historical Museum

MUSEUM | The Native American Wing of this museum contains a beautiful collection of northwestern California basketry. Artifacts from Eureka's Victorian, logging, and maritime eras fill the rest of the space. *✉ 240 E St. ☎ 707/443–1947 🌐 www.clarkemuseum.org 🎟 $5 🕒 Closed Mon.*

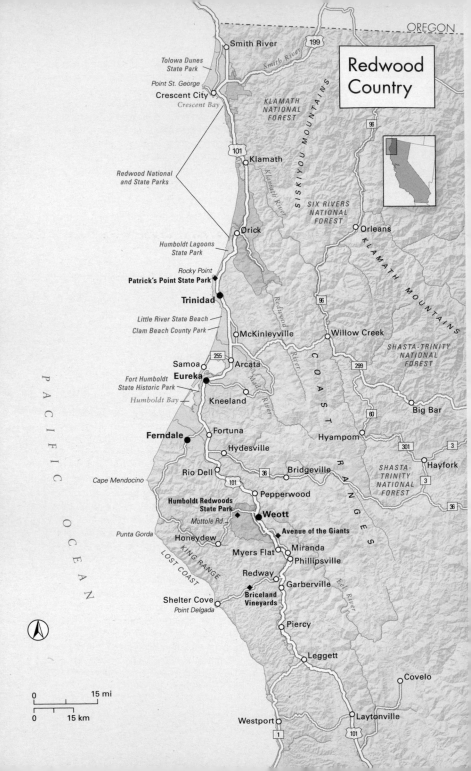

🍴 Restaurants

★ Brick & Fire Bistro
$$ | **MODERN AMERICAN** | Just about every seat in the darkly lighted, urbane dining room has a view of this downtown bistro's most important feature, a wood-fired brick oven used to prepare everything from roasted local Kumamoto oysters to a wild-mushroom cobbler topped with a cheesy biscuit—even the "fries," char-roasted potatoes tossed in olive oil and spices, come out of the oven. Creatively topped pizzas, sandwiches, and grilled meats and seafood round out the menu. **Known for:** house-made sausage pizzas; eggplant, brisket, and other sandwich fillings char-grilled in a wood-fired oven; house-made ginger ale. [$] *Average main: $19* ✉ *1630 F St.* ☎ *707/268–8959* 🌐 *www.brickandfirebistro.com* 🕒 *Closed Tues. No lunch weekends.*

Lost Coast Brewery and Cafe
$ | **AMERICAN** | This bustling microbrewery with surf-tropical decor accents is the best place in town to relax with a pint of ale or porter. Soups and salads, plus burgers, tacos, and light meals are served for lunch and dinner. **Known for:** outstanding beers; happy hour weekdays 4–6; brewery tours. [$] *Average main: $14* ✉ *617 4th St.* ☎ *707/445–4480* 🌐 *www.lostcoast.com.*

Samoa Cookhouse
$$ | **AMERICAN** | **FAMILY** | Waiters at this former cafeteria for local mill workers deliver family-style bowls—whatever is being served at the meal you've arrived for—to long, communal tables. For breakfast that means eggs, sausage, biscuits and gravy, and the like; lunch and dinner usually feature soup, potatoes, salad, and pie, plus daily-changing entrées such as pot roast and pork loin. **Known for:** hearty meals for carnivores; blast from the logging past atmosphere; museum in back. [$] *Average main: $18* ✉ *908 Vance Ave., near Cookhouse Rd., Samoa* ☎ *707/442–1659* 🌐 *www.samoacookhouse.net.*

🛏 Hotels

★ Carter House Inns
$$$ | **HOTEL** | Richly painted and aglow with wood detailing, the rooms, in two main Victorian buildings and several historic cottages, contain a mix of modern and antique furnishings; some have whirlpool tubs and separate sitting areas. **Pros:** elegant ambience; every detail in place; on-site Restaurant 301 ranks among town's best dining spots. **Cons:** not suitable for children; restaurant is a bit pricey; two-night minimum on weekends. [$] *Rooms from: $199* ✉ *301 L St.* ☎ *707/444–8062, 800/404–1390* 🌐 *www.carterhouse.com* 🛏 *32 rooms* 🍴 *Breakfast.*

🏃 Activities

Humboats Kayak Adventures
KAYAKING | You can rent kayaks and book kayaking tours that from December to June include whale-watching trips. Half-day river kayaking trips pass beneath massive redwoods; the whale-watching outings get you close enough for good photos. ✉ *Woodley Island Marina, 601 Startare Dr., Dock A* ☎ *707/443–5157* 🌐 *www.humboats.com* 🎟 *From $30 rentals, $55 tours.*

Trinidad

23 miles north of Eureka.

A mellow base for exploring the southern portion of Redwood National Park, coastal Trinidad got its name from the Spanish mariners who entered the bay on Trinity Sunday, June 9, 1775. Formerly the principal trading post for mining camps along the Klamath and Trinity rivers, these days Trinidad is a quiet and genuinely charming community with several beaches and ample sights and activities to entertain low-key visitors.

GETTING HERE AND AROUND

Trinidad sits right off U.S. 101. From Interstate 5, head west from Redding on Highway 299 and north on U.S. 101 north of Arcata. Redwood Transit System (⊕ www.redwoodtransit.org) provides bus service.

◉ Sights

Patrick's Point State Park

NATIONAL/STATE PARK | On a forested plateau almost 200 feet above the surf, the park has stunning views of the Pacific, great whale- and sea lion–watching spots, campgrounds, picnic areas, bike paths, and hiking trails through old-growth spruce forest. There are also tidal pools at Agate Beach, a re-created Yurok Indian village, and a small visitor center with exhibits. It's uncrowded and sublimely quiet here. Dogs are not allowed on trails or the beach. ⊠ 4150 Patrick's Point Dr. ✛ Off U.S. 101, 5 miles north of town ☎ 707/677–3570 ⊕ www.parks.ca.gov ⊠ $8 per vehicle.

⛱ Beaches

Clam Beach County Park and Little River State Beach

BEACH—SIGHT | FAMILY | These two adjoining oceanfront areas stretch for several miles south of Trinidad. The sandy beach here is exceptionally wide. Beachcombing and savoring fabulous sunsets are favorite activities. The two parks share day-use facilities. **Amenities:** parking; toilets. **Best for:** solitude; sunset; walking. ⊠ Clam Beach Dr. and U.S. 101, 6 miles south of Trinidad ☎ 707/445–7651 ⊕ www.parks.ca.gov ⊠ Free (day use).

⑪ Restaurants

★ Larrupin' Cafe

$$$$ | AMERICAN | Set in a two-story house on a quiet country road north of town, this restaurant—one of the best places to eat on the North Coast—is often thronged with people enjoying fresh seafood, Cornish game hen, mesquite-grilled ribs, and vegetarian dishes. The garden setting and candlelight stir thoughts of romance. **Known for:** garden setting; outside patio; smoked beef brisket. Ⓢ Average main: $31 ⊠ 1658 Patrick's Point Dr. ☎ 707/677–0230 ⊕ www.larrupin.com ☾ No lunch.

🛏 Hotels

Trinidad Bay Bed and Breakfast Inn

$$$ | B&B/INN | Staying at this small Cape Cod–style inn perched above Trinidad Bay is like spending the weekend at a friend's vacation house. **Pros:** great location above bay; lots of light; tall windows in Tidepool room. **Cons:** main house can feel crowded at full occupancy; expensive in summer; two-night minimum on weekends. Ⓢ Rooms from: $225 ⊠ 560 Edwards St. ☎ 707/677–0840 ⊕ www.trinidadbaybnb.com ⇩ 4 rooms ⑩ Free Breakfast.

Turtle Rocks Oceanfront Inn

$$$$ | B&B/INN | This comfortable inn has the best view in Trinidad, with the ocean and sunning sea lions seen from private, glassed-in decks in each room. **Pros:** great ocean views; comfortable king beds; surrounding landscape left natural and wild. **Cons:** no businesses within walking distance; interiors may be too spare for some guests; can be foggy here in summer. Ⓢ Rooms from: $280 ⊠ 3392 Patrick's Point Dr., 4½ miles north of town ☎ 707/677–3707 ⊕ www.turtlerocksinn.com ⇩ 6 rooms ⑩ Free Breakfast.

Chapter 20

SACRAMENTO AND THE GOLD COUNTRY

Updated by
Daniel Mangin

⊙ Sights	🍴 Restaurants	🛏 Hotels	🛍 Shopping	🍸 Nightlife
★★★★☆	★★★★☆	★★★★☆	★★★☆☆	★★★☆☆

WELCOME TO SACRAMENTO AND THE GOLD COUNTRY

TOP REASONS TO GO

★ **Gold rush:** Marshall Gold Discovery State Park is where it all started—it's a must-see—but there are historic and modern gems all along California Highway 49 from Nevada City to Mariposa.

★ **State capital:** Easygoing Sacramento offers sights like the Capitol and historic Old Sacramento.

★ **Bon appétit:** Sacramento has emerged as a foodie destination in the past decade, but its celebrations of food, drink, and culture date back to the gold-rush parade of immigrants.

★ **Wine tasting:** With bucolic scenery and friendly tasting rooms, the Gold Country's Shenandoah Valley has become an acclaimed wine-making region, specializing in Zinfandel.

★ **Rivers, sequoias, and caverns:** Natural beauty here is rich (stream beds are still lined with gold), high (sequoias in Calaveras Big Trees State Park), and deep (Moaning Cavern's main chamber is big enough to hold the Statue of Liberty).

The Gold Country is a large rural destination popular with those seeking a reasonably priced escape from Southern California and the Bay Area. Sacramento and Davis are in an enormous valley just west of the Sierra Nevada range. Foothill communities Nevada City, Auburn, Placerville, and Sutter Creek were products of the gold rush, and remain popular stopovers with travelers en route to Lake Tahoe.

1 **Sacramento.**

2 **Woodland.**

3 **Davis.**

4 **Lodi.**

5 **Nevada City.**

6 **Grass Valley.**

7 **Auburn.**

8 **Coloma.**

9 **Placerville.**

10 **Plymouth.**

11 **Amador City.**

12 **Sutter Creek.**

13 **Volcano.**

14 **Jackson.**

15 **Angels Camp.**

16 **Murphys.**

17 **Columbia.**

18 **Sonora.**

19 **Jamestown.**

20 **Mariposa.**

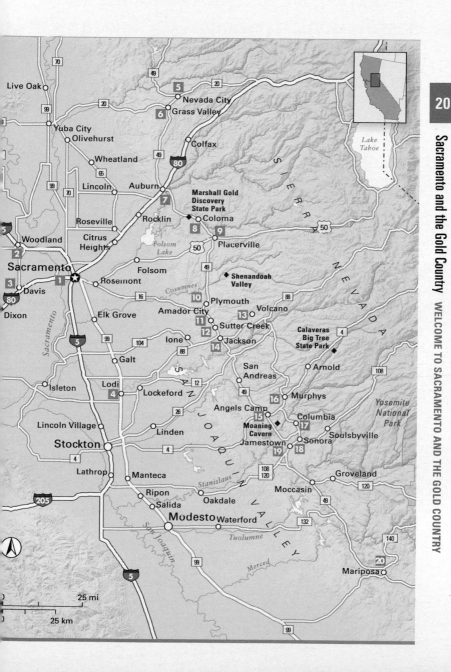

Live Oak
Nevada City
Grass Valley
Colfax
Yuba City
Olivehurst
Wheatland
Lincoln
Auburn
Roseville
Rocklin
Marshall Gold Discovery State Park
Coloma
Placerville
Woodland
Citrus Heights
Folsom Lake
Sacramento
Davis
Folsom
Rosemont
Shenandoah Valley
Dixon
Cosumnes
Plymouth
Volcano
Elk Grove
Amador City
Sutter Creek
Ione
Jackson
Isleton
Lodi
Lockeford
San Andreas
Calaveras Big Tree State Park
Arnold
Galt
Lincoln Village
Linden
Murphys
Angels Camp
Columbia
Soulsbyville
Sonora
Stockton
Moaning Cavern
Jamestown
Lathrop
Manteca
Groveland
Ripon
Salida
Oakdale
Moccasin
Modesto
Waterford
Tuolumne
Mariposa

SIERRA NEVADA
Lake Tahoe
Yosemite National Park
Sacramento
SAN JOAQUIN VALLEY
Stanislaus
San Joaquin
Merced

25 mi
25 km

The Gold Country is one of California's less expensive and more sublime destinations, a region of the Sierra Nevada foothills that's filled with natural and cultural pleasures. Visitors come for the boomtowns and ghost towns; to explore art galleries and shop for antiques; to savor "farm-to-fork" restaurants and delicious wine; and to rest at friendly, atmospheric inns.

Spring brings wildflowers, and in fall the hills are colored by bright red berries and changing leaves. Because it offers plenty of outdoor diversions, the Gold Country is a great place to take kids. Sacramento is an ethnically diverse city, with sizable Mexican, Hmong, and Ukrainian populations, among many others. Many present-day immigrants are relatively recent arrivals, but the capital city has absorbed several waves of newcomers since 1848, when James Marshall turned up a gold nugget in the American River. At the time, Mexico and the United States were still wrestling for ownership of what would become the Golden State. Marshall's discovery provided the incentive for the United States to tighten its grip on the region, and prospectors from all over the world soon came to seek their fortunes in the Mother Lode.

As gold fever seized the nation, California's population of 15,000 swelled to 265,000 within three years. The mostly young, male adventurers who arrived in search of gold—the '49ers—became part of a culture that discarded many of the button-down conventions of the eastern states. It was also a violent time. Yankee prospectors chased Mexican miners off their claims, and California's leaders initiated a plan to exterminate the local Native American population. Bounties were paid, and private militias were hired to wipe out the Native Americans or sell them into slavery. California was to be dominated by the Anglo.

The gold-rush boom lasted scarcely 20 years, but it changed California forever, producing 546 mining towns, of which fewer than 250 remain. The hills of the Gold Country were alive, not only with prospecting and mining but also with business, the arts, gambling, and a fair share of crime. Opera houses went up alongside brothels, and the California State Capitol, in Sacramento, was built partly with the gold dug out of the hills.

MAJOR REGIONS

Sacramento and Nearby. The gateway to the Gold Country, the seat of state government, and an agricultural hub, Sacramento plays many important contemporary roles. About 2½ million people live in the metropolitan area, which offers up more sunshine and lower prices than coastal California. The Sacramento area's mild climate and fertile soil are responsible for the region's current riches: fresh and bountiful food and high-quality wines. There's a growing local craft-beer scene, too. Visits to Sacramento and nearby towns like Woodland and Davis provide the broad agricultural perspective, Lodi the wine-making one. Wineries here earn national acclaim, yet they're without the high prices of Napa and Sonoma.

The Gold Country—South. South of its junction with U.S. 50, Highway 49 traces in asphalt the famed Mother Lode. The peppy former gold-rush towns strung along the road have for the most part been restored, many with money from a modern-day boom in vineyards and wineries.

The Gold Country—North. Old Sacramento's museums provide an excellent introduction to the Gold Country's illustrious history, but the region's heart lies along Highway 49, which winds the approximately 300-mile north–south length of the historic mining area past or near (from north to south) the following towns: Nevada City, Grass Valley, Auburn, Coloma, Placerville, Plymouth, Amador City, Sutter Creek, Jackson, Angels Camp, Murphys, Columbia, Sonora, Jamestown, and Mariposa. Some can be explored as easy day trips from Sacramento, but to immerse yourself in this storied setting, consider staying overnight at least a day or two, especially if you'll be stopping at the many wineries of the Sierra Foothills appellation. On days when it's not too hot or cold, the highway—a hilly, often twisting two-lane road—begs for a convertible with the top down.

Planning

When to Go

The Gold Country is most pleasant in spring, when the wildflowers are in bloom, and in fall. Summers can be hot in the valley (temperatures of 100°F are fairly common), so head for the hills. Sacramento winters tend to be cool, with occasionally foggy or rainy days. Throughout the year Gold Country towns stage community and cultural celebrations. In December many towns are decked out for Christmas.

Getting Here and Around

AIR TRAVEL
Sacramento International Airport (SMF) is served by Aeromexico, Air Canada, Alaska/Horizon, American, Delta, Frontier, Hawaiian, JetBlue, Southwest, United, and Volaris. A taxi from the airport to Downtown Sacramento costs about $40, but services like Lyft and Uber often cost much less. The Super Shuttle fare starts at $15. Public buses *(see Bus and Light-Rail Travel)* are also an option.

CONTACTS Sacramento International Airport. ✉ 6900 Airport Blvd., Sacramento ✛ 12 miles northwest of Downtown off I–5 ☎ 916/929–5411 ⊕ www.sacramento.aero/smf. **Super Shuttle.** ☎ 800/258–3826 ⊕ www.supershuttle.com.

BUS AND LIGHT-RAIL TRAVEL
Greyhound serves Sacramento from San Francisco and Los Angeles. Sacramento Regional Transit serves the capital area with buses and light-rail vehicles. Yolobus public buses Nos. 42A and 42B connect SMF airport and Downtown Sacramento, West Sacramento, Davis, and Woodland.

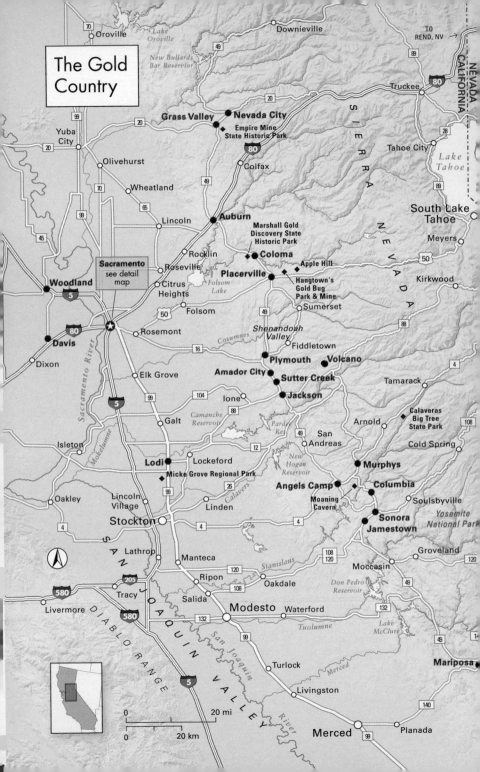

The Gold Country

Oroville
Lake Oroville
New Bullards Bar Reservoir
Downieville
TO RENO, NV
NEVADA
CALIFORNIA

Yuba City
Grass Valley
Nevada City
Empire Mine State Historic Park
Truckee
Tahoe City
Lake Tahoe

Olivehurst
Colfax

Wheatland
South Lake Tahoe
Meyers

Lincoln
Auburn

Rocklin
Marshall Gold Discovery State Historic Park
Coloma
Kirkwood

Woodland
Roseville
Placerville
Apple Hill

Citrus Heights
Folsom Lake
Hangtown's Gold Bug Park & Mine
Sumerset

Davis
Rosemont
Folsom
SIERRA
NEVADA

Dixon
Shenandoah Valley
Fiddletown

Elk Grove
Plymouth
Volcano
Tamarack

Amador City
Sutter Creek

Ione
Jackson
Calaveras Big Tree State Park

Galt
Camanche Reservoir
Pardee Res.
Arnold
Cold Spring

Isleton
San Andreas

Lodi
Lockeford
New Hogan Reservoir
Murphys

Oakley
Micke Grove Regional Park
Columbia
Soulsbyville

Lincoln Village
Linden
Angels Camp
Yosemite National Park

Stockton
Moaning Cavern
Sonora
Jamestown

Lathrop
Manteca
Groveland

Livermore
Tracy
Ripon
Oakdale
Moccasin

Salida
Don Pedro Reservoir

DIABLO RANGE
Modesto
Waterford
Lake McClure

Tuolumne

Turlock
Merced

Livingston

Merced
Planada

SAN JOAQUIN VALLEY

Mariposa

0   20 mi
0   20 km

CONTACTS Greyhound. ✉ *420 Richards Blvd.* ☎ *916/444–6858* ⊕ *www.grey-hound.com.* **Sacramento Regional Transit.** ☎ *916/321–2877* ⊕ *www.sacrt.com.* **Yolobus.** ☎ *530/666–2877, 916/371–2877* ⊕ *www.yolobus.com.*

CAR TRAVEL

Interstate 5 (north–south) and Interstate 80 (east–west) are the two main routes into and out of Sacramento. From Sacramento, three highways fan out toward the east, all intersecting with historic Highway 49: Interstate 80 heads northeast 34 miles to Auburn; U.S. 50 goes east 40 miles to Placerville; and Highway 16 angles southeast 45 miles to Plymouth. Two-lane Highway 49, one of America's great drives, winds and climbs through the foothills and valleys, linking the principal Gold Country towns. Traveling by car is the only practical way to explore the Gold Country.

TRAIN TRAVEL

On the Amtrak *California Zephyr,* you can ride the same route traveled by prospectors in the late 1800s. Amtrak trains also serve Sacramento and Davis from the Bay Area.

CONTACTS Amtrak. ✉ *401 I St.* ☎ *800/872–7245* ⊕ *www.amtrak.com.*

Restaurants

American, Italian, Chinese, and Mexican are common Gold Country fare, but chefs also prepare ambitious European, French, and contemporary regional cuisine based on seasonal local ingredients. Although fewer places make them these days, Grass Valley's meat- and vegetable-stuffed *pasties,* introduced by 19th-century gold miners from Cornwall, England, are one of the region's more unusual treats.

Hotels

Sacramento has plenty of full-service hotels, budget motels, and small inns. Larger towns along Highway 49—among them Auburn, Grass Valley, and Jackson—have chain motels and inns. Many Gold Country bed-and-breakfasts occupy former mansions, miners' cabins, and other historic buildings. *Hotel reviews have been shortened. For full information, visit Fodors.com.*

Visitor Information

EVENTS AND ENTERTAINMENT Sacramento 365. ⊕ *www.sacramento365.com.*

TOURISM AGENCIES Amador County Chamber of Commerce & Visitors Bureau. ✉ *115 Main St., Jackson* ☎ *209/223–0350* ⊕ *amadorchamber.com.* **El Dorado County Visitors Authority.** ✉ *542 Main St., Placerville* ☎ *530/621–5885* ⊕ *visit-eldorado. com.* **Grass Valley/Nevada County Chamber of Commerce.** ✉ *128 E. Main St., Grass Valley* ☎ *530/273–4667* ⊕ *www.grassvalleychamber.com.* **Tuolumne County Visitors Bureau.** ✉ *193 S. Washington St., Sonora* ☎ *209/533–4420, 800/446–1333* ⊕ *www. yosemitegoldcountry.com.* **Yosemite Mariposa County Tourism Bureau.** ✉ *5065 Hwy. 140, Suite E, Mariposa* ☎ *209/742–4567* ⊕ *www.yosemite.com.*

What It Costs			
$	$$	$$$	$$$$
RESTAURANTS			
under $16	$16–$22	$23–$30	over $30
HOTELS			
under $120	$120–$175	$176–$250	over $250

Sacramento

87 miles northeast of San Francisco, 384 miles north of Los Angeles.

All around the Golden State's seat of government you'll experience echoes of the gold-rush days, most notably in Old Sacramento, whose wooden sidewalks and horse-drawn carriages on cobblestone streets lend the waterfront district a 19th-century feel. The California State Railroad Museum and other venues hold artifacts of state and national significance, and historic buildings house shops and restaurants. River cruises and train rides are fun family diversions.

Due east of Old Sacramento is Downtown, where landmarks include the Capitol building and the surrounding Capitol Park. Golden 1 Center, the new sports and concert venue, is part of DOCO, short for Downtown Commons, which also includes shopping, restaurants, hotels, and a grassy and concrete gathering spaces.

Farther east, starting at about 15th Street, lies Midtown, a mix of genteel Victorian edifices, ultramodern lofts, and innovative restaurants and cozy wine bars. The neighborhood springs to life on the second Saturday evening of the month, when art galleries hold open houses. A few intersections are jumping most evenings when the weather's good; they include the corner of 20th and L streets in what's known as Lavender Heights, the center of the city's gay and lesbian community.

GETTING HERE AND AROUND

Most people drive to Sacramento and get around by car. Yellow Cab, Lyft, and Uber are reliable cab options.

Sacramento Regional Transit buses and light-rail vehicles serve the area. Bus 30 links Old Sacramento, Midtown, and Sutter's Fort.

Assuming that traffic is not a factor (though it often is), Sacramento is a 90-minute drive from San Francisco and a seven-hour drive from Los Angeles. Parking garages serve Old Sacramento and other tourist spots; on-street parking in Downtown can be difficult to find.

TRANSPORTATION CONTACTS
Sacramento Regional Transit. ☏ *916/321–2877* ⊕ *www.sacrt.com.* **Yellow Cab Co. of Sacramento.** ☏ *916/444–2222* ⊕ *www. yellowcabsacramento.com.*

ESSENTIALS

VISITOR INFORMATION Old Sacramento Visitor Information Center. ⊠ *1002 2nd St.* ☏ *916/442–7644* ⊕ *www.oldsacramento.com.* **Sacramento Convention and Visitors Bureau.** ⊠ *1608 I St., Downtown* ☏ *916/808–7777* ⊕ *www.visitsacramento.com.*

👁 Sights

California Automobile Museum
MUSEUM | More than 150 automobiles—from Model Ts, Hudsons, and Studebakers to modern-day electric-powered ones—are on display at this museum that pays tribute to automotive history and car culture. Check out a replica of Henry Ford's 1896 Quadracycle and a 1920s roadside café and garage exhibit. The docents are ready to explain everything you see. The museum is south of Downtown and Old Sacramento, with ample free parking. ⊠ *2200 Front St., Downtown* ☏ *916/442–6802* ⊕ *www.calautomuseum.org* 🖭 *$10* ⊗ *Closed Tues.*

California Museum
MUSEUM | FAMILY | Showcasing longtime and temporary residents who helped elevate the Golden State, this museum displays artifacts from the State Constitution to surfing magazines. Permanent exhibits cover topics like statehood, the experiences of California Indians, life for Japanese Americans in World War II internment camps, and the impact

of women. The California Hall of Fame honors Walt Disney, Jackie Robinson, Bruce Lee, Amelia Earhart, writer and Sacramento native Joan Didion, and other familiar names. ⊠ *1020 O St., at 11th St., Downtown* ☎ *916/653–7524* ⊕ *www.californiamuseum.org* ⤳ *$9* ⊘ *Closed Mon.*

★ California State Railroad Museum
MUSEUM | FAMILY | Sprawling over three floors and taking up the equivalent of 2½ acres of space, this museum celebrates the history of trains from their 19th-century English origins and the building of America's transcontinental railroad (Sacramento was its western terminus) to the pre–jet age glory days of rail travel and the high-speed trains in today's Europe and Asia. A permanent exhibit that debuted in 2019 for the 150th anniversary of the transcontinental railroad's completion details the contributions of Chinese laborers, and another section contains a cast gold "Last Spike," one of several spikes issued to commemorate the joining in Utah of the west-to-east Central Pacific and east-to-west Union Pacific lines. Twenty-two of the museum's railroad cars and engines—among them Pullman-style cars and steam locomotives—are on display at any one time, and there are interactive displays and a play area for kids. The exhibits of toy trains delight youngsters and adults. ⊠ *125 I St., at 2nd St., Old Sacramento* ☎ *916/323–9280* ⊕ *www.csrmf.org* ⤳ *$12.*

★ Capitol
GOVERNMENT BUILDING | Built in 1869 and topped by a 128-foot gilded dome, the Capitol functions as both a working museum and the active seat of California's government. Wander freely by reproductions of century-old state offices and into legislative chambers (in session from January to September) decorated in the style of the 1890s. Look for the abstract portrait of Edmund G. "Jerry" Brown, alongside those of fellow former governors Ronald Reagan (who succeeded Brown's father, Edmund G. "Pat" Brown) and Arnold Schwarzenegger. Guides conduct tours of the building and the 40-acre Capitol Park, which contains a rose garden, a fragrant display of camellias (Sacramento's city flower), and California Veterans Memorials. ∎TIP➔ **The Capitol's diverse trees include more than 1,000 trees from around the world.** ⊠ *10th St. and L St., Downtown* ☎ *916/324–0333* ⊕ *capitolmuseum. ca.gov* ⤳ *Free.*

Central Pacific Railroad Passenger Station
TRANSPORTATION SITE (AIRPORT/BUS/FERRY/ TRAIN) | FAMILY | At this reconstructed 1876 depot there's rolling stock to admire and a typical waiting room. Part of the year a train departs from the freight depot, south of the passenger station, making a 45-minute out-and-back trip that starts along the banks of the Sacramento River. ∎TIP➔ **Cookies and hot chocolate are served aboard sellout Polar Express rides between Thanksgiving and Christmas that include appearances by characters from the famous story.** ⊠ *930 Front St., at J St., Old Sacramento* ☎ *916/445–5995* ⊕ *www. csrmf.org/events/train-rides* ⤳ *Train rides from $12* ⊘ *Hrs vary.*

★ Crocker Art Museum
MUSEUM | Established in 1885 with a collection assembled by California Supreme Court judge E.B. Crocker (brother of Charles Crocker, of railroad-baron fame) and his wife, Margaret, Sacramento's premier fine-arts museum specializes in California art, European master drawings, and international ceramics. A highlight is the magnificent *Great Canyon of the Sierra, Yosemite* (1871) by Thomas Hill. Some works are displayed in two architecturally significant 19th-century structures, the original Italianate Crocker residence and the villa-like gallery the judge commissioned. A contemporary 125,000-square-foot space added in 2010 hosts outstanding traveling exhibitions. ∎TIP➔ **The museum stays open**

Sights ▼

1 California Automobile
  Museum **A4**
2 California Museum **B4**
3 California State Railroad
  Museum **A2**
4 Capitol. **C4**
5 Central Pacific Railroad
  Passenger Station...... **A3**
6 Crocker Art Museum... **A4**
7 Governor's Mansion..... **C3**
8 Huntington, Hopkins
  & Co. Store **A3**
9 Leland Stanford Mansion
  State Historic Park **B4**
10 Old Sacramento
  Schoolhouse
  Museum **A3**
11 State Indian Museum ... **E4**
12 Sutter's Fort **E4**

Restaurants ▼

1 The Bank 629 J.......... **B3**
2 Biba **E4**
3 Cafeteria 15L **C3**
4 Camden Spit
  & Larder **B3**
5 Ella **C3**
6 Hook & Ladder
  Manufacturing
  Company................. **C5**
7 The Firehouse........... **A3**
8 Kru **E4**
9 Magpie Cafe............. **C4**
10 Rio City Cafe............ **A3**
11 The Waterboy........... **D4**

Hotels

1 Amber House Inn of
  Midtown **D4**
2 Citizen Hotel **B3**
3 Delta King................ **A3**
4 Embassy Suites by Hilton
  Sacramento Riverfront
  Promenade **A3**
5 Hyatt Regency
  Sacramento **C3**
6 Kimpton Sawyer
  Hotel..................... **B3**

late on Thursday; pay what you wish on the third Sunday each month. ⊠ *216 O St., at 3rd St., Downtown* ☎ *916/808–7000* ⊕ *www.crockerartmuseum.org* ⊠ *$12* ☾ *Closed Mon.*

Governor's Mansion

HOUSE | This 15-room Italianate mansion was built in 1877 and used by the state's chief executives from the early 1900s until 1967, when Ronald Reagan vacated it in favor of a modern residence. Many of the interior decorations were ordered from the Huntington, Hopkins & Co. Hardware Store, one of whose partners, Albert Gallatin, was the original occupant. Following renovations completed in 2015, then-governor Jerry Brown began occupying the home, and in early 2019 his successor, Gavin Newsom, moved in—then announced he was decamping with his family to the Sacramento suburbs. You can view the mansion from outside, but it isn't open for tours. ⊠ *1526 H St., at 16th St., Midtown.*

Huntington, Hopkins & Co. Store

MUSEUM | Picks, shovels, and other paraphernalia used by gold-rush miners are on display at this re-creation of a 19th-century hardware store that also displays tools and accessories for households, farms, and machine shops. Though it's named for two of the Big Four railroad barons, their store was far more elaborate. ⊠ *113 I St., at Front St., Old Sacramento* ☎ *916/323–7234* ⊕ *www.csrmf.org* ⊠ *Free* ☾ *Closed Mon.–Wed.*

★ Leland Stanford Mansion State Historic Park

HOUSE | In 1856 this structure's original owner built a modest two-story row house purchased a few years later by Leland Stanford, a railroad baron, California governor, and U.S. senator who expanded it in 1862 and the early 1870s into a 19,000-square-foot mansion. The opulent space is open for touring except on days when California's governor hosts official events. Before Stanford's

wife and heir, Jane, died, she donated the mansion to Sacramento's Roman Catholic diocese, whose nuns ran it first as an orphanage and later a home for teenage girls. Luckily for the restoration efforts which began in 1986 after the state acquired the property, the nuns had stashed many original furnishings and fixtures in the attic and the renowned photographer Eadweard Muybridge had shot images in the 1870s that made clear what rooms looked like and where things belonged. ■**TIP**➔ **Guided tours of small groups depart hourly from 10 to 4.** ⊠ *800 N St., at 8th St., Downtown* ☎ *916/324–0575 recorded info, 916/324–9266 visitor center* ⊕ *www.parks.ca.gov/stanford-mansion* ⊠ *Free.*

Old Sacramento Schoolhouse Museum

MUSEUM | **FAMILY** | A kid-friendly attraction that shows what one-room schoolhouses were like in central California and the Sierra foothills in the late 1800s, this replica built in 1976 is a fun, quick stop a block from the waterfront. Some of the salient history is written on blackboards in chalk. ⊠ *1200 Front St., at L St., Old Sacramento* ⊕ *www.oldsacschoolhouse. org* ⊠ *Free.*

State Indian Museum

MUSEUM | Adjacent to Sutter's Fort, this small but engaging museum explores the lives and history of California's native peoples. Arts-and-crafts exhibits, a demonstration village, and an evocative video offer a fascinating portrait of the state's earliest inhabitants. ⊠ *2618 K St., at 26th St., Midtown* ☎ *916/324–0971* ⊕ *www.parks.ca.gov/indianmuseum* ⊠ *$5.*

Sutter's Fort

MUSEUM VILLAGE | **FAMILY** | German-born Swiss immigrant John Augustus Sutter founded Sacramento's earliest Euro-American settlement in 1839. A self-guided tour includes a blacksmith's shop, bakery, prison, living quarters, and livestock areas. Costumed docents sometimes reenact fort life, demonstrating crafts, food preparation, and firearms maintenance. ✉ *2701 L St., at 27th St., Midtown* ☎ *916/445–4422* 🌐 *www.suttersfort.org* 🎟 *From $5.*

🍴 Restaurants

The Bank 629 J

$$ | ECLECTIC | A sensitive restoration transformed a century-old neoclassical-style bank into a first-floor ensemble of food stations, a classy mezzanine bar, and (down in the former vault, its thick circular door the centerpiece) a self-serve taproom. Under gilded ceilings and ornate chandeliers on the main floor, the various purveyors serve Southern-tinged cuisine, burgers with an Asian-Cajun spin, poké bowls and sushi rolls, sandwiches and salads, vegan gelato, and other delights. **Known for:** sports on 18 TVs, many in the taproom; snacks, quick bites, full meals; near Golden 1 Center arena. [$] *Average main: $18* ✉ *629 J St., at 7th St., Downtown* ☎ *916/557–9910* 🌐 *www.thebank629j.com.*

★ Biba

$$$ | NORTHERN ITALIAN | Celebrity chef and owner Biba Caggiano's elegant yet comfortable haven of northern Italian cuisine, opened in 1986 near Sutter's Fort, stands tallest among the restaurants that elevated Sacramento's stature as a food town. The Capitol crowd flocks here for menus that change quarterly, with staples such as a 10-layer lasagna with Bolognese sauce (served only on Thursday and Friday), braised pork shoulder, and house-made gnocchi and pasta dishes. **Known for:** Sacramento institution still going strong; California and Italian wines; signature rum-soaked cake with chocolate ganache for dessert. [$] *Average main: $28* ✉ *2801 Capitol Ave., at 28th St., Midtown* ☎ *916/455–2422* 🌐 *www.biba-restaurant.com* 🕒 *Closed Sun. No lunch Mon. or Sat.*

Cafeteria 15L

$$ | AMERICAN | The exposed brick, reclaimed wood, mismatched chairs, and natural light streaming through large-paned windows of this easygoing hangout for comfort food make a great first impression on newbies and a lasting one on the many repeat local customers. Favorites like tater tots (in truffle oil), sloppy joes (from braised short ribs), and chicken and waffles (with pecan butter and Tabasco-and-black-pepper gravy) prove simultaneously familiar and intriguing. **Known for:** two outdoor patios; nostalgic food with a modern twist; weekend brunch. [$] *Average main: $21* ✉ *1116 15th St., at L St., Downtown* ☎ *916/492–1960* 🌐 *www.cafeteria15l.com.*

★ Camden Spit & Larder

$$$ | MODERN AMERICAN | Upscale London haberdasheries reportedly inspired the aesthetic of this impeccably designed, pressed-metal-ceilinged paean to spit-roasted, Brit-influenced meat dishes. Near Golden 1 Center and Downtown Commons, it's a place to share small offerings like sausage rolls, salt-cod fritters, local caviar (Sacramento is a center of caviar production), and Wagyu tartare, perhaps with a craft cocktail incorporating seasonal fruits, herbs, and vegetables, before proceeding to roasted half chicken or the house specialty, roast rib of beef with fermented horseradish. **Known for:** sea-salt fingerling fries with malt vinegar mayo; kitchen bar to watch chefs at work; wine, beer, and cider selections; inventive cocktails. [$] *Average main: $29* ✉ *555 Capitol Mall, at 6th St., Downtown* ☎ *916/619–8897* 🌐 *www.camdenspitandlarder.com* 🕒 *No lunch.*

Ella

$$$$ | MODERN AMERICAN | With fresh white calla lilies on the tables, ivory linen curtains, and distressed-wood shutters installed across the ceiling, this swank restaurant and bar near the Capitol is artfully designed and thoroughly modern. The stellar California–French farm-to-table cuisine served within changes seasonally, but typical dishes include steak tartare with garlic popovers and a farm egg, orange-anise marinated beet salad, a wood-fired pork chop, and bavette steak. **Known for:** fresh, seasonal local ingredients; waitstaff's attention to detail; cocktail and wine selection. [$] *Average main: $39* ✉ *1131 K St., at 12th St., Downtown* ☎ *916/443–3772* 🌐 *www.elladiningroomandbar.com* 🕑 *Closed Sun. No lunch.*

★ The Firehouse

$$$$ | **AMERICAN** | Sacramento's rich and famous including California governors going back to Ronald Reagan settle into the elegant spaces within the city's restored first brick firehouse to dine on award-winning contemporary cuisine. The creative fare ranges from carpaccio, seasonal oysters, and braised pork belly with sage bread pudding to delicately spiced pan-roasted sea bass and rack of lamb, rib eye, and other specialty meat cuts. **Known for:** steaks and seafood; chef's tasting menu; courtyard patio. [$] *Average main: $41* ✉ *1112 2nd St., at L St., Old Sacramento* ☎ *916/442–4772* 🌐 *www.firehouseoldsac.com* 🕑 *No lunch weekends.*

Hook & Ladder Manufacturing Company

$$$ | **MODERN AMERICAN** | Youthful and compelling, with found-art decorative elements and exposed vents, this historic former fire station is a favorite stop for cocktails, craft beers, and farm-to-fork fare. The area's year-round farmers' markets supply ingredients for the delectable salads and soups, and the carefully sourced beef, poultry, and seafood entrées are always good. **Known for:** carefully sourced ingredients; many local brews and wines; many vegan items. [$] *Average main: $26* ✉ *1630 S St., at 17th St., Midtown* ☎ *916/442–4885* 🌐 *www.hookandladder916.com.*

Kru

$$$ | **JAPANESE** | It's worth the drive a little past Sutter's Fort to this blond-wood mod-Japanese restaurant whose owner-chef fashions fresh and wildly creative sushi. Sit at blond-wood tables or the counter and order a sunshine roll, with spicy tuna, escolar, and shrimp tempura enlivened by the tart contribution of green apples and lemon, perhaps pairing it with cooked fare like smoked duck *kushiyaki* with plum-wine katsu sauce or hearty hot or cold ramen, including pork belly, poached shrimp, and mushroom broth. **Known for:** smart decor; nearly two dozen rolls; impressive sake, wine, and whiskeys. [$] *Average main: $28* ✉ *3135 Folsom Blvd., at Seville Way* ☎ *916/551–1559* 🌐 *www.krurestaurant.com* 🕑 *No lunch.*

★ Magpie Cafe

$$$ | **AMERICAN** | This Midtown eatery with a vaguely industrial look and a casual vibe takes its food seriously: nearly all the produce is sourced locally, and the chefs prepare only sustainable seafood. Roasted chicken for two with a chervil-ginger green sauce is a staple, as is the seafood skillet with seasonal vegetables. **Known for:** weekend brunch; happy-hour menu Tuesday–Friday; homemade ice-cream sandwiches. [$] *Average main: $25* ✉ *1601 16th St., Midtown* ☎ *916/452–7594* 🌐 *www.magpiecafe.com* 🕑 *Closed Mon. No dinner Sun.*

Rio City Café

$$$ | **AMERICAN** | Contemporary and seasonal Mediterranean and Californian cuisine, and huge floor-to-ceiling windows and an outdoor deck overlooking the river are the attractions of this restaurant designed to resemble a vintage steamship warehouse. The food—maple bourbon–marinated steaks, filet mignon Wellington, almond-crusted mahimahi, crab and shrimp Louie salads—is generally good, though the big draw is the setting. **Known for:** riverfront location; daytime water views; dinner starts at 4 pm. [$] *Average main: $25* ✉ *1110 Front St., at L St., Old Sacramento* ☎ *916/442–8226* 🌐 *www.riocitycafe.com.*

★ The Waterboy

$$$ | EUROPEAN | Rural French cooking with locally sourced, seasonal, high-quality often organic ingredients is the hallmark of this upscale white-tablecloth corner storefront restaurant that's as appealing for a casual meal with friends as it is for a drawn-out romantic dinner for two. Among the mains, try the steak du jour, coq au vin, or seasonal seafood, and save room for sweet (profiteroles) or savory (assorted cheeses) desserts. **Known for:** exceptional French cooking; quality local ingredients; welcoming chef. [$] *Average main: $30* ✉ *2000 Capitol Ave., at 20th St., Midtown* ☎ *916/498–9891* 🌐 *www.waterboyrestaurant.com* 🕒 *No lunch weekends.*

🛏 Hotels

★ Amber House Inn of Midtown

$$$ | B&B/INN | Veer from the beaten path of traditional lodging at Amber House Inn's two historic homes—one a 1905 Craftsman, the other an 1895 Dutch colonial–revival—just 1 mile from the Capitol. **Pros:** Midtown location; attentive service; full breakfast served in-room if desired. **Cons:** freeway access isn't easy; not exactly kid-friendly; lacks spa, fitness center, and other big-hotel amenities. [$] *Rooms from: $179* ✉ *1315 22nd St., Midtown* ☎ *916/444–8085* 🌐 *www.amberhouse.com* 🛏 *10 rooms* 🍴 *Free Breakfast.*

Citizen Hotel

$$$ | HOTEL | This boutique hotel built within the historic 1926 Cal Western Life building is dapper and refined, with marble stairs, striped wallpaper, and plush velvet chairs, lending the place a Roaring '20s charm. **Pros:** hip, sophisticated decor; smooth and solicitous service; terrific restaurant and bar. **Cons:** rooms near elevator can be noisy; rates vary widely depending on conventions, legislature, season; expensive parking. [$] *Rooms from: $208* ✉ *926 J St., Downtown* ☎ *916/447–2700* 🌐 *www.thecitizenhotel.com* 🛏 *198 rooms* 🍴 *No meals.*

Delta King

$$ | HOTEL | Wake up to the sound of geese taking flight along the river when you book a stay in one of Sacramento's most unusual and historic relics, a carefully restored riverboat hotel, permanently moored on Old Sacramento's waterfront. **Pros:** unique lodgings; steps from historic Old Town shopping and dining; period feel. **Cons:** slanted floors can feel a bit jarring; rooms are cramped; some noise issues. [$] *Rooms from: $154* ✉ *1000 Front St., Old Sacramento* ✣ *At end of K St.* ☎ *916/444–5464, 800/825–5464* 🌐 *www.deltaking.com* 🛏 *44 rooms* 🍴 *Free Breakfast.*

Embassy Suites by Hilton Sacramento Riverfront Promenade

$$$$ | HOTEL | Adjacent to Sacramento's iconic Tower Bridge, this property has huge common areas, updated large rooms, public art, and a reputation for customer service. **Pros:** best river view in town; proximity to Old Sacramento and Downtown; made-to-order breakfast included in rate. **Cons:** the atrium feels sterile; ho-hum guest-room style; high prices during events and when legislature is in session. [$] *Rooms from: $298* ✉ *100 Capitol Mall, Downtown* ☎ *916/326–5000* 🌐 *embassysuites3.hilton.com* 🛏 *242 suites* 🍴 *Free Breakfast.*

Hyatt Regency Sacramento

$$$ | HOTEL | With a marble-and-glass lobby and luxurious rooms, this multitiered, glass-dominated hotel across from the Capitol and adjacent to the convention center has a striking Mediterranean design. **Pros:** best rooms have Capitol Park views; some rooms have small balconies; excellent service. **Cons:** nearby streets can feel dodgy at night; somewhat impersonal; many corporate events. [$] *Rooms from: $220* ✉ *1209 L St., Downtown* ☎ *916/443–1234, 800/633–7313* 🌐 *sacramento.regency.hyatt.com* 🛏 *505 rooms* 🍴 *No meals.*

★ Kimpton Sawyer Hotel

$$$$ | HOTEL | Soft shades of brown and gray and furniture milled from California oak lend an haute-rustic feel to the spacious rooms and suites of this full-service hotel amid Sacramento's Downtown Commons (DOCO) shopping and entertainment complex. **Pros:** pool deck; "living room" lobby; convenient to Downtown and Old Sacramento. **Cons:** pricey in-season; no tubs in many rooms; may be too high-style for some guests. [$] *Rooms from: $254* ✉ *500 J St., Downtown* ☎ *916/545–7100 front desk, 877/678–6255 reservations* 🌐 *www.sawyerhotel.com* 🛏 *285 rooms* 🍴 *No meals.*

Nightlife

Dive Bar

BARS/PUBS | Live "mermaids" and "mermen" swim in a massive tank above the bar at this lively Downtown nightspot known for its extensive list of craft cocktails and local beers. ✉ *1016 K St., Downtown* ☎ *916/737–5999* 🌐 *divebarsacramento.com.*

Drakes: The Barn

BREWPUBS/BEER GARDENS | Drake's Brewing serves up beer, food, and musical and other events at a dramatically curving, cedar-shingled pavilion on 2 acres along the Sacramento River. The anchor food tenant, PizzaSmith, serves thin-crust New Haven–style pies; there are also resident and pop-up food trucks and a brewpub–beer garden (lawn-chair and other seating plus fire pits) pouring 50 Drake's brews on tap, including the potent Denogginizer Double IPA. The Barn is closed on Monday and Tuesday. ✉ *985 Riverfront St., at Garden St., West Sacramento* ✥ *Across Sacramento River from Downtown near Raley Field* ☎ *510/568–2739* 🌐 *drinkdrakes.com/barn.*

Harlow's

MUSIC CLUBS | This sceney restaurant draws a younger crowd to its art-deco bar-nightclub. They have an inviting patio plus live music after 9 pm from a diverse lineup. ✉ *2708 J St., at 27th St., Midtown* ☎ *916/441–4693* 🌐 *www.harlows.com.*

★ Midtown BierGarten

BREWPUBS/BEER GARDENS | The neighborhood feel and the selection of beers, ales, porters, stouts, sours, and ciders make a trip to this boisterous beer garden a fun occasion, with the garlic fries, fresh pretzels with mustard, old-fashioned hot dogs, and other small bites a definite bonus. A 40-foot cargo container holds the bar, and a 20-footer contains the bathrooms, with the rest of the setting alfresco. ✉ *2332 K St., at 24th St.* ☎ *916/346–4572* 🌐 *beergardensacramento.com.*

★ Midtown's Cantina Alley

BARS/PUBS | Flavorful, colorful, fruity cocktails, some served in hollowed-out pineapples or watermelons, are the specialty of this bar and restaurant whose equally rich-hued decor and corrugated-metal ceiling intentionally evoke similar spots throughout Mexico. While sipping sangria, a cerveza, one of several margaritas, or a Tijuana mule (made with tequila and delivered in a 128-ounce copper mug, it serves five), you can nibble on street tacos, posole, *elote* (corn on a stick, rolled in mayonnaise and topped with cheese and spices), and other small plates. ✉ *2320 Jazz Alley, Midtown* ✥ *Off 24th St. between J and K Sts.* ☎ *833/232–0639* 🌐 *www.cantinaalley.com.*

Punch Bowl Social

BARS/PUBS | This restaurant and entertainment complex offers bowling, billiards, table shuffleboard, karaoke, Giant Jenga, virtual reality, pinball, and Skee-Ball. After you've worked up an appetite, dine on updated pub grub and sip well-chosen craft beers, wine, specialty cocktails, or boozeless beverages. ✉ *500 J St., Downtown* ✥ *At 5th St.* ☎ *916/925–5610* 🌐 *www.punchbowlsocial.com/sacramento.*

Revival

BARS/PUBS | The poolside rooftop bar at the Kimpton Sawyer is a chic people-watching perch with views of Downtown Commons and the Golden 1 Center. They offer specialty cocktails and excellent bar bites, and host guest DJs after 9:30 pm Wednesday through Saturday (the bar is closed on other days except for special events). ⊠ *Kimpton Sawyer Hotel, 500 J St., Downtown* ☎ *916/545–7111* ⊕ *revival-sacramento.com.*

Streets Pub and Grub

BARS/PUBS | A favorite among Anglophiles, Streets is open until 2 am nightly, with lively karaoke on Wednesday night (with a band on month's second and fourth Thursday). ⊠ *1804 J St., at 18th St., Midtown* ☎ *916/498–1388* ⊕ *www.streetspubandgrub.com.*

Tiger

BARS/PUBS | Concrete walls and black-metal beams and railings reinforce the post-industrial mood at this two-level bar with zesty bites like paprika-spiced popcorn, pickled deviled eggs, and chicken-leek meatballs. The signature Tiger's Milk drink riffs off a piña colada with crème de cacao, gin, Frangelico, and coconut milk, and there are several other artisanal offerings and a few classics, including a Manhattan, plus beer and wine. ⊠ *722 K St., at 8th St., Downtown* ☎ *916/382–9610* ⊕ *www.tiger700block.com.*

🎭 Performing Arts

Broadway Sacramento

THEATER | This group presents Broadway shows at the Community Center Theater and produces summer musicals (think *Oklahoma, Annie*) at the theater-in-the-round Wells Fargo Pavilion. ⊠ *1419 H St., at 14th St., Downtown* ☎ *916/557–1999* ⊕ *www.broadwaysacramento.com.*

Crest Theatre

ARTS CENTERS | It's worth peeking inside the Crest even if you don't catch a show, just to see the swirling and flamboyant art-deco design in the foyer, or to dine at the Empress Tavern restaurant within. It's a beloved venue for classic and art-house films, along with concerts and other cultural events. ⊠ *1013 K St., at 10th St., Downtown* ☎ *916/476–3356* ⊕ *www.crestsacramento.com.*

🛍 Shopping

Downtown Commons (*DOCO*)

SHOPPING CENTERS/MALLS | As its name implies, this multiblock complex adjoining the Golden 1 Center aspires to be a gathering spot for locals and tourists as much as a place to shop, dine, catch a movie, or sip a cocktail. ⊠ *660 J St., Downtown* ✥ *Between 5th and 7th Sts., J and L Sts.* ☎ *916/273–8124.*

★ Kulture

GIFTS/SOUVENIRS | Two sons of migrant workers from Jalisco and Michoacán opened this vibrant shop that sells Mexican art, jewelry, and gifts, along with the duo's pithy Keepin It Paisa line of T-shirts, hoodies, and ball caps. Buoyed by the shop's success, the two expanded into the adjacent space where they and other vendors sell furniture, clothing, and other items. ⊠ *2331 K St., Midtown* ✥ *At 24th St.* ☎ *916/442–2728* ⊕ *kulturedc.wixsite.com/kulture* ☙ *Closed Mon.*

Scout Living

HOUSEHOLD ITEMS/FURNITURE | The members of this collective are specialists in home accessories and antique, vintage, and modern furniture. Even if you're not looking to redecorate, the shop's a wonder to walk through. ⊠ *1215 18th St., at L St., Midtown* ☎ *916/594–7971* ⊕ *www.scoutliving.com* ☙ *Closed Mon.*

Activities

American River Bicycle Trail
BICYCLING | The Jedediah Smith Memorial Trail, as it's formally called, runs for 32 miles from Old Sacramento to Beals Point in Folsom. Walk or ride a bit of it and you'll see why local cyclists and pedestrians adore its scenic lanes. Enjoy great views of the American River and the bluffs overlooking it. ■TIP→ Bring lunch or a snack. Pretty parks and picnic areas dot the trail. ⊠ Old Sacramento ⊕ www.americanriverbiketrail.com.

Sacramento Kings
BASKETBALL | The Sacramento Kings of the NBA play at the LEED-certified Golden 1 Center, which opened in 2016 as the centerpiece of the DOCO (Downtown Commons) complex of restaurants, hotels, and shops. ⊠ 500 David J. Stern Walk, Downtown ✛ At 5th and L Sts. ⊕ www.sacramentokings.com.

Sacramento River Cats
BASEBALL/SOFTBALL | FAMILY | The top minor-league affiliate of the San Francisco Giants plays before big crowds just across the Sacramento River from Downtown. ⊠ Raley Field, 400 Ballpark Dr., West Sacramento ✛ Across Sacramento River from Downtown ☎ 916/376–4700 ⊕ www.rivercats.com.

Woodland

20 miles northwest of Sacramento.

In its heyday, Woodland was among California's wealthiest cities. Established by gold seekers and entrepreneurs, it later became an agricultural gold mine. The legacy of the old land barons lives on in the restored Victorian and Craftsman architecture downtown; the best examples are south of Main Street on College, Elm, 1st, and 2nd streets. The town's top attractions pay tribute to car culture and motorized agriculture vehicles.

GETTING HERE AND AROUND
Yolobus (⊕ www.yolobus.com) serves Woodland from Sacramento, but it's far more practical to drive here via Interstate 5.

ESSENTIALS
VISITOR INFORMATION Woodland Chamber of Commerce. ⊠ 307 1st St., at Dead Cat Alley ☎ 530/662–7327 ⊕ www.woodlandchamber.org.

Sights

California Agriculture Museum
MUSEUM | FAMILY | This gigantic space provides a marvelous overview of the entire history of motorized agricultural vehicles through dozens and dozens of threshers, harvesters, combines, tractors, and more. A separate wing surveys the evolution of the truck, with an emphasis on ones used for farm work. ⊠ 1962 Hays La., off County Rd. 102 ☎ 530/666–9700 ⊕ www.CaliforniaAgMuseum.org ☞ $10 ⊗ Closed Sun. and Mon.

★ Reiff's Gas Station Museum
MUSEUM | Mark Reiff, an inveterate collector of gas-station pumps and signs, converted his home in a residential neighborhood into a joyful homage to 20th-century car culture. A yellow-and-orange "Roar with Gilmore" pump got Reiff going in 1999, and he's never stopped, adding more pumps and signs (Sinclair, Flying A, Sunray), along with a flood of nostalgia-inducing memorabilia. Reiff describes his creation as "labor of love and a butt load of fun"—and it is. Contact him to arrange a tour. ⊠ 52 Jefferson St., at McKinley Ave. ☎ 530/666–1758 ⊕ reiffsgasstation.com ☞ $7.

Woodland Opera House
ARTS VENUE | On the U.S. National Register of Historic Places, this 1896 structure hosted minstrel shows, John Philip Sousa's marching band, and early vaudeville acts before closing for six decades. Now restored, it hosts plays, musicals, and concerts year-round. If the box office is open, ask for a backstage tour or a

peek at the auditorium. ✉ *340 2nd St.* ☎ *530/666–9617* 🌐 *www.woodlandoperahouse.org.*

🍴 Restaurants

Kitchen428 and Mojo's Lounge
$$ | **AMERICAN** | Erected in 1891 to house luxury apartments, the Jackson building roared back to life as a showcase for locally sourced California cuisine from filet mignon to miso-marinated salmon. The menu at this stylish exposed-brick restaurant also includes vegetarian and vegan items. **Known for:** local and sustainable menu; cocktail bar with craft beers on tap; weekend brunch. [$] *Average main: $21* ✉ *428 1st St., off Main St.* ☎ *530/661–0428* 🌐 *www.mojoskitchen428.com.*

Davis

10 miles west of Sacramento.

Davis began as a rich agricultural area and remains one, but it doesn't feel like a cow town. It's home to the University of California at Davis, whose 38,000-plus students hang at downtown cafés, galleries, and bookstores (most of the action takes place between 1st and 4th and C and G streets), lending the city a decidedly college-town feel.

GETTING HERE AND AROUND

Most people arrive here by car via Interstate 80. In a pinch, you can get here via Yolobus (🌐 *www.yolobus.com*) from Sacramento. Downtown is walkable. Touring by bicycle is also a popular option—Davis is very flat.

ESSENTIALS

VISITOR INFORMATION Davis Chamber of Commerce. ✉ *640 3rd St.* ☎ *530/756–5160* 🌐 *www.davischamber.com.*

👁 Sights

University of California, Davis
COLLEGE | A top research university, UC Davis educates many of the Wine Country's vintners and grape growers, in addition to farmers, veterinarians, and brewmasters, too. Campus tours depart from Buehler Alumni and Visitors Center. On a tour or not, worthy stops include the **Arboretum,** the **Manetti Shrem Museum of Art,** and the **Mondavi Center,** a striking modern glass structure that presents top-tier performing artists. ✉ *Visitor Center, 550 Alumni La.* ☎ *530/752–8111 for tour information* 🌐 *visit.ucdavis.edu.*

🍴 Restaurants

Mustard Seed
$$$$ | **AMERICAN** | Many patrons at this restaurant serving eclectic seasonal California cuisine are attending performing-arts events at the Mondavi Center a short walk away or visiting their kids at UC Davis. With hardwood floors and tables topped with white linen, the dining room is cozy and romantic, but when the weather's fine, the tree-shaded patio out back is the best place to enjoy dishes like tomato bisque topped with a puff pastry and herb-crusted rack of lamb. **Known for:** lunchtime soups, salads, and sandwiches; smooth service; reasonably priced California wines. [$] *Average main: $32* ✉ *222 D St., Suite 11* ☎ *530/758–5750* 🌐 *www.mustardseeddavis.com* 🕒 *Closed Mon. No lunch weekends.*

🛏 Hotels

Aggie Inn
$$ | **HOTEL** | A 2016 renovation added a touch of style to this basic hotel less than a block from the UC Davis campus whose spacious cottages work well for families. **Pros:** great location; full breakfast with hot entrée; suites with kitchens. **Cons:** can get a little noisy; motel feel; lacks amenities. [$] *Rooms*

from: $155 ✉ *245 1st St.* ☎ *530/756–0352* 🌐 *www.aggieinn.com* 🛏 *33 rooms* 🍴 *Breakfast.*

Best Western Plus Palm Court Hotel
$$ | **HOTEL** | Rich accents of gold and cobalt blue add boutique flair to the spacious rooms of this dependable choice for business and leisure travelers. **Pros:** convenient location; good on-site restaurant; congenial staff. **Cons:** pricey during major UC Davis events; no pool; chain's usual free breakfast not offered. [$] *Rooms from: $163* ✉ *234 D St.* ☎ *530/753–7100* 🌐 *www.palmcourtdavis.com* 🛏 *27 rooms* 🍴 *No meals.*

Lodi

34 miles south of Sacramento.

With with more than 110,000 acres of mostly alluvial soils planted to more than six dozen grape varietals—more types than in any other California viticultural area—Lodi is a major grape-growing hub. Eighty-five or so wineries do business in Lodi, the self-proclaimed Zinfandel Capital of the World, and neighboring towns. (Although plenty of Zin grows here, these days farmers devote even more land to Cabernet Sauvignon.) Founded on agriculture, Lodi was once the country's watermelon capital. Today it's surrounded by fields of asparagus, pumpkins, beans, safflowers, sunflowers, melons, squashes, peaches, and cherries. Lodi retains an old rural charm. You can stroll downtown or visit a wildlife refuge, all the while benefiting from a Sacramento River delta breeze that keeps this microclimate cooler in summer than anyplace else in the area.

GETTING HERE AND AROUND

Most of Lodi lies west of Highway 99 and east of Interstate 5. Amtrak trains stop here frequently. GrapeLine (☎ *209/333–6806*) buses pass by many wineries, but touring by car is more efficient.

ESSENTIALS

VISITOR INFORMATION Lodi Conference & Visitors Bureau. ✉ *25 N. School St.* ☎ *209/365–1195, 800/798–1810* 🌐 *www.visitlodi.com.*

👁 Sights

Berghold Estate Winery
WINERY/DISTILLERY | The tasting room at Berghold recalls an earlier wine era with its vintage Victorian interior, including restored, salvaged mantlepieces, leaded glass, and a 26-foot-long bar. The wines—among them Viognier, Cabernet Sauvignon, Syrah, and Zinfandel—pay homage to French wine-making styles. ✉ *17343 N. Cherry Rd., off E. Victor Rd./Hwy. 12* ☎ *209/333–9291* 🌐 *bergholdvineyards.com* 🎟 *Tastings $10* 🕒 *Closed Mon.–Wed.*

Bokisch Vineyards
WINERY/DISTILLERY | This operation 11 miles outside of downtown comes highly recommended for its excellent Spanish varietals and warm hospitality. The Albariño white and Tempranillo and Graciano reds often receive favorable critical notice, but everything is well made, including the non-Spanish old-vine Zinfandel. ■ **TIP→ Bokisch welcomes picnickers; pick up fixings in town and enjoy vineyard views while you dine.** ✉ *18921 Atkins Rd.* ✥ *From Hwy. 99 head east on Hwy. 12, north on Hwy. 88, and east on Brandt Rd.* ☎ *209/642–8880* 🌐 *www.bokischvineyards.com* 🎟 *Tastings $10* 🕒 *Closed Tues.–Thurs.*

Harney Lane Winery
WINERY/DISTILLERY | The Harney family has grown grapes in Lodi since the 1900s dawned but only started a winery in 2006. Three Zinfandels star in a lineup that includes Albariño, Chardonnay, a multigrape rosé, Petite Sirah, Tempranillo, and an old-vine Zinfandel port-style dessert wine. Extend your tasting with a glass in the "forest" garden, where three-century-old cedars supply the

shade. ■TIP→ **Learn about the family and Lodi on the Grape to Glass tour.** ✉ *9010 E. Harney La.* ✛ *About 6½ miles south of downtown, Hwy. 99 to E. Harney La. exit* ☎ *209/365–1900* ⊕ *www.harneylane.com* ✉ *Tastings $10, tour $25.*

Jeremy Wine Co.

WINERY/DISTILLERY | Originally a downtown bank, its original floors unfinished and as timeworn as the centerpiece bar Trettevik bought on eBay, the place has the feel of a chic old-time saloon. Sangiovese, Tempranillo, and a few other reds, most from well-sourced Lodi appellation grapes, are the specialty here, with Chardonnay among the few whites, and a chocolate port-style dessert wine for anyone with a sweet tooth. ✉ *6 W. Pine St., at S. Sacramento St.* ☎ *209/367–3773* ⊕ *jeremywineco.com* ✉ *Tastings $10.*

Lodi Wine & Visitor Center

WINERY/DISTILLERY | A fine place to sample Lodi wines, the center has a tasting bar and viticultural exhibits. You can also buy wine and pick up a free winery map. The knowledgeable staff can suggest wineries to explore. ✉ *2545 W. Turner Rd., at Woodhaven La.* ☎ *209/365–0621* ⊕ *www.lodiwine.com* ✉ *Tastings $8.*

Lucas Winery

WINERY/DISTILLERY | David Lucas was one of the first local producers to start making serious wine, and today his Zinfandels are among Lodi's most sought-after vintages. In addition to Zin, Lucas makes a light Chardonnay with subtle oaky flavors. The 90-minute tour, for which reservations are required, will get you up to speed on the Lodi wine appellation. ✉ *18196 N. Davis Rd., at W. Turner Rd.* ☎ *209/368–2006* ⊕ *www.lucaswinery.com* ✉ *Tastings from $10, tour (includes tasting) $75* ⊙ *Closed Mon. and Tues.*

★ M2 Wines

WINERY/DISTILLERY | With its translucent polycarbonate panels, concrete floor, and metal framing, this winery's high-ceilinged tasting room strikes an iconoclastic, industrial-sleek pose along an otherwise relentlessly rural lane north of Lodi. The Soucie Vineyard old-vine Zinfandel and the Trio Red Wine blend are the flagships. ✉ *2900 E. Peltier Rd., Acampo* ✛ *Take Hwy. 99 north from downtown to Peltier Rd. exit and head west* ☎ *209/339–1071* ⊕ *www.m2wines.com* ✉ *Tastings $10.*

★ McCay Cellars

WINERY/DISTILLERY | Wine critics applaud owner-winemaker Michael McCay's pursuit of balance and restraint with his flagship TruLux Zinfandel and Faith Lot 13 Zin from century-old vines. A longtime grower who started his namesake label in 2007, McCay also makes several rosés and whites, plus reds from Spanish (Tempranillo), Rhône (Grenache, Syrah), and lesser-seen varietals like Cinsaut and Carignane. He's often on-site at his lively downtown tasting room. ✉ *100 S. Sacramento St.* ✛ *At W. Oak St.* ☎ *209/368–9463* ⊕ *www.mccaycellars.com* ✉ *Tastings $10.*

★ Michael David Winery

WINERY/DISTILLERY | *Wine Enthusiast* magazine anointed Adam Mettler of Michael David its winemaker of the year in 2018 in recognition of his skill at creating smooth but characterful red blends like Petite Petit (Petite Sirah and Petit Verdot) and Freakshow Zinfandel. Taste these and other wines at the sprawling roadside **Phillips Farms Fruit Stand,** where fifth-generation farmers turned winery owners Michael and David Philips also sell their family's gorgeous produce. ■TIP→ **Breakfast or lunch at the stand's café is a treat.** ✉ *4580 W. Hwy. 12, at N. Ray Rd.* ☎ *209/368–7384* ⊕ *www.michaeldavidwinery.com* ✉ *Tastings from $10.*

Micke Grove Regional Park

AMUSEMENT PARK/WATER PARK | **FAMILY** | This 258-acre, oak-shaded park has a Japanese tea garden, picnic tables, children's play areas, an agricultural museum, a zoo, a golf course, and a water-play feature. **Fun Town at Micke Grove,** a family-oriented amusement park, is geared toward younger children. ✉ *11793 N. Micke Grove Rd.* ✣ *Off Hwy. 99 Armstrong Rd. exit* ☎ *209/953–8800 park info* 🎟 *From $5.*

St. Amant Winery

WINERY/DISTILLERY | Although its estate vineyards are east of town in Amador County, St. Amant is among the wineries that helped raise the profile of Lodi as a wine-growing region. Known for Tempranillo, Zinfandel, and port-style wines, the winery hosts guests in an industrial-park facility. Turn right immediately after passing through the gate. ✉ *1 Winemaster Way, Suite I* ✣ *Take E. Turner Rd. east to N. Guild Ave. north; turn right after 100 feet* ☎ *209/367–0646* 🌐 *www.stamantwinery.com* 🎟 *Tastings $5* 🕓 *Closed Mon.–Wed.*

Van Ruiten Family Winery

WINERY/DISTILLERY | To experience what Lodi's hardworking old Zinfandel vines can produce, sample the Van Ruiten Old Vine Zin and the Reserve Sideways Lot 69 Old Vine Zin. Other wines of note include the Chardonnays and the Cabernet-Shiraz blend. ✉ *340 W. Hwy. 12* ✣ *¾ mile west of Lower Sacramento Rd.* ☎ *209/334–5722* 🌐 *www.vrwinery.com* 🎟 *Tastings $10.*

🍴 Restaurants

The Dancing Fox Winery and Bakery

$ | AMERICAN | A good downtown stop especially for lunch, the Dancing Fox also has a tasting room for its eponymous wines. The restaurant, with decor that shimmers with fairy-tale whimsy, sandwiches, salads, pizzas, burgers, and wraps and has more than a dozen beers on tap. **Known for:** Sunday brunch; many dishes baked in Spanish wood-fired oven; historic downtown setting. [$] *Average main: $14* ✉ *203 S. School St.* ☎ *203/366–2634* 🌐 *www.dancingfoxwinery.com* 🕓 *Closed Mon. No dinner Sun.*

Pietro's Trattoria

$$$ | ITALIAN | Lodi's go-to spot for Italian American classics wins fans for its quality ingredients, Tuscan-courtyard ambience, and plant-filled outdoor patio (reservations essential on weekends). Expect straightforward, well-executed renditions of chicken piccata and veal cacciatore, filling lasagna and fettuccine Alfredo (with chicken or prawns), pizzas, and the like, all delivered with informal good cheer by the cadre of servers. **Known for:** wine list focused on local vintages; Italian American classics; meatball and chicken pesto with cheese sandwiches for lunch. [$] *Average main: $23* ✉ *317 E. Kettleman La.* ☎ *209/368–0613* 🌐 *www.pietroslodi.com* 🕓 *Closed Sun.*

★ Towne House Restaurant

$$$$ | MODERN AMERICAN | Lodi power breakfasts and lunches and special-occasion dinners often take place in the distinguished rooms of this former residence behind, and part of, the Wine and Roses hotel. Painted in rich, textured hues offset by wide white molding, the rooms exude a subtle sophistication matched by seasonal dishes that might include a Niman Ranch pork chop with miso-molasses glaze or Hawaiian opah with nori risotto. **Known for:** dozens of local wines by the glass; nightly live music; fresh seasonal local ingredients. [$] *Average main: $38* ✉ *2505 W. Turner Rd., at Woodhaven La.* ☎ *209/371–6160* 🌐 *winerose.com/the-restaurant.*

🛏 Hotels

The Inn at Locke House

$$ | B&B/INN | Built between 1862 and 1882, the inn occupies a pioneer doctor's family home that rates a listing on the National Register of Historic Places. **Pros:** eager-to-please hosts; peace and quiet; local farm products in full breakfast. **Cons:** remote location; can be hard to find; lacks amenities of a full-service hotel. [$] *Rooms from: $149* ✉ *19960 Elliott*

Rd., Lockeford ☎ *209/727–5715* 🌐 *www.theinnatlockehouse.com* 🛏 *5 rooms* 🍴 *Free Breakfast.*

Wine & Roses Hotel

$$$ | **HOTEL** | Set on 7 acres amid a tapestry of informal gardens, this hotel has cultivated a sense of refinement typically associated with Napa or Carmel. **Pros:** luxurious setting; popular restaurant; spa treatments. **Cons:** expensive for the area; some guests mention that walls are thin; many events. [$] *Rooms from: $249* ✉ *2505 W. Turner Rd.* ☎ *209/334–6988* 🌐 *www.winerose.com* 🛏 *66 rooms* 🍴 *No meals.*

Nevada City

4 miles north of Grass Valley.

Nevada City, once known as the Queen City of the Northern Mines, is the most appealing of the northern Mother Lode towns. The iron-shutter brick buildings that line downtown streets contain antiques shops, galleries, boutiques, B&Bs, restaurants, a winery, and some tasting rooms. Gas street lamps add to the romance. At one point in the 1850s, Nevada City had a population of nearly 10,000—enough to support much cultural activity. Today, about 3,000 people live here, but the performing-arts scene remains vibrant.

GETTING HERE AND AROUND

You'll need a car to get here. Take Highway 20 east from Interstate 5 or west from Interstate 80. Highway 49 is the north–south route into town. Gold Country Stage vehicles (☎ *530/477–0103*) serve some attractions on weekdays.

ESSENTIALS

VISITOR INFORMATION Nevada City Chamber of Commerce. ✉ *132 Main St.* ☎ *530/265–2692* 🌐 *www.nevadacitychamber.com.*

👁 Sights

Firehouse No. 1

BUILDING | With its gingerbread-trim bell tower, Firehouse No. 1 has been one of the Gold Country's most distinctive buildings since 1861. The museum inside, worth a peek if it's open, houses artifacts from the gold rush, the Nisenan people, the ill-fated Donner Party, and the altar from a Chinese joss house (temple). ✉ *214 Main St.* ☎ *530/265–3937* 🌐 *www.nevadacountyhistory.org* 🎟 *Donation suggested* 🕓 *Closed Mon. and Tues. and Nov.–Apr.*

Nevada City Winery

WINERY/DISTILLERY | The area's oldest winery, established in 1980 in the Miners Foundry garage, pours its wines, many from Sierra Foothills grapes, in a newer nearby tasting room whose patio perches over the operation's current wine-making facility. Chardonnay is the best-seller, with Cabernet Franc and Rhône and Italian reds among the other specialties. ✉ *321 Spring St., at Bridge St.* ☎ *530/265–9463, 800/203–9463* 🌐 *www.ncwinery.com* 🎟 *Tastings from $8.*

Szabo Vineyards

WINERY/DISTILLERY | Taste for yourself what makes Sierra Foothills wines unique at the brick-walled sipping salon of owner-winemaker Alex Szabo. In addition to growing the grapes 7 miles west of his downtown tasting room and making the wines, Alex is often the one pouring them. His Zinfandel, Petite Sirah, Grenache, Syrah, and other wines impress with their soft tannins, ample acidity, and long finish. ✉ *316 Broad St., at York St.* ☎ *530/265–8792* 🌐 *www.szabovineyards.com* 🎟 *Tastings $9* 🕓 *Closed Mon.–Wed.*

Restaurants

Friar Tuck's

$$$ | EUROPEAN | Popular Friar Tuck's specializes in creative, interactive fondues and has an extensive menu of seafood, steaks, and pasta dishes. The sparkling interior has a late-19th-century ambience—it's one of Nevada City's best indoor spaces. **Known for:** cheese fondue; varied selection of mostly California wines; live music nightly. $ Average main: $28 ⊠ 111 N. Pine St. ☎ 530/265–9093 ⊕ friartucks.com ⊘ No lunch.

New Moon Cafe

$$$$ | AMERICAN | Although not eye-catching from outside, New Moon Cafe hugs you in an exquisite dining experience once you enter. Organic salads, homemade ravioli, fresh line-caught fish, and locally sourced beef, chicken, and pork dishes appear on the seasonally changing menu. **Known for:** a cosmopolitan meal in rural Gold Country; crème brûlée and other desserts; well-selected California and international wines. $ Average main: $32 ⊠ 203 York St. ☎ 530/265–6399 ⊕ www.thenewmooncafe.com ⊘ Closed Mon. No lunch weekends.

South Pine Cafe

$ | AMERICAN | Locals flock here at breakfast time for lobster Benedict, chorizo tacos, and other dishes that are anything but your ordinary eggs and pancakes. Imaginative burritos and burgers and more lobster in the form of a melt sandwich appear for lunch. **Known for:** homemade muffins; vegan and gluten-free options; additional Grass Valley location. $ Average main: $13 ⊠ 110 S. Pine St. ☎ 530/265–0260 ⊕ www.southpinecafe.com ⊘ No dinner.

Three Forks Bakery & Brewing Co.

$ | AMERICAN | Baked goods, wood-fired pizzas, excellent coffee (teas and kombucha, too), and microbrews made on-site draw locals and tourists to this redbrick spot with a high, heavy-beamed open ceiling. The food's ingredients come from nearby organic sources; the beers on tap range from a blonde and a pale ale to a double IPA and a porter. **Known for:** lunch and dinner menu changes with the seasons; breads, muffins, scones, cookies, and cakes; soups and salads. $ Average main: $14 ⊠ 211 Commercial St. ☎ 530/470–8333 ⊕ www.threeforksnc.com ⊘ Closed Tues.

Hotels

Deer Creek Inn

$$$ | B&B/INN | The main veranda of this cozy 1860 Queen Anne Victorian overlooks lush gardens that roll past a rose-covered arbor to the creek below (where you can pan for gold). **Pros:** relaxing creek sounds; afternoon wine gathering; gourmet breakfast. **Cons:** expensive for the area; minimum weekend-stay requirement; lacks full-service hotel amenities. $ Rooms from: $195 ⊠ 116 Nevada St. ☎ 530/264–7038 ⊕ www.deercreekinn.net ⇱ 4 rooms ⑩ Free Breakfast.

Madison House Bed & Breakfast

$$$ | B&B/INN | A convenient downtown location, filling breakfasts showcasing local organic products, and welcoming hosts who exceed expectations make for a winning combination at this northern Gold Country bed-and-breakfast inside a romantic Victorian house. **Pros:** landscaped garden and sun porch; homemade baked goods; historic, romantic atmosphere. **Cons:** no elevator to upper-floor rooms; some noise and sun in front rooms; weekend minimum-stay requirement. $ Rooms from: $185 ⊠ 427 Broad St. ☎ 530/470–6127 ⊕ www.themadisonhouse.net ⇱ 5 rooms ⑩ Free Breakfast.

Outside Inn

$ | HOTEL | FAMILY | It looks like a typical one-story motel, but the Outside Inn offers a variety of unique accommodations inspired by nature or activities in nature (there's a climbing wall in the rock-climbing suite), in an ideal location to enjoy Northern California's four seasons. **Pros:** fun reinvention of a motel; convenient to trails and hikes; affiliated Inn Town Campground for camping and glamping. **Cons:** rooms are on the small side; a half mile from town; weekend minimum-stay requirement. $ *Rooms from: $99* ⊠ *575 E. Broad St.* ☎ *530/265–2233* ⊕ *www.outsideinn.com* ⇥ *15 rooms* ⭘ *No meals.*

🎭 Performing Arts

Miners Foundry
ARTS CENTERS | The foundry, erected in 1856, produced machines for gold mining and logging. The Pelton Water Wheel, a power source for the mines (the wheel also jump-started the hydro-electric power industry), was invented here. The building is now used to stage art, dance, music, and film events. ⊠ *325 Spring St.* ☎ *530/265–5040* ⊕ *www.minersfoundry.org.*

Nevada Theatre
ARTS VENUE | Mark Twain, Emma Nevada, and Jack London have all appeared on stage at this 1865 redbrick edifice. The West Coast's longest continuously operating theater building, today it presents art and independent films, spoken-word artists, comedians, local theater groups, and live music. ⊠ *401 Broad St., at Commercial St.* ☎ *530/265–6161* ⊕ *www.nevadatheatre.com.*

Grass Valley

24 miles north of Auburn.

More than half of California's total gold production was extracted from mines around Grass Valley, including the Empire Mine, which, along with the North Star Mining Museum, is among the Gold Country's most fascinating attractions. Nearby Nevada City has better dining and lodging options, though.

GETTING HERE AND AROUND
You'll need a car to get here. Take Highway 20 east from Interstate 5 or west from Interstate 80. Highway 49 is the north–south route into town. Gold Country Stage (☎ *530/477–0103*) provides public transit. Expect a moderate wait.

⊙ Sights

★ Empire Mine State Historic Park
NATIONAL/STATE PARK | **FAMILY** | Starting with the "secret map" that mine management hid from miners, you can relive the days of gold, grit, and glory, when this mine was one of the biggest and most prosperous hard-rock gold mines in North America. Empire Mine yielded an estimated 5.8 million ounces of gold from 367 miles of underground passages. You can walk into a mine shaft and peer into dark, deep recesses, and almost imagine what it felt like to work this vast operation. Dressed-up docents portraying colorful characters who shaped Northern California's history share stories about the period. The grounds have the exquisite Bourn Cottage (call for tour times), picnic tables, and gentle trails—perfect for a family outing. ⊠ *10791 E. Empire St.* ☎ *530/273–8522* ⊕ *www.empiremine.org* ⊠ *$7.*

Holbrooke Hotel
HOTEL—SIGHT | A Main Street icon built in 1851, the hotel hosted entertainer Lola Montez and writer Mark Twain as well as Ulysses S. Grant and other U.S. presidents. New owners who took over in 2018 are renovating the property a section at a time. If it's open when you visit, the saloon is worth a peek as one of the oldest operating west of the Mississippi. ⊠ *212 W. Main St.* ☎ *530/273–1353* ⊕ *www.holbrooke.com.*

North Star Mining Museum
MUSEUM | **FAMILY** | Housed in a former power house, the museum displays the 32-foot-high Pelton Water Wheel, said

to be the largest ever built. It was used to power mining operations and was a forerunner of the modern turbines that generate hydroelectricity. Other exhibits, some geared to children, document life in the mines and the environmental effects mining had on the area. You can picnic nearby. ✉ *10933 Allison Ranch Rd.* ☎ *530/264–7569* 🌐 *www.nevadacounty-history.org* 🎟 *Donation requested.*

🍴 Restaurants

Cirino's at Main Street
$$ | ITALIAN | FAMILY | A family-owned spot with exposed brick walls, a tall ceiling, and a well-worn bar and floor, Cirino's serves up a vast menu of hefty Italian American favorites like Corsican rosemary chicken, steak à la Gorgonzola, and pork chop Milanese. The bar crew, which slings the signature Bloody Mary and other specialty cocktails, is as friendly as the rest of the team. **Known for:** house-made soups and sauces; family-friendly attitude; full-dinner "butcher shop" menu items with soup or salad, starch, and vegetable. [$] *Average main: $22* ✉ *213 W. Main St.* ☎ *530/477–6000* 🌐 *www.cirinosatmainstreet.com.*

Valentina's Organic Bistro & Bakery
$ | AMERICAN | The emphasis is on wellness and organic non–genetically modified ingredients at this wide-windowed, simply decorated roadside restaurant, whose owners' inspiration for providing healthful cuisine to their community grew out of the lengthy illness of one of their daughters. Locals love the pastries, burritos, quesadillas, waffles, and "wamlets" (omelets cooked in a waffle iron) for breakfast and the burgers, sandwiches, burritos, burrito bowls, and salads for lunch. **Known for:** coffee, chai and other teas, smoothies, and blended juices; muffins, scones, brownies, and cinnamon rolls; outdoor patio. [$] *Average main: $12* ✉ *841 Sutton Way* ☎ *530/272–4470* 🌐 *www.valentinasbistro.com* 🕒 *Closed Sun. No dinner.*

🍸 Nightlife

The Pour House
BARS/PUBS | The owners of this downtown bar across from the Holbrooke Hotel aim to please lovers of beer and wine with a dozen-plus pours of each, many from local and regional craft breweries and boutique wineries. The storefront space (closed Monday), with a long redbrick wall on the bar side, serves soups, dips, soft pretzels, and other comfort bites; there's live music some nights. ✉ *217 W. Main St., at Church St.* ☎ *530/802–5414* 🌐 *www.thepourhousegv.com.*

Auburn

18 miles northwest of Coloma, 34 miles northeast of Sacramento.

Halfway between San Francisco and Reno, Auburn convenient to gold-rush sites, outdoor recreation opportunities, and wineries. The self-proclaimed "endurance capital of the world" is abuzz almost every summer weekend with running, cycling, rafting or kayaking, and equestrian events. Old Town Auburn has its own gold-rush charm, with narrow climbing streets, cobblestone lanes, wooden sidewalks, and many original buildings. ■ **TIP→ Fresh produce, flowers, and baked goods are for sale at the farmers' market, held on Saturday morning year-round.**

GETTING HERE AND AROUND

Amtrak serves Auburn, though most visitors arrive by car on Highway 49 or Interstate 80. Once downtown, you can tour on foot.

👁 Sights

Bernhard Museum Complex
MUSEUM | Party like it's 1889 at this space whose main structure opened in 1851 as the Traveler's Rest Hotel and for 100 years was the residence of the Bernhard

family. The congenial docents, dressed in Victorian garb, describe the family's history and 19th-century life in Auburn. ✉ *291 Auburn–Folsom Rd.* ☎ *530/889–6500* 🌐 *www.placer.ca.gov* 🎫 *Free.*

Placer County Courthouse

MUSEUM | Visible from the highway, Auburn's standout structure is the Placer County Courthouse. The classic bronze-domed building houses the Placer County Museum, which documents the area's history—Native American, railroad, agricultural, and mining—from the early 1700s to 1900. Look for the wall safe housing gold nuggets valued at more than $300,000 today. ✉ *101 Maple St.* ☎ *530/889–6500* 🌐 *www.placer.ca.gov/departments/facility/placermuseums* 🎫 *Free.*

🍴 Restaurants

Auburn Alehouse

$ | **AMERICAN** | **FAMILY** | Inside the historic American Block building, which dates to 1856, you can see this craft operation's beers being made through glass walls behind the dining room, which serves burgers, nachos, salads, wraps, and other decent gastropub fare. Gold Country Pilsner, Old Town Brown, Gold Digger IPA, and Hop Donkey Red Ale are all Great American Beer Festival award winners. **Known for:** chicken, pork, and fish tacos; herb-brined buttermilk fried chicken; kids menu. [$] *Average main: $13* ✉ *289 Washington St.* ☎ *530/885–2537* 🌐 *www.auburnalehouse.com.*

Awful Annie's

$ | **AMERICAN** | **FAMILY** | One of Auburn's favorite old-time breakfast and lunch spots entices patrons with waffles, pancakes, Monte Cristo French toast, and a slew of egg dishes you can wash down with an award-winning Bloody Mary or two. Expect burgers, sandwiches, and more Bloody Marys for lunch. **Known for:** heartiest breakfast in the foothills; Grandma's bread pudding with brandy sauce; second location in nearby Lincoln. [$] *Average main: $12* ✉ *13460 Lincoln Way* ☎ *530/888–9857* 🌐 *www.awfulannies.com* 🕓 *No dinner.*

★ **Carpe Vino**

$$$ | **MODERN AMERICAN** | What started as a boutique wine retailer has become a must-visit experience for foodies who appreciate the hearty and imaginative French-inspired dishes served in this gem's charming setting, a restored 19th-century saloon. Sophisticated seasonal fare that always includes a vegan option is presented in a nonchalant, almost effortless way, as if ingredients rolled right from the farm basket onto your plate. **Known for:** extensive and varied wine list; impeccable service; 21-plus only. [$] *Average main: $27* ✉ *1568 Lincoln Way* ☎ *530/823–0320* 🌐 *www.carpevinoauburn.com* 🕓 *Closed Sun. and Mon. No lunch.*

The Pour Choice

$ | **AMERICAN** | Black subway tiles, contemporary bistro furniture, and a gray-marble counter lit by orb-shape Edison bulbs lend urban flair to this fine spot for a craft coffee or one of more than two dozen local, national, and international brews on tap. In a sliver of a space once occupied by a drugstore, the Pour Choice, which bills itself as Auburn's living room, serves light fare that might include a chèvre and Gouda grilled-cheese sandwich on ciabatta with bacon. **Known for:** upbeat vibe; talented baristas; outdoor terrace in good weather. [$] *Average main: $12* ✉ *177 Sacramento St.* ☎ *530/820–3451* 🌐 *thepourchoice.com.*

🛏 Hotels

Holiday Inn Auburn Hotel

$$ | **HOTEL** | **FAMILY** | Above the freeway across from Old Town, this hotel renovated in 2016 has a welcoming lobby and chain-standard but well-organized rooms. **Pros:** work areas in all

Almost 6 million ounces of gold were extracted from the Empire Mine.

rooms; suitable base for Gold Country exploring; on-site restaurant. **Cons:** lacks style; some traffic noise; can't walk to Old Town restaurants and shops. $ *Rooms from: $165* ✉ *120 Grass Valley Hwy.* ☎ *530/887–8787, 800/814–8787* ⊕ *www.auburnhi.com* ⇥ *96 rooms* ⦿ *No meals.*

★ Park Victorian

$$$$ | **B&B/INN** | A walking path leads down to Old Town Auburn from this boutique hotel inside a lavishly restored 1867 mansion set on 6½ secluded acres atop Snowden Hill. **Pros:** stunning views; within walking distance of Old Town restaurants; some original architectural details retained. **Cons:** pricey for the Gold Country but the gracious hosts deliver; minimum weekend-stay requirement; one room suitable for one adult only. $ *Rooms from: $295* ✉ *195 Park St.* ☎ *530/330–4411* ⊕ *www.parkvictorian. com* ⇥ *6 rooms* ⦿ *Free Breakfast.*

Coloma

On Hwy. 49 between Placerville (8 miles) and Auburn (18 miles).

The California gold rush started in Coloma. "My eye was caught with the glimpse of something shining in the bottom of the ditch," James Marshall recalled.

GETTING HERE AND AROUND

A car is the only practical way to get to Coloma, via Highway 49. Once parked, you can walk to all the worthwhile sights.

⊙ Sights

★ Marshall Gold Discovery State Historic Park

NATIONAL/STATE PARK | **FAMILY** | Most of Coloma lies within the historic park along the banks of the south fork of the American River. Though crowded with tourists in summer, Coloma hardly resembles the mob scene it was in 1849, when 2,000 prospectors staked out claims along the streambed. The town's population grew to 4,000, supporting seven hotels, three banks, and many stores and businesses. But when reserves of the precious metal dwindled, prospectors left as quickly as they had come. A working reproduction of an 1840s mill lies near the spot where James Marshall first saw gold. Trails lead to the mill, remnants of buildings and mining equipment, and a statue of Marshall with sublime views. ■ TIP→ For $7 per person, rangers give gold-panning lessons on the hour, year-round. ⊠ 310 Back St., off Hwy. 49 ☎ 530/622–3470 ⊕ www.parks.ca.gov/marshallgold ⊠ $8 per vehicle.

Placerville

44 miles east of Sacramento.

It's hard to imagine now, but in 1849 about 4,000 miners staked out every gully and hillside in Placerville, turning the town into a rip-roaring camp of log cabins, tents, and clapboard houses. The area was then known as Hangtown, a graphic allusion to the nature of frontier justice. It took on the name Placerville in 1854 and became an important supply center for the miners. (*Placer* is defined roughly as valuable minerals found in riverbeds or lakes.) Mark Hopkins, Philip Armour, and John Studebaker were among the industrialists who got their starts here. Today Placerville ranks among the hippest towns in the region, its Main Street abuzz with indie shops, coffeehouses, and wine bars, many of them inside rehabbed historic buildings.

GETTING HERE AND AROUND

You'll need a car to get to and around Placerville; it's a 45-minute drive from Sacramento via U.S. 50.

◉ Sights

Apple Hill

FARM/RANCH | FAMILY | From July to late December, Apple Hill Growers Association members open their orchards and vineyards for apple and berry picking, picnicking, and wine, cider, pressed-juice, and other tastings. With treasure hunts, pond fishing, pie making, and other activities, the area is a magnet for families, but there's plenty to entice adults as well. Stop at Wofford Acres Vineyard if only see the dramatic view of the American River canyon below. The Apple Hill website has a printable map and an up-to-date events calendar, or download the Official Apple Hill Growers app. ■ TIP→ Traffic often backs up on weekends, so take U.S. 50's Camino exit or visit during the week (although kids-oriented events are on weekends). ⊠ Placerville ✛ Starting 2 miles east of Hwy. 49, Exits 48–57 off U.S. 50 ☎ 530/644–7692 ⊕ www.applehill.com.

Boeger Winery

WINERY/DISTILLERY | Founder Greg Boeger's ancestors established a Napa Valley winery in the late 19th century. In 1972, he revived a gold rush–era farm that once supported fruit and nut orchards, a winery, and a distillery. These days Boeger produces estate wines from 30 varietals grown on two parcels totaling 100 acres, with Sauvignon Blanc and Barbera the best sellers and Zinfandel and Primitivo also worth seeking out. ■ TIP→ The creek-side picnic area fronting the tasting room hosts bands and food vendors on Friday evenings in summer (reserve space well ahead). ⊠ 1709 Carson Rd. ✛ Head north from U.S. 50, Exit 48, then northeast (right) on Carson Rd. ☎ 530/622–8094 ⊕ www.boegerwinery.com ⊠ Tastings from $5.

Hangtown's Gold Bug Park & Mine

MINE | FAMILY | Take a self-guided tour of this fully lighted mine shaft within a park owned by the City of Placerville. The worthwhile audio tour (included) makes clear what you're seeing. ■ **TIP→ A shaded stream runs through the park, and there are picnic facilities.** ✉ *2635 Goldbug La., Exit U.S. 50 at Bedford Ave. and follow signs* ☎ *530/642–5207* 🌐 *www.goldbugpark.org* 🎫 *Park free; mine tour $7* 🕒 *Closed weekdays Nov.–Mar. except for a few holidays.*

★ Holly's Hill Vineyards

WINERY/DISTILLERY | The founders of this woodsy hilltop winery 7 miles south of Apple Hill tasted Châteauneuf-du-Pape on their honeymoon, sparking a lifetime passion for Rhône wines made in classic French style. Mourvèdre is a specialty, by itself and in blends with Grenache, Syrah, or both. Carignane, Counoise, and other lower-profile Rhône reds are also made, along with whites that include the Roussanne-dominant Patriarche Blanc blend. Taste these beautifully crafted estate wines in a space with views that extend 75 miles on a clear day, and picnic outside when you're done. ✉ *3680 Leisure La., off Pleasant Valley Rd.* ✣ *From U.S. 50, Exit 49, follow Broadway east to Newtown Rd. and Pleasant Valley Rd. southeast* ☎ *530/344–0227* 🌐 *www.hollyshill.com* 🎫 *Tastings $5.*

★ Lava Cap Winery

WINERY/DISTILLERY | Nineteenth-century miners knew if they found the type of volcanic rocks visible everywhere on this winery's property that gold was nearby. These days the rocky soils and vineyard elevations as high as 2,800 feet play pivotal roles in the creation of fruit forward yet elegant wines with a hint of minerals. Zinfandel, Grenache, Cabernet Franc, and Petite Sirah star among the reds, Chardonnay and Viognier among the whites. ■ **TIP→ After a tasting you can picnic on the patio and enjoy Sierra foothills vistas.** ✉ *2221 Fruitridge Rd.* ☎ *530/621–0175* 🌐 *www.lavacap.com* 🎫 *Tastings from $5.*

Lewis Grace Winery

WINERY/DISTILLERY | A bright red 1890 barn greets visitors to this winery on land whose vineyards were replaced with apples during Prohibition. Wine critics praise the estate Tempranillo and Cabernet Sauvignon for their structure and elegance, with Grenache, Syrah, and Cabernet Franc the other noteworthy reds and Viognier and Pinot Gris the standout whites. Grapevines surround the high-ceilinged tasting room and adjacent patio on two sides, with views of the Crystal Range, its peaks snow-capped more than half the year, in the distance. ✉ *2701 Carson Rd.* ☎ *530/642–8424* 🌐 *gracepatriotwines.com* 🎫 *Tastings $5* 🕒 *Closed Tues.*

🍴 Restaurants

Allez

$$ | **FRENCH** | The tale of how the couple running this spot for to-go or dine-in French food came to be husband and wife says all one needs to know about their passion for beautifully crafted cuisine: he won her heart with his escargot sauce. In a casual space with ocher walls, six utilitarian stools at the wine bar, and a few tables inside and out, the two serve baguette sandwiches, salads, crepes, stews, and entrées like steak au poivre and wild-mushroom pasta. **Known for:** all-day prix-fixe menu (a deal), plus à la carte; sandwich, salad, and dessert lunch boxes; French pastries. [$] *Average main: $21* ✉ *4242 Fowler La., Diamond Springs* ✣ *Off Hwy. 49, 3 miles south of downtown Placerville* ☎ *530/621–1160* 🌐 *www.allezeldorado.com* 🕒 *Closed Sun. and Mon.*

Heyday Cafe

$$ | **AMERICAN** | Inside an exposed-brick 1857 former assay office where miners exchanged gold nuggets for the coin of the realm, the Heyday is a happy haven for salads, panini, and thin-crust pizzas at lunch and dinner entrées that might include seared salmon with coffee-smoked carrot puree and duck-fat confit half-roasted chicken. The mood here is casual, but the food is prepared with style. **Known for:** sherry-infused lobster bisque; local to international wine list; molasses gingerbread cake. [$] *Average main: $22* ✉ *325 Main St.* ☎ *530/626–9700* 🌐 *www.heydaycafe.com.*

★ Smith Flat House

$$$ | **MODERN AMERICAN** | Carefully sourced ingredients from local purveyors, meticulous execution, and a historic setting at a former mine site have made this restaurant 3 miles east of downtown a hit among locals, Gold Country tourists, and travelers heading to or from Tahoe. The seasonally changing menu might include crab ravioli, bouillabaisse, and the Black and White entrée of filet mignon and perfectly grilled prawns. **Known for:** waffle Benedict at Sunday brunch; salads, pizzas, burgers for weekend lunch; "hyper local, domestic, and international" wine list. [$] *Average main: $29* ✉ *2021 Smith Flat Rd.* ✣ *From U.S. 50, Exit 49, head north on Point View Dr. and Jacquier Rd. and east on Smith Flat Rd.* ☎ *530/621–1003* 🌐 *www.smithflathouse.com* 🕓 *Closed Mon. and Tues. No lunch Wed.–Fri.*

Solid Ground Brewing

$ | **ECLECTIC** | The chef at this brewpub with a no-nonsense industrial decor (high ceilings, concrete floor, huge garage doors) tailors the cuisine to the namesake beers produced by two Sierra foothills natives, one with an enology degree, the other with extensive experience in European beer making. Along with gastropub stalwarts like spicy wings, smoked bratwurst, and sliders (both with grass-fed beef, one with IPA bacon jam and Brie), chicken korma or salmon tartine might also appear on the menu. **Known for:** cheesy fried polenta tots; wine blended into some beers; live music at Sunday brunch and other times. [$] *Average main: $12* ✉ *553 Pleasant Valley Rd., Diamond Springs* ✣ *Off Hwy. 49, 3 miles south of downtown Placerville* ☎ *530/344–7442* 🌐 *solidgroundbrewing.com.*

🛏 Hotels

★ Eden Vale Inn

$$$$ | **B&B/INN** | **FAMILY** | Handcrafted by the owners, this lavish but rustic B&B occupies a converted turn-of-the-20th-century hay barn, the centerpiece of which is a 27-foot slate fireplace that rises to a sloping ceiling of timber beams. **Pros:** rooms are exceptionally plush; the patio and grounds are stunning; plenty of places outside for kids to run. **Cons:** expensive for the area; summer weekends book up far ahead; weekend minimum-stay requirement. [$] *Rooms from: $365* ✉ *1780 Springvale Rd.* ☎ *530/621–0901* 🌐 *www.edenvaleinn.com* 🛏 *7 rooms* 🍴 *Free Breakfast.*

★ Lucinda's Country Inn

$$$ | **B&B/INN** | Effusive but not intrusive hospitality is the trademark of this contemporary inn between Placerville and Plymouth whose spacious light-filled suites have views of the oaks, firs, and other trees surrounding the property. **Pros:** romantic setting; convenient for wine touring; filling breakfast and catered dinner option. **Cons:** some rooms sleep only two; long drive to Placerville or Plymouth restaurants; weekend minimum-stay requirement. [$] *Rooms from: $180* ✉ *6701 Perry Creek Rd., Fair Play* ☎ *530/409–4169* 🌐 *www.lucindascountryinn.com* 🛏 *5 rooms* 🍴 *Free Breakfast.*

Plymouth

20 miles south of Placerville.

The most concentrated Gold Country wine-touring area lies in the hills of the Shenandoah Valley, east of Plymouth—you could easily spend two or three days just hitting the highlights. Zinfandel is the primary grape grown here, but area vineyards produce many other varietals, from Rhônes like Syrah and Mourvèdre to Italian Barberas and Sangioveses. Most wineries are open for tastings at least on Friday and weekends, and some of the top ones are open daily; many welcome picnickers.

GETTING HERE AND AROUND

Highway 49 runs north–south through Plymouth's small downtown. Reach the Shenandoah Valley by heading east from the highway on Fiddletown Road and then north on Plymouth-Shenandoah Road. You will need a car to explore the valley and its vineyards.

👁 Sights

Amador Cellars

WINERY/DISTILLERY | Larry and Linda Long made wine out of their home in Truckee for 15 years before opening their down-home Amador County winery. Their son Michael is head winemaker, daughter Ashley his assistant. Estate-grown Zinfandel is the biggest seller, but this small operation also does well with Syrah, Barbera, Tempranillo, and the Portuguese varietal Touriga (one of the Port grapes), and there's a GSM (Grenache, Syrah, and Mourvèdre) Rhône-style blend. Just outside the modest tasting space, two oak trees shade a patio where guests are welcome to picnic. ⊠ *11093 Shenandoah Rd., Plymouth* ☎ *209/245–6150* ⊕ *amadorcellars.com.*

Bella Grace Vineyards

WINERY/DISTILLERY | For all the Gold Country's caverns and underground mines, few opportunities exist to taste wine in a cave, but at Bella Grace you can do so in one with vineyard views from the entrance while you sip. Barbera and old-vine Zinfandel earn the most critical acclaim; the Vermentino, Viognier, and Primitivo are worth checking out, too.

■ **TIP** ➔ **Cave tastings take place only three days a week (picnickers welcome), but the winery's downtown Sutter Creek space**

is open daily. ⊠ *22715 Upton Rd., off Steiner Rd., Plymouth* ☎ *209/418–5040* ⊕ *www.bellagracevineyards.com* ☾ *Closed Mon.–Thurs.*

Charles Spinetta Winery and Wildlife Gallery

WINERY/DISTILLERY | A casual, family-owned winery that appeals to non–wine drinkers with wildlife watercolors, sculptures, and other artworks and to lovers of sweet wines with orange and black muscats and the Zinfandel-based Zinetta, Charles Spinetta, in business since 1984, also makes dry reds. Petite Sirah, Barbara, Zinfandel, and its cousin Primitivo are among the latter ones that stand out. ⊠ *12557 Steiner Rd., off Shenandoah Rd., Plymouth* ☎ *209/245–3384* ⊕ *www.charlesspinettawinery.com* ☾ *Closed Tues. and Wed.*

★ Jeff Runquist Wines

WINERY/DISTILLERY | Judges at the 2018 San Francisco International Wine Competition bestowed Winery of the Year honors on this operation whose tasting room ranks among the Shenandoah Valley's jolliest. Known for elegant, fruit-forward wines with velvety tannins, Jeff Runquist specializes in Barbera, Zinfandel, and Petite Sirah but makes red wines from nearly two dozen varietals from Amador County, Lodi, Clarksburg, and several other appellations. ⊠ *10776 Shenandoah Rd., Plymouth* ☎ *916/245–6282* ⊕ *www. jeffrunquistwines.com* ⌸ *Free* ☾ *Closed Tues. and Wed.*

★ Scott Harvey Wines

WINERY/DISTILLERY | Owner-winemaker Scott Harvey helped elevate the profile of Amador County wines in the 1970s, later developing two wine programs in the Napa Valley before returning full time to the Sierra foothills. Harvey describes the foothills as similar to Italy's Piemonte region, where Barbera originated, but with one additional benefit: it's sunnier here, which this grape loves. Barbera, Zinfandel (one from vines planted in 1869), and Syrah are the focus, but you'll also find Cabernet Sauvignon and other reds along with Sauvignon Blanc, Riesling, and sparkling wine. ✉ *10861 Shenandoah Rd., Plymouth* ☎ *209/245–3670* 🌐 *www.scottharveywines.com* 🎫 *Tastings $7.*

Sobon Estate

WINERY/DISTILLERY | You can sip fruity, robust Zinfandels—old vine and new—and learn about wine making and Shenandoah Valley pioneer life at the museum here. This winery was established in 1856 and has been run since 1989 by the owners of Shenandoah Vineyards (whose wines you can also taste). To sample the best of the Zins, pay the modest fee for the reserve tasting. ✉ *14430 Shenandoah Rd., Plymouth* ☎ *209/245–4455* 🌐 *www.sobonwine.com* 🎫 *Tastings from $5.*

Terre Rouge and Easton Wines

WINERY/DISTILLERY | The winery of Bill Easton and Jane O'Riordan achieves success with two separate labels: terre Rouge, which focuses on Rhône-style wines, makes some of the area's best Syrahs. The Easton label specializes in Zinfandel from old and new vines, including an Amador County bottling. **■ TIP→ You can picnic on the shaded patio here, and there's a pétanque court nearby.** ✉ *10801 Dickson Rd., Plymouth* ☎ *209/245–4277* 🌐 *www.terrerougewines.com* 🎫 *Tastings $5* 🕒 *Closed Tues. and Wed.*

★ Turley Wine Cellars

WINERY/DISTILLERY | Zinfandel fans won't want to miss Turley, which makes a dozen and a half single-vineyard wines (collectors love them) from old-vine grapes grown all over California. Some of the wines, including a few from Amador County, are available only in the tasting room. Petite Sirah and Cabernet Sauvignon are two other emphases. Guests are welcome to purchase wine by the glass or bottle and picnic amid old olive trees when the weather's good, under an awning if not. **■ TIP→ Customized "focused tastings," offered twice daily by reservation, showcase wines from key vineyard sites.** ✉ *10851 Shenandoah Rd., Plymouth* ☎ *209/245–3938* 🌐 *www.turleywinecellars.com/amador* 🎫 *Tastings from $10.*

Vino Noceto

WINERY/DISTILLERY | Owners Suzy and Jim Gullett draw raves for their Sangioveses, which range from light and fruity to rich and heavy. They also produce small lots of Pinot Grigio, Barbera, Zinfandel, and other varietals. Tastings take place in the red barn where the couple began operations in the 1980s. ✉ *11011 Shenandoah Rd., at Dickson Rd., Plymouth* ☎ *209/245–6556* 🌐 *www.noceto.com* 🎫 *Tastings free, tour $18.*

🍴 Restaurants

Amador Vintage Market

$ | **AMERICAN** | Area caterer Beth Sogaard spiffed up Plymouth's original general store, transforming its handsome red- and sand-color brick building into a dandy stop for quiche and other breakfast fare and gourmet sandwiches and deli specialties like Muscovy duck confit, Dijon potato salad, and house-smoked salmon. A recent turkey meat loaf pepped up with blue cheese and porcini mushrooms is typical of Sogaard's reimagining of comfort-food staples you can enjoy on-site, at nearby wineries, or on picnic tables at the park next door. **Known for:** homemade truffle potato chips; selection of local wines (good way to tell where to go tasting); order for pickup or nearby delivery. [$] *Average main: $9* ✉ *9393 Main St., Plymouth* ☎ *209/245–3663* 🌐 *bethsogaard.com/vintage-market* 🕒 *No dinner.*

★ Taste

$$$$ | **MODERN AMERICAN** | A serendipitous find in downtown Plymouth, Taste serves eclectic modern dishes made from fresh local fare. Phyllo-wrapped mushroom "cigars" are a small-plate staple, and seared day boat scallops, rack of lamb, and duck confit are examples of owner-chef Mark Berkner's sustainably

Reliving the Gold Rush

When James W. Marshall burst into John Sutter's Mill on January 24, 1848, carrying flecks of gold in his hat, the millwright unleashed the glittering California gold rush with these immortal words: "Boys, I believe I've found a gold mine!" In short order, California's coastal communities began to empty as prospectors flocked to the hills, getting a jump on East Coasters, who didn't hear about the gold boom until the *New York Herald* reported it in mid-August. The gold rush began in earnest in 1849. Before it was over, Columbia's mines alone had yielded $87,000,000, and California's Mother Lode—a vein of gold-bearing quartz that stretched 150 miles across the Sierra Nevada foothills—had been nearly tapped dry.

Pure Vacation Treasure

The gold rush soon became the gold bust—by 1855 digging for the precious mineral had become increasingly difficult, and large corporations had monopolized mining operations— but today you can relive the era. Journey down the serpentine, nearly 300-mile-long Gold Country Highway,

a two-lane route appropriately numbered 49, to find pure vacation treasure: fascinating Mother Lode towns, rip-roaring mining camps, and significant strike sites.

Pan the Streams

In Placerville and other towns you can still pan the streams. Grab a non-Teflon-coated pan with sloping sides and head to the hills. Find a stream—preferably one containing black sand—you can stoop beside, and then scoop out sediment to fill your pan. Add water, then gently shake the pan sideways, back and forth. Doing this allows any gold to settle at the bottom. Pick out and toss away any larger rocks. Keep adding water, keep shaking the pan, and slowly pour the loosened waste gravel over the rim of the pan. If you're left with gold, yell "Eureka!" (California's state motto) then put it in a glass container. Your findings may not make you rich, but will entitle you to bragging rights. If you'd rather go with a guide, plenty of attractions and museums in the Gold Country will let you try your hand at prospecting.

sourced, creative entrées. **Known for:** superb beer and wine list; knowledgeable sommeliers; Monday prix-fixe menu. $ *Average main: $37* ⊠ *9402 Main St., Plymouth* ☎ *209/245–3463* ⊕ *www. restauranttaste.com* ⊙ *Closed Wed. No lunch Mon.–Thurs.*

Hotels

Amador Harvest Inn

$$ | **B&B/INN** | This B&B adjacent to the Deaver Vineyards tasting room occupies a bucolic lakeside spot in the Shenandoah Valley. **Pros:** rustic charm; hospitable

innkeeper; hearty breakfasts. **Cons:** no children allowed; somewhat spare decor; minimum weekend-stay requirement. $ *Rooms from: $150* ⊠ *12455 Steiner Rd., Plymouth* ☎ *209/245–5512, 800/217–2304* ⊕ *amadorharvestinn.com* ⌐ *4 rooms* ⧀ *Free Breakfast.*

★ Rest Hotel Plymouth

$$ | **B&B/INN** | The team behind Plymouth's Taste restaurant converted two adjacent run-down buildings into this boutique hotel whose individually decorated rooms rank among the area's finest. **Pros:** attention to detail; continental breakfast's baked goods; evening wine hour.

Did You Know?

You can still pan for gold, but any shiny stuff will usually be worthless iron pyrite. Here a young prospector tries his hand at Marshall Gold Discovery State Park.

Cons: minimum stay requirement some weekends; lacks big-city hotel amenities; some noise in street-side rooms. $ *Rooms from: $142* ✉ *9372 Main St., Plymouth* ☎ *209/245–6315* ⊕ *www.hotel-rest.net* ➵ *16 rooms* ❢❍❢ *Free Breakfast.*

Amador City

6 miles south of Plymouth.

The history of tiny Amador City (population 200) mirrors the boom-bust-boom cycle of many Gold Country towns. With an output of $42 million in gold, its Keystone Mine was one of the most productive in the Mother Lode. After all the gold was extracted, the miners cleared out, and the area suffered. Amador City now derives its wealth from tourists, who come to browse through its antiques and specialty shops.

GETTING HERE AND AROUND
Park where you can along Old Highway 49 (a bypass diverts Highway 49 traffic around Sutter Creek and Amador City), and walk around.

Hotels

Imperial Hotel
$$ | B&B/INN | An 1879 hotel on the bend in this one-block town, the Imperial charms its guests with six second-floor rooms whose antique furnishings include iron-and-brass beds, gingerbread flourishes, and, in one instance, art-deco appointments. **Pros:** history-evoking stay; good restaurant and bar; two rooms with balconies. **Cons:** hotel and bar are the town nightlife; rooms and hotel could use a refresh; noise issues in street-side rooms. $ *Rooms from: $130* ✉ *14202 Old Hwy. 49* ☎ *209/267–9172* ⊕ *www.imperialamador.com* ➵ *9 rooms* ❢❍❢ *Free Breakfast.*

Sutter Creek

2 miles south of Amador City.

Sutter Creek is a charming conglomeration of balconied buildings, Victorian homes, and neo–New England structures. At any time of year Main Street (formerly part of Highway 49) is worth a stroll for its shops selling antiques and works by local artists and craftspeople. Tasting rooms of note include Bella Grace and Scott Harvey. Sites like the 19th-century water-powered Knight Foundry and Monteverde Store Museum are worth a peek if you're in town on the rare days they're open, but always accessible is the open-air Miners' Bend Historic Gold Mining Park.

GETTING HERE AND AROUND
Arrive here by car on Highway 49. There's no public transit, but downtown is walkable. The visitor center organizes walking tours.

ESSENTIALS
INFORMATION Sutter Creek Visitor Center. ✉ *71A Main St.* ☎ *209/267–1344* ⊕ *www.suttercreek.org.*

Sights

Miners' Bend Historic Gold Mining Park
CITY PARK | A dedicated band of volunteers converted a parking lot into a compact open-air tribute to the area's mining legacy. Signs along the path describe 19th-century mining operations and the 16 pieces of equipment used to extract or process ore on display. ✉ *29 Old Hwy. 49* ☎ *209/560–6880* ⊕ *suttercreekfoundation.org* ➵ *Free.*

Monteverde Store Museum
MUSEUM | This store, opened 1896, is a relic from the past: its final owner walked out more than four decades ago and never returned. These days you can peruse what he left behind, including typical wares from a century ago, an elaborate antique scale, and a chair-encircled potbellied stove. ✉ *3 Randolph St.* ☎ *209/267–0493.*

🍴 Restaurants

Gold Dust Pizza
$$ | PIZZA | Zesty well-made pies like the Miner Moe's BBQ Chicken, with red onions, pineapple, bacon, and cheese make this casual spot a few steps off Main Street an excellent choice, particularly for lunch or a mid-afternoon snack. You can also build your own pizza or order a sandwich; there's some indoor seating, but when the weather's good most folks eat outside on the front patio or the creek-side one out back. **Known for:** ultracrispy crust; chicken wings and calzone; combo meals. [$] *Average main: $16* ✉ *20 Eureka St., off Main St., Davis* ☎ *209/267–1900.*

🛏 Hotels

Eureka Street Inn
$$ | B&B/INN | The lead- and stained-glass windows and the original redwood paneling, wainscoting, and beams lend a cozy feel to this 1914 Craftsman-style bungalow whose rooms, furnished with antiques, all have a gas stove or fireplace. **Pros:** quiet location; large bathrooms; engaging innkeeper. **Cons:** weekend minimum-stay requirement; lacks pool, room service, and other hotel amenities; old-time feel may not work for all travelers. [$] *Rooms from: $165* ✉ *55 Eureka St.* ☎ *209/267–5500* 🌐 *www.eurekastreet-inn.com* 🔑 *4 rooms* 🍴 *Free Breakfast.*

The Foxes Inn of Sutter Creek
$$$ | B&B/INN | The rooms in this 1857 yellow-clapboard house are handsome, with high ceilings, antique beds, and armoires; five have gas fireplaces. **Pros:** lovely inside and out; friendly owners; discounts at Helwig Winery for guests (same ownership). **Cons:** minimum weekend-stay requirement; pricey in season; per website inn is "most suitable" for children 12 and over. [$] *Rooms from: $199* ✉ *77 Main St.* ☎ *209/267–5882, 800/987–3344* 🌐 *www.foxesinn.com* 🔑 *7 rooms* 🍴 *Free Breakfast.*

Grey Gables Inn
$$$ | B&B/INN | Charming if you like lace and frills, this inn—with rooms named after British poets—brings the English countryside to Gold Country. **Pros:** English-manor feel; tasteful interiors and grounds; complimentary bottle of wine. **Cons:** adjacent town's busy main drag; minimum weekend-stay requirement; dated design. [$] *Rooms from: $220* ✉ *161 Hanford St.* ☎ *209/267–1039, 800/473–9422* 🌐 *www.greygables.com* 🔑 *10 rooms* 🍴 *Free Breakfast.*

Volcano

12½ miles northeast of Jackson, 13 miles east of Sutter Creek, 17 miles southeast of Plymouth.

Many roads, all of them winding, all of them scenic, lead to Volcano, an off-the-beaten-path former mining town of about 120 people, the entirety of which is a California Historical Landmark. Pick up a pastry at the Kneading Dough Bakery and head out any time of year to the main attraction, Black Chasm Cavern. In early spring, weather and other factors permitting, combine the cave visit with one to see Daffodil Hill's namesake flowers in bloom.

GETTING HERE AND AROUND

A car is the practical way to get to Volcano, via Highway 88 east from Jackson; Ridge Road and Highway 88 east from Sutter Creek (alternate route: Sutter Creek–Volcano Road, also east); or Fiddletown Road east from Plymouth to Shake Ridge Road southwest to Charleston Road southeast. GPS can be sketchy here, so plot and save your route when you have good coverage.

Sights

Black Chasm Cavern National Natural Landmark

CAVE | FAMILY | Guided 50-minute tours take you past stalactites, stalagmites, and rare formations of delicate helictites in three underground chambers, one of which also contains a lake. Black Chasm isn't the largest cave in the Gold Country, but its crystals dazzle both eye and camera—the Landmark Chamber, the tour's third stop, inspired a scene in the 2003 film *The Matrix Reloaded*. Outside is an area where kids can "pan" for crystals. ⊠ *15701 Pioneer Volcano Rd., Volcano* ✛ *¾ mile south of Volcano off Pine Grove–Volcano Rd.* ☎ *209/296–5007* ⊕ *blackchasmcavern.com* ⌧ *$19* ⊘ *Closed Mon.–Thurs. in Jan.*

Daffodil Hill

GARDEN | Each spring a 7-acre hillside east of Sutter Creek erupts in a riot of yellow and gold as (in a good year) hundreds of thousands of daffodils burst into bloom. The garden is the work of the McLaughlin family, which has owned this site since 1887. Daffodil plantings began in the 1930s. The display usually takes place between mid-March and mid-April. ■TIP→ **Call for daily weather updates.** ⊠ *18310 Rams Horn Grade Rd., Volcano* ✛ *From Main St., Hwy. 49, in Sutter Creek, take Shake Ridge Rd. east 13 miles* ☎ *209/296–7048* ⊕ *suttercreek. org/sutter-creek-events-daffodil-hill-amador-county* ⌧ *Free* ⊘ *Closed late Apr.–early Mar.*

 Restaurants

Kneading Dough Bakery

$ | AMERICAN | Breakfast entrées, soups, soufflés, and sandwiches are on the menu at this beloved spot for pastries, tarts, coffee cakes, scones, cookies, muffins, cupcakes, and other baked goods, all so well composed you'll wonder why your larger town doesn't have bakers this accomplished. Inside a 19th-century stone-and-wood building, the bakery has indoor and outdoor seating. **Known for:** enthusiastic owner and staff; Nana's Famous Cinnamon Rolls; order ahead (see website) for pickup or delivery to Sutter Creek or Jackson. Ⓢ *Average main: $9* ⊠ *16154 Main St., Volcano* ☎ *209/296–4663* ⊕ *www.kneadingdoughbakery.com.*

Hotels

Volcano Pub + Inn

$ | B&B/INN | The folks behind Plymouth's Taste restaurant and Rest hotel operate this four-room second-floor inn whose first incarnation, from the 1880s into the 1920s, was as a saloon and boardinghouse for miners and other mostly long-term guests. **Pros:** daily specials at pub; simple but pleasing decor; homemade full breakfast with egg dish, fresh fruit, and baked goods. **Cons:** per website "not suited for small children"; two rooms have a shower but no tub; minimum weekend-stay requirement. Ⓢ *Rooms from: $97* ⊠ *21375 Consolation St., Volcano* ☎ *209/296–7711* ⊕ *www.volcanounion.com* ⌫ *4 rooms* ⏹ *Free Breakfast.*

Jackson

8 miles south of Sutter Creek.

Jackson wasn't the Gold Country's rowdiest town, but the party lasted longer here than most anywhere else: "girls' dormitories" (aka brothels) and nickel slot machines flourished until the mid-1950s. Jackson also had the world's deepest and richest gold mines, the Kennedy and the Argonaut, which together produced $70 million in gold. Most of the miners who worked the lode were of Serbian or Italian origin, and they gave the town a European character that persists to this day. Jackson has pioneer cemeteries whose headstones tell the stories of local Serbian and Italian families. The city's official website (🌐 *ci.jackson.ca.us; click on "Visitor Center"*) has cemetery and walking-tour maps.

GETTING HERE AND AROUND

Arrive by car on Highway 49. You can walk to downtown sights but otherwise will need a car.

Sights

Kennedy Gold Mine

HISTORIC SITE | On weekends, docents offer guided 90-minute surface tours of one of the most prolific mines of the gold-rush era and one of the deepest gold mines in the world. Exhibits inside the remaining buildings illustrate how gold flakes were melted for shipment to San Francisco and how "skips" were used to lower miners and materials into the mile-long shaft and carry ore to the surface. ✉ *Kennedy Mine Rd., at Argonaut La.* ✥ *½ mile east of Hwy. 49* ☎ *209/223–9542* 🌐 *www.kennedy-goldmine.com* 🎟 *Free; guided tour $12* 🕓 *Closed weekdays year-round, weekends Nov.–Feb.*

Preston Castle

HISTORIC SITE | History buffs and ghost hunters regularly make the trip to this fantastically creepy 156-room Romanesque Revival structure erected in 1894 to house troubled youth. Having fallen into disrepair, the building is slowly undergoing a full restoration. On tours, which take place on many Saturdays between April and August, you'll hear all sorts of spine-tingling tales. ✉ *909 Palm Dr., Ione* ✥ *12 miles west of Jackson via Hwys. 88 and 104* ☎ *209/256–3623* 🌐 *www.prestoncastle.com* 🎟 *$20* 🕓 *Closed Sept.–Mar.*

Restaurants

Mel and Faye's Diner

$ | **AMERICAN** | **FAMILY** | Since 1956, the Gillman family has been serving up its famous "Moo Burger" with two patties and special sauce—so big it still makes cow sounds, presumably. Breakfast is available all day at this homey diner. **Known for:** loads of atmosphere; milk shakes and floats; freshly baked pies. [$] *Average main: $14* ✉ *31 Hwy. 88* ☎ *209/223–0853* 🌐 *melandfayes.homestead.com.*

Teresa's Place

$$ | **ITALIAN** | Ease back in time at this rustic roadside favorite of Gold Country residents and regulars that dates back to 1921, when its namesake, an Italian immigrant, opened a boardinghouse for local miners. Run by her descendants, the restaurant serves unfussy renditions of Italian American classics—pastas, wood-fired pizzas, veal and chicken dishes, and steak and seafood. **Known for:** full bar; local wines and microbrews; minestrone soup from family recipe. [$] *Average main: $21* ✉ *1235 Jackson Gate Rd.* ✥ *From downtown head north 1¼ miles on N. Main St.; from Hwy. 49 north of town take Jackson Gate Rd. east 1½ miles* ☎ *209/223–1786* 🌐 *www.teresas-place.com* 🕓 *Closed Wed. and Thurs. No lunch Sat.–Tues.*

Hotels

Hotel Léger

$ | **HOTEL** | A rowdy miners' haunt during the gold rush, this convivial saloon and hotel about 8 miles south of Jackson contains 13 rooms decorated with a mishmash of Victorian antiques and more utilitarian pieces. **Pros:** rich in history, including a 2013 "Hotel Impossible" makeover; individually decorated rooms with antiques and utilitarian pieces; on-site restaurant and saloon. **Cons:** creaky wooden floors; rooms above the saloon can be noisy; some rooms feel cramped. [$] *Rooms from: $110* ✉ *8304 Main St., Mokelumme Hill* ☎ *209/286–1401* 🌐 *www.hotelleger.com* 🔑 *13 rooms* 🍴 *No meals.*

Angels Camp

20 miles south of Jackson.

Angels Camp is famous chiefly for its May jumping-frog contest, based on Mark Twain's short story "The Celebrated Jumping Frog of Calaveras County." The writer reputedly heard the story of the jumping frog from Ross Coon, proprietor of Angels Hotel, which opened in 1856. Sidewalk plaques downtown à la the Hollywood Walk of Fame celebrate the winning frogs in the continuing competition. Either training's gotten way better, or something else is in play—the 1929 victor jumped only 4 feet, but for the last three decades most of the leaps have been from 18- to 20-plus feet. In addition to the contests, Angels Camp's draws include its explorable subterranean caverns and river and lake fishing spots for salmon, trout, and bass.

GETTING HERE AND AROUND
Angels Camp is at the intersection of Highway 49 and Highway 4. You'll need a car to get here and around.

◉ Sights

★ Angels Camp Museum
HISTORIC SITE | FAMILY | Learn a little bit about Mark Twain's "The Celebrated Jumping Frog of Calaveras County"—and Angels Camp's celebrated frog-jumping contests—at this museum's street-side facility, then head to the 3-acre spread behind it for a fascinating survey of gold rush–era mining history. The grounds include a carriage house with pre-automotive farming and passenger coaches and wagons, a large building with mining equipment, and, outside in its original mountings, the 27-foot-diameter water wheel that powered machinery at the area's Angels Quartz Mine. ⌂ *753 S. Main St.* ☏ *209/736–2963* ⊕ *angelscamp. gov/museum* ⊠ *$7.*

★ Moaning Cavern
CAVE | FAMILY | For a different sort of underground jewel, wander into an ancient limestone cave, where stalactites and stalagmites, not gold and silver, await. Take the 235-step Spiral Tour down a staircase built in 1922 into this vast cavern, or descend farther on the Expedition Tour caving adventure. Outside are zip lines and a climbing tower. ⌂ *5350 Moaning Cave Rd., Vallecito* ⊕ *About 2 miles south of Vallecito off Parrotts Ferry Rd.* ☏ *209/736–2708* ⊠ *Tours from $20, zip line $50.*

Murphys

10 miles northeast of Angels Camp.

Murphys is the Gold Country's most compact, orderly town, with enough shops and restaurants to keep families busy for at least a half day, and more than 20 tasting rooms within walking distance. To learn about the full lineup, drop by the Calaveras Wine Alliance's visitor center, whose staffers are good at pairing visitors with the right space, in some case providing discount passes. A well-preserved hamlet of white-picket fences and Victorian houses, Murphys exhibits an upscale vibe. Horatio Alger, Ulysses S. Grant, and other celebs passed through here, staying at what's now called the Murphys Historic Hotel & Lodge when they, along with many other 19th-century tourists, came to investigate the giant sequoia groves in nearby Calaveras Big Trees State Park.

GETTING HERE AND AROUND
Murphys is 10 miles northeast of Highway 49 on Highway 4. You'll need to drive here. Parking can be difficult on summer weekends.

CONTACT
Calaveras Wine Alliance
⌂ *202 Main St.* ☏ *209/728–9467* ⊕ *calaveraswines.org.*

👁 Sights

★ Calaveras Big Tree State Park

NATIONAL/STATE PARK | FAMILY | The park protects hundreds of the largest and rarest living things on the planet—magnificent giant sequoia redwood trees. Some are 3,000 years old, 90 feet around at the base, and 250 feet tall. There are campgrounds, cabin rentals, and picnic areas; swimming, wading, fishing, and sunbathing on the Stanislaus River are popular in summer. Enjoy the "three senses" trail, designated for the blind, with interpretive signs in braille that guide visitors to touch the bark and encourage children to slow down and enjoy the forest in a more sensory way. ✉ 1170 E. Hwy. 4, Arnold ✛ 15 miles northeast of Murphys, 4 miles northeast of Arnold ☎ 209/795–2334 ⊕ www.parks.ca.gov/calaverasbigtrees 🎫 $10 per vehicle.

DEA Bathroom Machineries

STORE/MALL | History resides inside this two-story plumbing shop, and not just because it occupies the 1901 former I.O.O.F. (International Order of Odd Fellows) Hall, constructed of lumber milled nearby. Though it exists primarily as a specialist in antique plumbing fixtures and vintage parts, the museumlike shop displays (all for sale) old tobacco tins, stereoscope cards, lamps, sewing machines, glassware, and similar items, plus souvenirs. ■TIP➔ **Be sure to slip upstairs to check out the deluxe porcelain toilets, some as ornate as fine china and selling in the thousands.** ✉ 495 Main St. ☎ 209/728–2031 ⊕ deabath.com.

Ironstone Vineyards

WINERY/DISTILLERY | Tours here take in spectacular gardens and underground tunnels cooled by a waterfall and include the automated performance of a restored silent-movie-era pipe organ. On display near the tasting room is a 44-pound specimen of crystalline gold. The winery, known for Merlot, Cabernet Sauvignon, Cabernet Franc, and old-vine Zinfandel, hosts concerts and other events. Its deli has picnic items. ■TIP➔ **Ironstone is worth a visit even if you don't drink wine.** ✉ 1894 6 Mile Rd. ✛ From Main St. in town, head south on Scott St. ☎ 209/728–1251 ⊕ www.ironstonevineyards.com 🎫 Tastings $5.

Lavender Ridge

WINERY/DISTILLERY | A stone building dating to 1859 houses this boutique winery's tasting room, which also sells artisanal cheeses and lavender products. Lavender Ridge's longtime owner-winemaker uses traditional French methods to craft wines from organically farmed Rhône grapes. The lineup includes single-varietal Viognier, Roussanne, and Grenache Blanc whites (also Rolle, aka Vermentino) and Grenache, Syrah, and Mourvèdre reds, single varietal and in a blend. Cheeses accompany all tastings, a nice touch. ✉ 425 Main St. ☎ 209/728–2441 ⊕ lavenderridgevineyard.com 🎫 Tastings from $10.

Mercer Caverns

CAVE | Light-hearted, well-informed guides lead 45-minute tours (208 steps down, 232 steps up) into caverns a prospector named Walter J. Mercer discovered in 1885. Millions of years in the making, the sheer, draperylike formations and aragonite crystals that resemble snowflakes enthrall visitors. ■TIP➔ **Dress in layers (even in summer) and wear nonskid closed-toe shoes for this mildly strenuous adventure.** ✉ 1665 Sheep Ranch Rd. ☎ 209/728–2101 ⊕ mercercaverns.net 🎫 $18.

Murphys Old Timers Museum

MUSEUM | A quirky blast from the past in a stone building that survived three 19th-century fires that destroyed downtown, the museum documents Murphys history with artifacts of the gold-rush period, the area's native people, and pioneer families, among them the town's namesake clan. ■TIP➔ **Historic walking tours take place on Saturday at 10 am.** ✉ 470 Main St. ☎ 209/728–1160 🎫 Free *(donation encouraged)* ⏲ *Closed Tues.–Thurs. and Mon. except holidays.*

Newsome Harlow Wines

WINERY/DISTILLERY | Single-vineyard Sierra Foothills Zinfandels are the passion of Newsome Harlow's part owner and winemaker Scott Klann. The ebullient Klann also makes Petite Sirah, Syrah, Carignane, and the Meritage blend of Cabernet Sauvignon and other Bordeaux varietals—whites include a Sauvignon Blanc on several local restaurants' wine lists. The lively in-town tasting room benefits from its upbeat staff, playful atmosphere, and indoor and outdoor tasting spaces, the latter with a fire pit and large sofa affectionately dubbed the Big A$$ Couch. ✉ *403 Main St.* ☎ *209/728–9817* 🌐 *nhvino.com.*

🍴 Restaurants

★ Alchemy Cafe

$$ | **AMERICAN** | A casual spot on the eastern edge of town with yellow walls and artsy French posters, Alchemy serves sturdy comfort food like braised lamb shank over fried polenta, drunken noodles with shrimp and Asian vegetables, and grilled Atlantic salmon. Pork belly, fried calamari with roasted jalapeños, and mussels with fries are among the starters that pair well with a bourbon rosemary sour specialty cocktail or perhaps the Alchemy Bloody Mary, hopped up with a splash of Firestone Pivo Pilsner. **Known for:** Calaveras County wines well represented; open continuously from lunch through dinner; mildly pricey but reliable. [$] *Average main: $22* ✉ *191 Main St.* ☎ *209/728–0700* 🌐 *alchemymurphys.com.*

Aria Bakery & Espresso Cafe

$ | **BAKERY** | For a place as small as it is, this bakery café often smelled before seen turns out a staggering array of sweet and savory pastries, sandwiches, salads, and desserts you can enjoy with a well-brewed (if not always swiftly made) coffee, espresso drink, or tea. The croissants are golden and flaky, the quiches moist and filling, and the scones large and flavorful; the breads for lunchtime sandwiches include sourdough, focaccia, and polenta wheat. **Known for:** limited seating inside and out; blueberry muffins, savory croissants, and other baked goods; vegetarian, vegan, gluten-free options. [$] *Average main: $12* ✉ *458 Main St., Suite B* ☎ *209/728–9250* ⏲ *Closed Tues. and Wed. in winter. No dinner.*

Dogwood

$$$ | **AMERICAN** | One of Calaveras County's shining stars serves fresh seasonal cuisine in a cabinlike white-walled space with an open kitchen and hardwood floors and tables. The meat-heavy menu might include grilled flat-iron steak, grilled pork porterhouse with bourbon-maple jus, and short ribs with caramelized shallot whipped potatoes, with grilled salmon and rice pilaf, three-cheese flamed-roasted pasilla pepper, and roasted cauliflower for those seeking lighter fare. **Known for:** woodsy setting; warm hospitality; alfresco dining in good weather. [$] *Average main: $29* ✉ *1224 Oak Circle, Arnold* ✣ *12 miles north of Murphys off Hwy. 4* ☎ *209/813–7101* ⏲ *No lunch.*

Grounds

$$ | **AMERICAN** | From potato pancakes for breakfast to grilled rib eye for dinner, this bustling bistro with a series of wainscoted rooms and an outdoor patio has something for all palates. Lighter grilled vegetables, chicken, sandwiches, salads, and homemade soups always shine here, as do heartier fare that might include elk medallions and prawns, manicotti with goat cheese and ricotta, and a robust cioppino. **Known for:** full bar; wines by local producers; attentive service. [$] *Average main: $22* ✉ *402 Main St.* ☎ *209/728–8663* 🌐 *www.groundsrestaurant.com* ⏲ *No dinner Mon. and Tues.*

Hotels

Dunbar House 1880

$$$ | **B&B/INN** | The oversize rooms in this elaborate Italianate-style home have brass beds, down comforters, gas-burning stoves, and claw-foot tubs. **Pros:** great breakfasts; colorful gardens; accommodating staff. **Cons:** expensive in-season; not kid-friendly; minimum-stay requirement on weekends. [$] *Rooms from: $186* ✉ *271 Jones St.* ☎ *209/728–2897* 🌐 *www.dunbarhouse.com* 🛏 *6 rooms* 🍴 *Free Breakfast.*

Murphys Historic Hotel & Lodge

$$ | **HOTEL** | Mark Twain, John Wayne, Susan B. Anthony, Ulysses S. Grant, and the guy who invented Lipton tea are among the past guests of this 19th-century throwback in the heart of Murphys that's intriguing more for its place in history than the pedestrian experience it delivers in the present. **Pros:** historic ambience; old-time saloon; proximity to shops, restaurants, and tasting rooms. **Cons:** original building lacks modern amenities; newer building has motel feel; restaurant can be noisy. [$] *Rooms from: $139* ✉ *457 Main St.* ☎ *209/728–3444, 800/532–7684* 🌐 *www.murphyshotel.com* 🛏 *29 rooms* 🍴 *No meals.*

Murphys Inn Motel

$ | **HOTEL** | Reasonably well run if steadfastly nondescript, this two-story motel built in the late 1990s has two things going for it: a convenient location on the edge of downtown and bargain rates most of the year. **Pros:** clean rooms; bargain rates; convenient location. **Cons:** thin walls; some road noise; lacks style and big-hotel amenities. [$] *Rooms from: $93* ✉ *76 Main St.* ☎ *209/728–1818, 888/796–1800 reservations* 🌐 *www.murphysinnmotel.com* 🛏 *37 rooms* 🍴 *No meals.*

Victoria Inn

$$ | **B&B/INN** | Decorated with contemporary furnishings with 19th-century accents, this inn benefits from a prime Main Street location within walking distance of restaurants, shops, and wine-tasting rooms. **Pros:** convenient location; romantic feel; filling continental breakfast. **Cons:** no TVs in rooms; minimum weekend-stay requirement; noise issues in some rooms. [$] *Rooms from: $161* ✉ *420 Main St.* ☎ *209/728–8933* 🌐 *www.victoriainn-murphys.com* 🛏 *23 rooms* 🍴 *Free Breakfast.*

Columbia

14 miles south of Angels Camp.

Columbia is the gateway for Columbia State Historic Park, one of the Gold Country's most visited sites. It's a great place for families to participate in living-history activities, like candle dipping and soap making on weekends. There are several inviting spots for a picnic in the area.

GETTING HERE AND AROUND

The only way to get here is by car, via either Highway 4 (the northern route) or Highway 49 (the southern) from Angels Camp.

Sights

★ **Columbia State Historic Park**

NATIONAL/STATE PARK | **FAMILY** | Columbia is both a functioning community and a historically preserved gold-rush town. Usually you can ride a stagecoach, pan for gold, and watch a blacksmith working at an anvil. Street musicians perform in summer. Restored or reconstructed buildings include a Wells Fargo Express office, a Masonic temple, an old-fashioned candy store, saloons, a firehouse, churches, a school, and a newspaper office. At times, all are staffed to simulate a working 1850s town. The park also includes the **Historic Fallon House Theater,** a gorgeous Victorian structure where Broadway-quality shows are performed. The town's two 19th-century historic lodgings, the Fallon Hotel ($) and City Hotel ($–$$) perch you in the past; reserve a room or cottage at ⊕ *www. reservecalifornia.com.* ⊠ *11255 Jackson St.* ☎ *209/588–9128* ⊕ *www.parks. ca.gov/columbia* ☑ *Free.*

🎭 Performing Arts

Sierra Repertory Theater Company
THEATER | The company, established in 1979, presents a full season of dramas, comedies, and musicals at the Historic Fallon House Theater and another venue in east Sonora. ⊠ *11175 Washington St.* ☎ *209/532–3120* ⊕ *www.sierrarep.org* ☑ *From $37.*

Sonora

4 miles south of Columbia.

Miners from Mexico founded Sonora and made it the biggest town in the Mother Lode. Following a period of racial and ethnic strife, the Mexican settlers moved on, and Yankees built the commercial city visible today. Sonora's historic downtown section sits atop the Big Bonanza Mine, one of the richest in the state. Another mine, on the site of nearby Sonora High School, yielded 990 pounds of gold in a single week in 1879. Reminders of the gold rush are everywhere in Sonora, in prim Victorian houses, typical Sierra-stone storefronts, and awning-shaded sidewalks. Reality intrudes beyond the town's historic heart, with strip malls, shopping centers, and modern motels.

If the countryside surrounding Sonora seems familiar, that's because it has been the backdrop for many movies over the years. Scenes from *High Noon, For Whom the Bell Tolls, The Virginian, Back to the Future III, Unforgiven,* and many other films were shot here.

GETTING HERE AND AROUND
Arrive in Sonora by car via Highway 49 (if coming from Columbia, drive south on Parrots Ferry Road). Parking can be difficult on the busy main drag, Washington Street (Highway 49).

👁 Sights

Tuolumne County Museum and History Centers
MUSEUM | The small museum occupies a historic gold-rush-era building that served as a jail until 1960. Vintage firearms and paraphernalia, gold specimens, and Me-Wuk baskets are among the many artifacts on display. ⊠ *158 Bradford St.* ☎ *209/532–1317* ⊕ *www.tchistory.org* ☑ *Free* ⊗ *Closed Sun.*

🍽 Restaurants

Diamondback Grill and Wine Bar
$ | **AMERICAN** | The bright decor and refined atmosphere suggest more ambitious fare, but massive half-pound burgers and sandwiches like the Ultimate Grilled Cheese with smoked bacon and tomato between three thick slices of sourdough bread are what this place inside a late-19th-century stone-walled building is about. Locals crowd the tables, especially after 6 pm, for the ground-meat patties, beer-battered onion rings, veggie burgers, and fine wines. **Known for:** garlic fries; wine bar and wine club; homemade desserts. Ⓢ *Average main: $13* ⊠ *93 S. Washington St.* ☎ *209/532–6661* ⊕ *diamondback-grillsonora.com.*

🛏 Hotels

Barretta Gardens Bed and Breakfast Inn
$$ | **B&B/INN** | Perfect for a romantic getaway or peaceful escape, this elegant 1904 inn evokes days gone by with three antiques-filled parlors but doesn't skimp on creature comforts in the well-tended guest rooms, also decorated in period

style. **Pros:** mature gardens; delicious breakfasts; great location. **Cons:** only eight rooms; minimum-stay requirement; period look may not appeal to all travelers. $ *Rooms from: $159* ✉ *700 S. Barretta St.* ☎ *209/532–6039* ⊕ *www.barrettagardens.com* ⇆ *8 rooms* ⦿ *Free Breakfast.*

Best Western Sonora Oaks Hotel & Conference Center

$$ | HOTEL | The standard-motel-issue rooms, some upgraded in 2019, are clean and spacious at this east Sonora establishment; the larger ones have outdoor sitting areas. **Pros:** clean rooms and public areas; great location for Gold Country and Stanislaus forest; suites have hillside views. **Cons:** front rooms can be noisy (ask for room away from highway); chain feel; minor housekeeping lapses in public areas. $ *Rooms from: $159* ✉ *19551 Hess Ave.* ☎ *209/533–4400, 800/780–7234* ⊕ *www.bwsonoraoaks.com* ⇆ *100 rooms* ⦿ *Breakfast.*

Jamestown

4 miles south of Sonora.

Compact Jamestown supplies a touristy view of gold-rush-era life. Shops in brightly colored buildings along Main Street sell antiques and gift items, and there are a couple of wine-tasting rooms, Inner Sanctum for Spanish varietals and Gianelli's for Italian ones. You can try your hand at panning for gold here or explore a bit of railroad history.

GETTING HERE AND AROUND

Jamestown lies at the intersection of north–south Highway 49 and east–west Highway 108. You'll need a car to tour here.

⊙ Sights

Gold Prospecting Adventures

TOUR—SIGHT | FAMILY | You'll get a real feel (sort of) for the life of a prospector on the three-hour gold-panning excursions (reservations recommended) led by this outfit's congenial tour guides. You might even strike gold at the Jimtown Mine. Even if you're not panning, it's fun to look at the gold-rush artifacts on display here. ✉ *18170 Main St.* ☎ *209/984–4653* ⊕ *www.goldprospecting.com* ✉ *Call for prices.*

★ Railtown 1897 State Historic Park

NATIONAL/STATE PARK | FAMILY | A must for rail enthusiasts and families with kids, this is one of the most intact early roundhouses (maintenance facilities) in North America. You can hop aboard a steam train for a 40-minute journey— bring along the family dog if you'd like. The docents entertain guests with tales about the history of locomotion. Listen to the original rotor and pulleys in the engine house and take in the smell of axle grease. Walk through a genteel passenger car with dusty-green velvet seats and ornate metalwork, where Grace Kelly and Gary Cooper filmed a scene in the epic Western *High Noon.* ■TIP→ **Polar Express excursions at Christmastime sell out quickly.** ✉ *18115 5th Ave.* ☎ *209/984–3953* ⊕ *www.railtown1897.org* ✉ *Roundhouse tour $5; rides from $15.*

🍴 Restaurants

Service Station

$$ | AMERICAN | Exposed brick walls and a pressed-metal ceiling lend an air of nostalgia that's heightened by this restaurant's theme, the golden age of road trips and automobile service stations. Half-pounder burgers and pulled-pork, tri-tip, and other sandwiches and wraps count among the menu's highlights, along with small plates like nacho fries and fried calamari and entrées that might include chicken, grilled salmon, or filet mignon. **Known for:** upbeat vibe; local wines, craft beers on tap; salads and vegetarian wraps and burgers for noncarnivores. $ *Average main: $20* ✉ *18242 Main St.* ☎ *209/782–5122* ⊕ *jamestown-servicestation.com.*

Hotels

Black Oak Casino Resort

$ | RESORT | About 12 miles east of Jamestown off Highway 108, this flashy, contemporary property appeals heavily to casino gamers, but it's also a nice place to stay, with well-outfitted rooms and a Gold Country location. **Pros:** clean and spacious rooms; diversions for kids and adults; lounge hosts talented acts on weekends. **Cons:** smoking permitted in some casino areas; nothing quaint or historic about the place; far from town. $ *Rooms from: $109* ✉ *19400 Tuolumne Rd. N, Tuolumne* ☎ *209/928–9300, 877/747–8777* ⊕ *www.blackoakcasino. com/lodging* ➡ *148 rooms* ⦿ *No meals.*

Jamestown Hotel

$$ | HOTEL | The spacious light filled rooms of this hotel that celebrated its 100th anniversary in 2019 are decorated simply but with flair, and all have updated bathrooms with a period feel. **Pros:** convenient to shops, restaurants, and tasting rooms; balcony overlooking Main Street; on-site dining. **Cons:** rooms lack refrigerators, microwaves, TVs, and other amenities; rooms are above saloon and restaurant (some noise bleeds though); no elevator. $ *Rooms from: $138* ✉ *18153 Main St.* ☎ *209/984–3902* ⊕ *www.thejamestownhotel.com* ➡ *8 rooms* ⦿ *No meals.*

McCaffrey House Bed and Breakfast Inn

$$$ | B&B/INN | Surrounded by trees on the edge of the Stanislaus National Forest, McCaffrey's appeals to travelers seeking a remote retreat, in this case run by innkeepers with an eye for detail and a zeal for green practices. **Pros:** rooms outfitted with stoves and Amish quilts; nearby hiking; romantically remote. **Cons:** too remote for some; lacks amenities of larger properties; weekend minimum-stay requirement. $ *Rooms from: $189* ✉ *23251 Hwy. 108, Twain Harte* ✛ *20 miles east of Jamestown* ☎ *209/586–0757,* *888/586–0757* ⊕ *www.mccaffreyhouse. com* ➡ *8 rooms* ⦿ *Free Breakfast.*

National Hotel and Restaurant

$$ | B&B/INN | In business since 1859, the National has survived the gold rush, gambling, prostitution, at least two fires, a ghost named Flo, and Prohibition, and stands today a well-maintained property with all the authentic character and charm its storied past suggests. **Pros:** authentic character—feels straight out of a Western movie; views from odd-numbered rooms (plus Room 2); popular restaurant (good brunches). **Cons:** some rooms are small; most even-numbered rooms have no view; some noise issues. $ *Rooms from: $150* ✉ *18183 Main St.* ☎ *209/984–3446* ⊕ *www.national-hotel. com* ➡ *9 rooms* ⦿ *Free Breakfast.*

Mariposa

50 miles south of Jamestown.

Mariposa marks the southern end of the Mother Lode. Much of the land in this area was part of a 44,000-acre land grant Colonel John C. Fremont acquired from Mexico before gold was discovered and California became a state. Many people stop here on the way to Yosemite National Park, about an hour's drive east on Highway 140.

GETTING HERE AND AROUND

If driving, take Highway 49 or Highway 140. YARTS (⊕ *www.yarts.com*), the regional transit system, can get you to Mariposa from the Central Valley town of Merced (where you can also transfer from Amtrak) or from Yosemite Valley. Otherwise, you'll need a car to get here and around.

🍴 Restaurants

Charles Street Dinner House

$$$ | AMERICAN | Centrally located Charles Street, its rustic decor heavy on the wood and Old West adornments, at once evokes gold-rush days and the 1980s, when it opened. The extensive straightforward menu includes hand-cut steaks, honey-barbecue baby back ribs, several pasta dishes, chicken, pork loin, lamb, a few well-adorned burgers, and some vegetarian options. **Known for:** excellent steaks; cheesecake, sundae, crème brûlée for dessert; local feel. $ *Average main: $27 ⊠ Hwy. 140 and 7th St. ☎ 209/966–2366 ⊕ www.charlesstreetdinnerhouse.net ⊗ No lunch weekends.*

Savoury's

$$ | **AMERICAN** | Seafood, pasta, and portobello mushrooms are some of the savory treats that draw high praise from locals at the kind of refined space you'd expect in an urban environment, not in mellow Mariposa. Contemporary paintings and photography set aglow by track lighting create a gallerylike atmosphere. **Known for:** well-prepared steak and seafood; full bar; vegetarian and vegan options. $ *Average main: $20 ⊠ 5034 Hwy. 140 ☎ 209/966–7677 ⊗ Closed Wed. No lunch.*

🛏 Hotels

Mariposa Lodge

$$ | **HOTEL** | Modern and tastefully landscaped, the lodge is a solid option for those who want to stay within 30 miles of Yosemite National Park without spending a fortune. **Pros:** convenient location; relatively inexpensive; clean rooms. **Cons:** no frills; lacks amenities of big-city properties; rooms near front pick up road noise. $ *Rooms from: $159 ⊠ 5052 Hwy. 140 ☎ 209/966–3607, 800/966–8819 ⊕ www.mariposalodge.com ⇥ 45 rooms ⑩ No meals.*

Chapter 21

LAKE TAHOE

Updated by
Daniel Mangin

⊙ **Sights** ⓘ **Restaurants** ⨂ **Hotels** ⊖ **Shopping** ⵠ **Nightlife**

★★★★★ ★★★★☆ ★★★★★ ★☆☆☆☆ ★☆☆☆☆

WELCOME TO LAKE TAHOE

TOP REASONS TO GO

★ **The lake:** Blue, deep, and alpine pure, Lake Tahoe is far and away the main reason to visit this High Sierra paradise.

★ **Skiing:** Daring black-diamond runs or baby-bunny bumps—whether you're an expert, a beginner, or somewhere in between, the numerous Tahoe-area ski parks abound with slopes to suit your skills.

★ **The great outdoors:** A ring of national forests and recreation areas linked by miles of trails makes Tahoe excellent for nature lovers.

★ **Dinner with a view:** You can picnic lakeside at state parks or dine in restaurants perched along the shore.

★ **A date with lady luck:** Whether you want to roll dice, play the slots, or hope the blackjack dealer goes bust before you do, you'll find round-the-clock gambling at the casinos on the Nevada side of the lake and in Reno.

In the Sierra Nevada range's northern section, the Lake Tahoe area covers portions of four national forests, several state parks, and rugged wilderness areas. Lake Tahoe, the star attraction, straddles California and Nevada and is one of the world's largest, clearest, and deepest alpine lakes.

1 **South Lake Tahoe.**

2 **Pope-Baldwin Recreation Area.**

3 **Emerald Bay State Park.**

4 **D.L. Bliss State Park.**

5 **Ed Z'berg Sugar Pine Point State Park.**

6 **Tahoma.**

7 **Tahoe City.**

8 **Olympic Valley.**

9 **Truckee.**

10 **Carnelian Bay to Kings Beach.**

11 **Incline Village.**

12 **Zephyr Cove.**

13 **Stateline.**

14 **Reno.**

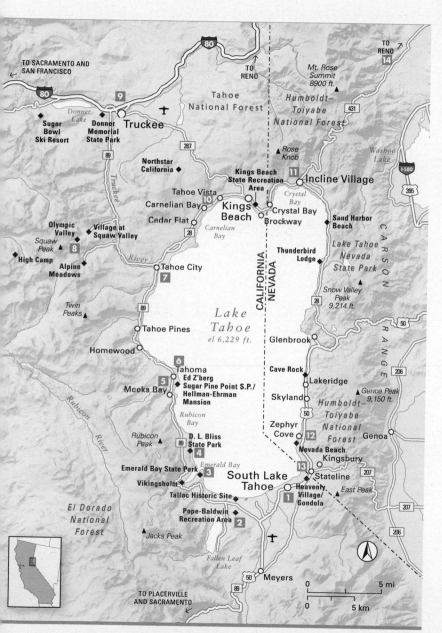

Whether you swim, fish, sail, or simply rest on its shores, you'll be wowed by the overwhelming beauty of Lake Tahoe, the largest alpine lake in North America. Famous for its cobalt-blue water and surrounding snowcapped peaks, Lake Tahoe straddles the state line between California and Nevada. The border gives this popular Sierra Nevada resort region a split personality: about half its visitors are intent on low-key sightseeing, hiking, camping, and boating; the rest head directly to the Nevada side, where bargain dining, big-name entertainment, and the lure of a jackpot draw them into the glittering casinos.

To explore the lake area and get a feel for its many differing communities, drive the 72-mile road that follows the shore through wooded flatlands and past beaches, climbing to vistas on the rugged southwest side of the lake and passing through busy commercial developments and casinos on its northeastern and southeastern edges. Another option is to actually go out *on* the 22-mile-long, 12-mile-wide lake on a sightseeing cruise or kayaking trip.

The lake, the communities around it, the state parks, national forests, and protected tracts of wilderness are the region's main draws, but other nearby destinations are gaining in popularity. Truckee, with an Old West feel and innovative restaurants, entices visitors looking for a relaxed pace and easy access to Tahoe's north shore and Olympic Valley ski parks. And today Reno, once known only for its casinos, attracts tourists with its buzzing arts scene, downtown riverfront, and campus events at the University of Nevada.

Planning

When to Go

A sapphire-blue lake shimmering deep in the center of an ice-white wonderland—that's Tahoe in winter. But those blankets of snow mean lots of storms that often close roads and force chain requirements on the interstate. In summer the roads are open, but the lake and lodgings are clogged with visitors seeking respite from valley heat. If you don't ski, the best times to visit are early fall—September and October—and late spring. The crowds thin, prices dip, and you can count on Tahoe being beautiful.

Most Lake Tahoe accommodations, restaurants, and even a handful of parks are open year-round, but many visitor centers, mansions, state parks, and beaches are closed from October through May. During those months, winter-sports enthusiasts swamp Tahoe's downhill resorts and cross-country centers, North America's largest concentration of skiing facilities. In summer it's cooler here than in the scorched Sierra Nevada foothills, the clean mountain air is bracingly crisp, and the surface temperature of Lake Tahoe is an invigorating 65°F to 70°F (compared with 40°F to 50°F in winter). This is also the time, however, when it may seem as if every tourist at the lake—100,000 on peak weekends—is in a car on the main road circling the shoreline (especially on Highway 89, just south of Tahoe City; on Highway 28, east of Tahoe City; and on U.S. 50 in South Lake Tahoe). Christmas week and July 4th are the busiest times, and prices go through the roof; plan accordingly.

Getting Here and Around

AIR TRAVEL

The nearest airport to Lake Tahoe is Reno–Tahoe International Airport (RNO), in Reno, 50 miles northeast of the closest point on the lake. Airlines serving RNO include Alaska, Allegiant, American, Delta, JetBlue, Southwest, United, and Volaris. Except for Allegiant, these airlines plus Aeromexico and Hawaiian serve Sacramento International Airport (SMF), 112 miles from South Lake Tahoe. North Lake Tahoe Express runs buses ($49 each way) between RNO and towns on the lake's western and northern shores, plus Incline Village, Truckee, Squaw Valley, and Northstar. South Tahoe Airporter runs buses ($29.75 one-way, $53 round-trip) between Reno–Tahoe Airport and resort hotels in the South Lake Tahoe area.

AIRPORT CONTACTS Reno Tahoe International Airport. ⊠ 2001 E. Plumb La., off U.S. 395/I–580, Reno ☎ 775/328–6400 ⊕ www.renoairport.com. **Sacramento International Airport.** ⊠ 6900 Airport Blvd., Sacramento ✛ Off I–5, 12 miles northwest of downtown ☎ 916/929–5411 ⊕ www.sacramento.aero/smf.

TRANSFER CONTACTS North Lake Tahoe Express. ☎ 866/216–5222 ⊕ www.northlaketahoeexpress.com. **South Tahoe Airporter.** ☎ 775/325–8944 ⊕ southtahoeairporter.com.

BUS TRAVEL

Greyhound stops in San Francisco, Sacramento, Truckee, and Reno. BlueGO ($2 per ride) provides year-round local service in South Lake Tahoe. On the north shore, Tahoe Area Regional Transit (TART; $1.75) operates buses between Tahoma and Incline Village and runs shuttles to Truckee. RTC RIDE buses ($2) serve the Reno area. All local rides require exact change.

In winter, BlueGO provides free ski shuttle service from South Lake Tahoe hotels and resorts to various Heavenly Mountain ski lodge locations. Most of the major ski resorts offer shuttle service to nearby lodging.

BUS CONTACTS Greyhound. ☎ 800/231–2222 ⊕ www.greyhound.com. **BlueGO.** ☎ 530/541 7149 ⊕ www.tahoetransportation.org/transit/south-shore-services. **RTC RIDE.** ☎ 775/348–7433 ⊕ www.rtcwashoe.com. **Tahoe Area Regional Transit (TART).** ☎ 530/550–1212, 800/736–6365 ⊕ www.placer.ca.gov/departments/works/transit/tart.

CAR TRAVEL

Lake Tahoe is 198 miles northeast of San Francisco, a drive of less than four hours in good weather and light traffic—if possible avoid heavy weekend traffic, particularly leaving the San Francisco area for Tahoe on Friday afternoon and returning on Sunday afternoon. The major route is Interstate 80, which cuts through the Sierra Nevada about 14 miles north of the lake. From there Highway 89 and Highway 267 reach the west and north shores, respectively.

U.S. 50 is the more direct route to the south shore, a two-hour drive from Sacramento. From Reno you can get to the north shore by heading south on U.S. 395/Interstate 580 for 10 miles, then west on Highway 431 for 25 miles. For the south shore, head south on U.S. 395/Interstate 580 through Carson City, and then turn west on U.S. 50 (56 miles total).

The scenic 72-mile highway around the lake is marked Highway 89 on the southwest and west shores, Highway 28 on the north and northeast shores, and U.S. 50 on the east and southeast. Sections of Highway 89 sometimes close during snowy periods, usually at Emerald Bay because of avalanche danger, which makes it impossible to complete the circular drive around the lake. Interstate 80, U.S. 50, and U.S. 395/Interstate 580 are all-weather highways, but there may be delays while snow is cleared during major storms.

Interstate 80 is a four-lane freeway; much of U.S. 50 is only two lanes with no center divider. Carry tire chains from October through May, or rent a four-wheel-drive vehicle. Most rental agencies do not allow tire chains to be used on their vehicles; ask when you book.

CONTACTS California Highway Patrol. ☎ 530/577–1001 South Lake Tahoe ⊕ www.chp.ca.gov. **Caltrans Current Highway Conditions.** ☎ 800/427–7623 ⊕ www.dot.ca.gov. **Nevada Department of Transportation Road Information.** ☎ 877/687–6237 ⊕ nvroads.com. **Nevada Highway Patrol.** ☎ 775/687–5300 ⊕ nhp.nv.gov.

TRAIN TRAVEL

Amtrak's cross-country rail service makes stops in Truckee and Reno. Amtrak also operates several buses daily between Reno and Sacramento to connect with coastal train routes.

TRAIN CONTACT Amtrak. ☎ 800/872–7245 ⊕ www.amtrak.com.

Restaurants

On weekends and in high season, expect a long wait at the more popular restaurants. And expect to pay resort prices almost everywhere. During the "shoulder seasons" (from April to May and September to November), some places may close temporarily or limit their hours, so call ahead. Also, check local papers for deals and discounts during this time, especially two-for-one coupons. Many casinos use their restaurants to attract gamblers. Marquees often tout "$8.99 prime rib dinners" or "$4.99 breakfast specials." Some of these meals are downright lousy and they are usually available only in the coffee shops and buffets, but at those prices, it's hard to complain. The finer restaurants in casinos deliver pricier food, as well as reasonable service and a bit of atmosphere. Unless otherwise noted, even the most expensive area restaurants welcome customers in casual clothes. *Restaurant reviews have been shortened. For full information, visit Fodors.com.*

Hotels

Quiet inns on the water, suburban-style strip motels, casino hotels, slope-side ski lodges, and house and condo rentals throughout the area constitute the lodging choices at Tahoe. The crowds come in summer and during ski season; reserve as far in advance as possible, especially for holiday periods when prices skyrocket. Spring and fall give you a little more leeway and lower—sometimes significantly lower, especially at casino hotels—rates. Check hotel websites for the best deals.

Head to South Lake Tahoe for the most activities and the widest range of lodging options. Heavenly Village in the heart of town has an ice rink, cinema, shops, fine-dining restaurants, and simple cafés, plus a gondola that will whisk you up to the ski park. Walk two blocks south from downtown, and you can hit the casinos.

Tahoe City, on the west shore, has a small-town atmosphere and is accessible to several nearby ski resorts. A few miles northwest of the lake, Squaw Valley USA has its own self-contained upscale village, an aerial tram to the slopes, and numerous outdoor activities once the snow melts.

Looking for a taste of Old Tahoe? The north shore with its woodsy backdrop is your best bet, with Carnelian Bay and Tahoe Vista on the California side. And across the Nevada border are casino resorts where Hollywood's glamour-stars once romped. *Hotel reviews have been shortened. For full information, visit Fodors.com.*

What It Costs

	$	$$	$$$	$$$$
RESTAURANTS				
	under $16	$16–$22	$23–$30	over $30
HOTELS				
	under $120	$120–$175	$176–$250	over $250

Outdoors and Backcountry Tips

If you're planning to spend any time outdoors around Lake Tahoe, whether hiking, climbing, skiing, or camping, be aware that weather conditions can change quickly in the Sierra. To avoid hypothermia, always bring a pocket-size, fold-up rain poncho (available in all sporting-goods stores) to keep you dry. Wear long pants and a hat. Carry plenty of water. Because you'll likely be walking on granite, wear sturdy, closed-toe hiking boots, with soles that grip rock. If you're going into the backcountry, bring a signaling device (such as a mirror), emergency whistle, compass, map, energy bars, and water purifier. When heading out alone, tell someone where you're going and when you expect to return.

If you plan to ski, be aware of resort elevations. In the event of a winter storm, determine the snow level before you choose the resort you'll ski. Often the level can be as high as 7,000 feet, which means rain at some resorts' base areas but snow at others.

BackCountry, in Truckee, operates an excellent website with current information about how and where to (and where not to) ski, mountain bike, and hike in the backcountry around Tahoe. The store also stocks everything from crampons to transceivers. For storm information, check the National Weather Service's website; for ski conditions, visit ⊕ *onthesnow.com.* For reservations at campgrounds in California state parks, contact Reserve California. If you plan to camp in the backcountry of the national forests, you'll need to purchase a wilderness permit, which you can pick up at the forest service office or at a ranger station at any forest entrance. If you plan to ski the backcountry, check the U.S. Forest Service's recorded information for conditions.

CONTACTS AND INFORMATION Back-Country. ⊠ *11400 Donner Pass Rd., at Meadow Way, Truckee* ☎ *530/582–0909 Truckee* ⊕ *www.thebackcountry.net.* **National Weather Service.** ⊕ *www.wrh. noaa.gov/rev.* **OntheSnow.com.** ⊕ *www. onthesnow.com/california/skireport.html.* **Reserve California.** ⊕ *www.reservecalifornia.com.* **U.S. Forest Service.** ⊠ *Office, 35 College Dr., South Lake Tahoe* ☎ *530/543–2600 general backcountry information, 530/587–3558 backcountry information recording after office hrs* ⊕ *www.fs.usda.gov/ltbmu.*

Skiing and Snowboarding

The mountains around Lake Tahoe are bombarded by blizzards throughout most winters and sometimes in fall and spring; 10- to 12-foot bases are common. Indeed, the Sierras often have the deepest snowpack on the continent, but because of the relatively mild temperatures over the Pacific, falling snow can be very heavy and wet—it's nicknamed "Sierra Cement" for a reason. The upside is that you can sometimes ski and board as late as May (snowboarding is permitted at all Tahoe ski areas). The major resorts get extremely crowded on weekends. If you're going to ski on a Saturday, arrive early and quit early. Avoid moving with the masses: eat at 11 am or 1:30 pm, not noon. Also consider visiting the ski areas with few high-speed lifts or limited lodging and real estate at their bases: Alpine Meadows,

Sugar Bowl, Homewood, Mt. Rose, Sierra-at-Tahoe, Diamond Peak, and Kirkwood. And to find out the true ski conditions, talk to waiters and bartenders—most of them are ski bums.

The Lake Tahoe area is also a great destination for Nordic skiers. Cross-country skiing at the resorts can be costly, but you get the benefits of machine grooming and trail preparation. If it's bargain Nordic you're after, take advantage of thousands of acres of public forest and parkland trails.

Tours

Lake Tahoe Balloons
BALLOONING | Take a hot-air balloon flight over the lake from mid-May through mid-October with this company that launches and lands its balloons on a boat. The four-hour excursion (the flight is 45–60 minutes) begins shortly after sunrise and ends with a traditional champagne toast. ⊠ *Tahoe Keys Marina, 2435 Venice Dr. E, South Lake Tahoe* ⌖ *Tahoe Keys Blvd. off Lake Tahoe Blvd.* ☎ *530/544–1221, 800/872–9294* ⊕ *www. laketahoeballoons.com* 🖅 *From $299.*

MS *Dixie II*
BOAT TOURS | The 520-passenger MS *Dixie II*, a stern-wheeler, sails year-round from Zephyr Cove to Emerald Bay on sightseeing and dinner cruises. ⊠ *Zephyr Cove Marina, 760 U.S. Hwy. 50, near Church St., Zephyr Cove* ☎ *800/238–2463* ⊕ *www. zephyrcove.com/cruises* 🖅 *From $65.*

North Lake Tahoe Ale Trail
SELF-GUIDED | Bike or walk one of North Lake Tahoe's dozens of trails, then reward yourself with a craft brew at an alehouse near the end of your chosen route. The largest concentration of beer stops is around Incline Village, but you'll find drinking spots in from Tahoma to Zephyr Cove. A dedicated website has an interactive map, descriptions, and short videos pairing trails and drinking spots. There

are also suggestions for paddleboarders and kayakers. ⊕ www.gotahoenorth.com/things/north-lake-tahoe-ale-trail.

Sierra Cloud

BOAT TOURS | The *Sierra Cloud*, a 41-passenger catamaran, departs from the Hyatt Regency beach at Incline Village and cruises the north and east shore areas for two hours. ⊠ *Hyatt Regency Lake Tahoe, 111 Country Club Dr., Incline Village* ☎ *775/831–4386* ⊕ *www.awsincline.com* ✆ *From $90* ⊗ *Closed Oct.–Apr.*

Tahoe Gal

BOAT TOURS | Docked in Tahoe City this old-style 120-passenger paddle wheeler departs daily from June through September and on some days in May on brunch, lunch, happy hour, and sunset tours of Emerald Bay and Lake Tahoe's north and west shores. Specialty excursions include ones with live music or other entertainment. ⚠ **Closed October–April and some days in May.** ⊠ *Departures from Lighthouse Center, 952 N. Lake Blvd., Tahoe City* ☎ *800/218–2464* ⊕ *www.tahoegal.com* ✆ *From $35.*

Tahoe Cruises

BOAT TOURS | This outfit operates cruises year-round on two boats, the *Safari Rose*, an 80-foot-long wooden motor yacht, and the *Spirit of Tahoe*, added in 2019. From mid-May to mid October, Tahoe Cruises offers barbecue lunch, happy-hour, sunset, and champagne cruises. Shuttle-bus pickup service is available. ⊠ *Ski Run Marina, 900 Ski Run Blvd., South Lake Tahoe* ☎ *888/867–6394* ⊕ *www.tahoecruises.com* ✆ *Call for prices.*

★ Thunderbird Lodge Cruise & Tour

BOAT TOURS | The captain of the *Tahoe*, a classic wooden boat, takes passengers on an east shore cruise whose highlights are a walking tour and picnic lunch at the Thunderbird Lodge, a historic mansion. ⊠ *Departures from Zephyr Cove Pier, 760 U.S. 50, Zephyr Cove* ☎ *775/230–8907* ⊕ *www.cruisetahoe.com/public-cruises* ✆ *$149.*

Visitor Information

CONTACTS Go Tahoe North. ☎ *530/581–6900* ⊕ *www.gotahoenorth.com.* **Tahoe South.** ☎ *775/542–4637 California, 800/588–4591 Nevada* ⊕ *tahoesouth.com.*

South Lake Tahoe

60 miles south of Reno, 198 miles northeast of San Francisco.

The city of South Lake Tahoe's raison d'être is tourism: the casinos of adjacent Stateline, Nevada; the ski slopes at Heavenly Mountain; the beaches, docks, bike trails, and campgrounds all around the south shore; and the backcountry of Eldorado National Forest and Desolation Wilderness. Less appealing are the strip malls, old-school motels, and low-rise prefab buildings lining U.S. 50, the city's main drag. Although in recent years a few jazzed-up motels and new boutique hotels have joined a few longtime high-quality inns, many places provide little more than basic accommodation. The small city's saving grace is its convenient location, bevy of services, and gorgeous lake views.

GETTING HERE AND AROUND

The main route into and through South Lake Tahoe is U.S. 50; signs say "Lake Tahoe Boulevard" in town. Arrive by car or, if coming from Reno airport, take the South Tahoe Express bus. BlueGO operates daily bus service in the south shore area year-round, plus a ski shuttle from the large hotels to Heavenly Mountain Resort in the winter.

ESSENTIALS

VISITOR INFORMATION Visit Lake Tahoe South. ⊠ *Visitor Center, 169 U.S. Hwy. 50, at Kingsbury Grade, Stateline* ☎ *775/588–5900* ⊕ *tahoesouth.com* ⊠ *Visitor Center, 3066 Lake Tahoe Blvd., at San Francisco Ave.* ☎ *530/541–5255* ⊕ *tahoesouth.com.*

Sights

★ Heavenly Gondola

VIEWPOINT | FAMILY | Whether you ski or not, you'll appreciate the impressive view of Lake Tahoe from the Heavenly Gondola. Its eight-passenger cars travel from Heavenly Village 2.4 miles up the mountain in 15 minutes. When the weather's fine, you can take one of three hikes around the mountaintop and then have lunch at Tamarack Lodge. ✉ *4080 Lake Tahoe Blvd.* ☎ *775/586–7000, 800/432–8365* 🌐 *www.skiheavenly.com* 🎫 *$61.*

Heavenly Village

STORE/MALL | This lively complex at the base of the Heavenly Gondola has good shopping, an arcade for kids, a cinema, a brewpub, a skating rink in winter, miniature golf in summer, and the Loft for magic shows and other live entertainment. Base Camp Pizza Co., Azul Latin Kitchen, and Kalani's for seafood stand out among the several restaurants. ✉ *1001 Heavenly Village Way, at U.S. 50* 🌐 *www.theshopsatheavenly.com.*

Restaurants

Artemis Lakefront Cafe

$$ | MEDITERRANEAN | A festive marina restaurant with a heated outdoor patio, Artemis reveals its Greek influences in breakfast dishes like baklava French toast and gyros and egg pita wraps. All day, though, the menus encompass more familiar options (eggs Benedict in the morning, burgers and grilled mahimahi later on). **Known for:** heated outdoor patio; outgoing staff; marina location. [$] *Average main: $19* ✉ *900 Ski Run Blvd.* ☎ *530/542–3332* 🌐 *www.artemislakefrontcafe.com.*

Blue Angel Café

$$ | ECLECTIC | A favorite of locals, who fill the dozen or so wooden tables, this cozy spot with Wi-Fi serves basic sandwiches and salads along with internationally inspired dishes like chipotle shrimp tacos and Thai curry. On cold days warm up with wine or an espresso in front of the stone fireplace. **Known for:** varied menu; daily 3–6 happy hour; easygoing staff. [$] *Average main: $17* ✉ *1132 Ski Run Blvd., at Larch Ave.* ☎ *530/544–6544* 🌐 *www.blueangelcafe.com.*

★ Evan's American Gourmet Cafe

$$$$ | ECLECTIC | Its excellent service, world-class cuisine, and superb wine list make this intimate restaurant the top choice for high-end dining in South Lake. Inside a converted cabin, Evan's serves creative American cuisine that might include pan-seared day boat scallops and meat dishes such as rack of lamb marinated with rosemary and garlic and served with raspberry demi-glace. **Known for:** intimate atmosphere; world-class cuisine; superb wine list. [$] *Average main: $38* ✉ *536 Emerald Bay Rd., Hwy. 89, at 15th St.* ☎ *530/542–1990* 🌐 *evanstahoe.com* 🕘 *No lunch.*

Kalani's at Lake Tahoe

$$$$ | ASIAN | The white-tablecloth dining room at Heavenly's sleekest (and priciest) restaurant is decked out with carved bamboo, a burnt-orange color palette, and a modern-glass sculpture, all of which complement Pacific Rim–influenced dishes like fillet of beef with miso-garlic butter and the signature Chilean sea bass with Thai-basil mash, wilted balsamic greens, and ponzu butter sauce. Sushi selections with inventive rolls and sashimi combos, plus less expensive vegetarian dishes, add depth to the menu. **Known for:** fresh-off-the-plane Hawaiian seafood; thoughtful wine selections; upscale setting. [$] *Average main: $37* ✉ *1001 Heavenly Village Way, #26, at U.S. 50* ☎ *530/544–6100* 🌐 *www.kalanis.com.*

My Thai Cuisine

$ | THAI | Fantastic flavors and gracious owners have earned this humble roadside restaurant with river-stone columns, pine-paneled walls and ceilings, Thai statues and ornamentation the loyalty of Tahoe residents and regular visitors. The aromatic dishes include crab pad Thai, basil lamb, sizzling shrimp, and numerous curries. **Known for:** many vegetarian options; lunch specials a steal; lively atmosphere. $ *Average main: $14* 2108 Lake Tahoe Blvd., ¼ mile northeast of "Y" intersection of U.S. 50 and Hwy. 89 530/544–3232 www. thairestaurantsouthlaketahoe.com.

Red Hut Café

$ | AMERICAN | A vintage-1959 Tahoe diner, all chrome and red plastic, the Red Hut is a tiny place with a wildly popular breakfast menu: huge omelets; banana, pecan, and coconut waffles; and other tasty vittles. A second South Lake branch has a soda fountain and is the only one that serves dinner, and there's a third location in Stateline. **Known for:** huge omelets; variety of waffles; old-school feel. $ *Average main: $10* 2723 Lake Tahoe Blvd., near Blue Lake Ave. 530/541–9024 www.redhutcafe.com No dinner.

Scusa! Italian Ristorante

$$$ | ITALIAN | This longtime favorite turns out big plates of veal scaloppine, chicken piccata, and garlicky linguine with clams—straightforward Italian American food (and lots of it), served in an intimate dining room warmed by a crackling fire on many nights. There's an outdoor patio that's open in warm weather. **Known for:** classic Italian American recipes; fritto misto, grilled radicchio, and fresh-baked mozzarella appetizers; sticky-bun bread pudding for dessert. $ *Average main: $23* 2543 Lake Tahoe Blvd., at Sierra Blvd. 530/542–0100 www.scusala-ketahoe.com No lunch.

★ Sprouts Natural Foods Cafe

$ | AMERICAN | If it's in between normal mealtimes and you're hungry for something healthful, head to this order-at-the-counter café for salads, overstuffed wraps, hot sandwiches, homemade vegan soups, all-day breakfasts, and the best smoothies in town. Dine at wooden tables in the cheery contemporary indoor space or out front on the patio, or just order food to go. **Known for:** fresh, healthy cuisine; vegan and vegetarian friendly; congenial staff. $ *Average main: $10* 3123 Harrison Ave., U.S. 50 at Alameda Ave. 530/541–6969 www.sprouts-cafetahoe.com.

Hotels

Base Camp South Lake Tahoe

$$ | HOTEL | This three-floor boutique hotel near the Heavenly Gondola, Stateline casinos, and several good restaurants provides solid value in a hip yet family-friendly setting. **Pros:** convenient location; great for groups; cool public spaces include rooftop hot tub with mountain views. **Cons:** communal dinners won't appeal to all travelers; near a busy area; not on the lake. $ *Rooms from: $129* 4143 Cedar Ave., off U.S. 50 530/208–0180 www.basecamptahoesouth.com 74 rooms Free Breakfast.

★ Black Bear Lodge

$$$ | B&B/INN | The rooms and cabins at this well-appointed inn feature 19th-century American antiques, fine art, and fireplaces; cabins also have kitchenettes—built in the 1990s with meticulous attention to detail, the entire complex feels like one of the grand old lodges of the Adirondacks. **Pros:** near Heavenly skiing; within walking distance of good restaurants; good for groups. **Cons:** no room service; lacks big-hotel amenities; social types may find setting too sedate. $ *Rooms from: $199* 1202 Ski Run Blvd. 530/544–4451 www.tahoeblackbear.com 9 rooms Free Breakfast.

Camp Richardson

$ | RESORT | FAMILY | The pluses of this old-fashioned family resort on 80 acres fronting Lake Tahoe are also its minuses: Camp Richardson earns retro cred for its 1920s rustic log cabin–style lodge, few dozen cabins, and small inn—all tucked beneath giant pine trees—but wins no style points for its straightforward accommodations and lack of amenities many travelers take for granted. **Pros:** lakeside location with wide choice of lodgings; great for families; inexpensive daily and weekly rates. **Cons:** dated style; lacks upscale amenities (and even phones and TVs in some rooms); some cabins available in summer only. $ *Rooms from: $105* ⌧ *1900 Jameson Beach Rd.* ☎ *530/541–1801, 800/544–1801* ⊕ *www.camprichardson.com* ⤳ *74 rooms* ⦿ *No meals.*

Hotel Azure

$$$$ | HOTEL | High-end motel meets boutique hotel at this totally revamped (to the tune of $3.5 million) property across the road from a beach. **Pros:** clean, spacious rooms; good work spaces and tech amenities; short drive to Heavenly Mountain. **Cons:** on busy Lake Tahoe Boulevard; no bell or room service; some sound bleed-through from room to room. $ *Rooms from: $262* ⌧ *3300 Lake Tahoe Blvd.* ☎ *530/542–0330, 800/877–1466* ⊕ *www.hotelazuretahoe.com* ⤳ *99 rooms* ⦿ *No meals.*

Marriott's Grand Residence and Timber Lodge

$$$ | RESORT | You can't beat the location of these two gigantic, modern condominium complexes right at the base of Heavenly Gondola, smack in the center of town. **Pros:** central location; great for families; near excellent restaurants. **Cons:** can be jam-packed on weekends; no room service; lacks serenity. $ *Rooms from: $195* ⌧ *1001 Heavenly Village Way* ☎ *530/542–8400 Marriott's Grand Residence, 800/845–5279, 530/542–6600 Marriott's Timber Lodge* ⊕ *www.marriott.com* ⤳ *431 rooms* ⦿ *No meals.*

Sorensen's Resort

$$ | RESORT | Escape civilization at this woodsy 165-acre resort within the Eldorado National Forest, 20 minutes south of town. **Pros:** gorgeous rustic setting; good on-site café serves three meals a day (nonguests welcome); outdoor activities.

Cons: nearest nightlife is 20 miles away; lacks amenities of larger properties; basic furnishings. $ *Rooms from: $145* ⌧ *14255 Hwy. 88, Hope Valley* ☎ *530/694–2203, 800/423–9949* ⊕ *www.sorensensresort.com* ⤳ *36 rooms* ⦿ *No meals.*

▽ Nightlife

Most of the area's nightlife is concentrated in the casinos over the border in Stateline. To avoid slot machines and blinking lights, try the California-side nightspots in and near Heavenly Village.

BARS

The Loft

THEMED ENTERTAINMENT | Crowd-pleasing magic shows and other entertainment and a casual-industrial setting keep patrons happy at this Heavenly Village bar and lounge where kids aren't out of place. The mood is upbeat, the specialty cocktails are potent, and if you're in the mood for dinner the kitchen turns out Italian fare more tasty than one might expect at such a venue. ⌧ *1001 Heavenly Village Way* ☎ *530/523–8024* ⊕ *www.thelofttahoe.com.*

Mc P's Taphouse & Grill

BARS/PUBS | You can hear live bands—rock, jazz, blues, alternative—on most nights at Mc P's while you sample a few of the 40 beers on draft. Lunch and dinner (pub grub) are served daily. ⌧ *4125 Lake Tahoe Blvd., Ste A, near Friday Ave.* ☎ *530/542–4435.*

🏃 Activities

FISHING

Tahoe Sport Fishing

FISHING | One of the area's largest and oldest fishing-charter services offers morning and afternoon trips. Outings include all necessary gear and bait, and the crew cleans and packages your catch. ⌧ *900 Ski Run Blvd., off Lake Tahoe Blvd.* ☎ *530/541–5448* ⊕ *www.tahoesportfishing.com* ⤳ *From $125.*

HIKING

Desolation Wilderness

HIKING/WALKING | Trails within the 63,960-acre wilderness lead to gorgeous backcountry lakes and mountain peaks. It's called Desolation Wilderness for a reason, so bring a topographic map and compass, and carry water and food. You need a permit for overnight camping (☎ 877/444–6777). In summer you can access this area by boarding a boat taxi ($14 one-way) at **Echo Chalet** (*9900 Echo Lakes Rd., off U.S. 50,* ☎ *530/659–7207,* ⊕ *www.echochalet.com*) and crossing Echo Lake. The Pacific Crest Trail also traverses Desolation Wilderness. ⊠ *El Dorado National Forest Information Center* ☎ *530/644–2349* ⊕ *www.fs.usda.gov/eldorado.*

Pacific Crest Trail

HIKING/WALKING | Hike a couple of miles on this famous mountain trail that stretches from Mexico to Canada. ⊠ *Echo Summit, about 12 miles southwest of South Lake Tahoe off U.S. 50* ☎ *916/285–1846* ⊕ *www.pcta.org.*

ICE-SKATING

Heavenly Village Outdoor Ice Rink

ICE SKATING | FAMILY | If you're here in winter, practice your jumps and turns at this rink between the gondola and the cinema. ⊠ *1001 Heavenly Village Way* ☎ *530/542–4230* ⊕ *www.theshopsatheavenly.com* ⊠ *$22, includes skate rental.*

South Lake Tahoe Ice Arena

ICE SKATING | For year-round fun, head to this NHL regulation–size indoor rink where you can rent equipment and sign up for lessons. ■ TIP→ **Hours vary; call or check website for public skate times.** ⊠ *1176 Rufus Allen Blvd.* ☎ *530/544–7465* ⊕ *tahoearena.com* ⊠ *$15; includes skate rental.*

KAYAKING

Kayak Tahoe

KAYAKING | Sign up for lessons and excursions (to the south shore, Emerald Bay, and Sand Harbor), offered from May through September. You can also rent a kayak and paddle solo on the lake. ⊠ *Timber Cove Marina, 3411 Lake Tahoe Blvd., at Balbijou Rd.* ☎ *530/544–2011* ⊕ *www.kayaktahoe.com* ⊠ *Rentals from $28, tours from $55.*

MOUNTAIN BIKING

Tahoe Sports Ltd.

BICYCLING | You can rent road and mountain bikes and get tips on where to ride from the friendly staff at this full-service sports store. ⊠ *Tahoe Crescent V Shopping Center, 4000 Lake Tahoe Blvd., Suite 7* ☎ *530/542–4000* ⊕ *www.tahoesportsltd.com.*

SKIING

If you don't want to pay the high cost of rental equipment at the resorts, you'll find reasonable prices and expert advice at Tahoe Sports Ltd. *(see Mountain Biking, above).*

★ Heavenly Mountain Resort

SKIING/SNOWBOARDING | Straddling two states, vast Heavenly Mountain Resort—composed of nine peaks, two valleys, and four base-lodge areas, along with the largest snowmaking system in the western United States—pairs terrain for every skier with exhilarating Tahoe Basin views. Beginners can choose wide, well-groomed trails, accessed from the California Lodge or the gondola from downtown South Lake Tahoe; kids have short and gentle runs in the Enchanted Forest area all to themselves. The Sky Express high-speed quad chair whisks intermediate and advanced skiers to the summit for wide cruisers or steep tree-skiing. Mott and Killebrew canyons draw experts to the Nevada side for steep chutes and thick-timber slopes.

The ski school is big and offers everything from learn-to-ski packages to canyon-adventure tours. Call about ski and boarding camps. Skiing lessons are available for children ages four and up;

there's day care for infants older than six weeks. Summertime thrill seekers participate in Epic Discovery—fun for the whole family that includes a mountain coaster, zip lines, a climbing wall, ropes courses, hiking opportunities, and a learning center. **Facilities:** 97 trails; 4,800 acres; 3,500-foot vertical drop; 28 lifts. ⊠ *Ski Run Blvd., off U.S. 50* ☎ *775/586–7000, 800/432–8365* ⊕ *www.skiheavenly.com* ⊠ *Lift ticket $154.*

Hope Valley Outdoors

SKIING/SNOWBOARDING | Operating from a yurt at Pickett's Junction, Hope Valley provides lessons and equipment rentals to prepare you for cross-country skiing and snowshoeing. The outfit has more than 60 miles of trails through Humboldt–Toiyabe National Forest, several miles of which are groomed. ⊠ *Hwy. 88, at Hwy. 89, Hope Valley* ☎ *530/721–2015* ⊕ *www.hopevalleycrosscountry.com.*

Kirkwood Ski Resort

SKIING/SNOWBOARDING | Thirty-six miles south of Lake Tahoe, Kirkwood is the hard-core skiers' and boarders' favorite south-shore mountain, known for its craggy gulp-and-go chutes, sweeping cornices, steep-aspect glade skiing, and high base elevation. But there's also fantastic terrain for newbies and intermediates down wide-open bowls, through wooded gullies, and along rolling tree-lined trails. Families often head to the Timber Creek area, a good spot to learn to ski or snowboard. Tricksters can show off in two terrain parks on jumps, wall rides, rails, and a half-pipe. The mountain gets hammered with an average of 354 inches of snow annually. If you're into out-of-bounds skiing, check out Expedition Kirkwood, a backcountry-skills program that teaches basic safety awareness. If you're into cross-country, the resort has 80 km (50 miles) of superb groomed-track skiing, with skating lanes, instruction, and rentals. Nonskiers can snowshoe, snow-skate, and go dog-sledding or snow-tubing. The children's ski school has programs for ages 3 to 12. **Facilities:** 86 trails; 2,300 acres; 2,000-foot vertical drop; 15 lifts. ⊠ *1501 Kirkwood Meadows Dr., Kirkwood* ⊕ *Off Hwy. 88, 14 miles west of Hwy. 89* ☎ *209/258–6000* ⊕ *www.kirkwood.com* ⊠ *Lift ticket $117.*

Sierra-at-Tahoe

SKIING/SNOWBOARDING | Wind-protected and meticulously groomed slopes, excellent tree-skiing, and gated backcountry skiing are among the draws at this low-key but worthy resort. Extremely popular with snowboarders, Sierra has several terrain parks, including Halfpipe, with 18-foot walls and a dedicated chairlift. For beginners, Sierra-at-Tahoe has more than 100 acres of learning terrain, and there are two snow-tubing lanes. **Facilities:** 46 trails; 2,000-plus acres; 2,250-foot vertical drop; 14 lifts. ⊠ *1111 Sierra-at-Tahoe Rd., Twin Bridges* ⊕ *12 miles from South Lake Tahoe off U.S. 50, past Echo Summit* ☎ *530/659–7453 information, 530/659–7475 snow phone* ⊕ *www.sierraattahoe.com* ⊠ *Lift ticket $110.*

Pope-Baldwin Recreation Area

5 miles west of South Lake Tahoe.

To the west of downtown South Lake Tahoe, U.S. 50 and Highway 89 come together, forming an intersection nicknamed "the Y." If you head northwest on Highway 89, also called Emerald Bay Road, and follow the lakefront, commercial development gives way to national forests and state parks. One of these is Pope-Baldwin Recreation Area.

GETTING HERE AND AROUND

The entrance to the Pope-Baldwin Recreation Area is on the east side of Emerald Bay Road. The area is closed to vehicles in winter, but you can cross-country ski here.

Sights

★ Tallac Historic Site

HISTORIC SITE | At this site you can stroll or picnic lakeside year-round, and then in late spring and summer you can also explore three historic estates. The **Pope House** is the magnificently restored 1894 mansion of George S. Pope, who made his money in shipping and lumber and played host to the business and cultural elite of 1920s America. The **Baldwin Museum** is in the estate that once belonged to entrepreneur "Lucky" Baldwin; today it houses a collection of family memorabilia and Washoe Indian artifacts. The **Valhalla** (⊕ valhallatahoe. com), with a spectacular floor-to-ceiling stone fireplace, was occupied for years by Walter and Claire Heller (tidbit: after their divorce, each visited the property on alternate weekends, though she held the title). Its Grand Hall, Grand Lawn, and a lakeside boathouse refurbished as a theater, host the summertime Valhalla Art, Music and Theatre Festival of concerts, plays, and cultural activities. Docents conduct tours of the Pope House in summer; call for tour times. ⊠ Pope Baldwin Recreation Area Hwy. 89 ☎ 530/541–5227 late May–mid-Sept., 530/543–2600 year-round ⊕ tahoeheritage.org ☜ Free, summer guided site walk $5, Pope House tour $10 ⊙ House and museum closed late Sept.–late May.

Taylor Creek Visitor Center

INFO CENTER | **FAMILY** | At this center operated by the U.S. Forest Service you can visit the site of a Washoe Indian settlement; walk self-guided trails through meadow, marsh, and forest; and inspect the Stream Profile Chamber, an underground display with windows right into Taylor Creek. In fall you may see spawning kokanee salmon digging their nests. In summer Forest Service naturalists organize discovery walks and evening programs. ⊠ Hwy. 89, 3 miles north of junction with U.S. 50 ☎ 530/543–2674 late May–Oct., 530/543–2600 year-round ⊕ www.fs.usda.gov ☜ Free.

Emerald Bay State Park

4 miles west of Pope-Baldwin Recreation Area.

You can hike, bike, swim, camp, scuba dive, kayak, or tour a lookalike Viking castle at this state park. Or you can simply enjoy the most popular tourist stop on Lake Tahoe's circular drive: the high cliff overlooking Emerald Bay, famed for its jewel-like shape and color.

GETTING HERE AND AROUND

The entrance to Emerald Bay State Park is on the east side of a narrow, twisting section of Highway 89. Caution is the key word for both drivers and pedestrians. The park is closed to vehicles in winter.

Sights

★ Emerald Bay State Park

NATIONAL/STATE PARK | A massive glacier millions of years ago carved this 3-mile-long and 1-mile-wide fjordlike inlet. Famed for its jewel-like shape and colors, the bay surrounds Fannette, Tahoe's only island. Highway 89 curves high above the lake through Emerald Bay State Park; from the Emerald Bay lookout, the centerpiece of the park, you can survey the whole scene. This is one of the don't-miss views of Lake Tahoe. The light is best in mid- to late morning, when the bay's colors really pop. ⊠ Hwy. 89 ☎ 530/525–7232 ⊕ www.parks.ca.gov ☜ $10 parking fee.

Vikingsholm

HOUSE | This 38-room estate was completed in 1929 and built as a precise copy of a 1,200-year-old Viking castle, using materials native to the area. Its original owner, Lora Knight, furnished it with Scandinavian antiques and hired artisans to build period reproductions. The sod roof sprouts wildflowers each

Fjord-like Emerald Bay is possibly the most scenic part of Lake Tahoe.

spring. There are picnic tables nearby and a gray-sand beach for strolling. A steep 1-mile-long trail from the Emerald Bay lookout leads down to Vikingsholm, and the hike back up is hard (especially if you're not yet acclimated to the elevation), although there are benches and stone culverts to rest on. At the 150-foot peak of Fannette Island are the ruins of a stone structure known as the Tea House, built so that Knight's guests could have a place to enjoy afternoon refreshments after a motorboat ride. The island is off-limits from February through mid-June to protect nesting Canada geese. The rest of the year it's open for day use—kayak and paddleboard rentals are available at Emerald Bay State Park's beach. ⊠ *Hwy. 89* ☎ *530/525–7232* ⊕ *www.vikingsholm.com* ✉ *Day-use parking fee $10; mansion tour $10* ⊗ *Closed late Sept.–late May.*

🏃 Activities

HIKING
Eagle Falls

HIKING/WALKING | To reach these falls, leave your car in the parking lot of the Eagle Falls picnic area (near Vikingsholm; arrive early for a good spot), and walk up the short but fairly steep canyon nearby. You'll have a brilliant panorama of Emerald Bay from this spot near the boundary of Desolation Wilderness. For a strenuous full-day hike, continue 5 miles, past Eagle Lake (a good spot for an alpine swim), to Upper and Middle Velma lakes. Pick up trail maps at Taylor Creek Visitor Center in summer, or year-round at the main U.S. Forest Service Office in South Lake Tahoe, at 35 College Drive. ⊠ *Hwy. 89 at Emerald Bay State Park.*

D.L. Bliss State Park

3 miles north of Emerald Bay State Park, 17 miles south of Tahoe City.

This park shares 6 miles of shoreline with adjacent Emerald Bay State Park, and has two white-sand beaches. Hike the Rubicon Trail for stunning views of the lake.

GETTING HERE AND AROUND
The entrance to D.L. Bliss State Park is on the east side of Highway 89 just north of Emerald Bay. No vehicles are allowed in when the park is closed for the season.

Sights

D.L. Bliss State Park
NATIONAL/STATE PARK | This park takes its name from Duane LeRoy Bliss, a 19th-century lumber magnate. At one time Bliss owned nearly 75% of Tahoe's lakefront, along with local steamboats, railroads, and banks. The park shares 6 miles of shoreline with Emerald Bay State Park; combined the two parks cover 1,830 acres, 744 of which the Bliss family donated to the state. At the north end of Bliss is Rubicon Point, which overlooks one of the lake's deepest spots. Short trails lead to an old lighthouse and Balancing Rock, which weighs 250,000 pounds and balances on a fist of granite. The 4.5-mile Rubicon Trail—one of Tahoe's premier hikes—leads to Vikingsholm and provides stunning lake views. Two white-sand beaches front some of Tahoe's warmest water. ⊠ *Hwy. 89 ✛ Entrance east side of Hwy. 89, 3 miles north of Emerald Bay State Park* ☎ *530/525–3345* ⊕ *www.parks.ca.gov* ⊠ *$10 per vehicle, day-use.*

Ed Z'berg Sugar Pine Point State Park

8 miles north of D. L. Bliss State Park, 10 miles south of Tahoe City.

Visitors love to hike, swim, and fish here in the summer, but this park is also popular in winter, when a small campground remains open. Eleven miles of cross-country ski and snowshoe trails allow beginners and experienced enthusiasts alike to whoosh through pine forests and glide past the lake.

GETTING HERE AND AROUND
The entrance to Sugar Pine Point is on the east side of Highway 89, about a mile south of Tahoma. A bike trail links Tahoe City to the park.

◉ Sights

Ed Z'berg Sugar Pine Point State Park
NATIONAL/STATE PARK | Visitors love to hike, swim, and fish in the summer at this park named for a state lawmaker who sponsored key conservation legislation, but it's also popular in winter, when a small campground remains open. Eleven miles of cross-country ski and snowshoe trails allow beginners and experienced enthusiasts alike to whoosh through pine forests and glide past the lake. Rangers lead full-moon snowshoe tours from January to March. With 2,000 densely forested acres and nearly 2 miles of shore frontage, this is Lake Tahoe's largest state park. ⊠ *Hwy. 89, 1 mile south of Tahoma* ☎ *530/525–7982 summer, 530/525–7232 year-round* ⊕ *www.parks. ca.gov* ⊠ *$10 per vehicle, day-use.*

Hellman-Ehrman Mansion
HOUSE | The main attraction at Sugar Pine Point State Park is the Hellman-Ehrman Mansion, a 1903 stone-and-shingle summer home furnished in period style. In its day the height of modernity, the mansion had electric lights and full indoor

plumbing. Also in the park are a trapper's log cabin from the mid-19th century, a nature preserve with wildlife exhibits, a lighthouse, the start of the 10-mile biking trail to Tahoe City, and an extensive system of hiking and cross-country skiing trails. If you're feeling less ambitious, you can relax on the sun-dappled lawn behind the mansion and gaze out at the lake. ■ **TIP→ Purchase tour tickets at the Sugar Pine nature center.** ✉ *Hwy. 89* ☎ *530/525–7982 summer, 530/525–7232 year-round* 🌐 *www.parks.ca.gov* 🎫 *$10 per vehicle, day-use; mansion tour $10.*

Tahoma

1 mile north of Ed Z'berg Sugar Pine Point State Park, 23 miles south of Truckee.

With its rustic waterfront vacation cottages, Tahoma exemplifies life on the lake in its quiet early days before bright-lights casinos and huge crowds proliferated. In 1960 Tahoma was host of the Olympic Nordic-skiing competitions. Today there's little to do here except stroll by the lake and listen to the wind in the trees, making it a favorite home base for mellow families and nature buffs.

GETTING HERE AND AROUND

Approach Tahoma by car on Highway 89, called West Lake Boulevard in this section. From the northern and western communities, take a TART bus to Tahoma. A bike trail links Tahoe City to Tahoma.

Hotels

Tahoma Meadows B&B Cottages

$$ | **B&B/INN** | **FAMILY** | With 16 individually decorated little red cottages sitting beneath towering pine trees, it's hard to beat this serene property for atmosphere and woodsy charm. **Pros:** lovely setting; good choice for families; close to Homewood ski resort. **Cons:** far from the casinos; may be too serene for some guests; old-style decor. [$] *Rooms from: $149* ✉ *6821 W. Lake Blvd.* ☎ *530/525–1553, 866/525–1553* 🌐 *www.tahomameadows.com* 🛏 *16 rooms* 🍴 *No meals.*

Activities

SKIING

Homewood Mountain Resort

SKIING/SNOWBOARDING | Schuss down these slopes for fantastic views—the mountain rises across the road from the Tahoe shoreline. This small, usually uncrowded resort is the favorite area of locals on a snowy day, because you can find lots of untracked powder. It's also the most protected and least windy Tahoe ski area during a storm; when every other resort's lifts are on wind hold, you can almost always count on Homewood's to be open. There's only one high-speed chairlift, but there are rarely any lines. The resort may look small as you drive by, but most of it isn't visible from the road. **Facilities:** 67 trails; 1,260 acres; 1,650-foot vertical drop; 8 lifts. ✉ *5145 W. Lake Blvd., Homewood* ✥ *Hwy. 89, 5 miles south of Tahoe City* ☎ *530/525–2992 information, 530/525–2900 snow phone* 🌐 *www.skihomewood.com* 🎫 *Lift ticket $129.*

Tahoe City

9 miles north of Tahoma, 14 miles south of Truckee.

Tahoe City is the only lakeside town with a charming downtown area good for strolling and window-shopping. Stores and restaurants are all within walking distance of the Outlet Gates, where water is spilled into the Truckee River to control the surface level of the lake.

GETTING HERE AND AROUND

Tahoe City is at the junction of Highway 28, also called North Lake Boulevard, and Highway 89 where it turns northwest toward Squaw Valley and Truckee. TART buses serve the area.

Sugar Pine Point State Park.

ESSENTIALS

VISITOR INFORMATION Go Tahoe North. ☎ *530/581–6900* 🌐 *www.gotahoenorth.com.*

👁 Sights

Gatekeeper's Museum

MUSEUM | This museum preserves a little known part of the region's history. Between 1910 and 1968 the gatekeeper who lived on this site was responsible for monitoring the level of the lake, using a winch system (still used today and visible just outside the museum) to keep the water at the correct level. Also here, the fantastic Marion Steinbach Indian Basket Museum displays intricate baskets from 85 tribes. ✉ *130 W. Lake Blvd.* ☎ *530/583–1762* 🌐 *www.northtahoemuseums.org* 🎟 *$5* 🕒 *Closed Mon.–Wed. early-Sept.–late May.*

Watson Cabin Living Museum

MUSEUM | In the middle of Tahoe City sits a 1909 hand-hewn log cabin, the town's oldest structure still on its original site. Now a museum open during the summer, it's filled with century-old furnishings and many reproductions. ✉ *560 N. Lake Blvd.* ☎ *530/583–1762* 🌐 *www.northtahoemuseums.org* 🎟 *Free* 🕒 *Closed Tues.–Wed. and early Sept.–May.*

🍴 Restaurants

Cafe Zenon

$ | **ECLECTIC** | Straightforward Vietnamese pho noodle soup is served all day at this restaurant at Tahoe City's public golf course, but the chef also prepares everything from poutine and kimchi hot dogs to green beans with pork or prawns. The Vietnamese French Dip, a local favorite, substitutes pho broth for the traditional beef. **Known for:** roasted-chicken, Polish sausage, and other sides; Hawaiian buns and gravy with fried egg at weekend brunch; golf course setting (skating rink in winter). [$] *Average main: $11* ✉ *251 N. Lake Blvd.* ✥ *Behind Bank of America building* ☎ *530/583–1517* 🌐 *www.cafezenon.com* 🕒 *Closed Tues.*

★ Christy Hill

$$$$ | **MODERN AMERICAN** | Huge windows reveal stellar lake views at this Euro–Cal restaurant serving seafood, beef, and vegetarian entrées, along with small-plate offerings. The extensive wine list and exceptional desserts earn accolades; the atmosphere is casual. **Known for:** tasting menu a good deal; romantic choice; dinner on the deck in fine weather. [$] *Average main: $37* ✉ *115 Grove St., at N. Lake Blvd.* ☎ *530/583–8551* 🌐 *www.christyhill.com* 🕑 *No lunch.*

Fire Sign Cafe

$ | **AMERICAN** | There's often a wait for breakfast and lunch at this great little diner with pine paneling, hardwood floors, and an exposed-beam ceiling, but it's worth it. The pastries are made from scratch, the salmon is smoked in-house, the salsa is hand cut, and there's real maple syrup for the many types of pancakes and waffles. **Known for:** pastries from scratch; many pancakes and waffles; fruit cobbler for dessert. [$] *Average main: $12* ✉ *1785 W. Lake Blvd.* ✥ *Hwy. 89, 2 miles south of downtown Tahoe City at Fountain Ave.* ☎ *530/583–0871* 🌐 *www.firesigncafe.com* 🕑 *No dinner.*

Wolfdale's

$$$$ | **ECLECTIC** | Consistent, inspired cuisine served in an elegantly simple dining room makes Wolfdale's one of the top restaurants on the lake, albeit among the most expensive. The imaginative entrées, many involving seafood, merge Asian and European cooking, and everything from teriyaki glaze to smoked fish is made in-house. **Known for:** multiple martinis and other cocktails; lake-view setting; happy hour wines and small plates (5–6:30 except Saturday and holidays). [$] *Average main: $39* ✉ *640 N. Lake Blvd., near Grove St.* ☎ *530/583–5700* 🌐 *www.wolfdales.com* 🕑 *Closed Tues. No lunch.*

Hotels

Basecamp Tahoe City

$$ | **B&B/INN** | **FAMILY** | A downtown motel for the 21st century, Basecamp charms its guests with a combination of industrial, retro, and rustic styles. **Pros:** lively public spaces; stylish rooms; convenient to commercial strip with restaurants and grocery stores. **Cons:** some road noise; lacks amenities of large properties; eight-minute walk to local beach. [$] *Rooms from: $149* ✉ *955 N. Lake Blvd.* ☎ *530/580–8430* 🌐 *www.basecamptahoecity.com* 🛏 *24 rooms* 🍴 *Free Breakfast.*

Cottage Inn

$$ | **B&B/INN** | Avoid the crowds by staying in one of these charming circa-1938 log cottages under the towering pines on the lake's west shore. **Pros:** romantic, woodsy setting; all rooms have gas fireplaces, some two-person tubs; private beach access. **Cons:** guests must be older than 12; most cottages accommodate two people maximum; minimum weekend-stay requirement. [$] *Rooms from: $150* ✉ *1690 W. Lake Blvd.* ☎ *530/581–4073, 800/581–4073* 🌐 *www.thecottageinn.com* 🛏 *22 rooms* 🍴 *Free Breakfast.*

Granlibakken Tahoe

$$ | **RESORT** | A condo community with its own snow-play area in winter, this secluded 74-acre resort's name means "a hillside sheltered by fir trees" in Norwegian—adventure fitness, and wellness activities are a key focus. **Pros:** range of lodging options, from studio condos to town houses; secluded location; pool and spa treatments. **Cons:** some guests find the location too secluded; more for families than romantic interludes; conference activities and weddings. [$] *Rooms from: $171* ✉ *725 Granlibakken Rd.* ☎ *530/583–4242 front desk, 800/543–3221 reservations* 🌐 *granlibakken.com* 🛏 *165 rooms* 🍴 *Free Breakfast.*

Mother Nature's Inn

$ | HOTEL | This Tahoe City bargain is a two-story, motel-style array of rooms behind a home-furnishings store. **Pros:** good value; comfortable rooms; in the middle of town near the beach. **Cons:** pet-friendly rooms may bother those with allergies; no views; rooms get little light. $ *Rooms from: $80* ✉ *551 N. Lake Blvd.* ☎ *530/581–4278* ⊕ *www. mothernaturesinn.com* �’ *8 rooms* ⦿ *No meals.*

★ **Sunnyside Steakhouse and Lodge**

$$$ | HOTEL | The views are superb and the hospitality gracious at this lakeside lodge 3 miles south of Tahoe City. **Pros:** complementary continental breakfast and afternoon tea; most rooms have balconies overlooking the lake; lively bar and restaurants. **Cons:** can be pricey for families; noisy in summer; pricey entrées at steak house. $ *Rooms from: $199* ✉ *1850 W. Lake Blvd.* ☎ *530/583–7200, 800/822–2754* ⊕ *www.sunny-sideresort.com* �’ *23 rooms* ⦿ *Free Breakfast.*

 Activities

RAFTING

Truckee River Rafting

WHITE-WATER RAFTING | FAMILY | In summer you can take a self-guided raft trip down a gentle 5-mile stretch of the Truckee River. This outfitter will shuttle you back to Tahoe City at the end of your two- to three-hour trip. ■TIP→ **On a warm day this makes a great family outing.** ✉ *175 River Rd., near W. Lake Blvd.* ☎ *530/583–1111* ⊕ *www.truckeeriver-rafting.com* ➘ *From $48.*

SKIING

Alpine Meadows Ski Area

SKIING/SNOWBOARDING | With an average 450 inches of snow annually, Alpine has some of Tahoe's most reliable conditions. It's usually one of the first areas to open in November and one of the last to close in May or June. Alpine isn't the place for show-offs; instead, you'll find down-to-earth alpine fetishists. The two peaks here are well suited to intermediate skiers, with a number of runs for experts only. Snowboarders and hot-dog skiers will find a terrain park with a super-pipe, rails, and tabletops, as well as a boarder-cross course. Alpine is a great place to learn to ski and has a ski school for kids and adults. On Saturday, because of the limited parking, there's more acreage per person than at other resorts. Lift tickets are good at neighboring Squaw Valley; a free shuttle runs all day between the two ski parks. **Facilities:** 100-plus trails; 2,400 acres; 1,802-foot vertical drop; 13 lifts. ✉ *2600 Alpine Meadows Rd.* ✛ *Off Hwy. 89, 6 miles northwest of Tahoe City, 13 miles south of Truckee* ☎ *530/583–4232, 800/403–0206* ⊕ *www.squawalpine.com* ✉ *Lift ticket $169.*

Tahoe Dave's Skis and Boards

SKIING/SNOWBOARDING | You can rent skis, boards, and snowshoes at this shop, which has the area's best selection of downhill rental equipment. ✉ *590 N. Lake Blvd.* ☎ *530/583–6415* ⊕ *www.tahoe-daves.com.*

Olympic Valley

7 miles north of Tahoe City to Squaw Valley Road; 8½ miles south of Truckee.

Olympic Valley got its name in 1960, when Squaw Valley USA, the ski resort here, hosted the Winter Olympics. Snow sports remain the primary activity, but once summer comes, you can hike into the adjacent Granite Chief Wilderness, explore wildflower-studded alpine meadows, or lie by a swimming pool in one of the Sierra's prettiest valleys.

GETTING HERE AND AROUND

Squaw Valley Road, the only way into Olympic Valley, branches west off Highway 89 about 8 miles south of Truckee. TART connects the Squaw Valley ski area

Squaw Valley USA has runs for skiers of all ability levels, from beginner to expert trails.

with the communities along the north and west shores, and Truckee, with year-round public transportation. Squaw Valley Ski Resort provides a free shuttle to many stops in those same areas.

👁 Sights

High Camp

VIEWPOINT | Ride the Squaw Valley Aerial Tram to this activity hub, which at 8,200 feet commands superb views of Lake Tahoe and the surrounding mountains. In summer, go for a hike, sit by the pool, or have a cocktail and watch the sunset. In winter you can ski or snow-tube. There's also a restaurant, a lounge, and a small Olympic museum. Pick up trail maps at the tram building. ✉ *Aerial Tram Bldg., Squaw Valley* ☎ *800/403–0206* 🌐 *www.squawalpine.com/events-things-do/aerial-tram-rides* 🎟 *Aerial Tram, $46.*

Village at Squaw Valley

COMMERCIAL CENTER | **FAMILY** | The centerpiece of Olympic Valley is a pedestrian mall at the base of several four-story ersatz Bavarian stone-and-timber buildings, where you'll find restaurants, high-end condo rentals, boutiques, and cafés. ✉ *1750 Village East Rd.* ☎ *530/584–1000, 800/403–0206 information* 🌐 *www.squawalpine.com/explore/about/squaw-valley-village-map.*

🍴 Restaurants

Fireside Pizza Company

$ | **PIZZA** | **FAMILY** | Adults might opt for the signature pear-and-Gorgonzola pizza at this modern Italian restaurant, but most kids clamor for the house favorite: an Italian-sausage-and-pepperoni combo with a bubbly blend of four cheeses. Salads and pasta dishes round out the menu at this family-friendly spot. **Known for:** inventive pizzas; good, inexpensive dining option in a pricey area; family friendly. [$] *Average main: $15* ✉ *The Village at Squaw Valley, 1985 Squaw Valley Rd., #25* ☎ *530/584–6150* 🌐 *www.firesidepizza.com.*

Graham's at Squaw Valley

$$$ | ECLECTIC | Sit by a floor-to-ceiling river-rock hearth under a knotty-pine peaked ceiling in this well-run restaurant's intimate dining room. The southern European–inspired menu changes often, but expect hearty entrées such as grilled beef tenderloin with wild mushroom sauce, along with lighter-fare small plates like quail with fig demi-glace or cassoulet. **Known for:** forest feel inside and out; highly regarded wine list; fireside bar for appetizers. $ *Average main: $30* ⊠ *Christy Inn Lodge, 1650 Squaw Valley Rd.* ☎ *530/581–0454* ⊕ *www. dinewine.com* ⊗ *Closed Mon. and Tues. No lunch.*

★ PlumpJack Cafe

$$$$ | AMERICAN | The menu at this silver-tone white-tablecloth restaurant whose wide windows reveal Squaw in all its glory changes seasonally, but look for rib-eye steak, seared diver scallops with risotto, and a filling, inventive vegetarian dish. Rather than complicated, heavy sauces, the chef uses simple reductions to complement a dish, resulting in clean, dynamic flavors. **Known for:** specialty cocktails; less expensive but equally adventurous bar menu; varied, reasonably priced wines. $ *Average main: $42* ⊠ *1920 Squaw Valley Rd.* ☎ *530/583–1578* ⊕ *www.plumpjackcafe. com* ⊗ *No lunch (except at bar).*

🛏 Hotels

★ PlumpJack Squaw Valley Inn

$$$ | HOTEL | Stylish and luxurious, this two-story, cedar-sided inn has a snappy, sophisticated look and laid-back sensibility, perfect for the Bay Area cognoscenti who flock here on weekends. **Pros:** small and intimate; loaded with amenities; personable and attentive service. **Cons:** not the best choice for families with small children; not all rooms have tubs; laid-back sensibility may not work for some guests. $ *Rooms from: $225* ⊠ *1920 Squaw Valley Rd.*

☎ *530/583–1576, 800/323–7666* ⊕ *www. plumpjacksquawvalleyinn.com* ⇥ *56 rooms* �○| *Free Breakfast.*

Resort at Squaw Creek

$$$ | RESORT | This Squaw Valley multifacility offers restaurants, a golf course, spa, heated swimming pool, ice skating rink, chairlift to the mountain, and groomed cross-country ski tracks on the property, plus all the amenities and services you could possibly want in the Tahoe area. **Pros:** every conceivable amenity; private chairlift to Squaw Valley USA for ski-in, ski-out; attractive furnishings. **Cons:** so large it can feel impersonal; high in-season rates; a lot of hubbub during ski season. $ *Rooms from: $219* ⊠ *400 Squaw Creek Rd.* ☎ *530/583–6300, 800/327–3353* ⊕ *www.squawcreek.com* ⇥ *405 rooms* ○| *No meals.*

The Village at Squaw Valley USA

$$$ | HOTEL | FAMILY | Right at the base of the slopes, at the center point of Olympic Valley, the Village's condominiums (from studio to three bedrooms) come complete with gas fireplaces, daily maid service, and heated slate-tile bathroom and kitchen floors. **Pros:** each condo sleeps at least four people; near Village restaurants and shops; at base of slopes. **Cons:** village often gets crowded on weekends; nicely appointed but not high style; lacks room service and other hotel amenities. $ *Rooms from: $199* ⊠ *1750 Village East Rd.* ☎ *530/584–1000, 888/259–1428* ⊕ *www.squawalpine.com/ lodging* ⇥ *198 rooms* ○| *No meals.*

🏃 Activities

GOLF

Resort at Squaw Creek Golf Course

GOLF | For beautiful views of Squaw Valley's surrounding peaks, play this narrow, challenging championship course designed by Robert Trent Jones Jr. The design emphasizes accuracy over distance, especially on the front nine. All fees include a golf cart plus valet parking;

rates drop after noon and again after 3 pm. ⊠ *400 Squaw Creek Rd.* ☎ *530/583–6300, 530/581–6637 pro shop* ⊕ *www.destinationhotels.com/squawcreek/recreation* ⌇ *From $89* ⅃ *18 holes, 6931 yards, par 71.*

SKIING

★ Squaw Valley USA

SKIING/SNOWBOARDING | Known for some of the toughest skiing in the Tahoe area, this park was the centerpiece of the 1960 Winter Olympics. Today it's the definitive North Tahoe ski resort and among the top-three megaresorts in California (the other two are Heavenly and Mammoth). Although Squaw has changed significantly since the Olympics, the skiing is still world-class and extends across vast bowls stretched between six peaks. Experts often head directly to the untamed terrain of the infamous KT-22 face, which has bumps, cliffs, and gulp-and-go chutes, or to the nearly vertical Palisades, where many famous extreme-skiing films have been shot. Fret not, beginners and intermediates: you have plenty of wide-open, groomed trails at High Camp (which sits at the *top* of the mountain) and around the more challenging Snow King Peak. Snowboarders and show-off skiers can tear up the five fantastic terrain parks, which include a giant super-pipe. Ski passes are good at neighboring Alpine Meadows; free shuttles run all day between the two ski parks. (By the early 2020s a gondola will connect them.) **Facilities:** 178 trails; 3,600 acres; 2,840-foot vertical drop; 30 lifts. ⊠ *1960 Squaw Valley Rd.* ✛ *Off Hwy. 89, 7 miles northwest of Tahoe City* ☎ *800/403–0206* ⊕ *www.squawalpine.com* ⌇ *Lift ticket $179.*

Tahoe Dave's Skis and Boards

SKIING/SNOWBOARDING | If you don't want to pay resort prices, you can rent and tune downhill skis and snowboards at this shop. ⊠ *3039 Hwy. 89, at Squaw Valley Rd.* ☎ *530/583–5665* ⊕ *www.tahoedaves.com.*

Truckee

13 miles northwest of Kings Beach, 14 miles north of Tahoe City.

Formerly a decrepit railroad town in the mountains, Truckee is now the trendy first stop for many Tahoe visitors. The town was officially established around 1863, and by 1868 it had gone from a stagecoach station to a major stopover for trains bound for the Pacific via the new transcontinental railroad. Every day, freight trains and Amtrak's *California Zephyr* still idle briefly at the depot in the middle of town. The visitor center inside the depot has a walking-tour map of historic Truckee.

Across from the station, where Old West facades line the main drag, you'll find galleries, gift shops, boutiques, a wine-tasting room, old-fashioned diners, and several good restaurants.

GETTING HERE AND AROUND

Truckee is off Interstate 80 between Highways 89 and 267. Greyhound and Amtrak stop here, and TART buses serve the area.

ESSENTIALS

VISITOR INFORMATION Truckee Donner Chamber of Commerce and the California Welcome Center. ⊠ *Amtrak depot, 10065 Donner Pass Rd., near Spring St.* ☎ *530/587–2757* ⊕ *www.truckee.com.*

◉ Sights

Donner Memorial State Park and Emigrant Trail Museum

NATIONAL/STATE PARK | The park and museum commemorate the 89 members of the Donner Party, westward-bound pioneers who became trapped in the Sierra in the winter of 1846–47 in snow 22 feet deep. Barely more than half survived, some by resorting to cannibalism. The absorbing Emigrant Trail Museum in the visitor center contains exhibits about the Donner Party, regional Native Americans, and railroad and transportation development in the area. In the park, you can picnic, hike, camp, and go boating, fishing, and waterskiing in summer; winter brings cross-country skiing and snowshoeing on groomed trails. ✉ *12593 Donner Pass Rd.* ✥ *Off I–80, Exit 184, 2 miles west of Truckee* ☎ *530/582–7892* 🌐 *www.parks.ca.gov/donnermemorial* 🎫 *$10 parking, day-use ($5 in winter).*

🍴 Restaurants

★ Cottonwood Restaurant & Bar

$$$ | **ECLECTIC** | Perched above town on the site of North America's first chairlift, this local institution has a bar decked out with old wooden skis, sleds, skates, and photos of Truckee's early days. The ambitious menu includes grilled steak, baby-back short ribs with chipotle barbecue jus, and house-special pasta dishes like chicken linguine. **Known for:** early-bird three-course dinner except in high season; wine selection; hilltop views from atmospheric bar. [$] *Average main: $28* ✉ *10142 Rue Hilltop Rd., off Brockway Rd., ¼ mile south of downtown* ☎ *530/587–5711* 🌐 *www.cottonwoodrestaurant.com* 🕒 *No lunch.*

FiftyFifty Brewing Company

$$ | **AMERICAN** | In this Truckee brewpub the warm red tones and comfy booths, plus a pint of the Donner Party porter (or a shot of bourbon), will take the nip out of a cold day on the slopes. The menu includes salads, burgers, inventive pizzas, barbecued ribs, pan-seared salmon, and the house specialty, a pulled-pork sandwich. **Known for:** high-quality burger beef; 2018 Brewery Group of the Year honors at top beer fest; après-ski action. [$] *Average main: $21* ✉ *11197 Brockway Rd., near Martis Valley Rd.* ☎ *530/587–2337* 🌐 *www.fiftyfiftybrewing.com.*

★ Marty's Cafe

$ | **AMERICAN** | You'd never know from this downtown café's laid-back decor that the namesake owner-chef's resume includes stints at fancy restaurants from Beverly Hills to Kennebunkport. Marty's hearty breakfasts (like the house-made granola or the fried egg sandwich with bacon and Gruyère on toasted French bread) and lunches—burgers, hoagies, "char dogs," sloppy joes, and a winning chicken-and-avocado BLT—are served from opening until closing. **Known for:** well-executed cuisine; daily specials and seasonal salads; ebullient hospitality. [$] *Average main: $15* ✉ *10115 Donner Pass Rd.* ☎ *530/550–8208* 🌐 *martyscafetruckee.com* 🕒 *No dinner.*

Moody's Bistro, Bar & Beats

$$$ | **ECLECTIC** | Head here for contemporary-Cal cuisine in a sexy dining room with pumpkin-color walls, burgundy velvet banquettes, and art-deco fixtures. The earthy, sure-handed cooking features organically grown ingredients: look for ahi poke, snazzy pizzas bubbling-hot from a brick oven, braised lamb shanks, pan-roasted wild game, fresh seafood, and organic beef. **Known for:** lighter fare for lunch; summer alfresco dining; live music in bar some nights. [$] *Average main: $27* ✉ *10007 Bridge St., at Donner Pass Rd.* ☎ *530/587–8688* 🌐 *www.moodysbistro.com.*

Pianeta Ristorante

$$$ | **ITALIAN** | A longtime town favorite, Pianeta serves high-style Italian cuisine in a warmly lit bi-level redbrick space on Truckee's historic main drag. Start with a beef carpaccio antipasto plate or perhaps house-made spicy-fennel and mild sausages, following up with a pasta course of ravioli Bolognese (both pasta and sauce made in-house), an entrée of ragout with spicy sausage and Mexican prawns—or both. **Known for:** welcoming atmosphere; tiramisu and panna cotta for dessert; West Coast and Italian wine selections. [$] *Average main: $29* ✉ *10096 Donner Pass Rd.* ☎ *530/587–4694* 🌐 *www.pianetarestauranttruckee.com* 🕒 *No lunch.*

Squeeze In

$ | **AMERICAN** | Meet the locals at Truckee's top choice for breakfast, thanks to the dozens of omelets and several variations on eggs Benedict along with banana-walnut pancakes and French toast oozing with cream cheese. At lunch savor homemade soups and sandwiches. **Known for:** cheeseburger omelet; homemade soups; gluten-free variations. [$] *Average main: $14* ✉ *10060 Donner Pass Rd., near Bridge St.* ☎ *530/587–9814* 🌐 *www.squeezein.com* ⏲ *No dinner.*

Truckee Tavern and Grill

$$$ | **AMERICAN** | The wood-fired grill in this second-floor downtown restaurant turns out steaks, chicken, and chops along with fish dishes that might include Mt. Lassen trout with white beans and mushrooms. As with the food, the decor is New West contemporary—bricks line the wall behind the bar, where mixologists craft wiggy drinks like the Salvador (as in Dalí, with rye, mescal, blood orange, and egg white), and, in tribute to Truckee's bootlegging past, pour artisanal small-batch gin and whiskey. **Known for:** buffalo tri-tip; pasta and fish entrées; deck overlooking downtown action. [$] *Average main: $26* ✉ *10118 Donner Pass Rd., near Spring St.* ☎ *530/587–3766* 🌐 *www.truckeetavern.com* ⏲ *No lunch Mon.–Wed.*

Hotels

Cedar House Sport Hotel

$$ | **HOTEL** | The clean, spare lines of the Cedar House's wooden exterior evoke a modern European feel, while energy-saving heating, cooling, and lighting systems emphasize the owners' commitment to sustainability. **Pros:** environmentally friendly; hip yet comfortable; heated-tile bathroom floors. **Cons:** some bathrooms on the small side; not all bathrooms have tubs; about a mile from historic downtown Truckee. [$] *Rooms from: $170* ✉ *10918 Brockway Rd.* ☎ *530/582–5655, 866/582–5655* 🌐 *www.cedarhousesporthotel.com* 🛏 *40 rooms* 🍴 *Free Breakfast.*

Northstar California Resort

$$$ | **RESORT** | The area's most complete destination resort entices families with its sports activities and concentration of restaurants, shops, and accommodations. **Pros:** array of lodging types; on-site shuttle; several dining options in Northstar Village. **Cons:** family accommodations can be pricey; lacks intimacy; some units not as attractive as others. [$] *Rooms from: $185* ✉ *5001 Northstar Dr.* ✣ *Off Hwy. 267, 6 miles southeast of Truckee* ☎ *530/562–1010, 800/466–6784* 🌐 *www.northstarcalifornia.com* 🛏 *250 rooms* 🍴 *No meals.*

★ Ritz-Carlton Highlands Court, Lake Tahoe

$$$$ | **RESORT** | Nestled mid-mountain on the Northstar ski resort, the plush accommodations of the four-story Ritz-Carlton have floor-to-ceiling windows for maximum views, along with fireplaces, cozy robes, and down comforters. **Pros:** superb service; gorgeous setting; ski-in, ski out convenience. **Cons:** in-season prices as breathtaking as the views; resort fee and mandatory valet parking add to cost of stay; must go off-site for golf and tennis. [$] *Rooms from: $342* ✉ *13031 Ritz-Carlton Highlands Court* ☎ *530/562–3000, 800/241–3333* 🌐 *www.ritzcarlton.com/laketahoe* 🛏 *170 rooms* 🍴 *No meals.*

River Street Inn

$$ | **B&B/INN** | On the banks of the Truckee River, this 1882 wood-and-stone inn has uncluttered, comfortable rooms that are simply decorated, with attractive, country-style wooden furniture and extras like flat-screen TVs. **Pros:** tidy rooms; good value; in historic downtown Truckee. **Cons:** parking is a half block from inn; decor is simple; noise from on-site restaurant and bar and nearby trains. [$] *Rooms from: $145* ✉ *10009 E. River St.* ☎ *530/550–9290 inn, 530/550–9222 restaurant* 🌐 *www.riverstreetinntruckee.com* 🛏 *7 rooms* 🍴 *Free Breakfast.*

Truckee Hotel

$$$ | HOTEL | A four-story hotel in business in various forms since 1873, the Truckee Hotel attracts history buffs and skiers, the latter for the reasonable rates when in-season prices skyrocket at Northstar, Sugar Bowl, and other nearby resorts. **Pros:** historic atmosphere; convenient to shops and restaurants; same owners operate a modern Hampton Inn nearby. **Cons:** no pool, fitness center, elevator; train and other noise issues (when booking ask for a quiet room); most rooms lack a private bathroom (though all have a sink). $ *Rooms from: $189* ✉ *10007 Bridge St.* ☎ *530/587–4444, 800/659–6921* ⊕ *www.truckeehotel. com* ⇆ *32 rooms, 24 with shared baths* ⦿ *Free Breakfast.*

 Activities

GOLF

Coyote Moon Golf Course

GOLF | With pine trees lining the fairways and no houses to spoil the view, this course is as beautiful as it is challenging. Fees include a shared cart; the greens fee drops at 1 pm and dips again at 3. ✉ *10685 Northwoods Blvd., off Donner Pass Rd.* ☎ *530/587–0886* ⊕ *www.coyotemoongolf.com* ⇆ *$175* ⦿ *18 holes, 7177 yards, par 72* ⊙ *Closed late fall–late spring.*

Northstar Golf

GOLF | Robert Muir Graves designed this course that combines hilly terrain and open meadows. The front nine holes here are open-links style, while the challenging back nine move through tight, tree-lined fairways. Rates, which include a cart, drop successively after 11, 1, and 4. ✉ *168 Basque Dr.* ✛ *Off Northstar Dr., west off Hwy. 267* ☎ *530/562–3290 pro shop* ⊕ *www.northstarcalifornia.com* ⇆ *$95 for 18 holes* ⦿ *18 holes, 6781 yards, par 72.*

MOUNTAIN BIKING

Cyclepaths Mountain Bike Adventures

BICYCLING | This combination full-service bike shop and bike-adventure outfitter offers instruction in mountain biking, guided tours, tips for self-guided bike touring, bike repairs, and books and maps on the area. ✉ *Pioneer Center, 10825 Pioneer Trail, Suite 105* ☎ *530/582– 1890* ⊕ *www.cyclepaths.net.*

Northstar California Bike Park

BICYCLING | From late May through September Northstar's ski slopes transform into a magnificent lift-served bike park with 100 miles of challenging terrain, including the aptly named Livewire trail. Guided tours, multiday retreats, and downhill, cross-country, and endurance races are available for riders of all abilities. ✉ *Northstar Dr., off Hwy. 267* ☎ *530/562–1010* ⊕ *www.northstarcalifornia.com* ⇆ *Lift $60.*

SKIING

★ **Northstar California**

SKIING/SNOWBOARDING | Meticulous grooming and long cruisers make this resort a paradise for intermediate skiers and a fine choice for families. Although the majority of the trails are intermediate in difficulty, advanced skiers and riders have access to Lookout Mountain's more than two dozen expert trails and 347 acres of gated terrain and steeps. The diversity of terrain in proximity makes it easier for families and groups with varying skills to hang out with each other. As for terrain parks, the ones here are considered among North America's best, with features that include a 420-foot-long super-pipe, a half pipe, rails and boxes, and lots of kickers. The Cross Country, Telemark and Snowshoe Center, located mid-mountain, is the starting point for a network of 35 km (22 miles) of groomed trails, including double-set tracks and skating lanes. The trails are also fat-bike friendly, so nonskiers can enjoy the park, too. The school has programs for skiers ages three and up, and on-site care is available for tots two and older. **Facilities:** 100 trails; 3,170 acres; 2,280-foot vertical drop; 20 lifts. ⊠ *5001 Northstar Dr.* ☎ *530/562–2267* ⊕ *www.northstarcalifornia.com* ⚑ *Lift ticket $160.*

★ Royal Gorge

SKIING/SNOWBOARDING | If you love to cross-country, don't miss Royal Gorge, which serves up 140 km (124 miles) of track for all abilities, six trail systems on a whopping 6,000 acres, a ski school, and nine warming huts. Because the complex, affiliated with Sugar Bowl, sits right on the Sierra Crest, the views are drop-dead gorgeous. ⊠ *9411 Pahatsi Dr., Soda Springs* ✛ *Off I–80, Soda Springs/ Norden exit* ☎ *530/426–3871, 530/426– 3871* ⊕ *www.royalgorge.com* ☞ *All-day pass $35.*

Sugar Bowl Ski Resort

SKIING/SNOWBOARDING | Opened in 1939 by Walt Disney, this is the oldest—and one of the best—resorts at Tahoe. Atop Donner Summit, it receives an incredible 500 inches of snowfall annually. Four peaks are connected by 1,650 acres of skiable terrain, with everything from gentle groomed corduroy to wide-open bowls to vertical rocky chutes and outstanding tree skiing. Snowboarders can hit two terrain parks with numerous boxes, rails, and jumps. Because it's more compact than some of the area's megaresorts, there's a gentility here that distinguishes Sugar Bowl from its competitors, making this a great place for families and a low-pressure, low-key place to learn to ski. It's not huge, but there's some very challenging terrain (experts: head to the Palisades). There is limited lodging at the base area. Facilities: 100 trails; 1,650 acres; 1,500-foot vertical drop; 12 lifts. ⊠ *629 Sugar Bowl Rd., Norden* ✛ *Off Donner Pass Rd., 3 miles east of I–80 Soda Springs/ Norden exit, 10 miles west of Truckee* ☎ *530/426–9000, 530/426–1111 snow phone* ⊕ *www.sugarbowl.com* ⚑ *Lift ticket from $118.*

Tahoe Dave's

SKIING/SNOWBOARDING | You can save money by renting skis and boards at this shop, which has the area's best selection and also repairs and tunes equipment. ⊠ *10200 Donner Pass Rd., near Spring St.* ☎ *530/582–0900* ⊕ *www. tahoedaves.com.*

Tahoe Donner Cross Country Ski Center

SKIING/SNOWBOARDING | Just north of Truckee, the center, which ranks among the nation's best cross-country venues for the skiing and the magnificent Sierra Crest views, includes 65 trails on 100 km (62 miles) of groomed tracks on more than 2,800 acres. In addition to cross-country skiing, there are fat-biking, dog, and snowshoeing trails. ⊠ *15275 Alder Creek Rd.* ☎ *530/587–9484* ⊕ *www.tahoedonner.com/xc.*

Carnelian Bay to Kings Beach

5–10 miles northeast of Tahoe City.

The small lakeside commercial districts of Carnelian Bay and Tahoe Vista service the thousand or so locals who live in the area year-round and the thousands more who have summer residences or launch their boats here. Kings Beach, the last town heading east on Highway 28 before the Nevada border, is full of basic motels and rental condos, restaurants, and shops.

GETTING HERE AND AROUND

To reach Kings Beach and Carnelian Bay from the California side, take Highway 89 north to Highway 28 north and then east. From the Nevada side, follow Highway 28 north and then west. TART provides public transportation in this area.

Beaches

Kings Beach State Recreation Area

BEACH—SIGHT | FAMILY | The north shore's 28-acre Kings Beach State Recreation Area, one of the largest such areas on the lake, is open year-round. The 700-foot-long sandy beach gets crowded in summer with people swimming, sunbathing, Jet Skiing, riding in paddleboats, spiking volleyballs, and tossing Frisbees. If you're going to spend the day, come early to snag a table in the picnic area; there's also a good playground. **Amenities:** food and drink; parking (fee); toilets; water sports. **Best for:** sunrise; sunset; swimming; windsurfing. ✉ *8318 N. Lake Blvd., Kings Beach* ☎ *530/546–7248* 🌐 *www.parks.ca.gov* 🎟 *$10 parking fee.*

Restaurants

Gar Woods Grill and Pier

$$$$ | ECLECTIC | The view's the thing at this lakeside stalwart, where you can watch the sun shimmer on the water through the dining room's plateglass windows or from the heated outdoor deck. Price wise, this is a better bet for lunch or weekend breakfast than for dinner, at which grilled steak and fish are menu mainstays, but specialties like crab chiles rellenos and pomegranate braised pork ribs also merit consideration. **Known for:** lake views; grilled steak and fish; specialty cocktails. [$] *Average main: $36* ✉ *5000 N. Lake Blvd., Carnelian Bay* ✣ *Hwy. 28, 2 miles west of Tahoe Vista* ☎ *530/546–3366* 🌐 *www.garwoods.com.*

Jason's Beachside Grille

$$ | AMERICAN | If the kids want burgers but you want bourbon, area mainstay Jason's has a full bar as well as steaks, 10 kinds of burgers, teriyaki chicken, and a big salad bar. The whole place is wood, from floor to ceiling, lending it an ultrarustic feel. **Known for:** salad bar; summer dining on deck overlooking the lake, tables by fireplace in winter. [$] *Average main: $19* ✉ *8338 N. Lake Blvd., Kings Beach* ☎ *530/546–3315* 🌐 *jasonsbeachsidegrille.com.*

Soule Domain

$$$ | ECLECTIC | Rough-hewn wood beams, a vaulted wood ceiling, and in winter, a roaring fireplace, lend high romance to this cozy 1927 pine-log cabin next to the Tahoe Biltmore casino. Chef-owner Charlie Soule's specialties include curried almond chicken, fresh sea scallops poached in champagne with a kiwi-and-mango cream sauce, and a vegan sauté judiciously flavored with ginger, jalapeños, sesame seeds, and teriyaki sauce. **Known for:** romance by candlelight; skillfully prepared cuisine; suave service. [$] *Average main: $30* ✉ *9983 Cove St., ½ block up Stateline Rd. off Hwy. 28, Kings Beach* ✣ *Restaurant is just west of Tahoe Biltmore casino at California-Nevada border.* ☎ *530/546–7529* 🌐 *www.souledomain.com* ⏲ *No lunch.*

Spindleshanks American Bistro and Wine Bar

$$$ | AMERICAN | A local favorite on the Old Brockway Golf Course, Spindleshanks serves mostly classic American cooking—ribs, steaks, and seafood updated with adventurous sauces—as well as house-made ravioli. Savor a drink from the full bar or choose a wine from the extensive list while you enjoy views of Lake Tahoe or the historic greens where Bing Crosby hosted his first golf tournament in 1934. **Known for:** classic American cooking; Lake Tahoe views; patio dining. [$] *Average main: $28* ✉ *400 Brassie Ave., Kings Beach* ✣ *At Hwy. 267 and N. Lake Tahoe Blvd.* ☎ *530/546–2191* 🌐 *www.spindleshankstahoe.com.*

Hotels

Ferrari's Crown Resort

$ | **HOTEL** | **FAMILY** | Great for families with kids and all travelers on a budget willing to trade style and amenities for below-average rates and (from some rooms) impressive water views, the family-owned Ferrari's has straightforward rooms in two formerly separate vintage-1950s motels, sitting side-by-side on the lake. **Pros:** family-friendly; lakeside location; a few rooms value-priced. **Cons:** older facility with unappealing exterior; thin walls; uninspired breakfast. [$] *Rooms from: $99* ✉ *8200 N. Lake Blvd., Kings Beach* ☎ *530/546–3388, 800/645–2260* 🌐 *www.tahoecrown.com* 🛏 *72 rooms* 🍴 *Free Breakfast.*

Mourelatos Lakeshore Resort

$$ | **B&B/INN** | At first glance this family-run waterfront property looks like a slightly above-average two-story motel, but with a private beach, two hot tubs, ceaselessly alluring lake and mountain vistas, and summertime barbecuing, kayaking, and other extras it legitimately lays claim to the title of resort. **Pros:** private beach; some rooms have full kitchens; summertime barbecuing and kayaking. **Cons:** decor a tad dated; books up quickly for summer; some rooms lack sufficient heat in winter. [$] *Rooms from: $160* ✉ *6834 N. Lake Blvd., Tahoe Vista* ☎ *530/546–9500* 🌐 *www.mlrtahoe.com* 🛏 *32 rooms* 🍴 *Free Breakfast.*

Rustic Cottages

$ | **HOTEL** | **FAMILY** | These charming clapboard cottages sit clustered beneath tall pine trees across the road from Lake Tahoe and a little beach. **Pros:** woodsy Old Tahoe feel; expanded continental breakfast; good value. **Cons:** older facility; some rooms are very small; lacks big-hotel amenities. [$] *Rooms from: $119* ✉ *7449 N. Lake Blvd., Tahoe Vista* ☎ *530/546–3523, 888/778–7842* 🌐 *www.rusticcottages.com* 🛏 *20 rooms* 🍴 *Free Breakfast.*

Incline Village

3 miles east of Crystal Bay.

Incline Village dates to the early 1960s, when an Oklahoma developer bought 10,000 acres north of Lake Tahoe. His idea was to sketch out a plan for a town without a central commercial district, hoping to prevent congestion and to preserve the area's natural beauty. One-acre lakeshore lots originally fetched $12,000 to $15,000; today you couldn't buy the same land for less than several million.

GETTING HERE AND AROUND

From the California side, reach Incline Village via Highway 89 or 267 to Highway 28. From South Lake Tahoe, take U.S. 50 north to Highway 28 north. TART serves the communities along Lake Tahoe's north and west shores from Incline Village to Tahoma.

ESSENTIALS

VISITOR INFORMATION Lake Tahoe Incline Village/Crystal Bay Visitors Bureau. ✉ *969 Tahoe Blvd.* ☎ *775/832–1606, 800/468–2463* 🌐 *www.gotahoenorth.com.*

Sights

Lakeshore Drive

SCENIC DRIVE | Take this beautiful drive to see some of the most expensive real estate in Nevada. The route is discreetly marked: to find it, start at the Hyatt hotel and drive westward along the lake. ✉ *Incline Village.*

★ **Thunderbird Lodge**

HOUSE | George Whittell, a San Francisco socialite who once owned 40,000 acres of property along the lake, began building this lodge in 1936, completing it in 1941. You can tour the mansion and the grounds by reservation only, and though it's pricey to do so, you'll be rewarded with a rare glimpse of a time when only the very wealthy had homes at Tahoe. The lodge is accessible via a bus from the Incline Village–Crystal Bay Visitors Bureau, several boats from the Hyatt in Incline Village, and a 1950 wooden cruiser from Zephyr Cove. ✉ *5000 Hwy. 28* ☎ *775/832–8750* 🌐 *www.thunderbird-tahoe.org/tours* 🎫 *From $50 for bus tour, $140 for boat tours.*

Beaches

Lake Tahoe–Nevada State Park and Sand Harbor Beach

BEACH—SIGHT | Protecting much of the lake's eastern shore from development, this park comprises several sections that stretch from Incline Village to Zephyr Cove. Beaches and trails provide access to a wilder side of the lake, whether you're into cross-country skiing, hiking, or just relaxing at a picnic. With a gently sloping beach for lounging, crystal-clear water for swimming and snorkeling, and a picnic area shaded by cedars and pines, **Sand Harbor Beach** sometimes reaches capacity by 11 am on summer weekends. A handicap-accessible nature trail has interpretive signs and beautiful lake views. Pets are not allowed on the beach from mid-April through mid-October. **Amenities**: food and drink; parking ($12 mid-April–mid-October, $7 rest of the year); toilets; water sports. **Best for**: boating; snorkeling; sunset; swimming; walking. ✉ *Sand Harbor Beach, Hwy. 28, 3 miles south of Incline Village* ☎ *775/831–0494* 🌐 *parks.nv.gov/parks/sand-harbor.*

Restaurants

Azzara's

$$ | **ITALIAN** | This dependable if not fabulous Italian family restaurant serves a dozen pasta dishes and many pizzas, as well as chicken, veal, shrimp, and beef. Prices initially might seem high, but once you factor in soup or salad and garlic bread, it's a pretty good value. **Known for:** family run; daily specials; excellent tiramisu. [$] *Average main: $22* ✉ *Raley's Shopping Center, 930 Tahoe Blvd., near Village Blvd.* ☎ *775/831–0346* 🌐 *www.azzaras.com* ⏲ *Closed Mon. No lunch.*

Fredrick's Fusion Bistro

$$$ | **ECLECTIC** | Copper-top tables lend a chic look to the dining room at this intimate bistro. The menu consists of a mélange of European and Asian dishes—braised short ribs, roasted duck with caramel-pecan glaze, fresh sushi rolls—most of them prepared with organic produce and free-range meats. **Known for:** chic and intimate; organic, free-range meat in most dishes; fireside tables. [$] *Average main: $24* ✉ *907 Tahoe Blvd., at Village Blvd.* ☎ *775/832–3007* 🌐 *fredricksbistro.com* ⏲ *Closed Sun. and Mon. No lunch.*

Le Bistro

$$$$ | **FRENCH** | Incline Village's hidden gem (this restaurant is hard to find, so ask for directions when you book) serves French-country cuisine in a romantic dining room with single-stem roses adorning linen-dressed tables. The five-course prix-fixe menu may include starters like flame-broiled eggplant with ratatouille or escargots, followed by one of several salads (try the gem lettuce Caesar) and lamb loin with lentils and tomato chutney or *coquille St.-Jacques* (scallops in cream sauce), paired with award-winning wines if you choose. **Known for:** romantic setting; five-course prix-fixe meal with wine pairings; gracious, attentive service. [$] *Average main: $65* ✉ *120 Country Club Dr., #29* ✥ *Off Lakeshore Blvd.* ☎ *775/831–0800* 🌐 *www.lebistrotahoe.com* ⏲ *Closed Sun. and Mon. No lunch.*

★ Mountain High Sandwich Company

$ | **AMERICAN** | A casual plank-floored all-natural deli serving breakfast and lunch, Mountain High may well be the only place in Tahoe to find coconut chia seed pudding and similar delicacies. More familiar fare—biscuits and sausage gravy for breakfast, house-smoked tri-tip sandwiches for lunch—is

Get to Sand Harbor Beach in Lake Tahoe–Nevada State Park early; the park sometimes fills to capacity before lunchtime in summer.

also on the menu, with many selections gluten-free and vegan or vegetarian friendly. **Known for:** grab-and-go items; inventive soups; sustainable practices. [$] *Average main: $10* ✉ *120 Country Club Dr., Suite 28* ☎ *775/298–2636* 🌐 *www.mountainhighsandwichco.com* 🕒 *Closed Mon. No dinner.*

Hotels

Hyatt Regency Lake Tahoe

$$$ | RESORT | A full-service destination resort on 26 acres of prime lakefront property, the Hyatt has a range of luxurious accommodations, from tower-hotel rooms to lakeside cottages. **Pros:** incredible views; low-key casino; luxurious accommodations. **Cons:** pricey (especially for families); feels corporate; smallish beach. [$] *Rooms from: $227* ✉ *111 Country Club Dr.* ☎ *775/832–1234, 888/899–5019* 🌐 *www.laketahoe.hyatt.com* 🛏 *422 rooms* 🍴 *No meals.*

Activities

GOLF

Incline Championship

GOLF | Robert Trent Jones Sr. designed this challenging course of tightly cut, tree-lined fairways laced with water hazards that demand accuracy as well as distance skills. Greens fee includes a cart, except for the 4:30 pm Super Twilight rate of $3 per hole (cart $25). ✉ *955 Fairway Blvd., at Northwood Blvd., north off Hwy. 28* ☎ *866/925–4653 reservations, 775/832–1146 pro shop* 🌐 *www.yourtahoeplace.com/golf-incline* 🎫 *$190 weekdays, $200 weekends* ⛳ *18 holes, 7106 yards, par 72.*

Incline Mountain

GOLF | Robert Trent Jones Jr. designed this executive (shorter) course that requires accuracy more than distance skills. The greens fee includes a cart. ✉ *690 Wilson Way, at Golfer's Pass, south off Hwy. 431* ☎ *866/925–4653 reservations, 775/832–1150 pro shop* 🌐 *www.yourtahoeplace.com/golf-incline* 🎫 *From $65* ⛳ *18 holes, 3527 yards, par 58.*

MOUNTAIN BIKING
Flume Trail Bikes

BICYCLING | You can rent bikes and get helpful tips from this company, which also operates a bike shuttle to popular trailheads. ⊠ *1115 Tunnel Creek Rd., at Ponderosa Ranch Rd., off Hwy. 28* ☎ *775/298–2501* ⊕ *www.flumetrailtahoe. com* ⊠ *From $45.*

SKIING
Diamond Peak

SKIING/SNOWBOARDING | Diamond Peak has affordable rates and many special programs. Snowmaking covers 75% of the mountain, and runs are groomed nightly. The ride up the 1-mile Crystal Express rewards you with fantastic views. Diamond Peak is less crowded than Tahoe's larger ski parks and provides free shuttles to nearby lodgings. A great place for beginners and intermediates, it's appropriately priced for families. Though there are some steep-aspect black-diamond runs, advanced skiers may find the acreage too limited. For snowboarders there's a small terrain park. **Facilities:** 30 trails; 655 acres; 1,840-foot vertical drop; 7 lifts. ⊠ *1210 Ski Way, off Country Club Dr.* ☎ *775/832–1177* ⊕ *www.diamondpeak.com* ⊠ *Lift ticket from $89.*

Mt. Rose Ski Tahoe

SKIING/SNOWBOARDING | At this park, ski some of Tahoe's highest slopes and take in bird's-eye views of Reno, the lake, and Carson Valley. Though more compact than the bigger Tahoe resorts, Mt. Rose has the area's highest base elevation and consequently the driest snow. The mountain has a wide variety of terrain. The most challenging is the Chutes, 200 acres of gulp-and-go advanced-to-expert vertical. Intermediates can choose steep groomers or mellow, wide-open boulevards. Beginners have their own corner of the mountain, with gentle, wide slopes. Boarders and tricksters have several terrain parks to choose from, on opposite sides of the mountain, allowing them to follow the sun as it tracks across the resort. The mountain gets hit hard in storms; check conditions before heading up during inclement weather or on a windy day. **Facilities:** 61 trails; 1,200 acres; 1,800-foot vertical drop; 8 lifts. ⊠ *22222 Mt. Rose Hwy., Reno* ⌖ *Hwy. 431, 11 miles north of Incline Village* ☎ *775/849–0704* ⊕ *www.skirose.com* ⊠ *Lift ticket $135.*

Tahoe Meadows Snowplay Area

SKIING/SNOWBOARDING | This is the most popular area near the north shore for noncommercial cross-country skiing, sledding, tubing, snowshoeing, and snowmobiling. ⊠ *Off Hwy. 431* ⌖ *From Hwy. 28 at Incline Village, head north about 6½ miles on Hwy. 431 toward Mt. Rose Ski Area.*

Zephyr Cove

22 miles south of Incline Village.

The largest settlement between Incline Village and the Stateline area is Zephyr Cove, a tiny resort. It has a beach, marina, campground, picnic area, coffee shop in a log lodge, rustic cabins, and nearby riding stables.

GETTING HERE AND AROUND
From the north shore communities, reach Zephyr Cove by following Highway 28 along the eastern side of the lake. From South Lake Tahoe, take U.S. 50 north and then west. Public transportation isn't available in Zephyr Cove.

⊚ Sights

Cave Rock
NATURE SITE | Near Zephyr Cove, this 75 feet of solid stone at the southern end of Lake Tahoe–Nevada State Park is the throat of an extinct volcano. The impressive outcropping towers over a parking lot, a lakefront picnic ground, and a boat launch. The views are some of the best on the lake; this is a good

spot to stop and take a picture. ⚠ **Cave Rock is a sacred burial site for the Washoe Indians. Climbing to it or through it is prohibited.** ✉ *U.S. 50, 4 miles north of Zephyr Cove* ☎ *775/831–0494* ⊕ *www. parks.nv.gov/parks/lake-tahoe-nevada-state-park-2* 🎫 *$10.*

🍴 Restaurants

Capisce?

$$$ | ITALIAN | The signature mushroom-and-tomato sauce is so thick it's called "gravy" at this roadside restaurant whose menu emphasizes old favorites from the Italian American side of the family that runs it. The mildly spicy concoction adds zest to cioppino (seafood stew), lasagna, and pasta dishes that include house-made ravioli that some diners prefer slathered instead with a velvety butter-and-Parmesan-cheese sauce. **Known for:** old family recipes; full bar patronized by many locals; desserts including gooey-wonderful cinnamon bun. 🅢 *Average main: $27* ✉ *178 U.S. 50* ☎ *775/580–7500* ⊕ *www.capiscelaketahoe.com* 🕐 *Closed Mon. No lunch.*

🛏 Hotels

Zephyr Cove Resort

$$$ | RENTAL | FAMILY | Beneath towering pines at the lake's edge stand 28 cozy, modern vacation cabins with peaked knotty-pine ceilings. **Pros:** family-friendly; cozy cabins; old-school ambience. **Cons:** lodge rooms are basic; can be noisy in summer; not all cabins have fireplaces. 🅢 *Rooms from: $209* ✉ *760 U.S. 50, 4 miles north of Stateline* ☎ *775/589–4906, 800/238–2463* ⊕ *www.zephyrcove.com* 🛏 *32 rooms* 🍴 *No meals.*

Stateline

5 miles south of Zephyr Cove.

Stateline is the archetypal Nevada border town. Its four high-rise casinos are as vertical and contained as the commercial district of South Lake Tahoe, on the California side, is horizontal and sprawling. And Stateline is as relentlessly indoors-oriented as the rest of the lake is focused on the outdoors. This small strip is where you'll find the most concentrated action at Lake Tahoe: restaurants (including typical casino buffets), showrooms with semi-famous headliners and razzle-dazzle revues, tower-hotel rooms and suites, and 24-hour casinos.

GETTING HERE AND AROUND
From South Lake Tahoe take U.S. 50 north across the Nevada border to reach Stateline and its casinos. If coming from Reno's airport, take U.S. 395/Interstate 580 south to Carson City, and then head west on U.S. 50 to the lake and head south. Or take the South Tahoe Express bus. BlueGO operates daily bus service.

⛱ Beaches

Nevada Beach

BEACH—SIGHT | Although less than a mile long, this is the widest beach on the lake and especially good for swimming (many Tahoe beaches are rocky). You can boat and fish here, and there are picnic tables, barbecue grills, and a campground beneath the pines. This is the best place to watch the July 4th or Labor Day fireworks, but most of the summer the subdued atmosphere attracts families and those seeking a less-touristy spot. **Amenities:** parking; water sports; toilets. **Best for:** sunrise; swimming; walking. ✉ *Elk Point Rd., off U.S. 50, 3 miles north of Stateline* ☎ *530/543–2600* ⊕ *www.fs.usda.gov/ recarea/ltbmu/recarea/?recid=11757* 🎫 *$8 day-use fee* 🐾 *Dogs permitted on leash in picnic areas but not on beach.*

🍴 Restaurants

★ Edgewood Tahoe

$$$ | AMERICAN | The three restaurants at Stateline's classy resort, all in impeccably designed spaces that make the most of the lakeside setting, offer some of the area's best dining, if on the pricey side. Head to the Bistro for casual-fancy breakfast, lunch, and dinner; Brooks Bar & Grill for inventive comfort food during lunch and dinner; and the Edgewood Restaurant for evening fine dining with views across the lake to Mt. Tallac. **Known for:** a venue for all moods; vegan and gluten-free options; golf-course views from outdoor deck at Brooks. Ⓢ *Average main: $27* ✉ *Edgewood Tahoe, 100 Lake Pkwy.* ☎ *775/588–2787* ⊕ *www.edgewoodtahoe.com/dine-imbibe.*

🛏 Hotels

Harrah's Tahoe Hotel/Casino

$ | HOTEL | The 18-story hotel's major selling point is that every room has two full bathrooms, a boon if you're traveling with family. **Pros:** lake and mountain views from upper-floor rooms; good midweek values; top-floor steak house with good views from all tables. **Cons:** can get noisy; uneven housekeeping; lacks intimacy. Ⓢ *Rooms from: $109* ✉ *15 U.S. 50, at Stateline Ave.* ☎ *775/588–6611, 800/427–7247* ⊕ *www.caesars.com/harrahs-tahoe* ⌦ *512 rooms* ⦿*| No meals.*

Harveys Lake Tahoe Resort Hotel and Casino

$ | HOTEL | This resort began as a cabin in 1944, and now it's Tahoe's largest casino-hotel; premium rooms have custom furnishings, oversize marble baths, minibars, and excellent lake views. **Pros:** live entertainment; 19 Kitchen and Sage Room Steakhouse restaurants; lake views from upper-floor rooms. **Cons:** can get loud at night; high summer rates; large property. Ⓢ *Rooms from: $119* ✉ *18 U.S. 50, at Stateline Ave.*

☎ *775/588–2411, 800/648–3361* ⊕ *www.caesars.com/harveys-tahoe* ⌦ *742 rooms* ⦿*| No meals.*

Lakeside Inn and Casino

$ | HOTEL | The smallest of the Stateline casinos, the property has good promotional room rates and simple, attractive accommodations in two-story motel-style buildings separate from the casino. **Pros:** daily dining specials; casino separate from accommodations; free Wi-Fi and no resort or parking fee. **Cons:** some rooms are dark and on the small side; motel-style buildings; despite name lake is a short walk away. Ⓢ *Rooms from: $109* ✉ *168 U.S. 50, at Kingsbury Grade* ☎ *775/588–7777, 800/624–7980* ⊕ *lakesideinn.com* ⌦ *124 rooms* ⦿*| No meals.*

★ The Lodge at Edgewood Tahoe

$$$$ | RESORT | The lodge, which debuted in mid-2017 on a prime lakefront parcel, makes a bold impression with its stone-and-walnut Great Hall, whose four-story wall of windows frames views across Lake Tahoe to grand Mt. Tallac. **Pros:** prime lakefront location; haute-rustic design; all rooms have balconies and fireplaces. **Cons:** high rates in-season; some rooms have no lake views; long walk to pool and hot tub from some rooms. Ⓢ *Rooms from: $400* ✉ *100 Lake Pkwy.* ☎ *775/588–2787, 888/769–1924* ⊕ *www.edgewoodtahoe.com/lodge* ⌦ *154 rooms* ⦿*| No meals.*

🍸 Nightlife

Each of the major casinos has its own showroom, featuring everything from comedy to magic acts to sexy floor shows to Broadway musicals.

LIVE MUSIC

Harveys Outdoor Summer Concert Series

CONCERTS | Headliners such as Robert Plant, Amy Schumer, Janet Jackson, and Keith Urban perform at this weekend concert series. ✉ *Harveys Lake Tahoe, 18 U.S. 50* ☎ *775/588–2411* ⊕ *www.caesars.com/harveys-tahoe/shows.*

South Shore Room

CABARET | Classic acts like Chris Botti and Todd Rundgren play Harrah's big showroom, along with the psychedelic Pink Floyd Laser Spectacular show and comedians like Sinbad. ⊠ *Harrah's Lake Tahoe, 15 U.S. 50* ☎ *775/586–6244 tickets, 775/588–6611* ⊕ *www.caesars.com/harrahs-tahoe/shows.*

Activities

GOLF

Edgewood Tahoe

GOLF | Golfers of all skill levels enjoy this scenic lakeside course that has four sets of tees, offering a variety of course lengths. The greens fee includes an optional cart. ⊠ *100 Lake Pkwy., at U.S. 50* ☎ *775/588–3566* ⊕ *www.edgewood-tahoe.com/golf* ☞ *From $150 (varies throughout season)* ⚐ *18 holes, 7529 yards, par 72.*

Reno

32 miles east of Truckee, 38 miles north-east of Incline Village.

Established in 1859 as a trading station at a bridge over the Truckee River, Reno grew along with the silver mines of nearby Virginia City and the transcontinental railroad that chugged through town. Train officials named it in 1868, but gambling—legalized in 1931—put Reno on the map. This is still a gambling town, with most of the casinos crowded into five square blocks downtown, but a thriving university scene and outdoor activities also attract tourists.

Parts of downtown are sketchy, but things are changing. Reno now touts family-friendly activities like kayaking on the Truckee, museums, and a downtown climbing wall. With over 300 days of sunshine annually, temperatures year-round in this high-mountain-desert climate are warmer than at Tahoe, though rarely as hot as in Sacramento and the Central Valley, making strolling around town a pleasure.

GETTING HERE AND AROUND

Interstate 80 bisects Reno east–west, U.S. 395 north–south (south of town the road is signed U.S. 395/Interstate 580). Greyhound and Amtrak stop here, and several airlines fly into Reno-Tahoe International Airport. RTC Ride provides bus service.

ESSENTIALS

BUS CONTACT RTC Ride. ⊠ *Transit Center, E. 4th and Lake Sts.* ☎ *775/348–7433* ⊕ *www.rtcwashoe.com.*

VISITOR INFORMATION Reno Tahoe Visitor Center. ⊠ *135 N. Sierra St.* ☎ *800/367–7366* ⊕ *www.visitrenotahoe.com.*

◉ Sights

★ National Automobile Museum

MUSEUM | FAMILY | An absolute delight filled with antique and classic cars with obscure and familiar names like Packard, Studebaker, Maxwell, Oldsmobile, and Lincoln, the museum, one of the best of its kind in the country, surveys automotive history. Celebrity vehicles include the Lana Turner Chrysler (one of only six made), an Elvis Presley Cadillac, and a Mercury coupe driven by James Dean in the movie *Rebel Without a Cause.* Hard to miss are the experimental and still futuristic-looking 1938 Phantom Corsair and a gold-plated 1980 DeLorean. ⊠ *10 S. Lake St., at Mill St.* ☎ *775/333–9300* ⊕ *www.automuseum.org* ☞ *$12.*

Nevada Museum of Art

MUSEUM | A dramatic four-level structure designed by Will Bruder houses this splendid museum's collection, which focuses on themes such as the Sierra Nevada/Great Basin and altered-land-scape photography. The building's exterior torqued walls are sided with a black zinc-based material that has been fabricated to resemble textures found in the

Black Rock Desert. Inside the building, a staircase installed within the central atrium is lit by skylights and suspended by a single beam attached to the atrium ceiling. ✉ *160 W. Liberty St., and Hill St.* ☎ *775/329–3333* 🌐 *www.nevadaart.org* 🎟 *$10* 🕓 *Closed Mon. and Tues.*

Riverwalk District

PROMENADE | A formerly dilapidated section of Reno's waterfront is now the toast of the town. The Riverwalk itself is a half-mile promenade on the north side of the Truckee River, which flows around Wingfield Park, where outdoor festivals and other events take place. On the third Saturday of each month, local merchants host a **Wine Walk** between 2 and 5. For $20 you receive a glass and can sample fine wines at participating shops, bars, restaurants, and galleries. In July, look for outdoor art, opera, dance, and kids' performances as part of the monthlong **Artown festival** (🌐 *artown.org*), presented mostly in Wingfield Park. Also at Wingfield is the **Truckee River Whitewater Park.** With activities for all skill levels, it's become a major attraction for water-sports enthusiasts. ✉ *North side of Truckee River between Lake and Ralston Sts.* 🌐 *www.renoriver.org.*

🍴 Restaurants

Beaujolais Bistro

$$$$ | **FRENCH** | Across from the Truckee River, this Reno favorite serves earthy, country-style French food—escargots, steak frites with red wine sauce, cassoulet, and crisp sweetbreads with Madeira, along with fish and vegetarian selections—with zero pretension. Wood floors, large windows, and brick walls with a fireplace create a welcoming and intimate atmosphere. **Known for:** inventive cocktails; intimate atmosphere; more casual experience at the bar. [$] *Average main: $35* ✉ *753 Riverside Dr., near Winter St.* ☎ *775/323–2227* 🌐 *www.beaujolaisbistro.com* 🕓 *Closed Mon. No lunch.*

★ **4th St. Bistro**

$$$ | **AMERICAN** | Tablecloths from Provence and a roaring fireplace in winter warm the dining room of this pert, petite bistro on the edge of town. The deliciously simple, smartly prepared cuisine might include oven-roasted fish with citrus beurre blanc or roasted duck breast with yams, tender kale, and port-poached tart cherries. **Known for:** desserts incorporating local fruit; global wine list; fireplace in winter, deck dining in summer. [$] *Average main: $30* ✉ *3065 W. 4th St.* ☎ *775/323–3200* 🌐 *www.4thstbistro.com* 🕓 *Closed Sun. and Mon. No lunch.*

🛏 Hotels

Eldorado Resort Casino

$ | **HOTEL** | In the middle of glittering downtown, this resort's huge tower has rooms overlooking either the mountains or the lights of the city. **Pros:** spacious rooms; skywalk connects hotel to Circus Circus and Silver Legacy casinos; amusingly kitschy decor. **Cons:** noisy atmosphere; some housekeeping lapses; faux-everything decor can overwhelm. [$] *Rooms from: $60* ✉ *345 N. Virginia St.* ☎ *775/786–5700, 800/879–8879* 🌐 *www.eldoradoreno.com* 🛏 *816 rooms* 🍴 *No meals.*

Peppermill Reno

$ | **HOTEL** | A few miles removed from downtown's flashy main drag, this property set a high standard for luxury in Reno, especially in the Tuscan Tower, whose 600 baroque suites have plush king-size beds, marble bathrooms, and European soaking tubs. **Pros:** luxurious rooms; casino decor; good coffee shop. **Cons:** deluge of neon may be off-putting to some; enormous size; mostly expensive dining. [$] *Rooms from: $109* ✉ *2707 S. Virginia St.* ☎ *775/826–2121, 866/821–9996* 🌐 *www.peppermillreno.com* 🛏 *1,623 rooms* 🍴 *No meals.*

☮ Nightlife

CASINOS

Eldorado Resort Casino

CASINOS | Action packed, with lots of slots and popular bar-top video poker, this casino also has good coffee-shop and food-court fare. Don't miss the Fountain of Fortune with its massive Florentine-inspired sculptures. ✉ *345 N. Virginia St., at W. 4th St.* ☎ *775/786–5700, 800/879–8879* ⊕ *www.eldoradoreno.com.*

Harrah's Reno

CASINOS | Occupying two city blocks, this landmark property has a sprawling casino and an outdoor promenade. ✉ *219 N. Center St., at E. 2nd St.* ☎ *775/786–3232, 800/427–7247* ⊕ *www.harrahsreno.com.*

Peppermill

CASINOS | A few miles from downtown, this casino is known for its excellent restaurants and neon-bright gambling areas. The Fireside cocktail lounge is a blast. ✉ *2707 S. Virginia St., at Peppermill La.* ☎ *775/826–2121, 866/821–9996* ⊕ *www.peppermillreno.com.*

Silver Legacy

CASINOS | A 120-foot-tall mining rig and video poker games draw gamblers to this razzle-dazzle casino. ✉ *407 N. Virginia St., at W. 4th St.* ☎ *775/325–7411, 800/215–7721* ⊕ *www.silverlegacyreno.com/gaming.*

Chapter 22

REDWOOD NATIONAL AND STATE PARKS

Updated by
Andrew Collins

👁 Sights	🍴 Restaurants	🛏 Hotels	🛍 Shopping	🍸 Nightlife
★★★★★	★★★★☆	★★★★★	★☆☆☆☆	★☆☆☆☆

WELCOME TO REDWOOD NATIONAL AND STATE PARKS

TOP REASONS TO GO

★ **Giant trees:** These mature coastal redwoods are the tallest trees in the world.

★ **Hiking to the sea:** The park's trails wind through majestic redwood groves, and many connect to the Coastal Trail, which runs along the western edge of the park.

★ **Rare wildlife:** Mighty Roosevelt elk favor the park's flat prairie and open lands; seldom-seen black bears roam the backcountry; trout and salmon leap through streams; and Pacific gray whales swim along the coast during their spring and fall migrations.

★ **Stepping back in time:** Hike mossy and mysterious Fern Canyon Trail and explore a prehistoric scene of lush vegetation and giant ferns—a memorable scene in Jurassic Park 2 was shot here.

★ **Getting off-the-grid:** Amid the majestic redwoods you're usually out of cell phone range and often free from crowds, offering a rare opportunity to disconnect.

U.S. 101 weaves through the southern portion of Redwood National and State parks, skirts around the center, and then slips back through redwoods in the north and on to Crescent City. The entire park spans about 50 miles north to south. The Kuchel Visitor Center, Humboldt Lagoons State Park, Prairie Creek Redwoods State Park, Tall Trees Grove, Fern Canyon, and Lady Bird Johnson Grove are in the southern section. In the central section, where the Klamath River Overlook is the dominant feature, the narrow, mostly graveled Coastal Drive loop yields ocean vistas. To the north are Mill Creek Trail, Enderts Beach, and Crescent Beach Overlook in Del Norte Coast Redwoods State Park, as well as Jedediah Smith Redwoods State Park, Stout Grove, Little Bald Hills, and Simpson-Reed Grove.

1 Del Norte Coast Redwoods State Park. The rugged terrain of this far northwestern corner of California combines stretches of treacherous surf, steep cliffs, and forested ridges. On a clear day it's postcard-perfect; with fog, it's mysterious and mesmerizing.

2 Jedediah Smith Redwoods State Park. Gargantuan old-growth redwoods dominate the scenery here. The Smith River cuts through canyons and splits across boulders, carrying salmon to the inland creeks where they spawn.

3 Prairie Creek Redwoods State Park. The forests here give way to spacious, grassy plains where abundant wildlife thrives. Roosevelt elk are a common sight in the meadows and down to Gold Bluffs Beach, where a short trail leads to Fern Canyon.

4 Orick Area. The highlight of the southern portion of Redwood National and State parks is the Tall Trees Grove. It's difficult to reach and requires a special pass, but it's worth the hassle—this section has some of the tallest coast redwood trees. The current world-record holder, a 379-footer named Hyperion, was discovered outside the grove in 2006.

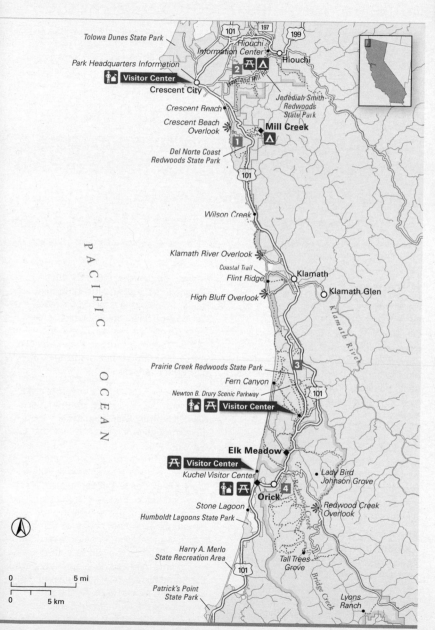

Tolowa Dunes State Park

Hiouchi
Information Center

Hiouchi

Park Headquarters Information

Visitor Center

Crescent City

Howland Hill Rd.

Jedediah Smith
Redwoods
State Park

Crescent Beach

Crescent Beach
Overlook

Mill Creek

Del Norte Coast
Redwoods State Park

101

Wilson Creek

Klamath River Overlook

Coastal Trail
Flint Ridge

Klamath

Klamath Glen

High Bluff Overlook

Klamath River

Prairie Creek Redwoods State Park

Fern Canyon

Newton B. Drury Scenic Parkway

Visitor Center

3

101

Elk Meadow

Visitor Center

Kuchel Visitor Center

Orick

4

Lady Bird
Johnson Grove

Redwood Creek Overlook

Stone Lagoon

Humboldt Lagoons State Park

Redwood Creek

Harry A. Merlo
State Recreation Area

101

Tall Trees
Grove

Bridge Creek

Lyons
Ranch

Patrick's Point
State Park

PACIFIC OCEAN

0   5 mi

0   5 km

Soaring more than 350 feet high, the coastal redwoods that give this park its name are miracles of efficiency—some have survived hundreds of years, a few more than two millennia. These massive trees glean nutrients from the rich alluvial flats at their feet and from the moisture and nitrogen trapped in their uneven canopy. Their thick bark can hold thousands of gallons of water, which has helped them withstand centuries of fires.

Planning

WHEN TO GO

Campers and hikers flock to the park from mid-June to early September. The crowds disappear in winter, but you'll have to contend with frequent rains and nasty potholes on side roads. Temperatures fluctuate widely: the foggy coastal lowland is much cooler than the higher-altitude interior.

The average annual rainfall is between 60 and 80 inches, most of it falling between November and April. During the dry summer, thick fog rolling in from the Pacific veils the forests, providing the redwoods a large portion of their moisture intake.

PLANNING YOUR TIME
REDWOOD IN ONE DAY

From Crescent City head south on U.S. 101. A mile south of Klamath, detour onto the 8-mile-long, narrow, and mostly unpaved **Coastal Drive** loop. Along the way, you'll pass the old **Douglas Memorial Bridge,** destroyed in the 1964 flood. Coastal Drive turns south above Flint Ridge. In less than a mile you'll reach the **World War II Radar Station,** which looks like a farmhouse, its disguise in the 1940s. Continue south to the intersection with Alder Camp Road, stopping at the **High Bluff Overlook.**

From the Coastal Drive turn left to reconnect with U.S. 101. Head south to reach **Newton B. Drury Scenic Parkway,** a 10-mile drive through an old-growth redwood forest with access to numerous trailheads. This road is open to all noncommercial vehicles. Along the way, stop at **Prairie Creek Visitor Center,** housed in a small redwood lodge. Enjoy a picnic lunch and an engaging tactile walk in a grove behind the lodge on the Revelation Trail, which was designed for vision-impaired visitors. Back on the parkway head north less than a mile and drive out on unpaved **Cal-Barrel Road,** which leads east through redwood forests. Return to the parkway, continue south about 2 miles to

AVERAGE HIGH/LOW TEMPERATURES

JAN.	FEB.	MAR.	APR.	MAY	JUNE
54/39	56/41	57/41	59/42	62/45	65/48
JULY	AUG.	SEPT.	OCT.	NOV.	DEC.
67/51	67/51	68/49	64/46	58/43	55/40

22

Redwood National and State Parks PLANNING

reconnect with U.S. 101, and turn west on mostly unpaved **Davison Road** (motor homes/RVs and trailers are prohibited). In about 30 minutes you'll curve right to **Gold Bluffs Beach.** Continue north to the **Fern Canyon** trailhead. Return to U.S. 101, and drive south to the turnoff for the **Thomas H. Kuchel Visitor Center.** Pick up a free permit—a limited number are granted daily—to visit the **Tall Trees Grove** and head north on U.S. 101 to the turnoff for **Bald Hills Road,** a steep route (motor homes/RVs and trailers are not advised). If you visit the grove, allow at least four hours round-trip from the Kuchel Visitor Center. You could also bypass the turnoff to the grove and continue south on Bald Hills Road to 3,097-foot **Schoolhouse Peak.** For a simpler jaunt, turn onto Bald Hills Road and follow it for 2 miles to the **Lady Bird Johnson Grove Nature Loop Trail.** Take the footbridge to the easy 1-mile loop, which follows an old logging road through a mature redwood forest.
■TIP→ Motor homes/RVs and trailers are not allowed on Coastal Drive, Cal-Barrel Road, and Davison Road, and are not advised on Bald Hills Road. Conditions on these roads can sometimes lead to closures or the requirement of high-clearance vehicles—check with the visitor centers before you set out.

GETTING HERE AND AROUND
AIR TRAVEL
United Airlines flies a few times daily between San Francisco and the most practical gateway, Arcata/Eureka Airport, between Trinidad and Arcata, about 16 miles north of Eureka. The regional carrier Contour offers daily service from Oakland to Del Norte County Regional Airport in Crescent City. Another option is Oregon's

Rogue Valley International Medford Airport, which is served by Alaska, Allegiant, American, Delta, and United, and is about a two-hour drive from the northern end of the park in Crescent City.

CAR TRAVEL
U.S. 101 runs north–south the entire length of the park. You can access all the main park roads via U.S. 101 and U.S. 199, which runs east–west through the park's northern portion. Many roads within the park aren't paved, and winter rains can turn them into obstacle courses; sometimes they're closed completely. Motor homes/RVs and trailers aren't permitted on some routes. The drive from San Francisco to the park's southern end takes about six hours via U.S. 101. From Portland it takes roughly the same amount of time to reach the park's northern section via Interstate 5 to U.S. 199.
■TIP→ Don't rely solely on GPS, which is inaccurate in parts of the park; closely consult official park maps.

PARK ESSENTIALS
PARK FEES AND PERMITS
Admission to Redwood National Park is free; several of the state parks collect day-use fees of $8, including the Gold Bluffs Beach and Fern Canyon sections of Prairie Creek Redwoods State Park, and the day-use areas accessed via the campground entrances in Jedediah Smith and Del Norte Coast state parks (the fee for camping overnight is $35). To visit the popular Tall Trees Grove, you must get a free permit at the Kuchel Visitor Center in Orick. Free permits, available at the Kuchel, Crescent City, and (summer only) Hiouchi visitor centers, are needed to stay at all designated backcountry camps.

PARK HOURS

The park is open year-round, 24 hours a day.

CELL PHONE RECEPTION

It's difficult to pick up a signal in much of the park, especially in the camping and hiking areas. If you need a public telephone, go to the Prairie Creek or Jedediah Smith visitor centers.

EDUCATIONAL OFFERINGS

RANGER PROGRAMS

All summer long, ranger-led programs explore the mysteries of both the redwoods and the sea. Topics include how the trees grow from fleck-size seeds to towering giants, what causes those weird fungi on old stumps, why the ocean fog is so important to redwoods, and exactly what those green-tentacled creatures are that float in tide pools. Campfire programs can include slide shows, storytelling, music, and games. Check with visitor centers for offerings and times.

Junior Ranger Program

TOUR—SIGHT | FAMILY | From June to early September, rangers lead one-hour programs for children between ages 7 and 12. Activities include nature walks and lessons in bird identification and outdoor survival. ☎ 707/465–7306 ⊕ www.nps.gov/redw.

Ranger Talks

TOUR—SIGHT | From mid-May through mid-September, state park rangers regularly lead discussions on the redwoods, tide pools, geology, and Native American culture. Check schedules at the visitor centers. ☎ 707/465–7335 ⊕ www.nps. gov/redw.

Redwood EdVentures

TOUR—SIGHT | FAMILY | Fun and engaging nature Redwood EdVentures scavenger hunts for kids, called Quests, include ones in the park. Visit the website for "treasure map" PDFs detailing the Quests, which typically take no more than an hour. Participants receive a patch upon completion. ⊕ www.redwood-ed-ventures.org.

RESTAURANTS

The park has no restaurants, but Eureka and Arcata have diverse dining establishments—everything from hip oyster bars to some surprisingly good ethnic restaurants. The dining options are more limited, though decent, in Crescent City, and there are a few good choices in Klamath, Orick, and Trinidad. Most small-town restaurants close early, around 7:30 or 8 pm.

HOTELS

The only lodgings within park boundaries are the Elk Meadow Cabins, near Prairie Creek Redwoods Visitor Center. Orick, to the south of Elk Meadow, and Klamath, to the north, have basic motels, and in Klamath there's the Requa Inn bed-and-breakfast. Elegant Victorian inns, seaside motels, and fully equipped vacation rentals are among the options in towns north and south of the park. In summer, try to book at least a week ahead at lodgings near the park entrance. *Hotel reviews have been shortened. For full information, visit Fodors.com.*

What It Costs			
$	$$	$$$	$$$$
RESTAURANTS			
under $12	$12–$20	$21–$30	over $30
HOTELS			
under $100	$100–$150	$151–$200	over $200

VISITOR INFORMATION

PARK CONTACT INFORMATION Redwood National and State Parks. ✉ *1111 2nd St., Crescent City* ☎ *707/465–7335* ⊕ *www. nps.gov/redw.*

VISITOR CENTERS

Crescent City Information Center

INFO CENTER | At the park's headquarters, this downtown visitor center with a gift shop and picnic area is the main information stop if you're approaching the Redwoods from the north. In winter, hours are limited and dependent on funding; call ahead to confirm. ⊠ *1111 2nd St., Crescent City* ☎ *707/465–7335* ⊕ *www. nps.gov/redw.*

Hiouchi Information Center

INFO CENTER | This small center at Jedediah Smith Redwoods State Park has exhibits about the area flora and fauna and screens a 12-minute park film. A starting point for ranger programs, the center has restrooms and a picnic area. ⊠ *U.S. 199* ⊹ *Opposite entrance to Jedediah Smith Campground, 9 miles east of Crescent City* ☎ *707/458–3294* ⊕ *www.nps.gov/redw.*

Jedediah Smith Visitor Center

INFO CENTER | Adjacent to the Jedediah Smith Redwoods State Park main campground, this seasonal center has information about ranger-led walks and evening campfire programs. Also here are nature and history exhibits, a gift shop, and a picnic area. ⊠ *U.S. 199, Hiouchi* ⊹ *At Jedediah Smith Campground* ☎ *707/458–3496* ⊕ *www.nps. gov/redw* ⊗ *Closed Oct.–May.*

★ Prairie Creek Visitor Center

INFO CENTER | **FAMILY** | In a small redwood lodge, this center has a massive stone fireplace. The wildlife displays include a section of a tree a young elk died beside. Because of the peculiar way the redwood grew around the elk's skull, the tree appears to have antlers. The center has information about summer programs in Prairie Creek Redwoods State Park, and you'll find a gift shop, a picnic area, restrooms, and exhibits on flora and fauna. Roosevelt elk often roam the vast field adjacent to the center, and several trailheads begin nearby. Stretch your legs with an easy stroll along **Revelation Trail,** a short loop that starts behind the lodge. ⊠ *Prairie Creek Rd., Orick* ⊹ *Off southern end of Newton B. Drury Scenic Pkwy.* ☎ *707/488–2039* ⊕ *www.nps.gov/redw.*

★ Thomas H. Kuchel Visitor Center

INFO CENTER | **FAMILY** | The park's southern section contains the largest and best of the Redwoods visitor centers. Rangers here dispense brochures, advice, and free permits to drive up the access road to Tall Trees Grove. Whale-watchers find the center's deck an excellent observation point, and bird-watchers enjoy the nearby Freshwater Lagoon, a popular layover for migrating waterfowl. Many of the center's exhibits are hands-on and kid-friendly. ⊠ *U.S. 101, Orick* ⊹ *Redwood Creek Beach County Park* ☎ *707/465–7765* ⊕ *www.nps.gov/redw.*

◉ Sights

SCENIC DRIVES

★ Coastal Drive Loop

SCENIC DRIVE | The 9-mile, narrow, and partially unpaved Coastal Drive Loop takes about one hour to traverse. Weaving through stands of redwoods, the road yields close-up views of the Klamath River and expansive panoramas of the Pacific. Recurring landslides have closed sections of the original road; this loop, closed to trailers and RVs, is all that remains. Hikers access the Flint Ridge section of the Coastal Trail off the drive. ⊠ *Klamath* ⊹ *Off Klamath Beach Rd. exit from U.S. 101.*

Howland Hill Road/Stout Grove

SCENIC DRIVE | Take your time as you drive this 10-mile route along Mill Creek, which winds through old-growth redwoods and past the Smith River. Trailers and RVs are prohibited on this route. ⊹ *Access from Elk Valley Rd., off U.S. 101.*

★ Newton B. Drury Scenic Parkway/Big Tree Wayside

SCENIC DRIVE | This paved 10-mile route threads through Prairie Creek Redwoods State Park and old-growth redwoods. It's open to all noncommercial vehicles. North of the Prairie Creek Visitor Center you can make the 0.8-mile walk to Big Tree Wayside and observe Roosevelt elk in the prairie. ⊠ *Orick* ✛ *Entrances off U.S. 101 about 5 miles south of Klamath and 5 miles north of Orick.*

SCENIC STOPS

Crescent Beach Overlook

VIEWPOINT | The scenery here includes views of the ocean and, in the distance, Crescent City and its working harbor. In balmy weather this is a great place for a picnic. You may spot migrating gray whales between November and April. ⊠ *Enderts Beach Rd.* ✛ *4½ miles south of Crescent City.*

Del Norte Coast Redwoods State Park

BEACH—SIGHT | This park southeast of Crescent City contains 15 memorial redwood groves and 8 miles of pristine coastline, which you can most easily access at Wilson Beach or False Klamath Cove. The old-growth forest extends down steep slopes almost to the shore. ⊠ *U.S. 101, Crescent City* ✛ *9 miles southeast of Crescent City* ☎ *707/465–7335* ⊕ *www.parks.ca.gov.*

★ Fern Canyon

CANYON | Enter another world and be surrounded by 50-foot canyon walls covered with sword, deer, and five-finger ferns. Allow an hour to explore the ¼-mile-long vertical garden along a 0.7-mile loop. From the northern end of Gold Bluffs Beach it's an easy walk, although you'll have to wade across or scamper along planks that traverse a small stream several times (in addition to driving across a couple of streams on the way to the parking area). But the lush, otherworldly surroundings, which appeared in *Jurassic Park 2,* are a must-see when creeks aren't running too high. Motor homes/RVs and all trailers are prohibited. You can also hike to the canyon from Prairie Creek Visitor Center along the moderately challenging West Ridge–Friendship Ridge–James Irvine Loop, 12½ miles round-trip. ⊠ *Orick* ✛ *2¾ miles north of Orick, take Davison Rd. northwest off U.S. 101 and follow signs to Gold Bluffs Beach.*

★ Jedediah Smith Redwoods State Park

NATIONAL/STATE PARK | Home to the Stout Memorial Grove, this park with 20 miles of hiking and nature trails is named after a trapper who in 1826 became the first white man to explore Northern California's interior. If coming from interior Oregon, this is your first chance to drive and hike among stands of soaring redwoods. ⊠ *U.S. 199, Hiouchi* ✛ *9 miles east of Crescent City* ☎ *707/458–4396* ⊕ *www.parks.ca.gov.*

Klamath River Overlook

VIEWPOINT | This grassy, windswept bluff rises 650 feet above the confluence of the Klamath River and the Pacific. It's one of the best spots in the park for spying migratory whales in early winter and late spring, and it accesses a section of the Coastal Trail. Warm days are ideal for picnicking at one of the tables. ⊠ *End of Requa Rd., Klamath* ✛ *2¼ miles west of U.S. 101.*

Lady Bird Johnson Grove

FOREST | One of the park's most accessible spots to view big trees, the grove was dedicated by, and named for, the former first lady. An easy 1-mile nature loop follows an old logging road through a redwood forest. ⊠ *Bald Hills Rd., Orick* ✛ *2 miles east of U.S. 101.*

★ Prairie Creek Redwoods State Park

NATIONAL/STATE PARK | **FAMILY** | Spectacular redwoods and lush ferns make up this park traversed by the stunning Newton B. Drury Scenic Parkway. Extra space has been paved alongside the parklands, providing fine places to observe herds of Roosevelt elk, which at one time neared extinction, in adjoining meadows. The park also includes famously spectacular Gold Bluffs Beach and Fern Canyon. If your time is limited, Prairie Creek is one of the best spots for a full day hiking and exploring. ⊠ *Prairie Creek Rd., Orick* ✛ *Off southern end of Newton B. Drury Scenic Pkwy.* ☎ *707/488–2039* ⊕ *www.parks.ca.gov.*

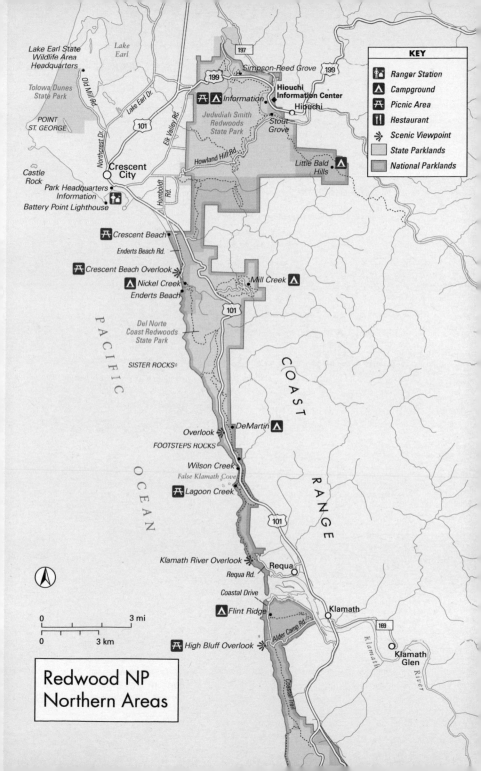

Redwood NP
Northern Areas

KEY

- 👥 Ranger Station
- ⛺ Campground
- 🏕 Picnic Area
- 🍴 Restaurant
- ✦ Scenic Viewpoint
- State Parklands
- National Parklands

Lake Earl State Wildlife Area Headquarters

Lake Earl

Tolowa Dunes State Park

Old Mill Rd.

Lake Earl Dr.

Simpson-Reed Grove

Hiouchi Information Center

Hiouchi

🏕 Information

Jedediah Smith Redwoods State Park

Stout Grove

POINT ST. GEORGE

Northcrest Dr.

Elk Valley Rd.

Howland Hill Rd.

Little Bald Hills ⛺

Crescent City

Castle Rock

Park Headquarters Information 👥
Battery Point Lighthouse

Humboldt Rd.

🏕 Crescent Beach

Enderts Beach Rd.

🏕 Crescent Beach Overlook ✦

⛺ Nickel Creek

Mill Creek ⛺

Enderts Beach

PACIFIC

Del Norte Coast Redwoods State Park

SISTER ROCKS

COAST

Overlook

DeMartin ⛺

FOOTSTEPS ROCKS

RANGE

Wilson Creek

False Klamath Cove

🏕 Lagoon Creek

OCEAN

Klamath River Overlook ✦

Requa

Requa Rd.

Coastal Drive

⛺ Flint Ridge

Klamath

Alder Camp Rd.

169

Klamath Glen

🏕 High Bluff Overlook ✦

Coastal Trail

Klamath River

0   3 mi
0   3 km

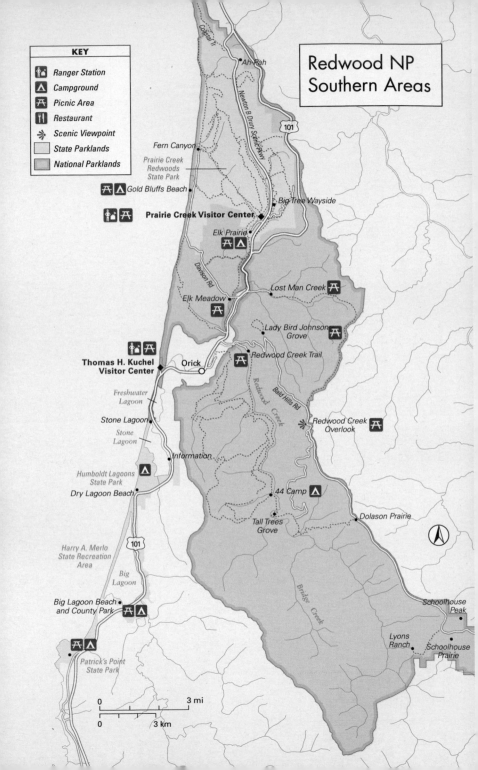

Redwood NP Southern Areas

KEY

- 🚻 Ranger Station
- 🏕 Campground
- ⛱ Picnic Area
- 🍴 Restaurant
- ⚡ Scenic Viewpoint
- ▢ State Parklands
- ▢ National Parklands

Coastal Trail

Ah-Pah

101

Newton B Drury Scenic Pkwy

Fern Canyon

Prairie Creek
Redwoods
State Park

⛱🏕 Gold Bluffs Beach

🚻⛱ **Prairie Creek Visitor Center**

Big Tree Wayside

Elk Prairie ⛱🏕

Davison Rd

Lost Man Creek ⛱

Elk Meadow ⛱

Lady Bird Johnson
Grove ⛱

**Thomas H. Kuchel
Visitor Center** 🚻⛱

Orick

⛱ Redwood Creek Trail

Freshwater
Lagoon

Redwood Creek

Bald Hills Rd

Stone Lagoon

Stone
Lagoon

Redwood Creek
Overlook ⛱

Information

Humboldt Lagoons
State Park 🏕

Dry Lagoon Beach

44 Camp 🏕

Dolason Prairie

Tall Trees
Grove

Harry A. Merlo
State Recreation
Area

101

Big
Lagoon

Bridge Creek

Big Lagoon Beach
and County Park ⛱🏕

Schoolhouse
Peak

Lyons
Ranch

Schoolhouse
Prairie

⛱🏕 Patrick's Point
State Park

0   3 mi

0   3 km

Plants and Wildlife in Redwood 👁

Coast redwoods, the world's tallest trees, grow in the moist, temperate climate of California's North Coast. The current record holder, topping out at 379 feet (or 386, depending on who's measuring), was found in the Redwood Creek watershed in 2006. These ancient giants thrive in an environment that exists in only a few hundred coastal miles along the Pacific Ocean. They commonly live 600 years—though some have been around for more than 2,000 years.

Diverse, Complex

A healthy redwood forest is diverse and includes Douglas firs, western hemlocks, tan oaks, and madrone trees. The complex soils of the forest floor support a profusion of ferns, mosses, and fungi, along with numerous shrubs and berry bushes. In spring, California rhododendron bloom all over, providing a dazzling purple and pink contrast to the dense greenery.

Old-Growth Forests

Redwood National and State parks hold nearly 50% of California's old-growth redwood forests, but only about a third of the forests in the park are old-growth. Of the original 3,125 square miles (2 million acres) in the Redwoods Historic Range, only 4% survived logging that began in 1850. A quarter of these trees are privately owned and on managed land. The rest are on public tracts.

Wildlife Species

In the park's backcountry, you might spot mountain lions, black bears, black-tailed deer, river otters, beavers, and minks. Roosevelt elk roam the flatlands, and the rivers and streams teem with salmon and trout. Gray whales, seals, and sea lions cavort near the coastline. More than 280 species of birds have been recorded in the parks, which are located along the Pacific Flyway.

Tall Trees Grove

FOREST | At the Kuchel Visitor Center you can obtain a free permit to make the steep 14-mile drive to this redwood grove that once contained the world-record holder for tallest tree. Rangers dispense a limited number per day, first come, first served. The hike from the trailhead parking lot is 4 miles round-trip. No trailers or RVs. ⊠ *Tall Trees Access Rd., off Bald Hills Rd., Orick* ✛ *Off Bald Hills Rd., 7 miles from U.S. 101, then 6½ miles to trailhead.*

🏃 Activities

BICYCLING

Besides the roadways, you can bike on several trails, many of them along former logging roads. Best bets include the 11-mile Lost Man Creek Trail, which begins 3 miles north of Orick; the 12-mile round-trip Coastal Trail (Last Chance Section), which starts at the southern end of Enderts Beach Road and becomes steep and narrow as it travels through dense slopes of foggy redwood forests; and the 19-mile, single-track Ossagon Trail Loop, on which you're likely to see elk as you cruise through redwoods before coasting ocean side toward the end.

BIRD-WATCHING

Many rare and striking winged specimens inhabit the area, including chestnut-backed chickadees, brown pelicans, great blue herons, pileated woodpeckers, northern spotted owls, and marbled murrelets.

FISHING

Deep-sea and freshwater fishing are popular here. Anglers often stake out sections of the Klamath and Smith rivers seeking salmon and trout. A single state license (⊕ www.wildlife.ca.gov/licensing/fishing) covers both ocean and river fishing. A two-day license costs about $24. You can go crabbing and clamming on the coast, but check the tides carefully: rip currents and sneaker waves can be deadly. No license is needed to fish from the long B Street Pier in Crescent City.

HIKING

★ Coastal Trail

HIKING/WALKING | This easy-to-difficult trail, depending on how much of it you tackle, runs most of the park's length; smaller sections that vary in difficulty are accessible at frequent, well-marked trailheads. The moderate-to-difficult **DeMartin section** leads past 6 miles of old-growth redwoods and through prairie. If you're up for a real workout, hike the brutally difficult but stunning **Flint Ridge section,** 4½ miles of steep grades and numerous switchbacks past redwoods and Marshall Pond (check ahead to be sure this section has reopened, following a closure as a result of bridge damage in 2018). The moderate 5½-mile-long **Klamath section,** which connects the Wilson Creek Picnic Area and the Klamath River Overlook, with a short detour to Hidden Beach and its tide pools, provides coastal views and whale-watching opportunities. *Moderate.* ⊠ *Klamath* ⊹ *Trailheads: DeMartin, U.S. 101 mile markers 12.8 (south) and 15.6 (north); Flint Ridge, Alder Camp Rd. at Douglas Bridge parking area, north end of Coastal Dr. (east), and off Klamath Beach Rd. (west); Klamath, Requa Rd. at Klamath River Overlook (south), Wilson Creek Picnic Area, off U.S. 101 (north)* ⊕ *www.nps.gov/redw.*

West Ridge–Friendship Ridge–James Irvine Loop

HIKING/WALKING | For a long, moderately strenuous trek, try this 12½-mile loop. The difficult West Ridge segment passes redwoods looming above a carpet of ferns. The difficult Friendship Ridge portion slopes down toward the coast through forests of spruce and hemlock and accesses iconic Fern Canyon. The moderate James Irvine Trail portion winds along a small creek and amid dense stands of redwoods. *Difficult.* ⊠ *Orick* ⊹ *Trailhead: Prairie Creek Visitor Center* ⊕ *www.nps.gov/redw.*

KAYAKING

With many miles of often shallow rivers, streams, and estuarial lagoons, kayaking is a popular pastime in the park.

Humboats Kayak Adventures

KAYAKING | You can rent kayaks and book kayaking tours that from December to June include whale-watching trips. Half-day river kayaking trips pass beneath massive redwoods; the whale-watching outings get you close enough for good photos. ⊠ *Woodley Island Marina, 601 Startare Dr., Dock A, Eureka* ☎ 707/443–5157 ⊕ *www.humboats.com* ⌦ *From $30 rentals, $55 tours.*

★ Kayak Zak's

KAYAKING | This outfit rents kayaks and stand-up paddleboards, good for touring the beautiful estuarial and freshwater lagoons of Humboldt Lagoons State Park. You can also book a guided nature paddle. Rentals at the Stone Lagoon Visitor Center take place year-round, and on most summer weekends Kayak Zak's sets up a trailer at nearby Big Lagoon. The lagoons are stunning. Herds of Roosevelt elk sometimes traipse along the shoreline of Big Lagoon; raptors, herons, and waterfowl abound in both lagoons; and you can paddle across Stone Lagoon to a spectacular secluded Pacific-view beach. ✉ *Humboldt Lagoons State Park Visitor Center, 115336 U.S. 101, about 5½ miles south of Orick, Trinidad* ☎ *707/498–1130* ⊕ *www.kayakzak.com* ✉ *From $30.*

WHALE-WATCHING

Good vantage points for whale-watching include Crescent Beach Overlook, the Kuchel Visitor Center in Orick, points along the Coastal Trail, and the Klamath River Overlook. From late November through January is the best time to see their southward migrations; from February through April the whales return, usually passing closer to shore.

Nearby Towns

Crescent City, north of the park, is Del Norte County's largest town (population about 6,700) and home to the Redwood National and State parks headquarters. Though it curves around a beautiful stretch of ocean, rain and bone-chilling fog often prevail. Very small **Klamath** is outside park boundaries though near to the middle section. The town has a few lodgings but not much dining. Roughly 50 miles south of Crescent City (20 miles north of Eureka), little **Trinidad** has a cove harbor that attracts fishermen and photographers. The picturesque town has a few notable dining and lodging options and is a good base for exploring Prairie Creek Redwoods State Park and other southerly attractions. Farther south, **Arcata** began life in 1850 as a base camp for miners and lumberjacks and had fewer than 1,000 residents until the early 1900s. Today this artsy, progressive town has about 17,200 citizens, plus another 8,500 students enrolled in Humboldt State University. Activity centers on the grassy Arcata Plaza, which is surrounded by restored buildings containing funky bars, cafés, and indie shops. Nearby **Eureka,** population 27,200 and the Humboldt County seat, was named after a gold miner's hearty exclamation. Its Old Town has an alluring waterfront boardwalk, several excellent restaurants and shops, and the region's largest selection of lodgings. The visitor center here is the area's best overall resource for tourism information. Strip malls dominate the city's outskirts, but the city center has much to recommend it.

VISITOR INFORMATION Arcata Humboldt Visitor Center. ✉ *1635 Heindon Rd., Arcata* ☎ *707/822–3619* ⊕ *www.arcatachamber. com.* **Crescent City/Del Norte County Chamber of Commerce.** ✉ *1001 Front St., Crescent City* ☎ *707/464–3174, 800/343–8300* ⊕ *www.delnorte.org.* **Eureka-Humboldt Visitors Bureau.** ✉ *322 1st St., Eureka* ☎ *707/443–5097, 800/346–3482* ⊕ *www. visitredwoods.com.*

👁 Sights

Battery Point Lighthouse

LIGHTHOUSE | Only during low tide, you can walk from the pier across the ocean floor to this working lighthouse, which was built in 1856. It houses a museum with nautical artifacts and photographs of shipwrecks. There's even a resident ghost. ✉ *Lighthouse parking, 235 Lighthouse Way, Crescent City* ☎ *707/464–3089, 707/464–3922* ⊕ *www.delnortehistory.org/lighthouse* ✉ *$5* ⊗ *Closed weekdays Oct.–Mar.*

Northcoast Marine Mammal Center

ZOO | The nonprofit center rescues and rehabilitates stranded, sick, and injured seals, sea lions, dolphins, and porpoises. Its facility isn't a museum or an aquarium, but placards and kiosks provide information about marine mammals and coastal ecosystems, and even when the place is closed you can observe the rescued animals through a fence enclosing individual pools. The gallery and gift shop is open on most weekends and some weekdays, especially in summer, and volunteers are often on hand to answer questions. It's worth calling the day of your visit to find out when feedings will take place. ✉ *424 Howe Dr., Crescent City* ☎ *707/465–6265* ⊕ *www.northcoastmmc.org* ✉ *Free.*

Sequoia Park Zoo

ZOO | FAMILY | Animal lovers of all ages appreciate visiting California's oldest zoo (it opened in 1907). A highlight here is strolling high above the forest on the nation's only redwood canopy walk. Although it's a relatively small zoo, it is conservation-focused and fully accredited, and it's developed a number of excellent new exhibits in recent years, Favorite areas for wildlife viewing include the red panda exhibit, a barnyard petting zoo, and a walk-in aviary with both local and exotic birds. ✉ *3414 W St., Eureka* ☎ *707/441–4263* 🌐 *www.sequoiaparkzoo.net* 🎟 *$10.*

Trees of Mystery

FOREST | FAMILY | Since opening in 1946, this unabashedly goofy but endearing roadside attraction has been doling out family fun. From the moment you pull your car up to the 49-foot-tall talking statue of Paul Bunyan (alongside Babe the Blue Ox), the kitschy thrills begin. You can then explore a genuinely informative museum of Native American artifacts, admire intricately carved redwood figures, and browse tacky souvenirs. For a fee you can ride a six-passenger gondola over the redwood treetops for a majestic view of the forest canopy, and stroll along several mostly easy trails through the adjacent forest of redwoods, Sitka spruce, and Douglas firs. ✉ *15500 U.S. 101 N, between Klamath and Del Norte Coast Redwoods State Park, Klamath* ☎ *707/482–2251* 🌐 *www.treesofmystery.net* 🎟 *Museum free, trails and gondola $18.*

🍴 Restaurants

IN THE PARK

PICNIC AREAS

Crescent Beach

RESTAURANT—SIGHT | This beach has a grassy picnic area with tables, fire pits, and restrooms. There's an overlook south of the beach. ✉ *Enderts Beach Rd., Crescent City* ✣ *4 miles south of Crescent City.*

Elk Prairie

RESTAURANT—SIGHT | In addition to many elk, this spot has a campground, a nature trail, and a ranger station. ✉ *Prairie Creek Redwoods State Park, 127011 Newton B. Drury Scenic Pkwy., Orick.*

★ High Bluff Overlook

RESTAURANT—SIGHT | This picnic area's sunsets and whale-watching are unequaled. A ½-mile trail leads from here to the beach. ✉ *Coastal Dr. loop, Klamath* ✣ *Off U.S. 1010, via Alder Camp Rd.*

OUTSIDE THE PARK

ARCATA

★ Cafe Brio

$$ | AMERICAN | With an inviting indoor dining room and outside seating overlooking bustling Arcata Plaza, this artisan bakery and restaurant is known for its savory and sweet breads. Notable noshes include ham-and-cheese breakfast croissants, focaccia sandwiches with avocado and Humboldt Fog goat cheese from Arcata's Cypress Grove creamery, and farm-to-table dinner fare. **Known for:** lemon cream tarts and other pastries available all day; small but terrific wine selection; Blue Bottle coffees. [$] *Average main: $14* ✉ *791 G St., Arcata* ☎ *707/822–5922* 🌐 *www.cafebrioarcata.com* ⏲ *No dinner Sun. and Mon.*

Wildberries Marketplace

$ | DELI | This market with juice and salad bars and a small café carries a great selection of deli items, cheeses, and picnic provisions, many of them produced regionally. **Known for:** burgers and jerk chicken sandwiches; organic produce; excellent pizzas, tarts, pies, and other baked goods. [$] *Average main: $8* ✉ *747 13th St., Arcata* ☎ *707/822–0095* 🌐 *www.wildberries.com* 💳 *No credit cards.*

CRESCENT CITY

Good Harvest Cafe

$$ | AMERICAN | The café, which serves great breakfasts and espresso drinks, lives up to its name with ample use of locally grown and organic ingredients.

Redwood trees, and the moss that often coats them, grow best in damp, shady environments.

For lunch and dinner there are salads, burgers, sandwiches, vegetarian specialties, and several fish entrées, plus a nice range of local beers and West Coast wines. **Known for:** fish-and-chips and other local seafood; hearty, delicious breakfasts; plenty of vegetarian items. [$] *Average main: $16* ✉ *575 U.S. 101 S, Crescent City* ☎ *707/465–6028.*

★ SeaQuake Brewing

$$ | **PIZZA** | Water from the cool and clean Smith River goes into the dozen or so beers poured at this microbrewery with a modern-industrial look. They pair well with wood-fired thin-crust pizzas that include one with grilled chicken, bacon, artichoke hearts, garlic cream sauce, and cheeses from the local Rumiano Cheese Company. **Known for:** tacos, wings, salads, and other starters; well-crafted beers on tap; the caramel stout sundae. [$] *Average main: $15* ✉ *400 Front St., Crescent City* ☎ *707/465–4444* 🌐 *seaquakebrewing.com* 🕒 *Closed Sun. and Mon.*

Vita Cucina

$ | **AMERICAN** | Although set in a nondescript downtown shopping center, this casual café, bakery, and takeout market serves fresh, creative food that's anything but ordinary. Come by in the morning for pastries, eggs, or quiche, or later on for fare that includes Vietnamese *banh mi* and sushi-grade-ahi sandwiches, whole smoked chicken with garlic-mashed potatoes, and barbecue-pork pizzas. **Known for:** great stop for picnic supplies before venturing into the park; daily-changing quiche (always with a vegetarian option); nice selection of fresh salads. [$] *Average main: $8* ✉ *1270 Front St., Crescent City* ☎ *707/464–1076* 🕒 *Closed Sun. No dinner.*

Hotels

IN THE PARK

★ Elk Meadow Cabins

$$$$ | **B&B/INN** | **FAMILY** | From the porches of these beautifully restored 1,200-square-foot former mill workers' cottages, guests often see Roosevelt elk meandering in the meadows. **Pros:** in a stunning part of Prairie Creek State Park yet conveniently located on U.S. 101; spacious enough for four to six guests; kitchens. **Cons:** a bit of a drive from most area restaurants; expensive for just two occupants, though reasonable for families or groups; furnishings are comfortable but plain. $ *Rooms from: $299 ⊠ 7 Valley Green Camp Rd., off U.S. 101 north of Davison Rd., Orick ☏ 707/488–2222, 866/733–9637 ⊕ www.elkmeadowcabins.com ⌁ 7 cabins* ⦿ *No meals.*

OUTSIDE THE PARK
CRESCENT CITY
Curly Redwood Lodge
$ | HOTEL | A single redwood tree produced the 57,000 board feet of lumber used to build this budget 1957 motor lodge. **Pros:** large rooms; several restaurants within walking distance; cool retro furnishings. **Cons:** road noise can be bothersome; very basic amenities; no breakfast. $ *Rooms from: $79 ⊠ 701 U.S. 101 S, Crescent City ☏ 707/464–2137 ⊕ www.curlyredwoodlodge.com ⌁ 36 rooms* ⦿ *No meals.*

Ocean View Inn & Suites
$$ | HOTEL | This clean, comfortable, and reasonably priced hotel doesn't have a lot of bells and whistles, but it does enjoy a great location on the edge of downtown Crescent City very close to the water. **Pros:** views of the water; many restaurants nearby; good value. **Cons:** on a busy road; cookie-cutter furnishings; nearby foghorn can be a little noisy. $ *Rooms from: $125 ⊠ 270 U.S. 101, Crescent City ☏ 707/465–1111, 855/623–2611 ⊕ www.oceanviewinn-crescentcity.com ⌁ 65 rooms* ⦿ *Free Breakfast.*

KLAMATH
★ Historic Requa Inn
$$ | B&B/INN | This serene 1914 inn overlooks the Klamath River a mile east of where it meets the ocean. **Pros:** serene; relaxing yet central location with river views; excellent restaurant. **Cons:** walls are thin; not a good choice for families with kids; not many dining options in the area. $ *Rooms from: $119 ⊠ 451 Requa Rd., Klamath ☏ 707/482–1425 ⊕ www.requainn.com ⌁ 12 rooms* ⦿ *Breakfast.*

Ravenwood Motel
$ | HOTEL | Attentive on-site owners converted a dowdy roadside motel into this class act consisting of 10 rooms and five suites—four with full kitchens—beautifully decorated with different themes. **Pros:** handy to park's central section; exceptionally clean rooms; a bargain. **Cons:** nonsuite rooms small; along a business strip with no view to speak of; no pets. $ *Rooms from: $75 ⊠ 151 Klamath Blvd., Klamath ☏ 707/482–5911, 866/520–9875 ⊕ www.ravenwoodmotel.com ⌁ 15 rooms* ⦿ *Breakfast.*

NEAR PARK'S SOUTHERN SECTION
Redwood Coast Vacation Rentals
$$ | RENTAL | Given the relatively limited number of hotels and inns close to the park, renting a vacation home in the area can be a good strategy, especially for groups of friends or families who appreciate kitchen facilities. **Pros:** properties for all budgets; all rentals have kitchens; many rentals have multiple bedrooms and baths. **Cons:** 10 am checkout; one-time cleaning fee adds a lot to the cost for travelers only staying a night or two; quality and furnishings vary from unit to unit. $ *Rooms from: $150 ⊠ McKinleyville ☏ 707/834–6555 ⊕ www.redwoodcoastvacationrentals.com ⌁ 75 units* ⦿ *No meals.*

Chapter 23

THE FAR NORTH

Updated by
Daniel Mangin

◉ Sights	🍴 Restaurants	🛏 Hotels	🛍 Shopping	🍸 Nightlife
★★★★☆	★★★☆☆	★★★☆☆	★★★☆☆	★★★☆☆

WELCOME TO THE FAR NORTH

TOP REASONS TO GO

★ **Mother Nature's wonders:** California's Far North has more rivers, streams, lakes, forests, and mountains than you'll ever have time to explore.

★ **Volcanoes:** With two volcanoes to view—Lassen and Shasta—you can learn firsthand what happens when a mountain blows its top.

★ **Fantastic fishing:** Whether you like casting from a riverbank or letting your line bob beside a boat, you'll find fabulous fishing in all the northern counties.

★ **Cool hops:** On a hot day there's nothing quite as inviting as a visit to Chico's world-famous Sierra Nevada Brewery. Take the tour, and then savor a chilled glass on tap at the adjacent brewpub.

★ **Shasta:** Wonderful in all its forms: lake, dam, river, mountain, forest, and town.

1 Chico. A state university and a famous brewery help set the mood in this city also known for its artisans and farmers.

2 Corning. Olive-oil tasting rooms have made this small town a fun stop for many travelers along Interstate 5.

3 Red Bluff. One of several gateway towns to Lassen Volcanic National Park, Red Bluff makes a good base for outdoor adventures.

4 Redding. A northern gateway to Lassen Volcanic National Park, Redding has several points of interest within city limits, and day trips to Weaverville, Shasta Dam, and Lake Shasta Caverns National Natural Landmark are easily undertaken from here.

5 Weaverville. A 19th-century temple erected by Chinese miners is the centerpiece of this laid-back town's historic district.

6 Shasta Lake. Caverns, Shasta Dam, and vacation houseboats count among this quiet town's draws.

7 Dunsmuir. The upper Sacramento River near Dunsmuir consistently ranks among the country's best fishing spots. Most of the accommodations at a popular resort here were formerly cabooses.

8 Mt. Shasta. The town named for the peak that towers above it lures outdoorsy types year-round—hikers and golfers in summer, skiers in winter.

9 Chester. The southern gateway to Lassen Volcanic National Park sits on the forested edge of Lake Almanor.

10 Mineral. Lassen's official address is this town within the 165-square-mile national treasure.

11 Burney. President Theodore Roosevelt was among the fans of two magnificent waterfalls here.

12 Tulelake. Hundreds of underground lava tube caves make this town's Lava Beds National Monument well worth the remote drive.

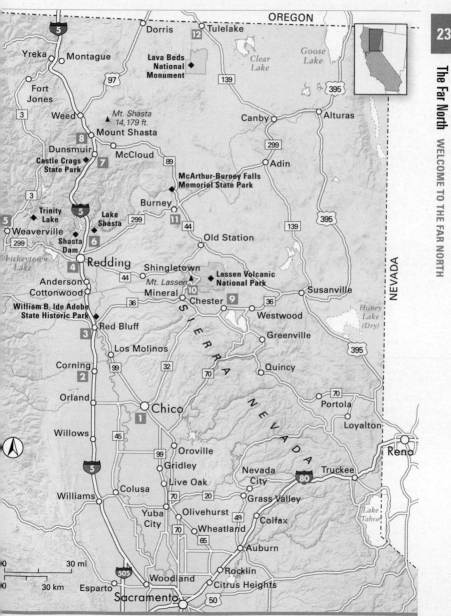

OREGON

Dorris Tulelake **12**

Clear
Lake

Goose
Lake

Yreka Montague

Fort
Jones

Lava Beds
National
Monument ◆

97

139

395

Weed

Mt. Shasta
14,179 ft. ▲

Canby

Alturas

8

Mount Shasta

Dunsmuir

McCloud

299

Adin

Castle Crags ◆
State Park

7

89

McArthur-Burney Falls
Memorial State Park

3

Trinity
Lake ◆

Burney

395

5

Weaverville

5 Lake
Shasta

299

11

44

Old Station

139

395

299

Shasta
Dam ◆

6

Whiskeytown
Lake

4 Redding

Shingletown

Anderson

44

Mt. Lassen ▲

Lassen Volcanic ◆
National Park

Susanville

Cottonwood

Mineral

10

Honey
Lake
(Dry)

William B. Ide Adobe
State Historic Park

36

Chester **9**

36

Westwood

3 Red Bluff

Los Molinos

Greenville

395

Corning

99

32

70

Quincy

2

Orland

Chico

70

Portola

1

45

Loyalton

Willows

Reno

99

Oroville

Gridley

Nevada
City

80

Truckee

Live Oak

Grass Valley

Williams

Colusa

70

20

Lake
Tahoe

Yuba
City

Olivehurst

49

Colfax

70

Wheatland

65

Auburn

Rocklin

30 mi

505

Woodland

Citrus Heights

30 km Esparto

Sacramento

50

NEVADA

The Far North's soaring mountain peaks, trail-filled national forests, alpine lakes, and wild rivers teeming with trout make it the perfect destination for outdoor enthusiasts, including hikers, cyclists, kayakers, and bird-watchers. You won't find many hot nightspots or cultural enclaves in this region, but you will discover crowd-free national and state parks, crystal-clear mountain streams, superlative hiking and fishing, plus small towns worth exploring. And the spectacular landscapes of Lassen Volcanic National Park and Mt. Shasta are sure to impress.

The wondrous landscape of California's northeastern corner is the product of volcanic activity. At the southern end of the Cascade Range, Lassen Volcanic National Park is the best place to witness the Far North's fascinating geology. Beyond the sulfur vents and bubbling mud pots, the park owes much of its beauty to 10,457-foot Mt. Lassen and 50 wilderness lakes. Mt. Lassen and another volcano, Mt. Shasta, draw amateur geologists, weekend hikers, and avid mountain climbers to their rugged terrain. An intricate network of high-mountain watersheds feeds lakes large and small, plus streams and rivers that course through several forests.

The most enduring image of the region, though, is Mt. Shasta, whose 14,179-foot snowcapped peak beckons outdoor adventurers of all kinds. There are many versions of Shasta to enjoy—the mountain, the lake, the river, the town, the dam, and the forest—all named after the Native Americans known as the Shatasla, or Sastise, who once inhabited the region.

MAJOR REGIONS
From Chico to Mt Shasta. The Far North is bisected, south to north, by Interstate 5, which passes through several historic towns and state parks, as well as miles of mountainous terrain. Halfway to the Oregon border is Lake Shasta, a favorite recreation destination, and farther north

stands the spectacular snowy peak of Mt. Shasta.

The Backcountry. East of Interstate 5, the Far North's main corridor, dozens of scenic two-lane roads crisscross the wilderness, leading to dramatic mountain peaks and fascinating natural wonders. Small towns settled in the second half of the 19th century seem frozen in time, except that they are well equipped with tourist amenities.

Note: Two of the most destructive fires in California history swept through the southern portions of this region in 2018, one centered just east of Chico, the other west of Redding. Collectively the two fires burned nearly 400,000 acres, destroying more than 20,000 structures, and killing 94 people. Although rebuilding efforts have begun and major tourist areas survived, you may see evidence of the blazes as you travel.

Planning

When to Go

Heat scorches the valley in summer. Temperatures above 110°F are common, but the mountains provide cool respite. Fall throughout the Far North is beautiful, rivaled only by spring, when wildflowers bloom and mountain creeks fed by the snowmelt splash through the forests. Winter is usually temperate in the valley, but cold and snowy in the high country. Some tourist attractions are closed in winter or have sharply curtailed hours.

Getting Here and Around

AIR TRAVEL

For the cheapest fares, fly into Sacramento and then rent a car—you'll need one anyway—and drive north. Redding, which is served by United Express, has a small airport. There's no shuttle service, but you can take a taxi for about $30 to downtown Redding, or rideshare starting at about $15.

AIR CONTACTS Redding Municipal Airport. ✉ *6751 Woodrum Circle, off Airport Rd., Redding* ☎ *530/224–4320* ⊕ *www.city-ofredding.org/departments/airports.*

GROUND TRANSPORTATION Anytime Taxi. ☎ *530/828–7962 for Chico transfers.* **Road Runner Taxi.** ☎ *530/241–7433 for Redding transfers* ⊕ *www.roadrunnertaxicab.com.*

BUS TRAVEL

Greyhound buses stop in Chico, Red Bluff, Redding, and Weed. TRAX buses serve Corning and Red Bluff. STAGE buses serve Dunsmuir and Mt. Shasta. Various other transit authorities provide local public transit *(see individual town listings for details).*

BUS CONTACTS Greyhound. ☎ *800/231–2222* ⊕ *www.greyhound.com.* **STAGE.** ☎ *530/842–8295* ⊕ *www.co.siskiyou.ca.us/generalservices/page/stage-schedule.* **TRAX.** ☎ *530/385–2877* ⊕ *www.taketrax.com.*

CAR TRAVEL

Interstate 5 runs up the center of California through Red Bluff and Redding. Chico is east of Interstate 5 where Highways 32 and 99 intersect. Lassen Volcanic National Park can be reached by Highway 36 from Red Bluff or (except in winter) Highway 44 from Redding. Highway 299 connects Weaverville and Redding. Check weather reports and carry detailed maps, warm clothing, and tire chains whenever you head into mountainous terrain in winter.

ROAD CONDITIONS Caltrans. ☎ *800/427–7623* ⊕ *www.dot.ca.gov.*

TRAIN TRAVEL

Amtrak serves Chico, Redding, and Dunsmuir.

TRAIN CONTACT Amtrak. ☎ *800/872–7245* ⊕ *www.amtrak.com.*

Restaurants

Redding, the urban center of the Far North, and college-town Chico have the greatest selection of restaurants. Cafés and simple eateries are the rule in the smaller towns. Dress is always informal.

Hotels

Chain hotels and motels predominate in this region, with the occasional small rustic or Victorian inn. Wilderness resorts close in fall and reopen in mid-spring after the snow season ends. In summer in towns such as Mt. Shasta, Dunsmuir, and Chester, and at camping sites within state or national parks, make lodging reservations well in advance. *Hotel reviews have been shortened. For full information, visit Fodors.com.*

What It Costs			
$	$$	$$$	$$$$
RESTAURANTS			
under $16	$16–$22	$23–$30	over $30
HOTELS			
under $120	$120–$175	$176–$250	over $250

Visitor Information

CONTACTS Shasta Cascade Wonderland Association. ✉ *Shasta Outlets, 1699 Hwy. 273, off I–5, Exit 667, Anderson* ☎ *530/365–7500* ⊕ *www.shastacascade.com.* **Trinity County Chamber of Commerce.** ✉ *509 Main St., Weaverville* ☎ *530/623–6101* ⊕ *www.trinitycounty.com.* **Visit Siskiyou.** ☎ *530/926–3696 Mt. Shasta Chamber of Commerce* ⊕ *visitsiskiyou.org.*

Chico

86 miles north of Sacramento.

The Sacramento Valley town of Chico (Spanish for "small") offers a welcome break from the monotony of Interstate 5. The Chico campus of California State University, the scores of local artisans, and the area's agriculture (primarily almond orchards) all influence the culture here. Chico's claim to fame, however, is the Sierra Nevada Brewery, which keeps beer drinkers across the country happy with its distinctive brews.

GETTING HERE AND AROUND

Highway 99, off Interstate 5 from the north or south, and Highway 32 east off the interstate, intersect Chico. Amtrak and Greyhound stop here, and Butte Regional Transit's B-Line buses serve the area. Chico's downtown neighborhoods are great for walking.

ESSENTIALS

BUS CONTACT B-Line. ☎ *530/342–0221* ⊕ *www.blinetransit.com.*

VISITOR INFORMATION Chico Chamber of Commerce. ✉ *180 E. 4th St., Suite 120* ☎ *530/891–5556, 800/852–8570* ⊕ *www.chicochamber.com.*

Bidwell Mansion State Historic Park
HOUSE | Built between 1865 and 1868 by General John Bidwell, the founder of Chico, this mansion was designed by Henry W. Cleaveland, a San Francisco architect. Bidwell and his wife, Annie, welcomed many distinguished guests to their pink Italianate home, including President Rutherford B. Hayes, naturalist John Muir, suffragist Susan B. Anthony, and General William T. Sherman. A one-hour tour takes you through most of the three-story mansion's 26 rooms. ✉ *525 Esplanade, at Memorial Way* ☎ *530/895–6144* ⊕ *bidwellmansionpark.com* 🎫 *$6* ⊗ *Closed Tues.–Fri.*

Bidwell Park

CITY PARK | The sprawling 3,670-acre Bidwell Park is a community green space straddling Big Chico Creek, where scenes from *Gone With the Wind* and the 1938 version of *Robin Hood* (starring Errol Flynn) were filmed. The region's recreational hub, it includes a golf course, swimming areas, and biking, hiking, horseback riding, and skating trails. Chico Creek Nature Center serves as the official information site for Bidwell Park. ✉ *1968 E. 8th St., off Hwy. 99* ☎ *530/891–4671* 🌐 *ccnaturecenter.org* 🎫 *Park free, nature center $4* 🕒 *Nature center closed Sun.–Tues.*

Chico Museum

MUSEUM | Immerse yourself in all things Chico at this small but engaging museum near Chico State University. Past exhibits have surveyed the city's Native American legacy, its former Chinatowns and agricultural past, and area movers and shakers. ✉ *141 Salem St., at 2nd St.* ☎ *530/891–4336* 🌐 *www.chicohistorymuseum.org* 🎫 *$5* 🕒 *Closed Mon.–Wed.*

Museum of Northern California Art

MUSEUM | After several years of successful pop-up exhibitions around town, this engaging museum found a permanent home in the Veterans Memorial Building, a handsome 1927 Classical Revival structure designed by the local architecture firm of Cole & Brouchaud. The focus is contemporary art produced from San Jose north to Oregon, some of it by area artists. ✉ *900 Esplanade, at E. Washington Ave.* ☎ *530/487–7272* 🌐 *www.monca.org* 🎫 *$5* 🕒 *Closed Mon.–Wed.*

National Yo-Yo Museum

MUSEUM | Cast aside images of a grand edifice and curators of renown: this yo-yo collection spanning multiple decades occupies the back of a downtown toy and novelty shop, itself a throwback to some era or another. If you've ever aspired to Walk the Dog or venture Around the World, you'll find this a diverting 15-minute stop. Highlights include the 256-pound No-Jive 3-in-1 yo-yo and comedian Tom Smothers's collection. ■ **TIP→ In the shop, don't miss the posters for years of Chico events.** ✉ *Bird in Hand, 320 Broadway, near W. 3rd St.* ☎ *530/893–0545* 🌐 *nationalyoyo.org* 🎫 *Free.*

★ Sierra Nevada Brewing Company

WINERY/DISTILLERY | This pioneer of the microbrewery movement still has a hands-on approach to beer making. Take the free Brewery Tour and see how the beer is produced—from the sorting of hops through fermentation and bottling, and concluding with a tasting. Other tours, for which there is a fee, focus on topics like hops, the brewery's history, and its sustainability initiatives. For the ultimate deep dive sign up for the 3½-hour Beer Geek Tour. ■ **TIP→ Tours fill up fast; reserve by phone or online before you visit.** ✉ *1075 E. 20th St., at Sierra Nevada St.* ☎ *530/345–2739 taproom, 530/899–4776 tours* 🌐 *www.sierranevada.com* 🎫 *Tours free–$50 (includes tasting).*

🍴 Restaurants

★ Bidwell Perk

$ | **AMERICAN** | It's name a play on nearby Bidwell Park, this clean and tidy many-windowed chain alternative for coffee (six different roasts daily) and pastries also serves full breakfasts and light lunches. Bagels, French toast, quiche, and croissant sandwiches in the morning give way to small plates, salads, bruschetta, and sliders as the day moves along. **Known for:** mostly small-batch beers and wines; outdoor patio; well-crafted espresso drinks. [$] *Average main: $9* ✉ *664 E. 1st Ave., at Mangrove Ave.* ☎ *530/899–1500* 🌐 *bidwellperk.com.*

★ 5th Street Steakhouse

$$$$ | STEAKHOUSE | Hand-cut steak is the star in this refurbished early 1900s building, the place to come when you're craving red meat, a huge baked potato, or some fresh seafood. Exposed redbrick walls warm the dining rooms, and a long mahogany bar catches the overflow crowds that jam the place on weekends. **Known for:** alfresco dining on outdoor patio; weekend crowds; prime cuts of beef with white-tablecloth service. $ *Average main: $35* ⊠ *345 W. 5th St., at Normal Ave.* ☎ *530/891–6328* ⊕ *www.5thstreetsteakhouse.com* ⊗ *No lunch Sat.–Thurs.*

Leon Bistro

$$$ | MODERN AMERICAN | The chef's experience at this local fave for romantic fine dining and special occasions includes a stint at the illustrious Chez Panisse restaurant in Berkeley, and her menu, based on locally sourced high-quality ingredients subtly spiced and presented with flair, reflects that influence. The main dining areas, with high-backed wooden booths in one section and tables and chairs elsewhere, is decorated with art by Dennis Leon, the chef's father, and a few other local artists of renown. **Known for:** mushroom fonduta and other starters; seasonal vegetable sampler a menu staple; Wagyu and elk burgers served with house-made potato chips. $ *Average main: $28* ⊠ *817 Main St., at E. 8th St.* ☎ *530/899–1105* ⊕ *www.leonbistro.com* ⊗ *Closed Sun.– Tues. No lunch.*

Red Tavern

$$$ | MEDITERRANEAN | With its burgundy carpet, white linen tablecloths, and mellow lighting, this is one of Chico's coziest restaurants. The Mediterranean-influenced menu, inspired by fresh local produce, with vegetarian and pescatarian fare in addition to meat and poultry dishes, changes seasonally— fettuccine with beef short-rib ragout and seared salmon with citrus beurre blanc are among recent offerings. **Known for:** California wine list; nightly specials; popular Sunday brunch. $ *Average main: $29* ⊠ *1250 Esplanade, at E. 3rd Ave.* ☎ *530/894–3463* ⊕ *www. redtavern.com* ⊗ *Closed Mon. No lunch Tues.–Thurs.*

Sierra Nevada Brewery Taproom

$$ | AMERICAN | An easy choice, especially if you've just done a tour and are steeped in company lore, the famous brewery's high-ceilinged, heavy-on-the-wood taproom bustles day and night with patrons washing down well-conceived gastropub grub with the best-selling Pale Ale and smaller-batch offerings, some of which are only available here. The open kitchen turns out burgers, wood-oven pizzas, and fish-and-chips (the fish's batter made with Pale Ale) with remarkable speed. **Known for:** beer-cheese and pretzels starters with mustard; soups and salads; no reservations except for large parties (come early to avoid the crowds). $ *Average main: $16* ⊠ *1075 E. 20th St.* ✛ *½ mile west of Hwy. 99, Exit 384* ☎ *530/345–2739* ⊕ *www.sierranevada.com/brewery/ california/taproom.*

🛏 Hotels

Hotel Diamond

$$ | HOTEL | Crystal chandeliers and gleaming century-old wood floors and banisters welcome guests into the foyer of this restored 1904 gem near Chico State University. **Pros:** downtown location; refined rooms, some with bay windows and fireplaces; Diamond Steakhouse. **Cons:** street scene can be noisy on weekends; some rooms are small; some rooms lack tubs. $ *Rooms from: $160* ⊠ *220 W. 4th St., near Broadway* ☎ *530/893–3100, 866/993–3100* ⊕ *www. hoteldiamondchico.com* ⤳ *43 rooms* ¶⊙¶ *Free Breakfast.*

Activities

Sacramento River Eco Tours

TOUR—SPORTS | Wildlife biologist Henry Lomeli guides boat tours on the Sacramento River to explore its diverse fish, fowl, and plant life. ⊠ *Chico* ☎ *530/864–8594* ⊕ *www.sacramentoriverecotours.com* 🖅 *From $85.*

Corning

29 miles northwest of Chico, 50 miles south of Redding.

Signs along Highway 99 and Interstate 5 beckon travelers to Corning, whose favorable soil and plentiful sunshine have made the town a center of olive cultivation and olive-oil manufacturing. At several tasting rooms you can sample olives, olive oil, and other products.

GETTING HERE AND AROUND

Corning lies just off Interstate 5 at Exit 631. From Chico take Highway 99 for 17½ miles and follow signs west to Corning. TRAX provides weekday bus service from Red Bluff.

⊙ **Sights**

★ Lucero Olive Oil

LOCAL INTEREST | As a brand Lucero dates back to the mid-2000s, but the family that started the company began farming olives in the Corning area in 1947. Lucero's extra-virgin olive oils have won countless awards in California and abroad. In the tasting room adjacent to the mill you can taste oils like Ascalona and Koroneiki and ones infused with lemon, chili, and other flavors, sometimes paired with excellent balsamic vinegars. ⊠ *2120 Loleta Ave., Corning* ✛ *Off Hwy. 99W, 1 mile south of Solano St.* ☎ *530/824–2190* ⊕ *www.lucerooliveoil.com* 🖅 *Tastings from $5.*

New Clairvaux Vineyard

WINERY/DISTILLERY | History converges in fascinating ways at this winery and vineyard whose tale involves pioneer-rancher Peter Lassen (Mt. Lassen is named for him), railroad baron Leland Stanford, newspaper magnate William Randolph Hearst, the Napa Valley's five-generation Nichelini wine-making family, and current owners the Trappist-Cistercian monks. In the 1890s the rambling redbrick tasting room, erected by Stanford, stored 2 million gallons of wine. These days hosts here pour Viognier, Tempranillo, Barbera, and other small-lot bottlings from grapes mostly grown nearby. The Syrah and Cabernet stand out, but everything's well made. The on-site chapel (the Hearst connection) has a convoluted story all its own. ⊠ *26240 7th St., Vina, Vina* ✛ *10 miles from Corning, Hoag Rd. east to Hill Rd. south to Rhode Island and South Aves. east* ☎ *530/839–2434* ⊕ *www.newclairvauxvineyard.com* 🖅 *Tastings $5.*

Olive Pit

FARM/RANCH | **FAMILY** | Three generations of the Craig family run this combination café, store, and tasting room where you can learn all about California olive production and sample olive products, craft beers and small-lot wines, and artisanal foods. Sandwich selections at the café include muffulettas and olive burgers. Wash your choice down with a balsamic shake in flavors that include peach, coconut, strawberry, and French prune. ■ TIP→ **The Olive Pit opens at 7 am and closes at 8 pm.** ⊠ *2156 Solano St., Corning, Corning* ✛ *Off I–5, Exit 631 (Corning Rd.)* ☎ *530/824–4667* ⊕ *www.olivepit.com* 🖅 *Tastings free for olive oil, $5 for beer and wine.*

Red Bluff

41 miles north of Chico.

Red Bluff is a gateway to Lassen Volcanic National Park. Established in the mid-19th century as a shipping center on the Sacramento River, and named for the color of its soil, the town, filled with dozens of restored Victorians, makes a good base for outdoor adventures in the area. The Tehama Country Visitor Center has information about wine tasting and other activities.

GETTING HERE AND AROUND

Access Red Bluff via exits off Interstate 5, or by driving north on Highway 99. Highway 36 travels east–west through town; east of the freeway it's called Antelope Boulevard, west of it Oak Street. Greyhound buses stop in Red Bluff and provide connecting service to Amtrak. TRAX (Tehama Rural Area Express) provides weekday bus service.

ESSENTIALS

VISITOR INFORMATION Tehama Country Visitor Center. ⊠ *250 Antelope Blvd., ¼-mile east of I–5* ☎ *530/529–0133.*

⊙ Sights

★ Gaumer's Jewelry

STORE/MALL | The Gaumer family has been making and selling jewelry in Red Bluff since the 1960s, and has been collecting rocks, gems, and minerals for even longer. When the jewelry shop is open, you can tour its fascinating museum, whose displays include crystals, gemstone carvings, fossils, and fluorescent minerals. ⊠ *78 Belle Mill Rd.* ⊹ *From I–5, Exit 649, head west on Hwy. 36 (Antelope Blvd.); make a right on Center Ave. and immediately make another right onto Belle Mill* ☎ *530/527–6166* ⊕ *www.gaumers.com* 🎫 *Free* ⊘ *Closed weekends.*

Red Bluff Round-up ⊙

Check out old-time rodeo at its best during the Red Bluff Round-Up. Held the third weekend of April, this annual event attracts some of the best cowboys in the country. For more information, visit ⊕ *redbluffroundup.com.*

Tuscan Ridge Estate Winery

WINERY/DISTILLERY | Depending on the day, this crowd-pleasing winery with a vineyard-view tasting room serves pizzas or antipasti to accompany some of the nearly two dozen reds and whites made here. Most of the grapes for them come from the Sierra foothills; the Zinfandel and Syrah in particular are worth seeking out. ■ **TIP → The winery opens in the late afternoon on Thursday and Friday.** ⊠ *19260 Ridge Rd.* ☎ *530/527–7393* ⊕ *www.tuscanridgeestate.com* 🎫 *Tastings $10* ⊘ *Closed Mon.–Wed.*

William B. Ide Adobe State Historic Park

NATIONAL/STATE PARK | Named for the first and only president of the short-lived California Republic of 1846, this peaceful park is on an oak-lined bank of the Sacramento River. The park's main attraction, an adobe home built in the 1850s and outfitted with period furnishings, reopened in 2019, completely renovated following damage that occurred when a giant oak tree fell on it during a 2015 storm. ⊠ *21659 Adobe Rd.* ⊹ *At Park Pl., ½ mile east of I–5* ☎ *530/529–8599* ⊕ *www.parks.ca.gov/ideadobe* 🎫 *$6 per vehicle* ⊘ *Visitor center and museum closed Mon.–Thurs.*

🍴 Restaurants

Green Barn Whiskey Kitchen

$$$ | **STEAKHOUSE** | In late 2018, new owners and a new chef renovated the dining room, revamped the menu, and added a layer of Kentucky charm to Red Bluff's premier steak house, which opened in 1959. As before, you're likely to find cowboys sporting Stetsons and spurs feasting on Angus beef steaks, tenderloin medallions, baby back ribs, and prime rib; for lighter fare, try the seafood dishes or entrée-size salads, and leave room for the bourbon-infused desserts. **Known for:** full bar; top-quality beef; convivial atmosphere. [$] *Average main: $25* ✉ *5 Chestnut Ave., at Antelope Blvd.* ☎ *530/527–3161* ⏲ *Closed Sun.*

🛏 Hotels

Hampton Inn & Suites Red Bluff

$$ | **HOTEL** | In a town filled with budget chain properties, this three-story hotel with clean, spacious rooms and a high-ceilinged lobby qualifies as the grande dame. **Pros:** clean, spacious rooms; Wi-Fi works well; pool and business and fitness centers. **Cons:** pricey for the area; on the north end of town away from most attractions; lacks personality. [$] *Rooms from: $133* ✉ *520 Adobe Rd.* ☎ *530/529–4178* 🌐 *www.hampton-inn3.hilton.com* 🔑 *97 rooms* 🍴 *Free Breakfast.*

Redding

32 miles north of Red Bluff on I–5.

A gateway to Lassen Volcanic National Park's northern entrance, Redding is an ideal headquarters for exploring the surrounding countryside.

GETTING HERE AND AROUND

Interstate 5 is the major north–south route into Redding. Highway 299 bisects the city east–west, and Highway 44 connects Redding and Lassen Park's north entrance. Amtrak and Greyhound stop here.

ESSENTIALS

BUS INFORMATION Redding Area Bus Authority. ☎ *530/241–2877* 🌐 *www.rabaride.com.*

VISITOR INFORMATION Redding Convention and Visitors Bureau. ✉ *Visitor center, 844 Sundial Bridge Dr.* ☎ *530/225–4100, 800/874–7562* 🌐 *www.visitredding.com.*

👁 Sights

Moseley Family Cellars

WINERY/DISTILLERY | Although its street name conjures up pastoral images, this winery whose grapes come from Napa, Sonoma, Lodi, and some local vineyards is actually in an industrial park. It's still worth a visit for its two Chardonnays and Syrah, Mourvèdre, old-vine Zinfandel, and other reds. ✉ *4712 Mountain Lakes Blvd., Suite 300* ☎ *530/229–9463* 🌐 *www.moseleyfamilycellars.com* 🎟 *Tastings $10* ⏲ *Closed Mon.–Wed. (except by appointment).*

Shasta State Historic Park

HISTORIC SITE | Six miles west of downtown lies the former town of Shasta City, which thrived in the mid- to late 1800s. The park's 19 acres of half-ruined brick buildings, accessed via trails, are a reminder of the glory days of the California gold rush. The former county courthouse building (whose exhibits include rare California landscape paintings), jail, and gallows have been restored to their 1860s appearance. The Litsch General Store, in operation from 1850 to 1950, is now a museum, with displays of items once sold here. Some trails and trees were damaged and a 1928 schoolhouse was destroyed when a 2018 fire burned through the park, though by early 2019 the main remaining structures, which include Shorty's Eatery (good sandwiches) had reopened. ✉ *15312 Hwy. 299* ☎ *530/243–8194* 🌐 *www.parks.ca.gov/*

shastashp 🎫 *Free to park, $3 Courthouse Museum* ⏲ *Courthouse Museum closed Mon.–Wed.*

★ **Turtle Bay Exploration Park**

CITY PARK | FAMILY | This park has walking trails, an aquarium, an arboretum and botanical gardens, and many interactive exhibits for kids. The main draw is the stunning Santiago Calatrava–designed **Sundial Bridge,** a metal and translucent glass pedestrian walkway, suspended by cables from a single tower, spanning a broad bend in the Sacramento River. On sunny days the 217-foot tower lives up to the bridge's name, casting a shadow on the ground below to mark time. Access to the bridge and arboretum is free, but there's a fee for the museum and gardens. ✉ *844 Sundial Bridge Dr.* ☎ *530/243–8850* 🌐 *www.turtlebay.org* 🎫 *Museum $16* ⏲ *Museum closed Mon. and Tues. early Sept.–mid-Mar.*

🍴 Restaurants

Armando's Gallery House

$$ | ECLECTIC | Dining is an enchanting adventure at Armando Mejorado's combination restaurant, art gallery, and occasional performance space in downtown Redding. The four-course menu, which changes weekly, has included everything from a modern take on shepherd's pie to Indonesian satay. **Known for:** fun, artsy, out of the ordinary; congenial host; à la carte and prix-fixe options. [$] *Average main: $20* ✉ *1350 Butte St.* ☎ *530/768–1241* ⏲ *Closed Sun.–Tues. No lunch.*

Clearie's Restaurant and Lounge

$$$$ | AMERICAN | The granddaughter of "Doc" Clearie, who ran a popular Redding restaurant long ago, returned the family name to fine-dining prominence with this white-tablecloth lounge and restaurant. Many guests begin with the signature blackberry lavender lemon drop "martini," bubbling like a cauldron courtesy of dry ice, and perhaps a baked Brie appetizer before, depending on the season, a main course like short-rib beef Stroganoff or pan-seared ahi tuna. **Known for:** white-tablecloth ambience; well-executed if not cutting-edge cuisine; great wine list. [$] *Average main: $32* ✉ *1325 Eureka Way* ☎ *530/241–4535* 🌐 *www.cleariesrestaurant.com* ⏲ *Closed Sun.*

From the Hearth Artisan Bakery & Café

$ | AMERICAN | A homegrown variation on the Panera theme, this extremely popular operation (as in expect a wait at peak dining hours) serves pastries, eggs and other hot dishes, and good coffee drinks, juices, and smoothies for breakfast, adding a diverse selection of wraps, panini, sandwiches, burgers, rice bowls, and soups the rest of the day. Some sandwiches are made with a bread that FTH bills as "Redding's original sourdough." **Known for:** baked goods; diverse selection; two other Redding locations (one downtown) plus another in Red Bluff. [$] *Average main: $11* ✉ *2650 Churn Creek Rd.* ☎ *530/424–2233* 🌐 *www.fthcafe.com.*

Jack's Grill

$$$ | STEAKHOUSE | The original Jack opened his grill (and an upstairs brothel) in 1938. Tamer these days but often jam-packed and noisy, this place is famous for its 16-ounce steaks and deep-fried shrimp and chicken dishes. **Known for:** 1930s atmosphere; great martinis; thick slabs of beef. [$] *Average main: $28* ✉ *1743 California St., near Sacramento St.* ☎ *530/241–9705* 🌐 *www.jacksgrillredding.com* ⏲ *Closed Sun. No lunch.*

Moonstone Bistro

$$ | AMERICAN | About 1½ miles southwest of downtown this light-filled restaurant in a strip mall prides itself on its use of seasonal organic produce, free-range meats, sustainable line-caught fish, and cage-free eggs. All day you can dine on fish tacos, a large mixed-greens salad, or burgers (standard, veggie, or teriyaki mushroom Swiss), with fish, chicken, and pasta dishes available at lunch, and heavier pork and beef dishes added for dinner. **Known for:** organic produce; all-day bistro menu; Sunday brunch. [$] *Average main: $22* ✉ *3425 Placer St., near Buenaventura Blvd.* ☎ *530/241–3663* 🌐 *www.moonstonebistro.com* 🕓 *Closed Mon. No dinner Sun.*

Nello's Place

$$$ | ITALIAN | Fine Italian dining and romantic old-style ambience go hand-in-hand at Nello's Place, where you'll find a varied selection of veal, chicken, beef, and pasta dishes along with lighter fish and vegetarian fare. For special presentations, order a Caesar salad prepared table-side for two, and bananas flambé for dessert. **Known for:** Caesar salad prepared table-side; cherries jubilee and bananas flambé for dessert; step-back-in-time feel. [$] *Average main: $28* ✉ *3055 Bechelli La., near Hartnell Ave.* ☎ *530/223–1636* 🌐 *www.nellosrestaurant.net* 🕓 *Closed Mon. No lunch.*

View 202

$$$ | MODERN AMERICAN | The view at this glass-walled hilltop restaurant is of the Sacramento River below the wide outdoor patio and well beyond the waterway to snowcapped mountains. It's best to stick with the least complicated preparations on the New American menu, which emphasizes grilled meats and fish from noted California purveyors but also includes bouillabaisse and house-made ravioli. **Known for:** gluten-free options; specialty cocktails; wine list among the North State's best. [$] *Average main: $26* ✉ *202 Hemsted Dr., off E. Cypress Ave.* ☎ *530/226–8439* 🌐 *www.view202redding.com.*

Vintage Public House

$$ | AMERICAN | A late-2018 decor refresh initiated by new owners added a touch of class to this comfort-food haven across from downtown's 1935 Cascade movie palace. The fare includes hearty soups, candied-bacon sliders, fish tacos, creative wraps, ahi wonton nachos, a locally revered mac and cheese, and plenty of burgers. **Known for:** patio dining; vegan selections; live music some days. [$] *Average main: $21* ✉ *1790 Market St., at Sacramento St.* ☎ *530/229–9449* 🌐 *vintageredding.com* 🕓 *No lunch Sat., no dinner Sun.*

Hotels

Best Western Plus Hilltop Inn

$$ | HOTEL | FAMILY | Comfortable Serta mattresses and strong free Wi-Fi are among the selling points of this hotel just off the freeway 3 miles southeast of downtown Redding. **Pros:** dependable chain property; comfortable beds; hot tub and pool area. **Cons:** rooms facing freeway can be noisy; microwave ovens only by request; minor housekeeping lapses. [$] *Rooms from: $140* ✉ *2300 Hilltop Dr.* ☎ *530/221–6100* 🌐 *www.thehilltopinn.com* 🛏 *114 rooms* 🍴 *Free Breakfast.*

★ Bridgehouse Bed & Breakfast

$ | B&B/INN | In a residential area a block from the Sacramento River and a ½-mile from downtown Redding, this inn contains six rooms in two side-by-side homes. **Pros:** easy hospitality; proximity to downtown and Turtle Bay; freshly baked scones at full breakfast. **Cons:** lacks pool, fitness center, and other standard hotel amenities; the two least expensive rooms are small; books up well ahead in summer. [$] *Rooms from: $119* ✉ *1455 Riverside Dr.* ☎ *530/247–7177* 🌐 *www.bridgehousebb.com* 🛏 *6 rooms* 🍴 *Free Breakfast.*

Fairfield Inn & Suites Redding

$$ | HOTEL | FAMILY | The three-story Fairfield's clean rooms, amiable service, 24-hour business center, mountain views from some rooms, and bright, chipper public areas make it the best choice among Redding's many chain properties. **Pros:** clean rooms; amiable service; many amenities. **Cons:** prices often higher than competitors; corporate feel; some rooms are small. $ *Rooms from: $136* ✉ *164 Caterpillar Rd.* ☎ *530/243–3200* ⊕ *www.marriott.com/hotels/travel/rddre* ⤳ *72 rooms* ❍❘ *Free Breakfast.*

🍸 Nightlife

Final Draft Brewing Company
BREWPUBS/BEER GARDENS | This spacious brick-walled brewpub opened in 2017 to high acclaim for its accessible ales and above-average pub grub. Try the beer-battered fish-and-chips with swirly fries instead of regular ones. While they're cooking, order a sampler flight to decide which of the brews to wash them down with. Monday night's trivia contests are wildly fun. ✉ *1600 California St., at Placer St.* ☎ *530/338–1198* ⊕ *www.finaldraftbrewingcompany.com.*

Wildcard Brewing Tied House
BREWPUBS/BEER GARDENS | At the mellow outpost of this brewery founded in 2012 you can sample an adventurous lineup that includes a pilsner, a red ale, several IPAs, and an almost chewy oatmeal porter. The flagship North State IPA's citrus notes are amped up to good effect in the Ruby Red Grapefruit, worth checking out if on tap when you visit. ✉ *1321 Butte St., at Pine St.* ☎ *530/255–8582* ⊕ *www.wildcardbrewingco.com.*

Woody's Brewing Company
BREWPUBS/BEER GARDENS | A fun downtown hangout with a party vibe, Woody's has built a loyal following for its Polish nachos (kettle chips, beer cheese, smoked sausage, and sauerkraut), special-recipe tater tots, and range of beers from fruited wheat ales to an unfiltered dry-hopped IPA and the Pray for Powder porter. The reasonably priced sampler flights provide a good introduction. ✉ *1257 Oregon St., at Shasta St.* ☎ *530/768–1034* ⊕ *www.woodysbrewing.com.*

Weaverville

46 miles west of Redding on Hwy. 299.

Chinese miners erected the 1874 Joss House that anchors Weaverville's impressive downtown historic district. The town, population about 3,600, is also a popular headquarters for family vacations and hiking, fishing, and gold-panning excursions.

GETTING HERE AND AROUND
Highway 299, east from the Pacific Coast or west from Redding, becomes Main Street in central Weaverville. Highway 36 from Red Bluff to Highway 3 heading north leads to Weaverville. Trinity Transit provides bus service.

ESSENTIALS
VISITOR INFORMATION Trinity County Visitors Bureau. ✉ *509 Main St.* ☎ *530/623–6101* ⊕ *www.visittrinity.com.*

👁 Sights

Trinity County Hal Goodyear Historical Park
HISTORIC SITE | For a vivid sense of Weaverville's past, visit this park, especially its **Jake Jackson Memorial Museum.** A blacksmith shop and a stamp mill (where ore is crushed) from the 1890s are still in use during certain community events. ✉ *780 Main St., at Bartlett La.* ☎ *530/623–5211* ⊕ *www.trinitymuseum.org* ⊙ *Museum closed various days Jan.–Apr. and Oct.–Dec.*

★ Weaverville Joss House State Historic Park
HISTORIC SITE | Weaverville's main attraction is the Joss House, a Taoist temple built in 1874 and called Won Lim Miao ("the temple of the forest beneath the clouds") by Chinese miners. The oldest continuously used Chinese temple in California, it attracts worshippers from around the world. With its golden altar, antique weaponry, and carved wooden canopies, the Joss House is a piece of California history that can best be

appreciated on a guided 30-minute tour. ✉ *630 Main St., at Oregon St.* ☎ *530/623–5284* 🌐 *www.parks.ca.gov/?page_id=457* 🎟 *Museum free; guided tour $4* ⏲ *Closed Mon.–Wed.*

🍴 Restaurants

Mamma Llama Eatery & Café

$ | AMERICAN | Tap into the spirit of 21st-century Weaverville at this mellow café that serves breakfast (all day) and lunch and in winter specializes in hot soups to warm body and soul. Expect all the usual suspects at breakfast along with Country Cheesy Potatoes (topped with green chili) and sausage between two biscuits topped with homemade sausage gravy; a spicy club wrap and several vegetarian sandwiches are among the lunch offerings. **Known for:** mellow vibe; good soups; espresso drinks. [$] *Average main: $8* ✉ *490 Main St.* ☎ *530/623–6363* 🌐 *www.mammallama.com* ⏲ *Closed Sun. No dinner.*

🛏 Hotels

Weaverville Hotel

$$ | HOTEL | Originally built during the gold rush, this beautifully restored hotel is filled with antiques and period furniture. **Pros:** gracious on-site owners; in heart of town's historic district; beautifully restored. **Cons:** no breakfast on-site; children under 12 not permitted; only one room has a TV. [$] *Rooms from: $140* ✉ *481 Main St., near Court St.* ☎ *530/623–2222, 800/750–8853* 🌐 *www.weavervillehotel.com* 🔑 *7 rooms* 🍽 *No meals.*

★ Whitmore Inn

$$ | B&B/INN | Amid Weaverville's historic district and shaded by black locust trees, this Victorian inn near shops and restaurants has five rooms, some with a shared bathroom. **Pros:** Victorian style with modern touches; convenient historic district location; innkeeper generous with sightseeing tips. **Cons:** some rooms share a bathroom; Victorian style in most rooms not for everyone; young children (age 5 and under) not permitted. [$] *Rooms from: $125* ✉ *761 Main St.* ☎ *530/623–2509* 🌐 *www.whitmore-inn.com* 🔑 *5 rooms* 🍽 *Free Breakfast.*

👜 Shopping

Highland Art Center Gallery

ART GALLERIES | Inside a historic Main Street home, this gallery showcases and sells painting, photography, fiber arts, ceramics, sculpture, and other handcrafted works produced by local artists and those from surrounding mountain communities. ✉ *691 Main St.* ☎ *530/623–5111* 🌐 *www.highlandart-center.org* ⏲ *Closed Sun. and Mon.*

🏃 Activities

Weaverville Ranger Station

HIKING/WALKING | Check here for maps, free wilderness and campfire permits, and information about local fishing and the 600 miles of hiking trails in the 500,000-acre Trinity Alps Wilderness. ✉ *360 Main St.* ☎ *530/623–2121.*

Shasta Lake

10 miles north of Redding.

The city of Shasta Lake, population about 10,000, is a portal to water, wilderness, dazzling stalagmites, and a fabulous human-made project, Shasta Dam, in the midst of it all.

GETTING HERE AND AROUND

Shasta Lake lies at the intersection of Interstate 5 and Highway 151. There is no local bus service.

👁 Sights

Lake Shasta

BODY OF WATER | Numerous types of fish inhabit the lake, including rainbow trout, salmon, bass, brown trout, and catfish.

The lake region also has California's largest nesting population of bald eagles. You can rent fishing boats, ski boats, sailboats, canoes, paddleboats, Jet Skis, and windsurfing boards at marinas and resorts along the 370-mile shoreline. ⊠ *Shasta Lake* ⊕ *www.shastacascade.com.*

★ Lake Shasta Caverns National Natural Landmark

NATURE SITE | FAMILY | Stalagmites, stalactites, flowstone deposits, and crystals entice visitors to the Lake Shasta Caverns. To see this impressive spectacle, you must take the two-hour tour, which includes a catamaran ride across the McCloud arm of Lake Shasta and a bus ride up North Grey Rocks Mountain to the cavern entrance. The temperature in the caverns is 58°F year-round, making them a cool retreat on a hot summer day. The most awe-inspiring of the limestone rock formations is the glistening Cathedral Room, which appears to be gilded. ■ TIP→ **In summer it's wise to purchase tickets online a day or more ahead of your visit.** ⊠ *20359 Shasta Caverns Rd., Lakehead* ✥ *Exit 695 off I–5, 13 miles north of Shasta Lake* ☎ *530/238–2341, 800/795–2283* ⊕ *www.lakeshastacaverns.com* ⌷ *$30.*

Shasta Dam

DAM | This is the second-largest concrete dam in the United States (only Grand Coulee in Washington is bigger). The visitor center has computerized photographic tours of the dam construction, video presentations, fact sheets, and historical displays. ■ TIP→ **Hour-long guided tours inside the dam and its powerhouse leave from the center every other hour from 9 to 3; arrive 30 minutes early.** ⊠ *16349 Shasta Dam Blvd., Shasta Lake* ✥ *From downtown Shasta Lake, take Hwy. 151 (Shasta Dam Rd.) west to Lake Blvd. north* ☎ *530/275–4463* ⊕ *www.usbr.gov/mp/ncao/dam-tours.html* ⌷ *Free.*

⛹ Activities

Bridge Bay Resort

BOATING | This resort 7½ miles north of Shasta Lake offers modest lakeside lodging, a restaurant, boat and Jet Ski rentals, and a full-service marina. The company's houseboats, available for rent, sleep from 8 to 13 people—before setting out you'll receive a short course in how to maneuver your launch. The resort outfits the boats with cooking utensils, dishes, and most of the equipment you'll need (you supply the food and linens). ⊠ *10300 Bridge Bay Rd., Redding* ✥ *Take I–5 Exit 690* ☎ *800/752–9669, 530/275–3021* ⊕ *www.bridgebayhouseboats.com* ⌷ *From $600 per night in summer, 2-night minimum.*

★ Shasta Marina at Packers Bay

BOATING | FAMILY | Packed with amenities, well maintained, and clean, this highly regarded operator's deluxe houseboats sleep from 14 to 16 people. Some even have a hot tub on board. ⊠ *16814 Packers Bay Rd., Lakehead* ✥ *West from I–5, Exit 693* ☎ *800/959–3359* ⊕ *shastalake. net* ⌷ *From $1250 per night in summer, 3-night minimum.*

Dunsmuir

10 miles south of Mt. Shasta.

Surrounded by towering forests and boasting world-class fly-fishing in the Upper Sacramento River, tiny Dunsmuir was named for a 19th-century Scottish coal baron who offered to build a fountain if the town was renamed in his honor. You can spend the night in restored cabooses at the fun Railroad Park Resort.

GETTING HERE AND AROUND

Reach Dunsmuir via exits off Interstate 5 at the north and south ends of town. Amtrak stops here; Greyhound stops in Weed, 20 miles north. On weekdays, STAGE buses serve Dunsmuir.

ESSENTIALS

VISITOR INFORMATION Dunsmuir Chamber of Commerce. ✉ *5915 Dunsmuir Ave., Suite 100* ☎ *530/235–2177* 🌐 *dunsmuir.com.*

Sights

★ Castle Crags State Park

NATIONAL/STATE PARK | Named for its 6,000-foot glacier-polished crags, which were formed by volcanic activity centuries ago, this park offers fishing on the upper Sacramento River, hiking in the backcountry, and a view of Mt. Shasta. The crags draw climbers and hikers from around the world. The 4,350-acre park has 28 miles of hiking trails, including a 2¾-mile access trail to **Castle Crags Wilderness,** part of the **Shasta-Trinity National Forest.** There are excellent trails at lower altitudes, too, including the ¼-mile Vista Point Trail (near the entrance), which leads to views of Castle Crags and Mt. Shasta. ✉ *6 miles south of Dunsmuir, Castella/ Castle Crags exit off I–5, 20022 Castle Creek Rd., Castella* ☎ *530/235–2684* 🌐 *www.castlecragspark.org* 🎟 *$10 per vehicle, day-use.*

Restaurants

Café Maddalena

$$$ | **MEDITERRANEAN** | The chef here gained experience working in top San Francisco restaurants before moving north to prepare adventurous Mediterranean fare with a French influence. Selections change seasonally but always feature a vegetarian dish, along with fish, beef, and chicken entrées. **Known for:** Euro-centric wine list; daily prix-fixe menu; outdoor dining under grape arbor. [$] *Average main: $27* ✉ *5801 Sacramento Ave.* ☎ *530/235–2725* 🌐 *www.cafemaddalena.com* 🕒 *Closed Mon.–Wed. and Jan.–mid-Feb. No lunch.*

Fine Fishing

The upper Sacramento River near Dunsmuir is consistently rated one of the best fishing spots in the country. Check with the chamber of commerce for local fishing guides.

Yaks on the 5

$$ | **AMERICAN** | Renowned for bacon-jalapeño and many other grass-fed burgers (which get a lot of love on social media), this festive joint, painted in bright colors and with a few interior murals and other artworks, wins most diners' hearts with its house-made ingredients (even buns), dozens of beers, and upbeat staff. You'll pay more than expected but will likely leave feeling you got your money's worth. **Known for:** garlic, duck-chili, barbecue, and other burgers; many beers on tap; upbeat decor and staffer. [$] *Average main: $18* ✉ *4917 Dunsmuir Ave.* ☎ *530/678–3517* 🌐 *www.yaks.com.*

Hotels

Railroad Park Resort

$$ | **HOTEL** | **FAMILY** | The antique cabooses here were collected over more than three decades and have been converted into 23 cozy motel rooms in honor of Dunsmuir's railroad legacy; there are also four cabins. **Pros:** gorgeous setting; unique accommodations; kitschy fun. **Cons:** cabooses can feel cramped; must drive to Dunsmuir restaurants; some guests find location too remote. [$] *Rooms from: $135* ✉ *100 Railroad Park Rd.* ☎ *530/235–4440* 🌐 *www.rrpark.com* 🛏 *27 rooms* 🍴 *No meals.*

Mt. Shasta

34 miles north of Lake Shasta.

While a snow-covered dormant volcano is the area's dazzling draw, the town of Mt. Shasta charms visitors with its small shops, friendly residents, and beautiful scenery in all seasons.

GETTING HERE AND AROUND

Three exits off Interstate 5 lead to the town of Mt. Shasta. When snow hasn't closed the route, you can take Highway 89 from the Lassen Park area toward Burney then northwest to Mt. Shasta. The ski park is off Highway 89. Greyhound stops at Weed, 10 miles north; Amtrak stops at Dunsmuir, 10 miles south. STAGE provides bus service.

ESSENTIALS

VISITOR INFORMATION Visit Mt. Shasta. ✉ *Visitor Center, 300 Pine St., at W. Lake St.* ☎ *530/926–4865, 800/926–4865* 🌐 *visitmtshasta.com.*

Sights

★ Mt. Shasta

VOLCANO | The crown jewel of the 2.5-million-acre Shasta-Trinity National Forest, Mt. Shasta, a 14,179-foot-high dormant volcano, is a mecca for day hikers. It's especially enticing in spring, when fragrant Shasta lilies and other flowers adorn the rocky slopes. A paved road, the Everitt Memorial Highway, reaches only as far as the timberline; the final 6,000 feet are a tough climb of rubble, ice, and snow (the summit is perpetually ice-packed). Hiking enthusiasts include this trek with those to the peaks of Kilimanjaro and Mt. Fuji in lists of iconic must-do mountain hikes. **■ TIP→ Always check weather predictions; sudden storms have trapped climbers with snow and freezing temperatures.** ✉ *Mt. Shasta* 🌐 *visitmtshasta.com/activities/mountaineering.*

🍴 Restaurants

Lilys

$$$ | ECLECTIC | This restaurant in a white-clapboard home, framed by a picket fence and arched trellis, offers an eclectic menu, starting with bourbon-glazed French toast for breakfast. Lunch and dinner selections vary seasonally but often include roasted beet salad, herb-stuffed fresh trout, a walnut garbanzo veggie burger, and marinated pork chops with cannellini beans. **Known for:** Wednesday sushi night; flavorful vegetarian options; weekend brunch. [$] *Average main: $24* ✉ *1013 S. Mt. Shasta Blvd., at Holly St.* ☎ *530/926–3372* 🌐 *www.lilysrestaurant.com.*

Poncho & Lefkowitz

$ | MEXICAN | The cuisine is Mexican and American at this small stand popular with locals and visitors for its burritos, quesadillas, fish tacos, tamales, sausages, and hot dogs. Order at the window and enjoy your meal at outdoor picnic tables with Mt. Shasta views (there's some indoor seating, too). **Known for:** fish tacos; strawberry lemonade; Mt. Shasta views. [$] *Average main: $8* ✉ *401 S. Mt. Shasta Blvd.* ☎ *530/926–1505* ⏲ *Closed Sun.*

Seven Suns Coffee and Cafe

$ | CAFÉ | A favorite gathering spot for locals, this small coffee shop in a stone building serves specialty wraps and burritos for breakfast and lunch (both served all day), plus soups and salad. Pastries, made daily, include muffins, cinnamon rolls, cookies, and scones (great blackberry ones in season). **Known for:** coffee, tea, chai, and spiced cider; outside patio; vegetarian offerings. [$] *Average main: $10* ✉ *1011 S. Mt. Shasta Blvd., at Holly St.* ☎ *530/926–9701* ⏲ *No dinner.*

Pacific Flyway

You don't need wings to catch the Pacific Flyway. All it takes is a car, a good map, and high-powered binoculars to follow the flight path of more than 250 bird species that migrate through far Northern California and stop at wildlife refuges on their way.

Eagles and hawks make their visits in winter; more than a million waterfowl pass through in fall. Returning migrants such as pelicans, cranes, and songbirds such as the marsh wren and ruby-crowned kinglet arrive in March, just in time to herald the spring; goslings, ducklings, and other newly hatched waterfowl paddle through the wetlands in summer.

February and March are especially good viewing times, when people are scarce but wildlife thrives in the cold climate. Many birds enter their breeding season during these months, and you can hear their unusual mating calls and witness aerial ballets as vividly plumed males pursue females.

One of the most impressive Pacific Flyway stopovers is on the California–Oregon border: the 50,092-acre Lower Klamath National Wildlife Refuge, established by President Theodore Roosevelt in 1908 as the country's first waterfowl refuge. The Klamath Basin area has the largest winter concentration of bald eagles in the lower 48 states. You can take a 10-mile auto tour through parts of the refuge, where the eagles feed from December through mid-March. (From Interstate 5 north of Mt. Shasta, take the U.S. 97 turnoff to Highway 161 and follow the signs.) Even if you're not already an avid birdwatcher, you likely will be after a visit to this special place.

—Christine Vovakes

Hotels

Best Western Tree House Motor Inn
$$ | **HOTEL** | The clean, standard rooms at this motel less than a mile from downtown Mt. Shasta are decorated with natural-wood furnishings. **Pros:** close to ski park; heated indoor pool; lobby's roaring fireplace is a big plus on winter days. **Cons:** not all lodging buildings have elevators; pricier than other chain properties (though it delivers more); some wear and tear. [$] *Rooms from: $165* ✉ *111 Morgan Way* ☎ *530/926–3101, 800/545–7164* 🌐 *www.bestwesterncalifornia.com/hotels/best-western-plus-tree-house* 🛏 *98 rooms* 🍴 *No meals.*

Inn at Mount Shasta
$$ | **HOTEL** | This two-story motel-style property conveniently located on Mt. Shasta's main drag wins points for its cleanliness, comfortable beds, and spacious rooms with Wi-Fi, microwaves, refrigerators, hair dryers, and flat-screen TVs with satellite HDTV. **Pros:** clean, spacious rooms; 500-square-foot family suite with three beds; convenient location. **Cons:** minimal style; few amenities; no elevator to second-floor rooms. [$] *Rooms from: $158* ✉ *710 S. Mt. Shasta Blvd.* ☎ *530/918–9292* 🌐 *innatmountshasta.com* 🛏 *30 rooms* 🍴 *No meals.*

Mount Shasta Resort
$$$ | **RENTAL** | Private chalets are nestled among tall pine trees along the shore of Lake Siskiyou, all with gas-log fireplaces. **Pros:** romantic woodsy setting with incredible views; full kitchens in many lodgings; largest chalets sleep up to six people. **Cons:** kids may get bored; must drive to Mt. Shasta restaurants; some hospitality lapses. [$] *Rooms from: $179*

✉ *1000 Siskiyou Lake Blvd.* ☎ *530/926–3030, 800/958–3363* ⊕ *www.mountshastaresort.com* ⇖ *65 rooms* ⦿ *No meals.*

🏃 Activities

Fifth Season Mountaineering Shop
CLIMBING/MOUNTAINEERING | This shop rents bicycles and skiing and climbing equipment, and operates a recorded 24-hour climber-skier report. ✉ *300 N. Mt. Shasta Blvd.* ☎ *530/926–3606, 530/926–5555 ski phone* ⊕ *www.thefifthseason.com.*

Jack Trout Fly Fishing
FISHING | The Upper Sacramento River is a world-class fly-fishing destination, and few anglers have as much experience fishing it as Jack Trout. He and his guides also book trips to several other Northern California rivers. ✉ *1004 S. Mt. Shasta Blvd.* ☎ *530/926–4540* ⊕ *www.jacktrout.com* ⊞ *Rates vary depending on trip, number of guests.*

Mount Shasta Resort Golf Course
GOLF | At a bit under 6,100 yards, the Mount Shasta Resort golf course isn't long, but it's beautiful and challenging, with narrow, tree-lined fairways and natural alpine terrain. Carts rent for $15; fabulous views are free. ✉ *1000 Siskiyou Lake Blvd.* ☎ *530/926–3052* ⊕ *www.mountshastaresort.com/course/* ⊞ *$45 weekdays, $60 weekends* 🎿 *18 holes, 6035 yards, par 70.*

Mt. Shasta Board & Ski Park
SKIING/SNOWBOARDING | FAMILY | Three-quarters of the trails at this ski park on Mt. Shasta's southeast flank are for beginning or intermediate skiers. A package for beginners, available through the ski school, includes a lift ticket, ski rental, and a lesson. There's twilight skiing on some nights for those who want to see the moon rise as they schuss. The base lodge has a bar, a few dining options, a ski shop, and a ski-snowboard rental shop. **Facilities:** 32 trails; 425 skiable acres; 1,435-foot vertical drop; 5 lifts.

✉ *4500 Ski Park Hwy.* ✛ *Hwy. 89 exit east from I–5, south of Mt. Shasta City* ☎ *530/926–8610 winter only, 530/926–8686 snow phone* ⊕ *www.skipark.com* ⊞ *Lift ticket $65.*

Mt. Shasta Forest Service Ranger Station
HIKING/WALKING | Check in here for current trail conditions and avalanche reports. ✉ *204 W. Alma St., at Pine St.* ☎ *530/926–4511, 530/926–9613 avalanche conditions* ⊕ *www.fs.usda.gov/main/stnf.*

Mt. Shasta Nordic Center
SKIING/SNOWBOARDING | This center, run by a nonprofit, maintains 15 miles of groomed cross-country ski trails. ✉ *Ski Park Hwy.* ✛ *North off Hwy. 89, 7 miles southeast of Mt. Shasta City* ☎ *530/926–2142* ⊕ *mtshastanordic.org.*

★ Shasta Mountain Guides
CLIMBING/MOUNTAINEERING | These guides lead hiking, climbing, and skiing tours to Mt. Shasta's summit. ✉ *Mt. Shasta* ☎ *530/926–3117* ⊕ *shastaguides.com.*

Chester

71 miles east of Red Bluff.

The population of this small town on Lake Almanor swells from 2,500 to nearly 5,000 in summer as tourists come to visit. Chester serves as a gateway to Lassen Volcanic National Park.

GETTING HERE AND AROUND
Chester is on Highway 36E, the main route from Red Bluff. When snow doesn't close Highway 89 in Lassen Park, visitors can take Highway 44 from Redding to Highway 89 through the park and to Highway 36E and onto Chester and Lake Almanor. Plumas County Transit provides local bus service.

ESSENTIALS
BUS INFORMATION Plumas County Transit. ☎ *530/283–2538* ⊕ *www.plumastransit.com.*

VISITOR INFORMATION Lake Almanor Area Chamber of Commerce. ✉ *278 Main St.* ☎ *530/258–2426* ⊕ *www.lakealmanorarea.com.*

Sights

Lake Almanor
BODY OF WATER | This lake's 52 miles of forested shoreline are popular with hikers, campers, swimmers, waterskiers, and anglers. At an elevation of 4,500 feet, the lake warms to above 70°F for about eight weeks in summer. ✉ *Off Hwys. 89 and 36* ☎ *530/258–2426* ⊕ *www.lakealmanorarea.com.*

★ **Volcanic Legacy Scenic Byway**
SCENIC DRIVE | A 500-mile scenic drive that connects Lassen with Oregon's Crater Lake National Park, the byway's southern loop begins in Chester and winds for about 185 miles through the forests, volcanic peaks, hydrothermal springs, and lava fields of Lassen National Forest and Lassen Volcanic National Park, providing an all-day excursion into dramatic wilderness. From Chester, take Highway 36 west to Highway 89 north, which within the park is called Lassen National Park Highway. Upon exiting the park, follow Highway 44 southeast to Highway 36, which leads you back to Chester and around Lake Almanor. Parts of this route are inaccessible in from mid-fall to mid-to-late spring. ✉ *Lassen Volcanic National Park* ☎ *800/474–2782* ⊕ *www.volcaniclegacybyway.org.*

🍴 Restaurants

★ **Cravings Cafe Espresso Bar & Bakery**
$ | **AMERICAN** | This casual breakfast and lunch place inside a white clapboard house satisfies diners' cravings with dishes like homemade slow-cooked corned-beef hash topped with two eggs and accompanied by a slice of sourdough bread. You can get breakfast and excellent pastries all day, with soups, salads, sandwiches, and burgers on

the menu for lunch. **Known for:** waffles with applewood-smoked bacon in the batter; vegetarian options; outdoor patio. **$** *Average main: $10* ✉ *278 Main St.* ☎ *530/258–2229* ⊙ *Closed Tues. and Wed. No dinner.*

Hotels

Best Western Rose Quartz Inn
$$ | **HOTEL** | Down the road from Lake Almanor and close to Lassen Volcanic National Park, this mid-range chain property is basically a motel, but the helpful staff (especially with touring plans) and amenities like good Wi-Fi, comfortable bedding, and spacious breakfast area make it a good choice for a short stay. **Pros:** within easy walking distance of town's restaurants; convenient to Lassen Volcanic National Park's southwest entrance; good Wi-Fi and other amenities. **Cons:** a little pricey for what you get; cookie-cutter decor; noise audible between rooms. **$** *Rooms from: $160* ✉ *306 Main St.* ☎ *530/258–2002* ⊕ *www.bestwestern.com* ➷ *50 rooms* ⦙⦙⦙ *Free Breakfast.*

★ **Drakesbad Guest Ranch**
$$$$ | **B&B/INN** | With propane furnaces and kerosene lamps, everything about this century-old property in the Lassen Volcanic National Park's remote but beautiful southeastern corner harks back to a simpler time. **Pros:** back-to-nature experience; great for family adventures; only full-service lodging inside the park. **Cons:** on a remote partially paved road 45 minutes' drive from nearest town (Chester); rustic, with few in-room frills; not open year-round. **$** *Rooms from: $384* ✉ *14423 Warner Valley Rd.* ☎ *866/999–0914* ⊕ *www.drakesbad.com* ⊙ *Closed mid-Oct.–early June* ➷ *19 rooms* ⦙⦙⦙ *All meals.*

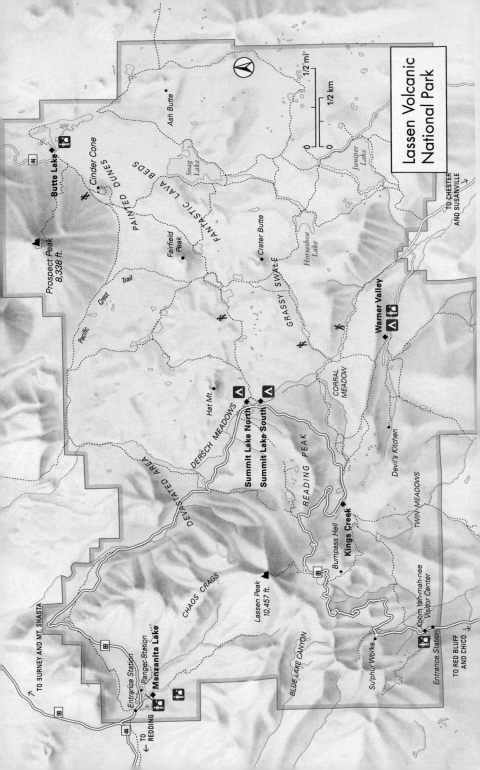

Lassen Volcanic National Park

1/2 mi
1/2 km

TO CHESTER
AND SUSANVILLE

Ash Butte

Butte Lake
44

Cinder Cone

Prospect Peak
8,338 ft.

PAINTED DUNES

Snag Lake

FANTASTIC LAVA BEDS

Fairfield Peak

Crater Butte

Juniper Lake

Horseshoe Lake

Pacific   Crest   Trail

GRASSY SWALE

Warner Valley

Hat Mt.

DERSCH MEADOWS

CORRAL MEADOW

Summit Lake North
Summit Lake South

DEVASTATED AREA

CHAOS CRAGS

READING PEAK

Devil's Kitchen

Lassen Peak
10,457 ft.

Bumpass Hell

TWIN MEADOWS

Kings Creek

Entrance Station

Ranger Station

Manzanita Lake

TO BURNEY AND MT. SHASTA

89

44

TO REDDING

89

BLUE LAKE CANYON

Sulphur Works

Kohm Yah-mah-nee
Visitor Center

Entrance Station

89

TO RED BLUFF
AND CHICO

Mineral

58 miles east of Redding, 42 miles east of Red Bluff.

Fewer than 200 people live in Mineral, the town that serves as Lassen Volcanic National Park's official address.

GETTING HERE AND AROUND

Whether coming from the west or the east, reach the park's southern entrance via Highway 36E, and turn onto Highway 89 for a short drive to the park. The northwest entrance is reached via Highway 44 from Redding. No buses serve the area.

Sights

★ Lassen Volcanic National Park

NATIONAL/STATE PARK | A dormant plug dome, Lassen Peak is the main focus of Lassen Volcanic National Park, but this 165 square-mile tract of dense forests and alpine meadows also abounds with memorable opportunities for hiking, camping, and wildlife photography. The famed peak began erupting in May 1914, sending pumice, rock, and snow thundering down the mountain and gas and hot ash billowing into the atmosphere. Lassen's most spectacular outburst occurred in 1915, when it blew a cloud of ash almost 6 miles high. The resulting mudflow destroyed vegetation for miles; the evidence is still visible today, especially in the Devastated Area. The volcano finally came to rest in 1921 but is not considered dormant: fumaroles, mud pots, lakes, and bubbling hot springs create a fascinating if dangerous landscape that can be viewed throughout the park, especially via a hiked descent into Bumpass Hell. Because of its significance as a volcanic landscape, Lassen became a national park in 1916. Several volcanoes—the largest of which is now Lassen Peak—have been active in the area for roughly 600,000 years. Lassen Park Road (the continuation of Highway 89 within the park) and 150 miles of hiking trails provide access to many of these wonders. The café at the main Kohm Yah-mah-nee Visitor Center, in the park's southern section, serves pizza, salads, sandwiches, burgers, and the like, along with coffee and hot cocoa, and beer (some of it from local producer Lassen Ale Works) and wine. ⚠ **Heed signs warning visitors to stay on the trails and railed boardwalks to avoid falling into boiling water or through thin-crusted areas.** ✉ *Mineral* 🌐 *www.nps.gov/lavo* 🎫 *$25 per car, $20 per motorcycle, $12 per person if not in motor vehicle* 🕒 *Visitor center closed Mon. and Tues. Nov.–Apr.*

Sulphur Works Thermal Area

NATURE SITE | **FAMILY** | Proof of Lassen Peak's volatility becomes evident shortly after you enter the park at the southwest entrance. Sidewalks skirt boiling springs and sulfur-emitting steam vents. This area is usually the last site to close in winter, but even when the road is closed, you can access the area via a 2-mile round-trip hike through the snow. ✉ *Lassen Park Hwy., Lassen Volcanic National Park* ✥ *1 mile from southwest entrance.*

Restaurants

★ Highlands Ranch Restaurant and Bar

$$$ | **AMERICAN** | Dining at the Highlands Ranch Resort's contemporary roadhouse restaurant is in a stained-wood, high-ceilinged room indoors, or out on the deck, which has views of a broad serene meadow and the hillside beyond. Among the few sophisticated eating options within Lassen Volcanic National Park's orbit, the restaurant serves updated classics like rib-eye steak (up to 22 ounces), balsamic-marinated Muscovy duck, and blackened ahi with carrot-cucumber slaw. **Known for:** striking views inside and out; small plates and burgers in the bar; inventive sauces and preparations. [$] *Average main: $25* ✉ *41515 Hwy. 36 E, Mill Creek* ☎ *530/595–3388* 🌐 *www.highlandsranchresort.com/restaurant* 🕒 *Closed Mon.–Wed. Nov.–late May.*

🛏 Hotels

★ Highlands Ranch Resort

$$$ | B&B/INN | On a gorgeous 175-acre alpine meadow 10 miles from Lassen's southwest entrance, this cluster of smartly designed upscale bungalows is peaceful and luxurious. **Pros:** stunning views; most luxurious accommodations near the park; friendly and helpful staff. **Cons:** pricey for the area (but you get a lot for what you pay); remote location 20 miles from Chester, the nearest big town; books up months ahead for summer stays. Ⓢ *Rooms from: $249* ✉ *41515 Hwy. 36 E, Mill Creek* ☎ *530/595–3388* ⊕ *www.highlandsranchresort.com* ⊘ *Closed Mon.–Wed. Nov.–late May* ⌫ *7 cottages* ⵀⵀ *Free Breakfast.*

🏃 Activities

★ Bumpass Hell Trail

HIKING/WALKING | Boiling springs, steam vents, and mud pots are the highlights of this 3-mile round-trip hike. Expect the loop to take about two hours. During the first mile there's a slight, gradual climb before a steep 300-foot descent to the basin. You'll encounter rocky patches, so wear hiking boots. Stay on trails and boardwalks near the thermal areas, as what appears to be firm ground may be only a thin crust over scalding mud. Due to ongoing trail rehabilitation, this hike may be fully or partially closed through 2020. *Moderate.* ✉ *Lassen Park Hwy., Lassen Volcanic National Park* ✛ *Trailhead: 6 miles from southwest entrance.*

★ Lassen Peak Hike

HIKING/WALKING | This trail winds 2½ miles to the mountaintop. It's a tough climb—2,000 feet uphill on a steady, steep grade—but the reward is a spectacular view. At the peak you can see into the rim and view the entire park (and much of California's Far North). Bring sunscreen, water, snacks, a first-aid kit, and, because it can be windy and cold at the summit, a jacket. *Difficult.*

✉ *Lassen Park Hwy., Lassen Volcanic National Park* ✛ *Trailhead: 7 miles north of southwest entrance.*

Burney

62 miles southeast of Mt. Shasta, 41 miles north of Lassen Volcanic National Park.

One of the most spectacular sights in the Far North is Burney Falls, where countless ribbon-like streams pour from moss-covered crevices. You have to travel forested back roads to reach this gem in a state park 10 miles north of the town of Burney, but the park's beauty is well worth the trek.

GETTING HERE AND AROUND

To get to the falls, head east off Interstate 5 on Highway 89 at Mt. Shasta. From Redding, head east on Highway 299 to Highway 89; follow signs 6 miles to the park.

👁 Sights

★ McArthur–Burney Falls Memorial State Park

NATIONAL/STATE PARK | FAMILY | Just inside this park's southern boundary, Burney Creek wells up from the ground and divides into two falls that cascade over a 129-foot cliff into a pool below. Countless ribbon-like streams pour from hidden moss-covered crevices; resident bald eagles are frequently seen soaring overhead. You can walk a self-guided nature trail that descends to the foot of the falls, which Theodore Roosevelt—according to legend—called "the eighth wonder of the world." On warm days, swim at Lake Britton; lounge on the beach; rent motorboats, paddleboats, and canoes; or relax at one of the campsites or picnic areas. ✉ *24898 Hwy. 89, 6 miles north of Hwy. 299, Burney* ☎ *530/335–2777* ⊕ *www.burneyfallspark.org* ⌫ *$10 per vehicle, day-use.*

Did You Know?

President Theodore Roosevelt supposedly called McArthur–Burney Falls "the eighth wonder of the world."

Tulelake

89 miles from Burney, 85 miles from Mt. Shasta City.

Lava Beds National Monument, the chief attraction of Tulelake, is so far north that one of the two main routes to it briefly passes into Oregon before looping back south into California. Stunning underground lava tube caves make the trip to this off-the-beaten-path geological site well worth the detour.

GETTING HERE AND AROUND

From McArthur-Burney state park, take Highway 89 south to Highway 299 east to Bieber-Lookout Road and Highway 139 north. At Forest Service Rte. 97 turn left (west) and follow signs. From Mt. Shasta City, take Highway 89 to Forest Service Routes 97 and 10. There's no public transportation.

◉ Sights

★ Lava Beds National Monument

NATURE SITE | FAMILY | Thousands of years of volcanic activity created this rugged landscape, which is distinguished by cinder cones, lava flows, spatter cones, pit craters, and more than 400 underground lava tube caves. During the Modoc War (1872–73), Modoc Indians under the leadership of their chief "Captain Jack" Kintpuash took refuge in a natural lava fortress now known as Captain Jack's Stronghold. They managed to hold off U.S. Army forces, which outnumbered them 20 to 1, for five months. When exploring this area, be sure to wear hard-soled boots and a bump hat. Bring a flashlight with you, although some are available for borrowing at the Indian Well Visitor Center, at the park's southern end. This is where summer activities such as guided walks, cave tours, and campfire programs depart from. ■ TIP→ **Lava Beds is extremely remote; see website for detailed driving instructions.** ✉ *1 Indian Well, Tulelake* ✛ *Take Forest Rte. 97 to Forest Rte. 10* ☎ *530/667–8113* ⊕ *www.nps.gov/labe* 🎫 *$20 per vehicle.*

Index

910

Photo Credits

Front Cover: Michael Ver Sprill/istockphoto [Description: Beautiful long exposure of the rushing water from Eagle Falls as it heads towards Lake Tahoe.] Back cover, from left to right: Pal Teravagimov/Shutterstock, PerseoMedusa/Shutterstock, Aneta Waberska/shutterstock. Spine: Gordon Swanson/Shutterstock. Interior, from left to right: Daniel Sanchez/istockphoto (2-3). **Chapter 1: Experience California:** Jaime Espinosa de los Monteros/istockphoto (8–9). Max Whittaker/Visit California (10). Charlie Blacker/istockphoto (11). Jill Krueger (11). Visit California/Carol Highsmith (12). California Travel and Tourism Commission dba Visit California..All rights reserved. (12). Hamilton Pytluk/Universal Studios Hollywood (12). Joseph Phelps (12). Visit California/Andreas Hub (13). David Livingston/The Hollywood Sign Trust (13). Jill Krueger (14). Jose Angel Astor Rocha/Shutterstock (14). Disney Enterprises, Inc. (14). TraceRouda/istockphoto (14). Jill Krueger (15). Visit California/Bongo (16). Jim Varley Photography/Alamy Stock Photo (16). Kelly vanDellen/istockphoto (16). Phillip Bond / Alamy Stock Photo (16). Courtesy L.A. Tourism (17). Michael Lauffenburger/shutterstock (17). Visit California/Blaise (18). Visit California/Robert Holmes (18). Visit California/thatgirlproductions.com/Jamie Williams (18). Briana Edwards/Paramount studios (18). Jill Krueger (19). Joshua Resnick (26). Courtesy Din Tai Fung USA (27). Matt Morris/Joseph Phelps Vineyards (28). Scribe Winery (28). Emma Morris/Ashes & Diamonds (28). Ridge Vineyards (28). Damion Hamilton Photographer 2018 (29). Kelly Puleio/Smith-Madrone Vineyards & Winery (29). The Donum Estate (29). Inglenook (29). Sebastien Burel/Shutterstock (30). Dancestrokes/Shutterstock (30). joseph s giacalone/Alamy Stock Photo (30). Julia Hiebaum/Alamy Stock Photo (31). Marcel Fuentes/Shutterstock (31). Jemny/Shutterstock (32). TJ Muzeni (32). ESB Professional/Shutterstock (32). Jill Krueger (32). Morenovel/Shutterstock (33). MNStudio/Shutterstock (33). Eug Png/Shutterstock (33). kropic1/Shutterstock (33). Pinz Bowling Center (34). www.nicholasnicholas.com (34). courtesy of the hollywood roosevelt (34). courtesy of the grove (34). Catch Hospitality Group (35). Henry Hargreaves (35). ROB STARK (35). courtesy of chateau marmont (35). **Chapter 3: California's Best Road Trips:** PauloZimmermann/istockphoto (51). **Chapter 4: San Diego:** Sierralara/shutterstock (75). alisafarov/Shutterstock (101). Dreyer Peter/age fotostock (101). Robert Holmes (102). Steve Snodgrass/Flickr, [CC BY 2.0] (103). Jim Epler/Flickr, [CC BY 2.0] (104). RENAULT Philippe/age fotostock (104). fPat (104). Chris Gotz/Shutterstock (104). fPat/Flickr, [CC BY 2.0] (104). Jose Angel Astor Rocha/Shutterstock (105). Howard Sandler/iStockphoto (120). **Chapter 5: Palm Springs:** Carol M. Highsmith/Visit California (131). sumikophoto/shutterstock (138). David Falk/iStockphoto (154). **Chapter 6: Orange County and Catalina Island:** Beach Media/shutterstock (171). www.ericcastro.biz/Flickr, [CC BY 2.0] (182). Robert Holmes (188). Scott Vickers/iStockphoto (193). www.rwongphoto.com/Alamy (194). Brett Shoaf/Artistic Visuals Photography (196). Lowe Llaguno/Shutterstock (198). Steve Heap/shutterstock.com (203). **Chapter 7: Los Angeles:** Jill Krueger (207). Jeff Morse/iStockphoto (210). wando studios inc/iStockphoto (211). Yelo34/Dreamstime.com (211). Paper Cat/shutterstock (217). Carl Yu (233). Adam Latham (243). **Chapter 8: Joshua Tree:** Eric Foltz/iStockphoto (283). Dennis Silvas/shutterstock (293). Greg Epperson/shutterstock (297). miroslav_1/istockphoto (298). **Chapter 9: Mojave Desert:** Sierralara/shutterstock (301). San Bernardino County Regional Parks (308). DebsG/shutterstock (312). Maksershov/Dreamstime.com (316). **Chapter 10: Sequoia and Kings Canyon National Parks:** Robert Holmes (321). urosr/Shutterstock (335). **Chapter 11: The Central Coast:** jamesh1977/istockphoto (349). Davidmschrader/Dreamstime.com (366). Aimee M Lee/Shutterstock (412). lucky-photographer/istockphoto (414-415). **Chapter 12: Monterey Bay Area:** haveseen/shutterstock (421). Nadezhdasarkisian/Dreamstime (430). Sergio TB/shutterstock (438). Wolterk/Dreamstime (448). Mike Brake/Dreamstime (460). **Chapter 13: Death Valley National Park:** Brian Brazil/shutterstock (471). kavram/shutterstock (481). LizzieMaher/istockphoto (483). **Chapter 14: Yosemite National Park:** Ershov_Maks/istockphoto (489). Sky_Sajjaphot/istockphoto (499). Jane Rix / Shutterstock (505). Simon Dannhauer (508). Katrina Leigh/Shutterstock (514-515). **Chapter 15: Eastern Sierra:** Glenn Pettersen/shutterstock (523). Mark Sayer/shutterstock (533). Zack Frank/shutterstock (543). Marc Venema (544). **Chapter 16: San Francisco:** San Francisco Travel Association/Scott Chernis (547). Walleyelj/Dreamstime.com (551). T photography/Shutterstock (551). San Francisco Travel Association/Scott Chernis (559). CURAphotography/Shutterstock (563). Brett Shoaf Artistic Visuals (564). Arnold Genthe (Public Domain) (564). Library of Congress Prints and Photographs Division (565). Sandor Balatoni (565). Library of Congress (566). canadastock/Shutterstock (583). Pius Lee/Shutterstock (585). San Francisco Municipal Railway Historical Archives (586). Andresr/Dreamstime.com (593). Robert Holmes (605). Aprillilacs (615). Rafael Ramirez Lee/iStockphoto (619). **Chapter 17: The Bay Area:** Gary Crabbe/Alamy Stock Photo (631). California Travel and Tourism Commission/Bongo (640). Nancy Hoyt Belcher/Alamy (642). Robert Holmes (663). **Chapter 18: Napa and Sonoma:** Infinity Visuals (673). Robert Holmes (680). Far Niente+Dolce+Nickel & Nickel (681). kevin miller/iStockphoto (681). Robert Holmes (682) (All). Domaine Carneros (683). star5112/Flickr, [CC BY 2.0] (683). Robert Holmes (684) (Top right). Robert Holmes (684) (Bottom Right). Gundolf Pftoenhauer (684). Robert Holmes (685) (All). Agence Images/Alamy (686). Cephas Picture Library/Alamy (686). PHILIPPE ROY/Alamy (686). Napa Valley Conference Bureau (687) (Top). Wild Horse Winery/ Forrest L. Doud (Second and Third from Top). Napa Valley Conference Bureau (687) (Fourth from Top). Panther Creek Cellars/Ron Kaplan (687) (Fifth from Top). Clos du Val (Marvin Coffin) (687) (Sixth from Top). Panther Creek Cellars/Ron Kaplan (687) (Seventh from Top). Warren H. White (687) (Bottom Right). Courtesy of the di Rosa Collection (690). Terry Joanis/Frog's Leap (704). Courtesy of Castello di Amorosa (712). Robert Holmes (723). **Chapter 19: The North Coast:** MWP/istockphoto (741). Robert Holmes (750). naturediver/istockphoto (756). Robert Holmes (764). **Chapter 20: Sacramento and the Gold Country:** heyengel/istockphoto (773). RickC/Flickr, [CC BY 2.0] (799). Ambient Images Inc./Alamy (806). **Chapter 21: Lake Tahoe:** MariuszBlach/istockphoto (819). Mblach/Dreamstime.com (834). thetahoeguy/shutterstock (837). Tom Zikas/North Lake Tahoe (840). Christopher Russell/iStockphoto (850). **Chapter 22: Redwood National and State Parks:** Ericliu08/istockphoto (857). iStockphoto (871). **Chapter 23: The Far North:** NPS (873). Stephen Moehle/shutterstock (897). **About Our Writers:** All photos are courtesy of the writers.

Fodor's CALIFORNIA

Publisher: Stephen Horowitz, *General Manager*

Editorial: Douglas Stallings, *Editorial Director*; Margaret Kelly, Jacinta O'Halloran, Amanda Sadlowski, *Senior Editors*; Kayla Becker, Alexis Kelly, Teddy Minford, Rachael Roth, *Editors*

Design: Tina Malaney, *Design and Production Director*; Jessica Gonzalez, *Graphic Designer*; Mariana Tabares, *Design & Production Intern*

Production: Jennifer DePrima, *Editorial Production Manager*; Carrie Parker, *Senior Production Editor*; Elyse Rozelle, *Production Editor*; Jackson Pranica, *Editorial Production Assistant*

Maps: Rebecca Baer, *Senior Map Editor*; Mark Stroud (Moon Street Cartography), David Lindroth, *Cartographers*

Photography: Jill Krueger, *Director of Photo*; Namrata Aggarwal, Ashok Kumar, Carl Yu, *Photo Editors*; Rebecca Rimmer, *Photo Intern*

Business & Operations: Chuck Hoover, *Chief Marketing Officer*; Robert Ames, *Group General Manager*; Tara McCrillis, *Director of Publishing Operations*; Victor Bernal, *Business Analyst*

Public Relations and Marketing: Joe Ewaskiw, *Senior Director Communications & Public Relations*; Esther Su, Senior *Marketing Manager*; Ryan Garcia, Thomas Talarico, Miranda Villalobos, *Marketing Specialists*

Fodors.com Jeremy Tarr, *Editorial Director*; Rachael Levitt, *Managing Editor*

Technology: Jon Atkinson, *Director of Technology*; Rudresh Teotia, *Lead Developer*; Jacob Ashpis, *Content Operations Manager*

Writers: Sarah Amandolare, Cheryl Crabtree, Paul Feinstein, Trevor Felch, Deb Hopewell, Marlise Kast-Myers, Denise M. Leto, Daniel Mangin, Rebecca Flint Marx, Kathy A. McDonald, Kai Oliver-Kurtain, Monique Peterson, Andrea Powell, Jeff Terich, Michelle Rae Uy, Claire Deeks van der Lee, and Candice Yacono.

Editors: Rachael Roth, Jeremy Tarr

Production Editor: Carrie Parker

33rd Edition

ISBN 978-1-64097-174-5

ISSN 0192–9925

Library of Congress Control Number 2019938463

All details in this book are based on information supplied to us at press time. Always confirm information when it matters, especially if you're making a detour to visit a specific place. Fodor's expressly disclaims any liability, loss, or risk, personal or otherwise, that is incurred as a consequence of the use of any of the contents of this book.

SPECIAL SALES

This book is available at special discounts for bulk purchases for sales promotions or premiums. For more information, e-mail SpecialMarkets@fodors.com.

PRINTED IN THE UNITED STATES OF AMERICA

10 9 8 7 6 5 4 3 2 1

About Our Writers

 Sarah Amandolare is a Los Angeles–based freelance journalist whose work has appeared in the *Los Angeles Times, the New York Times* online, *BBC Travel*, and *Salon,* among others. For this edition, she updated the Joshua Tree chapter.

 Native Californian **Cheryl Crabtree** has worked as a freelance writer since 1987 and regularly travels up, down, and around California for work and fun. She has contributed to *Fodor's California* since 2003 and also contributes to the *Fodor's National Parks of the West* guide. Cheryl is editor of *Montecito Magazine* and co-authors *The California Directory of Fine Wineries* book series, Central Coast and Napa, Sonoma, Mendocino editions. Her articles have appeared in many regional and national magazines. Cheryl updated the Central Coast, Monterey Bay Area, Palm Springs, Eastern Sierra, Yosemite National Park, The Mojave Desert, and Sequoia & Kings Canyon National Park chapters this edition.

Deb Hopewell lives, surfs, and cycles in Santa Cruz, California. Before embracing the life of a freelance writer, she was the travel editor at Yahoo for six years, and a longtime editor and columnist at the San Jose Mercury News before that. Her writing has appeared in Travel+Leisure, Outside, Architectural Digest, Sunset magazine, Yahoo, and Smarter Travel, among others. She updated the Death Valley chapter.

 Daniel Mangin returned to California, where he's maintained a home for three decades, after two stints at the Fodor's editorial offices in New York City, the second one as the editorial director of *Fodors.com* and the *Compass American Guides.* With several dozen wineries less than a half-hour's drive from home, he often finds himself transported as if by magic to a tasting room bar, communing with a sophisticated Cabernet or savoring the finish of a smooth Pinot Noir. For this edition, Daniel, the writer of *Fodor's Napa & Sonoma,* updated the Napa and Sonoma, North Coast, Redwood National Park, Far North, Sacramento & The Gold Country, Lake Tahoe, Best Road Trips, and Travel Smart chapters.

Updating our Los Angeles chapter was a team of writers from Fodor's Los Angeles: Paul Feinstein, Kathy A. McDonald, Candice Yarono and Michelle Rae Uy.

Updating our San Diego chapter was a team of writers from Fodor's San Diego: Marlise Kast-Myers, Jeff Terich, Kai Oliver-Kurtain, and Claire Deeks van der Lee.

Updating our San Francisco chapter was a team of writers from Fodor's San Francisco: Trevor Felch, Denise Leto, Daniel Mangin, Rebecca Flint Marx, Monique Peterson, and Andrea Powell.